MACWORLD

MUSIC &
SOUND BIBLE

By Christopher Yavelow

MACWORLD

MUSIC & SOUND BIBLE

By Christopher Yavelow
Composer, Multimedia Producer, and Educator

Foreword by Herbie Hancock
Recording Artist

IDG Books Worldwide, Inc.
An International Data Group Company
San Mateo, California 94402

Macworld Music & Sound Bible
Published by
IDG Books Worldwide, Inc.
An International Data Group Company
155 Bovet Road, Suite 610
San Mateo, CA 94402
(415) 312-0650

Library of Congress Catalog Card No.: 91-70290

ISBN 1-878058-18-5

Printed in the United States of America

10 9 8 7 6 5 4 3 2 1

Distributed in the United States by IDG Books Worldwide, Inc.
Distributed in Canada by Macmillan of Canada, a Division of Canada Publishing
Corporation; by Woodslane Pty. Ltd. in Australia; and by Computer Bookshops in
the U.K.

For information on translations and availability in other countries, contact Marc
Jeffrey Mikulich, Foreign Rights Manager, at IDG Books Worldwide.
Fax: (415) 358-1260.

For sales inquiries and special prices for bulk quantities, write to the address above
or call IDG Books Worldwide at (415) 312-0650.

Dedication

In loving memory of:
Karl Sighvatsson
and
Kimball Stickney

Acknowledgments

The Team

I was fortunate to have found a small group of people willing to help me complete a project of this scope and magnitude in a year. All of them worked under very arduous conditions.

- ❖ Jill Meschke
- ❖ Deborah Wagner
- ❖ Monique Fasel Yavelow
- ❖ Chris Berr
- ❖ Russell Steinberg
- ❖ Del Blake
- ❖ Peggy McAffee

Jill Meschke and Deborah Wagner were of great help with the graphics, often taking my seemingly indecipherable pencil sketches and turning them into works of art. Jill and Deborah also assisted with the creation of tables, testing of software, System 7, and verification of telecommunication services. Martha Catlin joined in at the last moment to assist with preparing the last few graphics.

Monique Fasel Yavelow proofread every word before anything was sent to Curt Roads and Craig Anderton for editing. When edited material was returned from Curt and Craig, she made sure that all the changes and corrections were implemented before the final drafts were sent to IDG. She also kept all research materials in order, took on any outside research that was required, and put both the Bibliography and the Telecommunography into final form. Additionally, Monique worked on the preparation of tables, translation of German and French manuals and correspondence, and anything else she could do to speed up the completion of the book.

Chris Berry and Monique organized the massive database of companies, correspondence, products received/required, and information sources. Peggy McAffee was responsible for organizing all of my communications with PAN. This included categorizing all the tips and bug reports in my FileMaker database of PAN messages. Russell Steinberg provided crucial and invaluable assistance on Chapters 20 and 29. Without his help, those chapters might very well have been dropped from the book due to time constraints. Russell, Deborah, Jill, and myself worked on the big notation software tables. Monique created the final tables from our notes.

Del Blake, Deborah, Monique, and myself worked together on the Manufacturers List. Del had the additional job of digging around in all the shareware and freeware programs with ResEdit to try to determine who wrote the software, since this information was often not available by any other means.

Technical Support

Virtually innumerable people have made contributions of all kinds to this endeavor. I am grateful to all of them.

I am much indebted to the outstanding work of the copy editor, Curt Roads, and the technical reviewer, Craig Anderton. They offered invaluable criticism, suggestions, and information, which helped mold my rough drafts into a book worthy of publication.

I express my deepest gratitude to Max and Madeleine Fasel, Brentano and Tobi Haleen, Laura Burggraf, Dominic Frontiere, Michael Johnson, Lincoln Johnson, and Gerry Kass, who provided assistance without which the book could never have been completed.

Thanks to Apple, Microtech, Digidesign, Opcode, Mark of the Unicorn, Roland, Panasonic, Akai, Steinberg-Jones, JL Cooper, Adams-Smith, Lone Wolf, Passport Designs, Articulate Systems, and Triangle Resources for providing hardware that made the project possible.

In particular, thanks are due to the individuals at those and other companies who provided additional assistance: Alan Kay, Keri Walker, Doedy Hunter, John Worthington, Martha Steffen, and Liz Gebhard (Apple); Randall Osborne and Delona Long (Microtech); Evan Brooks, Suz Howells, Toby Richards, and Tom Sherman (Digidesign); Paul de Benedictis and Keith Borman (Opcode); John Mavriades, Daniel Rose, and Jim Cooper (Mark of the Unicorn); Al Hospurs (Dr. T's); Jeff Junker (Adams-Smith); Anastasia Lanier and Dave Kusek (Passport Designs); Tom White (Roland); Chris Foreman (Panasonic); Lawrence Demarco (Korg); James Martin (Akai); Mark Lacas (Lone Wolf); and Stavros Cademenos (Articulate Systems).

Terry Kunysz of Casady & Greene supplied the Documentation font, and Wendy Carlos's Grace Notes and Crescendo fonts are used throughout the book. Additional thanks to Randall Bankert, whose last-minute loan of the LaserMaster plain paper typesetter and Macintosh IIci facilitated meeting the deadline. Finally, thanks to the several hundred software companies who sent evaluation copies of their software and soon-to-be-released software — I couldn't have done it without you.

Special Thanks

I am especially grateful to the following people:

Otto Laske and Curtis Roads for introducing me to the possibilities of computers and music; Karl Sighvatsson and Larry Scripp for the long-term loan of synthesizers and other devices that formed the basis of my first electronic music studio; and Curtis Roads and Don Byrd for encouraging me to write about computer music in the first place.

Jay Fenton, David Zicarelli, Don Byrd, Kimball Stickney, Nigel Redmond, Ric Ford, and Mark Lutton for always being available to answer technical questions about the inner workings of the Macintosh, software in general, and programming; Chet Graham, Bill Gardner, and Ralph Muha at Kurzweil Music Systems for answering all my questions about MIDI and sampling since the day I got involved with these things; Don Byrd for serving as my computer music notation mentor and clarifying my conceptions and misconceptions about the issue; Dominic Frontiere, Earl Hagen, Fred Karlin, and Bruce Miller for resolving many questions on film and video scoring; Laurie Spiegel and Joel Chadabe for explaining important concepts about intelligent instruments and interactive composition; and David Levitt for introducing me to object-oriented programming.

Mark Canter and the MacroMind beta-tester support group for assistance with Director; Bob Stein for showing me the true value of hypermedia; Kimball Stickney and Erfert Fenton for answering all my questions about PostScript and fonts; Peter and Coco Conn for answering my questions about video; Michael Lang for providing information from the inside of the scoring stage; Jeff Lorber for uncannily warning me about potential crashes often mere hours before I would have experienced them; and Joe DaVita and Steve Shannon for helping track down software that needed to be in the book.

Joyce McKeel for not paying any attention to me in 1969 when I declared that I would never become involved with any musical instruments that required electricity and forcing me to learn the basics anyway; Gardner Read for teaching me the intricacies of music notation and engraving over a period of four years, when neither of us anticipated that I would eventually put this knowledge to use with a computer; and David Lewin for teaching me about applications of probability theory to music; without this knowledge, I would never have been able to understand David Zicarelli.

I extend my gratitude to my students at Claremont Graduate School for bearing with my absolute exhaustion during the final stages of the project.

Finally, I apologize to my daughters, Celina and Stephanie, who put up with so many months of barely seeing their daddy.

(The publisher would like to give special thanks to Bill Murphy, without whom this book would not have been possible.)

About the Author

Christopher Yavelow received graduate degrees in composition and theory from both Boston University and Harvard University. During five years of postgraduate study in Europe he earned additional diplomas and certificates at Budapest's Franz Liszt Academy, the *Conservatoire Darius Milhaud*, the *Darmstadt Internationale Ferienkurse*, and the *Conservatoire Américain de Fontainebleau*. He has studied with Nadia Boulanger, David DelTredici, Zsolt Durko, Max Deutsch, Ernö Lendvai, György Ligeti, Mauricio Kagel, and Gardner Read.

Yavelow has held teaching positions at the University of Texas, Schiller College (where he was Chairman of the Department of Music), and Harvard University. Since 1988 he has been Professor of Graduate Composition at Claremont Graduate School. He also teaches at the American Film Institute's AFI-Apple Center for Film and Videomakers (for which he is an advisory board member) and the Center for Creative Imaging (Eastman Kodak). Additionally, he has held composer-in-residence posts at the MacDowell Colony, the Camargo Foundation, the Cummington Community of the Arts, the Windhover Center for the Creative and Performing Arts, and Paris's *Cité des Arts*.

Throughout the past two decades, 22 of Yavelow's works have received awards and prizes in national and international competitions, including the *Grand Prix à l'Unanimité* in the *Rencontres Internationales de Chant Choral*. During the same period he has been honored with 17 grants and fellowships such as the IREX Fellowship sponsored by the Social Science Research Council and the American Council of Learned Societies.

Most of his work in the 1970s was devoted to multimedia. His compositions have been commissioned by the Empire Brass Quintet, the Williams Trio, the Kodaly Musical Training Institute, the Modern Times Theater, Computer Professionals for Social Responsibility, and Collage — the Contemporary Ensemble of the Boston Symphony Orchestra. His interest in the theatrical aspects of music led to a 1981 National Endowment for the Arts grant to compose his three-act grand opera: *The Passion of Vincent Van Gogh*. In 1987 the Boston Lyric Opera commissioned a Macintosh-controlled opera about nuclear war — *Countdown* — under the auspices of Opera America's "Opera in the Eighties and Beyond" program. *Countdown* went on to win first prize in the 1988 Virginia Opera Society Competition. Recent multimedia activities include creating the Finale Guided Tour and music for the CD-ROM *Verbum Interactive*.

From the introduction of the Macintosh in 1984 until the present Yavelow has been a consultant and beta-tester for many companies developing music software for the Macintosh and for such hardware companies as Apple Computer, Kurzweil Music Systems, E-mu Systems, and Articulate Systems. He has been a member of the Apple Consultant Relations program since its inception.

A long-standing board member of NEWCOMP (the New England Computer Arts Association), upon moving to Los Angeles Yavelow assumed the directorship of MEGA (the Macintosh Entertainment Guild of America) for several years. He is currently on the board of the LAMG (the Los Angeles Macintosh Group).

His articles on computer-assisted composition, MIDI, and digital audio appear in *Macworld*, *Electronic Musician*, *Computer Music Journal*, *Verbum*, *NewMedia*, *The Journal of the Audio Engineering Society*, *Byte*, *MacWeek*, *Music Technology*, *MacInTouch*, and *Keyboards, Computers, and Software*.

Since 1985 he has been performing concerts of interactive computer music and lecturing extensively on the subject in the United States, France, Germany, Switzerland, and the Netherlands. In 1990 he and Brentano Haleen originated VADA: Voice Activated Digital Art, a new form of collaborative interactive multimedia performance art.

Christopher Yavelow's music is widely performed in North America and Europe and is available from *American Composers Edition* in New York and *Editions A Coeur Joie* in France.

President and Publisher
John J. Kilcullen

Publishing Director
David Solomon

Project Editor
Jeremy Judson

Production Director
Lana J. Olson

Copy Editor
Curtis Roads

Technical Reviewer
Craig Anderton

Text Preparation and Proofreading
Shirley E. Coe
Dana Bryant Sadoff
Megg Bonar
Mary Ann Cordova

Indexer
Matthew Spence

Book Design and Production
Peppy White
Francette M. Ytsma
(University Graphics, Palo Alto, California)

About IDG Books Worldwide

Welcome to the world of IDG Books Worldwide.

IDG Books Worldwide, Inc., is a division of International Data Group (IDG), the world's leading publisher of computer-related information and the leading global provider of information services on information technology. IDG publishes over 178 computer publications in more than 55 countries. Thirty million people read one or more IDG publications each month.

If you use personal computers, IDG Books is committed to publishing quality books that meet your needs. We rely on our extensive network of publications — including such leading periodicals as *Macworld, InfoWorld, PC World, Computerworld, Lotus, Publish, Network World, Computer Buying World,* and *SunWorld* — to help us make informed and timely decisions in creating useful computer books that meet your needs.

Every IDG book strives to bring extra value and skill-building instruction to the reader. Our books are written by experts, with the backing of IDG periodicals, and with careful thought devoted to issues such as audience, interior design, use of icons, and illustrations. Our editorial staff is a careful mix of high-tech journalists and experienced book people. Our close contact with the makers of computer products helps ensure accuracy and thorough coverage. Our heavy use of personal computers at every step in production means we can deliver books in the most timely manner.

We are delivering books of high quality at competitive prices on topics customers want. At IDG, we believe in quality and we have been delivering quality for 25 years. You'll find no better book on a subject than an IDG book.

John Kilcullen
President and Publisher
IDG Books Worldwide, Inc.

International Data Group's publications include: **ARGENTINA'S** Computerworld Argentina; **ASIA'S** Computerworld Hong Kong, Computerworld Southeast Asia, Computerworld Malaysia; **AUSTRALIA'S** Computerworld Australia, Australian PC World, Australian Macworld, Profit, Information Decisions, Reseller; **AUSTRIA'S** Computerwelt Oesterreich; **BRAZIL'S** DataNews, PC Mundo, Mundo IBM, Mundo Unix, Publish; **BULGARIA'S** Computerworld Bulgaria, Ediworld, PC World Express; **CANADA'S** ComputerData, Direct Access, Graduate Computerworld, InfoCanada, Network World Canada; **CHILE'S** Computerworld, Informatica; **COLUMBIA'S** Computerworld Columbia; **CZECHOSLOVAKIA'S** Computerworld Czechoslovakia, PC World Czechoslovakia; **DENMARK'S** CAD/ CAM WORLD, Communications World, Computerworld Danmark, Computerworld Focus, Computerworld Uddannelse, LAN World, Lotus World, Macintosh Produktkatalog, Macworld Danmark, PC World Danmark, PC World Produktguide, Windows World; **EQUADOR'S** PC World; **EGYPT'S** PC World Middle East; **FINLAND'S** Mikro PC, Tietoviikko, Tietoverkko; **FRANCE'S** Computer Direct, Distributique, GOLDEN MAC, InfoPC, Languages & Systems, Le Guide du Monde Informatique, Le Monde Informatique, Telecoms & Reseaux International; **GERMANY'S** Computerwoche, Computerwoche Focus, Computerwoche Extra, Computerwoche Karriere, edv aspekte, Information Management, Lotus Welt, Macwelt, Netzwelt, PC Welt, PC Woche, Publish, Unit, Unix Welt; **GREECE'S** Infoworld, PC Games, PC World Greece; **HUNGARY'S** Computerworld SZT, Mikrovilag Magazin, PC World; **INDIA'S** Computers & Communications; **ISRAEL'S** Computerworld Israel, PC World Israel; **ITALY'S** Computerworld Italia, Macworld Italia, Networking Italia, PC World Italia; **JAPAN'S** Computerworld Japan, Macworld Japan, SunWorld Japan; **KOREA'S** Computerworld Korea, Macworld Korea, PC World Korea; **MEXICO'S** Compu Edicion, Compu Manufactura, Computacion/Punto de Venta,Computerworld Mexico, MacWorld, Mundo Unix, PC Journal, Windows; **THE NETHERLAND'S** Computer! Totaal, Computerworld Netherlands, LAN Magazine, MacWorld Magazine; **NEW ZEALAND'S** Computer Listings, Computerworld New Zealand, New Zealand PC World; **NIGERIA'S** PC World Africa; **NORWAY'S** Computerworld Norge, C/world, Lotusworld Norge, Macworld Norge, Networld, PC World Ekspress, PC World Norge, PC World's Product Guide, Publish World, Student Guiden, Unix World, Windowsworld, IDG Direct Response; **PERU'S** PC World; **PEOPLE'S REPUBLIC OF CHINA'S** China Computerworld, PC World China, Electronics International; **IDG HIGH TECH** Newproductworld; **PHILLIPPINE'S** Computerworld, PC World; **POLAND'S** Computerworld Poland, Komputer; **ROMANIA'S** InfoClub Magazine; **RUSSIA'S** Computerworld-Moscow, Networks, PC World; **SPAIN'S** Amiga World, Autoedicion, CIM World, Communicaciones World, Computerworld Espana, Macworld Espana, PC World Espana, Publish; **SWEDEN'S** Affarsekonomi Management, Attack, CAD/CAM World, ComputerSweden, Digital/Varlden, Lokala Natverk/LAN, Mikrodatorn, Lotus World, MAC&PC, Macworld, Mikrodatorn, PC World, Publish & Design (CAP), Unix/Oppna system, Datalngenjoren, Maxi Data, Windows; **SWITZERLAND'S** Computerworld Schweiz, Macworld Schweiz, PC & Workstation; **TAIWAN'S** Computerworld Taiwan, PC World Taiwan; **THAILAND'S** Thai Computerworld; **TURKEY'S** Computerworld Monitor, Macworld Turkiye, PC World Turkiye; **UNITED KINGDOM'S** Lotus Magazine, Macworld; **UNITED STATES'** AmigaWorld, Cable in the Classroom, CIO, Computer Buying World, Computerworld, Digital News, DOS Resource Guide, Electronic News, Federal Computer Week, GamePro, inCider/A+, IDG Books, InfoWorld, Lotus, Macworld, Momentum, MPC World, Network World, NeXTWORLD, PC Games, PC World, PC Letter, Publish, RUN, SunWorld, SWATPro; **VENEZUELA'S** Computerworld Venezuela, Micro-Computerworld Venezuela; **YUGOSLAVIA'S** Moj Mikro.

Contents at a Glance

Tables at a Glance

Table of Contents

Foreword
by Herbie Hancock, Recording Artist

Perhaps the biggest change the Macintosh has brought to music is the opportunity for one to sit down at an instrument; compose music by playing it, or by conceiving something beforehand and checking it at the keyboard; and have the computer remember what was played — for example, using a sequencer. Add to this the flexibility of being able to play almost any sound from one or two keyboards (because we only have two hands) without having to run around the room. And to be able to change the connections of things, still sitting in the same chair, without having to physically get up and move wires. And then being able to print out the music without moving, too. In short — efficiency and speed.

Before the Macintosh, the physical act of writing a letter or music — just taking a pen in hand and having to manipulate it — slowed the process down. This is because it is possible to conceive musical ideas much faster than you can put them on paper.

Speed is the real issue because when you're writing music or text, your creativity should be able to flow freely, uninterrupted by hardware that can slow down that flow. The Macintosh lets you accomplish your task with fewer things slowing down the creative flow.

One issue we must constantly face is that the new technology provided by the Macintosh offers us so many more features — options that were, until now, impossible to even consider. These new alternatives give us access to a good deal more information, which means there are a lot more choices to make and many more parameters to deal with. This can slow us down, too. Human factors become very important. You can compare the problem to ergonomics in the sense that someone will have to come up with a system that deals with the human being and his or her interaction with all of this newly available information — organizational and retrieval techniques that go beyond simple patch librarians. But it's not just the librarians that are the issue. It's the complete integration of the human being with the devices and their options. This might consist of training ourselves in an organizational approach that is optimum for the current application.

Voice control is going to help. Speaking is one of the quickest methods a human being has for communicating. For example, with Articulate Systems's Voice Navigator you can control the Mac without having to physically type anything.

Digital audio is another area in which the Mac is significantly changing the way we work. At present, we are just seeing the beginning stages of digital audio, or at best, the latter part of the beginning. The next and intermediate stage will be sometime in the beginning of the next millennium. Solid-state crystal-based storage mediums for digital recordings are on the horizon. I'm not going to be around to see it when digital audio really gets into high gear. That's much later. By then we're going to be rid of wires and extraneous hardware. The last stage of wired cables is fiberoptics. First there'll be the integration of wires and fiberoptics, which is wires, but a slightly different concept of wires. Next will be the integration of fiberoptics and wireless.

Fiberoptics will be around for quite a while, because it's only a single cable but it can still handle much information over that one line. You can have all of your MIDI information, and control all of your instruments, digital audio information, video information, CDs, and SCSI coming down a single little fiberoptic cable all at the same time. Everything is traveling at the speed of light, and the data is clean, without any kind of distortion or change for about a mile and a half.

In the future you might have a single fiberoptic cable coming out of each instrument going to every next instrument. You might even have a box with different slots in it that interfaces with the Mac by a fiberoptic cable. Digidesign already markets the MacProteus and SampleCell as Macintosh cards. It's easy to envision a time when all your instruments will be plug-in boards.

As things continue to get smaller, the biggest problem will be that our hands and our bodies are too big. The interface will always have to be a certain size if it is manual. Later on, when synthetic organic implants become practical, that is, instead of using silicon for data, biological material will be used; you could actually have an implant in your brain. Then it will only be necessary to think your music and have it written out on a page. This will be very nice — if you can keep your mind still. It may necessitate training to keep your mind still enough to make it do what you want it to do.

The new visual programming languages have fantastic potential in this area. For example, my engineer, Will Alexander, is building a virtual mixer that integrates the three different mixers I have on my Audio Frame: the Audio Frame's built-in virtual mixer, the Yamaha DMP7 template, and the template for the Mark of the Unicorn 7S mixer. The DMP7 hardware has moving faders, so when I move the faders on the virtual mixer on the screen of the Audio Frame, it moves the faders of the DMP7. I can store all of the fader movements in Vision. This is not merely limited to fader movements; all the parameters have a MIDI number. In Vision, with its own set of MIDI-assignable faders, I can control the Q of the parametric equalizer and also record it. This is important because, while I can't physically put all those devices in front of me, I can have them all on-screen at one time. Finally, I have two Fadermasters that interface with the virtual mixers. This gives me a lot of flexibility because I can control all of them from one workstation.

The Macintosh's importance in managing the minor details of studio operation shouldn't be overlooked. As musicians, we don't deal with just music on the computer, there is phone-book and scheduling software, just to mention a few of the obvious. Even answering machine messages can be taken and stored on the Mac in a program such as Focal Point. In the field of music it's not only music and sounds that are controlled with the Mac, there are track sheets to deal with, cable and instrument assignments, as well as the organization of session time. Opcode's Cue film-scoring software has built-in features that facilitate copyright and royalty management. Programs to do your taxes have been available for quite some time.

Yavelow has got it all covered in this book. There are dozens of possible studio and workstation configurations diagrammed in this book with a complete discussion of hardware and software options. It's like a big thesaurus. He's found all of the software options. For example, I thought there were only three or four music fonts until now.

When I asked Yavelow how long he'd been working on this book, he replied "under a year so far." If he had said two years, I would have said "how could you get all this stuff together in only two years? It looks like about a five- or six-year job." He's got everything in this book!

Conventions Used in This Book

General Flow

I've taken every opportunity to make this book as user-friendly as possible. To this end, the book flows from setup to input to editing to output — mirroring the way you work. Consequently, if you are setting up your studio or workstation, you may want to thumb through the beginning of the book. If you are entering information, regardless of whether it is MIDI data, notation, digital audio, or anything else, turn to the second quarter of the book.

Likewise, when editing your music in any form, look for assistance about halfway through the book. And if you are at the output stage, regardless of whether you are turning out live music, going to tape or hard disk, or printing notation on paper, look at the third quarter of the book. Finally, if you are an educator or are looking to become a power user, the last quarter of the book will interest you.

The other element that occurs simultaneously, and therefore influences the general flow, is the progression of information from the beginner's level to the advanced level.

Part and chapter organization

After the introductory material, the 29 chapters of this book are organized into nine large parts and are followed by five appendixes. Each part opens with an introduction to the subject. At the beginning of each chapter, you will find a brief listing of the main topics covered in the chapter.

Most chapters are organized in one of two ways. Wherever possible, information flows from setup to input to editing to output. When this is not appropriate, chapters commence with detailed background information on the topic at hand and end with an application of these concepts in the context of specific software and hardware options.

Mini-forewords

Each of the nine large parts of the book begins with a foreword written by a noted authority on the topic at hand.

Icons

There are a number of icons in the page margins to help you navigate through the text.

 Special or unique feature.

 Technical information.

 Tip, shortcut, or clarification of a common myth.

 Shopping bargain.

 Warnings or alert.

 Read before proceeding.

Graphics
Studio setups and wiring diagrams

Studio setups are detailed diagrams of possible studio and workstation setups. Everything is drawn to scale. There are 22 main studio setup diagrams in Chapter 7. Many other chapters include additional setup diagrams devoted to specific tasks, for example, synchronization, live performance, and so on. The setup diagrams detail every aspect of hooking up your equipment as well as the data paths for the various types of information that get shuttled around during the applications discussed in this book (MIDI, SCSI, PostScript, ASCII, RS-422, digital audio, EBU, SMPTE, MTC, and so on). Consult the following figure for the key to data cable types used throughout this book.

———————	midi data = thin solid black line (arrow indicates the direction of data flow)
▬▬▬▬▬▬	midi snake = thick solid black line carrying many MIDI cables in both directions
———————	audio data = thin solid gray line (can represent stereo or mono; arrows where relevant)
▬▬▬▬▬▬	audio snake = thick solid gray line carrying many audio cabels in both directions
■-■-■-■-■	SCSI = medium dashed black line
———————	SMPTE = thinner medium gray line with diagonal slashes (data flow arrow if relevant)
·················	digital audio = thin dotted black line (signal flow arrow used if relevant)
׀׀׀׀׀׀׀׀׀׀׀׀׀	digital audio snake = thick dotted black line (signal flow arrow used if relevant)
– · – · – · –	video signal = thin dot-dash-dot-dash line (data flow arrow if relevant)
– – – – –	RS 422, AppleTalk, & other data = thin dashed black line (data flow arrow if relevant)

Flow charts

Flow charts illustrate the progression of steps one follows to execute a given musical task, to achieve a certain effect, or to solve a common problem. Usually, a flow chart can be thought of as a series of "step-by-steps" (see the following) and is often broken down into its individual step-by-step components.

Illustrations and screenshots

With the exception of one or two cases, all screenshots are taken from actual program operations rather than supplied by the manufacturer.

Tables
Feature tables

A feature table is a comparison listing of features and options showing one product in relation to a wide range of software or hardware packages that all accomplish the same general purpose. For some types of Macintosh applications, feature tables would be redundant. For example, we all expect a Macintosh word processor to allow for justified, centered, flush right, or flush left text, just as we assume that plain, boldface, and italic type styles are available. For such programs, a feature table listing only those features that are unique among the programs would be adequate. This is not the case with music software.

Music processing software is complex, and the approaches that developers have taken with respect to every musical issue are as different as the programs themselves. In general, you can make no safe assumptions about a music package other than the fact that it can open, close, and save files. From that point on, it's every program for itself. Because of this, most feature tables in this book have been constructed to be as thorough as possible.

Recommendations, requirements, and configurations tables

Some tables provide information about software or hardware configurations for the task at hand. Sometimes these address recommendations or possible options, and in other cases they illustrate specific hardware requirements.

Symbols

The following symbols are used consistently in both feature tables and tables of recommendations or requirements.

Symbol	Feature table	Recommendations, Requirements, and Configurations Tables
✪	Exceptional implementation (exceeds expectations or requirements)	Exceptional choice or solution (exceeds expectations or requirements) — Required
☆	Complete implementation *or* In some cases: Yes	Best choice — Required *or* In some cases: Yes
◗	Partial implementation (covers either most normal cases or only some cases usually discernable by the type of feature it is applied to)	Best alternative choice or solution *or* Recommended but not required
○	Not implemented *Note:* Used only if it is important to highlight that a specific feature is missing (otherwise, a blank box is used — see below) In some cases: No	Adequate alternative solution *or* In some cases: No
[Blank]	Not applicable *or* In some cases: Not implemented	Not applicable
①②③, or ❶ ❷❹, etc.	The numbers inside the boxes refer you to specific footnotes at the bottom of the table.	

Other common abbreviations found in a table include:

()   Somewhat or tentative. In feature tables, this can indicate a feature that is implemented in a pre-release version or an option that requires multiple user-actions, while it exists as a single operation in other software. In recommendations, requirements, or configurations tables, this can indicate an optional item.

L   Local in scope.

G   Global in scope.

UL or U   Unlimited in scope or quantity.

A   Automatic (the program takes care of this automatically).

M   Manual (you must perform specific actions for this to occur).

NA   Not applicable.

Command Concordances

Within some categories of applications, "command concordances" resolve differences between similar functions in two or more programs that use different commands or terminology for the same purpose. These are designed to facilitate effective communication between a user of one vendor's software and a user of another vendor's software.

Situations where the command concordances are helpful:

❖ You've decided to switch from one program to another and want to get up to speed on the new program as quickly as possible.

❖ You are working with people who are using a different product.

❖ You need to temporarily convert a file into another program's format to access certain features that are unavailable in the package that you normally use.

❖ You are required to use a certain software package, because everyone else working on the same project is using that package.

Step-by-steps

Step-by-steps are procedures for accomplishing a certain task that involves multiple menu accesses, mouse clicks, and dialog interaction.

Miscellaneous

The most current versions of all music, digital audio, and multimedia software and hardware are covered. In cases where an earlier version of a product is still in widespread use (for example, due to a hefty upgrade fee), these earlier releases are also treated as current in the text and indicated appropriately.

Products that are about to be released are also covered and clearly indicated as such in the text. In these cases, every effort has been made to distinguish between features that are "locked down" and guaranteed to be in the release version of a product and those that may be postponed for a future upgrade.

Other Titles To Enhance Your Mac Knowledge

As you travel in the Mac world, be sure to check out our other Mac books that are written by the experts on the topics you want to know:

The *Macworld Complete Mac Handbook,* by Jim Heid, is the ultimate Mac reference that includes hardware and software from soup to nuts and powerful tips and shortcuts.

The *Macworld Guide To System 7,* by Lon Poole, is loaded with valuable undocumented tips and secrets on the new Mac operating system — all you need to know about manipulating your hardware and software.

The *Macworld Read Me First Book,* edited by Jerry Borrell, gives you no-nonsense advice from the experts you trust on the hardware and software you need.

The *Macworld Guide To Word 5,* by Jim Heid, is a task-oriented guide to all the new features of Word 5 that includes helpful tutorials and valuable tips.

The *Macworld Guide To Excel,* by David Maguiness, is a task-oriented guide to all the new features of Excel 4, including helpful tutorials and valuable tips.

The *Macworld Guide To Works,* by Barrie Sosinsky, is a task-oriented guide to all the new features of Works 3, including helpful tutorials and valuable tips.

The *Macworld Networking Handbook,* by David Kosiur, Ph. D., is the only practical, hands-on guide that explains Macintosh networking from the ground up.

Introduction

The Mac is having a profound impact upon many aspects of music. Macs are found in recording studios, performance stages, orchestra pits, and in the classrooms of some of our most renowned institutions of musical learning. While the concept of the personal computer is not new, the concept of the personal-computer-controlled music studio is. For many composers, the Mac has replaced pencil and paper; for other musicians, it has replaced the orchestra; for some, it is replacing the tape-recorder; and for educators, the Mac is opening up new pedagogical strategies that have no corollary in traditional teaching methods.

Mac music software abolishes music industry distinctions that have fragmented the territory into various camps or genres: classical vs. pop, serious vs. commercial, and traditional vs. contemporary. This has caused an interesting phenomenon to emerge: People involved in pop/commercial music are discovering that they need to know more about the kind of theoretical information that used to make up the standard fare in a conservatory music education. On the other hand, conservatory-trained musicians, both performers and composers, are realizing that they need to know more about techniques that had previously been in the pop/commercial domain. After hundreds of years of a seemingly ever-widening gulf, the worlds of the pop, jazz, commercial, and classical musician are finally moving together again — the vehicle that is bringing them all to the same place is the Mac.

This book is designed to serve the needs of beginners through the most advanced professionals. Not only are all levels of users addressed, but also all types of users. There are no statistics available on how many people use their Mac for music or sound, but informed sources place the number in the mid- to upper-six figures. There could be as many as 750,000 of you out there.

I pay particular attention to the following topics (listed alphabetically):

- ❖ Algorithmic composition
- ❖ Digital audio and direct-to-hard disk (tapeless) recording
- ❖ Digital signal processing, equalization, and effects
- ❖ Education, computer-aided instruction, and scholarly research or analysis
- ❖ Film and video applications
- ❖ Interactive composition and performance
- ❖ MIDI software and hardware

❖ Multimedia
❖ Music utilities as well as nonmusic utilities used for music
❖ Networks, including music local area networks and related environments
❖ Notation by computer and music desktop publishing
❖ Performance (live)
❖ Sound design, sampling, patch editing, and so on
❖ Studio automation
❖ Synchronization, SMPTE, MTC, and so on

Whether you're a seasoned professional or have just bought your Mac and are toying with the idea of using it for music, you will find a wealth of useful information within this book.

First, I discuss historical background and categorize Mac applications to music. Next, I describe the state-of-the-art of each application, providing an overview, detailed analysis, and discussion of the impact of Mac music software and hardware for each category.

The greater part of the text flows from setup to input to editing to output, with all the related applications these activities require. This is exactly the order in which one works with music on the Mac. Multimedia aspects of all applications are incorporated into the general text, but there is also an entire section of the book dedicated specifically to this topic. Finally, I provide information aimed at increasing and enhancing musical productivity with the Mac.

To bring the technical discussions down to earth, examples of real-world applications and "celebrity" users are provided for some topics. These are in the form of interviews, profiles, and roundtable discussions. Each of the nine parts is preceded by a separate foreword written by a noted authority in the field to which the section is devoted.

I have attempted to cover every Mac music and audio product available, hardware and software alike. Product coverage extends beyond a mere list of products, features, and reviews, to a definitive applications-oriented reference/ handbook approach that you will probably want to keep within arm's reach of your Mac. To help you on-line, there is even a desk-accessory version of the index available so you can locate the right information in the book when you need it.

I've made available a software supplement to all purchasing the book. This set of disks contains numerous utilities and programs relating to the book's focus, including shareware, public domain, and proprietary software. See the coupon in the back of the book for ordering information.

For most activities covered by this book, a variety of software and hardware solutions are equally valid. We have reached a stage of development where most competing products offer the same basic functionality. Where they differ is in the areas of user interface and bells and whistles. It's somewhat like cars: They'll all get you where you are going, but some are made in Japan, painted metallic brown, and have tachometers and power doorlocks. I have made every effort not to let my preferences color my reporting on any of the products in this book (although I might try to persuade you to buy a Japanese car if you ask my opinion).

How This Book is Organized

This book is divided into nine main parts that roughly mirror the way you work, flowing from setup to input to editing to output. Outside of this principle some sections are devoted to special applications such as film, video, education, and multimedia.

Part One: The Basics covers the background information that you will need to understand the rest of the book, and also guides you through setting up your Mac music studio or workstation. Chapter 1 chronicles the history of Mac computer music with detailed discussions of synthesis methods, digital sampling, and everything you need to know about MIDI. Chapter 2 provides an overview of musical and audio applications for the Mac, organized into 12 categories. In Chapter 3 you will find basic information about setting up your Mac studio or workstation for MIDI, non-MIDI, or digital audio applications, with a special section on adding NuBus-based digital audio cards. If you haven't got a Mac yet, Chapter 4 will advise you on choosing the best Mac and peripherals for your musical tasks. Whether you have a Mac or not, the 25 purchasing tips in this chapter could save you a good deal of money on both your computer and music equipment purchases. Chapter 5 tells you what type of music and audio hardware you need and why, while Chapter 6 details your software options, organizing about 800 Mac music programs into application categories. Chapter 7 offers 22 sample Mac studio setups, complete with cabling diagrams and suggested equipment (with costs) configured at beginner, intermediate, and advanced levels. Once you have your studio or workstation configured, Chapter 8 covers routing data to, from, and within your Mac and external devices using Apple's MIDI Manager, Opcode MIDI System (OMS), Mark of the Unicorn's MIDI Time Piece, and Lone Wolf's MidiTap. Finally, Chapter 9 helps you understand the stages involved in transforming sound to music and how you can apply your Mac to the creative process.

Part Two: Sound deals with the most important ingredient for your Mac music-making activities — the sound materials you will be working with. Chapter 10 covers the sound-generating and playback capabilities of various Mac models.

You will also find detailed information on digitizing and editing 8- and 16-bit sounds in HyperCard. Chapter 11 is concerned with organizing your synthesizer sounds using both dedicated and universal patch librarians as well as database software. Chapters 12 and 13 deal with editing synthesized and sampled sounds, respectively — all current software options are covered in depth.

Part Three: Composition discusses applications of the Mac with respect to the creative process, making music on the Mac both with MIDI and without, sequencing, combining MIDI sequencing with digital audio, and both interactive and algorithmic composition. Chapter 14 presents 12 ways to use the Mac as a tool for computer-assisted composition. The focus of Chapter 15 is making music without MIDI with particular emphasis on HyperCard. Chapter 16 prepares you for all subsequent chapters concerned with MIDI through a discussion of the impact of MIDI on composition methodology and introduction to MIDI sequencing. Chapter 17 scrutinizes the features offered by six non-professional sequencers and five professional sequencers, while Chapter 18 looks at the latest rage: MIDI sequencers that offer digital audio tracks. Chapter 19 examines intelligent instruments and tools for interactive composition (both MIDI and non-MIDI) while Chapter 20 contrasts algorithmic composition with automatic composition, comparing software for "instant gratification" vs. programming-intensive software. Both Chapters 19 and 20 are illustrated with sample output in conventional music notation.

Part Four: Notation presents the capabilities of current-generation Mac music notation software. In Chapter 21 you will learn what to expect from notation software and the various options for input and editing notation data. Chapter 22 organizes notation software features into 20 categories and examines the capabilities of 14 notation programs in detail, letting you compare the printed output of a representative passage notated by all available Mac notation software.

Part Five: Performance tells you how to use the Mac to enhance live performance, including synchronizing the Mac to live performers, MIDI sequencing in live performance environments, interactive performance software, and using the Mac to control nonmusical performance parameters.

Part Six: Post-production is devoted to recording and editing digital audio and to automating both analog and digital mixing with the Mac. Chapter 24 describes available direct-to-hard disk recording systems. Special considerations for SMPTE synchronization in non-tape-based systems are addressed. Chapter 25 deals with approaches to MIDI-controlled mixing and virtual mixing using MIDI Volume, Pan, and Velocity. You will also learn how the Mac can be used for other tasks associated with studio production.

Part Seven: Film, Video, and Synchronization focuses on unique film and video applications to which the Mac can be applied. The various protocols and formats of synchronization are explained and Mac studio setup diagrams for all types of synchronization are provided. A large section in Chapter 26 covers cue sheet applications and utility software dedicated to film and video scoring.

Part Eight: Multimedia compares five multimedia authoring environments from the standpoint of their integration of music and audio. Chapter 27 includes tips, techniques, scripts, and syntax guides for digital audio and MIDI in multimedia. You will also find a discussion of multimedia legal issues and copyright law, sources for clip music as MIDI data, 8- and 16-bit soundfiles, and digital audio. Finally, a "Multimedia in Action" section analyzes different approaches to interactive magazines and interactive training.

Part Nine: Education focuses on computer-aided instruction from three points of view: the end user, the educator, and the developer. Chapter 28 covers the Mac as music teacher for self-guided learning and classroom instruction, including a detailed examination of 16 software options for ear training, theory, and applied instruction. The issues of Chapter 29 are nonlinear access and the implications of hypermedia for education. The latest tools for computer-based learning, interactive CD-ROMs, are evaluated. Two popular interactive CD-ROMs, *The Rite of Spring* and *The Ninth Symphony,* are compared.

Five appendixes give you useful supplemental information: (A) The MIDI Specification; (B) Bibliography for further reading; (C) Telecommunography listing dozens of music BBSs; (D) List of Manufacturers; and (E) a table giving the software versions used in the *Macworld Music & Sound Bible.*

Computer Rules To Live By

My overall philosophy for making music on the Mac (or for that matter, doing anything whatsoever with our favorite computer) often finds its way into the text. For the most part this is intentional, because I want to spare you the frustrations and headaches that I went through in developing my modus operandi.

Much of my philosophy about working with computers can be summed up in the following ten rules.

First Rule: The speed and power of a computer are directly proportional to one's functional efficiency and creative productivity.

Second Rule: Ease of upgrade, future viability, and expandability considerations rank foremost in purchase decisions.

Third Rule: The "if it ain't broke, don't fix it" axiom should never be applied to decisions about hardware or software upgrades, particularly system software upgrades.

Fourth Rule: The increase in efficiency and productivity gained by purchasing an item early in its life greatly exceeds the monetary gain obtained by "waiting until the price drops."

Fifth Rule: Most people use about 2 percent of their computer's power. The power user uses the other 98 percent, be it in the foreground, background, or while he or she is asleep.

Sixth Rule: Most software and hardware can be coaxed into accomplishing things never imagined or intended by their developers.

Seventh Rule: Just as the desire to compose music is not a reliable sign of talent, neither is the use of a computer capable of imparting creativity.

Eighth Rule: Any repetitive task that involves the collection, organization, processing, or retrieval of information should be delegated to a computer.

Ninth Rule: If you do not back up your hard disk, it will crash. If you do not back up your floppy disks, some day they will erase themselves.

Tenth Rule: Computers without hard drives should be illegal. Computers should be provided with the fastest, largest hard drive and the most RAM (Random Access Memory) affordable by the user. A hard drive, no matter how large in capacity, will become full much sooner than expected.

In researching this book, I personally met with representatives from nearly 90 percent of the companies included in this book. All companies were contacted by mail on at least two occasions, and notices about this book were posted on all the major telecommunications networks in the United States, in case there might have been a company or product of which I wasn't aware.

Incidentally, although the title of this book is the *Macworld Music & Sound Bible,* I have no official affiliation with *Macworld* magazine — it is one of the dozen or so magazines that regularly publish my articles.

When I started this project, I thought I had used most of the Mac music software products and hardware peripherals that were available. I was in regular contact with about 60 developers, although, granted, most of these were the mainstream, highly visible, and widely publicized products, about which I had written many magazine articles. What a pleasant surprise it was to find there were many more music and audio products available for the Mac than I had expected. Of course, this meant the book required much more work and time than I had originally planned for, especially when you consider that I had to learn all those new programs.

So writing this book has been almost as much a learning experience for me as I hope it will be for you reading it.

Christopher Yavelow
Studio City, California

Part One

The Basics

Part One

Foreword

by Craig Anderton

The Computer and the Musician

Looking over Part One, "The Basics," emphasized to me just how much lies ahead for those becoming involved with 1990s-style computerized music-making. From choosing a computer, to evaluating software, to setting up a music studio and learning how to use it efficiently, there's a lot to think about.

At first, you might wonder how you can possibly absorb the significance of all these options. But take heart: You couldn't have chosen a better time to get involved with computers. Paradoxically, the computer has matured to the point where it takes less effort to do even more powerful tasks.

Before the Macintosh there were two main computers for music, the Apple II and Commodore 64. Both were legacies of the days when computers worked solely on a text-oriented basis. When I tried to show musicians the wonders of computer-based sequencing in my little home studio, most of them tuned out during the process of entering the seemingly interminable lists of commands (not to mention the disk waits) needed just to get the thing to load a program and start functioning with some degree of efficiency. I kept telling my colleagues that computers were the wave of the future, as so many had said before me. Yet their complex operating systems were not a suitable match for people who had

spent much of their lives perfecting a non-verbal skill such as music.

Fast forward to 1984 and the introduction of the Macintosh. Musicians who had been terrified of computers suddenly had a machine that spoke their language: graphics-based, easy to use, and compact. One by one, musicians started migrating to the Mac. Forward-thinking companies like Digidrums (now Digidesign) and Opcode saw the Macintosh as the ideal computer for musicians and backed up that belief with software — primitive by today's standards, yet magical at the time. Dovetailing with the widespread adoption of MIDI, the Mac got a jump on the competition with respect to music that remains to this day. Although all major computers are supported by multiple companies making sophisticated music software, the Mac got there first, which is why the Mac — despite having a much lower installed user base than the IBM PC family — remains the computer of choice in many musicians' eyes (and, of course, ears).

There are many side effects that few would have predicted when musicians first started taking Macs into their studios (which is why you're holding a book and not a pamphlet!). When I became involved with musical applications for computers I certainly had no idea that eventually they would let you create a CD-quality recording at home with equipment costing a fraction of what it would cost to rent even a few hours of studio time . . . or that computers would open up entirely new career opportunities in sound creation and design because of the ease with which they can modify digital recordings and samples. Perhaps what surprised me the most was how wonderful a teacher a computer could be. Music became new again, as the computer provided the tools to manipulate the essence of music itself. With MIDI sequencing, every parameter of every note could be shaped and optimized. With synth editors, it became easier to create new and different sounds. When someone in my band needed to learn a part, the computer printed out the lead sheet in just a few minutes.

However, that's just the beginning. As Chapter 7 shows, a Mac music studio may veer off into professional audio, professional video, corporate multimedia, education, music publishing, and more. Many systems that started out half a decade ago with a simple sequencer have now grown to encompass digital audio recording and manipulation, and more recently, the ability to combine digital audio and MIDI sequences. Databases can locate particular sounds in seconds instead of minutes. As a bonus, just as many non-musicians have discovered music via the computer; musicians have learned about the joys of paint programs and Mac-style word processing. For me, the computer has become more and more a part of my life, even going so far as to patiently teach me

about harmony and music theory I'd previously glossed over.

In the interest of balancing out this glowing report, I should say there were times when using the Mac was so frustrating I felt like throwing it against the wall. But actually, I've spent very little time in "MIDI hell." There's usually a work-around to even the most confusing problem (and as the Mac's popularity grew, so did a network of experts whom I could tap for answers). However, you do need to realize that learning to use a computer is like learning a musical instrument; you can bang on a piano from day one and make noise, but playing the *Moonlight Sonata* takes practice. The more you educate yourself and the more time you put into your computer, the more you'll get out of it — which seems like a natural segue into the wealth of information that follows.

Just remember as you read this book that the ultimate goal of all this is to make music, so don't be overwhelmed by all the possibilities. As a friend of mine once said, a real musician can make music with two spoons and a glass of water, but all the equipment in the world won't help those who don't have music in their hearts. Think of the Mac as a way to amplify what's in your heart, and your relationship with this helpful little silicon-based life form will be off to a good start. ♩

Craig Anderton is founding editor of Electronic Musician Magazine.

Introduction to Part One

In this part of the book you'll learn all the general information that you will need to understand the rest of the book. "The Basics" is organized into sharply delineated sections, so you can easily skip over topics that you are already familiar with and focus in on exactly the information you need.

If you are not going to be doing MIDI applications or using analog tape, you may wish to skip the sections dedicated to those topics in Chapters 1, 3, 5, 6, and 7. If you already have a studio set up, you can skip Chapters 3 and 7 altogether. Conversely, if you are just setting up a studio or music workstation, you need only concern yourself with those portions of Chapters 3 and 7 that take the concept as far as you are planning to go for the time being. If you are an extremely advanced professional, you might even want to skip the nine chapters that make up "The Basics." You get the picture.

Part One discusses the elements of a Macintosh music studio that can be put under software control. These include synthesizers, digital signal processing effects, audio mixing boards, hard disk-based digital recorders, and sequencers that record MIDI information (i.e., performance information rather than acoustic information). Common peripheral devices include MIDI adaptors, mergers, thru boxes, hard disks, printers, modems, and devices dedicated to synchronization.

Categories of Macintosh music and sound applications are covered in detail, as are types of Macintosh musicians. Musical users don't fit into categories with any logical regularity. Five years ago, you would be hard-pressed to find a MIDI consultant, sound designer, or full-time programmer in the employ of a professional musician. Today, people of these job descriptions abound. The problem is, everyone seems to be doing a little bit of everybody else's job. It is difficult to find a sound designer who doesn't do some composing on the side. Similarly, most MIDI consultants are up to their elbows in sound designing as well. There are specialists out there, but the kind of power Macintoshes are putting at musicians' fingertips makes it awfully tempting to jump on this bandwagon a number of times and from a number of angles.

Part One closes with a wealth of information about setting up your Macintosh studio or workstation. Both hardware and software options are covered. Nearly two dozen equipment configurations are illustrated for you to use as models. These include general purpose setups at all user levels, as well as setups dedicated to a particular musical or audio task.

Chapter 1
Background

In this chapter...

✔ A brief history of computer music.

✔ A history of Macintosh computer music.

✔ An overview of electronic sound and acoustics.

✔ Detailed discussion of synthesis methods, digital sampling, and hybrid techniques.

✔ Everything you need to know about MIDI (the Musical Instrument Digital Interface).

✔ Tape and audio basics including digital audio.

Evolution of the Computer Music Revolution

The history of computer music is closely entwined with the history of electronic music. So here's a whirlwind review of electronic music at a pace of ten years per paragraph.

Experimentation with electronic instruments goes back to the end of the 19th century. Thaddeus Cahill built the world's first electric synthesizer in 1897. Cahill's massive Telharmonium generated sinusoidal tones and had a 36-note-per-octave keyboard. Leon Theremin's Theremin (1923) was the first widely publicized electronic instrument. The invention of recording equipment in the late 1930s paved the way for significant growth in this medium.

In the late 1940s and early 1950s, French composers Pierre Shaeffer and Pierre Henry experimented with the manipulation of recordings of natural sounds played backward, forward, and looped or spliced at various speeds, juxtapositions, and superimpositions. They called this type of music musique concrète due in part to the natural or concrète sources of the sound material.

Around the same time, other composers such as Karlheinz Stockhausen, one of the founders of the Studio for Electronic Music of the West German Radio (1951), were experimenting with sounds produced by purely electronic means, such as oscillators and sound generators.

The first electronic music concert in America is attributed to Otto Luening and Vladimir Ussachevsky at the Museum of Modern Art in New York, on

October 28, 1952. Luening and Ussachevsky collaborated on other works that combined live musicians with electronic sounds while they worked as codirectors of the Columbia-Princeton Center for Electronic Music.

Until the end of the '50s, the choice of sonic material, musique concrète, or electronic sound generation, somewhat divided electronic music into two schools of thought. Stockhausen's *Gesang der Jünglinge* (1956) is recognized as the first successful merging of both types of sonic material. By the mid-1960s, these two approaches began to be freely combined, and most serious electronic composers worked with both types of sound sources.

The first commercially available synthesizers started appearing in the late 1960s. The Moog Synthesizer, designed by Robert Moog, became publicly available in 1965 (see Figure 1-1).

In 1968, Walter Carlos released a record album of Johann Sebastian Bach's music called *Switched on Bach*. The music was performed on an early Moog synthesizer, and the commercial success of this record was a major factor in making the general public aware of the possibilities offered by electronic music.

Figure 1-1: Robert Moog (left) and Keith Emerson in front of Keith's custom Moog synthesizer, Rich Stadium, Buffalo, New York, July 1974.

By 1969, Don Buchla, who was also designing synthesizers around the same time as Moog, released a commercial modular synthesizer, the Buchla Electronic Music System. Other synthesizers would be introduced by Oberheim, Sequential Circuits, and E-mu Systems in the 1970s, and by the 1980s, the Japanese had entered the market full force.

Computers came onto the scene in the late 1950s. From the very beginning, experimentation focused in two directions: *computer-generated sound* (also known as computer sound synthesis) and *computer-assisted composition* (encompassing computer-generated music or algorithmic composition). Because synthesizers were not as widespread as they are now, computer-composed music was often transcribed to traditional notation and performed by live musicians playing traditional instruments. This practice continues to a lesser extent today.

Lejaren Hiller and Leonard Isaacson are credited with the first computer-generated composition, the *Illiac Suite* (1957), named after the ILLIAC computer at the University of Illinois, Urbana/Champaign. Although the notes were composed by the computer, the performance was realized by a traditional string quartet.

The first work in computer sound synthesis was initiated by Max Mathews at Bell Telephone Laboratories in 1959. In 1961 James Tenney became the first composer-in-residence at Bell Labs and used Mathew's MUSIC4 software to create his Stochastic String Quartet (1961). Subsequently, MUSIC4 was upgraded to MUSIC4B (and later to MUSIC5) by J.K. Randall and Hubert Howe. Bell Labs continued to attract composers such as Laurie Spiegel (see Chapter 19, "Interactive Composition and Intelligent Instruments"), and Mathews went on to develop (with Richard Moore) GROOVE (Generating Real-time Operations On Voltage-controlled Equipment).

Other computer sound synthesis research centers began to appear. One renowned institution is CCRMA (the Center for Computer Research in Music and Acoustics) at Stanford, which attracted the likes of John Chowning (inventor of FM synthesis), James A. Moorer (now with Sonic Solutions), and Leland Smith (programmer of SCORE in 1972). Paris's famous IRCAM (Institut de Recherches Coordination Acoustic Musique) was established. Newer labs include the Media Lab at MIT and CNMAT at Berkeley.

While all this was going on in America, things were happening in Europe too. Iannis Xenakis was making quite a sensation using FORTRAN IV to create what he termed "stochastic music." The Institute of Sonology (Utrecht) attracted computer composer Gottfried Michael Koenig, who developed PROJECT1 in 1964 and subsequently PROJECT2 in 1969. Koenig and his colleague and collaborator Otto Laske were the teachers of Barry Truax and William Buxton (creator of SCED in 1978). Laske, Truax, and Buxton returned to this continent to play a major role in computer sound synthesis and composition.

Nearly all of these people are alive today, with one exception: Vladimir Ussachevsky, who is often referred to as the father of American electronic music. It is interesting to note that near the end of his life, Ussachevsky embraced the Macintosh with great energy and enthusiasm, quickly graduating to the SE/30 (see Figure 1-2). Incidentally, the majority of the pioneers mentioned in this brief overview are now using Macintosh computers.

Brief History of Macintosh Computer Music
The first wave of Macintosh musicware: 1984 – 1986

❖ Notation software: First generation

❖ Software to control the Macintosh's   First generation
   internal synthesis capabilities:

Figure 1-2: Vladimir Ussachevsky at his Rhode Island studio in 1987. The Macintosh and Kurzweil are in sharp contrast to his collection of instruments from the fifties. The dials on some of the oscillators are almost as large as the Macintosh screen.

The first wave of Macintosh musicware focused primarily on *score editing* and secondarily on control of the early Macintosh's internal four-voice synthesizer.

Score editing, or using a Macintosh to deal with musical notes in a manner analogous to word processing, was released with varying degrees of success. In 1984, the year the Macintosh was introduced, Hayden Software's MusicWorks appeared as the first Macintosh music product. MusicWorks was created by Jay Fenton, who went on to program Video-Works and VideoWorks Interactive, the software that Apple used to author all of its interactive animated guided tours and that later evolved into MacroMind Director. The program included simple score

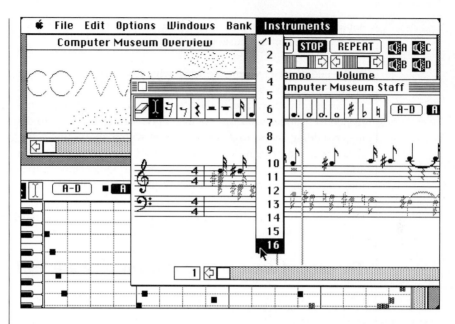

Figure 1-3: Hayden Software's MusicWorks — the first Macintosh music software (1984). The second version (1.1), pictured here, included MIDI but was never released commercially due to the concurrent collapse of Hayden Software. Notice that nearly all the user-interface features adopted by future music programs are already present in this early release. MusicWorks, the software, should not be confused with the company of the same name with which it has no association.

editing capabilities and the option to play these back through the Macintosh's built-in speaker using sounds that the user could edit (see Figure 1-3).

By the end of 1984, true first generation notation packages attempting to deal with music notation at a more professional level appeared, starting with Mark of the Unicorn's Professional Composer. This was followed shortly thereafter by Great Wave's Concertware, Utopian Software's MacMusic, and Triangle Resources's MusPrint. While only Mark of the Unicorn's Professional Composer provided score editing and printing capabilities that attempted to address the needs of serious musicians, other products such as Concertware, MacMusic, and MusicWorks integrated the Macintosh's internal synthesizer and score editing within one package.

First generation music processing packages found their niche among hobbyists and even many professional composers who were open-minded enough to put up with the monthly onslaught of bug-fixing updates. However, the serious publishing and engraving industry never really perceived these early attempts as anything more than toys. Even devoted Professional Composer users of impeccable musical qualifications were frustrated when they attempted to apply the program to music of even moderate complexity.

At the end of 1986, when Adobe Systems released its now famous Sonata font of PostScript music symbols, the music community held its breath in anticipation as literally every one of the aforementioned first generation products rushed to include PostScript compatibility. Sadly, they were to discover that merely adding access to a PostScript font within an existing software package didn't raise the program's capabilities up to a professional level any more than adding PostScript fonts to MacDraw's standard QuickDraw graphics brought it into competition with a true PostScript program like Illustrator.

One thing was certain, the introduction of PostScript into the music notation field marked the end of the first wave of Macintosh musicware.

The second wave of Macintosh musicware: 1987 – 1989

❖ MIDI sequencing software with 16 and   First generation
later 32 MIDI channels:

❖ Patch editing and sample editing   First generation
software for specific devices:

❖ Interactive composition packages: First generation

❖ Educational software for music: First generation

❖ MIDI programming languages: First generation

❖ Notation software incorporating   Second generation
PostScript and MIDI:

❖ Direct-to-hard disk recording   First generation
(Using an external peripheral
device instead of an internal card):

The second wave of music software for the Macintosh saw the release of the first music education products, a number of interactive composition programs, and several MIDI programming languages. However, the most progress was made in using the Macintosh to control external sound-generating devices from two different perspectives: editing of actual sounds (patches) of commercial synthesizers using MIDI and the recording of musical performance data via MIDI, commonly called MIDI sequencing.

MIDI sequencer software offering both MIDI input and MIDI output became available initially with Southworth's Total Music, and shortly thereafter with products such as Opcode's MIDIMac Sequencer, Mark of the Unicorn's Performer, and Great Wave's Concert Wave + MIDI. Some packages eventually provided for the conversion of MIDI data into CMN (conventional music notation). With respect to MIDI and sequencing, although these products appeared during the second wave of Macintosh musicware, the MIDI aspects were markedly first generation and all sequencers were limited to 16 MIDI channels.

While existing first generation notation software developers scrambled to release upgrades, new second generation music notation programs appeared, including HB Engraver (HB Imaging), Music Publisher (Graphic Notes), Finale (CODA), and Encore (Passport Designs). Two other products were announced, High Score and Nightingale. The former project was discontinued in 1990 due to the premature death of the programmer, Kim Stickney; the latter program is slated for release in 1991. The developers of all of these products assumed full PostScript compatibility as a prerequisite and, for some, this implied new PostScript music fonts in addition to or in conjunction with Adobe's Sonata font. Much was learned from the mistakes of the first generation packages; limitations were noted and remedied, professional publishers, engravers, and copyists were actually consulted, and every effort was made to fulfill their needs. Developers addressed the needs of composers, copyists, engravers, and publishers. The emerging desktop publishing and page layout packages were studied, and greater attention was paid to emulating the word-processing/ music-processing analogy. All this produced a quantum advancement in the state-of-the-art that continues to this day.

By the end of 1987, most sequencers had been updated so many times that they may be considered second generation products. Significant advancements were made in quantization and channel capacity. Manufacturers' upgrades began including the capability to output two sets of the standard 16 MIDI channels (for a total of 32), one group out the Macintosh's modem port and a second group out the printer port.

Until 1988, all commercially available sequencing software required that a performer play along with a metronomic "tick" generated by the computer as a reference frame for subsequent quantization. Starting in 1988, approaches to quantization began permitting the performer to play with *rubato* (expressive speeding up and slowing). These techniques employ either post-determination of beats and measures (by tapping on a specific key, for example), or pattern recognition processes to build a table of rhythmic relationships to determine intended durational values.

The third wave of Macintosh musicware: 1990 – present

❖ Direct-to-hard disk recording systems   Second generation
(using internal cards):

❖ MIDI sequencers with 512 channels   Second generation
and linked to patch libraries:

❖ MIDI sequencers begin to incorporate   Third generation
digital audio tracks:

❖ Patch librarians and sample editors   Second generation
become universal:

❖ Interactive software makes little progress: Still first generation

❖ Music education software includes   Second generation
interactive CD-ROMs:

❖ MIDI programming languages become   Second generation
visual:

❖ Notation becomes compatible with the   Second generation
Standard MIDI Files (SMF) format
and MIDI Manager:

The beginning of 1990 was a heyday for music software development. As much as the second wave had focused upon MIDI, the third wave focused on digital audio. Direct-to-hard disk recording appeared first in the IMS Dyaxis system now marketed by Studer Editech (requiring an external peripheral device and hard drive). This was followed almost immediately by Digidesign's two-channel Sound Tools package using their Sound Accelerator internal NuBus card and later with their four-channel Deck software using their Audiomedia card and their current 4- to 16-channel ProTools package. Initial input was analog, but direct digital input and output appeared very quickly.

Other areas focusing on digital audio included educational software with the introduction of interactive CD-ROMs (compact disc — read-only memory, see Chapter 4, "Choosing Your Mac") by the Voyager Company and Warner New Media. Educational music software has experienced a plethora of development since 1990.

MIDI programming languages became visual or icon-oriented with the release of Hip Software's HookUp! in 1990 and Opcode's Max in 1991. Max incorporated the control of CD-ROM drives, laser disc players, and other digital media right from the start. Even MIDI sequencers jumped on the digital audio bandwagon by allowing soundfile playback in synchrony with MIDI sequence playback.

By the middle of 1990, the MIDI channel capacity of MIDI sequencers had increased by orders of magnitude. Mark of the Unicorn's Performer began supporting up to 512 MIDI channels through novel use of unused MIDI message bytes and their MIDI Time Piece interfaces. Lone Wolf's MIDITap appeared, offering 65,000 MIDI channels to those who could afford its then $3,000 price tag.

Another advance in the realm of MIDI sequencers was the linking of patch name information to associated patch libraries and the capability to create virtual "instruments" by grouping of channel assignments that first appeared in Opcode's Vision. Mark of the Unicorn's Performer responded by increasing the capacity for virtual instruments from Opcode's 32 to a number only limited by available memory, and added other features.

By the end of 1990, MIDI sequencers entered their third generation with Opcode releasing StudioVision, the first MIDI sequencer to include digital audio tracks. Mark of the Unicorn and Steinberg followed in 1992 with Digital Performer and CuBase Audio, respectively. These programs all include digital audio of CD quality and work in conjunction with Digidesign's and other manufacturers' digital audio cards. Upgrades of existing MIDI sequencers providing compatibility with Mark of the Unicorn's 512 MIDI channel scheme began appearing in 1991, as did other interfaces supporting larger quantities of channels (such as Opcode's Studio 5). Passport Designs brought out Audio Trax, which also had digital audio (although at half the resolution of CD quality).

Due to the quantum leap that notation packages had made in their second generation, there was little progress in this third wave of Macintosh musicware other than the introduction of compatibility with SMFs and Apple's MIDI Manager. In fact, these two compatibility issues were addressed by nearly every other music software developer as well during this period. We are still waiting for the next generation of music notation packages to appear. The form these will take is discussed in Part Four, "Notation."

We have come from a single music product in 1984 to over 700 Macintosh music products in 1992. Even with only seven years of Macintosh musicware development, the sophistication of music software and hardware has reached a point where it is pretty easy to see where things are going. If the direction is not evident to you now, by the time you finish reading this book you should be equipped with enough information and foresight to draw your own conclusions.

Creating sound electronically

All musical instruments are merely reflections of the technology of the current historical period. When you think about it, there is little to distinguish electronic music instruments from acoustic instruments on a conceptual level.

In the 16th century, most instruments were made out of wood. By the 17th century, the technology of metal working had evolved to the point where more precise metal instruments could be made. By the 18th century, wood and metal technology had progressed sufficiently so that combining them in an instrument such as the piano was possible. By the middle of the 19th century, Adolphe Sax had thought enough about combining a wind instrument with a brass instrument to invent the saxophone. It is no wonder that in the 20th century, the technology of electricity has been harnessed for musical instruments. Nor is it surprising that when microprocessors appeared in the latter half of the 20th century, these should be incorporated into musical instruments as well. Electronic musical instruments are merely a product of the most advanced technology of this day, just as instruments created in earlier periods employed what was the state-of-the-art technology at that time, be it woodworking or metalworking.

Many observations that we can make about synthesizers also apply to acoustic instruments. The first correspondence concerns pitch range. In the early days of synthesis it was not uncommon to have bass synthesizers and lead synthesizers that were limited to the lower or upper range, respectively. Similarly, most acoustic instruments are limited in range. Bassoons, tubas, and cellos play best in the lower registers, while flutes, trumpets, and violins are limited to the upper registers. Similarly, many synthesizers have a limited range of only four- or five-octave keyboards. They can actually play a much wider range if controlled by computers or by way of a transposition button, if available. Nonetheless, the specifications of most synthesizers include the number of physical keys on the keyboard. This usually is stated as 49-, 61-, 76-, or 88-note, the four most common configurations of electronic keyboards.

While on the subject of keyboards, you should be aware that most electronic instruments are available in two formats: as keyboards or as modules that can be placed under the control of a separate keyboard or computer. The latter are sometimes referred to as rack-mountable modules, because there is an industry standard width of 19 inches (48 cm) for such devices that assures that they can be mounted in racks which have two mounting rails, 19 inches apart. The height of 1 rack space is measured in rack units, standardized at 1¾-inches (44 mm). As a general rule, the only thing different about a keyboard device and its rack-mountable module version is the keyboard. The interior sound-generating electronics should be identical.

One area of similarity concerns the number of notes that an instrument can play at one time. Although much more common in the early days of synthesis, even to this day some synthesizers are capable of playing only a single note at a time. These are called *monophonic*. Some acoustic instruments are also monophonic. Included among these are all brass instruments and woodwind instruments (although some woodwind players can produce more than one sound at a time using *multiphonics,* a term that is not employed in the discussion of electronic music).

Other synthesizers can play many notes simultaneously. Likewise, some acoustic instruments can play more than one note simultaneously. Examples of these are all stringed instruments, such as violins, violas, cellos, and basses, as well as guitars, pianos, and harps. Many percussion instruments can play more than a single note at a time too. These include xylophones, marimbas, and chimes. In the world of electronic instruments, the capability to produce more than one note at a time is referred to as *polyphony.*

Just as acoustic instruments have limits on the number of simultaneous notes they can sound at a time (usually equal to the number of strings an instrument has or the number of hands, fingers, or mallets that one uses to play them), so do electronic instruments normally have a finite number of notes that can be sounded simultaneously (often equal to the number of electronic oscillators that the instrument possesses). The word "voice" is used to refer to this: If an instrument is 12-voice polyphonic, that means that the instrument is capable of playing 12 notes simultaneously. Most synthesizers are capable of playing 8, 12, 16, 24, or 32 notes simultaneously. Because of the expense of each oscillator, most electronic instruments are capable of playing far fewer notes simultaneously than the number of keys they have. Many devices also have a monophonic mode in which they can play only a single note at a time. Monophonic mode is useful in simulating acoustic instruments and for solo lines where you might not want to have more than a single note at any given moment, as well as for guitar synthesizer applications (a guitar string plays only one note at a time).

Confusion arises because some electronic instrument manufacturers state the number of oscillators their instrument contains to indicate the theoretical upward limit of how many voices their device can have. This can be inaccurate because some devices require two, four, or more oscillators to produce a single pitch. To avoid accusations of impropriety in advertising, some of these same companies include a keyboard configuration that allows you to use a single oscillator for each pitch, although that particular sound is usually not as useful or as rich as multiple oscillator sounds.

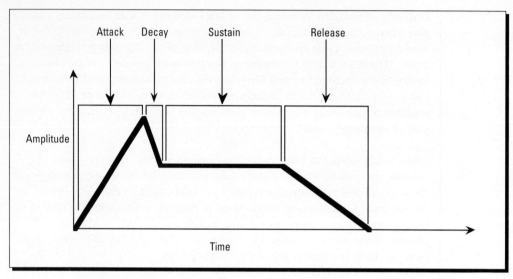

Figure 1-4: An ADSR (attack, decay, sustain, release) envelope.

You might be wondering what happens if you have an 8-voice polyphonic instrument and then play a ninth note while sustaining the previous eight. One note has to turn off to allow the new note to sound. The way this is accomplished in a device is referred to as its *channel-stealing algorithm.* Typical choices of what note to turn off are based upon different systems with different manufacturers. Some turn off the oldest note, some the softest note, some give preference to the highest or lowest note (high note or low note priority), and monophonic instruments often use last note priority (meaning that the last note to sound is the one that is played). Other schemes provide for the outer voices to be held at all costs or give preference to dropping notes of the same pitch as the new note. More sophisticated algorithms combine some or all of the above considerations.

Whether an instrument is monophonic or polyphonic, electronic or acoustic, any sound it produces changes its loudness or amplitude over time. The shape of this phenomenon is referred to as a sound's *envelope*. Envelopes on acoustic instruments are created by how fast or hard the performer blows into the instrument or drags the bow across its strings. In the acoustic world, these envelopes are sometimes referred to as articulations, dynamics, or a combination of the two. Envelopes in electronic instruments are created by *envelope generators* (EGs). Early envelope generators provided for four segments: an attack segment, a decay segment, a sustain segment, and a release segment (see Figure 1-4). For this reason they were known as ADSR envelope generators. It is now not uncommon for an electronic instrument to offer up to 256 segments (or stages) to its envelope.

Besides endowing an overall shape to the amplitude of a sound, many acoustic and electronic instruments have the capability of varying amplitude or pitch regularly or periodically over time. When an acoustic instrument varies its pitch regularly, we refer to that phenomenon as *vibrato*. When the same instrument varies its amplitude periodically, it is referred to as *tremolo*. Electronic instruments create vibrato and tremolo through the use of LFOs (low frequency oscillators). The frequency of an LFO is too low to be perceived as a distinct pitch, yet fast enough to be used to control another sound's amplitude or pitch.

One point where electronic instruments and acoustic instruments diverge is in the number of tone colors that can be played simultaneously. The musical word that refers to tone color is *timbre*. Acoustic instruments are capable of great nuance within a limited range of a single overall timbre, and some acoustic instruments can produce two timbres at once (for example, you can pluck a string of a violin with a finger on your left hand while bowing it with your right; you can bow a marimba while simultaneously striking it with a mallet).

On the other hand, since the end of the 1980s, most electronic instruments have been capable of producing a great number of radically different timbres simultaneously. Typical limits are 4, 6, 8, 10, 12, and 16. Greater numbers are possible using a technique called *layering,* where a single keyboard configuration (sometimes called a keyboard setup) actually has two to six or more different timbres on each key. This capability of playing more than one timbre at a time is referred to as *multitimbrality.* A 12-voice multitimbral instrument can play 12 different sounds simultaneously. Most instrument manufacturers just refer to their instrument as being multitimbral or not, without specifying the number of voices. This is particularly misleading, because some devices that are 16-voice polyphonic are only 8-voice multitimbral. Another area of confusion arises when synthesizers have separate outputs jacks for different sounds. Typical output configurations are 1 (mono), 2 (stereo), 4, 6, 8, and 12.

Multitimbrality should not be confused with the number of different sounds that an electronic instrument contains in its ROM or RAM, the capacity of the latter often being referred to as user presets. These days, it is not uncommon for an electronic instrument to contain 192 or more sounds, but still only be able to play a maximum of eight at any given moment. These sounds are referred to as patches (because early electronic instruments used electronic cables called patch cords to reconfigure their timbre). Other words used to refer to patches include preset, program, setup, and instrument. Unfortunately, some manufacturers use the word voice to refer to a patch. This is confusing because we use the word voice to refer to limits of polyphony and multi-timbrality.

To summarize, there are several parameters that are referred to regarding the capabilities of most electronic instruments: the number of keys, the number of voices that can be played at once, the number of different timbres that can be played at once, and the number of different sounds that the device is capable of storing in RAM or ROM.

With this in mind, an 88-note, 24-voice, multitimbral instrument with 192 patches and 128 user presets and separate outputs refers to a device with 88 keys (that can probably play a wider range when under computer control), limited to playing 24 notes simultaneously, probably capable of playing 8 different timbres simultaneously (no limit is specified, so 8 or 16 might be assumed), with 192 different sounds or tone colors permanently installed in its ROM and the possibility for the user to edit these, load in via computer, or otherwise create an additional 128 sounds for storage in the RAM. Unlike computers, the RAM in most electronic instruments does not disappear when the machine is turned off. It is kept alive by either a battery that is recharged whenever the instrument is turned on or by using a long-life, non-rechargeable battery technology. This type of RAM is technically referred to as "battery-backed RAM."

When a synthesizer is not a synthesizer

Many people call all electronic sound-generating devices synthesizers. This is not correct. There are now two general approaches to creating sound electronically: *synthesis* and *sampling*. There are also hybrid devices that create sounds by combining synthesis technology with sampling technology; this is the same underlying motivation that guided Adolphe Sax in combining woodwind and brass technology for his saxophone.

Synthesis refers to creating sounds electronically from electronically generated waveforms and signal processors. The instruments that do this are called synthesizers. While some synthesizers can be made to sound very much like acoustic instruments, there is always going to be a significant difference.

Sampling refers to re-creating sounds electronically from digital recordings of actual acoustic sounds, which are often, but not always, produced by real acoustical instruments. The instruments that take this approach are called *samplers* or *sample-players*. Although the word *sampler* is sometimes used to refer to both a device that can make digital recordings and one that can just play back digital recordings, this is technically incorrect. If there are no provisions for making the actual digital recording that is to be played back, the word sampler is a misnomer and the device is actually a sample player.

The following is a detailed discussion of the differences between synthesis and sampling.

Introduction to synthesis

There are two main approaches to electronic sound synthesis: *analog* and *digital*. These two categories embrace a large number of different techniques for the production of sound. There are even several types of hybrid synthesis that combine both analog and digital methods (the saxophone syndrome again).

The most important distinction to understand is the difference between the words *analog* and *digital*. Analog refers to something that is continuous, like a standard volume control. Digital refers to something that can be measured incrementally or represented by a series of numbers or discrete steps, like a rotary (stepped) switch. Analog things are made up of a theoretically infinite number of points, whereas digital things are made up of a finite number of points.

Analog synthesis is concerned with using voltages that can conceivably be set to any level to control musical parameters. Digital synthesis is concerned with using precise numbers to specify the values of musical parameters.

A common analogy is a glass filled with water and a glass filled with tiny beads (BBs, or ball bearings, if you like). We can measure and describe the number of beads in the glass as a finite number simply by counting them, but we cannot measure the number of "waters" in the glass (I suppose one could count the number of atoms or molecules, but it's close enough to infinite to be considered analog).

Vinyl records are analog because the variations in the grooves are continuous rather than varying by a series of measurable steps. CDs are digital, meaning that every point upon them represents a distinct number that is used to describe a measurement of sound. A photograph of a ball is analog — the number of points in the circumference is infinite. A video image of the same ball is digital because we can count the number of pixels on the video screen that make up its circumference.

Synthesis signal chain

The basic components of synthesis, whether analog or digital, are practically identical. The first item in the chain is a sound source capable of producing a continual electrical signal in the audible spectrum (20–20,000 Hz), which can be thought of as a soundwave. This element is called an *oscillator* (OSC). The user-specifiable parameters of an oscillator are usually wave form (sine, square, triangle, sawtooth, etc.) and pitch (see Figure 1-5). Usually, two or more oscillators are used to create a single voice.

Analog oscillators consist of an electrical circuit that generates a repeating (periodic or cyclical) oscillation (polarity fluctuation) of voltage. Digital

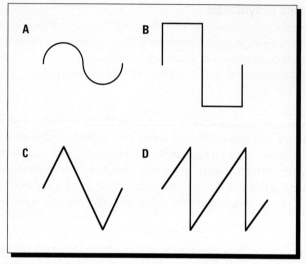

Figure 1-5: (A) Sine, **(B)** Square, **(C)** Triangle, and **(D)** Sawtooth waveforms.

oscillators store specific waveforms as a series of numbers that describe a single instance of the waveform's shape (sometimes called a wavetable). Repeatedly running through this series of numbers and converting them to analog voltage values (using a *digital-to-analog converter,* or DAC) produces a similar effect as an analog oscillator, but with very precise control.

Oscillators capable of being controlled by voltage are employed in analog synthesis and are called *voltage-controlled oscillators* (VCOs). Oscillators whose parameters may be specified by an exact number are used in digital synthesis and are called *digitally-controlled oscillators* (DCOs, sometimes DWOs, meaning *digital waveform oscillators).* The end result of controlling an oscillator digitally or with an analog voltage is similar, although, once again, digital control is much more accurate.

The next component in the chain is often a *filter* of some kind. Filters remove, reduce, or emphasize certain frequencies. They are crucial in establishing a sound's timbre because timbre is the product of a sound's frequency component. When it removes or reduces upper frequencies and passes through lower frequencies, the filter is referred to as a *low pass filter* (LPF). The opposite effect is achieved with a *high pass filter* (HPF). Other types of filters include *band pass filters* (BPFs), which only pass a specified frequency range. The opposite of a band pass filter is a *band reject filter* or *notch filter.* As with oscillators, filters may be controlled by analog voltages (in a *voltage-controlled filter,* or VCF) or digitally (in a *variable digital filter,* or VDF).

The final stage in the synthesis process is the *amplifier*. This will either be an analog *voltage-controlled amplifier* (VCA) or *variable digital amplifier* (VDA). This component is what determines the synthesized sound's loudness. It also alters a sound's volume over time.

Two other components are common to creating a synthesized sound: *low frequency oscillators* (LFOs) and *envelope generators* (EGs). When used in conjunction with an EG, the VCA is responsible for the sound's envelope, which can be as simple as a four-segment ADSR amplitude envelope or one of extreme complexity. Many synthesizers have at least one other EG that can be applied to the filter stage, although if there is only a single EG, there is often an option to choose to apply this to the VCA or VCF. More robust implementations provide for control of the oscillators by the EG or a dedicated EG.

The word *low* in low frequency oscillator, or LFO, refers to the fact that the oscillator's frequency is usually below the threshold of human hearing. The selection of waveforms is typically the same as for any oscillator. Thus, a sine wave LFO applied to a VCA produces amplitude tremolo, while an LFO applied to one of the primary oscillators produces a pitch vibrato.

To increase the versatility of LFOs many additional waveforms may be available besides the common sine, square, triangle, and sawtooth. Additional LFO waveforms that you will encounter include cosine, stair, and pulse along with the option to specify polarity (positive or negative) and direction, such as rising sawtooth or positive falling sawtooth.

Within the context of these five standard elements (VCO or DCO, VCF or VDF, VCA or VDA, EG, and LFO), it is possible to introduce any number of other modifiers, including *time variant filters* and *time variant amplifiers* (TVFs and TVAs), *mixers, inverters, negators, multipliers,* and *ring modulators*. The latter is a circuit that takes two input pitches and outputs two different pitches, one being the sum of the two input frequencies, the other being the difference. In some devices there are additional EGs and LFOs, which can be used locally (applied to a particular voice) or globally (applied to the device as a whole). In others, one oscillator may be used to control or modulate the frequency of another oscillator. Furthermore, analog and digital versions of each of the components can be mixed freely to create a variety of hybrid synthesis techniques.

Most synthesizers provide for any of the components to an individual sound to be dynamically controlled by the performer in real time. The most obvious example of this concept is the specification of pitch via a musical keyboard. Other common sources that are often linked to dynamic changes of the parameter values to any sound component are *attack velocity* (the speed a key is struck), *release velocity* (the speed at which a key is released), *pressure* (how

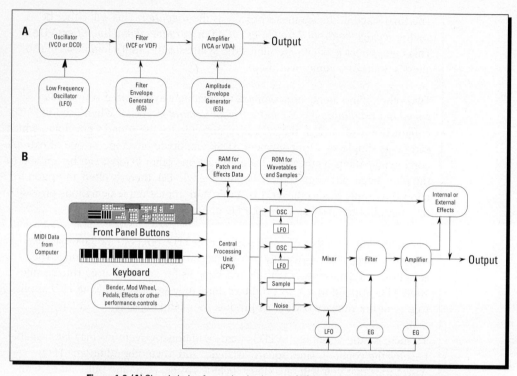

Figure 1-6: (A) Signal chain of a synthesized sound. **(B)** Synthesized sound in the context of an electronic instrument. Not all devices employ all the components pictured. For example, older instruments may not have any built-in DSP (digital signal processing) effects or capabilities to interact with an external effect before the signal reaches the output jacks. Devices with this latter capability have effects sends and returns on their back panels.

hard the key is pressed upon after it has reached the bottom of its normal travel distance), *pitch wheel, modulation wheel,* and various external pedals.

The entire process is shown in Figure 1-6.

With these fundamentals in mind, several types of synthesis are commonly found in commercially available synthesizers. Some devices incorporate more than one of these in a single unit, while others rename their synthesis techniques to differentiate themselves from competing manufacturers. Common approaches listed roughly in order of appearance or proliferation include:

❖ Subtractive synthesis
❖ Additive synthesis
❖ Frequency Modulation (FM) synthesis (also called algorithmic synthesis)

❖ Phase Distortion Synthesis (PDS)
❖ Resynthesized Pulse Code Modulation (RS-PCM) synthesis
❖ Karplus-Strong synthesis (also known as plucked string synthesis)
❖ Linear/Arithmetic synthesis (L/A)
❖ Advanced Integrated (AI) synthesis
❖ Advanced Vector (AV) synthesis
❖ Variable Architecture Synthesis Technology (VAST)

Subtractive synthesis

Many analog synthesizers use subtractive synthesis to generate sounds. The main principle at work in this form of synthesis is that you start with a very complex waveform, usually produced by one or two VCOs that are often mixed with *white* or *pink noise*. White noise is a random signal that theoretically contains an even distribution of all possible frequencies within a specified frequency range, and pink noise is an even distribution of all frequencies within each octave. The distinction is significant because in actuality, there are double the number of frequencies in each octave as one rises in pitch. There are also other "colors" of noise in use. These include red, green, blue, and azure. Regardless of its color, noise provides a rich harmonic content to the otherwise bland oscillator tones.

A VCF is the most important component to subtractive synthesis. Filters subtract specified harmonics from a noisy sound source. Because of the importance of the filter in this process, the type of filters any given manufacturer employed tended to provide the individual signature color of analog synthesizers. Once the sound has been reduced to its desired timbre, it is passed on to the VCA stage. All the previously mentioned possibilities of adding EGs and LFOs into the process are usually taken advantage of.

Most early analog synthesizers use this technique, as do some that are still commercially available. Notable recent examples of these are Oberheim's Matrix 6 and Matrix 1000, and Roland's JX10 and Alpha Juno. A big disadvantage of analog synthesizers is that an analog oscillator is not as precise as a digital oscillator with respect to its tuning.

Additive synthesis

Additive synthesis takes the opposite approach to that of subtractive. The principle that engendered additive synthesis was discovered by Jean Baptiste Fourier in the 19th century. Fourier's theory stated that any complex waveform could be reduced to a number of component sine waves, each with its own pitch and amplitude. In systems that provide for the variance of these component sine waves over time, each individual sine wave is assigned its own EG.

Many newer systems use digital wavetables for the creation of the large number of sine waves required. Early uses of additive synthesis are found in Hammond organs, which use electromechanical tone generators. More recent additive devices include the Kawai K5 and the Kurzweil K150. Additive synthesis is also available via Digidesign's Softsynth (see Chapter 10, "Sound Generation").

The introduction of wavetables had other ramifications in the industry. Because any series of numbers can function as a wavetable, an offshoot of this method of storage called *wavetable synthesis* was born and employed extensively by Korg and Ensoniq.

Frequency modulation

Frequency Modulation synthesis was one of the most important developments in electronic music. Created by John Chowning at Stanford University in California; it was licensed to Yamaha, after no American manufacturer had shown any interest in it; FM synthesis was the driving force behind their popular DX7 synthesizer.

If you find it confusing that FM radio uses the same acronym, you may rest assured that the same procedures are being used for both. The real confusing aspect of FM synthesis is that it dispenses with the oscillator-filter-amplifier model that many musicians find easy to grasp.

FM synthesis starts with two frequencies that are in the audible spectrum. One of the frequencies is then used to control (called modulate in this case) the other frequency. The waveform doing the controlling is called the *modulator* and the waveform being modulated is called the *carrier*. The amount of the modulator used to modulate the carrier and the difference in pitch between the frequencies of the two oscillators are the primary factors influencing the resultant timbre of the sound. In Yamaha parlance, both the modulators and carriers used in FM synthesis are referred to as *operators*. Yamaha makes 4- and 6-operator FM instruments.

An EG is sometimes applied to the carrier to provide for amplitude variance over time. Furthermore, most FM synthesis algorithms include a feedback loop that taps into the output of one of the operators and feeds it back to its own or another operator's modulator input (see Figure 1-7). There are many configurations of the operators possible with FM synthesis, but the real problem is that it is difficult to intuit what the effect of changing a parameter value will be.

Phase distortion synthesis

After Yamaha flooded the market with FM synthesizers, Casio released a new type of digital synthesis called Phase Distortion Synthesis (PDS) with the intent to provide the richness of timbre associated with FM but with the degree of control of subtractive synthesis.

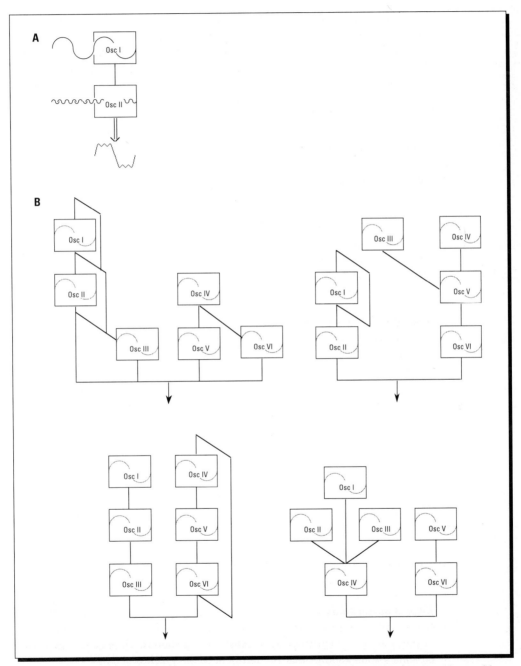

Figure 1-7: (A) Effect of a modulator upon a carrier wave. **(B)** Graphic representations of some of the common FM algorithms.

PDS is pretty easy to understand if you comprehend the concept of phase with respect to a regular soundwave such as a sine wave. When the sine wave reaches the peak of its positive curve, it is said to have a phase of 90 degrees. When it reaches the next zero point it is said to be at 180 degrees. When it reaches its negative peak it is said to be at 270 degrees, and when it finally returns to 0 again it is said to be at 360 degrees (equal to 0 degrees of the following period). With a sine wave, these points are all evenly spaced in time. PDS distorts the amount of time that it takes for each of these points to be reached, in the process making them irregularly spaced.

All that is necessary to synthesize sound in this manner are wavetables storing the regular waveform characteristics and waveshapers that dictate the rate at which each stage of the waveforms is to be reached. Filters are usually not a major component to PDS, and envelope generators, when used by Casio, have up to eight segments with one defined as a sustain segment. Because all envelope stages except the sustain segment are specified by indicating the rate at which the VCA reaches an indicated amplitude level, Casio refers to these as *rate-level envelope generators* (RLEGs).

Resynthesized Pulse Code Modulation

Roland recently introduced a form of synthesis that they call RS-PCM for Resynthesized Pulse Code Modulation.

Resynthesis of sound is related to additive synthesis. The heart of resynthesis is a *Fast Fourier Transform* (FFT) of a sampled sound, in this case, a sound recording using the *pulse code modulation,* or PCM technique. The resynthesizer then analyzes the FFT data to determine the frequency of the sine waves used to create the original sound. Depending upon the accuracy of this analysis, which, by the way, carries extreme computational overhead, the original sound may be re-created using additive techniques.

An important distinction between additive synthesizers and resynthesizers is the fact that resynthesizers often offer the same degree of flexibility of trans-forming the individual sine waves as a normal additive synthesizer. However, you are starting with a known quantity rather than building a sound from the bottom up.

Karplus-Strong synthesis

Karplus-Strong synthesis (named after Kevin Karplus and Alan Strong) is a type of physical modeling that creates realistic string sounds. The process involves creating a sound source that is equivalent to the pluck of a string and recirculating this sound through a filter that duplicates the time-varying spectrum of a vibrating string.

Karplus-Strong synthesis is very flexible for simulating plucked string and drum instruments. Any type of pluck, pick, or hammer at any force can be accommodated, as can any length of string and the location of the virtual pluck upon the virtual string. Sophisticated implementations provide for the sympathetic vibrations of adjacent strings and the resonance of the instrument's body (by simultaneously feeding some of the output of the original algorithm into other algorithms that model the characteristics of those elements). In this way you can model the exact sound that, for example, a two-ton sledge hammer would create if striking a string that was several miles in length. Physical modeling of sounds other than plucked strings is still in its infancy.

Introduction to digital sampling

Digital sound sampling is a new enough field that an explanation of the technique is in order. It can be easily understood by making an analogy to motion pictures. In a film, many consecutive still photographs of a continuous (analog) motion are projected rapidly to re-create the illusion of continuous motion. Sound also exists within an analog continuum, and sound sampling, or digitizing, captures "snapshots" of a sound (samples), which are subsequently played back at a rate normally between 5,000 and 100,000 samples per second in order to re-create the original sound. These sound snapshots are called samples and the process of recording these samples is known as *sampling* or *digitizing*.

Regarding questions of fidelity of the reproduction to the original, both sound and film share common concerns. Two specifications characterize sampling technology: *rate* and *resolution*. To clarify these two considerations I will return to the motion picture analogy. The size of a single frame in a film represents its resolution, and thus places actual physical limitations on the fidelity with which a film can reproduce visual information. Varying degrees of quality are dependent upon whether 8, 16, 35, or 70 millimeter film is used to capture the still photographs of analog motion.

Working hand-in-hand with resolution is the rate of speed at which the still photographs are projected. Typical 35mm film used in commercial movie-houses is projected at 24 frames per second and the general audience accepts this rate as adequate to achieve the illusion of continuous motion. If you have been fortunate enough to attend a projection of "Showscan" type movies, you will understand that film of a larger resolution, 70mm in this case, being projected at a rate which moves the film at nearly ten times the speed of conventional film projection, creates a vastly superior illusion of visual motion — an illusion similar to that of true 3-D projection without the glasses. This is certainly high fidelity with respect to film.

Sampling rate and resolution play an even larger role in determining the degree of credibility within the domain of sound reproduction. Average listeners are far less forgiving than filmgoers. The "size" (or resolution) of each sound sample is analogous to the size of film in a motion picture. Since a single sample consists of the measurement of an analog (i.e., continuous) voltage via an *analog to digital converter* (ADC), using a larger range of numbers for measuring this voltage permits a more accurate representation of the voltage.

Because digital computers use binary bits to represent numbers, the maximum number of bits available for each measurement determines the highest number that can be represented and thus, the incremental range within which all measurements must be scaled. The largest number that can be represented by 8 bits is 256; thus, 8-bit sampling requires that all voltages be rounded off to only 256 different values. 12-bit sampling offers resolution to 4,096 different steps and 16-bit sampling provides a range of 65,536. Theoretically, each additional bit adds approximately 6 dB (decibels) to the signal-to-noise ratio. However, in practice, many sampling devices, particularly those employing a technique known as "block-floating point," periodically send an additional 4, 6, or 8 bits of data along with their samples for the purpose of providing additional information about the sound's waveform. This information can be used to control VDAs and VDFs and may raise the dynamic range considerably.

The rate at which sound samples are captured as well as how fast they are output is almost as important as sample resolution when considering the fidelity of a digitally sampled sound to the original analog signal. A mathematician named Nyquist has proven, in what is now referred to as the Nyquist Theorem, that a minimum of two samples is necessary to represent a given soundwave. Therefore, to represent a pure sound with a frequency of 440 Hz, it is necessary to sample that sound at a minimum rate of 880 samples per second. In reality, most sounds are complex waveforms with overtones extending well beyond the average human range of hearing, or 20,000 Hz. Thus, for the accurate reproduction of most musical sounds, a minimum sampling rate of 40,000 samples per second is necessary. On the other hand, the degree to which overtones of frequencies higher than 10,000 to 12,000 Hz contribute to one's perception is debatable. These high overtones are of such low dynamic intensity (i.e., volume) that many people argue that a sampling rate of 25,000 samples per second is adequate, yet others feel sampling rates should be raised to 100 kHz or more in order to provide better high frequency response. Your point of view probably depends on how well you can hear high frequencies — both old age and hearing loss tend to affect high frequencies the most. As a reference point, the fundamental frequency of the highest note on a piano (C8) is 4,186 Hz.

Figure 1-8 shows a complete illustration of the sampled sound film analogy.

How Sampling Works: If you've ever looked closely at a compact disc you may have wondered where the grooves are that you used to see on analog vinyl LPs. In case you aren't aware of it, those grooves have been replaced by the same sort of ones and zeroes that your computer uses for everything it does. Here's how it works: Just like a motion picture creates the illusion of movement by playing back many consecutive still pictures at a rate so fast that our eye doesn't notice the separate images, digital audio plays back "snapshots" of sounds at a rate so fast your ear doesn't detect the separate samples, as they are called. While it only takes 24 frames of visual images per second to fool the eye with moving pictures, it takes 44,100 sound samples per second to replicate sound. Similarly, just as the size of each image affects realism in film (notice the difference between 8mm, 16mm, 35mm, and 70mm), the size of a digital audio sample contributes to its fidelity.

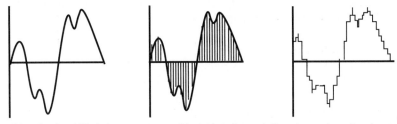

With respect to digital audio, a "sample" is, simply put, a measurement of the electrical voltage required to create a sound wave at any given moment — the more accurate these measurements are, the more convincing their subsequent re-conversion back into soundwaves will be. The conversion of sound into the digital domain is referred to as "analog to digital" conversion and is performed by chips referred to as "ADC"s (Analog to Digital Converters). Conversely, the re-conversion from the digital domain into the analog sound world is accomplished by "DAC"s (Digital to Analog Converters). In the above illustration, the rightmost diagram represents an analog waveform. The center diagram shows the samples (measurements of voltage) taken at regular intervals. The leftmost diagram shows the waveform reconstructed from the samples and illustrates why a greater number of samples per second results in a more accurate representation of the original sound.

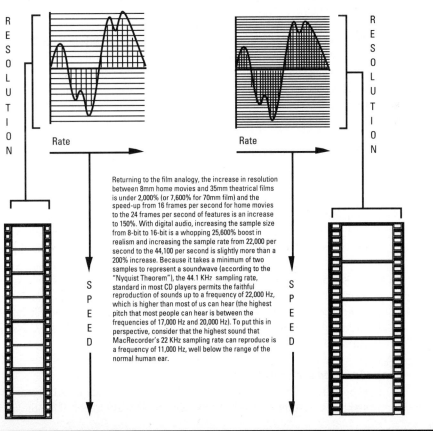

Returning to the film analogy, the increase in resolution between 8mm home movies and 35mm theatrical films is under 2,000% (or 7,600% for 70mm film) and the speed-up from 16 frames per second for home movies to the 24 frames per second of features is an increase to 150%. With digital audio, increasing the sample size from 8-bit to 16-bit is a whopping 25,600% boost in realism and increasing the sample rate from 22,000 per second to the 44,100 per second is slightly more than a 200% increase. Because it takes a minimum of two samples to represent a soundwave (according to the "Nyquist Theorem"), the 44.1 KHz sampling rate, standard in most CD players permits the faithful reproduction of sounds up to a frequency of 22,000 Hz, which is higher than most of us can hear (the highest pitch that most people can hear is between the frequencies of 17,000 Hz and 20,000 Hz). To put this in perspective, consider that the highest sound that MacRecorder's 22 KHz sampling rate can reproduce is a frequency of 11,000 Hz, well below the range of the normal human ear.

Figure 1-8: How sampling works.

Newer approaches to sound generation
Combining synthesis and sampling

The latest fashion among electronic instrument manufacturers is that of combining sampled sounds with synthesized sounds. Although most of these new techniques boil down to the same principles being marketed by different manufacturers under a different name, four approaches are referred to very frequently: L/A, AI, AV, and VAST.

Linear/Arithmetic synthesis

Linear/Arithmetic, or L/A, synthesis was introduced by Roland in 1987. It started the trend of combining digital samples (predominantly of attacks lasting a fraction of a second) with digital waveform tables. TVFs and TVAs ensured extremely fresh sounds, each with a unique evolution in the time domain. Ring modulators, popular in early analog synthesis, returned to play a major role in Roland's new synthesis. The reason that sampled attacks are used is that the attack portion of a sound is usually the most harmonically complex and difficult to synthesize, as well as providing the primary aural "cue" that differentiates instruments.

Two "partials" (meaning parts of the sound, not overtones, in Roland's terminology) are combined to make the raw material that will undergo TVF and TVA transformations. These two sources can be any combination of PCM sam-ples with digital waveforms (including two PCM samples or two digital wave-forms) that are mixed together or ring modulated. Besides PCM samples, both pitched and unpitched waveform loops are available, as are sound effect loops.

Advanced Integrated synthesis

In mid-1988, Korg's M1 and M1r, followed by their T1, T2, and T3 keyboards, introduced Advanced Integrated (AI) synthesis. AI (not to be confused with artificial intelligence) expanded upon Roland's L/A innovation of including sampled waveforms. Instead of just including sampled attacks, these devices brought in 4MBs of onboard 16-bit samples in ROM. Also included in the system are two multi-effects processors and a wide variety of routing possibilities.

While some of these are attack transients, others are attacks followed by a looped single-cycle waveform, and others are *multisamples*. Multisamples refer to keyboard setups where, instead of a single sampled soundfile having to be stretched over the entire keyboard, multisampled soundfiles are assigned at various intervals along the keyboard.

Advanced Vector synthesis

Korg followed their AI synthesis technology with Advanced Vector (AV) synthesis, first introduced in 1990 with their Wavestation. Like their AI devices, this type of synthesis includes both waveforms and 4MBs of 16-bit sampled soundfiles (though no multisamples) stored in ROM. Also included are 32 digital oscillators, each with its own VDF, VDA, EG, and a pair of LFOs, as well as two stereo digital dynamic multi-effects processors. The important departure from AI synthesis are wave sequencing (the capability of creating sequences of waveforms with up to 255 steps) and the inclusion of vector synthesis.

The original incarnation of vector synthesis was the Sequential Prophet VS. Korg's Wavestation development team was largely made up of ex-Sequential employees, so the incorporation of an advanced form of vector synthesis could be expected. There are several reasons for calling this reappearance of vector synthesis "advanced." First, there is the fact that the two to four sound sources involved can include any or all of the available ROM material, that is, sampled sounds, waveforms, and waveform sequences. Second, the sounds are 16-bit. Finally, the joystick-controlled voice-mixing occurs after the amplification stage. Contrast this to Sequential's earlier version of vector synthesis that used 12-bit sounds which did not include sampled sound and required the mixing of the waveforms prior to any processing.

Variable Architecture Synthesis Technology

In 1991, Kurzweil Music Systems, after having undergone bankruptcy and reorganization, was purchased by Young Chang Pianos. The influx of Korean capital into their R & D (research and development) division made possible the introduction of VAST (Variable Architecture Synthesis Technology) in the Kurzweil 2000. As with all the newer technologies, VAST combines sampled sounds with synthesized ones. The words *variable architecture* refer to the fact that Kurzweil's custom VLSI (very large scale integration) chips can be user-configured to accomplish just about any type of synthesis that has been or is currently being exploited, while providing the flexibility to realize new, as yet unthought of types of synthesis.

Along with an extremely open-ended synthesis engine, VAST includes an on-board sampler as well as 4MBs of ROM samples (of the impeccable standard established in their earlier products), RAM expandable to 64MBs using any combination of standard Macintosh SIMMS (1MB, 4MB, 8MB, or 16MB), SCSI (small computer system interface, see Chapter 4, "Choosing Your Mac") with option for a built-in hard drive, 1.4MB floppy disk drive capable of reading almost all encompassing variety of file formats, and digital inputs.

Impact of newer synthesis techniques

As each new synthesis technique appears, often the device that introduced it becomes the "hottest" piece of gear for a short period. This is easily attributable to the fact that the introduction of a new form of synthesis almost always heralds the introduction of a new palette of previously unheard sounds.

With this in mind, tracing the hottest synthesizers of each year usually corresponds to a timeline of reflecting the appearance of new synthesis techniques. When FM synthesis became commercially available, Yamaha's DX and TX series of instruments dominated the electronic music scene (roughly 1983 to 1986). When L/A synthesis became available in 1987, the hottest piece of gear was Roland's D-50 and other Roland models that exploited it. By mid-1988, Korg had introduced AI synthesis, and the devices that provided it (their M1 and T series instruments) dominated the market. Toward the end of 1990, Korg's own Wavestation with its advanced vector synthesis had eclipsed AI. While it is too early to tell at this time, many people expect that Kurzweil's new VAST synthesis will be the hit of 1992. Another contender is Peavey's Digital Phase Modulation synthesis, which includes interpolative sampling.

MIDI — The Musical Instrument Digital Interface

MIDI, the Musical Instrument Digital Interface developed in 1982, is an international specification used by musical instruments that contain microprocessors to communicate with other microprocessor-controlled instruments or devices (including computers such as the Macintosh, lighting controllers, mixers, and just about anything else). It is a sort of "synthesizer Esperanto."

The first synthesizer to speak MIDI was the Sequential Prophet 600 in 1983. Almost every electronic sound-generating device marketed since then has had MIDI capabilities. Indeed, it is in a manufacturer's interest to include MIDI in a product to ensure a certain degree of compatibility with all other manufacturers of similar products.

The MIDI Specification

The format of MIDI data was codified by representatives from synthesizer manufacturers Oberheim, Roland, and Sequential Circuits, who were subsequently joined by representatives from Kawai, Korg, and Yamaha. Shortly thereafter, two organizations were created to continue development of MIDI: The MIDI Manufacturers Association (MMA) and the Japan MIDI Standards Committee (JMSC). Their work is presented in a document called the MIDI Specification, often referred to as the MIDI Spec, which was made available to the general public in August of 1983.

The official information network for the MIDI industry is the International MIDI Association (IMA). The IMA is the exclusive distributor of the MIDI Specification document and related addenda. The organization also publishes a monthly bulletin that is a valuable resource. Anyone can become a member.

MIDI data flows over cables with standardized 5-pin DIN (Deutsche Industrie Norm) connectors serially, at a rate of 31.25 KBaud. The bits passing through MIDI cables are organized into MIDI "messages." MIDI cables carry MIDI data in one direction, hence there is a necessity to have both MIDI IN ports and MIDI OUT ports on most MIDI devices. A third MIDI THRU port for the purpose of immediately passing on information received at a device's MIDI IN port has become common enough to be considered standard. By using a device's MIDI THRU port, information not addressed to the specific device can be passed on to the appropriate device intended to respond to the information. In this manner, many devices can be "daisy-chained" together, all responding to a single MIDI controller, keyboard, computer, or other device capable of producing MIDI data.

One important rule is that MIDI OUTs are always connected to MIDI INs and MIDI INs are normally connected to MIDI OUTs, although they can be connected to MIDI THRUs.

Keep in mind that MIDI communicates performance data, not actual sound. MIDI can tell what note is being held down, how hard the key was struck, if any additional pressure was applied to the key after being struck, when and how quickly the key is released, and if any other controls such as sliders, wheels, switches, or pedals have been moved. It does not know anything about the sound that follows the key press, other than perhaps the patch number (or program number) of the sound. Because all devices use different numbering schemes, knowing the program number tells us nothing about the sound's actual timbre.

Addenda to the MIDI Specification

The original MIDI Specification has had several addenda. The first addendum occurred in 1986. This included more continuous controller definitions and a provision for system exclusive codes. System exclusive messages (called SysEx) are device specific and are reserved for special use by each manufacturer. When a SysEx message is sent down a MIDI cable, only devices made by the manufacturer whose SysEx ID is specified in the message will respond.

Also included in the 1986 addendum was a provision for something called the *sample dump standard* (SDS). SDS works in conjunction with a reserved SysEx code called Non-real time to allow the transfer of bulk samples between two devices.

In February of 1987, a "MIDI Time Code and Cueing Detailed Specification" was added as a supplement to the MIDI 1.0 Specification. *MIDI Time Code,* or MTC, is a way to specify absolute time for synchronization applications much in the same way the SMPTE (Society of Motion Pictures and Television Engineers) Time Code is used with video and film. The original MIDI Spec provided for a rudimentary form of relative synchronization that relies upon MIDI timing clocks being transmitted every $\frac{1}{24}$ of a quarter note. The location of an event using MIDI timing clocks is always specified as a certain number of measures, beats, and clocks relative to the beginning of the musical work (for example, the 4th beat of measure 12) rather than an absolute location as is the case with SMPTE (for example, 1 hour, 11 minutes, 17 seconds, and 8 frames). For most practical purposes, MTC corresponds to SMPTE with the exception being that, although accuracy to a quarter frame is assured, the complete SMPTE Time Code is only updated every two frames. Synchronization is discussed in detail in Part Seven, "Film, Video, and Synchronization."

A third major addition to the MIDI Spec occurred in July of 1988 and provided for Standard MIDI Files (SMFs). SMFs arose from the fact that one primary concern of MIDI is the recording of sequences of notes, including information about pitch, timing, on-velocity, off-velocity, patch-change, and various front panel synthesizer controls. Such recordings of MIDI data are called MIDI sequences. Before the implementation of SMFs, one of the problems facing microcomputer-controlled music studios was the fact that most software developers have a unique and often proprietary data format for saving information into files.

The option to save or open a MIDI sequence in the SMF format is often found in the "Save" and "Open" dialog boxes of music software. Some programs provide for this by offering a menu item named "Export..." or "Import...," both of which allow the passing of SMFs from one program to another. The advantages of SMFs for software manufacturers are similar to advantages of MIDI itself for hardware manufacturers. A file saved as an SMF in one person's MIDI sequencer can be opened, played, and edited with another software manufacturer's sequencer, notation program, or algorithmic composition tool. Patch data can also be saved in SMF format. Furthermore, SMFs are compatible across all computer platforms and therefore provide the only gateway to using MIDI sequence data captured by Macintosh software on an Atari, IBM, or other computer, in the rare event that such intercommunication were required.

MIDI's SDS and SMF have had a major impact upon telecommunications networks dedicated to music. For the first time, people with different manufacturers' sequencers and different brands of computers could communicate music and sound data to one another.

In 1990, a new Bank Select message was added to the MIDI Spec. Also added at this time was an extended definition of effect controllers.

In 1991, a "General MIDI mode message" protocol was added to the MIDI Spec at the urging of Roland and Microsoft. The incentive for this addition was to address issues in the ever-growing consumer and multimedia markets. The desire to be able to "plug and play" was also a contributing factor.

Among other things, General MIDI mode consists of a standardized list of patches that are all assigned to the same numbers, a universal patch location scheme if you will. This means that when a device is in General MIDI mode, for example, patch 1 is always an acoustic grand piano, patch 25 is a nylon stringed guitar, patch 41 is a solo violin, and so on. All 128 possible patch numbers have explicit assignments covering just about any instrument of the orchestra, as well as many standard electronic instruments, synthesizer timbres, and sound effects. Also specified by General MIDI mode is a standardized channel mapping of sounds for the first ten MIDI channels. For example, MIDI channel 10 is reserved for rhythm or drum parts.

Besides standardized patch numbers and channels, General MIDI mode also includes standardized voice parameters, including envelope. Perhaps the most welcome part of General MIDI is a standardized mapping of drum sounds to note numbers. Prior to this, playing a drum part on a different drum machine than the one it was created upon always resulted in cacophony, because there was no standardization of note numbers with respect to sound. On one device, Middle C might be a bass drum; on another, it might be an antique cymbal.

The ramifications of General MIDI are extensive. General MIDI may be a major player in the CD+MIDI Specification (a standard that includes a MIDI data track on audio CDs), as well as have an impact upon education applications where the set of available sound-generating devices can never be anticipated. While many professionals might never use it, consumers, multimedia producers, educators, and anyone who wants to be able to have their MIDI sequences play identically (or as closely as possible to their original intent), regardless of the synthesizer(s) that are used in playback, will welcome General MIDI as the solution to many problems that previously required additional hours of editing data for compatibility with devices other than those the data was created with.

Understanding MIDI messages

All MIDI messages consist of at least two bytes. The first part of the message is called the *status byte* and identifies what type of information is to follow. The next byte or bytes are called *data bytes,* because they provide the data indicating the actual value of the item specified in the status byte.

There are two main types of MIDI messages. These are called *Channel messages* and *System messages.* Channel messages usually include a MIDI channel number as the destination of the message. System messages do not include a channel number and are acted upon no matter what channel(s) a device is assigned to. Channel messages are further divided into *Channel Voice messages* and *Channel Mode messages.* System messages are divided into *System Exclusive messages, System Common messages,* and *System Real Time messages.*

Channel messages   To understand channel messages you must first understand an important concept, which is that most MIDI data is assigned to a
specific MIDI channel (one of sixteen possible). These are numbered from 1 to
16, and a MIDI cable can transmit information destined for any number of
MIDI channels simultaneously. It's sort of like what happens with cable
television. All the channels are there on the single cable, but you choose
which one you want to watch at any given moment.

Similarly, synthesizers and other devices can be instructed to listen for one or
more specific channels and to ignore data received on other channels. In this
way you can have a MIDI sequence playing a 16-track sequence with each
track set to a separate MIDI channel and 16 different synthesizers, each with a
different sound set to respond to data only if it is coming on a specified
channel. As noted in the section on synthesizers, many synthesizers and
samplers can be set to respond with a different sound on each MIDI channel.
Furthermore, it is becoming increasingly common for software to address more
than 16 MIDI channels by using special hardware interfaces that assign a
separate set of 16 MIDI channels to each of their MIDI outputs and provide a
means for specifying which cable to direct data to.

The other type of channel messages, Channel Voice messages, usually have
two data bytes. Table 1-1 illustrates the available channel.

Table 1-1: Channel Voice messages	
Note On	Key number (from 0 to 127 with middle C being 60)
	Key velocity (from 0 to 127 — how fast you pressed the key down)
Note Off	Key number (from 0 to 127 with middle C being 60)
	Key velocity (from 0 to 127 — how fast you release the key)
Channel Pressure	Aftertouch (from 0 to 127 — additional pressure applied to a key after it has traveled all the way down. Also called Monophonic Key Pressure because pressing down on any key while multiple keys are held is the same as applying the same amount of pressure to all keys held on the keyboard. Pressure can be linked to control any parameter of a sound that offers such control.)
Polyphonic Key Pressure	Key number (from 0 to 127 with middle C being 60)
	Aftertouch (from 0 to 127 — additional pressure applied to individual keys after the key has traveled all the way down. Because this requires a separate pressure sensor for every key, this is much less common than monophonic pressure. Pressure can be linked to control any parameter of a sound that offers such control.)

Table 1-1: Channel Voice messages (continued)

Program Change	Patch or program number (from 0 to 127 — indicates that a device should change to the sound associated with the program number.)
Bank Select	Bank Number (from 1 to 16,384 — switches to the specified patch bank. Very useful for devices that have more than 128 different sounds in them because the program change message itself is limited to 128 values; until the addition of the Bank Select message in 1990, you always had to give up a portion of your sounds if there were more than 128 in your device.)
Control Change	Controller Number (many controllers on the front panels of electronic instruments have specific numbers. Three control types exist and certain controller numbers are reserved for them. Control numbers 0 to 63 are continuous controllers, meaning that they can send full range of values. Control numbers 64 through 95 can be used for switches, meaning that they can be on or off; they can also be used for continuous controllers. Control numbers 96 and 97 are data increment controllers, meaning that pressing a button or turning a dial increments data directly. Some examples: Controller 1 is the Modulation Wheel, a continuous controller; Controller 64 is the Sustain Pedal, a switch.) Controller Value (from 0 to 127 — additional data can be added to extend the range to 16,384 values.)
Pitch Bend	The position of the Pitch Wheel (two bytes are sent to provide a value range of 16,384 settings.)

Channel Mode messages Channel Mode messages set the receiving mode for a device as a whole. There are four modes that a receiving instrument can be in, and each one affects the way incoming data is processed (see Table 1-2).

Table 1-2: Channel Mode messages

Omni On / Poly	Mode 1 (the device will respond polyphonically to incoming messages regardless of their channel assignment. If you have separate sounds assigned to separate MIDI channels, they will all sound simultaneously when your device is in this mode. Many synthesizers are set to this mode at the factory, so they will be in this mode the moment you power them on the first time.)
Omni On / Mono	Mode 2 (the device will respond monophonically to incoming messages regardless of their channel assignment. In essence, your synthesizer becomes a monophonic synthesizer. This is not a very useful mode and is seldom implemented.)

Table 1-2: Channel Mode messages (continued)

Omni Off / Poly	Mode 3 (the device responds polyphonically to data coming in on one or more user-specified MIDI channels. This is a very common setting both for instruments that are not multitimbral and those that are. In the latter case, sometimes the actual synthesizer will refer to this mode as "multi" mode. *Dynamic voice allocation* is a term often associated with this mode and a very desirable feature in electronic instruments.. This means that the instrument's processor determines on-the-fly, the optimum distribution of voices across the various MIDI channels, changing the number of voices assigned to a channel as necessary.)
Omni Off / Mono	Mode 4 (the device responds monophonically to data coming in on one or more user-specified MIDI channels. Essentially, each channel becomes an individual monophonic synthesizer.)

Some Channel Mode messages don't deal with the reception mode with respect to voice/channel assignments:

Local Control	On or Off (if local control is off, the keyboard of a synthesizer is, for all practical purposes, disconnected from the sound-generating electronics. The beauty of this is that the keyboard can be transmitting data on one MIDI channel while the synthesizer is receiving on another. In other words, pressing keys on the keyboard will not trigger sounds on the synthesizer connected to the keyboard, but will send out MIDI data to the MIDI OUT port.)
All Notes Off	(This message, if supported by the receiving synthesizer, turns off all notes on the receiving device. It is useful when notes become stuck, having somehow missed their Note Off command.)
Reset All Controllers	(Sets all MIDI controller values to zero.)

System messages System messages differ from channel messages in that there is no channel data attached to them. System messages are heard, and responded to if necessary, by all devices in the MIDI chain, regardless of channel assignment.

System Real Time messages System Real Time messages consist of a single byte that is sent regularly to synchronize two devices. The various types of system real time messages all deal with a specific aspect of synchronization. Remember that most synchronization is now accomplished using MIDI time code, and that is a system common message. Because of this, you may need to be aware of system real time messages in order to filter them out or otherwise turn them off so that they don't contribute to MIDI clog (see Table 1-3).

Table 1-3: Single Real Time messages

Timing Clock	A single byte (F8) that is sent out 24 times per quarter note. Devices that don't require this data ignore it.
Start	Instructs a sequencer (hardware or software) to start playing at the beginning of the current song (the current song is selected with the Song Select message that is a System Common message described below).
Stop	Instructs the sequencer to stop playing the current song.
Continue	Instructs the sequencer to resume playing the current song at the last point where it stopped playing. Contrast this to the Start command, which always starts at the very beginning of the sequence.
Active Sensing	On some devices this message is sent every 300 milliseconds. Once a device receives an active sensing message, it expects to get one every 300 milliseconds. If it doesn't, it assumes that a MIDI cable has accidentally become unplugged or the transmitting instrument has been turned off. When this happens, the receiving instrument will turn off all notes that might currently be sounding. This message was created because if a MIDI cable was inadvertently disconnected in between a note's ON command and its OFF command, the note or notes would continue to sound forever.
System Reset	Tells all devices connected to the transmitting device to return to its default settings, including channel mode and local control setting.

System Common messages   System Common messages are mainly concerned with getting a sequencer ready to play a song when it receives a Start message (see "System real time messages"). Because of this they are concerned with locating the song to play and specifying where the song should begin playing (see Table 1-4).

Table 1-4: System Common messages

Song Select	Number of Song (0 to 127 — this informs the sequencer which of 128 possible songs to load for playing. When the system real time message "Start" is received, playback of the song will commence.)
Song Position Pointer	Sixteenth note to start at (0 to 16,383 — locates a pointer to a specified position in the current song measure in 6-clock increments from the beginning of the song. Because there are 24 clocks per quarter note, 6 clocks equal one sixteenth note.)

Table 1-4: System Common messages (continued)

Tune Request	Causes devices that respond to this command to tune their oscillators. This was created for analog synthesizers, which often drifted out of tune. Digital synthesizers do not drift out of tune and therefore will not respond to a Tune Request.
EOX	End of System Exclusive: this informs all receiving MIDI devices that the transmission of a system exclusive message (see below) has ended and all devices can go back to normal operation.
MIDI Time Code	Frame Number (indicates the SMPTE frame number of the current film or video frame.)

System Exclusive messages System Exclusive messages permit manufacturers to expand the MIDI Spec to include commands that are only relevant to and recognized by their own devices. Each manufacturer is assigned an individual ID number that identifies the manufacturer. Only devices made by that manufacturer will respond to data following the SysEx ID number. When the SysEx status byte is sent, all devices receiving it will note the next byte, which is the manufacturer's ID, and if the ID is from a different manufacturer than their own, they will simply ignore all the rest of the data until they hear an EOX message (End of Exclusive, see above).

The uses of these messages are as varied as the manufacturers that use them. Some use them to transmit patch data or sample from one device to another or from a computer to a synthesizer. Others use them to transmit drum patterns or song data from one device to another. Still others use them to communicate front panel controls such as switches and buttons that are unique to their line of synthesizers and not part of the standardized set of controllers supported by MIDI.

MIDI clog

You will often hear about MIDI log jam or MIDI clog. This refers to the fact that MIDI can only communicate 31,250 bits of information per second. Because MIDI bytes are 8 bits long, and each bit includes 2 extra bits for error checking, there are 10 bits per MIDI byte. Thus, MIDI sends approximately 3 bytes of data per millisecond ($\frac{1}{1000}$ of a second). It takes about a millisecond to turn a note on and about a millisecond to turn it off. That means that MIDI can play about 500 notes per second.

You will notice a gap in the notes if they arrive more than 20 milliseconds apart. Therefore, the practical limit for the number of simultaneous notes that can be sent and heard as a chord is about 16. Of course, there are many other factors that come into play. The type of sound is significant. A chord assigned to a slow bowed string sound is not going to have a problem with audible gaps between the notes.

Where we get real problems is when there is a considerable amount of controller data being sent along with the notes. Pitch bend and other continuous controller events can clog the MIDI data stream to such an extent that notes that would be less than 20 milliseconds apart without controller data, are now farther than 20 milliseconds apart and we perceive them as slightly arpeggiated (not played simultaneously).

Surprisingly, this varies from synthesizer to synthesizer, so part of the problem can be blamed on the amount of time it takes the destination device to process the incoming MIDI data. There are CPUs (central processing units) in synthesizers just as there are in computers. A faster synthesizer CPU can mean that incoming MIDI data is processed more quickly, thus alleviating problems of MIDI data clog. Because CPUs are always getting faster and faster while at the same time becoming cheaper and cheaper, the role that they play in the MIDI clog picture is gradually disappearing.

There is a provision in the MIDI Spec that helps reduce MIDI clog when sequencers are controlling synthesizers. This provision is called *running status*. Running status refers to the feature in most sequencers that strips away unnecessary status bytes. For example, if 100 notes or 1,000 increments of the pitch wheel are being sent over the same MIDI channel or 1,000 increments of the pitch wheel, it is a waste of the MIDI bandwidth to send the channel designation with each note or each pitch wheel value. Because of this, most sequencers strip the status bytes from long strings of similar data and only send a new status byte when required; that is when the type of data changes.

Tape and audio basics

There are many good books on tape and audio basics listed in Appendix C, "Further Reading" so the introductory discussion here will be intentionally brief. Actual studio configuration diagrams are presented in Chapter 7, "Setting Up Your Mac Music Studio."

Sound

There are three primary aspects to sound: (1) creation or generation of *soundwaves,* (2) transmission or propagation of these soundwaves through the air, and (3) reception of these same soundwaves by a human ear, an electronic device such as a microphone, or a physical body such as a reflective surface.

Soundwaves or sound-pressure waves are generated by a vibrating body such as your vocal chords, a violin string, or a loudspeaker. These waves are very similar to ocean waves, except for the fact that they travel through the air rather than the water. The process involves periodic compression and subsequent rarefaction of air molecules by the vibrating body. Just like an ocean wave, the molecules themselves don't actually move, but displacement of air molecules happens in an outwardly direction from the source of vibration. This is called *propagation;* with sound, this motion travels at a fixed rate of speed (the speed of sound, or roughly 1,130 feet per second). A similar phenomenon occurs during the transmission of electrical energy through a wire, although instead of air molecules, electrons are the vehicle and they travel at the speed of light.

Any soundwave has a certain number of characteristics: *frequency, amplitude, envelope, phase,* and *harmonic content.*

Frequency is a number describing the rate at which a single wave cycle (called a period) occurs during a single second. It is usually equal to the number of times the sound generator is vibrating each second. Frequency determines our perception of pitch and is expressed in Hertz (Hz, meaning cycles per second). When something is vibrating at 440 Hz, we call that pitch "A." All multiples of this number are also called "A," although they are perceived to be higher and lower. Thus, 110 Hz, 220 Hz, 880 Hz, and 1,760 Hz are also called "A."

Amplitude is a number representing the loudness of a soundwave. It is calculated by determining the amount of pressure or displacement for a single instance of the soundwave when compared to the normal or equilibrium atmospheric pressure. The amount of displacement is usually between .00001 and .001 of an inch. Although this might seem to be a small distance, the human ear has a dynamic range that can distinguish millions of gradations within that framework. Because of this, a logarithmic scale is used to express amplitude. The unit of measurement is a decibel (dB). The threshold of human hearing is 0 dB, and the sound of a jet engine can be greater than 150 dB. The threshold of pain is 140 dB. Orchestras typically play within a 30 to 110 dB range, so their dynamic range is said to be 80 dB.

When a sound is produced, its amplitude usually changes over time. The first 300 milliseconds or so is the attack portion of the sound. During the attack the sound usually rises in volume, often to its greatest volume. In recognizing timbres, the attack portion is sometimes more important than the harmonic content (see below) of the sustain portion. The attack can be thought of as the signature of the timbre.

The attack may be followed by a slight decay in volume. Then there is a sustain segment where the sound maintains a relatively stable volume. Finally, there is a release segment, when the sound actually dies away. Many envelopes are more complex than this, but this *attack, decay, sustain, release envelope* (ADSR) is the model used in much electronic sound (see Figure 1-4).

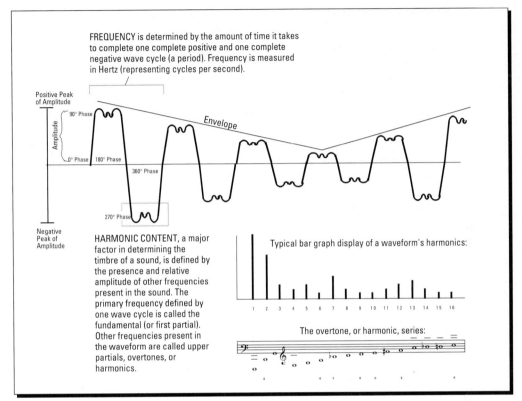

FREQUENCY is determined by the amount of time it takes to complete one complete positive and one complete negative wave cycle (a period). Frequency is measured in Hertz (representing cycles per second).

Positive Peak of Amplitude

90° Phase

Amplitude

Envelope

0° Phase 180° Phase

360° Phase

270° Phase

Negative Peak of Amplitude

HARMONIC CONTENT, a major factor in determining the timbre of a sound, is defined by the presence and relative amplitude of other frequencies present in the sound. The primary frequency defined by one wave cycle is called the fundamental (or first partial). Other frequencies present in the waveform are called upper partials, overtones, or harmonics.

Typical bar graph display of a waveform's harmonics:

1 2 3 4 5 6 7 8 9 10 11 12 13 14 15 16

The overtone, or harmonic, series:

Figure 1-9: Frequency, amplitude, envelope, phase, and harmonic content.

Phase refers to the phenomenon that occurs when two identical waveforms begin at slightly different times. This can happen due to the nature of the vibrating sound source, because the original soundwave is reflected off another source, or in the case of loudspeakers, because two sound sources are outputting identical waveforms, but there is a slight delay before the waveform arrives at the second sound source. Many special effects can be generated by shifting a waveform over time with respect to an identical copy of the same waveform (called phase-shifting). Phase is measured in degrees from 0 to 360. Consider the fact that a sine wave is essentially a circle that has been drawn on a moving piece of paper and you can locate where the various angles are. 0 degrees is the soundwave at equilibrium. 90 degrees is at the top of the positive side of the wave (the peak of the compression stage). 180 degrees is the point at which the wave passes through equilibrium again as it travels to the negative or rarefaction stage. 270 degrees represents the bottom of the negative side of the wave (or peak of the rarefaction stage). If a second soundwave begins when the first is just reaching the 90 degrees stage, the waves are said to be 90 degrees out of phase. Soundwaves that are 180 degrees out of phase cancel each other out and no sound is heard (see Figure 1-9).

Harmonic content partly determines the timbre of a sound. It is described by referring to other frequencies present in the sound as partials or overtones of that sound. Besides the lowest frequency wave, which is called the *fundamental* and which is usually the frequency that determines the overall pitch of the sound, most soundwaves have additional frequency content. The relative strengths of these upper partials or overtones provide the ear with information that can help distinguish one instrument from another. For example, a clarinet and violin can both play the note A 440 at an amplitude of 60 dB. If we cut off their characteristic attacks, the harmonic content of the sound is how we know by ear that one of the notes is being played by a clarinet and the other by a violin.

The sound recording chain

The conversion of soundwaves into electrical energy is the first step of the process of recording sound. Usually this is accomplished with a microphone, but in a synthesizer/sampler-based studio, analog audio data is routed directly into the recording hardware. As we have seen, most synthesis and sampling is now done digitally. Because of this, newer devices are appearing that can transmit audio data from one part of the recording chain to another without ever leaving the digital domain. This eliminates the need of having to go through a DAC to be converted into analog data and then through another ADC to reconvert the data back to digital form for the next stage of the chain.

Microphones   Most microphones work by providing an extremely thin sheet of conductive metal called the *diaphragm* that vibrates sympathetically with the soundwaves that hit it. This sheet of metal may be attached to a coil of wire (called a voice coil) or suspended (in the case of a ribbon microphone) within a magnetic field, such that its motion causes an interaction with the magnetic field to produce a small electrical current that varies in exactly the same manner as the soundwaves striking it. Other approaches, such as the one used for condenser microphones, also rely upon a stationary element interacting with a second element that vibrates sympathetically to incoming soundwaves.

Microphones come in many shapes and sizes and with different degrees of directionality. An omnidirectional microphone reacts identically, regardless of where the soundwave source is placed in relation to it. The field of sound that it will pick up is roughly in the shape of a sphere. Another common type of microphone is the bidirectional variety. These pick up sounds in front and behind the microphone in a figure eight pattern; the two spheres making up the "eight" meet at the sides of the microphone where nothing is picked up. Other directional characteristics exist. The most common of these are the *cardioid* (unidirectional), *supercardioid,* and *hypercardioid* (not to be confused or associated with SuperCard or HyperCard) response patterns, so named because of the overall relation to the shape of a heart.

Mixers The next part of the recording chain is either a *mixer,* if multiple sound sources are to be recorded simultaneously, or the recording device itself, if only a single sound source is to be recorded.

Besides allowing multiple sources to be mixed together in varying proportions, usually by moving faders (sometimes called sliders), mixers also provide a wide variety of other features. *Equalization, signal processing* (effects), and *panning* are among the more common of these.

Equalization (EQ) is the process of increasing or decreasing the amplitude or energy of specified frequency bands. EQ can range from simple tone controls (treble and bass) to parametric systems with many knobs that allow you to specify the width of the frequency band to boost, the center frequency in this band, and the amount of boost or cut.

Signal processing, often called effects, refers to the ability to route from a mixer or synthesizer, via a jack labeled "effects send" or "aux send," a controllable amount of the incoming signal to an external device for modification. The transformed signal is then sent back to the mixer, via a jack labeled "effects return" or "aux return." A knob on the mixer usually provides control over the proportion of the original signal that is mixed in with the returning processed signal. Typical signal-processing effects include reverberation (or reverb), digital delay lines (DDLs), chorusing, phase-shifting, flanging, pitch-shifting, compression, expansion, limiting, gating, spatialization, distortion, and signal enhancement (via a device such as an exciter).

These forms of signal processing and effects are discussed in Chapter 5, "Hardware Decisions," Chapter 23, "The Mac in Live Performance," and Chapter 24, "Direct-to-Hard Disk Recording."

Some mixers have no effects sends and returns, while others have four or more. With more than one effects send and return, you can route your audio signal to multiple types of signal processors.

Panning is another standard control found on a mixer. The pan knob allows you to specify the proportion of signal sent to either side of the stereo field at the final stereo output. Also, there is usually a mute and/or solo button that allows you to momentarily mute or solo an input.

Finally, all mixers provide some form of metering the incoming or outgoing signal level, either through VU (volume units) meters or LED (light emitting diodes) bars. In conjunction with these meters, you will often find a peak indicator that lights up if the signal gets too "hot" for the circuitry to handle (thus causing distortion in some cases).

Each of the above features of a mixer are normally associated with an individual mixer channel. Mixers typically have 8, 12, 16, 24, 32, 48, 64, or 96 channels, which can all be mixed down into a single stereo signal. There are so many controls on mixers because each channel requires the same number of meters, knobs, buttons, and faders.

Analog recorders   Recorders come in a variety of formats and record onto a variety of media. The most common format is a stereo (2-channel) analog tape recorder. Tape widths range from ⅛-inch for cassette to ¼-inch, ½-inch, 1-inch and 2-inch for open reel systems. Tape recorders divide tape horizontally into a number of tracks, 2 tracks being required for stereo recording. Other analog tape configurations include 3 (referring to 2-track with center timecode track), 4, 8, 16, and 24 tracks.

Full-track mono recorders record a single track over the full width of the tape. A half-track mono system records one track in one direction, and then the tape can be flipped over to record another track in the other direction. Two-track stereo recorders record 2 tracks in a single direction across the entire width of the tape, while quarter-track stereo recorders record 2 tracks in one direction and another 2 tracks in the other direction when the tape is flipped over.

The wider the tracks, the better the recording will be. Technically speaking, the signal-to-noise ratio increases by 3 dB whenever track width is doubled. ⅛-inch tape is used for stereo cassettes. Generally, ¼-inch tape is used for stereo or 4-track open reel recording, ½-inch tape for 4-track or 8-track recording, 1-inch tape for 8- or 16-track recording, and 2-inch tape for 16- or 24-track recording. Some manufacturers try to cram more tracks onto smaller width tapes (for example 4 or more tracks on a cassette, 8 or more tracks on a ¼-inch open reel), but these systems usually require sophisticated noise reduction circuits to make them professionally acceptable.

The speed at which a tape travels across its recording and playback heads ranges from 1⅞ inches per second (ips) and 3¾ ips for cassette recorders to 7½, 15, and 30 ips for open reel recorders. The faster the speed the more tape is required to record each second of sound. The more tape used to record each second of sound, the better the recording will be able to reproduce the original signal. This is because you can cram more information on a longer segment of tape than you can on a shorter one.

Analog tape recorders have three heads across which the tape travels. There is an erase head, a record head, and a playback head.

Sound is recorded by converting the incoming electrical signal back into a magnetic signal, which magnetizes the molecules of the recording tape. The tape

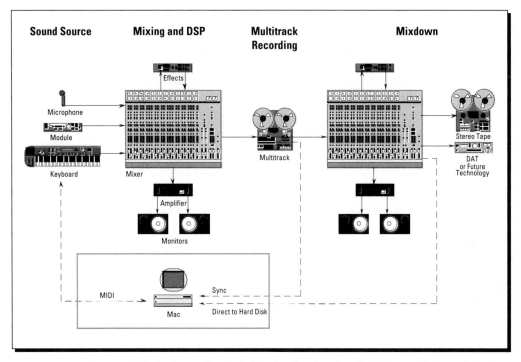

Figure 1-10: The basic recording chain. Note that the mixer does double duty so it is pictured twice in the illustration (2 mixers are not implied).

itself has a layer of magnetic oxide that is optimized for maintaining its magnetic orientation over a long period of time.

The playback process simply reverses the process. The now recorded tape passes by the playback head and induces an electrical current in coils of wire that form an integral part of the playback head. The resulting minute electrical signal can then be amplified.

Multitrack analog recorders duplicate this process, but provide for the recording of many tracks (see Figure 1-10). The two advantages of this system are that you may record additional material while listening to previously recorded material and that you may record individual instruments on separate tracks, so that these can be further processed or equalized during the mixdown process when all the tracks are combined into a single stereo mix.

Additional features that support multiple-take recording are found on multitrack recorders. These include the ability to play back tracks from the record head to assure that tracks being listened to synchronize with tracks being recorded. This feature is usually accessed by a button labeled "Sel-Sync," "Simul-Sync," or just "Sync."

Punch-in and punch-out also facilitate multiple-take recording. Using a footswitch or specifying a location using front panel controls, you can cause a track or tracks to go into record mode while the tape is rolling and out of record when the "punched-in" portion has been re-recorded. Many multitrack recorders include a return to zero (RTZ) button and possibly additional tape location memory buttons that can wind the tape to the zero point or other point indicated by the tape counter.

When multitrack recorders are used in conjunction with MIDI sequencers, one of their tracks is set aside to hold timing or synchronization information, usually in the form of SMPTE Time Code. This provides 30 absolute location addresses per second, which aids in device synchronization.

Some inexpensive tape recorders are available as mixer-recorder combinations that include a mixer and recording mechanism all in one box. Most of these are cassette systems, although some use larger cassettes (about the size of a Beta videotape) to provide for extra tracks. These systems are often a good choice for limited budget studios, because the problem of matching an appropriate mixer with a tape recorder has been solved by the manufacturer.

Finally, many tape recorders include noise reduction circuitry. In some cases this is defeatable (meaning that it can be bypassed), but in many cases there is no way to avoid the noise reduction circuitry. The most common types of noise reduction are dbx and Dolby. (They are available in several forms, the most popular of which are Dolby B and C — cassette only.) Dolby A and Dolby SR are expensive and therefore mainly found in professional facilities).

Studios that use multitrack tape recorders almost always have a separate recording deck known as the *mixdown deck* (see Figure 1-10). This is the final destination of all the recorded tracks after being passed through the mixer, once again to be mixed down into a stereo signal consisting of two channels. During the mixdown process, additional effects, signal processing, and EQ can be applied.

Mixdown decks vary according to the intended use of the final product. For many purposes, a 2-track stereo deck is used. Budget considerations may dictate that your mixdown deck be a cassette deck. Music intended for the accompaniment of film and video is usually mixed down to 4-track tape, where two of the tracks contain the stereo mix and a blank track separates the musical material from the fourth synchronization track (SMPTE track). There are 3-track systems available or stereo mixdowns with a special third center track set aside for synchronization. Occasionally, 8-track tapes are used for the final mix. In this case, there are three stereo pairs making up six of the tracks, and then a blank track separating the music from the eighth synchronization track.

In analog recording, every time a track is recorded on another device, there is at least 10 dB degradation added to the signal. Each separate recording is referred to as a "generation." A common procedure used with multitrack recorders when you begin to run out of tracks is to "bounce" several tracks down to a single track, so that the space they occupied can be reclaimed for additional tracks. Track bouncing also adds a generation to the recording. Bouncing down tracks that have already been bounced once adds yet another generation. Mixing down the multitrack recording to stereo counts as yet another generation. Finally, if you make cassette copies of your final mix, cut a record with it, or re-record it onto film or video, one more generation is added. After three generations, the degradation of the recording is noticeable to the average listener, so careful planning is required when recording. With digital recorders using digital input-output (I/O) to transfer audio data, no information is lost and no noise is added.

Amplifiers and loudspeakers   Amplifiers are the next to the last stage of the recording chain, and speakers (called monitors) are the final stage (see Figure 1-10). Audio signals coming from your tape recorder or mixer will need to be amplified to a level that is powerful enough to drive your loudspeakers.

With this in mind, the output level (in watts) of your power amplifier should be matched to the level of the speakers that you are going to use. Although your amplifier may be rated at less than the combined wattage of your speakers, it is very important that it not be rated higher than your speakers. This type of mismatching can quickly lead to blown speakers.

Budget studios can sometimes make do with having their home stereo system do the double duty of functioning as the amplification/speaker components to the Macintosh music system. Tighter budgets can dispense with speakers altogether and opt for headphone monitoring. Most professional studios have three sets of monitors.

The reason for having more than one set of monitors is so that you can use the best pair to listen to while you are mixing and the other pairs to simulate the equipment your intended audience will probably be listening on. If your music is going to be listened to predominantly on generic home stereo systems, it is a good idea to have a pair of monitors that will allow you to hear your music under those conditions. Some studios go so far as to have a set of speakers that are similar to those used in car radios for this same purpose.

Regardless of the number or expense of your monitors, the most important consideration is that they have a "flat" response, meaning that they don't tend to emphasize or deemphasize certain frequency ranges. If your speakers deemphasize the bass while you are recording, you may always crank the bass up to compensate. Then, when someone with a decent pair of speakers listens to the recording, the bass will sound disproportionately loud. Nearly all speakers come with a graph of their frequency response, and you should study this carefully before a purchase.

One final word of advice. Just like synthesis, recording is a chain of components. As with any chain, it is only as strong as its weakest link. Playing back a recording on a system that costs thousands of dollars through speakers that are not of commensurate quality is only going to sound as good as those cheap speakers. Likewise, recording sound with a high-end system will only sound as good as the microphone you are using.

State of the art: Digital audio

Digital recording tape has long been considered by many to be the best possible destination for a final mixdown. Early affordable systems (less than $1,000) often involved using an interface such as Sony's PCM-701 to transform a standard videocassette recorder into a digital audio recorder. The recent introduction of affordable DAT (digital audio tape) recorders has placed digital audio into the hands of just about anyone who wants it. Emerging digital recording technologies such as the Philips/Tandy Digital Compact Cassette (DCC) and Sony's Mini Disc (MD) promise to make digital audio even more cost effective.

When one refers to digital recordings, such as those available on CDs and DATs, the data on the actual disc or tape is encoded very much in the same way as one digitizes a sound with a sampler. The main difference is that we refer to the process as digital recording rather than sampling. CDs use a sampling rate of 44.1 KHz at a resolution of 16 bits. Because all CDs are stereo, meaning that there are two data words for each sample, it would seem that 1,411,200 bits of information are being output per second. Because of error correction and other information, the number of bits on a CD is actually triple that or about 4.3 million bits per second. An hour of stereo music requires 15.48 billion bits of data that gets reduced to 5 billion bits of audio sample data.

An interesting piece of CD trivia is that when the CD specification was being designed, Philips asked Herbert von Karajan how much music a CD should be able to hold. His response was that it should be able to hold a recording of his performance of Beethoven's *Ninth Symphony*. Current CDs have a maximum playing time of slightly over 74.5 minutes.

If you've ever looked closely at a compact disc, you may have wondered where the grooves are that you used to see on analog vinyl LPs. Those grooves have been replaced by the same sort of ones and zeroes that your computer uses for everything it does. Each group of 16 ones and zeroes represents $\frac{1}{44100}$ of a second.

With the introduction of CDs and finally consumer DATs, digital audio has become affordable for the average person. With the introduction of faster Macintoshes and faster hard drives, a new type of digital recording has become available to Macintosh musicians: direct-to-hard disk recording. (See Chapter 24, "Direct-to-Hard Disk Recording".)

Incidentally, one should always refer to this in print as direct-to-hard disk recording, rather than direct-to-disk recording, because New England Digital (NED), the makers of the Synclavier workstation (an expensive system that provides direct-to-hard disk recording) has trademarked the latter expression (I used the phrase "direct-to-disk" once in an article and NED sent some lawyers after me).

The hardware that makes direct-to-hard disk recording possible in a Macintosh music workstation requires the addition of a digital audio expansion card to one of the NuBus slots in Macintoshes that have such slots. Such cards provide for the conversion of sound into the digital domain, referred to as analog-to-digital conversion and performed by chips referred to as ADCs (analog-to-digital converters). The cards also provide for the reconversion of data from the digital domain into the analog sound world, a process that is accomplished by DACs (digital-to-analog converters).

Direct-to-hard disk recording has many advantages over recording onto digital tape. The most obvious example is that you have random access to all of your sound and can slip and slide regions of sound in ways that are simply impossible on a tape-based system, where all tracks are time-aligned to one another. Regions of any length can be defined at will and played in any order, because all the computer needs is a pointer indicating where a specific region of sound commences.

Editing direct-to-hard disk recordings offers many new options that were either unavailable with tape-based systems (whether analog or digital) or too time consuming to consider. Sound editing systems permit detailed control of sound texture. This fine control means the editor functions as a kind of sound "microsurgeon." Because all digital audio data is represented as binary numbers, many DSP (digital signal processing) algorithms, including digital EQ, were until now only available through dedicated hardware boxes, but are now achievable in software.

Having DSP built into the software means the sound data never has to leave the digital domain. When the digital effects unit does not have digital I/O ports, it is necessary to convert the digital data back into analog data. Then the external DSP device has to use its own ADC to convert input analog data into digital form for processing and then use its own DAC to reconvert the processed sound back into analog. Just like with re-recording analog tape tracks, each conversion of sound back and forth between the digital and analog worlds has as great a potential for degrading the signal. Eventually, the effect is similar to copying several generations of analog tape.

Regarding the question of bouncing tracks in the digital domain, there is no degradation of signal, no matter how many times the data is bounced. This is because mixing several tracks into a single entity merely requires adding together the numbers that represent the sample values. With non-hard-disk-based systems it is theoretically possible that a build-up of error correction signals might alter the sound, albeit imperceptibly.

Another significant difference to analog systems is the fact that much editing of direct-to-hard disk recording is nondestructive, meaning that the source material on your hard disk is not altered in any way. Such editing can take place in real time, on-the-fly during playback. Some editing operations are destructive; however, making a backup copy of your data is as simple as copying a Macintosh file.

The one stumbling block for direct-to-hard disk recording is that it takes about 10MBs of hard disk space to store a minute of stereo sound. You need a 600MB drive to record an hour of music. (In cases where you create a new mixdown file on the hard disk, you will effectively use 20MBs per stereo minute.) Also, your hard disk will need an access time of less than 28ms to make this all possible. This might seem prohibitive at first, but many of these systems will work with Syquest removable cartridge drives, and you can get almost four and a half minutes of high-quality digital audio on a single 44MB cartridge or nine minutes on an 88MB cartridge.

Although a relative newcomer to the Macintosh, by the end of 1990 CD-quality digital audio had reached a stage of development comparable to that of MIDI and notation. By 1991, the only thing left to do was to combine all three worlds in integrated software systems. This has already begun, and there are now many software options for the Macintosh musician that provide for the combination of digital audio data with MIDI data. Some of these also include conventional music notation as the representation of music data (see Chapter 18, "MIDI Sequencing with Digital Audio").

Perhaps one could go a bit further and wish that a time will come when MIDI data, digital audio data, and PostScript notation data can all travel down the same cable simultaneously, if only to alleviate the mass of different types of cables and connectors that one has to deal with in a studio. Well, that time is already upon us in the form of MediaLink (see Chapter 8, "Moving Data Around Your Music Network").

A final note

Now that you are aware of some of the possibilities of the personal computers for music, don't forget that we are not talking about just any personal computer, we are talking about the Macintosh. Regarding IBMs, Ataris, and Amigas, you recall the words of famed rap artist, Hammer: "You can't touch this!"

Summary

- Macintosh musicware has gone through three periods. The first wave of Macintosh musicware (1984–1986) focused primarily on score editing and secondarily on control of the early Macintosh's internal four-voice synthesizer. The second wave of Macintosh musicware (1987–1989) introduced MIDI sequencing, patch editing and sample editing software for specific devices, interactive composition packages, educational software for music, MIDI programming languages, notation software incorporating PostScript and MIDI, and direct-to-hard disk recording (using an external peripheral device instead of an internal card). The current third wave of Macintosh musicware (1990–present) offers direct-to-hard disk recording systems (using internal cards), MIDI sequencers with 512 channels and linked to patch libraries, MIDI sequencers with digital audio tracks, universal patch librarians and sample editors, interactive CD-ROMs for music education, visual MIDI programming languages, and notation software compatible with the Standard MIDI Files format and MIDI Manager.

- There are several important parameters regarding the capabilities of most electronic instruments: the number of keys, the number of voices that can be played at once, the number of different timbres that can be played at once, and the number of different sounds that the device is capable of storing in RAM or ROM.

- Many people call all electronic sound-generating devices synthesizers. This is not strictly correct. There are now two general approaches to creating sound electronically: synthesis and sampling. There are also hybrid devices that create sounds by combining synthesis technology with sampling technology. Synthesis refers to creating sounds electronically from electronically generated waveforms and signal processors. The instruments that do this are called synthesizers. While some synthesizers can be made to sound very much like acoustic instruments, there is always going to be a significant difference. Sampling refers to re-creating sounds electronically from digital recordings of actual acoustic sounds, which are often, but not always, produced by real acoustic instruments. The instruments that take this approach are called samplers or sample-players.

- There are two main approaches to electronic sound synthesis: analog and digital. The distinction is important. Analog refers to something that is continuous, like a standard volume control. Digital refers to something that can be measured incrementally or represented by a series of numbers or discrete steps, like a rotary (stepped) switch. Analog things are made up by a theoretically infinite number of points, whereas digital things are made up of a finite number of points.

- MIDI, the Musical Instrument Digital Interface developed in 1982, is an international specification used by musical instruments that contain microprocessors to communicate with other microprocessor-controlled instruments or devices (including computers such as the Macintosh, lighting controllers, mixers, and just about anything else). It is a sort of "synthesizer Esperanto."

✔ MIDI data flows over cables with standardized 5-pin DIN connectors serially, at a rate of 31.25 KBaud. The bits passing through MIDI cables are organized into MIDI "messages." MIDI cables carry MIDI data in one direction, hence there is a necessity to have both MIDI IN ports and MIDI OUT ports on most MIDI devices. A third port called MIDI THRU for the purpose of immediately passing on to another device, information received at a device's MIDI IN port has become common enough to be considered standard. One important rule is that MIDI OUTs are always connected to MIDI INs and MIDI INs are normally connected to MIDI OUTs, although they can be connected to MIDI THRUs.

✔ MIDI communicates performance data, not actual sound. MIDI can tell what note is being held down, how hard the key was struck, if any additional pressure was applied to the key after being struck, when and how quickly the key is released, and if any other controls such as sliders, wheels, switches, or pedals have been moved. It does not know anything about the sound that follows the key press, other than perhaps the patch number (or program number) of the sound. Because all devices use different numbering schemes, knowing the program number tells us nothing about the sound's actual timbre.

✔ There are two main types of MIDI messages, each consisting of at least two bytes: a status byte and a data byte. The two types of messages are called Channel messages and System messages. Channel messages usually include a MIDI channel number as the destination of the message. System messages do not include a channel number and are acted upon no matter what channel(s) a device is assigned to. Channel messages are further divided into Channel Voice messages and Channel Mode messages. System messages are divided into System Exclusive messages, System Common messages, and System Real Time messages.

✔ There are three primary aspects to sound: (1) creation or generation of soundwaves, (2) transmission or propagation of these soundwaves through the air, and (3) reception of these same soundwaves by a human ear, an electronic device such as a microphone, or a physical body such as a reflective surface. Any soundwave has a certain number of characteristics: frequency, amplitude, envelope, phase, and harmonic content.

✔ The recording is a chain of components just like the synthesis chain. As with any chain, it is only as strong as its weakest link. Playing back a recording on a system that costs thousands of dollars through speakers that are not of commensurate quality is only going to sound as good as those cheap speakers. Likewise, recording sound with a high-end system will only sound as good as the microphone you are using.

✔ Digital recording tape has long been considered by many to be the best possible destination for a final mixdown. The recent introduction of affordable DAT recorders has placed digital audio into the hands of just about anyone who wants it. Emerging digital recording technologies such as the Philips/Tandy Digital Compact Cassette and Sony's Mini Disc promise to make digital audio even more cost effective.

Chapter 2
Music and Sound on the Mac

In this chapter . . .

✔ An overview of musical and audio applications of the Macintosh.

✔ A brief review of the evolution of Macintosh music and sound applications.

✔ Categorization of the twelve types of Macintosh music and sound applications.

✔ Examples of Macintosh applications in sound design, composition, notation, performance, post-production, film and video, multimedia, networking, education, musical and acoustical analysis, programming, and ancillary tasks.

✔ Flow charts illustrating the hierarchy of some of the Macintosh music and sound applications.

The Stepping Stones to Mac Music and Sound

Applications of the Macintosh to music and sound can be grouped into twelve classifications.

- ❖ Sound design
- ❖ Notation
- ❖ Post-production and digital audio
- ❖ Multimedia
- ❖ Education
- ❖ Programming for music

- ❖ Composition
- ❖ Performance
- ❖ Film and video
- ❖ Networking
- ❖ Music and acoustical analysis
- ❖ Ancillary tasks

Each category builds on or grows out of the previous stage(s) of development. Expressed as a more literal model, composers first desire to represent their musical ideas, then hear them, then analyze and modify the sounds they hear, then construct and realize creations of greater complexity, and finally, teach all this to others.

Additionally, each specific stage, once initiated, continued to evolve. As the overall progression unfolds, so does both the quantitative and qualitative scope of control. Score editors added more and more staves, symbols, and automatic correction features. The number of independent sounds that could be controlled expanded from 1 to 4 to 6 to 16 to 32 to 96 to the current 512, while variety of control over individual events multiplied. Sound design capabilities progressed by expanding the number of objects used for synthesis and increasing the resolution of sampled sounds. Control of algorithmic composition increased in complexity as it became possible to group descriptions of smaller portions of works into modules that could be worked with independently and themselves grouped together into modules.

During this increase of quantitative scope, two types of growth along qualitative lines are observed: first, continually greater externalization occurs. Score editors are developed that communicate with larger external music typesetting machines. Control of sound extends from controlling the Macintosh's internal synthesizer to controlling external synthesizers through MIDI. Sound design progresses from internal additive synthesis and sampling to the editing of sounds sampled on external devices. Second, at every stage the degree of interactivity increases.

In reading the following, keep in mind that the twelve applications categories have been placed in an order dictated by increasing interdependence and increasing externalization. A simple representation of this organization might be something like the following.

Composers must first have *sound* before they can compose. After *composition* there is a need for *notation*. Notation and other representations of musical compositions can then be performed or realized synthetically. *Performances* of music can further be modified and enhanced at the post-production stage. *Post-production* activities involving digital signal processing and other digital audio applications can render the music into a format suitable for film, video, or multimedia. The finished *film, video, multimedia* or other music or sound object can be distributed via networks. *Networks,* whether WANs (Wide Area Networks), MLANs (Music Local Area Networks), or DANs™ (Distributed Audio Networks), can be used to create and communicate projects of increasingly greater complexity. In order to ensure the continued evolution and improvement of these tools, concepts, and activities, musicians develop systems to *educate* greater numbers of participants. The end result of more educated musicians results in progressively more powerful *analytical* and *programming* tools to further the cause. Finally, to achieve greater efficiency, the computer is used for all the *ancillary tasks* associated with this continuum (see Chapter 9, "The Journey Between Sound and Music").

While it is convenient to break the music industry into large categories, keep in mind that many musicians now fit into many categories simultaneously — some days one area predominates, on other days another does.

Sound Design

The Macintosh is used as a sound-generating/patch or soundfile editing/analyzing device. This activity is often referred to as sound design. Sound

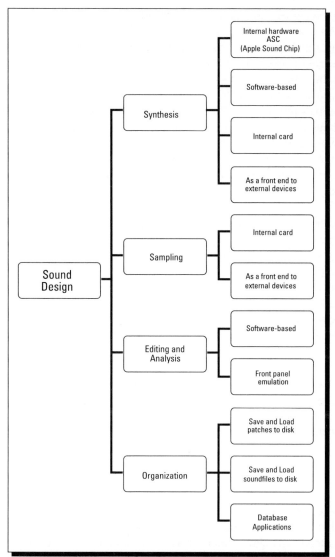

Figure 2-1: Hierarchy of elements associated with sound design.

design may involve software dedicated to all or some of the following tasks (see Figure 2-1):

- ❖ Sound sampling
- ❖ Sound organization
- ❖ Sound synthesis
- ❖ Sound editing and analysis

The field of sound design encompasses a wide variety of activities, ranging from going out to the countryside and recording natural sounds for later sampling to programming synthesizers. Occasionally, the term sound design is applied to setting up complex performing configurations that maximize musicians' control over these sounds.

Although a sound designer is usually hidden away in the studio, the new sounds that this work gives birth to often provide the essential ingredient necessary for communicating the subliminal impact of a movie scene. A sound designer's new creation may supply the unforgettable characteristics to a corporate sound logo, in this case referring to a small identifiable musical theme that is associated with a corporation or advertising campaign, usually under six seconds in length and over five figures in price — sound logos are not jingles, but they may be included in a company's jingle. Finally, where in the past a pop group's unique sound might have been attributed to its recording engineer or producer, in the present it is often traceable to the raw material provided by the sound designer. To understand sound designing, it is necessary to recall the distinction between the two main ways in which electronic instruments get the sounds they produce: sampling and synthesis.

Sampling, you will remember from the previous chapter, refers to making a digital recording of sound (called a *soundfile*) for later playback. The process is similar to creating a moving picture from a series of still photographs projected at a high rate of speed. Sound sampling takes a number of "snapshots" (*samples*) of the sound and plays these back at a very fast speed to re-create the sound (usually between 32,000 and 50,000 samples per second, although 44,100 samples per second is becoming standard due to its prevalence in the digital audio industry). Because all the information is stored as numbers, it is easy to manipulate and transform these sounds (digital effects processing). Even though sampled soundfiles usually utilize elegant data compression, they still require a vast amount of memory (often hundreds of thousands of bytes).

The other way that electronic instruments produce sound is by configuring parameters of a variety of front panel buttons, knobs, sliders, and controls to create altogether new, unnatural sounds. The terms FM (Frequency Modulation) synthesis, additive synthesis, PCM (Pulse Code Modulation), and LA (Linear Arithmetic) synthesis are used to describe popular methods of digital synthesis. A synthesizer configuration that you can recall for future musical playback is referred to as a *patch*. Since patches don't record any sound data, but merely the parameter settings needed to re-create a specific sound, patch information does not require very much computer memory.

The Macintosh can enter the sound designing picture at many stages. Perhaps the most primal level is using the Macintosh to actually generate sounds in software without providing any pre-existing sonic material. This can be accomplished at many resolutions, ranging from the creation of 8-bit soundfiles that play out through the Mac's own speaker to the creation of CD-quality 16-bit soundfiles that can be loaded into commercial samplers or played through a Macintosh equipped with internal cards supporting that level of fidelity.

Notable tools in this area include both Digidesign's SoftSynth (a synthesizer in software, as the name suggests) and TurboSynth (a modular synthesizer in software with the added capability of utilizing sampled soundfiles for its raw material). Both programs are capable of generating sounds from nothing and outputting these sounds to 8-bit or 16-bit soundfiles that can be played directly from the Macintosh or from an external sampler. See Chapter 10, "Sound Generation."

Applying the concept of generating new sounds to external devices, many software-based patch editors and librarians now provide ways to algorithmically generate new patches with minimal user interaction. For example, Opcode patch librarians provide three features for this task. Their "Shuffler" takes an inspiration bank of patches and generates a new bank where each byte of each patch is taken from the same location in one of the inspiration bank's patches selected randomly. Their "Shades" option produces a gradual transformation from one inspiration patch to another inspiration patch with as many steps in between as the particular type of synthesizer bank will hold. "Constrained Random" also produces a new bank of patches from two inspiration patches. However, instead of mapping a smooth transition from the first patch to the second over the entire bank, it uses the parameter values of the inspiration patches as the upper and lower limits for randomly generated parameter values. This topic is covered in more detail in Chapter 10, "Sound Generation."

In the realm of sampled soundfile editing and analyzing, both Digidesign and Passport Designs market software capable of manipulating sounds sampled on nearly all commercially available samplers as well as sounds sampled by the Mac. See Chapter 13, "Editing Sampled Sound."

In the domain of *patch editing* (the creation of new sounds using an external synthesizer), Macintosh software can greatly simplify the user interface to such external sound-generating devices' sound manipulation capabilities. This is because many more controls can be simulated on a Macintosh screen than are economically feasible to expect on a hardware device. Also, virtual controls that have no correlation in the physical world may be implemented. For example, manipulating graphic representations of such obtuse concepts as amplitude envelopes makes it easier to conceptualize corresponding complex editing procedures. In this area, Opcode Systems dominates the market by virtue of covering the most number of devices, although Dr. T, Hybrid Arts, Sound Quest, and Zero One also have formidable editors for the devices they support. See Chapter 12, "Editing Synthesized Sound."

Finally, the creation of all these new sounds, either through direct Macintosh synthesis or sampling or by using the Macintosh as a front end for creating new sounds on an external synthesizer or sampler, eventually precipitates the need to organize these new sounds for later retrieval. There are two approaches to this issue: libraries made up of the actual sound objects themselves (or the data required to reconfigure the target device to produce a particular sound) and libraries made up of descriptions of the sound objects with or without the ability to retrieve and pass on the actual objects.

Patch librarians store actual data capable of reconfiguring a device to produce a sound because a snapshot of the device's control settings is a very small object (with respect to size in kilobytes) in the library. On the other hand, sampled sound often requires a thousand times more memory than patch information; therefore, the organization of sampled sound libraries is typically left to database software capable of quickly locating sounds matching detailed search criteria. See Chapter 11, "Sound Organization."

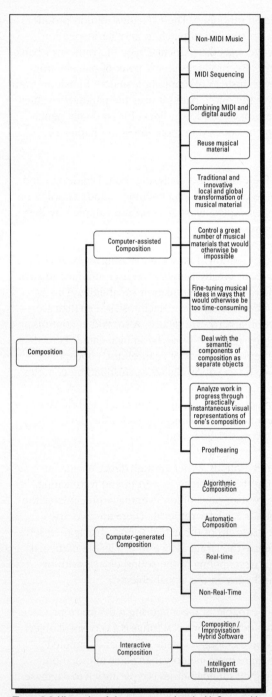

Figure 2-2: Hierarchy of elements associated with Composition.

Items outside the scope of this text, though nonetheless significant sound design applications, include using Macintosh software and hardware tools intended for music and sound in the realm of science and industry (for example, using Digidesign's Sound Tools package to analyze airplane engine performance). While these scientific and industrial endeavors certainly are novel uses of Macintosh musicware, the emphasis of this book is on applications applied to musical creativity.

Composition

Besides simplifying the interface to sound manipulation, the Macintosh can simplify the process of creating musical compositions. This includes musical data stored as MIDI sequences or as digital audio files and the generation of music both interactively and algorithmically. Macintosh musical applications dedicated to composition generally fall into three classes (see Figure 2-2):

❖ Computer-assisted composition
❖ Computer-generated composition
❖ Interactive composition

Computer-assisted composition

In the class of computer-assisted composition (sometimes referred to as CAC), the Macintosh can enhance creative efficiency and productivity in seven basic ways.

Supporting the reusability of musical material. The Macintosh provides for experimentation within an immense set of transformations of your musical material — for example, to quickly experiment with many alternate juxtapositions of musical material through cut, copy, and paste operations both in the horizontal (temporal) and vertical (textural) domains.

Providing for both traditional and innovative transformations of musical material on both a local and global level. The Macintosh can greatly increase the speed at which both simple and complex editing procedures are accomplished. The speed at which operations can be executed is so great that transformational operations that would otherwise not be experimented with become viable. On a simple level, it is possible to listen to a composition at any desired transposition or tempo almost instantaneously. Such sweeping global edits can also be applied to individual elements on a local level. More complex edits such as inverting all the pitches between C2 and F3 with rhythmic values greater than a sixteenth note but smaller than a dotted eighth note are also relatively easy to accomplish when the data is stored as a MIDI sequence.

Allowing the control of a massive number of musical materials. In this instance, musical materials may be considered as consisting of multiple synthesizers, multiple musical themes, or motives. Synchronization applications come into play here as well. One widely practiced application is the process of recording tracks individually onto a multitrack recorder with the assurance that everything will line up in the final mix. Another common use of Macintosh synchronization capabilities is that of creating "virtual tracks" that are played in synchrony with pre-recorded tracks, often due to having run out of analog tracks to record on.

Enabling the fine-tuning of musical ideas in ways that would otherwise be too time-consuming. Examples of this are the possibility of testing numerous alternate orchestrations through the simple reassignment of MIDI channels (or patches) or of testing numerous alternate rhythmic or articulation patterns.

Offering a means for dealing with the components of your work as separate objects. The manipulation of your musical material, or the processes that generate your musical material, as distinct objects permits the shaping of these components into a finished composition from a level of abstraction that more closely resembles actual creative thought processes. Many MIDI sequencers now support "chunking" or "chaining" of individual musical components that may be as small as a single note, chord, motive, or theme and as large as your available RAM. Reorganization of overall form from a global level can be as simple as typing a string of letters, where each individual letter represents a complete musical idea. Alternatively, you can often rearrange iconic representations of your musical ideas simply by dragging them around with the mouse.

Permitting the chance to analyze your work in progress through instantaneous visual representations of your performance either in graphic notation or conventional music notation.   Most Macintosh software tools for composition now support some form of graphic representation of musical data. Visual representations of your ideas, whether as a graph or in conventional music notation, not only provide you with instant feedback of the shape of your ideas, but also can highlight crucial relationships and avenues for exploration that might otherwise go unnoticed.

Supporting proofhearing.   Perhaps most importantly, the Macintosh provides the immediate opportunity to hear, in real time, a rendition of a complex work which, either due to considerations of tempo, rhythmic complexity, or the sheer number of simultaneous interdependent parts, would be impossible except during an actual performance. In the words of my teacher Nadia Boulanger: "Nothing can replace the ear!"

Computer-generated composition

New software tools are bringing computer-generated composition capabilities to the Macintosh (sometimes referred to as algorithmic composition) that have hitherto been available only with the most powerful mainframe computers. With computer-generated composition, typically a set of rules, constraints, or conditional algorithms are defined by the composer. Armed with this information, the system proceeds to generate a complete musical composition with no additional human intervention. To generate passable or usable music, the systems must provide tools that are generalized enough to handle the needs of a vast body of users, while at the same time provide enough malleability to meet individual requirements of a specific nature. Algorithmic composition systems are generally of two types: those that generate music in real time, making all compositional decisions on-the-fly (sort of a computer-generated improvisation), and those that generate music in non-real time, allowing for the testing of alternate consequences to their "decisions" and backtracking or branching where necessary, finally outputting a finished composition to a usable file that may be realized electronically or converted to notation for performance by traditional acoustic instruments. See Chapter 20, "Algorithmic Composition."

Interactive composition

Interactive composition straddles the boundaries separating composition and improvisation. Three essential elements that contribute to making interactive composition practical on a large scale, have recently fallen into place. First, the Macintosh provides us with the ability to make extremely complicated compositional decisions at speeds approaching literally millions of decisions in the space between two notes — for all practical purposes in real time. Second, the Macintosh can keep track of all the necessary musical rules and aesthetic principles inherent to musical composition, providing the benefits of knowledge equivalent to years of advanced musical training built right into software programs. Finally, the Macintosh's "friendly" user interface is permitting people with relatively little knowledge of computer programming to explore realms of creativity that were, until now, open only to people with advanced degrees in computer science. A sort of hybrid creative process has developed. This hybrid, referred to as *interactive composition,* combines many of the concepts of composition and improvisation, adding to them a myriad of hitherto unexplored creative options made possible by the speed at which computers can process complex information. See Chapter 19, "Interactive Composition and Intelligent Instruments."

Notation

The Macintosh is rapidly evolving toward realizing the dream of the music processor as analogous to the word processor. There are two fundamental reasons to use music notation software: the manipulation of preexisting music and the creation of new music. The first category includes publishing, engraving, copying, and, to a certain extent, arranging and orchestration. The second category includes composition and musical realization. The impact of notation software on the music industry is felt in three main areas (see Figure 2-3):

❖ Music score processing
❖ Music desktop publishing
❖ Mass distribution of musical information in notation format

With this in mind, Macintosh music notation software is used to:

❖ Produce a final legible copy for the purposes of publication or distribution
❖ Extract parts required for performance
❖ Create new versions in different keys
❖ Quickly create a new arrangement by using tools
❖ Simplify the manipulation of musical ideas using software tools
❖ Create an electronic realization of an acoustical score
❖ Create an electronic realization as an end in itself

The entry and editing of scores for eventual printout uses the Macintosh keyboard, mouse, graphics tablet or dedicated peripheral device, or uses the transcription performance information obtained from a MIDI keyboard or converted from pitch-tracking devices.

Music score processing

Using a Macintosh for music score processing offers many advantages. Cutting and pasting are two operations that lend themselves very well to music processing; due to repetition and modified repetition, much musical information is reusable within the same piece. Just like spellchecking in a word processor, automatic proofreading of rhythm and instrumental ranges is greatly simplified with a computer. Interactive proofhearing and ease of editing go

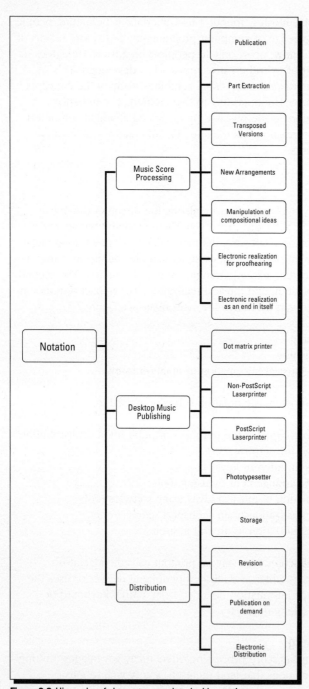

Figure 2-3: Hierarchy of elements associated with notation.

without saying. The chance to analyze your work in progress through the availability of practically instantaneous visual representations of your performance either in graphic notation or conventional music notation can be quite constructive.

Music desktop publishing

The fields of music desktop publishing and music publishing in general share many of the advantages of music processing. Notation software makes it possible for several people to work on the same job, with the computer substituting for manual dexterity and, to a certain extent, musical knowledge. The time traditionally wasted in copying out musical scores and extracting parts is completely eliminated. As a tool for scholars and educators, the impact of music desktop publishing is equal in magnitude to that of desktop publishing for text.

Mass distribution of musical information in notation format

The distribution of musical information has traditionally presented such obstacles for publishers that much of their work becomes a labor of love rather than a financially profitable enterprise. The decision to have a work of music engraved and mass produced has become more a question of economics than artistic merit. With manually prepared music, revisions and corrections are often as costly as the original engraving. With the emergence of useable music software, the main concern of publishers may be reduced to how much manual polishing (if any) the score will require, rather than how many copies they can afford to print and store in their warehouse.

The advantages of mass storage and publication on demand are obvious. Musical notation stored as computer data is far more practical than a single master copy or set of printing plates, which require storage in a climate-controlled vault after having been used for printing a sizable inventory that must itself be carefully stored and carries no reasonable assurance of eventual sale. With notation information stored as computer data, backup copies are identical to the original, and new masters may be produced quickly and automatically. Maintaining an inventory of printed output is becoming less and less a necessity, as publication on demand becomes a reality. The speed, quality, and flexibility of output devices are beginning to make it possible for publishers to merely print music on an order-by-order basis with the confidence that each copy will be of identical quality.

Now that the same tools for manuscript preparation are in the hands of the composers, the decision to publish a work is not strictly dependent on issues of engraving, duplication, and storage costs. Newer notation programs let a publisher customize files received from composers to conform to the "house style" of engraving, a look that may have been developed and cultivated over a period of time, in some cases a century.

Finally, reseller distribution is a matter of merely sending out entire music catalogs on CD-ROMs, optical cartridges, or magnetic tape. Print output is being taken care of at the point of sale. The updating of this media (except in the case of CD-ROMs) via telecommunications is also becoming increasingly feasible, and with the wide-scale implementation of ISDN (Integrated Services Digital Network), such point-of-sale updating may not even be necessary, as retrieval of notational data can be directed to a single storage source.

Some companies are carrying this idea even further with the manufacture of music kiosks that will permit sheet music purchasers on-screen preview and musical auditioning before selecting a work for printing in whatever key desired. Naturally, the possibility exists for such kiosks to dispense not only printed output but also MIDI data. Because film composers are using the same software in increasing numbers, such kiosks, when updated via telecommunications, present the opportunity for a person, after viewing a film on the day of its release, to merely walk across the mall and purchase the sheet music for the theme song.

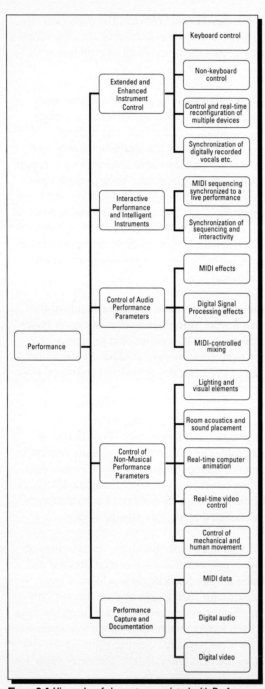

Figure 2-4: Hierarchy of elements associated with Performance.

Performance

In live performance situations, MIDI controllers of any kind as well as software-based MIDI sequencers are used to control sound-generating devices, MIDI effects processors, DSP effects processors, and other performance elements such as lighting and real-time control of video animation or other visual effects. As an aid in a live performance situation, the Macintosh is typically assigned to one or more of the following four roles (see Figure 2-4):

❖ Extended and enhanced device control
❖ Intelligent instruments and interactive performance
❖ Control of audio performance parameters
❖ Control of non-musical performance parameters

Extended and enhanced device control

As the Macintosh becomes more powerful and synthesizers and samplers less expensive, performance applications become more and more elaborate. Performance applications use the Macintosh either as a sound-storage device or as a sequencer. First and foremost, the Mac provides a useful place to store sample files, synth patches, MIDI configurations, or other information that changes from piece to piece. The RAM in most synthesizers and samplers is not big enough to hold enough patches or soundfiles for an entire evening. Many setups require reloading all devices between songs — in some cases, assistants are loading unused synthesizers during a song.

Using the sequencing capabilities of the Macintosh in live performance is not as common, except in situations where there are not enough musicians to play all the parts or where sequencers were used in a recording of the work and the intent is to re-create the record on stage. The same rationale applies when samplers are used to re-create background vocals and other special effects that an audience has come to expect from repeated exposure to a widely played recording of the same work.

The Macintosh and MIDI are also used in live performance situations to synchronize other devices, such as drum machines and MIDI sequencers, or to convert audible triggers, for example, from a bass drum, into synchronization codes that can then be used to keep other devices in sync with the rest of the ensemble. Such applications also provide for sequenced material to be kept in time with a conductor's beat during a *musico-dramatic* performance where singers, dancers, or other human performers are being directed by the conductor.

Finally, samplers are occasionally used by symphony, ballet, and opera orchestras to provide for a little used instrument (for example, the cimbalom) or to simplify transportation (for example, a harpsichord or boys' choir) while on tour.

Intelligent instruments and interactive performance

Some of the characteristics of interactive computer music were mentioned above under "Composition." All of the same factors making interactive composition feasible apply here as well. The difference is that in an interactive performance the powers of interactive music software are focused more on the improvisation side of the spectrum rather than the act of musical composition. Because the object is to create a credible musical work on-the-fly instead of a file that can be subsequently realized electronically or output to paper, interactive performance also tends to capitalize upon alternate controllers and intelligent instruments rather than merely on manipulating on-screen software controls.

An intelligent instrument takes incoming information and processes it prior to passing it on for output. Processing of incoming data has become so fast that most of the systems currently in use appear to be operating in real time. Many interactive composition software packages provide for remote control of all or most of their transformational options to be accomplished from the external MIDI controller. On the other hand, many alternate controllers allow performers to pass more types of information simultaneously to the computer than would be humanly possible with a normal MIDI controller. The Macintosh mouse is also used as the controller for communicating information to the computer for real-time processing into music.

Control of audio performance parameters

Other common elements to be placed under Macintosh control in a real-time performance situation include MIDI routing, merging, processing, filtering, MIDI-controlled audio mixers, and perhaps more than anything else, MIDI-controllable DSP devices used to create such effects as delays, reverberation, flanging, filtering, and chorusing.

MIDI routing, merging, and filtering "patches" can be called up by a single patch change sent to devices with capabilities to respond appropriately to such commands. This permits your entire MIDI network configuration to be changed almost instantaneously, often with the press of a single button, which can be executed between the space of two notes or while one note or chord is sustaining, making the process completely imperceptible to the audience.

MIDI-controlled audio mixers are becoming increasingly popular, and dedicated MIDI controllers to interface with them are also becoming widespread. Some systems include the facility to take "snapshots" of all applicable settings on a mixing board and recall these remotely with a single command, while others provide for gradual changes over user-specified or predefined time periods.

The most popular type of audio control used in a live performance situation is the association of a distinct DSP effects setting with an individual sound or group of sounds. When sending the patch change to call up the desired sound, the same data is passed on to MIDI-controllable effects processors that have particular settings associated with that patch number. Some more sophisticated sound modules provide the option for remapping the received patch change to a new number as it is passed along the MIDI THRU port. The use of a MIDI processor can permit any instrument to perform this same reassignment.

Control of non-musical performance parameters

The Macintosh, via both MIDI and proprietary interfaces, is frequently called upon to control inherently non-musical elements in a performance situation. In this category are lighting, lasers, real-time animation, and video processing as well as other visual effects. In one case the Macintosh is used to configure the entire acoustical properties of the concert space through the rotation of wall and ceiling panels. See Part Five, "Performance."

Post-production

Post-production applications of the Macintosh, although long available, are only recently becoming widespread due to dropping prices of requisite software and hardware peripherals. The Macintosh has penetrated three areas of specialization:

❖ Studio automation
❖ Direct-to-hard disk recording
❖ Digital signal processing

Studio automation

As in live performance situations, Macintosh and MIDI-automatable mixing boards are being put under software control. In these cases, more emphasis is placed upon precision and non-real-time editing rather than real-time operation and instantaneous recall of predefined configuration. DSP devices are also being automated in this fashion, just as they are during live performances.

Direct-to-hard disk recording

Professional hard-disk-based digital recording systems and the digital mixing of material recorded with it have also moved into the domain of the Macintosh. Digital audio capabilities, previously requiring investments in the mid- to high-six figures, are now well within the reach of even modest home studios. For well under $5,000 for the appropriate Macintosh tools, you can now record, edit, and mix down audio of CD-quality and produce a master without ever leaving the digital domain. In this fashion, it is possible to produce a musical product that has never entered the analog domain until the end user plays the recording on a CD or DAT player.

Digital signal processing

The same systems that provide for direct-to-hard disk digital recording also permit digital signal processing without ever entering the analog domain. Filtering, EQ, noise reduction, normalization, envelope editing, and other DSP effects are some of the things that can be more faithfully achieved when the data does not have to be continually converted to and from the analog to digital domains.

Film and Video

The film and video segment of the entertainment industry was one of the first groups of professionals to embrace Macintosh music and sound technology. The Macintosh is widely applied to four tasks (see Figure 2-5):

❖ Scoring
❖ Synchronization of multiple devices or of music to television or film
❖ Automated dialog replacement (ADR)
❖ Sound effects (SFX)

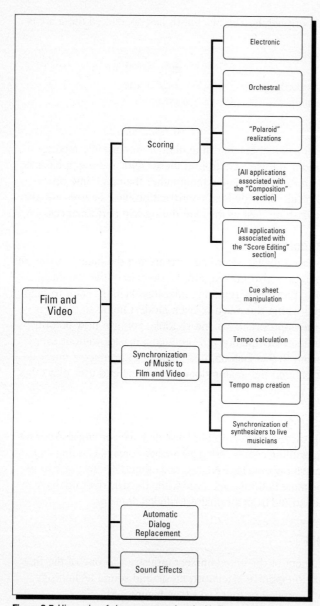

Figure 2-5: Hierarchy of elements associated with film and video.

Scoring

The Macintosh is used in many capacities in film and video scoring, regardless of whether the item being scored is a 30-second commercial or a three-hour feature film. Naturally, all the applications listed under the heading of "Composition" apply to this type of scoring, but even before the composition commences, Macintoshes are used to stripe videotape with time code, to capture and identify crucial visual "cuts" and "hits," to create "cue sheets," and to search tempos that allow "catching" the maximum number of these cuts and hits.

If the score is to be recorded acoustically, there is software that will print out blank score paper complete with timing information, hit points marked, descriptions of the action where it occurs in the score, and dialog. If the score is going to be realized electronically, the same software can be used to generate tempo maps with subtle timing changes that guarantee that each hit will be caught precisely. These tempo maps can be exported into most commercial MIDI sequencers that are commonly used to create the music in these cases. In either situation, the use of electronic devices to continually preview your evolving score precisely synchronized with the picture can be an invaluable aid to the scoring process for some composers.

Some film and video composers are even becoming facile enough with Macintosh notation software to be able to use Mac-printed scores and parts during scoring sessions. This practice can be motivated by considerations of time (if you are extremely fast with your notation software) and copying costs.

Synchronization of multiple devices or of music to television or film

The synchronization of music to film or video is one of the most common applications of the Macintosh in this industry. Fortunately, the Society of Motion Picture and Television Engineers has adopted a time code standard, appropriately called SMPTE Time Code, that facilitates synchronization. Through the use of imported tempo maps described above, it is possible to ensure that every desired musical event is perfectly synchronized with its appropriate visual event. But synchronization may also be used earlier in this process in a similar role as that described under the heading "Composition" — that is, for the recording of tracks individually onto a multitrack recorder or for the employment of virtual tracks.

One very common use of the Macintosh's synchronization capabilities is to synchronize MIDI-sequenced music being output by synthesizers and samplers to live musicians on the scoring stage. Here, as discussed before under the heading "Performance," an audible event is converted to sync pulses that drive the MIDI sequencers. However, in this case, the audible event is not the attack of the bass drum, but merely the metronomic click that is being fed to the live musicians through their headphones.

Finally, one obscure use of the Macintosh in this area is for "Polaroiding" film scores. This refers to the creation of an electronic rendition of a score that will eventually be performed by live musicians. Synchronizing the synth realization of the picture permits a producer and director to audition the music for the purposes of making suggestions and offering constructive criticism prior to incurring the major financial expense of recording an entire orchestra.

ADR and SFX

Both the fields of ADR (Automated Dialog Replacement) and sound effects are coming under the sway of the Macintosh. With software supporting EDLs (edit decision lists, also called playlists) — frame-address-locked lists that trigger specified events, in this case, music or audio — digital audio recordings as well as MIDI-triggered samplers can be used to automate these time-consuming activities that once relied upon a razor blade and tape-splicing block.

Multimedia

Multimedia has become the buzzword of the 1990s. Actually, serious artists have been creating works combining various media including music, film, slides, and live performers since the early '50s and have even been calling these works "multimedia works" or, to a lesser extent, "mixed media," "intermedia," or "happenings." The sudden embrace of multimedia by the business community has finally brought this concept to the attention of the masses. Unfortunately, it has also taken the acceptance of multimedia by these same corporations to somehow validate multimedia as a legitimate form of expression or communication.

In general, corporate America has come to describe as multimedia practically anything produced by computers that uses both sounds and images — if a human can direct the flow of this "multimedia" or navigate a patch of seemingly infinite variety through the thing in question, it is often called "interactive multimedia" and is elevated accordingly in the eyes of the beholder.

Considering the Macintosh as a multimedia tool leads one to several classifications of endeavors, not necessarily in any particular order:

❖ Multimedia in the business environment
❖ Desktop video with desktop audio
❖ Multimedia "art"

Multimedia in the business environment

Among other things, multimedia is employed in business for employee training, presentations (both in-house and public), advertising, interactive product demonstrations, and end-user training. Some innovative uses of multimedia in the corporate world include résumés of individuals and annual reports of entire companies. Interactive multimedia is useful wherever random or non-linear access to cross-referenced information is desired, or where multiple representations, analogies, or metaphors of concepts can benefit or expedite comprehension. In fact, multimedia can be effective in any instance where a picture is worth a thousand words ... just add music.

With the maturation of desktop publishing (DTP), businesses have become quite proficient at turning out flashy charts, graphics, and slide presentations. Give people a Macintosh, some graphics software, and in a couple of weeks they're producing first-class ad layouts.

The problem is that the DTP and graphics analogies don't hold for music, and corporate multimedia has raised many legal issues, largely precipitated by considerations of musical copyrights. You can't hold the Shift key down to write a beautiful melody (Yet!). So people get in the habit of just ripping off whatever music they need from commercial recordings. Fortunately, there are solutions. Clip music (a trademarked term of Dr. T's), which is analogous to clip art, is available in a variety of formats, both as prelicensed audio data and as MIDI data (see Part Eight, "Multimedia").

Desktop video with desktop audio

When corporate multimedia becomes slick and the people producing it start using more sophisticated tools, they cross an invisible line into the world of desktop video and desktop audio rather than multimedia. Somewhere along the line people arrived at the conclusion that interactive multimedia is hipper than non-interactive multimedia and that desktop video and audio is even cooler still. Actually, all of these fields are interrelated, but I will honor the distinction that desktop video and audio require slightly more formidable tools and expertise.

Multimedia "art"

Multimedia for art's sake is a vast territory, the explorations of which began hundreds if not thousands of years ago. After all, what is opera, if not multimedia? This not withstanding, I will limit this discussions to those artistic applications utilizing the Macintosh as the primary enabling technology empowering creative innovation (see Chapter 28, "Computer-Aided Instruction").

Networking

Most people on networks push around data on AppleTalk cables or similar wires. Modems, which operate via telephone lines, often figure into the scenario too. Just as musicians have an additional 88 keys (and often hundreds or thousands more buttons) to deal with than other computer users, the types of data they have to push around is considerably more diverse. Musicians encounter two types of networking: Telecommunications and Music LANs.

Telecommunications

Telecommunications is becoming a standard part of the Macintosh music studio. Excluding all of the normal uses of modems, they are also valuable to musicians for communicating with music networks and BBSs (bulletin board services) dedicated to the archiving of sample files, patches, and utilities for downloading, for remote MIDI control, and for distant collaboration.

Music LANs

Even in a mid-range Macintosh music setup, you confront a wide variety of data: MIDI, SMPTE, MTC, SCSI, ASCII, PostScript, analog audio, digital audio, video, and a variety of proprietary RS-422 formats. MIDI is for music and event control, SMPTE and MTC for synchronization, SCSI for storage of Macintosh-readable data as well as for proprietary sample formats, ASCII for typing, PostScript for printing music, both analog and digital audio for sound, and video for the normal purposes as well as for audio recording. As if that weren't enough, many synthesizers and samplers maintain proprietary data protocols via RS-422 lines. Finally, it is becoming increasingly common for advanced users to work with more than one computer to maintain a network in the traditional sense of the word.

Most of the data mentioned above requires its own type of cable. Data of the same class may additionally require elaborate hardware switching, routing, or patching devices. Two recent advances in this field are Mark of the Unicorn's MIDI Time Piece network, which increases the number of available MIDI channels from 16 or 32 to 512, while eliminating the need for any MIDI mergers, thru boxes, switchers, routers, or processors, and also provides for multiple Macintoshes on the network. An even more ambitious undertaking, Lone Wolf's MediaLink and MIDITap, provides for sending all the above mentioned data types down the same cable (a twisted pair or fiber optic) in both directions simultaneously.

Education

The presence of the Macintosh in music education is growing exponentially, spurred on by Apple's generous academic discounts and seeding. While the Macintosh can aid scholars and educators with many non-musical tasks (see Part Nine, "Education"), applications dedicated to instruction are divided into three general categories:

❖ Classroom
❖ Self-guided/interactive
❖ CD-ROMS, Compact Disc Interactive (CDI) and Interactive Videodiscs (IVD)

Classroom

Popular Macintosh CAI (computer-aided instruction) applications include ear training (with automatic pacing), harmony instruction (with error detection and feedback), orchestration (with sampling devices used as an orchestral "sketch pad"), performance practice monitoring, as well as music history and appreciation. HyperCard-based and dedicated applications generators provide software authoring tools that require minimal knowledge of programming — in other words, programming for the rest of us. Voyager's CD AudioStack provides educators with simple tools to create interactive instructional courseware using virtually any compact disc.

Self-guided/interactive

The Macintosh's role in self-guided education is growing as fast as its role in the classroom. In fact, many of the same programs are adaptable to both contexts (see Part Nine, "Education").

CD-ROMS, CDI, and IVD

HyperCard has stimulated much development in music education, including sophisticated CAI interfaces to educational videodiscs for the creation of IVDs (Interactive Videodiscs), CD-ROMs, and standard CDs (compact discs) that can be played on a CD-ROM player supporting audio output.

By placing a videodisc under Macintosh control, it is possible to address any individual frame or series of frames on the disc. Similarly, when a standard CD is played through a CD-ROM drive, playback can start at any point on the disc rather than at the beginning of a track as would be the case with an audio CD player. Development toolkits for both these media automate the creation of buttons or controls in HyperCard and other supported environments. You simply indicate what you want the button or control to do — start playing at frame 26468, play frames 13476 through 31790, or define a number of non-contiguous events to play back sequentially — and the authoring toolkit creates the button or control that will initiate the desired function.

While the above-mentioned methods permit nearly unlimited interactivity with a CD or VD, CDI (Compact Disc Interactive) is a standard unto itself for interactive CD-ROMs that can contain both audio and video data. These discs require dedicated CDI players, and the development systems are currently beyond the reach of individuals. The disadvantage of CDI is that no computer is required, therefore limiting interaction to a pointing device such as a joystick.

Musical and Acoustical Analysis

The development of Macintosh software for musical and acoustical analysis has lagged well behind all other categories of musical applications. While many cataloging and statistical applications are being accomplished with generic third-party database software, the real power of the Macintosh in this context is to actually analyze musical data gathered either in the form of notation or performance data. The vast majority of software in this area is being written for non-Macintosh computers. This is largely due to the fact that in nearly every case, custom applications are required and the task of programming the Macintosh up until very recently has not been trivial.

Another stumbling block holding up this type of development is the interminably slow-moving codification of a musical representation standard. Standard MIDI Files (SMF), unless the MIDI specification is extended to cover basic graphic notation elements (e.g., dynamics, articulations, and expressive markings) and context-dependent descriptions (e.g., whether a note is a sharp or a flat), will never be able to fulfill these needs. Fortunately, the American National Standards Institute committee on Musical Information Processing (MIPS) hopes to present a first draft of the proposed Standard Music Description Language (SMDL) by mid-1992. Once this standard is defined, MIDI translators and conversion utilities that facilitate the development of analytical software tools on the Macintosh will certainly appear.

The delay of a standardized representation of musical data should not be seen as an obstacle to musical and acoustical analysis. New software tools such as

EarLevel Engineering's Hyper MIDI can easily be adapted to accommodate for data missing from the SMF spec and will undoubtedly stimulate growth along these lines. Current development that has opted for forging ahead in spite of these obstacles is generally limited to four areas:

- ❖ Pedagogical research
- ❖ Musicological analysis and research
- ❖ Acoustical analysis
- ❖ Psychoacoustical analysis and research into musical perception

Programming for Music

Programming for Macintosh music applications is a rich field with opportunities available to individuals of all levels of programming abilities. Most of the other categories of Macintosh applications to music would not exist without software support. Development tools are available for three types of programming:

- ❖ Traditional programming languages
- ❖ Object-oriented languages
- ❖ Visual programming languages

Traditional programming languages

Most MIDI programming for commercial applications is done in the C language, and several MIDI extension packages take care of many of the MIDI routines and thus leave you free to concentrate on matters of functionality and interface. Pascal is used less and less. Special forms of Basic and Pascal are available, aptly named "MIDI Basic" and "MIDI Pascal." Likewise, there are at least two Lisp extensions dedicated to MIDI programming. There are even some versions of Forth optimized for MIDI development. Apple's own MacApp has been used to develop some of the most successful commercial music applications. Finally, there are always some people who prefer to program in 68000 assembly language directly, regardless of the difficulty.

Object-oriented languages

HyperCard, SuperCard, and Plus are often referred to as object-oriented programming (OOP) languages. This means that the operation of a program relies on the transmission of *messages* between *objects*. They are also referred to as *event-driven* environments because typically, an object will not take an action (technically called a *method*) unless an event triggers it. Other OOP concepts that are covered in this text include *properties, hierarchy,* and *inheritance.* Where HyperCard, SuperCard, and Plus differ from traditional OOP languages is that program code may be placed in actual visual objects.

Because these systems provide the ability to create objects using natural language (for example, if the mouse is down, then play the MIDI file "my masterpiece"), they have been touted as tools allowing programming for the rest of us. There is a good deal of truth in this claim. If you are under the impression that computer programming is a complex, tedious endeavor requiring considerable knowledge of an esoteric language, then these OOP tools are for you. Within hours you will discover that programming can be a fun and rewarding activity with plenty of opportunities for instant gratification.

There are some rather new MIDI extensions to HyperCard and related environments. EarLevel Engineering's HyperMIDI 2.0 offers the most complete set of MIDI tools available in this domain. Opcode's MIDIPlay and Passport's HyperMusic offer similar functionality without implementation of MIDI input.

Visual programming languages

Visual programming languages (sometimes called "icon-based" programming languages) are even easier than OOP languages for some people. Programs are constructed entirely by using the mouse to connect icons together. Rube Goldberg-looking networks are created, and in some cases these elaborate schematics may be collapsed into a single new icon with appropriate inputs and outputs for connecting to other icons.

Typical examples of visual programming languages include VPL's HookUp! and Lone Arranger (both formerly distributed by Hip Software), Opcode's Max, and Serius's Serius.

Ancillary Tasks

The Macintosh can perform a number of ancillary tasks for musicians. Surprisingly, many of these are often overlooked by users who consider their Macintosh to be a dedicated MIDI or music tool. Because the main focus of this book is on applications for musical creativity, coverage is limited in the ancillary tasks area. However, because one of the concerns of this book is to use the Macintosh to increase creative productivity, there are certain topics that increase your overall efficiency in dealing with the non-musical tasks in your life so as to free up additional time for creative endeavors.

❖ Business
❖ Organizational
❖ Utilities

Business

Commercial software exists to automate nearly every aspect of the business side of your musical life. With respect to accounting, the Macintosh can easily handle everything from balancing your checkbook to managing the billing and payroll of even the largest professional studios. You can use the Macintosh for all your word processing, to generate personalized form letters through mail merge software, and to create print ads with desktop publishing software. Graphics software can be used to great advantage in configuring the layout of your studio from determining optimum placement of rack-mounted modules to designing the entire structure to house your studio. Using the Macintosh to create wiring diagrams and data routing flow charts can save you plenty of time when it becomes necessary to track down a problem. If the Macintosh is used to its fullest capacity, there is little need to use a pencil and paper again.

Organizational

Database and related programs are a natural for the Macintosh music studio, regardless of size. These can be used to catalog everything from samples, patches, sequence setups, track sheets, and recordings to tracking clients and leads and maintaining a personal address book. Time management software is another must for musicians. Calendar and project management software is available for both single- and multi-user environments. There are a number of wonderful reminder utilities that can interface with some of the popular calendar programs.

Utilities

Utilities is a special category. There are those dedicated to musical tasks, those dedicated to non-musical tasks, which can easily be adapted to musical tasks, and those dedicated to enhancing overall speed, productivity, and efficiency, no matter what type of activity you are engaged in. There are five main types of utilities: desk accessories, INITs, cdevs, FKeys, and dedicated programs that fulfill a utilitarian function.

Exploiting the available utility enhancements of your Macintosh computing environment is possibly the single most important determinant in increasing your overall creative productivity. For more on music and general utilities, see the coupon in the back of the book.

Summary

✔ The Macintosh is now being employed in every possible area of music and sound: sound design, composition, notation, performance, post-production, film and video, multimedia, networking, education, musical and acoustical analysis, programming, and ancillary music business tasks.

✔ At the beginning of the process, sound design applications of the Macintosh included synthesis, sampling, sound editing and analysis, and organization. Other sources of sound material include telecommunications networks, commercial libraries, and sounds stored in the ROM chips of external devices.

✔ After accumulating sound material, Macintosh applications supporting creative input include computer-assisted composition, computer-generated composition, and interactive composition, all of which are available to both the MIDI and non-MIDI musician. The impact of the Macintosh upon composition rivals that of the printing press upon text.

✔ While desktop music publishing is now within reach of every Macintosh user, notation software has evolved to the professional level required by the world's most renowned publishers. The concepts of "publication on demand" and electronic distribution of music are now a reality.

✔ On the performance stage, the Macintosh is being used to automate both musical and non-musical parameters of real-time performance. The latter includes lighting, signal processing, room acoustics, and real-time computer animation and video. Some musicians use the Macintosh to record their performances as MIDI or digital audio data.

✔ The presence of the Macintosh in post-production is becoming more prevalent with the less expensive systems dedicated to direct-to-hard disk recording, digital signal processing, and studio automation.

✔ Film, video, and multimedia are areas where the Macintosh has become the de facto standard. Film scoring, synchronization, automatic dialog replacement, and sound effects are but a few common tasks now placed under Macintosh control. Clip music (prelicensed music) is a growing resource for multimedia production.

✔ Networking and telecommunications are very important to the Macintosh music community. Anyone with a synthesizer, MIDI interface, and Macintosh has the beginnings of a Music Local Area Network. Many telecommunications networks and BBSs focus on Macintosh music. It is now possible to "jam" with a colleague over a modem.

✔ Nearly every aspect of music education now has Macintosh software support. There is software available from multiple vendors for ear training, music theory, music history and appreciation, composition, orchestration, and even monitoring instrumental practice. The Macintosh has engendered entire new forms of interactive and self-guided music learning tools. The Macintosh also provides a wealth of new tools for music educators, scholars, and researchers.

✔ The Macintosh is used to dealing with the business aspects of music too. Common uses range from client and project management, bookkeeping, accounting, and desktop publishing to sound databases and studio design.

Chapter 3

Mac Music Studio Basics

In this chapter . . .

✔ Setting up a Macintosh-based music studio or workstation.

✔ An overview of non-MIDI-oriented setups including those dedicated to 8-bit and 16-bit digital audio, music desktop publishing, multimedia, and education.

✔ An overview of MIDI-oriented setups and workstation setups.

✔ A chart illustrating every possible configuration of Macintosh NuBus cards dedicated to synthesis, sampling, digital signal processing, and direct-to-hard disk recording.

Getting Set Up for Your Studio Setup

In this and the next four chapters you will discover what you need to know about setting up a Macintosh-based music studio or workstation. Even if you already have a setup for Macintosh music, you may find it useful to review some of this information. It is easy to determine which information you can skip over, allowing you to zoom in on exactly what pertains to your particular setup.

In this chapter I examine the three general directions you can take in this respect and what the essential ingredients are depending upon your intended application.

In the next three chapters you will find information about the extent of financial outlay you can expect, calculated by considering both your expected level of use and your projected activities. Included are some helpful tables for determining these figures.

Approaches

There are three main approaches to using your Macintosh for music, sound, and multimedia:

❖ Non-MIDI-oriented setups
❖ MIDI-oriented setups
❖ The Macintosh as a self-contained workstation

Non-MIDI-oriented Setups

It may come as a surprise to you if you're used to thinking of music and the Macintosh as something revolving around MIDI, but there are plenty of musical applications for the Macintosh that do not involve MIDI. There are possibilities in the following areas:

❖ 8-bit non-MIDI music
❖ 16-bit digital audio
❖ Education
❖ Music desktop publishing
❖ Multimedia

8-bit non-MIDI music

First, you can get pretty deeply involved in music and the Macintosh without making any additional purchases beyond your computer. I refer to using HyperCard to create music with 8-bit sampled sounds. It is possible to amass entire hard disks full of public domain sounds that you can manipulate entirely within HyperCard — and everyone gets HyperCard free with their Macintosh.

You can significantly expand your horizons in this area by purchasing an input device in the form of an 8-bit digitizer (sampler) such as MacroMind-Paracomp's MacRecorder or Articulate Systems's VoiceLink. The newer Macintoshes (Macintosh Classic, Macintosh LC, and Macintosh IIsi) all have built-in digitizing capabilities. Finally, you can even build a digitizer for very little expense; the complete schematics for such a device are provided in Chapter 10, "Sound Generation." Using a digitizer, you will be able to create your own soundfiles for use in HyperCard or other applications that can make use of 8-bit soundfiles.

Finally, if you decide to spend some money on software in this area, you have a number of choices:

❖ Studio Session
❖ Jam Session
❖ Super Studio Session
❖ HyperComposer

8-bit digital audio with the Macintosh is often referred to as "low-end digital audio" in this book, as opposed to 16-bit digital audio, which is often referred to as "high-end digital audio."

Music desktop publishing

Many notation software packages provide for proofhearing through the Macintosh's internal sound-generating capabilities. Most notation packages also offer alternatives to entering music via MIDI in the form of clicking notes on staves with the mouse or remapping the Macintosh keyboard into something resembling a musical keyboard. These packages are discussed in Part Four, "Notation."

Table 3-1 shows just how prevalent music desktop publishing is.

Table 3-1: Notation software and music desktop publishing features		
	Proofhear through Macintosh speaker	Note-entry with mouse	Note-entry with keyboard emulation, on-screen keyboard, or ADB (Apple Desktop Bus) peripheral
ConcertWare	●	●	●
Deluxe Music	●	●	●
Encore	○	●	●
Finale	●	●	●
HB Engraver	○	●	○
Lime	●	○	●
Music Publisher	●	○	●
Music Writer	○	●	○
MusicProse	●	●	●
Nightingale	●	●	○
NoteWriter	○	●	●
Professional Composer	●	●	●
SpeedScore	○	●	○

16-bit digital audio

With the introduction of Studer Editech's Dyaxis and Digidesign's Sound Accelerator and Audiomedia NuBus cards, it has become possible to work with CD-quality audio on the Macintosh. CD-quality, you recall, refers to 16-bit samples with a sample rate of 44.1 KHz or greater. Direct-to-hard disk recording is one possibility with these systems.

While high-end professionals often use these cards in conjunction with MIDI, where MIDI is used to synchronize digital audio data to film and video, there is a world of applications employing these cards in the realms of multimedia and education, not to mention mastering compact discs using the Macintosh as a dedicated digital recorder.

Multimedia

Whether 8-bit or 16-bit digital audio, the Macintosh can inject sound and music into multimedia presentations and interactive applications without ever requiring MIDI. Examples of authoring software to produce these presentations are: MacroMind Director, Apple HyperCard, Silicon Beach's SuperCard, and Serius's Programmer or Developer. One particularly useful feature of Digidesign's Audiomedia and Sound Designer software is the ability to save soundfiles in a "chunky" format, which will play back at 16-bit if accessed on a Macintosh equipped with a Sound Accelerator or Audiomedia card, and will revert to 8-bit playback through the Macintosh speaker if no card is present. The same is true of Passport Designs's Alchemy, which uses the Sound Accelerator or Audiomedia card if it's present. See Part Eight, "Multimedia" for more information about these applications.

Education

Today, there are probably more non-MIDI applications of the Macintosh within education than there are MIDI applications. However, this imbalance is rapidly changing. At present, educational applications are predominantly based around the following platforms:

❖ HyperCard   ❖ SuperCard
❖ Director   ❖ Serius
❖ Authorware   ❖ IVDs (Interactive Videodiscs)
❖ Interactive CD-ROMs

In general, these applications are dedicated to ear training, music history, and appreciation, as well as music theory and analysis.

MIDI-oriented Setups

Macintosh music setups centering around MIDI are legion, and the greater part of this book is given over to these types of setups and applications. Suffice it to say that MIDI-oriented setups can play a major role in all the activities categories discussed in Chapter 2. The primary items include:

❖ Music desktop publishing (including notation)
❖ MIDI music (including composition and performance)
❖ 16-bit digital audio
❖ Film and video
❖ Multimedia
❖ Education

The Macintosh as a Self-contained Workstation

Using Macintosh's NuBus slots for music and digital-audio cards can turn your Macintosh into a veritable MIDI or digital audio workstation of formidable power.

The cards available at this time include Studer Editech's Dyaxis plus Excellerator DSP card, Digidesign's Sound Accelerator (included with their Sound Tools package), Audio Card (included with their ProTools package), Audiomedia, MacProteus, SampleCell, Mark of the Unicorn's Digital Wareboard, and Symbolic Systems's Kyma Interface Card (required to access their Capybara DSP box), all of which offer 16-bit digital signal processing and/or direct-to-hard disk recording at professional sampling rates. In the 8-bit world there is Passport Designs's innovative Sound Exciter, a virtual MIDI sample player existing entirely in software.

With a Macintosh II, IIx, or IIfx, you have six NuBus slots, five of which can be dedicated to music and digital audio (you need to reserve one for the video card). On a Macintosh IIcx or IIci, you have three NuBus slots, two of which may be used for music and digital audio cards on the IIcx, and on the IIci all three may be used, if you are using its built-in video rather than a NuBus video card. On an SE/30 or IIsi, you have a single NuBus slot. There are slot expansion chassis available for many Macintosh models, although these are currently extremely expensive.

MIDI, if used in any of these configurations, can be routed entirely through Apple's MIDI Manager or OMS (see Chapter 8, "Moving Data Around Your Music Network"), without requiring any additional hardware such as an external MIDI interface.

The following list indicates some of the configurations that are possible, if you use all available slots. The cards are:

MacProteus   MIDI-controlled 32-voice ROM sample player

Sound Accelerator   DSP card with 2-track direct-to-hard disk capabilities
                        (Sound Tools)

Audio Card   DSP card with 4-track direct-to-hard disk capabilities
                        (Sound Tools Pro)
                        (Up to four may be installed, but if you install more
                        than a single Audio Pro card you need Digidesign's
                        System Accelerator card to manage SCSI output)

Audiomedia   DSP card with 4-track direct-to-hard disk capabilities

SampleCell   MIDI-controlled 16-voice, 8 out, 8MB RAM sample player (Up to four may be installed)

Kyma Interface Card Required to access the Capybara DSP box

Excellerator   DSP card for real-time digital EQ, sample rate conversion, time compression and expansion, etc.
(Up to two may be installed, a Dyaxis is required for direct-to-hard disk capabilities)

Each dot in Table 3-2 represents the possibility of installing a NuBus card. There are other variations that have been omitted because of their infrequency. For example, you could fill all slots with MacProteus cards if you really like the sound and want to increase its polyphony. Likewise, multimedia developers who want to cover all the bases might want to have two types of direct-to-hard disk recording cards such as the Sound Accelerator and the Audiomedia card. Table 3-2 lists only the most logical configurations.

Table 3-2: NuBus card configurations

MacProteus	Sound Accelerator	Audio Card	Audiomedia	SampleCell	Kyma Interface	Excellerator
Mac II, IIx, IIfx						
•	•			•••		
•		•		•••		
•		••①		••		
•		•••①		•		
•			•	•••		
•				•••	•	
•				••••		
•	•			••		•
•	•			•		••
•				•••		•
	•			••		••
	•			•••		•
	•			••••		
		•		•••		•

Table 3-2: NuBus card configurations (continued)

MacProteus	Sound Accelerator	Audio Card	Audiomedia	SampleCell	Kyma Interface	Excellerator
		●		●●		●●
		●		●●●●		
		●●①		●		●
		●●①		●●		
		●●●①		●		●
		●●●●①				
			●	●●		●●
			●	●●●		●
			●	●●●●		
				●●	●	●●
				●●●	●	●
				●●●●	●	

Mac IIci (built-in video)

MacProteus	Sound Accelerator	Audio Card	Audiomedia	SampleCell	Kyma Interface	Excellerator
●	●			●		
●	●					●
●		●		●		
●		●				●
●			●	●		
●			●			●
●				●	●	
●					●	●
●				●		●
●						●●
	●			●		●
	●			●●		
	●					●●
		●		●		●
		●		●●		
		●				●●

Table 3-2: NuBus card configurations (continued)

MacProteus	Sound Accelerator	Audio Card	Audiomedia	SampleCell	Kyma Interface	Excellerator
		●●①				
			●	●●		
			●			●●
				●	●	●
				●●	●	
					●	●●
				●●		●
				●		●●
				●●●		

Mac IIci (with video card) or Mac IIcx

MacProteus	Sound Accelerator	Audio Card	Audiomedia	SampleCell	Kyma Interface	Excellerator
●	●					
●		●				
●			●			
●				●		
●					●	
●						●
	●			●		
	●					●
		●		●		
		●				●
			●	●		
			●			●
				●	●	
				●●		
					●	●
						●●

Mac IIsi or SE/30

MacProteus	Sound Accelerator	Audio Card	Audiomedia	SampleCell	Kyma Interface	Excellerator
●						
	●					

Table 3-2: NuBus card configurations (continued)

MacProteus	Sound Accelerator	Audio Card	Audiomedia	SampleCell	Kyma Interface	Excellerator
		●				
			●			
					IIsi	
						IIsi

Note: ① indicates System Accelerator card is required if more than a single Digidesign Audio Card (from the Sound Tools Pro package) is present.

One important fact to keep in mind when installing multiple cards in a single Macintosh is that accessing more than one or two cards simultaneously may require the speed of a Macintosh IIci or IIfx. Only a Macintosh IIfx, Quadra, and other future 68040-based CPUs are guaranteed to be able to handle as many cards as you can install. Alternatively, you can install a CPU accelerator to provide the required speed, but be sure to check that it is compatible with the cards you want to install. Of course, there are still reasons to install multiple cards even if they can't be accessed simultaneously — it is standard operating procedure to use one card or combination of cards on one project and another on a different project.

Taking the first setup as a model (a Macintosh II, IIx, or IIfx with a MacProteus card, a Sound Accelerator card, and three SampleCell cards), might be a typical configuration of MIDI Manager that would use all these devices under the control of a sequencer such as Opcode's StudioVision. (See Figure 3-1.)

This is clearly an instance of the Macintosh as an extremely powerful self-contained workstation and one that does not require any additional external devices, except for an amplifier and speakers. One would probably want to add a mixer with EQ and some effects for going out to tape or DAT and for direct-to-hard disk recording. A MIDI controller for MIDI sequence entry would be another obvious addition.

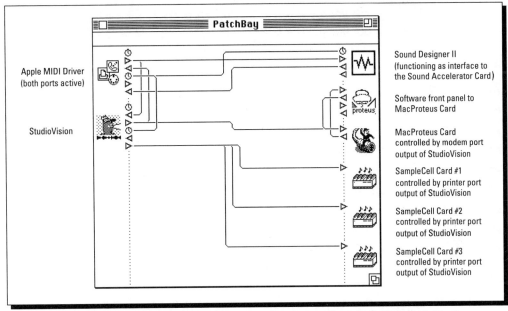

Figure 3-1: This is a typical MIDI Manager configuration for a 6-slot Macintosh loaded with Digidesign's MacProteus card, Sound Accelerator card, and three SampleCell cards. Opcode's StudioVision is controlling the show. Its modem port outputs are routed to the MacProteus and its printer port outputs are routed to the three SampleCells. Digidesign's Sound Designer II is providing access to their Sound Accelerator card and the MacProteus Front Panel program is being used as a virtual front panel to the MacProteus card.

Summary

✔ There are an equal number of non-MIDI and MIDI music applications for the Macintosh. Non-MIDI music applications include 8-bit and 16-bit digital audio, music desktop publishing, multimedia, and education.

✔ Most music notation software does not require MIDI. Proofhearing can be accomplished through the Macintosh's built-in speaker or audio output jack. Alternatives to MIDI entry of notation data include note-entry using the mouse, through the Macintosh keyboard emulating a musical keyboard, through an on-screen musical keyboard, or dedicated ADB peripheral.

✔ Using current digital signal processing and direct-to-hard disk recording cards, there are at least 73 possible configurations of Macintosh IIs and SE/30s if you fill all available slots. Many of these configurations transform your Macintosh into a music workstation as powerful as those costing literally hundreds of times as much just a few years ago.

✔ Accessing more than one or two digital audio cards simultaneously may require the speed of a Macintosh IIci, IIfx, Quadra, and other future 68040-based CPUs. Alternatively, you can install a CPU accelerator to provide the required speed. There are still reasons to install multiple cards even if you cannot access them simultaneously — it is standard operating procedure to use one card or combination of cards on one project and another on a different project.

Chapter 4

Choosing Your Mac

In this chapter...

✔ Descriptions of the hardware characteristics of all Macintosh models.

✔ Reasons favoring faster Macintoshes.

✔ Recommended Macintoshes organized by usage level.

✔ Enhancing your Macintosh.

✔ Hard drives, backup systems, SCSI, and storage media alternatives.

✔ Everything you need to know about RAM and RAM expansion.

✔ FPUs, PMMUs, virtual memory, upgrades, and accelerators.

✔ Twenty-five purchasing tips for computer and music gear.

What Do You Want to Do With Your Mac?

This chapter advises you on what type of Macintosh to purchase from several standpoints: first, based upon your level or the level you wish to attain, and second, based upon the focus of your activities — I have delineated seven types:

❖ 8-bit non-MIDI music
❖ Desktop music publishing (including notation)
❖ MIDI music (including composition and performance)
❖ 16-bit digital audio
❖ Film and video
❖ Multimedia
❖ Education

In some cases these activities overlap. One example is that if you are using MIDI for computer-assisted composition, there is a great probability that you may want to do notation. Likewise, you may already know that you will be using your Macintosh in a variety of categories.

I have omitted "programming for music" from this list of activities for obvious reasons. If you are writing software for music, the object of your labors will certainly fall within one of the above types of activities, and therefore you should examine those sections to determine the setup that your intended users may be expected to possess.

Macintosh Models, Macintosh Decisions

The type of Macintosh you need will depend entirely upon how far you want to take your Macintosh music and sound activities. As I mentioned in the "Introduction," the speed and power of your computer is directly related to creative productivity. With this in mind, I strongly suggest that you get the fastest Macintosh that you can afford.

It is surprising how many studios I visit that contain between $100,000 and a million dollars worth of synthesizers, video and audio equipment, and yet have everything under the control of a single Macintosh Plus. Even more surprising is the resistance to the suggestion that they upgrade to a computer more in league with the rest of their gear.

If you are serious about doing anything with a Macintosh, never forget that a faster model is going to mean that you spend less time looking at the watch cursor and consequently have more time for creativity. The seconds and milliseconds add up very quickly. If it takes you 40 seconds to save a file with a slower computer and 10 seconds to save with a faster computer, and you save your files about every ten minutes (which is about the longest amount of time you should allow between file saves), then you are saving three minutes every hour. If you work in the studio for ten hours straight, that adds up to a half hour a day or 3.5 hours a week, or 14 hours a month. And this is only when file saves are taken into consideration. If you also add in the time saved booting up your computer, launching and quitting applications, opening and closing files, reaction to menu selections, scrolling within windows and dialogs, even the time it takes a dialog to appear on the screen and the screen redrawing itself, you can save a staggering amount of time each day by bumping up to a faster computer or accelerating your current computer. I am talking about saving literally several hours each day merely by doubling the speed of your processor; for example, upgrading an SE to an SE/30.

I don't want anyone to think that this discussion is meant to denigrate owners of less powerful Macintoshes or in any way project a negative connotation regarding the slower machines. The point is more for shock value and to emphasize the recommendation that instead of buying another synthesizer module, the money might be better spent in bringing your Macintosh up to a level consistent with your abilities and the rest of your equipment. A large number of the people working with faster models today achieved a great many significant accomplishments with a Macintosh Plus and even with a 128K and 512K. In fact, if you own a Plus and follow the power user techniques available in the products mentioned in the coupon in the back of the book, as well as the specific tips you find in the intervening nine sections, you will even be able to run rings around less informed owners of the most powerful Macintosh IIfx!

With this in mind, Table 4-1 presents recommendations for the computer I consider to be the minimum requirement for 12 levels of usage as listed below.

Levels 1 to 3   Beginner through amateur
Levels 4 to 6   Hobbyist through intermediate
Levels 7 to 9   Semi-professional through professional
Levels 10 to 12   Advanced professional through power-user

The Macintosh models are listed roughly in order of speed. I have included computers that have been discontinued, because many of you will own a discontinued model and others of you may find extremely good deals on purchasing a used Macintosh from the group that has been discontinued.

My position on discontinued computers is, don't buy one unless you really have to (remember the second and third rules from the "Introduction"). The exceptions to this are cases where you might want to purchase a discontinued model in order to upgrade the logic board to a current, faster model because this can sometimes be cheaper than purchasing the newer model outright. For example, the discontinued Macintosh II and IIx models can be upgraded to a Macintosh IIfx at a great savings over purchasing a IIfx outright. The Macintosh IIcx can be upgraded to a IIci, and Apple has promised 68040 upgrades for the IIci in the future.

Table 4-1: Mac user levels

Macintosh	1	2	3	4	5	6	7	8	9	10	11	12
Plus (discontinued)	●											
SE (discontinued)	●	●										
Classic	●	●	●									
Portable	▸	▸	▸	▸								
LC	▸	●	●	●	▸							
Classic II		▸	▸	●	●	●	▸					
II (discontinued)		▸	●	●	●	▸	▸	▸	①	①	①	①
SE/30		▸	▸	●	●	●	▸					
IIcx (discontinued)		▸	●	●	●	▸	▸		②			
IIx (discontinued)		▸	●	●	●	▸	▸	▸		①	①	①
IIsi				●	●	●	●	●	▸	▸		
IIci					▸	●	●	●	●	▸	▸	
IIfx						▸	▸	●	●	●	●	●

① Indicated as a good choice because of the comparatively low cost to upgrade to a IIfx.
② One redeemable quality of the IIcx at this level is the upgrade path to the IIci (and further when Apple releases new CPUs).

Recommended Macintosh Enhancements

When I bought my first Macintosh, a 128K, in 1984 (for over $2,000, even after having driven all the way to New Hampshire to avoid paying sales tax), the salesperson sweetened the deal by throwing in three free (400K) floppy disks, at the same time informing me that these would hold somewhere between 1,500 and 2,000 pages of data. "After all," he continued, "they add up to almost ten times the entire memory of the computer." I thanked him profusely for the freebies and, after doing some quick calculations on the amount of music and letters I wrote in any given year, naively replied, "Well these three disks should last me at least a year." I couldn't have been more wrong.

Now I have nearly 5,000 floppy disks, 20 removable 45MB cartridges, and almost 1.5 gigabytes of hard drives (2 gigabytes if you count the CD-ROM drive) attached to my computer at all times. And if I need more room, which I sometimes do, I shoot files over AppleTalk to the hard drives attached to one of the other two systems on the network.

Hard drives

One of the members of the original Macintosh development team once stated, "A Macintosh without a hard drive is like a car without a gas tank," and that continues to be a valid concept. A hard drive is required to run System 7.

The first peripheral you should consider adding to your Macintosh is a hard drive. For anyone involved in Macintosh music and sound in any form, I recommend an absolute minimum capacity of 40MB. Most 40MB hard drives run at least seven and often nine or ten times faster than a floppy disk.

One word of caution: There are still some non-SCSI hard drives floating around in the used equipment classified ads. These are to be avoided at all cost. If you purchase a used Apple hard drive, make sure it has "HDSC" in the model number and not just "HD." The original Apple HD ran through the extremely slow external floppy disk drive port.

SCSI

SCSI, pronounced "scuzzy," stands for Small Computer System Interface, a high speed data transfer protocol. The Mac Plus was the first Macintosh to include a SCSI port, and every Macintosh since then has one on the back. The most common SCSI devices are hard drives, but many other devices also communicate with the Macintosh via SCSI. These include CD-ROM players, scanners, samplers, tape backup systems, external digital audio systems (such as Studer Editech's Dyaxis system and Symbolic Technologies's Kyma system), non-PostScript laser printers, and at least one voice recognition device (Articulate Systems's Voice Navigator).

Up to eight SCSI devices can be linked together on the SCSI bus. When multiple devices are attached along the bus, this is referred to as a daisychain. Because the Macintosh itself counts as a SCSI device, that leaves you room for up to seven peripherals.

Every device on the SCSI chain must have a unique SCSI address or ID ranging from 0 to 7. This can't be stressed strongly enough. Put in another way, it means that no two devices can have the same ID number. If you are unsure of the ID numbers of any devices, do not include them in the chain until you are sure.

The Macintosh itself is always SCSI ID 7, and any internal hard drives are supposed to be preset to ID 0. The order of ID numbers of the devices on the SCSI chain is irrelevant, although some people claim that if you are booting off an external hard drive, it is better to have that drive set to SCSI ID 6. I have used every possible order and configuration of SCSI addresses and can detect no difference whatsoever by setting the boot drive to ID 6.

The first and last device in a SCSI chain must be terminated. This refers to the first and last devices as they are arranged along the cable, not with respect to their ID numbers that can be in any order. Observe the following rules:

❖ If you have a single external hard drive and no internal drive, then your external drive should be terminated. For the record, I have run many unterminated drives in a single SCSI device system without any ill effects.

❖ If you have two external devices and no internal drive, theoretically you should terminate both of them (that is why a terminator has room to plug a cable into it). In practice, I've run many two-drive systems where only the last drive was terminated and never experienced any problems.

❖ If you have more than two external devices and no internal drive, then the first and last device must be terminated, and all intervening devices (there could be up to four) must be unterminated.

❖ If you have an internal drive (you can assume it is terminated) and a single external drive, you should terminate the external drive. For the record, I have run many unterminated drives in systems that include terminated internal drives without any ill effects.

❖ If you have an internal drive and two or more external devices, the very last device must be terminated. All intervening devices must be unterminated. An easy way to check if everything is all right is to see if there are any SCSI ports with nothing connected to them. This will be the last device on the chain and requires a terminator.

❖ If you have a Macintosh IIfx, you must use a special black external terminator that you can obtain from Apple (don't even think about hooking up external SCSI devices to a Mac IIfx without this special black terminator!).

❖ Never have more than two terminators on the SCSI chain. This can draw excessive current from the SCSI controller chip in the computer and damage it.

Of course, the above is a moot point if you never turn off your Macintosh or external SCSI devices. For years the Macintosh community has vacillated back and forth about the advisability of leaving your Macintosh on all the time. The current prevailing school of thought about this is to never shut down your Macintosh. The reasoning is that booting up places extra stress on all electrical components as well as hardware components in external devices (such as drive motors). Furthermore, there are many good arguments about the effect of changes of temperature upon chips and drive platters.

SCSI 2

Current Macintoshes use SCSI 1 protocol to transfer data to SCSI devices. The SCSI implementation of the Macintosh limits the transfer rate to 1.5MB per second, although some models such as the Macintosh IIci can achieve transfer rates up to 2MB per second. SCSI 2 provides for between 2.1 and 4.4MB per second transfer rates.

Storage media alternatives

Hard drives aren't the only SCSI mass storage media available. Nowadays your options include removable magnetic cartridges, WORM drives, optical drives, CD-ROM drives, tape, battery-backed RAM drives, and flopticals.

Removable cartridges are of particular interest to Macintosh musicians, because many samplers and sample players now support SCSI hard drives. The problem is that these musical devices require that the drives be formatted in proprietary formats. With a normal fixed hard drive this means that once it is formatted for a particular sampler, it cannot be used for anything else without completely erasing its entire contents. Removable media permits individual cartridges to be formatted each for a separate device. You can have some cartridges formatted for your Kurzweil, Emulator, or S1000, while others are formatted for use with the Macintosh: the best of both worlds. There is even no reason to have to plug and unplug cables to change devices, because inexpensive SCSI switch-boxes are now available that allow you to have all your devices on-line at all times and merely switch to the destination device and insert the appropriately formatted cartridge.

The most popular forms of removable magnetic cartridge drives in the Macintosh community are based upon the 45MB Syquest mechanism (usually formatted to between 42- and 44MB). While Syquest itself does not market a cartridge drive, many vendors market drives using its technology. These range from $500 to $1,500 for a single cartridge device, to $2,500 for a double cartridge device. Most include a cartridge or two when you purchase them. Additional cartridges cost between $65 and $100 (less if purchased in quantities), depending upon which manufacturer's name is on the box. That's like getting a 45MB hard drive for $75 and you can't beat that.

Syquest-based drives have other advantages besides price and multiple functionality. Averaging a 25-millisecond access time, they are as fast as many fixed drives and even fast enough to support direct-to-hard disk digital audio systems. They are extremely portable and an excellent backup medium. It's much easier to eject a cartridge and slip it into your briefcase than to unplug a fixed drive and pack it up for transportation. Finally, because so many Macintosh owners use them, it is easy to bring data to another location with the assurance of compatibility between cartridge players of different manufacturers (sometimes you will have to bring along the INIT that came with your drive as well).

The competing format to Syquest, the Bernoulli technology, although predating Syquest by years, has not fared so well with the Macintosh community. Bernoulli cartridges come in 10-, 20-, and 44MB capacities and are more durable than Syquest (if you can believe the company's claims). You probably could throw them across the room without worry. The problem is that they are more expensive than Syquest mechanisms; the cartridges themselves are more expensive, and very few musicians use them. You should only consider a Bernoulli box if you don't ever want to exchange data with friends and colleagues or if you happen to live in a community where everyone else is in the Bernoulli camp.

Several companies are starting to push a new 50MB Ricoh mechanism cartridge technology at the time of this writing, and 88MB Syquest cartridges are now available from many vendors. With the immense installed base of the 45MB Syquest systems, it will be difficult for this new standard to capture a significant market share, at least with respect to the Macintosh music community. You should survey your friends and colleagues and consider the benefits of compatibility.

The first type of optical drive to appear, the WORM (write-once read-many) drive, can hold up to one gigabyte of data. They have little popularity with mainstream Macintosh musicians, because they are not erasable. Also, they are expensive (over $3,000) and slow. I can't think of any use for them whatsoever, except perhaps to archive a completed album project or something of that nature. After all, what good is data if you can't play with it? There are many non-musical applications for these machines, because many scientific, business, and information management tasks require that every version of a particular file be preserved for future scrutiny. Since these drives can't be erased even if you wanted to, they are perfect for such chores.

The type of removable media that gets the award for most promising new storage technology is the *magneto-optical* drive. For many years the slowest of all alternatives, recent advances have resulted in speeds that finally support direct-to-hard disk digital audio recording (i.e., just under 28-ms access time). This speed increase is generally limited to the recently introduced 3.5-inch magneto-opticals, so make sure that this is the dimension of the optical drive you are considering. While this is still at least 50 percent slower (considering both access time and transfer rate) than most fixed hard drives, it is certainly tolerable for many people.

Optical cartridges generally have a capacity of around 600MB (give or take 50MB), 225MB to 325MB per side, and they are cheap, averaging about $160 to $220 a piece. I'll do the math for you: For the price of 90MB of removable Syquest cartridges, you can get 600MB of optical storage. The bad news is that the drive mechanism itself is over $4,000. In addition, removable opticals are not compatible across all vendors' drive mechanisms. Personally, I'm waiting for these to get down in price and start showing access times closer to the less than 15 ms I've come to expect from the Microtech 1.2GB drive I'm using before I consider purchasing one.

Tape drives have been around longer than SCSI itself. Because access to data on tape is serial rather than random, they are primarily used for backup and archiving purposes. A confusing number of formats are available from many different manufacturers: Teac (60- or 150MB), DC600 (250MB), DC2000 (40-, 60-, 80-, or 120MB), 4mm helical scan or DAT (1.2GB), and 8mm helical scan (2.2GB). Note that the last two use standard DAT tapes and 8mm videotapes respectively, so the price per megabyte is extremely low. The cost for the mechanisms goes up as the price per megabyte drops. Teac mechanisms run between $600 and $1,000; DC2000 mechanisms range from $1,000 to $1,500; 4mm DAT mechanisms run between $2,000 and $3,000; and 8mm systems are generally over $4,000.

The DAT format is becoming increasingly popular, and the prices are dropping to reflect this. The price per megabyte is about $1.50, and this is reduced to about 75¢ when you buy your second tape. Transfer speed is fast (I average nearly 10MB per minute with Microtech's DAT backup system). Reliability is high (provided you are using reliable backup software) and automation is extremely easy. Finally, 4mm DAT cartridges, smaller than audio cassettes, are extremely transportable. It can make you feel extremely secure to have a reliable backup copy of your entire computing life that you can carry around in your shirt pocket.

The newest form of storage media is the *floptical disk,* which is about the same size as a standard floppy (with a mechanism about the same size as a floppy disk drive), yet with capacities up to 25MB. These are not commercially available at the time of this writing, but may well be in the stores by the time you read this.

Many storage enhancements have begun to appear in the '90s. These include SCSI "accelerators," "disk-suplexing," "disk-mirroring," and combination devices that package a fixed hard drive and a backup system in the same box. Combination drives are available for hard drives in any size from 40MB to 2GB, with the backup mechanism being anything from a 45MB magnetic cartridge or 650MB optical cartridge to any form of tape system discussed above.

RAM

RAM (random-access memory) is the next area of expansion that you should consider as early as possible. More RAM will let you use MultiFinder to load several programs into memory simultaneously, run current generation programs that require additional room to flex their true strengths, run more INITs and cdevs that will increase the overall speed, power, and efficiency of your Mac, and finally, take full advantage of Apple's System 7.0, which requires a minimum of 2MB of RAM.

The Mac Plus and SE can each hold up to 4MB of RAM (excluding third-party add-on expansion boards), while most other Macintoshes can hold at least 8MB, and in some cases much more.

Most people don't understand the fact that to expand to a 4MB machine from a 1MB machine does not mean buying three more megabytes of memory — it means buying 4MB of memory. This is because Macintoshes have either two, four, or eight slots for memory, each group of four slots referred to as a *bank*. Memory comes in five SIMM (single in-line memory module) configurations: ¼MB SIMMs, 1MB SIMMs, 2MB SIMMs, 4MB SIMMs, and 16MB SIMMs. One-half MB SIMMs are made but hard to find. With some exceptions noted below, it is necessary to have one or both banks' slots entirely filled with SIMMs. Generally, these SIMMs should be the same size throughout each bank (except when going from 1MB to 2½MB).

Breaking the 8MB barrier requires both System 7.0 and either a PMMU chip or a 68030 processor (which has the PMMU built in). Thus, some Macs may be coaxed into accepting larger quantities of RAM by adding third-party 68030 upgrades or accelerator boards. Note that PMMU capability is required to take full advantage of System 7.0.

Virtual memory

Since the release of System 7 there has been a good deal of publicity about *virtual memory*. Virtual memory refers to using part of your hard drive as if it were RAM. This is important because in System 7 there is no unifinder, only MultiFinder —meaning you can always run as many programs simultaneously as your RAM capacity will support. When you switch a program to the foreground, it swaps its disk-based virtual memory with your actual physical RAM. With virtual memory, a Macintosh that only has 2MB of physical RAM can perform as if it has up to 14 or more megabytes of RAM installed.

Don't be too concerned with virtual memory. Virtual memory is slow and it is not compatible with most music applications.

To use virtual memory you need System 7 (or a third-party virtual memory INIT for System 6.x), a PMMU chip (you may retrofit some Macintosh models with a 68551 PMMU chip) or a 68030- or 68040-based CPU with the same memory management built into the processor, and a large contiguous block of space on your hard drive. This reserved area of your hard drive is where the virtual memory swap file will reside. The Macintosh really only operates on physical RAM so there is a considerable amount of swapping (known as paging) between this swap file and the physical RAM. You should carefully weigh the trade-off in giving up valuable hard drive space for virtual memory.

Macintoshes without 32-bit clean ROMs (SE/30, LC, II, IIx, IIcx) are limited to 14MB of Finder RAM (minus 1MB for every NuBus card installed). Macintoshes with 32-bit clean ROMs (IIci, IIsi, IIfx) can access up to 1GB of RAM (virtual or physical). The Mac Plus, SE, Classic, and Portable cannot use virtual memory because their ROMs do not include the necessary code.

If your Macintosh supports 32-bit addressing (Macintosh IIsi, IIci, IIfx, and future Macintoshes), be careful when enabling this feature. Many existing programs are not compatible with 32-bit addressing. It's a good idea to check with the manufacturer about this and always be aware of whether 32-bit addressing is enabled or disabled at any moment.

FPUs, upgrades, and accelerators

FPUs (numeric coprocessors, or math coprocessors, as they are sometimes called) are standard on the SE/30 and all Mac IIs, although it is an option on the IIsi. These SIMMs speed up math calculations, often by a factor of 100. In fact, floating point calculations on a Mac IIfx (which has a Motorola 68882 math coprocessor running at 40 MHz) are a full 200 times faster than on a Mac without an FPU. This has a great impact upon programs that route their calculations to the FPU, such as spreadsheets and some page layout programs. However, almost no music software uses the math coprocessor, the reason being that such programs would not be compatible with Macs that do not contain an FPU, such as the

Mac Plus and SE. A good rule of thumb is that if a music program claims compatibility with the Plus and SE, it probably does not access the FPU.

Some music programs such as Finale allow you the option to execute an operation using floating-point arithmetic and thus accessing the math coprocessor. Selecting Recalc while pressing the Option key will force a floating-point recalculation of the page layout. Surprisingly, this is actually slower than normal non-FPU recalculation.

The types of upgrades you might consider for applicable Macintoshes are the addition of a 68551 PMMU chip (less than $200), the addition of an FPU (if you use programs that access it), and the upgrade to a 68030 processor (which has the PMMU built in). Notice that the word here is "upgrade." Generally, upgrades will not significantly speed up your Macintosh, but merely increase compatibility with System 7.0. Some companies market upgrades for the Mac Plus in the exact same boxes as their accelerator cards and advertise these upgrades in the same ads as their accelerators. Many people have been unpleasantly surprised to find that after putting a 16 MHz 68030 upgrade in their Mac Plus, they are not running twice as fast as they had expected, but only marginally faster, if that. It will save you a lot of time to check and make sure that what you are buying actually says "accelerator" on it and not merely "upgrade."

Accelerators are available from numerous third-party vendors and range from $450 to more than $3,000. With respect to accelerators, price is usually an accurate indicator of performance. A $450 Dove Marathon 33 MHz 68030 accelerator will speed up a Mac II by about 65 percent, and a $3,000 50 MHz 68030 Siclone or DayStar card will speed you up by at least 300 percent (to just short of the speed of the IIfx). If you own a IIci, you have an additional acceleration path available, that of a static RAM cache card that plugs into your processor direct slot (PDS). These are available from Apple and less expensively from third parties. Typical speed increases with a cache card run at least 30 percent.

There are several utilities for testing the speed of your Macintosh. Speedometer and CheckTicks are shareware programs that provide pretty accurate results. For more on music and general utilities, see the coupon in the back of this book.

Purchasing Tips (For Both Computer-Related and Music-Related Gear)

If you have come up with a large figure after doing the calculations at the end of the previous section, or large in proportion to your personal financial resources, don't worry. You may be able to get the number down to a manageable amount by following some of the tips listed below.

Purchasing tip number 1: With some exceptions that will be discussed in the following, you should never pay list price for anything. Retail outlets get most of their wares at least 30 percent and usually 40 percent (or more, if they purchase in large quantities) off the posted list price. Thus, there is some room for negotiation. Depending on the store, location, and matters of competition, you can generally expect to pay between 20 and 25 percent below list price, even 30 percent below list in special cases. But remember, storefront dealers have lots of overhead such as rent, employees, flooring plans, and advertising that they must try to recoup from their profit margin.

Purchasing tip number 2: Some items are so "hot" that you will merely be wasting your and the salesperson's time trying to negotiate a lower cost. Noted examples of this were periods of between three to six months following the introduction of the synthesizer with the most revolutionary sound of the year, for example, DX7, Roland's D50, Korg's M1, Emu's Proteus, and Korg's Wavestation (for more information, see Tip 19).

Purchasing tip number 3: Some stores are willing to beat another advertised price or catalog price (including mail order, if the mail order company also operates a retail store outlet), even if they do not publicize this as store policy. On the other hand, some stores or mail order companies that conspicuously display or advertise the fact that they will beat any advertised price, have all their products priced at list price. The trick is that because of the attention called to the fact that the store is willing to beat any advertised price, many people assume that the store's items are already priced with that in mind and don't bother to check any other sources. Because of this, these stores rarely have to honor that guarantee as they rake in the money by charging list price for everything.

Purchasing tip number 4: Try before you buy. Or if that is not possible, attend a demonstration at a trade show or conference, clinic or seminar at a local computer or music store, or study a friend or colleague using the same program. If you are going to try something out in a store, make sure you try it out using a configuration that is identical to your own.

Purchasing tip number 5: Future viability (from the Second Rule). This week's hot product could be next year's doorstop. But how do you determine the future viability of a product? First of all, if it is a synthesizer, you can try using your ears. For most other matters, some research is required (see Tip 22). Of course, if you can accurately determine that owning the product immediately is going to more than pay for itself, then future viability becomes less of an issue.

Purchasing tip number 6: Take into account compatibility with the hardware and software of your circle of friends, colleagues, and clients when making purchase decisions. Along these same lines, most of the electronic music magazines periodically publish equipment lists of well-known professionals and studios. You should study these lists carefully because, although many of these personalities can afford to purchase every new toy that comes along, they are also in a financial position to cast aside things that turn out to be relatively useless. With this in mind, taking note of what items these people don't have can be extremely informative.

Purchasing tip number 7: When treading in unfamiliar waters or making the decision to be the first person on your block with a new product, consider how important product support is going to be and where you are going to get it.

Purchasing tip number 8: Know what you want before entering a retail facility. If you aren't completely certain, you risk being sold something that isn't exactly right for your application. Don't waste money on anything that you aren't 100 percent certain you will use. This goes double for software.

Purchasing tip number 9: It is usually to your advantage to put together a package deal from a single sales outlet rather than buying numerous components from different sources. For a sale involving several or more items, the seller is often willing to give you a better break on the savings amortized over the entire group of items that you are purchasing. This can be a double-edged sword, if you are not aware of the list price of everything that makes up the package. It is very easy for a dealer to throw something into a package that looks like it should be expensive, when in fact that item is offsetting all the other supposed savings you are making on all the other items. If you know the list price of every item in the package and then take off 25 percent from that, and the price of the package is still lower, it is probably a good deal.

Purchasing tip number 10: Be wary of statements like, "And I'll even throw in this MIDI transmogrifier absolutely free." Be especially wary of service contracts, extended warrantees, etc., unless the gear you are buying is in the upper five or six figures or you happen to be accident-prone. Most states require at least a one-month return policy, and some require vendors to provide a 90-day return policy. With microprocessor-controlled devices like computers and sound devices, if it doesn't break in the first month, it's probably going to last long enough that any repairs you require will still cost less than an extended warranty. However, the greater the number of mechanical or moving parts in the product, the more you should consider purchasing an extended warranty or service contract. For example, if you do a heavy volume of printing, you should always take this option when purchasing a dot-matrix printer.

Purchasing tip number 11: If you are making an extremely large purchase, consider hiring a consultant to help in the decision-making process. Spending a couple of hours with a qualified consultant will usually more than pay for his or her fee in savings over the entire purchase.

Purchasing tip number 12: Keep your eye out for periodic sales and try to get on as many store mailing lists as possible, so that you have advance knowledge of such sales. But be forewarned that some sales are really just ploys to get you into the store — the retailer might only have one of the advertised items at the "sale" price and that will usually have been sold by the time you arrive.

Purchasing tip number 13: Look for money-back guarantees and guarantees that, if the price drops within a given period (often one or two months), you will receive a refund of the difference between what you paid for it and the new price. Some stores even go so far as to provide a guarantee that, if a competing store drops the price within the specified time period, they will still refund the difference.

Purchasing tip number 14: Don't expect people working in retail outlets to have anything more than a limited surface knowledge of the products they are selling. Occasionally, you will find a dedicated sales person who has done his or her homework. If you find such an individual, you should feel extremely fortunate and seriously consider any advice he or she gives you.

Purchasing tip number 15: It is better to spend a little more for a product if doing so ensures you better-than-average after-sales support. If you are lucky enough to find a dealer who understands the product you are buying and is willing to answer your questions regarding its operation, you will probably find that this dealer's prices are slightly higher. With many products, the difference in price is well worth it because of the time that you will save getting up to speed with the product's operation. This is a strong argument against mail order.

Purchasing tip number 16: Do not be intimidated by salespersons who purposely throw around a lot of jargon and terms that you don't understand just to confuse you. Either ask to speak to someone else or just put up with it. Remember, nine times out of ten, if the offending salesperson really did know so much more than you, he or she wouldn't be working as a salesperson. In all fairness, there are salespersons who actually possess considerable knowledge about the things they sell. However, you will usually find that these individuals also possess the personal skills to know how to talk to you at your level without talking down to you.

Purchasing tip number 17: Buy music gear in a music store and computer gear in a computer store (with the possible exception of hard drives and extra RAM). Unless you know what you are doing, or have absolute confidence in the person you are dealing with, or have researched the topic and made your decision in advance, do not buy a hard drive from a music outlet and be wary of buying a hard drive from some computer stores.

Purchasing tip number 18: Non-storefront dealers exist, although they are often hard to locate. A non-storefront dealer is a person authorized by a company to sell their products without maintaining a retail storefront. Often, these people are required to purchase the items they sell at less of a mark-off than a retail outlet. Because of this, prices of non-storefront dealerships tend to be slightly higher than most retail outlets. On the other hand, non-storefront dealers typically do not advertise, so they do not have to calculate those expenses into the purchase price. The same goes for the expenses of store rental and staffing. Usually, a non-storefront dealer is either selling the products that he or she works with on a daily basis or is a consultant who has become a non-storefront dealer for the purpose of serving his or her clientele. In either case, better after-sales support can often be expected from non-storefront dealers, and that's what you are paying the higher price for. So if they don't advertise, how do you find one? The best way is to call the manufacturer and inquire if there are any such dealers in your area.

Purchasing tip number 19: Mail-order purchases carry as many risks as advantages. For many products, including computers, it is possible to find better prices through mail-order outlets. You may save on sales tax if the firm is out of state. On the other hand, you have to add in the expense of shipping. Furthermore, after-sales support is virtually non-existent when dealing with mail-order firms. You'll probably need to use a credit card to purchase through mail-order houses, but using a credit card has its own advantages. First, if the product is not what you were led to believe you were purchasing or if it is defective, you usually have a legal right to a refund from your credit card company rather than the dealer. Second, many credit cards offer additional buyer protection such as extending the manufacturer's warranty. Always determine whether the item you want is in stock when dealing with a mail-order company. This is especially important when purchasing the current year's most fashionable synthesizer. Most manufacturers are responding to complaints of undercutting from storefront dealers by doling out products very slowly to mail-order houses that sell too cheaply. Because of this, you may have to get on a waiting list for these types of items, with no guarantee that your order will be filled within a reasonable amount of time (two to four months seems about normal in these cases). Finally, make sure that your credit card is not billed until the item is shipped (if that's not possible, then cross that firm off your list). Keep in mind that federal trade regulations require that mail-order firms deliver your products within 30 days or provide you with the option to refund your money.

Purchasing tip number 20: Used microprocessor-controlled equipment is an exceptionally delicate issue. Generally, if there is anything even minutely out of line with computers, they won't boot up. Similarly, synthesizers simply won't play if something is out of whack. With respect to the electronics and, in particular, the electronics concerned with digital data, it's safe to assume that it is just as impossible for a device to be "half dead" as it is for a human. Unfortunately, the same doesn't hold for the hardware or analog electronic components (for example, the power supply). While it is easy to determine if a hardware control (for example, a key or slider) is not functioning, it is impossible to determine if something is only intermittently failing. Your best approach is to have someone with the appropriate diagnostic tools examine the used item before you purchase it. The amount you spend for such a service will almost always be less than future repairs or the difference between the cost of the used item and its cost new.

Purchasing tip number 21: Don't hesitate to offer old equipment as a trade-in. Even if the store does not have a "used gear" area, chances are that one of the salespersons or someone else who happens to overhear you making the offer, might be looking for such an item.

Purchasing tip number 22: Research. Research. Research. Exploit every resource to find out as much as you can about what you are considering for purchase. This means magazines, newsletters, users groups, and BBSs. Don't trust a single reviewer's opinion unless you have found through past experience that you agree with everything he or she has to say. It is better to look at reviews of the same product appearing in competing magazines for a second opinion. Try to keep track of the good reviews a certain company keeps getting in a magazine in proportion to the amount of advertising space that the same company purchases in the magazine. If a music manufacturer does not advertise in a certain magazine (few music manufacturers advertise in computer magazines), then a good review in that magazine can generally be given more credibility. Research prices as well. While it is convenient to deal with the store that happens to be on the corner of your block, you would be well advised to call every dealer in town as well as a number of mail-order companies to determine what the going rate is for the item you want. In other words, shop around!

Purchasing tip number 23: A company's size or visibility through advertising is not a reliable indicator of the quality of that company's product, after-sales support, upgrade policies, or service department.

Purchasing tip number 24: Don't expect any software company to notify you of upcoming free upgrades. This is a case where continuing research may be the only way you will avoid being three versions behind the rest of the world. Some companies, even if they have sent you an announcement of a free upgrade, won't send the upgrade unless they receive a call or letter requesting it. Finally, on the subject of upgrades, don't assume that a program or device is completely incompatible with your Macintosh just because it always crashes. Many software and hardware companies have unpublicized ROM or software versions that are designed to assure compatibility with your specific Macintosh model.

Purchasing tip number 25: If a software or hardware product fails to perform the way you were led to believe it would from advertising or by a store representative, do not hesitate to demand your money back. With this in mind, it is a good idea to familiarize yourself with the store's return policy prior to making any purchases whatsoever. Remember, if you purchase the item with a credit card, the law guarantees you certain rights that are not available if you purchase it with cash (see Tip 19).

Another tip that goes without saying is not to place any significance in a product name. Names like Professional Composer can be misleading because some people infer that other products are not "Professional" and that is simply not the case. One assumes that Coda chose the name Finale to imply that this was the final word in music notation software, although shortly thereafter Passport came out with a notation package named Encore, implying perhaps that the software goes one step beyond Finale. While this may be true for certain users, it certainly should not be an *a priori* assumption.

To illustrate the kind of reasoning that goes into the naming of a product, an example from my own experience can drive the point home. HB Imaging once asked me to think of a name for their music font, telling me that they wanted something musical like *Sonata,* but Adobe had already laid claims to that name. I had recently been performing John Cage's *Sonatas and Interludes,* so I said, "Whenever I think of the word *Sonata,* I think of the word *Interlude."* Although I explained the reason for this, they decided to go with the name and marketed their font as Interlude.

One final word about purchasing. Don't skimp on your Macintosh. If used efficiently, your Macintosh will be the single most powerful tool that you can use for your creative productivity, and ultimately the most important piece of equipment in your setup.

Summary

✔ The type of Macintosh you need depends entirely upon how far you want to take your Macintosh music and sound activities. The speed and power of your computer are directly related to creative productivity. With this in mind, the fastest Macintosh that you can afford is strongly recommended.

✔ The seconds and milliseconds add up very quickly. On slower Macintoshes you waste crucial time booting up your computer, launching and quitting from applications, opening, saving, and closing files, menu selection response time, scrolling within windows and dialogs, the time it takes a dialog to appear on the screen and the screen redrawing itself. Bumping up to a faster computer or accelerating your current computer can save you several hours each week.

✔ CPU accelerators and cache cards are often the most economically practical approach to increasing your computing speed. Alternatively, you can save money by buying a discontinued Macintosh and installing an official Apple logic board upgrade.

✔ The first peripheral you should consider adding to your Macintosh is a hard drive. One of the members of the original Macintosh development team once stated, "A Macintosh without a hard drive is like a car without a gas tank." System 7 requires a hard drive. For anyone involved in Macintosh music and sound in any form, the minimum recommended capacity is 40MB. Most 40MB hard drives run at least seven, and often nine or ten, times faster than a floppy disk.

✔ There are many storage media alternatives. Some of the more popular options include removable magnetic cartridges, WORM drives, optical drives, CD-ROM drives, DAT, 8mm and other tape, battery-backed RAM drives, and flopticals.

✔ RAM is available in 150, 120, 100, 80, and 70 nanosecond speeds. The speed must match your Macintosh's requirements. The IIfx requires special 64-pin, 80-nanosecond SIMMs.

✔ Virtual memory, available in System 7, refers to using part of your hard drive as if it were RAM. This is important because in System 7 there is no unifinder, only MultiFinder — meaning you can always run as many programs simultaneously as your RAM capacity will support. Virtual memory is slow and it is not compatible with most music applications, especially those that use timing information such as MIDI sequencers, some notation programs, and digital audio software.

✔ There are at least 25 ways (listed in this chapter under "Purchasing tips") that you can save a substantial amount of money on the purchase of computer-related and music-related gear.

Chapter 5
Hardware Decisions

The Essential Ingredients

The essential ingredients for a Macintosh-based music setup fall into two categories: hardware and software. Hardware includes a Macintosh and other peripherals, both musical and Macintosh-related (unless you are going with the most basic setup described in Chapter 3 under "Non-MIDI-oriented Setup"). You interact with the Macintosh hardware by means of musical applications programs.

Your needs should define your choice of hardware. After deciding whether to purchase a digital synthesizer or a digital sampling keyboard, the main considerations are *velocity sensing, number of note polyphony,* and *multitimbral capabilities.* Velocity sensing, which allows you to play at varying and multiple levels of volume, adds several hundreds of dollars to the price. If you are an amateur, hobbyist, or merely using the synthesizer for input (that is, you will be using live musicians reading from your printed score) you might not need this feature. If you are going to use the synthesizer as an output device, even if only for proofhearing, you will want to consider how many notes can be sounded simultaneously (referred to as *n-voice polyphony*) and whether or not the synthesizer is *multitimbral* (which refers to the capability of playing several different types of sounds, or patches, simultaneously). Finally, your specific applications may require that you forego digital synthesizers altogether in favor of digital samplers, in which case you may have to dig even deeper into your pocket.

Choosing the Rest of Your Equipment

The rest of the equipment you need depends entirely on the applications you intend to run. Table 5-1 gives a general idea of the items you will probably need to purchase, categorized by application area. If you plan to use your setup for more than one application, you should read across the rows and take note of all the required items for all your planned activities (you may want to make a check mark next to each row that describes equipment you will need). In some categories, particularly multimedia and education, keep in mind the distinction between end-user and producer/creator while making selections.

Following this table is a similar one giving price ranges for the various items organized by level of involvement (beginning, intermediate, advanced, and professional). The blank column is there for you to enter the budget figure you want set for a particular item or category of items based upon your selections or checklist from the table.

Table 5-1: Other necessary equipment

	8-bit Non-MIDI music	Desktop Music publishing	MIDI Music	16-bit digital audio	Music for film, video	Music for multimedia	Music education
Macintosh peripherals							
RAM	2 to 4	2.5 to 5	4 to 8	8 to 128	8	8 to 32	2 to 4
Hard drive	▶	●	●	●	●	●	▶
Backup system				●	▶		
CD-ROM				▶		▶	●
Printer		●	▶	▶	▶	▶	●
PostScript printer		▶	▶			▶	▶
Scanner							
8-bit digitizer	●						▶
Modem		▶	▶	▶	▶	▶	
Software							
Sound design	▶		●	●	●	●	
MIDI sequencer		▶	●	▶	●	▶	
Non-MIDI sequencer	●			▶		●	▶
Algorithmic			▶		▶		
Notation		●	▶		▶		
Interactive			▶		▶		
Direct-to-hard disk				●	▶	▶	
Synchronization			▶	▶	●	▶	
Multimedia	▶					●	▶
Education							●

Table 5-1: Other necessary equipment (continued)

	8-bit Non-MIDI music	Desktop Music publishing	MIDI Music	16-bit digital audio	Music for film, video	Music for multimedia	Music education
Internal card							
Sound generating		◗	◗		◗	◗	◗
Sampler			◗		◗	◗	
Digital audio				●	◗	◗	
NTSC video					◗		
Interfaces							
16-chan MIDI		◗		◗		◗	◗
32-chan MIDI	◗	●	◗		●	◗	◗
>32-chan MIDI		●			●	◗	◗
SMPTE converter		◗	◗		●		
VITC converter					◗		
Lock-up system					◗		
Sound generating devices							
Synthesizer	◗	●	◗		●	◗	◗
Sample player	◗	●	◗		●	◗	◗
Sampler			◗	◗	◗	◗	◗
MIDI controller	●	●	◗		●	◗	◗
Audio and DSP							
Effects/EQ			◗	●	●	◗	
Mixer			◗	●	●	◗	◗
Amplifier	●	◗	●	●	●	●	●
Speaker	●	◗	●	●	●	●	●
Network							
MIDI patchbay			◗		◗	◗	
Audio patchbay			◗	◗	◗	◗	
Data switchers			◗		◗	◗	
Analog recorder							
Cassette	◗		◗	◗	●	◗	◗
Multitrack			◗	◗	◗	◗	
Mixdown deck			●	◗	●	◗	

Table 5-1: Other necessary equipment (continued)

	8-bit Non-MIDI music	Desktop Music publishing	MIDI Music	16-bit digital audio	Music for film, video	Music for multimedia	Music education
Digital recorder							
Direct-to-hard disk			●	◗	◗		
DAT			◗	●	◗	◗	
Video							
Deck & monitor					●	◗	●
Laserdisc player					◗	◗	

Table 5-2 indicates price ranges for equipment that you may need to purchase, depending upon your planned activities. The price ranges are broken down into four user levels. You should transfer to the "worksheet" column the appropriate figures you want to budget for any of the items you marked on the previous column. You can total this at the bottom of the page to see what your investment is going to be.

Remember, you won't need gear from every category. What you will need is entirely dependent upon your applications. A good approach would be to examine the previous table and determine which items are necessary and which items are optional for your intended activities. Then, circle or otherwise make note of those figures in the appropriate column on the next table to quickly see the areas in which you might have to make an investment.

A word about the figures: Wherever applicable, figures chosen are for products with the maximum longevity, upgradability, and future viability (see Second Rule in the Introduction). The lower number of each price range has been determined by consulting and averaging prices from various mail order houses. The high end of each range indicates an average of list prices for the items in question. Many of the figures in the "Professional" and "Advanced" columns represent multiple items (for example, with respect to software the assumption is that you may need similar products from competing vendors to round out your data manipulation options). Consult the tables in Chapter 7, "Setting Up Your Mac Music Studio," for more detailed price breakdown. You will probably want to pick a figure somewhere between these two extremes to enter into your worksheet column. You may even want to do the calculations three times: once for the minimum, once for the maximum, and once for your ideal setup. For further information on purchasing strategies, see "Purchasing tips" at the end of the previous chapter.

Table 5-2: Expense worksheet

	Beginner through Amateur	Hobbyist through Intermediate	Semi-pro through Professional	Advanced Pro through Power User	Worksheet
Macintosh peripherals					
Additional RAM	$0-200	$0-400	$200-1,500	$400-4,000	
Hard drive	0-300	300-800	300-1,500	1,500-4,000	
Backup system	50-600	50-600	600-2,000	2,000-3,000	
CD-ROM	500-1,000	500-800	800-1,200	800-1,200	
Printer	500-1,000	500-1,500	500-1,500	500-1,500	
PostScript printer	1,500-3,000	1,500-3,000	1,500-3,000	3,000-60,000	
Scanner	400-1,500	400-1,500	1,500-3,000	3,000-6,000	
8-bit digitizer	160-270	160-270	320-540	320-540	
Modem	100-500	100-500	500-1,200	500-1,200	
Software					
Sound design	250-400	400-700	1,000-1,500	1,000-2,000	
MIDI sequencer	150-500	250-500	500-1,000	1,000-2,000	
Non-MIDI sequencer	25-100	100-1,000	130-1,000	1,000-2,000	
Algorithmic	100-200	100-150	250-600	600-1,200	
Notation	150-400	150-400	400-600	400-600	
Interactive	100-200	100-250	250-600	600-1,200	
Direct-to-hard disk	400-1,000	400-1,000	1,000-2,000	1,000-2,000	
Synchronization	300-600	300-600	600-1,000	1,600-2,500	
Multimedia	300-700	700-1,500	1,500-7,000	5,000-20,000	
Education	150-300	500-1,500	1,500-8,000	6,000-15,000	
Internal card					
Sound generating	800-900	800-900	800-1,800	800-1,800	
Sampler	1,500-2,400	1,500-4,800	1,500-7,000	1,500-9,400	
Digital audio	800-3,300	800-3,300	3,000-6,300	5,000-40,000	
Special video	500-1,000	500-1,000	1,500-4,700	4,000-9,000	

Table 5-2: Expense worksheet (continued)

	Beginner through Amateur	Hobbyist through Intermediate	Semi-pro through Professional	Advanced Pro through Power User	Worksheet
Interfaces					
16-chan MIDI	$60-100	$60-100	$60-100	$60-100	
32-chan MIDI	200-380	200-380	200-380	200-380	
>32-chan MIDI	380-500	380-500	380-2,000	380-20,000	
SMPTE converter	150-170	(150-400)	(150-1,200)	(400-1,200)	
VITC converter	1,000-1,200	1,000-1,200	1,000-1,200	1,000-3,500	
Lock-up system	2,800-3,200	2,800-5,500	2,800-7,500	5,500-15,000	
SGD					
Synthesizer	500-1,500	800-3,000	3,000-10,000	5,000-18,000	
Sample player	500-1,500	500-3,000	1,500-8,000	3,000-12,000	
Sampler	350-1,500	1,500-6,000	2,500-12,000	5,000-25,000	
MIDI controller	300-1,500	1,500-2,600	1,500-2,600	1,500-2,600	
Audio and DSP					
Effects/EQ	200-500	500-1,200	1,500-4,000	5,000-25,000	
Mixer	250-800	800-2,500	4,000-25,000	25,000-600,000	
Amplifier	300-600	600-900	750-1,500	750-3,000	
Speakers	100-500	500-1,200	1,500-5,000	2,500-12,000	
Network					
MIDI patchbay	90-300	300-1,000	500-1,200	1,200-6,000	
Audio patchbay	90-200	200-800	400-1,200	800-2,500	
Data switchers	80-150	80-150	80-300	150-500	
Analog recorder					
Cassette	200-400	250-800	500-1,200	800-2,500	
Multitrack	300-1,200	750-5,000	2,500-15,000	8,000-80,000	
Mixdown deck	200-750	1,000-2,500	2,500-5,000	5,000-15,000	
Digital recorder					
Direct-to-hard disk	800-3,300	800-4,300	3,300-11,000	6,300-60,000	
DAT	1,200-1,600	1,600-4,500	1,600-8,000	4,500-22,000	

Table 5-2: Expense worksheet (continued)

	Beginner through Amateur	Hobbyist through Intermediate	Semi-pro through Professional	Advanced Pro through Power User	Worksheet
Video					
Deck & monitor	$700-1,200	$1,400-2,500	$3,600-15,000	$3,600-60,000	
Laserdisc player	900-1,200	1,000-2,000	1,000-2,000	1,000-2,000	

Total: Macintosh peripherals with music and sound equipment: _____

Total: Macintosh system (CPU, monitor, and keyboard only): _____

Sales tax if any: _____

Shipping if any: _____

TOTAL _____

(Add 10% of total for cables, media, racks, accessories) **+10%** _____

GRAND TOTAL _____

Hardware Categories in Detail

You have many hardware options. The following discussion breaks down the general hardware categories and explains why you should or should not purchase them. See Appendix D, "List of Manufacturers," for detailed company information.

Macintosh peripherals

Storage media

It is important to understand the distinctions between the numerous types of storage media for your Macintosh.

- ❖ Floppy disks
- ❖ Hard drives
- ❖ Removable cartridge drives (45MB, 50MB, 88MB)
- ❖ Optical drives
- ❖ Magneto-optical drives
- ❖ Silicon disks
- ❖ Flopticals

Computer programs with their associated data usually must reside in the computer's RAM before they can be worked with, and the quicker access time of a hard disk means that programs and data stored on the disk are loaded into the computer's RAM at speeds of often six to 24 times that of floppy disks. To get a picture of how much data 20MB is, consider the following: 1 kilobyte (1,024 bytes) is often thought of as being equivalent to a single double-spaced typewritten page — thus 20MB theoretically provide enough storage capacity for 20,000 pages. Actually, because of overhead required by most software in the form of file headers and other proprietary data associated with a file, the number is significantly less.

Although a hard disk is vastly more speedy and spacious than a floppy (but often not much bigger in physical size), you interact with a hard disk in much the same way as with a floppy: Files can be created, examined, modified, and deleted. The files on a hard disk can contain MIDI sequencing information, synthesizer patches, sounds, programs, and actual digital audio recordings equal or superior in quality to that of CDs. Soundfiles for commercial sampling keyboards can be very memory hungry (a single one of the four RAM banks of the Kurzweil 250 holds 658 kilobytes of samples). As with the computer memory chips mentioned above, hard disks continue to be less expensive and of larger capacity — 40MB to 80MB hard disks are becoming more and more popular among serious home computer users.

Drive manufacturers often publicize the access times (measured in milliseconds) of their hard drives as being a measure of their drive's performance. Access times range from 5 ms to over 100 ms (faster is better). This is somewhat misleading, as the actual performance of a hard drive is also related to the speed at which it can transfer data (called the data transfer rate, usually between 780K per second to 1.5MB per second when using the Macintosh's native SCSI port and controller) and to the interleave factor of the drive.

Access time is an average of seek time and latency time. Seek time is the average amount of time it takes the drive head to move to the track containing the desired data. Latency time is the average amount of time it takes the required sector to move into position once the drive head is located at the appropriate track. Data transfer rate refers to how fast the desired data can be transferred into RAM once it is located.

Backup systems

Backup systems use the following media for archiving and backup:

- ❖ Tape (formats: Teac, DAT [4mm], Videotape [8mm], DC600, DC2000)
- ❖ Removable cartridge drives (45MB or 50MB)
- ❖ WORM drives
- ❖ Optical drives
- ❖ Magneto-optical drives
- ❖ Disk duplexing
- ❖ Disk mirroring

As the size of hard disks continues to grow, the question of how to back up your hard disk is becoming a major consideration. "Backing up" refers to the process of saving a copy of your data as a precautionary measure against the ever-present possibility of losing irreplaceable work due to a hardware malfunction. Sometimes a file or floppy disk can become corrupted for no apparent reason, but the most common way to lose data is through a hard disk crash. It can happen all of a sudden, with no prior warning whatsoever: You turn on your Macintosh and the computer is no longer able to access the hard disk. This is referred to as a crash. In the Macintosh community, such crashes are relatively common, and the larger the hard disk, the more you stand to lose in the event of this dreaded system failure. Some hard disk crashes are not as terminal as they might first seem when you are staring at a blank screen speculating that you may have lost all your data. Procedures for recovering from some of these less fatal crashes are discussed in the material in the coupon in the back of this book.

Whereas the periodic copying of the contents of 10MB or 20MB hard drives onto floppy disks (a popular method for backing up the disk) usually takes about an hour, with an 80MB disk drive it can take up to four hours to complete the feeding of the 100 floppies into the disk drive required to copy all the data (high-density 1.4MB floppies would require only 50 floppies). Using Syquest 45MB removable cartridges as backup media is an alternative that can save considerable time.

Fortunately, most backup software provides incremental backup capabilities, so that after you back up your disk the first time, each subsequent backup will only involve replacing the files that have changed since the previous session (most backup software keeps track of this automatically). Consequently, every subsequent backup will require substantially less time. Because it is advisable to back up the drive once a day (to ensure that only a single day's work might be lost), backup systems that can run without human supervision are becoming more popular. In this category, tape backup systems offer the most value per dollar.

Some people keep two identical drives online at all times, "incrementally" backing up the main drive by manually copying the files that have been modified during the day's computing onto the dedicated backup drive. Because recent advances in backup software include utilities that can transfer 80MB of data between two identically sized SCSI drives in less than ten minutes or perform an incremental backup in even less time, and the price of hard drives has plummeted, the practice of having two identical hard disks is becoming more feasible.

Carrying this concept even further, the latest rages are *disk duplexing* and *disk mirroring*. Both provide for continuous backup of your data by maintaining an identical copy of your primary drive, automatically, at all times.

Disk mirroring involves writing the same data to two drives on the Macintosh SCSI port and is a software solution. The problem is that because the data must be written twice, it can take twice as long to perform writes. On the other hand, reads are sped up because the software is intelligent enough to read from the drive whose head is closest to the required data. Usually, if one drive in the pair fails, the backup drive kicks in automatically. Companies providing disk mirroring software are listed in the next chapter.

Disk duplexing is a hardware solution that requires both software and a NuBus card that provides an additional SCSI bus upon which to attach the duplexed or "twin" drives. Because data is intercepted on its way to the Macintosh's native SCSI port and simultaneously routed to the twin drive on the additional SCSI bus, the impact upon write times is insignificant, never slowing down the data transfer process by more than 5 percent. This makes disk duplexing the preferred method of fault-tolerant continuous backup. Normally, the twin drives do not appear on the desktop, unless you intentionally mount them. When the primary drive fails, you merely move the twin drive over to the Macintosh's native SCSI bus and continue right where you left off.

Both disk duplexing and disk mirroring can be solutions to continuous backup, but there are still some risks involved. Because both the primary and secondary (or twin) drive are kept identical, if you accidentally erase the primary drive, you also will have erased its twin. Likewise, if the primary drive becomes infected by a virus or the directory gets corrupted, the twin drive will have identical problems. Disk duplexing can get around these problems, because you have the option not to continually twin your primary drive but to do so only when you initiate the process. Because of the additional SCSI NuBus card, data transfer from the primary drive to the twin can be as fast as 30MB per minute (about 2½ minutes to duplicate an 80MB drive).

CD-ROM drives
❖ With audio capabilities
❖ Without audio capabilities
❖ Jukebox

CD-ROM stands for compact disc read-only memory. CD-ROMs look exactly like audio CDs, except that they store data instead of digitized sound (some store digitized sound as well; read on). Such discs cannot be written to . . . yet! CD-ROM drives are available both with and without audio playback capabilities, meaning that besides providing access to up to 650MB of data, they can also play back normal audio CDs. You should not dismiss a CD-ROM player with audio because you already own a CD player. CD-ROM drives with audio offer many possibilities for music applications that are simply not available by combining a dedicated CD player with a CD-ROM drive.

CD-ROM drives are extremely slow. Data transfer cannot exceed 153K (kilo-bytes!) a second because of limits defined in the CD standard set by Sony and Philips about a decade ago (compare SCSI's current maximum transfer rate of 1.5MB per second, about ten times faster; then consider that new SCSI implementations of accelerators and SCSI II achieve rates up to and exceeding triple that). With this in mind, the difference in speed of CD-ROM drives is more related to access time than transfer rate (although some CD-ROM drives can't even get up to the meager 153K maximum transfer speed defined in the specification). This is exactly the opposite of hard drives, where data transfer rates are equal to or more important than access times in determining overall drive performance. Access times on CD-ROM drives range from just over 100 ms to over 1,000 ms. Pretty slow!

If it's so slow, what's it good for, you are probably wondering. CD-ROMs retail between about $59 and over $1,000, depending upon what's on them. Typical contents include public domain software libraries, clip art, clip music, font libraries, reference books (even the Whole Earth Catalog), maps, whole encyclopedias, dictionaries, games, and multimedia educational programs that teach everything from music appreciation to Japanese. Multimedia authoring systems such as MacroMind's Director, MacroMind-Paracomp's MediaTracks, and Authorware's Authorware are being distributed on CD-ROMs because of the amount of disks required for these multimedia development systems and the possibility of including a vast amount of examples within the 600MB to 650MB of storage space on a CD-ROM.

Musicians should be particularly interested in CD-ROM drives because of the growing number of libraries of sampled sounds available in that format and the availability of excellent interactive music education resources on CD-ROMs.

Apple's original CD-ROM had one of the slowest access times available. Their newer drive has almost doubled this speed, making Apple's new drive a major contender in this market. The Toshiba mechanism often comes in first in speed tests. CD-ROM drives using Toshiba's mechanism include those from Toshiba (XM-3201), CD Technology (Porta Drive), and ProCom (HiPerformance).

Printers and other output devices

❖ Dot-matrix
❖ Inkjet
❖ Non-PostScript laser
❖ 300 dots per inch (dpi) PostScript laser
❖ 300 dpi TrueType laser
❖ High resolution (400+ dpi) PostScript laser
❖ Phototypesetters
❖ Slidewriters

There are many people making music with personal computers who get along fine without a printer in their setup. However, if you require conventional music notation or part extraction, a printer of some kind is necessary. A dot-matrix printer or inkjet printer is the cheapest solution to musical printing requirements. Other kinds of printers, called "daisy wheel" or "impact" printers, are designed for letter writing and do not provide the graphic capabilities required by conventional musical notation. Even if you believe that you will never need to do notation or graphics of any kind, you should think very seriously before considering the purchase of an impact or daisy-wheel printer. The price of higher resolution laser printers has plummeted to well below $1,000 and, accordingly, many musical users are finding that the quality offered by such machines is well worth the money.

A major influence favoring a laser printer for music is the versatile device-independent page description language known as PostScript, and the availability of a wide variety of publishing-quality PostScript music fonts. Unlike earlier bitmapped music fonts, PostScript fonts define symbols as vectors and Bezier curves. Using a PostScript music font in conjunction with notation software, a music file may be printed for proofing on a bitmapped dot-matrix printer and finally output to either a 300-dpi PostScript printer or a phototypesetter (1,270 and 2,540 dpi) for publishing-quality printing. Apple's TrueType imaging technology, part of System 7, is an alternative to PostScript and is the first serious attempt to challenge the supremacy of PostScript in the professional imagesetting world.

Even if you are not planning on doing any music notation, a printer is useful for other tasks around the studio. Applications range from printing tracksheets, wiring diagrams, and the contents of sound libraries, to all the utilitarian requirements of managing the business end of your musical life, such as billing and correspondence. In all cases, the higher the resolution of your printer, the more professional your output will appear.

Before buying a laser printer always check how often you have to replace the engine. Most Apple laser printers can print 150,000 pages before requiring an engine change. Some new low-cost PostScript laser printers require an engine change every 15,000 pages. At about $300 for the replacement engine, by the time you reach 150,000 pages, you will have spent an additional $3,000 on the laser printer that seemed to be such a good deal.

Scanners

- ❖ Black-and-white
- ❖ Color
- ❖ Sheetfed
- ❖ Handheld
- ❖ Imagewriter-based
- ❖ Gray-scale
- ❖ Flatbed
- ❖ Overhead
- ❖ Handheld with built-in OCR
- ❖ Slide scanners

A scanner is to a still image as a sampler is to a single soundwave. The process of digitizing an analog visual image is remarkably similar to digitizing an analog sound.

Scanners come in a variety of types and provide an equally wide range of capabilities. All scanners serve the same purpose: transferring an external image into a graphics file that you can manipulate within the Macintosh just as you might any other graphics file. Scanners usually have the capability of writing to more than one file type: EPS, Paint, PICT, or TIFF. These file types are to graphics software as SMFs are to MIDI software.

The first obvious difference between different scanner types is whether they digitize in black-and-white, gray-scale, or color. The next difference is the maximum size of the scannable image — handheld scanners offer a much smaller image area than other scanners. Finally, all scanners digitize images at different resolutions — analogous to audio sample resolutions (see Chapter 1, "Background"). Scanner resolutions range from 75 to 1,200 dpi, although most hover between 300 to 600 dpi. The resolution of slide scanners is measured in pixels, with $1,024 \times 1,500$ at the low end and $4,096 \times 6,144$ at the high end.

All scanners can be used in conjunction with OCR (optical character recognition) software to convert text, which has been scanned in as a graphic into actual editable text. At least one new scanner, Caere's Typist, puts state-of-the-art OCR technology into a chip within a handheld scanner. Using this device (the price is under $500), you can scan printed text at up to 500 words per minute, just as if you were typing it.

Scanners will be most useful to you if you are creating multimedia productions that are handling both the musical and visual elements. If you are an educator, you may find a scanner extremely handy in the preparation of course materials. For both multimedia producers and educators, the sophistication of your scanner (color, gray-scale, black-and-white, etc.) depends upon your needs and your budget.

Scanners can find many applications in a Macintosh music studio. You might want to scan in pages from synthesizer manuals, wiring diagrams, recording session notes, or even menus of nearby restaurants. Combining OCR with scanning offers many advantages to a studio. For example, if you purchase a large sound effects or sample library and get a 200-page catalog of the sounds, you will probably want to enter new sounds into the database where you keep track of all of your other sounds. This allows you to categorize, search, and otherwise organize your library. If, as in the present example, your sound effects or sample library has just increased by 10,000 sounds, you can see how much easier it will be to transfer the data from the printed catalog to your database using scanning and OCR.

8-bit audio digitizers

❖ Commercial external
❖ Home-made
❖ Built into Macintosh

An 8-bit audio digitizer can be thought of as simply a low-resolution sampler or hard-disk recorder such as those discussed in Chapter 1, "Background." You will recall that professional 16-bit hard-disk recording and sampling rates are 44.1 KHz or 48 KHz — 8-bit digitizers typically use 22 KHz as the maximum sample rate. The difference in quality is striking.

8-bit sample files are useful for many multimedia applications. They can be edited and looped with the same degree of flexibility as CD-quality 16-bit sounds. There are even sound and music libraries available that consist entirely of 8-bit soundfiles. Interactive authoring environments thrive on 8-bit sound-files. HyperCard, SuperCard, Authorware, and Director are just a few of the development systems that offer extensive 8-bit soundfile support. The Authorware package even comes with an 8-bit digitizer.

The number of Macintosh programs that use 8-bit soundfiles is staggering, especially to MIDI musicians who sometimes think that MIDI software is all that is out there. Chapter 15, "Making Music without MIDI," provides a listing of many of these applications. For you MIDI musicians, Passport Designs even has an 8-voice software-based synthesizer, which utilizes 8-bit soundfiles that can be controlled by any MIDI program via Apple's MIDI Manager — great if you need to work on something when your gear is at another location.

Finally, there is at least one program (MasterTuner) that lets you use an 8-bit digitizer as the microphone for extremely accurate intonations applications.

At present, there are not many options to choose from among 8-bit digitizers. You can build your own, buy a Macintosh LC or IIsi, or buy one of the two commercial packages. Keep in mind that the built-in digitizers on the Macintosh LC and IIsi provide monophonic sampling only, whereas when using two third-party digitizers, one on each serial port, you can actually create 8-bit 22 KHz stereo soundfiles.

MacroMind-Paracomp's MacRecorder 8-bit digitizer has enjoyed such widespread popularity that it is considered to be the industry standard. Buy two and you can sample in stereo. Articulate Systems's VoiceLink is a recent challenger to the MacRecorder dynasty. Although these digitizers are relatively inexpensive, you can reduce your financial outlay even more by building your own digitizer.

Modems

- ❖ 1200-baud
- ❖ 2400-baud
- ❖ 9600-bps
- ❖ 14,400-bps
- ❖ 19,200-bps
- ❖ Fax modems
- ❖ Net modems

Once you've tuned into the bitstream with a modem, you can get to the point where you feel like telecommunicating is a "seventh sense" — if your modem is on the fritz it can induce feelings similar to losing any other one of your senses. The acuteness of this added sense is measured in *baud* (short for Baudot — Emile Baudot developed a practical printing telegraphy system in 1874), often equated to bits per second, although this is not completely accurate. Baud rate is generally used to represent the maximum speed of data transfer you can achieve over the telephone lines.

Modems (short for *mo*dulation *dem*odulation) provide you with a gateway to thousands of online services around the world. There are networks and BBSs (bulletin board services) that focus on just about any topic you can think of. There are countless systems dedicated to the Macintosh and quite a few to music and MIDI (see Appendix C, "Telecommunography").

On-line services provide vital information literally months before you will ever read about it in the press. You can learn about bugs, work-arounds, hidden features, and tips for every piece of gear and software you possess. A wealth of soundfiles and patches float around on telecommunications networks, not to mention a preponderance of public domain (PD) software and shareware that can save you hundreds, even thousands of dollars. You may find commercial software updates long before the manufacturer gets around to sending you a notice of a new version. Finally, you may discover a community of other "modemers" that can become lasting friends, although you might never meet any of them in the flesh.

Telecommunications received quite a bit of bad press when computer viruses started appearing. Many of the early viruses were inadvertently spread via the file libraries associated with BBSs. For the most part, this was limited to the IBM world. I have been telecommunicating for almost a decade and troubleshooting viral infections for clients since the first computer virus appeared. My personal experience has been that the overwhelming majority of viral infections can be traced back to two sources: (1) computer stores that offer clients system software updates and PD programs from the Macintoshes they have on display, and (2) manufacturers who innocently duplicate an infected upgrade and then send it out to all their registered users. One thing is certain, I have downloaded gigabytes of data from online services and been called to disinfect hundreds of hard drives, and I have never been able to trace a virus to an online service. The unfounded sensationalism linking viruses to telecommunications has had at least one good effect: On-line services are now meticulously thorough in the screening of all data that is available for downloading. Furthermore, whenever a new virus is discovered, the tools to inoculate you from it appear on online services before anywhere else.

As with the other aspects of your computing environment, I seriously recommend getting the fastest modem you can afford. The times that you are going to appreciate your modem the most are those situations in which you need something right away in order to get on with what you are doing. You may need a friend or colleague to transfer a soundfile, patch bank, disk utility, or system software update at a crucial point in a project when the clock is ticking. You don't want to be staring at the wristwatch, especially if you are working under a deadline.

For a real-world dramatic illustration of how modem speed can affect you, consider the following statistics. When I first got into telecommunications at a speed of 300 baud, it took 12 hours to transfer a megabyte of data. The following year, when I got my first 1200-baud modem, that same transfer required only three hours. For almost four years I used a 2400-baud modem, which could zip that megabyte from one computer to another in 90 minutes. Now, I use a 19,200-bps modem and can transfer a megabyte in just over 11 minutes.

When most people had 300-baud modems, 1200-baud modems were called high-speed modems. When everyone got 1200-baud modems, then 2400-baud modems began to be referred to as high-speed modems. 9600-bps modems are what one means when speaking of high-speed telecommunications. While nearly every modem from 9600-bps on down is compatible with one another, the two higher speed configurations, 14,400-bps and 19,200-bps, although compatible at speeds of 9600-bps and below, are not compatible with each other when their throttles are let out completely.

Besides the single-user data modem that the vast majority of us use, there are several other types of modems you should be aware of. A *net-modem* is a special type of data modem that can be shared by many users on a LAN (local area network). A *fax modem* is a modem that can be used to send and receive faxes. These features are beginning to be combined in one box. There are net-fax modems, fax/data modems, and net/fax/data modems will probably be the next rage.

While it may seem like the ultimate in computer integration to be able to fax a document from your computer with the same ease that you direct a document to your printer, there are some trade-offs. First of all, while your computer is sending or receiving a fax, it either can't be used for anything else, or, if you have a system that can run in the background, the operation of your Macintosh will be sluggish at best. Second, printing out a received fax is excruciatingly slow. Finally, there is no way to write on a document and then fax it. You cannot make revisions, add comments, or sign your name to a contract because you can only fax data that can appear on your Macintosh screen. If you want to fax something else, you need to have a scanner and scan the item in before faxing it.

I bought the very first fax modem available for the Macintosh and have since lived to regret it. On the other hand, when I used to fax people documents with my AppleFax modem, I often received calls from people asking "How did you get my fax machine to print out so nicely?" No one has ever asked me that since I started using a dedicated fax machine, even when I transmit in high-resolution mode.

Nowadays, you shouldn't have to spend more than $120 for a 2400-baud modem. Zoom's 2400-baud modems are often available for less than $100. Hayes and U.S Robotics are the most popular 9600-bps modems. In the high-speed lane, the U.S. Robotics 14,400-bps HST and 19,200-bps Telebit T-2500 are in hot competition. U.S. Robotics's advertisements often claim a throughput of 38,400-bps although this figure is vastly inflated and applies only to special types of files (most of which you will never encounter). The 9600-bps modem protocols are now standardized, but if you are thinking about purchasing a higher speed modem, it is important to consider what model is owned by the people with whom you will be telecommunicating. This includes networks, BBSs, and service bureaus (for example, at the time of this writing, Kinko's is putting a Telebit T-2500 in every one of its offices). Dove Computer's DoveFax series is without contest the most popular line of fax modems available. An alternative is Orchid Technology's OrchidFax.

Macintosh monitors

- ❖ Black-and-white
- ❖ Gray-scale
- ❖ 8-bit color
- ❖ 24-bit color
- ❖ NTSC
- ❖ Multisync

There are three main categories of Macintosh monitors: color, gray-scale, and monochrome. While external monitors are generally thought of as applying to Macintoshes without built-in screens, larger monitors are also available for compact Macintoshes such as the Plus, Classic, SE, and SE/30. Color monitors are not available for the Plus, as there is no provision for color in its ROMs.

Nearly all monitors require the addition of a video card (see the section "Macintosh internal cards" in this chapter), and not all video cards support all monitors. Exceptions to this are certain monitors that are compatible with the built-in video support of the Macintosh IIci, LC, and IIsi. Even in these cases, you would be well advised to purchase a monitor that does not rely upon the built-in video capabilities of those computers, because using built-in video reduces the amount of RAM available to your system and may also slow down your Macintosh.

Another reason to buy an external monitor for the IIci, LC, or IIsi concerns System 7. The provision that System 7 requires 2MB of RAM is affected by these three Macintoshes that use part of the system memory to deal with video. If you are using the built-in video with a IIci, LC, or IIsi, you will need more than 2MB of RAM to take full advantage of System 7. However, with a monitor driven by its own video card, you can still get by with 2MB of RAM to run System 7 on these machines. Of course, if you already have more than 2MB of RAM, this is not as important a consideration.

Color (or gray-scale) is not a strong selling point for music applications, although some programs are beginning to take advantage of color for displaying different types of data on the same screen. Because all music developers want to remain compatible with compact Macintoshes for marketing reasons, it is unlikely that a music program will ever actually stipulate a color monitor as a requirement for its operation.

Monitors are available in many sizes. The built-in monitors found with compact Macintoshes are 9 inches on the diagonal (512 pixels wide × 384 pixels high). The smallest screen that Apple markets as an external monitor is 12 inches (640 pixels wide × 480 pixels high for monochrome and 512 × 384 pixels for RGB color). Prior to 1991 most Apple color monitors were 13 inches on the diagonal (also 640 × 480 pixels). The display area of many 13-inch Apple monitors that are being driven by Apple video cards can often be increased to 704 × 512 pixels by using a public domain INIT called MaxApple-Zoom (see coupon in the back of this book). None of these monitors allow you to view an entire 8½ × 11 inch page. Some third parties market displays in this category with a 14-inch diagonal.

When the diagonal dimension exceeds 14 inches, a monitor is often referred to as a portrait display. Portrait-size monitors can display a full 8½ × 11 inch page. These are sometimes referred to as single-page displays. The typical diagonal measurement is 15 inches and the horizontal width is still 640 pixels, but the vertical dimension is increased to 870 pixels.

Two-page displays (sometimes called landscape displays) are found in 19- and 21-inch diagonal configurations and can typically display at least the print area of two 8½ × 11 inch pages. The horizontal measurement for two-page displays is usually at least 1,024 pixels. Apple's two-page display is 1,152 × 870 pixels, although third-party vendors sell monitors in this category that increase the dimensions up to 1,280 × 960 pixels and therefore are capable of displaying two full 8½ × 11 inch pages with the margins of the pages shown as well.

Screen real estate is always going to have an impact upon the efficiency with which you can work with a piece of software. Fortunately, most developers still program their software with the idea that a large part of the user base will have compact Macintoshes with 9-inch screens. Fewer than 1 percent of Macintosh music programs require a large screen, although many will take advantage of the extra display area if they detect the presence of a larger screen. The real problem arises through multiple windows being open under MultiFinder. To get around this, Apple has a provision in System 7 to hide all windows except those pertaining to the currently active program. Many people have already been doing this for several years using an INIT called Tablecloth.

You should seriously consider purchasing a large screen monitor (i.e., full-page or two-page display) if you are going to be involved in multimedia production, soundfile editing, or notation. For multimedia production, a large screen means that you can keep authoring tools visible and accessible without obscuring the window that displays the project at the size your end-users will most likely be using. If your multimedia productions are going to involve video, you might also consider purchasing an NTSC monitor so that you can see how your Macintosh RGB graphics are going to appear on a composite video screen. Ideally, you could use a multisync monitor for this. Multisync monitors allow you to switch back and forth between composite video and RGB.

Because more and more notation programs operate within or offer the option to operate within the context of a virtual page or pages, if your primary activity is music notation, much time can be saved with a larger screen.

Finally, you should keep in mind that the Macintosh provides easy support of multiple monitors. This gives you the option of keeping your authoring or notation tools on one screen and displaying the current document on a second screen.

Input devices

❖ **Keyboard**
Normal
Extended
Third-party

❖ **Mouse**
Mechanical
Optical
The HeadMouse

❖ **Trackball**
Standard
Felix

❖ **Graphics tablet**
Without pressure-sensitivity
With pressure-sensitvity
The UnMouse

❖ **Other**
Voice recognition systems
CS-1 (Control Station)
Presto keypad

The primary devices that you use to interact with the Macintosh are its keyboard and pointing device. Typically, the pointing device is a mouse, although there are many alternatives to this. With one exception, nearly all input devices in this category are ADB devices, meaning that they connect to the computer via the Apple Desktop Bus, which utilizes small, rounded four-pin connectors.

There are several "official" Apple Macintosh keyboards, including the standard keyboard and the extended keyboard. Both include numeric keypads, but the extended version adds a number of useful keys. No commercial software requires an extended keyboard, although many programs take advantage of the presence of one by mapping certain functions to single keystrokes, giving access to a feature that would necessitate a menu call with a standard keyboard.

A number of third-party keyboards provide the same keys found on the Apple extended keyboard at a significantly lower price. But Apple keyboards are quite durable. On two occasions I have entered my studio to find that a leaky roof has dropped about a cup of water into my Apple extended keyboard. On both occasions, I simply poured the water off and let the keyboard dry out for several hours. As testimony to Apple's keyboard durability, there were no ill effects. I have never seen an Apple keyboard break down but I have seen many third-party keyboards malfunction — typical symptoms seem to be the command or option keys being internally stuck in the down position. There is one ingenious third-party keyboard that allows you to actually configure the layout of the keys themselves. I know of a number of people with this configurable keyboard and have never heard of any problems with it.

The main input device with the most alternatives is the Macintosh's pointing device, traditionally a single-button mouse. Most mice are mechanical, meaning that they track your hand motion on a surface by incorporating a rolling ball element. Some mice are optical, meaning that they have no moving parts and track your hand movement with a small light source being reflected off a special mouse pad. Wireless mice are available. At least one wireless hand mouse is marketed and another "head mouse" mounts on a headband and tracks mouse movement in direct relation to your eye movements. In the case of the head mouse, mouse clicks are issued by pressing a little bar that mounts across the front of your keyboard. Both systems require infrared (line of sight) communication with the Macintosh.

The most popular alternative to the mouse is a trackball. The principle is similar to an upside down mouse. Instead of you rolling the mouse's built-in ball across a surface, you roll your hand across a ball incorporated into a stationary holder. Trackballs are very popular among musicians because they require the least amount of dedicated surface area. When you are trying to keep your computer keyboard as close as possible to your Macintosh keyboard and mouse, a fixed and mountable element such as a trackball makes much more sense than a free standing, dangling mouse that requires a considerable amount of surface area. At least one trackball, Curtis's MVP Mouse, has three buttons to which you can assign just about any function and an optional footswitch which is also assignable in function.

While a trackball requires rolling your palm across a ball the size of a billiard ball, Felix uses the same principle with an extremely small moving element that you can control with a single finger or grasp like a pencil.

Graphics tablets are a special type of input device optimized, as you might expect, for graphics entry. You control cursor movement on a graphics tablet with a special pen. Writing or drawing on the tablet maps a corresponding analog of your pen activity to appear on the screen. Some graphics tablets such as the Wacom tablet now offer pressure sensitivity. In these cases, pressing the pen harder onto the surface of the graphics tablet has the same effect that pressing a felt-tip pen or paintbrush would have on a traditional drawing surface. The UnMouse is similar to a graphics tablet, except that it is smaller and you usually use your finger in place of a pen. Graphics tablets can be very effective for non-MIDI entry of music into notation software. At least one program, Passport's NoteWriter, includes a built-in handwriting recognition system that translates scrawled notation symbols into their intended PostScript characters and therefore lends itself to a graphics tablet/pen style input device.

Voice recognition systems are increasingly popular input devices for the Macintosh. I have been using Articulate Systems's Voice Navigator for years and it only gets better and better. Voice recognition systems are generally not used to dictate letters as you might imagine. Their main purpose is to assign a voice command to a mouse or keyboard action or series of mouse/keyboard actions. One effective use of such devices is when you are step-entering music into a sequencer or notation program. If you need to keep both hands on your MIDI keyboard, rather than jumping back and forth to the Macintosh keyboard to change rhythmic durations, you can simply say "sixteenth note," "eighth note triplet" to change the step duration. Voice recognition used in conjunction with a mouse can save much time as well. For example, when you are adding ancillary markings to a score in a notation program, rather than calling up an ancillary symbol palette or dialog box and then selecting the next symbol from it, you can keep your mouse fixed at the current position on the staff and simply say, for example, "up slur," "tenuto mark," or "mezzo forte" to change the cursor to the next type of marking you wish to enter. Another advantage of voice recognition devices is that a single voice command can initiate a complex series of actions, combining multiple mouse movements, menu, and dialog interactions into one macro-like event.

Two ADB input devices are specifically dedicated to musical applications. Music Publisher's Presto Pad (discussed in Chapter 21, "Score Input and Editing") sits beside your Macintosh keyboard and is used to specify pitch within their accompanying notation program. JL Cooper's CS-1 is an innovative ADB controller that maps virtual software controls onto hardware buttons and knobs (see the section "MIDI controllers" in this chapter).

Most ADB input devices can be daisychained, meaning that you can have multiple types of input devices connected to a single Macintosh. Warning: Never plug or unplug an ADB device while the computer is powered up.

Macintosh internal cards
Audio cards
❖ ROM-based sample player
❖ RAM-based sample player
❖ Digital audio card (for DSP and Direct-to-hard disk recording)

All three types of audio cards available for the Macintosh are marketed by Digidesign, clearly the leader in digital audio workstation technology for micro-computers (see Table 5-3). Their MacProteus card puts an E-mu Systems Proteus/1 sample player inside your Macintosh. Their SampleCell card puts an 8MB to 40MB sampler inside your Macintosh (8MB if you have one card using 1MB SIMMs and 40MB if you have five cards). Both of these NuBus cards provide audio connectors to the back of the Macintosh chassis. Instead of using an external hardware MIDI interface to pass on your MIDI data, you can simply make all the connections internally, in software, with Apple's MIDI Manager (see Chapter 8, "Moving Data Around Your Music Network").

Internal digital audio cards are used to make and edit direct-to-hard disk record-ings and as an adjunct to sound design and editing for external samplers or the internal SampleCell. With an internal digital audio card, you can turn your Macintosh into a self-contained compact-disk mastering system.

Combining these three types of cards, ROM sample player, RAM sample player, and digital audio, you can assemble a dedicated music workstation of formidable power. You may need a IIfx or accelerated Macintosh to use all three types of cards simultaneously, although many projects may require accessing only one of your installed cards. You can dispense with dozens of external boxes, cables, and support devices. This approach is discussed extensively in Chapters 15, 18, and 27.

Table 5-3: Macintosh internal cards — Audio cards

Company	Product	List price	Description and specifications
Digidesign	MacProteus	900	ROM Sample Player
Digidesign	SampleCell	2,000	RAM Sample Player (add cost of up to 8MB RAM to this price). Up to 5 may be installed.
Digidesign	Audiomedia	1,000	Four channels, analog input/output
Digidesign	Sound Accelerator	3,285	A/D System: AD-IN

Table 5-3: Macintosh internal cards — Audio cards (continued)

Company	Product	List price	Description and specifications
		3,285	Digital I/O System: DAT I/O
		4,280	A/D & Digital I/O System: AD-IN, DAT I/O
		5,285	Pro Analog System: Pro I/O
		6,280	Pro Analog & Digital I/O System: Pro I/O, DAT I/O
Digidesign	ProTools Audio Card	11,000	(provides 4 channels of digital recording per card)
Mark of the Unicorn	Digital Waveboard	1,500	Four Channel, digital input/output

Video cards

❖ Monochrome
❖ 4-bit
❖ 8-bit
❖ 24-bit
❖ Graphics acceleration cards
❖ Composite video and NTSC

Unless you are using a compact Macintosh, LC, IIci, or IIsi, you will need a video card to drive your monitor. Even if you are using an LC, IIci, or IIsi, you may want to consider substituting a video card in place of its on-board video capabilities (which uses up precious system RAM) for reasons stated above in the section on monitors.

Because more bits means more money, buy a video card that will support the kind of monitor you can afford in the future.

Composite and NTSC video cards are important if you are working on the visual side of multimedia production. One extremely important consideration is that Macintosh graphics appear on your screen completely differently than they do on an interlaced composite or NTSC video screen — a very clear example of WYSINWYG (What You See Is Not What You Get). Single pixel dissolves and transitions created in MacroMind's Director, which work perfectly on the Macintosh's RGB screen, are nauseating when converted to NTSC due to the interlaced scanning technique of the ancient NTSC technology.

The variety of internal cards targeted at this market can make it very confusing as to which card to buy. The types of features include frame-grabbing (being able to grab a frame of video from an external source), video overlay (being able to combine Macintosh-generated graphics with an external video source), full-motion display (being able to display an external source inside a Macintosh window), composite output (being able to output video to an external VCR or display system), frame-by-frame output (being able to output Macintosh-created animations a frame at a time in broadcast quality), and video compression (being able to compress still video images and/or full motion video into more manageable file sizes). Some boards integrate many of these capabilities, while others are dedicated to doing a single one of these tasks extremely well. No current video cards offer all of these options, so you should be very sure about what you are going to need before making an investment, since these cards are not cheap.

On the other hand, video acceleration cards, originally aimed at the Macintosh graphics community, are becoming popular with Macintosh musicians engaged in notation. For example, Apple's 8•24 GC card can accelerate screen redrawing by 3,000 percent. This is the aspect of notation software that holds you back the most — waiting for the screen to redraw. Screen redrawing is such a bottleneck for notation programs that some manufacturers have added an option to only redraw the screen when you specifically request a display update. The disadvantage of this kluge is that while you are working, you are never really seeing the page of music as it will appear the next time you redraw the screen.

Internal video cards and their various bells and whistles are discussed in Chapter 7, "Setting Up Your Mac Music Studio" (see the first table in that chapter for a list of popular options).

Accelerator cards

Macintoshes can be sped up by adding an internal accelerator. Besides the graphics accelerators listed above, there are three main types of add-on cards that can speed up your Macintosh:

- ❖ CPU accelerators
- ❖ Cache cards
- ❖ SCSI accelerators

CPU accelerators replace the existing Macintosh processor (from the 68000 family) with a processor running at a faster clock speed. These can be added to any Macintosh whether or not the Macintosh has an internal slot. Macintoshes with soldered-on processors (Plus, SE, Classic) must use CPU accelerators specifically manufactured for the particular Macintosh model, whereas Macintoshes with logic boards that have their 68000 (020, 030, 040) CPU socketed in place are easier to upgrade.

CPU accelerators come in many speeds. Some merely replace the processor with a speedier version without moving the Macintosh's RAM onto the accelerator board, thus creating a speed bottleneck by forcing the computer to continue to access its RAM at the original speed while CPU operations are sped up to the extent of the processor having to wait for the RAM (called a "wait state"). More expensive accelerators move the RAM to their own board to ensure that it can be driven at the speed provided by the new processor. In either case, a math coprocessor (also referred to as a floating point unit, or FPU) may be included on the accelerator board. This adds floating point capabilities to Macintoshes that originally had no math coprocessor. In some cases a speedier FPU can be added to Macintoshes with native FPUs.

Musicians need not worry too much about math coprocessors when running software that is compatible with the Plus, SE, Classic, or LC, because these computers don't have math coprocessors, so you can be confident that the software does not require one or run faster with one. It is not in the interest of the marketing department of a software developer to create programs that require an FPU, because doing so is not a factor in about 80 percent of their possible sales.

In some cases a PMMU (Page Memory Management Unit) is included on the accelerator board to assure compatibility with virtual memory features of System 7. This is not necessary if the accelerator board uses an 030 or 040 processor because the PMMU is built into these chips. You should not take this to imply that all 030- or 040-based accelerators will be compatible with the virtual memory features of System 7. First of all, the results aren't in yet regarding third-party accelerators and System 7 compatibility. Second, even among Apple's own machines, only those Macintoshes with "32-bit clean" ROMs will be able to access more than 14MB of virtual memory, up to 4 gigabytes more, to be exact. The only currently available 32-bit clean Macintoshes are the IIci, IIfx, and IIsi. You can get around this by using Apple's Startup Document called Mode32. This patches the ROMs on unclean 68030-based Macintoshes so that they function as if they were 32-bit clean.

RAM cache cards are available for most Macintoshes, particularly the IIci and specifically for its PDS (processor direct slot). The IIsi and IIfx also have PDSs. Cache cards generally provide 32K or 64K of static RAM (SRAM). At 25 nanoseconds, SRAM is much faster than the DRAM (dynamic RAM) used for the main memory of Macintosh computers. A RAM cache stores the most recently used or frequently needed data, as well as "nearby" data, just in case the CPU might need it again. The "hit ratio" on these cards is usually 90 percent or so, so it's very likely that information *near* the most recently used will be accessed again. The Macintosh General cdev contains a RAM caching option. This cache in the control panel utilizes the main RAM of the Macintosh and thus delivers data at between 70 to 150 nanoseconds depending on what Macintosh model you are using. The speed of the SRAM on dedicated cache cards is what makes them increase overall performance so significantly — by 15 to 30 percent. Many of the better CPU accelerator cards include an SRAM cache too.

SCSI expansion cards

❖ Disk duplexing cards
❖ Additional SCSI bus cards

Some SCSI enhancement cards, whether speeding up the SCSI data transfer rate or not, have the added attraction of providing a second or third set of SCSI addresses, allowing you to increase the number of SCSI peripherals connected to your Macintosh accordingly.

A disk duplexing SCSI card is a special case. While these do provide you with another set of SCSI addresses, the only purpose of this second set of addresses is to continually back up designated drives from your primary SCSI bus (see the section "Backup systems" in this chapter).

Interfaces
MIDI

❖ 16-channel
❖ 32-channel
❖ Greater-than-32-channel
❖ Interfaces with built-in synchronization, routing, merging, and processing

Your MIDI interface is perhaps the most important piece of MIDI gear you will purchase if you plan to use MIDI in any way whatsoever (see Figure 5-1 for an illustration of a basic MIDI setup). To control external MIDI devices from your Macintosh, you need a MIDI interface to convert MIDI data that exists in a format your Macintosh can understand to a format that your external MIDI devices can understand, and vice versa. Your synthesizer's MIDI IN and OUT cables plug into one side of this box (using 5-pin DIN cables) and your Macintosh plugs into the other side (using a single 8-pin connector or a db9 connector for the 512K Macintosh).

MIDI interfaces come in three types: those that support a single set of 16 MIDI channels, those that support two sets of 16 MIDI channels (sometimes referred to as dual interfaces), and those that manipulate the MIDI specification to support greater than 32 channels. Dual interfaces do not violate the 16-channel MIDI specification because they simply send a separate set of 16 channels out of each of the Macintosh's serial ports. However, greater than 16-channel interfaces must employ MIDI messages that are not yet officially sanctioned by the IMA. There is nothing wrong with taking advantage of this sort of hardware ingenuity.

Basic MIDI interfaces provide one MIDI IN port and one MIDI OUT port and are connected to the Macintosh with a single cable. You will recall from Chapter 1 that this doesn't limit you to a single sound-generating device. Your

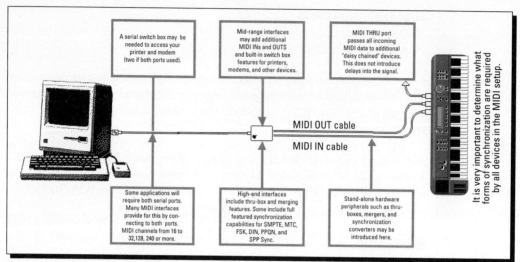

Figure 5-1: The most basic MIDI setup requires a Macintosh, MIDI Interface (Apple's is pictured), and a single MIDI synthesizer. Specific applications and individual hardware preferences will determine what type of interface is required as well as the kinds of interface peripherals needed. In general, options in the boxes in the upper half of the diagram will tend to be less costly than those in the bottom half.

MIDI instruments have a third MIDI port labeled "MIDI THRU," which passes information received at the MIDI IN ports to additional devices. With older devices, distortion introduced between each MIDI IN and THRU port limits the practical length of such a MIDI daisychain to four devices. This is not a problem with newer MIDI gear.

If you have or are planning to have more than four MIDI devices, several 16-channel MIDI interfaces include more than one MIDI OUT port. These also allow for "star" networks (see Chapter 8, "Moving Data Around Your Music Network") to be assembled with a smaller number of devices.

Most professional interfaces connect to both Macintosh serial ports simultaneously. This permits MIDI software to address two separate sets of 16 MIDI channels at MIDI's standard 32.25 Kbaud. In this increasingly popular configuration it is possible to have 32 MIDI channels accessing 32 different sounds at a single time. These interfaces provide two MIDI IN ports, permitting multiple devices to send data to the Macintosh simultaneously.

Because your serial port(s) need to be dedicated to the MIDI interface, you might wonder how to access your modem or printer without continually swapping cables. For single-cable interfaces, you'll need a serial switch box. Fortunately, all interfaces that usurp both serial ports provide built-in switching functions on their front panels. However, if you want more than two serial devices to be accessible by one or more of your serial ports, you will still need a serial data switcher in between your MIDI interface and Macintosh. Keep in mind that most MIDI interfaces require separate power cords.

Many MIDI interfaces include built-in synchronization features. It is also possible to add a peripheral synchronization box to an interface without built-in sync capabilities. Such boxes are covered under their own heading. There are many reasons why you might synchronize your MIDI synthesizers and Macintosh to non-MIDI devices like certain drum machines, tape-recorders, and VCRs. Because few of these devices support MIDI, sound-generating devices accompanying them, or dedicated to laying down sequences a track at a time, eventually drift apart.

Synchronization methods have become increasingly more precise. Early TTL, DIN, and PPQ sync gave way to more accurate "intelligent" sync methods. Later, software developers started to implement synchronization features of the MIDI specification (Start, Stop, and Continue commands). Nonetheless, the first versions of MIDI sync still required that all devices be started from the beginning of the sequence or tape during each recording pass, thus wasting precious time. This was remedied through software support of MIDI Song Position Pointer (SPP), which permits devices to calculate elapsed 16th notes so that one device can instruct others to start at a specific point on the track.

SMPTE Time Code, originally developed for NASA (the National Aeronautics and Space Administration), is the industry standard for synchronizing audio with video. Rather than recorded pulses, SMPTE Time Codes contain exact location information: hour, minute, second, and frame. Initial SMPTE-to-MIDI interfaces relied upon the conversion of SMPTE into SPP, but since the adoption of MIDI Time Code (MTC), it is possible to effectively send SMPTE information over MIDI. Because of MTC's data requirements (meaning that it requires a significant portion of MIDI's fixed 31.25 KBaud bandwidth), a less data hungry, "Direct Time Lock" SMPTE-to-MIDI synchronization protocol has been adopted by several manufacturers.

Several other functional enhancements are sometimes found in MIDI interfaces. These include MIDI THRU box functions, MIDI merging, and MIDI data processing. These features are noted in Table 5-4. However, because there are so many MIDI black boxes dedicated to these particular functions, you are referred below to the corresponding headings for their definitions and how to determine whether you need such capabilities.

There are two greater-than-32-channel interfaces: Mark of the Unicorn's MIDI Time Piece and Opcode's Studio 5. Both employ different techniques to get around MIDI's 16-channel limitations. Both also include all the synchronization, THRU box, merging, and processing features you will probably ever need. A single MIDI Time Piece (often abbreviated as MTP) provides eight input and output ports, each of which can be assigned a discrete set of 16 MIDI channels. The terminology used equates each input and output with a "cable" (e.g., "Cable 6, Channel 12"). Therefore, with one of these interfaces you have 128 MIDI channels available if your software can address them (and many newer programs can). Any combination of inputs can be merged together and any input can be mapped to any output or outputs. Finally, each of the channels and each of the inputs and outputs can have their own set of MIDI processing assignments. A network of up to four MTPs can be assembled, providing you with 32 MIDI IN and MIDI OUT ports and a grand total of 512 MIDI channels. A single Opcode Studio 5 starts out resembling two MTPs in functionality. There are 15 MIDI INs and OUTs for a grand total of 240 channels. Two Studio 5s can be attached to your Macintosh, so a network of 480 channels is possible. Nearly all of the features found in the MTP are present in the Studio 5, and there are many new features. Furthermore, the Studio 5 can support Mark of the Unicorn's proprietary cabling codes while the converse is not true. See Chapter 8 for a thorough examination of these all-in-one devices.

When you purchase an interface, you should consider the number of MIDI inputs and outputs you currently require and then add an ample amount in anticipation of future acquisitions. Next, consider the number of MIDI channels that you want to access. Because the prices are so close, the question of whether to get a single (16-channel) or dual (32-channel) interface should be weighed carefully. The only situations where I would recommend settling for a 16-channel interface are in entry level setups, setups for notation where MIDI will only be used for data entry andperhaps proofhearing, and certain multimedia production setups. If you anticipate the need to control a large number of multitimbral devices, you should seriously consider a greater-than-32-channel interface. Finally, the question of whether you require synchronization features or will require them in the future should be answered.

No single product has all possible options, but you won't require every feature for your specific setup or applications. If you're new to MIDI and want to take the plunge with a functional, inexpensive, easy-to-setup, compact interface with no external power requirements, Apple's own MIDI interface might be a good beginning — it comes with two MIDI cables (a value of $10 – $25) so you can get to work the moment you open the box (unless you own a IIfx, which is incompatible with Apple's own MIDI interface!). And where else can you get MIDI cables with the Apple logo on them?

Table 5-5 helps you compare interfaces on a feature-by-feature basis. Related devices that work in conjunction with your MIDI interface are found later in this chapter under the headings "SMPTE converters," "Lockup systems," and "MIDI networking and processing."

Table 5-4: MIDI Interfaces

Company (numbers refer to Table 5-5)	Product and version	List price $	Description and specifications
Altech (1)	ALTECH MIDI Interface	100	16-chan, 1 In, 3 Out, self-powered
Altech (2)	ALTECH Dual Interface	150	32-chan, 2 In, 6 Out (switchable to 1 In, 6 Out)
Apple (3)	MIDI Interface	100	16-chan, 1 In, 1 Out, self-powered (IIfx incompatible)
Austin Development (4)	MIDIFace II	130	32-chan, 2 In, 6 Out (switchable to 1 In, 6 Out)
JL Cooper (5)	MacNexus	70	16-chan, 1 In, 1 Out, self-powered
JL Cooper (6)	Sync•Link	200	32-chan, 2 In, 2 Out. SMPTE-to-MTC or DTL. Smart FSK, SPP, Audio Click. Jam Sync/Regeneration. Read and write SMPTE (24, 25, 30, 30df).
JL Cooper (7)	SyncMaster	350	32-chan, 2 In, 6 Out. SMPTE-to-MTC or DTL. Smart FSK, SPP, Audio Click. Jam Sync/Regeneration and reshaping. Read and write SMPTE (24, 25, 30, 30df).
Mark of the Unicorn (8)	MIDI Time Piece	500	128-chan cableized (networkable to 512-chan), 8 In, 8 Out. SMPTE-to-MTC or DTL. Regenerate. Merge, process, and filter MIDI data.
Opcode (9)	MIDI Translator	60	16-chan, 1 In, 3 Out, self-powered
Opcode (10)	Studio Plus 2	200	32-chan, 2 In, 6 Out (switchable to 1 In, 6 Out)
Opcode (11)	Studio 3	380	32-chan, 2 In, 6 Out (assignable). SMPTE-to-MTC or DTL. Audio Click. Jam Sync, Regeneration, Flywheel. Read and write SMPTE (24, 25, 30, 30df).
Opcode (12)	Studio 5	1,295	240-chan, 15 In, 15 Out. SMPTE-to-MTC or DTL. Audio Click. Jam Sync, Regeneration, Flywheel. Read and write SMPTE (24, 25, 30, 30df).
Passport (13)	MIDI Transport	460	32-chan, 1 In, 3 Out plus 1 In, 1 Out (merged with sync). SMPTE-to-MTC, DTL, or Smart FSK. Read and write SMPTE (24, 25, 30, 30df). Writes FSK.

Table 5-5: MIDI interfaces feature comparisons

(See Table 5-4 for key to numbers)	1	2	3	4	5	6	7	8	9	10	11	12	13
Ins and Outs													
Number of Inputs	1	2	1	2	1	2	2	8	1	2	2	15	2
Number of Outputs	3	6	1	6	1	2	6	8	3	6	6	15	4
Number of channels supported													
Per box	16	32	32	16	16	32	32	128	16	32	32	240	32
Per maximum network configuration								512					
THRU box features													
Assign all Outputs to a single Input		●		●			●	●		●	●	●	
Assign any Input(s) to any Output(s)								●			●	●	
Save Setups								●			●		
Built-in serial port switcher		●					●	●		●	●	●	●
Input merging													
Any two Inputs								●				●	
Any combination of Inputs								●				●	
Processing features													
Remap Input channels								●				●	
Remap Output channels								●				●	
Mute events by channel								●				●	
Mute events by cable								●				●	
Different Input and Output muting								●				●	
Mutable events (channel messages):													
Note ons and offs								●				●	
Monophonic pressure (aftertouch)								●				●	
Polyphonic pressure								●				●	
Pitch Bend								●				●	
Patch Change								●				●	
Controllers								●				●	

Table 5-5: MIDI interfaces feature comparisons (continued)

(See Table 5-4 for key to numbers)	1	2	3	4	5	6	7	8	9	10	11	12	13
Processing features (continued)													
Mutable events (system messages):													
System Reset								●				●	
System Realtime								●				●	
Tune Request								●				●	
Active Sensing								●				●	
System Exclusive								●				●	
MIDI Time Code								●				●	
Data thinning													
Synchronization													
FSK sync						●	●					●	●
MTC (MIDI Time Code)						●	●	●			●	●	●
DTL (Direct Tme Lock)						●	●				●	●	●
DTLe (Direct Tme Lock Enhanced)								●				●	
SMPTE Formats read (LTC)													
24 frame, 25 frame						●	●	●			●	●	●
30 non-drop, 30 drop						●	●	●			●	●	●
29.97												●	
Stripe SMPTE (LTC)													
Set audio level of output signal						●	●	●			●	●	●
Regenerate (Jam sync)						●	●	●			●	●	
Echo sync at specified output								●				●	
Echo sync at multiple outputs								●				●	
Sync to Audio Click						●	●				●	●	
Utilities													
Configure from Macintosh						●	●	●			●	●	●
Configure with Front panel												▶	
Configurations stored in Macintosh								●				●	
Configurations stored in Interface													●
Macintosh SMPTE Display						●	●	●			●	●	●

Part One: The Basics

Table 5-5: MIDI interfaces feature comparisons (continued)

(See Table 5-4 for key to numbers)	1	2	3	4	5	6	7	8	9	10	11	12	13
Additional specifications													
Settings are battery backed												●	
MIDI status lights													
Input						●	●	●		●	●	●	●
Output						●	●	●		●	●		●
Cable activity								●				●	
SMPTE Lock							●	●		●	●	●	●
Dedicated MIDI controller input										●	●		
No power supply required		●		●		●			●				

SMPTE converters

❖ LTC converter
❖ VITC converter

Use SMPTE Time Code to synchronize MIDI software running on your Macintosh with an external tape recorder or video deck. With synchronization you can record many audio tracks in multiple passes with the assurance that every note will be aligned with the appropriate notes on other tracks. Synchronization is a necessity when composing or realizing music for film or video, because it is usually important that audio events align with corresponding visual events.

Unlike early formats of MIDI synchronization, which relied upon counting identical timing messages relative to a particular starting point, SMPTE provides a system where a unique address is written to an audio or video tape up to 30 times per second. The important concept to keep in mind is that MIDI sync, SPP, pulse sync and other early methods are based on relative time, whereas SMPTE (and MTC) is based upon absolute time.

SMPTE addresses are expressed as HH:MM:SS:FF where HH = hours, MM = minutes, SS = seconds, and FF = frames, at the prevailing frame rate. Because each SMPTE address uses 80 bits to describe an individual address, some software and even hardware devices are capable of referencing each individual bit as a separate address, thus providing a timing resolution of $\frac{1}{2400}$ of a second, about $\frac{1}{10}$ of a millisecond.

There are five SMPTE frame rates in widespread use: 24, 25, 30 non-drop, 30 drop, and 29.97 frames per second. The most popular rates used in the United States are 30 drop and 29.97. The distinctions between the various frame rates are discussed in Chapter 26, "Film and Video Applications."

LTC and VITC are the two systems for recording SMPTE Time Code on magnetic tape. Longitudinal Time Code (LTC) is treated just like any other kind of audio and is recorded horizontally onto one of the audio tracks of a video tape or onto an unused audio track of an audio tape (usually a track on the edge and often with a blank track in between so that noise of the time code does not spill over into tracks used for music). In order for LTC to be sensed by a synchronization device, the tape must be rolling. When a video tape is paused, the last SMPTE address to be transmitted is not always the correct address of the frame paused upon. Vertical Interval Time Code (VITC) is recorded directly into the helically scanned video signal of a video tape (VITC is not available for audio tape). The advantage of VITC is that while a video tape is paused and a single frame is repeatedly scanned (because the time code is embedded in the video signal), it continues to be sent out repeatedly, just as if the tape was rolling. And the frame number is accurate, which is not the case with LTC.

Many MIDI interfaces have LTC converters built into them (see the section "MIDI interfaces" in this chapter). No current MIDI interfaces have VITC capabilities. Because of these two facts, if your MIDI interface does not have SMPTE conversion hardware built into it or you want to use VITC, you will need an external converter (see Table 5-6).

Table 5-6: Interfaces — SMPTE converters

Company	Product	List price $	Description and specifications
Aphex	Studio Clock	700	SMPTE-to-MIDI, Click, Tempo map; Macintosh editor available for $90.
JL Cooper	PPS-2	170	SMPTE-to-MTC or DTL. Smart FSK, SPP, MIDI Click. Jam Sync/Regeneration. Read and write SMPTE (24, 25, 30, 30df). 1 In, 1 Out. Merges time code with incoming MIDI.
JL Cooper	PPS-100	400	SMPTE-to-MTC or DTL. Smart FSK, SPP, PPQN, DIN Sync, MIDI clock, Audio Click. Pulse outputs. Read and write SMPTE (24, 25, 30, 30df). 1,000 event memory. Can offset sync.
Mark of the Unicorn	Video Time Piece	1,200	SMPTE (VITC and LTC)-to-MTC or DTLe. NTSC or PAL/SECAM. Audio Click. House sync. Jam Sync and Regeneration, Flywheel. Genlock. Display and burn Time Code window on video, Download graphics to video, Display streamers on video.
Opcode	Timecode Machine	150	SMPTE-to-MTC or DTL. Jam Sync. Read and write SMPTE (24, 25, 30, 30df). 1 In, 1 Out. Merges time code with incoming MIDI.

Lockup systems

A *lockup system* is a box that allows two or more hardware devices to lock together as if they were running off the same motor. A single machine acts as a "master" to one or more "slave" devices. A SMPTE Time Code track on every device being locked together is used as a reference. Because SMPTE offsets can be entered into the lockup device, it is not necessary that the time code on the master video tape, for example, correspond exactly to the time code on slaved tape recorders. By entering a SMPTE offset, all devices are kept in sync.

Lockup systems are expensive, but they do have certain advantages. For example, if you are composing for film or video, it is easy to slave your Macintosh software to a SMPTE track on the video tape using a MIDI interface with built-in SMPTE conversion or in conjunction with an external SMPTE converter. In this way you can continually audition your music against the picture in absolute synchronization. Using the same devices, it is easy to slave your Macintosh software to a multitrack audio recorder as you lay down your tracks one at a time. The SMPTE track on your audio tape can later be used to synchronize music to the video and everything will align just as it did while you were slaved to the video tape. The one thing that you cannot do is slave the audio tape recorder to the video tape recorder so that you can watch the picture in synchronization with the multitrack recording. A lockup system provides for just this.

Note that while it may be helpful to watch the picture in sync with the multi-track during the mixdown process, the only other cases where such a system will aid in the composition process are: (1) when there are so many different sounds, instruments, or tracks being used that a true sense of the music cannot be obtained without adding the real tracks (on the tape recorder) with the virtual tracks (on the Macintosh); (2) when live musicians enter the picture. Even in these cases, for years composers have worked without the benefit of true machine lockup, so you should carefully consider the purchase of such an expensive system. Keep in mind that lockable video decks and tape recorders are more expensive than non-lockable ones and the cables that go between the various lockable devices can cost over $200 and each device requires its own custom cable.

The most popular lockup systems are those by Adams Smith and Lynx. A viable alternative that may save you some expense is available from Fostex.

Networking devices

MIDI networking and processing

- ❖ MIDI THRU box
- ❖ MIDI patcher
- ❖ MIDI merger
- ❖ MIDI processor
- ❖ MIDITap (MediaLink)

In a moderately advanced system, you will probably need a MIDI THRU box (or a more sophisticated version such as a MIDI patcher, MIDI matrix switcher, or MIDI router) to re-route outgoing MIDI information to different destinations. If you are simply playing your synthesizers, you only need a MIDI cable connected to their MIDI IN port. However, if you are planning to edit patches or transfer new patch banks to your synthesizer, most devices require that their MIDI OUT port also be connected to your Macintosh. As noted in the section "Interfaces," mid-range interfaces include limited THRU-box capabilities, and higher-end interfaces (greater-than-32-channel) offer extensive THRU box features as well as merging.

MIDI THRU boxes can help overcome the signal distortion introduced by daisychaining MIDI devices as data is passed from a device's MIDI IN port to its MIDI THRU port. Status LEDs are often provided so you can tell at a glance what mode your interface is in or where MIDI data is being routed.

You may also want to have a MIDI merger (to combine two incoming MIDI data streams — "Y connectors" are not permitted), which uses a microprocessor to mix several incoming MIDI data streams into a single MIDI data stream. MIDI merging is sometimes necessary for recording new MIDI data while simultaneously syncing to a third device. MIDI merging is always required if you want to record from more than two devices. Finally, because patch-editing requires that a module's MIDI OUT be routed to your interface's MIDI IN, you may require a MIDI merger if you want to play a module while simultaneously editing its patches. Note that unlike the data coming into a device's MIDI input, a device's MIDI output is not echoed at its MIDI THRU port. If you are using a dual interface, you can get around some of these problems since there are two MIDI inputs — one directing data to the Macintosh's modem port and the other directing data to the printer port. If you are using a greater-than-32-channel interface, you won't have any of these problems because the number of mergeable MIDI cables is equivalent to the number of MIDI IN ports on the interface.

Common features on MIDI processors and THRU boxes with processor-like capabilities include the option to filter out certain types of MIDI data, mute specified channels, re-map channels, and thin out types of data that might overload the system or clog up the cables. All such features are accessible in real time. Most MIDI processors provide for the merging of at least two incoming MIDI data streams. Some MIDI THRU boxes that include processing provide options to initialize each channel on separate outputs with a specific patch. More versatile processors can produce, for example, echoes by delaying and/or retriggering incoming information.

Many MIDI processors allow you to save setups to battery-backed RAM in the device. These setups can be recalled via front-panel controls. This is an important feature because, unless you are using a greater-than-32-channel interface, you will want to have several configurations, one for inputting MIDI data to the Macintosh and separate configurations for each external device whose patches you want to edit. For live performance situations, the ability to recall a large number of saved configurations is often a necessity.

Most newer boxes provide the option to recall setups via MIDI. Typically, a specified range of program numbers on a specified channel is mapped to the various configurations saved in the battery-backed RAM of the device. Some go so far as to allow you to specify which input these designated special program changes will be received on. Simply sending a patch change command on the assigned channel (and cable in some devices) causes the MIDI THRU box to switch to the desired configuration.

Mark of the Unicorn's MIDI Time Piece and Opcode's Studio 5 include nearly all the features typically found in MIDI THRU boxes, routers, mergers, and processors. And they also function as MIDI interfaces to the Macintosh. As if that weren't enough, they also include built-in SMPTE converters and support for hundreds of cableized MIDI channels.

Lone Wolf's MidiTap is a special type of MIDI network device that provides for an almost unlimited number of MIDI devices to be addressed individually. Configurations of your MIDI network called "LanScapes" can be saved, recalled, and edited graphically. See Table 5-7 for details of all MIDI network devices.

For more information on the topic of MIDI networks, see Chapter 8, "Moving Data Around Your Music Network."

Table 5-7: MIDI network devices (excluding interfaces)

Company	Product	List Price $	Description and specifications
360 Systems	MIDI Patcher	300	8 × 8 MIDI patchbay with merging and processing
360 Systems		350	MIDI patchbay w/100 set-up memories
Akai		150-200	MIDI data processors
Akai		200-300	Programmable MIDI patchbays
Akai		400	MIDI-programmable mix bay
Anatek Microcircuits	MIDI Widgets	50-150	Mergers, splitter, transposer, mini-sequencer
Anatek Microcircuits		400	8 × 1 MIDI merger
Aphex Systems		800	Rhythm "humanizer"
Digital Music Corp.	MX8	90-150	6 × 8 MIDI patchbay with merging and processing
Forte Music		1,000	6 × 6 MIDI data processor

Table 5-7: MIDI network devices (excluding interfaces) (continued)

Company	Product	List Price $	Description and specifications
Hinton Instruments		3,000-6,000	8- to 24-point MIDI patchbay
Ibanez		350	MIDI patchbay, 5 effects loops, 128 presets
Intone		900	MIDI programmable audio and MIDI patching
Intone		500-1,000	7 × 8 MIDI patchbay, 6 controller inputs, SMPTE, MTC, Macintosh interface w/optional 16 × 16 audio patchbay
JL Cooper	Nexus	100	3 × 8 MIDI patchbay
JL Cooper	Nexus Plus	160	2 × 8 MIDI merger/processor
JL Cooper	MSB+	390	8 × 8 MIDI patchbay/processor
JL Cooper	MSB Plus Rev2	390	8 × 8 MIDI patchbay/processor with Macintosh editor and remote control
JL Cooper	MSB 16/20	1,000	16 × 20 MIDI patchbay/processor, 3-way merge, Macintosh editor and remote control
JL Cooper	Synapse	1,200	16 × 20 MIDI patchbay/processor
Kawai		140	4 × 8 out MIDI patchbay
KMX	MIDI Central	579	15 × 16 MIDI patchbay with merging
Lone Wolf	MidiTap	1,600	High-speed MIDI network extender
MidiMix		44	MIDI THRU, splitter, merge boxes
MidiMix		400	4 × 5 MIDI merger w/ clock input
Roland		360	MIDI filter/processor

Audio networking
❖ Patchbay
❖ Digital patchbay
❖ MIDI-controllable patchbay

Audio patchbays route audio signals much in the same way that MIDI THRU boxes or patchers route MIDI data. It is advantageous for all audio input and output cables to be present at and routed via the audio patchbay. Patchbays usually consist of two rows of audio jacks. The rear side may have audio jacks or places for connections to be soldered.

There are several types of patchbays (see Figure 5-2). An *un-normaled patchbay* requires a cable to be connected between every vertical pair of plugs in order for the cables arriving at the patchbay to be connected to one another. A *normaled patchbay* connects every vertical pair of jacks (cables) automatically, provided there are no plugs in either jack — plugging a cable in either

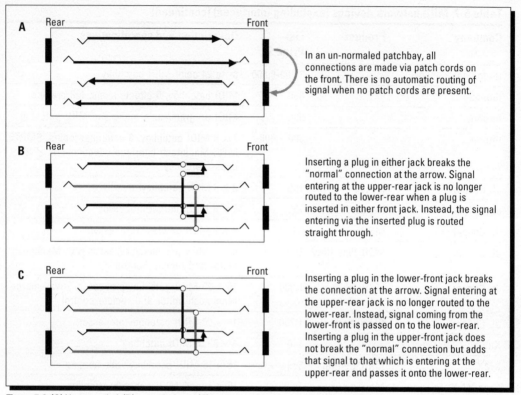

A

Rear   Front

In an un-normaled patchbay, all connections are made via patch cords on the front. There is no automatic routing of signal when no patch cords are present.

B

Rear   Front

Inserting a plug in either jack breaks the "normal" connection at the arrow. Signal entering at the upper-rear jack is no longer routed to the lower-rear when a plug is inserted in either front jack. Instead, the signal entering via the inserted plug is routed straight through.

C

Rear   Front

Inserting a plug in the lower-front jack breaks the connection at the arrow. Signal entering at the upper-rear jack is no longer routed to the lower-rear. Instead, signal coming from the lower-front is passed on to the lower-rear. Inserting a plug in the upper-front jack does not break the "normal" connection but adds that signal to that which is entering at the upper-rear and passes it onto the lower-rear.

Figure 5-2: (A) Un-normaled, **(B)** normaled, and **(C)** half-normaled patchbays showing the effect upon signal routing when a cable is plugged into either the upper or lower of each pair of jacks.

jack severs the connection. A *half-normaled patchbay* only disconnects the incoming data when a cable is plugged into the lower jack.

Most patchbays deal with analog signals, although digital patchbays are starting to appear. Like just about everything else in the world of music, a number of patchbays are now being marketed that respond to MIDI. These can save various routing configurations and assign them to a MIDI program number for later recall. With such devices you can completely change your audio routing configuration by simply sending a MIDI program change message to your patchbay.

When considering patchbays and other audio connections you should understand the distinction between *balanced* and *unbalanced lines*. Balanced lines use cables that have two conductors and a third separate shield for the ground. Signal traveling on each of the conductors is identical but with opposite polarity. When the signal arrives at its destination a simple circuit sums the two signals (which cancel each other out being of opposite polarity) and removes any differences. Because the signals started out being identical, these differences at the destination amount to noise that was introduced while the signal traveled along the cable (possible by RFI — radio frequency interference or ambient electric or magnetic fields). Balanced lines usually use XLR connectors. Unbalanced lines have only two conductors: one that transmits the signal and the other employed as ground (and often doubling as the shield). Unbalanced lines generally use RCA or ¼-inch (phono) connectors.

It is also a good idea to understand the concept of *line level*. Line level signals average about +4 dB at 0 dBVU on professional audio gear. Many electronic devices operate at -10 dB which is the level of home stereo equipment (referenced to 0 dBVU on professional audio gear). The outputs and inputs of some devices are switchable between +4 and -10. Microphones and magnetic instrument pickups operate at a level of -40 to -60 dB (referenced to 0 dBVU on professional audio gear). You may use an inexpensive device called a direct box to convert a -10 dB level output to +4 dB to make up for incompatibilities between your inputs and outputs.

Sound-generating devices and controllers

❖ **Synthesizers (analog, digital, and other)**
Module
Keyboard

❖ **Sample player**
Module
Keyboard

❖ **Sampler**
Module
Keyboard

❖ **Sampler/sample player combinations**
Module
Keyboard

❖ **Synthesizer/sample player, synthesizer/ sampler combinations**
Module
Keyboard

❖ **Drum machine**
Module
Keyboard

❖ **Third-party hardware modifications**

As you recall from Chapter 1, there are three main types of MIDI sound-generating devices used in conjunction with the Macintosh: synthesizers, samplers, and sample players. A few hybrid conglomerations exist. The main distinction between them is in the manner by which the devices create sound.

Synthesizers "synthesize," or create, new sounds through the manipulation of digital or analog oscillators. Synthesized sounds may attempt to imitate naturally occurring sounds, but synthesizers have not evolved to the point where the actual reproduction of complex natural waveforms is possible — their forte is the creation or design of new sounds not normally found in nature. On the other hand, sample players and samplers have the ability to "play back" sounds that have been digitally recorded from the real world (or from other synthesizers for that matter) and to modify this output with much the same flexibility as a synthesizer. Sample players play back soundfiles stored on their ROM chips or loaded in their RAM chips. Samplers have the capability of both recording and playing back sounds and some have a complete set of factory-supplied soundfiles permanently stored in their ROM chips.

Whether synthesizer, sample player, or sampler, the main differences between hardware sound-generating devices come down to the following features: velocity sensing, number of note polyphony, multitimbral capabilities, and pressure sensitivity (monophonic or polyphonic).

Velocity sensing is the capability of playing at varying and multiple levels of volume. Many amateurs, hobbyists, or those using the synthesizer for input (for notation purposes) do not need this feature.

Monophonic pressure, often called Aftertouch or Channel Aftertouch, is a series of MIDI messages that are sent by continuing to exert pressure on a keyboard key after it has reached the bottom of its travel range and the note has already sounded. Monophonic aftertouch takes an average of the pressure being applied to all keys currently down. This information can be used for expressive articulation purposes such as changing the degree of LFO modulation (which might be mapped to vibrato or tremolo), changing the amplitude, filter cutoff, or pitch bend. Not all devices are capable of sending or responding to this information.

Polyphonic pressure differs from monophonic Aftertouch in that pressure messages are sent for each note individually rather than averaged across all notes being held down. Naturally, this consumes a considerable amount of the MIDI bandwidth.

To use the synthesizer as an output device, even if only for proofhearing, raises the issues of polyphony and multitimbrality. While a traditional acoustic piano may sound 88 notes together, until very recently, most synthesizers and samplers were restricted to 4- to 16-voice polyphony with more devices being required for thicker textures. Some newer devices stretch these limits to 32 voices and beyond.

After considerations of polyphony, multitimbrality, that is whether or not a device may output more than one type of sound at a time, becomes of tantamount importance. Where in the past the vast majority of commercially available electronic sound-generating devices were restricted to playing back a single sound at a time, now, with a multitimbral synthesizer or sampler, it is possible for a single instrument to respond to specific MIDI channels, each assigned to a separate patch or soundfile, and thus utilize a single device to produce different sounds or timbres played simultaneously. Unitimbral synthesizers and samplers have all but disappeared.

Most sound-generating devices are available in two versions, either with a piano-style keyboard or as a rack-mountable module without keyboard. All rack-mountable devices come in a standard 19-inch width (48.25 cm) for mounting together in racks. The vertical dimension is also standardized as a multiple of 1 rack-unit, meaning 1.75 inches (44 mm).

It is common to control a network of modular synthesizers and/or samplers with a "dumb" keyboard, generally known as a MIDI keyboard controller. Such controllers, while having no sound-generating capabilities themselves, are generically designed for the purpose of optimizing interaction with a large body of existing modular devices. See the section "MIDI controllers."

MIDI controllers

- ❖ Keyboard
- ❖ Wind
- ❖ Guitar
- ❖ Drum
- ❖ Pitch tracker
- ❖ Other

Because modular sound-generating devices do not have a keyboard, an external controller of some kind is used to play them. Dumb (non-sound-generating) keyboards are manufactured for this purpose, but it is also perfectly normal to control a module with a keyboard that has built-in sound-generating capabilities. It is equally viable for one keyboard to control another.

For people without keyboard ability, many non-keyboard oriented MIDI controllers are available. These range from guitar controllers aimed at the large market of guitar players who desire to manipulate external devices and electronic wind or valve instruments, spawned by similar considerations, to pitch trackers which can convert a normal audio sound source into the appropriate MIDI note codes.

Using a pitch tracker, any singer or instrumentalist may control a MIDI device without having to know anything about the traditional piano keyboard. This does not mean that you could play symphonic audio recordings through a pitch tracker and have all the notes transcribed into their appropriate MIDI codes. Current pitch tracking technology is really only successful at tracking a single solo melodic line under very controlled conditions at best. Accurately tracking multi-voiced polyphonic textures in real time is something to dream about.

Other artists, such as Holland's Michel Waisvisz, are inventing new MIDI controllers, which have no resemblance whatsoever to traditional musical instruments. For his own work, Waisvisz uses a pair of glove-like "hands," which include mercury switches sensing their angle relative to the horizon, sonars to sense the proximity of the gloves to one another, and a number of switches under each finger.

Finally, the Macintosh mouse itself can be employed as an alternative MIDI controller, provided the software supports this usage. Notable examples include Ovaltunes, Music Mouse, Jam Factory, and M, all distributed by Dr. T's Music Software. These programs are discussed in Chapter 19, "Interactive Composition and Intelligent Instruments."

Newer hardware controllers have appeared whose sole purpose is to control non-pitch elements via MIDI. Hardware boxes providing faders (sliders) that can be mapped to any continuous MIDI controller are increasingly common. JL Cooper's Fadermaster provides eight assignable hardware faders. You can use two of these inexpensive MIDI devices together to build a 16-channel MIDI mixer. Assigning the MIDI output of these faders to controller 7 (MIDI volume) on 16 different channels and routing that into your sequencer lets you record multiple volume mixes of a MIDI sequence. Virtual faders are now a common feature in many sequencers and all have provisions to map onscreen faders to just about any external controller. The main advantage to this is that you can move several hardware faders simultaneously, whereas you can only move one virtual fader at a time since there is only one cursor. Another way of looking at this is that the mouse-controlled cursor provides you with a single on-screen "finger" as it were, forcing you to become a "unidextor." External hardware MIDI faders have the added bonus that the faders can be assigned to output any type of MIDI data, thus giving you real-time dynamic control over many other musical and sound-synthesis parameters.

On the other hand, JL Cooper's CS-1, while not a MIDI controller per se, can be adapted for use with just about any music program that involves the recording of MIDI events. The CS-1 provides hardware play, stop, record, rewind, and fast forward buttons, as well as a jog wheel and function keys, all of which may be mapped onto their corresponding virtual controls in a MIDI sequencer or digital audio software environment. Rather than taking up a MIDI cable or channel, it connects to the Apple Desktop Bus (ADB).

Signal processors

❖ **Effects**
Reverberation
DDLs
Chorusing, phasing, and flanging
Pitch shifting
Auto panning
Stereo processing
Other dedicated effects devices
Multi-effects processor

❖ **Equalization (filtering)**
Digital
Analog
Parametric
Graphic

❖ **Audio enhancement**
Compressors and limiters
Exciters and other signal enhancers
Noise gates
Noise reduction
Sonic spatializers

The term *signal processor* refers to a wide range of devices that are used to alter an audio sound or signal. Signal processing can be employed in a real-time performance situation, as a sound (electronic or otherwise) is being recorded, at the mixdown stage, or when recorded sound is played back. When you adjust the treble or bass controls of your stereo system, you are signal processing.

Signal processors fall into three large categories: those dedicated to special effects, those dedicated to equalization (filtering), and those dedicated to enhancing sound quality. Many signal processors are capable of operating in one or more of these categories, and some can apply multiple types of processing simultaneously. These are often referred to as multi-effects devices.

Effects devices add or apply reverberation, digital delays, chorusing, phasing, flanging, pitch-shifting, panning, and similar transformations to an audio signal. Your mixer may have an "effects send" jack to send a portion of the incoming signal to the effect processor. The processed sound comes back to the mixer through an "Effects return" jack and is mixed in various proportions with the original signal.

Equalizers (EQ) are sophisticated descendants of the treble and bass controls on your stereo system, cassette recorder, or CD player. They boost or cut a specified frequency, frequencies, or range of frequencies with precise control.

Finally, *sound enhancers* are signal processors that compress or limit the dynamic range of an audio signal, to excite or otherwise enhance a sound's harmonic content, to control the three-dimensional placement of a sound in physical space, and to remove or lessen the amount of noise associated with an audio signal.

Signal processors can be analog or digital. The increasingly popular digital variety uses an ADC to convert the incoming signal to digital data prior to processing and a DAC to convert the processed data back to an analog format. Because digital recording has become widespread, newer digital signal processing devices are available that do not require the conversion and reconversion of the sound from analog to digital and back, but simply keep the sound in its digital format at all times.

It is becoming common for a signal processor to be MIDI controllable. This permits dynamic control of signal processing in real time by a sequencer or hardware device capable of sending out the appropriate MIDI messages.

Audio gear

❖ **Mixer**
    Keyboard mixers and submixers
    General purpose
    Automation (MIDI and non-MIDI)
    Digital

❖ **Amplifier**
    Preamplifier
    Headphone amplifier
    Power amplifier

❖ **Speakers**

The most significant difference between electronic instruments and acoustic instruments is that the former require some sort of audio system in order to produce sound. Certain manufacturers provide headphone outputs to get around this. In a modest setup you can even use your home stereo system in place of a dedicated sound reinforcement system for your electronic instruments. However, the best solution is a dedicated audio system. In most cases your primary components will be a mixer, amplifier, and speakers.

Mixers come in just about any size and configuration imaginable. There are single rack-space units whose sole purpose is to balance gain and pan settings (and occasionally provide limited EQ features, but rarely include effects sends and returns), and there are multiple rack-space mixers that provide many of the features of a tabletop or console-type mixer.

The most important consideration in purchasing a mixer is the number of channels — not to be confused with the number of inputs, since many mixers offer several types of inputs for each individual channel, including balanced, unbalanced, ¼-inch (phone jack), RCA, XLR (three-pin connecter), mono, or stereo. Your mixer should provide enough channels so that there can be an individual channel dedicated to every single audio output of your system. You should include all your signal processors in this calculation, because it is common practice to route effects returns into unused mixer channels for greater mixing flexibility. Next, you should have a few open channels for live instruments that you might want to record. Finally, you should allow yourself a realistic number of extra channels to be used for future instrument purchases and the occasions where you rent an additional piece of gear or borrow something from a friend.

The other considerations in your mixer purchase will be the type of built-in EQ, number of effects sends and returns, type of metering, and, most importantly, the noise threshold expressed as the signal-to-noise ratio. At the higher end, mixer automation may also come into the picture.

Some relatively low-cost mixers provide for automation via MIDI. These are generally rack-mountable and come in two varieties: (1) mixers with an equal number of inputs and outputs that don't actually "mix" audio signals but simply allow you to control attenuation (gain) via MIDI on the way to a dedicated mixer; and (2) full-blown MIDI mixers that include control over gain, pan, effects mix, and EQ. MIDI-controlled mixers take two approaches to automation. The first approach is to store a limited number of "snapshots" of mixer settings and provide a limited control over the transitions from one snapshot to another. The second approach is that of continuous control.

For situations where you are dealing with predominantly electronic sound sources, rack-mountable mixers can easily suffice. However, rack-mountable mixers rarely exceed 16 channels, and with most current-generation multi-timbral electronic instruments offering four to 12 individual outputs that can be assigned to a specific sound, two synthesizers can eat up all the channels on a rack-mountable unit. Fortunately, most mixers of this type offer features that allow you to chain several of the same manufacturer's units together and have them function as one large mixer. If you are on a budget, you can employ single rack-space units as submixers for multiple-output electronic instruments before sending the signal on to your primary mixer.

Line mixers are usually rack-mountable (one or two rack spaces) and used as effects return mixers, keyboard sub-mixers, and the like. These usually have knobs instead of faders and provide eight mono or stereo inputs and a stereo or mono output. All include gain controls and some add pan, effects, basic EQ controls, and output LED (light-emitting diode) meters. A nice feature is an auxiliary link for chaining several such mixers together.

Tabletop mixers and mixing consoles can be configured with all the inputs you will ever need, and many are designed to allow the future addition of more input modules should you need them. Non-rack-mountable mixers are significantly more expensive than those discussed in the previous paragraph. The fact that they generally have a better signal-to-noise ratio also contributes to their cost.

Commercial music studios generally have at least three pairs of monitor speakers: a very highly rated pair to listen to during recording and mixing down, and one or two other pairs to simulate the average listener's home system or the average car stereo system. Three pairs of monitor speakers are not generally used in classical CD mastering studios, where a single high-end pair such as B & W 801s is common. For many years, Yamaha's NS-10Ms were the industry standard, all-purpose monitors; however, Tannoys are gradually being substituted in their place. Auratones are another popular alternative for "reality checkers." Naturally, the maximum power rating of your amplifier should be matched closely to your pair of speakers that have the maximum power requirements.

If you are going to be doing a lot of sampling, you will probably want to add a standard audio CD player to your audio gear. Many commercial source banks for building sample libraries are distributed on standard CDs. For obvious reasons, a CD player with digital outputs is preferable. With such a player, you can transfer sound directly to DAT or to a digital audio card in the Macintosh without entering the analog domain. You can then convert sounds captured in this way to soundfiles that are in the native format of your sampler. Check the output format carefully when purchasing a CD player for this purpose. Many use optical connectors, whereas your DAT or digital audio card might require AES/EBU or SPDIF connectors.

Analog recorders

Cassette decks

❖ Single
❖ Dual

Cassette decks are useful in the studio because everyone seems to own one, so a cassette is a convenient format for distributing music with guaranteed compatibility. Dual cassette decks are handy for making multiple copies of, for example, your demo tape. In a budget system, a cassette deck might be used as a final mixdown device. Some cassette decks have built-in mixers and features that allow them to be used as multitrack recorders (see the section "Integrated mixer/recorder" in this chapter).

Multitracks

❖ 4-track   ❖ 16-track
❖ 8-track   ❖ 24-track

Multitrack analog recorders are becoming less and less of a standard feature in studios, as the power to manipulate virtual sequencer tracks is enhanced. In MIDI's infancy, analog recorders were necessary due to limitations imposed by the technology. Nowadays, because of advances in MIDI and electronic instrument technology, it is becoming increasingly popular to accomplish all mixing in the Macintosh and record the final mix in one pass.

In the early days there were only 16 MIDI channels, and most sound-generating devices were not multitimbral. Consequently, if you wanted to use two different sounds on the same (unitimbral) device, you had to record these in separate passes onto separate tracks of a multitrack recorder. This was also a factor if you wanted to build up a complex sound consisting of a number of different devices, but here you were also restricted by MIDI's paltry 16 channels.

The advance to dual interfaces providing access to 32 channels helped alleviate the situation somewhat. More people started to do their mixing completely in software and outputting the final mix in one pass directly to stereo (two tracks). But as multitimbrality became standard, even 32 channels could only support two fully multitimbral devices. Enter the greater-than-32-channel MIDI interfaces.

With the advent of MIDI interfaces that provide simultaneous control of up to 512 MIDI channels, the necessity of laying analog tracks down one at a time has been virtually eliminated — except of course for acoustic sound sources. Using one of these interfaces you can simultaneously address all 16 channels on up to 32 fully multitimbral devices. The necessity to record onto multitrack because of lack of MIDI channels is no longer a consideration. Virtual faders, hardware MIDI faders, and MIDI-controlled mixers remove the need to use a sophisticated mixing console's faders during mixdown. The fact that MIDI fader data is viewable and editable even makes them preferable over a non-automated standalone mixer.

One remaining argument in favor of multitracking is that of being able to get by with a limited number of signal processing effects. Because you are making multiple recording passes, you can re-use the same effects device with different settings at each recording pass. With the price of effects devices dropping on a daily basis and more and more synthesizers including built-in effects devices, even this consideration is becoming less important. The fact that most signal processors are now MIDI controllable means that you can even record, edit, and automate the adjustments that you would in earlier times have been forced to attempt in real time while recording. This makes it a simple matter to output multiple tracks in one pass directly to the final mix.

Finally, even the necessity for tape multitracking when coupling live instrumentalists with electronic tracks is rapidly disappearing. More and more MIDI sequencers are providing for the inclusion of digital audio tracks directly within a MIDI sequence so, unless you are dealing with a group of live musicians, you end up with greater control over your program material by confining all your multitracking to software running on the Macintosh.

Last but not least, don't forget that going to multitrack and then mixing down to a stereo master always adds a generation to the recording, and unless your gear is digital, this will always result in signal degradation.

So what, you may ask, are the advantages of multitracking? Excluding the obvious necessity of multitracking for situations involving several acoustic musicians, essentially it is six of one and a half dozen of the other. Multitrack recorders are expensive, but you can save money on signal processors and EQ, since many of these outboard boxes can do double and triple duty. If you want to apply a $15,000 signal processor, for example, a reverb, at different settings to every device, then it makes sense to record the tracks individually. Having 512 MIDI channels is not going to solve problems of an electronic instrument's limited polyphony, nor will it have any impact on older unitimbral sound-generating devices, which you may have come to love. There is also no way to get around situations where you have to load different patch libraries or sample soundfiles into a device (not an uncommon situation). These cases are still going to require recording multiple tracks in separate passes. One final reason for using multitrack recording involves the professional recording industry. Often many alternate mixes of a multitrack recording are required — different producers and engineers may mix and remix the same source tracks over and over. Sometimes different mixes of the same tune are used for the CD, the EP, and for the music video.

Mixdown decks

❖ 2-track
❖ 3-track
❖ 4-track

Mixdown decks are necessary regardless of whether you are mixing multitrack recordings down to stereo or outputting a final mix in a single pass. ¼-inch or ½-inch tape is the most common medium used for mixdown, with DAT coming on strong.

Two-track stereo decks are popular unless you require SMPTE track. When your music is going to be later synchronized to film or video, a popular format is one allowing for two-channel stereo plus a SMPTE track. Four-track record-ers are often used for this purpose because a blank guard track can separate the outer-edge SMPTE track from the music tracks, assuring that no SMPTE noise bleeds through the program material. Three-track recorders that have a center channel for SMPTE are equally popular for stereo mixdowns. They have the advantage of being compatible with half-track recorders.

In the film and video industry, music is often mixed down to three channels instead of two-channel stereo. Soloists are placed on the third channel to provide some flexibility at the dubbing stage when the music is mixed with the dialog and sound effects. Such three-channel mixes can be accomplished with a 4-track recorder, although this places music directly next to the time code track, so great care must be exercised. In rare instances, three stereo pairs are requested. Here you would use an 8-track recorder with the first six tracks dedicated to the three stereo pairs, then a blank guard track between the music and the outer edge SMPTE track.

DAT recorders are becoming increasingly popular for mixdowns. DAT recorders are discussed below.

Integrated mixer/recorder

❖ Cassette
❖ Other formats

Analog multitrack recorders with a built-in mixer offer an effective alternative for someone who does not wish to invest in a large console and stand-alone recorder. These are available in standard cassette formats (although the transport speed is generally significantly higher than a normal cassette recorder to provide for a greater dynamic range).

Many integrated mixer/recorders use proprietary tape formats marketed by the same company that manufactures the hardware. For example, Akai's MG1214 is a professional 14-track recorder with a built-in mixer. Twelve tracks are available for audio and the remaining two tracks consist of an address track and a synchronization track. The MG1214 uses cassettes that resemble Beta video-cassettes but are only available from Akai.

Digital recorders

- ❖ Hard-disk-based
  - Macintosh-based
  - Standalone

- ❖ Multitrack
  - DASH
  - Other formats

- ❖ PCM
  - Beta
  - VHS

Digital audio is certainly the buzz word of the latter 20th century. It took relatively little time for sales of compact discs to outdistance those of analog vinyl LPs. Digital recording systems can be disk-based or tape-based.

Tape-based digital audio systems are similar to analog tape, with the exception that audio data is represented by ones and zeros rather than voltage fluctuations. Early tape-based digital audio recorders employed PCM encoders to record digital audio onto standard video cassettes using standard VCRs. These were limited to 2-channel stereo, although some attempts were made to gang up several synchronized systems to create a pseudo multitrack environment. Because so much recording was done using these methods, it is not uncommon to see support of some of these formats, such as Sony's PCM-F1 or PCM-1630.

Tape-based systems now support at least eight tracks and more expensive recorders sport 32 and 48 tracks. Two methods are in common use: *rotary head recording* and *stationary head recording*. There are two formats for stationary head recording: DASH (digital audio stationary head) and ProDigi. Editing is significantly easier using stationary head systems (unless you happen to own a Macintosh and a direct-to-hard disk recording system). A relatively inexpensive newcomer in this arena is Alesis's ADAT system.

Rotary head digital recording is a descendant of video tape recording where a helical scanning rotating record head is also used. Some consumer-level video-8 cameras record their audio in stereo PCM format on the helical scan tracks.

Tape-based digital audio systems share some of the same problems found in analog systems. The tracks are linearly aligned with one another, making it very difficult to shift things around in the temporal domain. Hard-disk-based digital audio has the advantage of providing random access to all recorded sound data. Hard-disk-based recording systems thus provide the most flexible medium for digital audio editing. While optical drives have been used as backup systems for direct-to-hard disk recordings since the technology emerged, in 1991 it became possible to substitute optical drives as the primary recording medium.

There are two types of hard-disk recording systems available to the Macintosh: those based upon internal digital audio cards installed on the Macintosh NuBus, and stand-alone units consisting of hard drives with built-in digital audio recording hardware. The latter type often uses the Macintosh as a front end to control and edit via proprietary software supplied by the manufacturer. Digidesign dominates the Macintosh-based direct-to-hard disk arena with their Sound Accelerator and Audiomedia cards.

The fact that one of the world's most respected analog record manufacturers, Otari, simply repackages Digidesign's Sound Accelerator running on a Macintosh within the innards of their digital audio workstation is an indication of Digidesign's standing in this area.

DAT

❖ Consumer
❖ Professional (with and without SMPTE synchronization)

DAT (digital audio tape) recording represents the pinnacle of consumer recording technology. Because it was built from scratch and the designers had full knowledge of the mistakes made by earlier recording technologies, when DAT recording was finally released it represented a triumph in technological achievement.

Serious development of R-DAT (rotary head digital audio tape) began in 1981 and at the DAT conference in August of 1986, 81 companies agreed on the R-DAT standard. The first R-DAT machines were introduced less than a year later. The word DAT is now used in place of R-DAT. The format for S-DAT (stationary head digital audio tape) has also been standardized. Consider the rigorous specifications of R-DAT:

❖ **Track width**	13.591 microns
❖ **Track length**	23.501 millimeters
❖ **Recording density**	114,000,000 bits per square inch
❖ **Audio data rate**	1,536,000 bits per second (16-bit, 48 KHz stereo)
❖ **Overall data rate**	2,770,000 bits per second (including error correction and subcodes)

DAT decks are becoming the standard for professional music studios, and their rapidly dropping prices have brought them full force into the consumer market. The first advantage of DAT decks is that many can record at the 44.1 KHz sampling frequency used by compact discs. In fact, virtually identical electronics are used in the playback stage of a DAT and a CD. Second, when DAT tapes are copied to one another in the digital domain, there is theoretically no degradation from copy to copy. Finally, because DAT is a standard (the manufacturers learned their lessons with Beta and VHS VCRs), tapes will play identically on any DAT machine without having to worry about tape type, noise reduction, or bias settings. DAT tape itself, which averages around $12 a cassette ($7 in Japan), looks just like a miniature VHS tape rather than an audio cassette and often carries a "Full Lifetime Warranty" that it will "perform to your satisfaction for your lifetime!"

With two DAT machines or a DAT combined with a direct-to-hard disk recording system (Macintosh-based or standalone), the concept of digitally bouncing tracks without signal loss becomes a reality. Bouncing tracks is a standard operating procedure in the analog tape world where one can run out of available tracks on a multitrack tape recorder rather quickly. Traditionally, when faced with this situation, musicians bounce (mix) down any number of tracks to either a single mono track or two tracks for stereo in order to free up the tracks that have been bounced for additional material. Unfortunately, in the analog tape world, this technique adds a generation to the recording process and results in progressively greater distortion with each bounce. With digitally bounced tracks there is no distortion added, no matter how many bounces are involved.

The main problems with DAT so far have been engendered by the fact that DAT recording is so perfect. Record and CD companies are justifiably very worried that DAT recorders will make it possible to eat into their profits. In fact, with a CD player capable of outputting digital data and a DAT recorder capable of recording digital data, it is possible to rip off an exact copy of the digital information that was used to master the CD. This issue gained such prominence at the end of the 1980s that Congress actually put a temporary halt to the importing of consumer market DAT recorders (virtually all DAT machines are made in Japan).

In 1990 consumer DAT recorders were given the seal of approval for importation into the United States, and CDs now have a "copy inhibit" bit in their subcodes that limit digital recording of their data (note that the copy inhibit scheme does not prevent analog recording by a DAT or any other machine). This form of copy protection is vastly superior to the one that almost got approved. For some time CBS was lobbying for a "notch" copy-protection scheme that would have removed the high 'B' to 'Bb' frequency band from all recorded music whether on CD, vinyl, cassette, or DAT. In this method, DAT recorders would sense the missing frequency band and simply not go into record mode.

With the current copy inhibit scheme, you can make one digital copy of a CD, presumably for use with the DAT deck in your car, but that's as far as it goes. Any attempt to make a second copy of that DAT recording will be thwarted because a DAT recorder will simply not record digital data from another DAT when it encounters the copy inhibit bit. Fortunately, for those of us who want to make multiple copies of our own music on DAT, professional models have implemented an incrementable copy inhibit counter that allows you to set the number of copies that can be made from your original. This is not unlike the "hard disk installation" copy protection method most users of commercial music software are accustomed to, where you are allotted a specified number of hard disk installs (usually one or two). Still, even on pro models, it will not be possible to make more than a single copy from a CD that has been digitally recorded onto a DAT.

The first DAT recorders had no provision for synchronization and were therefore not extremely popular in the film and video industry. Because so many synchronizable DAT machines (also known as time code DATs) appeared at the beginning of the 1990s, the practicality of DAT as a mixdown media for film and video is growing.

Keep in mind that DATs were not originally intended for professional use although many are now considered to be professional "non-consumer" models. Some DATs do sound better than others. Tapes are fragile and mechanisms can go out of alignment. Tape drop-outs increase with the number of times a tape is played, not merely recorded.

Sony recently announced a new Mini Disk technology that records up to 74 minutes of stereo at CD-quality rates onto 2½-inch magneto-optical disks. Sony hopes that these devices will eventually render all compact cassette tapes obsolete. Certainly the random access audio and synchronization options implicit in such a system make it attractive. Only time will tell what impact this will have on DAT technology.

Video gear
Decks
- ½-inch
- ¾-inch
- 1-inch

If you are going to get into film and video composition, a video deck is an absolute necessity. Other uses of a video deck in the Macintosh music studio include the archiving of digital audio masters. With the advent of DAT, previously expensive PCM encoders can be had for a song, so as an interim storage device while you are saving up for a DAT your VCR can do double duty.

One of the most important considerations for your video deck is that it have separate left and right channel outputs because video tape delivered for scoring will normally have SMPTE on one channel and dialog on the other. Next, you should seriously consider getting a deck with a jog (sometimes called shuttle) wheel. This allows you to scrub through an area for the purpose of noting SMPTE times. A frame-advance feature can be tolerated in place of a jog wheel.

Half-inch VHS is a very popular format for the delivery of film or video to be scored. Recording and playback at anything but the fastest speed is not a requirement because SMPTE is unreliable at slower speeds. Likewise, the ability to play back hi-fi channels is not required because SMPTE will almost never be recorded on those tracks. S-VHS (Super VHS) is a popular consumer format, but not a requirement in the film and television industry.

Video to be scored can be delivered in ¾-inch and 1-inch tape formats if requested, although you will not be expected to own decks of this tape width. If you are mastering multimedia productions at a very high level, you may wish to have a deck that uses one of these formats. One-inch tape is considered broadcast quality.

Two other important considerations may influence your purchase of a video deck: whether it is lockable and whether it supports "Control-L" (LANC) remote control.

Lockup systems were discussed earlier in the section "Lockup systems." These systems allow the motor of your video deck to be synchronized to the motors of external tape machines. It is a high-end feature that you may wish to consider if your main occupation is composing for film and video.

Control-L, or LANC, refers to a protocol that many Macintosh multimedia systems support to provide for semi-accurate control of consumer VCR decks by multimedia authoring systems. NEC's PC-VCR uses a slightly more accurate serial control system that is also supported by most multimedia authoring environments. If you are into multimedia production, you should definitely consider purchasing a Control-L or serial-controlled deck.

Miscellaneous video devices

❖ CDI player
❖ CD+G
❖ CD+M

❖ DVI player
❖ Video distribution amplifier

If you are serious about multimedia, a videodisc player that can be placed under Macintosh control is a must. Similarly, you may wish to own a CD player that supports one or more of the newer CD formats. These include:

❖ *CDI:* Compact Disc Interactive. A new CD-ROM technology that includes storage and random access of audio, video, graphics, text, and data. There are five grades of audio quality including one that allows 16 parallel channels.

❖ *CD+G and CD+M:* Compact Disc Plus Graphics and Compact Disc Plus MIDI. Both of these standards capitalize upon the unused 25MB of space on an audio CD (6 bits per each 8-bit subcode frame). CD+G can combine still graphics with the CD audio. CD+M can output 16 channels of MIDI data synchronized with the CD audio. Innovative combinations of both can provide for scrolling conventional music notation displays during MIDI output.

❖ *DVI:* Digital Video Interactive. DVI combines full-motion video with CD audio (an hour of each). This system requires a computer for playback.

CDI players will play back traditional audio CDs but not vice versa. CD+Gs and CD+Ms can be played on audio CD players, but the graphic and MIDI data is ignored. Traditional audio CDs can also be played back on CD+G and CD+M players.

If you have a large number of video devices, you may wish to purchase a video distribution amplifier to take care of the switching and routing tasks much in the same way that you use a MIDI patcher or audio patchbay. Mark of the Unicorn markets a rack-mountable unit for this purpose.

Summary

✔ The essential ingredients for a Macintosh-based music setup fall into two categories: hardware and software. Hardware includes a Macintosh and other peripherals, both musical and Macintosh-related. Your needs should define your choice of hardware.

✔ Macintosh peripherals include storage media, backup systems, CD-ROM drives, printers and other output devices, scanners, audio digitizers, modems, monitors, and input devices. Also in this category are internal cards for the Macintosh including accelerators, SCSI expansion cards, digital audio cards (ROM- and RAM-based sample players, direct-to-hard disk recording systems), and special video cards.

✔ External music peripherals include MIDI interfaces (16-, 32-, and greater-than-32-channel), SMPTE converters, VITC converters, lockup systems, MIDI patchbays, sound-generating devices (synthesizers, samplers, sample players, and drum machines), MIDI controllers, signal processors (effects, EQ, and other audio enhancement devices), mixers, amplifiers, speakers, and audio patchbays.

✔ Other peripherals you may need include cassette recorders, multitrack recorders, mixdown decks, direct-to-hard disk recording systems, DAT recorders, video decks and monitors, and laserdisc players.

✔ After deciding whether to purchase a digital synthesizer or a digital sampling keyboard, the main differences between hardware sound-generating devices come down to the following features: velocity sensing, number of note polyphony, multitimbral capabilities, and pressure sensitivity (monophonic or polyphonic).

✔ Velocity sensing, which allows you to play at varying and multiple levels of volume, adds several hundreds of dollars to the price. If you are an amateur, hobbyist, or merely using the synthesizer for input (that is, you will be using live musicians reading from your printed score) you might not need this feature.

✔ If you are going to use the synthesizer as an output device, even if only for proofhearing, you will want to consider how many notes can be sounded simultaneously (referred to as n-voice polyphony) and whether the synthesizer is multitimbral (which refers to the capability of playing several different types of sounds, or patches, simultaneously). Finally, your specific applications may require that you forego digital synthesizers altogether in favor of digital samplers, in which case you may have to dig even deeper into your pocket.

✔ Most sound-generating devices are available in two versions, either with a piano-style keyboard or as a rack-mountable module without keyboard. All rack-mountable devices come in a standard 19-inch width (48.25 cm) for mounting together in racks. The vertical dimension is standardized as a multiple of one rack-unit, meaning 1.75 inches (44 mm).

✔ It is common to control a network of modular synthesizers and/or samplers with a "dumb" keyboard, generally known as a MIDI keyboard controller. Such controllers, while having no sound-generating capabilities themselves, are generically designed to optimize interaction with a large body of existing modular devices.

✔ For people without keyboard ability, many non-keyboard oriented MIDI controllers are available. These range from guitar controllers aimed at the large market of guitar players who desire to manipulate external devices and electronic wind or valve instruments, spawned by similar considerations, to pitch trackers that can convert a normal audio sound source into the appropriate MIDI note codes.

Chapter 6

Software Options

In this chapter . . .

- What software is and why your Macintosh needs it.
- The many forms of software.
- A look at the different categories of software.
- Types of Macintosh copy protection schemes.
- Purchasing tips and recommendations.
- Annotated tables organizing over 800 Macintosh music programs into application categories.

What Is Software?

Software is required for any microprocessor-controlled hardware device to function for its intended purpose. Hardware devices in this context include the Macintosh itself, synthesizers, samplers, DSP effects devices, and just about anything with silicon chips inside of it. Software is fundamentally different from hardware in that it does not exist in any tangible form. Software is merely a group of ones and zeros (bytes) that are organized by the programmer or user in such a way that it facilitates the execution of a specific task. Software controls hardware to allow both to be controlled by "jelly-ware" (the human brain).

A wide range of applications software is necessary to manage the variety of musical situations that recur on a day-to-day basis. This includes software for purposes such as MIDI sequencing, SoundEditing and/or generation, sound and sequence library management, conventional music notation, digital mixing, algorithmic composition, and telecommunications.

Most commercially available software packages have reached the point where one can accurately use the term "second generation" to describe the state of development in the microcomputer software industry. This implies that the musical community has entered a stage where the responses to, and capabilities of, initial software releases have all been tallied, and current undertakings endeavor both to learn from early mistakes and address a wide body of user responses and requests.

Recent formidable advances in object-oriented programming, data-compression, and searching techniques engendered by Apple's new HyperCard software authoring package (bundled with all Macintosh computers) are changing the face of the industry by putting the power to create extremely sophisticated applications into the hands of people with little or no actual programming knowledge. With HyperCard, and similar programming environments such as SuperCard and Plus, the dream of computers writing their own programs based upon near natural (English) language input from the user has finally been fulfilled. The ramifications of this concept are just beginning to be realized by the music software industry.

Software exists in many forms:

❖ **Functional categories**
  System software
  Applications software
  Utility software
  Development systems
  Data (and "documents")
  Dedicated software

❖ **Distribution categories**
  Commercial
  Proprietary
  Shareware (or honorware)
  Freeware
  Public Domain
  Pirate

❖ **Other distinctions**
  Stand-alone applications
  Copy-protected software
  Firmware

Functional categories

Software can be grouped into six main categories with respect to function: system software, applications software, utility software, development systems, data, and dedicated software.

System software is a special type of software that permits a device to operate, hence it is sometimes referred to as the "operating system." The function of system software is usually invisible to the user. In other words, the computer or external device requires the software in order to operate, but you do not need to know much (if anything) about the software in order to use the device it controls. The Macintosh System and Finder are examples of system software. System software often provides a platform or environment within the context of which other types of software may be utilized.

Applications software is also referred to as programs or simply as applications. Applications can create or manipulate data or control external peripherals (including synthesizers and samplers). Data created by applications is usually referred to as a "file" or "document." Applications are usually launched by double-clicking their icons with the mouse. Data or documents are created, opened or read by their parent application. MIDI sequencers, notation packages, and patch editor/librarians are all examples of applications.

Utility software comes in many forms: DAs, INITs, cdevs, FKeys, rdevs, startup documents, XCMDs, and XFCNs.

Utility software is used to configure or enhance the operation of either system software, applications software, data, RAM, or storage media. Usually, utilities don't create documents themselves other than usage reports, although there are some exceptions. Some utilities, desk accessories in particular, are functionally identical to applications and can save files and manipulate data in similar manners. The difference is that these mini-applications can be run concurrently with normal applications software without requiring MultiFinder. Examples of utilities are macro systems, backup software, file compression programs, virus protectors, spelling checkers, file conversion utilities, disk and resource editors, and diagnostic and data recovery systems.

Development systems are used to create applications, utilities, or documents that function as applications when coupled with a software engine or interpreter. Most development systems are applications or groups of applications themselves. Often, a development system includes a "compiler" for the purpose of generating stand-alone applications or documents (see the section "Stand-alone applications" in this chapter). Development systems include programming languages or environments, authoring systems, and applications generators. Examples of development systems include traditional programming languages such as C, Basic, Lisp, and Pascal; object-oriented programming languages such as HyperCard, SuperCard, and Smalltalk; and visual programming languages such as Sirius and Authorware.

Data is a special type of software that can be utilized and/or manipulated by applications, utilities, development systems, and external peripherals. Data of this kind is usually referred to as "files" or "documents." Typically, data files or documents can only be accessed by the parent application that created it, unless the data is in a format that has become standardized for a specific class of applications (e.g., Standard MIDI Files and ASCII text files). Examples of data files are MIDI sequences, notation files, patch files (which can be loaded into synthesizers), soundfiles (which can be loaded into samplers and sample players), and documents created by word processing or graphics applications.

Dedicated software is sometimes used to refer to applications, utilities, or data that is dedicated to manipulating a specific external device and has no functional value, unless it is used in conjunction with the device it is intended for. Sometimes, this is contrasted with "universal" software such as a universal patch librarian, as opposed to a dedicated patch librarian. The first will deal with just about any device on the market, while the second is dedicated to managing patches on a single device. Nowadays, the word "dedicated" is used more often to refer to hardware devices that are designed to perform a single function, such as a dedicated hardware sequencer or a dedicated direct-to-hard disk recording system.

Distribution categories

There are six categories of distribution through which you may obtain software, although only five are legal: commercial, proprietary, shareware, freeware, PD (public domain), and pirate.

Much of the software that you use is *commercial* software. Commercial software is sold through retail outlets, such as computer stores, music stores, and mail order houses. Occasionally, you will find smaller companies that require you to purchase directly from the company, which has no distribution channels, or which has only a single retail outlet source that may include a chain of stores such as ComputerWare, Egghead, Businessland, and so on. You should consider purchasing commercial software from the manufacturer only when there is no other alternative. The reason for this is that when a manufacturer has normal distribution channels, but also sells directly to the end user, that manufacturer is usually required to sell products at list price, whereas retail outlets are allowed to discount (often heavily) the same products.

Proprietary software is a program developed for a particular company for use in-house, and is not sold via normal retail channels. Typically, you will not need proprietary software, unless you are employed by a company that uses it, or you commission the creation of such software for your own personal use. The term proprietary software is sometimes misused to refer to beta software or software that ships with a particular device and is dedicated to the control of that device or task exclusively.

Shareware, sometimes called honorware, refers to software that is distributed for free, with the understanding that if you use it you will send a small payment to the author. If you don't use it, you will either pass it on to a friend or destroy it. The fee and address to send it to is usually accessible via a menu item in the program or listed at the end of the "Read-Me" file (if any). Payment of shareware fees is really a matter of conscience on behalf of the user. Typically, your payment will entitle you to free upgrades of the product and/or technical support. Because the fees are so small, you really should pay them if you find yourself using the product, because this will ensure both further development of that specific product and also impact the general continuation of the shareware principle in general. Shareware is often distributed by user groups, BBS systems, and companies that specialize in the distribution of shareware.

Freeware is similar to shareware, except that there is no fee requested by the author. Distribution channels are the same: user groups, BBS systems, and companies that specialize in the distribution of shareware. Freeware authors retain the copyright to their software, and often stipulate that their software may not be distributed in such a fashion that another company ends up making a profit on it. An example of freeware is Disinfectant.

Public Domain software, sometimes called PD software, is uncopyrighted software that the author has placed in the public domain, thereby giving up all rights to the program. You do not need to compensate the author for PD software.

Pirate software refers to the illegal practice of using software that you have not paid for. It is actually stealing and therefore illegal in the eyes of the law (as well as an affront to your conscience), often carrying hefty fines and even prison sentences if you are caught. Because much software is not copy-protected (see the section "Copy-protected software" in this chapter), it is often exchanged freely between friends. Sometimes this is done with the understanding that you will purchase the program if you find it satisfactory (sort of a try-before-you-buy philosophy). Of course you will not have the documentation, and in my neighborhood, there is not a single photocopy store that will copy software documentation because they are aware that it is probably being used for piracy. Without the documentation, you can't use the software to its greatest advantage. Besides not having the documentation, if you use pirated software you are not entitled to any upgrades or technical support from the developer.

Despite the high price of certain software items, most music software will eventually pay for itself many times over if used correctly. If you want to inspect a program before you purchase it, you should request a demo version of the product from the company if one exists. Finally, in recognition of the high cost of certain music products, some companies allow you to split the purchase with a friend if you can't afford the program outright. It's your conscience.

Other distinctions

There are three other software descriptors that you need to know about: stand-alone applications, copy-protected software, and firmware.

Stand-alone applications

Stand-alone applications are programs that can be run by themselves without requiring any other software engine besides the general Macintosh operating system. They are sometimes referred to as "double-clickable" applications, because they can be launched by double-clicking on them. This is contrasted to programs that require their parent application to be present on the disk in order to run. The vast majority of commercial software products that you will use can be expected to be stand-alone applications. Examples of programs that require an engine (sometimes referred to as a run-time engine or player) or their parent (or creator) application in order to function are HyperCard stacks, SuperCard projects, Director Documents, uncompiled Basic programs, and the like. Some development systems offer the option to create stand-alones by several means. Compilers are available for programming languages such as Basic that really do create stand-alone applications out of documents, and these usually run faster than their interpreted counterparts. Director and SuperCard both offer an option to merge their run-time player engine into your document to create a pseudo double-clickable application. Unfortunately, because the run-time engine is merely merged into the document, no increase of speed is realized.

Copy-protected software

You can't make a functional copy of a *copy-protected* program. You can duplicate the disk, but the program won't run from the duplicated disk. Although copy protection is frowned upon by the Macintosh community and is rapidly disappearing, many music programs still employ some form of copy protection.

The most common protection scheme is to allow you to copy the program onto a hard disk, but then require that you insert the master disk (referred to as the key disk) into the disk drive when the program is launched in order for the program to function. Some schemes require inserting the disk merely once a day (or until your Macintosh is shut down), while others demand key-disk insertion whenever the program is launched. If something happens to your key disk, you are out of luck. Because of this, many companies that use this form of copy protection provide you with a backup key disk in case something happens to your original.

Another common form of copy protection is the "hard disk installation" scheme. In this method, you are allowed to install one (or sometimes two) copies of the software onto your hard drive, either by running the application from its unlocked master disk or by running a special installer program. Once the software is installed in this manner on your hard disk, you can run it from the hard disk without inserting a key disk. Invisible key files are created on your hard disk that unlock the program. While these files are invisible, they can be seen by many disk management utilities such as DiskTop or DiskTools. You should never delete or move any invisible files that you notice when using those utilities, because if you delete the invisible key file, you have lost your "install" completely, and the program will not run without the key disk anymore. These files often have boxes in their names (e.g., ☐☐☐☐) or the word "key" appended to their name.

One major problem with the hard disk installation form of copy protection is that because you cannot move the invisible key files, it is difficult to optimize or defragment your hard drive without first de-installing the programs. Disk Express II (version 2.04 or greater) is the only disk optimizer that will anchor these files and still defragment your hard drive, although because these invisible key files must be anchored, complete defragmentation is often not possible. At least you do not lose your installs.

Copy protection is a particular problem with the IIfx. Some key disk and hard disk installation methods will not work with a IIfx. In fact, with respect to the hard disk installation method, for certain programs, the only way to run copy-protected software from a IIfx is to attach its hard drive to any other Macintosh and then install the programs while the hard drive is attached to the other computer. After they have been installed, you can return the hard drive to the IIfx and run the programs as you would normally. If the software supports key-disk insertion copy protection exclusively, without the possibility of hard disk installation, you often can't run it on a IIfx at all. Some manufacturers have found ways to implement both types of protection schemes on the IIfx and before long, there should be no need to install programs with the hard drive temporarily attached to another computer (note that some programs may never be updated in this respect).

Firmware

The last type of software that you will read about in this book is *firmware*. Firmware refers to software that is "burned" into ROM chips. Firmware can contain operating systems (in the case of a computer or synthesizer) or digital audio samples (in the case of a sample player). Because firmware is on ROM, the instructions or data are not lost when the computer or other type of device is powered down. Firmware utilizes several types of chips. These include PROMs (programmable read-only memory — these cannot be erased), EPROMs (erasable programmable read-only memory — these can be erased and rewritten by someone with an expensive EPROM burner or by the manufacturer of your device), and EEPROMs (electrically erasable programmable read-only memory — these can be updated without the use of an EPROM burner, even via modem).

Normally you will have little interaction with firmware other than to take advantage of the capabilities it adds to your computer or sound-generating device. Sometimes, manufacturers update their firmware, and you may receive a new ROM, PROM, EPROM, or EEPROM in the mail for replacing in your device. Because these chips are socketed, the replacement is usually quite simple. Another type of firmware that you may come into contact with is found in ROM cards and can be plugged into many synthesizers to expand their sound libraries.

Software categories related to application categories

The following outline further breaks down the general software categories.

Sound design

❖ Sound generation
❖ Sample editors
❖ Patch librarians
❖ Universal patch librarians
❖ Patch editors and editor/librarians
❖ Patch data
❖ Sample data
❖ Sound databases

Composition

❖ Non-MIDI sequencers and interactive software
❖ MIDI sequencers
❖ MIDI sequencers with digital audio
❖ Interactive composition software
❖ Algorithmic composition software

Notation

❖ Notation software
❖ Music fonts

Performance

❖ Interactive performance software
❖ Software for control of additional performance parameters

Post-production

❖ Direct-to-hard disk recording software
❖ Studio automation
❖ Digital signal processing

Film and video

❖ Synchronization

Multimedia

❖ Production environments
❖ Clip "music"

Networking

❖ Music local area networks
❖ Telecommunications

Education

❖ CAI: ear training
❖ CAI: theory and analysis

❖ CAI: applied instruments
❖ CAI: history and appreciation
❖ Education: miscellaneous

Musical and acoustical research
❖ Pedagogical research
❖ Musical logical analysis and research
❖ Acoustical analysis and research
❖ Psychoacoustical analysis and research

Programming
❖ Traditional programming languages
❖ Object-oriented programming "for the rest of us"
❖ Visual programming languages
❖ Other programming environments

Ancillary tasks
❖ Software for hardware
❖ Business and organizational
❖ Utilities (programs)
❖ Utilities (DAs, FKeys, cdevs (control panels), INITs, startup documents, system extensions)

Software Categories in Detail

The following tables provide examples of software organized by category. See Appendix D, "List of Manufacturers" for detailed company information.

Every item is listed alphabetically by company, except for one table. In Table 6-7, "Sound design software — Patch data," items are listed by synthesizer model name to make it easier to find sound for the particular instruments you own. Another thing to note about Table 6-7 is that firmware is not listed, that is, patches that are marketed on RAM or ROM cards are omitted — only patch data marketed on Macintosh floppy disks, in data formats readable by patch-librarian software in wide circulation, has been listed. For information on patch data marketed on RAM or ROM cards, see the advertisements in any issue of *Electronic Musician* or *Keyboard* magazines, or check out *Keyboard* magazine's annual buyers' guide.

Several software packages are listed on two tables because they function with equal effectiveness in two categories.

Many tables have a column heading "S, F, PD." These refer to shareware, freeware, and public domain software, respectively. All other products are commercially available. A very small number of programs include the annotation "product discontinued" or "company out of business." These are included because most of these items can still be purchased in many music stores or through mail order sources.

Some software includes the comment "HyperCard Stack." Many of these are as powerful as stand-alone applications, a testament to Apple's HyperCard environment truly offering programming for the rest of us.

On a Budget?
Configure your system with freeware and shareware

Consult Table 6-38 for shareware, freeware, and public domain options that apply to almost every category of software covered by this book. Notation and 16-bit direct-to-hard disk recording are about the only areas of Macintosh musical endeavor for which non-commercial alternatives are lacking. See Tables 6-1 through 6-8 for company information.

Table 6-1: Sound design software — Sound generation (see Chapter 10)

Company	Product	Comments	S, F, PD
Digidesign	SoftSynth	Akai S950, S900, S700, S7000	
		Dynacord Add On (SDS)	
		E-mu SP-1200, Emax, Emulator II	
		Ensoniq Mirage, Multisampler	
		Korg DSS-1, DSM-1	
		Oberheim DPX-1	
		Peavey DPM 3, DPM V3, DPM 3se (SDS)	
		Roland S-10, S220, S-50, S-550, MKS-100	
		Sequential Prophet 2000, 2002	
		Simmons SDX (SDS)	
		Yamaha TX-16-W (SDS)	
		12-bit SDS	
		16-bit SDS	
Digidesign	SoftSynth SA	Akai S1000, S1000PB, S950, S900, S700, S7000	
		Casio FX1, FZ-10M	
		Dynacord Add One (SDS), ADS	
		E-mu SP-1200, Emax, Emax II	
		E-mu Emulator II, Emulator III	
		Ensoniq Mirage, Multisampler, DSK, EPS	
		Forat F-16	
		Korg DSS-1, DSM-1	
		Oberheim DPX-1	
		Peavey DPM 3, DPM V3, DPM 3se (SDS)	
		Roland S-10, S220, S-50, S-550, MKS-100, S-330	

Table 6-1: Sound design software — Sound generation (continued)

Company	Product	Comments	S, F, PD
Digidesign (cont.)	SoftSynth SA (cont.)	Sequential Prophet 2000, 2002 Yamaha TX-16-W 12-bit SDS 16-bit SDS	
Digidesign	TurboSynth	Akai S1000, S1000PB, S950, S900, S700, S7000 Casio FX1, FZ-10M Dynacord Add One (SDS), ADS E-mu SP-1200, Emax, Emax II E-mu Emulator II, Emulator III Ensoniq Mirage, Multisampler, DSK, EPS Forat F-16 Korg DSS-1, DSM-1 Oberheim DPX-1 Peavey DPM 3, DPM V3, DPM 3se (SDS) Roland S-10, S220, S-50, S-550, MKS-100, S-330 Sequential Prophet 2000, 2002 Yamaha TX-16-W 12-bit SDS 16-bit SDS	
John F. Duesenberry	DX_PIG	Incremental Patch Generator	Shareware
Opcode Systems	[See Tables 6-3 and 6-5]	Patch Factory option in most Opcode librarians and editors algorithmically generates new patches	
Symbolic Sound	Kyma	Requires card and external Capybara box	

Table 6-2: Sound design software — 16-bit sample editors (see Chapter 13)

Company	Product	Comments	S, F, PD
Digidesign	Sound Designer II	Akai S1000, S1000PB Akai S950, S900, S700, S7000 Casio FX1, FZ-10M Dynacord Add One (SDS), ADS E-mu SP-1200, Emax, Emax II E-mu Emulator II, III Ensoniq Mirage, Multisampler Ensoniq DSK, EPS Forat F-16 Korg DSS-1, DSM-1 Peavey DPM 3, DPM V3, DPM 3se (SDS) Oberheim DPX-1 Roland S-10, S220, S-50, S-550, MKS-100, S-330 Sequential Prophet 2000, 2002 Yamaha TX-16-W 12-bit SDS 16-bit SDS	

Table 6-2: Sound design software — 16-bit sample editors (continued)

Company	Product	Comments	S, F, PD
Digidesign	Sound Designer II SK	(see compatible samplers listed under Sound Designer II)	
Digidesign	Sound Designer Universal	(non stereo samplers — see list for Sound Designer II SK)	
MacroMind Paracomp	SoundEdit Pro		
Passport Designs	Alchemy	Akai S1000, S1000PB, S950, S900 Casio FX1, FZ-10M Dynacord Add One (SDS) E-mu SP-1200, Emax, Emax II, Emulator III Ensoniq Mirage, Multisampler Ensoniq EPS, EPS 16 Plus Oberheim DPX-1 Peavey DPM 3, DPM V3, DPM 3se (SDS) Roland S-50, S-550, S-330 Sequential Prophet 2000, 2002 Yamaha TX-16-W 12-bit SDS 16-bit SDS	
Passport Designs	Sound Apprentice	[see sampler compatibilities under Alchemy]	
Stephen Knight	SignalEditor	AIFF Files and other 8-, 12-, and 16-bit file formats	Shareware

Table 6-3: Sound design software — Patch librarians (see Chapter 11)

Company	Product	Comments	S, F, PD
B. Chrétien	SBX-80 Librarian		Shareware
Cliffhanger Productions		PROfiler Proteus Storage Librarian (for Proteus 1 and 2)	
Curt Bianchi	Korg M1 Librarian		Shareware
David Foster	Yamaha SY-77 Librarian		Shareware
David Schenfeld	SendBank (Yamaha YS100 and YS200)		Shareware
E-mu	Emulator Three Remote Controller/Librarian		
EarLevel Engineering	D50 Lister	Included with HyperMIDI 2.0	
Gary Becker	S-10 Librarian		Shareware
James Chandler Jr.	DX 7 Librarian (all DX/TX series)		Freeware
Kurzweil	ObjectMover (K1000, K1200)		
Kurzweil	QLS (K250)		
Larry Mistrot	D110 File System	HyperCard Stack	Freeware

Table 6-3: Sound design software — Patch librarians (continued)

Company	Product	Comments	S, F, PD
Mac Media	DX/TX/RX Voicepatch Librarian		
Michael Clemens	Yamaha PSS-680 Librarian	HyperCard Stack	Shareware
Mike Cohen	CZ Lib (Casio CZ 101, 1000, 5000)		Shareware
Opcode Systems	Casio CZ series with RZ-1 drum samples		
Opcode Systems	Ensoniq ESQ-1/SQ-80		
Opcode Systems	Fender Chroma, Polaris		
Opcode Systems	Kawai K-1, K-3, K-5, KM5		
Opcode Systems	Korg M-1, T1/M1/M3r		
Opcode Systems	Linn Drum	does not include Patch Factory	
Opcode Systems	Oberheim Matrix 6/1000, OB-8		
Opcode Systems	Oberheim Xpander/ Matrix 12		
Opcode Systems	Prophet VS		
Opcode Systems	Roland Alpha Juno 1 & 2		
Opcode Systems	Roland D-50, Juno 106		
Opcode Systems	Roland JX-8P		
Opcode Systems	Roland Super Jupiter		
Opcode Systems	Yamaha DX7 II/TX802/Bulk	(supports all 6-operator devices: DX7, TX7, TX816)	
Opcode Systems	Yamaha DX11/TX81z and DX21/27/100		
PostModern Productions	Kawai K-1 Librarian Kawai K-4 Librarian		Shareware
Robert E. Otto	U110 Patch Report		Shareware
Steve Makohin	E-mu Sp-12 Librarian		Shareware
Zero-One	D-50 Patch Librarian		
Zero-One	M1 Librarian		

Table 6-4: Sound design software — Universal patch librarians (see Chapter 11)

Company	Product	Comments	S, F, PD
Beaverton Digital	Universal MacPatch Librarian	[company out of business] (SysEx Bulk Dumps)	
Benoît Widemann	MIDI Test	(SysEx Bulk Dumps)	Shareware
Christopher Watson	Benson	(SysEx Bulk Dumps)	Shareware
EarLevel Engineering	Bulk Librarian	Included with HyperMIDI 2.0 (SysEx Bulk Dumps)	
Kevin Rosenberg	YLib		Shareware
Michael Williams	MIDILib DA		Freeware
Mike Collins	EQ SysEx Snapshot	HyperCard Stack (SysEx Bulk Dumps)	Shareware
Multimedia Artis	MIDI Mix 3D		

Table 6-4: Sound design software — Universal patch librarians (continued)

Company	Product	Comments	S, F, PD
Opcode Systems	Galaxy		
Opcode Systems	Opcode PatchLib	DA	
Pixel Publishing	Super Librarian		
Pixel Publishing	Super Librarian Accessory	DA	
Thomas W. Inskip	MIDI Ex	(SysEx Bulk Dumps)	Shareware

Table 6-5: Sound design software — Patch editor librarians (see Chapter 12)

Company	Product	Comments	S, F, PD
Altech	Casio Voice Editor		
Altech	DX Voice Editor		
Beaverton Digital	D-50 Editor Librarian	[company out of business]	
Beaverton Digital	ESQ1, SQ80 Editor Librarian	[company out of business]	
Beaverton Digital	FB-01 Editor Librarian	[company out of business]	
Beaverton Digital	L/A Universal Editor Librarian	[company out of business]	
Beaverton Digital	TX81Z, DX11 Editor Librarian	[company out of business]	
Bokonon Technologies	PatchMaster PROteus		
Bokoton	Tiresias (EPS and EPS16)		
Breakertech Software	Korg DW8000, EX8000		
Christopher Watson	MAX70 (PCM 70)		Shareware
Digital Music Services	DX7II PRO		
Digital Music Services	FB PRO-M		
Digital Music Services	TX81Z PRO	(includes earlier DX II PRO)	
Digital Music Services	TX802 PRO		
Don Box	K1000 (Editor)/Librarian	HyperCard Stack	Freeware
Doug Wyatt	DX WIT		Freeware
Dr. T's	Caged Artist D-50 Editor/Librarian		
Dr. T's	Roland D-10, 110, 20		
Dynaware	Ballade Roland MT-32 Editor Librarian		
EarLevel Engineering	SPX90 Editor/Librarian	Included with HyperMIDI 2.0	
Freq Sound	Kurzweil MIDIBoard		
Fumitaka Anzai	KAMIKAZE DX (DX, TX series)		
Galanter Productions	ART Multiverb III		
Galanter Productions	ART SGE Multi-effect		
Galanter Productions	Proteus/2, 2-XR		
Galanter Productions	Roland GP-8		
Galanter Productions	Roland GR-50		
Galanter Productions	Xpander and Matrix-12		
Harold Long	MT 32 Editor	HyperCard Stack	Shareware
Interval Music Systems	Kawai K1 Editor Librarian		

Table 6-5: Sound design software — Patch editor librarians (continued)

Company	Product	Comments	S, F, PD
Interval Music Systems	Kawai K4 Editor Librarian		
Interval Music Systems	Protezoa		
James Chandler Jr.	Kawai K4 Editor Librarian		Shareware
James Chandler Jr.	Korg M1 Editor Librarian		Shareware
James Chandler Jr.	Yamaha DX7, TX7 Editor Librarian		
Kurzweil	Kbd Mover (K250)		
Kurzweil	Seq Mover (K250)		
Kurzweil	Kurzweil 150 Sound Modeling Program		
Larry Mistrot	D110 Data System	HyperCard Stack	Shareware
Lexicon	LXP Programmer Stack	HyperCard Stack	Freeware
Multi Media Arts	Korg M1 Orchestrator Editor Librarian		
Multi Media Arts	Roland D-10, 110, 20 Editor Librarian		
Multi Media Arts	Roland D-50 Editor Librarian		
Multi Media Arts	Roland MT-32 Editor Librarian		
Musical Systems	Lexicon LXP 1, LXP 5	HyperCard Stack	
Opcode Systems	Casio CZ Series		
Opcode Systems	E-mu Proteus		
Opcode Systems	Ensoniq ES-1, SQ-80		
Opcode Systems	Kawai K-1		
Opcode Systems	Korg T1/M1/M3r		
Opcode Systems	Kurzweil 1000		
Opcode Systems	Oberheim Matrix 1000/Matrix-6		
Opcode Systems	Roland D-50/D-550, MT-32		
Opcode Systems	Roland Multi-D Series	Supports D10, D10, D20, MT-32	
Opcode Systems	Yamaha DX7 II/TX802/Bulk DX7, TX7, TX816	Supports all 6-operator devices:	
Opcode Systems	Yamaha DX11/TX81z and DX21/27/100		
Opcode Systems	Yamaha FB-01		
PhyShy	Proteus Editor		Shareware
Russel Salerno	MKS 50 Editor	HyperCard Stack	Shareware
SONUS	D-50 Design	[company out of business]	
Sound Quest	Quest Series of synthesizer specific editor librarians		
Steven S. Dimse	TX81Z Patch Editor/Librarian		
Sweetwater Sound	K250 Editor Librarian		
Tanya Rust	Music Scales		Shareware
Time of Your Life Music	LXP 5 Editor	HyperCard Stack	Shareware
Valhalla	Roland D-50 Editor Librarian		
Valhalla	Roland D10, 110, 20 Editor Librarian		

Table 6-5: Sound design software — Patch editor librarians (continued)

Company	Product	Comments	S, F, PD
Valhalla	Roland MT-32 Editor Librarian		
Valhalla	Roland R-8 Editor Librarian		
Valhalla	Yamaha SY77 Editor Librarian		
Valhalla	Yamaha TX81Z Editor Librarian		
Zero-One	Korg M1, M3r, T1, T2, T3, Librarian/Orchestrator		
Zero-One	D-50 Editor		

Table 6-6: Sound design software — Universal editor librarians (see Chapter 12)

Company	Product	Comments	S, F, PD
Beaverton Digital	L/A Universal Editor/Librarian	[company out of business]	
Benoît Widemann	MIDI Control	DA	Shareware
Computer Business Associates	Mac MIDI Master		
Dr. T's Music Software	XOR		
Hybrid Arts	GenEdit Universal Editor Librarian		
Opcode Systems	Galaxy Plus Editors		
Sound Quest	MIDI Quest Universal Editor Librarian		

Table 6-7: Sound design software — Patch data (see Chapters 11 and 12)

Note: Only sounds on Mac disks are listed — not RAM or ROM cards.
(Listed alphabetical by device.)

Synthesizers	Company
CZ-1, 101, 1000, 3000, 5000	Leister, Patch/Works
E-mu Proteus/1, 2	Sardonic Sounds, Sound Source
E-mu Proteus/1	Galanter Productions
Ensoniq ESQ-1, ESQ-M, SQ-80	Danler Music, ManyMIDI, Patch/Works, PatchMan Music, Valhalla
Ensoniq VFX, VFX-SD	Navarrophonic, Sound Source
K250 Sound Library	Kurzweil Music
Kawai K1. IM, IR	Kawai, ManyMIDI, Sound Source, Leister
Kawai K4	Sound Source
Kawai K5	James Chandler Jr.
Korg DW8000, EX8000	Livewire
Korg M1	Electron Artistries, Leister, ManyMIDI, Patch/Works, Soundsations, Sound Source, Valhalla
Korg T1, T2, T3	Soundsations
Korg Wavestation	Sound Source
Kurzweil 1000	Key Connection

Table 6-7: Sound design software — Patch data (continued)

Note: Only sounds on Mac disks are listed — not RAM or ROM cards.
(Listed alphabetical by device.)

Synthesizers	Company
Oberheim Matrix 6/1000	PatchMan Music
Oberheim Xpander/M12	Galanter Productions
Roland D-10, 110, 20	Navarrophonic, Leister, ManyMIDI, PatchMan Music, Sound Source, Valhalla
Roland D-50, D-550	Leister, Livewire, ManyMIDI, Navarrophonic, Patch/Works, Sound Source, Superior Sounds, Valhalla, Zero One
Roland D-70	Sound Source
Roland MC-500	Danlar Music
Roland MT-32	Digital Informative, Dr. T's, Leister, Livewire, ManyMIDI, Navarrophonic, Sound Source
Roland R-8	Navarrophonic, PatchMan Music, Sound Source
Roland U-20. 220	Sound Source
Yamaha DX 11	Livewire, ManyMIDI, Soundsations, Sound Source, Valhalla
Yamaha DX 21	Livewire, PatchMan Music, Soundsations, Sound Source, Valhalla
Yamaha DX7, TX7	Leister, Livewire, ManyMIDI, Soundsations, Sound Source
Yamaha DX7IIFD, IID, S	Livewire, ManyMIDI, Soundsations, Sound Source, Valhalla
Yamaha DX27, 27S, 100	Digital Informative, Livewire, PatchMan Music, Sound Source
Yamaha FB01	Leister
Yamaha TX81Z	Livewire, ManyMIDI, PatchMan Music, Soundsations, Sound Source, Superior Sounds, Valhalla
Yamaha TX81z/DX11	Galanter Productions
Yamaha TX802	Livewire, ManyMIDI, Soundsations, Sound Source, Superior Sounds
Yamaha V-50	Valhalla

Table 6-8: Sound design software — Sample data for samplers (see Chapter 13)

Company (supported samplers too numerous to list)

Digidesign
E-mu
Ear Works
East-West
GreytSounds
InVision Interactive
Korg
McGill University
NorthStar
Optical Media
ProSonus

Table 6-8: Sound design software — Sample data for samplers (continued)

Company (supported samplers too numerous to list)

Sound Ideas
Sound Source
Ubershall
Valhalla

Table 6-9: Sound design software — Sound databases (see Chapter 11)

Company	Product	Comments
Dr. T's Music Software	XOR	Universal patch editor/librarianwith built-in sound database
E-mu	Emulator Three Remote Controller/Librarian	Requires and Emulator Three
Gefen Systems	M&E Library	Comes pre-configured with standard sound effects or production music libraries including New England Digital optical disk listings.
MM Software	SoundFinder	HyperCard Stack
YAV Digital Music	SFX Organizer	Part of the *Macworld Music & Sound Bible* Software Supplement
YAV Digital Music	SoundTracker	Part of the *Macworld Music & Sound Bible* Software Supplement

Table 6-10: Composition software — Non-MIDI music (see Chapter 15)

Company	Product	Comments	S, F, PD
Addison Wesley	HyperComposer	HyperCard Stack	
Apple	Audio Palette		Freeware
Apple	MultiTrack		Freeware
Bogas Productions	Studio Session		
Bogas Productions	Super Studio Session		
Brøderbund	Jam Session		
Chuck Walker	Cheap Sequencer	HyperCard Stack	Freeware
Coda	Mac Drums		
Chris Reed	SoundEditor	ResEdit Template	Freeware
Dennis Fleisher	AudioData		Freeware
Digidesign	Live List, Master List, Radio Cart		
Digidesign	SoftSynth, TurboSynth		
Fractal Software	SoundCap		
GreatWave	ConcertWare	Instrument Maker	
Hiezer Software	Digital Audio Suite		
Jerry C. Welsh	HyperRap	HyperCard Stack	Freeware
Joe Pavone	HyperTunes	HyperCard Stack	Shareware

Table 6-10: Composition software — Non-MIDI music (continued)

Company	Product	Comments	S, F, PD
MacroMind-Paracomp	HyperSound	Part of the MacRecorder System	
MacroMind-Paracomp	SoundEdit	Part of the MacRecorder System	
Passport Designs	Alchemy		
Passport Designs	Audio Trax		
Passport Designs	Sound Exciter		
Pentallect	MacTunes	HyperCard Stack	Shareware
Primera	Different Drummer		
STAX	Sound Effects Studio	HyperCard Stack	Shareware
Stephen Knight	SignalEditor	AIFF Files and other 8-, 12-, and 16-bit file formats	Shareware
Steve Drazga	Sound Studio		Shareware
Unknown	Drum Machine	SuperCard Application	
Various vendors	SoundWave		

Table 6-11: Composition software — MIDI sequencers (see Chapter 17)

Company	Product	Comments	S, F, PD
Dr. T's Music Software	Beyond		
Dynaware	Ballade		
Electronic Arts	Deluxe Recorder		
Freq Sound	MIDI Paint		
Freq Sound	One Step		
Green Oak Software	Rhapsody		
Mark of the Unicorn	Performer		
Opcode Systems	EZ-Vision		
Opcode Systems	Vision		
Passport Designs	MasterTracks Pro	[will continue to be sold until stock is exhausted]	
Passport Designs	Pro-4.5, Pro 5		
Passport Designs	Trax		
Robert Patterson	MIDI Companion	DA	Shareware
Steinberg	CuBase		

Table 6-12: Composition software— MIDI sequencers with digital audio (see Chapter 18)

Company	Product	Comments	S, F, PD
Digidesign	Deck	Requires Audiomedia card (16-bit)	
Dr. T's Music Software	Beyond	Requires 16-bit digital audio card	
Mark of the Unicorn	Digital Performer	Requires 16-bit digital audio card	
Opcode Systems	Studio Vision	Requires 16-bit digital audio card	

Table 6-12: Composition software — MIDI sequencers with digital audio (continued)

Company	Product	Comments	S, F, PD
Passport	Audio Trax	8-bit digital	
Steinberg	CuBase 2	[forthcoming]	

Table 6-13: Composition software — Interactive composition (see Chapter 19)

Company	Product	Comments	S, F, PD
Dr. T's Music Software	Interactor		
Dr. T's Music Software	Jam Factory		
Dr. T's Music Software	M		
Dr. T's Music Software	Music Mouse		
Dr. T's Music Software	Ovaltune		
Dr. T's Music Software	UpBeat		
Hotz Instruments Technology	Hotz MIDI Translator	[forthcoming — software and hardware versions]	
Nebulous Enterprises	MacMuse	Software emulation of Hal Chamberlin's Muse Machine	Freeware
Primera	Different Drummer		

Table 6-14: Composition software — Algorithmic composition (see Chapter 20)

Company	Product	Comments	S, F, PD
Butch Mahoney	Evolution		
Butch Mahoney	Music Box		
Dr. T's Music Software	KCS Level II	Programmable Phrase Generator feature	
EarLevel Engineering	Algorithms	Included with HyperMIDI 2.0	
EarLevel Engineering	Fractal Music Generator	Included with HyperMIDI 2.0	
Frog Peak	Compose		
Frog Peak	HMSL		
Kurzweil Foundation	Cybernetic Composer		Shareware
Malmö College of Music	Music Lines		Shareware
Steinberg	CuBase	Interactive Phrase Synthesizer and Logical Editor features	

Table 6-15: Notation software (see Chapter 22)

Company	Product	Comments	S, F, PD
C.E.R.L.	Lime		
Coda	Finale		
Coda	MusicProse		

Table 6-15: Notation software (continued)

Company	Product	Comments	S, F, PD
David Palmer	Subtilior	HyperCard Stack (optimized for mensura notation)	Shareware
Electronic Arts	Deluxe Music Construction Set		
Euterpe	Euterpe		
Great Wave Software	ConcertWare +		
Great Wave Software	ConcertWare + MIDI		
Mark of the Unicorn	Professional Composer		
Music Krafters	ExampleKrafter	[company out of business]	
Music Krafters	NoteKrafter	[company out of business]	
Music Writer	Music Writer	[distribution system]	
MusicNet	MusicNet	[distribution system]	
Passport Designs	Encore		
Passport Designs	Note Writer		
Pyware	Music Writer		
Repertoire	Music Publisher		
Sun Valley Software	Toccata	[company out of business]	
Temporal Acuity	Nightingale	[forthcoming]	
ThinkWare	SpeedScore	[forthcoming] (optimized for fretted instrument notation)	
Vendor in transition	HB Engraver		

Table 6-16: Notation software — Music fonts (see Chapter 22)

Company	Product	Comments	S, F, PD
Adobe	Sonata		
Butch Mahoney	Mozart		
C.E.R.L.	Marl, Tufa		
Cassady & Greene	Crescendo, GraceNotes		
Chord Type	ChordType		
Coda	MIDICom, Newport, Petrucci, Rameau, Seville		
David Rokowski	Shpfltnat		Shareware
DVM	MetronomeFont, MetTimes		
E & R	Tabula — Lute & Fretted	Instrument Font	
ergo sum	AkkordeonRegister, Susato		
Great Wave	ConcertWare		
HB Imaging	Interlude		
Mark of the Unicorn	ChordFont, MusicFont		
Music Publisher	Repertoire		
Note Ware	FretFinder		
Note Ware	NameThatChord	(formerly called ChordSyms)	

Table 6-16: Notation software — Music fonts (continued)

Company	Product	Comments	S, F, PD
Passport Designs	Frets		
Prime Music Engraving	HagenChords, HagenGuitarCreator		
Prime Music Engraving	HagenGuitarFlats, HagenGuitarSharps		
Prime Music Engraving	HagenHand, HagenKorea, WriterMusic		
Think Ware	Musical		

Table 6-17: Performance software — Interactive performance (see Chapters 19 and 23)

Company	Product	Comments	S, F, PD
Dr. T's Music Software	Interactor		
Dr. T's Music Software	Jam Factory		
Dr. T's Music Software	M		
Dr. T's Music Software	Music Mouse		
Dr. T's Music Software	Ovaltune		
PG Music	Band-in-a-Box		
Scorpion Systems	sYbil		
Unknown	The Shearing Grid		Freeware

Table 6-18: Performance software — Control of additional performance parameters (see Chapter 23)

Company	Product	Comments	S, F, PD
Allen Goodwin and J. Steven Moore (distributed by ECS)	Advantage Showare (charting)	Marching band drill creation software	
Calaban	Calaban		
Crown	IQ	Speaker and EQ Automation	
Digidesign	Q-Sheet AV	JL Cooper MLC-1 (lighting controller) Sunn PLC 816 (lighting controller)	
LabanWriter	LabanWriter	Labanotation	
Pyware	ChartMaster	Marching band drill creation software	

Table 6-19: Post-production software — Direct-to-hard disk recording (see Chapter 24)

Company	Product	Comments	S, F, PD
Digidesign	Audiomedia	Requires Audiomedia Card (included with Audiomedia card)	
Digidesign	Deck	Requires Audiomedia Card	
Digidesign	Sound Access	[See next entry]	

Table 6-19: Post-production software — Direct-to-hard disk recording (continued)

Company	Product	Comments	S, F, PD
Digidesign	Sound Designer II	Included with the following packages: Sound Tools A/O (Sound Accelerator Card and AD IN) Sound Tools Digital I/O (Sound Accelerator Card and DAT I/O) Sound Tools A/D & Digital I/O (Sound Accelerator Card, AD IN, and DAT I/O) Sound Tools Pro Analog (Sound Accelerator Card and Pro I/O) Sound Tools A/O (Sound Accelerator Card and AD IN) Sound Tools Pro Analog & Digital I/O (Sound Accelerator Card, Pro I/O, and DAT I/O) Pro Tools (Pro Tools Audio Card and related peripherals)	
Mark of the Unicorn	Digital Performer	Requires digital audio card	
Opcode Systems	Studio Vision	Requires digital audio card	
Roland	DM-80 Front End	Macintosh Software for Roland's DM-80 external direct-to-hard disk recorder	
Steinberg-Jones	Cubase Audio	Requires digital audio card	
Studer Editech	MacMix	For the Dyaxis external direct-to-hard disk and digital audio system	
Symmetrix	Symmetrix	Requires digital audio card	

Table 6-20: Post-production software — Studio automation (see Chapter 25)

Company	Product	Comments	S, F, PD
B. Chrétien	SBX-80 Librarian		Shareware
Digidesign	Q-Sheet AV	Mixing Boards/Controllers: Akai MPX 820 IOTA Midifader JL Cooper SAM & MAGI Peavey PKM 8128 Simmons SPM 8:2 Twister Engineering Yamaha DMP-7 Audio Patch bays: Akai DP2000, DP3200 Tantek M4100 MIDI Patchbays: JL Cooper MSB+	
Digital Music Services	DMP7 PRO		
Erik G. Hanson	Music Production Package	Filemaker Templates	
Freq Sound	MIDI Mixer 7		

Table 6-20: Post-production software — Studio automation (continued)

Company	Product	Comments	S, F, PD
JL Cooper	CS-1 Editor Librarian		
JL Cooper	FaderMaster		
Missing Byte Software	TrackSheet		
Musically Intelligent Devices	MegaMix		
Opcode Systems	Akai MPX820 Mixer Editor Librarian		
Opcode Systems	JL Cooper MSB Librarian		
Opcode Systems	Track Chart		
Studio Master Computer Systems	Outboard Master		
Studio Master Computer Systems	Studio Master		
Studio Master Computer Systems	Track Master		
Wachter Software	Assistant Engineer		
Zero-One	MIDIMix 3D	DA	

Table 6-21: Post-production software — Digital signal processing (see Chapter 26)
(See also effects editors included with universal editor librarians)

Company	Product	Comments	S, F, PD
Digidesign	FX-Designer		
Digidesign	Q-Sheet AV	ADA MQ-1	
		AST 01	
		ART IEQ	
		Alesis MIDIverb	
		Alesis MIDIverb II	
		Alesis MIDIfex	
		Korg DRV 3000	
		Korg DVP-1	
		Lexicon PCM 70	
		Lexicon 480	
		Lexicon 224 (with clarity retrofit)	
		Roland DEP-5	
		Yamaha SPX-90, SPX-90 II	
		Yamaha Rev1, Rev5, Rev7	
		Yamaha D1500	
EarLevel Engineering	SPX90 Editor/Librarian	Included with HyperMIDI 2.0	
Galanter Productions	ART Multiverb III Editor/Librarian		
Galanter Productions	ART SGE Multi-effect Editor/Librarian		
Lexicon	LXP Programmer Stack	HyperCard Stack	Freeware
Musical Systems	Lexicon LXP 1, LXP 5	HyperCard Stack	
Opcode Systems	Lexicon PCM-70 Librarian		

Table 6-21: Post-production software — Digital signal processing (continued)

Company	Product	Comments	S, F, PD
Opcode Systems	Yamaha Rev5 Reverb Librarian		
Opcode Systems	Yamaha SPX-90 Effect Librarian		
Time of Your Life Music	LXP 5 Editor	HyperCard Stack	Shareware

Table 6-22: Film and video software — Synchronization (see Chapter 26)
(See also above under studio automation and below under utilities)

Company	Product	Comments	S, F, PD
B. Chrétien	SBX-80 Librarian		Shareware
HyperSong	Tracksheet		
Opcode Systems	Cue		
Passport Designs	Clicktracks		
Softhansa	Time Calculator	DA	

Table 6-23: Multimedia software — Production (see Chapter 27)

Company	Product	Comments	S, F, PD
Addison Wesley	Hyper Composer	HyperCard Stack	
Apple	QuickTime		Freeware
Apple	Video cdev		Freeware
Authorware	Authorware Professional		
Bright Star Technologies	InterFACE		
Claris/Apple	HyperCard		
Digidesign	Sound Installer		
EarLevel Engineering	HyperMIDI	HyperCard Stack	
Farallon	MediaTracks		
MacroMind	Director		
MacroMind	Media Maker		
Motion Works	Add Motion	HyperCard Stack	
Opcode Systems	MIDI Play	HyperCard Stack	
Passport Designs	HyperMusic	HyperCard Stack	
Robertson Reed Smith	StackStarter		Freeware
Serius	Serius Programmer		
Silicon Beach	SuperCard		
Spinnaker	Plus		
Steve Drazga	Developer Stack	HyperCard Stack	Shareware
Voyager	VideoDisc Accessory Series		
Voyager	VideoStack 8000	HyperCard Stack	

Table 6-23: Multimedia software — Production (continued)

Company	Product	Comments	S, F, PD
Voyager	Voyager CD AudioStack	HyperCard Stack	
Voyager	Voyager VideoStack	HyperCard Stack	
VPL	HookUp!		

Table 6-24: Multimedia software — Clip music (see Chapter 27)

Company	Product	Comments	S, F, PD
B & B Soundworks	Sound Resources Library	8-bit soundfiles in HyperCard format	
Berkeley Mac Users Group	BMUG Sound Library	8-bit soundfiles on floppy disks	PD
Bogas Productions	Music Disks	8-bit soundfiles on floppy disks	
Boston Computer Society	StackSounds	8-bit soundfiles on floppy disks	PD
Desktop Music	Music CD-ROM	8-bit soundfiles on CD-ROM	
Dietrich Gewissler	HeadStart	SMF Database of rhythm patterns	
Digidesign	Clip Tunes	16-bit production music on CD-ROM	
Dr. T's Music Software	MIDI Clips	SMFs on floppy disks	
Gemini Marketing	Performer Music files	Mark of the Unicorn	PD
Golden MIDI Music	Golden MIDI Sequences	SMFs on floppy disks	
Great Wave Software	ConcertWare+ Music	ConcertWare files on floppy disks	
Great Wave Software	Terpsichore (ConcertWare)	ConcertWare files on floppy disks	
Mac Media	MIDI Minus One	SMFs on floppy disks	
Navarrophonic	Drum patterns for HR16		
Opcode Systems	MIDI Play	MIDIPlay (see above) includes 46 SMFs	
Passport Designs	Music Data	Hundreds of SMFs in all styles	
Tactic Software	Sound Clips	8-bit soundfiles on floppy disks	
YAV Digital Music	YAVClips	8-bit soundfiles on floppy disks (Part of the *Macworld Music & Sound Bible* Software Supplement)	

Table 6-25: Networking software — Music local area networks (see Chapter 8)

Company	Product	Comments	S, F, PD
Apple	MIDI Manager	System software	
Freeware			
Grame	MIDIShare		
Lone Wolf	Virtual Studio	Requires MidiTap hardware	
Mark of the Unicorn	MIDI Time Piece DA	Requires MIDI Time Piece(s)	
Opcode System	OMS	Includes OMS setup and many INITs and drivers (see below)	
Passport Designs	DAN: Distributed Audio Network	A feature found in Passport's Alchemy and Sound Apprentice	
Steinberg	M•ROS		

Table 6-26: Networking software — Telecommunications

Company	Product	Comments	S, F, PD
Aladdin	Stuffit Deluxe	Compression/Archival software	
Aladdin	Stuffit 1.6	Compression/Archival software	Shareware
Bill Goodman	Compactor	Compression/Archival software	Shareware
David P. Alverson	ZTerm	Telecommunications software	Shareware
FreeSoft	White Knight	Telecommunications software	
PAN	PAN Messenger	Telecommunications software	
Salient	Disk Doubler	Compression/Archival software	
Scot Watson	Red Ryder	Telecommunications software	Shareware
Software Ventures	Microphone	Telecommunications software	

Table 6-27: Education software — Ear training (see Chapter 28)

Company	Product	Comments	S, F, PD
Andromeda	Master Tuner		
Antelope Engineering	TuneUp		
Ars Nova	Practica Musica		
Brad Needham	Interval		PD
Educational Courseware Systems (ECS)	Tune It II		
EduCorp	Pitcher		
Electronic Courseware Systems	Keyboard Chords MIDI		
Imaja	Listen		
Indiana University	Encore		
Kirk Austin	Ear Tutor		PD
Lawrence Gallagher	Ear Trainer		Shareware
Mac Media	BigEars		
Mac Media	Perfect Pitch		
Marion Williamson	GOATS Interval Drill		
Mayfield Publishing	MacGamut: Intervals, Scales and Chords		
Mayfield Publishing	MacGamut: Melodic Dictation		
RMI	Perceive		
Soul Support Software	7th Heaven		
Wingtip Software	Ear Training	HyperCard Stack	Freeware

Table 6-28: Education software — Theory and analysis (see Chapter 28)

Company	Product	Comments	S, F, PD
Academic Courseware Exchange	Voice		
Alfred	Music Achievement Series		
Alfred	Practical Theory		

Table 6-28: Education software — Theory and analysis (continued)

Company	Product	Comments	S, F, P
Carnegie Mellon University	MacVoice		
Dartmouth College	AppleTones		
Dartmouth College	Mozart		
Dartmouth College	Palestrina		
Educational Courseware Systems	Early Music Skills		
Educational Courseware Systems	Note Speller		
Elvin S. Rodriguez	NoteHangMan		Shareware
Hip Software	Harmony Grid		
Janis Kindred	Tutorial/Drill: Program for Music Theory		
MacBEAT	Compose Yourself	HyperCard Stack	
Mayfield Publishing	Explorations		
MiBAC	MiBAC Music Lessons		
Micro Works Corp.	CampsE	HyperCard Stack	
New England Conservatory	A Walk Through Functional Harmony		
Northwestern University at Evanston	Imager		
Project Zero	SongSmith		
Soundscape	JI Calc	HyperCard Stack	Shareware
Teachnology	Audio/Graphic Dictionary of Harmony	HyperCard Stack	
University of Northern Arizona	MMP Chords		Freeware
University of Northern Arizona	MMP Harmonic Analysis		Freeware
USERsoft microSYSTEMS	MacChanges		Shareware
YAV Digital Music	Nadia Boulanger	Harmony à la the teachings of Nadia Boulanger (Part of the *Macworld Music & Sound Bible* Software Supplement)	

Table 6-29: Education software — Applied instruments (see Chapter 28)

Company	Product	Comments	S, F, PD
Alfred	Basic Adult Piano Theory		
Alfred	Basic Piano Theory		
Baudville	Chord Wizard		
Baudville	Fretboard Wizard		
Baudville	Guitar Wizard		
Baudville	Scale Wizard		
Coda	Practise Room		
Electronic Courseware Systems	Keyboard Blues MIDI		
Electronic Courseware Systems	Keyboard Extended Jazz Harmonies MIDI		
Electronic Courseware Systems	Keyboard Fingerings MIDI		

Table 6-29: Education software — Applied instruments (continued)

Company	Product	Comments	S, F, PD
Electronic Courseware Systems	Keyboard Intervals MIDI		
Electronic Courseware Systems	Keyboard Jazz Harmonies MIDI		
Electronic Courseware Systems	Keyboard Kapers MIDI		
Electronic Courseware Systems	Keyboard Namegame MIDI		
Electronic Courseware Systems	Keyboard Note Drill MIDI		
Electronic Courseware Systems	Keyboard Tutor MIDI		
Electronic Courseware Systems	MIDI Jazz Improvisation		
Kawai	Interactive Software for most Kawai Keyboards		
Kawai	Virtual MIDI Lab		
Mac Media	Virtuoso Pianist		
Max Stax	Banjo Chord & Scale Builder		
MiBAC	MiBAC Jazz Improvisation Software		
Nappo Software	Guitar Tutor		
P G Software	Band-in-a-Box		
Playing Hard to Get	Guitarist	HyperCard Stack	Shareware

Table 6-30: Education software — History and appreciation (see Chapters 28 and 29)

Company	Product	Comments	S, F, PD
Charles Boody	Delaware 3	Videodisc	
CIMI	Name That Guitarist	HyperCard Stack	
CNMAT	Country Blues in Hypermedia		
Dr. T's Music Software	Adventures in MusicLand		
Heizer Software	Worldwide Old Time Melodies	HyperCard Stack	
Illinois State University	Toney Music Games	CD-ROM	
Joel Zobkiw	Electronic Music Encyclopedia	HyperCard Stack	Shareware
Kawai	Opera Construction Set		
Northwestern University at Evanston	Big Ears	CD-ROM	
Opcode Systems	The Book of MIDI	HyperCard Stacks	
Robert Winter	Parsifal	HyperCard Stack	Shareware
The Music Society	Understanding MIDI Protocol	HyperCard Stack	Shareware
Voyager	Beethoven: Ninth Symphony		
Voyager	J.S. Bach: Brandenburg	HyperCard Stack	
Voyager	Stravinsky: The Rite of Spring		
Voyager	Schubert: Trout Quintet	[forthcoming]	
Voyager	Strauss (Richard): Three Tone Poems	[forthcoming]	
Voyager	Dvorak: New World Symphony	[forthcoming]	
Voyager	Bartok: Music for Strings, Percussion, and Celeste	[forthcoming]	

Table 6-30: Education software — History and appreciation (continued)

Company	Product	Comments	S, F, PD
Voyager	Johnny Green's Body and Soul	[forthcoming]	
Voyager	Mozart: The Dissonant Quartet		
Warner New Media	Bach: The Art of the Fugue	[forthcoming]	
Warner New Media	Beethoven String Quartet #14		
Warner New Media	Beethoven: Seventh Symphony	[forthcoming]	
Warner New Media	Berlioz: Symphonie Fantastique	[forthcoming]	
Warner New Media	Brahms Requiem		
Warner New Media	Britten: Young Person's Guide to the Orchestra		
Warner New Media	Mozart: Symphony #40	[forthcoming]	
Warner New Media	Mozart: The Magic Flute		
Warner New Media	Mussorgsky: Pictures at an Exhibition	[forthcoming]	
Warner New Media	Rachmaninoff: Second Piano Concerto	[forthcoming]	
Warner New Media	Strauss: Also Sprach Zarathustra	[forthcoming]	
Warner New Media	Stravinsky: The Rite of Spring	[forthcoming]	
Warner New Media	Tchaikovsky: The Nutcracker Suite	[forthcoming]	
Warner New Media	Vivaldi: The Four Seasons	[forthcoming]	

Table 6-31: Education software — Miscellaneous (see Part Nine)

Company	Product	Comments	S, F, PD
Allen Goodwin and J. Steven Moore (distributed by ECS)	Advantage Showare (charting)	Marching band drill creation software	
Coda	Finale Guided Tour	[by Christopher Yavelow]	
ergo sum	Finale Praxis		
Illinois State University	HyperCard Etudes	HyperCard Stack	
Kawai	KiMMS Classroom	Kawai Music Management System for classroom music	
Navarro Software	Jim Heid's Sound Stack	HyperCard Stack	
Pyware	ChartMaster	Marching band drill creation software	
Pyware	Music Charting Aid		
Software Guild	Music Library System		
W.W. Norton	The Music Kit	HyperCard Stack	

Table 6-32: Musical and acoustical research software (see Part Nine)

Company	Product	Comments	S, F, PD
Andromeda	Master Tuner	Uses MacroMind-Paracomp's MacRecorder	
Barbara Jesser	Interaktive Melodieanalyse		

Table 6-32: Musical and acoustical research software (continued)

Company	Product	Comments	S, F, PD
Barbara Kwiatkowska	Universal Analytical Music Notation System		
Bose Corp	Modeler		
Bose Corp	SpeakerCAD		
Christoph Schnell	AlphaTIMES		
Dimitris Gianelos	Automated transcription and analysis system		
Igor Popvic	Analytical Layers		
Illinois State University	Psychomusicology Tutor	HyperCard Stack	
James Kippen	Bol Processor		
Jeanne Bamberger	Project Athena		
John Roeder	Declarative Analysis of Non-tonal Music	Graphics-based Music Analysis System	
Robert Freuwald	Music Manager		
University of Milan	Intelligent Music Workstation		

Table 6-33: Programming and visual programming software

Company	Product	Comments	S, F, PD
Act Informatique	MIDI Lisp		
Altech	MIDIBASIC		
Altech	MIDIBASIC Q Lib		
Altech	MIDIPascal		
Altech	MIDIWrite		
Apple	HyperCard		
Applied Digital Arts	Keynote		
Carnegie Mellon	CMU MIDI ToolKit		
EarLevel Engineering	HyperMIDI		
Eric Huffman	Megalomania		Freeware
Grame (MIDIShare)	MIDIShare Stack		
Heizer Software	CompileIt!	Compiles HyperCard scripts into XCMDx	
Opcode Systems	MAX		
Opcode Systems	PatchTalk	Included with Opcode patch librarians and editors	
Richard Boulanger	C-Sound		
Silicon Beach	SuperCard		
Sound Quest	MIDI Quest Development System		
University of Melbourne	Music4C		
VPL	HookUp!		

Table 6-34: Ancillary tasks — Software for hardware (see Chapters 8 and 10)

Company	Product	Comments	S,F,PD
Altech	ESQ Filer	DA	
Altech	TX81Z Filer	DA	
Aphex Systems	Studio Clock Editor	Program	
Aphex Systems	Studio Clock	DA	
Digidesign	MacProteus Front Panel		
Digidesign	SampleCell Editor		
Digidesign	.MIDI port Fix	INIT	
Digidesign	.Sound Accelerator	INIT for Sound Accelerator	
Digidesign	Diskable DA	DA	
Digidesign	MacProteus Batteries	INIT for MacProteus	
Digidesign	SampleCell Driver	Driver for SampleCell	
E-mu	Emulator Three Remote Controller/Librarian		
FreqSound	JamBox DA		
FreqSound	JamBox Manager		
FreqSound	JamBox On/Off DA		
FreqSound	JamBox Tempo Librarian		
FreqSound	MIDIMIXER7		
JL Cooper	FaderMaster	DA	
JL Cooper	CS-1 Editor Librarian		
JL Cooper	FaderMaster Librarian	DA and program	
JL Cooper	PPS-Que	DA and program	
Kevin Rosenberg MD	Kurz 1000 OM List		Shareware
Kurzweil Music	KbdMover		
Kurzweil Music	Object Mover		
Kurzweil Music	QLS		
Kurzweil Music	SD Convert		
Kurzweil Music	SeqMover		
Lone Wolf	MT Downloader	HyperCard Stack	
MacroMind-Paracomp	MacRecorder Driver	Driver to use MacRecorder as a microphone à la the IIsi	
Mark of the Unicorn	MTP DA		
Mark of the Unicorn	VTP DA		
Mark of the Unicorn	MIDI Mixer 7 DA		
Opcode Systems	OMS Setup		
Opcode Systems	Studio 3 DA		
Opcode Systems	TimeCode DA		
Panasonic SV-3900	SV-3900 Serial Controller	HyperCard Stack	
Passport Designs	Setup transport DA		
Steven Dimse	JamBox Saver		

Table 6-34: Ancillary tasks — Software for hardware (continued)

Company	Product	Comments	S,F,PD
Zero-One	D-50 Editor	DA	
Zero-One	D-50 Librarian	DA	
Zero-One	D-50 Librarian Editor Plus	DA	

Table 6-35: Ancillary tasks software — Business and organization

Company	Product	Comments	S, F, PD
SmokeTree Studios	HyperStudio	HyperCard Stacks	
Erik G. Hanson	Music Production Package	FileMaker Templates	
Grover Wilkins	MusicFile Cataloging System		
Logical "Berlioz"	Berlioz		
Summit Software	Track Sheet		
The Software Guild	Music Library System		
Words & Deeds	Archie Studio Management System		

Table 6-36: Ancillary tasks software — Music utilities (programs)

Company	Product	Comments	S, F, PD
Adam Shabtach	MacMuse		Freeware
Aesthetic Engineering	MIDI Terminal		Shareware
Altech Systems	MIDI Tracer		
Andromeda Computer	MasterTuner		
Anonymouse	Conformer		Freeware
Apple	HourGlass	MIDI Manager sample program	Freeware
Apple	MIDIArp	MIDI Manager sample program	Freeware
Apple	Patchbay	MIDI Manager	Freeware
Apple	SimpleKey	MIDI Manager sample program	Freeware
Apple	SquidCakes	MIDI Manager sample program	Freeware
Apple	Wuliax		Freeware
Articulate Systems	MIDI Voice Waves	Command list files for Voice Navigator	
Beaverton Digital	SCFileConverter	[company out of business]	
Benoît Widemann	MIDITest		Shareware
Bob Lafleur	DX/TX converter		Freeware
Bogas Systems	S.S.M.U. (Studio Session MIDI Utility)		
Bose Corp	RackMaker		
Chas Turner	ToneRows		
Chris Reed	PlayAIFF		Freeware
Christian Teuscher	MIDI Chord HIASL		Freeware
CTM Development	MIDIPack		
David Lichtman	DX Unique		Shareware

Table 6-36: Ancillary tasks software — Music utilities (programs) (continued)

Company	Product	Comments	S, F, PD
Dennis Fleisher	AudioData		Freeware
Digidesign	DATa		
Don Box	Strum		Freeware
Don Harris	StudioCalc		Shareware
Don Harris	DelayCalc		Shareware
Doug Wyatt	MIDI Reclock		Shareware
Doug Wyatt	DX Patch Sorter		Shareware
Doug Wyatt	MIDI TypeCaster		Freeware
EarLevel Engineering	Delay FX	Included with HyperMIDI 2.0	
EarLevel Engineering	EQ SYSEX Snapshot		
EarLevel Engineering	Key Strummer	Included with HyperMIDI 2.0	
EarLevel Engineering	Keyboard Analyzer	Included with HyperMIDI 2.0	
EarLevel Engineering	MIDI File Player	Included with HyperMIDI 2.0	
EarLevel Engineering	MIDI Utilities	Included with HyperMIDI 2.0	
EarLevel Engineering	MIDIcalc	Included with HyperMIDI 2.0	
EarLevel Engineering	Strummer	Included with HyperMIDI 2.0	
Entropy Engineering	Channeler		Freeware
Entropy Engineering	Watcher		Shareware
Freq Sound	Matrix 12, Xpander Text Convert	HyperCard Stack	Shareware
Grame	BarGraph	MIDIShare sample program	
Grame	Cquencer	MIDIShare sample program	
Grame	Display	MIDIShare sample program	
Grame	Echo	MIDIShare sample program	
Grame	Ef1 DMP7	MIDIShare sample program	
Grame	Ef2 DMP7	MIDIShare sample program	
Grame	Façade	MIDIShare sample program	
Grame	MIDI Bench	MIDIShare sample program	
Grame	Midi Connection	MIDIShare sample program	
Grame	Midi Life	MIDIShare sample program	
Grame	Midi Space	MIDIShare sample program	
Grame	MIDIShare		
Grame	Pan DMP7	MIDIShare sample program	
Grame	Panel	MIDIShare sample program	
Grame	Universal Ctrl	MIDIShare sample program	
Grame	Vol DMP7	MIDIShare sample program	
Grame	Volumes	MIDIShare sample program	
Harmony Systems	SL_to_SD		Shareware
Insanely Great Software	Play All Sounds		Freeware
James Chandler Jr.	DinoSwitch		Shareware

Table 6-36: Ancillary tasks software — Music utilities (programs) (continued)

Company	Product	Comments	S, F, PD
Jeff Smeenge	Aural Organization	FileMaker Template	
Jim Moore	Sound/Pict Thief		Shareware
Jim Nitchals	MIDI CD		Freeware
Joe Zobkiw	Sound Æ Res		Shareware
Joe Zobkiw	SoundConverter (to Sys 7)		
John Raymonds	SuperPlay		Shareware
John Worthington	T2C2	HyperCard Stack	Freeware
Kelly Major	Sound Convert	HyperCard Stack	Freeware
Ken McLeod	MusicCard	HyperCard Stack	Freeware
Kurzweil	SD Convert		
Kurzweil (Ralph Muha)	MIDI Scope		PD
Lee Story	MIDI Display		PD
Lee Story	MIDI Echoe		PD
Mac Media	MIDI Works		
MacroMind-Paracomp	MacRecorder Hacker Kit		
Mason Bliss	MusicBase		Freeware
MaxStac	MusicCards	HyperCard Stack	
Michael Pelz-Sherman	Twelve-Tone	HyperCard Stack	Shareware
North Shore Computers	Sound Manager		Shareware
Opcode Systems	OMS Setup		
Opcode Systems	M1 File Converter		
Opcode Systems	MIDI Logger		
Opcode Systems	Track Chart		
Paul Ferguson	Chroma		Shareware
Paul Ferguson	Lefty		Freeware
R.S.I.	Rhyme Design		
Riccardo Ettore	Sound Æ snd		Shareware
Riccardo Ettore	Sound Mover		Shareware
Russ Wetmore	SoundCap Æ snd		Shareware
SCABAJAK Software	Music Tracker	HyperCard Stack	Freeware
Summit Software	MetroGnome		Shareware
Terry Bertram	MacKeyboard		Shareware
Unknown	Hypersong-Tracksheet	HyperCard Stack	
Unknown	MIDI File Fixer		PD
Unknown	The Shearing Grid		Shareware
Wette Enterprises	FinaleFontReport	HyperCard Stack	Freeware
YAV Digital Music	MacMusic Articles	Database of all articles on Macintosh Music, MIDI, Digital Audio, and Multimedia published in popular Macintosh and Music magazines for the past four years (Part of the *Macworld Music & Sound Bible* Software Supplement)	

Table 6-36: Ancillary tasks software — Music utilities (programs) (continued)

Company	Product	Comments	S, F, PD
YAV Digital Music	MacMusic Products and Resources	Database of Macintosh Music, Digital Audio, and Multimedia Products and Resources (Part of the *Macworld Music & Sound Bible* Software Supplement)	
YAV Digital Music	MacMusic Companies	Database of Music, MIDI, Digital Audio, and Multimedia Software and Hardware Companies (Part of the *Macworld Music & Sound Bible* Software Supplement)	
YAV Digital Music	*Macworld Music & Sound Bible* Glossary	Database (non-DA version) of the terms found in this book (Part of the *Macworld Music & Sound Bible* Software Supplement)	
YAV Digital Music	*Macworld Music & Sound Bible* Online Index	Online index (non-DA version) to the *Macworld Music & Sound Bible* (Part of the *Macworld Music & Sound Bible* Software Supplement)	
YAV Digital Music	Rack Designer	HyperCard Stack (Part of the *Macworld Music & Sound Bible* Software Supplement)	
YAV Digital Music	Synth and Audio Art	Hundreds of popular devices in object-oriented graphics format, all to scale (Part of the *Macworld Music & Sound Bible* Software Supplement)	
Zedcor	CassetteLabeler		

Table 6-37: Ancillary tasks software — Music utilities (DAs, FKeys, cdevs, INITs)

Company	Product	Comments	S, F, PD
Altech	Sys-X Filer	DA	
Apple	IIfx Serial Switch	cdev	Freeware
Apple	Mac II Video Card Utility	cdev	Freeware
Apple	MIDI Manager (with Apple MIDI Driver)	INIT	Freeware
Apple (MIDI Manager)	PatchBay	DA	Freeware
Apriori Software	QuickRhyme	DA	
Austin Development	MIDI Mode	DA	
Austin Development	MIDI Program Select	DA	
Austin Development	MPS II (MIDI Program Select)	DA	
Bruce Tomlin	Sound Master	cdev	Shareware
Bruce Tomlin	SoundPlay	DA	PD
Chip Burwell	Orchestrator	DA	Shareware
David Lewis	Midi Control Numbers	DA	Freeware
Don Box	Delay Calc	DA	
Don Box	Studio Calc	DA	
EarLevel Engineering	MIDI Mangler	cdev	Freeware
Grame	MIDI Thru	DA (MIDIShare)	

Table 6-37: Ancillary tasks software — Music utilities (DAs, FKeys, cdevs, INITs) (continued)

Company	Product	Comments	S, F, PD
Grame	MIDIShare	cdev (MIDIShare)	
Greg Smith	Finder Sounds	cdev	Freeware
Interval Music Systems	LoadaZoa	DA (included with Protezoa)	
Joe Zobkiw	MIDI Bytes	DA	Shareware
Joe Zobkiw	MIDI Controller #s	DA	Shareware
M.J. Williams	Tapper	DA	
Mark Erickson	MIDIHz	DA	Shareware
Mark Erickson	Trax	DA	Shareware
Michael Williams	MIDI Lib	DA	Shareware
Opcode Systems	OMS (Opcode MIDI System)	INIT includes MIDI Time Piece OMS driver, SampleCell OMS driver, Standard Interface OMS driver, Standard Interface OMS driver, Studio 5 OMS driver	
Opcode Systems	Opcode MIDI INIT	cdev (functionally equivalent to MIDI Mangler by EarLevel Engineering listed above)	
Opcode Systems	Patch Librarian (universal)	DA	
Opcode Systems	"Up Your(FCB)s"	INIT	
Passport Designs	Sound Exciter	INIT creates a virtual synthesizer	
Riccardo Ettore	SndControl	cdev	Shareware
Riccardo Ettore	StartupSndINIT	INIT	Shareware
Robert L. Mathews	Speed Beep	cdev	Shareware
Robert Patterson	MIDI Companion	DA	Shareware
Robert Patterson	MIDI Companion	DA	Shareware
Softhansa	Time Calculator	DA	
Unknown	MusicMaker	DA	
YAV Digital Music	Clix to BPM	DA (Part of the *Macworld Music & Sound Bible* Software Supplement)	
YAV Digital Music	Factory Patches	Set of DAs with factory patch lists for many electronic instruments (Part of the *Macworld Music & Sound Bible* Software Supplement)	
YAV Digital Music	HyperMIDI Syntax	DA (Part of the *Macworld Music & Sound Bible* Software Supplement)	
YAV Digital Music	MIDI Troubleshooter	DA (Part of the *Macworld Music & Sound Bible* Software Supplement)	
YAV Digital Music	*Macworld Music & Sound Bible* Glossary	DA providing many of the terms found in this book (Part of the *Macworld Music & Sound Bible* Software Supplement)	

Table 6-37: Ancillary tasks software — Music utilities (DAs, FKeys, cdevs, INITs) (continued)

Company	Product	Comments	S, F, PD
YAV Digital Music	*Macworld Music & Sound Bible* Online Index	Online index in a DA to the *Macworld Music & Sound Bible* (Part of the *Macworld Music & Sound Bible* Software Supplement)	
YAV Digital Music	Music Fundamentals	DA (Part of the *Macworld Music & Sound Bible* Software Supplement)	
YAV Digital Music	Music Macros	Sets of macros in various macro-utility formats for a variety of popular music programs (Part of the *Macworld Music & Sound Bible* Software Supplement)	
YAV Digital Music	Musicians Addressbook	DA (Part of the *Macworld Music & Sound Bible* Software Supplement)	
YAV Digital Music	Notator Calculator	DA (Part of the *Macworld Music & Sound Bible* Software Supplement)	
YAV Digital Music	Orchestration	DA (Part of the *Macworld Music & Sound Bible* Software Supplement)	
YAV Digital Music	Patch Editing Tips	DA (Part of the *Macworld Music & Sound Bible* Software Supplement)	
YAV Digital Music	Sample Editing Tips	DA (Part of the *Macworld Music & Sound Bible* Software Supplement)	
YAV Digital Music	Sequencer Calculator	DA (Part of the *Macworld Music & Sound Bible* Software Supplement)	
YAV Digital Music	Shortcuts	Set of DAs with shortcuts for a variety of popular music programs (Part of the *Macworld Music & Sound Bible* Software Supplement)	
YAV Digital Music	Synchronization Calculator	DA (Part of the *Macworld Music & Sound Bible* Software Supplement)	
YAV Digital Music	The MIDI Spec	DA (Part of the *Macworld Music & Sound Bible* Software Supplement)	
YAV Digital Music	The Ultimate MIDI DA	DA (Part of the *Macworld Music & Sound Bible* Software Supplement)	
YAV Digital Music	Time Converter	Rhythm to Clock to PPQN converter DA (Part of the *Macworld Music & Sound Bible* Software Supplement)	
YAV Digital Music	Tunings	DA (Part of the *Macworld Music & Sound Bible* Software Supplement)	
YAV Digital Music	WYSIWYP	"What You Say Is What You Play" Sets of Voice Navigator commands for a variety of popular music programs (Part of the *Macworld Music & Sound Bible* Software Supplement)	
Zero-One	MIDI MIX 3D	DA	

Table 6-38: Shareware, Freeware, and Public Domain software

Musical tasks	Product	S	F	PD
16-bit sample editing	SignalEditor	●		
8-bit sample editing	SoundEditor		●	
8-bit sample editing	Audio Data		●	
Dedicated patch librarian	See Table 6-3 for 13 options	●	●	
Universal patch librarian	MIDILib DA		●	
Universal patch librarian	YLib	●		
Universal patch librarian	See Table 6-4 for six options	●	●	
Dedicated patch editor/librarian	See Table 6-5 for 12 options	●	●	
Universal patch editor/librarian	MIDI Control	●		
Music in HyperCard	MacTunes	●		
Music in HyperCard	See Table 6-10 for additional options	●	●	
MIDI sequencer	MIDI Companion	●		
Interactive composition	MacMuse		●	
Algorithmic composition	Cybernetic Composer	●		
Algorithmic composition	Music Lines	●		
Notation (mensural only)	Subtilior	●		
Postscript music font	Shpfltnat	●		
Interactive performance	The Shearing Grid		●	
Effects editing	LXP Programmer Stack		●	
Effects editing	LXP-5 Editor (HyperCard stack)	●		
Tempo map librarian	SBX-80 Librarian	●		
Clip sounds for multimedia	BMUG, BCS			●
Clip MIDI data	Gemini Marketing			●
Ear training	Interval			●
Ear training	Ear Tutor			●
Ear training	Ear Trainer	●		
Ear training	Ear Training (HyperCard stack)		●	
Theory	JICalc	●		
Theory	MMP Chords and Harmonic Analysis		●	
Theory	MacChanges	●		
Guitar	Guitarist (HyperCard stack)	●		
Reference	Electronic Music Encyclopedia (HyperCard stack)	●		
Reference	Understanding MIDI Protocol	●		
Reference	Parsifal	●		
Visual MIDI programming	Megalomania	●		
Music utilities	See Tables 6-36 and 6-37 for over 60 options	●	●	●

Summary

✔ Microprocessor-controlled hardware devices require software to function for their intended purpose. Hardware includes the Macintosh itself, synthesizers, samplers, DSP effects devices, and just about anything with silicon chips inside it. Software is different from hardware in that it does not exist in any tangible form. Software is merely a group of ones and zeros (bytes) organized by the programmer or user in such a way that it facilitates the execution of a specific task.

✔ A wide range of applications software is necessary to manage the variety of musical situations that recur on a day-to-day basis. This includes software for purposes such as MIDI sequencing, SoundEditing and/or generation, sound and sequence library management, conventional music notation, digital mixing, algorithmic composition, and telecommunications.

✔ Recent formidable advances in object-oriented programming, data-compression, and searching techniques engendered by Apple's new HyperCard software authoring package (bundled with all Macintosh computers) are changing the face of the industry. HyperCard puts the power to create extremely sophisticated applications into the hands of people with little or no programming knowledge.

✔ Software falls into two main categories relating to its function and distribution. Functional categories include system software, application software, utility software, development systems, data, and dedicated software. Distribution categories include commercial, proprietary, shareware (or honorware), freeware, public domain, and software piracy. The last is illegal.

✔ Stand-alone applications (sometimes called "double-clickable" applications) are programs that run by themselves without requiring any other software engine besides the general Macintosh operating system. This is contrasted with programs that require their parent application to be present on the disk in order to run. Examples of programs that require an engine or their parent (or creator) application in order to function are HyperCard stacks, SuperCard projects, and Director Documents.

✔ You can't make a functional copy of a copy-protected program. You can duplicate the disk, but the program won't run from the duplicated disk. The Macintosh music community frowns on copy protection and this practice is rapidly disappearing. Nonetheless, many music programs still employ some form of copy protection.

Chapter 7

Setting Up Your Mac Music Studio

In this chapter ...

✔ Twenty-two Macintosh studio setups, complete with signal flow charts and suggested equipment.

✔ Possible studio configurations at three levels: entry level, intermediate, and advanced.

✔ The seven types of Macintosh studio setups: 8-bit non-MIDI music, desktop music publishing, MIDI music, 16-bit digital audio, film and video, multimedia, and education.

✔ Estimated costs (high and low) for each setup.

✔ Principles for optimal signal routing in each type of setup.

✔ Budget-stretching tips.

Making Sense of the Studio Setups

This chapter provides 22 sample Macintosh studio setups, complete with signal flow charts and suggested equipment lists. You can use these as models in setting up your own music computing environment.

These setups are grouped according to the musical tasks they are expected to perform. Each setup is optimized for one primary task, but some are multi-functional. The seven categories are 8-bit non-MIDI music, desktop music publishing, MIDI music, 16-bit digital audio, film and video, multimedia, and education. For each of these types of activities, examples are provided that illustrate possible configurations at three levels: entry level, intermediate, and advanced.

You can easily create hybrid setups combining two or more types of activities by noting where the diagrams overlap and where they are different.

The chapter closes with a section illustrating the author's setup with commentary.

Each setup diagram consists of three parts: comments about the setup, a list of equipment shown in the diagram, and the diagram of the setup.

If you are interested in a specific application, it would be to your advantage to read the comments for all the setups in that application category. This is because each one builds upon the one from the previous level, and the relevant comments are often not repeated as you move up the ladder.

Estimated costs

The minimum and maximum dollar figures provided for the price ranges are calculated as follows:

❖ Lower figure = the cost of the setup with the italicized items omitted.

❖ Higher figure = the cost of the setup with the italicized items added in.

Items not figured into the calculations:

❖ The Macintosh itself, meaning the CPU, monitor (and standard video card if applicable), keyboard, and RAM. This is because you will probably purchase the first items at the same time and place and possibly the RAM as well. Even if you purchase the RAM from a third-party vendor, the prices fluctuate so greatly that including its cost in the calculation might be misleading. All other Macintosh peripherals (including the hard drives) are included in the calculations. Where a range of hard drive capacities is listed, the cost used for calculating the lower figure is the cost of the lowest capacity drive. The cost used in the higher figure is the cost of the highest capacity drive for the range listed. Where special video or audio cards are required, these are also figured into the calculations. So, how much should you budget for your Mac CPU, monitor, keyboard and RAM? As the expense of the peripheral gear rises, the proportionate cost of the Macintosh drops. Figure on an additional 50 percent to 200 percent for the entry level configurations, an additional 25 percent to 50 percent for the intermediate setups, and an additional 10 percent to 25 percent for the advanced systems.

❖ Software. Because software selection is a personal matter and prices are so varied, software is not included in the calculations. Be prepared to spend a minimum of an additional 15 percent to 25 percent of the total cost of the setup on software for the entry level setups; an additional 10 percent to 15 percent for the intermediate level setups; and an additional 5 percent to 10 percent for the advanced level setups. These software guidelines refer to music and audio software exclusively. You may want to purchase additional software for other applications such as word processing or managing a database.

❖ Furniture, floppy disks, removable cartridges, cables, and racks. Once again, these are omitted from the calculations because these items are a personal matter and the prices are so varied. Be prepared to spend an additional

2 percent to 10 percent of the total cost of any setup on these types of items — less if you build some of the furniture and racks yourself.

❖ Tax and shipping.

In all cases, prices used for calculation purposes are based upon 80 percent of list price. Also, many of the items I have selected are in the upper echelon of their class, and the prices used for calculations do not take into account rumored or expected reductions coming about through the release of newer models by the same manufacturer or the ever-dropping costs of high technology devices in general. Because of this intentional over-conservativism, you may be pleasantly surprised to discover that many of the setups can be configured at a considerably lower price.

Finally, if you are a shrewd bargainer, you can probably do much better than this. If you pick up some of the equipment used, you can configure any setup at a substantially lower cost.

Remember that hard drives are included in the estimated cost of each setup. Figures used for these drives are based upon typical list prices from high quality vendors such as Microtech. If you already have a hard drive or are planning to purchase a Macintosh with an internal drive, then you can reduce your expenses even more.

Reading the equipment tables

There are five columns in the equipment tables. The first indicates the type of device. The second indicates the example pictured in the diagram. The third suggests possible areas where you might expand the setup. The fourth and fifth provide alternates for the devices pictured in the setup diagram or offered as suggestions for expansion.

❖ Anything in the Pictured column appears in the diagram.

❖ Italicized entries in the Pictured column indicate optional equipment.

❖ Items in the Pictured column are followed by the superscripted number 1 to 6 and a letter. These match up to their appropriate counterparts in the diagram. See Figure 7-1 for the distinctions between the numbers 1 through 6.

❖ The Expansion column suggests items you might want to consider for expanding the setup, depending upon your budget.

❖ The Alternate 1 and Alternate 2 columns illustrate a few alternatives to the pictured item and occasionally alternatives to the Expansion column item if there is no corresponding pictured item. The distinctions are evident. Usually, both alternates are equally valid; however, in many cases, Alternate 1 items will be less expensive than Alternate 2 items. In some cases, an alternative will consist of more devices than the original one for which it is an alternate. For example, an alternate for one pair of powered speakers might consist of separate amplifier and speaker components.

The equipment lists and setup diagrams include many actual product suggestions. These suggestions represent products with which I have had personal experience. The potential for expandability and maximum compatibility within the industry are considerations in all cases.

Key to last 7 columns of Table 7-1

M = MIDI Data
A = Audio Data
S = SCSI Data
T = Time code Data
D = Digital Audio
R = RS-422 and other (inc. AppleTalk)
C = Device Category (see Figure 7-1)

Table 7-1: Devices and data types

Devices used in the setup diagrams			Data types						
Devices [ ]=discontinued but generally available	Devices Pictured in Illustrations	Unpictured Alternate Solutions	M	A	S	T	D	R	C
Macintosh	Compact Mac representing: [Mac Plus] [Mac SE] Mac Classic Mac LC Mac SE/30 Mac II CPU representing: Mac II — 1-slot Mac II si Mac II — 3-slot [Mac II cx] Mac II ci Mac II — 6-slot [Mac II] [Mac IIx] Mac IIfx Mac Standard Kbd Mac Extended Kbd Mac Internal Slots			●	●			●	1
Mac peripherals									
RAM	(not pictured, but 1 to 128MB)								
Monitor	Apple 13" Monitor Apple Full-Page Display Apple 2-Page Display							●	1
Hard drive	Microtech N40 thru N650 Drives Microtech N1000 Gigabyte Drive [Jasmine 80MB Drive]					●			1

Table 7-1: Devices and data types (continued)

Devices used in the setup diagrams			Data types						
Devices [ ]=discontinued but generally available	Devices Pictured in Illustrations	Unpictured Alternate Solutions	M	A	S	T	D	R	C

Backup system	Microtech R-45
	  Cartridge Drive
	Microtech T1200 DAT
	  Backup System
	Microtech OR 650
	  Optical Drive
	Golden Triangle Disk
	  Twin (Disk Duplexing
	  System)
		Microtech T150
		  (TEAC CT-600N tape
		  backup system)
		Genius 8mm tape
		  backup system
					●				1

CD-ROM	Apple CD-ROM Drive	Toshiba XM 3201 CD-ROM Drive			●				1
Printer	Apple ImageWriter LQ (dot matrix) Apple StyleWriter							●	5
PostScript printer	Apple LaserWriter Plus Apple LaserWriter II SC Apple LaserWriter II NT LaserMax 1200	Apple Personal LaserWriter NT TI MicroLaser						●	5

Scanner	Handheld Scanner
	  (generic)
	Apple Flatbed Scanner
	Sharp JX-600 scanner
	  (color)
		La Cie Silverscanner
		  (color)
					◗			●	3

8-bit digitizer	MacroMind-Paracomp
	MacRecorder
		Articulate Systems
		  VoiceLink
		SID (Sound Input
		  Device)
								●	3

Misc. input devices	USR Courier 2400 baud
	  modem
	Telebit T2500 19,200
	  baud modem
	Articulate Systems
	  Voice Navigator
					◗			●	1

Table 7-1: Devices and data types (continued)

Devices used in the setup diagrams			Data types						
Devices [ ]=discontinued but generally available	Devices Pictured in Illustrations	Unpictured Alternate Solutions	M	A	S	T	D	R	C
Video digitizer	Digital Visions Computer Eyes Pro (Video Digitizer)	Koala MacVision Aapps Micro TV, DigiVideo, or DigiVideo Color Orange Micro Personal Vision						●	3
Internal card									
Sample player	Digidesign MacProteus			●					3
Sampler	Digidesign SampleCell			●			●		3
Digital audio	Digidesign Audiomedia Digidesign Sound Accelerator Digidesign AD-IN Digidesign DAT I/O Digidesign Pro I/O			●			●		5
CPU accelerator		16 MHz to 50 MHz CPU accelerators CacheCard			●			●	1
SCSI Enhancement	Daystar SCSI Accelerator	Micronet NuPort			●				1
Video card	8-bit Apple Video Card 8-bit Video Card (generic) 24-bit Apple Video Card 24-bit Video Card (generic)							●	1
Graphics accelerator	Apple 8•24 GC (Graphics Accelerator)	SuperMac graphics accelerator						●	1
Video compression		C-Cube Compression JPEG Compression (note: daughter-board option for RasterOps 364) SuperMac VideoSpigot and VideoSpigot Pro (QuickTime)						●	1

Table 7-1: Devices and data types (continued)

Devices used in the setup diagrams			Data types						
Devices [ ]=discontinued but generally available	Devices Pictured in Illustrations	Unpictured Alternate Solutions	M	A	S	T	D	R	C
Overlay graphics and video		TrueVision NuVista, NuVista+ Mass MicroSystems ColorSpace IIi and ColorSpace FX VideoLogic DVA-4000							
Full-motion display (rw = resizable window)	VideoLogic DVA-4000	RasterOps 364 Mass Micro systems ColorSpace FX Workstation Moon- raker Radius TV TrueVision NuVista+						●	1
Frame grabber	RasterOps 364	Computer Friends ColorSnap 32 TrueVision NuVista+ Mass Micro QuickImage 24, ColorSpace IIi, or ColorSpace FX RasterOps 232/SFX or 24L VideoLogic DVA-4000 Radius TV						●	3
Composite output	TrueVision NuVista, NuVista+	Apple 8•24 GC Mass Micro Easy Video8 or ColorSpace Computer Friends TV ProducerPRO Generation X TV Box RasterOps 232/SFX or 24L VENT Mac Video						●	1
Frame-by-frame output	TrueVision NuVista+ with Diaquest DQ-Animaq	Advanced Digital Imaging MacVac PC VCR						●	5

Table 7-1: Devices and data types (continued)

Devices used in the setup diagrams			Data types						
Devices [ ]=discontinued but generally available	Devices Pictured in Illustrations	Unpictured Alternate Solutions	M	A	S	T	D	R	C
Video processing		VENT Video Master IMT-8000 Digital F/X Video F/X Avid Avid1 Media Composer NewTek Video Toaster						●	1
Interfaces									
16-chan MIDI	Opcode MIDI translator	Apple MIDI Interface Altech MIDI Interface JL Cooper Nexxus series	●					●	2
32-chan MIDI	Opcode Studio 3	Altech MIDI Interface JL Cooper Nexxus series Passport MIDI Transport	●	◗		◗		●	2
>32-chan MIDI	MOTU MTP (MIDI Time Piece)	Opcode Studio 5	●	◗		◗		●	2
SMPTE converter	Opcode Time code Machine	JL Cooper PPS series Roland SBX-1000	●			●			2
VITC converter	MOTU VTP (Video Time Piece)		●			●		●	2
Lock-up system	Adams Smith Zeta-3	Lynx Lockup System	●			●		●	2
SGD & controller									
Kbd controller	Roland PC-200 Roland A-80	Kurzweil MIDIBoard Elka Keyboard Controller	●						3
Analog synth Kbd		Oberheim Matrix-12	●	●					3
Digital synth Kbd		Roland D-20 Yamaha V-50 Yamaha SY-77	●	●					3
Hybrid synth Kbd	Korg Wavestation Korg M1	Roland D-50 Roland D-70	●	●					3

Table 7-1: Devices and data types (continued)

Devices used in the setup diagrams			Data types						
Devices [ ]=discontinued but generally available	Devices Pictured in Illustrations	Unpictured Alternate Solutions	M	A	S	T	D	R	C
Sample player Kbd	Korg T1	Roland U-20 Korg T2 Korg T3 Kurzweil K1200-88 Kurzweil K1200-76	●	●					3
Sampler Kbd	Kurzweil K250	Ensoniq EPS Korg W-30 E-mu E-III Akai S1000KB	●	●	▶			▶	3
Synth/sample Kbd	Kurzweil K2000	E-mu Emax II	●	●	▶		▶	▶	3
Analog module	[Roland MKS-70] Oberheim Matrix-1000	Oberheim Xpander	●	●					3
Digital module	Roland D-550	Roland MT-32 Roland D-110 Yamaha TX-802 Yamaha TG-77	●	●					3
Hybrid module	Roland CM-64 (or other CM Series) Korg M1 Korg M1rex Korg Wavestation A/D	Korg M3r Roland Sound Canvas	●	●					3
Sample player mode	E-mu Proteus/1 E-mu Proteus/2 E-mu Proformance Kurzweil 1000 PX Kurzweil 1000 SX Kurzweil 1000 HX Kurzweil 1000 GX Kurzweil 1200 Pro I Kurzweil 1200 Pro II Kurzweil 1200 Pro III	Roland U-220 Roland Sound Canvas	●	●					3
Sampler module	Roland S-550 Akai S1000	Roland S-330l Roland S-770 Ensoniq EPS (rack mount version)		●	▶			▶	3

Part One: The Basics

Table 7-1: Devices and data types (continued)

Devices used in the setup diagrams			Data types						
Devices [ ]=discontinued but generally available	Devices Pictured in Illustrations	Unpictured Alternate Solutions	M	A	S	T	D	R	C
Synth/sample mode		E-mu Emax II (rack mount version)	●	●					3
Drum machine	Alesis HR and SR series Roland R-8	Roland R-8M Simmons SD series Akai MPC60	●	●					3
Other controller	JL Cooper Fadermaster Lexicon MRC Niche MAS Fadermonster JL Cooper CS-1 Roland CA-30, CA-50, or RA-50		●					▸	3
Audio and DSP									
DSP effects	Lexicon LXP-1 Lexicon LXP-5 Lexicon LXP-15 Lexicon PCM-70 Lexicon 300 Lexicon 480 Lexicon 480 LARC [Roland SRV-2000] Roland SDE-3000 Yamaha SPX-900	Alesis MIDIverb III Alesis Quadraverb Korg A-3 Korg DRV-3000 Roland R-880 LAMS RMX-16 TC Electronics TC1126 Eventide H-3000	●	●				▸	4
Other Signal Processing	BBE 422 or 822A (Sonic Maximizer) DBX 160XT (Compression/Limiter) Rane MPE14 (MIDI EQ)	DBX 165A DBX 166 DBX F-900 Rane DC-24 Dolby A and SR Roland RSS Spatializer Drawmer M-500 (Dynamics Processor) Aphex 612 (Expander/Gate) Orban 764A (MIDI EQ) Roland E-660 (MIDI EQ)	▸	●				▸	4

Table 7-1: Devices and data types (continued)

Devices used in the setup diagrams			Data types						
Devices [ ]=discontinued but generally available	Devices Pictured in Illustrations	Unpictured Alternate Solutions	M	A	S	T	D	R	C
Mixer	Boss BX-8 or BX-80 (8 channel) Roland M-160 (16 channel) Roland M-16E (16 chan with EQ)	Alesis 1622 (16 channel) Hill Audio (16-20 channel) Speck mixers (many configs)		●					4
MIDI-controlled Mixer	MOTU MM7 (MIDI Mixer 7) Niche ACM (Audio Control Module) Yamaha DMC1000 (digital)	Yamaha DMP7 Akai MPX820 Yamaha DMP7D (digital)	●	●			▸		4
Console	24 channel Console (24 chan) 48+ channel Console (greater than 24 chan)		▸	●		▸	▸	▸	4
Amplifier	Amplifier (generic)			●					4
Speaker	Yamaha NS-10M JBL 44-12	Tannoy (near field monitors) Auriton T6 Subcompact		●					4
Powered Speakers	Roland CS-10 Roland MA-12C			●					4
Microphone	Microphone (generic)			●					3
Network									
MIDI Patchbay	KMX MIDI Central	JL Cooper MSB series Lone Wolf MidiTap	●						2
Audio Patchbay	Furman PB-40 Tascam PB-32 Switchcraft TT	360 Systems Audio Matrix-16 Akai Digital Patchbay DP3200	▸	●					4
Speaker Switchbox	Speaker switchbox (generic)			●					4
Serial Data Switcher	Dataspec Serial Switchbox							●	2

Table 7-1: Devices and data types (continued)

Devices used in the setup diagrams			Data types						
Devices [ ]=discontinued but generally available	Devices Pictured in Illustrations	Unpictured Alternate Solutions	M	A	S	T	D	R	C
SCSI Data Switcher	Computer Friends SCSI Switchbox				●				2
Analog Recorder									
Cassette	AIWA WX808 Dual Cassette Deck			●					5
Multitrack	Tascam ATR-60/8 or 60/8HS (8-track) / Tascam 48 or 58 (8-track)] / Fostex G16 (16-track) / Otari MTR-80-24 or MTR-100A (24-track)			●		●		●	5
Integrated Mixer/Deck	Fostex 280 / Akai MG1214	Akai MG14D / Tascam 246 Portastudio / Tascam 688 MIDI Studio		●		●		●	5
Mixdown Deck	Fostex E2			●		●		●	5
Digital Recorder									
DtHD (Mac/external)		Studer Dyaxis / Roland DM-80 / Lexicon Opus / Akai DD1000	►	●		►	●	●	5
Digital MTR		Akai DR1200 / DASH MTR - Sony or Studer		●		►	●	●	5
DAT	Panasonic SV-3700 / Sony PCM-7050 (time code)	Panasonic SV-3900 / JVC DSDT900 (time code) / Fostex D-20 (time code)		●		►	●	►	5
Video									
Deck	JVC BR-7700U (½") / Sony VOS-9850 (¾")	AIWA 900 (½") / JVC 2000 (¾")		●		●		●	6

Table 7-1: Devices and data types (continued)

Devices used in the setup diagrams			Data types						
Devices [ ]=discontinued but generally available	**Devices Pictured in Illustrations**	**Unpictured Alternate Solutions**	**M**	**A**	**S**	**T**	**D**	**R**	**C**
Serial-controlled Deck (LANC Protocol aka Control-L)	Sony EVS-900 (Hi8) Sony SLV-757 (VHS)	Sony EV-C3 (8mm) Sony SLV-676 (VHS) Sony SLV-R5UC (SVHS) NEC PC-VCR (SVHS)		●				●	6
Serial-controlled Videodisc Player	Pioneer LVP-8000	Pioneer LVP-4200 Pioneer LVP-2200 Sony LDP-2000		●				●	6
Monitor	JVC 27" Monitor (NTSC) Sony GVM-1300 (multisync)	Sony Trinitron Monitor Mitsubishi Monitor							
Camera	Sony V-101 (Hi-8) Sony Mavica (still digital camera)	Sony TR5 (8mm) Sony V-5000 (Hi8)		●				●	6

Yes, a super-studio would contain at least one of each of the items listed above.

Reading the setup diagrams

In general, the setup diagrams read from left to right with respect to input, editing, and output. Going one level deeper, you will see that the data path often describes a circle or spiral with the Mac at the beginning. When viewed in this way, there are up to six main areas on the diagrams. These are:

1. The Macintosh area
2. The interface area
3. The input and sound-generating area
4. The mixing and processing area
5. The output and recording area
6. The video area

These numbers also correspond to the superscripts in the table provided with each diagram and are used to label the actual items on the diagram itself. See Figure 7-1.

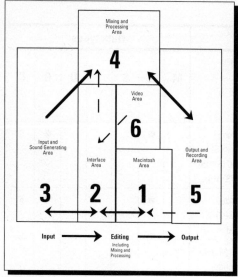

Figure 7-1: Setup Flow (basic).

In most cases, the actual devices themselves are located in the area corresponding to their device category. There are some exceptions. For example, digital audio direct-to-hard disk recording cards and their associated interfaces (technically area 5 items) are located in the Macintosh area (area 1) along with the extended chassis representing an opened Macintosh CPU. The same holds for internal sound-generating cards, which are labeled with area 3 superscripts.

These six areas are further broken down into sub-areas as indicated in Figure 7-2.

Keep in mind that not all setups require gear in all these categories. In these cases, rather than spread everything out inordinately, for considerations of readability, the diagrams are collapsed into a smaller space with the various components in the same general relationship to the Macintosh.

Seven different types of data paths are indicated. Three of these data paths are available as single cables or as "snakes" (larger cables made up of many grouped single cables). Therefore, ten different types of cables are represented. The key to reading this cabling symbology is provided in Figure 7-3.

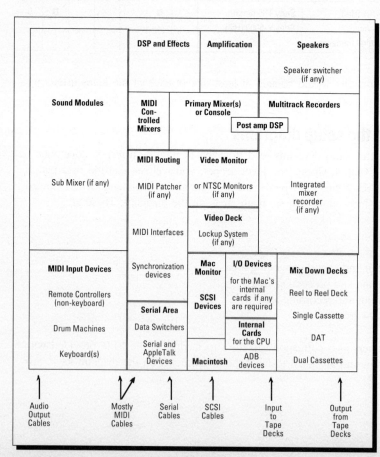

Figure 7-2: Setup Flow (detail).

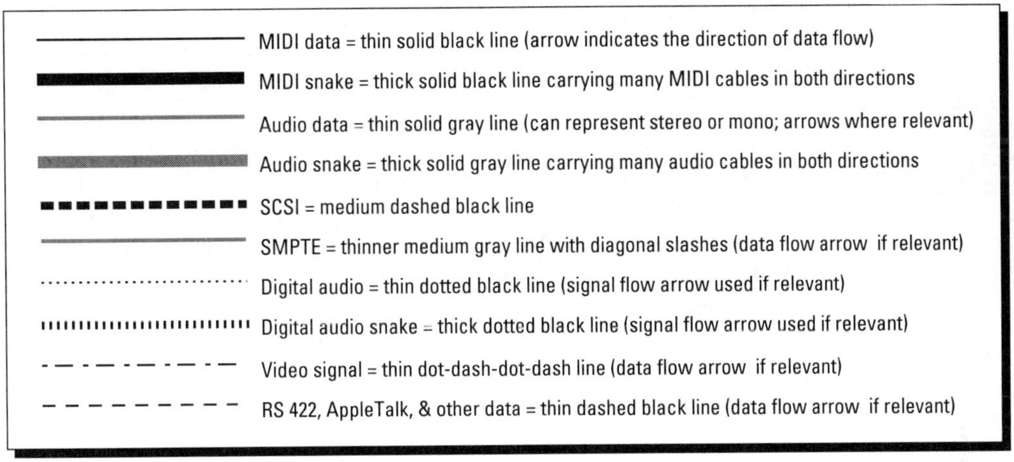

————————	MIDI data = thin solid black line (arrow indicates the direction of data flow)
████████████	MIDI snake = thick solid black line carrying many MIDI cables in both directions
————————	Audio data = thin solid gray line (can represent stereo or mono; arrows where relevant)
▓▓▓▓▓▓▓▓▓▓	Audio snake = thick solid gray line carrying many audio cables in both directions
▪ ▪ ▪ ▪ ▪ ▪ ▪ ▪ ▪	SCSI = medium dashed black line
————————	SMPTE = thinner medium gray line with diagonal slashes (data flow arrow if relevant)
· · · · · · · · · · · · ·	Digital audio = thin dotted black line (signal flow arrow used if relevant)
‖‖‖‖‖‖‖‖‖‖‖‖‖‖	Digital audio snake = thick dotted black line (signal flow arrow used if relevant)
– · — · — · — · —	Video signal = thin dot-dash-dot-dash line (data flow arrow if relevant)
– – – – – – –	RS 422, AppleTalk, & other data = thin dashed black line (data flow arrow if relevant)

Figure 7-3: Cable Keys.

Pre-planning and final points to consider

The setup of configurations are purposely very general and planned to cover a wide variety of situations. Your personal needs and budget may steer you into one direction or another.

After considering which particular Macintosh to purchase, that is, if you haven't got one already, in most cases, your next most important consideration is the master MIDI controller that you will use as a primary musical input device.

In the setup diagrams, I have normally indicated a "dumb" (possesses no sound-generating capabilities) MIDI keyboard controller in this capacity. However, if you are not a keyboard player, you may substitute a MIDI guitar, violin, EWI, EVI, or whatever your instrument happens to be. MIDI guitar experts seem to believe that certain modules respond better than others to this type of controller. Notable among these are the Oberheim Xpander, Yamaha TX81Z and TX802, and the Ensoniq EPS 16 Plus.

On the other hand, you may want to substitute a sampled or digital piano with MIDI for any of the MIDI controllers listed below. Most of these range from $3,000 to $5,000, except for Yamaha's DiskClavier, which lists for about $20,000. Many include additional sounds besides just a piano and also include built-in amplifier and speakers. Following are some popular models, all with 88 weighted keys.

❖ Bachmann WS400   ❖ Technics SX-PX66M
❖ Kawai MR3000   ❖ Yamaha CVP-50 Clavinova
❖ Korg SGX Sampling Grand ❖ Yamaha DiskClavier
❖ Kurzweil Mark IV

Most of the intermediate and advanced setups assume an 88-note keyboard as the controller. However, you should be aware that there are often 76-note and/or 61-note alternatives to many of the models listed.

Conversely, many of the entry level setups use a Roland PC-200 as the controller keyboard for purposes of illustration. Although the PC-200 has only 49 unweighted keys, there is an octave shift button. It is velocity-sensitive and provides a minimum set of MIDI remote control functions. Its light weight makes it perfect for traveling. The fact that it can be run on batteries makes it a perfect choice for someone with a Macintosh Portable and an unpowered MIDI interface (such as Apple's own) to take to the beach or mountaintop and compose their next symphony in peace. There aren't any velocity-sensitive keyboards even close to the price of the PC-200, which I have seen at well below $300.

Although I have, for purposes of illustration, often used a dumb keyboard controller as the primary MIDI device, you might just as easily substitute a synthesizer, sampler, or sample-playing keyboard as your primary controller. In all cases, I have provided for this approach in the "alternate" columns.

When substituting a sound-generating keyboard for a dumb MIDI controller, you may want to consider adding a module to complement the type of synthesis in your sound-generating controller. Therefore, if you choose a synthesizer as your main MIDI keyboard controller, you should consider a sampler or sample-player as your first modular device. Likewise, if you choose a sampler or sample-player as your main MIDI keyboard controller, consider a synthesizer as your first module. Of course, if you are only interested in creating music that sounds like acoustic instruments, you may want all your modules to be of the sampler/sample-player variety.

Carrying the idea of a complementary sound palette a bit further, many of the intermediate and advanced setups include representatives from many different types of synthesis. With this in mind, as the setups become more complex, each type of synthesis becomes filled in (analog, digital, hybrid, sampler, sample-player, and synthesizer/sampler). When you have a well-rounded system that contains most of these categories, then you should look into expanding into multiple devices within a single synthesis category.

Similarly, for purposes of illustration, I have been conservative on the number of effects and digital signal processing devices included in each diagram. This, once again, is a personal and financial matter and it is an area where one person might want the same number of effects as sound-generating devices, another person might require five or six times the number of effects as their number of sound-generating devices, and yet another can get by on a single effect.

Audio patchbays have been omitted from the diagrams because they would obscure the actual data path for the purposes of illustration. All audio input and output cables would simply arrive at the audio patchbay and you would not be provided with any information about the actual destinations. Many setups list the audio patchbay as "not pictured," which is to say that one would be highly recommended in that situation. Knowing the actual sources and destinations of all the cables provides you with the most crucial information needed for configuring a normaled or half-normaled patchbay.

Budget-stretching tips

The following are some tips for cutting down on the price of many of the sample setups:

❖ Omit some or all of the italicized items.

❖ Substitute your home stereo system for the audio reinforcement components.

❖ Eliminate the audio reinforcement components entirely by using a pair of headphones.

❖ Substitute a sound-generating keyboard in place of a dumb keyboard controller.

❖ Cut down on the number of effects.

❖ Don't purchase a MIDI interface with synchronization features unless you need it.

❖ Use virtual tracks in place of additional analog tape-recorder tracks. With the expansion of the available polyphony and multitimbrality of current sound-generating devices and the number of MIDI channels concurrently available (to 512 if you have four MIDI Time Pieces), many people are finding that it is possible to record directly to the final stereo mix rather than recording a track at a time on an expensive analog multitrack recorder and then mixing down to stereo from there. An advantage of this is that you omit one recording generation.

❖ Exploit the virtual mixer capabilities of your sequencer instead of buying a full-blown outboard mixer. Careful editing of velocity and volume (controller 7) data can reduce the need for a sophisticated mixer; a simple line mixer might do the job. Similarly, repeatedly copying and merging MIDI data with a slight offset can often substitute for a digital delay line (DDL).

❖ Rent little-used equipment when you need it. For example, if you are doing lots of MIDI sequenced music, you may be able to get away without a multitrack recorder, only renting one for a day or two when you finally have everything perfect. If you prefer to work with a multitrack recorder during the composition process, consider renting a mixdown deck rather than purchasing mixdown gear. The same thing goes for effects. You can rent a $15,000 reverberator for a weekend when you are doing the final mix and have an extra $14,800 to play with. If you carefully consider exactly what proportion of your time will be spent using a specific device, you may find that the number of days you actually use your recording and mixdown devices is relatively insignificant compared to the amount of time you spend using your actual sound-generating devices.

❖ Rent time on expensive equipment. If you are doing notation, there are many service bureaus that rent time on laser printers or phototypesetting machines. Kinko's is one nationwide chain that provides such a service. If there is no Linotronic output bureau in your city, there are many available via modem. Similarly, there are enough studios completely dedicated to the mixdown process that you can rent some time whenever necessary.

❖ Find and utilize compatible studios where you can simply bring a floppy disk or hard drive with your files on it and output your music on a million dollars' worth of gear.

❖ Substitute a lower-priced unit for the one listed in either the "Pictured" column or the "Alternate 1" and "Alternate 2" columns. One good example of this is that for setups that list a video deck, I have used the JVC BR7700U ($3,200) in all cases. The reasons for this are (1) based upon my own survey of intermediate to professional studios; and (2) because this model has "lock-up" capabilities (thus fulfilling my upwardly compatible requirement). It is possible to find less expensive video decks that have a jog wheel or frame advance in the $800 range (for example, the AIWA 900). Likewise, for the ¾-inch deck you could substitute a JVC 2000 ($3,000) for the Sony 5050 ($6,000). Another example is the setups that feature interactive videodisc players. I have listed the Pioneer 8000 ($2,000) because it is the industry-preferred model for development situations. For non-development purposes, you could get by with a Pioneer 4200 ($1,000) or even a Pioneer 2200 ($750).

❖ Become aware of the interdependency of devices. Removing one of the devices may allow you to forego another one or two related purchases. For example, samplers like the K250 that support external hard drives are some-times paired with Syquest-based cartridge drives and SCSI switch boxes. The logic behind this is that, by using a SCSI switch box, you can make the

Syquest drive perform double duty, meaning that some of the cartridges can be formatted for the Macintosh and some for the sampler, a highly recommended alternative to purchasing a dedicated hard drive for a sampler. Instead of spending a thousand dollars on the dedicated drive, all you need is another $65 Syquest cartridge formatted for the specific sampler. Note that some samplers such as the Akai S1000, Ensoniq EPS, and E-mu EIII can be installed directly on the Macintosh SCSI bus without the need of a SCSI switch box. Nonetheless, you may still want to use a SCSI switch box to increase your number of available SCSI addresses or to solve problems that may arise when such devices are introduced into the SCSI chain. Concerning MIDI data, substituting a MIDI interface with a built-in switch that can reroute the Macintosh serial port to your modem can eliminate the need for a serial switch box. Similarly, the Lexicon MRC, although configurable for a wide variety of tasks, really shines when used in conjunction with a Lexicon effects processor. If you already have an ample number of non-Lexicon effects, you could easily drop the MRC from any of the setups.

Macintosh Music Setups

8-bit non-MIDI music

(For a detailed discussion see Parts Two and Three.)

Entry level	**$500 – $1,000**
Intermediate	**$1,800 – $4,200**
Advanced	**$4,800 – $10,600**

If your focus is on 8-bit non-MIDI music you can expect to achieve results with the lowest financial outlay.

The first thing that you will want to purchase is a device capable of digitizing external sounds into 8-bit samples. Next you will need a sound system of some kind to plug into your Macintosh's audio output port. Finally, you may want to invest in some recording equipment and effects to widen the possibilities for audio input or to capture your creations for posterity.

Setup 1: Entry level 8-bit non-MIDI music
($500 – $1,000)
This setup provides for sound digitization with MacroMind-Paracomp's MacRecorder and playback through Roland's CS-10 powered speaker combination (see Table 7-2).

Table 7-2: Setup 1 — Entry level 8-bit non-MIDI music

	Pictured	Expansion	Alternate 1	Alternate 2
Macintosh	Compact Mac [1a]		Mac LC	
Mac Peripherals				
RAM	2 to 4MB	5 to 8MB		
Hard Drive		40 to 80MB Drive		
Backup System		Syquest		
CD-ROM		CD-ROM w/ audio		
Printer		Dot Matrix Printer		
8-bit Digitizer	MacroMind-Para-comp MacRecorder [3a]		VoiceLink	SID
Misc. Input Devices	*USR Courier 2400 baud modem* [1b]			
Internal Card				
CPU Accelerator		16 to 32 MHz card		
Audio and DSP				
Amplifier				Amplifier
Speaker				NS-10M
Powered Speakers	Roland CS-10 [4a]		Roland MA-12C	
Network				
Serial Data Switcher	*Dataspec Serial Switchbox* [2a]			
Analog Recorder				
Cassette	*AIWA WX808 Dual Deck*[5a]			
Integrated Mixer/Deck		Fostex 280	Fostex 280	

You may want to add a modem for the purpose of collecting soundfiles from on-line services where you will find them overflowing the data libraries. Adding a modem might prompt you to add a serial switch box so that you can switch between the modem and the sound input device with the press of a button.

The optional cassette recorder provides you with line-input to your digitizer and expands the sound palette you have at your disposal. You may also choose to add a dual cassette to facilitate making copies of your creations (see Figure 7-4).

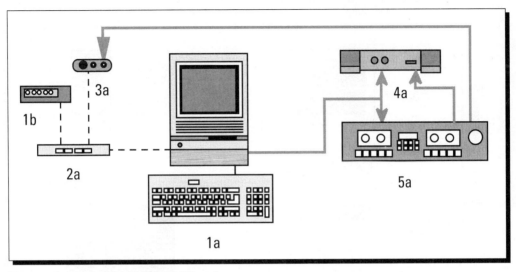

Figure 7-4: Setup 1: Entry level 8-bit non-MIDI music.

Both SoundEdit and SoundWave provide editing tools that allow you to transform your soundfiles in many of the ways you would using 16-bit soundfiles with tools that require investments of ten or more times your investment here. However, many of the techniques you can acquire working with these programs will provide you with much of the background needed in the 16-bit digital audio world.

You can use your 8-bit sounds and music tracks in HyperCard, SuperCard, or Director or make instruments out of them to expand the offerings of Studio Session and Jam Session. Both Music Mouse and Ovaltunes are as fun without MIDI as they are with MIDI, and the education package Practica Musica is also serviceable in a non-MIDI environment.

If you already have a cassette recorder or a sound system, you can reduce your expenses accordingly.

Setup 2: Intermediate 8-bit non-MIDI music
($1,800 – $4,200)

This configuration adds multitrack recording via the Fostex 280 (integrated mixer and multitrack cassette deck) to the capabilities of setup 1 and assumes that you will be on-line with a modem downloading sounds (see Table 7-3). An optional CD-ROM drive is included because some third parties are beginning to market 8-bit samples and clip music on CD-ROMs, and many multimedia pieces that you will want to study are available in this format too.

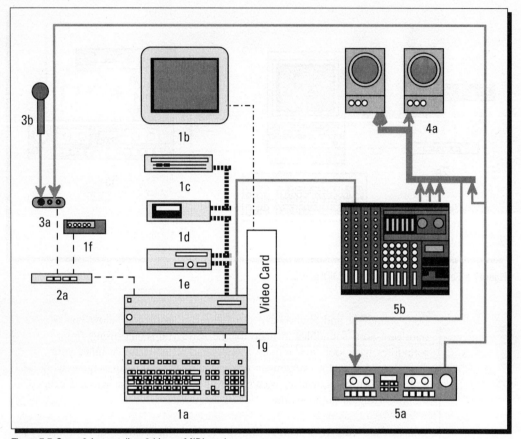

Figure 7-5: Setup 2: Intermediate 8-bit non-MIDI music.

Because both the multitrack recorder, CD-ROM drive, and the modem will greatly increase your sound library, a hard drive has been added to increase your storage capacity. A Syquest removable cartridge drive is suggested as a backup and also because you may start creating soundfiles that no longer fit onto floppy disks; Syquest 45MB or 88MB cartridges are an excellent way to transport your work from one location to another.

Having moved up to this intermediate level, you will probably want to use a higher quality microphone than the one built into your 8-bit digitizer. Having the microphone will also increase your versatility for source material that you can record into the Fostex 280.

In Figure 7-5, the sound playback system has been upgraded to a pair of Roland MA-12C powered speakers.

You may want to consider a sound-editing program that can handle both 8-bit and 16-bit soundfiles such as Passport's Sound Apprentice to add the sophisticated editing features normally associated with 16-bit digital audio.

Table 7-3: Setup 2 — Intermediate 8-bit non-MIDI music			
	Pictured	**Expansion**	**Alternate 1**	**Alternate 2**
Mac Peripherals				
RAM	4 to 8MB	More than 8MB		
Monitor	Apple 13" Monitor [1b]		Apple Full-page Display	Color
Hard Drive	Microtech 40-200MB [1c]		Additional Storage	
Backup System	Microtech Syquest [1d]		Microtech T150	
CD-ROM	Apple CD-ROM Drive [1e]			
Printer		Dot Matrix Printer		
PostScript Printer			LaserWriter SC	
8-bit Digitizer	MacroMind-Para-comp MacRecorder [3a]		Articulate Systems VoiceLink	SID
Misc. Input Devices	USR Courier 2400 baud modem [1f]			
Internal Card				
CPU Accelerator		32-50 MHz card	CacheCard	
Video Card		Color Video Card		
Audio and DSP				
Amplifier		Amplifier		
Speakers		Yamaha NS-10M	Tannoy	
Powered Speakers	Roland MA-12C [4a]			
Microphone	Microphone [3b]			
Network				
Serial Data Switcher	Dataspec Serial Switchbox [2a]			
Analog Recorder				
Cassette	AIWA WX808 Deck [5a]			
Integrated Mixer/Deck	Fostex 280 [5b]			

Setup 3: Advanced 8-bit non-MIDI music
($4,800 – $10,600)

If you are going to take 8-bit audio this far, you will want to be using a more powerful Macintosh with a larger screen. Your soundfiles are going to get bigger and the larger screen will allow you to view more for editing purposes. Of course, with your soundfiles getting larger you will need a larger capacity hard drive and definitely a removable 45MB or 88MB Syquest drive for transporting them.

As a serious 8-bit sound designer, a CD-ROM drive is mandatory, as is a modem. A dot matrix printer is suggested at the very least, if only because you will want to keep your sounds organized and categorized and such organization implies the printing of reports and indexes. However, if you are going to make this kind of financial commitment to expanding the musical capabilities of your Macintosh, you will probably find many other uses for the printer as well.

The scanner, which makes up $1,800 of the cost, is suggested for those who are developing HyperCard stacks or SuperCard projects for multimedia or educational purposes.

At this level, you may want to start utilizing a MIDI keyboard controlling a sound-generating device such as Roland's CM-64 (pictured) or one of their CM-32 modules to record sounds or music into your 8-bit digitizers (see Table 7-4). There are two digitizers suggested to provide for stereo input. The drum machine is also suggested as a useful adjunct.

Considering the possibility of actually performing the music you are digitizing, several effects devices have been suggested. The first is a Lexicon LXP-1 that will provide you with a variety of reverbs, delays, and many other interesting DSP effects. A BBE Sonic Maximizer is also pictured. This DSP device performs time-alignment of the upper partials of your sounds and can restore or add realism to any sound you put through it.

Notice that the MIDI gear is not interfaced to the Macintosh. This is because the setup is geared toward 8-bit non-MIDI music. The simple addition of a single-input low-cost interface (around $80) and appropriate MIDI software would convert this setup to a dual purpose 8-bit non-MIDI plus MIDI music system.

You can still do some MIDI music with this setup without a MIDI interface. By using Apple's MIDI Manager in conjunction with Passport's virtual synthesizer, the Sound Exciter, you can play back music from most MIDI sequencers by patching their output to the Sound Exciter's input. Because the Sound Exciter is a synthesizer created in software, no external MIDI connections are required. Furthermore, you can create new instruments for this software synthesizer using the 8-bit sound-digitizing tools required by each of these first three setups.

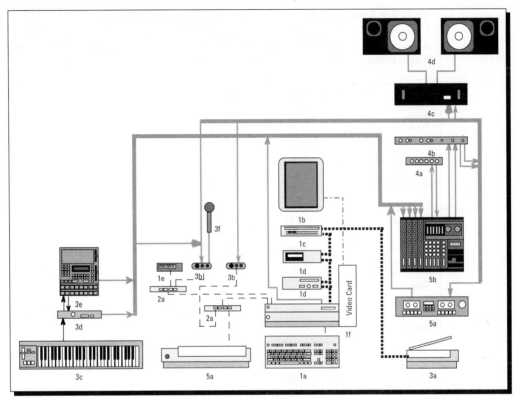

Figure 7-6: Setup 3: Advanced 8-bit non-MIDI music.

Once again, the sound playback system has been upgraded, this time to a separate amplifier and a pair of professional Yamaha NS-10M speakers. This audio setup will also serve you well should you expand your setup to a multifunction one (see Figure 7-6).

Table 7-4: Setup 3 — Advanced 8-bit non-MIDI music

	Pictured	Expansion	Alternate 1	Alternate 2
Macintosh	Mac II — 3- or 6-slot [1a]		Mac II — 6-slot	
Mac Peripherals				
RAM	8MB	More than 8MB		
Monitor	Apple Full-page Display [1b]		Apple 2-page Display	Color
Hard Drive	Microtech N40 thru N650 Drives [1c]	Additional Storage		

Table 7-4: Setup 3 — Advanced 8-bit non-MIDI music (continued)

	Pictured	Expansion	Alternate 1	Alternate 2
Backup System	Microtech Syquest [1d]	Microtech T150	Microtech T150	Golden Triangle DiskTwin
CD-ROM	Apple CD-ROM Drive [1d]			
Printer	*Apple Imagewriter LQ* [5a]		LaserWriter II SC	
PostScript Printer			LaserWriter II	
Scanner	*Apple Flatbed Scanner* [3a]			
8-bit Digitizer	2 MacroMind-Para-comp MacRecorders [3b]		Articulate Systems VoiceLink	SID
Misc. Input Devices	USR Courier 2400 baud modem [1e]	Articulate Systems Voice Navigator		

Internal Card

Sample Player		Digidesign MacProteus		
CPU Accelerator		32-50 MHz card	CacheCard	
Video Card	Video Card [1f]	Color Video Card		

SGD & Controller

Kbd Controller	*Roland PC-200* [3c]			
Hybrid Synth Kbd			Korg M1	
Sample Player Kbd			Roland U-20	Kurzweil K1200-88 Korg T1
Hybrid Module	*Roland CM-64 (or other CM series)* [3d]		Korg M1r	Roland Sound Canvas
Samp. Play. Mod.		E-mu Proteus/2	Kurzweil K1200 series	
Drum Machine	*Alesis SR-16* [3e]	Alesis SR-16B	Roland R-8	

Audio and DSP

DSP Effects	*Lexicon LXP-1* [4a]	Lexicon LXP-5	Roland SRV-2000	Roland SPX-900
Other Signal Processing	*BBE 422 or 822A* [4b]	DBX 160XT		
Amplifier	Amplifier [4c]			
Speakers	Yamaha NS-10M [4d]	Full-size monitors	Tannoy	
Powered Speakers		Roland MA-12C		
Microphone	Microphone [3f]			

Table 7-4: Setup 3 — Advanced 8-bit non-MIDI music (continued)

	Pictured	Expansion	Alternate 1	Alternate 2
Network				
Serial Data Switcher	Dataspec Serial Switchbox [2a]			
Analog Recorder				
Cassette	AIWA WX808 Dual Deck [5a]			
Multitrack		Tascam 48		
Integrated Mixer/Deck	Fostex 280 [5b]			

Desktop music publishing

(For details see Part Four, "Notation.")

Entry level $1,600 – $2,500

Intermediate $4,900 – $7,200

Advanced #1 $13,800 – $26,200

Advanced #2 $22,500 – $35,000

To get into desktop music publishing, all you really need is software that allows you to enter notes on the screen with a click of the mouse, or to "play" the Macintosh keyboard in a mode that remaps the letter keys to musical pitches. This notwithstanding, there are a few add-ons that will make your task much simpler.

The first add-on you should consider is a printer of some kind. At the lower end, you may want to stick with a dot matrix printer such as the Apple ImageWriter LQ or StyleWriter, because you can always take your music to outside service bureaus when you need PostScript output. Having a printer at home will allow you to proofread your music before taking it to a service bureau.

Nowadays, most notation packages provide for MIDI input and you can enter music with a musical keyboard much faster than with a mouse.

Using a MIDI keyboard doesn't require that you have any MIDI sound-generating devices because many notation packages provide for non-MIDI proofhearing. Similarly, as suggested in setup 3, you can use Passport's Sound Exciter to enhance the playback capabilities of MIDI-Manager-compatible notation programs.

Of course, the best proofhearing comes when you can hear the notated score with some approximation of the instruments that are going to be playing it. Because of this, the intermediate and advanced desktop music publishing setups contain sample playback modules and more sophisticated sound systems.

Setup 4: Entry level desktop music publishing
($1,600 – $2,500)

Notation files tend to be large, so even this entry level setup includes a hard drive.

A dot matrix printer is recommended for proofreading. An Apple ImageWriter LQ can be used for final output if you are using a notation program that supports fonts for which you have one triple in size of the one used by the program (see Table 7-5). This is because the printer uses the larger sized font to scale down a high quality version of your music font at actual size. An Apple StyleWriter uses outline fonts, so font-scaling is not required.

Having a modem is a good idea if you are planning to transfer your files to output service bureaus for printing with 300 or greater dpi laser printers and phototypesetters. A modem can also come in handy if you are going to set yourself up in business converting SMFs into notation, because many notation programs now provide for the direct conversion of SMFs into CMN.

Finally, if you are going to be entering a large amount of music into notation software, a MIDI keyboard can speed up the process significantly. If you are not planning on ever doing anything else with your MIDI entry controller, you may wish to substitute a Roland PC-100 for the keyboard pictured in Figure 7-7 (a Roland PC-200), because the PC-100 does not transmit velocity, and velocity sensing is something that you may not be concerned with when strictly entering notes for music notation rather than playback.

No sound-generating devices are included in this setup. It is assumed that at this level you will use the Macintosh speaker-based proofhearing capabilities of the notation software rather than external devices or simply proofread your music rather than proofhear it. If you go with the former strategy, a set of powered speakers is recommended.

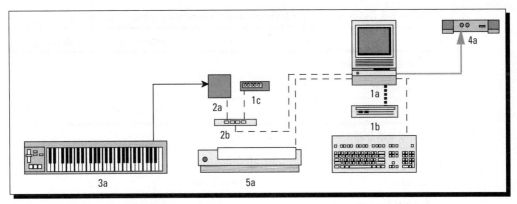

Figure 7-7: Setup 4: entry level desktop music publishing.

Table 7-5: Setup 4 — Entry level desktop music publishing

	Pictured	Expansion	Alternate 1	Alternate 2
Macintosh	Compact Mac preferably SE/30 [1a]		Mac II series	
Mac Peripherals				
RAM	2.5 to 4MB			
Monitor		Larger monitor	Apple 13" Monitor	Full-page display
Hard Drive	40-80MB [1b]	Additional storage		
Backup System		Microtech Syquest		
Printer	Apple ImageWriter LQ [5a]	Non-PS Laserprinter		
PostScript Printer			PS Laserprinter	
Misc. Input Devices	*USR Courier 2400 baud modem* [1c]	Articulate Systems Voice Navigator		Presto Pad (for Music Publisher Software)
Internal Card				
Sample Player		Digidesign MacProteus		
CPU Accelerator		16-32 MHz card		
Interfaces				
16-chan MIDI	*Opcode MIDI translator* [2a]			
32-chan MIDI		Opcode Studio 3	Altech MIDI Interface	Passport MIDI Transport

Table 7-5: Setup 4 — Entry level desktop music publishing (continued)

	Pictured	Expansion	Alternate 1	Alternate 2
SGD & Controller				
Kbd Controller	Roland PC-200 [3a]			
Sample Player Kbd			Kurzweil K1200-88	
Audio and DSP				
Amplifier		Outboard Amplifier		
Speakers		Yamaha NS-10M		
Powered Speakers	Roland CS-10 [4a]		Roland MA-12C	
Network				
Serial Data Switcher	Dataspec Serial Switchbox [2b]			

Setup 5: Intermediate desktop music publishing
($4,900 – $7,200)

This setup is similar to setup 4, except that it is assumed that you will require a PostScript output device capable of at least 300 dpi. Output at that resolution is acceptable for many purposes, even, in some cases, as publication masters.

One important item to check when buying a laser printer is how often you have to replace the engine. Most Apple laser printers can print 150,000 pages before requiring an engine change. At least one new low-cost PostScript laser printer that is getting rave reviews in the press, requires an engine change every 15,000 pages. At $289 for a replacement engine, by the time you reach 150,000 pages, you will have spent an additional $2,890 on the laser printer that seemed to be such a good deal. Most reviewers fail to take this into consideration and it is not in a manufacturer's best interest to place such information in their advertisements.

Because you will often be using software that allows you to view your music and edit in a Page View, you should have a monitor capable of displaying at least a single full page at a size you do not need a magnifying glass to read.

The facility for proofhearing your notation is standard at this level. An E-mu Proteus/2 is recommended because it is 16-channel multitimbral and provides for 32-voice polyphony. Also, the Proteus/2 includes credible samples of virtually every instrument in the orchestra, and because the vast majority of notated music is concerned with eventual performance by live musicians on acoustic instruments, this module will serve you well in most situations.

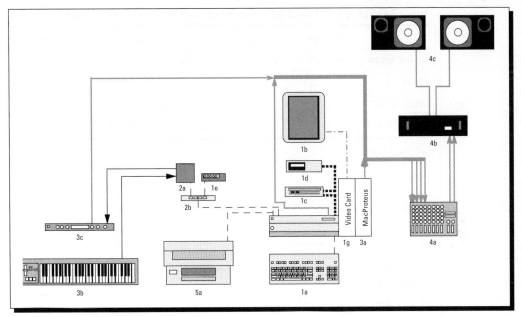

Figure 7-8: Setup 5: Intermediate desktop music publishing.

The one instrument missing from the Proteus/2 is a piano and that explains the suggestion in the Expansion column (see Table 7-6) of a piano module such as the E-mu Proformance or the internal MacProteus card (which also includes a piano sound). Another solution would be to have the MacProteus card as your sole sound-generating device and thus create a self-contained music notation workstation within your Macintosh. The disadvantage of the MacProteus is that it is a Proteus/1 rather than a Proteus/2 and is missing a large number of the acoustic instruments that you are likely to require.

Because of these proofhearing considerations, the sound system has been up-graded from that suggested at the entry level (see Figure 7-8).

Table 7-6: Setup 5 — Intermediate desktop music publishing

	Pictured	Expansion	Alternate 1	Alternate 2
Macintosh	Mac IIsi or ci [1a]		Other Mac II	
Mac Peripherals				
RAM	4 to 5MB			
Monitor	Apple Full-page Display [1b]		Apple 2-page Display	
Hard Drive	40 to 80MB [1c]			

Table 7-6: Setup 5 — Intermediate desktop music publishing (continued)

	Pictured	Expansion	Alternate 1	Alternate 2
Backup System	Microtech Syquest [1d] Golden Triangle DiskTwin			
Printer			Non-PS Laserprinter	
PostScript Printer	PS Laserprinter [5a]			
Misc. Input Devices	Modem [1e]		Articulate Systems Voice Navigator	

Internal Card

	Pictured	Expansion	Alternate 1	Alternate 2
Sample Player	Digidesign MacProteus [3a]			
CPU Accelerator		32-50 MHz card		
SCSI Enhancement				
Video Card	Video Card [1g]			

Interfaces

	Pictured	Expansion	Alternate 1	Alternate 2
16-chan MIDI	Opcode MIDI Translator [2a]			

SGD & Controller

	Pictured	Expansion	Alternate 1	Alternate 2
Kbd Controller	Roland PC-200 [3b]		Roland A-80	
Sample Player Kbd			Roland U-20	Kurzweil K1200
Samp. Play. Mod.	E-mu Proteus/2 [3c]	E-mu Proformance	Roland U-220	Roland Sound Canvas

Audio and DSP

	Pictured	Expansion	Alternate 1	Alternate 2
DSP Effects		Lexicon LXP-1		
Mixer	Boss BX-8 or BX-80 [4a]			
Amplifier	Amplifier [4b]			
Speakers	Yamaha NS-10M [4c]			
Powered Speakers			Roland MA-12C	

Network

	Pictured	Expansion	Alternate 1	Alternate 2
Serial Data Switcher	Dataspec Serial Switchbox [2b]			

Setup 6: Advanced desktop music publishing

$13,800 – $26,200 (for a 1,000 x 1,000 dpi printer)
$22,500 – $35,000 (for a 1,200 x 1,200 dpi and 11 x 17-inch printer)

The greater portion of your budget in an advanced desktop music publishing setup will be spent on a printer of greater than 600 dpi resolution. Fortunately, there are now alternatives to buying $60,000 to $100,000 phototypesetters to achieve greater than 1,000 dpi or that print on paper up to 11 x 17-inches (see Table 7-7). The one pictured in Figure 7-9 is the LaserMax 1200, which lists for about $18,000. Of course if you really require 2,540 dpi you may still want to take your files to a Linotronic service bureau.

Table 7-7: Setup 6 — Advanced desktop music publishing

	Pictured	Expansion	Alternate 1	Alternate 2
Macintosh	Mac IIfx [1a]		Accelerated Mac II series	
Mac Peripherals				
RAM	8MB or more			
Monitor	Apple 2-page Display [1b]			
Hard Drive	100MB to 300MB [1c]			
Backup System	Microtech Syquest [1d]		Microtech DAT	
PostScript Printer	>600 dpi printer e.g., LaserMax 1200 [5a]			
Telecommunication	Modem of 2400 baud or greater [1e]			
Misc. Input Devices	*Articulate Systems Voice Navigator* [1f]			
Internal Card				
Sample Player	*Digidesign MacProteus* [3a]			
CPU Accelerator		50MHz or more		
SCSI Enhancement	*Daystar SCSI Accelerator* [1g]			
Video Card	Video Card [1h]			
Graphics Accelerator		Apple 8•24 GC		
Interfaces				
32-chan MIDI	Opcode Studio 3 [2a]		Altech MIDI Interface	Passport MIDI Transport
>32-chan MIDI		MOTU MTP	Opcode Studio 5	

Table 7-7: Setup 6 — Advanced desktop music publishing (continued)

	Pictured	Expansion	Alternate 1	Alternate 2
SGD & Controller				
Kbd Controller	Roland A-80 [3b]			
Sample Player Kbd			Kurzweil K1200-88	Korg T1
Samp. Play. Mod.	E-mu Proteus/2 [3c]	E-mu Proformance		
Sampler Module	*Akai S-1000* [3d]			
Synth/Sampler Mod.				Kurzweil K2000
Other Controller	*JL Cooper CS-1* [2b]			
Audio and DSP				
DSP Effects	Lexicon LXP-5 [4a]	Roland SRV-2000	Yamaha SPX-900	
Other Signal Processing	*BBE 422 or 822A* [4b]	DBX 160XT		
Mixer	Boss BX-8 or BX-80 [4c]			
Amplifier	Amplifier [4d]			
Speakers	JBL 44-12 [4e]			
Network				
MIDI Patchbay	*KMX MIDI Central* [2c]			
Analog Recorder				
Cassette	AIWA WX808 Dual Deck [5b]			
Multitrack	*Tascam 48* [5c]			
Integrated Mixer/Deck			Fostex 280	Akai MG1214
Mixdown Deck			Fostex E2	
Digital Recorder				
DAT	*Panasonic SV-3700* [5d]			

At this level you will not want to settle for anything less than a two-page display monitor and the speed of your Macintosh will be critical. For these reasons a Mac IIfx is recommended with a SCSI accelerator. CPU and graphics accelerators are recommended for future expansion.

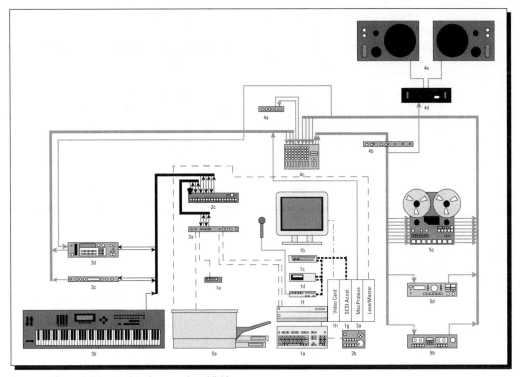

Figure 7-9: Setup 6: Advanced desktop music publishing.

Besides for your own personal use, this setup is also ideal for an output service bureau, publisher, or contract engraver. If you are setting up such an office, you will want a modem to be able to accept files electronically from clients.

With an advanced setup such as this you will also require a full 88-note controller keyboard for MIDI entry. Articulate Systems's Voice Navigator voice recognition system is highly recommended for anyone to whom speed is of paramount importance. When entering music from a MIDI keyboard in conjunction with the Voice Navigator, you are free to keep your hands on the musical keyboard and issue all other commands by voice rather than moving your hands off the MIDI keyboard to the Macintosh keyboard and then back. Moving the hands back and forth from the two types of keyboards requires continual re-orientation of your fingers, which eats up precious seconds that quickly add up to hours.

Expanded audio options are also recommended. Clients may wish to hear a "Polaroid" version of the work you are notating. With this in mind, I have suggested the same devices mentioned at the intermediate level setup and the addition of a modular sampler such as the Akai S-1000 to provide for any exotic instruments that may be found in the score you are notating. These added devices should make you seriously consider a 32-channel MIDI interface in place of the 16-channel ones suggested for the entry- and intermediate-level setups.

You or your clients may desire a full-blown realization of the printed score, so a number of tape output devices are also pictured in Figure 7-9. Because of the option for realizing a notation file via sampled sounds onto tape, a minimum number of DSP effects are suggested — a reverb such as the LXP-5 at the very least.

Some people prefer to use a notation program in place of a MIDI sequencer because they are more comfortable reading CMN. If you are one of these, you may wish to consider this setup without the costly printer, substituting instead a 300-dpi laser printer, to bring the price down considerably.

MIDI music
(For details see Part Three, "Composition.")

Entry level	$2,500 – $4,400
Intermediate	$18,200 – $34,700
Advanced	$63,000 – $87,000

To get involved with MIDI you need a controller capable of communicating via MIDI. Typical MIDI-compatible sound-generating keyboards range from about $299 for a Casio CZ1000 digital synthesizer (multitimbral, 8-voice polyphonic, non-velocity sensitive) up to $500,000 for a Synclavier (perhaps the most expensive Macintosh peripheral available). If you are only going to use a single keyboard in the setup, you should decide early on whether it will be of the synthesizer, sampler, sample-player, or dumb MIDI controller variety.

After deciding whether to purchase a synthesizer or a sampler/sample player keyboard, your main considerations are velocity sensing (perhaps aftertouch or pressure too), number of note polyphony, and multitimbral capabilities. *Velocity sensing* (or the capability of playing at varying and multiple levels of volume) adds to the price. If you are going to use the synthesizer as an output device, even if only for proofhearing, you will want to consider how many notes can be sounded simultaneously (referred to as *n*-voice polyphony) and whether or not the synthesizer is multitimbral (which refers to the capability of playing several different types of sounds or patches simultaneously). The greater polyphony and multitimbrality that you possess, the more you can use virtual tracks instead of audio tape tracks.

You will need a hardware MIDI interface to translate your synthesizer's MIDI data into a format readable by the Macintosh. Macintosh MIDI interfaces run from $49 to $900 and are marketed by Altech Systems, Apple Computer, JL Cooper, Mark of the Unicorn, Opcode Systems, and Passport Designs. At the upper end some interfaces have built-in synchronization features while lower-priced models may require an additional SMPTE converter for synchronization.

If you are using your musical data to control sound-generating devices for realizing your compositions, you will need some sort of tape recorder, ideally one with multiple tracks. Most music software at the intermediate to advanced level will be able to send and receive synchronization information. This allows you to lay down your analog tracks one at a time, with the assurance that they are time-aligned, thereby getting around such device limitations as a restrictively small number of polyphonic voices or the inability to output several different sound timbres at the same time.

In the three setups that follow, you will notice a rather wide jump in costs. You should take this to imply that there are many configurations in between the three levels illustrated. Because expandability and upgradability are considerations, if your budget falls somewhere between the higher cost of one setup and the lower cost of the next level up, you should consider cross-pollinating your configuration with appropriate additions from the next higher setup. Naturally, the non-italicized items are the first candidates for such considerations.

Setup 7: Entry level MIDI music
($2,500 – $4,400)

For the entry level MIDI music setup, all you really need is a MIDI keyboard, a sound-generating device, and a MIDI interface to translate MIDI data into a form that your Macintosh software can understand (see Table 7-8). The MIDI interface also allows your Macintosh to transmit data back to your sound-generating device(s) in a format they will expect (MIDI data).

I suggest the Roland PC-200 because it is the least expensive velocity-sensing dumb MIDI controller.

As a sound-generating device, Roland's CM-64 provides for both sampled and synthesized sounds, offering a whopping 63-voice polyphony and 15-channel multitimbrality. There is even a built-in drum machine. The L/A (linear arithmetic) synthesis sounds can be assigned to MIDI channels 1 through 8, the drum parts to channel 9, and the PCM (pulse code modulation) sampled sounds to channels 10 through 15. It is really an extremely flexible all-in-one box. The sounds may be expanded by adding U-110 PCM cards.

The CM-64 is essentially a combination of Roland's CM-32L L/A synthesis module (which includes the 8 synth parts and 1 drum part) and their CM-32P module (which represents the sampled sound section). If you're leaning toward synthesis, you might want to substitute the less expensive CM-32L. Conversely, if your leanings are toward sampling, you might substitute the less expensive CM-32P or possibly an E-mu Proteus/2 if you are planning on building a more sophisticated setup in the future.

If you would rather use a controller that is a sound-generating device unto itself, the keyboard versions of the CM-32L and CM-32P are the D-10 and U-20 models, respectively (the rack-mountable versions are the D-110 and U-220). If you're looking for higher-end keyboards with expandability in mind, you might consider the Korg M1 or Kurzweil 1200 keyboards in place of the Roland models.

On the other hand, if you do stick with the Roland gear and have little arranging abilities, you can expand the setup by adding Roland's RA-30, RA-50, or Pro-E intelligent arranger devices. These are uncannily able to process your single-line melodies and output credible accompanimental arrangements to their CM-series modules, and these arrangements can easily be captured by your Macintosh sequencer.

Although the CM-64, CM-32L, D-10, K1200, and M1 all contain drum sounds, I suggest augmenting the setup with a drum machine, primarily because of the pad interface, built-in patterns, and wider range of sounds found in such a dedicated device.

Because the setup pictured in Figure 7-10 handles a maximum of 16 MIDI channels and the alternate setups do not exceed 17 MIDI channels, I recommend a single 16-channel MIDI interface.

You will want at least one effects device. The Lexicon LXP series and its remote controller, their MRC, is something that can also serve you if you expand your setup by adding additional devices.

Table 7-8: Setup 7 — Entry level MIDI music				
	Pictured	**Expansion**	**Alternate 1**	**Alternate 2**
Macintosh	Compact Mac [1a]		Mac LC or si	Mac II series
Mac Peripherals				
RAM	2 to 4MB			
Monitor				Apple 13" Monitor
Hard Drive	*40 to 80MB HD* [1b]			
Backup System		Microtech Syquest		
CD-ROM		CD-ROM w/audio		
Printer		Apple ImageWriter LQ		
8-bit Digitizer			MacroMind-Para-comp MacRecorder	Articulate Systems VoiceLink
Misc. Input Devices	*USR Courier 2400 baud modem* [1c]			
Internal Card				
Video Card				Video Card
Interfaces				
16-chan MIDI	Opcode MIDI Translator [2a]		Apple MIDI Interface	Altech MIDI Interface
SGD & Controller				
Kbd Controller	Roland PC-200 [3c]		Roland U-20 or Roland D-20	
Hybrid Synth Kbd			Korg M1	
Sample Player Kbd			Kurzweil K1200-88	
Digital Module	Roland CM Series [3a]		Roland D-110	
Samp. Play. Mod.			E-mu Proteus/2 Roland U-220	Kurzweil 1200 Pro I, II, or III Roland Sound Canvas
Drum Machine	*Alesis SR-16* [3b]			
Other Controller	*Lexicon MRC* [3d]	Roland RA-50	JL Cooper Fadermaster	

Table 7-8: Setup 7 — Entry level MIDI music (continued)

	Pictured	Expansion	Alternate 1	Alternate 2
Audio and DSP				
DSP Effects	Lexicon LXP-1 [4a]	BBE 422 or 822A	Lexicon LXP-5	Yamaha SPX-900
Mixer		8-channel mixer		
Amplifier			Amplifier	
Speakers			Yamaha NS-10M	
Powered Speakers	Roland MA-12C [4b]			
Network				
Serial Data Switcher	Dataspec Serial Switchbox [2b]			
Analog Recorder				
Multitrack		8-track ½"		
Integrated Mixer/ Deck	Fostex 280 [5a]		Akai MG12-14	

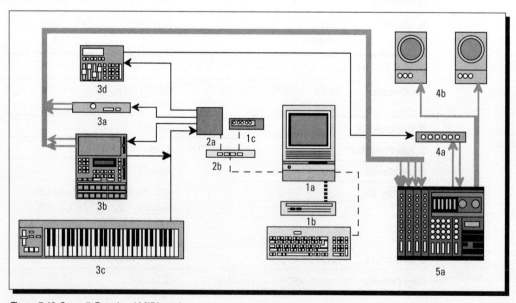

Figure 7-10: Setup 7: Entry level MIDI music.

Setup 8: Intermediate MIDI music
($18,200 – $34,700)

Don't be frightened by the $18,200 lower cost estimate of the intermediate MIDI configuration. If you are willing to assemble this setup in stages, you can easily cut the price in half or more.

You can stretch your budget by holding off or making substitutions in the DSP (digital signal processing) effects and output devices area (see Table 7-9). You may very well be able to get along without a 16-track analog recorder and prefer to mix down directly to DAT (digital audio tape) (rather than the high 3-track pictured in Figure 7-11) or even to cassette. Some of the bells and whistles in the MIDI controller area can be cut back, such as the Fadermaster, MRC, and MIDI-controlled mixer.

Also look for Macintosh peripherals to omit. If you are willing to religiously back up your data onto floppy disks, you could forego the Syquest cartridge drive. You may be able to get along without a printer or CD-ROM, too. As always, you may cut your costs considerably by going with a sound-generating keyboard as your main controller.

Finally, a digital audio card is suggested due to the recent proliferation of MIDI sequencers that provide for digital audio tracks along with MIDI data. If your output is not going to involve live players, you may want to hold off on purchasing the digital audio card.

In the intermediate range MIDI setup, an 88-note primary MIDI controller is recommended. A second keyboard can also be used to great advantage. You will notice a strong tendency for increased representation of the different types of synthesis. The devices suggested are all professional and will continue to be useful as your setup grows.

Because this setup, at the upper end, is geared to producing output at the professional level, higher-end DSP effects devices are suggested and the output devices are upgraded accordingly.

Table 7-9: Setup 8 — Intermediate MIDI music

	Pictured	Expansion	Alternate 1	Alternate 2
Macintosh	Mac II — 3-slot [1a]		Mac si	Mac II — 6-slot
Mac Peripherals				
RAM	4 to 8MB			
Monitor	Apple 13" Monitor [1b]		Apple Full-page Display	Apple 2-page Display

Table 7-9: Setup 8 — Intermediate MIDI music (continued)

	Pictured	**Expansion**	**Alternate 1**	**Alternate 2**
Hard Drive	80 to 200MB [1c]	More storage		
Backup System	Microtech Syquest [1d]	2nd Microtech Syquest	Microtech T150	Microtech DAT
CD-ROM	*Apple CD-ROM Drive* [1e]			
Printer	Apple ImageWriter LQ [5a]	Non-PS Laserprinter		
PostScript Printer			PS Laserprinter	
8-bit Digitizer	*MacroMind-Para-comp MacRecorder* [3a]		Articulate Systems VoiceLink	SID
Misc. Input Devices	USR Courier 2400 baud modem [1f]			

Internal Card

	Pictured	**Expansion**	**Alternate 1**	**Alternate 2**
Sample Player	*Digidesign MacProteus* [3b]			
Digital Audio	*Digidesign Audiomedia* [5b]		Digidesign Sound Accelerator	
CPU Accelerator		32 to 50 MHz		
Video Card	Video Card [1g]		8-bit Apple Video Card	24-bit Apple Video Card

Interfaces

	Pictured	**Expansion**	**Alternate 1**	**Alternate 2**
32-chan MIDI	Opcode Studio 3 [2a]		Altech MIDI Interface	Passport MIDI Transport
>32-chan MIDI		MOTU MTP	Opcode Studio 5	
SMPTE Converter			Opcode Time code Machine	JL Cooper PPS1

SGD & Controller

	Pictured	**Expansion**	**Alternate 1**	**Alternate 2**
Kbd Controller	A-80 [3c]		Kurzweil MIDI Board	Elka Keyboard Controller
Analog Synth Kbd		Oberheim Matrix-12	Oberheim Matrix-12	
Digital Synth Kbd		Roland D-20	Roland D-20	Yamaha V-50
Hybrid Synth Kbd	*Korg M1* [3d]	Roland D-70	Roland D-50 or	Korg Wavestation, Roland U-20 Korg M1, Roland D-70 or Yamaha SY-77

Table 7-9: Setup 8 — Intermediate MIDI music (continued)

	Pictured	Expansion	Alternate 1	Alternate 2
Sample Player Kbd			Kurzweil K1200-88	Korg T1
Sampler Kbd		Akai S1000KB	Ensoniq EPS	Korg W-30 or E-mu E-III
Synth/Sample Kbd		Kurzweil K2000	E-mu Emax II	
Analog Module	Oberheim Matrix-1000 [3e]	Roland MKS-70	Roland MKS-70	Oberheim Expander
Digital Module		Roland MT-32 or Roland D-550	Yamaha TX-802	Roland D-110
Hybrid Module	Korg M1rex [3f]	Korg Wave-station A/D	Korg M3r or Yamaha TG-77	Korg Wave-station A/D
Samp. Play. Mod.	E-mu Proteus/2 [3g] (and E-mu Proformance) [3h]	Kurzweil 1200 Pro I, II, and/or III	Roland U-220	Roland Sound Canvas
Sampler Module	Akai S1000 [3i]	Add hard disk	Roland S-550 Ensoniq EPS (rack mount version)	Roland S-770
Synth/Sample Mod.			E-mu Emax II (rack mount version)	
Drum Machine	Alesis HR or SR series [3j]	Roland R-8	Roland R-8M	Simmons SD series or Akai MPC60
Other Controller	JL Cooper Fadermaster [3k] Lexicon MRC [3l]	JL Cooper CS-1		Niche MAS Fadermonster

Audio and DSP

Effects	Lexicon LXP-15 [4a]	Lexicon 300	Lexicon LXP-5 Lexicon PCM-70	Korg A-3 Roland R-880 or Lexicon 480L
Other Signal	BBE 422 or 822A [4b] and 2 DBX 160XTs or DBX 166) [4c]	Aphex 612	Drawmer M-500	Rane DC-24
Mixer	Roland M-16E [4d]			
MIDI-controlled Mixer	Niche ACM [4e]	MOTU MM7	MOTU MM7	Yamaha DMP7
Console		24-channel Console		
Amplifier	Amplifier [4f]			

Table 7-9: Setup 8 — Intermediate MIDI music (continued)

	Pictured	Expansion	Alternate 1	Alternate 2
Speakers	Yamaha NS-10M [4g]	Bigger Monitors	Tannoy	
Microphone	Microphone [3m]			

Network

MIDI Patchbay	KMX MIDI Central [2b]			
Audio Patchbay	(not pictured)			
Speaker Switchbox				
Serial Data Switcher	Dataspec Serial Switchbox [2c]			
SCSI Data Switcher	Computer Friends SCSI Switchbox [2d]			

Analog Recorder

Cassette	AIWA WX808 Dual Deck [5c]			
Multitrack	Fostex G16 [5d]		Tascam 48 or 58	
Integrated Mixer/Deck			Fostex 280	Akai MG1214 or Akai MG14D
Mixdown Deck	Fostex E2 [5e]			

Digital Recorder

DAT	Panasonic SV-3700 [5f]		Panasonic SV-3900	

Setup 9: Advanced MIDI music
($63,000 – $87,000)

Like the intermediate setup, this configuration can be assembled in stages as your budget allows.

The primary concern at both ends of the advanced MIDI spectrum is maximum flexibility — the capability to handle the widest range of MIDI music situations that may arise (see Table 7-10). Although the focus is upon MIDI composition and realization, the setup also supports, to a certain extent, the activities of notation, scoring for film, video, and multimedia with lock-up capabilities, realizing

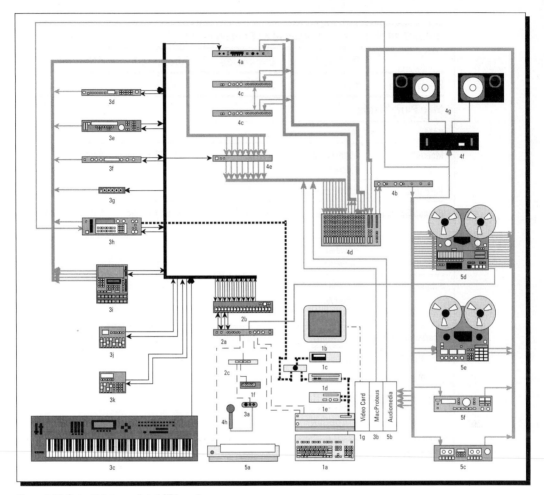

Figure 7-11: Setup 8: Intermediate MIDI music.

other people's projects at your facility, adequate support of digital audio, sweetening, and especially outputting master-quality recordings for any purpose, including records, film, video, CD-ROM, and other interactive media.

You can significantly reduce your expenses by eliminating some of the ancillary tasks provided for in this configuration (see Figure 7-12). Identify those activities that fulfill your personal requirements rather than the broad spectrum of endeavors the entire setup facilitates, then carve up the setup accordingly.

Table 7-10: Setup 9 — Advanced MIDI music

	Pictured	Expansion	Alternate 1	Alternate 2
Macintosh	Mac IIfx [1a]	Second Mac	Mac IIci	
Mac Peripherals				
RAM	8MB or more			
Monitor	Apple Full-page Display [1b]		Apple 13" Monitor	Apple 2-page Display
Hard Drive	300MB to 1GB [1c]	Additional Storage		
Backup System	Microtech Syquest [1d]	Microtech T150	Golden Triangle DiskTwin	Microtech DAT
CD-ROM	*Apple CD-ROM Drive* [1e]			
Printer	Non-PS Laserprinter (LaserWriter II SC pictured) [5a]			
PostScript Printer		PS Laserprinter		
8-bit Digitizer	*MacRecorder* [3a]		Articulate Systems VoiceLink	
Misc. Input Devices	USR Courier 2400 baud modem (or greater) [1f]			
Internal Card				
Sample Player	*Digidesign Mac Proteus* [3b]			
Sampler	Digidesign SampleCell [3c]			
Digital Audio	*Digidesign Audiomedia* [5b]		Digidesign Sound Accelerator	
CPU Accelerator		50+ MHz CPU accelerator		
SCSI Enhancement		Daystar SCSI Accelerator		
Video Card	8-bit Apple Video Card [1g]		24-bit Apple Video Card	

Table 7-10: Setup 9 — Advanced MIDI music (continued)

	Pictured	Expansion	Alternate 1	Alternate 2
Interfaces				
>32-chan MIDI	2 MOTU MTPs [2a]	3rd MOTU MTP	Opcode Studio 5	
Lock-up System	*Adams Smith Zeta-3* [2b]			
SGD & Controller				
Kbd Controller	Roland A-80 [3d]	2nd Kbd controller	Kurzweil MIDIBoard	Elka Keyboard Controller
Analog Synth Kbd		Oberheim Matrix-12	Oberheim Matrix-12	
Digital Synth Kbd		Yamaha V-50	Roland D-20	Yamaha V-50
Hybrid Synth Kbd		Korg M1 or Roland D-70	Roland D-50 or Roland U-20	Korg Wavestation, Korg M1 or Roland D-70 or Yamaha SY-77
Sample Player Kbd			Kurzweil K1200-88	Korg T1
Sampler Kbd		Akai S1000KB	Ensoniq EPS	Korg W-30 or E-mu E-III
Synth/Sample Kbd	*Kurzweil K2000*		E-mu Emax II	
Analog Module	Roland MKS-70 [3f] *Oberheim Matrix-1000* [3g]	Roland MKS-70	Roland MKS-70	Oberheim Expander
Digital Module	Roland D-550 [3h]	Yamaha TX-802	Yamaha TX-802	Roland D-110 or Yamaha TG-77
Hybrid Module	Korg Wave-station A/D [3i]	Korg M1r	Korg M3r	Korg M1r
Samp. Play. Mod.	E-mu Proteus/1 [3j] E-mu Proteus/2 [3k] E-mu Proformance [3l]	Kurzweil 1200 Pro I, II, and/or III or 2nd E-mu Proteus/2	Roland U-220	Roland Sound Canvas
Sampler Module	Akai S1000 [3m]	Add hard disk	Roland S-550 Ensoniq EPS (rack mount version)	Roland S-770
Synth/Sample Mod.			E-mu Emax II (rack mount version)	
Drum Machine	Roland R-8 [3n]	Simmons SD series	Simmons SD series	Akai MPC60

Table 7-10: Setup 9 — Advanced MIDI music (continued)

	Pictured	Expansion	Alternate 1	Alternate 2
Other Controller	Niche MAS Fadermonster [3o] JL Cooper CS-1 [3p] Lexicon MRC [3q]		2 JL Cooper Fadermasters	

Audio and DSP

	Pictured	Expansion	Alternate 1	Alternate 2
DSP Effects	Lexicon 300 [4a] Lexicon LXP-15 [4b] Roland SDE-3000 [4c]	Lexicon PCM-70 Lexicon 480L	Lexicon PCM-70, Korg A-3, or Eventide H-3000	Roland R-880 or Lexicon 480L
Other Signal Processing	BBE 822A [4d] 2 DBX 160XTs [4e] Rane MPE14 [4f]	2 DBX 165As Orban 764A Roland RSS Spatializer	Drawmer M-500 Orban 764A	Dolby A or S DBX F-900 Roland E-660
Mixer	Roland M-16E [4g] (drum & Kbd submixer)	2nd rackmount mixer	Alesis 1622	Hill Audio
MIDI-controlled Mixer	MOTU MM7 [4h] (or Niche ACM)	2nd MOTU MM7 or Niche ACM	Yamaha DMP7	Akai MPX820
Console	48+ channel Console [4i]			
Amplifier	Amplifier [4j]			
Speakers	Yamaha NS-10M [4k] JBL [4l]			
Microphone	At least 2 [3r]			

Network

	Pictured	Expansion	Alternate 1	Alternate 2
MIDI Patchbay		KMX MIDI Central [2c]	JL Cooper MSB series	
Audio Patchbay	(not pictured)	DMS MIDI controllable patchbay		
Speaker Switchbox	Speaker switchbox [4n]			
Serial Data Switcher	Dataspec Serial Switchbox [2d]			
SCSI Data Switcher	Computer Friends SCSI Switchbox [2d]			

Table 7-10: Setup 9 — Advanced MIDI music (continued)

	Pictured	Expansion	Alternate 1	Alternate 2
Analog Recorder				
Cassette	AIWA WX808 Dual Deck [5c]			
Multitrack	Otari MTR-80-24 or MTR-100A [5d]	2nd 24-track	Other Otari MTR formats	
Integrated Mixer/Deck			Akai MG1214	
Mixdown Deck	2-track of choice [5e]			
Digital Recorder				
DtHD (Mac/ext)		Studer Dyaxis	Roland DM-80	
Digital MTR		Akai DR1200	DASH MTR - Sony or Studer	
DAT	2 Panasonic 3700s [5f]			

16-bit digital audio

(For details see Parts Two and Six.)

Entry level $8,700 – $18,400

Intermediate $26,800 – $40,000

Advanced $45,000 – $90,000

Getting into 16-bit digital audio is really not as expensive as it once was, thanks to Digidesign. The digital audio boards themselves are not that expensive. The real expenses come from the storage and output devices.

Stereo digital audio requires about 10MB per minute of direct-to-hard disk recording. The hard disk must have a maximum access time of 28 ms. With this in mind, be prepared to purchase a fast, large-capacity drive. Because of the size of the files that you will be making, you will require more robust backup systems, such as optical drives and DAT systems.

The other area of expense is in the type of recorders, analog or digital, that you will want as output destinations for your direct-to-hard disk recordings. Because your direct-to-hard disk recordings will be of CD-quality or better, you will want the recorders at the end of the chain to be worthy of your digital data.

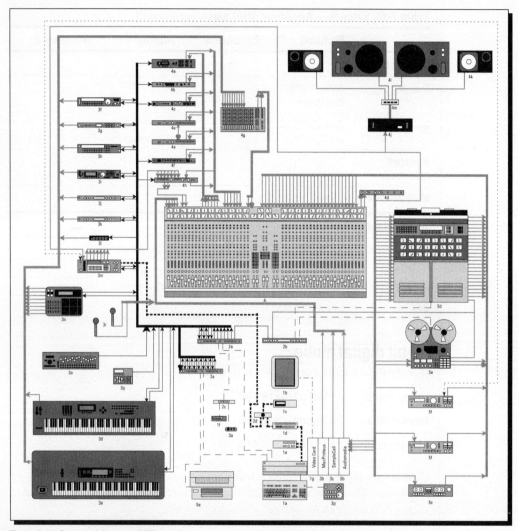

Figure 7-12: Setup 9: Advanced MIDI music.

If you are doing digital audio for film purposes, synchronizable digital output devices must be considered. If you are making digital masters that will eventually end up on CDs, you may seriously want to consider configuring your system so that your audio never enters the analog domain until it is played back on the consumer's CD player.

Setup 10: Entry level 16-bit digital audio
($8,700 – $18,400)

While the Audiomedia card, which provides for four tracks of digital audio, costs only $1,000, the bulk of the expenses in this configuration are related to storage and output devices (see Table 7-11). If you already have sufficient storage and recorders, you can reduce your expenses accordingly.

On the other hand, if you are only going to be recording less than four to eight minutes of music at a time, you can even get by with a Syquest removable cartridge as your digital audio storage medium. Most clock in at just under the required 28 ms access time. The 45MB removables hold slightly over four minutes of stereo digital audio, and you can squeeze almost nine minutes onto the newer 88MB removable cartridge drives. See Figure 7-13 for storage considerations.

If you are using the Syquest as a backup medium, consider it an interim measure. Backing up a 30-minute direct-to-hard disk recording will take seven of the 45MB cartridges or four of the 88MB removables. In either case, you will be out nearly $700 and after backing up two hours of digital audio you might as well have purchased a DAT backup system instead. You can fit 1300MB (over two hours of digital audio) on a $10 DAT cassette, and every next two hours of music will merely require purchasing another DAT cassette rather than $700 worth of additional Syquest cartridges.

Table 7-11: Setup 10 — Entry-level 16-bit digital audio

	Pictured	**Expansion**	**Alternate 1**	**Alternate 2**
Macintosh	Mac II — 3-slot [1a]		Mac II — 6-slot	
	w/ Mac Extended Kbd		w/ Mac Extended Kbd	
Mac Peripherals				
RAM	4MB	5MB or more		
Monitor	Apple 13" Monitor [1b]		Apple Full-page Display	Apple 2-page Display
Hard Drive	Microtech N300 to N600 [1c]	Additional Storage		
Backup System	Microtech Syquest [1d]	Microtech DAT backup	Microtech OR 650 Optical Drive	
Printer	Apple ImageWriter LQ [5a]		Non-PS LaserWriter	
PostScript Printer		PSLaserprinter		
Misc. Input Devices	USR Courier 2400 baud modem [1f]			

Table 7-11: Setup 10 — Entry-level 16-bit digital audio (continued)

	Pictured	Expansion	Alternate 1	Alternate 2
Internal Card				
Sampler		Digidesign SampleCell		
Digital Audio	Digidesign Audiomedia [5b]		Digidesign Sound Accelerator	
CPU Accelerator	*32-50 MHz accelerator* [1h]		CacheCard (IIci)	
SCSI Enhancement		Micronet NuPort	Daystar SCSI Accelerator	
Video Card	Video Card [1i]	Color Video Card		
SGD & Controller				
Other Controller	*JL Cooper CS-1* [3a]	JL Cooper Fadermaster	Lexicon MRC	
Audio and DSP				
DSP Effects	*Lexicon LXP-5* [4a]	Lexicon LXP-15	Yamaha SPX-900	Roland SRV-2000 Lexicon 300 Lexicon 480L
Other Signal Processing	*DBX 160XT* [4b]	BBE 422 OR 822A		
Mixer	*Roland M-16E* [4c]	24-chan mixer		
MIDI-controlled Mixer		Niche ACM	MOTU MM7	
Amplifier	Amplifier [4d]			
Speakers	Yamaha NS-10M [4e]	JBL	Tannoy	
Microphone	Microphone [3b]			
Analog Recorder				
Cassette	*AIWA WX808 Dual Deck* [5c]			
Multitrack	*Tascam ATR-60/8 or 60/8HS* [5d]		Fostex G16	Otari MTR-80-24 or MTR-100A
Integrated Mixer/Deck			Akai MG1214	
Mixdown Deck	Fostex E2 [5e]			
Digital Recorder				
DtHD (Mac/ext)			Roland DM-80	
DAT	Panasonic SV-3700 [5f]			

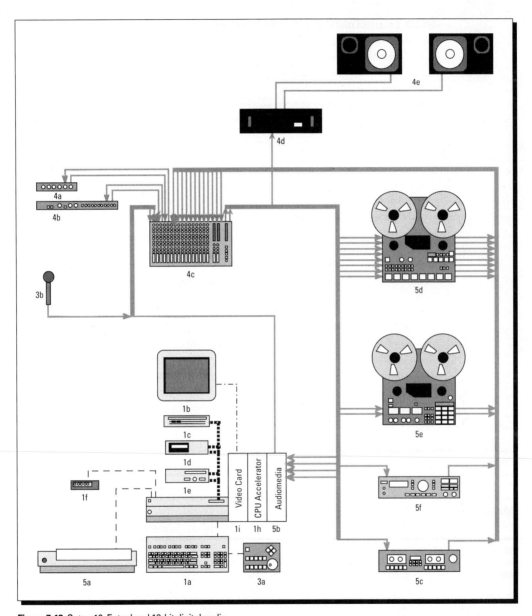

Figure 7-13: Setup 10: Entry level 16-bit digital audio.

Setup 11: Intermediate 16-bit digital audio
($26,800 – $40,000)

At the intermediate level, you will probably require some of the more sophisticated DSP capabilities of Digidesign's Sound Accelerator over their Audiomedia
card (see Table 7-12). If you require the Audiomedia features missing from the
Sound Accelerator, there is no reason why you shouldn't have both cards installed.
An obvious expansion is upgrading to digital I/O capabilities by adding a DAT I/O
box.

Assuming that some of your digital audio endeavors involve sound design for
samplers, the configuration provides for the possibility of adding MIDI to your
setup. A Roland A-80 controller keyboard used in conjunction with an Akai S-1000
and Digidesign's SampleCell card is pictured in Figure 7-14, but you could just as
well substitute a K2000 in their place.

At this level you will be using Sound Designer as your primary direct-to-hard disk
recording interface, and therefore a logical purchase is JL Cooper's CS-1 ADB
controller that provides hardware controls for many of Sound Designer's functions.

A 24-channel console is suggested to provide ample flexibility for recording live
musicians. If you are going to be recording electronic instruments predominantly,
you could get by with less. Also influencing the console considerations are your
decisions as to whether to use multitrack tape as an interim media prior to
mixdown or whether you will be outputting your digital audio data in a single
pass. In either case, you may want to consider owning two DAT recorders for the
purpose of making copies of your final mix without leaving the digital domain.

Table 7-12: Setup 11 — Intermediate 16-bit digital audio

	Pictured	**Expansion**	**Alternate 1**	**Alternate 2**
Macintosh	Mac II — 3- or 6-slot [1a] w/ Mac Extended Kbd		Mac IIfx w/ Mac Extended Kbd	
Mac Peripherals				
RAM	8MB	More than 8MB		
Monitor	Apple Full-page Display [1b]		Apple 2-page Display	
Hard Drive	600 to 1200MB [1c]	Additional storage		
Backup System	Microtech OR 650 Optical Drive [1d]	Microtech DAT	Microtech DAT	
CD-ROM	Apple CD-ROM Drive [1e]			

Table 7-12: Setup 11 — Intermediate 16-bit digital audio (continued)

	Pictured	Expansion	Alternate 1	Alternate 2
Printer	*Non-PS Laserprinter* [5a]			
PostScript Printer		PS Laserprinter	PS Laserprinter	
Misc. Input Devices	*USR Courier 2400 baud modem (or greater)* [1d]			

Internal Card

	Pictured	Expansion	Alternate 1	Alternate 2
Sampler	*Digidesign SampleCell* [3a]			
Digital Audio	Digidesign Sound Accelerator [5b] with AD-IN [5c]	Digidesign DAT I/O for Sound Accelerator, Audiomedia	Digidesign PRO I/O for Sound Accelerator	Digidesign ProTools
CPU Accelerator	*32-50 MHz accelerator* [1e]			
SCSI Enhancement		Micronet NuPort	Daystar SCSI Accelerator	
Video Card	Video Card [1f]	Color Video Card		

Interfaces

	Pictured	Expansion	Alternate 1	Alternate 2
32-chan MIDI	*Opcode Studio 3* [2a]		Altech MIDI Interface	Passport MIDI Transport
>32-chan MIDI		MOTU MTP or Opcode Studio 5		
SMPTE Converter			JL Cooper PPS	Opcode Time code Machine
VITC Converter		MOTU VTP		

SGD & Controller

	Pictured	Expansion	Alternate 1	Alternate 2
Kbd Controller	*Roland A-80* [3b]	2nd Kbd Controller	Kurzweil MIDIBoard	Elka Keyboard Controller
Analog Synth Kbd			Oberheim Matrix-12	
Digital Synth Kbd			Yamaha V-50	Roland D-20
Hybrid Synth Kbd		Korg M1 or Wavestation	Roland D-50 or Roland D-70	Yamaha SY-77
Sample Player Kbd			Kurzweil K1200-88	Korg T1
Sampler Kbd		Akai S1000KB	Ensoniq EPS	Korg W-30 or E-mu E-III
Synth/Sample Kbd		Kurzweil K2000	E-mu Emax II	

Table 7-12: Setup 11 — Intermediate 16-bit digital audio (continued)

	Pictured	Expansion	Alternate 1	Alternate 2
Analog Module		Roland MKS-70	Oberheim Matrix-1000	Oberheim Expander
Digital Module		Roland D-550	Yamaha TX-802	Roland D-110 or Yamaha TG-77
Hybrid Module		Korg Wavestation A/D	Korg M1rex	Korg M3r
Samp. Play. Mod.		E-mu Proteus/1 and/or Proteus/2 and/or E-mu Proformance	Kurzweil 1200 Pro I, II, and/or III	Roland U-220 Roland Sound Canvas
Sampler Module	Akai S1000 [3c]	Add hard disk	Roland S-550 Ensoniq EPS (rack mount version)	Roland S-770
Synth/Sample Mod.			E-mu Emax II (rack mount version)	
Drum Machine		Roland R-8	Alesis HR and SR series	
Other Controller	JL Cooper CS-1 [3d]	JL Cooper Fadermaster	Lexicon MRC	

Audio and DSP

	Pictured	Expansion	Alternate 1	Alternate 2
DSP Effects	Lexicon LXP-15 [4a]	Lexicon PCM-70 or Lexicon 300	Roland SRV-2000 or Yamaha SPX-900	Lexicon 300 Lexicon 480L
Other Signal Processing	DBX 160XT [4b] BBE 422 or 822A [4c]	Rane MPE14		
MIDI-controlled Mixer		Niche ACM	MOTU MM7	
Console	24-channel Console [4d]			
Amplifier	Amplifier [4e]			
Speakers	Yamaha NS-10M [4f]	JBL 44-12	Tannoy	
Microphone	at least 2 [3d]			

Network

	Pictured			
MIDI Patchbay	KMX MIDI Central			
Audio Patchbay	(not pictured)			
Speaker Switchbox	Speaker switchbox			
SCSI Data Switcher	Computer Friends SCSI Switchbox [2b]			

Table 7-12: Setup 11 — Intermediate 16-bit digital audio (continued)

	Pictured	**Expansion**	**Alternate 1**	**Alternate 2**
Analog Recorder				
Cassette	AIWA WX808 Dual Deck [5d]			
Multitrack	Fostex G16 [5e] or 16-track of choice		Tascam ATR-60/8 or 60/8HS	Otari MTR-80-24 or MTR-100A
Integrated Mixer/Deck			Akai MG1214	
Mixdown Deck	2-, 3-, or 4-track of choice [5f]			
Digital Recorder				
DtHD (Mac/ext)			Studer Dyaxis	Roland DM-80
Digital MTR			Akai DR1200	DASH MTR - Sony or Studer
DAT	Panasonic SV-3700 (or 2) [5g]			

Setup 12: Advanced 16-bit digital audio
($45,000 – $90,000)

The advanced level digital audio system presumes that every component in the system will be of the highest professional caliber.

The major differences between this setup and the intermediate one include the substitution of Digidesign's top-of-the-line Pro I/O analog interface for their AD-IN, with the understanding that their DAT I/O is no longer an option but a requirement.

Italicized options that represent diverging avenues of digital audio endeavors favor devices that can communicate entirely in the digital domain. With this in mind, the Lexicon 300 is recommended as the primary DSP effects device, and a Yamaha all-digital DCM1000 mixer rounds out the system (see Table 7-13).

With the same object of keeping your data in the digital domain, Kurzweil's K2000, a synth/sampler keyboard with digital inputs (or alternatively, the digital I/O card for Akai's S1000), and Digidesign's SampleCell card are recommended for sound design.

At this level you may want one of your DAT machines to include a time code track and be synchronizable. The Sony PCM 7050 has these features. A lock-up system for the DAT and 24-track is suggested if you go this route. The lock-up system and synchronizable DAT can be used in conjunction with video applica-

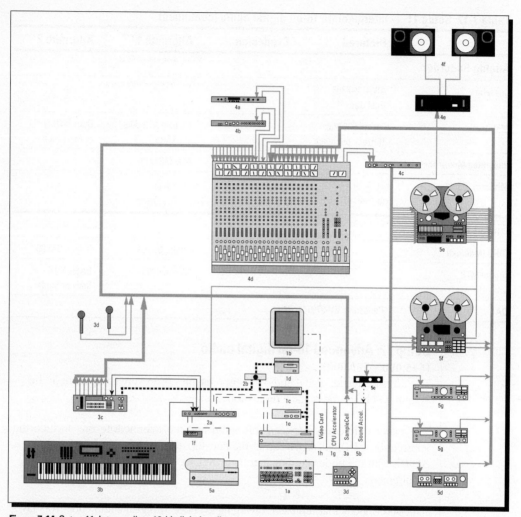

Figure 7-14: Setup 11: Intermediate 16-bit digital audio.

tions if you expand the system to include a lockable deck such as the JVC BR7700U (½") or Sony VOS 9850 (¾-inch) pictured in Figure 7-15.

Finally, if you ever need to push any digital data through the phone lines, the size of the files you will be dealing with will require a 19,200 bps modem such as the Telebit T2500, or a 38,400 bps modem as they become available.

Table 7-13: Setup 12 — Advanced 16-bit digital audio

	Pictured	Expansion	Alternate 1	Alternate 2
Macintosh	Mac IIfx [1a]	Second Mac	Accelerated Mac	
Mac Peripherals				
RAM	> 8MB	More RAM		
Monitor	Apple 2-page Display [1b]			
Hard Drive	Gigabyte or more [1c]	More storage		
Backup System	Microtech DAT [1d]	Microtech or 650 Optical Drive	Microtech or 650 Optical Drive	
CD-ROM	Apple CD-ROM Drive [1e]			
Printer	*Non-PS Laserprinter* [5a]			
PostScript Printer		PS Laserprinter	PS Laserprinter	
Misc. Input Devices	Telebit T2500 19,200 baud modem [1f]			
Internal Card				
Sample Player				
Sampler	Digidesign SampleCell [3a]			
Digital Audio	Digidesign Sound Accelerator [5b] with Pro I/O [5c] and DAT I/O [5d]	Digidesign Audiomedia	Substitute the Digidesign AD-IN box for the Digidesign Pro I/O	Digidesign ProTools
CPU Accelerator		50 MHz or greater		
SCSI Enhancement		Micronet NuPort	Daystar SCSI Accelerator	
Video Card	8-bit Apple Video Card [1g]		24-bit Apple Video Card	
Interfaces				
>32-chan MIDI	*MOTU MTP* [2a]		Opcode Studio 5	
VITC Converter		MOTU VTP		
Lockup System	*Adams Smith Zeta-3* [2b]			
SGD & Controller				
Kbd Controller	*Roland A-80* [3b]	2nd Kbd Controller	Kurzweil MIDIBoard	Elka Keyboard Controller
Analog Synth Kbd			Oberheim Matrix-12	

Table 7-13: Setup 12 — Advanced 16-bit digital audio (continued)

	Pictured	Expansion	Alternate 1	Alternate 2
Digital Synth Kbd			Yamaha V-50	Roland D-20
Hybrid Synth Kbd		Korg M1 or Korg Wavestation	Roland D-50 or Roland D-70	Yamaha SY-77
Sample Player Kbd			Kurzweil K1200-88	Korg T1
Sampler Kbd		Akai S1000KB	Ensoniq EPS	Korg W-30 or E-mu E-III
Synth/Sample Kbd	Kurzweil K2000 [3c]		E-mu Emax II	
Analog Module		Roland MKS-70	Oberheim Matrix-1000	Oberheim Expander
Digital Module		Roland D-550	Yamaha TX-802	Roland D-110 or Yamaha TG-77
Hybrid Module		Korg Wavestation A/D	Korg M1rex	Korg M3r
Samp. Play. Mod.		E-mu Proteus/1 and/or Proteus/2 and/or E-mu Proformance	Kurzweil 1200 Pro I, II, and/or III	Roland U-220 Roland Sound Canvas
Sampler Module	Akai S1000 [3d]	Add hard disk	Roland S-550 Ensoniq EPS (rack mount version)	Roland S-770
Synth/Sample Mod.			E-mu Emax II (rack mount version)	
Drum Machine		Roland R-8	Alesis HR and SR series	
Other Controller	JL Cooper CS-1 [3e] Niche MAS Fadermonster [3f]	JL Cooper Fadermaster	Lexicon MRC	

Audio and DSP

	Pictured	Expansion	Alternate 1	Alternate 2
DSP Effects	Lexicon 300 [4a] Rane MPE14 [4b]	Lexicon 480L	Korg A-3 Eventide H-3000	Roland R-880 Roland E-660
Other Signal Processing	BBE 422 or 822A [4c] 2 DBX 160XTs [4d]	Orban 764A Roland RSS Spatializer	Orban 764A Drawmer M-500	DBX F-900 Dolby A or SR
MIDI-controlled Mixer	Yamaha DMC1000 [4e] Niche ACM [4f]	Additional MIDI-controlled mixers	2 MOTU MM7s	Yamaha DMP7D
Console	24-channel Console [4g]	48+ channel Console		
Amplifier	Amplifier [4h]			
Speakers	Yamaha NS-10Ms [4i] JBL 44-12 [4j]			
Microphone	At least 2 [3e]			

Table 7-13: Setup 12 — Advanced 16-bit digital audio (continued)

	Pictured	Expansion	Alternate 1	Alternate 2
Network				
MIDI Patchbay		KMX MIDI Central		
Audio Patchbay	(not pictured)	360 Systems Audio Matrix-16	Akai Digital Patchbay DP3200	Yamaha Digital Patchbay
Speaker Switchbox	Speaker switchbox [4l]			
Serial Data Switcher	*Dataspec Serial Switchbox* [2c]			
SCSI Data Switcher	*Computer Friends SCSI Switchbox* [2d]			
Analog Recorder				
Cassette	AIWA WX808 Dual Deck [5e]			
Multitrack	*Otari MTR-80-24* [5f]	2nd 24-track		
Mixdown Deck	2-, 3-, or 4-track of choice [5g]			
Digital Recorder				
DtHD (Mac/ext)		Studer Dyaxis	Roland DM-80	Lexicon Opus Akai DD1000
Digital MTR		Akai DR1200	DASH MTR Sony or Studer	
DAT	Panasonic SV-3700 [5h] Sony PCM-7050 [5i]	Synchronizable DAT	JVC DSDT900 (time code)	
Video				
Deck	*JVC BR-7700U* [6a]	Sony VOS 9850		
Monitor	*JVC 27" Monitor* [6b]			

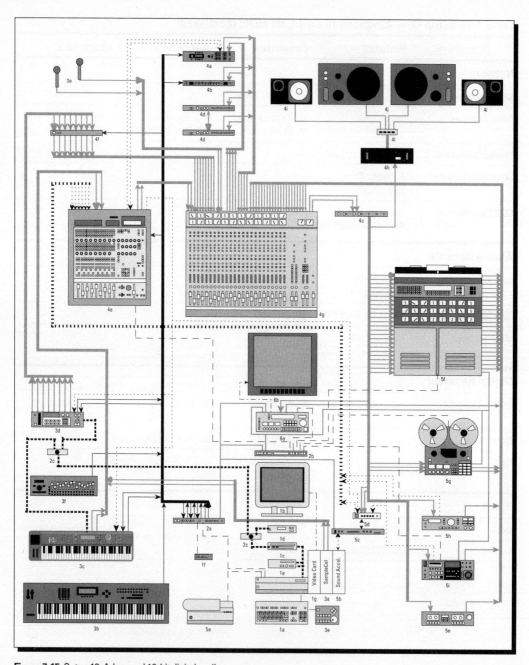

Figure 7-15: Setup 12: Advanced 16-bit digital audio.

Film and video

(For details see Part Seven, "Film, Video, and Synchronization.")

Entry level $15,500 – $28,000

Intermediate $35,200 – $54,000

Advanced $83,500 – $108,000

All the film and video setups begin with the assumption that your product will be broadcast or enjoy a theatrical release. If you are just scoring your family's home video tapes, you can certainly make do with considerably less gear.

The three setups provide for the creation of a synth score as the primary concern and because of this, you will notice the correspondence of some elements to those presented in the MIDI music section (setups 7, 8, and 9). Other product delivery formats are included as alternatives.

Of course, in all cases you are going to require a video deck and monitor. I have included a synchronizable deck in each setup to provide for the eventual upgrading of your system. Non-lockable video decks are considerably less expensive. The most important consideration about the deck is that it have a jog-wheel or, at the very least, a frame-advance feature, and that it have separate audio outs for the right and left channels. This is because during the scoring process you will almost always have SMPTE Time Code on one of the audio tracks and dialog on the other. At the higher end, two luxury options you may want to consider are VITC compatibility and a lock-up system such as the Adams Smith Zeta III or a Lynx.

Provision for scores performed by live musicians is provided from two standpoints. First, a printer is included in most setups for the purpose of printing out scores and parts. Naturally, if all your music is to be performed by live musicians, you may want to look closely at the setups included in the section on music desktop publishing (setups 4, 5, and 6) and cut down on the sound-generating capabilities of the setups in the present section to the minimum necessary for proofhearing or to provide directors and producers with a rough sketch (often referred to as a Polaroid) of your work in progress.

The second auxiliary task provided for by the intermediate and advanced systems is combining MIDI tracks with direct-to-hard disk digital audio recordings of live musicians. If digital audio is going to make up the major portion of your scoring activities, you may want to look back to the previous section (setups 10, 11, and 12) for additional suggestions on expanding in this direction.

The tape format for delivery of your music is a unique situation in this category. Although you might be able to get by in some situations with a non-time code DAT (some people claim that a DAT merely needs to start at the right SMPTE frame rather than be continually locked up), at the higher end of the business you will want to deliver your product on an analog three-track tape (center SMPTE track) or four-track tape (with SMPTE separated from the audio by a blank track). If you can afford it, a synchronizable DAT is preferable, although until their presence becomes more widespread, you may find that you have to bring your own machine to the final dubbing session.

The MIDI interface in the film and video setups is an extremely important consideration. While I have configured the setups as progressing from 16- to 32- to greater-than-32-channel interfaces for purposes of illustration, if you are serious about electronic scoring of film and video, you would be well advised to start out with the highest-capacity interface. The MIDI Time Piece and the Studio 5 both have built-in professional time code conversion, and their greater-than-32-channels "cable" implementations mean that you can often dispense with a MIDI patchbay if the number of your devices would seem to require one.

Setup 13: Entry level film and video
($15,500 — $28,000)
This setup provides for synchronizing your MIDI sequencer to the LTC (Longitudinal Time Code) SMPTE track on the video deck (see Figure 7-16). Because you may not require more than 16 MIDI channels, and 16-channel MIDI interfaces do not normally provide for time code conversion, you will need a separate converter box such as the Opcode TimeCode Machine (see Table 7-14). If you are planning on building a setup that will grow over time, for an extra $100 or so you might want to substitute a 32-channel interface with built-in time code conversion or even a greater-than-32-channel interface.

Most of the same comments stated in the MIDI music section (setups 7, 8, and 9) apply here.

Table 7-14: Setup 13 — Entry level film and video

	Pictured	Expansion	Alternate 1	Alternate 2
Macintosh	Compact Mac [1a]		Mac LC or si	Mac II series
Mac Peripherals				
RAM	2 to 4MB	4 to 8MB		
Monitor		Apple Full-page Display	Apple Full-page Display	Apple 2-page Display
Hard Drive	40 to 80MB [1b]	Additional storage		

Table 7-14: Setup 13 — Entry level film and video (continued)

	Pictured	Expansion	Alternate 1	Alternate 2
Backup System	*Microtech Syquest* [1c]	Microtech T150	Microtech T150	Microtech DAT
Printer	Apple Image-Writer LQ [5a]	Non-PS laserprinter	Non-PS laserprinter	
PostScript Printer		PS Laserprinter	PS Laserprinter	
Misc. Input Devices	USR Courier 2400 baud modem [1d]			

Internal Card

	Pictured	Expansion	Alternate 1	Alternate 2
CPU Accelerator		32 to 40 MHz accelerator		

Interfaces

	Pictured	Expansion	Alternate 1	Alternate 2
16-chan MIDI	Opcode MIDI Translator [2a]		Apple MIDI Interface	Altech MIDI Interface
32-chan MIDI		Opcode Studio 3	JL Cooper Nexxus series	Passport MIDI Transport
>32-chan MIDI		MOTU MTP	Opcode Studio 5	
SMPTE Converter	Opcode Time code Machine [2b]		JL Cooper PPS series	Roland SBX-1000

SGD & Controller

	Pictured	Expansion	Alternate 1	Alternate 2
Kbd Controller			Roland A-80	Kurzweil MIDIBoard or Elka Keyboard Controller
Analog Synth Kbd			Oberheim Matrix-12	
Digital Synth Kbd			Roland D-20	Yamaha V-50
Hybrid Synth Kbd	Korg T1 [3a] (or T2 or T3)		Korg M1 or Roland D-50	Korg Wavestation, Roland D-70, Roland U-20 or Yamaha SY-77
ample Player Kbd			Kurzweil K1200-88 or Kurzweil K1200-76	
Sampler Kbd			Akai S1000KB or Ensoniq EPS	Korg W-30 or E-mu E-III
Synth/Sample Kbd			E-mu Emax II	Kurzweil K2000
Analog Module	*Oberheim Matrix-1000* [3b]	Roland MKS-70	Roland MKS-70	Oberheim Expander

Part One: The Basics

Table 7-14: Setup 13 — Entry level film and video (continued)

	Pictured	Expansion	Alternate 1	Alternate 2
Digital Module		Roland MT-32 or Roland D-550	Yamaha TX-802	Roland D-110
Hybrid Module		Korg M1rex or Korg Wavestation A/D	Korg M3r or Yamaha TG-77	Korg Wavestation A/D
Samp. Play. Mod.	E-mu Proteus/2 [3c] (and E-mu Proformance) [3d]	Kurzweil 1200 Pro I, II, and/or III or E-mu Proteus/1	Roland U-220	Roland Sound Canvas
Sampler Module	Roland S-550 [3e]		Akai S1000 Ensoniq EPS (rack mount version)	Roland S-770
Synth/Sample Mod.			E-mu Emax II (rack mount version)	
Drum Machine	Alesis HR or SR series [3f]	Roland R-8	Roland R-8M	Simmons SD series or Akai MPC60
Other Controller	JL Cooper Fadermaster [3g]	Lexicon MRC, JL Cooper CS-1	Lexicon MRC	Niche MAS Fadermonster

Audio and DSP

	Pictured	Expansion	Alternate 1	Alternate 2
DSP Effects	Lexicon LXP-1 [4a] (or LXP-5)	Lexicon LXP-15 or PCM-70	Lexicon LXP-15 or PCM-70	Lexicon 300 or Korg A-3
Other Signal Processing	BBE 422 or 822A [4b]	2 DBX 160XTs or DBX 166	2 DBX 160XTs or DBX 166	Drawmer M-500
Mixer	Roland M-16E [4c]			
MIDI-controlled Mixer	MOTU MM7 [4d] (or Niche ACM)	2nd MIDI-controlled mixer	Yamaha DMP7	Akai MPX820
Console		24-channel Console	48+ channel Console	
Amplifier	Amplifier [4e]			
Speakers	Yamaha NS-10M [4f]	Larger monitors		

Network

	Pictured	Expansion	Alternate 1	Alternate 2
MIDI Patchbay	KMX MIDI Central [2c]			
Audio Patchbay	(not pictured)	360 Systems Audio Matrix-16		
Serial Data Switcher	Dataspec Serial Switchbox [2d]			

Analog Recorder

	Pictured	Expansion	Alternate 1	Alternate 2
Cassette	AIWA WX808 Dual Deck [5b]			

Table 7-14: Setup 13 — Entry level film and video (continued)

	Pictured	Expansion	Alternate 1	Alternate 2
Multitrack	Tascscam ATR-60/8 or 60/8HS [5c]		Fostex G16	24-track
Integrated Mixer/Deck			Akai MG1214	
Mixdown Deck	*Fostex E2* [5d]			
Digital Recorder				
DAT	*Panasonic 3700* [5e]			
Video				
Deck	JVC BR-7700U [6a]			
Monitor	JVC 27" Monitor [6b]			

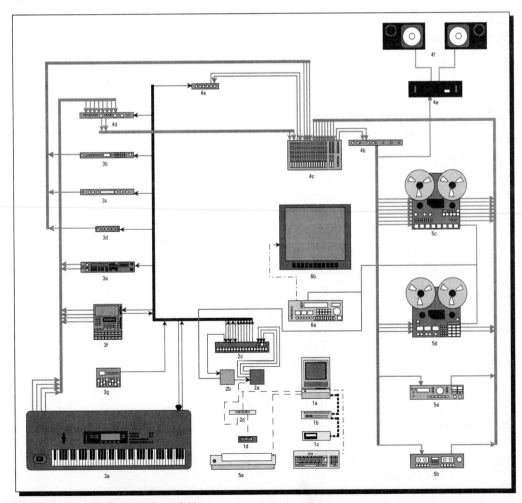

Figure 7-16: Setup 13: Entry level film and video.

Setup 14: Intermediate film and video
($35,200 – $54,000)

Like the intermediate MIDI music setup (setup 8), this intermediate film and video scoring setup adds digital audio capabilities and additional sound-generating devices (see Table 7-15). Output devices and DSP effects are also upgraded accordingly. To cut the cost by about $15,000, you might want to substitute the Akai MG12-14 (12-track integrated mixer-recorder) in place of the 16-track machine and mixing console pictured in Figure 7-17. The number of prime time television shows and made-for-TV movies being scored with the Akai machine are a testament to its viability in these areas.

Table 7-15: Setup 14 — Intermediate film and video

	Pictured	Expansion	Alternate 1	Alternate 2
Macintosh	Mac II — 3-slot [1a]		Mac IIsi	Mac II — 6-slot
Mac Peripherals				
RAM	4 to 8MB	More than 8MB		
Monitor	Apple 13" Monitor [1b]	Apple Full-page Display	Apple Full-page Display	Apple 2-page Display
Hard Drive	100 to 300MB [1c]			
Backup System	*Microtech Syquest* [1d]	Microtech T150	Golden Triangle DiskTwin	Microtech DAT
CD-ROM	*Apple CD-ROM Drive* [1e]			
Printer	Non-PS Laserprinter [5a]			
PostScript Printer			PS Laserprinter	
Misc. Input Devices	USR Courier 2400 baud modem (or greater) [1f]			
Internal Card				
Sample Player		Digidesign MacProteus		
Sampler		Digidesign SampleCell		
Digital Audio	*Digidesign Sound Accelerator* [5b] *with AD-IN* [5c]	Digidesign DAT I/O for Sound Accelerator		
CPU Accelerator		32-50 MHz accelerator		
SCSI Enhancement		Daystar SCSI Accelerator	Micronet NuPort	Daystar SCSI Accelerator
Video Card	*8-bit Apple Video Card* [1g]	Color Video Card		

Table 7-15: Setup 14 — Intermediate film and video (continued)

	Pictured	Expansion	Alternate 1	Alternate 2
Interfaces				
16-chan MIDI				
32-chan MIDI	Opcode Studio 3 [2a]		JL Cooper Nexxus series	Passport MIDI Transport
>32-chan MIDI		MOTU MTP or Opcode Studio 5		
VITC Converter	*MOTU VTP* [2b]			
SGD & Controller				
Kbd Controller	Roland A-80 [3a]	2nd Kbd controller	Kurzweil MIDIBoard	Elka Keyboard Controller
Analog Synth Kbd		Oberheim Matrix-12	Oberheim Matrix-12	
Digital Synth Kbd		Yamaha V-50	Roland D-20	Yamaha V-50
Hybrid Synth Kbd	Korg Wavestation [3b]	Korg M1 or Roland D-70	Roland D-50 or Roland U-20	Korg M1 or Roland D-70 or Yamaha SY-77
Sample Player Kbd			Kurzweil K1200-88	Korg T1
Sampler Kbd		Akai S1000KB	Ensoniq EPS	Korg W-30 or E-mu E-III
Synth/Sample Kbd		Kurzweil K2000	E-mu Emax II	
Analog Module	Roland MKS-70 [3c] *Oberheim Matrix-1000* [3d]	Roland MKS-70	Roland MKS-70	Oberheim Expander
Digital Module	Roland D-550 [3e]	Yamaha TX-802	Yamaha TX-802	Roland D-110 or Yamaha TG-77
Hybrid Module	Korg M1r [3f]		Korg M3r	Korg Wavestation A/D
Samp. Play. Mod.	E-mu Proteus/1 [3g] *E-mu Proteus/2* [3h] E-mu Proformance [3i]	Kurzweil 1200 Pro I, II, and/or III or 2nd E-mu Proteus/2	Roland U-220	Roland Sound Games
Sampler Module	Akai S1000 [3j]	Add hard disk	Roland S-550 Ensoniq EPS (rack mount version)	Roland S-770
Synth/Sample Mod.			E-mu Emax II (rack mount version)	
Drum Machine	Roland R-8 [3k]	Simmons SD series	Simmons SD series	Akai MPC60
Other Controller	JL Cooper Fadermaster [3l] Lexicon MRC [3m]	Niche MAS Fadermonster JL Cooper CS-1	2 JL Cooper Fadermasters	Niche MAS Fadermonster JL Cooper CS-1

Table 7-15: Setup 14 — Intermediate film and video (continued)

	Pictured	Expansion	Alternate 1	Alternate 2
Audio and DSP				
DSP Effects	Lexicon LXP-15 [4a] Roland SDE-3000 [4b]	Lexicon PCM-70 Lexicon 300	Lexicon PCM-70, Korg A-3, or Eventide H-3000	Roland R-880 or Lexicon 480L
Other Signal Processing	*BBE 822A* [4c] 2 DBX 160XTs [4d]	Rane MPE14 or Orban 764A	Drawmer M-500 Orban 764A	Dolby A or S DBX F-900 Roland E-660
MIDI-controlled Mixer	*MOTU MM7* [4e] *(or Niche ACM)*	2nd MIDI-controlled mixer	Yamaha DMP7	Akai MPX820
Console	24-channel Console [4e]	48+ channel Console		
Amplifier	Amplifier [4f]			
Speakers	Yamaha NS-10M [4g] JBL 44-12 [4h]			
Microphone	Microphone [3n]			
Network				
MIDI Patchbay	KMX MIDI Central [2c]			
Audio Patchbay	(not pictured)	360 Systems Audio Matrix-16		
Speaker Switchbox	Speaker switchbox [2d]			
Serial Data Switcher	*Dataspec Serial Switchbox* [2e]			
SCSI Data Switcher	*Computer Friends SCSI Switchbox* [2f]			
Analog Recorder				
Cassette	AIWA WX808 Dual Deck [5d]			
Multitrack	Fostex G16 [5e]		24 track	
Integrated Mixer/Deck			Akai MG1214	
Mixdown Deck	3- or 4-track of choice [5f]			
Digital Recorder				
DtHD (Mac/ext)		Studer Dyaxis	Roland DM-80	Lexicon Opus
Digital MTR		Akai DR1200	DASH MTR - Sony or Studer	

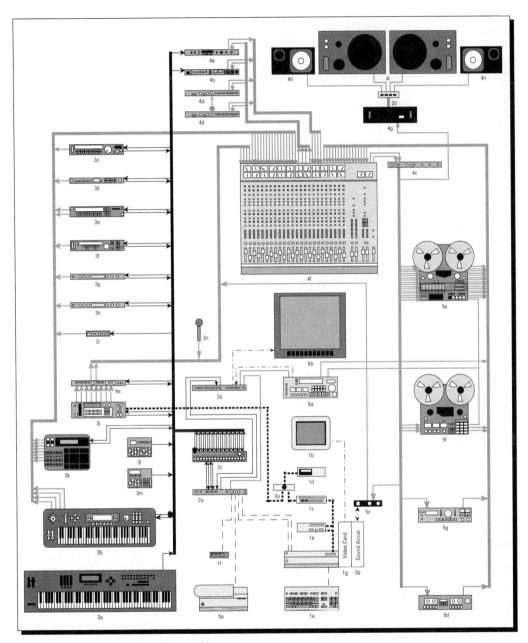

Figure 7-17: Setup 14: Intermediate film and video.

Table 7-15: Setup 14 — Intermediate film and video (continued)

	Pictured	Expansion	Alternate 1	Alternate 2
DAT	*Panasonic 3700* [5g]	Synchronizable DAT	JVC DSDT900 (time code)	
Video				
Deck	JVC BR-7700U [6a]			
Monitor	JVC 27" Monitor [6b]			

Setup 15: Advanced film and video
($83,500 – $108,000)

The advanced setup pictured is merely a point of departure. At this level you could easily have two of almost everything pictured in Figure 7-18 and listed in Table 7-16 (and quadruple the number of DSP effects) and still feel the need to expand. The more sound-generating devices you have, the larger your virtual orchestra. The more output formats you support, the greater your marketability. Many professional setups include two 24-track machines locked together with a synchronizer such as the Adams Smith pictured in Figure 7-18. For similar reasons, you may wish to include a ¾-inch video deck in your setup such as the industry-standard Sony VOS-9850. The large console pictured in this setup is included both to handle the 24-track machine and because, at this level, you will probably be dealing with live performers from time to time.

Table 7-16: Setup 15 — Advanced film and video

	Pictured	Expansion	Alternate 1	Alternate 2
Macintosh	Mac IIfx [1a]	Second Mac	Mac accelerated to close to or beyond IIfx speed	
Mac Peripherals				
RAM	More than 8MB	More RAM		
Monitor	Apple 2-page Display [1b]			
Hard Drive	Gigabyte or more [1c]	More storage		
Backup System	Microtech DAT [1d]	Microtech OR 650 Optical Drive	Microtech OR 650 Optical Drive	
CD-ROM	Apple CD-ROM Drive [1e]			
Printer			Non-PS Laserprinter	
PostScript Printer	PS Laserprinter[5a]			

Table 7-16: Setup 15 — Advanced film and video (continued)

	Pictured	Expansion	Alternate 1	Alternate 2
Misc. Input Devices	Telebit T2500 19,200 bps modem [1f]			

Internal Card

Sampler	*Digidesign SampleCell* [3a]			
Digital Audio	Digidesign Sound Accelerator [5b] with AD-IN [5c]	Add Digidesign DAT I/O or PRO I/O to Sound Accelerator	Digidesign ProTools	
CPU Accelerator		50 MHz or greater		
SCSI Enhancement		Micronet NuPort	Daystar SCSI Accelerator	
Video Card	8-bit Apple Video Card [1g]		24-bit Apple Video Card	

Interfaces

>32-chan MIDI	MOTU MTP [2a] (or Opcode Studio 5)	2nd, 3rd, or 4th MOTU MTP or Opcode Studio 5		
VITC Converter	MOTU VTP [2b]			
Lock-up System	Adams Smith Zeta-3 [2c]			

SGD & Controller

Kbd Controller		2nd Kbd controller	Kurzweil MIDIBoard	Elka Keyboard Controller
Analog Synth Kbd		Oberheim Matrix-12	Oberheim Matrix-12	
Digital Synth Kbd		Yamaha V-50	Roland D-20	Yamaha V-50
Hybrid Synth Kbd		Korg M1 or Roland D-70	Roland D-50 or Roland U-20	Korg Wavestation, Korg M1, Roland D-70 or Yamaha SY-77
Sample Player Kbd	Korg T1 [3b]		Kurzweil K1200-88	Korg T1
Sampler Kbd		Akai S1000KB	Ensoniq EPS	Korg W-30 or E-mu E-III
Synth/Sample Kbd	*Kurzweil K2000* [3c]		E-mu Emax II	
Analog Module	Roland MKS-70 [3d] *Oberheim Matrix-1000* [3e]	Roland MKS-70	Roland MKS-70	Oberheim Expander
Digital Module	Roland D-550 [3f]	Yamaha TX-802	Yamaha TX-802	Roland D-110 or Yamaha TG-77

Table 7-16: Setup 15 — Advanced film and video (continued)

	Pictured	Expansion	Alternate 1	Alternate 2
Hybrid Module	Korg Wavestation A/D [3g]	Korg M1r	Korg M3r	Korg M1r
Samp. Play. Mod.	*E-mu Proteus/1* [3h] *E-mu Proteus/2* [3i] *E-mu Proformance* [3j]	Kurzweil 1200 Pro I, II, and/or III or 2nd E-mu Proteus/2	Roland U-220	Roland Sound Canvas
Sampler Module	Akai S1000 [3k]	Add hard disk	Roland S-550 Ensoniq EPS (rack mount version)	Roland S-770
Synth/Sample Mod.			E-mu Emax II (rack mount version)	
Drum Machine	Roland R-8 [3l]	Simmons SD series	Simmons SD series	Akai MPC60
Other Controller	Niche MAS Fadermonster [3m] *JL Cooper CS-1* [3n] *Lexicon MRC* [3o]		2 JL Cooper Fadermasters	

Audio and DSP

	Pictured	Expansion	Alternate 1	Alternate 2
DSP Effects	Lexicon 300 [4a] *Lexicon LXP-15* [4b] *Roland SDE-3000* [4c]	Lexicon PCM-70 Lexicon 480L	Lexicon PCM-70, Korg A-3, or Eventide H-3000	Roland R-880 or Lexicon 480L
Other Signal Processing	BBE 822A [4d] 2 DBX 160XTs [4e] *Rane MPE14* [4f]	2 DBX 165As Orban 764A Roland RSS Spatializer	Drawmer M-500 Orban 764A	Dolby A or S DBX F-900 Roland E-660
Mixer	Roland M-16E [4g] (drum & kbd submixer)	2nd rackmount mixer	Alesis 1622	Hill Audio
MIDI-controlled Mixer	MOTU MM7 [4h] (or Niche ACM)	2nd MOTU MM7 or Niche ACM	Yamaha DMP7	Akai MPX820
Console	48+ channel Console [4i]			
Amplifier	Amplifier [4j]			
Speakers	Yamaha NS-10M [4k] JBL 44-12 [4l]			
Microphone	At least 2 [3n]			

Network

	Pictured	Expansion	Alternate 1	Alternate 2
MIDI Patchbay			KMX MIDI Central	JL Cooper MSB series
Audio Patchbay	(not pictured)	360 Systems Audio Matrix-16		

Table 7-16: Setup 15 — Advanced film and video (continued)

	Pictured	Expansion	Alternate 1	Alternate 2
Speaker Switchbox	Speaker switchbox [2d]			
Serial Data Switcher	Dataspec Serial Switchbox [2e]			
SCSI Data Switcher	Computer Friends SCSI Switchbox [2f]			
Analog Recorder				
Cassette	AIWA WX808 Dual Deck [5d]			
Multitrack	Otari MTR-80-24 [5e]	2nd 24-track	Other Otari MTR formats	
Integrated Mixer/Deck			Akai MG1214	
Mixdown Deck	3- or 4-track of choice [5f]			
Digital Recorder				
DtHD (Mac/ext)		Studer Dyaxis	Roland DM-80	
Digital MTR		Akai DR1200	DASH MTR - Sony or Studer	
DAT	Panasonic SV-3700 [5g] *Sony PCM-7050* [5h]		JVC DSDT900 (time code)	
Video				
Deck	JVC BR-7700U [6a] *SonyVOS-9850* [6b]			
Monitor	JVC 27" Monitor [6c]			

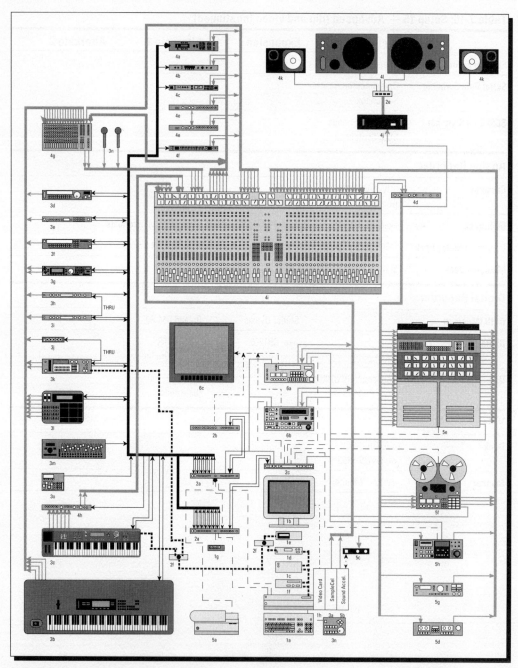

Figure 7-18: Setup 15: Advanced film and video.

Multimedia

(For details see Part Eight, "Multimedia.")

Entry level $2,100 – $3,900

Intermediate $7,500 – $20,000

Advanced #1 $46,000 – $75,000

Advanced #2 $58,000 – $87,000

Multimedia, as the name suggests, requires a multiplicity of media, both as input and as output. There are many avenues to take if you want to become involved in this recently acclaimed field. Multimedia can be interactive or passive and include any or all of the following in just about any juxtaposition or superimposition:

❖ Music
  8-bit digital audio (via the Macintosh audio port)
  16-bit digital audio (via internal digital audio cards)
  MIDI synthesizers, samplers, and sample players

❖ Static Mac-created graphic images
  Black-and-white
  8-bit and 24-bit color
  3-D black-and-white and color

❖ Static graphic images acquired through external devices
  Images scanned in with a B & W or color scanner
  Frames grabbed from a video camera
  Frames grabbed from a VCR
  Frames grabbed from a videodisc

❖ Animation
  Sequences of Mac-created graphics
  Sequences of graphics acquired from external devices
  Animation documents produced by Mac-based animation software

❖ Full-motion video
  From a VCR or video camera
  From a laserdisc
  From a CD-ROM
  From a hard disk (by way of Apple's QuickTime)

❖ External device control
   MIDI instruments and other MIDI devices
   CD-ROM drives
   Compact disc players (audio)
   Videotape players
   Videodisc players

Output media include any combination of the following:

❖ The Macintosh monitor and audio port
❖ The Macintosh monitor and digital audio card output
❖ Slides
❖ Videotape (real time)
❖ Videotape (frame-by-frame)
❖ CD-ROM
❖ Laserdisc
❖ Video presentation device (such as a video or slide projector)
❖ Any of the above in real- or non-real-time combination with any number of external devices that can be placed under Macintosh control. These include:

   ❖ MIDI instruments and other MIDI devices
   ❖ CD-ROM drives
   ❖ Compact disc players (audio)
   ❖ Videotape players
   ❖ Videodisc players

As a consumer of multimedia, you can get by with a single CD-ROM drive and add a laserdisc player. However, the configurations pictured in this section all provide for multimedia authoring and other creative endeavors as well. Because of this, a wide variety of media are supported in each setup. Your own interests will guide you in paring down the systems for the type of input and output you are most comfortable with.

First, you have to decide whether you are interested in becoming a multimedia producer or simply producing music for multimedia. Don't discount the thought of becoming a multimedia producer, even if you are primarily a musician. If you've got the ideas, you'd be surprised how easy they can be realized with a Macintosh equipped with the right tools. To paraphrase multimedia visionary Marc Canter:

"Before the Macintosh there were paintbrushes and musical keyboards — now everything is possible from a single platform, the Macintosh."

Assuming that most of you are musicians, you may notice a slight bias toward configuring the three multimedia setups for the musical aspect of multimedia as the primary objective with the other types of multimedia production illustrated in lesser detail. For example, you may need such things as video distribution amplifiers, special effects, character generators, dedicated cable interfaces, video conversion boxes (e.g., RGB to NTSC or back), slidewriters, and other task-specific devices introduced into the video loop. Just as I have omitted audio patchbays from the audio loop, I have omitted these items for the sake of illustration.

If you are going to get into the production side, meaning not just the music but the visual content as well, you should select your video card or cards very carefully. There are a number of factors to consider: 8-bit or 24-bit, with or without graphics accelerator, and with or without image compression.

Next, you need boards that will, with respect to the visual element, function analogously to the tools for sound manipulation that form the basis of your interaction with your synths and samplers. Most video boards of this kind provide many desirable features, but no one board may provide all the features you need at the level you require. Features of high-end video boards include overlaying Macintosh graphics with video, displaying full-motion video in a fixed or resizable window on your computer monitor, grabbing frames from external video sources, outputting full-motion composite (in the U.S. this means NTSC) video to an external video recorder, outputting single frames one at a time to an animation recorder, providing an interface to video-processing devices, and supporting Apple's QuickTime direct-to-hard disk digital video.

One reason why your choice of video boards is crucial is that you will prob-ably want at least two in your Macintosh. Putting extra boards in a Macintosh is an easy thing for a computer graphics artist or animator, but for a musician there are other concerns. The problem is that your Macintosh may already be crammed full of cards of the digital audio persuasion. You may have a MacProteus, Sound Accelerator, or Audiomedia card in there, plus a SampleCell or two or four — a veritable digital music workstation all within your Macintosh CPU. Not to mention that you might also have a disk-duplexing card in there along with a SCSI accelerator (thank goodness most CPU accelerators don't install on the NuBus). Non-musicians working in multimedia don't have such a wide array of choices and never seem to be running out of slots. Of course, there are NuBus expansion chassis that will provide you with a number of additional slots. And many professional musi-cians who are getting into multimedia find themselves seriously considering such NuBus expansion chassis; they are not cheap, running about $2,000.

Setup 16: Entry level multimedia setup
($2,100 – $3,900)

This setup is in many respects similar to setup 1, the entry level 8-bit non-MIDI music setup (see Table 7-17 and Figure 7-19). From a musician's standpoint the primary concern is with 8-bit non-MIDI music.

Many impressive presentations can be created with a single MacRecorder and HyperCard running the MacroMind animation engine. If you have seen the award-winning interactive universe "Cosmic Osmo," you can see the power of these two simple tools.

Add a scanner to the setup and you have all that was necessary to create Opcode's wonderful interactive "Book of MIDI" HyperCard stack set.

Add MacroMind Director as an authoring tool and you have the tools to create just about any guided tour that you have ever seen, including those of Apple Computer. MacroMind already has two CD-ROMs of interactive multimedia presentations available, including documents, the vast majority of which could have been created with this entry level setup.

Speaking of CD-ROMs, if you bring Voyager's AudioStack interactive CD-ROM authoring software into the picture, you have everything you need to create an interactive presentation using any 16-bit compact disc as the sound source. Outstanding examples of this medium are Voyager's own *Beethoven's Ninth* and *The Rite of Spring* packages and Warner New Media's *The Magic Flute* and *Beethoven's 14th String Quartet*. While you are at it, you should check out *Verbum Magazine*'s CD-ROM edition, "Verbum Interactive" (a two-disc set).

As you can see, even with this entry level setup, the possibilities are virtually limitless.

Table 7-17: Setup 16 — Entry level multimedia

	Pictured	Expansion	Alternate 1	Alternate 2
Macintosh	Compact Mac [1a]		Mac LC	MAC IIsi
Mac Peripherals				
RAM	2 to 4MB			
Monitor			Apple 13" Monitor	Apple Full-page Display or Apple 2-page Display
Hard Drive	40-80MB [1c]			
Backup System		Microtech Syquest		
CD-ROM	Apple CD-ROM Drive [1c]			

Table 7-17: Setup 16 — Entry level multimedia (continued)

	Pictured	Expansion	Alternate 1	Alternate 2
Printer	Apple Image-Writer LQ [1d]	Non-PS Laserprinter		
PostScript Printer			PS Laserprinter	
Scanner	*Handheld scanner* [3a]			
8-bit Digitizer	MacroMind-Para-comp MacRecorder [3b]		Articulate Systems VoiceLink	SID
Misc. Input Devices	USR Courier 2400 baud modem [1f] *Digital Visions Computer Eyes Pro* [3c]		Koala MacVision	Digital Visions Computer Eyes Pro

Internal Card

	Pictured	Expansion	Alternate 1	Alternate 2
CPU Accelerator		16 to 40 MHz accelerator		
Video Card	8-bit Apple Video Card [1e]		24-bit Apple Video Card	
Frame Grabber		ColorSnap 32		

Audio and DSP

	Pictured	Expansion	Alternate 1	Alternate 2
Amplifier				Amplifier
Speakers				Yamaha NS-10M
Powered Speakers	Roland CS-10 [4a]		Roland MA-12C	
Microphone	*Microphone* [3d]			

Network

	Pictured	Expansion	Alternate 1	Alternate 2
Serial Data Switcher	*Dataspec Serial Switchbox* [2a]			

Analog Recorder

	Pictured	Expansion	Alternate 1	Alternate 2
Cassette	AIWA WX808 Dual Deck [5a]			
Integrated Mixer/Deck		Fostex 280	Fostex 280	

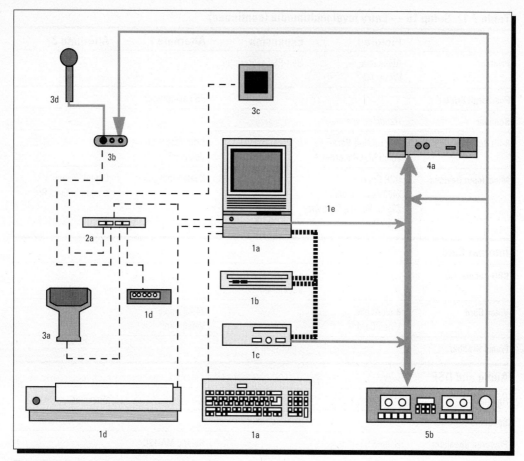

Figure 7-19: Setup 16: Entry level multimedia.

Setup 17: Intermediate multimedia
($7,500 – $20,000)

The intermediate level setup adds to 8-bit digital audio the option to bring your own MIDI music into the picture and suggests the upgrading to Digidesign's Audiomedia card for true 16-bit CD-quality digital audio. In either case, your 8- or 16-bit soundfiles are going to require the hefty storage and backup systems pictured.

Even if you aren't a trained musician, if you can at least pick out a tune, the pictured CA-30 Intelligent Arranger from Roland can take your input and turn it into a full band or orchestral arrangement. This also helps you avoid any copyright infringement charges if you succumb to the temptation of digitizing OPM (other people's music).

Although the MIDI features are all in italics to highlight the fact that they are optional in case you need them, the DSP effects and integrated mixer/cassette deck are not italicized (see Table 7-18). This is to urge you to get involved in some of the effects that you can achieve by running your sound source through a DSP device and using basic multitracking techniques on the way to the MacRecorder or Audiomedia card.

Additional audio support devices have been added to the setup to provide for expanded audio capabilities (see Figure 7-20).

For those of you who want to exercise your visual creativity, a general-purpose TrueVision NuVista+ is recommended, because it provides a resizable full-motion video window from which you can grab frames and also provides for overlaying Mac-created graphics with video and outputting the result in composite video to any NTSC (other formats available) device such as a VCR. The wealth of features found in this single board means that you won't have to use up more than one additional NuBus slot. The optional video camera and deck are both LANC (Control-L) compatible to facilitate their interface to MacroMind MediaMaker.

Table 7-18: Setup 17 — Intermediate multimedia

	Pictured	Expansion	Alternate 1	Alternate 2
Macintosh	Mac II — 3-slot [1a]		Mac II — 6-slot	
Mac Peripherals				
RAM	4 to 8MB			
Monitor	(See below under video) [1b]		Apple Full-page Display	Apple 2-page Display
Hard Drive	80 to 600MB [1c]	Additional storage		
Backup System	Microtech Syquest [1d]	Microtech T150	Microtech DAT Golden Triangle DiskTwin	Microtech or 650 Optical Drive
CD-ROM	Apple CD-ROM Drive [1e]			
Printer	Non-PS Laserprinter [5a]			
PostScript Printer		PS Laserprinter	PS Laserprinter	
Scanner	Apple Flatbed Scanner [3a]			
8-bit Digitizer	MacroMind-Para-comp MacRecorder [3b]		Articulate Systems VoiceLink	SID

Table 7-18: Setup 17 — Intermediate multimedia (continued)

	Pictured	**Expansion**	**Alternate 1**	**Alternate 2**
Misc. Input Devices	USR Courier 2400 baud modem [1f] *Digital Visions Computer Eyes Pro* [3c]		Koala MacVision	Digital Visions Computer Eyes Pro

Internal Card

	Pictured	**Expansion**	**Alternate 1**	**Alternate 2**
Digital Audio	*Digidesign Audiomedia* [5b]			Digidesign Sound Accelerator
CPU Accelerator		32-40 MHz Accelerator	CacheCard	
SCSI Enhancement		Daystar SCSI Accelerator		
Video Card	8-bit Apple Video Card [1g]			
Graphics Accelerator		Apple 8•24 GC		
Video Compression		JPEG Compression	C-Cube Compression	
Composite Output	*TrueVision NuVista, or NuVista+* [3d]			
Full-motion Display			Workstation Moonraker	Radius TV or VideoLogic DVA-4000
Frame Grabber	(included w/above)		Aapps Micro TV, DigiVideo, or DigiVideo Color RasterOps 364	Mass Micro QuickImage 24 or Orange Micro Personal Vision

Interfaces

	Pictured	**Expansion**	**Alternate 1**	**Alternate 2**
16-chan MIDI			Altech MIDI Interface	Opcode MIDI Translator
32-chan MIDI	*Opcode Studio 3* [2a]		Altech MIDI Interface	Passport MIDI Transport

SGD & Controller

	Pictured	**Expansion**	**Alternate 1**	**Alternate 2**
Kbd Controller	*Roland PC-200* [3e]		Roland A-80	Kurzweil MIDIBoard or Elka Keyboard Controller
Hybrid Synth Kbd			Korg M1	Korg T1
Sample Player Kbd			Roland U-20	Kurzweil K1200-88
Sampler Kbd			Akai S1000KB	Ensoniq EPS
Synth/Sample Kbd			Kurzweil K2000	E-mu Emax II

Table 7-18: Setup 17 — Intermediate multimedia (continued)

	Pictured	Expansion	Alternate 1	Alternate 2
Analog Module		Oberheim Matrix-1000		
Digital Module		Roland D-550	Yamaha TX-802	Roland D-110
Hybrid Module	*Roland CM Series* [3f]		Korg M1rex	Korg Wavestation A/D
Samp. Play. Mod.		E-mu Proteus/1 and/or Proteus/2	Kurzweil 1200 Pro I, II, or III	Roland Sound Canvas
Sampler Module	*Roland S-550* [3g]	Akai S1000	Akai S1000	Roland S-770
Synth/Sample Mod.				
Drum Machine	*Alesis HR or SR* [3h]	Roland R-8	Roland R-8	
Other Controller	*Roland CA-30* [3i]	Niche MAS Fadermonster	Lexicon MRC	

Audio and DSP

	Pictured	Expansion	Alternate 1	Alternate 2
DSP Effects	Lexicon LXP-5 [4a]	Lexicon LXP-15	Lexicon LXP-15 Yamaha SPX-900	Lexicon PCM-70 Roland SRV-2000
Other Signal Processing		DBX 166 BBE 422 or 822A	DBX 166 BBE 422 or 822A	Drawmer M-500 Aphex 612
Mixer	Boss BX-8 or BX-80 [4b]		Roland M-16E	
Amplifier	Amplifier [4c]			
Speakers	Yamaha NS-10M [4d]	Bigger speakers such as JBL 44-12	Tannoy	
Powered Speakers			Roland MA-12C	
Microphone	Microphone [3j]			

Network

	Pictured	Expansion	Alternate 1	Alternate 2
Serial Data Switcher	*Dataspec Serial Switchbox* [2b]			

Analog Recorder

	Pictured	Expansion	Alternate 1	Alternate 2
Cassette	AIWA WX808 Dual Deck [5c]			
Multitrack		Tascam ATR-60/8 or 60/8HS	Tascam ATR-60/8 or 60/8HS	Fostex G16
Integrated Mixer/Deck	Fostex 280 [5d]		Akai MG1214	
Mixdown Deck		Fostex E2		

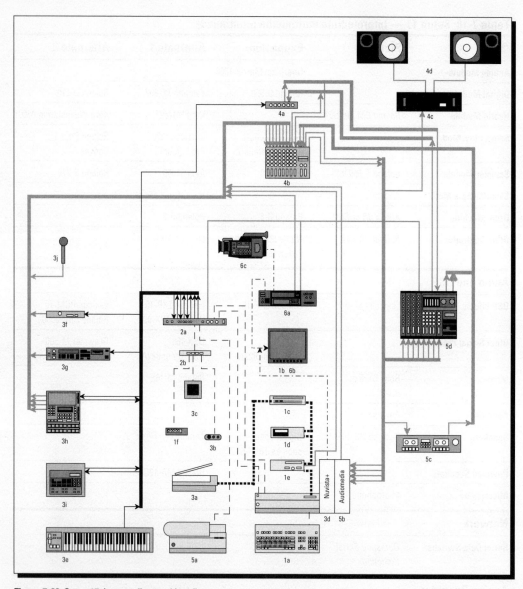

Figure 7-20: Setup 17: Intermediate multimedia.

Table 7-18: Setup 17 — Intermediate multimedia (continued)

	Pictured	Expansion	Alternate 1	Alternate 2
Digital Recorder				
DAT		Panasonic SV-3700		
Video				
Deck (LANC protocol)	*Sony SLV-757* [6a]	Sony EVS-900 NEC PC-VCR		
Monitor	Sony GVM-1300 [6b]			
Camera	*Sony V-101* [6c]			

Setup 18: Advanced multimedia

($46,000 – $75,000 without frame-by-frame or slide output)
($58,000 – $87,000 with frame-by-frame or slide output)

This setup, more than any other one in this chapter, is by far the most flexible, providing, in some way or another, for just about any single Macintosh music application — all you need is the right software. If you want to get involved in every aspect of Macintosh music you should examine setup 18 (both the pictured and expansion columns) in relation to the intermediate and advanced configurations of the other applications discussed in this chapter (see Table 7-19).

There aren't many italicized options here, suggesting that at this level you are definitely going to want to become involved in multimedia in its entirety, not just from the musical side of things. You may want to look at this setup as the foundation of a full-service multimedia production facility.

Dropping the graphics and video support devices from the configuration will leave you with everything that you need to provide the music for any multimedia project, be it an interactive CD-ROM, laserdisc, or some future medium yet to appear on the scene.

Conversely, the video input and editing devices have been considerably expanded from the intermediate setup. Now two LANC decks are suggested (one a Hi8 and the other an S-VHS), and a Sony Mavica still video camera has been added.

Two items not pictured in Figure 7-21 are a frame-by-frame output system and a slide-output system. Both of these add significantly to the cost of your setup (see above), so you may want to consider using service bureaus for the time being when you need these forms of output. Don't forget, such items are rentable and the bulk of your time is going to be spent in creative matters as opposed to output (meaning your output devices might be sitting gathering dust a good deal of the time). Now even recordable videodiscs can be rented inexpensively.

Table 7-19: Setup 18 — Advanced multimedia

	Pictured	Expansion	Alternate 1	Alternate 2
Macintosh	Mac IIfx [1a]		Accelerated Mac II — 3- or 6-slot	
Mac Peripherals				
RAM	8MB or more			
Monitor	19" Color [1b]			
Hard Drive	600 to 1.2 Gig [1c]	Additional storage		
Backup System	Microtech DAT [1d]		Microtech OR 650 Optical Drive	8mm
CD-ROM	Apple CD-ROM Drive [1e]			
Printer				
PostScript Printer	PS Laserprinter [5a]			
Scanner	Color Scanner [3a]		La Cie Color scanner	Sharp JX-600 Color scanner
8-bit Digitizer	*Articulate Systems VoiceLink* [3b]		MacroMind-Paracomp MacRecorder	
Misc. Input Devices	Telebit T2500 19,200 bps modem [1f] *Digital Visions Computer Eyes Pro* [1g]		Koala MacVision	Digital Visions Computer Eyes Pro
Internal Card				
Sample Player	*Digidesign MacProteus* [3c]			
Sampler	*Digidesign SampleCell* [3d]			
Digital Audio	Digidesign Sound Accelerator [5b] with AD-IN [5c] and DAT I/O [5d]		Digidesign Audiomedia	Digidesign PRO I/O for the Sound Accelerator
CPU Accelerator		50 MHz or more		
SCSI Enhancement		Daystar SCSI Accelerator Micronet NuPort		
Video Card	24-bit Apple Video Card (with accelerator) [1h]			
Graphics Accelerator	(on video card)			
Video Compression		Compression card	JPEG Compression	C-Cube Compression

Table 7-19: Setup 18 — Advanced multimedia (continued)

	Pictured	Expansion	Alternate 1	Alternate 2
Full-motion Display			RasterOps 364 Workstation Moonraker	Radius TV or VideoLogic DVA-4000
Frame Grabber	RasterOps 364 [3f]		Aapps Micro TV, DigiVideo, or DigiVideo Color	Mass Micro QuickImage 24 or Orange Micro Personal Vision
Composite Output	TrueVision NuVista+ [5e]		VENT Mac Video, Mass Micro Easy-Video8 or ColorSpace, Computer Friends TV ProducerPRO, Generation X TV Box	RasterOps 232/SFX TrueVision NuVista+
Frame-by-frame Output		Frame-by-frame output device	PC-VCR Diaquest DQ-Animaq	Advanced Digital Imaging MacVac
Video Processing		Video processor	VENT Video Master IMT 8000	Digital F/X Video F/X, Avid Avid1 Media Composer

Interfaces

	Pictured	Expansion	Alternate 1	Alternate 2
16-chan MIDI				
32-chan MIDI			Opcode Studio 3	Passport MIDI Transport
>32-chan MIDI	2 MOTU MTPs or Opcode Studio 5s [2a]	2nd MOTU MTP or Opcode Studio 5		
VITC Converter		MOTU VTP		
Lock-up System		Adams Smith Zeta-3		

SGD & Controller

	Pictured	Expansion	Alternate 1	Alternate 2
Kbd Controller	Roland A-80 [3h]	2nd Kbd controller	Kurzweil MIDIBoard	Elka Keyboard Controller
Analog Synth Kbd		Oberheim Matrix-12	Oberheim Matrix-12	
Digital Synth Kbd		Yamaha V-50	Roland D-20	Yamaha V-50
Hybrid Synth Kbd		Korg M1 or Roland D-70	Roland D-50 or Roland U-20	Korg Wavestation, Korg M1, Roland D-70, or Yamaha SY-77
Sample Player Kbd			Kurzweil K1200-88	Korg T1
Sampler Kbd		Akai S1000KB	Ensoniq EPS	Korg W-30 or E-mu E-III

Part One: The Basics

Table 7-19: Setup 18 — Advanced multimedia (continued)

	Pictured	Expansion	Alternate 1	Alternate 2
Synth/Sample Kbd		Kurzweil K2000	E-mu Emax II	
Analog Module	*Roland MKS-70* [3i] *Oberheim Matrix-1000* [3j]	Roland MKS-70	Roland MKS-70	Oberheim Expander
Digital Module	*Roland D-550* [3k]	Yamaha TX-802	Yamaha TX-802	Roland D-110 or Yamaha TG-77
Hybrid Module	*Korg Wavestation A/D* [3l]	Korg M1r	Korg M3r	Korg M1r
Samp. Play. Mod.	*E-mu Proteus/1* [3m] *E-mu Proteus/2* [3n] *E-mu Proformance* [3o]	Kurzweil 1200 Pro I, II, and/or III or 2nd E-mu Proteus/2	Roland U-220	Roland Sound Canvas
Sampler Module	Akai S1000 [3p]	Add hard disk	Roland S-550 Ensoniq EPS (rack mount version)	Roland S-770
Synth/Sample Mod.			E-mu Emax II (rack mount version)	
Drum Machine	*Roland R-8* [3q]	Simmons SD series	Simmons SD series	Akai MPC60
Other Controller	*Niche MAS Fadermonster* [3r] *JL Cooper CS-1* [3s] *Lexicon MRC* [3t]		2 JL Cooper Fadermasters	

Audio and DSP

	Pictured	Expansion	Alternate 1	Alternate 2
DSP Effects	Lexicon LXP-15 [4a]	Lexicon 300 Roland SDE-3000	Lexicon PCM-70, Korg A-3, or Eventide H-3000	Roland R-880 or Lexicon 480L
Other Signal Processing	BBE 822A [4b] *2 DBX-160XTs* [4c]	2 DBX 165As Rane MPE14 Roland RSS Spatializer	Drawmer M-500 Orban 764A	Dolby A or S DBX F-900 Roland E-660
Mixer	Roland M-16E [4d]	2nd rackmount mixer	Alesis 1622	Hill Audio
MIDI-controlled Mixer	*MOTU MM7 (or Niche ACM)* [4e]	2nd MOTU MM7	Yamaha DMP7 or Niche ACM	Akai MPX820
Console	*24-channel Console* [4f]			
Amplifier	Amplifier [4g]			
Speakers	Yamaha NS-10M [4h] JBL 44-12 [4i]			
Microphone	At least 2 [3u]			

Table 7-19: Setup 18 — Advanced multimedia (continued)

	Pictured	Expansion	Alternate 1	Alternate 2
Network				
MIDI Patchbay			JL Cooper MSB series	
Audio Patchbay	(not pictured)	360 Systems Audio Matrix-16		
Speaker Switchbox	Speaker switchbox [4k]			
Serial Data Switcher	Dataspec Serial Switchbox [2b]			
SCSI Data Switcher	Computer Friends SCSI Switchbox [2c]			
Analog Recorder				
Cassette	AIWA WX808 Dual Deck [5f]			
Multitrack	*Fostex G16* [5g]	2nd Otari MTR	Tascam ATR-60/8 or 60/8HS	Otari MTR-80-24
Integrated Mixer/Deck			Akai MG1214	
Mixdown Deck	2-, 3-, or 4-track of choice [5h]			
Digital Recorder				
DtHD (Mac/ext)		Studer Dyaxis	Roland DM-80	
Digital MTR		Akai DR1200	Studer DASH MTR	
DAT	Panasonic SV-3700 [5i]	Sony PCM-7050	JVC DSDT900 (time code)	
Video				
Deck (first 2 support LANC protocol)	Sony EVS-900 [6a] Sony SLV-757 [6b] *Sony VOS-9850* [6c]	NEC PC-VCR		
Serially-controlled Videodisc Player	Pioneer LVP-8000 [6g]			
Monitor	Sony GVM-1300 [6d]			
Camera	Sony V-101 [6e] *Sony Mavica* [6f]			

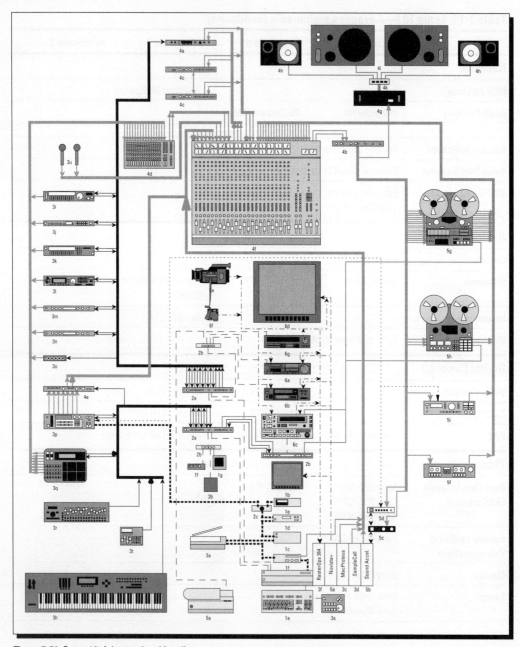

Figure 7-21: Setup 18: Advanced multimedia.

Education

(For details see Part Nine, "Education.")

Entry level $700 – $1,600

Intermediate $3,500 – $10,000

Advanced $15,000 – $38,000

Using the Macintosh as an educational tool can take many forms. Two subcategories are self-guided learning and institutional instruction. In an institutional setting, a properly configured Macintosh can be used by the instructor alone, by the instructor and the students, or simply by the students in conjunction with appropriate direction. Related activities for an educator include scholarly research and analysis and the creation of personal teaching tools.

The three setups in this category are organized so they can easily be adapted to function as a single workstation viable at home for self-guided learning, as a single workstation in a classroom, or as multiple workstations in an institutional computer music lab. In the latter case, it is often desirable to have multiple workstations networked together. Such networking can deal with computer data alone (providing for students to transmit their assignments to the instructor's centralized file server), or with MIDI data (providing for the sharing of resources and offering the possibility to combine a number of complementary workstations into a single entity for larger projects).

Besides the obvious use of a Macintosh-based music workstation in the teaching of electronic music, education applications now embrace ear-training, music theory, history and appreciation, orchestration, composition, and performance. Software is available that is appropriate for every grade level from kindergarten to graduate school. The systems in this section attempt to support as many of these activities as possible, yet they are modular enough that components that are inapplicable to the specific educational environment can be dropped accordingly.

Having taught at and consulted for many educational institutions, I am well aware of the budgetary obstacles that can hinder the establishment of a computer learning station, particularly one exclusively dedicated to music. Because of this, cost has been a serious consideration in building the setups in this section.

Although there may be some barriers to breach in bringing state-of-the-art educational tools to your institution, Apple has many academic discounts when it comes to purchasing the computers themselves, some hardware companies have similar education incentives, and many software companies provide low-cost site licenses where multiple copies of their programs are going to be used by a group of students.

Setup 19: Entry level education
($700 – $1,600)

This setup provides for both interactive disk-based and CD-ROM instruction, and a variety of non-MIDI CAI (computer-aided instruction) software (see Table 7-20). MacroMind-Paracomp's MacRecorder is included as a tool to use for some authoring systems, but it also can be used as an excellent introduction to principles of digital audio (see Figure 7-22).

Table 7-20: Setup 19 — Entry level education

	Pictured	Expansion	Alternate 1	Alternate 2
Macintosh	Compact Mac [1a]		Mac LC	
Mac Peripherals				
RAM	2 to 4MB			
Hard Drive	40 - 80MB [1b]			
Backup System		Microtech Syquest		
CD-ROM	Apple CD-ROM Drive [1c]			
Printer		Apple ImageWriter LQ	Non-PS Laserprinter	
PostScript Printer			PS Laserprinter	
8-bit Digitizer	MacroMind-Paracomp MacRecorder [3a]		Articulate Systems VoiceLink	SID
Misc. Input Devices	USR Courier 2400 baud modem [1d]			
Audio and DSP				
Amplifier				Amplifier
Speakers				Yamaha NS-10M
Powered Speakers	Roland CS-10 [4a]		Roland MA-12C	
Network				
Serial Data Switcher	Dataspec Serial Switchbox [2a]			

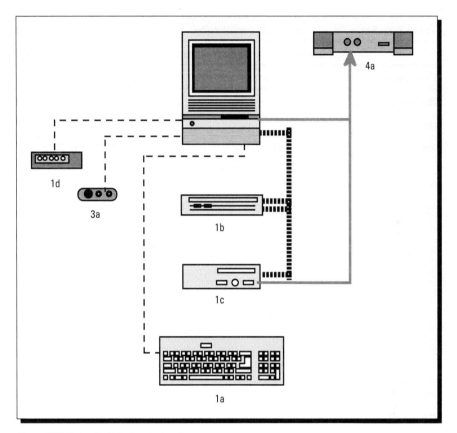

Figure 7-22: Setup 19: Entry level education.

Setup 20: Intermediate education
($3,500 – $10,000)

This setup builds upon the entry level setup adding printing capabilities for music notation, basic MIDI devices, additional authoring tools (e.g., the scanner), and a cassette recorder for saving student projects (see Table 7-21 and Figure 7-23).

In addition to the possibilities offered by the CD-ROM drive, the interactive videodisc player expands these into an area that is only just beginning to be explored by developers of education music software.

Table 7-21: Setup 20 — Intermediate education

	Pictured	Expansion	Alternate 1	Alternate 2
Macintosh	Mac II — 3-slot [1a]		Mac II — 6-slot	
Mac Peripherals				
RAM	4 to 8MB			
Monitor	Apple 12" or 13" Monitor [1b]		Apple Full-page Display	Apple 2-page Display
Hard Drive	80 to 100MB [1c]	Additional storage		
Backup System	*Microtech Syquest* [1d]	Microtech T150	Golden Triangle DiskTwin	
CD-ROM	Apple CD-ROM Drive [1e]			
Printer	*Non-PS Laserprinter* [5a]			
PostScript Printer		PS Laserprinter	PS Laserprinter	
Scanner	*Handheld scanner* [3a]		Apple Flatbed Scanner	
8-bit Digitizer MacRecorder [3b]	MacroMind-Paracomp	VoiceLink	Articulate Systems	SID
Misc. Input Devices	*USR Courier 2400 baud modem* [1f]			
Internal Card				
CPU Accelerator		32-40 MHz Card	**CacheCard**	
SCSI Enhancement		Daystar SCSI Accelerator		
Video Card	8-bit Apple Video Card [1g]			
Interfaces				
16-chan MIDI	*Opcode MIDI Translator* [2a]			
32-chan MIDI		Opcode Studio 3	Altech MIDI Interface	Passport MIDI Transport
SGD & Controller				
Kbd Controller	*Roland PC-200* [3c]		Roland A-80	Kurzweil MIDIBoard or Elka Keyboard Controller
Sample Player Kbd			Roland U-20	Kurzweil K1200-88
Hybrid Module	*Roland CM Series* [3d]		Roland Sound Canvas	

Table 7-21: Setup 20 — Intermediate education (continued)

	Pictured	**Expansion**	**Alternate 1**	**Alternate 2**
Samp. Play. Mod.		E-mu Proteus/2 E-mu Proformance	E-mu Proteus/2 E-mu Proformance	Kurzweil 1200 Pro I, II, or III

Audio and DSP

	Pictured	**Expansion**	**Alternate 1**	**Alternate 2**
DSP Effects	*Lexicon LXP-1 or* *Lexicon LXP-5* [4a]	Lexicon LXP-15	Lexicon LXP-15 Yamaha SPX-900	Lexicon PCM-70 Roland SRV-2000
Mixer	*Boss BX-8 or* *BX-80* [4b]			
Amplifier	*Amplifier* [4c]			
Speakers	*Yamaha NS-10M* [4d]	Bigger speakers such as JBL 44-12	Tannoy	
Powered Speakers			Roland MA-12C	
Microphone	*Microphone* [3e]			
Network				
Serial Data Switcher	*Dataspec Serial* *Switchbox* [2b]			

Analog Recorder

	Pictured	**Expansion**	**Alternate 1**	**Alternate 2**
Cassette	*AIWA WX808* *Dual Deck* [5b]			
Integrated Mixer/Deck		Fostex 280	Fostex 280	Akai MG1214
Mixdown Deck		2-, 3-, or 4-track of choice		

Video

	Pictured	**Expansion**	**Alternate 1**	**Alternate 2**
Monitor	*JVC 27" Monitor* [6a]			
Serial-controlled **Videodisc Player**	*Pioneer LVP-8000* [6b]			

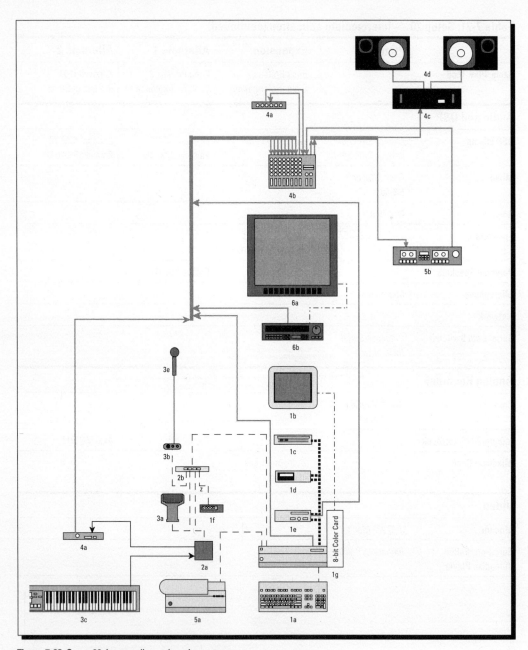

Figure 7-23: Setup 20: Intermediate education.

Setup 21: Advanced education
($15,000 – $38,000)

Although some wealthier institutions provide multiple workstations in this price range, a single workstation (pictured in Figure 7-24) could be modularized in such a way that it could serve as the basis of a computer or electronic music studio and also serve in a variety of other educational settings. Many of the italicized options represent an expansion of the authoring capabilities provided for in the intermediate setup (see Table 7-22).

Were an institution to configure multiple workstations based upon Figure 7-24, a practical strategy to follow might include the substitution of Fostex 280s (integrated mixer/cassette decks) for the Akai MG12-14, and the replacement of some of the sound reinforcement gear with headphones. This of course is because using anything else in a lab with multiple workstations would preclude the possibility of multiple users taking advantage of the facility simultaneously.

In such a situation, each workstation might have the three main sound-generating devices, referring to the Korg T-1 hybrid synthesizer (which also serves as the controller), the Proteus/2 sample player, and the S-550 sampler, while only a single workstation is completely decked out with the SampleCell and Audiomedia cards. Similarly, each workstation could have a lower-capacity (80MB) hard drive, while the fully configured one would need a large-capacity drive to deal with the digital audio requirements. Naturally, there need only be one laser printer on the network.

Table 7-22: Setup 21 — Advanced education

	Pictured	Expansion	Alternate 1	Alternate 2
Macintosh	Mac II — 3-slot [1a]		Mac II — 6-slot	
Mac Peripherals				
RAM	4 to 8MB [1b]			
Monitor	Apple 12" or 13" Monitor [1c]		Apple Full-page Display	Apple 2-page Display
Hard Drive	80 to 600MB [1d]	Additional storage		
Backup System	Microtech Syquest [1e]	Microtech T150	Microtech DAT	Microtech or 650 Optical Drive
CD-ROM	Apple CD-ROM Drive [1f]			
Printer			*Non-PS Laserprinter*	
PostScript Printer	PS Laserprinter [5a]			
Scanner	*Apple Flatbed Scanner* [3a]			

Table 7-22: Setup 21 — Advanced education (continued)

	Pictured	**Expansion**	**Alternate 1**	**Alternate 2**
8-bit Digitizer	MacroMind-Para-comp MacRecorder [3b]		Articulate Systems VoiceLink	SID
Misc. Input Devices	USR Courier 2400 baud modem [3c]			
Video Digitizer	*Digital Visions Computer Eyes Pro* [3d]		Koala MacVision	Aapps Micro TV, DigiVideo, DigiVideo Color, Orange Micro Personal Vision

Internal Card

	Pictured	**Expansion**	**Alternate 1**	**Alternate 2**
Sample Player	*Digidesign MacProteus* [3e]			
Sampler	*Digidesign SampleCell* [3f]			
Digital Audio	Digidesign Audiomedia [5b]			Digidesign Sound Accelerator
Video Card	8-bit Apple Video Card [1g]		24-bit Color	
Frame Grabber	*TrueVision NuVista+* [3g]		Mass Micro QuickImage 24	

Interfaces

	Pictured	**Expansion**	**Alternate 1**	**Alternate 2**
32-chan MIDI	Opcode Studio 3 [2a]		Altech MIDI Interface	Passport MIDI Transport
>32-chan MIDI		MOTU MTP or Opcode Studio 5		

SGD & Controller

	Pictured	**Expansion**	**Alternate 1**	**Alternate 2**
Kbd Controller			Kurzweil MIDIBoard	Roland A-80 or Elka Keyboard Controller
Hybrid Kbd	Korg T1 [3h]			
Sample Player Kbd			Kurzweil K1200-88	
Samp. Play. Mod.	E-mu Proteus/2 [3i] *E-mu Proformance* [3j]	2nd E-mu Proteus/2 or Kurzweil 1200 Pro I, II, III	Kurzweil 1200 Pro I, II, III	Roland U-220 Roland Sound Canvas

Table 7-22: Setup 21 — Advanced education (continued)

	Pictured	Expansion	Alternate 1	Alternate 2
Sampler Module	*Roland S-550* [3k]		Akai S1000	Roland S-770
Synth/Sample Mod.			Kurzweil K2000	
Other Controller	*JL Cooper Fadermaster* [3l]	Lexicon MRC JL Cooper CS-1	Niche MAS Fadermonster	

Audio and DSP

	Pictured	Expansion	Alternate 1	Alternate 2
DSP Effects	Lexicon LXP-15 [4a]	Lexicon 300	Lexicon PCM-70	Korg A-3
Mixer	*Roland M-16E* [4b]			
Console		24-channel Console		
Amplifier	Amplifier [4c]			
Speakers	Yamaha NS-10M [4d] *JBL 44-12* [4e]			
Microphone	*At least 2* [4g]			

Network

	Pictured	Expansion	Alternate 1	Alternate 2
Serial Data Switcher	*Dataspec Serial Switchbox* [2b]			

Analog Recorder

	Pictured	Expansion	Alternate 1	Alternate 2
Cassette	AIWA WX808 Dual Deck [5c]			
Multitrack			Tascam ATR-60/8 or -60/8HS	Fostex G16
Integrated Mixer/Deck	*Akai MG1214* [5d]		Fostex 280	
Mixdown Deck	2-, 3-, or 4-track of choice [5e]			

Digital Recorder

	Pictured	Expansion	Alternate 1	Alternate 2
DAT	*Panasonic SV-3700* [5f]			

Video

	Pictured	Expansion	Alternate 1	Alternate 2
Monitor	JVC 27" Monitor [6a]			
Serial-controlled Videodisc Player	Pioneer LVP-8000 [6b]			

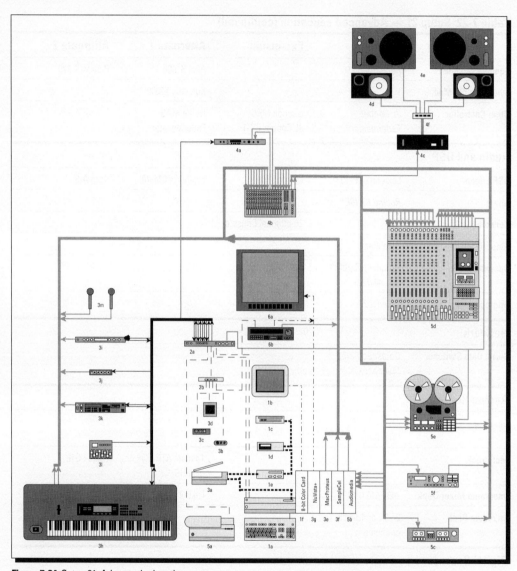

Figure 7-24: Setup 21: Advanced education.

The Author's Multi-Purpose Setup

Prior to the introduction of the Macintosh, my involvement with computers and electronic music was limited to the gear available at the educational institutions I attended. On the computer side, this consisted of IBM mainframes. On the electronic music side, this consisted of Arp 2500 and 2600 synthesizers and several 2-track ¼-inch tape decks.

Studio evolution

In 1984, I started with a 128K Macintosh (and an ImageWriter) that I bought expressly for the purpose of running Mark of the Unicorn's Professional Composer and MacroMind's MusicWorks, which were, at that time, the only music programs available for the Macintosh. The rest of my gear consisted of a Roland VK-09 synthesizer (non-MIDI), a Fender Rhodes (non-MIDI) electric piano, a Yamaha DX7, a Roland MSQ-100 hardware sequencer that stored sequence data on audio cassettes, a nameless graphics equalizer, a dbx noise reduction box, a Teac 4-track ¼-inch tape recorder, a Sony TC-153 SD cassette deck, a Fender guitar amplifier, and a pair of headphones. From time to time, I would borrow a friend's Yamaha TX 816.

In 1985, I had become tired of FM synthesis and having been a classically trained musician from the start, I started shopping around for something that sounded more like the instruments that I had been accustomed to. I decided to put all my eggs in one basket and purchase a Kurzweil 250 (I was the 700th person to do so if the serial number can be believed). In 1985, I also purchased a Tascam-48 ½-inch 8-track recorder and a Boss 8-channel mixer to go with it. As every new Macintosh came out, I upgraded to it immediately. Likewise with Macintosh peripherals: I purchased an external 400K disk drive when they appeared and finally a 10MB internal GCC Hyperdrive (the first hard drive to appear for the Macintosh). Finally, a friend sold me a used 300-baud modem.

In 1986, I continued to pour money into Kurzweil upgrades, discovered the cost of decent ½-inch tape, and bought my first effects processor, a Yamaha SPX-90 reverb. As each new Opcode MIDI interface came out, I upgraded to it (and continue to do so). Toward the end of the year I began to get more sophisticated in the realm of synchronization and purchased a used Roland SBX-80 as well as a Southworth Systems JamBox. I continued to upgrade my Macintosh as every new model was released. Mac peripherals continued to soak up financial resources as well: I traded up my 400K external drive for an 800K drive, and the 10MB Hyperdrive for one of the first 20MB external drives, a SuperMac DataFrame. The ImageWriter I became an ImageWriter II and I traded up to a used 1200-baud modem. My setup also required purchasing several serial data switch boxes, first a MacNifty and later a DataSpec. Eventually, I purchased a second Yamaha SPX-90.

In 1987 and 1988, the bulk of my synthesizer acquisitions consisted of one each of the Kurzweil 1000 modules in the order they appeared: the 1000PX, 1000SX, 1000HX, and 1000GX. This necessitated the purchase of a MIDI switcher, a Digital Music Corp MX-8 (6-input, 8-output, with MIDI data processing features). I wrangled a long-term loan of an amplifier and professional studio monitors from a friend. I added a BBE-402 Sonic Maximizer to my effects. I continued to upgrade my MIDI interface as every new model came out and added an Opcode Timecode Machine for other MTC (MIDI Time Code) compatibility. As always, I continued to upgrade my Macintosh at every new release. In fact, by late 1988 I was running two Macintoshes in sync to one another for the purpose of having access to 64 MIDI channels. My ImageWriter became a LaserWriter Plus and I sold my 1200-baud Prometheus modem to buy a 2400-baud U.S. Robotics modem. My hard drive became a Jasmine 80MB and eventually a second Jasmine 80 was added purely as a backup system. As it became clear that I needed both of my 80MB drives as primary devices, I purchased one of the first 45MB removable cartridge drives from Microtech, both as a backup device and to use for my then recently acquired SCSI option to the Kurzweil 250. This dual purpose drive required the purchase of a SCSI switch box.

By 1989, my ears were begging for something besides sampled sounds. All five of my sound-generating devices were either sample-players or samplers. I found that the sampler was being used more and more to play back sounds of synthesizers, so I decided the time was right to get back into synthesis. By the summer of 1989 my studio configuration stabilized. The only minor changes and additions in 1990 included gear that was only released in 1990, like the Korg Wavestation, the E-mu Proteus/2, the Mark of the Unicorn MIDI Time Piece, and a few other items.

Annotated studio figures

Figure 7-25 shows the actual physical location of the workstation I built to house all my equipment. The Macintosh keyboard slides out from beneath the MIDI keyboard.

There are a total of about 1,200 buttons, knobs, and faders. Naturally, the ones that I need to adjust the least are placed out of arm's reach. Because the master controller Kurzweil 250 has a mode in which I can control all four Kurzweil modules and view their readouts in the screen on the K250, these four modules are placed the farthest from my seat.

There is a two-foot area behind the workstation to facilitate reconfiguring cables when the need arises. This does not happen very often because all audio ins and outs are present at the 200-point half-normaled patchbay within arm's reach beside my right leg. Likewise, the MIDI INS and OUTS all terminate at the interface area, within arm's reach above my left shoulder.

Figure 7-26 illustrates how the overall signal and data flow describes an outward spiral with the Macintosh and input devices at the origin and output devices at the end.

Figure 7-27 is a wiring schematic organized according to the same principles as the previous 21 setups. See Table 7-23 for a listing of the author's network device types.

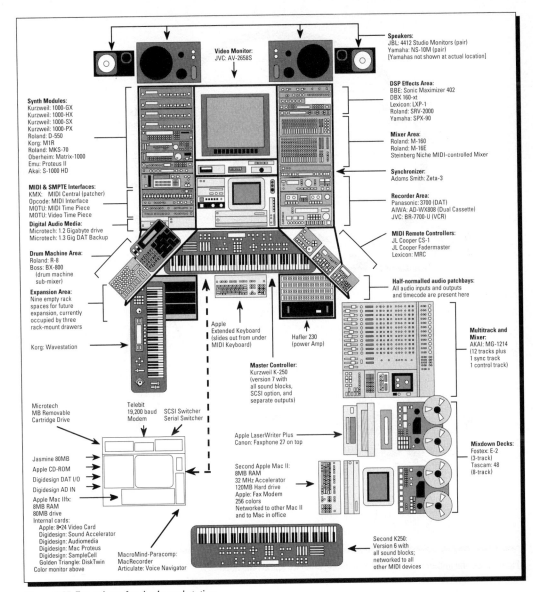

Speakers:
JBL: 4412 Studio Monitors (pair)
Yamaha: NS-10M (pair)
[Yamahas not shown at actual location]

Video Monitor:
JVC: AV-2658S

DSP Effects Area:
BBE: Sonic Maximizer 402
DBX 160-xt
Lexicon: LXP-1
Roland: SRV-2000
Yamaha: SPX-90

Synth Modules:
Kurzweil: 1000-GX
Kurzweil: 1000-HX
Kurzweil: 1000-SX
Kurzweil: 1000-PX
Roland: D-550
Korg: M1R
Roland: MKS-70
Oberheim: Matrix-1000
Emu: Proteus II
Akai: S-1000 HD

Mixer Area:
Roland: M-160
Roland: M-16E
Steinberg Niche MIDI-controlled Mixer

Synchronizer:
Adams Smith: Zeta-3

MIDI & SMPTE Interfaces:
KMX: MIDI Central (patcher)
Opcode: MIDI Interface
MOTU: MIDI Time Piece
MOTU: Video Time Piece

Recorder Area:
Panasonic: 3700 (DAT)
AIWA: AD-WX808 (Dual Cassette)
JVC: BR-7700-U (VCR)

Digital Audio Media:
Microtech: 1.2 Gigabyte drive
Microtech: 1.3 Gig DAT Backup

MIDI Remote Controllers:
JL Cooper CS-1
JL Cooper Fadermaster
Lexicon: MRC

Drum Machine Area:
Roland: R-8
Boss: BX-800
   (drum machine
   sub-mixer)

Half-normalled audio patchbays:
All audio inputs and outputs
and timecode are present here

Expansion Area:
Nine empty rack
spaces for future
expansion, currently
occupied by three
rack-mount drawers

Korg: Wavestation

Apple
Extended Keyboard
(slides out from under
MIDI Keyboard)

Hafler 230
(power Amp)

Multitrack and Mixer:
AKAI: MG-1214
(12 tracks plus
1 sync track
1 control track)

Master Controller:
Kurzweil K-250
(version 7 with
all sound blocks,
SCSI option, and
separate outputs)

Microtech
MB Removable
Cartridge Drive

Telebit
19,200 baud
Modem

SCSI Switcher
Serial Switcher

Apple LaserWriter Plus
Canon: Faxphone 27 on top

Mixdown Decks:
Fostex: E-2
(3-track)
Tascam: 48
(8-track)

Jasmine 80MB

Apple CD-ROM

Digidesign DAT I/O

Digidesign AD IN

Second Apple Mac II:
8MB RAM
32 MHz Accelerator
120MB Hard drive
Apple: Fax Modem
256 colors
Networked to other Mac II
and to Mac in office

Apple Mac IIfx:
8MB RAM
80MB drive
Internal cards:
   Apple: 8•24 Video Card
   Digidesign: Sound Accelerator
   Digidesign: Audiomedia
   Digidesign: Mac Proteus
   Digidesign: SampleCell
   Golden Triangle: DiskTwin
Color monitor above

MacroMind-Paracomp:
MacRecorder
Articulate: Voice Navigator

Second K250:
Version 6 with
all sound blocks;
networked to all
other MIDI devices

Figure 7-25: Front view of author's workstation.

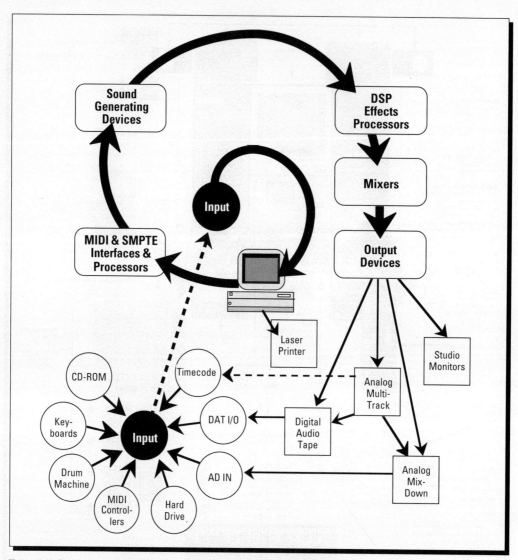

Figure 7-26: The author's workstation illustrating outward spiral data flow.

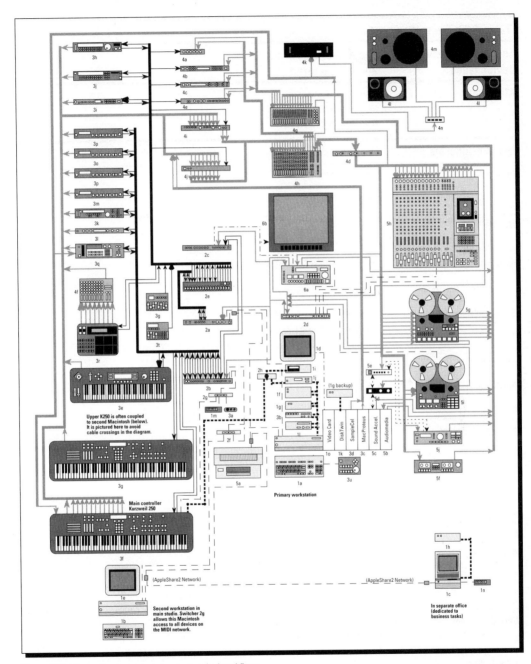

Figure 7-27: The author's workstation network signal flow.

Table 7-23: The author's network

The author's network device types	The author's network devices pictured
Macintosh	Mac IIfx [1a] Mac II (33 MHz Accel) [1b] MacPlus (16 MHz Accel) [1c]
Mac Peripherals	
RAM	Mac IIfx = 8 Mac II = 8 Mac Plus = 4
Monitor	Apple 13" Monitor [1d] Apple 13" Monitor [1e]
Hard Drive	Microtech N1000 Gigabyte [1f] Jasmine Direct Drive 80 [1g] Jasmine Direct Drive 80 [1h]
Backup System	Microtech R-45 Syquest Drive [1i] Microtech T1200 DAT Backup System [1j] Golden Triangle DiskTwin (Disk Duplexing) [1k]
CD-ROM	Apple CD-ROM Drive [1l]
PostScript Printer	LaserWriter Plus [5a]
8-bit Digitizer	MacroMind-Paracomp MacRecorder [3a]
Misc. Input Devices	Telebit T2500 19,200 baud modem [1m] Apple Fax Modem [1n] Articulate Systems Voice Navigator [3b]
Internal Card	
Sample Player	Digidesign MacProteus [3c]
Sampler	Digidesign SampleCell [3d]
Digital Audio	Digidesign Audiomedia [5b] Digidesign Sound Accelerator [5c] Digidesign AD-IN [5d] Digidesign DAT I/O [5e]
CPU Accelerator	Video Card 24-bit Apple Video Card [1o] 8-bit Apple Video Card [1p]
Interfaces	
32-chan MIDI	Opcode Studio 3 [2a]
>32-chan MIDI	MOTU MTP (MIDI Time Piece) [2b]

Table 7-23: The author's network (continued)

The author's network device types	The author's network devices pictured
VITC Converter	MOTU VTP (Video Time Piece) [2c]
Lock-up System	Adams Smith Zeta-3 [2d]

SGD & Controller

Hybrid Synth Kbd	Korg Wavestation [3e]
Sampler Kbd	Kurzweil K250 [3f]
	Kurzweil K250 [3g]
Analog Module	Roland MKS-70 [3h]
	Oberheim Matrix-1000 [3i]
Digital Module	Roland D-550 [3j]
Hybrid Module	Korg M1r [3k]
Samp. Play. Mod.	E-mu Proteus/2 [3l]
	Kurzweil 1000 PX [3m]
	Kurzweil 1000 SX [3n]
	Kurzweil 1000 HX [3o]
	Kurzweil 1000 GX [3p]
Sampler Module	Akai S1000 [3q]
Drum Machine	Roland R-8 [3r]
Other Controller	JL Cooper Fadermaster [3s]
	Lexicon MRC [3t]
	JL Cooper CS-1 [3u]

Audio and DSP

DSP Effects	Lexicon LXP-1 [4a]
	Roland SRV-2000 [4b]
	Yamaha SPX-90 [4c]
Other Signal Processing	BBE 422 (Sonic Maximizer) [4d]
	DBX 160XT (Compression/Limiter) [4e]
Mixer	Boss BX-8 (8-channel) [4f]
	Roland M-160 (16 channel) [4g]
	Roland M-16E (16 channel with EQ) [4h]
MIDI-controlled Mixer	MOTU MM7 (MIDI Mixer 7) [4i]
	Niche ACM (Audio Control Module) [4j]

Table 7-23: The author's network (continued)

The author's network device types	The author's network devices pictured
Amplifier	Hafler 230 [4k]
Speaker	Yamaha NS-10M [4l] JBL 44-12 [4m]

Network

MIDI Patchbay	KMX MIDI Central [2e]
Audio Patchbay	Furman PB-40 (four)
Speaker Switchbox	Speaker switchbox (generic) [4n]
Serial Data Switcher	Dataspec Serial Switchbox [2f] Dataspec Serial Switchbox [2g]
SCSI Data Switcher	Computer Friends SCSI Switchbox [2h]

Analog Recorder

Cassette	AIWA WX808 Dual Cassette Deck [5f]
Multitrack	Tascam 48 (8 track) [5g]
Integrated Mixer/Deck	Akai MG1214 [5h]
Mixdown Deck	Fostex E2 [5i]

Digital Recorder

DAT	Panasonic SV-3700 [5j]

Video

Deck	JVC BR-7700U (1/2") [6a]
Monitor	JVC 27" Monitor (NTSC) [6b]

Summary

- As the expense of your peripheral gear rises, the proportionate cost of the Macintosh drops. After purchasing your music hardware, when budgeting for your Macintosh, figure on an additional 50 to 200 percent for the entry level configurations, an additional 25 to 50 percent for the intermediate setups, and an additional 10 to 25 percent for the advanced systems.

- Be prepared to spend a minimum of an additional 15 to 25 percent of the total cost of the setup on software for the entry level setups; an additional 10 to 15 percent for the intermediate level setups; and an additional 5 to 10 percent for the advanced level setups. These software guidelines refer to music and audio software exclusively. You may want to purchase additional software for other applications such as word processing or managing a database.

- You should budget an additional 2 to 10 percent of the total cost of any setup for furniture, floppy disks, removable cartridges, cables and racks — less if you build some of the furniture and racks yourself.

- After the consideration of which particular Macintosh to purchase, that is, if you haven't got one already, in most cases, your next most important consideration is the master MIDI controller that you will use as a primary musical input device. A dumb keyboard controller is often the primary MIDI device but you might just as easily substitute a synthesizer, sampler, or sample-playing keyboard as your primary controller.

- When substituting a sound-generating keyboard for a dumb MIDI controller, you may want to consider adding a module to complement the type of synthesis in your sound-generating controller. Therefore, if you choose a synthesizer as your main MIDI keyboard controller, you should consider a sampler or sample-player as your first modular device. Likewise, if you choose a sampler or sample-player as your main MIDI keyboard controller, consider a synthesizer as your first module. Of course, if your main interest is creating music that sounds like acoustic instruments, you may want all your modules to be of the sampler and/or sample-player variety.

- You can stretch your budget by substituting your home stereo system for the audio reinforcement components, using a pair of headphones, or cutting down on the number of signal processors. You shouldn't purchase a MIDI interface with synchronization features unless you need it.

- Use virtual tracks in place of additional analog tape-recorder tracks. With the expansion of the available polyphony and multitimbrality of current sound-generating devices and the number of MIDI channels concurrently available, many people are finding that it is possible to record directly to the final stereo mix rather than recording a track at a time on an expensive analog multitrack recorder and then mixing down to stereo from there. An advantage of this is that you omit one recording generation.

- Exploiting the virtual mixer capabilities of your sequencer can save you the expense of a full-blown outboard mixer. Careful editing of velocity and volume (controller 7) data can reduce the need for a sophisticated mixer. Similarly, repeatedly copying and merging MIDI data with a slight offset can often substitute for a digital delay line.

- It is important to become aware of the interdependency of devices. Removing one device may allow you to forego another one or two related purchases.

Chapter 8

Moving Data Around Your Music Network

In this chapter . . .

✔ Routing data to, from, and within your Macintosh and among external devices.

✔ Apple's MIDI Manager, QuickTime, Opcode MIDI System (OMS) MIDIShare, and M•ROS.

✔ Various approaches to MIDI multitasking.

✔ Elements of the MLAN (music local area network) and network topologies.

✔ Automating network reconfiguration for sound design.

✔ Mark of the Unicorn's MIDI Time Piece network.

✔ Lone Wolf's MediaLink and the MidiTap.

✔ An interview with Mark Lacas, co-developer of MediaLink and the MidiTap.

Following the Flow of Network Information

Setting up your studio or workstation forces you to consider the flow of a variety of types of data and the paths these follow. This chapter opens with an introduction to routing MIDI data through the Macintosh, including simply getting your data to and from its serial ports. The remainder of the chapter is devoted to the routing of your data once it has left your Macintosh by discussing various approaches to music local area networks (MLANs).

When you interconnect the Macintosh with peripheral devices, you use hardware cables of a wide variety of formats. When you interconnect applications and devices within your Macintosh, you often use virtual cables defined in software. Besides costing absolutely nothing, virtual cables offer many other fringe benefits.

Routing MIDI Data To and From Your Mac

One task that MIDI software takes care of is getting your data to and from the Macintosh. Many programs include a built-in MIDI driver to facilitate communication with the MIDI interface hooked up to one or both of your Macintosh's serial ports. Such programs merely need to know the speed of your MIDI interface and what port or ports it is connected to (see Figure 8-1). If you use synchronization, you may need to also inform your software as to which port synchronization information will arrive at and what format this data will be in.

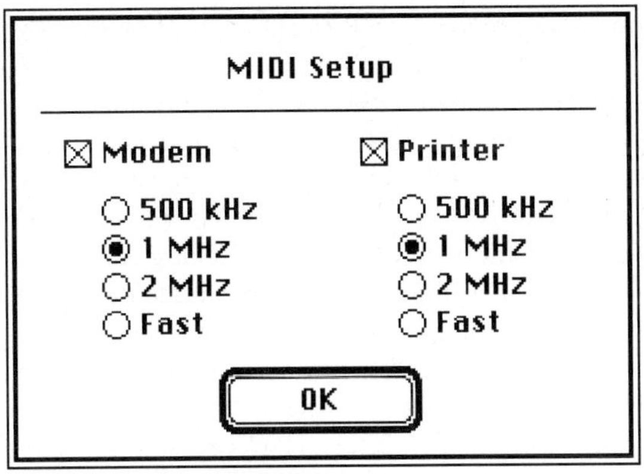

```
┌─────────────────────────────────────────┐
│  ┌───────────────────────────────────┐  │
│  │           MIDI Setup              │  │
│  │  ─────────────────────────────    │  │
│  │                                   │  │
│  │  ☒ Modem          ☒ Printer       │  │
│  │     ○ 500 kHz        ○ 500 kHz    │  │
│  │     ⦿ 1 MHz          ⦿ 1 MHz      │  │
│  │     ○ 2 MHz          ○ 2 MHz      │  │
│  │     ○ Fast           ○ Fast       │  │
│  │                                   │  │
│  │        ┌─────────────────┐        │  │
│  │        │       OK        │        │  │
│  │        └─────────────────┘        │  │
│  └───────────────────────────────────┘  │
└─────────────────────────────────────────┘
```

Figure 8-1: Typical MIDI Setup dialog box for configuring a MIDI program's built-in MIDI driver.

No matter what model Macintosh you have, if you use the Macintosh's printer port for MIDI data, you always need to know whether or not AppleTalk is active. You must turn AppleTalk on to use many types of printers, standard networking software such as Tops or AppleShare, and various other peripheral devices.

Polite MIDI programs automatically deactivate AppleTalk when they are launched and then restore the AppleTalk setting to its previous state when you quit the program. Many programs remind you to do so manually as they are booting up. In most of these cases, once you access the Chooser under the Apple Menu and deactivate AppleTalk, the printer port becomes available for MIDI. Less elegant programs may require that you re-launch them with AppleTalk turned off before they will address the printer port. Some programs simply assume that you have deactivated AppleTalk, so they don't even warn you if it is on, they simply refuse to send or receive MIDI via the printer port.

Usually, the AppleTalk setting you were using when you last shut down your Macintosh is the one recalled the next time you restart the computer. However, certain versions of the Macintosh system software combined with certain Macintosh models don't remember this setting, so that every time you reboot your Macintosh, AppleTalk is active.

Because your PRAM (parameter RAM) stores the AppleTalk setting, if you zap the PRAM, AppleTalk defaults to its active state. The clock battery keeps the PRAM alive in most Macintoshes. Therefore, if your battery goes dead, AppleTalk cannot remember its previous setting and will always be active when you boot up your Macintosh.

If you suspect that your PRAM has become scrambled, you can execute a procedure called "zapping the PRAM." Zapping the PRAM can often restore a misbehaving Macintosh to normalcy. To zap the PRAM on any Macintosh running a version of System 6, simply select the Control Panel DA while holding down the Command, Shift, and Option keys. A common myth is that you cannot do this in MultiFinder. The solution for MultiFinder is to drag the mouse down to the Control Panel menu item without holding down the Command, Shift, and Option keys, then hold the three keys down immediately prior to releasing the mouse. Another myth is that this technique does not work on the Macintosh Plus but instead you must take out the clock battery for five minutes. Taking out the clock battery will always zap the PRAM but it is not necessary. To zap the PRAM in System 7 you need Apple's PRAM Zapper utility. Zapping the PRAM resets some system defaults such as the default boot-up device (if you have a System folder on more than one hard drive), the mouse tracking settings, and the IIfx Serial Switch settings (Macintosh IIfx only). It does not reset the clock unless you resort to removing the clock battery.

All Macintoshes follow the same rules regarding the routing of MIDI data, with two important exceptions:

❖ If you have a Macintosh Portable, you must use Apple's MIDI Manager or Opcode's OMS to route data to your serial ports.

❖ If you have a Macintosh IIfx, you must obtain a cdev called the IIfx Serial Switch (see Figure 8-2). This must reside in your System folder (System 6.x) or in your Control Panels folder (System 7). Unfortunately, Apple does not ship this little piece of software with any Macintosh, so you have to find it on your own. You can obtain it from many on-line telecommunications services, most authorized Apple dealers, user groups, APDA (Apple Programmers and Developers Association), and even on many commercial software disks of MIDI software that is IIfx-compatible.

Apple's MIDI Manager

Apple's MIDI Manager is an increasingly popular alternative to using a program's built-in MIDI driver. It has become the preferred method for the internal routing of MIDI data, so more and more programs that rely exclusively on Apple's MIDI Manager are beginning to appear (see Figure 8-3). Such programs often do not include their own built-in MIDI drivers, therefore requiring MIDI Manager for their operation. The flexibility of MIDI Manager for the internal routing of MIDI and timing data is having a major impact on the configuration of external MIDI LANs.

With MIDI Manager you deal with logical or virtual MIDI ports. Connecting IN ports to OUT ports is as simple as drawing a line that functions as a virtual MIDI cable between ports (see the section "Using MIDI Manager" in this chapter). But before we jump in and start using MIDI Manager, a brief examination of its place within the Macintosh operating system is in order.

Figure 8-2: Apple's IIfx Serial Switch cdev. You access this as you would any other control panel. In order to use MIDI programs, make sure it is set to "Compatible," as in this illustration. You must reboot your Macintosh for the new setting to become active. If MIDI starts malfunctioning or MIDI software freezes your screen, check here first to see if the switch has been accidentally set to "Faster" mode (this can happen for no apparent reason). Note that zapping the PRAM (parameter RAM) will usually reset this switch back to "Faster" mode.

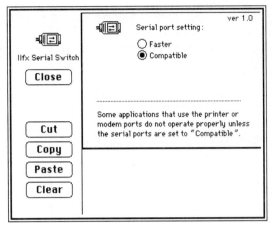

The Macintosh managers

You have probably noticed that the Macintosh user interface is pretty consistent. One reason for this is that Apple supplies many managers in the ROMs of the Macintosh. There is a memory manager, font manager, printing manager, resource manager, file manager, slot manager, sound manager, window manager, and SCSI manager, to name a few. Apple added the sound input manager starting with System 6.0.7 to deal with the input of digitized sound. Programmers can call upon these managers to handle certain essential elements to program operation rather than having to struggle to write routines for their own programs to accomplish the same goals.

Besides the collection of managers that Apple provides in its Toolbox for software developers, another type of system resource is common. These resources are called *drivers*. You use them to facilitate and standardize communication between the Macintosh and peripheral devices. Some drivers are built into the ROM chips.

It took Apple quite some time to realize that it would be helpful for them to write a driver to facilitate serial communication with MIDI devices. In the meantime, every MIDI software developer had to write their own driver to handle communication via the serial ports. Opcode Systems was nice enough to supply their MIDI drivers to many other companies, even their competitors. However, because there were still a large number of developers who had written their own drivers, the situation was far from standardized. To complicate matters further, because timing information is critical to MIDI, each programmer had to figure out a unique way to interface with the T1 timer on the Macintosh's 6522VIA chip — the only sufficiently accurate timing clock available in the Macintosh's hardware.

A
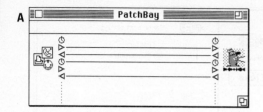

B
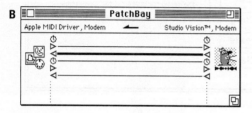

C
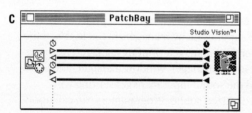

D
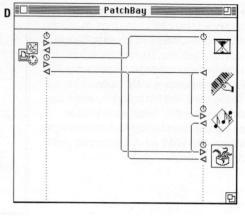

Figure 8-3: (A) A MIDI Manager patch involving a single program, StudioVision. The Macintosh's modem port input and output are patched to the corresponding input and output of StudioVision. The Macintosh's printer port is receiving data from StudioVision's printer port output. Timing information is being received at the Macintosh's printer port and routed to StudioVision. **(B)** Clicking on a cable in PatchBay's window displays information about the connection under the window's title bar, including source, destination, and direction of data flow. **(C)** Clicking on a program icon in PatchBay's window causes all of its connections to be highlighted. **(D)** A relatively simple MIDI Manager patch using the sample applications that come with the official version: Simple Keyboard, MIDIArp, SquidCakes, and Hour Glass. Notes that you play on the Simple Keyboard are sent through MIDIArp, which adds arpeggiations. The output of MIDIArp is routed both to the printer port and to SquidCakes, which records the data and can loop it if desired. SquidCakes's output is routed out the printer port as well. MIDI input arriving at the modem port merges with the data arriving at SquidCakes's input. This allows you to play along with the arpeggiations MIDIArp creates, which may or may not be looping. Hour Glass monitors timing information received at the printer port and converts it into any display format you might desire.

MIDI multitasking

When MultiFinder became popular, it was not uncommon for people to run several MIDI applications simultaneously. Running a sequencer together with a notation program or a patch editor/librarian, or all three together, became the normal state of affairs for people with enough RAM to allow it. As RAM dropped in price, this group of people grew larger. Before MIDI Manager, when two MIDI programs were running under MultiFinder and you switched from one application to another, the first application had to de-install its serial port drivers and the new foreground application had to install its drivers. The problem was that not all programs provided for this. Such conflicts didn't mean that the offending program was not compatible with MultiFinder, but merely that it wasn't friendly with other MIDI applications under MultiFinder.

There is another disadvantage of running multiple MIDI programs under MultiFinder (before MIDI Manager): Since each program took over the T1 timer when the program was brought to the foreground and each application sent to the background had to relinquish control of the T1 timer, there was no way for two programs to use the timer simultaneously. The implications of this were that only one program could be outputting MIDI data (requiring accurate timing) simultaneously. Another way to say this is that there could be no true multitasking, because the timer couldn't be shared.

Apple's MIDI Manager solved all these problems and others, while at the same time opening up a whole new world of Macintosh MIDI capabilities. A side effect was the Macintosh's enhancement of the MIDI powers significantly beyond those of any other personal computer.

Apple's MIDI Manager is a piece of system software consisting of an INIT, a driver, and a program called PatchBay (PatchBay is also available as a desk accessory). By providing a standard driver and common timing clock, developers no longer had to concern themselves with addressing the serial port or taking over the T1 timer. All their programs had to do was send their data to MIDI Manager and let Apple take care of the details.

MIDI Manager provides extensive timer support, including internal and external synchronization capabilities. The same clock drives all applications, and MIDI Manager can represent timing information in whatever format a client program requires — milliseconds, beats, or MTC (MIDI Time Code). Because of this, true MIDI multitasking in MultiFinder is achievable. This is significant, because in System 7 there is no more unifinder, only MultiFinder. Multitasking with MIDI Manager fulfills the definition of the word "multitasking" so perfectly that it is probably the most highly developed example of a multitasking environment yet to appear on the Macintosh. With MIDI Manager it is possible to route the output of one MIDI application into another while both communicate with the serial ports of yet a third or fourth application. The possibilities are practically infinite.

Another advantage of MIDI Manager is that when Apple releases new computers or operating systems, they merely have to provide a new version of the MIDI Manager to assure that all existing software remains compatible. This is exactly the approach that Apple takes with its printer drivers, CD-ROM drivers, and scanner drivers.

Making the transition to MIDI Manager

Musicians and developers of music software should be flattered that, in developing MIDI Manager, Apple is raising their support of music to the same status as their support of printed text. However, there is a transition period going on at this time, and it will probably extend well into 1992.

Many programs are still not MIDI-Manager-compatible, meaning that they require and install their own MIDI drivers, while at the same time taking control of the T1 timing chip. Others have a software switch, so you can select whether or not to use MIDI Manager or the program's built-in MIDI drivers. Instead of providing a software toggle switch, some programs that support MIDI Manager require you to reboot your Macintosh without the MIDI Manager INIT before you can use the software's own driver. This is a poor solution to the issues of MIDI Manager compatibility.

Two reasons for supporting both standards are that not every Macintosh musician will own MIDI Manager (even though it is free) and that slower Macintoshes such as the Plus, Classic, and SE sometimes perform better when bypassing MIDI Manager. The latter consideration may not apply for long as every version of MIDI Manager to be released has been significantly faster than the previous one — meaning that it has required significantly less CPU time. At the time of this writing, version 2.01 of MIDI Manager is current and noticeably faster than even version 2.0.

Another reason for supporting both MIDI Manager and a program's proprietary driver is due to the MIDI Specification. MIDI Manager is intended to be 100 percent compatible with the official MIDI Specification. Software and hardware that break some of the official rules in the Specification will naturally require their own custom driver to permit this. One important example is Mark of the Unicorn's Performer software and their MIDI Time Piece interface. At the time of this writing Mark of the Unicorn is working closely with Apple to achieve MIDI Manager compatibility.

Running a MIDI-Manager-compatible program in MultiFinder with one that is not MIDI-Manager-compatible can present problems. When you switch to the non-compatible application, it installs its own MIDI drivers to control the serial port. When you switch back to the MIDI-Manager-compatible application, even if the other program removes its drivers when it goes to the background, MIDI Manager doesn't necessarily re-install its drivers.

This problem is not the fault of MIDI Manager. Remember that MIDI Manager is meant to facilitate MIDI multitasking. With this in mind, it has strong reasons for keeping its driver alive when you switch from application to application in Multi-Finder, and it assumes that its driver will be active when you bring a compatible application to the foreground. Thus, when you switch back to the MIDI-Manager-compatible application from the non-compatible application, you may find that the MIDI Manager program can no longer send or receive MIDI. Fortunately, some programs such as Interval Systems's Protozoa, provide a "Sign In/Sign Out" option. This forces the MIDI-Manager-compatible program to sign into MIDI Manager every time it is brought to the foreground, thus re-installing Apple's MIDI driver.

Although this "Sign In/Sign Out" option is a polite concession to developers who have not updated their software to MIDI Manager compatibility, this defeats the whole purpose of MIDI Manager. It is an interim solution while other programs are making the transition to MIDI Manager.

This phenomenon is sometimes referred to as "Port Wars." Sometimes the MIDI-Manager-compatible application wins the war and sometimes the other program wins. Occasionally, you end up with your serial ports so "trashed" that you can't use them for anything, even after rebooting. Printers and modems can become inaccessible. When this happens, many people bring their Macintosh to a dealer for repair. This is absolutely unnecessary. You can reset your serial ports by following these steps:

1. Reboot the Macintosh with an ImageWriter driver in your System folder.
2. Open the Chooser DA.
3. Select the ImageWriter driver (icon).
4. Click back and forth on the icons representing the modem and printer ports.

Alternatively, you can use a cdev called MIDI Mangler to reset your serial ports and even write the new setting to the PRAM that is kept alive by your Macintosh clock battery.

Eventually, most MIDI programs running on the Macintosh will be MIDI-Manager-compatible. It may take longer for some companies to update their software than others. A few may even decide to stay in the Macintosh MIDI stone age and never offer MIDI Manager support. The advantages for developers, users, and the entire Macintosh music community are so great that there will surely come a time when manufacturers who do not support MIDI Manager will either have to jump on the bandwagon or give up any hope of continuing to sell their wares.

There are some minor disadvantages of MIDI Manager. The most widely voiced criticism is that it requires more of the Macintosh's CPU time to run an application with MIDI Manager than using a program's built-in MIDI driver. This is not a problem on faster Macintoshes, but slower machines such as the Plus, Classic, and SE may perform unacceptably, even when only a single MIDI-Manager-compatible program is running. Newer versions of MIDI Manager will undoubtedly remedy this issue.

Of course, if you are using SampleCell, MacProteus, or Sound Exciter, you must run MIDI Manager, because the only way to communicate with these NuBus cards and software-based synthesizers is via the virtual MIDI cables that MIDI Manager provides (Note: OMS and Performer version 3.63 can communicate with SampleCell). As more programs drop the practice of including their own proprietary MIDI drivers, there will be no alternative.

Apple is strongly advising developers to support MIDI Manager in order to remain compatible with other MIDI software and future Macintoshes, which may not support MIDI through any other manufacturer-specific drivers.

Using MIDI Manager

You interact with MIDI Manager by way of the PatchBay DA or application. Here MIDI-Manager-compatible programs and cards automatically appear as icons, complete with virtual inputs, outputs, and timing ports ready to plug into one another with a mere drag of the mouse. You can sever a connection by holding the mouse down until it becomes a knife and using the knife to cut the desired connection.

Double-clicking an icon in PatchBay typically brings up that program's control panel if one exists. A single program can have up to 16 virtual ports. You can save collections of connections as patches and reload them later. MIDI-Manager-compatible programs often configure their PatchBay connections automatically upon launching. In this case, you don't have to interact with PatchBay at all.

Following is a step-by-step tour of configuring a MIDI Manager patch.

When PatchBay opens, you see the Apple MIDI Driver icon with two sets of MIDI input and output ports (represented as little triangles). You will only see one set of ports if you forgot to disable AppleTalk from the Macintosh's printer port before launching PatchBay. A timing port may also be visible (resembling a little clock). You can drag the Apple MIDI Driver icon to either side of the PatchBay's window (see Figure 8-4).

When you select an icon in PatchBay's window, the icon becomes highlighted. Then, you may select Open Panel from the PatchBay menu. Alternatively, you can simply double-click on an icon to bring up its control panel (provided one exists). See Figure 8-5 for more details.

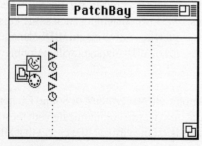

Figure 8-4: PatchBay window with Apple MIDI Driver icon.

If you have internal sound-generating cards installed, these also appear as icons in PatchBay's window. In fact, because these devices provide virtual MIDI ports only, MIDI Manager is the only way to route MIDI data to them in order to play them. Only two such cards exist at this time, Digidesign's MacProteus (ROM-based sample player) and their SampleCell (RAM-based sample player). Opcode's OMS (see the section "The Opcode MIDI System (OMS)" in this chapter) is an alternative

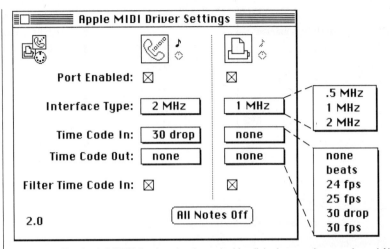

Figure 8-5: The Apple MIDI Driver icon has been double-clicked to open its control panel. Note that when you select an icon, its name appears at the top of its column. The control panel provides a number of pop-up menus, as illustrated in this diagram. With these menus and the check boxes within the control panel, you can create just about any configuration desired for communication with the outside world. For example: which (physical) ports you will be using for MIDI, the speed of your hardware MIDI interface, separate time code formats for the inputs and outputs, and whether or not to filter time code received at a particular port. There is even an All Notes Off button for remedying stuck notes problems that can occur if the corresponding note-off message does not follow a note-on message.

solution to routing MIDI data to SampleCell but not MacProteus. As the advantages to this delivery format for sound-generating devices are recognized, other manufacturers surely will follow Digidesign's example. Instead of having to choose between a rack-mounted or keyboard version of a device, the possibility of a NuBus card version may exist.

Another type of device requiring MIDI Manager for control is a virtual synthesizer, that is, a synthesizer that is created completely in RAM. At this time, Passport Designs's Sound Exciter is the only such virtual synthesizer commercially available (the shareware program MIDI CD offers some of the same features as Sound Exciter without the use of MIDI Manager — see Chapter 15, "Making Music without MIDI"). Although it is referred to as a synthesizer, the Sound Exciter is technically a RAM sample player, because it uses 8-bit soundfiles as its sound material (see Figure 8-6).

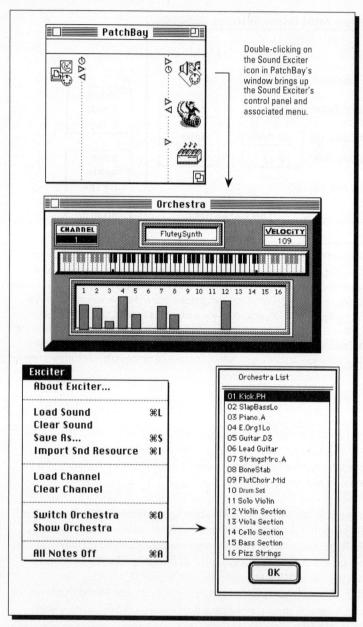

Double-clicking on the Sound Exciter icon in PatchBay's window brings up the Sound Exciter's control panel and associated menu.

Figure 8-6: The PatchBay window with icons for Digidesign's internal cards and Passport Designs's virtual synthesizer. Double-clicking Sound Exciter's icon brings up the control panel as indicated. SampleCell and MacProteus don't have any control panels that are accessible from MIDI Manager. Instead, they require dedicated applications.

When you launch a MIDI-Manager-compatible application, its icon, complete with software inputs and outputs, appears in Patchbay's window. When an appropriately designed program signs into MIDI Manager, virtual cables automatically connect it to the appropriate virtual ports. In this manner, you can launch the applications dedicated to controlling the SampleCell and MacProteus, and they are automatically wired to their associated NuBus cards, as Figure 8-7 illustrates. Note that PatchBay does not have to be active for this to happen. It is only necessary for the MIDI Manager INIT to be active.

When you launch additional MIDI-Manager-compatible programs (for example, MIDI sequencers, patch editors, algorithmic tools, and notation programs), their icons will appear in PatchBay's window or their auto-connections will be made, if PatchBay is not open.

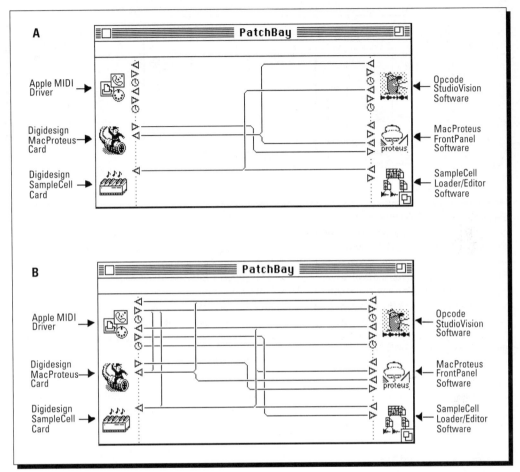

Figure 8-7: The front panels of SampleCell and MacProteus are stand-alone applications. When you launch these programs, the necessary connections to their associated cards are made, as this illustration shows. PatchBay's window does not have to be open for these automatic connections to take place. **(A)** The MacProteus and SampleCell cards are connected to their virtual front panels. StudioVision is controlling both cards. The Apple MIDI Driver (upper left) is not connected, indicating that the Macintosh's serial ports are not in use — MIDI sequencing and playback without a MIDI interface. **(B)** This configuration is identical to the above, however, the connections to the Apple MIDI Driver bring all the cards and software under the control of external devices. Likewise, MIDI output can be directed to external devices with this patch. An external MIDI interface is required.

Wiring up your MIDI Manager patch is as simple as using the mouse to drag virtual patch cords from virtual input to output and vice versa. To sever connections, you simply hold the mouse button down until the cursor becomes a knife, at which time you can use this virtual knife to cut your virtual cables. Alternatively, you can click on a cable to select it and choose Break Connection from PatchBay's menu.

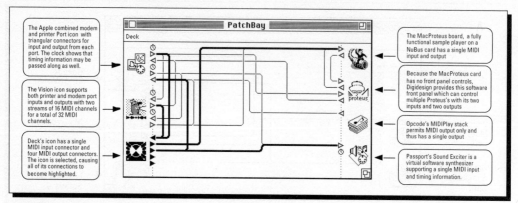

Figure 8-8: A complex PatchBay configuration. In this example, Deck records MIDI data coming in from the Mac's Modem port and passes it and previously recorded data to the MacProteus card and Passport's Sound Exciter. The Proteus's software "front panel" is also wired up to the Proteus card and connects to the Mac's printer port to control an external Proteus. Vision can receive and send MIDI data from either of the Mac's serial ports and can also send data from its modem side to Deck and from its printer side to the MacProteus. Besides being routed to Vision, MIDI data coming in from the Mac's printer port is passed to the Sound Exciter, as are an additional 16 channels controlled by Deck. MIDI Play, Opcode's HyperCard MIDI stack, is set up to output its data out the Macintosh's printer port. During this whole process, Deck is playing back three digital audio tracks and recording a fourth audio track, all at CD-quality. Selecting an application in PatchBay causes that application's connections to be highlighted, as is the case with Deck in this illustration.

Connecting two or more outputs to a single input automatically merges their data. You do not need any additional merging hardware. See Figure 8-8 for an example of a complex PatchBay configuration.

To aid you in visualizing the connections, clicking on a device's or program's icon causes all of its cables to become highlighted, and the device's name appears above the column. Clicking on a port (little triangle) identifies its function and device. Clicking on a cable displays both its source and destination above each column as well as the direction that data is flowing in (see Figure 8-8).

Now that you have made all the connections, you can save this PatchBay configuration as a patch file. The next time you need to run these programs simultaneously, simply launch all the programs and then open PatchBay (the program or the DA) and load the patch you saved. Future versions of MIDI Manager may include the capability of automatically launching the applications required when you load the patch itself.

MIDI Manager ideas

Applications running in MIDI Manager do not stop running when you send them to the background under MultiFinder. This is largely because all applications involved share the timing clock — no single program has to take it over. Similarly, all the programs share the Apple MIDI driver — no single program has to install its own driver when it comes to the foreground.

This state of affairs opens up an infinite number of possibilities for MIDI on the Macintosh. You can combine groups of programs from different manufacturers as if they were simply modules in a larger MIDI processor.

Sometimes your aggregate applications turn out to be interim solutions that will eventually be supported by individual applications. A good example of this is capturing the data from a program that does not support Standard MIDI Files (SMFs) to a sequencer that does. In all probability the first program will eventually support SMFs at some later date. However, until that day arrives, you can use MIDI Manager to record the data in real time into a program with SMF support. Then, you simply need to save the file as an SMF and you are free to do whatever you want with it — convert it to notation, use it as source material in an algorithmic program, and so on.

Process MIDI data as it is recorded into and/or output from a MIDI sequencer

There are many ways to process MIDI data as it is being sent to your sequencer. You can even process MIDI data as it is being output from your MIDI sequencer. If you want, using MIDI Manager you can do both at once. The simple MIDIArp arpeggiator is an option. Steinberg's Cubase has a pretty powerful MIDI processor built into it, which you can access from other programs through MIDI Manager by running both programs simultaneously. Megalomania is MIDI-Manager-compatible. You can use it to create real-time MIDI processors of extreme complexity. You can also employ HookUp! and MAX for these purposes.

Capture the output of interactive or algorithmic programs with a MIDI sequencer or notation program

Although most algorithmic and interactive composition programs can save SMFs by now, those that don't can easily be interconnected with a sequencer that has the required capabilities. Using HookUp! or MAX, you can create just about any kind of MIDI data processor you can imagine. You can also create interactive and algorithmic composition software of extreme sophistication. It's a simple task to route the output of these programs to a MIDI-Manager-compatible sequencer.

Run an interactive composition program together and in sync with a sequencer

If you've ever wished that your sequencer had interactive capabilities, it's a simple matter to add them by running an interactive program together with a sequencer. In this way, you can listen to pre-recorded sequencer tracks while recording into and interacting with your favorite interactive composition program. Connecting the timing ports of the programs involved guarantees that everything will remain in sync. If the participating programs support it, you can route some of your sequencer's pre-recorded tracks into the interactive software at the same time. Of course, you may want to introduce a MIDI processor such as Megalomania or one you design yourself with HookUp! or MAX somewhere into the loop. You could even record the combined MIDI output of all these programs back into another sequencer or some additional tracks in the sequencer already engaged in this MIDI Manager patch.

Create algorithmically generated graphics

Install MIDI XCMDs into an animation program such as Director or a program that supports animation such as Serius. Then link MIDI inputs of the animation to an interactive or algorithmic composition program and write the required scripts to interpret incoming MIDI data. Voilà, you're watching algorithmically generated animation. Or if you are interconnecting an interactive program, you can trigger the associated graphics in real time.

Add external non-MIDI device control to any MIDI program

Drivers for Director, Serius, HyperCard, and SuperCard allow these programs and others to control such external non-MIDI devices as CD-ROM players (which double as audio CD players), video disc players, VCRs, video cameras, and the like. Because these programs import MIDI-Manager-compatible MIDI XCMDs, you can now place such devices under the control of MIDI sequencers or interactive and algorithmic composition software.

Record patch data editing into a MIDI sequencer to allow real-time control of the sound modification capabilities of a device during playback

If you've ever wanted to be able to control the patch-editing capabilities of your sound-generating devices during the playback of a MIDI sequence, MIDI Manager provides a way to do this. Simply record the output of the appropriate patch editor/librarian on a record-enabled track of your sequencer. Then, when you play back the sequence, the recording of your parameter editing will play back along with the note data. If you like, you can use this method to record complete patch data into sequence tracks, thereby allowing you to load new patches on-the-fly, during playback.

Run several copies of a program to enhance its capabilities

One of the best examples of this is Jam Factory (see Chapter 19, "Interactive Composition and Intelligent Instruments"). Jam Factory provides four sequencer modules that you "teach" during a setup stage or in real time, during a performance. If you want to double your forces, you can run and synchronize two copies of Jam Factory simultaneously. Now you have eight interactive modules. Because the developers realized this possibility, they built certain features into the program to enhance this sort of activity. For example, you can control the software by MIDI-keyboard-activated macros and presets — but there is a feature that allows you to pass on to the second copy of Jam Factory a trigger for a different macro or preset.

Synchronize MIDI sequencers to direct-to-hard disk recording programs

You can record digital audio tracks into the MIDI sequencer StudioVision, but suppose you want to play back more than two digital audio tracks simultaneously. Instead of waiting for the developers of StudioVision to include this feature, you can simply run a program that already supports direct-to-hard disk recording and playback of four tracks of audio together with a MIDI-Manager-compatible sequencer of your choice. For example, Dr. T's MIDI sequencer Beyond and Digidesign's Deck 4-track direct-to-hard disk recording system permit this when running together and synchronized in MIDI Manager. Another rationale for this scenario might be that you are already used to a certain MIDI sequencer — one that has no digital audio capabilities in and of itself.

Install MIDI XCMDs into any program to add complete MIDI functionality to software that doesn't have MIDI support yet

The number of programs that support XCMDs continues to grow. Many presentation programs already allow the importation of XCMDs. HyperMIDI provides an excellent set of MIDI XCMDs that you can use for this. Even Affinity Systems's powerful macro software, Tempo, supports imported XCMDs. It is possible to build Tempo macros that can execute, at lightning speed, just about anything you can accomplish yourself by interacting with the Macintosh. Imagine triggering complex macros by playing notes on your keyboard controller.

Just about anything else you can conceive of

If your Macintosh is fast enough, you might be able to construct a hybrid of all the above configurations and make it work as a single entity.

Running applications in the background

Some programmers create MIDI-Manager-compatible applications that don't run in the background. You can make simple alterations to a program using ResEdit or Resorcerer that occasionally remedy this. You may even want to try this for programs that are not MIDI-Manager-compatible.

For example, before Finale became MIDI-Manager-compatible, I used the following trick to force parts of the program to work in the background. Pasting in a large amount of data might take up to a half hour if the file was a 500-measure symphony movement. Other massive edits sometimes take equally long — for example, transposing several hundred measures or applying a new beat positioning chart upon an entire work. By forcing Finale to operate in the background, I was able to initiate these operations and then bring another program to the foreground, where I would work on something else while Finale continued in the background. Often, even the programmer is amazed to find that this is possible (as was true in this example).

To force a program to support background operation with ResEdit or Resorcerer, you must open the program in either application and double-click on the SIZE

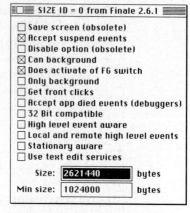

```
┌─────────────────────────────────────────┐
│▤□▤▤  SIZE ID = -1 from Finale 2.6.1  ▤▤▤│
├─────────────────────────────────────────┤
│ Save screen      ◉ 0   ○ 1           ⬆   │
│ (Switcher)                               │
│                                          │
│ Accept           ○ 0   ◉ 1               │
│ suspend                                  │
│ events                                   │
│                                          │
│ Disable          ◉ 0   ○ 1               │
│ option                                   │
│ (Switcher)                               │
│                                          │
│ Can              ○ 0   ◉ 1               │
│ background                               │
│                                          │
│ MultiFinder      ○ 0   ◉ 1               │
│ aware                                    │
│                                          │
│ Only             ◉ 0   ○ 1               │
│ background                               │
│                                          │
│ Get front        ◉ 0   ○ 1           ⬇   │
│ clicks                                   │
└─────────────────────────────────────────┘
```

Figure 8-9: This is the standard ResEdit SIZE resource editor. Simply set the following attributes to "1": Accept suspend events, Can background, and MultiFinder aware.

```
┌─────────────────────────────────────────┐
│▤□▤  SIZE ID = 0 from Finale 2.6.1  ▤▤▤▤ │
├─────────────────────────────────────────┤
│ ☐ Save screen (obsolete)                 │
│ ☒ Accept suspend events                  │
│ ☐ Disable option (obsolete)              │
│ ☒ Can background                         │
│ ☒ Does activate of FG switch             │
│ ☐ Only background                        │
│ ☐ Get front clicks                       │
│ ☐ Accept app died events (debuggers)     │
│ ☐ 32 Bit compatible                      │
│ ☐ High level event aware                 │
│ ☐ Local and remote high level events     │
│ ☐ Stationary aware                       │
│ ☐ Use text edit services                 │
│                                          │
│    Size:  │ 2621440      │ bytes         │
│ Min size: │ 1024000      │ bytes         │
└─────────────────────────────────────────┘
```

Figure 8-10: This is the alternate ResEdit SIZE resource editor template by Chris Reed (freeware). Simply check the following checkboxes: Accept suspend events, Can background, and Does activate of FG switch.

resource, so that you can edit it (see Figures 8-9 through 8-11). Whenever you edit a program with ResEdit or Resorcerer, be sure to work on a copy of the software, because you can inadvertently render a program useless with these tools.

The Opcode MIDI System (OMS)

The Opcode MIDI System (OMS) is a software environment for running multiple MIDI applications. Because OMS is so new, there are many misconceptions floating around. The most prevalent of these are that OMS is a replacement for MIDI Manager or that Opcode has created a new standard that will require you to make a choice between MIDI Manager and OMS. There is no truth to these rumors.

OMS consists of an INIT, a setup application called OMS Setup, and a folder of drivers. At this time, OMS includes drivers for most standard dual MIDI interfaces, Mark of the Unicorn's MIDI Time Piece, Opcode's own Studio 5 interface, and Digidesign's SampleCell. The final driver is an OMS-compatible replacement for Apple's MIDI Manager. Lone Wolf has an OMS driver for its MidiTap (see the section "MediaLink and the MidiTap").

OMS and MIDI Manager contrasted

OMS accomplishes many of the same things that Apple's MIDI Manager does. In some ways it is similar to MIDI Manager. The most blatant similarity is that it makes the necessary connections between MIDI programs and the Macintosh's

```
┌─────────────────────────────────────────────────────┐
│ ▓▓▓▓▓▓▓▓▓▓▓  SIZE -1 from Finale 2.6.1  ▓▓▓▓▓▓▓▓▓▓▓ │
│ Application Capabilities:                             │
│                                                      │
│   ☒ MultiFinder aware      ☐ 32-Bit compatible       │
│   ☒ Accepts Suspend/Resume ☐ Get "Child Died" events │
│   ☒ Can Background                                   │
│   ☐ Only Background         ☐ Save Screen             │
│   ☐ Get front clicks        ☐ Option switch           │
│   ┌─ ≥ System 7.0 only ─────────────────────────┐    │
│   │ ☐ Accepts high level events                  │    │
│   │ ☐ Accepts both local & remote high-level events│  │
│   │ ☐ Stationery-aware when opening documents     │    │
│   └──────────────────────────────────────────────┘    │
│                                                      │
│ Preferred Partition Size: │1000│ (K bytes)           │
│                                         ┌──────────┐ │
│ Minimum Partition Size:   │1000│ (K bytes)│  Cancel  │ │
│                                         └──────────┘ │
└─────────────────────────────────────────────────────┘
```

Figure 8-11: This is the Resorcerer SIZE resource editor. Simply check the following checkboxes: MultiFinder aware, Accepts Suspend/Resume, and Can Background.

serial ports. It also can make automatic connections behind the scenes between OMS-compatible applications, much as MIDI Manager does when correctly written programs are launched under MultiFinder or in Finder 7.

OMS achieves all the routing of MIDI data without requiring a desk accessory like MIDI Manager's PatchBay. Of course the disadvantage of not having the sort of "under the hood" access that PatchBay provides means that you can't alter the connections that OMS makes automatically. However, you can use PatchBay with OMS for certain cases (see the section "Using OMS together with MIDI Manager").

Like MIDI Manager, you can also use OMS to route MIDI data to internal NuBus cards. At the time of this writing, only Digidesign's SampleCell card is supported. You can still transmit data to the MacProteus card if you have one, by resorting to OMS's tap into MIDI Manager.

One important advantage of OMS is that it requires much less CPU time than MIDI Manager. This means that musicians with slower Macintoshes may find that OMS removes some of the blockades that might have seemed impassable were MIDI Manager the only option.

Unlike Apple's MIDI Manager, OMS does not provide a centralized timing source for all currently running applications to synchronize to. Because of this, only one MIDI program can use the T1 timer (see the section "MIDI multitasking") at a time. This does not mean that you can't run multiple MIDI applications simultaneously, only that you cannot run multiple MIDI applications that require timing information together. With this stipulation, you can run as many editor/librarians as you want while a sequencer is using the timing clock to play or record a sequencer. And the provisions to operate MIDI Manager and OMS together will allow application synchronization in some cases.

Also in sharp contrast to Apple's MIDI Manager, OMS does not provide for IAC (Interapplication Communication). However, it does incorporate Opcode's own "publish and subscribe" protocol, which can achieve many of the same results if the programs involved are OMS-compatible.

One area that MIDI Manager does not even attempt to address is the routing of your data once it has left your Macintosh. OMS excels in this department. OMS can be taught the complete characteristics of your entire external MIDI setup. It can learn which device connects to which port of your MIDI interface or patchbay. It can learn which MIDI channels are active on any device. It can even learn all the various configurations that you have stored in your MIDI patcher.

Telling OMS about your MIDI setup

Before you can use OMS you must supply it with detailed information about your MIDI setup. You do this by using the OMS Setup program (see Figure 8-12). In most cases you need only do this once. Afterwards, you simply inform OMS about any new gear that you have added to your network or any changes you have made in the physical cabling.

Although only one studio setup may be active at a time, you can save as many studio setups as you want. This might be advisable if you work in different studios or if your own studio configuration changes regularly. Other cases where your basic configuration might change include having a transportable rack of devices that you take with you to sessions in other studios or to performances, providing for gear that you rent or borrow from time to time, and situations where you might want several individuals to have access to subsets of the available devices, for example, in an academic computer music lab.

Once you've told OMS which serial ports you will be using for MIDI, the setup program is intelligent enough to look down the cables and see what type of MIDI interface you have: a standard 16-channel, dual 32-channel, or greater-than-32-channel interface. The window that appears looks a bit like PatchBay's main window.

After you have told OMS about your interfaces, you then define the devices that are connected to your interfaces. OMS knows about most of the MIDI instruments out on the market, so once you have selected the manufacturer's name, the next pop-up menu lists individual devices marketed by that company. When you select a specific device, you will find that OMS has even more information about the individual device, including whether it is multitimbral or might be a controller. You may also specify what channels each device is listening to. If you have two or more of the same type of device, you assign a unique ID to each one. OMS attaches an appropriate icon to every device, but you may override this assignment (see Figure 8-13). See Figure 8-14 for an example of typical OMS with a standard dual interface and no MIDI patcher.

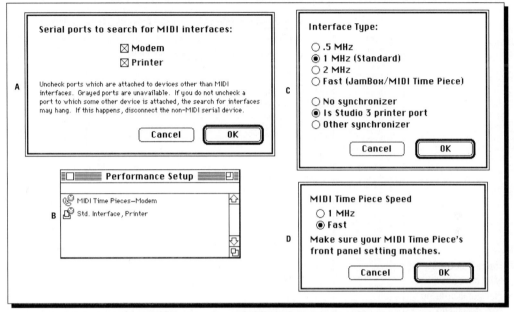

Figure 8-12: OMS Setup's main configuration window. The first step in defining an OMS studio setup. This illustration progresses as you normally would during the setup process. **(A)** First you tell OMS which serial ports to search for MIDI interfaces. **(B)** The result of the search is displayed and OMS has determined that there is a standard interface connected to the printer port and a MIDI Time Piece connected to the Modem Port. Note: OMS cannot determine if you have more than one MIDI Time Piece networked off of a single serial port, but you can tell OMS about it. **(C)** Double-clicking on the standard interface icon brings up this port configuration dialog box. In most cases, MIDI Time Piece will have already entered the correct settings for you. **(D)** Double-clicking the MIDI Time Piece icon presents you with a dialog box that asks you to verify the setting of the front panel's speed switch.

OMS has provisions for MIDI patchers. The patcher icon is introduced between the device icons and the interface icon. OMS expects that the default (boot up) patcher configuration (in the quadrangle to the left of the patcher name) will allow the Macintosh to transmit to all devices connected to the patcher and will allow the master controller to input data to the Macintosh (see Figure 8-15).

If a MIDI Time Piece or Studio 5 interface is connected to the Macintosh, OMS will know it and display the correct name. OMS will also have installed the driver required to communicate with these two greater-than-32-channel interfaces. Unlike the previous example, OMS will understand that all devices connected to the interface can be in two-way communication with the Macintosh simultaneously (see Figure 8-16).

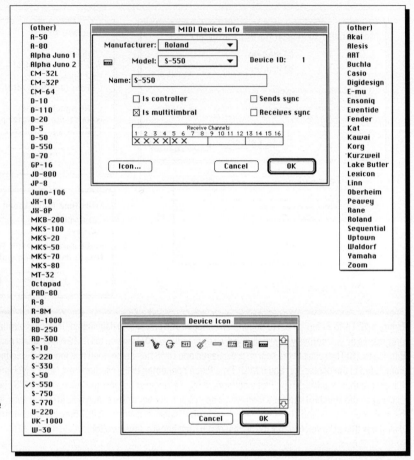

Figure 8-13: OMS's MIDI device configuration dialog box. The pop-up menu Manufacturers is displayed on the right for purposes of illustration. The collection of possible icons displayed at the bottom appears when you click the Icon... button.

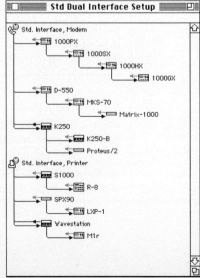

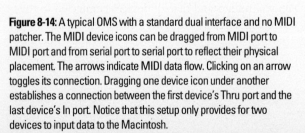

Figure 8-14: A typical OMS with a standard dual interface and no MIDI patcher. The MIDI device icons can be dragged from MIDI port to MIDI port and from serial port to serial port to reflect their physical placement. The arrows indicate MIDI data flow. Clicking on an arrow toggles its connection. Dragging one device icon under another establishes a connection between the first device's Thru port and the last device's In port. Notice that this setup only provides for two devices to input data to the Macintosh.

Figure 8-15: An OMS configuration with a MIDI patcher connected to the modem port interface. It is strongly recommended that each patcher input port is connected to the same device as its corresponding output. Even if your actual physical setup has an output from your interface connected to a device and the corresponding output from that device connected to the patcher, you must represent the cables as if they are connected to the patcher in pairs, that is, both the output and the input. The display is a bit misleading, because the arrows seem to imply that all devices are in constant two-way communication with the interface. OMS understands the setup to mean that when a specific patcher configuration is called up via MIDI program change (the numbers indicated in the left-hand quadrangles), that setup will permit two-way communication with the device immediately to the number's right. This would have been the author's OMS setup if OMS had been released before the MIDI Time Piece.

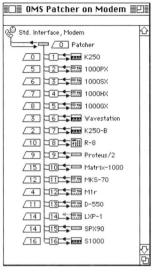

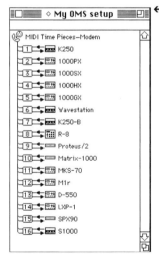

← **Figure 8-16:** An OMS setup for two MIDI Time Pieces networked off the modem port. There are always 256 MIDI channels available, and all devices are in constant two-way communication with the Macintosh. This is the author's current OMS setup.

Using OMS

The OMS has three modes of operation. One mode allows you to run OMS-compatible applications only. Another mode lets you run both OMS- and non-OMS-compatible programs. The third mode lets you run OMS-compatible programs and most MIDI-Manager-compatible software (see Figure 8-17). There are advantages and disadvantages of each mode.

Using OMS-compatible applications only

If a program is OMS-compatible life is very simple. OMS makes all the necessary MIDI connections behind the scenes, and you don't have to worry about anything beyond configuring your initial OMS studio setup document. At the time of this writing, only Opcode software is OMS-compatible and only a small number of their programs. These are: Vision, StudioVision, Galaxy Plus Editors, Max, and Track Chart.

With Vision, StudioVision, and Galaxy Plus Editors, there will obviously be no fighting over the Macintosh timing clock. You would never have any reason to run Vision and StudioVision simultaneously, and Galaxy Plus Editors does not require timing information.

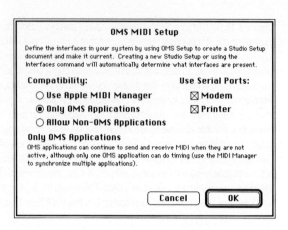

Figure 8-17: OMS's mode selection dialog box. Here you must decide whether to allow non-OMS-compatible programs or whether to provide MIDI Manager support. You can change these settings any time. You do not have to reboot the Macintosh; OMS simply installs the appropriate driver as soon as you press the OK button.

Galaxy Plus Editors is optimized for use with Vision and StudioVision using the OMS system. OMS keeps the three programs updated with respect to all your port and channel assignments, interface types, device IDs, and other necessary information. The Publish and Subscribe links between the various Galaxy modules and Visions allow you to refer to patches by name in MIDI sequences. You can be confident that any changes that you make to patch information in Galaxy will be updated in Vision or StudioVision.

Do not confuse Opcode's proprietary Publish and Subscribe protocols with those of the same name found in System 7 — they have nothing to do with one another.

OMS allows Vision or StudioVision to know what devices are assigned to what ports and channels. It will automatically insert the correct names wherever you might have had to make a channel assignment in the past. In other words, destination devices are referred to by name rather than MIDI channel number, making it easy to see at a glance where your data is going.

Finally, OMS provides compatibility between Opcode's software products and Mark of the Unicorn's MIDI Time Piece 128- to 512-channel interface network, something that the music community begged for from the moment Mark of the Unicorn released their greater-than-32-channel interface.

When you are in OMS-compatible mode, you can achieve best results by running only OMS-compatible applications. Your OMS-compatible applications are able to communicate with each other, even when one or more of the programs are in the background. A timing-dependent program that you may be running, such as Vision or StudioVision, can continue to run in the background, provided that the foreground application does not require the Macintosh timer. This allows you to run a MIDI sequence in the background, then bring Galaxy

Plus Editors into the foreground and edit the sounds of all your instruments while the sequence continues to play.

In this mode you can start up a non-OMS-compatible application and run it (provided that it is not a MIDI-Manager-dependent program). The newly launched software will simply remove OMS's serial driver and install its own. This means that when you return to the OMS-compatible program or programs that you were initially running, they will no longer function.

You can get around this by tricking OMS into reinstalling its driver. Simply select the OMS setup menu option in your OMS program and click back and forth between the radio buttons when the dialog box appears (see Figure 8-17). When you press the OK button, OMS will reinstall its drivers and you can continue. However, the next time you switch back to the non-OMS-compatible program, it will again replace its drivers for OMS's. An easier solution is to allow for non-OMS-compatible applications in the first place.

Allowing non-OMS-compatible applications

When OMS is in its "Allow Non-OMS-Compatible Applications" mode, you can have the advantages of intercommunication between OMS programs and still run non-OMS-compatible software. The only stipulation is that the non-OMS programs not be MIDI-Manager-dependent. In that case you should be in OMS's "Use Apple MIDI Manager" mode.

This mode assumes that other programs will be replacing the OMS serial port driver. Thus, every time you switch to and from an OMS program, that is, bring it to the foreground or send it to the background, the OMS driver will be politely loaded or removed as required.

Using OMS together with MIDI Manager

OMS includes a mode that allows it to work together with Apple's MIDI Manager. To take advantage of this, you must be sure that the MIDI Manager extension (INIT) is loaded when you boot up your Macintosh. OMS substitutes its own driver in place of the Apple MIDI Driver. In fact, it's a good idea (but not absolutely necessary) to remove the Apple MIDI Driver from your System Folder if you are going to use OMS's version.

In this mode, OMS-compatible applications communicate with one another behind the back of MIDI Manager. You still use PatchBay to set up the connections between MIDI Manager-compatible applications.

After opening PatchBay, when you double-click on the OMS MIDI Manager icon, the control panel is significantly different from that of Apple's MIDI Driver (see Figure 8-18). The OMS MIDI Manager control panel allows you to set up to

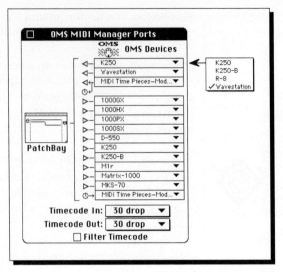

Figure 8-18: Double-clicking on OMS's MIDI Driver icon in PatchBay brings up its control panel. Here you create the input and output ports for the driver. You can designate one of each as a timing port, too. The only way you can determine what a virtual port is actually connected to is by clicking it. This displays the name of the device connected to that port above PatchBay's window. Note that there is no way to determine whether that device is connected to the physical modem or printer port. In fact, there is no reason to know this — you have already informed OMS of the physical connections between your devices and your Macintosh using the OMS Setup program. This is why OMS can present you with a list of devices here.

11 destination devices and three source devices, one of each can be a timing port. Because OMS knows everything there is to know about your devices, it is able to provide pop-up menus for each of these 14 ports.

The setup displayed in the previous figure provides for 11 destinations to the OMS MIDI Driver. If you have more devices, you are out of luck if you want to access them in this mode. As you can see in Figure 8-19, you may still make many additional connections between all the MIDI-Manager-compatible applications you may be running at any time. Furthermore, don't forget that your OMS-compatible programs are automatically connected to each other behind MIDI Manager's (and PatchBay's) back.

Alternatives for internal routing

MIDIShare and M•ROS are two alternatives for the internal routing of data. The advantages that these environments might provide are offset by the drawback that not many programs support them. This shouldn't prevent you from using them. Additionally, you should not get the impression that the use of MIDIShare or M•ROS-based systems excludes you from running MIDI Manager or OMS programs, or even programs that fall outside the boundaries of any of the approaches. In the worst case, you might have to reboot your Macintosh in order to load a required serial driver or system extension.

MIDIShare (Grame)

MIDIShare is France's answer to MIDI Manager and HyperMIDI all bundled together. It offers the same multitasking, timer-sharing MIDI environment as MIDI Manager and has the added advantage of being a multiplatform development

Figure 8-19: The OMS MIDI Driver icon is shown here in PatchBay as it appears after configuration (see Figure 8-18). Note that the OMS SampleCell Driver is being used to communicate with Digidesign's SampleCell NuBus card, while Apple's MIDI Manager is being used to communicate with their MacProteus card. OMS communicates with the SampleCell "behind the back" of MIDI Manager so it is not necessary to draw any virtual cable connections. In fact, the only reason that SampleCell's icon appears in PatchBay's window in this illustration is because its MIDI Manager driver was present in the

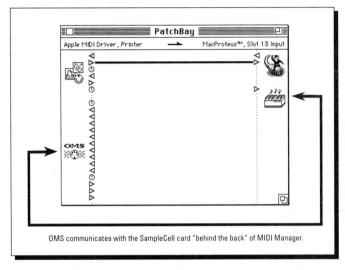

OMS communicates with the SampleCell card "behind the back" of MIDI Manager.

System Folder. This allows you to connect non-OMS-compatible applications to the SampleCell. Removing SampleCell's standard driver would still allow OMS to communicate with the card (OMS has its own SampleCell driver), although MIDI Manager and MIDI-Manager-compatible (non-OMS) programs would not be able to send data to SampleCell if its standard driver was removed. Note that leaving SampleCell's standard driver in the System Folder would seem to allow you to connect both MIDI Manager programs and OMS programs to the SampleCell simultaneously. If you try to do this, some MIDI messages may be ignored.

system — it is available for the Atari computer as well as the Macintosh. This is not surprising, considering the fact that Atari computers are considerably more popular than Macintoshes among European musicians because of the price difference; however, the Macintosh is starting to increase its market share in Europe, due to the introduction of lower-cost machines such as the Classic, LC, and IIsi.

Like MIDI Manager, MIDIShare includes a system extension (a cdev instead of an INIT) that allows MIDI programs to run simultaneously, synchronized to a single clock and sharing a common serial port driver. Programs may run simultaneously both in the background and foreground. MIDIShare's MIDI Connection program replaces MIDI Manager's PatchBay. MIDI Connection lets you set up virtual connections between MIDIShare-compatible programs. There can be up to 256 virtual ports, and any program can loop back to itself.

Also like MIDI Manager, a programmer must develop his or her application specifically for the MIDIShare environment. The package comes with some five dozen routines for MPW and ThinkC to aid you in this. There are also HyperCard XCMDs and XFCNs that allow you to create MIDIShare stacks just as you do with HyperMIDI. Finally, like MIDI Manager, the software ships with a number of sample programs.

M•ROS (Steinberg)

Steinberg is another European company making impressive inroads into the American computer music industry. Their Cubase MIDI sequencer, one of the most popular Atari sequencers, was ported to the Macintosh in late 1990 (see Chapter 17, "MIDI Sequencing").

M•ROS stands for MIDI Real-time Operating System and is designed to be a platform for interapplication communication and synchronization. This is all very well for the Atari community, where there exist multiple M•ROS-compatible applications, but for Macintosh musicians Steinberg's own Cubase represents the sole M•ROS program. Nonetheless, you may find M•ROS helpful if you are a Cubase user.

M•ROS is a virtual MIDI port, to which you can direct MIDI data by way of "invisible MIDI cables." Were there other M•ROS-compatible Macintosh programs, they could interconnect to Cubase via M•ROS. But you can use this extra virtual MIDI port to reroute MIDI data from Cubase to itself with such flexibility that it is surprising that no other Macintosh sequencers provide such a feature. Note that the M•ROS port does not appear in PatchBay.

You can set any Cubase track to receive input from or output to M•ROS's virtual MIDI port, just as you would assign a physical MIDI port to a track. Cubase's powerful built-in MIDI processor can also tap into M•ROS. You can route incoming data to the MIDI processor and then send it along M•ROS's invisible MIDI cables to a track set to receive on its M•ROS port. Similarly, you can set tracks to output to M•ROS, which might in turn direct their data through the MIDI processor.

The principles behind M•ROS relate to those of all the virtual MIDI routing systems available — meaning MIDI Manager, OMS, and MIDIShare. Only time will tell whether Steinberg's solution will engender any wide-scale third-party support.

Routing Data Among External Devices

Now that you are familiar with all the possibilities available for routing MIDI within your Macintosh, I'll discuss routing data, MIDI and otherwise, among your external devices. So far you have dealt with logical or virtual ports — your external devices are connected with physical ports. To do this effectively, you must understand the workings of networks, and in particular, local area networks (LANs).

Elements of the Music LAN

The moment you connect two devices via MIDI, you have begun to establish a LAN for music. You will probably end up pushing a lot of other kinds of data around through cables attached to your Macintosh and external peripherals, MIDI and otherwise. When you stop to think about it, the sheer number of different data formats you have under your control is quite impressive: MIDI, SMPTE, MTC, SCSI, ASCII, AES/EBU, SPDIF, RGB, and NTSC, not to mention the data you send to your printer, your modem, or proprietary RS-422 protocols used by many samplers for high-speed soundfile transfer and by lockup systems for hardware synchronization. If you have several Macintoshes, you may be on a Tops or AppleShare network already. Add to this the audio data that you're sending to your mixer from all your sound-generating devices.

Some of these data formats use the same types of cables; for example, you can send MIDI and MTC down MIDI cables; SMPTE and analog audio use audio cables. Most other data formats require their own types of cabling. Whereas it is normal that cables of non-musical networks such as AppleTalk carry data in both directions simultaneously, MIDI cables require one cable for each data direction. That is why you have separate MIDI IN cables and MIDI OUT cables.

MLANs and standard LANs contrasted

MIDI networks differ from traditional computer networks in the following ways:

❖ MIDI has unidirectional cabling (referred to as "simplex" communication). Information can only travel in one direction.

❖ MIDI is limited to transmitting 16 channels of information on each cable. Because of the general trend toward fully multitimbral devices, taking advantage of the full potential of a single device can require all 16 channels.

❖ It is very difficult to know or retrieve the name of the device that is receiving the data you are sending. You need a considerable amount of effort and setup time to assure that the data you send will actually arrive at the device you want to receive it. Finally, there are no built-in provisions for a device to verify that it has indeed received the data intended for it. A new addition to the MIDI Specification, Identity Request and Reply, may alleviate some of these problems when electronic instrument manufacturers begin supporting it. This will eventually facilitate the possibility of configuring every device in an entire MIDI network by issuing a single command.

❖ When devices are daisychained, every added device subtly alters the signal. This does not affect small MIDI systems, but daisychaining more than four or five devices can potentially cause problems. Traditional computer networks simply slow down when too much data is being pumped down the cables, whereas MIDI devices can drop messages at random. Because music inherently requires precise timing, any distortion of the data stream is unacceptable.

❖ Merging of data streams is difficult. MIDI Y connectors are not allowed. MIDI was designed to have one device transmitting upon a single cable at a time. Until recently, the merging of more than two MIDI data streams was difficult, and a merging of even two data streams required additional hardware. It is also extremely difficult to install more than a single computer on a MIDI network.

❖ The 31.25 KBaud data rate of MIDI is relatively slow when compared to other networking protocols. For most people, this presents no problems, but for those of us who need faster communication, there are no MIDI accelerators available.

❖ The MIDI specification limits cable length to 50 feet. While a conservative figure, now that MIDI can control everything from lighting consoles to mixers and signal processors, this limitation means that most MIDI LANs may need to be more local than you would like.

Some people are adapting ready-made networking software. Berklee College of Music in Boston, has created a network of digital music workstations. Each station has a Macintosh, a Kurzweil MIDI keyboard controller, modular synthesizers and samplers, including a fully loaded Kurzweil Expander, Yamaha RX-11 Drum Machine and TX-816 modular synthesizer, an Oberheim Expander, a Kamlet Matrix MIDI switch box, a Yamaha SPX-90 digital effects processor and D-1500 digital delay, a multi-channel mixer, and a multitrack recorder. Using 3Com's EtherMac network, each computer connects to a central file server, which automatically backs itself up to tape every night at 2 a.m. (a file server is a large hard disk storage area accessible to a number of computers). All the workstations' MIDI devices are networked together, so that a single workstation can control several others if necessary. Finally, the audio output from each workstation can be routed to any other workstation or group of workstations.

Network topologies

There are three standard configurations of LANs: bus, ring, and star. A variation of the bus topology is sometimes referred to as a tree topology.

MLAN basics

When you connect MIDI devices via their THRU ports, you are creating a *bus topology*. When you use a MIDI Thru box or patchbay, the box assumes the role of a hub in a star network. There are variations. You can daisychain devices off of a MIDI Thru box. You can even use two or more MIDI patchbays to act as separate hubs for a hybrid star, bus, or tree configuration (see Figure 8-20).

Eliminating MIDI data distortion with a MIDI Thru box

Most Macintosh musicians begin to purchase networking support hardware to make up for some of the inherent limitations to the MIDI Specification. In order to eliminate data distortion experienced when devices are daisychained using their THRU ports, many people purchase a MIDI Thru box or patcher to make sure that the same data arrives at all designated destinations simultaneously.

 Perhaps the most significant and widely published yet unfounded rumor about MIDI is that timing delays are introduced whenever you daisychain MIDI devices.

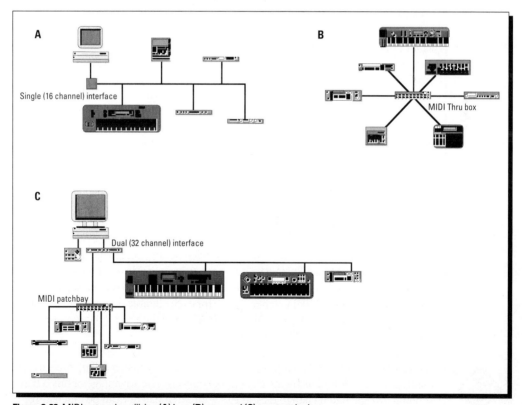

Figure 8-20: MIDI networks utilizing **(A)** bus, **(B)** star, and **(C)** tree topologies.

This misconception started due to a typo in an article in the January 1986 issue of *Keyboard Magazine*. The article stated that MIDI Thru ports introduced a 3 millisecond delay into a daisychained MIDI path. The correct figure should have been three-microseconds. Concern arose because it takes 1 millisecond to send a MIDI note-on message and 1 millisecond to send a MIDI note-off message — five daisychained MIDI devices, each adding a 3 millisecond delay could bring the timing errors into the audible range. However, 3 microseconds are insignificant. Any perceptible delays that you hear are created by the speed at which a specific synthesizer processes data it receives, not how many devices are daisychained by way of their THRU ports. The real problem is that the opto-isolators at the THRU port have a slew rate requiring several nanoseconds to go from full on to full off. On a daisychain of many devices this could conceivably distort MIDI data (see Figure 8-21), for example, by effectively flipping a bit from 1 to 0 or dropping a bit altogether. With newer devices employing newer opto-isolators, this is not a problem.

Patch editing without a MIDI patchbay

Because MIDI patchers usually have an equal number of inputs and outputs, they can greatly facilitate the use of patch editors and librarians. Patch editing and librarian software allows you to control the innards of most MIDI devices easily. Patch librarians permit you to save, organize, and load individual patches as well as entire banks of sounds. Such software can also deal with all other user-configurable elements of a MIDI device. Examples are tuning, program maps, effects settings, output routes, and velocity curves, to name a few. Most synthesizers and samplers require duplex (two-way) communication for these operations (see Figure 8-22). Similarly, Macintosh patch editors and librarians require that the device being edited be placed under remote control of the Macintosh. It also should be able to send information back to the software. This means that the device's MIDI IN port must be set up to receive information from the Macintosh while the device's MIDI OUT port is set up to send data back to the Macintosh.

Network patch editing with a MIDI patchbay

Until very recently, the easiest way to achieve the necessary duplex communication between the Macintosh and the MIDI device being edited was to employ a MIDI patcher (see Figure 8-23). The output of every editable device is returned to an input on the patcher. In this scenario it is only necessary to create separate configurations of your MIDI patcher — one for each editable device — that route the appropriate input back to the Macintosh. You can then recall the required setup when you want to edit a specific device.

If the MIDI patcher used responds to program change, you can call up the various configurations without using the front panel buttons. The advantage of this is that sending a single patch change message to your MIDI patcher can be much faster than manually pressing a button to scroll through the patcher's setup list until the

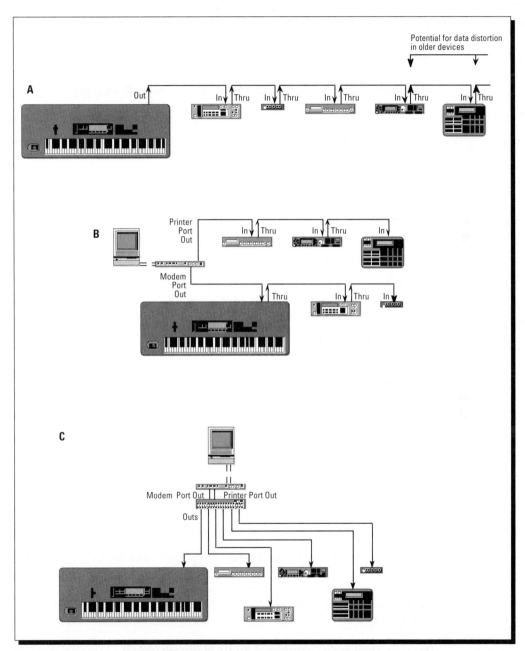

Figure 8-21: (A) Daisychaining vs. **(B)** standard dual interface approach vs. **(C)** a MIDI Thru box star configuration. In the daisychained setup, data distortion may be introduced at the indicated points.

appropriate setup is located. Normally, a specified MIDI channel or range of patch numbers on a specified MIDI channel is reserved for reconfiguring the MIDI patcher remotely.

Automating network reconfiguration for sound design

When you can recall MIDI patcher configurations via program change messages, it is only logical to expect Macintosh software to take care of reconfiguring the patcher automatically, the moment you indicate which device you intend to edit. In this area, current-generation software makes a strong distinction between editors and librarians for synthesizers as opposed to those for samplers. This division will undoubtedly disappear as technology advances.

Synthesizer patch editors and librarians

It is now common for both universal and dedicated patch editors and librarians to automate MIDI patcher reconfiguration.

Some dedicated or device-specific patch librarians and editor/librarians automatically switch your MIDI patcher to the configuration required upon launching the software. This is accomplished by designating the appropriate program change message for the software to send to your MIDI patcher when you begin patch editing.

Automatic network reconfiguration is becoming a standard feature in the increasingly popular universal patch librarians and editor/librarians. This state of affairs has been indirectly brought about by the ever-dropping prices of electronic instruments. The realization that many people now have multiple devices led software developers to concentrate on universal software instead of separate programs dedicated to specific devices. Universal librarians and editor/librarians have kept pace with emerging devices and have grown to the point where a single program can manage the sound libraries as well as edit the patches of nearly every synthesizer currently in use, including many that are no longer on the market.

Once you have set up a universal librarian or editor/librarian to automatically reconfigure your MIDI network, you are free to deal with the software without having to worry about setting up the appropriate data routing via your MIDI patcher. The software takes care of that transparently, behind the scenes (see Figure 8-24).

Passport Designs's Distributed Audio Network (DAN)

Passport's Alchemy and Sound Apprentice sample editing software (see Chapter 13, "Editing Sampled Sound") provides the flexibility of automated network reconfiguration (discussed in the previous section with regard to synthesizers) to the world of samplers. These programs are optimized for use

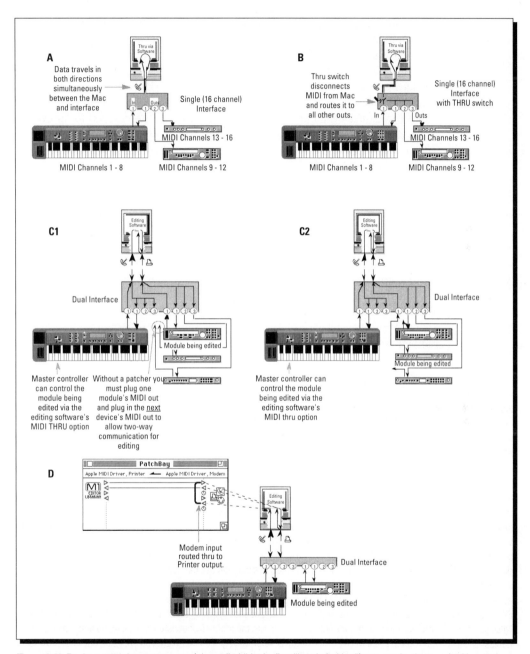

Figure 8-22: Basic approaches to two-way (also called "duplex" or "hand-shaking") communication required by patch editors and librarians without using a MIDI patcher. **Setup A:** You use this configuration for playing devices from *(continued)*

with a MIDI-controllable MIDI patchbay, that is, one that can change its configuration in response to MIDI program change messages received on a specified channel.

The idea behind Passport's Distributed Audio Network (DAN) has wider implications than similar approaches applied to synthesizers. You can edit all your sampled soundfiles without regard to which device they are destined for or even which device created them. This allows you to create and organize a master sample library that you can load into any of your samplers rather than having to keep track of soundfiles in separate formats.

When you want to transfer a soundfile to a sampler, simply indicating the destination sampler causes the software to send a program change command to your MIDI patcher. The MIDI patcher then calls up the required configuration (usually, this will be a setup providing for two-way communication). Because the software knows the characteristics of most samplers, it can execute any required sample rate or format conversion on-the-fly, as it is transferring the sound to each device.

The DAN requires a minimal amount of setup. You must teach Alchemy or Sound Apprentice which MIDI patcher configurations are required for communicating with each sampler.

Figure 8-22 (continued): the master controller. MIDI data is looped through the Macintosh by turning on the software's "Patch Thru" option or by using MIDI Manager (see below). This setup allows you to play your devices or input data into a Macintosh MIDI program whenever you are using software that has a "Patch Thru" option. When you do not have a MIDI program booted up, playing your instruments may necessitate using MIDI Manager to route incoming MIDI data or create a patcher configuration that bypasses the Macintosh completely. Alternatively, you could use Setup B. Because none of the modules' outputs are returned to the Macintosh, the only device you can edit is your master controller. **Setup B:** Many MIDI interfaces have a "Thru" switch on their front panels, which routes MIDI data received at its MIDI IN port directly to all outputs. Note that this often disconnects MIDI communication to the Macintosh, but also has the advantage of allowing you to play external modules when your Macintosh is not powered on. **Setups C1 and C2:** When you add a dual interface, that is, one that connects to both of the Macintosh's serial ports, you have two MIDI inputs to play with. Most software can handle the echoing of master-controller data received at one serial port out the serial port designated to the device currently being edited (C2). Notice that you can use this setup to edit a single module and simultaneously control it from your master controller. If your master controller happens to be a sound-generating device as well, you can edit its sounds without having to change any cables. To edit any other modules connected to the interface's outputs requires unplugging the first module's output and replaying it with the second device's output cable. MIDI patchers and greater-than-32-channel interfaces alleviate the problem of constantly unplugging and replugging cables whenever you want to edit a MIDI device. **Setup D:** Alternatively, if the software you are using does not provide for echoing MIDI data from one port to the other, but does support MIDI Manager, you can use MIDI Manager to achieve the same result. An example MIDI Manager patch for this setup is shown with the setup.

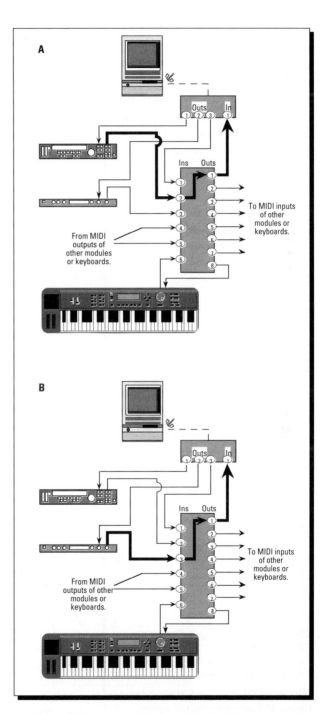

Figure 8-23: Approaches to duplex communication required by patch editors and librarians when a MIDI patcher is introduced into the network. A single (16-channel) MIDI interface is used in these illustrations. **Setup A:** Adding a MIDI patcher to the network allows you to bring all your devices' outputs back to the Macintosh to establish duplex communication required by patch editor/librarians. In this example, you would be able to edit the top module pictured. Notice that your master controller is no longer able to send data to the Macintosh unless you are using a MIDI interface that supports 32 or more channels. **Setup B:** This setup allows you to edit the bottom module pictured. To edit other devices, apply the same logic to configuring the patchbay. If you have a dual interface, you can configure both Setups A and B to provide for your master controller, using the same strategies illustrated in the previous figure.

Figure 8-24: Typical setup dialog boxes for automating network reconfiguration with universal editors and librarians.

MIDI merging

Many MIDI devices can receive new patches and other parameter configurations when you send them to the device's MIDI input, without concern about the device's MIDI output. On the other hand, editing sounds with patch editing software usually needs full duplex communication between your Macintosh and the device you want to edit. Because the vast majority of MIDI interfaces only provide for a single MIDI input per Macintosh serial port, this often creates a situation where your master controller keyboard is no longer in the communication loop. You cannot merge MIDI data by using MIDI Y connectors — ones that meet the MIDI Specification don't exist (Micro-W markets a MIDI Y connector that does not meet the MIDI Spec but does work in some situations). Enter the hardware MIDI merger.

True MIDI mergers process one or more MIDI data streams in such a way that the individual MIDI messages do not get jumbled together (see Figure 8-25). They make sure that a MIDI message from one of the sources is finished transmitting before inserting the next MIDI message from the other source into the merged data stream. Although with MIDI Manager this is as simple as connecting two or more virtual MIDI cables to the same port, in the physical world you must employ a hardware box that supports MIDI merging.

Hardware with MIDI merging capabilities come in three general varieties. The first is a little merge box that you use in conjunction with a MIDI interface patchbay to merge two incoming MIDI streams into one. These boxes often have two inputs and a single merged output through which the merged data passes.

The second common merging configuration involves using a MIDI patcher with built-in merging functions. These come in two varieties. One type provides two inputs that are always merged together. The other type allows you to merge any two inputs (see Figure 8-26).

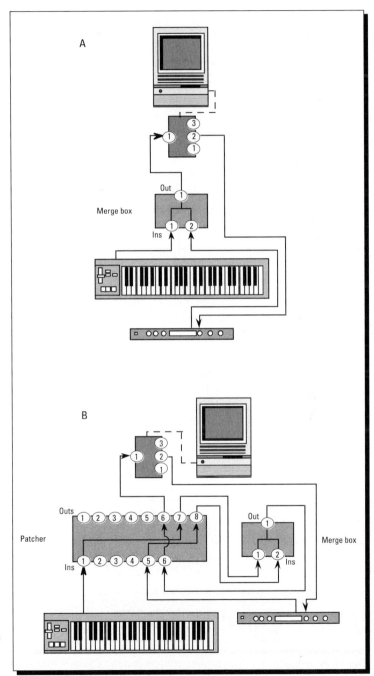

Figure 8-25: Configurations using a standard 2-to-1 merger. **Setup A:** Merge box with MIDI interface. In this setup the outputs of two devices go to the two inputs of the merge box. The merge box's output goes to the input of a single MIDI interface. **Setup B:** Merge box with MIDI patchbay. Although you could simply introduce the merge box between the devices you desire to merge and a single input on the patcher, there are better solutions, particularly one that will enable you to merge any two devices coming into the patcher. In this illustration, two of the patcher's outputs go to the merger's inputs, and the merger's output returns to one of the patcher's inputs. To merge any two inputs, you simply route them to the outputs that route them to the merger.

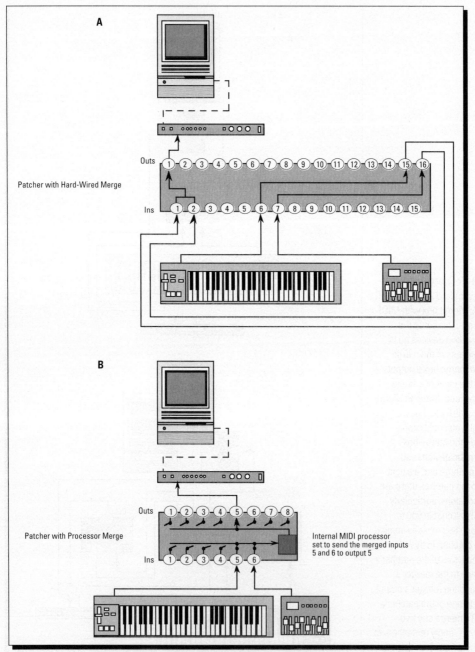

Figure 8-26: Configurations of MIDI patchers with built-in merging. **Setup A:** Patcher with two hard-wired merge inputs. In this case, the best solution is similar to the one described in Figure 8-25. Connect the two hard-wired merging inputs to two outputs. Any data that you route to these two ouptuts will return to the two merging inputs and reappear at whatever output you assign to those inputs. **Setup B:** Patcher/processor with the capability of merging any two inputs. Sometimes it is necessary to route the incoming data into a built-in processor that has been set to its merge mode. You can then direct the output of this internal processor to whatever physical output you desire.

The third type of merger commonly available is a MIDI interface with built-in merging capabilities. The two contenders in this arena are Mark of the Unicorn's MIDI Time Piece and Opcode's Studio 5. These are discussed below.

Total network reconfiguration

One of the dreams of a computer musician that MLANs are on their way to fulfilling is that of reconfiguring an entire studio with a single command. At least one high end system, Lone Wolf's MediaLink, already offers this and all with a single cable to boot (see the section "MediaLink and the MidiTap").

As you have seen in the studio diagrams in Chapter 7, there are many other types of data than MIDI that need to be organized on your MLAN. There are also many other devices besides sound generators that you may need to configure.

Signal processors represent a class of non-sound-generating devices that you will probably want to configure on your network. Fortunately, many of these now respond to MIDI. There are even some editor/librarian programs available for the more common effects devices. You can simply add these to your MIDI network, like any other MIDI keyboard or module.

The routing of audio data is an area that might, at first glance, seem to elude remote control. Usually one envisions elaborate patchbays with a spaghetti of patch cords directing the data from patch point to patch point. Another scenario, if you are using a normaled or half-normaled patchbay, is a patchbay with no patch cords connected to it, or perhaps very few — the cord spaghetti is all hidden behind it.

MIDI-controllable audio patchbays are now available. With these hardware devices, you make all audio connections by configuring a matrix display, without having to plug or unplug a single patch cord. You can save different configurations as setups and recall them via MIDI program change messages. Some MIDI-controllable audio patchbays even provide for internal merging of audio signals. With either kind, your audio patchbay merely becomes another device on your MIDI network.

One command — one configuration

When you are working on a Macintosh music project, you will often have all your sound-generators set to receive certain information on particular channels. Each channel may be set to a certain sound (patch or sample, depending upon whether the device is a synthesizer or sampler). Your signal processors will have been configured to precise settings that support your current sound configuration. Finally, your audio patchbay may have the patch cords in the exact unique arrangement required for the project.

If you need or want to start a new project before you have finished another project, you face the necessity of making voluminous notes about what cord was hooked up where, which devices were listening to which channels, and which sounds were assigned to each channel. It would be very convenient to be able to take a snapshot of your entire network configuration that could be used at a later date to reconfigure the entire network back to the state required for the previous project.

A similar situation arises when you have established a general-purpose configuration of the devices you normally work with, and then a project comes up that requires complete reconfiguration of your network. You'd like to be able to return to your normal configuration with a single command.

If you use a MIDI patcher that can itself be controlled through MIDI in conjunction with a MIDI-controllable audio patchbay, you already have the tools to exercise single-command reconfiguration. If you use MediaLink (see the section "MediaLink and the MidiTap"), the process is even simpler.

Many people place patch changes and other MIDI messages (e.g., MIDI volume settings) at the beginning of each MIDI sequencer track. The moment you start the sequence, all the devices switch to the required sounds or, in the case of signal processors, the required effects. If your network includes a MIDI-controllable audio patchbay, then your sequencer can send a command to configure your audio routing as well. Some sequencers provide for an initial or default patch to be sent out at the beginning of each track. You can transmit other global device settings along with this program change message. Some people create a special "initialization" sequence to bring all the devices to a known state.

The problem with the procedure outlined in the previous paragraph is that it assumes that all of your devices have the same sounds loaded into them that were there when you created your setup. Usually this isn't the case. Because of this, many people started recording patch information in the form of a complete SysEx data dump onto sequencer tracks. This guaranteed that the synthesizers would have the expected patches associated with program changes sent at the beginning of the sequence. Newer sequencers such as Mark of the Unicorn's Performer have provisions for attaching a default SysEx dump to a device for just this purpose.

Universal patch librarians and editor/librarians such as Opcode's Galaxy and Galaxy Plus Editors allow you to create aggregate "bundles" that consist of the exact state of all your devices. To accomplish this with a single command, you will need a greater-than-32-channel or dual interface or MIDI-controllable patcher that can set up the necessary two-way communications. With a MIDI Time Piece or Studio 5 interface, the process is simplified, because all devices are in constant two-way communication with the Macintosh. With a MIDI-controllable patcher, Galaxy or Galaxy Plus Editors will reconfigure the patcher sequentially as the entire memory of each device is dumped into the Macintosh.

There are still some problems with the techniques described in the previous two paragraphs. First, when using the "SysEx data on sequencer track" procedure, it can be difficult to set up the sequence in such a way that all the necessary devices receive their SysEx dumps. Staggering the data on different tracks solves some of these problems, but experimentation, often with a stop watch, may be required. The other disadvantage of this method is that there is no easy way to take a snapshot of the entire network and retrieve all the SysEx information from each device. You must capture the state of each device or patch individually, often by using the font panel controls of your keyboards and modules.

The aggregate bundle solution à la Galaxy is capable of taking the required snapshot of the system — that is, successively retrieving all the SysEx information from each device on the network and providing for the subsequent reloading of all devices en masse. Galaxy only deals with the data that it can retrieve via SysEx. Sometimes, this does not include other types of information you might put at the head of a sequencer track, such as channel volume, mod wheel setting, or bender setting. While Galaxy comes very close to our model, it ends up not being a single-command solution. You may still need an initialization sequence to configure specific parameters Galaxy did not save and devices Galaxy did not support. Even among support devices, you don't want to have to do a complete bulk dump to all your devices merely to set channels to their normal patches. Therefore, you must add a few more steps.

The biggest problem with both solutions is that they make no provisions for samplers. With very few exceptions, most sample soundfiles used by professional samplers are not communicable via MIDI. While there is a MIDI Sample Dump Standard (SDS) that does take care of a few devices, many people own non-SDS samplers and sample players.

At the present time, the only way to achieve single-command reconfiguration of your entire network is to automate the process using a macro utility. This is exactly how many professionals, including myself, get around the limitations of current software. Popular macro utilities include Genesis Micro Software's Automac III, Affinity Systems's Tempo II Plus, or CE Software's QuicKeys 2. Articulate Systems's LanguageMaker, which ships with their Voice Navigator speech recognition system, offers macro-making at a level comparable to these three dedicated utilities. Although Tempo II Plus is by far the most powerful macro utility for the Macintosh, any of these programs can record your steps as you open various programs and files and load them to their intended devices, including samplers. Such recordings, called *macros*, can be triggered by a single keystroke command or by a voice command in the case of the Voice Navigator.

Solutions for Music Networks

Three alternative packages offer sophisticated MIDI networking support. Each consists of a hardware box or boxes and a semi-proprietary communications protocol. The contenders are Mark of the Unicorn's MIDI Time Piece, Opcode's Studio 5, and Lone Wolf's MidiTap (their gateway to the company's innovative MediaLink network communications protocol).

The MIDI Time Piece and Studio 5 are relatively inexpensive. The MidiTap is significantly more expensive, although its cost merely represents the price of its power.

The most promising aspect of these three emerging technologies is that they can all work together in just about any combination. Despite healthy competition between these developers, there is an increasing amount of cooperation. Rather than divide the music community by forcing a choice among three standards, the presence of three options offers you the benefit of being able to tailor your approach exactly to your needs. You have the assurance that, should your needs change, you can add other boxes accordingly, knowing that you won't have wasted your prior investment.

Mark of the Unicorn's MIDI Time Piece

Mark of the Unicorn rocked the industry when they introduced their MIDI Time Piece in early 1990. The box was developed by members of the team that had designed the ill-fated Southworth JamBox. Attendees of the 1990 Winter NAMM (National Association of Music Merchants) show were amazed to see a single Macintosh driving 512 independent MIDI channels, quite a step up from the paltry 32 channels that had truly seemed like maximum limit to any rational person entering the Anaheim Convention Center at the opening of the show.

The MIDI Time Piece system is based upon the concept of cables. Individual cables can each have their own set of 16 MIDI channels. An individual MIDI Time Piece has eight pairs of MIDI input and output ports. Eight times 16 equals 128, meaning that each box can support 128 channels. Up to four MIDI Time Pieces can be networking to a single Macintosh (or several Macintoshes if desired). The normal configuration for four boxes is to have two connected to the Macintosh's printer port and two connected to the modem port. In any case, four MIDI Time Pieces provide for 512 MIDI channels (4 times 128).

The principle behind the MIDI Time Piece's operation is easy to understand. Along with every channel message, a cable identification byte is sent that tells the MIDI Time Piece which cable to send the data out on or, with respect to MIDI input, which cable data is coming in from. Of course, to accommodate the relatively limited bandwidth of MIDI (31.25 KHz), these cable identification messages are only sent when required, that is, when the destination or source cable changes. If a stream of 100 MIDI messages are being sent out the same port, there is no reason to clog up the MIDI stream with 100 extra cable identification messages — it is only necessary to inform the MIDI Time Piece when data is directed to a different cable.

At the time of this writing, the MMA (MIDI Manufacturers Assoc.) does not officially sanction the cable message that the MIDI Time Piece utilizes. However, it is among the group of MIDI messages that the MMA considers "unused" (for the time being).

Advantages of increasing the number of MIDI channels

The first advantage of 128 channels (or 256, 384, or 512 channels, depending on the number of MIDI Time Pieces you have) is that you can keep every channel on each one of your multitimbral devices active at all times. It is no longer necessary to remember what instrument is set to respond on what channel.

Consider the typical scenario with a simple MIDI setup and a 16-channel interface. You can communicate with up to 16 unitimbral devices. The moment you get a multitimbral instrument, you are stuck. For example, if you have an M1 as a controller (8-channel multitimbral) and a D-550 (unitimbral), you can assign the M1 to MIDI channels 1 through 8 and the D-550 to channel 9. Great, you have seven channels left over. Now you purchase a Proteus/2, which is 16-channel multitimbral. You can only activate seven of the Proteus/2's 16 channels. In other words, you are giving up nine channels on the Proteus/2.

To alleviate the situation, you purchase a second 16-channel interface to attach to the Macintosh's remaining serial port. Alternatively, you might just trade up to a 32-channel dual interface. Now you can access all 16 channels of the Proteus/2, and you still have seven channels to spare on the original interface. You could add seven more unitimbral devices before you grow out of this setup, but adding another multitimbral device will again require you to give up nine of its channels. If you want to control your signal processing effects via MIDI, you can subtract more channels.

The problem is that more and more sound-generating devices are multitimbral. The chances are very good that you will have three or more multitimbral devices in a modest setup. If two of these are 8-channel multitimbral and the remaining one is fully multitimbral, things might work out fine for a while — of course, for every signal processor that you want to control via MIDI you would have to give up a channel on one of your instruments. And forget about buying another multitimbral device — you're simply out of channels.

Several years ago, in order to get around the 32-channel limitation, you would have had to resort to a method that several of my colleagues and I employed. When we needed more MIDI channels, we simply synchronized two Macintoshes running the identical MIDI sequence, one slaved to the other. Each Macintosh had its own 32-channel dual interface, so at least we could access 64 channels. An alternative solution was to dump sequences to a workstation's on-board sequencer and sync it to the Mac. In many cases the hardware sequencer will be more accurate, but offer less resolution.

Enter the MIDI Time Piece with its 128-channel solution. Now you can have up to eight fully multitimbral devices on a single interface and you can expand to up to 32 similar devices by adding one, two, or three more MIDI Time Pieces to your network. Each one provides an additional 128 channels. If you need more than 512 channels, you can probably afford to purchase a second Macintosh and employ the synchronization technique discussed in the previous paragraph to access 1,024 channels!

Be forewarned that there are many programs that cannot take advantage of the vast number of channels provided by a MIDI Time Piece, although their number is dwindling. Because of this, the front panel of the MIDI Time Piece offers a switch to make it function as a simple 32-channel dual interface. Even when the MIDI Time Piece assumes this other identity, many of the other features that it provides are still available.

Say goodbye to MIDI patchbays, Thru boxes, mergers, processors, and synchronization converters

The MIDI Time Piece is not merely a multi-channel interface, it is also a MIDI patchbay, Thru box, merger, and processor. Its features are very robust in these areas. Consider the topic of merging. The MIDI Time Piece can selectively merge any combination of up to eight MIDI data streams (most stand-alone MIDI mergers are limited to two MIDI data streams). Two MIDI Time Pieces can merge up to 16 MIDI data streams. Additionally, the MIDI Time Piece can convert the four most common forms of SMPTE into MTC (MIDI Time Code) or DTLe (Direct Time Lock enhanced), which means that you can use it for syncing with any existing MIDI software that supports synchronization. It also reads and writes SMPTE in the four formats and has the added advantage of automatically regenerating SMPTE received at its Audio In jack and passing it out the Audio Out jack.

If the price of a MIDI Time Piece seems high (list $495, street $385), consider the fact that you won't need to purchase any of that additional gear. On top of everything, the MIDI Time Piece can serve as the expandable foundation upon which you can build a powerful MLAN.

You can configure the MIDI Time Piece via the MIDI Time Piece DA. This powerful Apple Menu Item lets you monitor the network configuration, interconnect cables, merge data streams, remap channels, filter (mute) specific kinds of MIDI data on a per-channel basis, and stripe and read SMPTE time code. The DA also lets you save as many different configurations as you want for later recall. Figures 8-27 through 8-33 take you through a tour of these features.

Possible MIDI Time Piece network physical connections

Each MIDI Time Piece (MTP) has a computer port and a network port. There are some simple rules to follow:

❖ Never connect a Macintosh serial port to an MTP network port unless its computer port is also connected to the same Macintosh.

❖ Never connect an MTP computer port to another MTP's network port.

❖ Certain configurations, as indicated in Table 8-1, may require connecting a standard interface to an MTP computer port.

Figure 8-27 next page: Selecting Network Configuration displays your MIDI Time Piece (MTP) network. You can include up to four MTPs in a single network. Many of the setups pictured incorporate a standard interface. The reason for this is that many of you might be adding an MTP or two to your existing setup. However, you don't have to retire your old interface — these illustrations show you how to put it to use in the new context. Note that in configurations where two MTPs are connected via their network ports, the cable connecting them can be up to 1,000 feet long. **Setup A:** A single MTP connected to the Macintosh's modem port and set to Fast mode (provides 128 channels, 1 MHz mode provides for 16 channels). The option connection between the Macintosh's printer port and the MTP's network port lets the MTP emulate a 32-channel interface in 1 MHz mode. **Setup B:** A single MTP connected to both Macintosh serial ports (128 channels available at either port in fast mode, 32 channels available in 1 MHz mode). **Setup C:** A single MTP connected to the Macintosh's modem port with a standard 16-channel interface connected to the printer port (fast mode provides 144 channels, 1 MHz mode provides for a total of 32 channels). **Setup D:** A single MTP and a 32-channel dual interface. The MTP's network port is connected to the "left over" Macintosh port on the standard interface. This configuration provides for 160 channels in fast mode and 32 channels in 1 MHz mode. **Setup E:** Two MTPs attached to the Macintosh's modem port. The MTPs are connected via their network ports. This provides for 256 channels in fast mode and still only 16 channels in 1 MHz mode. You may wonder why you wouldn't simply connect a single MTP to each of the Macintosh's ports. The answer to this is that the devices attached to one MTP would not be able to be routed and merged with devices connected to the other MTP. To get around this, you can optionally connect the Macintosh's printer port to the computer port on the second MTP. This allows you to emulate a 32-channel interface and still be able to interconnect all devices, regardless of which MTP they are physically attached to. In this case, you have to be extremely careful when you use software that allows you to refer to devices by name. **Setup F:** Two MTPs and a 32-channel dual interface. This setup provides for 288 channels in fast mode and 32 channels in 1 MHz mode. When you introduce a third MTP between the standard interface and the Macintosh's printer port (connect the third MTP's network port to the standard interface), the channel count increases to 416. **Setup G:** Four MTPs. This configuration provides for 512 individually addressable channels. Of course, you may still emulate a 32-channel standard interface in 1 MHz mode. Optionally you could connect a standard interface to either or both of the boxes assigned to cables 9 to 16. One additional standard interface would provide a total of 518 channels and two would bring the total up to 544 channels. **Setup H:** Four MTPs networked to two Macintoshes. Both computers have complete access to all 512 channels simultaneously. Variations on this configuration are possible with two or three MTPs, but a single MTP cannot be shared with another Macintosh.

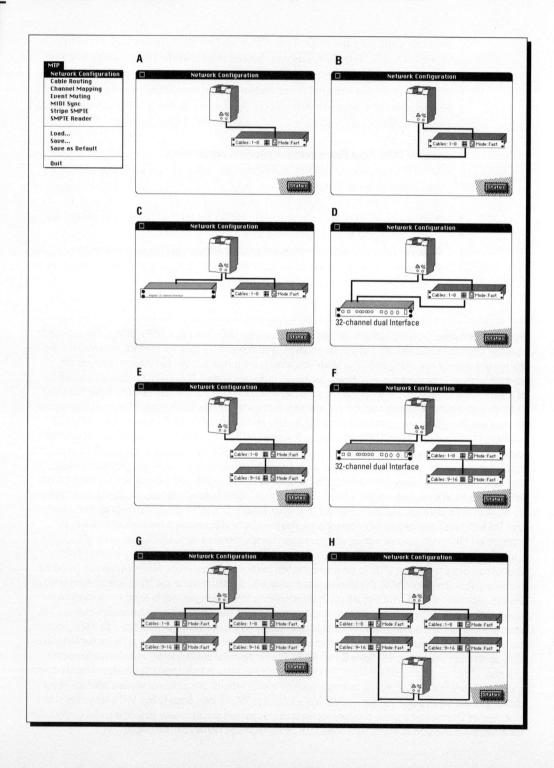

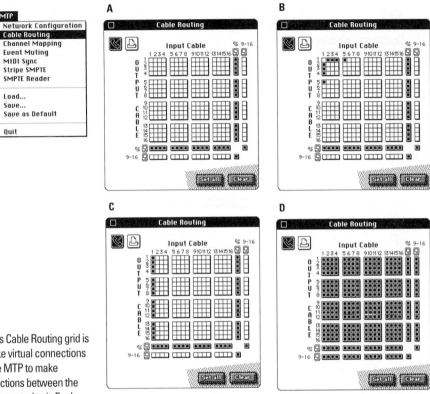

Figure 8-28: This Cable Routing grid is where you make virtual connections that instruct the MTP to make physical connections between the MIDI cables connected to it. Each MTP has 8 MIDI inputs and 8 MIDI outputs. If you have one MTP, only rows and columns 1 through 8 are active. If you have two MTPs, all cells on the grid are active. If you have any MTPs connected to your printer port, you can use the printer port button to pull up a separate grid for its configuration. The additional rows and columns in each grid (with the little Macintosh identifier) are provided to route data to and from the Macintosh. Like most Mark of the Unicorn configuration grids, clicking on the number representing the row or column (in this case the input and output cables) will toggle every box in that row or column on or off. Some typical setups follow: **Setup A:** When you use MIDI software, you will probably want only the boxes next to the little Macintoshes highlighted. This assumes that the MIDI software will handle the routing and/or thru configurations of all your data. **Setup B:** This configuration merges the inputs of cables 2 through 5 and sends them to cable 1. It also routes the output of the device connected to cable 1 to cables 2 through 5. Use this setup if you have a K250 connected to cable 1 and 4 K1000 modules connected to cables 2 through 5. You will then be able to bring up the display of the K1000 modules in the K250's LED and control them remotely using the K250's front panel buttons (this requires two-way communication with each K1000, which is why you need to set up the merging situation). **Setup C:** This setup directs the data arriving at cable 1 (assumed to be your master controller) to all the output cables. Your master controller can then play all the devices connected to the output cables simultaneously. Variations on this scheme are useful when you want to play a single module from your master controller and you are not running a MIDI software program. You simply highlight the row corresponding to the module you want to play from your controller (this box should be highlighted in the master controller's column). Sometimes, you might want to do this when you are running patch editor/librarian software that does not provide for echoing your master controller's input to the device being edited. To get around this sort of program deficiency, simply route the master controller to the device you are editing. Your master controller data will merge with all patch-editing data that your software is sending to the device you are editing. **Setup D:** In this setup, all data arriving at all input cables is merged and routed to all output cables.

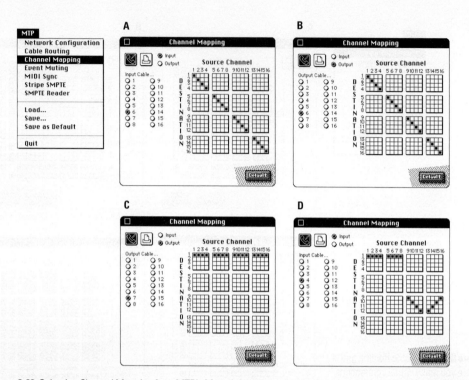

Figure 8-29: Selecting Channel Mapping from MTP's Menu brings up a window that contains up to 64 embedded grids. There is an individual channel map for data coming in from each cable connected to a modem port MTP and for data going out to a cable connected to a modem port MTP. A similar situation exists for any MTPs connected to the printer port. You will only have to deal with the number of grid boxes corresponding to the total number of inputs and outputs on all the MTPs you are using. Naturally, the only grids you will concern yourself with are those that are linked to cables actually in use. You toggle from grid to grid by clicking on the cable selection radio buttons running down the left side of the screen — each brings up a new grid (although you may not notice this if the new grid resembles the previous one). First select the input cables with the Input-Output radio buttons at the top of the screen. After going through your input cables in this manner, you get to the next set of grids by clicking the Output radio button at the top of the screen. If you have MTPs connected to your printer port, click the Printer port icon at the upper left and repeat the whole procedure. Remapping (re-channelizing) a MIDI channel to a cable is as simple as clicking the box in the column corresponding to the source channel at the row that corresponds to the destination channel. Data flows from the top down and toward the left. Remember, you can configure this individually for each input and output cable you are using. Normally, you will probably want to keep these grids in their default mode (diagonal line from upper left to lower right). This represents non-rechannelization. A few other possible configurations are displayed in this illustration. **Setup A:** Default configuration for modem port input cable 6 (no channel remapping). **Setup B:** Default configuration for modem port output cable 6 (no channel remapping). **Setup C:** Source data on any channel is remapped to channel 1 for modem port cable 7. This configuration (and similar ones for the remaining cables) is sometimes used by session musicians who want to communicate instantly with all their devices on channel 1. **Setup D:** For input cable 4, source data on channels 1 through 8 is remapped to channel 1. The remaining channels are inverted: 16 to 9, 15 to 10, 14 to 11, and 13 to 12.

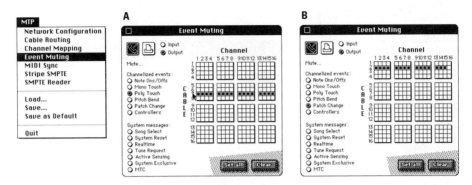

Figure 8-30: The MTP's Event Muting option is a powerful filter containing up to 52 grids. Each grid corresponds to a filter for a specific type of data that you can apply on a per-channel, per-cable basis. You can do this at the input or output stage by choosing between the Input and Output radio buttons at the top of the screen. **Setup A:** Poly Touch (pressure) is being removed from all channels outputting to cable 7. This assumes that the device assigned to cable 7 does not respond to Poly Touch messages. There is no reason to overload the MIDI bandwidth with messages that will be ignored anyway.
Setup B: Patch Change is being ignored by the device attached to output cable 2 unless it appears on channel 16. **Setup C:** All incoming Active Sensing messages are filtered from all cables on all channels. You should consider doing this, because Active Sensing is rarely useful anymore and simply clogs up the available MIDI bandwidth. **Setup D:** Incoming Mono Touch (pressure) is being filtered from the master controller. This can be used if you are working with MIDI software that does not provide an input filter and you wish to thin out the MIDI data stream. **Setup E:** Song Select messages are being filtered from data being sent out cable 4. This would be a good idea if the cable 4 device was a drum machine and you were working in a MIDI sequencer that provided for chaining sequences into songs. Sometimes triggering a song in such a program sends out a song select message. Such a message might cue up a song or pattern that was stored in the drum machine's memory. **Setup F:** Incoming Note Ons and Offs are being filtered from the device connected to cable 8. I sometimes use this when one of my daughters comes into the studio and starts trying to play the keyboard connected to cable 8 while I am working.

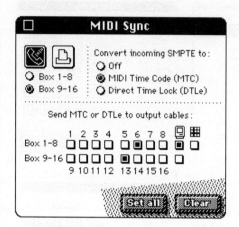

Figure 8-31: MTP's MIDI Sync dialog box has four imbedded screens, one for each MTP on the network. Each allows you to convert incoming SMPTE to MTC or DTLe. The latter is a proprietary SMPTE synchronization protocol employed by Mark of the Unicorn's own Performer sequencer and several other programs. The converted synchronization data can be routed to any combination of output cables, the Macintosh (this is normal), or the MTP network port (and thus, the interface or device connected to that port).

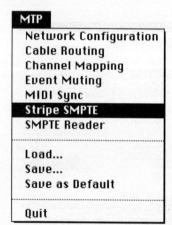
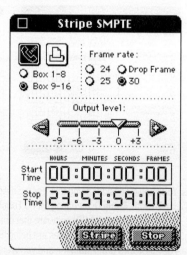

Figure 8-32: The MTP's SMPTE striping dialog box is unique in that it lets you set the output level (referenced to –10 dB when the slider is set to 0) of the audio SMPTE data being output at the MTP's Audio Out jack. Toggling the radio buttons and icons in the upper left selects a specific MTP as the SMPTE striper for networks including more than a single MTP. The other set of radio buttons lets you switch between the four common SMPTE formats. Once you start striping you can continue with other work on the Macintosh — striping will continue from the MTP without requiring any Macintosh CPU time.

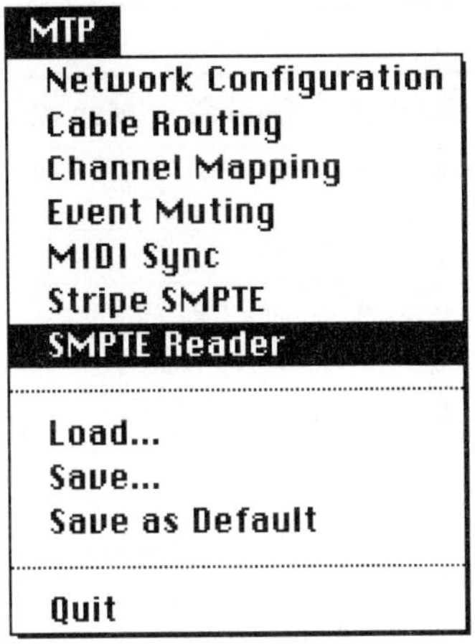

MTP
> **Network Configuration**
> **Cable Routing**
> **Channel Mapping**
> **Event Muting**
> **MIDI Sync**
> **Stripe SMPTE**
> **SMPTE Reader**
>
> **Load...**
> **Save...**
> **Save as Default**
>
> **Quit**

Figure 8-33: The MTP's SMPTE Reader automatically detects the frame rate of incoming SMPTE and displays it and a running update of SMPTE addresses. The current conversion format is also displayed (MTC or DTLe). Also displayed are the serial port and MTP cable, if any, that the converted SMPTE is passed on to. For the reader to function, converted SMPTE must be passed on to the Macintosh (see Figure 8-32). Note: the SMPTE Reader only updates while it is the active (front or foremost) window. You may keep it open and continue with other tasks. Every time you click on it to bring it to the front, it starts updating again.

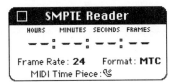

Use Table 8-1 to check your MTP network. Place an "x" in every box that represents a physical connection on your network. If you have an "x" in any of the empty boxes, you are doing something wrong.

Addressing channels and cables by name

With the possibility for up to 512 active MIDI channels you may find it hard to remember what data is going where. Because of this, most software that supports cableized MIDI channels also provides for associating a name with a particular cable and channel. With such a system, if you want to send data on channel 4 to, for example, a Wavestation attached to cable 6, you may assign a name to cable 6, channel 4. You might assign the name "Wavestation-4" or "Wavestation Strings" if you have reserved the Wavestation's channel 4 for string type sounds. Instead of looking up what cables and channels a device is assigned to and typing in that information, you simply select "Wavestation-4" from a pop-up menu or scrolling list of device possibilities (see Figure 8-34).

Opcode's Studio 5

Opcode announced the Studio 5 interface in 1991 (about a year after the MIDI Time Piece). This interface provides many of the same features of the MIDI Time Piece, but there are some significant differences.

Where each MIDI Time Piece provides you with a total of 128 channels, each Studio 5 provides for 15 cables, each with its own set of MIDI channels for a grand total of 240 MIDI channels per box.

The Studio 5 includes other features that were present in Opcode's previous high-end interface, the Studio 3 (note: there was no Studio 4). These include the ability to read and convert momentary and continuous audio footswitches to MIDI data.

Table 8-1: Possible MIDI Time Piece network physical connections

Primary Macintosh	Mac #1		MTP 1		MTP 2		MTP 3		MTP 4		Dual #1		Dual #2		Mac #2	
	M	P	C	N	C	N	C	N	C	N	M	P	M	P	M	P
Modem			●					○			○	○	○	○		
Printer				●	○		●				○	●	○	●		
MTP 1																
Computer	●										●	○	○	○		
Network		●				●										
MTP 2																
Computer		○									●	○	○	○	●	
Network				●												
MTP 3																
Computer			●													
Network	○								●		○	●	○	●		●
MTP 4																
Computer													○	●		
Network								●								●
Dual #1																
Modem	○	○	●		●			○							●	
Printer	○	●	○		○		●									●
Dual #2																
Modem	○	○		○	○		○		○						●	
Printer	○	●		○	○		●		●							●
Mac #2																
Modem					●						●		●			
Printer							●		●			●		●		

Key to Table 8-1

M	Macintosh Modem port
P	Macintosh Printer port
C	MIDI Time Piece Computer port
N	MIDI Time Piece Network port
●	Represents a normal connection
○	Represents an unlikely, but nonetheless possible connection

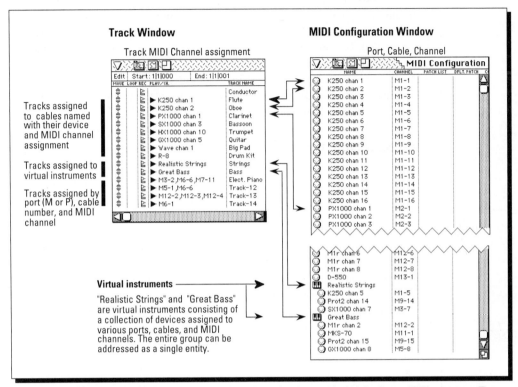

Figure 8-34: Mark of the Unicorn's approach to cableized channel assignment in their Performer MIDI sequencer. Three types of channel-to-track assignments are illustrated: by device name (representing a serial port, cable, and channel), by virtual instrument (representing a collection of devices), and alphanumerically (by port, cable, and channel numbers). You can see why addressing devices by name or function is desirable, particularly if you have a large number of multitimbral devices.

Opcode's interface also includes a very important addition to the standard synchronization features: that of being able to synchronize to an incoming audio pulse such as audio drum track or an audio click. Such clicktracks are sent to musicians' headsets during film and video scoring sessions.

One distinct advantage of the Studio 5 over the MIDI Time Piece is relevant to studio musicians and session players. The Studio 5 contains a decent amount of battery-backed RAM. In fact, you can store all your network configurations in the Studio 5 itself and recall them by MIDI. This means that you do not have to bring a Macintosh to a recording date. Conversely, because you configure the MIDI Time Piece by its MTP DA and you save and load all configurations with your Macintosh, any reconfiguration of a MIDI Time Piece requires you to have a computer present at all times.

Naturally, the Studio 5 offers extensive OMS support because both are Opcode products. The Studio 5 also offers complete compatibility with the MIDI Time Piece as well. Be forewarned that the documentation of many software packages erroneously states that a MIDI Time Piece is required to access more than 32 channels or to "cableize data." This is simply because these manuals were written before the Studio 5 was publicly announced. You can substitute an Opcode Studio 5 in practically all of these cases.

MediaLink and the MidiTap

Lone Wolf's MediaLink is a high speed networking protocol designed for the real-time simultaneous transmission of all forms of digital media information. A single fiber optic cable can carry over a half-million MIDI channels in both directions simultaneously. This eliminates the need for multiple cables and snakes. You don't need to connect MediaLink devices in any particular order because the software knows the identity of every device on the network.

The MIDI Specification limits the length of MIDI cables to 50 feet, but MediaLink fiber optic cables can span about a mile and a half. If you merely need long distance remote control and can live without the other features of MediaLink, use Lone Wolf's FiberLink system to connect MIDI devices over the same distance. Each FiberLink system provides two boxes with a single MIDI input and output and two fiber optic ports.

Because data is traveling at a speed ranging from 2 MBit to 100 MBit per second, there is no perceptible signal delay. Current MidiTaps (see the section "The MidiTap" below) communicate at 2 MBit per second which is 64 times MIDI speed — future Taps will communicate at 3,000 times MIDI's speed. Fiber optic cables have the added advantage that they are practically indestructible and completely immune to ground loops, hums, and RFI (radio frequency interference).

The protocol can also communicate analog and digital audio, video, SMPTE, SCSI, AppleTalk, and other forms of digital data, but the hardware for supporting this is still being designed at the time of this writing. MediaLink can also communicate MIDI data over the telephone lines allowing for virtual studios, parts of which may be in other cities or on other continents.

Lone Wolf's motto is "One button, one cable." MediaLink supports 65,536 groups of 16 MIDI channels. Half (32,768) of these are user definable and the remaining groups are tagged with specific manufacturer IDs. All 524,288 MIDI channels can be sent simultaneously and bidirectionally down a single fiber optic cable. A single button press or Macintosh command can reconfigure the entire network. All channels are truly mergeable. You can merge data that is all on the same MIDI channel and the type of data makes no difference (MediaLink can merge SysEx data with note data — something that most MIDI mergers don't allow).

You should be aware of the fact that MediaLink is not intended to be a replacement for MIDI as some rumors have stated. It is a MIDI support system that makes up for many of MIDI's deficiencies such as cable length, minimal number of channels, and the distribution of extremely dense real-time data to a large number of devices. It does not use any non-standard MIDI messages to communicate with the instruments on a network. Its primary function is to distribute and deliver data (MIDI data in this case), not to interpret or modify such data.

The MidiTap

MediaLink is a set of rules that are used to arbitrate access to a single bus connectivity system. The MidiTap uses that set of rules.

To use MediaLink for MIDI you must have at least one of Lone Wolf's hardware MidiTaps. The MidiTap is a single rackspace unit and the first one on your network normally connects to the serial port of your Macintosh. You can use the MidiTap as a MIDI interface although there are no built-in synchronization conversion features. It is more accurate to think of the MidiTap as an interface between MIDI and MediaLink.

Each MidiTap has four MIDI inputs and outputs, each of which provides a unique set of 16 channels. Therefore, each MidiTap can address 64 discrete MIDI channels. Each port, channel, and arbitrary group of ports and channels across your network (spanning any number of MidiTaps) can be given a unique name, address, and MIDI processing configuration. You may want to have more than one MidiTap in your network. MediaLink provides for up to 253 MidiTaps on a network.

Each MidiTap has two fiber optic ports. You use these to connect one MidiTap to another or to connect a MidiTap to another MediaLink device such as an AudioTap (which can handle 24 channels of digital audio simultaneously). The fiber optic ports are identical — it doesn't matter which one you plug into. Audio and MIDI can coexist on the same fiber optic cable without getting in the way of each other.

You can connect MidiTaps in a bus topology or, using Lone Wolf's FiberHub which provides eight MediaLink fiber optic ports, you can implement a star topology. You can hang bus topologies off star topologies and these can connect to additional star topologies. For example, if you hang four of the 16 × 16 MidiHubs off one MidiTap it can ultimately support 64 ports, each one with 16 channels. It gets quite big quite fast. The connection order simply doesn't make any difference. Nor is proximity a factor in making network configurations.

Finally, each MidiTap has one high-speed RS232 interface port to which you can connect computers, modems, printers, or any other RS232 device. The RS232 port communicates at 150-38.4 Kbaud asynchronously and 9600 to 250 Kbaud synchronously.

The MidiTap's front panel has a 16-character × 2-line LED-backlit LCD. There are also three LED indicators that display network mode, Tap status, and the degree of MIDI channel usage. The front panel also has four buttons and a knob from which you can edit and scroll through network configurations known as LanScapes.

There are three main forms of communication between networked MidiTaps. Using *node-to-node* communication, any individual MidiTap can control and configure any other individual MidiTap on the network. *Broadcast* communication allows any MidiTap to send data to all other MidiTaps on the network at the same time. *Multi-cast* transmissions involve any number of MidiTaps sending to separate groups of receivers simultaneously.

While you can connect thousands of MIDI devices to a MediaLink network, you may also connect any number of computers to the network. MediaLink currently supports all Macintosh, IBM, and Atari computers.

MidiTaps and modems

The MidiTap stores its firmware on EEPROMs (electronically erasable program-mable read-only memory chips). This means that Lone Wolf can send software updates via modem from Lone Wolf directly to your MidiTap. You can also download software revisions from an on-line service and transfer them to your MidiTaps from the Macintosh. Finally, any MidiTap can connect to another MidiTap and update the EEPROMs directly. This doesn't imply that there are bugs in the MidiTap. Even the very first MidiTaps shipped bug-free. All the updates so far have been to add features, mainly at the request of MidiTap users.

You can control MidiTaps by modem too. This is advantageous for collaborative projects, troubleshooting, and consulting. You can even share resources and jam via modem (see the section "Working with LanScapes").

Setting up LanScapes

A LanScape is a very important concept to MediaLink. It is a configuration of physical or virtual devices, including their interconnections. You may have as many LanScapes as you like, each one representing an entire configuration of your system. Before you can create a LanScape, you must teach MediaLink about all your devices. This is essentially a setup mode similar to that of Opcode's OMS environment.

MediaLink needs to know the names of the instruments you have connected to every MidiTap port on your network. You can do this from the MidiTap or from the Macintosh. You can associate a graphic object with each physical instrument. These graphics are much larger and more descriptive than those supplied with OMS. Furthermore, you can create your own graphics. You can even use scanned photos of your actual gear if you want.

The beauty of this system is that you needn't concern yourself with ports, cables, or channels as you do with OMS and a MIDI Time Piece network. With MediaLink you deal with your physical boxes. It doesn't matter if you interconnect the fiber optic cables in any new configuration.

You use the Virtual Studio setup application to create LanScapes. Here you can view your instruments on a screen that displays your instruments. You can drag these around the screen to emulate their physical locations in your studio if you like. You interconnect devices by drawing cables from device to device much like with Apple's PatchBay. There are no limitations to the number of cables that can run between devices and you do not have to concern yourself with how the devices connect physically, as long as their respective MidiTaps are linked by way of a fiber optic cable.

A LanScape can introduce additional parameter control in the form of device definitions for each of its nodes. Devices can consist of a Tap, port, and channel address or a group of any number of these items. You can assign one or more categories to each device and you define the categories. Sample categories might include digital synthesizer, analog synthesizer, sampler, drum machine, virtual instrument, computer, signal processor, my gear, my friend's gear, or co-owned gear (see Figure 8-35). You will see how important these categories can be as we delve deeper into creating a LanScape.

Each device definition may include such information as patch and channel assignment (patch name and number are visible). Each MIDI channel can have 16 other configuration parameters such as volume, pan, and mod setting. You may also indicate a transposition for each device. Finally, each device definition can include an input and output filter as well, much like those provided by the MTP DA (see Figure 8-36).

Better yet, you can create virtual devices consisting of a collection of channels spanning multiple MidiTaps if you like. You might have a killer bass sound made up of a certain patch on channel 3 of your M1, in combination with another patch on channel 6 of your D-550, in combination with several samples on different channels of your Proteus. This collection of sounds can itself be defined as a virtual device. You can even assign a graphic of a bass guitar to this combination of sounds and have it appear in your LanScape ready to have cables drawn to and from it. Any conditions that you apply to this aggregate virtual device apply to

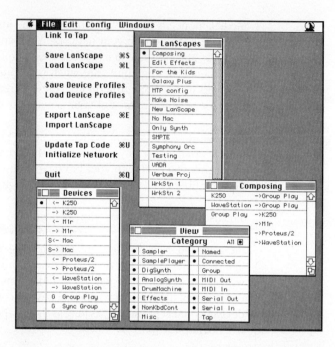

Figure 8-35: Virtual Studio's various configuration windows. You assign your devices to MidiTap ports in the Devices window. The LanScapes window provides a list of stored LanScapes and allows you to switch instantly from one to another (the currently active LanScape has a bullet next to it). The View window filters what devices will be shown in the Virtual Studio Window (not pictured in this illustration, but see Figures 8-37 and 8-38). The Connection window is titled with the name of the current LanScape (in this case "Composing") and displays a text listing of all the connections indicating all sources and destinations.

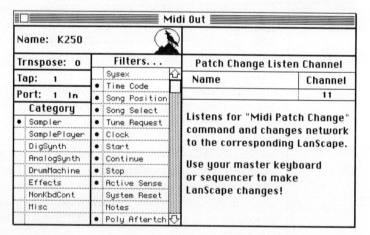

Figure 8-36: The Virtual Studio's device setup screen. Double-clicking a device brings up this configuration screen or the option to create a new virtual device. Double-clicking a virtual cable allows you to set up a new device that consists of any combination of channels on that cable.

all its constituent parts. Thus, in one fell swoop you can specify a transposition or set of filters for the virtual device that applies to all the sounds making up the virtual device.

Carrying the virtual instrument idea in the other direction, you can assign each individual channel of a physical device to be a separate virtual device. Of course you can also specify groups of channels to be a virtual device as well. For example, with a Proteus/2 you might assign particular patches to each MIDI channel for every instrument of the orchestra. Then you could designate that each channel be a separate virtual instrument and assign the appropriate graphic to it: flute, oboe, clarinet, bassoon, French horn, and so on. You could then set up your LanScape to resemble the traditional orchestral seating diagram. In other words, you can decouple your channels from their physical device associations and create a realistic representation of your "orchestra."

Another use of this feature would be to create a virtual replication of the physical locations of all your devices at the relative locations they occupy in your "real" studio. Such a representation could include multiple rooms or buildings (see Figures 8-37 and 8-38).

Every MidiTap on your network contains all the information necessary for it to fulfill its purpose in the LanScape, but the Macintosh can store the entire LanScape as a single entity. Because each MidiTap knows the part it plays in a given LanScape and knows the name of each LanScape, reconfiguration is instantaneous. The Macintosh does not have to transmit a large file of configuration data — it simply sends the name of the LanScape out to the network. Furthermore, because the MidiTaps themselves store the LanScape parameters, switching any MidiTap to a specific LanScape causes all the MidiTaps on the network that participate in the particular LanScape to call up the required settings.

Figure 8-37: A MidiTap LanScape prior to making any interconnections between devices. In this illustration, device outputs appear at the left and inputs at the right. You can drag any device to any location on the screen. This illustration shows all devices on the network. The View filter allows you to hide specified categories of devices if you want. Normally, you would set some connections to always appear in your default New LanScape window.

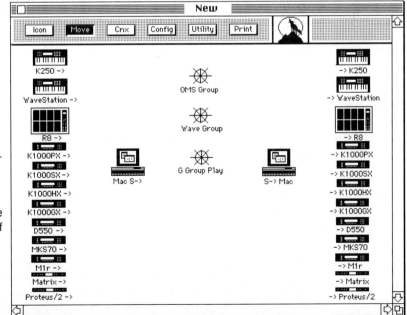

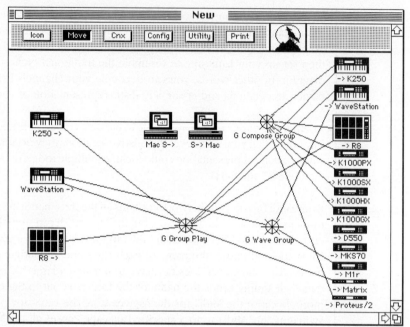

Figure 8-38: A typical MediaLink LanScape after drawing the desired connections between devices. You can print this or save it as a text file that you can edit in plain English with any word processor. The View filter has been used to hide all non-controllers from the input side of the configuration (left side).

A level above LanScapes enhances collaboration with a group of people who all have their own MidiTap networks. In this mode, individual MediaLink networks joined for a performance can still maintain some degree of independence. A technician or designated individual can trigger a certain "song" LanScape that causes everyone's MidiTap to load a collection of LanScapes. Some members of the ensemble might employ 20 different personal LanScapes throughout the song whereas others only require two or three different reconfigurations throughout the duration. A performing ensemble or band might employ this mode.

The LanScape can be filtered. Remember that you have designated that each device is in one or more categories. You can request that the display be limited to only samplers, only synthesizers and samplers, only your friend's devices, only the synthesizers that you and your friend jointly own, only virtual devices that consist of a combination of analog synthesizers and digital synthesizers, and so on. Thus, your landscape information can serve as a device database that can be searched and manipulated with the same flexibility you expect from a traditional database.

Working with LanScapes

LanScapes are much more powerful than you might expect. Once you have exported a LanScape to a text file, you can take that file to another studio and load it into its MediaLink network. The Virtual Studio software will automatically make all the necessary connections between devices that have the same name and it will ask you what you want to substitute for any missing devices. This generates a map file so that whenever you load one of your LanScapes at this studio, it will automatically make any substitutions that you specified the first time. Alternatively, you could modem the LanScape ahead and include patch dumps with the information.

A large studio facility can set up LanScapes that span different rooms, buildings, and towns. A single fiber optic cable can link the various locations. Some LanScapes can deal with the devices that are physically present in the same room while others can include devices in different rooms and buildings. Those different rooms and buildings can also have their own LanScapes that deal with only the physically present devices. Naturally, you can filter your view of the LanScape to include only those rooms or buildings you want to concern yourself with at any given moment.

When combined with a modem, LanScapes are even more powerful. You can define a LanScape that includes devices that are only accessible via modem. Double-clicking on one of these devices in the LanScape could cause your modem to dial up the remote location and retrieve patches or soundfiles from the remote device. Virtual Studio does not require going through the MidiTap to do this — only that a modem be connected to the remote MediaLink network.

You can jam with your friends via modem too. The only requirement is that you have the same or similar devices. A simple scenario might have you and a friend both playing on an M1 keyboard. Your friend is performing on channel 4 and you are performing on channel 1. You hear your performance mixed with the data that he is sending you over the modem. Likewise, your friend hears his or her M1 mixed with the data being sent to you over the modem. 2400 baud communications can handle this because two people playing in real time can't come close to overloading MIDI's bandwidth, unless they use pitchbend or pressure. Of course, with faster 9600 bps modems, using v.32bis, MNP, or PEP data compression schemes, you can achieve full MIDI speed over a modem. It doesn't require any special hardware because the MidiTap takes care of sorting all the data out at either end.

With a more complex setup you and your friend might have different instruments. The chances are that you can substitute something on your LanScape that comes pretty close to what your friend is hearing and vice versa.

Another scenario might have a remote colleague manipulate an interactive composition program that is controlling various devices in your studio. You could play along with this and capture the whole performance as a MIDI sequence or an audio performance.

You can even communicate with several different people via modem simultaneously. For example, if three people were jamming by modem, the two on each end of the hookup would only need a single phone line, but the person in the middle would need two phone lines and two modems. With five people, the three people in the middle would all need two lines and two modems.

Collaborating via modem is also possible between two continents. You can't jam but you can do zero-delay recording. Assuming that you have a common piece of gear, you send the music and the MIDI clocks to your friend on the other continent. For purposes of this example the musician is going to lay down a synthesizer line for you. Your friend gets the music and the clocks after x amount of delay, but doesn't hear this delay and just plays along with the music being heard. This performance data is sent back to you, combined with the original music and timing information. The playing and the clocks get back to you in sync, and you record based on your incoming clock with no delay.

Incorporating MediaLink into your existing setup

MediaLink doesn't necessarily obsolete your existing patchbays and interfaces. Notice that neither MediaLink or the MidiTap includes any SMPTE conversion features. Although MediaLink can carry SMPTE time code, or any other synchronization data for that matter, you will probably want to keep your current interface to provide for the conversion of SMPTE into MTC or DTLe.

You can sync to SMPTE by having the first of your MediaLink devices connected to your modem port and connect a standard interface with a built-in sync converter to your printer port. Alternatively, you could attach a MIDI Time Piece to your modem port and attach your first MediaLink device to its network port. Another solution would be to use a dedicated SMPTE converter such as Opcode's MIDI Time Code Machine to introduce MTC as MIDI data inputting directly to one of the MIDI ports on your MidiTap. All three of these solutions allow you to introduce MTC into the MediaLink network for the synchronization of remote devices connected to MidiTaps.

Fortunately the MidiTap has both MIDI Time Piece and OMS compatibility modes that allows you to take advantage of all the cableization features of software optimized to work in conjunction with Mark of the Unicorn's and Opcode's interface.

The future of MediaLink

Because the MidiTap responds to MIDI program change for reconfiguration, Passport's DAN works well with the system as do most universal patch editor/librarians that use program change messages to set up two-way communications with the device being edited. Complete MIDI Manager, OMS, Studio 5, and MIDIShare compatibility is under development and may be available when you read this. Because MediaLink is fundamentally a delivery system, adding support for these third-party products is rather simple.

Lone Wolf is working on ScsiTaps, AudioTaps, VideoTaps, and "you-name-it"-Taps. Both an ISDN and a MediaLink point-to-point protocol are being developed to allow modem bridges to link remote studios and permit them to function more efficiently as a single entity.

MediaLink is well on its way to transforming an external MIDI network into something that is as easy to deal with as a workstation. In fact, with MediaLink all your devices can function as if they are one huge workstation.

Interview with Mark Lacas, co-developer of MediaLink

Yavelow: What do you think about MLANs?

Lacas: I feel that they're essential. I know that my own frustration in the studio was the necessity that created my invention. Orchestrating all the music is the creative aspect; orchestrating all the connections and all the gear is the technical aspect. I wanted to minimize or streamline the technical aspect in my studio, and I'm sure that many people feel that way, so that they can stick to the creative aspect.

Yavelow: How did MediaLink develop?

Lacas: When we first set out to do this, we were going to use a standard protocol, because the whole reason for a standard is that everyone could adapt to it. But the more we searched among all the standard protocols of the world, the more we found out that they were all inadequate in various ways, and in fact had fatal flaws when it came to the real-

time aspect. And not only the real-time aspect, but the fault-tolerant nature of what's necessary for its performance situation. Basically, you don't want to be playing with Pink Floyd standing in front of 50,000 people and have your network reconfigure, shutting things down for a second right in the middle of your performance.

Typical protocols on the market are the Carrier Sense type protocols (CSMA), which are like EtherNet. They work fine when you have just a little bit of traffic, and there is not much loading, just the same as two or three people in a room can talk quite pleasantly without needing an arbitrator. Carrier Sense means you listen for someone else talking, and when you sense that no one is talking, that there is a gap, you can jump in and say what you have to say.

As soon as you start getting too many people with opinions on what to say in a short time, you start needing arbitration. In such a situation Carrier Sense doesn't work — there are too many interruptions and collisions, so to speak. So CSMA networks are out, as far as the real-time and fault-tolerant natures of networking.

The obvious solution for arbitration in human conversation is to have a chairman with a gavel, who picks which people are allowed to talk. That's a polled system, or a master-oriented system. Well, those work fine; they are very fast, they are very efficient, but the main problem is that when you lose the master, you lose the whole system. And I think that's unacceptable in my design.

The other aspects of a polled system are that you waste network bandwidth polling each device to see if it has something to say, and whether it should be allowed to say it. So we counted that out immediately.

Then there are the token-oriented systems. A token-oriented system operates much like when you have a group of people in a room and you have a pencil or a baton and you pass the baton around, and whomever has the baton is allowed to talk. The problem is, there is a latency in getting the baton around the room to you, which uses up critical time and efficiency.

Also, if there are only two people in a heated discussion and there are 20 people in the room, you're wasting 18 people's worth of time passing the baton through them, because the baton can't collectively go from node to node; it passes in numerical order among the nodes of the network. In a typical music or audio situation you are going to grow to a very large network, because of all the light stage left, light stage right, light stage center, drum kit, keyboard, hydraulics, flash spots,

you name it, that you need for multimedia control. In essence, you may have only one or two computers controlling all that. So why pass a token to all the hundreds of nodes that are only receivers or have nothing to say? — a terrible waste of network efficiency.

From all of this, and from all our analysis of the various standard network protocols, we deemed that none of them was acceptable. We also noticed the opportunity to create one that did work. We feel that ours is so simple and has such general-purpose capabilities that it would be hard for someone to come up with anything more efficient than what we're doing.

For example — and this is unheard of in the networking world — MediaLink can get up to 99 percent efficiency under certain conditions, and that's incredible. Plus, MediaLink has the other unique characteristic of being able to be fault-tolerant — that's very critical. But in a token system, when you lose the token or when you have a new node enter or leave the network, you have to shut down the entire network to rebuild the logical ring. Again, this is unacceptable in a performance situation.

So, MediaLink has the characteristics of being real time, only passing the arbitration among those guys who have something to say, so you don't waste any efficiency in that regard, plus, as you load MediaLink, the amount of network latency and delay is hardly affected until you reach saturation — a very important characteristic. You don't notice any change in its operation until the thing just gets blown away; and then it's like a brick wall, it degrades totally, whereas most LAN protocols degrade linearly, which means you have 50 percent more data, it's 50 percent worse.

Another couple of interesting aspects involved in MediaLink that I don't want to leave out, are that MediaLink is the only network protocol that allows network-wide real-time synchronization, which is critical in entertainment audio markets — whether it's MIDI Time Code or SMPTE or Video Frame Lock, or whatever — you need to accurately guarantee that everything in the network will be operating off a common timebase. MediaLink is the only one that has this capability built in. To add to that, when you are using the built-in synchronization, it statistically affects the efficiency of the network about zero — you don't lose anything for using it.

We can guarantee, at least with the first implementation of the MediaLink chip, 200 nanoseconds resolution network-wide, which is about three orders of magnitude better than SMPTE.

Yavelow: Could you contrast the MidiTap with other types of MediaLink "taps."

Lacas: The MidiTap is exactly what it says: a tap for MIDI into MediaLink, as the AudioTap will be a tap for audio into the network, and the SCSITap and the SMPTETap, and any other form of Tap becomes a gateway into MediaLink. An interesting way to describe MediaLink, so that people understand it instantly, is to say: As far as anyone sending data to MediaLink is concerned, be it a tape deck or audio system or MIDI thing, consider MediaLink to be FedEx — you just put the stuff in a little box and put an address on it, and you don't worry about how it gets to the other end, and you know that it will get there in a certain time frame — take it out of the box, and the original data is just the way you put it in. That's the way MediaLink can be used — it's a high-speed delivery system for data.

A person with four synths and one MidiTap and one AudioTap could plug all his audio connectors into the AudioTap and all the MIDI into the MidiTap, and have one cable coming out of that rack. Then you have AudioTap and MidiTap by the console, and just tap in and extract those signals right there. You don't get the ground loops, you don't get the hum, and you don't have any electrical biases to worry about.

Yavelow: Even if some audio signals work on a +4 dB protocol while others work at -10 dB?

Lacas: It doesn't matter. That's just a matter of padding. Our AudioTap will do digital and/or analog simultaneously too.

Yavelow: Really? Because most synths output analog signals.

Lacas: Right. And the AudioTap has eight ins and eight outs, that is, four stereo ins and outs. So one MidiTap with its four ports and one AudioTap with its four stereo jacks make a perfect combination for synths, they're little building blocks.

Yavelow: And that's even while other data is going down the same cable.

Lacas: That's the whole point. The other distinction that MediaLink has, that other ones don't, is that MediaLink has a built-in multi-cast capability. With most networks, I send you a packet and you say "aha" and acknowledge it, so that's an acknowledged transmission, which all networks operate on. The problem is, the only other kind of transmission that other networks have is called broadcast, but when you say broadcast, it's to everybody. So there is either broadcast or directed to one guy. If you want to send, say, a video feed to five guys, you can't send it broadcast, because it would go to everyone; you can't send it as a datagram, because then you'd have to send it individually to each of the five, and you'd use five times the network bandwidth to get that one signal through. MediaLink has 65,000 channels of multicast, which means I could be listening from my specific address for data sent right to me, and I am going to acknowledge all those with an acknowledgment. But I could also be listening to a multiplicity of broadcast channels, so I could distribute video to five guys as a zone, so to speak. And I could distribute audio. For example, if you were to stick AudioTaps in a major airport, which there is a plan to do, you can logically zone the audio instead of zoning it by which wire you send it down. So, if I want to say, all of the marketing officers are zone 5, and all of the sales officers are zone 6, and Bob's office is Bob's node number, and the whole airport is zone 100, so it's just by the address that I put in the packet of the audio data of which zone it is, it would automatically come out only those speakers, without having to have a separate wire to each location. It would go on one common fiber.

Yavelow: *Would you be using your Virtual Studio software for this type of setup?*

Lacas: Yes. The beauty is that our VirtualStudio software, if it's told to connect through a network through our RS-232 connection, appears the same to the user. So if someone is out on the road with a rig, and they need some consulting, because something is not working right or they want to add some new setups to write a new song, their techno guru doesn't have to fly out there to fix it. Instead, he can dial them up, run the software through the phone lines and adjust their network accordingly. These

are the things that make our system totally and uniquely different from other manufacturers' music MIDI products. By being packet- rather than TDM- or connection-oriented, it gives us a great deal of flexibility for the multicast, the zoning, and all the other attributes of the system.

Being an object-oriented system, as ours is, as opposed to just "here is a box and you connect these ports," the ports (for example, MidiTap 3, MidiPort 3) have an object that represents them within the network, which you can interrogate and set up. Also it's a distributed MIDI database. So, every object in the network can be interrogated: "What kind of devices are out there?" — and they all answer: "Well, I'm a synth; I'm digital; I'm an analog synthesizer," and so on, and they respond as entities, which again separates us from the rest of the masses in that we have distributed intelligence and database capability.

When you set up a MediaLink and MidiTap system from the computer, you don't have to have the computer to use it. You unplug it from the computer and go out on the road; your patches and volumes and names and everything go with you, because they are embedded in the electrically erasable ROMs in the MidiTap.

Another point I want to bring up right now, which I think is extremely important — and again I'm being vocal about it so that other products will change and hopefully follow our lead — every electronic music device on the market these days has a computer in it, a microprocessor. But the manufacturers haven't enlisted the computers to do important user interface stuff. For example, we alphabetize all of your LanScapes and all of your devices in the network on-the-fly. And when you dial through on the front panel or when the computer deals with it for you, you see them in the order that logically your brain can deal with. Otherwise, when you call something a number, then you have to have a cheat sheet to look up what that number is. I don't know how many countless hours I've wasted with today's current generation of products going through one at a time until I found the sound I wanted. If it happened to be number 99 out of a hundred, well, I went through 99 before I found it.

Yavelow: Now, the fiber optic thing . . . how sturdy are those, if people step on them or drop a road case on one?

Lacas: They're as sturdy as MIDI connectors. Our armored fiber has two layers of keflar, which is what they make bulletproof vests out of . . . so I can truly say that our cables are bulletproof. And they have stainless steel connectors — we've jumped on them, and you can't break them.

Yavelow: How long did it take to develop MediaLink?

Lacas: One of the things that really surprised us is that we developed MediaLink and created the product in less than a year. When we got customer feedback for the product we had shipped — even in its first software revision — it felt as if it had been on the market for at least three years, because we've only had about five or ten bug reports from day one of shipping the product, and none of them were critical bugs, they were just annoyances. We have never had a product crash in the field. We have never had a return from an unhappy customer. All of our customers have become disciples after using the darn thing.

Yavelow: I can attest to that!

Summary

- One task that MIDI software takes care of is getting your data to and from the Macintosh. Many programs include a built-in MIDI driver to facilitate communication with the MIDI interface hooked up to one or both of your Macintosh's serial ports. Such programs merely need to know the speed of your MIDI interface and what port or ports it connects to. If you use synchronization, you may need to inform your software as to which port synchronization information will arrive at and what format this data will be in.

- Apple's MIDI Manager is an increasingly popular alternative to using a program's built-in MIDI driver. It has become the preferred method for the internal routing of MIDI data, so more and more programs that rely exclusively on Apple's MIDI Manager are beginning to appear. Such programs often do not include their own built-in MIDI drivers, therefore requiring MIDI Manager for their operation. With MIDI Manager you deal with logical or virtual MIDI ports. Connecting IN ports to OUT ports is as simple as drawing a line that functions as a virtual MIDI cable between ports.

- The Opcode MIDI System (OMS) is a software environment for running multiple MIDI applications. The most common misconceptions about OMS are that it is a replacement for MIDI Manager or that Opcode has created a new standard that will require you to make a choice between MIDI Manager and OMS. There is no truth to these rumors. OMS accomplishes many of the same things that Apple's MIDI Manager does. The most blatant similarity is that it makes the necessary connections between MIDI programs and the Macintosh's serial ports.

✔ MIDIShare and M•ROS are two alternatives for the internal routing of data. The advantages that these environments might provide are offset by the drawback that not many programs support them. This shouldn't prevent you from using them. Additionally, you should not get the impression that the use of MIDIShare or M•ROS-based systems excludes you from running MIDI Manager or OMS programs, or even programs that fall outside the boundaries of any of the approaches. In the worst case scenario, you might have to reboot your Macintosh to load a required serial driver or system extension.

✔ The moment you connect two devices by way of MIDI, you have begun to establish a local area network (LAN) for music. You will probably end up pushing a great deal of other kinds of data around through cables attached to your Macintosh and external peripherals, MIDI and otherwise.

✔ Most Macintosh musicians purchase networking support hardware to make up for some of the inherent limitations to the MIDI Specification. To eliminate data distortion experienced when devices are daisychained using their THRU ports, many people purchase a MIDI Thru box or patcher to make sure that the same data arrives at all designated destinations simultaneously.

✔ MIDI Time Piece and Studio 5 networks are based upon the concept of cables. Individual cables can each have their own set of 16 MIDI channels. An individual MIDI Time Piece has eight pairs of MIDI input and output ports so each box can support 128 channels. Up to four MIDI Time Pieces can be networking to a single Macintosh (or several Macintoshes if desired) providing for 512 MIDI channels (4 times 128). One advantage of such a large number of MIDI channels is that you can keep every channel on each one of your multitimbral devices active at all times. It is no longer necessary to remember what instrument is set to respond on what channel.

✔ Lone Wolf's MediaLink is a high speed networking protocol designed for the real-time simultaneous transmission of all forms of digital media information. A single fiber optic cable can carry over a half-million MIDI channels in both directions simultaneously. This eliminates the need for multiple cables and snakes. You don't need to connect MediaLink devices in any particular order because the software knows the identity of every device on the network. Lone Wolf's motto is "One button, one cable." A single button press or Macintosh command can reconfigure the entire network. MediaLink can also communicate MIDI data over the telephone lines allowing for virtual studios, parts of which may be in other cities or on other continents.

Chapter 9

The Journey Between Sound and Music

In this chapter . . .

✔ The stages involved in transforming sound to music.

✔ Applications of the Macintosh to the creative process.

✔ Overview of the generation, accumulation, editing, and organization of sound material.

✔ Creative input and subsequent manipulation.

✔ Mixing, signal processing, synchronization, and output.

Conceptualizing Your Creative Process

Once you have your studio or workstation set up, it is important that you have a strong conceptual model of exactly how your musical ideas, your musical materials or data, will flow through the setup during the creative process. To establish an effective working methodology, you always need to be aware of what stage you are in with respect to the overall endeavor.

The control of sound and the manipulation of musical ideas with a Macintosh often requires a wide range of software during the creative process. The developmental stages of this process encompass three transformations: Sound resources are manipulated, organized into music, and then expressed as sound.

Before the sound is actually transformed into music, a Macintosh may have been instrumental in its creation, editing, and organization within a sound library. Once sounds exist, they may then be organized into music with a MIDI sequencer, a non-MIDI sequencer, or notation package, or other appropriate software. Typically, this involves one of four input methods: real-time, step-time, interactive, or algorithmic.

In the final transformation, the whole assemblage is turned back into sound as the Macintosh controls the various synthesizers, effects devices, and mixers. If this output is to be recorded onto multitrack tape, a synchronization device is often necessary to maintain the temporal alignment of the separate tracks when they are recorded in multiple passes (a once standard procedure that is now giving way to music directly recorded to two or more tracks in a single pass).

Conversely, the output may be recorded using the increasingly more common (and inexpensive) "direct-to-hard disk" method. In this case, you have another chance to "fix it in the mix" using state-of-the-art digital mixing and DSP (digital signal processing) software. Newer direct-to-hard disk digital audio systems permit digital audio tracks to be aligned with MIDI data tracks, so that additional MIDI sequenced parts can be synchronized to real audio information and for controlling additional sound-generating devices and/or automating mixers and effects devices that respond to MIDI.

A simplified model of the entire three-stage process (sound→music→sound) encompasses the following six activities:

1. Accumulation of sound material
2. Sound editing and organization
3. Creative input
4. Shaping input into music
5. Mixing and signal processing
6. Output

Figure 9-1 illustrates this continuum.

Accumulation of Sound Material

Music that is played using electronic instruments usually draws its material from one of two domains: sampling or synthesis. The first possible introduction of a Macintosh into the musical process is in the actual creation or capturing of sonic material through the techniques of sound generation or sound sampling or a combination of the two.

While software and analog-to-digital devices exist that allow the Macintosh to function as a veritable digital sampling machine, until very recently, the Macintosh was not capable of attaining the minimum level of fidelity required by professionals (i.e., sounds sampled at a resolution of 16 bits, with a 44.1 KHz sampling rate). The 32-bit Macintosh II running with a MC68020 CPU was the first model to challenge this limitation. Its "open architecture" stimulated third-party developers to produce digital audio cards that could be plugged into one or more of the Macintosh's slots or attached by means of the SCSI port. This transformed the Macintosh II into a complete high-quality digital-audio workstation — and all at a fraction (roughly $\frac{1}{100}$) of the cost for such technology prior to this point in technological history.

Now, with a relatively inexpensive (under $1,000) internal digital audio card, the Macintosh can function as a sampler rivaling dedicated external devices that cost considerably more. These cards allow for individual samples to be accessed from an external MIDI keyboard or from a sequencer running on the Macintosh and

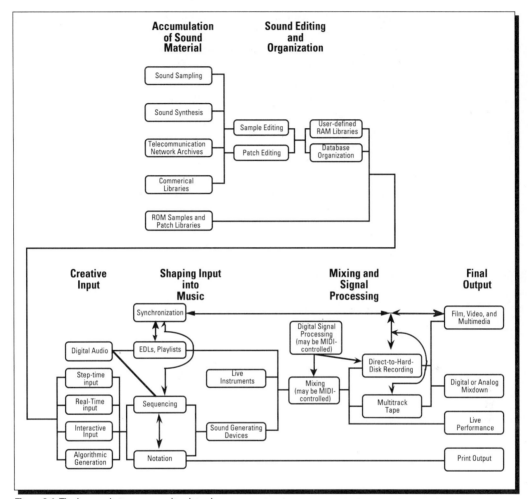

Figure 9-1: The journey between sound and music.

routed to the card via Apple's MIDI Manager. But, more importantly, most internal digital audio cards permit direct-to-hard disk recording of longer passages and can therefore form the basis of an entire soundtrack for a multimedia presentation.

Professional 16-bit sound notwithstanding, 8-bit sound sampling has been available on the Macintosh for quite some time through MacroMind-Paracomp's MacRecorder and now through Articulate's VoiceLink. The SID kit is a do-it-yourself 8-bit digitizer that performs some of the same functions as the commercial products. Eight-bit sampled sound has a wide range of uses in multimedia and educational software.

On the other hand, the Macintosh's 32-bit CPU is perfectly capable of synthesizing high quality complex sound using popular synthesis techniques such as additive, subtractive, or FM synthesis. Sounds created in this manner may sometimes be tested using the hardware of the Macintosh generating them, but due to physical limitations, they are not often played back for musical purposes by the computer that created them, unless the Macintosh is equipped with an internal card (such as Digidesign's Sound Accelerator, Audiomedia, or SampleCell) capable of reproducing the sound to specifications comparable to those of external devices.

Ironically, a sort of hybrid process is necessary. Most sounds synthesized on the Macintosh must be transformed into a file that is compatible with a digital sampling keyboard or module's file format. Typically, a sound synthesized in this manner is converted into an accurate reproduction of what the resultant sampled soundfile would have been, had the sound been sampled from the real world. This permits the sound to be transferred into a sampling keyboard or module for playback later — in essence, "tricking" the device into thinking that the file is one which it created itself. A similar situation exists when using internal digital audio cards. Digidesign's TurboSynth and SoftSynth software-based synthesis programs can output sounds directly from the Macintosh by way of internal digital audio cards.

Actually, using the Macintosh as the sound-generating or sound-sampling device is not the predominant method involved in the accumulation of sound material. The vast majority of musical uses of the Macintosh rely on external sound-generating devices (synthesizers, samplers, and sample players) for sound material. With external devices, the Macintosh is used as a front-end to the editing capabilities of the external device or as an organizational storage medium for patches or soundfiles.

Sound Editing and Organization

In most cases, the first software introduced into the computer-assisted musician's creative process is used to edit or manipulate the acoustical properties of the sound material itself. Depending upon the source of a musician's sonic material — sampled or synthesized — the editing procedure may include modifying sampled soundfiles using an on-screen graphic waveform editor, or it may mean editing the patches of a synthesizer in real-time via an on-screen simulation of the physical controls of the synthesizer.

Many external sound-generating devices use a limited number of buttons and controls that may function in a variety of ways, depending on the parameter being edited or the "mode" that the device is currently set to. However, the computer simulation of a device's front panel, which appears on-screen, is not similarly limited: Each separate editing function may have its own simulated control (or virtual control), including ongoing visual feedback that often provides a far easier and more efficient interface to the sound-modification potential of the device than the manufacturers have built into the physical hardware. This is due to the size of most external devices' front panels, which have only enough room for a small number of controls such as knobs, buttons, and faders, and even less room for a visual display.

Editing may be as simple as boosting a sound's gain or creating an envelope, to microscopically examining and altering single sound samples in a file consisting of a half million samples. In the latter case, the edit base, historically defined by the width of the razorblade used to cut and splice analog tape together, can be as small and accurate as $\frac{1}{48000}$ of a second (many analog recorders transport tape at $7\frac{1}{2}$-inches per second — imagine trying to cut a $7\frac{1}{2}$-inch piece of tape into 0.00015625-inch strips with a razorblade).

A boon to the creative use of Macintosh-controlled devices that cannot be over-stressed is the speed at which complex editing operations can be accomplished, coupled with the convenience of being able to edit numerous devices without leaving one's position in front of the computer screen. This has had an impact on music-making similar to the introduction of the word processor to writers.

Sound libraries

After creating the sounds that are to be used, either through sampling, synthesis, or the creation and editing of sounds found in external devices, the next function of the Macintosh is to manipulate the sound library. Although most sound-generating devices include stock patches (referred to as *presets*) or sampled soundfiles in their ROM chips, most of these devices also provide RAM into which user-defined banks or libraries of edited sounds can be stored or loaded individually or as a unit. In the case of samplers and sample players, these objects consist of individual user-sampled soundfiles or collections of soundfiles. In the case of synthesizers, these objects are user-created parameter settings known as *patches*.

Librarian software serves several purposes. First and foremost it organizes soundfiles or patches into larger groups or banks, which are associated together on the basis of musical considerations. This is important, because the amount of available RAM within a given device places physical limitations upon the number of patches or soundfiles that may be stored in it — usually around 64 user setups. This capacity is invariably exceeded by the number of available patches or soundfiles that you might create or collect from outside sources. Typical sources for sounds include those you create with your own sound editing, public domain libraries, user groups, or those you purchase from sound designers or soundware manufacturers.

As RAM becomes cheaper, many devices are providing on-board storage space for more sound objects than MIDI is capable of handling. MIDI expects there to be 128 different sound "programs" (numbered 0 to 127), and that is the maximum number that can be addressed with most devices. It is becoming increasingly common for a device to have more than 128 sounds on-line in immediately accessible RAM — but any sound numbered greater than 128 may not be called up by MIDI in a Program Change message. To take care of this anomaly, many synthesizers provide for the creation of a user-defined patch list that remaps higher numbered (greater than 127) patches onto numbers 127 or less. Librarian software facilitates rapid mapping of the 128 MIDI program numbers to a user-specified subset of the sounds available online.

A new addition to the MIDI Spec, "Bank Switching," now permits synthesizers to recognize a command that switches the patch list to a new bank of sounds. Theoretically, each bank of sound can have up to 127 patches, and there can be 127 banks. Because this is a relatively new addition to the MIDI Spec, not many devices support it. Prior to the implementation of a standardized bank switching command, a few ambitious synthesizer manufacturers, whose devices always contained many more than 127 sounds, had provided for bank switching in their software by specifying that if two patch change messages were received in a row, the first message would switch the bank and the second would call up the patch in the new bank. Kurzweil Music Systems took this approach in its 1000 and 1200 series of rack-mount modules, and Oberheim employed a similar scheme with its Matrix 1000.

Many sound-generating devices allow you to create libraries consisting of con-figurations of the instrument's keyboard mapping. In such cases, the musical keyboard can be divided at "split points" into separate regions, each of which may have different patches or soundfiles associated with it. Because of this, the actual musical keys begin to lose their scale-associated, do-re-mi-fa-sol-la-ti-do orientation and become merely triggers. Consider an extreme case, the Kurzweil 250. This sampling keyboard allows each of its 88 keys to be tuned to any frequency (expressed in cents), triggering any instrument or sound, and having its own "effects file" (a group of its own unique digital processing effects) associated with it. As if that were not enough, Kurzweil keyboard setups may include configurations that consist of up to six layers, each of which may be divided into 88 regions in the same manner. With 449 configura-tions online in a fully loaded machine, librarian software is a welcomed aid.

Beyond libraries dedicated to sounds, patches, keyboard-mappings, and MIDI assignments, you can also find software that you can use to organize libraries of melodies, motives, themes, and patterns — in other words, musical ideas. Bogas Productions's Studio Session is a good example of this (see Chapter 15, "Making Music without MIDI"). Once musical fragments and ideas have been identified as separate entities within such a database, these tools provide composers and arrangers with a way to assemble and manipulate their material from increasingly greater levels of abstraction, with results far more efficient and effective than addressing each musical note as an individual event. Such methodology is often much closer to the way that composers actually conceptualize a work of music.

The simplest solution to the organization of musical ideas is the ever more common implementation of chaining in the context of a MIDI sequencer. With this approach, individual sequences are defined as "sub-sequences" (in Vision, StudioVision, EZ Vision, and Beyond) or "chunks" (in Performer) or "clip files" (in Finale), and these can easily be strung together into "songs," as the combination of such sub-sequences are often called. Some software even go as far as allowing the songs to be linked together into larger supersets.

Similarly, digital audio packages such as Sound Designer and Audiomedia are beginning to offer such capabilities through options that define portions of soundfiles or direct-to-hard disk recordings as "regions," which can be assembled into "playlists." In effect, the soundfile serves as a database; material within the file can be reordered at will, nondestructively.

In both these initial attempts at the organization of musical ideas, objects can usually be reused as many times as desired within their destination songs or playlists, and often, changes or edits to the source object are reflected in all their subsequent occurrences. Certain packages, however, offer options to defeat this, thereby breaking the links to the source object. While this type of manipulation of musical ideas as objects can greatly simplify the compositional process, there are many standard database operations missing from current implementations. Foremost among these omissions is the ability to search for ideas fulfilling user-specified criteria such as key, tempo, duration, meter, or keyword. Also missing are options to search on the basis of sonic properties such as loudness, timbre, attack type, and so on. This is a big unsolved problem of present-day digital audio workstations. You have hundreds or thousands of files all on one level. A sound database system is urgently needed.

Finally, at the vanguard of computer music software is that which permits the creation of a library of processes that generate music rather than the actual music itself. Commercial software in this area has already become general enough to address the needs of composers of many different and essentially philosophically incompatible genres and styles. Research in this area has led many to speculate that the codification of "style templates" is just around the corner. Such templates would allow you to manipulate the stylistic and emotional elements of musical material with a great amount of control. Consider, for example, the processing of musical ideas through a sieve that filters out all influences of Schoenberg, replacing them with modules from a Bartokian style template, combining with this a 23 percent bias toward Debussy's aesthetics derived from a specific period, say 1911 to 1913, and finally orchestrating the material à la late 19th-century romanticism with an intermingling of 1960s jazz. CDI (Compact Disc Interactive) promises to provide access to such capabilities through controllers similar to the joysticks used in computer games.

Creative Input

The Macintosh handles two common types of musical data: MIDI data and digital audio data. With few exceptions, notation data is merely a representation of MIDI data.

MIDI data

The most common use of MIDI information is to record and store sequences of musical events played on a Macintosh-controlled sound-generating device such as a synthesizer or sampler. Both hardware devices and software programs that record MIDI data are called MIDI sequencers. Notation software packages are offering more and more of the functionality of MIDI sequencers. Another use is to store and edit parameter settings for synthesizers and effects.

When MIDI data is recorded as a MIDI sequence, it is often compared to piano-roll data. Like player piano rolls, MIDI sequences do not record actual sounds, only the information that triggers a sound. Thus, each playing of a MIDI sequence results in an actual re-performance of what was played initially and carries the implication that there will be no signal degradation from multiple-generation recording.

Besides channel designation (MIDI translates this data over 16 discrete MIDI channels simultaneously), MIDI communicates such information as pitch, key-on and -off velocity, duration, program (patch or soundfile) change, and the status of a variety of front panel controls. Furthermore, because MIDI data consists entirely of numerical information, any mathematical operation or calculation that can be applied to a number or a string of numbers may be applied to MIDI data as well. This permits MIDI data to be edited and manipulated in numerous ways.

Most MIDI sequencer software and some notation software operates like a typical multitrack tape recorder. Many software sequencers emulate the front panel of a tape recorder on the computer screen — complete with familiar play, record, pause, rewind, and fast forward controls. The main difference between analog tape recorders and MIDI sequencers is that the latter may have hundreds of tracks upon which the data can be edited very quickly and easily. The scope and type of editing operations that you can apply to MIDI data greatly exceeds that available upon analog devices. Furthermore, the cost of professional MIDI sequencer software is minuscule compared to multitrack tape recorders. There are some limitations to this methodology. It doesn't by itself account for voice or acoustic instruments. Since MIDI is such a weak protocol for timbre, you get the "freeze-dried" sounds of commercial synthesizers, drum machines, and the lock-step rhythms of mechanical devices.

As mentioned above, there are four fundamental ways to record musical ideas as MIDI data: real-time, step-time, interactive, and algorithmic.

Real-time

In this case, the term "real-time" indicates recording in a manner identical to analog recording (although no sound is recorded, only trigger information — note name, key velocity, and duration — for the re-creation of the performance). Usually, real-time input is from a MIDI synthesizer or keyboard controller, although other types of MIDI controllers make it possible for people with no musical keyboard ability to have notes played on any instrument (or sung) accurately converted into MIDI information. Techniques borrowed from the tape recorder world, such as automatic punch-in and punch-out, are also available.

Step-time

"Step-time" refers to a popular entry method that allows music to be recorded in "non-real" time — the playback rhythmic value of every note is specified manually upon entry. Often, this method allows you to choose a note's duration, such as quarter note, from a palette on the computer screen. Then, until a new rhythmic value is selected from the palette, every succeeding note played from that point on will have the designated temporal value, regardless of whether it is actually held for $\frac{1}{10}$ of a second or 10 minutes.

Another approach to step-time entry popularized with notation software and now finding its way into MIDI sequencers is that of clicking notes onto the screen with the mouse. Once again, the rhythmic value is specified in advance, and pitch is specified by mouse location.

Interactive

Data can be entered into the Macintosh through the use of interactive software. Interactive software processes incoming MIDI data in real time, so that new data is generated or existing data is transformed. In addition to composition applications, interactive software is often used in live performance. The main problem with interactive software is providing an interface that is general enough to support a large number of different users with different ideas about what their music should sound like after real-time processing. Newer interactive software packages come close to solving these problems.

Algorithmic

The final method for entering musical material is through generating a stream of MIDI data algorithmically, which is to say, from a mathematical formula. This is becoming increasingly popular, as computers become more user-friendly, and the user interface to complex compositional algorithms becomes simpler. Indeed, graphic user interfaces permit the precise creation and manipulation of such algorithms without ever having to refer to numbers or mathematical operations — further evidence of the trend for computers to write programs for themselves based upon interpretations of input from humans who are not expected to have any knowledge of computer programming. Available Macintosh software permits the generation of credible music from probabilistic, cyclical, and statistical distributions of user input pitches, rhythms, dynamic (loudness) patterns, and articulations (subtle performance techniques such as accents).

Digital audio data

Unlike MIDI data, which consists of triggering information and no sound data, digital audio data is purely sound data without any triggering information. Digital audio data can be brought into the Macintosh in two ways: through direct-to-hard disk recording, or by transferring soundfiles from an external device, such as a dedicated sampler, CD-ROM library, or other storage device. Sample resolutions range from 8-bit to 16-bit.

On the cutting edge of technology for entering and manipulating musical ideas are software packages that combine MIDI data with digital audio data, either through the incorporation of digital audio tracks into MIDI sequencers, or through the incorporation of MIDI sequencer data tracks into direct-to-hard disk recording systems.

Shaping Input into Music

No matter how your musical ideas are recorded into the Macintosh (as MIDI data or digital audio data), the real strength of the Macintosh is how the data can be edited once it is in the computer.

Editing practices such as Cut, Copy, Paste, Merge, and Insert are powerful operations possible with MIDI sequencers, notation packages, and digital audio software alike. All have analogies in the analog world in the form of splicing tape and bouncing tracks.

With a MIDI sequencer or notation package, note correction is child's play, as are transposition and tempo changes. Even though these simple editing operations require mathematical operations, such calculations are considered to be "invisible to the end user." A single example will clarify this statement. Consider the act of transposing a piece of music up one key. The internal operation of the soft-ware will look at the note numbers of each note event and add '1' to them. However, the user will merely specify the beginning and end of the edit region and issue a completely musical command such as "transpose up one semitone" — the computer takes care of all the calculations behind the scenes, hence the concept, "invisible to the end user."

Rhythmic correction or quantization is a standard operating procedure. Quantizing a passage automatically "rounds off" performance data to a user-specified rhythmic grid (typically, the smallest rhythmic duration in the piece). Various methods of quantization displacement or sensitivity are employed to counteract the inhuman machine-like quality of music played back with perfect rhythmic accuracy.

Until very recently, all commercially available sequencing and notation software required that a performer play along with a metronomic "tick" generated by the computer to serve as a reference frame for subsequent quantization. Some sequencers allowed you to specify a small set of possible rhythmic values in advance of performance in order to speed up the quantization process. Newer strategies do not require performance to a given beat or the performer to play without rubato (a normal expressive type of speeding up and slowing down the tempo). Instead, these allow you to tap in the beat while you are playing (for example, using a foot pedal), provide for post-determination of beats and measures (by tapping on a specific key while your recorded music plays back, for example), or use advanced pattern-recognition processes to build a table of rhythmic relationships and then apply this information to input data for the purpose of determining intended durational values from a human performance including variations of tempo.

Most MIDI sequencers provide for the translation of MIDI data into conventional music notation by way of saving sequences in the Standard MIDI File format, which can then be imported into a notation program. Notation software often includes such features as automatic transposition, instrumental range proofreading, rhythmic error detection, and part extraction.

In general, when MIDI sequencing, notation, or digital audio software is introduced into the studio music-making setup, fundamental activities such as recording, editing, and effect-synchronization are performed with increasing time efficiency. In an industry where time is often equated with money, these savings can be significant.

Mixing and Signal Processing

In stage three, when the input and subsequently edited data is converted back into sound, pre-programmed signal processing effects are often triggered by MIDI commands sent to external devices or, in the case of digital audio, EQ (equalization) and effects algorithms can be applied to the soundfiles. In either case, the processing can take place in real time, on-the-fly, or during the playback processes.

Most newer signal processors include MIDI IN ports, through which particular effects, either ROM-based or user-defined, may be assigned to particular patch numbers to be triggered by MIDI program change messages. In the simplest implementation, a specific synthesizer patch or soundfile may have its own associated effects such as flanging, chorusing, reverberation, echo, or delay. This is called up at the same time the MIDI program change command is sent from the sequencer to the synthesizer. In this fashion, each of the 128 possible program changes may trigger its own associated reverb, flange, chorusing, delay, or other digital effect.

Using MIDI data itself to generate effects that mimic those created by digital signal processing is also common. Software-based MIDI effects generators take incoming MIDI data and juggle the numbers before they pass them on to the sound-generating device. For example, in such a setup it is a simple matter to delay repetitions while progressively decreasing velocity (loudness) to create echo effects, add constants to incoming MIDI note numbers to create chorusing or harmonization, or change the channel numbers for pre-assigned pitch ranges to affect real-time orchestration via intelligent keyboard splitting. Rather than through digital signal processing, these effects are produced entirely from the multiple retriggering of notes to which patterns or offsets may or may not be applied.

Automation, the most desirable feature of astronomically expensive mixing boards, is being brought into the financial range of the typical Macintosh-controlled music studio. The front panel of many MIDI-able mixing boards and effects panels can be emulated on the computer's screen. You simply manipulate virtual controls such as graphic knobs, buttons, and faders. During playback, these sliders, knobs, and buttons animate in real time as they send the appropriate data to the external device.

Another approach to this type of automation is to use dedicated external devices capable of sending MIDI data or unused controls on synthesizers to manipulate on-screen fader consoles available in most newer MIDI sequencers or digital audio systems. In the case of virtual mixing controls in a MIDI sequencer, new data is generated that modifies existing data for the purpose of producing the desired output effect during playback.

Output

In stage three, MIDI data or digital audio data is converted back into sound, and notation data is converted either into sound or output to paper. Audio output will usually end up on multitrack analog tape, digital recording tape, or on a hard drive (in the case of direct-to-hard disk recording systems).

Multitrack tape

By recording on multiple tracks with multiple passes, it is possible to greatly exceed the number of musical parts dictated by the number of audio channels in the various synthesizers. When it becomes necessary to record separate analog tape tracks of MIDI music at different times, the only way to assure that the events on each track will line up on the audio track is to use some form of synchronization: Pulse sync (also known as PPQN, PPQ, MIDI sync, or MIDI clock sync), SPP sync, SMPTE sync, MIDI Time Code, or Direct Time Lock.

Synchronization

Pulse sync locks together two MIDI devices; it does not provide a device with any way of knowing where it is in a sequence. Therefore, when using this method, it is absolutely necessary to start each recording pass at the very beginning, even if the current track being synchronized doesn't actually produce any sound until a half hour later.

SPP sync (Song Position Pointer) gets around this problem by including Start, Stop, Continue, and Song Position Pointer codes to allow two MIDI devices to "lock up" and function as a single unit with some degree of accuracy, locating to various parts of the sequence as required.

FSK sync (Frequency Shift Keying) is a process that translates various forms of Pulse sync and SPP sync into audio tones that can be recorded onto tape, so that the tape recorder becomes the master device to control external sound generators. A "sync track" consisting of evenly spaced pulses is recorded onto audio tape and used as a master temporal reference to slaved MIDI sequencers. Some systems provide for the encoding of SPP codes onto the FSK track as well.

The video industry standard, SMPTE Time Encoding, provides very precise information about the location or address of any particular point in time with respect to any point on an analog or digital audio tape. SMPTE is used to effectively lock together MIDI sequencer software with multitrack analog or video tape — guaranteeing that when one device is rewound or fast-forwarded, the other device will "chase" it to the same point in time.

Finally, the MMA (MIDI Manufacturers Association) and JMSC (Japanese MIDI Standards Committee) approved MIDI Time Code (MTC) in 1988. It adds greater precision to SMPTE-to-MIDI lockup and opens the doors to applications that used MTC in place of SMPTE Time Code as a way of achieving synchronization precision close to that of SMPTE at much less expense. Unfortunately, the drawback to MTC is that it requires a large portion of the MIDI bandwidth to send time location information, about eight times the amount required by other forms of synchronization. Therefore, this reduces the amount of musical information that can be sent during the 3,125 ten-bit bytes that are being transmitted every second.

As a solution to the limiting bandwidth of MTC, even before the MTC standard was officially accepted into the MIDI Spec, the JamBox 4, a SMPTE/MIDI interface from Southworth Music Systems, introduced a type of SMPTE synchronization called Direct Time Lock (DTL). DTL vastly reduces the amount of data required to send synchronization information, thus freeing up the MIDI data path for more musical information. Many interfaces now support DTL, although only Mark of the Unicorn's Performer sequencer software is able to synchronize to it.

Hard disk-based digital recording

Perhaps the most impressive personal Macintosh peripherals now available are relatively inexpensive, yet are extremely high quality direct-to-hard disk digital audio systems. These are 16-bit, 44.1 KHz (i.e., CD-mastering quality), n-track systems that take advantage of the SCSI port on the Macintosh to provide access to hard drives upon which data brought in through NuBus cards is stored. The maximum recording time of these systems is limited only by the size of the hard disk storage medium, and 2 gigabyte SCSI drives are available, providing for up to four hours of stereo audio. The Macintosh becomes an interface to digital mixing of tracks recorded on a hard disk, providing a means for testing and saving mix scores.

Live performance

If the sound output is in the context of a live performance, some less obvious uses of MIDI data can come into play. These include the control of lighting (specific notes, patches, or songs assigned to specific lighting configurations or effects), the control of animation or video processing, tape-recorded material, and the control of special effects.

A Macintosh is even being used in Paris to control the acoustics of the main performance hall (l'éspace de projections) at IRCAM. The room's walls and ceilings have 171 motorized three-part panels, each of which can be rotated to exhibit one of three main acoustic properties (reflection, diffusion, or absorption) and three mixed properties (reflection-diffusion, reflection-absorption, or diffusion-absorption). Theoretically, the room may be "tuned" to enhance the resonance of a specific musical key. The operator uses the mouse to "paint" the desired acoustics on the screen of the Macintosh, which displays a representation of the room as it would look if the walls were flattened out.

Summary

✔ There are six stages involved in using the Macintosh to transform sound into music: (1) The accumulation of sound material, (2) Sound editing and organization, (3) Creative input, (4) Shaping input into music, (5) Mixing and signal processing, and (6) Final output, including digital or analog recording, live performance, film, video, and multimedia, and printed notation.

✔ Music employing electronic instruments usually draws its material from one of two domains: sampling or synthesis. The first possible introduction of a Macintosh into the musical process is in the actual creation or capturing of sonic material through the techniques of sound generation or sound sampling or a combination of the two.

✔ Depending upon the source of a musician's sonic material — sampled or synthesized — the ensuing editing process may include modifying sampled soundfiles using an on-screen graphic waveform editor, or it may mean editing the patches of a synthesizer in real time through an on-screen simulation of the physical controls of the synthesizer.

✔ The next function of the Macintosh is to manipulate the sound library. Although most sound-generating devices include stock patches (referred to as presets) or sampled soundfiles in their ROM chips, most of these devices also provide RAM into which you can load and store banks or libraries of edited sounds. In the case of samplers and sample players, these objects consist of individual user-sampled soundfiles or collections of soundfiles. In the case of synthesizers, these objects are user-created parameter settings known as patches.

✔ The Macintosh handles two common types of musical data: MIDI data and digital audio data. With few exceptions, notation data is merely a representation of MIDI data. The most common use of MIDI information is to record and store sequences of musical events played on a Macin-tosh-controlled, sound-generating device such as a synthesizer or sampler. Both hardware devices and software programs that record MIDI data are called MIDI sequencers. There are four fundamental ways to record musical ideas as MIDI data: real-time, step-time, interactive, and algorithmic.

✔ Regardless of whether you are dealing with MIDI data or digital audio data, the real strength of the Macintosh is how you can edit the data once it is in the computer. Editing practices such as Cut, Copy, Paste, Merge, and Insert are powerful operations possible with MIDI sequencers, notation packages, and digital audio software alike. Note correction is child's play, as are transposition and tempo changes. Rhythmic correction or quantization is a standard operating procedure. Quantizing a passage automatically "rounds off" performance data to a user-specified rhythmic grid (typically, the smallest rhythmic duration in the piece).

✔ When creative input and subsequently edited data is converted back into sound, pre-programmed signal processing effects are often triggered by MIDI commands sent to external devices or, in the case of digital audio, EQ and effects algorithms can be applied to the soundfiles. In either case, the processing can take place in real time, on-the-fly, or during the playback processes.

✔ MIDI data or digital audio data is converted back into sound, and notation data is converted either into sound or output to paper. Audio output will usually end up on multitrack analog tape, digital recording tape, or on a hard drive (in the case of direct-to-hard disk recording systems).

Part Two

Sound

Part Two
Foreword
by Frank Seraphine

Sound

I first used a computer for the movie *Tron* in 1982. All we had were two 16-track tape recorders synchronized to a video machine. We had a few ways to edit sound, but I became very adept at flying everything in, like a musician, right to the picture. If the timing was off a little bit, we just had the sound editors cut it when it was transferred to Mag. I used to have my staff spend most of their time cataloging sounds, trying to organize everything by hand. For *Tron*, we worked for a year just organizing the sound library.

With the Macintosh, everything is controllable. In the past you could use a database to catalog sounds, but that's where it ended. The catalog couldn't interact with the sound data itself. Now you can control your sounds while you see them. You can also assemble libraries so big that it would be impossible to handle them in any other way.

The Macintosh screen display is a great advantage. One nice thing about librarian programs is that they let you see a full page of your sounds, for example, an entire bank. Just being able to see a page of all of your synthesizers makes your life ten times better. This wasn't possible before computers entered the picture. On the front panel of the actual devices, you had to scroll up and down in a tiny window, and often the sounds were just numbers without names. Just associating a name with the numbers

has been a great boon for synthesis. It's also helpful to be able to print all that information out.

At this point, one of the most progressive applications in the areas of sound effects, sound design, organization, and storage is the Remote Controller/Librarian for the Emulator III. The unique thing about the program is that it automatically creates and catalogs its own library. You just push the Catalog button on the screen, and the software locates everything that you've done and loads it into the Macintosh. You come back a half hour later and it's all automatically organized into a library listing. You don't have to do any work. This is incredible automation for sound editing, because it's typical to make four or five banks of sounds and twenty presets or so every night. The clients can use the program's Browser feature to quickly audition the sounds on each disk.

Of course it is necessary to convert all the sounds to a single format. I am still going through my PCM F1 library, and having to resample everything that I've done on older media. I am finding that a lot of my analog tapes won't even run anymore, they are so old — for example, the sound effects for *Star Trek* are 12 to 15 years old — they won't even rewind. If I can rewind a tape by exercising it, the sound turns out fine, which lets me sample them into the digital domain before they're gone. Everything that I have on

¼-inch tape as well as everything that I've done on PCM F1 and DAT and other sampler formats is being transferred to the Emulator III and cataloged by its librarian to maximize control.

To facilitate this process, Passport's Alchemy offers a great way to trade sounds from other synthesizers. Alchemy can act as a handshake program with sounds from other 16-bit formats using their Distributed Audio Network. You can preview every sound in a single sampler and then send them back to the Macintosh. When I'm developing sounds for other companies, I give them my sounds on Alchemy and they convert that data to burn their chips.

For the organization of patches that are not automated by software like the Emulator III's librarian, it's relatively easy to set up a custom database in a program like Microsoft Works with different fields for category, description, and comments about how the sound was used, where it originated, and how much memory is left. Include all the specs: if it's ¼-inch, 15 ips, stereo 2-track, Dolby SR, and so on. Grading all the sounds from A to F is a good idea too. If you set things up correctly you can do searches for any criteria that one can possibly imagine about a sound.

Effects devices offer a way to edit sounds that is often overlooked. Oftentimes it's easier to get an effect out of the Eventide H3000 than through direct editing. This is the approach I took in the movie *Lawnmower Man* — creating the sounds on analog synthesizers, manipulating them with the Eventide, and finally sampling them in the Emulator III so I can edit them in the digital domain and add SMPTE Time Code numbers. Once the sounds are in sample form, we edit them to the picture. Opcode's Galaxy Plus Editors

has had a major impact in this respect, because it has templates for Lexicon and other effects devices that make it possible to, for example, synchronize reverberation effects to timecode.

It's great that things have moved away from tape and razor blades. Even in the *Tron* days we had to do a lot of programming, particularly timecode numbers. It was maddening. Now with Opcode's Vision, you can scroll your sequence up to where the picture is — if you have VITC on the tapes, it scrolls right to your picture in-point when you roll the video. Then you drag your sound up to the appropriate frame number, and that becomes the beginning of your sound. Then you jog the picture to the out-point and stretch your sound to that length in the graphic editing window and you're in and out, it's as easy as that. With VITC, you don't think of a SMPTE number, you just pull the sound until it reaches the point where you are in the video.

The future for massive sound libraries is in 650MB cartridge juke box changers — trays with disks, able to access all of the sounds on those disks and load them in as required. When you daisy chain these cartridge changers together, you have a massive library that you can control in seconds through the Macintosh. Librarian software is a necessity to control mass storage media easily, because you can go crazy trying to insert this disk or that disk, as you look for a particular disk you need. We shouldn't have to touch any disks anymore, just store them all in a bank somewhere and push a button to load them.

The Macintosh is going to play the most important role in sound design. It's the intelligent interface to everything that we do. ♩

Frank Seraphine is founder and president of Seraphine F/X.

Introduction to Part Two

Before you can create music with the assistance of the Macintosh, it is necessary to have sound material to work with. The Macintosh can assume a critical role at all stages in the generation and accumulation of sound material. There are several types of sound you will want to place under Macintosh control:

❖ Sounds synthesized by the Macintosh
❖ Sounds sampled by the Macintosh
❖ Factory-preset sounds (patches) in external synthesizers
❖ Factory-preset sounds (samples or soundfiles) in external samplers
❖ User-created and/or -edited sounds in external synthesizers
❖ User-created and/or -edited sounds in external samplers
❖ Loadable sounds, banks, and libraries for external synthesizers
❖ Loadable sounds, banks, and libraries for external samplers

In the above list, external devices can be thought of as being peripheral to the Macintosh as it is shipped from Apple. With this in mind, we will treat internal cards that are added to the Macintosh to provide sampling or synthesis capabilities as if they were external devices.

The Macintosh has had built-in sound since the very beginning. The DAC on all Macintoshes is made by Sony. A single DAC, like the one found on the Macintosh Plus, SE, Classic, Classic II, and LC, is capable of playing 8-bit monophonic sound. The Macintosh II series (including the IIsi), the SE/30, Mac Portable, Power Books, and Quadras all contain Sony sound chips that are able to provide stereo output (still at 8-bit). Furthermore, with the exception of the LC, these models also contain an Apple Sound Chip (ASC) that enhances audio output considerably. The LC provides for ASC emulation. Finally, the Classic II, IIsi, LC, Power Book 140, Power Book 170, and Quadra models include a microphone input for recording sound directly into the Macintosh (at a maximum 8-bit sampling rate).

Editing synthesized sounds is a branch of sound design commonly referred to as patch editing. The programs that allow you to edit synthesized sounds are called patch-editors. Patch editors greatly simplify the control of the internal sound manipulation capabilities of MIDI devices. Nearly all synthesizers allow you to modify their sounds by way of controls on their front panels. Other types of MIDI devices, such as MIDI-controllable effects, MIDI mixers, and MIDI controllers, provide similar editing options. Unfortunately, although most MIDI devices offer vast capabilities for sound design of this kind, they only provide a limited number of controls. On the other hand, the Macintosh permits the simulation of hundreds of virtual controls on-screen, and these always remain assigned to the same function. The main issue boils down to user interface. Software can provide a better user interface than hardware, and we know that user interface is one area in which the Macintosh excels.

The *raison d'être* of most sample-editing programs is exactly the same as for patch-editing programs: The devices themselves often do not provide adequate user interfaces to their own internal sound-editing capabilities. Although samplers tend to have considerably more front panel controls than do synthesizers, the opportunity for additional virtual controls to be simulated by sample-editing software still exists. Both patch editors and sample editors share the same advantages of hard disk storage. But unlike patch-editing software, sample-editing software provides the further advantage of being a unifying point by which sounds of incompatible samplers can share sample libraries. On the Macintosh's screen, a visual representation of a soundfile's waveform communicates information that is orders of magnitude beyond anything native to the sampler itself, while at the same time providing for on-screen manipulation of wave data in ways that are simply unavailable without such a display. However, non-waveform parameter manipulation (e.g., envelopes) may be simpler by way of the front panel controls of certain samplers.

In the area of sound organization, you will find librarian software for the loading, retrieval, and organization of such ephemeral items as individual tone parameters, individual patches, banks of groups of patches, individual sampled soundfiles, entire sample RAM, global settings or master parameters, program maps or lists, velocity maps, pressure maps, intonation tables or micro tunings, reverbs, DSP effects parameters, and sequences (if the device has a built-in sequencer).

The four chapters in this section describe sound sources available to your Macintosh and take you through all types of sound generation (internal and external), editing (of synthesized and sampled sounds), and organization (both through librarians and sound databases).

Chapter 10
Sound Generation

In this chapter . . .

✔ Sound-generating and playback capabilities of various Macintosh models.

✔ The Apple Sound Chip, Sound Manager, and MACE compression/decompression scheme.

✔ Approaches to algorithmic sound generation with the Macintosh and available software options.

✔ Using 8-bit digital audio with the Macintosh.

✔ The interaction of sound with HyperCard and ResEdit.

✔ Sampling 8-bit sound with the Macintosh using external digitizers.

✔ Complete instructions and schematics to build your own sound input device.

✔ Editing 8-bit sampled sounds with the Macintosh.

✔ Customizing your Macintosh environment with sound.

✔ Turning the Macintosh into a MIDI instrument for sampled sound playback.

✔ NuBus cards for ROM and RAM sampling vs. virtual sampling.

Overview

The Macintosh is a formidable sound-generating device in its own right. All Macintoshes have built-in 8-bit sound capabilities and these are exploited by many products. The Macintosh can play sound through its internal speaker or out the audio port on the back panel, which will accept a ⅛-inch mini plug (stereo for all Macintosh IIs and beyond, otherwise mono). You can add a NuBus card to provide for 16-bit sound from any Macintosh with NuBus slots.

There are four ways to create sound with a Macintosh:

❖ Synthesize sounds with the Macintosh's built-in synthesizers. These can be played back by way of the Macintosh's built-in sound capabilities.

❖ Sample sounds using the Macintosh's built-in sampling features (only available with certain models). These can be played back by way of the Macintosh's built-in sound capabilities or a dedicated NuBus card.

❖ Sample sounds using an external digitizer attached to the Macintosh's serial or SCSI ports. These can be played back by way of the Macintosh's built-in sound capabilities or a dedicated NuBus card.

❖ Algorithmically generate sampled sounds for playback by way of the Macintosh's built-in sound capabilities or a dedicated NuBus card.

The Macintosh as a Sound-Generating Device
Internal sound capabilities of various Macintoshes

Since the beginning, the Macintosh has had built-in sound. Rumor has it that a member of the original Macintosh development team approached Steve Jobs with a third-party chip. The person allegedly claimed that it would be possible to add the sound chip to the Macintosh for under $3 a machine. According to the same rumor, this happened on a Friday. Steve Jobs replied that if this person could get all the bugs out of it and have a working prototype by Monday morning, he'd consider including sound in the Macintosh. It seems as though this programmer was able to deliver, because every Macintosh has had sound capabilities since January 24, 1984 (the Macintosh's birthday).

The DAC (digital-to-analog converter) on all Macintoshes is made by Sony. A single DAC, found on the Macintosh Plus, SE, Classic, and LC, is capable of playing 8-bit monophonic sound. When these computers encounter stereo sound data, they play only the right channel (this is true with certain early models of the original Macintosh II). The Macintosh II series (including the IIsi), the SE/30, and the Macintosh Portable all contain two of these Sony sound chips and are thus able to provide stereo output (still at 8-bit). Furthermore, with the exception of the LC, these models also contain an Apple Sound Chip (ASC) that enhances audio output considerably. The LC provides for ASC emulation. Finally, the IIsi and LC models include a microphone input for recording sound directly into the Macintosh (at a maximum 8-bit sampling rate). From System 6.0.7 onward, many programs have taken advantage of this microphone input to provide for voice mail and document voice annotation.

You needn't have a Macintosh IIsi or LC to reap these System 6.0.7 benefits. There are several third-party drivers that, when placed in your 6.0.7 System Folder, allow you to use MacroMind-Paracomp's MacRecorder digitizer, Articulate Systems's Voice Impact Pro (formerly VoiceLink), or even a homemade digitizer in place of the microphone included with the IIsi and LC. MacroMind-Paracomp's MacRecorder Driver is the most popular of these.

The moment you load MacroMind-Paracomp's driver and reboot, any applications that have built-in sound-recording capabilities display those options on their menus. For third-party programs that have no built-in hooks for the Sound Manager, you can use MacroMind-Paracomp's driver or the Macintosh's native driver in conjunction with Praxitel's Read My Lips to add voice annotations and sounds.

You can even record sound directly in the control panel (see Figure 10-1).

Figure 10-1: The Sound control panel showing both the standard and MacRecorder sound drivers. You can use sounds recorded here as your System beep. Certain utilities like SuitCase II, MasterJuggler, and SoundMaster let you assign these sounds to other events. Typical among these events are Startup sounds and Shutdown sounds. The second dialog box shown is the Sound Manager's standard Record interface.

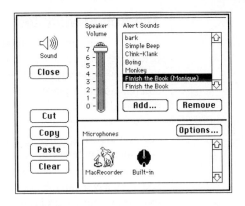

Due to hardware limitations of the Sound Driver (ROM-based) in early Macintoshes (particularly the Plus and SE), the highest frequency the Macintosh can currently produce is 11,116 Hz. An early version of "Inside Macintosh" gives the following explanation for this limitation:

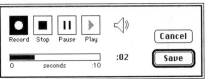

The Sound Driver and disk-motor speed-control circuitry share a 740-byte buffer, of which the Sound Driver uses the 370 even-numbered bytes. Every horizontal retrace interval (every 44.93 microseconds — when the beam of the video screen moves from the right edge of the screen to the left), the MC68000 automatically fetches 2 bytes from this buffer and sends the high order byte to the speaker. Thus, all frequencies generated by the Sound Driver are multiples of this 44.93-microsecond period. The highest frequency physically possible for the Sound Driver is twice this period, or 89.96 microseconds, which translates to a frequency of 11,116 Hz. Likewise, every vertical retrace interval (every 16.6 milliseconds), the Sound Driver fills its half of the 740-byte buffer with the next set of values. The sampling rate is limited to 22.254 KHz (remember the Nyquist Theorem from Chapter 1: The highest frequency representable equals ½ the sample rate).

These conditions may not be identical in current-generation Macintoshes, but the sampling rate remains at about 22,254 samples per second, with a resolution of 8 bits. The internal speaker of the Macintosh is unable to handle sound of this quality, although it makes a formidable effort and is satisfactory for many purposes. The back-panel audio output jack can send the Macintosh's audio signal to an external amplifier such as a typical home stereo system. For purposes of comparison, most CDs use a 44.1 KHz sampling rate with 16-bit sample resolution.

The Sound Manager

Any Macintosh can create, modify, and play sounds without requiring external hardware. This is accomplished by a piece of software called the Sound Manager. For those of you who have been using the Macintosh prior to System 6.x, this Sound Manager replaces the older Sound Driver. In fact, Apple no longer supports the Sound Driver.

The Sound Manager first appeared with System 6.0. Since then, Apple has continued to enhance it. The Sound Manager runs on all Macintoshes, but all its capabilities are not available for certain models (see the section "Summary of Sound Manager capabilities" in this chapter). The Sound Manager provides routines, resources, and drivers that handle all the recording, playback, saving, and storing of sound on the Macintosh. Even the System beep is now a Sound Manager routine. The Sound Manager can also synthesize sound and speech and synchronize multimedia presentations.

Some features of the Sound Manager are available only if you have the ASC found in the Macintosh II series, the SE/30, the Macintosh Portable, and the LC. These include continuous multichannel playback of sampled sounds from your hard drive. Before System 7, the Macintosh could only play a single channel of sampled sounds at a time. With the System 7 Sound Manager, programs can play several channels of sound concurrently, and multiple applications can each open their own sound channels. Note that at this time only Macintoshes with ASCs can play multichannel sound.

The Macintosh's built-in synthesizers

The Sound Manager plays back sounds using synthesizers that control the ASC. These synthesizers reside in the System File as resources of type 'snth '. In computers that do not have an ASC, the Sound Manager does its best to use synthesizers that provide the highest quality sound possible for the machine.

The Macintosh currently has three types of synthesizer 'snth ' resources. There are three of each type in the Sound Manager: three square-wave synthesizers, three wavetable synthesizers, and three sampled sound synthesizers. Of each group of three synthesizers, one is a general type for any Macintosh, one is optimized for a Macintosh with an ASC, and the final one is for the Macintosh Plus and SE.

The note synthesizer or square-wave synthesizer

The note synthesizer, also known as the square-wave synthesizer, can play simple sounds described by frequency or pitch, amplitude, and duration. This synthesizer takes the least CPU time. The standard System beep uses this synthesizer.

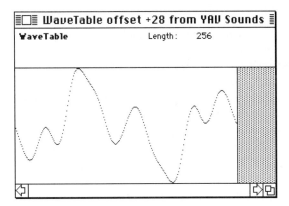

WaveTable offset +28 from YAU Sounds

WaveTable   Length: 256

Figure 10-2: A wavetable for a moderately complex sound.

The wavetable synthesizer

The wavetable synthesizer creates sound by using a single wave cycle (or period). As you know from Chapter 1, such a table is called a wavetable (see Figure 10-2). You can open a maximum of four wavetable channels at once, meaning that you can have up to four-voice polyphony with this synthesizer. The Macintosh's wavetables are 512 bytes long. Each byte represents a sample of a single wave cycle. Because these are 8-bit samples, each byte can represent 256 values (that is, 0 plus the number 1 through 255). Just as with traditional wavetable synthesis and digital oscillators, the sampled waveform loops repeatedly to create a continuous sound.

The sampled sound synthesizer

The sampled sound synthesizer (Apple's terminology) is the most interesting of the three. This is what the Macintosh uses to play back digitally recorded sounds as well as sounds that are computed on-the-fly. The sampled sound synthesizer can play sounds stored as 'snd ' resources, AIFF files, or AIFF-C files (compressed AIFF files). AIFF stands for audio interchange file format, a standard created by Apple and several cooperating third-party developers. AIFF and AIFF-C files are preferable for longer samples. Both AIFF and AIFF-C files are also useful in cases where different applications are intended to play the same files, because it is easier for programs to share files than resources. If your Macintosh has an ASC, you can play all three formats directly from disk.

AIFF-C files have some advantages. AIFF-C files can read, write, and store non-compressed sounds, but AIFF files can only hold non-compressed audio data. Both AIFF formats can also contain MIDI data.

All three sound formats can be either stereo or mono, but AIFF and AIFF-C sounds can be multichannel. Three-channel sounds are used for left, right, and center. Four-channel sounds are used for left, center, right, and surround (rear). A variation on four-channel sound is quadrophonic sound — front left, front right, rear left, and rear right. Finally, six-channel sounds have channels for left, left center, center, right, right center, and surround. You can specify additional channels for certain cases, but don't forget that the Sound Manager currently supports only six audio channels.

There are two types of 'snd ' resources, namely format 1 and format 2 'snd ' resources. Any of the Macintosh's synthesizers can play format 1 'snd ' resources.

A format 1 'snd' resource might be a sampled sound, a wavetable, or a sequence of commands that describe a tune and no other sound data. Format 2 'snd' resources always contain samples and are used by HyperCard (HyperCard versions prior to 2.0 required format 2 sound resources). Only the sampled sound synthesizer can play them. All 'snd' resources in the System File are format 1. Note that HyperCard (version 1.2.1 and earlier) incorrectly labeled 'snd' resources as format 1. If you are using ResEdit to play with 'snd' resources, you should know that 'snd' resource IDs in the 0 to 8191 range are reserved for use by Apple Computer. Of these, the 'snd' resources 1 through 4 comprise the standard system alert sounds.

As is common with musical samplers and sample players, the Macintosh's sampled sound synthesizer can play back samples at different rates to change the sample's pitch. Only the sampled sound synthesizer can play back multichannel sounds, and when it does, no other synthesizers can operate.

The MIDI synthesizer

A fourth internal 'snth' resource available to developers is the MIDI synthesizer. This provides a standard interface for programs that need to control external MIDI devices. At the current time, few manufacturers support this resource.

Other 'snth' synthesizers

Several of Digidesign's products that rely on their digital audio boards include a utility called Sound Installer. It allows you to add and remove both 'snd' and 'snth' resources to a document or program. It also provides for playback of both 8-bit and 16-bit mono or stereo sounds through Digidesign's Sound Accelerator NuBus card. Finally, the program automatically converts Sound Designer and AIFF files into 'snd' resources.

Digidesign's software introduces two new types of 'snd' resources: *chunky* and *interleaved*. An interleaved 'snd' resource is a 44.1 KHz, 16-bit stereo sound. A chunky 'snd' resource contains both a 16-bit, 44.1 KHz version of a sound and an 8-bit, 22 KHz version of the sound.

If one of Digidesign's digital audio cards is inside your Macintosh, you can play these sounds just as if they were 8-bit sounds, for example, from HyperCard or Director. Note that interleaved 'snd' resources require that a digital audio card be installed. The advantage of chunky 'snd' resources is that they will play back at 16-bit resolution if there is a Sound Accelerator card present, but they will also play back at 8-bit resolution if no card is installed. This makes them extremely desirable for multimedia presentations that you want to be able to execute on Macintoshes with or without a digital audio card.

It is necessary to use Digidesign's Sound Installer to install a special 'snth' resource into the program that will be playing back an interleaved or chunky 'snd' resource (alternatively, you can install Digidesign's 'snth' resource directly into your System File). At the time of this writing, Digidesign's 'snth' resource will only play back 'snd' resources that can fit into RAM. It will not play back files from disk. This 'snth' resource should only be installed in programs that already support the playback of traditional 'snd' resources such as HyperCard, Director, and SuperCard.

Digidesign has other provisions for playing files from disk, including AIFF, Sound Designer, and Sound Designer II files. These are XCMDs and XFCNs that you can install in any software supporting such externals. For example, they work very well with HyperCard and SuperCard. Note that in the case of HyperCard, it is not possible to have both the play-from-disk XCMDs and Digidesign's 'snth' resource installed simultaneously. You must choose one or the other or maintain two copies of HyperCard, one with the 'snth' resource installed, the other with the XCMD set installed.

Interaction with the Sound Manager

Unless you are a programmer, you don't need to interact directly with the Sound Manager — but you can if you want to. You may be recording and playing back sounds every day using the sound input capabilities of programs supporting the new Sound Manager, HyperCard, MacroMind-Paracomp's SoundEdit, or simply the control panel. In these cases, the Sound Manager's activities are often hidden "under the hood" of your software's interface (its operation is invisible to the end user).

A ResEdit sound editor template by Chris Reed is available through many online services. At the time of this writing, the current version is 2.0a2. You can use ResEdit to paste this wonderful tool into ResEdit itself.

Reed's Sound Editor template for ResEdit provides access to many of the parameters used by the Sound Manager to play 'snd' resources. You can examine and alter sample files and wavetables. You can change the synthesizer the Macintosh uses to play a sound. You can also insert commands that process a sound during playback. You can change the formats of sounds and reset loops, sample rates, base note, and duration of the sample data. You can also preview sounds in the original format or as they would sound using HyperCard (see Figures 10-3 through 10-5).

MACE

MACE, short for Macintosh audio compression and expansion, was developed to reduce the vast storage requirements of sound. You will recall from Chapter 1 that a minute of stereo CD-quality sound takes up over 10MB. A minute of stereo 8-bit sound, sampled at the Macintosh's highest sampling rate of 22 KHz, occupies slightly more than 2.5MB, and a minute of the same sound in mono form takes about 1.3MB.

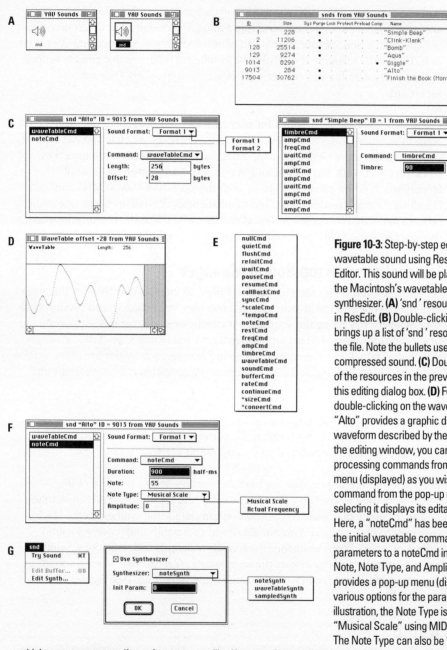

Figure 10-3: Step-by-step editing of a wavetable sound using ResEdit's Sound Editor. This sound will be played back using the Macintosh's wavetable sound synthesizer. **(A)** 'snd' resource as it appears in ResEdit. **(B)** Double-clicking the 'snd' icon brings up a list of 'snd' resources stored in the file. Note the bullets used to indicate a compressed sound. **(C)** Double-clicking one of the resources in the previous list brings up this editing dialog box. **(D)** For example, double-clicking on the wavetable resource "Alto" provides a graphic display of the waveform described by the wavetable. **(E)** In the editing window, you can add as many processing commands from the pop-up menu (displayed) as you wish. **(F)** Inserting a command from the pop-up menu and then selecting it displays its editable parameters. Here, a "noteCmd" has been inserted to play the initial wavetable command. The parameters to a noteCmd include Duration, Note, Note Type, and Amplitude. Note Type provides a pop-up menu (displayed) of the various options for the parameter. In this illustration, the Note Type is referenced as "Musical Scale" using MIDI note numbers. The Note Type can also be "Frequency," in which case you can specify any frequency you like. However, frequencies above 11 KHz are not recommended, because that is the highest frequency allowed for the Macintosh's 22 KHz sampling rate as determined by the Nyquist Theorem. **(G)** The Edit Synth... menu option provides this dialog box with a pop-up menu (displayed) for selecting the desired 'snth' resource (spelled "synth" on the menu).

Figure 10-4: Step-by-step editing of a sampled sound (called "Finish the book (Monique)") using ResEdit's Sound Editor. Naturally, this sound will be played back using the Macintosh's sampled sound synthesizer. **(A)** The sampled sound's dialog box is similar to the one we came to at step C. **(B)** Double-clicking the "bufferCmd" or "soundCmd" displays a graphic representation of the sample with the loop, if any, highlighted. **(C)** Selecting the Edit Header… option from the Buffer menu (displayed), which appears when you open the sample display, brings up this dialog box for you to set the sample's length, sample rate, base note, loop start, and loop end. **(D-1)** The editing window for the Macintosh's "Clink Clank" beep. Note that two notes are played. These correspond to the Clink and the Clank of the sound. The source sample is the same for both notes. **(D-2)** The note parameters for Clink Clank. **(D-3)** Resetting the note numbers to those displayed here results in a Clank Clink beep. As you can see, the pitches have been reversed.

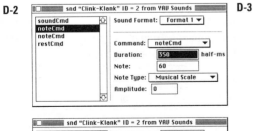

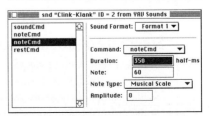

A

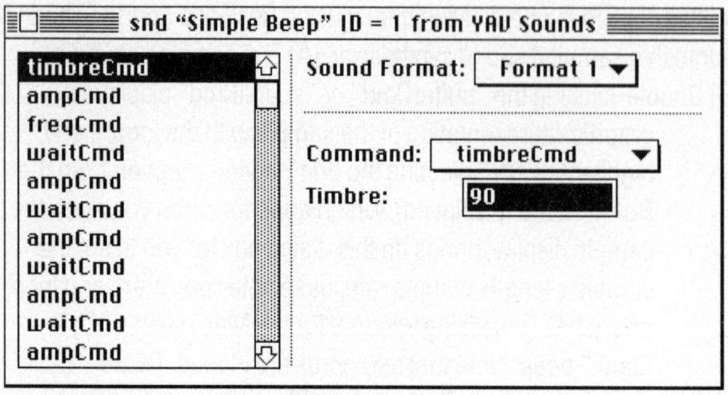

snd "Simple Beep" ID = 1 from YAU Sounds	
timbreCmd	Sound Format: Format 1 ▼
ampCmd	
freqCmd	
waitCmd	Command: timbreCmd ▼
ampCmd	
waitCmd	Timbre: 90
ampCmd	
waitCmd	
ampCmd	
waitCmd	
ampCmd	

B

timbreCmd	90	
ampCmd	224	
freqCmd	69 (1.0)	Musical Scale (Actual Frequency)
waitCmd	40	half-ms
ampCmd	200	
waitCmd	40	half-ms
ampCmd	192	
waitCmd	40	half-ms
ampCmd	184	
waitCmd	40	half-ms
ampCmd	176	
waitCmd	40	half-ms
ampCmd	168	
waitCmd	40	half-ms
ampCmd	160	
waitCmd	40	half-ms
ampCmd	144	
waitCmd	40	half-ms
ampCmd	128	
waitCmd	40	half-ms
ampCmd	96	
waitCmd	40	half-ms
ampCmd	64	
waitCmd	40	half-ms
ampCmd	32	
waitCmd	40	half-ms
ampCmd	0	

Figure 10-5: Step-by-step editing of a sound destined for the Macintosh's note synthesizer (also known as the square-wave synthesizer) using ResEdit's Sound Editor. This sound is the Macintosh's own default system beep. **(A)** Going through steps A and B of Figure 10-3 brings up the editor dialog box. You can see that the "Simple Beep" is really a complex sound with 27 commands describing the sound's envelope. **(B)** This is a listing of the parameters that produce the Simple Beep. A sound destined for the note synthesizer usually begins with a timbreCmd that is essentially a lowpass filter similar to the tone control on a stereo system.

Apple's MACE scheme can compress sounds to ⅓ or ⅙ of their original size. This allows a minute of Macintosh monophonic 22 KHz sound to be stored in 667K or 222K, respectively. Beware of the fact that fidelity is lost using 3:1 compression, although it may be suitable for certain musical applications. The 6:1 compression ratio is only useful for speech.

One very helpful aspect of the MACE scheme is that you can decompress sounds in real time during playback. Macintosh IIs and their successors can convert sample rates during real-time decompression (see Table 10-1).

Table 10-1: MACE compatibility

	Real-time 3:1 and 6:1 Compression	3:1 and 6:1 Decompression and Playback	Stereo Decompression and Playback	Sample-rate Conversion
Plus, SE, and Portable		●		
Macintosh II and successors	●	●	●	●

Summary of Sound Manager capabilities

❖ Play a sequence of simple frequencies
❖ Play complex waveforms stored as wavetables
❖ Play sampled (digitally recorded) sounds
❖ Record or sample sounds using appropriate sound input hardware

❖ Mix and synchronize up to six channels of sound (with System 7)
❖ Process sounds on their way to the Macintosh speaker or audio jack
❖ Play sounds continuously from disk while executing other tasks
❖ Play an alert sound
❖ Perform 3:1 and 6:1 sound compression using MACE
❖ Decompress compressed sounds in real time during playback
❖ Obtain and provide information about sound channels
❖ Monitor and limit CPU time consumed by sound-related activities

Algorithmic sound synthesis on the Macintosh

Several Macintosh programs let you synthesize sounds that you can save as 8-bit or 16-bit soundfiles for playback by the Macintosh's own hardware, an external sampler, or an internal digital audio card. Although the products of these labors are sampled soundfiles, the processes used to create them are deeply entrenched in traditional sound synthesis. At least one program takes the wavetable approach.

InstrumentMaker

Great Wave's ConcertWare includes a utility called InstrumentMaker (see Figure 10-6). With InstrumentMaker you can create a waveform in two ways, by drawing it with a pencil tool or by computing it from values entered for the first 20 harmonics. The program can automatically scale the computed waveform if it would result in clipping.

Besides drawing waveforms, you can also draw envelopes and vibratos (see Figure 10-7). You can set a sustain loop for an envelope, just like you might set one for a sampled soundfile.

SoundEdit

MacroMind-Paracomp's SoundEdit software is normally thought of as the front end to their MacRecorder hardware digitizer (see next section and next chapter). But SoundEdit also has built-in synthesis capabilities. You can do single-operator FM synthesis, generate white noise, and synthesize pure tones at a specified frequency, amplitude, and duration using sine waves, square waves, or triangle waves. Because SoundEdit has extensive signal-processing capabilities, including sophisticated mixing of up to four soundfiles, the sounds you synthesize can serve as building blocks for more complex waveforms.

Used in combination with ResEdit's Sound Editor, you have complete musical control over sounds you synthesize with SoundEdit (see Figure 10-8). You can also use HyperCard to create music with these sounds. Finally, you might want to use sound synthesized in this way as source material for any of the 8-bit music-making programs discussed in Chapter 15, "Making Music without MIDI."

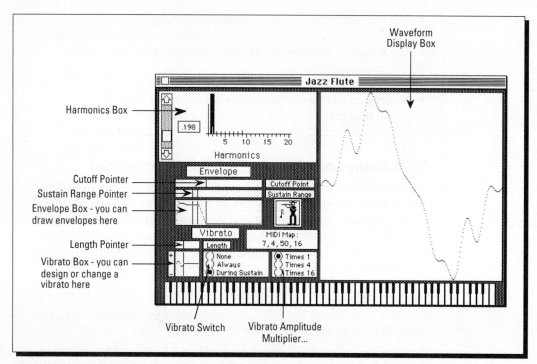

Figure 10-6: ConcertWare's InstrumentMaker lets you design waveforms in this window. Although each sound you create consists of a single waveform that is continually repeated, you have extensive control over the sound's envelope and vibrato.

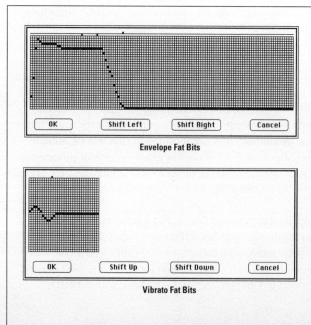

Figure 10-7: InstrumentMaker provides similar controls for setting a waveform's envelope and vibrato. Here you see the envelope's "fat bits" window compared to the vibrato's "fat bits" window. You can compute a vibrato if you want using the dialog box. Note that there are options to set other vibrato parameters in the main window (see Figure 10-6). These allow you to specify when the vibrato will occur (for example, only in the sustain loop) or whether to use a multiplier for the vibrato shape (1x, 4x, or 16x).

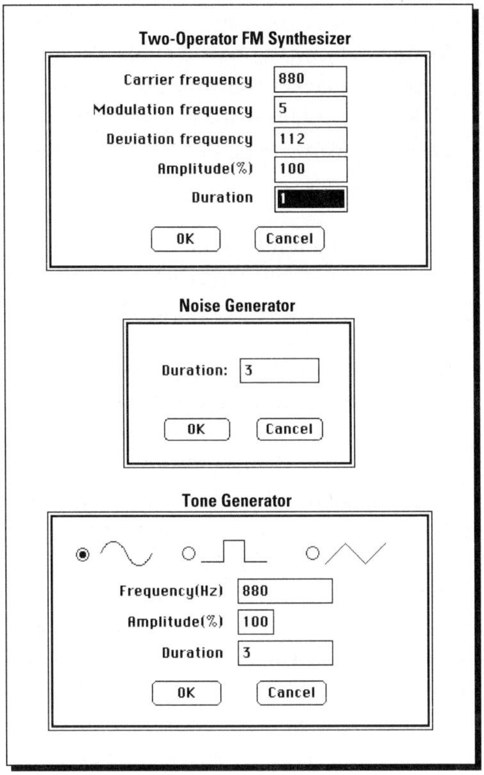

Two-Operator FM Synthesizer

Carrier frequency | 880
Modulation frequency | 5
Deviation frequency | 112
Amplitude(%) | 100
Duration | 1

OK   Cancel

Noise Generator

Duration: | 3

OK   Cancel

Tone Generator

Frequency(Hz) | 880
Amplitude(%) | 100
Duration | 3

OK   Cancel

Figure 10-8: SoundEdit's three little-known software synthesizers are controlled through these dialog boxes. They are the two-operator FM Synthesizer, the Noise Generator, and the Tone Generator.

SoundWave

SoundWave is distributed both with the Authorware multimedia development system (which includes a MacRecorder in the package) and the Articulate Systems's Voice Impact Pro (formerly VoiceLink) digitizer. SoundWave has multiple distribution arrangements that call for the bundling of it in the previously mentioned packages. There may be more bundled versions of this software when you read this.

While the program does not provide extensive synthesis capabilities, it does offer an interface for programmers to add synthesis modules to SoundWave's Custom menu. The Tone Generator is a sample of one of these custom modules that ships with the product (see Figure 10-9).

SoftSynth

SoftSynth is a fascinating and powerful additive synthesizer that supports carrier/modulator synthesis as well. The SoftSynth program is, in fact, a simulation of a digital additive synthesizer. Sounds that you create with this software-based synthesizer can be previewed at 8-bit resolution through the Macintosh's internal speaker or at 16-bit resolution if you have one of Digidesign's digital audio cards installed in your Macintosh and are using SoftSynth SA.

You can save synthesized files created with SoftSynth as soundfiles and load them into most samplers supported by Digidesign's other software. These include the Akai S700, S7000, and S900; the Casio FZ-1; E-mu's Emax and Emulator II; the Ensoniq Mirage, Multisampler, EPS, and EPS (SCSI); Korg's DSS-1 and DSM-1; Roland's S-10, S-220, MKS-100, Peavey S-50, S-550, and S-330; the Yamaha TX16W; and any sampler supporting the MIDI 12-bit or 16-bit Sample Dump Standard.

When you save a soundfile from SoftSynth, it synthesizes the sound and creates a 16-bit Sound Designer file. When you load the sound into a sampler supported by SoftSynth, the program does the required resolution conversion, if any (for example, to 12-bit or 8-bit). Like most of Digidesign's programs, SoftSynth includes a normalize function to guarantee that the sound's peak amplitudes are as high as possible without clipping.

```
≡≡≡≡≡ Tone Generator ≡≡≡≡≡
   This utility will          Length  2225
generate up to four sine
waves of different
frequency and amplitude.    Wave  period   amplitude
   Length is entered in        1     11        127
bytes. A value of 22255
produces one second of         2     22        108
sound.
                               3     44        64
   Period is entered in
bytes. Twenty-two bytes        4     48        92
gives a 1 kHz tone.

   Amplitude should be
from 0 to 127.               [ Cancel ]   [   OK   ]
```

Figure 10-9: SoundWave's Tone Generator module is accessed through the Custom menu. You can write your own synthesis modules for installation under the same menu.

Alternatively, you can save a SoftSynth configuration as a parameter file. Parameter files take very little memory (about 31K) and contain all the information required to re-create the sound that they describe.

Traditional additive synthesis mixes sine waves while controlling each sine wave's amplitude envelope over time. Each sine wave represents a single partial to the sound's spectrum. SoftSynth allows you to choose between other waveforms as your building blocks and to use up to 32 partials (the fundamental and up to 31 overtones). Besides sine waves, SoftSynth offers square, triangle, white noise, and band-limited noise (white noise filtered to a bandwidth of approximately 500 Hz centered on a partial's frequency). If you want, every partial of a sound can use a different waveform. Furthermore, you do not have to restrict the ratio between each partial to that of the harmonic overtone series, but can use any ratio that you want. The partials do not have to be aligned on harmonic frequencies in additive synthesis.

SoftSynth's main screen displays the envelopes of all the partials making up your sound (see Figure 10-10). The display is the equivalent of an FFT (Fast Fourier Transform) of your sound, showing the loudness of each partial as it evolves over time. You can set the overall amplitude of each partial by adjusting the 32 faders at the bottom of SoftSynth's main screen.

Clicking on the partial number located under its associated fader on the main screen (see Figure 10-10) brings up the single partial editor for that partial. Here you can edit the amplitude envelope, tuning contour (frequency envelope), wave type, and ratio (to the fundamental) of each partial on an individual basis.

SoftSynth provides a separate envelope for every partial making up a sound. While traditional analog synthesizers usually allow a four-stage ADSR envelope, SoftSynth's envelopes can include up to 40 stages and you can adjust each stage with an accuracy of 2 milliseconds.

As if that weren't enough, each SoftSynth partial has a unique tuning contour that acts as a frequency envelope (see Figure 10-11). This allows you to set pitch deviations of up to ±50 percent. You can adjust tuning contours with the same flexibility as amplitude envelopes. The tuning contours can contain up to 15 stages. There are two scales. The 2 percent deviation scale allows precise tuning changes within 2 percent of the partial's base frequency. The

Figure 10-10:
SoftSynth's main screen showing a 32-partial sound. You can view it from all four angles; it is the equivalent of rotating the 3-D FFT display to each of its four sides. This allows you to see envelopes that might be hidden by other partials when viewed from a certain angle.
You use the faders at the bottom of the main screen to adjust the overall amplitude of individual partials.

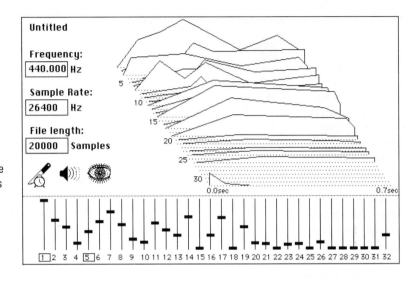

The speaker icon plays back the sound. The eye icon updates the screen. The knife icon takes you to Time-Slice mode. Partial numbers with boxes around them function as modulators within the context of SoftSynth's carrier/modulator synthesis patch.

50 percent deviation scale provides for greater pitch adjustments. Once you have adjusted the frequency envelope in the 50 percent setting, you should not attempt to switch back to the 2 percent setting.

SoftSynth provides for selective copying and pasting of any of the parameters associated with one partial onto those of one or more other partials. You can copy any combination of the amplitude envelope, frequency contour, wave type, or ratio.

Time slice editing gives you access to the overall amplitude envelope of the entire sound. The time slice display also shows "timbre events." Each timbre event corresponds to a breakpoint in the individual partial's envelopes (see Figure 10-12).

Besides additive synthesis, SoftSynth offers a powerful implementation of carrier/modulator synthesis (see Figure 10-13). If you understand FM synthesis, you will find it very easy to grasp the concepts behind SoftSynth's carrier/modulator synthesis, where a modulator is a waveform that modulates any other waveform (the carrier).

Digidesign's implementation allows any or all of SoftSynth's 32 partials to function as a modulator, carrier, or both. Each partial can still use an individual 40-stage

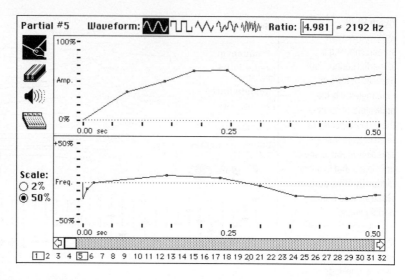

Figure 10-11: This screen, known as "single partial editing mode," appears when you click any of the main screen's partial numbers. The amplitude envelope appears at the top. The tuning contour (frequency envelope) appears at the bottom. The lines indicating the envelope are like elastic bands; you can stretch them in any direction by pulling on a breakpoint with the cursor. The eraser tool is there to remove a breakpoint. You click the speaker icon to audition the individual partial displayed on this screen.

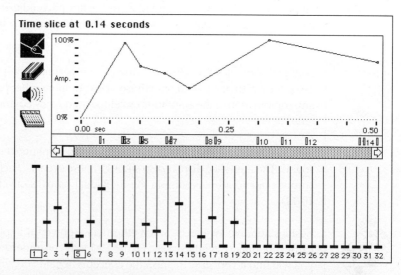

Figure 10-12: SoftSynth's Time Slice editing mode. Here you can adjust the contour of the amplitude envelope for the entire sound in the same way that you do for individual partials (see Figure 10-11). Timbre events are shown just above the horizontal scroll bar. You can move them forward and backward in time. Furthermore, you can create new timbre events simply by clicking between two existing events. Clicking any timbre event displays the amplitude settings for that event by configuring the amplitude faders to correspond to their settings for that particular event (point in time). Note that some of the faders are gray when the program is in real-time mode. Because changes to sounds are recalculated instantly in real-time mode, only changes to the first eight partials or so are allowed. You can switch to batch mode to edit other partials and then resynthesize the sound out of real time.

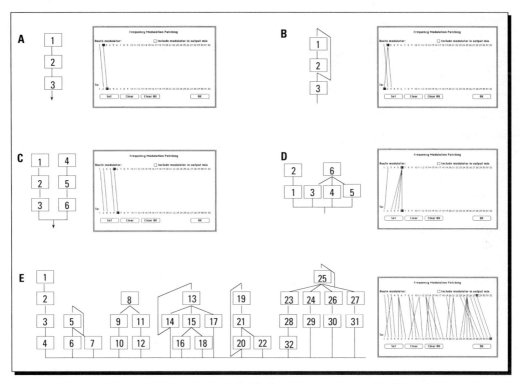

Figure 10-13: Four simple carrier/modulator patches in SoftSynth and one complex algorithm. The patches are shown in two forms: as a block diagram and as the SoftSynth setup screen that the block diagram represents. **(A)** Stack of two modulators and a single carrier. **(B)** Two modulators with a single carrier and feedback. **(C)** Parallel stacks, each consisting of two modulators and one carrier. **(D)** Four carriers, the first of which is modulated by a single modulator. A second modulator is applied to the remaining three carriers. The second modulator feeds back to itself. **(E)** A carrier/modulator patch involving all 32 of SoftSynth's partials.

amplitude envelope, 15-stage frequency envelope, and a different waveform. Carrier/modulator patches are called algorithms. Partials assigned to function as a modulator appear with boxes around their partial numbers on SoftSynth's main screen. In those cases, the main screen fader is used to adjust the modulation amount of that particular partial (or, more accurately, modulator, because the partial is functioning as a modulator).

SoftSynth also includes an intelligent SmartSynth function. This allows you to specify a general description of the sound you want (see Figure 10-14). The SmartSynth randomizes parameters within the ranges that you specify in the SmartSynth setup menu. This way you can create a sound that is a rough model of what you envision and then use SoftSynth's single partial editor to tweak each of the sound's components into a precise reflection of the sound you imagined.

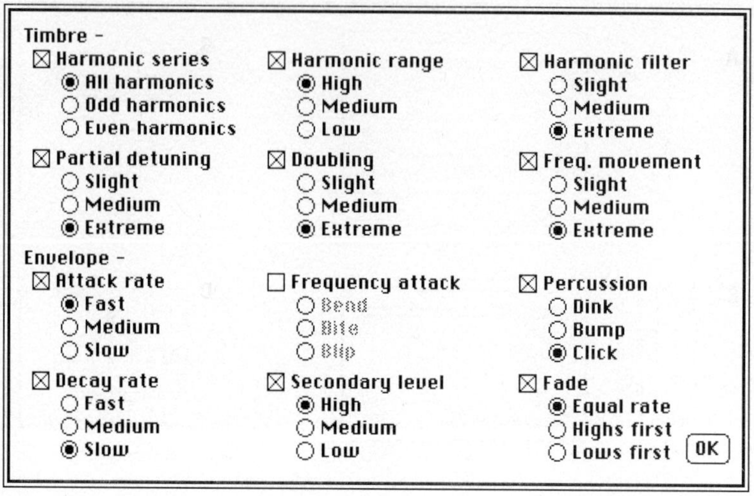

Figure 10-14: SoftSynth's
SmartSynth function lets
you quickly create a
sound based upon your
general description of the
various parameters
making up the sound.
The SmartSynth
randomizes the various
parameter settings within
the limits you specify.
You can also use
SmartSynth to process
an existing sound that
you have created in any
of the other ways
available through

```
┌──────────────────────────────────────────────────────────────┐
│ Timbre -                                                       │
│ ☒ Harmonic series    ☒ Harmonic range    ☒ Harmonic filter    │
│    ◉ All harmonics       ◉ High              ○ Slight          │
│    ○ Odd harmonics       ○ Medium            ○ Medium          │
│    ○ Even harmonics      ○ Low               ◉ Extreme         │
│ ☒ Partial detuning   ☒ Doubling          ☒ Freq. movement     │
│    ○ Slight              ○ Slight            ○ Slight          │
│    ○ Medium              ○ Medium            ○ Medium          │
│    ◉ Extreme             ◉ Extreme           ◉ Extreme         │
│ Envelope -                                                     │
│ ☒ Attack rate        ☐ Frequency attack  ☒ Percussion         │
│    ◉ Fast                ○ Bend              ○ Dink            │
│    ○ Medium              ○ Bite              ○ Bump            │
│    ○ Slow                ○ Blip              ◉ Click           │
│ ☒ Decay rate         ☒ Secondary level   ☒ Fade              │
│    ○ Fast                ◉ High              ◉ Equal rate      │
│    ○ Medium              ○ Medium            ○ Highs first     │
│    ◉ Slow                ○ Low               ○ Lows first  [OK]│
└──────────────────────────────────────────────────────────────┘
```

SoftSynth. Typically, you
would deactivate all but the one or two parameters you want involved in the processing. You can even process sounds
created by SmartSynth. You can also repeatedly process the same sound to transform it progressively toward the
crystallization of your goal.

SmartSynth also lets you selectively process individual parameters of a sound you
have already created through additive or carrier/modulator synthesis. In this
application you might turn off all of the SmartSynth's parameters except the one
that you want to apply to your existing sound.

In either case, you can include two types of parameters in you model, *timbre
parameters* and *envelope parameters*. Timbre parameters include the harmonic
series (all, odd, or even), the harmonic range (highest partial), the harmonic filter
(degree to which upper partials are lowered in amplitude), partial detuning, partial
doubling, and frequency movement (function of the tuning contour by up to 2
percent). Envelope parameters include attack, decay, and fade rates, sustain level,
frequency attack tuning contour (by up to 50 percent), and a percussion parameter that adds band-limited noise, sine, square, or triangle waves to partial number
32 at the beginning of the sound.

TurboSynth

Digidesign's TurboSynth is a modular synthesis program. It provides for the
manipulation of digital synthesis, sampling, and signal processing within a
context that emulates the traditional approach to analog synthesis, where
modules were interconnected with patch cords. With TurboSynth, the various
modules are represented as icons on the screen. You plug inputs into outputs
simply by drawing a virtual patch cord on-screen with the mouse.

You can use TurboSynth for additive and subtractive synthesis. The program also supports AM (amplitude modulation) and carrier/modulator synthesis. In addition, you can apply most of TurboSynth's editing features to sampled sounds. In fact, when used to modify sampled soundfiles, TurboSynth leaves some of the dedicated sample editors in the dust.

A large segment of the Macintosh music community is unaware of TurboSynth, but don't let its low profile fool you — this program is a sound designer's dream come true.

As with the SoftSynth program, you can preview sounds created with TurboSynth at 8-bit resolution through the Macintosh's internal speaker or at 16-bit resolution if you have one of Digidesign's digital audio cards installed in your Macintosh. With Digidesign's Sound Accelerator card installed, you can sample sounds directly into TurboSynth.

You can save (synthesize) TurboSynth files as soundfiles and load them into most samplers supported by Digidesign's other software. These include the Akai S700, S7000, S900, and S950; the Casio FZ-1 and FZ-10M; E-mu's Emax, Emulator II, Emulator II; Ensoniq's Mirage, Multisampler, EPS, EPS (MIDI and SCSI), and EPSM (MIDI and SCSI); Korg's DSS-1 and DSM-1; Roland's S-10, S-220, MKS-100, S-50, S-550, and S-330; and any sampler supporting the MIDI 12-bit or 16-bit Sample Dump Standard. Another way to work with TurboSynth is to mix the soundfiles it creates, using a sample editing program such as those discussed in Chapter 13, "Editing Sampled Sound."

TurboSynth includes the traditional modular synthesis components (oscillators, filters, and amplifiers), but augments these with a variety of DSP (digital signal processing) modules not normally available with a hardware modular synthesizer. These include a spectral inverter, digital delay, time stretcher, time compressor, pitch shifter, frequency envelope editor, amplitude envelope editor, resonator, mixer, wave-reshaper, and general AM-FM-PM (pitch modulation) modulator.

You operate TurboSynth by manipulating synthesis modules with the six primary tools appearing in the upper portion of the tool palette (see Figure 10-15). These same tools or a subset thereof are also found in all the module windows. The module windows do not require the patch tool or the "Mac to Sampler" tool, but sometimes add additional tools where appropriate.

Before you start creating a new sound with TurboSynth, you must set some basic parameters (see Figure 10-16). Because you are interconnecting a variety of virtual sound modules and modifiers with virtual patch cords, TurboSynth must know whether to convert data appearing at a module's inputs to a default sample rate or to have the module "inherit" its sample rate from the sound it is

Figure 10-15:
TurboSynth's main screen showing a typical sound patch. You use the six tools at the top of the palette to manipulate the other icons. With the exception of the Output Module (which appears automatically) the various modules are dragged onto the working area from the lower 15 icons on the palette. The arrow tool moves modules. The patch cord tool connects one module to another. Each module has an output, and most have at least one input. The eraser removes entire modules and breaks connections made with the patch cord. Clicking on the speaker plays the current sound as it will appear at the output jack. (Note that clicking speaker icons in the windows of other modules generally plays the sound as it would appear if the output jack were placed immediately after that window, allowing you to audition the sound up until that point in the sound patch.) The "Mac to Sampler" icon transfers the current sound to the sampler selected under the Sampler menu. Finally, the "Info" icon tells you how much memory is free and how much is used and provides an option to compact the memory and/or release the memory taken up by sound on the Clipboard.

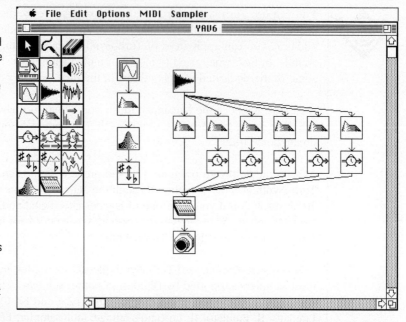

receiving at an input. Likewise, because certain modules can alter the duration of a sound, you must inform TurboSynth about whether each module is to always keep the same soundfile length, or inherit the length of a sound from the sound it is receiving at an input, or alter the length dynamically based upon a sum of all the operators modifying the current sound.

The 15 icons making up the lower portion of TurboSynth's palette are the synthesis modules that you use to create sounds. You incorporate modules into a sound patch by using the cursor to select the module and drag a copy of it out into the main part of the window. Once in the main workspace, double-clicking any module will open it up, so that you can tweak all the parameters relevant to the specific module. Opening up some modules reveals smaller sub-modules. They, in turn, can be double-clicked to present their own inner controls, like a Chinese box within a box within a box. In TurboSynth, the smallest boxes define the characteristics of the boxes that enclose them, and so on up in a hierarchical pattern.

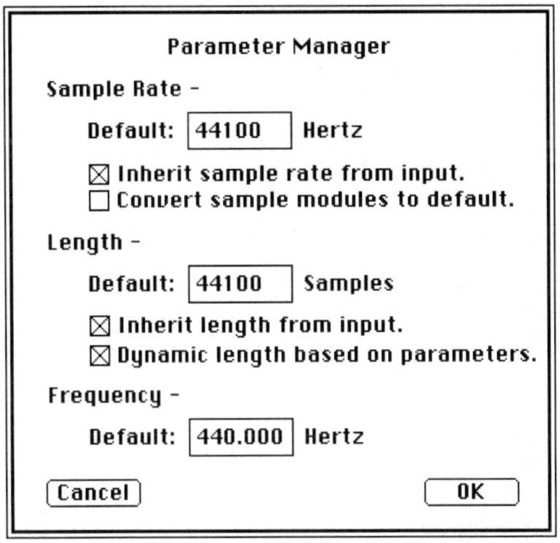

```
┌─────────────────────────────────────┐
│          Parameter Manager          │
│  Sample Rate -                       │
│     Default:  │ 44100 │  Hertz       │
│     ☒ Inherit sample rate from input.│
│     ☐ Convert sample modules to default.│
│  Length -                            │
│     Default:  │ 44100 │  Samples     │
│     ☒ Inherit length from input.     │
│     ☒ Dynamic length based on parameters.│
│  Frequency -                         │
│     Default:  │ 440.000 │  Hertz     │
│  (Cancel)                  (  OK  )  │
└─────────────────────────────────────┘
```

Figure 10-16: TurboSynth's Parameter Manager lets you specify the overall terms of communication between the modules involved in a patch. A real-world analogy to this dialog box would be an "intelligent" audio input, including a switch that allowed you to specify that signal received by the input was (1) always converted to +4 dB, or (2) always permitted to pass at the original level, regardless of whether it was +4 or -10 dB.

The upper-three modules represent the three types of raw sound material that you can use as the basis of any sound. These are oscillators, sampled soundfiles, and noise, corresponding to the third row of icons reading across. Because these are the building blocks of complex sounds, they accept no inputs.

The Oscillator Module has a *Waveform Mode* and a *Harmonic Mode* (see Figure 10-17). In the Waveform Mode, sounds are represented in the standard fashion as a plotting of amplitude over time. In Harmonic Mode, each waveform is represented as an FFT spectrum displaying its first 64 harmonics. When you switch back and forth between Waveform and Harmonic Mode, TurboSynth performs a Fourier Transform or Inverse Fourier Transform as required.

You have 11 presets — waveforms or harmonic spectra, depending upon the mode — and a 12th option to retrieve previously saved waveforms. In addition, you can use the pencil cursor to draw or edit any existing waveforms. You can drag any number of waveforms or harmonic spectra out into the oscillator's workspace/timeline, just as you drag oscillators themselves out into TurboSynth's main workspace. Once on the timeline, double-clicking on an individual sonic event opens it up for editing. When multiple waveforms are on the timeline, TurboSynth effects a smooth crossfade from one waveform to the next.

The Sample Module lets you import any Sound Designer format soundfile into a TurboSynth patch to become one of the raw components of the sound patch. Dragging a Sample Module out into the TurboSynth workspace presents you with a standard SF GetFile dialog box, where you can select a soundfile from your hard disk. Alternatively, if you have one of Digidesign's Sound Accelerator cards in your Macintosh, you can sample sounds directly into TurboSynth.

Once the sampled sound is present in the TurboSynth's window, double-clicking it opens up a window that constitutes a comprehensive sample editor (see Chapter 13). In addition to standard Cut, Copy, and Paste editing, you have tools for sample-rate conversion, gain scaling and normalization, envelope removal (removes the amplitude envelope and leaves the sample at continuous maximum volume — as if the sound was heavily compressed), and a number of tools for

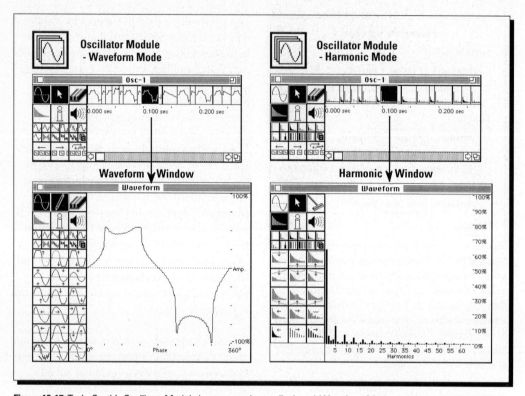

Figure 10-17: TurboSynth's Oscillator Module has two modes as displayed: Waveform Mode and Harmonic Mode. Each mode provides 11 preset waveforms or harmonic spectra and the option to import a previously saved waveform. Once you drag a waveform or harmonic spectrum into the oscillator's workspace (timeline), double-clicking an individual sonic event opens it up for minute editing. In Waveform Mode, this brings up a palette of 18 tools that allow you to increase or decrease amplitude, stretch, compress, smooth, or roughen the wave's shape, and add or remove noise. You can apply each tool to different parts of the waveform. The icons representing these functions give a much better picture of what they are used for than a verbal description (see lower portion of palette in left side of diagram). Harmonic Mode provides 15 tools for editing the harmonic spectrum. With them you can increase or decrease harmonic amplitude, stretch, compress, or otherwise reshape harmonic spacing, and add or remove individual harmonics. Again, the icons are self-explanatory (see lower portion of palette in right side of diagram). Both modes allow you to use the pencil tool to edit the graphic representation of the sound directly. If you create something that you want to use as a component in another sound, it is a simple matter to save that element as a file that you can recall from within the Oscillator Module.

manipulating the soundfile's loop. Loop tools include loop extension (repeatedly copying the loop as actual sound data to fill the required duration), crossfade looping, a full-fledged loop window like those discussed in Chapter 13, and the option to save the looped portion as a waveform file. You can access waveform files in the Oscillator Module as discussed in the previous paragraphs.

Having the option to use a sample soundfile as a component to a TurboSynth patch opens up many possibilities. You can use a sample as a modulator or carrier in FM-

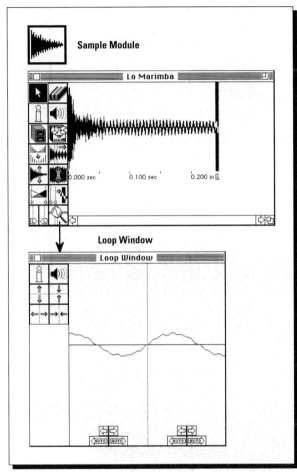

Sample Module
Loop Window

Figure 10-18: TurboSynth's Sample Module lets you use a soundfile (or soundfiles) in Sound Designer format as raw material for a TurboSynth patch. Furthermore, with one of Digidesign's digital audio cards, you can sample sounds directly into TurboSynth. Once you have brought a sampled soundfile into the domain of TurboSynth, double-clicking on it opens up a full-fledged sample editor as shown in this illustration.

style synthesis. You can emulate the new types of hybrid synthesis used by the Roland D-50 and D-550, the Korg M1, M1r, and T-series, and Kawai K-1, which combine a sampled attack with a synthesized sound. You can use a sampled sound as a point of departure for both additive or subtractive synthesis. Or you can apply tools traditionally associated with digital synthesis to complex sampled sounds rather than simple digital oscillators.

Don't forget that the use of Sound Designer format files can be a two-way street. Any sounds that you create in TurboSynth can subsequently be edited with any software that supports Sound Designer format soundfiles (see Chapter 13). Thus, you can take advantage of the whole range of traditional sample-editing tools after creating your sound — then bring that sound back into TurboSynth for further processing and go back and forth as much as you like, ad infinitum (see Figure 10-18).

No synthesizer, virtual or otherwise, would be complete without a noise generator. TurboSynth provides one in the guise of its Noise Oscillator Module (see Figure 10-19). Although you would probably not use noise as the entire basis of a sound, you will find many uses for noise that you have processed with some of TurboSynth's other modules, including amplitude envelopes, filter envelopes, resonators, and the like.

TurboSynth's 12 digital signal processing modules all have at least one input and output. These provide complete graphic control over the amplitude, filter, and frequency envelopes, spectral inversion, delays, time compression, selective frequency expansion, modulation of one sound by another (FM, AM,

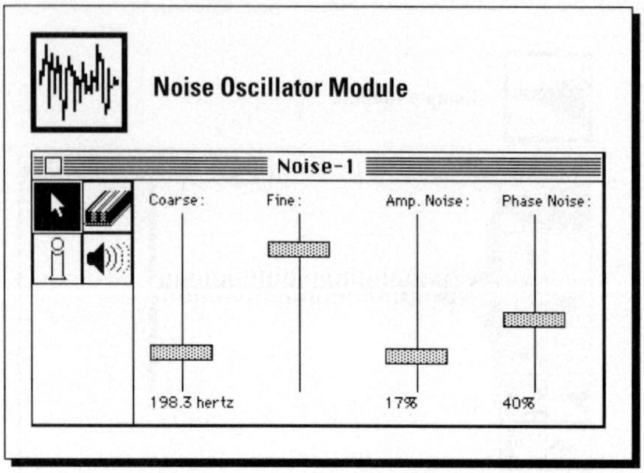

Figure 10-19: TurboSynth's Noise Oscillator Module lets you set the frequency of the perceived pitch of the noise, the amplitude noise (the degree to which the amplitude points of the noise are varied), and the phase noise (the degree to which the phase of the noise is varied).

or PM), resonance, and phase-reshaping of the waveform applied on-the-fly (see Figure 10-20). Finally, a Mixer Module accepts up to 32 inputs from other modules and lets you mix them using on-screen faders to specify their levels as a percentage value. Like all other TurboSynth modules, the Mixer Module is subject to normalization (optional) to assure that the final mix does not result in any clipping or, conversely, that the highest peaks of the final mix reach maximum amplitude.

One particularly elegant feature of TurboSynth is that you can "collapse" a patch at any module into a soundfile that is equivalent to the sound up to that point in the chain (see Figure 10-21). You might use this if you were running out of memory, or merely running out of screen real estate. You can do this at the end of the signal chain if you want — meaning the Output Module — and then use the resulting sampled soundfile as a Sample Module at the beginning of a new TurboSynth sound patch. But you don't have to do this at the end of the chain, you can do it anywhere. You might have many "branches" leading into a Mixer Module. It is easy to select the last modules of each branch before they connect to the mixer and then save each one as a separate soundfile. The same sound can then be synthesized by patching the soundfiles constituting what had formerly taken an entire branch directly into the mixer. Now that they have been reduced to a single icon, you might want to introduce additional modules between these composite modules and their inputs to the mixer. You can repeat this ad infinitum. Of course, there is no signal or generation loss, because this is all being accomplished with digital samples.

A fundamental limitation of TurboSynth version 2 is that it can only handle and generate 32 seconds of sound at 44.1 KHz. This has nothing to do with the amount of memory you have. It's because of an arbitrary programming decision to set the limit to one million samples. Another drawback of TurboSynth is that it is a computationally intensive program with no way to feed it a parameter script. Once you have a patch, to create 20 variations you need to point, click,

Figure 10-20:
TurboSynth's 12 digital signal processing modules laid out exactly as they appear on the main palette. In this illustration, each module has been double-clicked on to reveal the controls "under its hood." Unlike the Oscillator, Sample, and Noise Modules, which provide outputs only, most of these 12 processors provide for multiple output taps and at least one input. The 13th module, the Output Module at the bottom, is the overall output for the entire patch. Because of this, the module only accepts inputs — its output is sent to the Macintosh speaker, the Sound Accelerator card, directly to a sampler selected in the Sampler menu, or saved as a file for subsequent editing in another program. Note that the Output Module also provides a loop window just like the one available in the Sample Module. A loop at this stage is applied to the entire aggregate sound arriving at the output. Crossfade looping is also available.

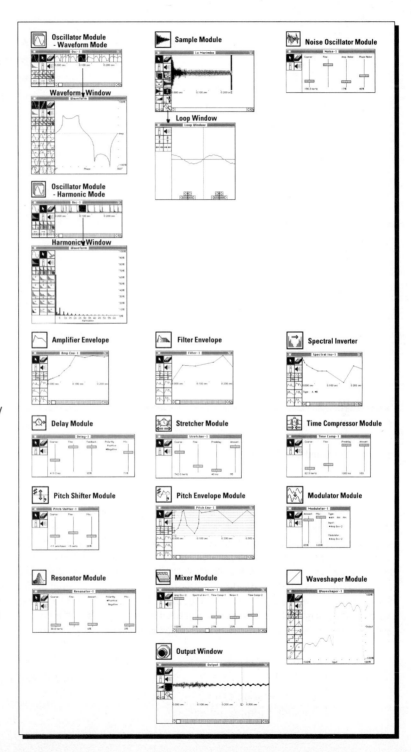

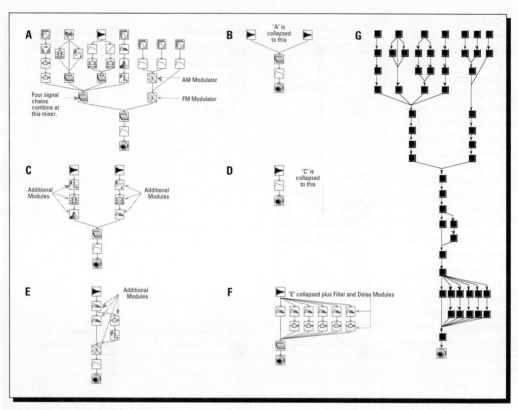

Figure 10-21: TurboSynth's capability for "perpetual patching" by continually collapsing portions of the signal chain into individual modules. **(A)** The first component of this sound consists of four signal chains arriving at a mixer. Several other oscillators are routed to a Modulator Module being used for FM synthesis. The outputs of this modulator and the original mixer are themselves mixed on the way to the final output. **(B)** Here, each of four original signal chains has been collapsed to individual soundfiles that are passed on to the first mixer. The modules involved in the FM side of the original patch have also been reduced to a soundfile. So far, the final output is the same for configurations A and B. **(C)** Additional processing modules have been introduced into the early stages of sound patch. The final output is no longer identical to that of A or B. **(D)** Here, every component of the sound up to the final mixer has been converted to a single sampled soundfile. The final output is identical to that of C. **(E)** Additional modules have been introduced into the final stages of the signal processing chain. The final output is not equivalent to A, B, C, or D. **(F)** The sound patch displayed in E has been converted to a sampled soundfile at E's output jack. On the way to the new output jack, it has been patched through some Delay Modules to create a reverb effect. If the Delay Modules were removed, the final output would be identical to that of E. Note that this soundfile can be used as a point of departure to construct an entirely new sound patch. **(G)** This is a simplified tree diagram of the entire sound represented by the sampled soundfile in F as it would have appeared if none of the original components were converted to soundfiles along the way.

point, click, type, click, point, etc., dozens of times. You have to walk through each new sound variation's creation, step by step. Here's a case which shouldn't require interaction.

Kyma

Unlike the other programs discussed in this chapter, Symbolic Technologies's Kyma System requires their dedicated outboard digital audio box and a NuBus card. However, the nature of its operation mandates its inclusion in this section.

In other chapters of this book, I make a strong case for equating the relationship between sound design and computer-assisted composition to that of traditional instrument design and traditional composition. For the vast majority of cases, this analogy holds. However, there are a number of composers for whom the creation of new sounds is inseparable with the compositional process, which means the unfolding of the music and the unfolding of the sound may be interdependent. For this group, Kyma offers the tools to work with sound creation and music creation as a single entity. An element in one world (for example, the transformation of a musical motive) can influence or define an element in the other world (such as the transformation of an audible sound). With Kyma, either element can shape the other.

Many composers consider a musical work as an organized continuum of individual sound events. Kyma, on the other hand, allows you to deal with a musical work as if it were a single complex sound event. To facilitate this, it consolidates the activities of software synthesis, real-time sound processing and editing, event structuring, and algorithmic composition into a single process (see Figure 10-22).

In Kyma you use "sounds" as building blocks. A Kyma sound, at any level of a composition, can be anything from a single sample, a timbre, a note, a motive, a phrase, a section, to an entire composition. Kyma does not force you to make a distinction between the concepts of instrument and score (although you can if you want). You can see that this is not merely a compositional system but an entire philosophy of musical aesthetics. Because of this, hard-core advocates of the system tend to appear to be fanatics. Furthermore, literature and documentation are obscured by a hefty amount of proselytizing and metaphysics. Still, once you get to the meat of the matter, Kyma really does offer substantial creative tools.

Kyma places a strong priority upon real-time interactivity at all levels. Because the Macintosh is unable to handle the immense computational overhead required by such a system, Kyma provides for real-time digital signal processing through its hardware component, the Capybara.

The Capybara connects to your Macintosh via its own single NuBus card or SE/30 PDS card. The internal Macintosh card contains a single Motorola 56001 DSP chip and the external Capybara box can hold up to eight additional cards, each with its own MC 56001 chip. The Motorola 56001 chip is the heart of most digital audio

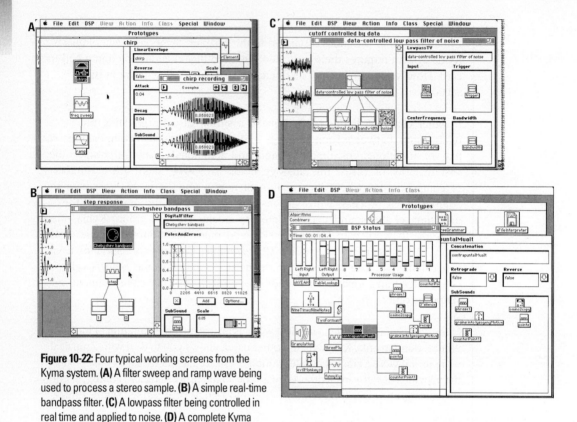

Figure 10-22: Four typical working screens from the Kyma system. **(A)** A filter sweep and ramp wave being used to process a stereo sample. **(B)** A simple real-time bandpass filter. **(C)** A lowpass filter being controlled in real time and applied to noise. **(D)** A complete Kyma score containing objects required to generate instruments (sounds) in real time and other objects representing algorithms that perform the virtual instruments. Note the real-time display of DSP processor usage.

cards for the Macintosh (and other computers for that matter), including Digidesign's Sound Accelerator and Audiomedia cards. The Kyma system cannot address the Digidesign cards, although Kyma is completely compatible with AIFF soundfiles.

The Capybara box operates all the MC 56001 DSP chips in parallel. When all eight slots are filled, it can achieve speeds of 94.5 MIPS (million instructions per second). In comparison, a stock Macintosh IIfx operates at under 10 MIPS. The rack-mountable box has balanced and unbalanced stereo inputs and outputs (greater than 90 dB signal-to-noise-ratio), a MIDI IN, OUT, and THRU, and a connection to its companion NuBus card. A/D and D/A converters are included with sample rates ranging from 11 KHz to 48 KHz (with oversampling the output rates can go to 96 KHz). Each expansion card includes 768K of dynamic RAM and 24K of no-wait-state static RAM. Thus, a fully configured system provides 6MB of dynamic RAM (for sampling) and 216K of static RAM. The software automatically detects the presence of each expansion card.

Kyma's roots can be traced back to the Music-N software synthesis languages developed by Max Mathews and others. The early mainframe synthesis programs, such as Music I through Music V, Music 4BF, Music 4C, and Music 11, relied upon a command line interface (CLI) and offline compilation. It was first necessary to build an "orchestra" by compiling complex instrument definitions, then write a score, usually in obscure IBM-type code, then link the score to the orchestra, and finally compile the entire composition before you could get any audible feedback. In other words, those early languages represent everything that the Macintosh environment has striven with great success to rectify in the realm of computer human interface (CHI). Kyma puts the power of those pioneer music languages into a graphic user interface, adding to it the real-time capabilities provided by the Capybara box and interactive MIDI control.

Kyma is obviously well suited for certain types of music. If you compose such types of music, you should definitely consider Kyma. The manufacturer makes it easy to examine their product by selling the complete manual separately. For a serious musician, perusing the actual users' manual is significantly more revealing than playing with the demo disks that so many other developers use for the same purpose.

Other options

Csound and Music 4C are two additional options for the Macintosh musician enamored with the Music IV/Music V paradigm. While Music 4C is essentially a Macintosh version of Music 4BF, Csound is its own language.

Csound is a Macintosh implementation of Barry Vercoe's Music 11 software (which was used exclusively on DEC PDP-II computers running Unix) that was originally written by Richard Karstens for a VAX and later ported to the IBM PC before coming to the Macintosh. Richard Boulanger of the Berklee School of Music was on the team that ported the program and is handling its distribution (Dan Ellis and Bill Gardner were the other two people involved in the port).

Among other things, Csound supports linear prediction, vocoding, granular synthesis, formant synthesis (derived from IRCAM's Chant) — approaches to synthesis that are unavailable with any other Macintosh system. The package includes unlimited virtual oscillators and a variety of instruments created by many renowned Music 11 aficionados. Don't let the "C" in Csound mislead you — you don't need to know how to program in C (however, be forewarned that Csound is more difficult than C!).

Music 4C was written by Grame Gerrard at the University of Melbourne. Unlike Csound, you really do need to know C to use it, since the orchestra file is a C program.

Both Csound and Music 4C let you hook synthesis modules together. Both can use Sound Designer and AIFF files. Unfortunately, both require that you do so by typing text instructions rather than patching together graphic modules like TurboSynth and Kyma. Csound and Music 4C offer Macintosh users offline synthesis of the type that is embraced by traditional computer music ideologies based upon non-real-time software synthesis with a text-based interface.

Programs like Csound and Music 4C continue to live because synthesizer manufacturers continue to take the closed "black-box" approach to their devices. Once you have mastered these programs, they offer a means to accomplish things that would be impossible with any other single program. For the musician who can program, Csound and Music 4C offer the ultimate in precision and flexibility, at the expense of difficulty in use.

Although Csound and Music 4C are text-based, user-friendly interfaces to these tools may possibly appear in the future. Some universities already offer graphical front-end programs to Music N languages. These let users combine the ease-of-use of visual programming with the precision and flexibility of the Music N model. They make it possible to generate a text file that is compiled like a normal Music N job.

Both packages could be very useful for educators involved in teaching historical approaches to computer music. As faster Macintoshes are introduced, it is possible that these two programs may offer a more real-time interactive approach. On the other hand, because real-time digital signal processing is already a reality in other products, Csound and Music 4C may have a hard time finding recruits for their camp.

The Macintosh as a Sampler

The Macintosh can function as a sampler with 8- or 16-bit resolutions. Depending upon the model Macintosh you have, sampling at 8-bit resolution may or may not require purchasing or building an external digitizer. Sampling at 16-bit resolution will always require the addition of a NuBus card (for the Macintosh II series) or a PDS card (for the SE/30). You can expect to pay proportionately more for higher resolution sampling. Whether you are doing 8- or 16-bit sampling, once you start using your Macintosh for sound digitization, you have taken the first step toward transforming your Macintosh into a serious digital audio workstation.

Eight-bit digitizers

Eight-bit digitizers are often referred to as "low-end," because the limitations on their resolution and sampling rate (typically a maximum of 22 KHz) restricts them from ever approaching professional audio quality. Nonetheless, don't underestimate the usefulness of 8-bit soundfiles sampled at 22 KHz. Such sounds can be ideal for multimedia presentations, interactive media, and educational purposes.

Because of their limited storage requirements, they are also useful for voice annotations, voice mail, and previewing 16-bit sounds. Finally, as you will see in Chapter 15, there are many programs dedicated to using these sounds in a compositional environment — both with and without MIDI. When sampled carefully, the quality of these soundfiles can be remarkably convincing. Consider that the original $30,000 Fairlight Series II used 8-bit sound.

Tapping into the Sound Manager with HyperCard

The Macintosh IIsi and LC both have microphone inputs, and a microphone is included in the box when you buy one of these models. Apple has indicated that all future Macintoshes will include a sound input jack. If you don't have one of these models, you can use MacroMind-Paracomp's MacRecorder (see the section "MacRecorder and SoundEdit" in this chapter) in place of the Apple microphone, providing that you have their sound driver in your system folder and are running System 6.0.7 or later.

HyperCard 2.1 (and later) comes with an Audio Palette that is accessible from the Edit menu or by typing **AudioPalette** in the HyperCard's Message box. If you want to access the Audio Palette without making the actual palette visible, you can type **AudioPalette invisible.** For the Audio Palette to function completely you must have system 6.0.7 or greater and appropriate sound input hardware as described in the previous paragraph (the Audio Palette will function with recording disabled if you are using System 6.0.5).

You can use the Audio Palette to add sounds to HyperCard stacks (see Figure 10-23). There is no easier way to accomplish this. The Audio Palette also provides limited sound-editing tools. You can cut, copy, and paste any sound or portion of a sound and you can remove sounds that have already been saved into a stack. Sounds that you create with the Audio Palette are sorted as format 2 'snd ' resources in the resource fork of whatever stack was active when you opened the Audio Palette.

HyperCard is fertile ground for digitized sound. HyperCard stacks have been able to play back sounds since the original release of the software. The number of multimedia and educational stacks grows on a daily basis and by some accounts, the words "interactivity" and "HyperCard" are now practically synonymous. Voice annotations are merely one example of the use of digitized sound in HyperCard.

Because of HyperCard's principle of inheritance (see the copuon in the back of this book), sounds that are recorded or otherwise moved into your Home stack are accessible from within any HyperCard stack. However, sounds that are in any other stack are only accessible when that stack is in use. This is easy to

A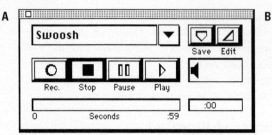

B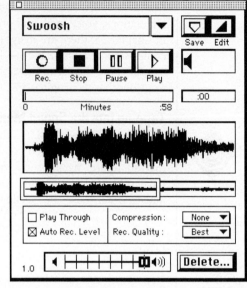

Figure 10-23: HyperCard's Audio Palette is accessible as a menu option in HyperCard 2.1 (or later), providing that you are running System 6.0.7 (or later) and have a Macintosh IIsi or LC. The feature becomes available with other Macintoshes if you have an alternative sound input device, such as MacroMind-Paracomp's MacRecorder, and a driver for the device in your system folder. **(A)** The Audio Palette has controls that emulate those of a typical analog recorder. The little speaker on the right functions as an input LED. The memory bar at the lower left shows you a running update of how much RAM the current sound is consuming. **(B)** Clicking on the Edit button at the upper right opens up the Audio Palette to display the rest of its controls. These include an overview of the entire waveform. Dragging over a portion of this overview moves it to the miniature selection display window immediately above the overview. Other pop-up menus and control buttons are self-explanatory.

This is easy to verify by opening the Audio Palette in various stacks. Whenever you're not in the Home stack, you will still see all the sounds installed in the Home stack listed in the Audio Palette's pop-up menu.

If you want to use a sound in more than one stack, it makes much more sense to install the sound in your Home stack rather than to copy it into all the stacks you might be intending to use it in. If you do make a habit of storing the bulk of your sounds in the Home stack, you should remember to copy any necessary sounds back into the stacks that use them if you are developing a stack or project for distribution. There are many ways to move sounds from one stack to another (see Figure 10-24). Refer to the sidebar, "Editing 'snd' resources with Digital Audio Suite" and Figure 10-25 for more information on managing 'snd' resources.

MacRecorder and SoundEdit

MacroMind-Paracomp's MacRecorder package has set the standard for 8-bit digitizers since its introduction by Farallon in 1987. Version 2.05 was current at the time of this writing. The hardware component is a Macintosh-colored box about the size of a television remote control, including a built-in microphone and also jacks for an external microphone and line input. The only control is a single input level knob. A standard 8-pin DIN cable plugs into either of the Macintosh's

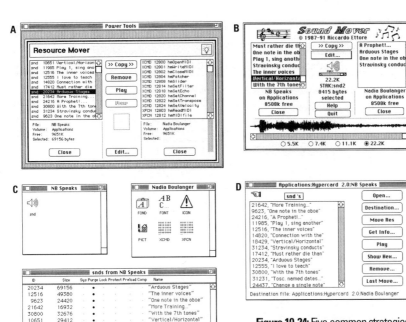

Figure 10-24: Five common strategies for moving sounds from stack to stack. **(A)** If you have the HyperCard Development Kit, you can use the Resource Mover card in the Power Tools stack. Apple's HyperCard Resource Mover (formerly known as ResCopy or the ResCopy SCMD) is also available as a separate stack through many online services. **(B)** Ricardo Ettore's shareware Sound Mover allows you to move sounds from one document or application to another the same way that you use Apple's Font/DA Mover to move fonts and DAs. Note that this utility is often distributed under the name of "The Sound Manager Package." Do not confuse this with Apple's own Sound Manager. **(C)** Apple's ResEdit can be used to copy any sound resource from one place to another. Other resource editors such as Mathemaesthetics's Resourcerer can be employed for the same purpose. Note: To enhance sound performance in HyperCard, check the "PreLoad" attribute in the Get Info box for a sound. **(D)** Miles Calbaum's shareware ResMaster DA provides many of the same features as Resource Mover (see A in this illustration). **(E)** Digidesign's Sound Installer, besides moving sounds from stack to stack, can convert Sound Designer (16-bit mono) or AIFF (8- or 16-bit mono or stereo) files into 'snd ' resources for installation into programs that can use them such as HyperCard. This utility can also install a special 'snth ' resource that will permit the Sound Manager to route 8- or 16-bit mono or stereo 'snd ' resources directly to their Sound Accelerator card if one is detected in the current environment. All five of these utilities are not restricted to moving sound resources among HyperCard stacks. You can use them to extract sound resources from any program or file (HyperCard or otherwise). ResEdit always displays all program or document resources but with Resource Mover or Sound Mover, you must hold the option key down while clicking the Open button to display programs in the file list. Any of these utilities can access the resources in currently open stacks provided that the stack is not the foreground document. However, only Resource Mover can access resources in other programs or documents *while* the programs or documents themselves are open. Finally, with the exception of Sound Mover, these utilities may be used to move any other type of resources you might want to manipulate.

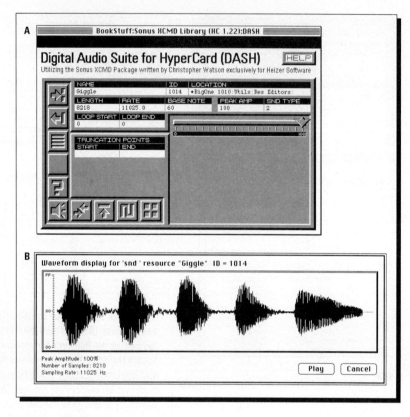

Figure 10-25: (A) The main card of Christopher Watson's Digital Audio Suite (Heizer Software) allows you to edit 8-bit 'snd' resources with great flexibility. **(B)** The Display Waveform button brings up a graphic overview of the current 'snd' resource.

serial ports. No external power is required. The rest of the package consists of a program, SoundEdit, and two HyperCard stacks, HyperSound and HyperSound ToolKit.

The MacRecorder package supports stereo sampling on just about any Macintosh. To record in stereo, you will need two of the MacRecorder digitizers; connect one to the printer port and one to the modem port. While the IIsi and LC provide a microphone for sampling into the Macintosh, they do not support stereo sampling, so you may even want to own a MacRecorder if you have one of these newer Macintoshes. The possibilities of employing a MacRecorder to tap into the features offered by the IIsi and LC's microphone, without owning a IIsi or LC, are discussed earlier in this chapter.

As a sample editor, SoundEdit provides the same caliber of features for manipulating 8-bit sampled soundfiles as the professional sample editors discussed in Chapter 13 provide for 16-bit sounds. SoundEdit packs a lot of power.

The MacRecorder system is very similar to professional direct-to-hard disk recording systems except that all sampling is done into RAM (SoundEdit Pro,

Editing 'snd' resources with Digital Audio Suite

The Sonus Externals Library is a collection of external functions (XCMDs and XFCNs) and commands dedicated to the management and manipulation of 'snd' resources and the data they contain.

You can retrieve and modify the sound resource's wavedata and header information. This set of externals allow you to alter the actual sonic content of the resource, as well as edit the sampling rate, base note value, loop points, name and ID, plus display the waveform on the screen. The waveform for the sound can be reversed, scaled, optimized, truncated, or sectioned. The data for the waveform can also be displayed as hexadecimal values or graphically. About the only thing you can't do with these externals is record the actual sound. There are many other options for recording 8-bit 'snd' resources discussed elsewhere in this chapter.

XCMDs and XFCNs provided in the Sonus Externals Library

RemoteOpen (XFCN):	Opens the resource fork of a specified file.
RemoteClose (XCMD):	Closes the resource fork of a specified file.
GetSounds (XFCN):	Displays a list of all the sounds in the open resource file. The list displays the ID, name, and size of each 'snd' resource in the file.
GetData (XFCN):	Returns hexadecimal data representing each byte within the waveform.
RemotePlay (XCMD):	Plays the current 'snd' resource.
RemoteRename (XCMD):	Renames the 'snd' resource in the open resource file.
RemoteRenum (XCMD):	Renumbers the 'snd' resource in the open resource file.
GetRate (XFCN):	Returns the sampling rate of the 'snd' resource.
GetNote (XFCN):	Returns the base note value of the 'snd' resource.
GetLoop (XFCN):	Retrieves both the start and end loop points.
GetLength (XFCN):	Returns the total number of samples in the 'snd' resource.
GetType (XFCN):	Returns the format (type 1 or 2) of the 'snd' resource. This is the only Sonus External that deals predictably with type 1 'snd' resources.
GetPeak (XFCN):	Returns the percentage value of the greatest amplitude of the waveform for the 'snd' resource.
SetLoop (XCMD):	Sets new start and end loop points.
SetNote (XCMD):	Sets the base note value (0 to 127) held within a 'snd' resource's header data.
SetRate (XCMD):	Sets the sampling rate for the 'snd' resource.
ReverseSnd (XCMD):	Reverses the wavedata of the 'snd.'
ScaleSnd (XCMD):	Allows you to scale the amplitude of the waveform of a sound within a range of 25 percent to 200 percent.
SectionSnd (XCMD):	Splits a sound into smaller equal parts, each a separate 'snd' resource.
TruncateSnd (XCMD):	Snips bytes off the start and/or end of a sound's wavedata.
OptimizeSnd (XCMD):	Normalizes the amplitude of a 'snd' to the maximum possible amplitude without clipping (zero values are unchanged).
DisplaySnd (XCMD):	Displays the entire waveform of the 'snd' as a graphic representation of the waveform, including the sampling rate, peak amplitude, and sample length.

discussed in Chapter 24, records directly to hard disk). Because of this, the maximum sampling time is about 45 seconds per megabyte of RAM at 22 KHz. Lower sampling resolutions increase the maximum sound length up to three minutes per megabyte at a sampling resolution of 5.5 KHz. These times are halved for stereo soundfiles.

SoundEdit provides for 8-bit sampling at four resolutions: 22 KHz, 11 KHz, 7.3 KHz, and 5.5 KHz. Mono 22 KHz soundfiles may be sampled with non-MACE 3:1, 4:1, 6:1, and 8:1 compression (Note: Compression is not available for stereo soundfiles). While this increases the maximum duration of a soundfile significantly, compression greatly limits the playback fidelity and once a soundfile has been compressed, none of SoundEdit's signal processing effects may be applied to it (you may still cut, copy, and paste the data). Fortunately, sample rate conversion (down sampling) and compression may be applied after a sound has been sampled and edited.

Downsampling is as simple as pasting a soundfile into a new file set at a lower sampling rate. You will achieve much better results by sampling at 22 KHz and then pasting the resulting soundfile into a new 11 KHz file than by recording the same sound initially at the 11 KHz sampling rate. This is very important for multimedia applications: Do not sample at 11 KHz; paste a 22 KHz file into an 11 KHz file to decrease the file size while retaining as much fidelity as possible.

Because you are dealing with 8-bit samples, calculating the storage requirements of a soundfile is easy. Each sample is equal to one byte. Therefore, sampling at 22 KHz (22,000 samples per second) will take exactly 22K of disk space.

SoundEdit can open and save files in four formats, any of which may include a loop:

❖ *SoundEdit:* SoundEdit's native format can be opened by SoundEdit, SoundCap, SoundWave, MacroMind Director, MediaMaker, MediaTracks, Authorware, and others. Note that this format saves the sound in the data fork of the file so the sound is not visible to ResEdit or other resource editors. However, it can be manipulated with Sound Mover.

❖ *Instrument:* This format can be used as a Studio Session, Jam Session, or Sound Exciter Instrument (see Chapter 15). Note that this format saves the sound in the data fork of the file so the sound is not visible to ResEdit or other resource editors. However, it can be manipulated with Sound Mover. Instrument format sounds must be sampled at 11 KHz with a maximum length of 32,767 samples. If the instrument includes a loop, the minimum length of the sound is 1,480 samples.

❖ *Resource:* This can be used by HyperCard, SuperCard, MacroMind Director, Sound Exciter, or any other software that supports 'snd' resources. When you save the resource into a HyperCard stack, it is automatically converted to a type 2 'snd' resource, otherwise it is saved as a type 1 resource.

❖ *AIFF:* The audio interchange file format is described elsewhere in this chapter. Besides saving sounds in this format, SoundEdit can also open 16-bit AIFF files although in doing so the program discards eight bits of data for every sample, effectively converting the 16-bit sound into an 8-bit sound.

SoundEdit does not try to emulate traditional analog recorder controls, instead you click the microphone icon to record and the speaker icon to play back. There are two significant aids to recording. First, you can display a continuous reading of the input amplitude envelope, which serves as an extremely accurate input level meter. Second, you can display a continuous real-time spectrum analysis of the signal coming into the MacRecorder showing the amplitude of component frequencies on a scale of 0 to 5 KHz or 0 to 10 KHz. This can provide some insight into what the optimum sampling rate would be for the sound being analyzed (see Figure 10-26).

Once you have sampled or otherwise opened a soundfile, SoundEdit's real power can be exploited (see Figure 10-27). All the standard Macintosh cut, copy, and paste operations are available. You can apply any number of digital signal processing effects to the entire sound or a selected region. DSP options are found under the Effects menu (see Figure 10-28). Refer to the sidebar, "For programmers and hackers" for information on adding items to the Effects menu.

The two remaining components of the MacRecorder package will be important to you if you plan to use sampled sound in HyperCard. HyperSound is an interface to the MacRecorder digitizer built within HyperCard. It has been slightly obsoleted by System 6.0.7 and 7.0's Audio Palette (see the section, "Tapping into the Sound Manager with HyperCard" in this chapter), but it does offer a few features that the Audio Palette lacks.

While the Audio Palette lets you manipulate sounds in the current stack and the Home stack, HyperSound can provide import and export sounds to any stack without having to open the stack in question (see Figure 10-29). You can also copy sounds to the clipboard. The Audio Palette lets you record at 22 KHz and 11 KHz. HyperSound adds 7.3 KHz and 5.5 KHz to these. The Audio Palette provides access to 3:1 and 6:1 MACE compression. HyperSound adds 4:1 and 8:1 (non-MACE) compression.

Figure 10-26: SoundEdit can display as many sounds as your RAM can hold. The display is read from left to right with the horizontal axis representing time and the vertical axis representing amplitude. You can zoom out to see overall amplitude envelope of an entire soundfile or zoom in far enough that individual samples can be edited. In this illustration, the same 2.91-second sound is shown at three different magnifications. The intermediate zoom is displaying the first .89 seconds of the sound (the cursor is located .67 seconds into the sound). The lowest display is zoomed out to the sample level. The display units used in the info boxes (lower-right corner) have been switched to samples. The sound is revealed to be 64,706 samples in length and the portion showing is the first 619 samples of the sound, or about 281 milliseconds.

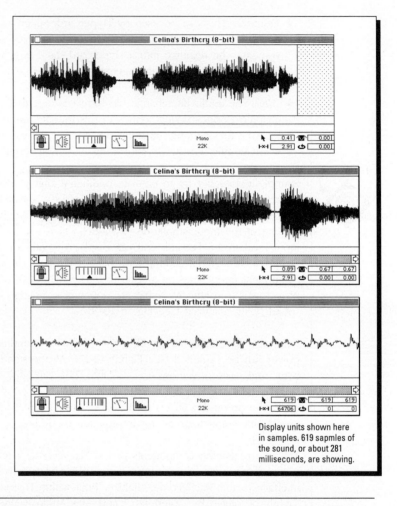

Display units shown here in samples. 619 sapmles of the sound, or about 281 milliseconds, are showing.

Figure 10-27 (at right): This composite illustration shows all the digital signal processing effects available with SoundEdit via the Effects menu and their associated controls. Amplify…changes gain by a percentage. Backwards reverses sample order. Bender… provides an elastic contour delimiter upon which you can insert as many breakpoints as you desire. You use the radio buttons to set the range to 1 or 2 octaves. Echo… lets you specify delay time in milliseconds and echo strength as a percentage of the previous amplitude. Envelope… provides an elastic contour with unlimited breakpoints that you shape into a new amplitude envelope. The scale can be set from zero to any maximum multiplier you desire. Filter… offers a five-band graphic equalizer. The vertical bars delineating the frequency bands may be dragged to change the width of any band and the new center frequency is displayed during adjustment. The horizontal boost/cut bars display their values in dB while you drag them. Flanger applies a flanging algorithm over which you have no control. FM Synthesis… (See above under "Algorithmic sound synthesis on the Macintosh.") Noise… (See above under "Algorithmic sound synthesis on the Macintosh.") Ping Pong gradually interchanges the left and right channels of a stereo sound. The effect is similar to turning the pan knob on a mixer from left to right for the left channel while you simultaneously turn the right channel's pan knob from right to left. Reverb… offers four reverberation algorithms. Silence sets the values of the selected samples to zero. Smooth… allows you to smooth jagged edges, clips, and pops in a sound. It is essentially a fast lowpass filter. Sonogram… computes a sonogram of the region (should be viewed in

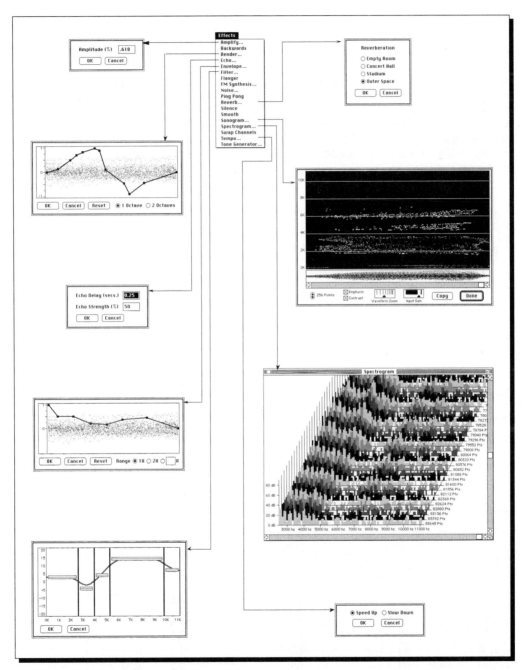

color). Spectrogram... computes a 3-D FFT of the region plotting over time the changing of the amplitudes to a selected number of frequency bands. Swap channels exchanges the right and left channels for the selected region.

Tempo compresses or expands the duration of the selected region without changing the pitch. Slow Down doubles the duration and Speed Up halves the duration. Tone Generator... (See "Algorithmic sound synthesis on the Macintosh.")

Figure 10-28: Using this Set Pitches dialog box, you can set the playback pitch of any sound relative to the pitch at which it was recorded. This is useful when saving sounds as Instruments for use in Studio Session, Jam Session, or Sound Exciter. This is also required if you plan to control sounds musically in HyperCard, that is, by specifying sounds to play at particular pitches. Remember that sounds saved as Instruments (not HyperCard sounds) cannot be longer than 32,767 samples and must be sampled at 11 KHz. If they contain a loop, the minimum soundfile size is 1,480 samples.

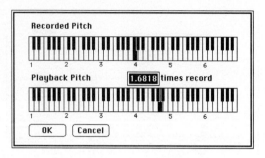

HyperSound ToolKit

MacroMind-Paracomp's HyperSound Toolkit provides the tools you need if you want to control the MacRecorder from within HyperCard scripts (or from within any program supporting XCMDs for that matter). The stack includes six XCMDs and six XFCNs .

❖ *CopySnd* (XCMD): This XCMD copies a sound to the Clipboard. You can then paste that sound into another HyperCard stack (using the PasteSnd XCMD), the Scrapbook, SoundEdit, or any other file that accepts sound resources.

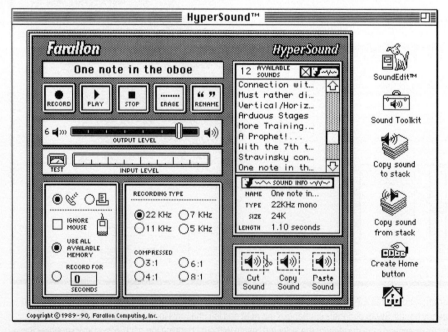

Figure 10-29: The main control card for MacroMind-Paracomp's HyperSound stack. Although the digital signal processing effects available with SoundEdit are missing, you can manage HyperCard sounds with great flexibility.

❖ *DuplicateSnd* (XCMD): This XCMD copies a sound directly from one file to another, without using the Clipboard. You can copy to and from files of any type, not just HyperCard stacks. If the specified destination file does not exist, DuplicateSnd creates a new file.

❖ *EraseSnd* (XCMD): This XCMD removes a sound resource from the currently active stack.

❖ *Fplay* (XCMD): This XCMD lets you play and stop playing compressed and uncompressed sounds from a HyperCard stack. Fplay can queue up sounds in the same way as the HyperCard play command. Putting *continuous* at the end of the list will play the last sound continuously. Fplay does not have the tempo and note specification features of the HyperCard Play command.

❖ *Fsound* (XFCN): This function returns the name of the currently playing sound (if the sound is being Fplayed), or "done," just like the HyperTalk function "the sound."

❖ *InputLevel* (XFCN): This function returns a value between 0 and 100 that indicates the input level from the MacRecorder with zero being silence, and 100 indicating the maximum input level. Optionally, the input level can be shown graphically on the card as a level meter.

❖ *PasteSnd* (XCMD): This XCMD pastes a sound from the Clipboard into the current stack.

❖ *Record* (XFCN): This function has seven arguments, all of which are optional except the first. You can specify the name of the sound to be recorded, the recording type (sampling rate and compression type), serial port that MacRecorder is connected to, the length of recording time in 60ths of a second, whether or not mouse or keyboard activity will interrupt recording, a user-defined function indicating how long to wait before initiating recording, and the name of a HyperCard field the rectangle of which specifies the boundaries of a recording progress indicator. The rectangle must be 16 pixels wide and its left edge must be an integer multiple of 16. As recording proceeds, the rectangle will be filled from the bottom up to indicate recording progress.

❖ *RenameSnd* (XCMD): This XCMD is used to change the name of a sound resource.

❖ *SndInfo* (XFCN): This function returns a comma-separated list of three items: sound size (in bytes), sound type (sample rate or compression ratio), and sound length (in 60ths of a second).

❖ *SndList* (XFCN): This function returns a return-delimited list of all the sounds in a stack. Optionally, it will also return the size of each sound, separated from the sound name by a comma.

❖ *Volume* (XFCN): This function sets the speaker volume to a level between 0 and 7 or returns the current speaker volume setting.

Editing sounds with SignalEditor

Stephen Knight's shareware SignalEditor is a program for sound editing and analysis in the time and frequency domains (see Figure 10-30). Input can come from either previously digitized files or by recording directly into SignalEditor with MacroMind-Paracomp's MacRecorder sound digitizer.

Cut, Copy, Paste, and Extraction are supported. The software can read and write several file formats: MacroMind-Paracomp's SoundEdit 1.0 and SoundEdit 2.0, GWI's SpeechLab files, and data files consisting of signed-short samples. Files can be in 8-, 12-, or 16-bit resolution. Multiple channel files are supported.

Some of the options include waterfall spectral displays, Linear-Predictive-Coding (LPC) scatterplots with frequency marking, slice or frame, displays and marking, export of all FFT and LPC results to standard text files, and printing. You can configure FFT points, spectrum drawing scale, smoothing, number of waterfall FFTs, and LPC autocorrelation order/poles.

The results of the Waterfall, Slice, and LPC computations can be exported to a text file or copied as a picture to the Clipboard. Note that copying display areas to the Clipboard (the To Clipboard item under the Edit menu) will not display the actual picture when the Clipboard is displayed or when the Clipboard is pasted to the Scrapbook. When pasted to MacDraw, the picture will display correctly.

Saving FSSD (common file format) files as SpeechLab files and vice versa changes their sampling rate. SignalEditor tries to come as close as possible to the sampling rate, but analyzing an FSSD file that was originally a SpeechLab file will create inconsistent results (that is, frequency values and timing will not be accurate). SignalEditor is also not capable of changing the timing relationships between channels.

Voice Impact Pro and SoundWave

Articulate Systems's Voice Impact Pro (formerly called VoiceLink) is an external 8-bit digitizer that offers on-board MACE compression (unlike MacRecorder). Because the MACE compression is built into the hardware, users of system versions earlier than 6.0.7 can still use this valuable option with all its implications (such as background recording without keyboard or mouse interruption). The non-

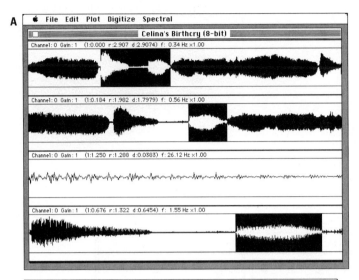

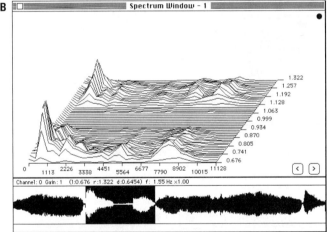

Figure 10-30: (A) SignalEditor's main screen displaying waveforms at various resolutions. **(B)** SignalEditor's spectrum analysis of the selected region in the uppermost waveform of A above.

"Pro" version, simply called Voice Impact, is lacking the built-in MACE compression. Both are controlled by Articulate Systems's Voice Record DA, which is quite powerful, offering graphic waveform display, cut, copy, paste, merge, and gain changing options. However, if you want to get into the real nitty-gritty of 8-bit soundfile editing, you can easily bring the files into the SoundWave software that comes with Voice Impact Pro (see Figures 10-31 and 10-32).

Although SoundWave ships with Voice Impact Pro, it is not linked to any particular digitizer in the way that SoundEdit is associated with the MacRecorder digitizer (see Figure 10-33). Because of this, the program is included with other packages that support 8-bit sounds. For example, the Authorware multimedia package, which includes the MacRecorder hardware, comes with SoundWave in place of SoundEdit.

Just like SoundEdit, SoundWave offers recording at 22 KHz, 11 KHz, 7.5 KHz, and 5.5 KHz. However, if you are using System 6.0.7 or greater and accessing the Sound Manager, either because you have a IIsi or LC, or because you are using the MacroMind-Paracomp MacRecorder driver (as described above), your recording possibilities are strictly 22 KHz with optional 3:1 or 6:1 MACE compression. Later, you can use SoundWave's Resample option to convert the

Figure 10-31: Articulate Systems' Voice Impact Pro 8-bit audio digitizer.

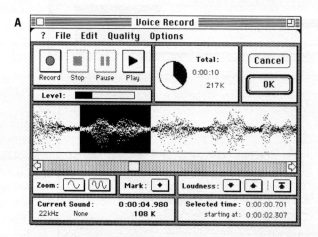

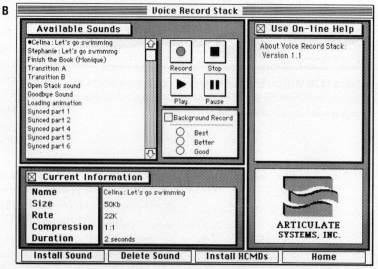

Figure 10-32: (A) Articulate Systems's Voice Record DA ships with their Voice Impact and Voice Impact Pro. The Voice Record DA will accept input from MacroMind-Paracomp's MacRecorder and the microphone that Apple includes with the IIsi and LC. **(B)** Articulate's hardware comes with this Voice Record stack that allows you to control sound input and output from HyperCard.

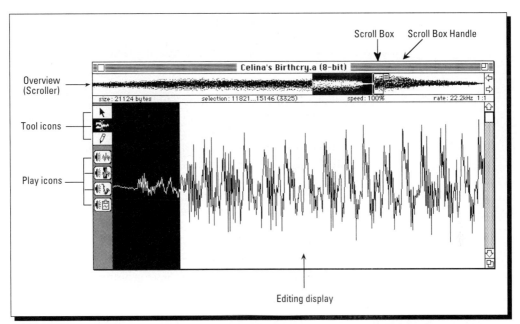

Scroll Box   Scroll Box Handle

Celina's Birthcry.a (8-bit)

Overview
(Scroller)

size: 21124 bytes   selection: 11821...15146 (3325)   speed: 100%   rate: 22.2kHz 1:1

Tool icons

Play icons

Editing display

Figure 10-33: SoundWave's main screen. Note: The overview is always present and the portion of the sound in the current window is shown as a box in the overview and the current selection is highlighted both in the overview and the main window. There are only two zooms, full in to the individual sample level and full out to display the entire sound. The overview window is always fully zoomed out and the editing window is always fully zoomed in. The tool icons along the side of the window include a redundant arrow cursor for scrolling and operating menus and dialog boxes; a selection cursor for selecting regions for editing; and a pencil for actually drawing in changes on your waveform (this feature is noticeably lacking in SoundEdit). The play icons include buttons to play the entire soundfile, play the selected region, play the soundfile as a Studio Session or Jam Session Instrument, and play the Clipboard.

sample rate, providing that the sound is uncompressed. To record into SoundWave without accessing the Sound Manager, you must reboot with the MacroMind-Paracomp MacRecorder driver disabled.

SoundWave can open and save all the same file types as SoundEdit with the exception of 16-bit AIFF files (it can open 8-bit AIFF files). SoundWave does provide an additional, rather innovative file format called "Numeric." A Numeric file is a return-delimited text file that can be opened by any text editor or spreadsheet. You could also create a custom application in HyperCard or any other environment to read in the values of such a file. With a SoundWave Numeric file you can use a spreadsheet to analyze sample data or even process the data through your own custom algorithms. In this capacity, the usefulness of this unique file format cannot be overstressed.

SoundWave offers a limited number of signal processing effects and all of these are also found in SoundEdit. Besides the continual overview display and the option to save a soundfile as numeric data, SoundWave offers several other options not found in SoundEdit. These include printing the screen (or a selection thereof) and fading in and out (Note: Fading in and out can also be achieved in SoundEdit's Envelope option or by adding Jim Nitchal's NSFX resource as described above). SoundWave also provides a custom menu where you can install your own modules such as effects or sound-generating functions (see Figure 10-34). The program comes with documentation and sample source code for MPW (Macintosh Programmers Workshop), Lightspeed C, Lightspeed Pascal, and others. The Tone Generator described above under "Algorithmic sound synthesis on the Macintosh" is an example of such an extension.

SoundWave also provides options for mixing soundfiles (although only a single soundfile or selection may be mixed with data on the clipboard), setting the pitch for soundfiles destined to be Studio Session or Jam Session instruments, and spectrum analysis (see Figure 10-35).

SoundCap

Fractal Software's SoundCap was a very popular early 8-bit sound-editing program for the Macintosh. Originally bundled with the MacNifty Audio Digitizer (offering sampling rates at 22 KHz, 11 KHz, 7.4 KHz, and 5.5 KHz), it went all the way to version 4.3 before distribution was officially discontinued. There are many people still using the MacNifty Audio Digitizer, and there are many SoundCap sounds available through user groups and online services. A number of utilities are available to convert these sounds into formats that were introduced after the program stopped being supported by its developers.

MacMike

Premier Technology's MacMike is a digitizer that some of you may remember from the early days of the Macintosh. After a brief period of moderate popularity, the company, based in New York at the time, disappeared. In late 1991, MacMike resurfaced in San Francisco. Besides its extremely low cost ($60), this digitizer is unique because it includes all the digitization hardware in the handle of the microphone. The software emulates Apple's built-in microphone on the IIsi and LC, thus assuring compatibility with programs that expect to see those input devices. A utility called Sound Pad, designed for the quick recording and playback of voice memos, comes with the digitizer. Like Articulate Systems's Voice Impact Pro, the recording features of the microphone are operated from a DA. Similarly, Apple's Sound Manager is a requirement.

Build your own digitizer

The Sound Input Device (SID+) is a do-it-yourself audio digitizer designed for the Macintosh computer. It produces a continuous stream of digitized samples

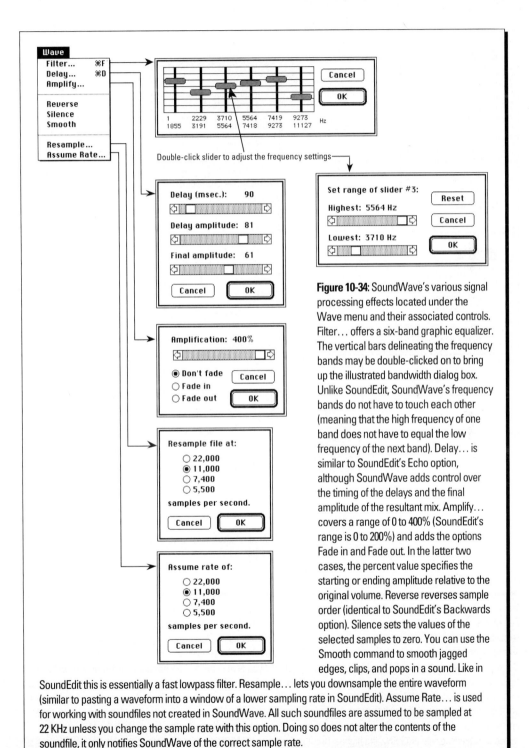

Double-click slider to adjust the frequency settings

Figure 10-34: SoundWave's various signal processing effects located under the Wave menu and their associated controls. Filter... offers a six-band graphic equalizer. The vertical bars delineating the frequency bands may be double-clicked on to bring up the illustrated bandwidth dialog box. Unlike SoundEdit, SoundWave's frequency bands do not have to touch each other (meaning that the high frequency of one band does not have to equal the low frequency of the next band). Delay... is similar to SoundEdit's Echo option, although SoundWave adds control over the timing of the delays and the final amplitude of the resultant mix. Amplify... covers a range of 0 to 400% (SoundEdit's range is 0 to 200%) and adds the options Fade in and Fade out. In the latter two cases, the percent value specifies the starting or ending amplitude relative to the original volume. Reverse reverses sample order (identical to SoundEdit's Backwards option). Silence sets the values of the selected samples to zero. You can use the Smooth command to smooth jagged edges, clips, and pops in a sound. Like in SoundEdit this is essentially a fast lowpass filter. Resample... lets you downsample the entire waveform (similar to pasting a waveform into a window of a lower sampling rate in SoundEdit). Assume Rate... is used for working with soundfiles not created in SoundWave. All such soundfiles are assumed to be sampled at 22 KHz unless you change the sample rate with this option. Doing so does not alter the contents of the soundfile, it only notifies SoundWave of the correct sample rate.

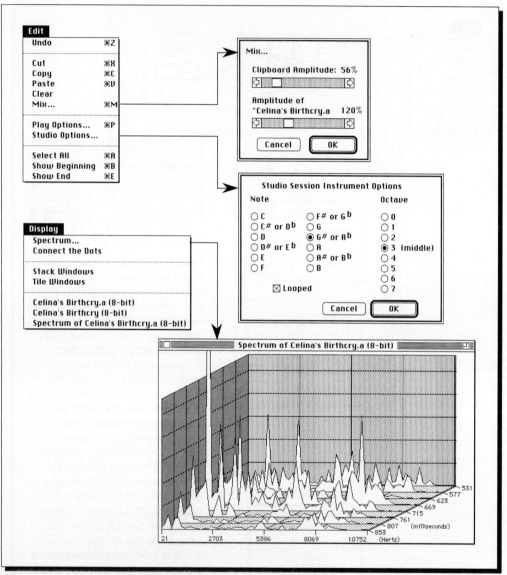

Figure 10-35: SoundWave's Mix, Studio (set pitch), and Spectrum options found under the Edit and Display menus. Edit Menu: Mix... lets you mix a sound on the Clipboard with the region selected in the main window. You can set the relative proportions of each waveform as a percentage. Studio Options... allows you to set the playback pitch of any sound relative to the pitch at which it was recorded. This is useful when saving sounds as Instruments for use in Studio Session, Jam Session, or Sound Exciter. This is also required if you plan to control sounds musically in HyperCard, that is, by specifying sounds to play at particular pitches. Remember that sounds saved as Instruments (not HyperCard sounds) cannot be longer than 32,767 samples and must be sampled at 11 KHz. If they contain a loop, the minimum soundfile size is 1,480 samples. Display Menu: Spectrum... computes and displays an FFT of the soundfile or selected region divided into regions of 1,000 samples. You can set the highest and lowest frequencies to be displayed. With the Macintosh's maximum sampling rate of 22 KHz, the highest possible frequency is 10,752 Hz and the lowest is 21 Hz. You can choose to display the spectrum in two or three dimensions.

at 22 KHz and is software-compatible with other existing audio digitizer software. SID+ was developed by Jeffrey Siegel, Dave Fleck, and Eric Gould. This freeware package is available from most online services.

Tables 10-2 and 10-3 identify the available 8-bit sound types and compatible applications discussed in this chapter and in Chapters 19 and 27.

Table 10-2: 8-bit sound formats	
File format	**File type**
'snd' resource (format 1)	rsrc
'snd' resource (format 2)	rsrc
Instrument (Studio Session, Jam Session, Sound Exciter)	DEWF
SoundEdit, SoundWave, SoundCap (sound is in data fork)	FSSD
AIFF (8-bit)	AIFF
AIFF (16-bit)	AIFF
Sound Designer	SFIL
Dyaxis	MSND
SoundLab, MacKeyboard (sound is in data fork)	WAVE
Super Studio Session	DEWF
MacDrums	MSWF
Crystal Quest	SMSD
World Builder	ASND
Dark Castle	SOUN
QuarterStaff	wave
Gauntlet	GSND

Table 10-3: Applications using 8-bit sound				
Program	'snd' resource	AIFF (8-bit)	Instruments type: DEWF	type: FSSD SoundEdit, SoundWave SoundCap	type: WAVE SoundLab
Authorware	●			●	
Director	●	●		●	
HookUp!	●			●	
HyperCard	●				
Jam Session			●	●	
Different Drummer				●	
MediaMaker	●	●		●	
MediaTracks	●	●		●	
Ovaltune			●		
Serius	●				
Sound Exciter			●		
SoundMaster	●				
Studio Session			●		
Super Studio Session			●		
SuperCard	●			●	
System (beep)	●				

Professional digital audio (16-bit)

By adding a digital audio card such as Digidesign's Sound Accelerator or
Audiomedia to one of the Macintosh's internal slots you can sample and record
direct-to-hard disk at true CD rates and resolution, that is 16-bit samples at a
sampling rate of 44.1 KHz. Besides hard-disk-based recording, these cards are often
used in sound design as an adjunct to sound editing software and sound synthesis
software for previewing purposes.

More and more programs are taking advantage of the capabilities of Digidesign's
digital audio cards if they are installed. Notable among these are Digidesign's Sound
Designer II, Audiomedia, Deck, Q-Sheet A/V, TurboSynth, and SoftSynth, Passport
Design's Alchemy and Sound Apprentice, Opcode's StudioVision, Mark of the
Unicorn's Digital Performer, and Steinberg's
Audio Cubase.

Digidesign's Sound Accelerator and Audiomedia cards and related software are discussed in Chapters 13, 18, and 24.

The Macintosh as a MIDI Instrument

There are other ways to get digital audio out of your Macintosh than playing back sound files from your hard disk. Equipped with the appropriate cards, your Macintosh can function as a ROM- or RAM-based sample player. Installing such cards is another step in converting your Macintosh into a stand-alone music workstation. You use Apple's MIDI Manager to route data to such digital audio NuBus cards. Chapter 8, "Moving Data Around Your Music Network" includes a detailed discussion of the interaction of MIDI Manager and all the cards discussed below.

The Macintosh as a ROM-based sample player
MacProteus

In a joint venture with E-mu Systems and Opcode, Digidesign is marketing the MacProteus, a NuBus card version of E-mu's Proteus/1 sound module (not to be confused with the Proteus/2 module), one of the most popular MIDI instruments of the past two years (see Figure 10-36). The MacProteus is a sample player with a library made up of real instruments and synthesizer-type sounds, sampled at 39 KHz with 16-bit resolution. The sounds are stored in 4MB of ROM chips on the NuBus card. The MacProteus contains 192 instruments (128 ROM presets and 64 RAM presets) and is capable of playing back 32 notes simultaneously. Furthermore, it is 16-channel multitimbral. When combined with Sound Tools or Deck and AudioMedia, the MacProteus becomes part of the "Digidesign Desktop Music Production System."

The main difference between E-mu's stand-alone Proteus and Digidesign's MacProteus card is that the number of output jacks has been reduced from six to two. Naturally, there is no front panel with buttons and knobs on it, but the card comes with a software "front panel" that is even easier to manipulate than its hardware counterpart. Besides contributing to this software front panel, Opcode markets a full Proteus Editor/Librarian that allows you to transform the sounds in any way imaginable and then save these edits in patch libraries.

You can play the MacProteus with any MIDI keyboard or access it with almost any MIDI software as well as with HyperCard, SuperCard, and Director. What you won't need is a hardware MIDI interface because instead of plugging in MIDI cables, you use Apple's MIDI Manager to connect the components. With one of these in your Macintosh, there are at least three items you don't have to carry on the plane — a peripheral sound module, MIDI interface, and cables.

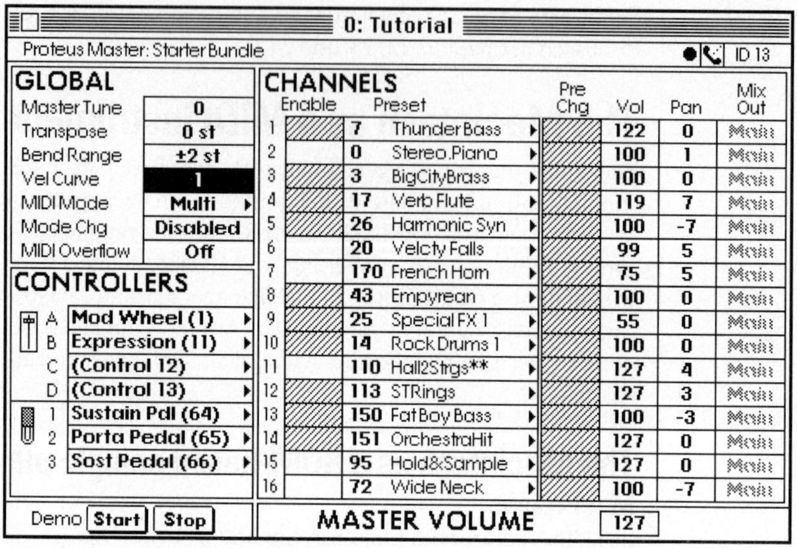

Figure 10-36: The software-based front panel for Digidesign's MacProteus NuBus card. Although the card itself has no physical controls, this virtual front panel allows you to interact with the MacProteus with greater flexibility than the physical controls found on an external rack-mounted Proteus/1. Selecting sounds and assigning them to MIDI channels is particularly easy because clicking on any patch name brings up a pop-up menu of all available patches. The software, developed by Opcode, is also a fully functional librarian for the MacProteus card.

0: Tutorial

Proteus Master: Starter Bundle — ID 13

GLOBAL

Master Tune	0
Transpose	0 st
Bend Range	±2 st
Vel Curve	1
MIDI Mode	Multi
Mode Chg	Disabled
MIDI Overflow	Off

CONTROLLERS

A	Mod Wheel (1)
B	Expression (11)
C	(Control 12)
D	(Control 13)
1	Sustain Pdl (64)
2	Porta Pedal (65)
3	Sost Pedal (66)

CHANNELS

Enable	Preset		Pre Chg	Vol	Pan	Mix Out
1	7	Thunder Bass		122	0	Main
2	0	Stereo.Piano		100	1	Main
3	3	BigCityBrass		100	0	Main
4	17	Verb Flute		119	7	Main
5	26	Harmonic Syn		100	-7	Main
6	20	Velcty Falls		99	5	Main
7	170	French Horn		75	5	Main
8	43	Empyrean		100	0	Main
9	25	Special FX 1		55	0	Main
10	14	Rock Drums 1		100	0	Main
11	110	Hall2Strgs**		127	4	Main
12	113	STRings		127	3	Main
13	150	FatBoy Bass		100	-3	Main
14	151	OrchestraHit		127	0	Main
15	95	Hold&Sample		127	0	Main
16	72	Wide Neck		100	-7	Main

Demo **Start** **Stop**

MASTER VOLUME 127

The Macintosh as a RAM-based sample player
SampleCell

Digidesign's SampleCell is a NuBus card that turns your Macintosh (II series and beyond) into a 16-voice polyphonic, fully multitimbral, 16-bit, stereo, RAM-based sample player supporting sampling rates up to 48 KHz, with eight polyphonic outputs. The SampleCell is based on the same chip that was the basis of the Dynacord ADS sampler. You can install up to 8MB of RAM on a SampleCell card using standard Macintosh SIMMs. A Macintosh can accommodate up to five SampleCell cards, resulting in an 80-voice, 40-output sampler with up to 40MB of RAM to load sounds into. Like MacProteus, SampleCell is controlled with MIDI Manager; you don't need a hardware MIDI interface unless you want to control the card by an external device. With the SampleCell, you also have the option to use OMS (see Chapter 8, "Moving Data Around Your Music Network") as an alternative to MIDI Manager (however, in general, OMS is not a substitute for MIDI Manager).

SampleCell comes with a CD-ROM containing 630MB of sampled instruments. A number of third-party sound library CD-ROMs are available from such vendors as Prosonus (who created the original SampleCell CD-ROM), Greytsounds, Bob Clearmountain, and OSC. The board supports Sound Designer and AIFF. The card also includes a special version of Digidesign's Sound Designer software. Using this or another version of Sound Designer (or other sample editor such as Alchemy) you can import, export, and edit soundfiles to and from almost any other sampler.

Although the SampleCell card does not provide for direct sampling by itself, if you have a Sound Accelerator or Audiomedia card, you can use it to bring sounds into a SampleCell. Likewise, you can use TurboSynth or SoftSynth to create sounds for SampleCell.

The SampleCell Editor included with the card allows you to load sounds into SampleCell and perform a wide variety of standard editing operations found on dedicated hardware samplers (see Figure 10-37). Editing sample playback parameters with the SampleCell Editor is considerably easier and faster than with a dedicated hardware sampler. Furthermore, editing with the SampleCell Editor is non-destructive. It does not alter your original soundfile; when you reload a bank of samples into SampleCell, all edits you have stored with the bank are preserved.

LiveList

Digidesign's LiveList is part of their Sound Tools utility package. It lets you assign any soundfile of Sound Designer I, Sound Designer II, or AIFF format to be triggered by a MIDI event — not necessarily a note — or even a Macintosh keyboard key (see Figure 10-38). Playback is by way of the Sound Accelerator card. Triggering typically originates from an external controller. Because entire soundfiles or regions of playlists (see Chapter 24, "Direct-to-Hard Disk Recording") can be triggered, this little program is very effective in a live performance situation.

The Macintosh as a virtual synthesizer
Sound Exciter

Passport's Sound Exciter also turns your Macintosh into a MIDI instrument, but it does so purely with software (see Figure 10-39). Because it uses the Macintosh's internal hardware for digital-to-analog conversion, it is limited to 22 KHz 8-bit samples. You can create these sounds with MacroMind-Paracomp's MacRecorder or any of the programs mentioned in this chapter. In addition to the sounds that come with the package, it can play back any instruments from Jam Session, Studio Session, or Super Studio Session. Although Sound Exciter will respond to all 16 MIDI channels complete with MIDI velocity, this software sample player is limited to playing eight notes at a time — but these can be eight different sounds (that is, 8-voice polyphonic, 8-channel multitimbral), and a different group of eight MIDI channels can be used for each event. Like the MacProteus, it relies on Apple's MIDI Manager, so you can play it from a MIDI keyboard or you can patch directly to it from any MIDI Manager-compatible software. What's really amazing is that nobody ever thought of doing this before.

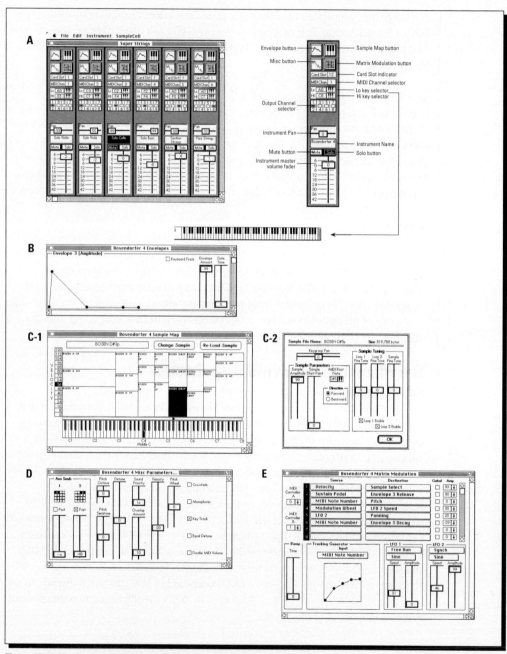

Figure 10-37: You load and edit SampleCell sounds with Digidesign's SampleCell Editor program. **(A)** The main window of the SampleCell editor allows you to load instruments into a bank. A bank can consist of as many samples as can fit into your SampleCell. The four buttons at the top of each sound bank bring up the following four powerful editing options. **(B)** The Envelope window provides access to three ADSR envelopes, the most important of which is the amplitude envelope (only one per instrument). You can set envelopes to track the keyboard, so that their overall durations decrease

Figure 10-38: LiveList's setup window lets you create a list of soundfiles or regions of soundfiles to which you assign MIDI or Macintosh keyboard triggers called "Start Events." You must also assign "Stop Events" that halt playback of a sound. In the case of a MIDI note, this will usually be the Note-Off message. A special

#	Start Event	Name	Preload	Loop	Finish	Stop Event
		Yet Another Drum Kit				
1	C2 on, chan 1	Hi Hat Closed	X		X	Next Start
2	D2 on, chan 1	Hi Hat Open/Close	X	X		Next Start
3	E2 on, chan 1	Short Crash	X		X	Next Start
4	F2 on, chan 1	Short Tamborine	X			Next Start
5	G2 on, chan 1	Tama Kick	X		X	Next Start
6	A2 on, chan 1	Tama Snare	X		X	Next Start
7	B2 on, chan 1	Wood Block	X		X	Next Start
8	C3 on, chan 1	808 Claps	X			Next Start
9	Mac key "d"	Bongo	X		X	Next Start
10	Mac key "f"	Finger Snap	X			Next Start
11	Mac key "g"	Pearl Tom V short	X		X	Next Start
12	Mac key "h"	Syn Tom	X		X	Next Start
13	D3 on, chan 1	Bushack				Next Start

type of trigger is "Previous Stop." This causes the sound to commence immediately at the end of the preceding event. You can set each soundfile to loop until the stop event occurs. Sounds can also be set to "Finish," meaning that they will always play through to their ends. There is an Automatic Advance option that causes a single Start Event to step through an entire list of sounds.

Figure 10-37 (continued) progressively and uniformly as the pitch gets higher. You can assign triggers to the other two envelopes in the Matrix Modulation window (see item E). **(C-1)** The Sample Map window lets you assign individual soundfiles to up to 20 specific regions or individual notes of the MIDI keyboard. Each region (called a Key Group in SampleCell terminology) can have up to three samples assigned to it. Each sample assigned to a Key Group can be assigned to a specified velocity zone, so that a different sample will be triggered depending on the velocity of the note triggering the sample. You can also use this window as a MIDI monitor that highlights the triggered sample and displays the incoming velocity and pitch. **(C-2)** Clicking the Sample Name box or double-clicking on an individual sample brings up a dialog box for editing additional parameters such as sample panning, amplitude, start point, root note, direction (forward or backward), and fine tuning the entire sample, the sustain loop, and the release loop. **(D)** The Miscellaneous window lets you set auxiliary sends for each channel of an instrument, complete with control over signal level and a pre/post toggle. Here you can also set the octave and semitone transposition of the entire instrument as well as the detune. Sound Priority lets you set the priority of an instrument when SampleCell must play more than its allotted 16 voices (this is also known as a channel-stealing algorithm). Other miscellaneous parameters accessible here include response to MIDI velocity, MIDI volume (Controller 7), pitch wheel range, and crossfade. **(E)** The Matrix Modulation window allows you to configure how each instrument responds to incoming controller information as well as SampleCell's own built-in LFOs, wave generator, and tracking generator. For every instrument there can be 16 modulation patches, each of which consists of a source, destination, gate attribute, and modulation amount (referring to the amount of change you designate to be under your control).

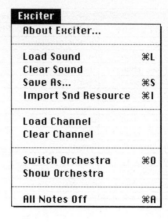

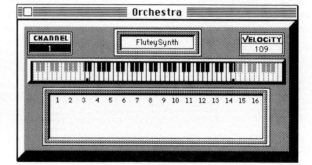

Figure 10-39: Passport's Sound Exciter is a software-based sample player that you can control with MIDI Manager. This illustration shows its control panel, which you bring up by double-clicking the Sound Exciter icon in MIDI Manager's PatchBay. Also pictured are Sound Exciter's menu and orchestra configuration display. Chapter 8, "Moving Data Around Your Music Network" contains additional information on using Sound Exciter.

Summary

✔ Since the beginning, the Macintosh has had built-in sound. All Macintoshes have built-in 8-bit sound capabilities and these are exploited by many products. The Macintosh can play sound through its internal speaker or out the audio port on the back panel, which will accept a ⅛-inch mini plug (stereo for all Macintosh IIs, otherwise mono). You can add a NuBus card to provide for 16-bit sound from any Macintosh with NuBus slots.

✔ There are four ways to create sound with a Macintosh: (1) Synthesize sounds with the Macintosh's built-in synthesizers for playback by way of the Macintosh's built-in sound capabilities; (2) Sample sounds using the Macintosh's built-in sampling features (only available with certain models); (3) Sample sounds using an external digitizer attached to the Macintosh's serial or SCSI ports for playback by way of the Macintosh's built-in sound capabilities or a dedicated NuBus card; (4) Algorithmically generate sampled sounds for playback by way of the Macintosh's built-in sound capabilities or a dedicated NuBus card.

✔ Any Macintosh can create, modify, and play sounds without requiring external hardware. This is accomplished by a piece of software called the Sound Manager which first appeared with System 6.0. This Sound Manager replaces the older Sound Driver. The Sound Manager runs on all Macintoshes, but all its capabilities are not available for certain models. The Sound Manager provides routines, resources, and drivers that handle all the recording, playback, saving, and storing of sound on the Macintosh. Even the System beep is now a Sound Manager routine. The Sound Manager can also synthesize sound and speech and synchronize multimedia presentations. Some features of the Sound Manager are available only if you have the Apple Sound Chip found in the Macintosh II series, the SE/30, the Macintosh Portable, and LC.

✔ You needn't have a Macintosh IIsi or LC to reap the benefits of the new Sound Manager. There are several third-party drivers that, when placed in your 6.0.7 System Folder, allow you to use MacroMind-Paracomp's MacRecorder digitizer, Articulate Systems's Voice Impact Pro, or even a homemade digitizer in place of the microphone included with the IIsi and LC. MacroMind-Paracomp's MacRecorder Driver is the most popular of these.

✔ The Sound Manager uses MACE, short for Macintosh audio compression and expansion, developed to reduce the vast storage requirements of sound. Apple's MACE scheme can compress sounds to 1/3 or 1/6 of their original size. This allows a minute of Macintosh monophonic 22 KHz sound to be stored in 667K or 222K, respectively. Beware of the fact that fidelity is lost using 3:1 compression, although it may be suitable for certain musical applications. The 6:1 compression ratio is only useful for speech. MACE can decompress sounds in real time during playback. Macintosh IIs and their successors can convert sample rates during real-time decompression.

✔ Several Macintosh programs let you synthesize sounds that you can save as 8-bit or 16-bit soundfiles for playback by the Macintosh's own hardware, an external sampler, or an internal digital audio card. Although the products of these labors are sampled soundfiles, the processes used to create them are deeply entrenched in traditional sound synthesis. At least one program takes the wavetable approach.

✔ There are other ways to get digital audio out of your Macintosh. Equipped with the appropriate cards, your Macintosh can function as a ROM- or RAM-based sample player. Installing such cards is another step in converting your Macintosh into a stand-alone music workstation. You use Apple's MIDI Manager to route data to such digital audio NuBus cards.

Chapter 11
Sound Organization

In this chapter . . .

✔ Explanations of various types of sound data.

✔ The importance of System Exclusive data for patch librarians.

✔ An overview and brief history of patch librarian software.

✔ The difference between dedicated and universal librarian software.

✔ System configuration issues for data transfer.

✔ Hierarchical levels of data organization within devices contrasted to those available with software.

✔ Dedicated and universal librarians examined in detail (commercial, shareware, and freeware).

✔ Utilities to enhance patch librarian activities and bulk dump utilities.

✔ Table of devices supported by universal librarians.

✔ Approaches to generating new patches algorithmically.

✔ Limitations of current-generation librarian software.

✔ Sound database solutions for patches, samples, and other types of audio information.

Sensible Storage for Sound Data

Musical data that is not readily retrievable is practically useless. This consideration leads one to seek out librarian software for the loading, retrieval, and organization of such ephemeral items as:

❖ Individual tone parameters
❖ Individual patches
❖ Banks of groups of patches
❖ Individual sampled soundfiles
❖ Entire sample RAM
❖ Global settings or master parameters
❖ Program maps or lists

❖ Velocity maps
❖ Pressure maps
❖ Intonation tables or micro tunings
❖ Reverberation parameters
❖ DSP effects parameters
❖ Sequences (if the device has a built-in sequencer)

Some programs provide similar features for musical phrases and, recently, for the very processes that one uses to create music (see Chapters 15 and 19). Of course, you can also use your Macintosh to organize your record or CD collection (see the section "Commercial sound organizers" in this chapter).

Most electronic instruments, with the exception of RAM-based sample players, contain sounds known as factory presets. Usually, there are between 50 and 192 such presets, with 128 being the most common number. These presets are either stored in the device's ROM chips (so that you cannot edit them directly) or in battery-backed RAM. Sometimes a device will originally include a copy of its ROM-based patches in its RAM so that you can edit them. Other manufacturers ship their instruments with a completely different set of sounds in their instrument's RAM, so if you want to create new sounds you have to erase some of the sounds the instrument came with. Finally, a few instruments have all their sounds in battery-backed RAM rather than ROM chips.

Nearly all synthesizers include some RAM where you can create and save new sounds. Room for 64 user-defined patches is typical, although instruments with "extended RAM" often provide more space. If your synthesizer is the type that came with all of its factory presets in RAM or some in RAM and some in ROM, you will probably want to save some or all of these sounds before you start creating new ones. In any case, once you have started editing sounds and saving them in your synthesizer's RAM, you will eventually run out of space to hold your creations and require some kind of off-line storage. This can happen sooner than you think. The moment a friend comes over with a cartridge or disk full of fantastic sounds, you are confronted with the storage dilemma.

In the early days of synthesis, if you made changes to a sound using a device's front panel controls, you were lucky if the manufacturer gave you any means to save your sonic creations. Often, a cassette interface was provided that allowed you to transfer the data to a standard audio cassette, an intrinsically unreliable backup method. Later, it became popular for synthesizers to provide a slot into which you could insert a RAM cartridge and transfer *en masse* your edited sounds from the device's RAM to the cartridge. Because the manufacturers were often the exclusive source of these cartridges, they could charge whatever they liked for them — and they did. Prices often ranged from $50 to $100 for a cartridge that would only hold a single bank of sounds. A single RAM cartridge for the Kurzweil 250 cost a whopping $700, and each of these cartridges only held half a bank of the Kurzweil's RAM (the instrument could be configured with up to four RAM banks, so you'd need to spend $5,600 on cartridges to save the entire contents of a K250 with the expanded RAM option).

Besides their ridiculous expense, one major problem of the RAM cartridge approach is that you often have to deal with entire banks of patches rather than individual sounds. Creating a single cartridge consisting of your favorite patches from all your other cartridges is sometimes impossible.

Patch data is system exclusive data

Fortunately, the creators of the original MIDI Specification realized that individual synthesizer manufacturers had different ways of dealing with the inner programming capabilities of their various devices. A special type of MIDI message called System Exclusive (referred to as SysEx) was included in the specification to deal with the idiosyncrasies of different devices (see Chapter 1, "Background"). SysEx messages are often used to transmit patch data and other information that you might want to store for future recall.

The first item in a SysEx message is a status byte (Hex "F0") identifying the fact that the ensuing information will be of the System Exclusive variety. The next piece of information is the manufacturer's ID number (every manufacturer has a unique SysEx ID). All the data following the manufacturer's ID is relevant only to specific devices made by that manufacturer. Devices made by other manufacturers that might receive this message (e.g., because they are daisychained on the same MIDI cable) simply ignore it.

Here is a down-to-earth description of a case where you might have four synthesizers daisychained on a single MIDI cable, either by way of the individual devices' THRU ports or possibly a MIDI THRU box. The four instruments are an E-mu Proteus/2 sample player, a Roland D-550 synthesizer module, a Korg M1R synthesizer module, and a Korg Wavestation keyboard used as a controller. When the F0 byte comes down the cable, all the devices stop what they are doing and wait to see if the following messages are for them. They don't have to wait long because the next significant piece of information is the manufacturer's ID. Korg's ID (Hex 42) comes down the cable, so the E-mu and Roland devices stop paying attention from that point on, but the two Korg devices are still wondering who the SysEx message is for. Next comes a Family Code message of Hex 19, which designates the M1 family, so the Wavestation (the Hex 28 family) stops listening. Then a Member Code message (Hex 01 in this case) is sent for the Korg M1R to be sure that the ensuing information is for it. Now comes a stream of data that only the M1R can understand, but by this point, the M1R is the only device paying any attention to the data flow anyway. Finally, an "End of Exclusive" message (Hex F7, commonly referred to as EOX) comes down the cable, and the M1R knows that its personal SysEx data transmission has ended.

SysEx data is what makes librarian software possible. It is only necessary for a computer program to understand a device's SysEx implementation, meaning the structure of the data that can be accessed and manipulated once a device has received its manufacturer's ID, Family Code, and Member Code. Most synthesizer manuals publish their unique SysEx implementation chart at the back of their manual. If you've ever looked at one of these, you'll be glad that there are programmers out there who have created interfaces to these data structures, so that we never have to deal with these numbers ourselves.

It is common for companies to employ a single librarian program shell for a wide variety of devices. The only thing that needs to change is how the shell interprets the SysEx data for each specific device. This is accomplished through relatively little pieces of program code or resources, which may be internal or external to the program shell itself. Depending upon the manufacturer, these are called drivers, configuration files, modules, resources, templates, or profiles. Sometimes they are just labeled with the name of the device that they support. This is the case with Opcode Systems librarians, which keep their profiles in a folder named "Consult Manual."

When computers and MIDI instruments began communicating it became possible to store SysEx data on floppy disks and hard drives. A $1 800K floppy disk can often hold the equivalent of 20 RAM cartridges that might have cost you $1,000. Because librarian software is usually inexpensive, it can easily pay for itself very quickly. This doesn't necessarily mean that RAM cartridges are obsolete. In live performance situations, it is easier to swap RAM cartridges than to load a bank from the Macintosh, unless you must load a large number of devices at once. Also, if your Macintosh or hard drive crashes during a performance, having your sounds available on RAM cartridge could save the show.

The evolution of librarian software

The evolution of librarian software has progressed through a number of stages. First, there were small programs that could send and retrieve the entire SysEx memory (often referred to as a "bulk dump") of a device. This type of software does not let you manipulate the individual items in the SysEx data.

Next to appear was librarian software dedicated to individual synthesizers. These programs only understand the SysEx data from a specific device or, occasionally, a group of related devices that have compatible patch formats (e.g., Yamaha DX7, TX7, and TX816). For the device whose data they understand, they often provide many ways to organize and reorganize items in your library, whether they are patches or intonation tables. In this case, you need a separate librarian for each type of synthesizer you own. Because such programs are dedicated to servicing specific devices, they are referred to as *dedicated librarians.*

Shortly after dedicated librarians became popular, people began demanding a means to edit the items in their libraries that went beyond merely rearranging them. Early on, Opcode began including a "Patch Factory" option with their librarians that could algorithmically generate new sounds based on existing sounds in your libraries. However, the real strength of the Macintosh's user interface was put to bear on patch editing software. Initially, patch editors and patch librarians were separate programs. Like librarians, the first generation of patch editors were also dedicated to individual devices and therefore referred to as dedicated patch editors (see Chapter 12, "Editing Synthesized Sound").

It didn't take long for patch editors and librarians dedicated to the same synthesizers to become integrated into a single entity. These programs are called *dedicated editor/librarians*.

As the price of electronic instruments dropped, people began to have more devices and therefore require more dedicated librarians or dedicated editor/librarians. Before MultiFinder and inexpensive Macintosh memory, working with several electronic devices required opening and closing a multitude of different programs. To solve this problem, *universal patch librarians* appeared on the scene. A universal librarian usually comes with device profiles, templates, or modules for a large number of synthesizers, MIDI controllers, signal processors, reverbs, MIDI mixers, and even MIDI patchbays. These profiles provide the information necessary for the universal librarian to communicate with all the MIDI devices they support. As hardware manufacturers release new devices, the universal librarian software developers only need to add new profiles to their software rather than write entirely new programs. Many companies maintain telecommunications bulletin board systems (BBSs) with a repository. Most universal librarians provide for generic bulk dumps to handle devices not included with the manufacturer's set of profiles (often because the software developer has deemed the missing devices as "dinosaurs"). Some companies such as Opcode and Sound Quest provide programming tools for you to create your own device profiles for gear not covered in the software's standard profile library.

As you might guess, *universal patch editor/librarians* became available. These integrate universal librarians with the editors corresponding to the devices supported by the universal librarian (see Chapter 12).

Some patch librarians include options to control a device remotely (see Figures 11-11 and 11-12). You can edit sounds using such programs, however, they are not technically editor/librarians because you are not editing the sounds with the Macintosh, you are only pushing the device's front panel buttons remotely. Programs of this type can be referred to as *remote controller/librarians* rather than editor/librarians.

Many music software manufacturers market both product-specific dedicated librarians, editors, and editor/librarians as well as universal librarians and editor/librarians. How long this will continue is questionable, because for the price of a universal editor/librarian that may support up to a hundred devices, you can only buy two or three dedicated editor/librarians. The same goes for universal librarians and dedicated librarians. Many music stores have already seen the writing on the wall. Shortly after universal editor/librarians became available I started seeing some music stores advertising blow-out sales of dedicated editors and librarians — librarians that originally listed for $50 to $100 being offered for

$5 or $10 and editors that were originally priced at well over $100 being offered for $10 to $20.

Dedicated Librarians

Dedicated librarians only function with the electronic instrument for which they have been created. In the current era of universal librarians and universal editor/librarians the main selling point of dedicated librarians is low cost. Such programs are also the obvious choice for musicians with a small number of devices. In any event, there are a vast number of Macintosh musicians who would rather leave the sound designing to companies who are in that business and therefore have little need for an editor/librarian, dedicated or universal.

One of the most powerful aspects of dedicated librarians is the option to reorganize existing banks of synthesizer objects such as patch data and global data. Moving individual items from one bank to another using RAM cartridges is often difficult. These programs also make it extremely easy to create patch maps (see below).

Patch data might include data about what waveforms are being used, the settings of the instrument's oscillators (including LFOs), filters, envelope generators, and amplifiers, keyboard mapping, layering, and splits, coarse and fine tuning, pan settings, and, if the device includes internal DSP effects, how these are being applied to the particular sound. The name of the patch is also included.

Global data can contain such information as the master transposition or tuning setting of the entire instrument, a global velocity map, the intonation table being used, channel-stealing algorithm settings (if available), individual channel characteristics (such as polyphonic limit, note range, or channel volume), the program map in use (if multiple maps are provided for), output settings (if the instrument has options for mono, stereo, or separate outputs), and global controller settings such as pitch bend range and modulation wheel assignment.

Each patch has a unique program number; these numbers can extend into the thousands, even though MIDI can only transmit 128 different patch numbers (the relatively new MIDI Bank Select message can get around this limitation for devices that support it). Program maps or program lists provide a way of reassigning the sounds in an instrument so that they all fall within the 1-to-128 or 0-to-127 range and are thus addressable by MIDI program change messages.

Most librarians let you retrieve from your synthesizer individual objects or banks of objects of the same type. Banks of patches retrieved this way may or may not include ROM-based patches. Usually a bank will hold 50, 64, 92, or 128 patches, and some instruments support multiple banks. Some librarians allow you to retrieve, in one fell swoop, files consisting of every object in the device. The latter are often referred to as "bundles," a term coined by Opcode Systems. It is so appropriate that I will use it generically within this text to refer to the files of that type. With newer Opcode librarians, bundles can contain data for more than one device.

Transferring data

The act of transferring objects such as patches to and from a MIDI device like a synthesizer is often called *uploading* (transferring the data from the synthesizer to the Macintosh) and *downloading* (sending the data from the Macintosh to the synthesizer). Note that the use of these words may appear to be exactly the opposite of what you are accustomed to with telecommunications. When you are on a telecommunications network or BBS, downloading refers to retrieving data from the host system you are connected to and uploading refers to sending data to the host. It's not really the opposite, though, because in the case of transferring data to and from a synthesizer, the Macintosh functions as the host.

To accomplish data transfers of the type required by patch librarians, you will usually need bidirectional communication between your Macintosh and the device with which you are currently working. This is also referred to as "hand-shaking" or "full duplex" communication. In other words, the device's MIDI IN and MIDI OUT ports will both need to be recognized by the Macintosh. For a detailed discussion of the various approaches to this type of bidirectional hookup see Chapter 8, "Moving Data Around Your Music Network."

Levels of organization

There are many levels of grouping objects (such as sounds) within devices. Most devices allow you to transfer individual objects. Because many types of individual objects (for example, patches) are often grouped into banks, most devices let you transfer entire banks of objects at a time. There is usually a provision to transfer the entire current state of a device including all its objects and banks. Macintosh software usually refers to this as a "bundle" or "performance." Universal librarians and editor/librarians can group multiple devices into a higher level structure called a multi-device bundle or performance. Furthermore, most Macintosh software dealing with sound organization and editing lets you agglomerate objects into libraries (see Figure 11-1), a concept that has no counterpart within the devices themselves.

Once patches have been transferred from your synthesizer to the Macintosh, many patch librarians provide features to combine many banks of patches into higher-level objects called "libraries" (Note: Some manufacturers call a bank a library). With typical capacities running in the thousands, libraries can hold many more objects than can be loaded into your synthesizer at one time.

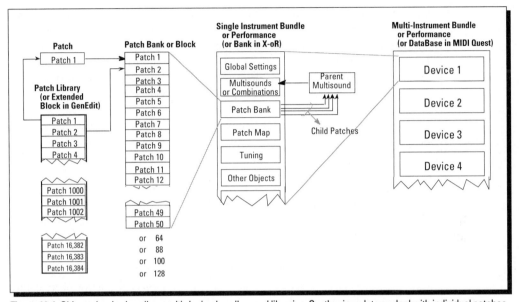

Figure 11-1: Objects, banks, bundles, multi-device bundles, and libraries. Synthesizers let you deal with individual patches or banks of patches. Macintosh software usually refers to the entire state of a device as a bundle or performance. Multi-device bundles or performances are only available with software capable of dealing with more than one device — particularly universal librarians and editor/librarians. Libraries are a level of organization provided by such Macintosh software and, having no counterpart in hardware devices, are usually not transferable *en masse* (although individual objects may be transferred between libraries and devices). Instead, libraries are used to impose a certain order on objects you retrieve from external devices.

Libraries are very useful for organizing your sounds. Many programs automatically sort all new patches added to a library. When you add a patch to a library, nearly all programs check to see if a patch of the same name exists, but some software even checks the data to see if the patch is already in the library under a different name.

Some programs allow you to open multiple libraries simultaneously, so that you could have one master library of all your patches and then organize them into *sublibraries*, each dedicated to a different type of sound — for example, flute sounds, string pads, lead synths, favorite sounds, or any other criteria you can imagine. In these cases, there is usually no limit on the size of a sublibrary either. In fact, most programs don't make a distinction — a library is a library.

Programs that only allow you to open a single library at a time can still organize your sounds by logical or timbral criteria. They simply require that you organize your sounds into banks rather than additional libraries. Because you can often copy patches from bank to bank as easily as you can from library to bank or from library to library, there is very little functional difference. The disadvantage to this approach is that the number of patches a bank can hold is determined by the synthesizer manufacturer. If you are gathering all 40 of your marimba-like sounds into a single bank for a synthesizer that restricts bank sizes to 50 patches and you suddenly acquire another 30 marimba-like sounds, you have to start a new bank. Now you have things in two places, so alphabetization is going to become a problem (unless you do it manually or label one bank *Marimba-like Sounds A thru L* and the other one *Marimba-like Sounds M thru Z*).

Moving patches from the master library or a sublibrary to a patch bank that can be loaded into your synthesizer is usually as simple as pointing to the patch name with the mouse and dragging the item into the list designating the individual patch banks. A similar click-drag interface moves patches from the master library to other libraries and also moves patches from banks into libraries. For software that does not support dragging patches from one window to another, the Macintosh's standard Cut, Copy, and Paste options perform the same job.

Because individual patch data is usually a relatively small number of bytes, many programs let you send the patch to the synthesizer the moment its name is clicked on the Macintosh screen. The transmission is essentially instantaneous and this feature allows you to quickly audition new sounds. This can be very useful for the task of organizing your master library into logical sublibraries prior to creating banks.

Commercial Librarian Software

There are at least 43 dedicated patch librarians available for the Macintosh. These cover most of the popular synthesizers and some other types of MIDI devices. Thirteen of these 43 are shareware or freeware (see the section "Shareware and freeware solutions" in this chapter). To see if there is a dedicated librarian for your synthesizers, check the tables in Chapter 6, "Software Options."

Korg M1 Librarian

Opcode Systems markets dedicated librarians for dozens of popular synthesizers and MIDI devices (see Figures 11-2 through 11-6). Their librarian interface is roughly identical, regardless of the synthesizer. The manuals for all their librarians are virtually identical, with the exception of a supplement providing information that is idiosyncratic to the particular librarian you have purchased.

Because of the user-interface consistency between their various librarians, an examination of one example, in this case, their Korg M1 Librarian, will suffice to illustrate the workings of all the others. This is truly a case of "if you've seen one, you've seen them all." However, this axiom does not hold for Opcode's editor/librarians.

Figure 11-2: When you choose Open from an Opcode Librarian File menu you are presented with a list of all the file types recognized by the librarian. Clicking any file type "filters" the display so that only files of that type are visible. In this illustration, only Programs are showing. This includes both banks and libraries of programs.

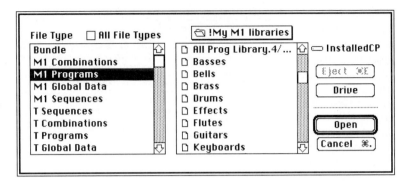

Figure 11-3: The main screen of Opcode's M1 Librarian with all the components to a typical M1 Bundle open. The actual Bundle file is at the upper right. Double-clicking any object in the Bundle's window brings up the window for that object. The large Programs window and the three behind it are all banks. The MouseKeys keyboard at the bottom of the screen lets you audition sounds, record little sequences, and set MIDI channels and ports — all without an external MIDI keyboard.

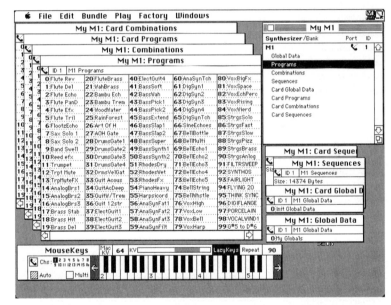

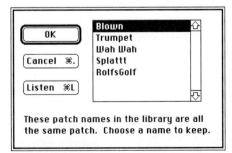

Figure 11-4: Opcode Librarians have an option to delete duplicate patches. The program determines if the patch data is the same, even if the name is different. This dialog box asks you to decide what to do in these cases.

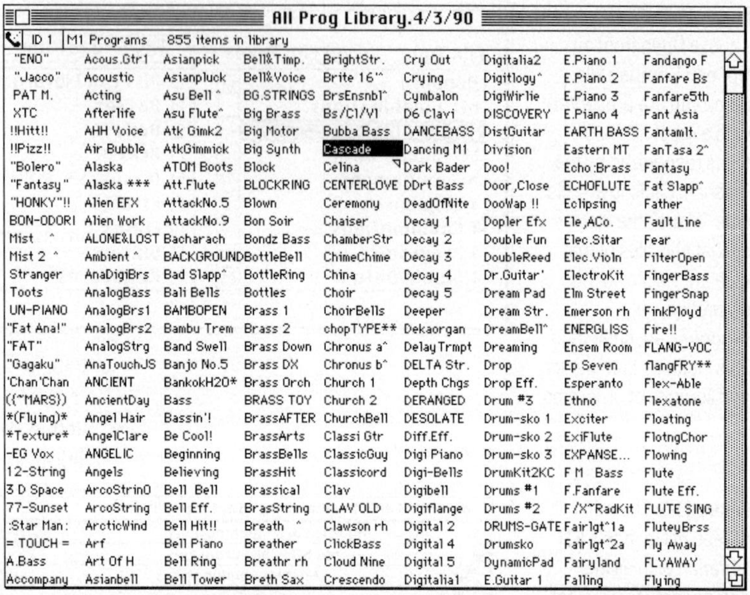

Figure 11-5: An Opcode M1 Librarian Program library file. This M1 program library has 855 patches in it. Notice that they are automatically sorted. The little triangle by the patch named "Celina" (directly under the highlighted patch) indicates that there are comments associated with that sound. These comments can be viewed by way of the Get Info menu item. Unfortunately, there is no searching capabilities, so if you wanted to categorize sounds using the comment option, you have no easy way of locating your categories.

Figure 11-6: Because the Opcode Librarians let you open many files at once, it is easy to categorize your sounds into separate libraries. In this illustration, the master library is at the top of the screen and sublibraries, each representing a different instrument or timbre, are arranged across the bottom of the screen. When you select a patch from the master library, it is automatically loaded for auditioning. The patches can be dragged to their appropriate storage location by holding the option key down while clicking a patch name.

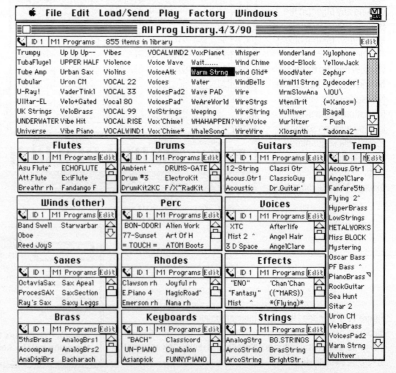

A

▣▤ ▤ Harmonic & STRAWBERRY (shade) ▤▤

🔍 ID 1	M1 Programs	50 items in library			
01Harmonic	11Harmonic	21HarmonER	31HarmWBER	41HaRAWBER	⬆
02Harmonic	12Harmonic	22HarmonER	32HarmWBER	42HaRAWBER	
03Harmonic	13HarmoniR	23HarmonER	33HarmWBER	43HaRAWBER	
04Harmonic	14HarmoniR	24HarmoBER	34HarmWBER	44HaRAWBER	
05Harmonic	15HarmoniR	25HarmoBER	35HarAWBER	45HaRAWBER	
06Harmonic	16HarmoniR	26HarmoBER	36HarAWBER	46HTRAWBER	
07Harmonic	17HarmoniR	27HarmoBER	37HarAWBER	47HTRAWBER	
08Harmonic	18HarmonER	28HarmoBER	38HarAWBER	48HTRAWBER	⬇
09Harmonic	19HarmonER	29HarmWBER	39HarAWBER	49HTRAWBER	
10Harmonic	20HarmonER	30HarmWBER	40HaRAWBER	50HTRAWBER	

B

▣▤ ▤ Harmonic & STRAWBERRY (consRdm) ▤▤

🔍 ID 1	M1 Programs	50 items in library			
EBRiARa	aTiESisEWs	imsomaASno	rcRSTSYs T	SmmSaEYBsT	⬆
manSRmr r	AYioRRiRSW	iTSERRRHro	RRmmosonsR	SnoEanSSar	
nRYRTaARR	BRHBYRRRo	mTSorRcRRn	RrR RAEmRS	sRRERREWar	
sBaBSTrmr	BRRTrWWnEa	n TaSRoRnY	rRTWscBHEc	TAmABsscRa	
aBSnRARSHa	EarioTrArs	nAmiBrc AT	RTBcWHYHRs	TBcWRYnnBr	
aciRBcRRSn	EmmRSE oRs	nSBcRHmmBn	RTmcAaTS a	WnWTBm aS	
aHABTRAm s	EYRRrBroEs	ocRBRSnRWR	RY rRacEBY	Y HrEB SsR	
AinmTnnHWW	EYSAHcRRHn	oHWrccTocT	RYRYRBYiiS	YBYmnaSHaA	
AmYiisrW A	HAHRiiEso	omSTiYAoTc	SaiYcTERs	YmmWEmmrRY	⬇
ATEAoWsSrs	iAYRaWiRRA	R RiTRABiT	SERanSWaEn	YoBRracHRW	

Figure 11-7: The names of patches algorithmically generated by Opcode's Patch Factory option reflect the process used to create them. In this illustration, the source patches chosen from the inspiration library were called *Harmonic* and *STRAWBERRY*. **(A)** Shading assigns names to the generated patches that gradually transform from the word *Harmonic* to the word *STRAWBERRY*, just as the sounds themselves do. **(B)** Constrained Random assigns names to the generated patches that simply pull characters at random from the names of the source patches.

Although Opcode's dedicated librarians are primarily concerned with organizing your sounds, as an added bonus they provide a Patch Factory feature with three options for generating new patches algorithmically: Shuffler, Shades, and Constrained Random (see Figure 11-7). All of these options require an "inspiration" bank or library file that you have already created or acquired.

The Shuffler takes an "inspiration" bank or library of patches and generates a new collection of sounds where each byte of each generated patch is selected randomly from the same location as one in the inspiration bank's patches. For example, suppose your inspiration bank is called "InsBank." The Shuffler generates a bank in which one of the patches is called "GenPatch." The first byte of GenPatch will be the same as the first byte of one of the patches in InsBank. The second byte in GenPatch will be identical to the second byte of another patch in InsBank, and so on.

The Shades option requires that you first select two individual patches in your inspiration bank or library. These are the start and end points of your shading. The Shades option produces a gradual transformation from one of these patches to the other, with as many steps in between as you desire. It is very easy to hear the smooth change from the start and end patches you chose from your inspiration bank or library.

Constrained Random also requires you to select two patches from your inspiration bank or library. However, instead of generating a smooth transition from the first patch to the second over the entire bank, it uses the parameter values of the inspiration patches as the upper and lower limits for randomly selected parameter values in the generated patches. This gives you more control than you might at first imagine. For example, suppose you only want to randomly vary certain parameters of a sound, but not others. If you want to leave the envelopes of the patches untouched, all you have to do is make sure that the envelopes of the two inspiration patches are identical. Because the Constrained Random option uses the two envelope settings as the upper and lower limits for random selection, and in this case — they are identical — no changes will be made to the envelope.

Because Opcode's librarian shell is identical for all synthesizers, if you own more than one of the company's librarians you can combine them into a single program. You can install version 4 librarian profiles into version 5 librarians but not vice versa (exceptions are the Yamaha TX816 and Yamaha DX7/TX librarians, which require version parity). The program will alert you if you attempt to make an improper installation. By installing several librarian profiles into a single program, in essence you have created a "multi-librarian" capable of dealing with several devices without switching programs. It's not a "universal librarian" (see the section "Universal Librarians" in this chapter), but it's getting close.

Opcode PatchLib desk accessory

If you own one or more of Opcode's librarians you can access your patch banks and libraries by way of Opcode's desk accessory (see Figure 11-8). You can install your librarian profiles into the desk accessory. If you have multiple librarians installed in your main librarian shell, then this desk accessory can function as a multi-librarian too. The desk accessory can open multiple files and copy between files. With some other MIDI programs such as sequencers, especially those from Opcode, you can even transfer patches while a sequence is playing. Some features found in Opcode's librarian programs are not available in the desk accessory. For example, you cannot create new files nor can you retrieve data from a device, you can only transmit data to a device.

Figure 11-8: Opcode's PatchLib desk accessory can access any patch banks or libraries created by dedicated Opcode librarians that you own. Notice that there is now an option to create a new file and that the Get Program and Get Bank menu options are disabled. These are not disabled temporarily — they're simply not available from the desk accessory.

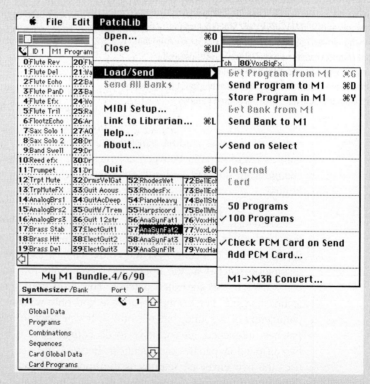

Software Gallery

Korg M1 Librarian

M1 Lib 1.0
FILES
XFR
Cmbi
Prog
Seq
RCV
M
ly M1 Bundle.4/6/9
8
FILES
SineEchoes
FlootzEcho
AnalogBrs3
BassSlap1
AnaSynFat1
WahBrass
Bambu Ech
Flute Rev
DynaFusion
8
M1 Librarian
Midi Map
1
1 2 3 4 5 6 7 8 →
OFF
Apples Midi Manager
SYS

Figure 11-9: Zero-One's patch librarians in desk accessory (DA) format. This particular illustration is of their M1 Librarian. An M1 combination bank is open. Limited editing is available for combinations. An M1 combination consists of up to eight individual programs. The individual programs making up this particular combination called "DynaFusion" are listed above its name. The little arrows on either side of the names of the sounds making up the combination allow you to scroll through your available patches and thereby alter the combination itself. Because combinations may be set to respond to their constituent patches on separate channels, the lower window provides controls to set the channels assigned to each patch making up the combination. Zero-One patch librarian DAs work particularly well while MIDI sequencers are running. With System 6.x you may have to hold the option key down while opening the DA to force it to open "within" your active application rather than in DA Handler. Zero-One also markets a D-50 librarian in a DA with a similar interface.

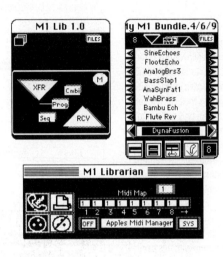

Kurzweil 1000/1200 Series Object Mover

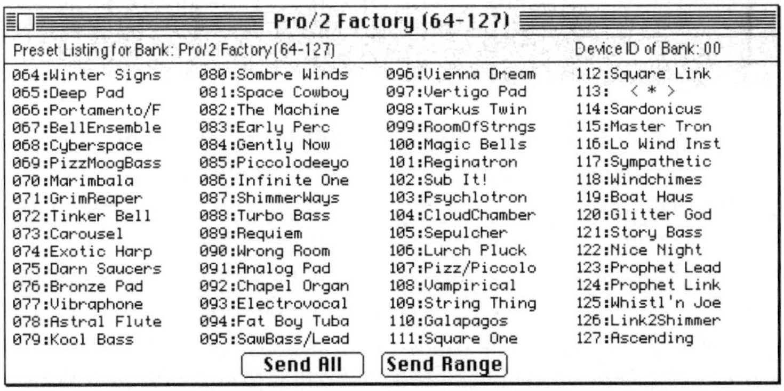

Pro/2 Factory (64-127)
Preset Listing for Bank: Pro/2 Factory (64-127)
Device ID of Bank: 00
064:Winter Signs 080:Sombre Winds 096:Vienna Dream 112:Square Link
065:Deep Pad 081:Space Cowboy 097:Vertigo Pad 113: < * >
066:Portamento/F 082:The Machine 098:Tarkus Twin 114:Sardonicus
067:BellEnsemble 083:Early Perc 099:RoomOfStrngs 115:Master Tron
068:Cyberspace 084:Gently Now 100:Magic Bells 116:Lo Wind Inst
069:PizzMoogBass 085:Piccolodeeyo 101:Reginatron 117:Sympathetic
070:Marimbala 086:Infinite One 102:Sub It! 118:Windchimes
071:GrimReaper 087:ShimmerWays 103:Psychlotron 119:Boat Haus
072:Tinker Bell 088:Turbo Bass 104:CloudChamber 120:Glitter God
073:Carousel 089:Requiem 105:Sepulcher 121:Story Bass
074:Exotic Harp 090:Wrong Room 106:Lurch Pluck 122:Nice Night
075:Darn Saucers 091:Analog Pad 107:Pizz/Piccolo 123:Prophet Lead
076:Bronze Pad 092:Chapel Organ 108:Vampirical 124:Prophet Link
077:Vibraphone 093:Electrovocal 109:String Thing 125:Whistl'n Joe
078:Astral Flute 094:Fat Boy Tuba 110:Galapagos 126:Link2Shimmer
079:Kool Bass 095:SawBass/Lead 111:Square One 127:Ascending
Send All
Send Range

Figure 11-10: Cliffhanger Productions's PROfiler is a librarian for E-mu's Proteus series of sample players (all versions supported). You can send and retrieve entire banks and also send individual patches or ranges of patches. You can send ranges of patches to new locations, but you cannot copy patches from bank to bank.

PROfiler Proteus Storage Librarian

Figure 11-11: Kurzweil's
Object Mover is a remote
controller/librarian that
borrows its interface from
Apple's Font/DA Mover.
You can only open two
banks at once and copy or
remove objects from one
to another. The Remote
button calls up a remote
virtual front panel that you
can manipulate exactly
like you would the real
thing. You can edit sounds
remotely with this front
panel, although you do not
save any steps in doing
so. That is to say that you
have to press the mouse
button or Macintosh
keyboard keys the same
number of times you
would have to physically
press the front panel
buttons.

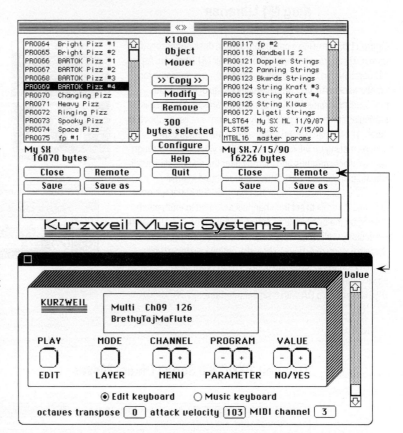

E-mu Emulator Three Remote Controller/Librarian

E-mu Systems's Emulator Three Remote Controller/Librarian is different from the
librarians examined so far in that it deals with sampled soundfiles rather than
synthesizer patches (see Figure 11-12). Like those of most samplers, the files of
the Emulator III are so large that options to instantaneously audition files in
libraries are not possible, although soundfiles can be transferred from the Macintosh to the E-III rather quickly by way of the SCSI connection between the two
devices. Note: Alchemy's Open Special… dialog box provides a Listen option
with which you can audition E-III files (see Chapter 13, "Editing Sampled
Sound").

Unlike the Kurzweil 1000 remote controller described in Figure 11-11, this software saves steps when you control the E-III remotely from the Macintosh. For
example, although all the buttons on the screen operate exactly like their hardware counterparts, there are many menus that allow you to jump directly to a
function without multiple navigation actions.

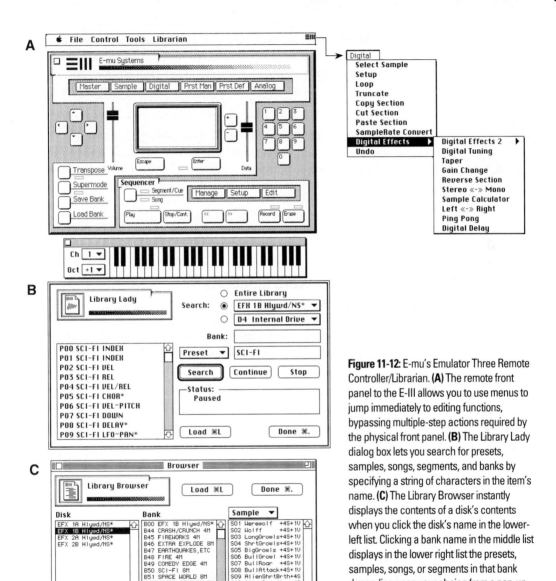

Figure 11-12: E-mu's Emulator Three Remote Controller/Librarian. **(A)** The remote front panel to the E-III allows you to use menus to jump immediately to editing functions, bypassing multiple-step actions required by the physical front panel. **(B)** The Library Lady dialog box lets you search for presets, samples, songs, segments, and banks by specifying a string of characters in the item's name. **(C)** The Library Browser instantly displays the contents of a disk's contents when you click the disk's name in the lower-left list. Clicking a bank name in the middle list displays in the lower right list the presets, samples, songs, or segments in that bank depending upon your choice from a pop-up menu directly over the lower-right window. Objects can be loaded into the E-III directly from this screen.

The remote controller also has a macro-recording mode that allows you to go through time-consuming actions purely for the purpose of recording a macro. Such time-intensive calculations include many DSP functions such as normalization, compression, and EQ. In this mode the E-III does not respond to your remote commands, although whatever macro utility you are using will accurately record the steps. There are no built-in macro features in the software so you have to use a third-party utility such as QuickKeys, Tempo, AutoMac, or MacroMaker. You can use looping macros to process many files unattended, for example, to compress a large number of soundfiles.

Several features of this librarian are missing in most other librarians. For example, it provides searching and printing capabilities within its sound database. Searches are limited to finding strings within filenames. Cataloging of soundfiles is automatic, although it can take three to ten minutes per disk. Because the catalog of sounds and their pertinent information is stored as a separate file on your hard drive, searches are extremely fast. This also permits the location of sounds residing on off-line media such as CD-ROMs, cartridges, and other removable media.

Shareware and freeware solutions
Yamaha SY-77 Librarian

David Foster's shareware ($5) SY-77 Librarian offers many of the functions you expect in a commercial librarian. You can open multiple banks and cut, copy, and paste between banks. When you select a patch the software does not send the patch data, but instead sends a program change message that corresponds to the bank location clicked on. This means you must be sure that the active window contains the sounds currently loaded in your SY-77. You use menu commands to send the actual patch or bank data rather than clicking a patch name.

S-10 Librarian

Gary Becker's shareware ($35) S-10 Librarian is a utility for transferring samples to and from the Roland S-10. Although the author calls it a librarian, it has no other librarian functions per se.

CZ Lib

MIDIBasic was the development system for Mike Cohen's shareware CZ Lib (librarian for Casio's CZ101, CZ1000, and CZ5000).

Yamaha DX/TX Librarian

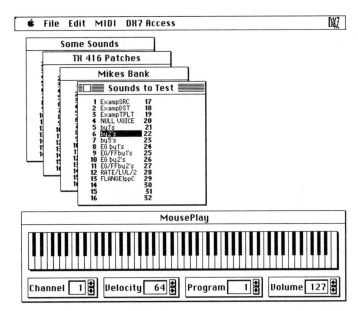

Figure 11-13: James Chandler's DX7 Librarian is compatible with most Yamaha DX and TX series instruments. Up to ten banks may be opened simultaneously and you can copy and paste between banks. Transfer is done by bank rather than individual patch. The file format is compatible with early Opcode (pre-version 4) editors and librarians. A Bulk SysEx menu option can transfer MidiEx-compatible SysEx dumps of up to 128K. The software provides a seven-octave on-screen keyboard.

Kawai K-1 Librarian and Kawai K-4 Librarian

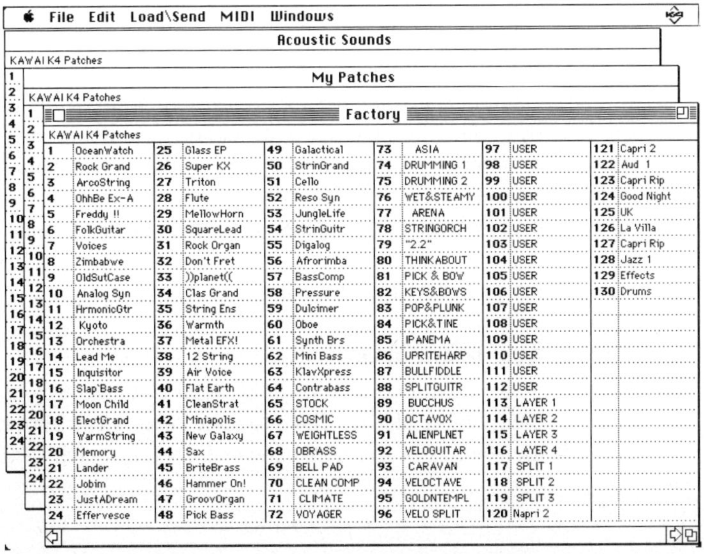

Figure 11-14: PostModern Production's Kawai K-1 and K-4 Librarians have nearly identical interfaces. Note the similarity with the interfaces of commercial librarians such as those by Opcode Systems. There are only so many ways to represent a bank of patches. PostModern provides for multiple banks to be open at once and copying and pasting between them.

Korg M1 Librarian

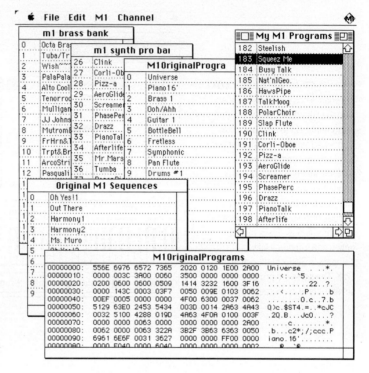

Figure 11-15: Curt Bianchi's M1 Librarian is a very serviceable shareware ($15) offering for M1 programs, combinations, and sequences. The software supports Cut, Copy, and Paste between multiple banks and libraries for both programs and combinations. The window at the bottom lets you examine the Hex data for any patch or combination.

Other utilities

Many types of utilities besides patch editors can work in conjunction with a patch librarian. Occasionally utilities are required to convert from one file format to another even with programs of the same manufacturer. Although this doesn't happen often, Opcode's M1 File Converter was required to convert files from their old M1 librarian format to their newer format. Opcode also provides a utility to update older librarians so that they can be used by the Opcode PatchLib DA described above. Several examples of stand-alone programs follow.

Kurz 1000 OM List

Kevin Rosenberg's Kurz 1000 OM List utility will open files created by Kurzweil's own Object Mover. The program creates text reports (see Figure 11-16), detailing the settings of every parameter for every patch in the file.

```
Program #65 analg brass48mod
OutputProg 0, StealingOption 0, PolyLimit 0
        Layer 1
        KeyMap 58, LoKey 12, HiKey 120, Transp 0, Detune 1, Delay 0, Volume 253
        Stereo 0, CompEFX #0, CompEFXlink 0, Enable 127
        AltStart 127, DynamRng 60, kbTilt 0, Balance 0
        SoftPedalRng 6, PitchWhlRng 4, compEFX 0
        V1 Trig Off, level = 0. V2 Trig Off, level = 0
        Ignore Release      Off     Ignore Sustenuto      Off      Ignore Sustain      Off
                Ignore Suspend      Off
        P-Wheel Disable      Off     P-Wheel Key Only      Off      Volume Disable      Off
                Touch Disable      Off                   Balance Sense      Off


                ENV 1: #Attacks 3, #Releases 1
                        Attack 1: Level 100, Time 1
                        Attack 2: Level 80, Time 125
                        Attack 3: Level 0, Time 0
                        Release 1: Level 0, Time 23
                EFX 2: 00 12 6f 7e bb a6 00 00 00 00 00 00 00 00
                ENV 2: #Attacks 3, #Releases 1
                        Attack 1: Level 100, Time 0
                        Attack 2: Level 0, Time 16
                        Attack 3: Level 0, Time 0
                        Release 1: Level 0, Time 150
```

Figure 11-16: A text report created by the Kurz 1000 OM List utility.

Roland U-110 Patch Report

Robert E. Otto's Roland U-110 Patch Report was also developed using MIDIBasic. The software provides a similar parameter report as Kevin Rosenberg's Kurz 1000 OM List described above. Note the difference in parameter complexity of a single patch between the Kurz 1000 (see Figure 11-16) and the U-110 (see Figure 11-17).

```
Patch #60          Multi-Set1                  1        2        3        4        5        6
Output Mode #50    M8                          M8       7        8        4        4
Chorus Rate and Depth         1         1      Tremolo Rate and Depth    0        0


                   BASIC      |        LEVEL   |       PITCH    |        LFO
Pa  Cd  Tn  Name   Ou In Pc Mp Lo  Hi  Prt Vl  Ea Er Ps Cr Fn Bn Dd Ps  Rt Ad Dt Rt Md Mr Cs Ps
1   0   99  DRUM   3  10 1  1  0   127 127 15  0  0  0  0  0  2  0  0   50 0  0  0  5  2  0  0
2   0   51  AB VM  4  2  0  1  0   127 127 15  0  7  0  0  0  2  0  2   50 0  0  0  5  2  0  0
3   0   2   AP2VM  1  1  0  1  0   127 127 15  0  0  0  0  0  2  3  0   50 0  0  0  3  2  0  0
4   0   24  AG SN  1  3  0  1  0   127 127 15  0  0  0  0  0  2  3  0   50 0  0  0  5  2  0  0
5   0   79  T& SN  5  4  0  1  0   127 127 15  0  0  0  0  0  2  3  0   50 0  0  0  5  2  0  0
6   0   85  SX SN  6  5  0  1  0   127 127 15  0  0  0  0  0  2  3  0   50 0  0  0  3  2  0  0
```

Figure 11-17: Roland U-110 Patch Report.

DX/TX Patch Converter

Bob Lafleur's DX/TX Patch Converter is a freeware program that converts from the extinct MusicWorks Inc.'s DX/TX Patch Editor to Opcode's pre-version 4 file format.

DX-Unique

Robert Lichtman's DX-Unique is a utility program to use in conjunction with Opcode's Yamaha DX7 patch librarians and editors. It scans existing libraries and banks of patches and creates a new library in which no two patches have the same name, nor do two names have the same patch. If the software encounters patches with the same name and different data, you are prompted for a new name. Likewise, if the program discovers patches with the same data but different names, you are asked to choose one name to keep.

DX-Wit

Doug Wyatt's shareware DX-Wit is like a stand-alone version of the Constrained Random option in the Patch Factory feature found in most of Opcode's librarians (see the section "Commercial Librarian Software" in this chapter). This is not surprising, as Doug was one of the developers of the Opcode librarians. Although DX-Wit may not work with Opcode's new file format, it does have one option not currently found in Patch Factory. The software includes a randomization setting that lets you specify a percentage chance of using a random operator to select a parameter value rather than taking the operator from one of the inspiration patches. You will recall that the Constrained Random feature to Opcode's Patch Factory requires an "inspiration" bank from which to randomly select parameter values.

DX-Patch Sorter

Doug Wyatt's freeware DX-Patch Sorter opens "old format" Opcode DX7, TX, and TX816 banks and libraries and creates a new sorted library. The program first chooses a patch at random and then finds the patch with the fewest different parameters, continuing to do so until the patches are sorted in order of similarity. This type of sorting is useful in detecting patches that are only different in insignificant respects.

DX_PIG

John Duesenberry's DX_PIG generates a specified number of Opcode format patches that are all variations of a single source patch. PIG is an acronym for patch incremental generator. The reason for the name is that the software generates new patches by incrementing and decrementing parameter values from the source patch, just as you might by pressing the front panel buttons of the DX7. To operate DX_PIG you specify a source patch and destination patch that tell the software the boundaries or limits of its incrementing and decrementing. The program creates a specified number of patches that gradually transform from the source patch to the destination patch. What makes this different from the Opcode Patch Factory's Shades option is that you can also specify a "template" or "increment list" patch if you want. The values of each non-zero parameter in this template are taken as the step values that will be added or subtracted to source patch parameter values as it moves toward the destination patch. If you only want to change a single operator you can set all the parameter values of the template patch to zero, except those for the operator you want to increment or decrement. DX_PIG provides an option that lets you display and edit the values used in the source, destination, and template patches.

Universal Librarians

You can think of a *universal librarian* as a combination of multiple librarians in a single program. Some dedicated librarians such as those marketed by Opcode Systems allow you to install multiple profiles into one program shell, but once you have done this with three or four dedicated librarians, it would have been more cost effective to simply have purchased a universal librarian.

With the growing number of universal editor/librarians (see Chapter 12, "Editing Synthesized Sound") and their ever dropping price, if you have more than two or three synthesizers you might want to consider simply purchasing a universal editor/librarian rather than a universal librarian. As long as you don't choose the Edit option, your universal editor/librarian will function exactly as a universal patch librarian. Even if you aren't planning on doing any sound design at this time, you might get the urge in the future, and with an editor/librarian you'll be ready. Of course, once a manufacturer adds editing features to its librarian, the price rises significantly. Universal librarians are always going to be much less expensive than universal editor/librarians, so if you're on a tight budget, take this into consideration.

Commercial software

Excluding shareware options (see the section "Shareware and freeware solutions" in this chapter), there are only two major players in the commercial universal librarian market for Macintoshes: Opcode Systems's Galaxy and Pixel Publishing's Super Librarian. Most software developers are now concentrating their efforts on universal editor/librarians, so it's doubtful whether there will be any future universal librarians to compete with these two products.

Setup stage

Both Galaxy and Super Librarian require a setup stage for telling the software what devices you will be working with. Most popular synthesizers are supported. For a complete list of devices compatible with each program, see Table 11-1 that follows this section. Both programs allow you to specify a list of device types to be installed (see Figure 11-18). The main difference is that

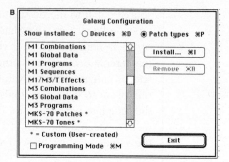

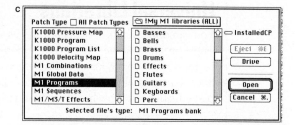

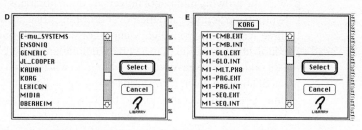

Figure 11-18: (A) In Galaxy this dialog box gives you the choice of installing devices consisting of all their associate patch types or just individual patch types from specific devices. **(B)** Choosing Patch Types displays this list for the selected device. **(C)** Once you have installed device modules into Galaxy, they appear in the Open... dialog box. Here you can view all supported objects or use the scrolling list as a "filter" (clicking an object name filters the right hand list so that only objects of that type are displayed as is the case in this illustration). **(D)** In Super Librarian's device installation dialog box, double-clicking a device name (or pressing the Select button) brings up a list of its available data type Profiles — see E below. **(E)** Super Librarian's list of Profiles available for the Korg M1. These are equivalent to patch types in Opcode's terminology — see B above.

Galaxy can be configured with an unlimited number of devices available when you launch the software, and Super Librarian imposes another level of organization above what is available when you launch the program. Super Librarian requires that you install devices into Setups, each of which can consist of up to 16 objects. These objects each represent individual types of data, for example, patch data, tuning data, or global data. You can have multiple setup files open simultaneously.

Network considerations

After you have installed all the required modules or profiles into your software, you must inform the program what Macintosh serial port each device is connected to and what MIDI channel each is listening to (see Figure 11-19).

Figure 11-19: (A) Setting the Macintosh serial port and MIDI channel in a Galaxy bundle window. The port name is a toggle button and the channel number is a "numerical." A numerical is an interface item that lets you change numerical values in a field by holding the mouse down on the field and dragging upwards to increment the values (dragging downwards decrements the values). Note that changes you make here are updated

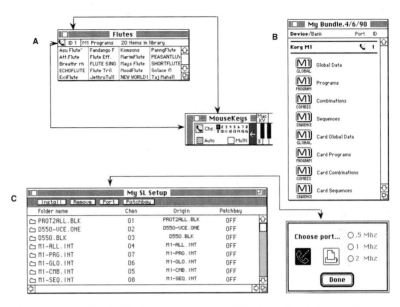

on the MouseKeys on-screen keyboard. **(B)** Setting the Macintosh serial port and MIDI channel in a Galaxy bundle window. Note, changes here do not update MouseKeys. **(C)** Setting the Macintosh serial port and MIDI channel in a Super Librarian setup window.

If you are using a MIDI patchbay that responds to program change messages, you may want to inform your software whether or not to send a program change message to your MIDI patchbay when you initiate a data transfer (to call up the configuration that permits bidirectional communication with the device. See Figure 11-20). A complete discussion of MIDI patchbays and their use in conjunction with librarian and editor/librarian software is found in Chapter 8, "Moving Data Around Your Music Network."

Banks and setups

In Galaxy, a bank is a collection of data of a similar type (see Figure 11-21). A good example is a patch bank. Super Librarian also uses the term bank to refer to such a collection of objects. However, with respect to data types that you might find within a bank, Super Librarian and Galaxy differ significantly. Galaxy uses the same terms to refer to synthesizer data types as the manufacturers themselves do. Super Librarian, as a remnant from its original IBM incarnation, uses two- and three-letter profile name extensions to identify data type.

Bundles and performances

A bundle in Galaxy is a set of banks that may all be from the same instrument or from different instruments. Super Librarian refers to this as a performance. Using a bundle of banks in Galaxy or a Super Librarian performance, you can

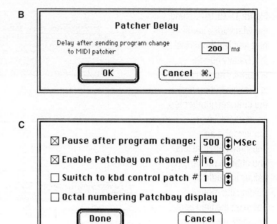

Figure 11-20: Because the transferral of SysEx information usually requires bidirectional communication between the Macintosh and the MIDI device, librarian software provides for automatically switching your MIDI Patchbay to the configuration required for the active device. **(A)** In Galaxy you set the MIDI patchbay program change numbers in the System Configuration dialog box. **(B)** Galaxy provides this dialog box to specify a pause after sending a program change to the patchbay to allow time for the patchbay to configure itself. **(C)** In Super Librarian you set the MIDI patchbay program change numbers right in the Setup window. Super Librarian's Patchbay Pause dialog box lets you specify a "Keyboard Control" patch to switch back to after transferring data to and from your devices, so that you can immediately begin playing the newly loaded sounds.

send and receive all specified data to and from your devices by issuing a single command (see Figure 11-22).

Reorganizing sounds

Both Galaxy and Super Librarian allow you to cut, copy, and paste data freely between compatible banks using the Edit menu or its keyboard shortcuts. Both also allow you to reorganize patches in a bank by dragging their names with the mouse, and support discontiguous patch selection.

Galaxy goes one step further. If you hold the option key down while clicking a patch name, you can drag it into another bank or library window. If there are additional objects associated with the patch (such as "child" patches to a "parent" multisound) and you are dragging the item to a bundle window, all the necessary objects are copied too (see below).

Auditioning sounds

Galaxy and Super Librarian have different approaches to auditioning sounds. Both provide for the playing of a sequence (see below) as well as a MIDI THRU option that lets you test newly loaded sounds with your MIDI controller.

A
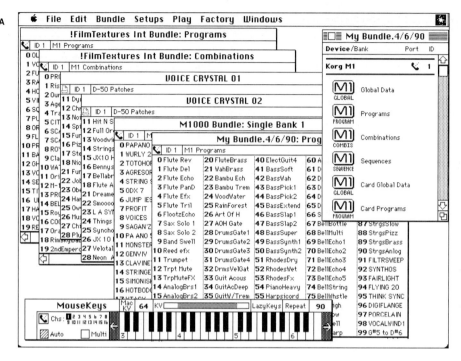

B
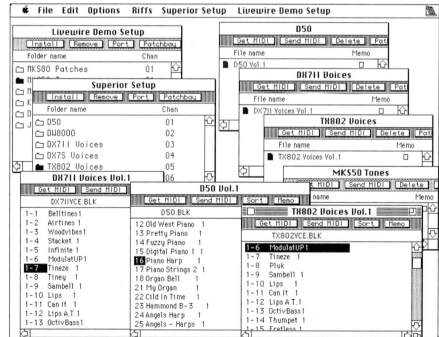

Figure 11-21: (A) The main screen of Galaxy with a number of banks open. **(B)** The main screen of Super Librarian with a number of banks open.

A
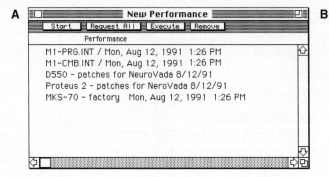

B
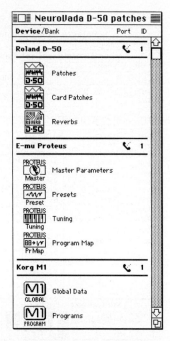

Figure 11-22: (A) A multiple-device "performance" in Super Librarian.
(B) A multiple-device "bundle" in Galaxy. Bundles and performances are
functionally equivalent.

Galaxy includes an on-screen MIDI keyboard called MouseKeys, which you
can play with the mouse to audition the current patch. There are also two
other menu options that help you audition sounds. Send on Select sends the
patch data to your synthesizer the moment you click a patch name in a bank
or library, making it the currently active patch for immediate audition. Play on
Select first sends the patch data and then plays the current MIDI sequence (see
below) whenever you click on the name of a patch in a bank or library
window.

Super Librarian's approach is to send the patch *number* (as a program change
message) to your synthesizer when you click a patch name. This difference
between Super Librarian and Galaxy is important. Because Super Librarian does
not send the actual patch data, only the patch number, you must always be sure
that the bank loaded into your device is identical to the currently active bank
on the Macintosh screen.

Sequences and riffs

Galaxy lets you record a MIDI sequence by way of your MIDI controller or the
on-screen MouseKeys keyboard that you can then play to audition sounds. The
sequence can be looped, so you can try different sounds by simply clicking
their names (with Send on Select and Loop enabled). You can even import a
MIDI sequence in SMF format for this purpose.

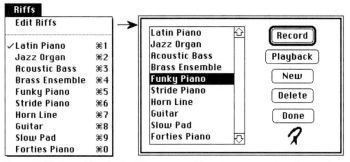

Figure 11-23: Super Librarian's Riffs menu provides 10 sequences in various styles for testing sounds. You can substitute your own music by way of the Edit Riffs menu item.

Super Librarian's implementation of this feature is more extensive. The software comes with 10 pre-recorded sequences in a number of styles that you start to play back when you select them from the Riffs menu (see Figure 11-23). You can replace these sequences with your own recordings if you like.

Programming modules and profiles

Both Galaxy and Super Librarian offer built-in programming utilities to create your own device modules (Galaxy) or profiles (Super Librarian). Opcode calls its programming language PatchTalk and Pixel calls it MOS (MIDI Operating System). You can use these features to create profiles for any devices that aren't currently supported by Galaxy or Super Librarian. These could include devices so old or rare that Opcode or Pixel are unlikely to offer modules or profiles for them, as well as devices that are too new to be supported by the software. In the latter case, Opcode or Pixel will probably eventually write a module or profile to support the device. Finally, you can write modules or profiles to support custom-designed or one-of-a-kind MIDI devices.

PatchTalk and MOS are partially menu- and dialog-box-driven, so programming is a little easier than if you were starting from scratch with a text editor. It will help to be familiar with hexadecimal numbers, the MIDI Specification, and the system exclusive section of the manual for the device you want to write a module or profile for. Some knowledge of programming is also helpful (a working knowledge of HyperTalk, HyperCard's built-in scripting language, will probably suffice for PatchTalk, because the two languages are similar).

Be forewarned that both PatchTalk and MOS will require some effort and experimentation on your part.

Unique features

Galaxy and Super Librarian each have some unique features that may make one program or the other more suitable for your particular applications. First and foremost, you should consider the devices supported by the librarian. Consult Table 11-1 at the end of this section. Other unique features follow.

Galaxy

Some of Galaxy's unique features have been mentioned above. These include MouseKeys and the ability to import MIDI sequences in SMF format as well as compatibility with libraries and other files from other Opcode software, Patch Factory, Delete Duplicates option, and the No Duplicate Patches in Libraries option. These were discussed above in the section about Opcode's dedicated Korg M1 Librarian. Two other special features bear mentioning.

Galaxy handles *parent* and *child* paths particularly well. A Parent patch is a sound made up of additional patches or data types that reside in another type of library or RAM object. The components making up the Parent patch are its Child patches. For example, M1 combinations are Parents and the programs that make them up are their Child patches. Because combinations and programs are different data types, Galaxy automatically attaches the relevant Child patch (or other associated data) to the Parent when you copy a Parent object from one bundle to another. If you copy a Parent object to anything but a bundle, the little triangle appears at the upper right of the Parent's name, indicating that Child objects *were* associated with the parent, but does not bring the necessary data into the new bank. Choosing Patch Info from the File menu will provide you with enough information to locate the missing pieces.

Galaxy can be linked to Opcode's MIDI sequencers Vision and StudioVision (see Chapters 17 and 18). This allows you to refer to patches by name from a pop-up menu in the sequencer environment rather than by program number. You can use these names in Vision or StudioVision wherever program numbers can be entered. This includes all List and Graphic windows, the Control Bar, and the Metronome Sound dialog box. You can even assign names to individual notes for drum machines. Vision and StudioVision can also automatically generate their "Instrument Lists" (corresponding to MIDI channel assignments in the MIDI Instruments window) from the information you provide by linking them to Galaxy.

Linking Galaxy patch names is a two-step process. First you must "publish" the bundle that contains the patch names you want to make available to Vision or StudioVision. To do this you simply select the bundle window and choose Publish Names from the Edit menu. (Note: You can only publish names from bundles, so if you have a stand-alone library or bank, put it into a bundle file before publishing it.)

Next, you must "subscribe" to the publication. In Vision or StudioVision choose Program and Note Names from the Setups menu. In the ensuing dialog box, select the channels that correspond to the devices in the bundle you want to subscribe to. Finally, choose Subscribe from the Names menu or by way of the Modify button. After you have subscribed to all the necessary bundles, they will appear in a pop-up menu accessible by clicking the little triangle in the Device/Name List column of the Program and Note Name dialog box.

Now whenever you change a name of a patch in Galaxy and save the bundle, the patch name is automatically updated in Vision or StudioVision. You might simply rename a patch in Galaxy or the patch location might have acquired a new name because you pasted a more appropriate sound into the same location.

Rather than setting up a dynamic link between Galaxy and Vision or StudioVision, you also have the option to simply copy the patch names over to the sequencer. In this case, changes you make to the Galaxy bundle are not reflected in Vision or StudioVision.

Note that Opcode's Publish and Subscribe option is proprietary. It is not the same as System 7's Publish and Subscribe feature. The features mentioned in the previous paragraphs were "broken" in some early versions of Galaxy and Vision. If Publish and Subscribe don't work the first time you try it (following the steps above), you probably need an upgrade.

Super Librarian

Some of the unique features of Super Librarian include a provision to edit the Help files (press command-shift-H), an option to enter performance comments that are always visible (see Figure 11-22(A)), a constant display of a bank's last modification date, and options to stack or overlap all open windows (a very desirable feature, since a universal librarian encourages you to have many windows open at one time).

While both Galaxy and Super Librarian can print the contents of banks and some other windows, Super Librarian has the added feature of being able to save this information as a text file, which you can edit with a word processor or import into a database.

Free Trade is Super Librarian's option to copy files from one device folder to another, even if the profile origins don't match (e.g., DX7 and TX7).

Like Opcode's PatchLib DA, Super Librarian includes a desk accessory that can load banks and performances. Like Opcode's DA, Pixel's will not retrieve data from an external device.

Table 11-1: Supported devices

Company	Device	Opcode	Pixel
Akai	S700, S612		●●
Alesis	HR16, MIDIVerb III, MMT8, QuadraVerb	○●○●	◗○◗●
Art	Multiverb II		●
Casio	CZ-1, 1000, 101, 3000, 5000, RZ-1, VZ-1	●●●●●●●	●●●●○○○●
Digital Music	MX8 Patch Bay		●
Digitech	DSP128, DSP 128+		◗●
E-mu	Proteus/1 and /2, XR	●●	●●
Ensoniq	ESQM, ESQ1, SQ-1, SQ-80, SQ-R, VFX, VFX SD	●●●●●●●	●●○●○●○
Fender	Chroma, Polaris	●●	
JL Cooper	MSB+, MSB16/20 Patch Bay	●●	●●
Kawai	K1, K1m, K1r, K3, K3m, K4, K4m, K5, K5m	●●●●●●●●	●●●●●●●●
Korg Poly 800, Wavestation	707, DW-6000, DW-8000, EX-800, EX-8000, P3,	○○●○●○●●	●●●◗●●●○
Korg	M1, M1R, M1-EX, M1R-EX, M3R, T1/2/3	●●●●●●●●	●●●●●●●●
Kurzweil	1000 (PX, PX Plus, HX, SX, GX, AX Plus), K1000 (SE, SE extended, SE II, SE II extended), K1200 (Pro 1, Pro 2, Pro 3)	●●●●●●● ●●●●●●	○○○○○○
Lexicon	LXP-1, LXP-5, PCM-70	●○●	●●●
Linn	LinnDrum	●	
MIDIA	Music Box		●
Oberheim	Xpander, Matrix-6, Matrix-12, Matrix 1000, OB-8	●●●●●	●●○●●
Peavey	DPM-3	●	●
Rane	MPE 14, MPE 28, MPE 47	●●●	
Roland	CM series (32L, 32P, 64)	●	
Roland	D-10, D-110, D-20, D-5, D-50, D-550, D-70	●●●●●●●	●●●●●●●
Roland	GP-8, GP-16, Juno-106, JX8-P, JX-10	○●●●●○	●○○●●
Roland	MKS-50 Alpha Juno, MKS-70, MKS-80 Super Jupiter	●●●	●●●
Roland	MT-32, PAD-80, Rhodes 660, R-8, R-8M, S-10, S330 SBX-80	●○○●●○●○	●●●●●◗●◗
Roland	TR707, TR727, U-110, U-20, U-220	○○○○●	◗◗●●●
Sequential	Drumtrax, Prophet 600, Prophet VS	○○●	◗◗◗
360 Systems	MIDI Patchbay		◗
Yamaha	DX1, 100, 5, 7, 7-E!, 7II, 7IIE!, 7S, 11, 21, 27, 27s	●●●●●● ○●●●●●	○●●●●● ●●●●●○
Yamaha	FB-01, KX76, REV5, RX5, RX7, RX11, RX17, RX21	●○○●○○ ○○○●●	●◗◗○◗●◗◗●○
Yamaha	SPX90, SPX90 II, SY55, SY77	●●○●	●○●●

Table 11-1: Supported devices (continued)

Company	Device	Opcode	Pixel
Yamaha	TG33, TG55, TG77, TX216, TX7, TX802, TX81Z, TX816	●●●●●●●●	○●○●●●●○
Yamaha	V50, YS200		●●
Generic SysEx	(Generic Bulk Dump)	●	●

Shareware solutions
YLib

Kevin Rosenberg's YLib is a very ambitious shareware MIDI universal librarian with a professional-looking interface rivaling commercial offerings. Multiple-device windows can be open simultaneously. When you bring a window to the front, a menu appears informing you what objects are supported for that particular MIDI device. There is even a built-in text editor for taking notes.

YLib-compatible devices include the Yamaha TX81Z (Voices, Performances, Effects, Program changes, Microtunings), Yamaha DX7II (Voices — Full DX7II, Performances, Microtunings), Roland D-110 (internal bank Tones, Timbres — banks a & b, Patches), Roland GR-50 (internal bank Tones, Timbres — banks a & b, Patches), Kawai K1 (Single- and Multipatches from internal or external banks), Korg P3 (Multipatch data), Alesis QuadraVerb (Patch data), Digital Music MX-8 (Patch data), and Bulk data (saves multiple messages in one bulk file that is MIDIEX compatible if you set the file type to BINA using ResEdit or another utility).

Bulk dump utilities

Bulk dump utilities allow you to capture the entire state of your MIDI device or certain banks of specified data types. Usually such utilities do not organize or display the individual objects within a bulk dump — for example, patches within a bulk dump of a patch bank. However, you can capture an individual patch as a bulk dump if your device can transmit single patches. Some bulk dump utilities include options to send and receive MIDI Sample Dump Standard (SDS) files as well as synthesizer patches. Often, you have to write your own device driver to accomplish a bulk dump. This isn't as difficult as it may sound (see the following example).

MidiLib DA

Michael Williams's freeware MidiLib is a desk accessory that can send and receive MIDI SysEx data to and from MIDI devices. Just like the commercial universal librarians described above, you need profiles for the instruments you want to address. In MidiLib terms, these are referred to as *driver files*. You may need to devote some time writing profiles for your instruments in order to use them.

MidiLib drivers are written in an English-like script language and can be edited with any word processor by importing the drivers as TEXT files. A MidiLib driver consists of command lines that begin with a keyword and end with a return. The driver must contain a valid MidiLib ID followed by a valid Driver ID. It must also contain both Backup and Restore script markers and must end with the End script marker (see Table 11-2).

Table 11-2: MidiLib driver command set

Command	Data	Description	Comments
.MidiLib	version number	MidiLib ID	required
.Driver ID	four character ID	Driver ID (filetype)	required
.Backup		Backup script marker	required
.Restore		Restore script marker	required
.End		End script marker	required
.Send	<HEX><HEX>	Send hex string	
.SendFile	number of characters	Send from file	
.Delay	number of ticks	Delay (tick = 1/60 sec)	
.Match	<HEX><HEX>	Match incoming string	
.WriteFile	number of characters	Write incoming chars to file	

The software comes with sample drivers for Roland's MT32 and Yamaha's TX81Z.

Incidentally, MidiLib must always use the modem port for communication to your devices.

MidiEx Mac

If you've ever used another type of computer for music you've probably heard of the MIDI Exclusive file format commonly referred to as MidiEx. Thomas W. Inskip's MidiEx Mac is the first Macintosh implementation of this utility. It can store any type of SysEx data except sequences (see Figure 11-24).

MidiEx saves and opens files in standard TEXT file format. It has an Open Other option that allows it to open SysEx files created by other programs such as MIDI sequencers (these are not guaranteed to work, but they usually do).

Because of the wide number of computers that support the MidiEx format, it can be very useful for sharing files with people who do not have Macintoshes. If you do this via modem, which is the normal way to transfer MidiEx and SMF files from computers of different types, you should upload them using a binary format such as XMODEM or YMODEM, but you need to disable MacBinary in

Figure 11-24: MidiEx Mac lets you easily add new devices and data types. **(A)** You simply type the data request that you find in the back of your synthesizer manual into the Add Message dialog box and give it a name. **(B)** This device or data type is automatically added to the Message menu. Subsequently, selecting the item from this menu initiates a transfer (to the Macintosh) of banks, individual objects, or the entire state of your synthesizer. **(C)** Retrieved data appears in a window where you can give it a name. You can send all the data in this window with one command if you like.

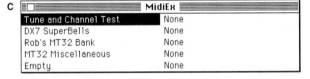

your telecommunications program. When MacBinary is enabled in a modem transfer, Finder-related information is written to the file header that only Macintoshes can understand. If you forget to disable MacBinary, the person receiving the file can still use it by stripping the opening 128-byte file header.

Other options

Several other options exist. EQ SysEx Snapshot by Mike Collins is a HyperMIDI-based HyperCard stack (for bulk dumps from effects devices such as Yamaha's SPX90 and Lexicon's PCM70), the Bulk Librarian Stack that comes with EarLevel Engineering's HyperMIDI 2.0, and Benoît Widemann's MIDI Test application. These utilities are purely generic bulk dump capturing/loading applications — you must initiate the transfer from the device in question.

Sound Databases

Most sound databases are distributed as HyperCard stacks (meaning that you need HyperCard to run them) or database templates (meaning that you often need the corresponding database program to make use of them). Popular database formats include FileMaker (and FileMaker Pro), Panorama, database, and others. HyperCard is free with every Macintosh, but with most other database software some sort of investment is involved.

Commercial sound organizers

Sound Finder

MM Software's SoundFinder takes a graphic approach to categorizing your sounds (see Figure 11-25). To speed up your cataloging, this HyperCard stack can import sound names from Opcode format files (pre-version 5).

SoundTracker

SoundTracker is part of the *Macworld Music & Sound Bible* Software Supplement (see coupon at the back of the book). It is offered in three formats: as a Hyper-Card Stack, as a FileMaker Pro Template, and as a DAtabase-format desk accessory. SoundTracker is available in two versions: Empty (you fill in all the data) or Presets (the database includes all the factory patches for most popular MIDI devices). Sets of macros for popular macro utilities are included to speed up cataloging your sounds. SoundTracker lets you organize your synthesizer sounds and print reports in a variety of formats (see Figure 11-26).

Once you have organized your sounds, SoundTracker lets you print out a variety of reports. Reports can be displayed on the screen or printed by way of the buttons on the right side of the data entry screen. These features are also available from a menu. Many of the reports assume that you have specified a rating (on a scale of 0 to 9) for each sound, because the report wants to select sounds that are only of a specified rating or greater. Some typical report options follow:

❖ *Main Data* (by device): All applicable information appearing on the main data screen sorted by device. Within each device heading the sounds are also sorted by patch name.

❖ *Main Data* (orchestra): All sounds (list form) with all applicable information sorted by name in the order the instrument names appear on an orchestral score. Within each instrument the sounds are also sorted by device, and within each device they are sorted by patch name.

❖ *Main Data* (by name): All sounds (list form) with all applicable information sorted by name.

❖ *All Sounds* (by device): All sounds (list form) sorted by device. Within each device heading the sounds are also sorted by patch name.

❖ *All Sounds* (orchestra): All sounds (list form) with all applicable information sorted by name in the order the instrument names appear on an orchestral

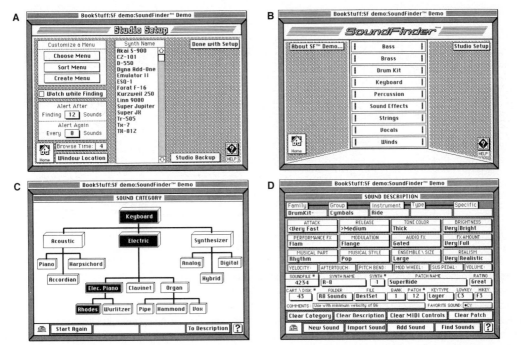

Figure 11-25: (A) The SoundFinder Setup card lets you customize some of the menus that you will later use to categorize your sounds. You can create your own menus of devices in your studio, descriptive terms for tones, and descriptive terms for effects. **(B)** The navigation card of SoundFinder is where you jump to the nine main sound categories listed in the middle of the card. **(C)** Sound Category cards are displayed graphically like this one. Clicking a category at the end of a branch highlights the branch leading to that type of sound. **(D)** Pressing the To Description button on one of the nine Category cards (see C) takes you to the Sound Description card, where you can enter information about the sound. Most information is entered by way of pop-up menus that appear when you click any field. Some information is automatically entered when you import sound names from an early-version Opcode format file.

score. Within each instrument the sounds are also sorted by device, and within each device they are sorted by patch name.

❖ *All Sounds* (by name): All sounds (list form) with all applicable information sorted by name.

The following reports are also available sorted by device, by name, or by orchestral position, similar to the above. For the "Rating of 8+" and "Rating of 7+" the final level of the sort is by rating number. These last three types of reports are also available in two printed formats: as a one-column list (see below) and as a two-column list with slightly less information.

❖ *Device-Name* (best): All sounds for the specified device with a rating of 9.
❖ *Device-Name* (8+): All sounds for the specified device with a rating 8 or better.
❖ *Device-Name* (7+): All sounds for the specified device with a rating 7 or better.

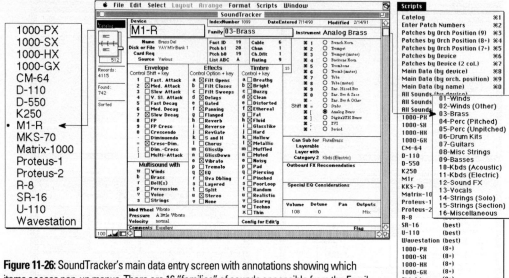

Figure 11-26: SoundTracker's main data entry screen with annotations showing which items access pop-up menus. There are 16 "families" of sounds accessible from the Family pop-up menu. When you select a Family from this menu, 16 possible family subcategories appear next to radio buttons at the upper right. In other words, SoundTracker offers 256 categories and subcategories as the main level of sound classification. The checkboxes allow you to enter such sound attributes as envelope, effects, timbre, and multitimbre. SoundTracker is part of the *Macworld Music & Sound Bible* Software Supplement.

SFX Organizer

SFX Organizer is part of the *Macworld Music & Sound Bible* Software Supplement. It is also offered in three formats: as a HyperCard Stack, as a FileMaker Pro Template, and as a DAtabase-format desk accessory. Sets of macros for popular macro utilities are included to speed up cataloging your sound effects. SFX Organizer lets you organize your sound effects and print reports in a variety of formats (see Figure 11-27).

Once you have organized your sound effects, SFX Organizer lets you print out a variety of reports. Reports can be displayed on the screen or printed in a variety of formats. These features are found on a special navigation screen and are also available from a menu. Like SoundTracker (above), options are available to limit your reports to a certain rating or above. Some typical report options follow:

❖ Sort/Display/Print by Location
❖ Sort/Display/Print by Source
❖ Sort/Display/Print by Name
❖ Sort/Display/Print by Category (see Figure 11-28)

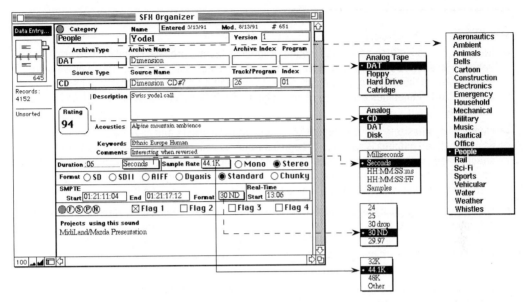

Figure 11-27: SFX Organizer's main data entry screen with annotations showing which items access pop-up menus. Pop-up menus make it easy to enter SFX category, source, and archive location. Other pop-up menus are for duration and SMPTE information, both in a variety of formats. The checkboxes and radio buttons allow you to enter other important attributes. SFX Organizer is part of the *Macworld Music & Sound Bible* Software Supplement.

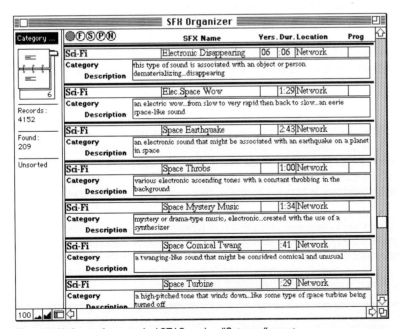

Figure 11-28: A page from a typical SFX Organizer "Category" report.

Summary

🗸 Most electronic instruments contain sounds known as factory presets. Usually, there are between 50 and 192 such presets, with 128 being the most common number. These presets are either stored in the device's ROM chips (so that you cannot edit them directly) or in battery-backed RAM. Sometimes a device includes a copy of its ROM-based patches in its RAM so that you can edit them.

🗸 Nearly all synthesizers include some RAM where you can create and save new sounds. Room for 64 user-defined patches is typical, although instruments with "extended RAM" often provide more space. Once you have started editing sounds and saving them in your synthesizer's RAM, you will eventually run out of space and require some kind of off-line storage. This can happen sooner than you think, and when it does you can use librarian software to solve the storage problems.

🗸 Librarian software exists for the loading, retrieval, and organization of such ephemeral items as individual tone parameters, individual patches, banks of groups of patches, individual sampled soundfiles, entire sample RAM, global settings or master parameters, program maps or lists, velocity maps, pressure maps, intonation tables or micro tunings, reverberation parameters, DSP effects parameters, and sequences.

🗸 There are many levels of grouping objects (such as sounds) within devices. Many types of individual objects (for example, patches) are often grouped into banks. Most devices let you transfer either individual objects or entire banks of objects at a time. There is usually a provision to transfer the entire current state of a device, including all its objects and banks. Macintosh software usually refers to this as a "bundle" or "performance." Universal librarians and editor/librarians can group multiple devices into a higher-level structure called a multi-device bundle or performance. Furthermore, most Macintosh software dealing with sound organization and editing lets you agglomerate objects into libraries, a concept that has no counterpart within the devices themselves.

🗸 Dedicated librarian programs only understand the SysEx data from a specific device or, occasionally, a group of related devices that have compatible patch formats (e.g., Yamaha DX7, TX7, and TX816). If you are using dedicated librarian software, you need a separate program for each type of synthesizer you own.

🗸 Many librarian programs include options to generate new sounds algorithmically based on existing sounds in your libraries. However, the real strength of the Macintosh's user interface was put to bear on patch editing software. Initially, patch editors and patch librarians were separate programs. The first generation of patch editors was also dedicated to individual devices and therefore referred to as dedicated patch editors. It didn't take long for patch editors and librarians dedicated to the same synthesizers to become integrated into a single entity called a dedicated editor/librarian.

🗸 A universal librarian allows you to deal with many different types of devices from within a single program. These programs usually come with device profiles, templates, or modules that provide the information necessary for the universal librarian to communicate with all the MIDI devices they support. Some companies provide programming tools for you to create your own device profiles for gear not covered in the software's standard profile library.

Chapter 12
Editing Synthesized Sound

In this chapter . . .

✔ Front-panel editing and Macintosh editing contrasted.

✔ Relating synthesizer sound parameters to their corresponding acoustic properties.

✔ Dedicated and universal editor/librarians examined in detail (commercial, shareware, and freeware).

✔ Devices supported by dedicated and universal editor/librarians.

✔ Utilities to enhance patch-editing activities.

✔ Patch-editing software feature tables.

The Sound-Editing Interface 'For the Rest Of Us'

Editing synthesized sound is a branch of sound design commonly referred to as *patch editing*. The programs that allow you to edit synthesized sounds are called *patch editors*. Patch editors greatly simplify the control of the internal sound manipulation capabilities of MIDI devices.

Nearly all synthesizers allow you to modify their sounds by way of controls on their front panels. Besides synthesizers, other types of MIDI devices such as MIDI-controllable effects, MIDI mixers, and MIDI controllers provide similar editing options. Unfortunately, although most MIDI devices offer vast capabilities for sound design of this kind, they only provide a limited number of controls, often a single knob, numeric keypad, several function buttons, possibly a data slider or two, some arrow keys for scrolling, and a very tiny display (usually little more than a 24- to 48-character LCD, although larger displays are starting to appear).

In most cases, all the hardware controls on a MIDI device are multi-functional; they do different things depending on what mode you are in. Often there are dozens of modes and it is very difficult to keep track of what mode you are in, hence it is sometimes difficult to predict the effect any given control will have if you manipulate it.

On the other hand, the Macintosh permits the simulation of hundreds of virtual controls on-screen and these always remain assigned to the same function. The main issue boils down to user interface. Software can often provide a better user interface than hardware and it is well known that user interface is one area in which the Macintosh excels. One exception should be noted: JL Cooper's CS-1 control station box (an ADB device mentioned in many chapters of this book) provides a hardware interface for many on-screen controls that can greatly speed up your editing in many programs.

A simple example will clarify the importance of hardware vs. software user interface. Suppose you want to change the waveform of a particular low frequency oscillator (LFO) for a patch using the front panel controls of your synthesizer.

It could require hundreds of manipulations of the front panel controls to your synthesizer — just to change an LFO waveform! To grasp the difficulty of dealing with such a system, imagine a typewriter that only displays 24 characters at a time and only has six keys functioning in 20 modes rather than the traditional two (upper and lowercase). Such a typewriter might require you to press a key to go into "number" mode, and then repeatedly press an arrow key until the desired number appears. It would have similar keys to get into vowel, consonant, and punctuation modes.

With Macintosh-based patch-editing software you can usually accomplish the above with three steps:

1. Double-click the name of the patch (e.g., in a bank window) that you want to edit.

2. Select the new LFO waveform from a menu, pop-up menu, or group of radio buttons.

3. Save the edited version.

That's all there is to it. The software takes care of all the other steps instantaneously, and without your having to know anything about them. Editing efficiency increases because much more information is available on a computer screen than in a 24-character LCD, and clumsy navigation through your synthesizer's menu tree is made invisible.

This chapter will introduce you to patch editors, paying particular attention to editor/librarians. Editor/librarians that combine both patch-editing and librarian functions in one program are rapidly becoming the standard format for such software. Like librarians (see Chapter 11, "Sound Organization"), there are two types of editors and editor/librarians: dedicated and universal.

Because the vast majority of options in this area are editor/librarians rather than just editors, it would be a very good idea to review the sections on librarians in

Chapter 11 so that you understand the basic principles of librarian software. For the most part, these will not be repeated in this chapter. However, for reasons known only to the software programs, most universal editor/librarians have considerably more sophisticated librarian features than dedicated librarians or universal librarians. These features will be covered in this chapter.

While you are reviewing librarians and universal librarians, you should also look at the discussion of SysEx data in the same chapter.

General Principles

Because SysEx data is what defines the characteristics of the sounds in your synthesizer, the editor/librarian's main concern is with creating an intelligible and editable representation of this SysEx data. The other concern of this type of program is to present on-screen controls to manipulate SysEx data.

You will recall that, in the case of librarian software, programs use little pieces of code or resources to interpret how the software deals with specific devices of different manufacturers. With librarians, these can be called drivers, configuration files, modules, resources, templates, or profiles. Editor/librarians also require similar data. There is one important distinction. In the context of an editor/librarian the word "template" almost always refers to a second chunk of data required by the software in addition to the driver or profile that defines a device's SysEx communication parameters. Sometimes these two items (profile and template) are combined into one data file that your software loads during the configuration stage (in the case of a universal editor/librarian) or that is built into the software (as is often the case in dedicated editor/librarians).

Editor/librarians use their templates to define the graphic user interface to SysEx data editing, the format of which is defined by the device profile or driver. The reason that different templates are required is that different devices offer manipulation of different patch parameters. For example, a synthesizer that does not allow you to apply an envelope to a filter will not require a graphic interface for controlling the filter envelope to be built into its template. This carries an underlying implication of another important concept: Not all synthesizers allow you to edit all types of data.

Understanding patch parameters

The sound parameters of synthesizer patches are often labeled with esoteric-sounding terms; they actually refer to common sound characteristics that you probably already understand. It's a good idea to be able to relate your conceptual model of a sound to the synthesizer parameters that affect such a sound. Table 12-1 should assist you in making the connection.

Table 12-1: Sound parameters of synthesizer patches

Synthesizer parameter	Sound characteristic	Comments
Amplitude envelope attack rate	Attack, attack speed	Usually the first segment of the envelope
Amplitude envelope release rate	Decay	Fade-out speed
Amplitude envelope	Amplitude transformation	Temporal changes of volume
Channel volume	Amplitude (overall)	Volume (loudness)
Chorus	Ensemble	Effect of several identical sound sources playing simultaneously
Chorus delay	Multiple attacks	Effect of several identical sound sources playing slightly out of sync (adds realism to samples). In the extreme, can be used to simulate echo effects.
Controller assignment or performance controller assignment	Articulation	For example, assigning after-touch to a pitch LFO would bring in vibrato as you apply pressure to your keyboard's keys after note sounds
Detune amount	Beating or overtone	Effect of two identical sound sources playing slightly out of tune (adds realism to samples). For synthesizer sounds, can create beating effects or add harmonic complexity.
Envelope	Articulation	When applies to amplitude, defines the characteristics of the attack, decay, sustain, and release. See below for applications to other parameters.
Filter cutoff	Brightness	Defines amplitude of high frequency components
Filter envelope	Timbral transformation	Temporal development of timbre
Keyboard scaling of timbre or timbre scaling	Brightness in upper registers	For example, a piano gets brighter as the notes get higher
LFO applied to amplitude	Tremolo	Amplitude modulation
LFO applied to frequency	Vibrato	Pitch modulation
LFO depth setting	Vibrato/tremolo width	Pitch/amplitude modulation range
LFO rate setting	Vibrato/tremolo speed	Vibrato/tremolo rate
MIDI volume	Amplitude (overall)	Volume (loudness)
Noise	Unpitched	Generally refers to white noise containing a random distribution of every frequency at equal volume within a specified frequency range. Can be used to add such effects as bow noise to a string sound or breath noise to a wind sound.
Pan	Localization	Location in stereo field
Partial	Timbre	Harmonic spectrum or harmonic content
Pitch bend range	Glissando	Sliding pitch, not necessarily between notes
Portamento range	Glissando	Sliding pitch between notes
Reverberation	Spatial source distance	Select different types of reverberation and depths of reverberation
Tone	Timbre	Harmonic spectrum or harmonic content
Tuning (or coarse tuning or fine tuning)	Pitch	Frequency
VCA envelope or TVA setting	Amplitude transformation	Temporal changes of amplitude

Table 12-1: Sound parameters of synthesizer patches (continued)

Synthesizer parameter	Sound characteristic	Comments
VCA envelope attack rate	Attack, attack speed	Usually the first segment of the envelope
VCA envelope decay rate	Percussive quality	Attack transients
VCA envelope release rate	Decay	Fade out speed
VCA envelope sustain length	Duration	Staccato vs. legato articulation
VCF envelope or TVF setting	Timbral transformation	Temporal development of timbre
Volume	Amplitude (overall)	Volume (loudness)
Waveform	Timbre	Spectrum or harmonic content (could be an inharmonic spectrum)
Waveform oscillator	Timbre	Harmonic spectrum or harmonic content

It is important to understand the unique way in which your synthesizer refers to the parameters that modify sounds, because most patch editors address parameters by the names found in the internal workings of the device they are editing.

Several exceptions to this rule exist. When editing envelopes (be they filter envelopes, amplitude envelopes, or any other envelopes your synthesizer provides), it is now a relatively standard feature for an editor/librarian to provide a graphic picture of an envelope with little handles where the segments change. Envelope editing can be accomplished by using the mouse exclusively to reshape the on-screen graphic representation by way of its handles — the software converts the resultant new graphic shape into the appropriate MIDI data that will generate an envelope identical to the picture on your screen. Often it sends the corresponding value changes in real time to your synthesizer and also updates the parameter value indicators on the screen, if they exist. Such graphical interfaces for the manipulation of parameters that lend themselves toward a graphically expressed model increase your "conceptual contact" with the sound data you are working with.

Dedicated Editor/Librarians

Like dedicated librarians, dedicated editor/librarians only function with the electronic instrument for which they have been created. Also like librarians, dedicated editor/librarians are less costly than universal editor/librarians (until you need more than four or five such programs).

There are Macintosh-dedicated editor/librarians available for over 60 different models of synthesizers and sample players. Consult Table 12-2 at the end of this section to see if there is an editor/librarian for yours. If not, you might find it in Table 12-3 at the end of the section on universal editor/librarians.

Commercial software

The varying approaches to the representation of internal instrument parameters are easy to see by comparing the interfaces of the following three Proteus editor/librarians with the Proteus editing templates offered by the universal editor/librarians (see the section "Universal Editor/Librarians" in this chapter).

PatchMaster Proteus editor/librarian

Bokonon's PatchMaster Proteus uses the typical spreadsheet style display of patch banks and libraries and has a very graphical interface to editing (see Figure 12-1). Unlike many dedicated editor/librarians, PatchMaster Proteus provides for libraries that can hold as many patches as you like. An on-screen keyboard is available. This editor/librarian is very powerful and easy to navigate, although there aren't a lot of frills such as algorithmic patch generation, duplicate patch checking, and data comparison.

All editing is accomplished by pop-up menus and scroll arrows (see Figure 12-2). The program adds some enhancements to scrolling through values. If you hold the option key down while you click a scroll arrow, the scrolling speeds up. If you hold down the command key, the numbers increase by values of 100 or, for many parameters, the values immediately jump to their maximum setting.

Protezoa Proteus editor/librarian

Interval Music Systems's Protezoa will edit any E-mu Proteus (including 1, 2, 1+2, 1+Protologic board, and XR versions). The software has a very graphical approach. Clicking just about anything on the screen brings up a menu, sub-editor, or toggles that option on or off. The program saves files in its own format or Opcode's format.

Some special features include the option to assign one of your controller keyboard's continuous controllers to be a data entry slider for the software and the ability to play chords from its on-screen keyboard. It also has a patch-generating feature. Rudimentary database options let you categorize sound by attributes to quickly locate all sounds of a specified kind within a bank.

The software comes with a LoadaZoa desk accessory that lets you load various types of data into your Proteus. (See Figures 12-3 through 12-6 for more information on Protezoa.)

Proteus Editor/Librarian

PhySy's Proteus Editor/Librarian is compatible with E-mu's Proteus/1 and /XR. The software has an interface feature that may come as a surprise to seasoned Macintosh users: scrolling windows that contain pop-up menus, checkboxes, and other data-entry controls. Dr. T's X-oR takes a similar approach (see the section

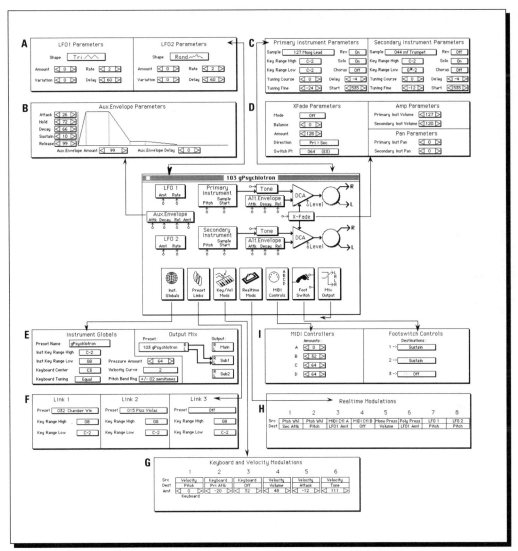

Figure 12-1: Bokonon's PatchMaster Proteus Editor/Librarian's interface to individual patch editing. This main screen provides an intuitive representation of the signal flow that the Proteus employs internally to create a sound. Clicking any element brings up its associated editor. **(A)** The LFO Parameters Editor is accessed by clicking either LFO 1 or LFO 2. **(B)** Envelope Editors like this are available by clicking Aux. Envelope or either of the Alt. Envelopes (primary or secondary). Although no "handles" appear on the graphic representation of the envelope, it can still be reshaped with the mouse. **(C)** The Primary and Secondary Instrument Parameters Editor is accessed by clicking either of those elements in the main display. **(D)** The Xfade and DCA (digitally controlled amplifier) Parameters Editor. The seven large buttons running along the bottom of the main window bring up additional editors. **(E)** Instrument Globals and Output Mix Editor (clicking either the Inst. Globals or Mix Output buttons calls this up). **(F)** The Preset Links Editor. **(G)** The Keyboard and Velocity Modulation Editor. **(H)** The Realtime Modulation Editor. **(I)** The MIDI Controls and Footswitch Editor (accessed by clicking either button).

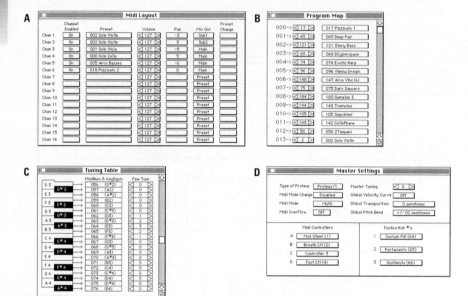

Figure 12-2: PatchMaster Proteus offers its global editors by way of the Windows menu. **(A)** MIDI Layout Editor (for editing channel assignments, etc.). **(B)** Program Map Editor. **(C)** Tuning Table Editor. **(D)** Master Settings Editor.

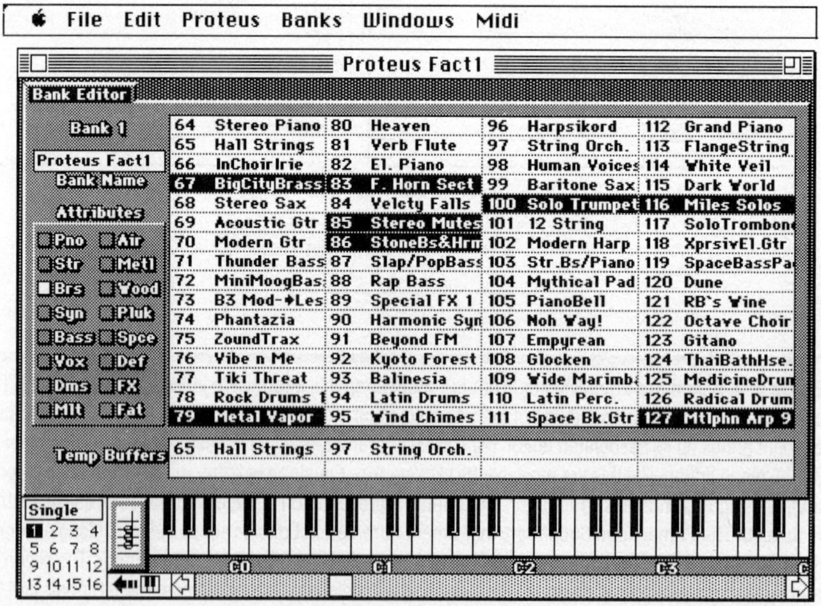

Figure 12-3: A bank window in Protezoa. You can assign one or more of sixteen attributes to a sound. In this illustration, "Brs" has been clicked, resulting in all brass sounds being highlighted. Like most editor/librarians you can drag patches around with the mouse to reorganize them. The Windows menu lets you access editors for individual presets (see Figure 12-4), links, globals (see Figure 12-5), patch maps, tuning tables, and also offers the "Rand-O-Rama" option (see Figure 12-6).

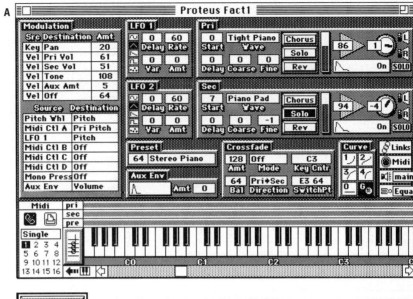

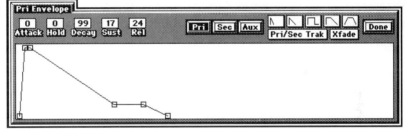

Figure 12-4:
(A) Just about everything on Protezoa's Preset Editor screen is a switch or pop-up menu. The output stage (upper right) includes rotatable knobs to set panning and LED-style level indicator/controls. **(B)** Clicking any of the envelopes brings up the Pri Envelope Editor.

Figure 12-5:
Protezoa's Globals Editor lets you set almost every parameter that you would access from the Master button on the Proteus front panel. Volume is set using on-screen sliders. The Pan Parameter uses rotatable on-screen knobs. Clicking the preset names above the knobs brings up a menu of all available presets.

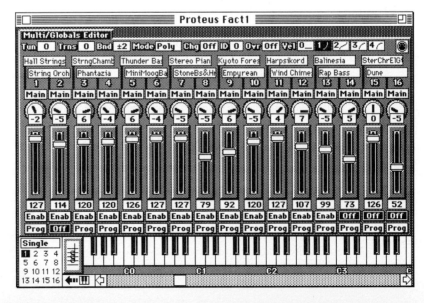

Figure 12-6:
Protezoa's Rand-O-
Rama option lets
you quickly gene-
rate a single preset
or bank of new
patches for your
Proteus. You have
the option to Ran-
domize values
completely or
Interpolate
between two
selected patches
(as shown in this
figure). Unhigh-
lighted parameters
are not affected by
the operation. This
lets you insulate
certain parameters
from the generation process.

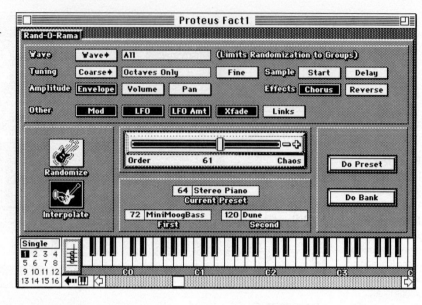

"Universal Editor/Librarians" in this chapter). Most Macintosh users do not expect to see checkboxes or pop-up menus in a scrolling field. About the only other place you will find such an interface is in certain documents created by Claris's FileMaker Pro.

PhySy's Proteus Editor/Librarian can edit any patch parameter except a patch's linking configuration. Also, there is no way to edit global data in the Proteus.

Korg M1 Editor/Librarian (Opcode)

Opcode Systems markets patch editors for almost every make and model of synthesizer currently in widespread use (see Table 12-2). The main screens of these editors pack quite a bit of data in their displays — often equivalent to what other programs require several screens for (see Figures 12-7 and 12-8).

The librarian portion of their editor/librarians has a very consistent interface from synthesizer to synthesizer, and all the standard features of the Opcode librarian shell are usually available (see Chapter 11). These include bundles and groups of bundles from different synthesizers, PatchFactory (for algorithmic patch genera-tion), unlimited size library files, on-screen keyboard (MouseKeys), importation, recording, and playback of MIDI sequences, delete duplicates options, duplicate data search options, parent/child patch handling, and a simple mouse-dragging approach to moving and copying files.

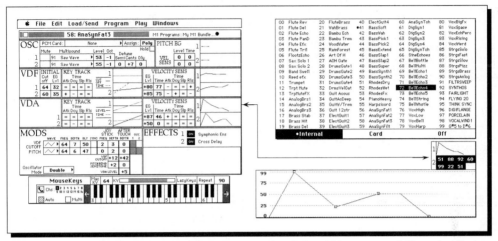

Figure 12-7: Opcode's M1 Editor/Librarian's individual patch-editing window. All the parameter fields can be edited as numericals or by typing values from the Macintosh keyboard. Once you have made some edits, the Compare menu option lets you toggle back and forth between the edited and unedited version of your sound. Clicking any of the small envelope graphics brings up the envelope-editing window pictured below the parameter window. As is typical of Macintosh editor/librarians, you use the little square envelope handles to reshape the envelope. There is an option to display envelope data numerically on the main parameter window (rather than the small graphic thumbnails pictured here). When you choose this, you can really see all parameter values of a patch at a single glance.

Because of the unique characteristics of each device, the editing interface of every Opcode editor/librarian has a completely different appearance. Opcode has now combined all their editors into a single universal editor/librarian. For an example of how different the interfaces to different synthesizers can be, see the section "Galaxy Plus Editors" in this chapter.

Roland D-50 Editor/Librarian (Valhalla)

Valhalla's D-50 Editor/Librarian (developed by Steven Dimse — see below under TX81Z Editor/Librarian) provides an excellent model of most of the features that form the standard set of options we have come to expect in such programs.

The software can save patches in larger libraries, algorithmically generate patches (using Shade or Shuffler — see Opcode's M1 Librarian in Chapter 11 for a discussion of these techniques), an on-screen keyboard, play, record, and loop sequences for patch auditioning, and it offers a very intuitive graphical interface to parameter editing including envelopes that are reshapable by way of the mouse.

A unique feature is its Patch Sheet Editing option (see Figure 12-9). This displays all patch parameters and their values organized logically into a scrolling list. Here you can type in values directly from the Macintosh keyboard. These individual patch parameter listings can also be printed, a feature sorely missing from nearly all other programs.

Figure 12-8: Other editing screens of Opcode's M1 Editor/Librarian. **(A)** MultiSound Editor. You use the little triangles to access pop-up menus like the one pictured at the upper right of Figure 12-7. Because there are so many options, the pop-up menu is in multiple columns. Furthermore, dragging the mouse down to one of the bold-face options at the bottom of the menu presents an entirely new set of items. **(B)** Effects Editor. This is available from the main parameter editor screen (see Figure 12-7) and from the multisound editor. **(C)** Global Data Editor. Here you can set many of the parameters that you would access by pressing the M1's Global button. **(D)** Double-clicking one of the Drum Kit buttons in the Global data editor brings up a Drum Kit editing window like this one. Clicking a drum sound name — Tom2 in this illustration — displays the note or range of notes that the sound is assigned to. Similarly, clicking a note on the miniature musical keyboard displays the sound assigned to it. With a sound name selected, you can drag along the on-screen musical keyboard to set its range. It is possible to overlap or duplicate ranges, in which case the other sound's assignment changes to "DUP." Fortunately, the editor provides a Reassign Duplicates option that moves all duplicate assignments to the top of the keyboard for reassignment.

Roland D-50 Editor/Librarian (Dr. T)

Dr. T's Roland D-50 Editor/Librarian can open up to four banks at a time with the standard bank display seen on most of the librarians covered in Chapter 11.

The software provides a very innovative way for auditioning sounds called Mouse-Play. This bears some similarities to Dr. T's MusicMouse software discussed in Chapter 19, "Interactive Composition and Intelligent Instruments." Rather than an on-screen keyboard, you use the mouse button (with the command key down) to play notes on your synthesizer. The note number is relative to the mouse's horizontal position, and the velocity is relative to the mouse's vertical position. Holding the option key down while you do this will transmit modulation values. You can assign this feature to Mod Wheel, Aftertouch, Breath, or Foot controllers. There is also a "Glissando" mode accessible by holding down the shift key that allows mouse motion to continually trigger notes without you having to press the mouse button down for each new attack.

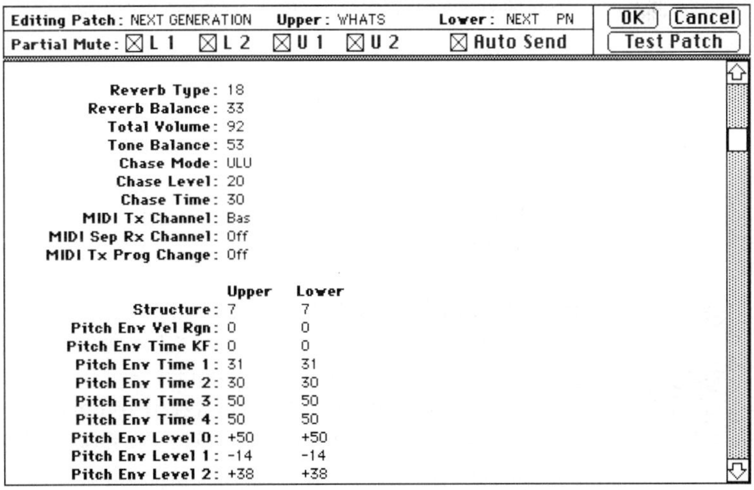

Figure 12-9:
(A) Typical parameter-editing windows from Valhalla's D-50 Editor/Librarian. These are accessed by double-clicking a patch name in a bank or library window. There are eight such windows for each patch although only one can be displayed at a time. Pictured are the Patch Upper Common Editor and the Upper Partial 1 Editor. The envelope in the Upper Partial 1 window has been clicked to bring up the Envelope Editor pictured below. **(B)** The lower window is Valhalla's unique Patch Sheet Editor. This lists all the parameter values associated with the patch being edited in a scrolling window. You can type new values if you want or print the entire list.

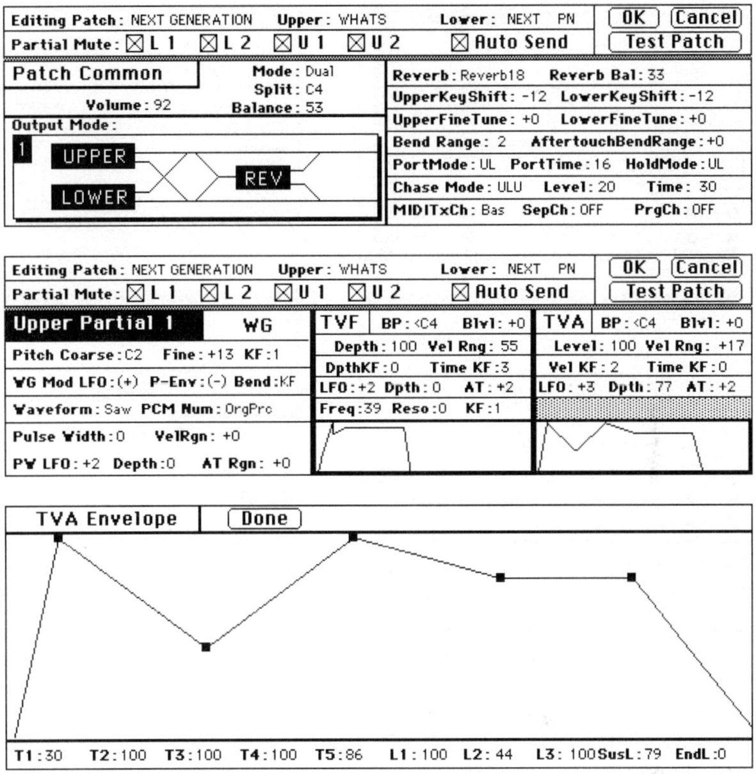

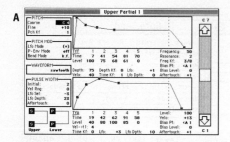

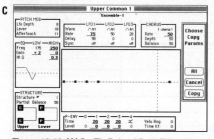
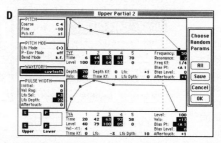

Figure 12-10: (A) Dr. T's Roland D-50 Editor/Librarian's Upper Partial 1 editing screen. All parameters function like Opcode-style "numericals" — dragging upward on them with the mouse button pressed increments the values and dragging downward decrements them. **(B)** A special Copy/Swap dialog box lets you interchange data between various components of a patch. **(C)** Regardless of which screen you are currently viewing, you can compare the data to any other patch in your library or to the current patch in its unedited state. Parameters that have different values from the one you are editing are underlined. A Copy button is available to copy those parameters *en masse* to the Clipboard. **(D)** The Random Mask is also available in any editing screen. Here you can highlight any parameters that you want to be randomized the next time you use the Randomize command to generate new patches. You also have the option to set a Randomization percentage parameter to control the percent of randomization within each parameter's range.

Seven separate screens are required to display the parameters of an individual patch: Upper Partial 1, Upper Partial 2, Upper Common, Lower Partial 1, Lower Partial 2, Lower Common, and Patch. These are selectable from the Windows menu. You can copy selected parameters between these various screens (see Figure 12-10).

Yamaha TX81Z Editor/Librarian

Steven S. Dimse's Yamaha TX81Z Editor/Librarian is a bargain, since it has many of the features found in programs costing two or three times its price. Besides the on-screen keyboard, the program can record and play back sequences. There is a Randomize Bank option that functions like the Opcode PatchFactory's Shuffler option (see Chapter 11).

Kurzweil 250 Sequence Mover

The Kurzweil 250 is one of many MIDI instruments that offer an internal (hardware-based) sequencer. There are not many editor/librarians for hardware-based

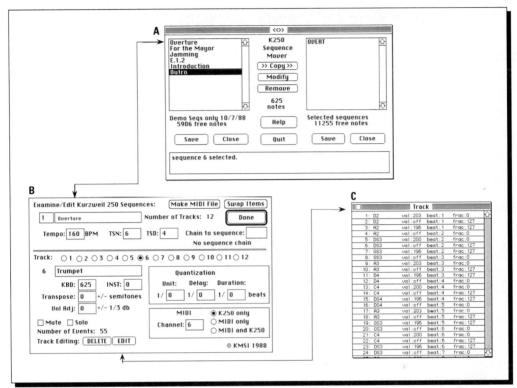

Figure 12-11: Kurzweil Music Systems's Sequence Mover is an editor/librarian for the internal (hardware-based) sequencer within their Kurzweil 250 sampler/sample player. **(A)** The main screen provides an interface borrowed from Apple's Font/DA Mover. Here you can copy sequences from library to library or remove sequences. You can have up to 40 sequences in a library or 12,000 notes — whichever comes first. **(B)** Selecting a sequence for editing brings up this Track Attributes Editor that lets you edit global attributes of each track. Tracks are selected by way of the radio buttons in the center of the window. **(C)** Clicking the Edit button in the Track Attributes Editor brings up this display of the data on the selected track. "Val" refers to velocity. The reason some of these numbers exceed 127 is because the velocity resolution of the K250 has 256 increments (double that of MIDI's 127). "Frac" refers to the fractional portion of the beat (256 fractions per beat). MIDI sequencers usually refer to this as "tick" or "clock."

sequencers, because it is usually an easy task to transfer the data to a software-based MIDI sequencer for editing.

The advantage of an editor such as Kurzweil Music Systems's K250 Sequence Mover is largely in the area of live performance, where you will be using the hardware sequencer on stage (see Figure 12-11). If you are working with a lot of files for this purpose, it may be more efficient to use this editor/librarian, because the files remain in their native K250 format. Note that the program does provide an option to convert their proprietary file format into an SMF.

Shareware and freeware solutions

Considering the programming complexity of editor/librarians, it is surprising that there are many shareware and freeware offerings. Many of these are HyperCard-based and thus can be found in the coupon in the back of the book.

Utilities
KAMIKAZE DX

Fumitaka Anzai's freeware KAMIKAZE DX is primarily an algorithmic patch generator for the DX7, TX7, and TX816. You can send and receive patches from your DX/TX instrument and their parameters and envelopes are displayed. The software provides very flexible controls for patch generation (see Figure 12-12).

MultiMaker

Command Development's (in conjunction with Korg USA) MultiMaker is a freeware sample mapping utility for the Korg T1, T2ex, and T3ex (see Figure 12-13). If you have a T2 or T3, you must have the RAM option installed in order for it to receive sample dumps. This option (known as EXK-T) is available at any authorized Korg service center for the suggested installed price of $250. The T1, T2ex, and T3ex come with this option already installed.

MultiMaker does not actually send samples to T-series keyboards. You can use Sound Designer, Alchemy, or a MIDI Sample Dump utility to transfer the samples to your instrument. MultiMaker simply maps samples that are already in RAM.

Normally, samples that are sent to the T-series keyboard are only accessible through the use of a drum kit. The main disadvantage of this approach is that there are only four drum kits in a T-series keyboard. Dedicating a drum kit to map samples uses up one of your drum kits. In addition, only one drum kit is playable at a time (in a program).

MultiMaker allows you to create and send up to 40 fully mapped *multisounds* that are independent of the four drum kits and offer more flexibility for mapping your samples across the keyboard (a Top Key parameter is provided). Furthermore, a program can have up to two multisounds assigned to it.

A multisound is a collection of samples, mapped out on a keyboard. For example, suppose you have eight violin samples. Instead of calling up each of the eight samples, simply call up the multisound "violin" which has all eight samples, each mapped to their correct pitches.

When you map samples with MultiMaker you should be aware of the following practical limits that are imposed by a soundfile's sample rate:

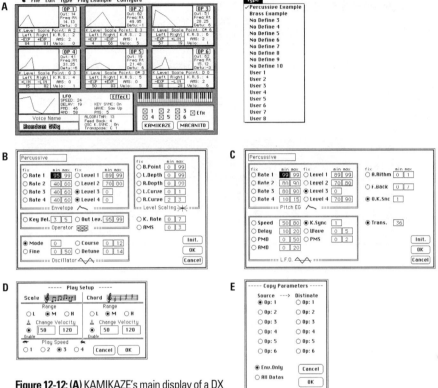

Figure 12-12: (A) KAMIKAZE's main display of a DX or TX patch. Note that you cannot edit the values on this screen. The software's primary function is to generate new patches. The checkboxes at the lower right let you insulate certain operators or the effects from patch generation activities. The KAMIKAZE button executes your generation algorithm. The MACINITO button does the same thing, but allows you to include a deviation factor specified as a percentage. **(B)** The Operator Configuration dialog box. This is where you set the randomization limits for the Operators that you have chosen to have for parameter value generation. Most parameters let you specify a minimum and maximum value for the extremes of the randomization range. The radio buttons, when enabled, lock in specific values for their parameters. **(C)** The Effects Configuration dialog box. Here you supply additional effects information for the patch generation algorithm. Interaction with this dialog box is similar to that of the Operator Configuration dialog box (see B). **(D)** Once you have generated a patch, you can audition it with a scale or chord. This dialog box lets you specify some parameters to auditioning playback. **(E)** This Copy Parameters dialog box lets you copy parameters from one operator to another.

❖ 48 KHz samples can be stretched to about a quartertone short of an octave.
❖ 44.1 KHz samples can be stretched to one octave and a half-step.
❖ 32 KHz samples can be stretched to one octave and a fifth.
❖ 24 KHz samples can be stretched to just under two octaves.
❖ 16 KHz samples can be stretched to two octaves and a fifth.

Figure 12-13:
MultiMaker lets you create 40 Multisound sample mappings for Korg T-series instruments. You can set five parameters for each sample making up a Multisound: Level, Tuning, Decay, Filter, and Transpose On/Off. These settings allow you to balance each sample relative to the others to create smooth transitions. The software saves files which you can use to instantly reconfigure your instrument.

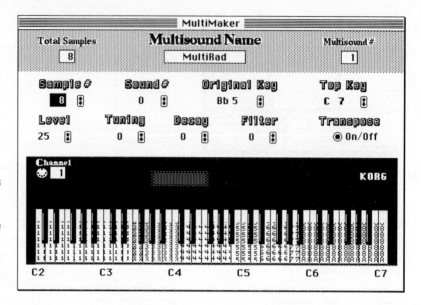

Music Scales

Tanya Rust's shareware Music Scales allows you to define your own scales for the Yamaha DX7II, TX81Z, DX7S, and TX802 and configure the physical layout of these on your MIDI keyboard. Of course, you can send these scales to your synthesizers.

Scales can be entered in this program in three linear formats — Hertz, ratios, and decimals, and also in exponential units that you define. Specification by Hertz is obvious — you specify frequency of the pitches. Ratios are typically just intonation and non-tempered-style ratios: 3/2, 9/8, 16/15, and so on. Decimal entry simply allows you to enter the ratio in decimal format. For example, the ratio 3/2 would be entered as 1.5.

The final type of scale entry is exponential, usually used to represent tempered tunings. First you define the number of units desired in moving from the unity to the octave. These units are then considered as "equal" exponential steps. Specifying pitches in Cents is an exponential system using 1200 units.

The scales you create don't necessarily have to ascend from left to right in the normal manner. They can descend, go backwards, or be randomized across the keyboard. With the latter option you must specify the number of octaves of the scale you wish to randomize. You may have up to 127 notes in any of your scales. This lets you ignore the concept of an octave or of any replication and enter a mathematical sequence or series.

Most traditional scales are defined within an octave (2/1), with their pattern repeating at the next octave. Music Scales lets you define your own octave span to be whatever you want. A MIDI note number table reference window is available.

Scales do not have to be assigned to consecutive keys on your MIDI keyboard. Assigning a scale to keys is as simple as pressing the notes on your keyboard for each scale tone. The last key press defines where the scale will restart. If you skip keys, they are left alone, allowing you to pass through the program again and assign another scale to the remaining keys.

All the scales you create may be displayed as decimals, Hertz, or exponentially. You can also print these windows as either the original scale or the last conversion you made. Finally you can save and load scale configuration files to and from disk.

Patch editor/librarians sorted by device

Table 12-2 lists all the editor/librarians available and their respective company. Company names in brackets are out of business, although their products are still in stores. A single line including multiple device names means that a single program supports all devices on that line.

Table 12-2: Patch editor/librarians

Company	Supported devices
Sound Quest	(Quest Series)
Galanter Productions	ART Multiverb III
Galanter Productions	ART SGE Multi-effect
Opcode Systems	Casio CZ Series
Altech	Casio Series
Bokoton Technologies	E-mu Proteus
Interval Music Systems	E-mu Proteus
Opcode Systems	E-mu Proteus
PhySy	E-mu Proteus (Shareware)
Galanter Productions	E-mu Proteus/2, 2-XR
Bokoton Technologies	Ensoniq EPS, EPS16
Opcode Systems	Ensoniq ESQ1, SQ80
[Beaverton Digital]	Ensoniq ESQ1, SQ80

Table 12-2: Patch Editor/Librarians (continued)

Company	Supported devices
Interval Music Systems	Ensoniq VFX
Opcode Systems	Kawai K1
Interval Music Systems	Kawai K1
Interval Music Systems	Kawai K4
James Chandler Jr.	Kawai K4 (Shareware)
Interval Music Systems	Kawai XD5
Interval Music Systems	KMX MIDI Central
Breakertech Software	Korg DW8000, EX8000
Multi Media Arts	Korg M1
James Chandler Jr.	Korg M1 (Shareware)
Zero-One	Korg M1, M3r, T1, T2, T3
Opcode Systems	Korg T1, M1, M3r
Kurzweil Music Systems	Kurzweil 150
Kurzweil Music Systems	Kurzweil 250 Keyboards
Kurzweil Music Systems	Kurzweil 250 Sequences
Opcode Systems	Kurzweil 1000
Sweetwater Sound	Kurzweil K250
Don Box	Kurzweil K1000 (Freeware HyperCard Stack)
Freq Sound	Kurzweil MIDIBoard
Lexicon	Lexicon LXP (Freeware HyperCard Stack)
Time of Your Life Music	Lexicon LXP 1 (Shareware HyperCard Stack)
Musical Systems	Lexicon LXP 1, LXP 5 (HyperCard Stack)
Christopher Watson	Lexicon PCM 70 (Shareware)
Opcode Systems	Oberheim Matrix 1000/Matrix-6
Galanter Productions	Oberheim Xpander, Matrix-12
Dr. T's	Roland D-10, 110, 20
Multi Media Arts	Roland D-10, 110, 20
Zero-One	Roland D-50
[Beaverton Digital]	Roland D-50
Dr. T's	Roland D-50
Multi Media Arts	Roland D-50
[SONUS]	Roland D-50
Valhalla	Roland D-50
Opcode Systems	Roland D-50/D-550
Valhalla	Roland D10, 110, 20

Table 12-2: Patch Editor/Librarians (continued)

Company	Supported devices
Opcode Systems	Roland D10, D110, D20, MT-32
Larry Mistrot	Roland D110 (Shareware HyperCard Stack)
Galanter Productions	Roland GP-8
Galanter Productions	Roland GR-50
[Beaverton Digital]	Roland L/A Devices
Russel Salerno	Roland MKS 50 (Shareware HyperCard Stack)
Harold Long	Roland MT 32 (Shareware HyperCard Stack)
Dynaware	Roland MT-32
Multi Media Arts	Roland MT-32
Opcode Systems	Roland MT-32
Valhalla	Roland MT-32
Valhalla	Roland R-8
Interval Music Systems	Sequential Prophet VS
Altech	Yamaha DX Series
Tanya Rust	Yamaha DX Series (Shareware)
Fumitaka Anzai	Yamaha DX, TX series
Opcode Systems	Yamaha DX7 II, TX802, DX7, TX7, TX816
James Chandler Jr.	Yamaha DX7, TX7
Digital Music Services	Yamaha DX7II
Opcode Systems	Yamaha DX11, TX81z, DX21, 27, 100
[Beaverton Digital]	Yamaha FB-01
Digital Music Services	Yamaha FB-01
Opcode Systems	Yamaha FB-01
EarLevel Engineering	Yamaha SPX90
Valhalla	Yamaha SY77
Digital Music Services	Yamaha TX81Z
Steven S. Dimse	Yamaha TX81Z
Valhalla	Yamaha TX81Z
[Beaverton Digital]	Yamaha TX81Z, DX11
Digital Music Services	Yamaha TX802

Universal Editor/Librarians

A universal editor/librarian is a combination of multiple editor/librarians into a single program. Like dedicated librarians, some dedicated editor/librarians (such as those marketed by Opcode Systems) allow you to install multiple profiles into one program shell, but once you have done this with three or four dedicated editor/librarians, it would have been more cost-effective simply to purchase a universal editor/librarian.

You can expect to find the following features in most of the choices available:

❖ Add groups of device profiles simultaneously during the setup stage.
❖ Auto-configure your MIDI patchbay to facilitate bidirectional communication.
❖ Transfer individual patches, groups of objects of the same data type, all objects for a specific device, and groups of objects for multiple devices.
❖ Take a "snapshot" of the entire configuration of all your devices with a single command (and reload this snapshot with a single command).
❖ Organize objects into libraries for storage and classification purposes.
❖ Drag patches from window to window.
❖ Send patch data to device by clicking the patch name with the mouse.
❖ Do graphic-parameter editing rather than typing in values.
❖ While parameter editing, simultaneously update the device being edited.
❖ Copy and paste individual parameters and groups of parameters.
❖ Compare two patches or an edited patch with its pre-edited version.
❖ Generate algorithmic patches.
❖ Audition patches by way of an on-screen keyboard.
❖ Audition patches by playing a sequence.
❖ Record and loop sequences from within the program.
❖ Play a note or sequence automatically after each parameter edit.
❖ Print a list of the patch names of a library or bank.
❖ Use online help.
❖ Create new profiles in a utility language.
❖ Provide compatibility with files on other computer platforms.

Some features that are very desirable but only available from a couple of manufacturers include:

❖ Duplicate patch searching.
❖ Individual components of multisounds travel with the multisound.
❖ Save patch data as MIDI files.
❖ Assign attribute keyword to individual patches.
❖ Sort and search libraries based on a variety of criteria.

Room for improvement

There is a good deal of room for development in universal editor/librarians. Many important features are missing from most current programs. For example, only X-oR provides database features of any degree of sophistication. A few other things to look for in the future include:

❖ *The option to print listings of the parameter values to individual patches.* This should be possible without simply taking a screen dump — screen dumps take too long and are uneditable with a text editor.

❖ *Options to save library and bank listings to a disk file.* Such files could be used to import your library contents into a database. They would also give you the option to reformat the printout in a way that was consistent with all your other studio-related documents.

❖ *Options to locate patches based upon parameter similarity.* This might present a list of patches that are of a specified degree of similarity for auditioning and quick deletion. MIDIQuest offers a rudimentary implementation of this type of feature.

❖ *Sophisticated database options.* Only X-oR provides a level of database manipulation commensurate with the requirements of most users of universal editor/librarians, although Opcode plans to include some similar features in a future release of Galaxy Plus Editors.

❖ *An auto-assign attributes (or keywords) option that looks at the patch data itself.* It would be very easy for the software to look at the data of a patch as it is received or loaded into a library. All it has to do is look at the amplitude envelope to assign such keywords as "slow attack," "medium attack," "fast attack," "slow decay," or "fast decay." Similarly, it could look for an LFO applied to amplitude or frequency to assign "tremolo" or "vibrato" keywords. It could even look at the speed and depth of the LFO and further distinguish between "fast vibrato" or "wide vibrato." Detecting the pan setting would permit the software to assign keywords like "panned full right" or "panned left center." It could even look at the filter cutoff to determine a keyword related to brightness. Finally, it could look at the effects settings and insert observations like "heavy reverb" or "slightly flanged." This sort of thing is child's play for a computer.

❖ *An auto-assign performance comments option that looks at the patch data itself.* Like the previous example, such an option would allow the software to automatically insert such comments as "aftertouch controls vibrato," "mod wheel controls tremolo rate," or "sustain pedal is disabled."

❖ *Analytical and interactive attribute assignment.* Carrying this concept of an "intelligent" universal editor/librarian a little further, the software could make the above two features analytical and interactive. This would allow you to request that all the patches with (for example) "fat," "metallic," or "analog" in their keywords or comments be analyzed for parameter similarity. The software could then compare subsequent additions to the library against the parameter value ranges it had determined for those descriptors and then automatically add the descriptor to the patch name or comment. A similar operation could be constructed to determine instrument type — "fat strings," "analog brass," or "sax pad," for example. This and the two preceding features, besides being indispensable in the general organization of your existing sound collection, could be used to quickly categorize banks of randomly generated patches.

❖ *Keyword re-mapping utilities.* With software that allows keyword attributes to be assigned to patches, the transfer of libraries to other people's systems could be greatly enhanced. X-oR does try to match keywords between libraries when trading sounds with other people, but a problem exists if the keywords are not identical. For example, what if you have a keyword "SnareDrum" and your friend's keyword is "Snare Drum" with a space between the words. A utility should compare patch data against two lists of keywords. If the software detected that your keyword for a long amplitude release segment was "Fast Decay" and your friend's keyword for the same parameter was "Quick Cutoff," the program should make the translation. You should be able to create a "map" file like those used for other purposes in Lone Wolf's Virtual Studio (see Chapter 8, "Moving Data Around Your Music Network"), so that whenever you exchange patches with that friend again, the software simply looks at the map file to translate your keywords into your friend's terminology.

❖ *Parameter-editing-screen layout mirroring signal path.* This is an area where there is much room for improvement. Editing screens that are laid out according to the actual signal flow within a device make it much easier for us to visualize the editing required to arrive at the sound we are imagining. PatchMaster Proteus (see the section "PatchMaster Proteus editor/librarian" at the beginning of this chapter) makes an attempt at this. Many other editor/librarians provide similarly intuitive approaches to editing effects that are built into certain synthesizers. This concept could easily be applied to the entire sound. It would make editing more efficient, because we would come to expect effects, VCA, Pan, and output routing to be toward the right side of the editing window and oscillators and LFOs on the left. Envelopes and filters would probably be somewhere in the middle of such a screen, and linked sounds would be across the bottom as a metaphor for the layering they create. This approach would also help people develop an inner sense of what is actually going on when they edit a parameter, how that edit fits into the overall scheme of things in the device's synthesis process, and most importantly, how to visualize a sound with respect to the editing that will be required to create that sound.

❖ *Configurable parameter-editing control layouts.* You should be able to rearrange the parameter controls on the editing screens in a universal editor/librarian. Some people never touch the effects settings of a patch, while others never concern themselves with envelope editing. Because of this, individual controls should be user-configurable on the main patch-parameter-editing screens. There is no need to clutter up a window with objects that you are never going to manipulate. This feature would be particularly useful for sounds that require multiple editing screens due to the number of editable parameters. In such cases, you should be able to move all the controls that you use the most to one screen for instant access. Many notation programs already offer user-configurable palettes for the same reasons.

❖ *Options to combine editing controls for different synthesizers onto a single screen.* The next logical step beyond user-configuration of the editing screen layout is the option to combine editing controls for different synthesizers onto a single screen. Beyond the concept of multisounds within an individual device, in practice many sounds are made up of layers of patches being played by different instruments (sequencers already provide for grouping these as virtual instruments that are addressable by a single name). If you want to tweak the overall envelope of this multi-device composite sound, it should be possible to bring the relevant envelope controls for each of the participating patches (regardless of what device they reside in) onto a single screen. Such a screen might also have an option to place all the envelopes under a single master envelope control link. Reshaping the master envelope would then reshape all the component envelopes accordingly. Such custom screen layouts could be automatically installed under a menu where they would appear with names such as "Group Envelope Editor" or "Group LFO Editor." Choosing one of these items could automatically install all the required components of the group of selected patches into the group editing window.

Commercial editor/librarian software

There are five commercial universal editor/librarians available. Because the previous chapter covered librarian software in detail, the following discussions will focus on the editing capabilities of the available universal editor/librarians. Special attention is paid to unique elements. Consult Chapter 11 and Table 12-4 at the end of this section for information on detailed librarian options.

One of your first concerns will be whether or not a universal editor/librarian supports the devices you own. Use Table 12-3 to make this determination. Don't be too concerned if a synthesizer you own is not on this list. Table 12-3 only indicates device profiles that shipped with the programs at the time of this writing. Most manufacturers add more profiles on an ongoing basis. Some even maintain BBSs, where you can download new profiles or profiles created by other users for rare instruments. Furthermore, all universal editor/librarians provide utilities to create new profiles and editing templates for devices that are not included with the program.

Table 12-3: Supported devices

Note: ◗ = Librarian features only (limited or no editing)

Company	Device	Galaxy Plus Editors	GenEdit	MIDI Master	MIDI-Quest	X-oR
360 Systems	8x8 Patcher					●
Akai	MB76					●
Akai	S700					
Akai	S612					
Alesis	HR16		●		●	●
Alesis	MIDIVerb III	◗				
Alesis	MMT8					
Alesis	QuadraVerb	◗				●
Art	Multiverb					●
Art	Multiverb II					●
Casio	CZ-1	◗	●			
Casio	CZ-1000	◗	●		●	●
Casio	CZ-3000	◗	●			●
Casio	CZ-5000	◗	●		●	●
Casio	CZ-101	◗	●		●	●
Casio	CZ-230S		●			
Casio	RZ-1	◗				
Casio	VZ-1				●	●
Casio	VZ-10M					●
Digital Music	MX8 Patch Bay			●	●	●
Digitech	DSP128				●	●
Digitech	DSP 128+					
E-mu	Proteus/1	●	●	●	●	●
E-mu	Proteus/2	●			●	●
E-mu	Proteus XR	●	●			●
Ensoniq	ESQ-M	●	●		●	●
Ensoniq	ESQ-1	●	●	●	●	●
Ensoniq	SQ-1	●			●	●
Ensoniq	SQ-80	●	●		●	●
Ensoniq	SQ-R	●				●
Ensoniq	VFX	◗			●	●
Ensoniq	VFX SD	◗				●

Table 12-3: Supported devices (continued)

Note: ▶ = Librarian features only (limited or no editing)

Company	Device	Galaxy Plus Editors	GenEdit	MIDI Master	MIDI-Quest	X-oR
Eventide	Harmonizer				●	
Fender	Chroma	▶				
Fender	Polaris	▶				
JL Cooper	MSB+	▶		●	●	●
JL Cooper	MSB16/20 Patch Bay	▶		●	●	
Kawai	K1	▶	●	●	●	●
Kawai	K1m	▶	●			
Kawai	K1r	▶	●			
Kawai	K3	▶			●	
Kawai	K4	▶		●	●	●
Kawai	K5	▶	●		●	●
Kawai	K5m	▶	●			
Kawai	R-50				●	
KMX	15x16 Patcher					●
Korg	707					●
Korg	DDD-5				●	
Korg	DFS-1					●
Korg	DS-8			●	●	●
Korg	DVP-1				●	●
Korg	DW-6000				●	●
Korg	DW-8000	▶		▶	●	●
Korg	EX-800				●	
Korg	EX-8000	▶		▶	●	●
Korg	M1	●	●	●	●	●
Korg	M1-EX	●				●
Korg	M1R	●	●		●	●
Korg	M1R-EX	●				●
Korg	M3R	●		●	●	●
Korg	P3					●
Korg	Poly 6					●
Korg	Poly 800				●	
Korg	SDD-3300				●	

Table 12-3: Supported devices (continued)

Note: ◗ = Librarian features only (limited or no editing)

Company	Device	Galaxy Plus Editors	GenEdit	MIDI Master	MIDI-Quest	X-oR
Korg	Symphony					●
Korg	T1	●	●	●	●	●
Korg	T2	●	●	●	●	●
Korg	T3	●	●	●	●	●
Korg	Wavestation	●				●
Korg	Z3					●
Kurzweil	1000 (PX, PX Plus, HX, SX, GX, AX Plus)	●	●			
Kurzweil	K1000 (SE, SE extended, SEII, SEII extended)	●	●			
Kurzweil	K1200	●	●			
Kurzweil	K1200 (Pro 1, Pro 2, Pro 3)	●	●			
Lexicon	LXP-1	◗	●	●	●	●
Lexicon	LXP-5		●			●
Lexicon	PCM 70	◗	●			●
Linn	LinnDrum	◗				
MIDIA	Music Box					
Oberheim	Xpander	◗	●			●
Oberheim	Matrix-6	●		●	●	●
Oberheim	Matrix-6R	◗			●	●
Oberheim	Matrix-12	◗	●	●		●
Oberheim	Matrix-1000	●		●	●	●
Oberheim	OB-8	◗				
Peavey	DPM-3	◗				●
Rane	MPE 14	◗				●
Rane	MPE 28	◗				●
Rane	MPE 47	◗				●
Roland	Alpha Juno 1	◗				●
Roland	Alpha Juno 2	◗				
Roland	CM series (32L, 32P, 64)	◗				
Roland	D-10	●	●	●	●	●
Roland	D-110	●	●	●	●	●
Roland	D-20	●	●		●	●
Roland	D-5	●	●		●	

Table 12-3: Supported devices (continued)

Note: ◗ = Librarian features only (limited or no editing)

Company	Device	Galaxy Plus Editors	GenEdit	MIDI Master	MIDI-Quest	X-oR
Roland	D-50	●	●	●	●	●
Roland	D-550	●	●			●
Roland	D-70	●			●	
Roland	DEP-5					●
Roland	E-20				●	
Roland	GM-70					●
Roland	GP-8					●
Roland	GP-16	◗				
Roland	GR-50				●	●
Roland	Juno-106	◗			●	●
Roland	JX-8P	◗			●	●
Roland	JX-10					
Roland	MKS-20					●
Roland	MKS-50 Alpha Juno	◗				
Roland	MKS-70	◗				●
Roland	MKS-80 Super Jupiter	◗		●		●
Roland	MT-32	●	●	●	●	
Roland	PAD-80	◗				
Roland	Rhodes 660					
Roland	R-8	◗			●	●
Roland	R-8M	◗			●	●
Roland	S10					
Roland	S330 (names only)	◗				
Roland	SBX80					
Roland	TR707					
Roland	TR727					
Roland	U-10			●		
Roland	U-110				●	●
Roland	U-20				●	●
Roland	U-220	◗			●	●
Sequential	Drumtrax				●	●
Sequential	Max					●
Sequential	MultiTrk				●	

Table 12-3: Supported devices (continued)

Note: ◗ = Librarian features only (limited or no editing)

Company	Device	Galaxy Plus Editors	GenEdit	MIDI Master	MIDI-Quest	X-oR
Sequential	Prophet 5				●	●
Sequential	Prophet 10				●	
Sequential	Prophet 600				●	●
Sequential	Prophet T8				●	
Sequential	Prophet VS	◗				
Sequential	SixTrk				●	●
Waldorf	Microwave	◗				●
Yamaha	DMP7				●	●
Yamaha	DX100	◗		●	●	●
Yamaha	DXII				●	
Yamaha	DX5	◗			●	
Yamaha	DX7	●	●	●	●	●
Yamaha	DX7-E!	◗				
Yamaha	DX7II	●	●			●
Yamaha	DX7II-D	●			●	
Yamaha	DX7II-E!	◗				
Yamaha	DX7II-FD	●			●	
Yamaha	DX11	●			●	
Yamaha	DX21	●		●	●	●
Yamaha	DX27	●		●	●	●
Yamaha	DX27S	◗				●
Yamaha	FB-01	◗			●	●
Yamaha	KX76					●
Yamaha	KX88					●
Yamaha	REV5	●				
Yamaha	RX5					
Yamaha	RX7				●	
Yamaha	RX11				●	●
Yamaha	RX17				●	
Yamaha	RX21		●			
Yamaha	RX21L				●	
Yamaha	SPX90	●			●	●
Yamaha	SPX90 II	●				●

Table 12-3: Supported devices (continued)

Note: ❘ = Librarian features only (limited or no editing)

Company	Device	Galaxy Plus Editors	GenEdit	MIDI Master	MIDI-Quest	X-oR
Yamaha	SY22				●	
Yamaha	SY55	❘			●	
Yamaha	SY77	●			●	●
Yamaha	TF01				●	
Yamaha	TG55	❘			●	
Yamaha	TG77	●			●	●
Yamaha	TX416	●		●		
Yamaha	TX7	●		●	●	●
Yamaha	TX802	●	●	●	●	●
Yamaha	TX81Z	●	●	●	●	●
Yamaha	TX816	●		●		
Yamaha	V50				●	●
Yamaha	YS200					
Generic SysEx	(Generic Bulk Dump)	●		●	●	

Galaxy Plus Editors

Opcode's Galaxy Plus Editors combines all their earlier editor/librarians into a single program. The software requires their OMS (Opcode MIDI System). OMS comes with Galaxy Plus Editors, so that is not a problem. You can read all about OMS in Chapter 8, "Moving Data Around Your Music Network."

OMS makes Galaxy Plus Editors very easy to install. Because you have told OMS all about the configuration of your system with the OMS Setup program, Galaxy Plus Editors can use that information to configure itself. Of course, if you are using OMS for the first time, having just received it with Galaxy Plus Editors, you will still need to go through OMS's setup stage (see Chapter 8 for details).

Galaxy Plus Editors's Easy Configure option installs all the modules (profiles) for your system with the push of a single button. OMS tells Galaxy Plus Editors what devices you have, what serial port, cable, or channel they are assigned to, which configuration of your MIDI patchbay is required for bidirectional communication with each device (if you are using a MIDI patchbay), the speed and type of your MIDI interface, and, if you have several devices of the same make and model, what their respective IDs are. Then Galaxy Plus Editors simply asks you to insert the disks with its modules on them one after another. It installs all the required modules automatically. That's all there is to it.

Many of Galaxy Plus Editors's strong points regarding its librarian capabilities are identical to those of Galaxy (without editors), as discussed in Chapter 11. Special features to recall include PatchFactory (a very robust algorithmic patch generator), an elegant approach to the handling of duplicate patches and duplicate patch data, a strong Parent/Child (multisound) implementation, publishing patch names so that Vision and StudioVision can Subscribe to them to create dynamic links between the two programs, and the option to save files in several formats (Galaxy, Librarian version 5, and Old Librarian formats). The latter feature facilitates sharing data with friends and colleagues who may not own Galaxy Plus Editors. To share files with people who don't own Opcode products, you can capture any data that you send to your devices to an SMF. Be careful with this option, because anything you click might send data that you don't want included in the SMF.

Galaxy Plus Editors differs from the available universal editor/librarians in that there is very little consistency between the appearance of the various editing templates (see Figure 12-14). This is partly because Galaxy Plus Editors's templates were created over a number of years as dedicated editor/librarians and simply all brought together into the universal editor/librarian. For an example of an Opcode editor interface, see the section "Korg M1 Editor/Librarian (Opcode)."

I liken each of Galaxy Plus Editors's editing screens to a different work of art by artists of the same school — and from a visual standpoint, many of these screens resemble works of art. There are definitely similarities, but the differences outnumber these significantly. There are valid arguments on both sides of Galaxy Plus Editors's interface inconsistency issue. I like it because after hours of staring at the screen, each new editor provides a different and refreshing graphic to wake me up, re-stimulate my creative juices, and provide a new perspective for thinking of the sound capabilities of the specific synthesizer any screen is dedicated to. Others prefer to see the same interface on all the parameter-editing screens, regardless of the device being edited. These people argue that the learning curve is faster because only one set of operating methods must be mastered. People on the other side of the fence maintain that once you are familiar with the interface of each of Galaxy Plus Editors's editors you always know instantly what device you are editing when you have multiple device windows open on the screen and that there is a danger of losing track of which window goes with which device when the interfaces are too consistent. It's an important issue, and the ramifications on the speed at which you can accomplish your sound-designing activities are significant.

Opcode plans to incorporate a powerful Find command into Galaxy Plus Editors by 1992 (in beta-test at the time of this writing). The new version includes the option to assign keywords (grouped into categories) to any patch (see Figure 12-15). It has over 1,500 factory presets, pre-tagged with keywords (courtesy

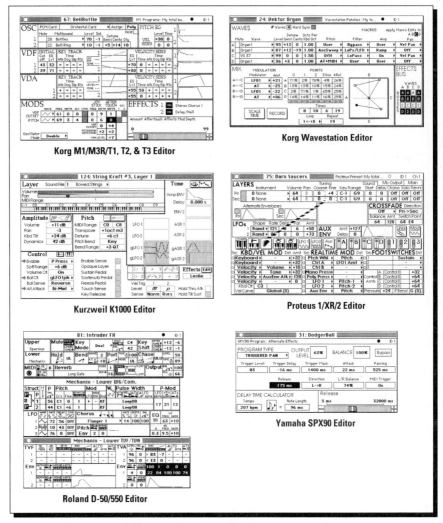

Figure 12-14: Opcode's Galaxy Plus Editors. Six different editing templates. Note the widely varied approach to the interface to synthesizers, even those of the same manufacturer. Compare the Roland D-50 and Proteus templates to those of other manufacturers pictured in earlier figures in this chapter.

Korg M1/M3R/T1, T2, & T3 Editor

Korg Wavestation Editor

Kurzweil K1000 Editor

Proteus 1/XR/2 Editor

Roland D-50/550 Editor

Yamaha SPX90 Editor

of Sound Source Unlimited), but you are free to modify these as you like and create your own categories and keywords. You can also assign comments to individual patches. Boolean searches are supported (see the section "X-oR").

GenEdit

Hybrid Arts's GenEdit is a recent port of their popular Atari software. Consequently, some tactics and terminology are slightly different from what you might expect. For example, what most programs refer to as banks, GenEdit calls blocks. A library is not a separate type of object, it is merely a block for which you have

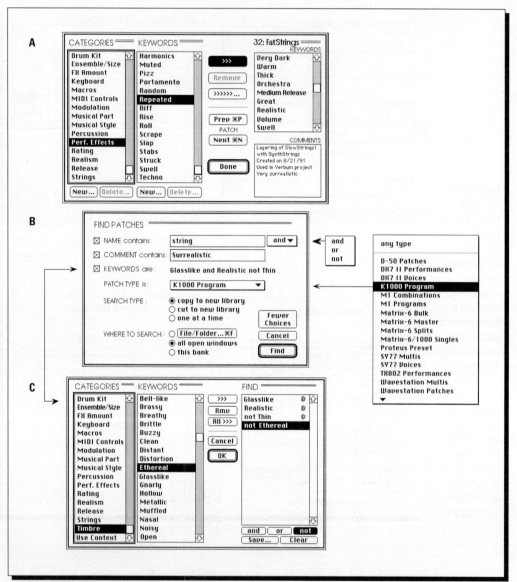

Figure 12-15: Galaxy Plus Editors's forthcoming keyword assignment and searching features (due for release in 1992). Note: The appearance of these dialog boxes may change slightly (they are in beta-test at the time of this writing). **(A)** You assign keywords and comments using this Patch Info dialog box. Selecting a category in the scrolling list at the far left brings up the keywords associated with that category. Assigning a keyword to a patch uses the Apple Font/DA mover interface. You select the keyword and press the >>> button. **(B)** Once you have assigned keywords to your sounds, you use this dialog box to locate patches for gathering into a new library by way of copying or cutting from the source libraries or banks. You may search by Name, Comment, or Keywords with Boolean And, Or or Not operators using the little pop-up menu at the upper right. The Patch Type pop-up menu brings up a list of all the patch types that you have currently installed in Galaxy Plus Editors. **(C)** If you include keywords in your search, you use this Find Keywords dialog box to choose a number of keywords with Boolean operators. These appear next to the "KEYWORDS are:" checkbox in the Find dialog box as indicated in this illustration by the arrow.

specified an increase in size and capacity. Although the number of profiles included with the software is quite large, a big portion of the software is devoted to Hybrid Arts's profile development system and their driver-creating language called CNX.

GenEdit provides a unique approach to patch generation (see Figure 12-16). You can "average" up to six patches using the software's Make Patch option. For each patch participating in the software, you can set the level (the relative proportion that will contribute to the generated patch) and the distortion (the amount by which the specific source patch will be distorted).

GenEdit provides a visual programming environment that makes it very easy to create new templates. You can simply drag desired controls from a palette onto the main window and then stretch them to whatever size you want. Double-clicking any of these items brings up its Value Edit dialog box (see Figure 12-17). Using this utility it is possible (though difficult) to create editors that address more than one device at a time. So you can have a single editor that controls only the TVFs of all your devices that have TVFs.

Surprisingly, editing templates are very easy to churn out. You can also call up the tool palette and customize any of the editors that come with the software. GenEdit comes with drivers for most manufacturers, but if you want to create your own, the program comes with CNX, a programming language for drivers.

MIDI Master

Computer Business Associates's MIDI Master is another port from the non-Macintosh world, in this case the IBM. Parameter editing is accomplished by way of sliders (see Figure 12-18). Sliders are used for everything, even on/off switches. Like GenEdit, the software comes with a user-friendly template editor for creating your own custom editing templates (see Figure 12-19). A random patch generator lets you select up to four Parent patches, anchor up to 26 parameters so that they are not affected by randomization, and then generate new patches by randomizing unanchored parameters. The program also includes a SysEx recorder window that captures, displays, and saves to disk any SysEx information you send to it.

MIDIQuest

Sound Quest's MIDIQuest is yet another port from the other computing world, in this case the world of IBMs, Ataris, and Amigas. In addition to all the standard features found in other programs, MIDIQuest adds a few unique options not found in any other program (see Figure 12-20).

Unique MIDIQuest features include the option to import banks or other groups of files *en masse* into a library directly from disk and the ability to sort files by manufacturer, instrument, or file size (you can also sort by name, date, or keyword).

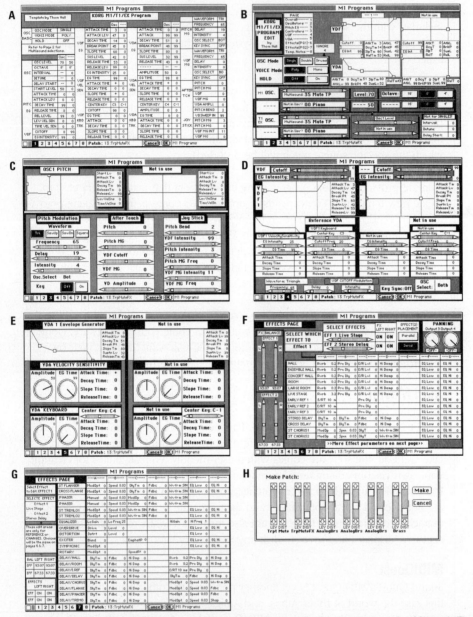

Figure 12-16: Hybrid Arts's GenEdit. Seven screens are required to edit all the parameters of an M1 patch. These are labeled A through G in this illustration. You can jump from screen to screen using the buttons running across the bottom of each window. A typical Make Patch dialog box is pictured at the lower right (H). Here, you can average up to six patches that you have selected in a Block window. The controls set the level and individual distortion that will be applied to each patch during the averaging process.

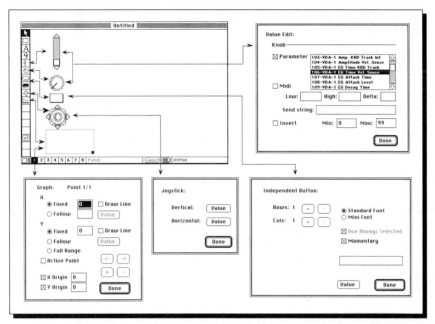

Figure 12-17: GenEdit's template creation screen. The palette on the left (which can be moved to the right if desired) is an unlimited well of graphic symbols. You drag these to any location in the window. You can then freely resize the graphics. Double-clicking a graphic element brings up its Value Edit dialog box, where you enter the information you want the control to transmit as well as minimum/maximum control values, and other characteristics of the graphic. The Value Edit dialog for sliders and knobs are identical. Note the little arrows in the Graph Value Edit dialog box. With these you can scroll through the various points (which would appear as handles, for example, if the graphics were used to edit envelopes). The plus and minus buttons are there to add and delete graphics segment points.

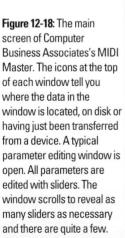

Figure 12-18: The main screen of Computer Business Associates's MIDI Master. The icons at the top of each window tell you where the data in the window is located, on disk or having just been transferred from a device. A typical parameter editing window is open. All parameters are edited with sliders. The window scrolls to reveal as many sliders as necessary and there are quite a few.

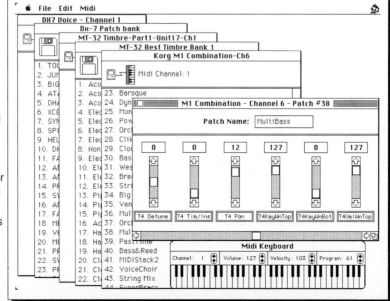

A — Edit Instrument: M1 Combination - Channel 6

Template Name	Data Type	Midi Channel
M1 Combination - Channel	8 Bit #1	1

Manufacturer ID	66	Memory Mapped Device Information	
Device ID	25	Bytes in Address & Size	3 Bytes
Model ID	0	Starting Address	0 0 0
Number of Parameters	154	Data Size	0 0 0

Buttons: GNRL INFO, PATCH INFO, PARAM DEF, EDIT MSG, Midi Master™

B — Edit Instrument: M1 Combination - Channel 6

Number of patches in bank	100	☐ Acknowledge Message
Bytes per patch	124	☐ Manual patch bank dump
Bytes per individual dump	0	☒ Send patch when selecting
Bytes before data starts	6	☒ Select patch w/program chg
Characters in patch name	10	☐ Multiple patch dumps
Patch name offset in data	0	☐ Multiple dump requests
Patch name parameter #	0	☐ Program chg per request
		☐ Send write message

Buttons: GNRL INFO, PATCH INFO, PARAM DEF, EDIT MSG, Midi Master™

C — Edit Instrument: M1 Combination - Channel 6

Combi Type

Name	Number	Offset	Mask	Minimum Value	Maximum Value	Display Offset
Combi Type	10	10	127	0	4	0
Effect 1 #	11	11	127	0	33	0
Effect 2 #	12	12	127	0	33	0
Eff1 L Bal	13	13	127	0	100	0
Eff1 R Bal	14	14	127	0	100	0
Eff2 L Bal	15	15	127	0	100	0
Eff2 R Bal	16	16	127	0	100	0

Buttons: GNRL INFO, PATCH INFO, PARAM DEF, EDIT MSG, Midi Master™

D — Popup menu:
✓ Acknowlege
Single Patch Request
Bulk Patch Request
Parameter Change
Single Tx
Bulk Tx
Write Complete
Device ID

Edit Instrument: M1 C...

Message Under Edit:

240 66 0 0 0 0 0 0
0 0 0 0 0 0 0 0

Marker	Dec	Hex	Marker	Dec	Hex
Insert patch data here	255	FF	Insert absolute program #	250	FA
Start checksum calculation	254	FE	Insert program # + offset	249	F9
End checksum calculation	253	FD	Insert device ID message	248	F8
Address to follow	252	FC	End of exclusive message (EOX)	247	F7
Insert param num here	251	FB			

Buttons: GNRL INFO, PATCH INFO, PARAM DEF, EDIT MSG, Midi Master™

Figure 12-19: MIDI Master's Template Editor/Creator uses four windows to create an instrument template. You can jump from one window to another using the buttons at the bottom left of any of the windows. **(A)** The General Information window is where you enter header information such as Manufacturer ID, Device ID, Model ID. Note that Data Type, MIDI Channel, and Bytes In Address & Size are pop-up menus. **(B)** The Patch Information window is where you specify such information as the number of patches in a bank, bytes per patch, patch name offset in data, and other related information required by the editor. **(C)** The Parameter Definition editor lets you set values for each parameter that you will later edit with sliders in MIDI Master. The minimum and maximum values define the range of the individual sliders. **(D)** The Message editor lets you create and modify various messages that you access from the pop-up menu at the top of the screen. Messages that MIDI Master is concerned with in this case include Single Patch Request, Bulk Patch Request, Parameter Change, Write Complete, Program Number Marker, and so on.

MIDIQuest actually looks at the data in the data's associated driver to find the manufacturer's name and the device name (by translating the SysEx IDs).

A very desirable feature, shared only with X-oR at the time of this writing, is that libraries can be searched by a variety of criteria. To the standard patch name, key-word, and test-string-in-comments found in X-oR, MIDIQuest adds "by similarity" (which you specify by a percentage value) and "by byte value." The latter is useful only to programmers. A rudimentary implementation of Boolean Ands and Nots are allowed in searches (see Figure 12-25). Searches can be executed in multi-instrument bundles that the program appropriately calls "Data Bases."

MIDIQuest takes Super Librarian's approach to auditioning sound with sequences (see Chapter 11). You can have up to ten sequences loaded into the program to play back whenever you want. The playback controls are pretty sophisticated for this type of environment. The playback window lets you mute selected channels and includes a graphic display of channel activity.

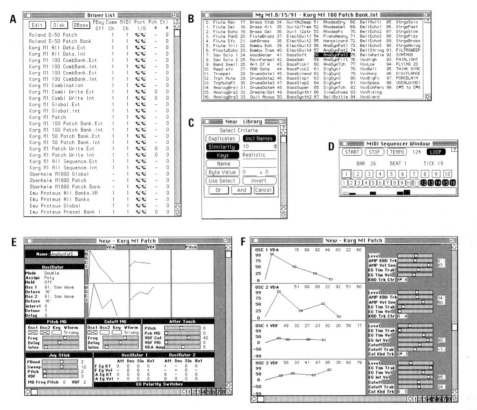

Figure 12-20: (A) MIDIQuest driver list. **(B)** MIDIQuest bank window. **(C)** The Search Criteria dialog box. What appear to be buttons in this window actually function as checkboxes (one of MIDIQuest's many alterations of the standard Macintosh user interface). When they are highlighted, it indicates that the item is part of the search criteria. Most of the options are self-explanatory. Exceptions include Use Select — this takes a selected patch in the library as the model for the search criteria. The Boolean Or and And buttons refer to all the criteria enabled above those buttons. And means that the search will find patches that fulfill all the highlighted criteria. Or means that the search will find patches that fulfill any of the highlighted criteria (even just one). The Invert button functions sort of like the Boolean Not operator. When highlighted, the search will find all patches that do not fulfill the specified criteria. Invert (Not) can be combined with And or Or, but it makes no sense to combine And and Or in a search. **(D)** The SMF Sequence Player window. You use the upper row of ten buttons to select from up to ten sequences you may have loaded into the program. The lower row of 16 buttons is used to mute MIDI channels. The bar at the bottom of the window displays channel activity beneath each channel button. Height is equivalent to velocity **(E)** and **(F)** Typical MIDIQuest patch-editing windows. There is really only one scrollable window but you can jump from screenful to screenful with the buttons at the lower right. You edit data in three ways: by typing new values, by manipulating the graphic controls (such as sliders, knobs, and envelope handles) with the mouse, and by using the plus or minus keys. Note the vertical scroll bar. You can use this to scroll to different "pages" of the editor. It is faster yet to click on the buttons at the lower right in order to jump immediately to a specific part of the editor.

Other unique features include auto-backup of files and four-level undos. The multiple-undo is accomplished with buffers. Each patch has four buffers to which you can save work in progress. These can then be restored with a menu command. "Swap patches" is a very useful feature that X-oR also shares. When this option is turned on, dragging a patch from one bank or Data Base to another swaps the source and destination patches.

Unlike all most other available universal editor/librarians for the Macintosh, Sound Quest requires that you purchase its template designer separately.

Although the company has made an impressive port of their IBM software to the Macintosh world, there are many holdovers from the earlier version that will take some time getting used to. For example, this is the only Macintosh program I have ever seen that assigns Command-period to a keyboard shortcut for a menu item (Mix All). If you are used to pressing Command-period a couple of times to abort an operation, you may find yourself in for a long wait while you watch a number of new banks be inadvertently generated.

X-oR

Dr. T's X-oR is the newcomer to the Macintosh universal editor/librarian scene. As you can see from Table 12-4, X-oR is the most feature-laden program of the five universal editor/librarians available. This may be because it has a lot of history behind it. It has been a popular program in the IBM, Atari, and Amiga worlds for years and is already up to version 3.0 on those platforms. The Macintosh version is significantly enhanced (see Figures 12-21 through 12-23).

There is some terminology that you should know for understanding X-oR. An X-oR patch refers to a collection of parameters, whether a voice patch or a micro-tuning patch. X-or banks equate to Opcode single-instrument bundles. Like Super Librarian (see Chapter 11), a collection of banks is called a performance (equivalent to a multi-instrument bundle in Galaxy).

X-oR supports Mark of the Unicorn's multicable (greater-than-32-channel) MIDI Time Piece interface without having to use OMS, as Galaxy Plus Editors does. Furthermore, it is MIDI Manager-compatible. Its MIDI-Manager-compatibility is so strong that the programmer felt it was not necessary to include a built-in sequencer in the software. The manual suggests running your sequencer in the background under MIDI Manager to achieve the same results. See Chapter 8 for more information on the MIDI Time Piece, OMS, and Apple's MIDI Manager.

X-oR has many unique features, perhaps the most fascinating of which is its long-awaited (by the Macintosh community), fully implemented database functions (see below). Some unique options are courtesy features that speed up your editing and librarian activities.

Figure 12-21: Dr. T's X-oR. A typical Performance window (referred to as a multi-instrument bundle by some other programs). Note the quantity of information displayed. In the channel column "--" indicates devices that respond on multiple MIDI channels, and "xx" indicates that if that module is selected, the mode of the instrument will be changed (making other modules inactive if necessary — for example, the M1 can be in Combination or Program mode, but not both). The checkmark indicates patches that have been edited but not saved. A question mark may appear in this column if X-oR thinks that the module's patch data might be out of sync with the actual data in the physical instrument. The last column shows where the patch came from (patch file, performance, bank, library, or "received," meaning from the external instrument). Note: this displays the most recent source, which is not necessarily the original source.

<table>
<tr><td>🍎</td><td>File</td><td>Edit</td><td>Library</td><td>MIDI</td><td>Play</td><td>Windows</td></tr>
</table>

Performance : Perf.7/19/91

Port	Ch	Instrument	Area	✓	Patch Name	Source
13	1	Roland D-50	Patch		Fantasia	Received
6	1	Wave Station	multiset	?	UNNAMED multiset	Received
6	off	Wave Station	perform	?	UNNAMED perform	Received
6	off	Wave Station	patch	?	UNNAMED patch	Received
6	off	Wave Station	wave seq	?		Received
12	1	Korg M-1	Combi		FilmScore	Received
12	1	Korg M-1	Program	✓	Flute Rev	Received
12	--	Korg M-1	Drum Kit	?	Init Drum Kit	Received
12	--	Korg M-1	Global		Unnamed Global	Received
9	1	Emu Proteus2	Setup	?	Default Setup	Received
9	1	Emu Proteus2	Preset	?	--Default--	Received
9	--	Emu Proteus2	Prog.Map	?		Received
9	--	Emu Proteus2	Tune Tbl	?		Received
8	1	Roland R-8	Feel Pat	?		Received
0	1	Roland R-8	Pattern	?		Received
8	1	Roland R-8	Song	?		Received
8	1	Roland R-8	MIDI	?		Received
8	1	Roland R-8	Sounds	?		Received
8	1	Roland R-8	ROM Card	?		Received
11	1	Super JX	Patch		ELECTRIC PIANO	Received
11	1	Super JX	Tone 1	?		Received
11	1	Super JX	Tone 2	?		Received

M1P Main Library

Name	Date	Comment
AnalogBrs1	7/20/91 4:20	Analog
AnalogBrs2	7/20/91 4:20	Analog
AnalogBrs3	7/20/91 4:20	Analog (got from Pat H. and then edited)
Band Swell	7/20/91 4:19	Neuro VADA
FlootzEcho	7/20/91 4:18	Neuro VADA
Flute Del	7/20/91 4:17	For VADA2
Flute Echo	7/20/91 4:17	For VADA2
Flute Efx	7/20/91 4:17	For VADA2
Flute PanD	7/20/91 4:17	For VADA2
Flute Rev	7/20/91 4:17	For VADA2
Flute Tril	7/20/91 4:17	For VADA2
Reed efx	7/20/91 4:19	Neuro VADA
Sax Solo 1	7/20/91 4:18	Neuro VADA
Sax Solo 2	7/20/91 4:18	Neuro VADA
TrpMuteFX	7/20/91 4:19	My Edits
Trpt Mute	7/20/91 4:19	My Edits
Trumpet	7/20/91 4:19	My Edits

717 patches

Figure 12-22: A library window in X-oR. X-oR libraries display much more information than other universal editor/librarians. Patch name, keyword, comments, and last modification date are displayed. Libraries can be sorted by name or by last modification date (which takes the time into consideration). The width of the columns can easily be changed by dragging the column divider tabs.

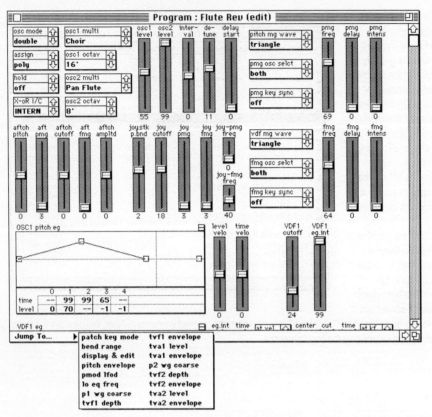

Figure 12-23: A typical parameter-editing screen from X-oR. Note that the window scrolls both horizontally and vertically to reveal more controls. In fact it can scroll quite extensively. The parameter-editing interface is very consistent between synthesizers and all editors resemble this one. The Jump To pop-up menu at the bottom left of the window lets you jump to particular areas immediately, rather than having to scroll for relocation. The Jump To pop-up menu, rather than listing nameless page numbers, contains the names of the screen areas as pictured in this illustration.

❖ Store window locations for subsequent recall.
❖ Be able to open files from competing manufacturers.
❖ Name banks within performances (multi-instrument bundles).
❖ Format the text of a library (with standard Macintosh tabs) for printing (printed output includes names, keywords, comments, and creation dates).

One special feature that speeds up parameter editing significantly is X-oR's option to map a physical control on your synthesizer or MIDI controller to the on-screen controls. Anywhere you need to scroll through values when you are parameter-editing, all you need to do is move the controller on your keyboard, perhaps the data slider or modulation wheel, to manipulate the values on the screen.

Like Dr. T's Roland D-50 Editor/Librarian discussed above, X-oR implements MousePlay for auditioning sounds. You will recall that this allows you to use the mouse button (with the command key down) to play notes on your synthesizer. The note number and velocity are mapped to the mouse's horizontal and vertical positions. Holding the option key down while you do this transmits modulation values. X-oR's MousePlay feature is enhanced to allow you to assign any continuous controller you want to this function. The "Glissando" (MousePlay with the shift key down) continually triggers notes without any new mouse button presses. A new feature in X-oR is the option to constrain MousePlay to one of 13 scales: chromatic, major, natural minor, harmonic minor, melodic minor, whole-tone, diminished (octatonic), pentatonic, pentatonic minor, enigma, Neapolitan, Neapolitan minor, and Hungarian.

X-oR takes patch comparison to a higher level; it offers a byte-level comparison expressed as a percentage, which indicates the similarity of the raw physical data bytes making up the objects being compared.

The handling of parent and child patch relationships (see Chapter 11 under "Galaxy") is particularly well implemented. X-oR is constructed so that there is no way that a parent patch can lose track of its child patches.

Online help in X-oR is editable with a standard word processor, so if you have any special notes pertaining to your setup that you want to add to the online help, you can do it.

X-oR's patch generation algorithms are the most flexible of all the available universal editor/librarians (see Figure 12-24). X-oR's blend option interpolates new patches between two selected patches (similar to the shade option in Galaxy Plus Editors). X-oR also provides a random parameter swap called mingle (similar to the shuffler option in Galaxy Plus Editors). To both of these features, X-oR adds the option to gradually introduce specifiable degrees of randomness. The program also lets you include parameters that are not editable by any other means in the patch generation process.

In answer to many people's prayers, X-oR includes extensive library searching capabilities. The program comes with predefined keywords that are organized in groups, but you can edit these to your heart's content. You can assign up to eight keywords to a patch. The process is simplified by way of hierarchical pop-up menus that display the available groups with their associated keywords as submenus. You can also assign a separate comment to every patch. When you are adding groups of similar patches to a library, you can specify that selected keywords are automatically attached to the patches as they are entered in the library.

After you've assigned keywords and comments to your sounds, use the Find Patches dialog box to locate patches that fulfill criteria you specify. The Find

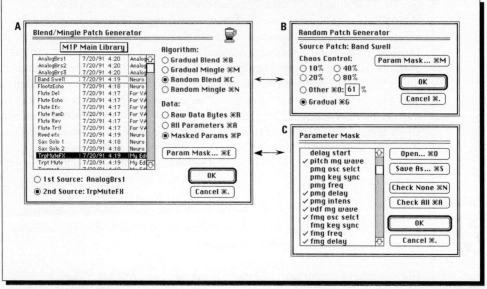

Figure 12-24: X-oR provides three types of algorithmic patch generation to create banks of new patches: **(A)** X-oR's Blend and Mingle dialog box. **(B)** X-oR's Randomize dialog box. **(C)** X-oR's Parameter Mask dialog box (available with blending, mingling, and randomizing) lets you exclude parameters from the patch generating algorithm by unchecking them from a scrolling list.

Patches option lets you create a search rule. The search rule can include a text string to search for in patch comments. Or the search rule can include keywords (also accessed via hierarchical pop-up menus). You can also attach Boolean operators (accessed from pop-up menus as well) to create a very precise search rule (see Figure 12-25). You can even place a Boolean operator between a text string search (aimed at the patch comments) and the keyword list.

Boolean operators are And, Or, and Not. And finds patches that have both the first keyword and the second keyword. Or finds patches that have either keyword, but not necessarily both. Not finds patches that do not have the indicated keyword. Or takes precedence over And and Not.

Following is an example applied to X-oR, which provides for five Boolean operators:

	Strings
	Solo
AND	Solo
AND	Violin
OR	Viola
OR	Cello
NOT	Synth

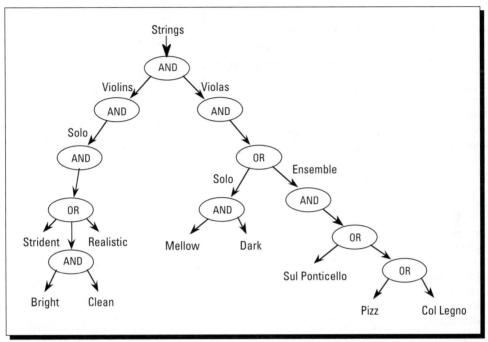

Figure 12-25: A complex example of Boolean operators used in a search criterion. Find: Strings AND (Violins AND (Solo AND (Strident OR Realistic OR (Bright and Clean)))) AND (Violas AND ((Solo AND Mellow AND Dark) OR Ensemble AND ((Sul Ponticello) OR (Pizz OR Col Legno)))).

would find all string sounds that are solo violins, violas, or cellos, but not synth-type.

	Strings
	Strings
AND	Solo
AND	Violin
OR	Viola
AND	Realistic
OR	Tremolo

would find all string sounds that are solo violins or violas and are either realistic or tremolo (see Figure 12-26).

Table 12-4 is a list of all the features found in the available universal editor/librarians.

Figure 12-26: X-oR provides powerful library searching features. **(A)** First you use the Keyword Setup dialog box to create your keywords. X-oR comes with dozens already made for you and they are excellent choices, but you may want to modify or add to them. **(B)** When you copy patches into a library, the Library Patch Information dialog box appears. If you choose the Comment option (lower left), all the patches you are currently copying into the library will have the same keywords and comments. This is a very useful feature.

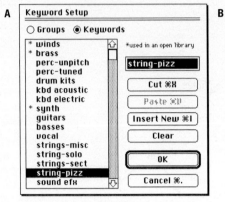

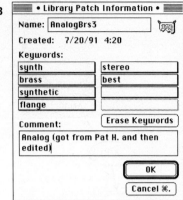

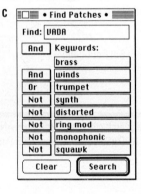

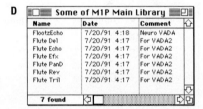

For example, it's easy to select all sounds from a bank that have the same timbre, assign the keyword one time, and then use the Comment option to assure that all the patches have those keywords and comments associated with them in the library. **(C)** The Find Patches menu option brings up this dialog box. Here you can specify a text string to search for in the comments associated with each patch and up to eight keywords to include in the search criteria. Each item has a Boolean operator pop-up menu beside it (see text for explanation). **(D)** This is the result of a typical search. The number of found items appears at the lower left. A single menu command toggles between the found items and the rest of the library.

Table 12-4: Universal editor/librarian features

❶ = Announced for 1992
② = Information unavailable at the time of this writing

Feature	Galaxy Plus Editors	GenEdit	MIDI Master	MIDI-Quest	X-oR
Setup					
Add multiple profiles at a time	●	●		●	●
Configure launch to auto-open	●				●
Specified libraries	●				●
Specified bundle/performance	●				●
Empty bundle, bank, library	●●●				
Specify Middle C is C3 or C4	●				
User-assignable keyboard shortcuts		●			
Specify reduced MIDI speed option for problem instruments		●			
Windows					
Windows menu displays open windows	●				●
Store and recall window locations					●
Stack or tile					
Move to next window command	●				●
Save all (saves all edits in all open windows)	●				
Close all	●				
MIDI communication					
Single interface (16 channels)	●	●	●	●	●
Dual interface (32 channels)	●	●		●	●
Multicable interface (> 32 channels)	●				●
Auto-configure MIDI patchbay	●	●		●	●
MIDI Manager-compatible, required		●○			●○
OMS-compatible, required	●●				
Transferring data					
Filter Open File dialog box display by data or file type	●		●		●
Get/send individual patches	●	●		●	●
Get/send individual data types (banks)	●	●		●	●
Get/send all banks of individual instruments	●	●		●	●
Get/send all banks of multiple instruments	●			●	●

Table 12-4: Universal editor/librarian features (continued)

❶ = Announced for 1992
② = Information unavailable at the time of this writing

Feature	Galaxy Plus Editors	GenEdit	MIDI Master	MIDI-Quest	X-oR
Transferring data (continued)					
Send on select option	●	●		●	●
Option to exclude specified devices in multi-instrument bundle load				●	
Save as SMF option	●			●	
Open files from other manufacturers					●
Save files in other manufacturers' formats					
MidiEx-compatible				●	
Send any MIDI message					●
Organizing data					
Drag patches to copy and paste within bank or library	●			●	●
Drag patches to copy and paste from library or bank to another library or bank	●			●	●
Edit menu copy, cut, paste	●	●	●		●
Option to swap source with destination patch			●	●	
Multi-instrument bundles or performance	●				●
Name banks within bundles					●
Handling of duplicate patches					●
Option to delete duplicate patches	●			●	
Option to not permit copying duplicate patches into library	●				●
Audition patch in duplicate notification dialog box	●				
Option to auto-rename when duplicate names are encountered	●				
Parent/Child Patches					
Child info available in libraries auto-entry	●●				
Child patches travel with parent from bank to bank	●				●
Child patches travel with parent from library to library					●
Child patches travel with parent on transfer to synthesizer	●				●

Table 12-4: Universal editor/librarian features (continued)

❶ = Announced for 1992
② = Information unavailable at the time of this writing

Feature	Galaxy Plus Editors	GenEdit	MIDI Master	MIDI-Quest	X-oR
Libraries	●	●		●	●
Import files *en masse* into library				●	
Sort by name, date, keyword				●●●	●●○
Sort by manufacturer, instrument, file size				●●●	
Auto sort, disable auto sort	●○				●●
Auto creation assign dates and time				●	●
Assign keywords to patches	❶			●	●
Keywords organized into larger "groups"	❶				●
Number of keywords (per individual program)	②				8
Auto assign keywords	②				●
Assign same keyword to all patches selected	②				●
Assign comments to patches	❶				●
Auto assign comments	②				●
Assign comments to banks	②				●
Assign comments to libraries	②				●
Display keywords, comments, dates in main library window (along with names)	②				●●●
Searchable?	❶			●	●
Search by patch name	❶			●	●
Search by keyword	❶			●	●
Search by string in comment	❶			●	●
Search by data similarity	②			●	
Search by byte value	②			●	
Boolean searches	❶			▸	●
AND, OR, NOT	❶			▸▸▸	●●●
Number of levels (criteria)	②			(6)	8
Toggle display between last search and show all	②			●	●
Format library text display (comments, dates, etc.)					●
Print library or bank contents	●	●		●	●

Table 12-4: Universal editor/librarian features (continued)

❶ = Announced for 1992
② = Information unavailable at the time of this writing

Feature	Galaxy Plus Editors	GenEdit	MIDI Master	MIDI-Quest	X-oR
Parameter editing					
Numericals, pop-up menus, toggle switches	●●●	●○●		○●●	●●●
Sliders, knobs, envelope "handles"	●○●	●●●	●○○	●●●	●○●
Text values are continually updated when dragging envelope handles	●				●
Copy and paste individual parameters	●			●	●
Copy and paste groups of parameters	●			●	●
Comparison option (compare edited with unedited or any two patches)	◗			●	●
Display byte-level similarity as percentage					●
Map physical continuous controller to on-screen controls				●	
Assign MIDI keyboard event to select the next or previous patch	●				
Consistency of on-screen controls for different devices		◗	●	●	●
Generation of patches					
Gradual transformation (interpolation) from source patch to destination patch	●			●	●
Introduce randomness				●	●
Specify degree				●	●
Random parameter swap	●		●	●	●
Gradually increase randomness					●
Use two patches as upper and lower parameter value constraints for randomization	●				
Average multiple patches together		●			
Set level and distortion of each participating patch			●		
User control					
Exclude specified parameters	◗	●	●	●	●
Specify min/max parameter values for random generation	●	◗			
Include non-editable parameters					●
Generate banks or libraries of user-specified size	●			●	●

Table 12-4: Universal editor/librarian features (continued)

❶ = Announced for 1992
② = Information unavailable at the time of this writing

Feature	Galaxy Plus Editors	GenEdit	MIDI Master	MIDI-Quest	X-oR
Auditioning					
Echo or MIDI THRU	●	●	●	●	●
On-screen keyboard	●		●		●
Auto repeat notes	●				
On-screen or other transmittable continuous controllers				●	●
Sequences	●	●		●	
Play, record, loop	●●●	●●○		●●●	
Import SMF	●			●	
Load multiple sequences				●	
Mute MIDI channels				●	
Play chords	●			●	●
MousePlay (screen coordinates mapped to pitch and velocity)				●	●
Constrain to scale, key					●●
Play After Edit option	●	●		●	●
Miscellaneous					
Copy-protected	●	●			
Link patch names to MIDI sequencer	●				
Online help, editable?	●○			●○	●●
Multiple undo buffers				●	
Create new profiles	●	●	●	●	●
System included with program	●	●	●		
Must be purchased separately				●	
MIDI monitor window text, graphic		●○		●●	●○
All notes off command	●				●
Auto backup				●	
Program exists on other computers		●	●	●	●
IBM			●	●	●
Atari		●		●	
Amiga				●	●
Files are compatible between other manufacturers' computers		●	●	●	

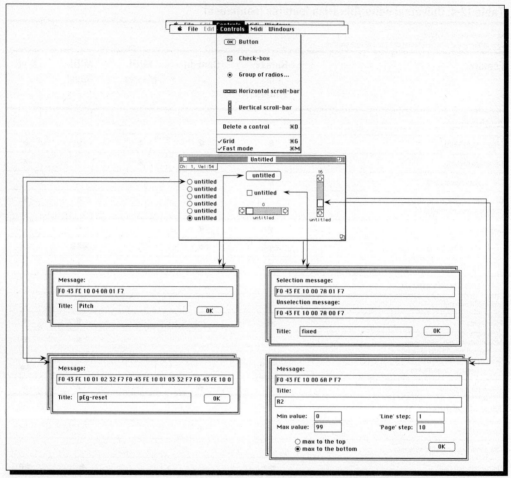

Figure 12-27: Benoît Widemann's shareware MIDI Control, like GenEdit's Template Editor, lets you select interface controls from the Control menu and place them on a screen. After an object has been placed, clicking it with the Shift key pressed lets you resize it, clicking it with the Option key pressed lets you reposition it, and clicking it with the Command key pressed lets you set its attributes including name, MIDI message, minimum and maximum values (or selected and unselected state for checkboxes). Clicking an object without any modifier keys pressed sends the MIDI message assigned to that object.

Shareware and freeware solutions
MIDI Control

Benoît Widemann's shareware MIDI Control is a visual programming language that lets you create patch editors for any device for which you have the MIDI implementation chart. See Figure 12-27. The program does not deal with libraries, but you can save individual patches which average in size from about 1K to 3K (they can get as large as you need).

> It is very easy to create a patch editor with MIDI Control. Likewise, it is an easy matter to create editors that address multiple devices from the same screen.

Summary

✔ Editing synthesized sounds is a branch of sound design commonly referred to as patch editing. The programs that allow you to edit synthesized sounds are called patch editors. Patch editors greatly simplify the control of the internal sound manipulation capabilities of MIDI devices. Editor/librarians that combine both patch-editing and librarian functions in one program are rapidly becoming the standard format for such software. Like librarians, there are two types of editors and editor/librarians: dedicated and universal. There are at least 78 dedicated editor/librarians and five universal editor/librarians available. Over 150 devices are supported by at least one editor/librarian.

✔ Nearly all synthesizers allow you to modify their sounds by way of controls on their front panels. Besides synthesizers, other types of MIDI devices such as MIDI-controllable effects, MIDI mixers, and MIDI controllers provide similar editing options. Unfortunately, although most MIDI devices offer vast capabilities for sound design of this kind, they only provide a limited number of controls, often a single knob, numeric keypad, several function buttons, possibly a data slider or two, some arrow keys for scrolling, and a very tiny display.

✔ In most cases, all the hardware controls on a MIDI device are multi-functional; they do different things depending on what mode you are in. Often there are dozens of modes and it is very difficult to keep track of what mode you are in. That's why it is sometimes difficult to predict the effect any given control will have if you manipulate it.

✔ The Macintosh permits the simulation of hundreds of virtual controls on-screen, and these always remain assigned to the same function. The main issue boils down to user interface. Software can often provide a better user interface than hardware, and user interface is one area in which the Macintosh excels.

✔ The sound parameters of synthesizer patches are often labeled with esoteric-sounding terms; they actually refer to common sound characteristics that you probably already understand. It's a good idea to be able to relate your conceptual model of a sound to the synthesizer parameters that affect such a sound, because most patch editors address parameters by the names found in the internal workings of the device they are editing, rather than as the acoustical property they control.

✔ Like dedicated librarians, dedicated editor/librarians only function with the electronic instrument for which they have been created. Also like librarians, dedicated editor/librarians are less costly than universal editor/librarians (until you need more than four or five such programs).

✔ A universal editor/librarian combines multiple editor/librarians into a single program. Like dedicated librarians, some dedicated editor/librarians allow you to install multiple-device profiles into one program shell.

Chapter 13

Editing Sampled Sound

Looking at the Packages Involved

The focus of this chapter is on software capable of editing sampled sounds of greater than 8-bit resolution. Software for editing 8-bit sounds was discussed in Chapter 10, "Sound Generation." You will recall that there are five popular options for editing 8-bit soundfiles:

❖ MacroMind-Paracomp's SoundEdit
❖ SoundWave (various vendors, including Authorware and Articulate Systems)
❖ Fractal Software's SoundCap
❖ Heizer's Digital Audio Suite
❖ Stephen Knight's Signal Editor

There are five Macintosh software packages that can edit sounds sampled on external devices:

❖ Digidesign's Sound Designer SK
❖ Digidesign's Sound Designer II
❖ Digidesign's TurboSynth
❖ Passport's Alchemy (originally marketed by Blank Software)
❖ Passport's Sound Apprentice

All of these packages can also edit certain types of 8-bit sounds as well as edit most direct-to-hard disk recording soundfiles. Of the five packages listed above, only Sound Designer II can record directly to hard disk. Discussions of direct-to-hard disk recording applications of these and other software packages are presented in Chapter 24, "Direct-to-Hard disk Recording." Also found in Chapter 24 is Digidesign's Audiomedia, which, although it can edit most of the same file types as the other products, is excluded from the present discussion because there is no provision for sending and retrieving sounds to and from an external sampler.

In the past, custom sample editor programs were available for each type of sampler. Standardization of file formats coupled with advances in software design have brought about a situation where all currently available sample editors can be considered universal in that they support most samplers commonly in use.

General Principles

The *raison d'être* of most sample-editing programs is exactly the same as for patch-editing programs: The devices themselves often do not provide adequate user interfaces to their own internal sound-editing capabilities. Although samplers tend to have considerably more front panel controls than do synthesizers, the opportunity for additional virtual controls to be simulated by sample-editing software still exists.

Both patch editors and sample editors share the same advantages of hard disk storage. But unlike patch-editing software, sample-editing software provides the further advantage of being a unifying point by which sounds of incompatible samplers can share sample libraries. This should not be confused with the MIDI SDS, which also provides a way for samplers to share files. Sample-editing software employs the SDS for many conversions, but most are not limited to SDS-compatible samplers for converting files to the formats of other manufacturers. This is because when a sample-editing package is editing a soundfile, generally that soundfile has been internally converted into one of several standard formats that can be easily reconverted into formats required by individual devices. These formats are:

❖ Sound Designer I
❖ Sound Designer II (mono)
❖ Sound Designer II (stereo)
❖ AIFF

One benefit of this has been the creation of whole libraries, including some CD-ROMs, of files in the generic Sound Designer format and, recently, of devices that provide playback access to those files and therefore many competing manufacturers' sampled sounds.

The display of a commercial sampler does not compare to the functionality of that of the Macintosh. A visual representation of a soundfile's waveform communicates information that is orders of magnitude beyond anything native to the sampler itself, while at the same time providing for on-screen manipulation of wave data in ways that are simply unavailable without such a display. However, non-waveform parameter manipulation (e.g., envelopes) may be simpler with the front panel controls of certain samplers.

Software Options

There are several options for sample-editing software. TurboSynth is an algorithmic sound generator/editor and because of this warrants a separate discussion. Sound Designer II and Sound Designer SK are functionally identical, except for the fact that the latter program has the direct-to-hard disk recording features stripped out of it. Likewise, Sound Apprentice is functionally identical to Alchemy, except it is missing compatibility with the Emulator III, time compression, pitch shifting, envelope editing, and SCSI transfer features.

This leaves us with two primary sample-editing packages to examine: Sound Designer II and Alchemy. Both programs provide a complete set of basic features for editing, processing, and loading sounds into your sampler from your hard disk. That is where the similarity ends. The "bells and whistles" offered by the two manufacturers are so different that many people would be wise to consider owning programs from both companies.

Just as various painting and graphics programs offer different features, making it desirable to own more than one, so Sound Designer II and Alchemy are complementary.

General Interface Issues

Both the Digidesign and Passport products center around a waveform window that includes a tool palette, horizontally oriented in the case of Sound Designer and vertically oriented in the case of Alchemy (see Figure 13-1). Each program can open up as many files as your RAM will support, and with Sound Designer, each window has its own tool palette. Alchemy uses a single tool palette that applies to all windows.

The main difference between these two approaches is that in the multipalette format of Sound Designer, every open window (i.e., each open soundfile) can utilize different horizontal and vertical axis units. The vertical axis, representing volume, can be set to units representing a percent of the maximum or the actual sample value. The horizontal axis can be time in seconds, time notated as hours:minutes:seconds:milliseconds, SMPTE in five formats, decimal or hex sample number, film feet and frames, or bars and beats. Alchemy's single-control

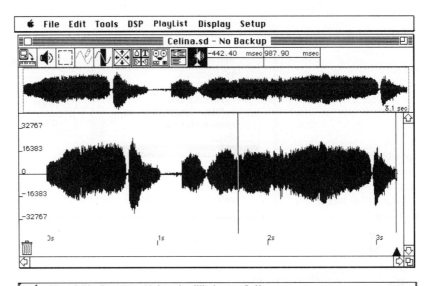

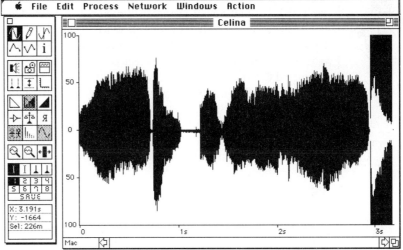

Figure 13-1: Sound Designer's main screen (top) compared to Alchemy's main screen (bottom). At first glance it appears that Alchemy has many more tools than Sound Designer, however, many of these "missing" tools are present as menu options.

palette requires all open files/windows to utilize the same reference scales (the vertical axis is percent of maximum volume, the horizontal axis can be time in seconds, 30 non-drop SMPTE, or sample number in decimal or hex).

The difference between the palettes for Sound Designer and Audiomedia is that the latter is missing the far left icon (Send to Sampler), because Audiomedia has no direct sampler compatibility. Likewise, the difference between the palettes for Alchemy and Sound Apprentice is that the latter is missing the second from the top row of icons (which access the time compression, pitch shifting, and envelope-editing features).

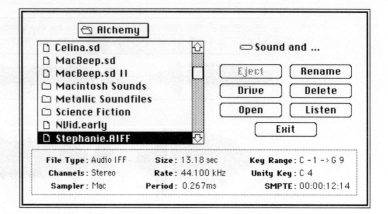

Figure 13-2: Alchemy's Open Special... dialog box allows you to audition and open files one after another without leaving the dialog box.

Opening files

Both Alchemy and Sound Designer support the standard Open File dialog box, but Alchemy adds a very useful bit of functionality to this menu option (see Figure 13-2). This is the Open Special... option that allows you to open many files one after another without having to re-access the menu command (or press Command-O). This is augmented with a great deal of information about the selected file, including the file type, number of channels, original sampler, size (length in seconds), sample rate, period, key range, unity key (original pitch of sample or pitch you have designated as the unity key), and SMPTE offset (if you have designated one). Furthermore, you can audition sounds prior to opening them with the Listen button and rename them with the Rename button.

Waveform overview

A *waveform overview* can be a very helpful way to navigate around a sample of even moderate length. In all cases, the overview displays an uneditable representation of the entire waveform scaled to the size of the current window, no matter how far zoomed out you are in the editable portion of the window.

Alchemy and Sound Designer have different approaches to this (see Figure 13-3). The waveform overview is always present in Sound Designer, but it must be called up in Alchemy by clicking the overview button found on the tool palette. Not displaying the overview has some advantages when dealing with longer samples or direct-to-hard disk recordings: Calculating the overview display can take time — about one second for every six seconds of wave data in Sound Designer on a Macintosh IIfx (rates on slower machines are considerably longer). While the results are pretty instantaneous when dealing with files that you might send to your sampler, for direct-to-hard disk recordings, that works out to about two minutes for every 12 minutes of stereo soundfile. This is why the waveform

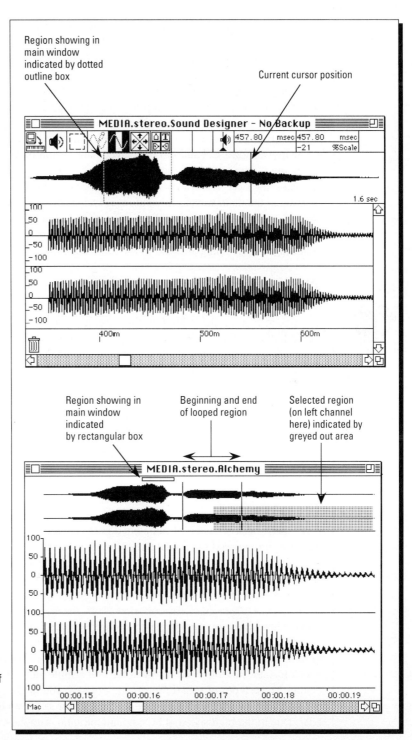

Figure 13-3: Anatomy of the overview windows of Sound Designer and Alchemy.

overview is optional in Alchemy and also why Sound Designer's Time Line is simply a line with the time divisions in the currently selected durational units marked upon it. The Time Line overview takes no time whatsoever to calculate.

In either program, it is easy to visualize the entire sound using the overview and also extremely easy to jump from point to point in a large sound by merely clicking in the overview. There are some differences. With Sound Designer, you can initiate playback from any portion of the soundfile by simply clicking in the overview, and the main waveform will jump to the played back region of the file when you release the mouse button (provided that the file is long enough to warrant it). In both programs, the overview always indicates the portion of the soundfile currently showing in the main waveform window as well as the current cursor location. Alchemy adds to this a display of the currently selected region, even if the selection is not visible in the main waveform window, and also displays two vertical bars indicating the beginning and end of the looped region, if any.

Working with files

With sample-editing software it is sometimes necessary to work with files that are too large to fit in available RAM. In this case, files are opened and edited on disk, sort of like virtual memory without System 7. Unless you are using System 7 or some other form of virtual memory, the current version of Alchemy can only accomplish this type of editing with files originating from the Studer Dyaxis direct-to-hard disk system. On the other hand, Sound Designer provides a way to get around the destructive editing of this process by offering a Use Backup Files option. With this turned on, an exact copy of the file is created (providing that you have enough room on your hard drive) and all your edits are performed on the copy. When you save the file, you are given the option of undoing your edits by discarding the changes you have made, in which case the copy of the file is erased and your original file is preserved without the edits. If you do want to save the changes, the edited copy is swapped for the original file.

Fortunately, most commercial samplers do not create files that are anywhere near big enough to exceed the available RAM of your Macintosh. If your sampler does create big files, you need merely expand the RAM in your Macintosh to the required amount. At the time of this writing, 4MB and 16MB SIMMs let you expand your RAM up to 128MB of Finder memory on many Macintosh models.

While editing files you can choose to audition sounds through the Macintosh's speaker at a fixed or variable sampling rate up to 22 KHz. Better yet, if you happen to have a Digidesign Sound Accelerator or Audiomedia card installed, you can audition sounds in full 16-bit clarity at the real sample rate of the soundfile you are editing. These types of sound previewing can save you hours of transfer time because you don't need to wait to send files to your sampler before hearing your edits. Due to the high speed of SCSI communication, samplers that support this protocol alleviate some of the wait states if you don't have an internal digital audio card in your Macintosh and often provide the capability of continually updating the soundfile in your sampler's RAM for immediate preview.

File Conversion

Sampled soundfiles can exist in many different formats, although the vast majority will be in Sound Designer (see Table 13-1) or AIFF. To confuse matters, there are several types of Sound Designer files.

Table 13-1: Sampled soundfile formats

File type	Sound Designer, Sound Designer SK	Alchemy, Sound Apprentice
8-bit snd resource	●	●
8-bit Sound Lab		●
16-bit snd resource	●	
Chunky (8-bit plus 16-bit interleaved)	●	
16-bit Sound Designer (I)	●	●
16-bit Sound Designer II (mono)	●	
16-bit Sound Designer II (stereo)	●	
16-bit Audio Interchange File Format (AIFF)	●	●
16-bit Dyaxis Format		●

Obviously, the common ground here for 16-bit files is the original Sound Designer for mono files and the AIFF designed by Apple. Regardless of whether your sampler's resolution is 12-bit, 16-bit, or something else, during the editing process your software will be manipulating the samples in the Sound Designer or AIFF. During transmission of the soundfiles back to the sampler, they are reconverted to the format required by that specific sampler.

Alchemy's compatibility with the Dyaxis file format is a useful feature, especially if you have a Dyaxis stand-alone direct-to-hard disk studio system. Its flexible multi-format direct digital interface provides a gateway to many additional file formats (most of which are meaningful only in the world of direct-to-hard disk recording): DASH, ProDigi, PCM 1610, 1630, and 601, S/PDIF, and Yamaha Digital Cascade.

Sample Dump Standard

The MMA 12-bit and 16-bit Sample Dump Standard (SDS) was created to allow for samples to be transferred over MIDI. Due to the size of most soundfiles and the speed of MIDI, this will tend to be slow. Samples can be sent to a device in either an open loop system (one way communication — a MIDI OUT connected to a MIDI IN) or a closed loop system (MIDI IN and OUT of one device connected appropriately to the MIDI OUT and IN of the other device). Closed loop systems provide for handshaking to improve speed and facilitate error checking and recovery.

SDS supports sample resolutions from eight to 28 bits and is also able to communicate loop points and loop types. Some important data is not communicated in an SDS soundfile transfer. This includes whether or not the file is stereo, what key range the sample is assigned to, and what the unity or root pitch is. By far the most common resolutions for SDS files are 8-bit, 12-bit, and 16-bit, all supported by Alchemy (Sound Designer supports 12-bit and 16-bit SDS). Alchemy requires that loop points be turned on (with the Loop Cursors icon on the palette) for all sounds retrieved via SDS.

You should be aware of several important omissions from the SDS that can affect the way you interact with SDS-compatible samplers:

❖ *"Not Sampled" sounds:* SDS has no provision for determining via MIDI the fact that a sound location is available, but as of yet not sampled.

❖ *"Nonexistent" sounds:* SDS has no way of determining via MIDI the number of sampled soundfiles available in a sampler. For example, SDS cannot determine that there is no "sound #65" in a sampler that can only hold 64 sounds.

❖ *Sound replacement:* SDS has no way of determining via MIDI whether a sampler will replace a sound at an occupied location or not.

❖ *Transfer to empty locations:* SDS cannot determine via MIDI whether a sampler will transfer to a currently unoccupied location or not.

Sampler intercommunication

You can transfer soundfiles between the Macintosh and external samplers in one of five ways:

❖ MIDI (proprietary via SysEx messages)
❖ MIDI (12-bit SDS)
❖ MIDI (16-bit SDS)
❖ RS-422 (proprietary cables)
❖ SCSI

Before you can transfer files to and from your Macintosh and your sampler, there is a simple setup procedure required. With Sound Designer this involves selecting Sampler... from the Setup menu and adding devices to the list of available samplers (see Figure 13-4). Many device parameters are automatically attached to the device name, so all you have to do is double-click its name to

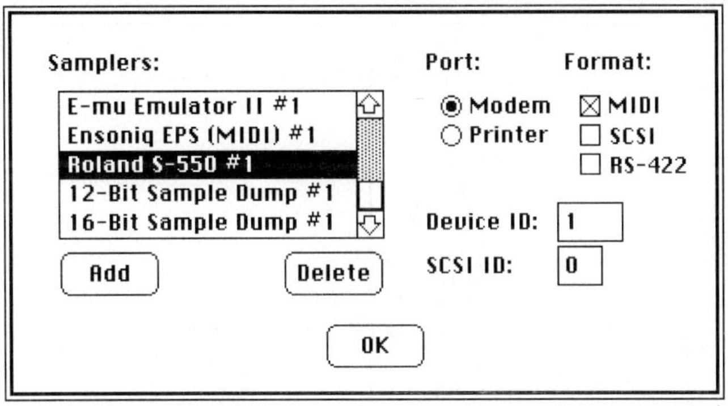

Figure 13-4: Once you have added recognizable devices using Sound Designer's Add button, you can select which device you want to work with in this Sampler dialog box.

add it to the device list. Exceptions are devices that support two different transfer protocols (in which case you have to select which one you will use) and cases where you have more than one of the same sampler on your network (in which case you will have to specify separate ID numbers). Similarly, you may have to set the SCSI ID to the correct value if your sampler communicates via SCSI.

Alchemy takes a significantly different approach to sampler intercommunication. Passport's DAN (Distributed Audio Network) feature automates your entire sampler network by speeding up the process of sending and retrieving sounds to and from various samplers (see Figure 13-5). Besides storing the appropriate communications protocols for each of your samplers, the DAN configuration stores the patch data to send to a MIDI-controllable MIDI patchbay (most MIDI patchbays can change their own internal routing configurations upon the receipt of a patch change message assigned to that setup and transmitted upon a designated channel). This is an extremely useful feature in that you never have to remember to switch your MIDI patchbay when sending sounds to and from your samplers. However, you do have to remember to reset your MIDI patcher's configuration to what it was prior to the sample dump.

Table 13-2 indicates compatible samplers with the five programs under examination.

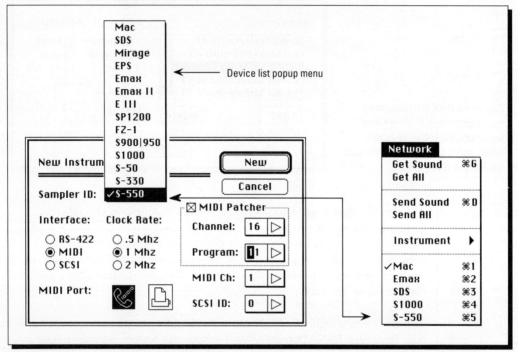

Figure 13-5: Sounds added to Alchemy's DAN are automatically appended to the Network menu for quick selection. Note the MIDI Patcher option for associating a particular configuration of your MIDI-controllable MIDI patcher with a particular sampler. When sending or receiving soundfiles from the sampler is selected in the Network menu, this assures the proper configuration of your MIDI patchbay.

Table 13-2: Sampler compatibilities

	Sound Designer, Sound Designer SK, TurboSynth	Alchemy, Sound Apprentice
Akai S700,X7000 (MIDI)	●●	
Akai S950, S900 (MIDI)	●●	●●
Akai S1000, S100PB (via 16-bit SDS or SCSI)	●●	●●
Casio FX-1, FZ-10M (MIDI)	●●	●●
Digidesign Sound Accelerator, Audiomedia	●●	●●
Dynacord ADD-one (via 16-bit SDS)	●	●
Dynacord ADS (via 16-bit SDS)	●	
E-mu EII (RS-422)	●	
E-mu EIII (SCSI)	●	●

Table 13-2: Sampler compatibilties (continued)

	Sound Designer, Sound Designer SK, TurboSynth	Alchemy, Sound Apprentice
E-mu Emax, Emax II (RS -422)	●●	●●
E-mu SP-1200 (via 12-bit SDS or MIDI)	●	●
Ensoniq DSK	●	
Ensoniq EPS (MIDI or SCSI)	●	●
Ensoniq Mirage (MIDI)	●	●
Forat F16 (16-bit SDS)	●	●
Korg DSS-1, DSM-1 (12-bit SDS)	●●	●●
Oberheim DPX-1 (12-bit SDS)	●	●
Peavey DPM^{SE} (16-bit SDS)	●	●
Roland MKS-100 (MIDI)		●
Roland S-10 (MIDI)		●
Roland S-50, S-550 (MIDI)	●	●
Roland S-220 (MIDI)		●
Roland S-330 (MIDI)	●	●
Roland S-770 (16-bit SDS)	●	●
Sequential Prophet 2000, Prophet 2002 (SDS)	●●	●●
Simmons SDX (16-bit SDS)	●	●
Studer Dyaxis (SCSI)		●
Yamaha TX-16W (12-bit SDS)	●	●
12-bit SDS, 16-bit SDS	●●	●●
Send to sampler options		
Mono/Stereo (L & R)/Select L or R	●●●	●●○
Send all windows		●
Auto-resample on send (with prompt)		●

Direct-to-hard disk recording conversion

Any direct-to-hard disk recording can be used as source material for a sample-editing program. Keep in mind that with the Passport software, you will have to be able to fit the file into your available RAM, unless it is coming from the Dyaxis.

I have witnessed many composers struggling with creating instruments directly in their samplers from a source such as the McGill University library available on standard CDs. An easier process is to employ a direct-to-hard disk recording system, such as the Dyaxis or Digidesign's Sound Tools or Audiomedia, in conjunction with a CD player that has digital outputs. In this manner it becomes possible to record direct-to-hard disk the entire range of the desired instrument in one pass without entering the analog domain. Then you can go in with your sample-editing software and divide each note into a separate soundfile for cleaning up on the Macintosh using the editing options of your software.

Resampling options

Both Passport's and Digidesign's software provide resampling options. Usually, resampling is required for translating soundfiles from one sampler's format to another's.

The quick and dirty way to change a soundfile's sample rate is to type a new rate into the Soundfile Info box associated with the soundfile. With this method, because you are merely changing the speed of sample playback, your sample will not play back at the original pitch or duration. If you type in a number that is half the original sample rate, the sound will play back an octave lower and be twice as long.

The preferred method for changing a soundfile's sample rate retains the original pitch and duration of the soundfile. There are a variety of algorithms to calculate the values of samples to add when increasing the sample rate and what samples to drop when decreasing the sample rate.

Sound Designer's SR Convert option allows you to specify the new sample rate either by typing in its value in Hertz or by providing the ratio between the new sample rate and the original sample rate. Converting a soundfile's rate from 44100 Hz to 22050 Hz can be accomplished by specifying 22050 as the new sample rate or by specifying that the new sample rate will be 0.5 the value of the original rate. Sound Designer can perform sample rate conversions downward to 0.5 the original rate and upward to 8 times the original rate (but not exceeding 96.2 KHz).

Alchemy's Resample… option also allows you to specify the new sample rate, but instead of offering you an option to specify the new sample rate's ratio to the original sample rate, it provides you with the option to specify the new soundfile length in samples and displays the resulting ratio. There are no downward limits to the sampling rate (within reason), and the upward sample rate can be as high as 100 KHz.

One important distinction in the approaches to sample rate conversion between the two companies is that with Sound Designer, performing a sample rate conversion always requires creating a new soundfile, leaving your original intact, whereas in Alchemy, the conversion process edits the actual soundfile in the active window — so keep a copy if you are going to need the file at the original rate.

Mono/stereo conversion

Alchemy has menu options named Mono to Stereo and Stereo to Mono. These are pretty straightforward in their operation. Mono to Stereo considers the original mono file to be the left channel and makes a copy of it into the right channel. Stereo to Mono simply deletes the right channel.

Sound Designer does not provide mono/stereo conversion options directly from the menus, but there are several ways to accomplish the same effect. First, if you are working with an AIFF or Sound Designer II format mono file, you can select Add channel from the Display menu and copy the contents from the original channel into the newly added channel. The other option is to create a mix file using the same mono soundfiles for the inputs to the right and left channels of the mix file and designating that the resulting soundfile will be stereo. In this latter case, you are required to save a new soundfile to disk. Either method will achieve the same result as Alchemy's Mono to Stereo option.

To create a mono file from an existing stereo file in Sound Designer always requires using the Mix menu option and designating that the resulting mix file will be mono. This provides considerably more flexibility than Passport's method of simply deleting the right channel. When in the Mix dialog box (see the section "Mixing" in this chapter), you can specify the various levels, pans, and delays of the two input channels, and this can have a profound effect upon the resulting mono soundfile.

Regional Reorganization of Sound Data
Standard Cut, Copy, Paste, and Clear

One area of editing where software-based sample editors greatly surpass the built-in editing of dedicated external devices is in the Cut, Copy, and Paste operations that we all have come to take for granted in the Macintosh user interface. As with sequencers and some notation programs, there are some additional related operations added to the standard three. Take careful note of the different results from Paste operations depending upon the manufacturer of the software in the following descriptions:

❖ Cut: Removes the selected region and places it on the Clipboard; then closes up the resulting gap by shifting the waveform to the right (what had been the end) of the selected region back to the end of the waveform at the left (what had been the beginning) of the selected region.

❖ Copy: Copies the selected region to the Clipboard, leaving the original intact.

❖ Paste (Alchemy):

1. At insertion point: Replaces all data to the right of the insertion point with the Clipboard.

2. To a selected region smaller than the Clipboard: Replaces as much material as possible of the selected range with the Clipboard, ignoring that portion of the Clipboard that exceeds the duration of the selected region.

3. To a selected region larger than the Clipboard: Replaces the portion of the selected destination that is as long as the Clipboard with the Clipboard. The portion that exceeded the duration of the Clipboard is unchanged.

4. With the option key down: Begins the Paste operation from the end of the selected region — this is called *outpoint editing,* a very useful feature.

5. With a mono Clipboard being pasted to a stereo region: Prompts for the stereo pan of the material onto both channels with a slider to adjust the panning.

6. With a stereo Clipboard being pasted to a single channel of a stereo file: The like channel of the Clipboard is pasted to the like channel of the destination.

7. With a stereo Clipboard being pasted to a mono file: Pastes uppermost channel only.

In all cases, the pasted material remains selected after the operation.

❖ Paste (Sound Designer):

1. At insertion point: Inserts the Clipboard at the insertion point, shifting all data originally after the insertion point to the right.

2. To a selected region: Deletes the region, even if the region is larger than the Clipboard, then inserts the Clipboard into the deleted area, pushing all data originally after the selected region to the right, if necessary.

3. With a mono Clipboard being pasted to a stereo region: Prompts for a channel destination for the paste operation if the insertion point or selected region encompasses both channels of the destination.

4. With a stereo Clipboard being pasted to a mono file or a single channel of a stereo file: Mixes the contents of the Clipboard together prior to pasting.

In all cases, the pasted material *does not* remain selected after the operation.

❖ Clear (Alchemy):

> or

❖ Silence (Sound Designer): Deletes the selected portion of the waveform without moving the material to the Clipboard and without closing up the space left by the deletion. Can also be thought of as setting all the sample values for the selected region to zero.

❖ Clear (Sound Designer): The selected portion of the waveform is deleted and the material to the right of the selected region is shifted to close up the resulting space (equivalent to Cut in Alchemy).

❖ Extract (Alchemy):

> or

❖ Trim (Sound Designer): Deletes all data prior to and following the selected region, thus setting the soundfile equal to the "extracted" selection.

Passport adds to these standard commands the following:

❖ Insert: Inserts the Clipboard at the location of the insertion point (cursor) or immediately in front (to the left) of a selected region, sliding all ensuing samples to the right to make room for the inserted material. The former case produces the same result as Digidesign's Paste 1. operation.

❖ Replicate: Fills a region with as many copies (one after another) of the Clipboard as will fit in the selected range. Useful for creating long sounds from single wave periods to simulate echo effects.

Digidesign adds to these standard commands the following:

❖ Replace:

1. At insertion point: Replaces all data to the right of the insertion point with the Clipboard.

2. To a selected region smaller than the Clipboard: Replaces as much material as possible of the selected range with the Clipboard, ignoring that portion of the Clipboard that exceeds the duration of the selected region.

3. To a selected region larger than the Clipboard: Replaces the portion of the selected destination that is as long as the Clipboard with the Clipboard. The portion that exceeded the duration of the Clipboard is unchanged.

These are identical to Alchemy's Paste 1., 2., and 3. operations.

Because cutting and pasting sound data can result in two parts of a waveform being unmatched with respect to their slope — therefore causing a pop or click sound — both Passport and Digidesign provide switchable options to avoid these situations.

Alchemy provides an Auto Zero option that causes all selected ranges to be adjusted to start and stop at zero-crossings. When you drag the mouse over a waveform region, the beginning and ending points of the region you dragged over will snap to the closest zero-crossings. This is particularly useful in selecting regions for potential loops. Alchemy provides an additional switchable option called Blending. With Blending on, all edit splice points, whether resulting from Cut, Paste, or Insert, are automatically crossfaded with each other to produce a smooth transition. Actually, a small portion of the waveform (defined in the Edit Options dialog box) is overlapped before and after each splice point. This tends to decrease the total duration of the current soundfile.

Sound Designer provides a Smoothing toggle that alters the sample values at splice points to smooth the transitions created by Cuts, Pastes, Clears, and Replaces. Smoothing also kicks in when you execute a gain change, reverse a sound, or perform just about any other operation that could result in a jagged waveform splice point.

Mixing

Mixing and merging two or more sounds together is a powerful option available with Macintosh-based sample-editing software. Essentially, during either of these operations, the source sample values are added to the destination sample values. When sample values are added together, the possibility of exceeding the maximum sample value range is ever-present, and the result is *clipping*. Sound Designer scales the mixed sounds so that clipping can never occur, but Alchemy requires careful monitoring of the source and destination regions to avoid clipping. With Alchemy it may be necessary to change the gain of either the source or destination to assure that the resultant mix is not clipped.

Alchemy provides a single flexible and intuitive Mix menu option that mixes the contents of the Clipboard with the selected destination region. Alchemy's actual Mix operation functions identically to its Paste operation:

1. At insertion point: Mixes all data to the right of the insertion point with the Clipboard.

2. To a selected region smaller than the Clipboard: Mixes as much material as possible of the selected range with the Clipboard, ignoring that portion of the Clipboard that exceeds the duration of the selected region.

3. To a selected region larger than the Clipboard: Mixes the portion of the selected destination that is as long as the Clipboard with the Clipboard. The portion that exceeds the duration of the Clipboard is unchanged.

4. With the command key down: Begins the mix operation from the end of the selected region — called outpoint editing.

5. With a mono Clipboard being mixed to a stereo region: Prompts for the stereo pan of the material onto both channels with a slider to adjust the panning.

6. With a stereo Clipboard being mixed to a single channel of a stereo file: The like channel of the Clipboard is mixed to the like channel of the destination.

7. With a stereo Clipboard being mixed to a mono file: Mixes uppermost channel only.

In all cases, the mixed material remains selected after the operation.

Sound Designer's Mix options are considerably more robust than Alchemy's. First, Sound Designer makes a distinction between Mixing, which can accept up to four sources and produce a stereo or mono mix, and Merging, which crossfades one soundfile into another. The latter option may require a calculator to determine the merge points.

Digidesign's Mixing capabilities are best understood through an examination of the Mix dialog box available in both Sound Designer and Audiomedia (see Figure 13-6).

A-B comparisons

Nearly all editing that you will perform with a Macintosh-based sample-editing program provides for making quick A-B comparisons using Undo and Redo. Because Sound Designer can perform some larger edits directly onto the data on the hard disk and these cannot be undone, you will be alerted with a dialog box if you are about to perform such an edit. Of course, if you have selected the Use Backup Files option, you can always revert to the original unedited state of the current soundfile, regardless of the scope of your edit.

Figure 13-6: Digidesign's Mix dialog box will accept up to four files for input. These can freely intermix mono and stereo file types, the only requirement being that all the files to be mixed are currently open. Source channel (for stereo soundfiles) is specified at the top through a pop-up menu. Reading down, the next option is a fader or faders to indicate the desired percentage (in terms of amplitude) of the source file (or channel of the source file) to be mixed into the output file. Under the faders is a sliding triangular indicator to specify

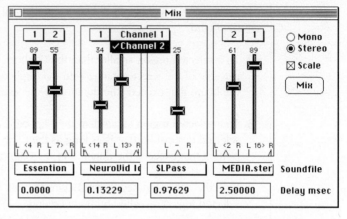

the amount of pan toward the right or left channel that the applicable file or channel will be mixed to. There are 16 degrees of pan in either direction. Below the fader console is another pop-up menu listing all open files. This is where you choose the file pertaining to the fader configuration above. Finally, beneath the filename are fields where you type the delay in milliseconds before the indicated soundfile enters the mix process. The type of output file, mono or stereo, is indicated using the radio buttons at the upper right. In all cases, a new file is created, so you never have to worry about altering any of the data in the source files. The Scale checkbox is a very useful option. Checking this box assures that no amplitudes resulting from the mixing of the selected files exceed 100 percent of the maximum playback amplitude. In other words, you will never have to worry about a mix resulting in clips, as you might with Alchemy. However, unlike Alchemy, it is difficult to mix two sounds in the middle of two files.

Frequency-dependent Editing
Parametric EQ

Parametric EQ is a precise method of boosting or cutting the volume of specified frequencies.The treble and bass tone controls on consumer audio gear are very primitive analog examples of equalization (shelving, to be precise — see below). In professional audio, parametric EQ normally has three controls: One to specify the frequency or center frequency of a particular range of frequencies, a second to specify the degree of boosting or cutting to be applied to that frequency or range of frequencies (usually specified in dB), and a third to specify the bandwidth or range of frequencies to be affected by the boost or cut. To understand parametric EQ, it is necessary to understand the different types of EQ filters that are tradition-ally associated with parametric EQ. Because Sound Designer offers nearly all of the standard forms of EQ filters and the icons associated with these types are quite appropriate, these have been used for illustrative purposes in Figure 13-7.

The beauty of parametric EQ in the digital domain is that it is possible to set the required values (frequency, boost or cut amount, and bandwidth) with absolute precision. Sound Designer's parametric EQ dialog box is shown in Figure 13-8. Alchemy offers low-shelf, high-shelf, and peak/notch EQ as shown in Figure 13-9.

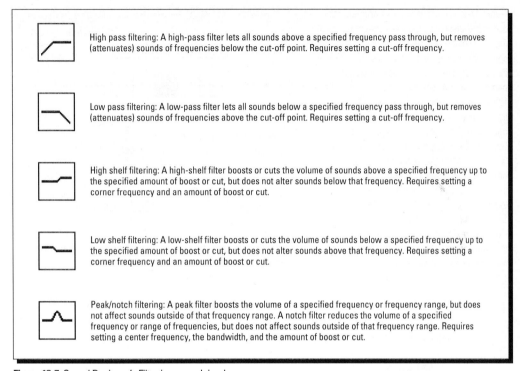

High pass filtering: A high-pass filter lets all sounds above a specified frequency pass through, but removes (attenuates) sounds of frequencies below the cut-off point. Requires setting a cut-off frequency.

Low pass filtering: A low-pass filter lets all sounds below a specified frequency pass through, but removes (attenuates) sounds of frequencies above the cut-off point. Requires setting a cut-off frequency.

High shelf filtering: A high-shelf filter boosts or cuts the volume of sounds above a specified frequency up to the specified amount of boost or cut, but does not alter sounds below that frequency. Requires setting a corner frequency and an amount of boost or cut.

Low shelf filtering: A low-shelf filter boosts or cuts the volume of sounds below a specified frequency up to the specified amount of boost or cut, but does not alter sounds above that frequency. Requires setting a corner frequency and an amount of boost or cut.

Peak/notch filtering: A peak filter boosts the volume of a specified frequency or frequency range, but does not affect sounds outside of that frequency range. A notch filter reduces the volume of a specified frequency or range of frequencies, but does not affect sounds outside of that frequency range. Requires setting a center frequency, the bandwidth, and the amount of boost or cut.

Figure 13-7: Sound Designer's Filter icons explained.

The fundamental musical problem with software EQs of these types is that they have no envelope. You can't "fade in" the EQ like you can on a mixing console. These software versions can only be switched on or off, not a very flexible implementation considering the power of the Macintosh.

Graphic EQ

Only Sound Designer offers digital graphic equalization (see Figure 13-10). Ten bands are available for mono soundfiles and five bands are available for stereo soundfiles (down from 14 and seven in pre-2.0 versions of Sound Designer II).

Hum removal

If your system is not properly grounded, you may encounter a 60-cycle hum (50 cycles in some parts of the world). This is an artifact created by the actual current coming out of your wall. As might be expected, in many cases additional artifacts will be located at multiples of 60 Hz. Digidesign's Deck software (see Chapter 24, "Direct-to-Hard disk Recording") includes a specific hum-removal menu option that uses a complex non-real-time algorithm, you can approximate the same effect by using a high-pass filter to remove frequencies below 60 Hz.

Figure 13-8: Sound Designer's Parametric EQ. dialog box displays a graphic representation of the effect of the selected filter upon the harmonic spectrum of the waveform. In this illustration, a Peak/Notch filter has been selected with a center frequency of 8202 Hz and a bandwidth of 1200 Hz (600 Hz above and below the center frequency). Frequencies in this band will be boosted by 8 dB (the number typed in the Boost/ Cut box). The volume is automatically set to 50 percent when you enter this dialog box in order to provide some headroom for boosting frequencies. The Process button applies the EQ. to the selected region, actually altering the data. Settings may be saved directly into Sound Designer and thus are available for all files, or

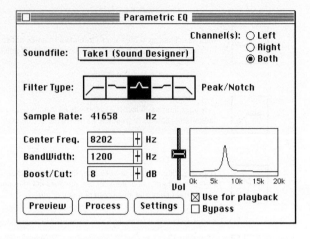

they may be saved only with the current file. Use for playback is an option that mainly pertains to direct-to-hard disk recording applications, allowing the EQ. to be applied upon output rather than altering data in the soundfile.

With Alchemy you can use the Harmonic Spectrum display to create a deep notch pseudo-filter to remove the hum. Unfortunately, all of these techniques can be destructive in the case of music with frequencies below 60 Hz.

Waveform inversion

Inverting a waveform merely replaces all positive sample values with negative values and vice versa. This can be thought of as multiplying all the sample values by -1. This should produce no audible effect upon the soundfile. Waveform inversion is useful in creating certain types of loops and mixes. For example, if you want to create a mirror crossfade loop, you will reverse a portion of the sound. The waveform of the reversed sound will need to be inverted so that the slopes match at the splice points.

Figure 13-9: In this parametric EQ setting in Alchemy, a notch filter is being created with a center frequency of 880 Hz and a bandwidth of 40 Hz. The frequencies between 840 Hz and 920 Hz will be cut in volume by 12 dB. Note: When selecting a Low Shelf or High Shelf, the frequency parameter is still labeled "Center Freq," although what you are really setting is the corner frequency, since bandwidth is not relevant in these cases.

Digital EQ		OK
		Cancel
Center Freq:	880.00 (hz)	Filter Type:
Cut/Boost:	-12.00 (dB)	○ Low Shelf
Width:	40.00 (hz)	○ High Shelf
		⦿ Peak/Notch

Figure 13-10: (A) Sound Designer's Programmable Graphic EQ dialog box, like its Parametric EQ dialog box, allows you to preview your settings in real time if you have a Sound Accelerator or Audiomedia card installed. The amount of cut or boost is always indicated beneath each band, as is the center frequency. Like its Parametric EQ option, you can name and save settings either with Sound Designer itself or with the current soundfile by pressing the Settings button. **(B)** Sound Designer also allows for setting the center frequency and bandwidth of each of the bands in the graphic equalizer. Clicking the frequency number below any band brings up the Parameters dialog box for that particular band. Here, the center frequency for band 5 is set to 325 Hz, and the bandwidth is 187 Hz (93.6 Hz above and below the 325 Hz center frequency).

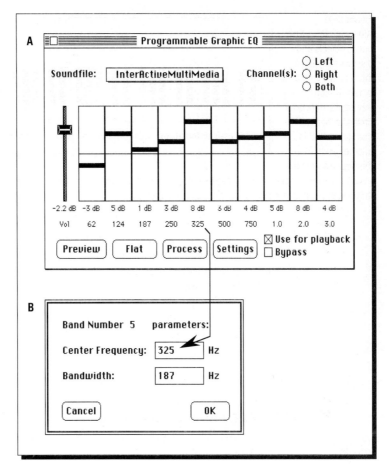

Pitch shifting

Both Alchemy and Sound Designer allow you to change the pitch of a soundfile or region of a soundfile with the choice of either preserving the original duration (time correction) or not preserving the duration. Without preserving duration, a soundfile that has undergone a pitch shift will merely sound like a tape recording that has been sped up.

Alchemy's approach is from the standpoint of pitch transposition, and the interface is a piano keyboard as in Figure 13-11. Pitch shifting is not available in Passport's Sound Apprentice.

Sound Designer's pitch shifting features are considerably more powerful than Alchemy's (see Figure 13-12). Like Alchemy, the fundamental pitch of the selected

Figure 13-11:
Alchemy's Pitch Shift option detects and displays the pitch of the selected soundfile or region, highlighting this pitch in dark gray on the keyboard (G4 in this figure). Clicking another pitch (E4 in this figure) enters the

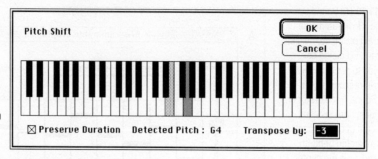

transposition amount in the Transpose by field (-3 semitones in this case). You have the option of preserving the original duration by clicking in the Preserve Duration checkbox.

region is detected and displayed in Hertz. Pitch shifting is possible by semitones and cents ($\frac{1}{100}$ of a semitone), and the time correction (preserve duration) option displays the actual ratio between the original and shifted soundfile. As with most of Digidesign's DSP options, it is possible to preview the sound while adjusting the controls. However, in this case, the previewed sound will not reflect the time correction, because the associated algorithm cannot be applied in real time.

Current "pitch detection" algorithms such as those used in Alchemy and Sound Designer are really "pitch guessing." They are quite often incorrect.

Frequency envelope editing

Frequency envelope editing is only available in Alchemy. It is a powerful feature that can add nuance and expressivity to a sound. The frequency envelope of any soundfile can be auto-traced, edited, copied, and applied to another soundfile. Once a frequency envelope has been traced and copied to the Clipboard, it can be treated as a frequency envelope, as an amplitude envelope, or as actual wave data. Note that when a frequency envelope is treated as an amplitude envelope, all negative values are converted to positive values, because amplitudes below zero do not exist.

Envelopes can be edited by drawing with the pencil cursor or by dragging break-point knobs that you can specify or have automatically placed by the software following an auto-trace. The frequency range may be specified as two octaves, one octave, or a single semitone. Figure 13-13 uses a range of one octave. Applying either a drawn envelope or a copied envelope to a soundfile produces an effect similar to moving the pitch bend lever on a synthesizer through the course outlined by the envelope.

Figure 13-12: Sound Designer's Pitch Shift dialog box is particularly suited to the fine tuning of instrumental and vocal sounds. After the Master Tuning reference is set (A = 440 Hz, 441.3 Hz, or whatever), clicking the Note pop-up menu brings up a keyboard where you can set a pitch to listen to as a tuning reference while you are previewing the shifting accomplished by the two center sliders (previewing is only available with the Sound Accelerator or Audiomedia cards installed). Playing the tuning reference while you move the sliders to tune your soundfile allows for extremely accurate tuning of the pitch prior to actually processing the shift (i.e., transforming the samples of the current soundfile).

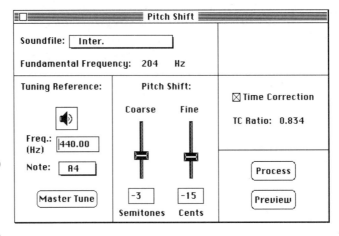

Figure 13-13: Four Alchemy files are open illustrating several of its frequency enveloping features. The frequency envelope of the upper-left soundfile (MEDIA...) has been auto-traced and pasted upon the Slow Attack Brass soundfile in the lower right. An envelope has been drawn onto the Slap Bass soundfile at the upper right with the pencil tool. After the envelope was drawn, the pencil was toggled into "knob" mode to display the breakpoints or knobs of the envelope. These function as handles that can be stretched elastically as you would in any object-oriented drawing program. The effect on the slap bass sound will be to start about an octave higher than the original sample and bend down to six semitones below the original sample, ending with a bend back up to the pitch of the original sample. Finally, the Loop Sine frequency envelope has been auto-traced to illustrate that a pure waveform of a single pitch results in an absolutely flat frequency envelope.

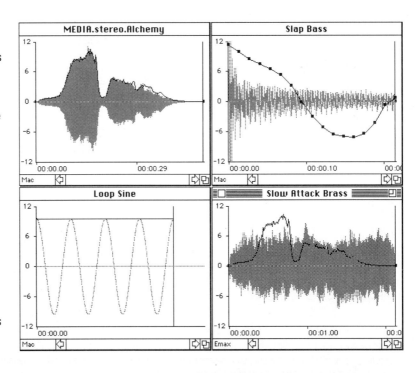

Spectrum analysis and resynthesis

Any sound can be described as a product of the interaction of a number of sine waves. FFTs (Fast Fourier Transforms) are representations of the frequency spectrum of a sound reduced to these component sine waves (see Figure 13-14). The amplitudes of the sine waves can then be calculated and displayed with respect to their transformations over a given period of time.

Sound Designer displays FFTs in dazzling 3-D (plotting frequency, amplitude, and time). Unfortunately these cannot be edited. They do provide information that may be useful in determining the appropriate EQ settings for a sound under extremely

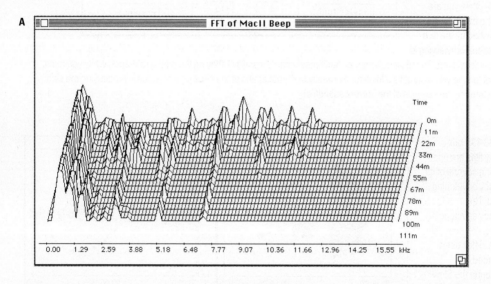

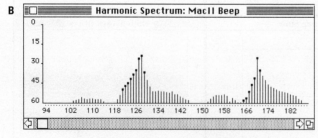

Figure 13-14: (A) Digidesign's FFT is displayed in impressive 3-D, showing how the amplitudes (volume, indicated by relative height of the peaks) of the various frequencies (horizontal axis) making up the selection transform over time (vertical axis, in milliseconds). This data is not directly editable upon the display — it can, however, be used to determine correct EQ settings, although it's probably better to use your ear.

(B) Alchemy's display of the same soundfile extends to 8,192 frequency bands, accessible with the lower scroll bar. Displays are limited to 32,768 samples, slightly under a second of sound sampled at 44.1 KHz. Individual frequency bands or groups of contiguous or discontiguous bands may be selected for editing (selected frequencies are indicated by the little black boxes in the illustration). Frequency bands can be cut, copied, pasted, cleared, and mixed. The amplitude of individual bands may be adjusted simply by dragging its selection box up or down. When a single frequency band is selected, the Clear Above and Clear Below Edit menu options become enabled and can be used to clear all bands above or below a selected frequency.

rare conditions. On the other hand, Alchemy's FFTs are in 2-D (the time axis is not present), but you can edit the amplitude of the component sine waves.

When any band or range of bands is selected, the information about that band (or highest band of a selected region) is provided in the palette's numeric display, as shown in Figure 13-15.

No edits are actually executed until the Resynthesize icon on the tool palette is clicked on or Resynthesize is selected from the Process menu. Keep in mind that Alchemy's resynthesis generates a steady-state tone — all time variations may become smeared. This is usually only a minor problem.

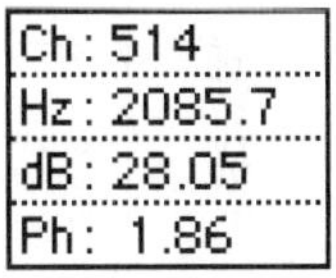

Figure 13-15: Spectrum information about a single band selected in Alchemy's Harmonic Spectrum display. The channel number (Ch) refers to the number of the band counting from the lowest frequency present. The next numbers are the selected band's frequency in Hertz followed by its volume in decibels and finally its phase.

```
Ch: 514
Hz: 2085.7
dB: 28.05
Ph: 1.86
```

Amplitude-dependent Editing

Clipping and drawing

Clipped segments of waveforms are those parts of the wave that exceed the available headroom for recording. The effect is unpleasant, and merely reducing the overall volume for the affected segment is usually not enough to repair it. Often a click or pop is heard. Sample-editing software includes tools for actually drawing in the waveform window to change the waveform (see Figure 13-16). Clipping and drawing work together because, while you can draw waveforms for a variety of reasons, the most common reason will be to remove clipping. Considering the fact that there are over 44,000 samples per second, you may have to devote a good deal of time to this depending upon the length of the clipped region.

Gain control

Changing the gain (or amplitude) of a soundfile is very easy to do in software because it only requires multiplying the sample values by a constant (see Figure 13-17). Decreasing the gain will usually not cause any problems. However, increasing gain can lead to clipping.

Alchemy's implementation of gain changing (called *scaling*) prevents you from accidentally clipping samples, because you specify gain changes by indicating the maximum sample value as a percentage of the total sample value range. Since you cannot specify a sample value greater than 100 percent of the available range, clipping avoidance is taken care of automatically.

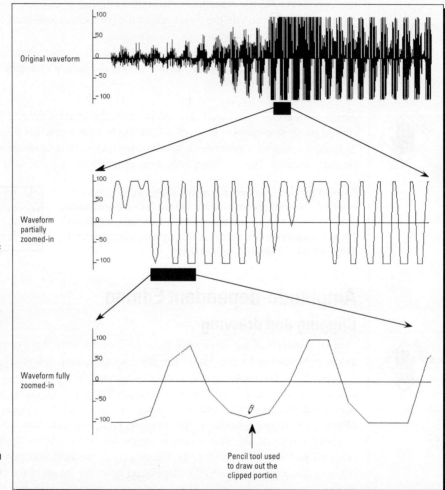

Figure 13-16: Three views of a clipped region of a soundfile. The pencil tool has been used to reshape the clipped samples at the bottom. This portion of the waveform initially re-sembled the clipped portion immediately to the right of it.

Original waveform

Waveform partially zoomed-in

Waveform fully zoomed-in

Pencil tool used to draw out the clipped portion

Figure 13-17: Sound Designer allows you to specify gain change by percentage or by dB (in 100ths of dB increments). If you are decreasing gain you won't run into problems, but if you are boosting gain it requires doing a little math to figure out if your boost is going to result in clipping. You can click the Peak Value to find out the highest sample value as a percentage of the amplitude range. One way to determine the highest gain change is to divide 100 by the Peak Value (as a decimal percent, in this case 0.40236) and then subtract 100 from the result. In this example, the formula reads (100 ÷ 0.40236) - 100 = 148.533, meaning that 148.533 percent is the highest gain change percentage that will not result in clipping for the selected region. Actually changing the gain by this maximum value has the same effect as the Normalize menu command.

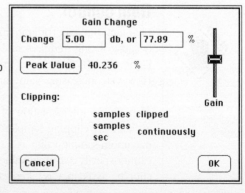

To change gain or scale a region or soundfile in Alchemy, you must first turn on Show Threshold from the Action menu. Once the threshold indicators are present, you can drag them up and down to specify the desired amount of increase or decrease in sound. While you are dragging the threshold indicators, the percentage of increase or decrease is shown in the numeric display on the palette next to the word Scale. Note that when you move the cursor back over the waveform proper, the Scale indication will disappear. After you have set the scaling threshold in this manner, selecting Scale from the Process menu or clicking the Scale icon on the palette executes the operation. You must have the threshold indicators showing in order to scale the amplitude to anything other than peak value (100 percent, i.e., what Sound Designer refers to as *normalizing*).

Sound Designer's approach to changing gain requires you to be a bit more careful, because it is possible to boost the volume into the clipping range.

Normalization

Normalizing a waveform refers to scaling the amplitude of a waveform (usually upward), so that the peak value of the waveform or selected region is set to the peak amplitude value allowed by the program. Although normalization will have no effect on zero-value samples, it may amplify any noise present in the sample — be careful.

In Alchemy, normalization is accomplished by setting the amplitude threshold to 100 percent and then performing the Scale operation either from the Process menu or by clicking the Scale icon on the palette. A shortcut to this is performing the Scale operation without displaying the amplitude threshold, because 100 percent is always used when the threshold is not visible.

Sound Designer's Normalize menu command increases the volume of a selected region so that the original highest value peaks at 100 percent of the available amplitude range. If no region is selected, the entire soundfile is normalized.

Fade in, Fade out

Fading in and out are handled differently by Alchemy and Sound Designer. Fading in and out have musical analogies (crescendo and decrescendo), with one distinction: Fade outs always go from 100 percent of the original amplitude to zero volume, and fade ins always go from zero amplitude to 100 percent of the pre-fade value of the final selected sample. It is possible to get around this limitation in Alchemy by manually drawing a fade while editing the waveform's amplitude envelope.

Sound Designer's fade in and fade out options perform linear fades (see Figure 13-18).

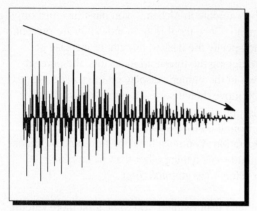

Figure 13-18: With linear fadeouts, like those employed by Sound Designer, every next wave cycle is reduced in volume linearly, so that the peaks of each waveform describe a straight line.

Alchemy does not provide for linear fade ins and fade outs, except via manually drawing such fades while editing the waveform's amplitude envelope. Alchemy's fade in and fade out options always use the fade curve's slope defined in the Edit Options dialog box (see Figure 13-19).

Crossfade

Crossfading refers to fading in one soundfile or region of a soundfile while another soundfile or region thereof is fading out.

Alchemy crossfades material on the Clipboard with the selected region of the active file. The material on the Clipboard is faded out while the existing selected region gets faded in. The selected region becomes the sum total of the crossfade, and any sound on the Clipboard that does not fit into the target selected region is ignored. As with most Clipboard options, holding the option key down while performing the crossfade commences from the end of the selected region and fades the

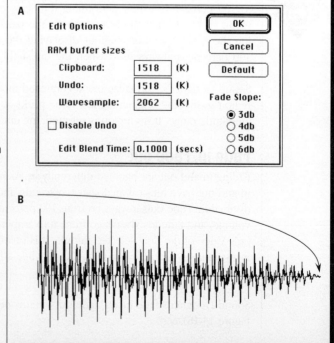

Figure 13-19: (A) Alchemy's Edit Options dialog box provides for four fade slopes from 3 dB to 6 dB. Each fade slope uses a curve that boosts the amplitude by the selected amount at the center of the curve. The 3 dB curve is the same as Sound Designer's Equal Power slopes used in crossfades but unavailable in simple fade ins and fade outs.
(B) Alchemy's fade out using a 3 dB slope boosts the amplitude by 3 dB at the center of the fade curve. This ensures that the amplitude halfway through the fade is 7/10 of its former value. Such a curve is very useful when dealing with complex waveforms.

Figure 13-20: Sound Designer's Merge option crossfades two soundfiles smoothly into one another. The merge length given in samples and milliseconds defaults to the maximum setting, so make sure you don't increase this number. You can, however, decrease this number if you want — this has the same effect as shifting the Merge Start marker. Finally, you can specify a linear crossfade or an Equal Power crossfade, which uses a curve designed to boost the volume by 3 dB at the crossfade center.

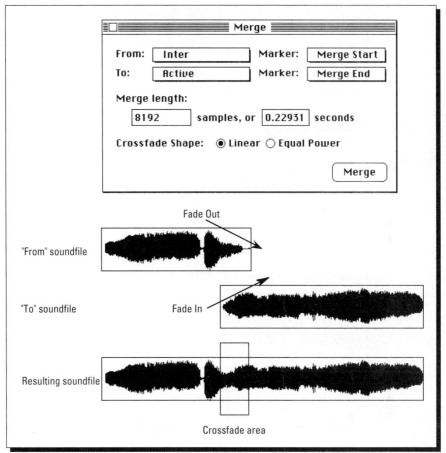

Clipboard in rather than out. The fade slope used is always the currently selected curve in the Edit Options dialog box described above (see Figure 13-19).

Sound Designer does not have a crossfade option per se, however, the Merge operation crossfades two soundfiles smoothly from one to another (see Figure 13-20). A new soundfile is created from the two source soundfiles (both of which must be open before commencing a merge). In this way you can create a sound that starts out as a trumpet and gradually transforms into a violin. The creative uses of this feature are many.

After opening the two soundfiles, you must place a marker (using the marker tool from the tool palette) at the point in the first soundfile where the merge is to begin and a marker where the merge is to end in the second soundfile. These markers can be named anything you want, however, naming them "Merge

Start" and "Merge End" will simplify matters. In the Merge dialog box, you are presented with pop-up menus for both the beginning and ending soundfiles and a pop-up menu listing all the markers in each selected soundfile. In practice this operation may require a considerable amount of planning. It may be helpful to draw the merge on paper to study the relationship between the markers and crossfade time.

Noise gating

Noise gating is an option available only in Sound Designer at the time of this writing. A noise gate allows you to specify an amplitude level above which all signals will pass through. When the amplitude of the input signal drops below the specified level, no signal passes through.

Noise gates are effective in those soundfiles including silent sections for removing tape hiss, radio frequency interference, and other noise added by gear between the input source and the input to the DSP board that inevitably enter the signal chain when the program material is not present.

Most noise gates offer user adjustment of the speed at which sound is turned on and off (attack and release time). These are very crucial adjustments, because some settings will produce a disagreeable breathing or pumping effect. Sound Designer adds a Detect control at the input stage (ranging from Peak to Average) and an output level setting in decibels. Sound Designer's Noise Gate option is part of its Dynamics dialog box shown under the next section.

Compression/limiting, expanding

Like noise gating, compression, limiting, and expanding are standard options only in Sound Designer at the time of this writing (see Figure 13-21). It is possible to compress, expand, and limit in Alchemy, but this is a more tedious and convoluted process involving either cycle-by-cycle normalization or amplitude envelope drawing. Compression is a type of signal processing that can be thought of as an automatic volume fader. When the input signal exceeds the user-specified threshold, the gain is reduced, lowering the volume continually according to the slope determined by the compression ratio.

Compression ratios describe the amount of increase in input required to produce a specified output. A compression ratio of 6:1 indicates that every 6 dB increase in input signal will produce a 1 dB increase in the output level. The result of compression is to increase the volume of soft sections and decrease the volume of loud sections, so that the overall dynamic range is decreased. As with a noise gate, the speed at which the gain is reduced (after the input threshold is exceeded) and recovered (after the input signal drops below the threshold) is normally controlled by the user (attack time and release time). As with noise gating, these settings are crucial for avoiding a pumping or breathing effect.

Figure 13-21: Sound Designer's Dynamics dialog box provides access to its compressor/limiter, expander, and noise gate functions. For compressing/limiting, the ratio setting ranges from 1:1 to 100:1. When the Expander function is selected, the range is from 1:1 to 1:10. When Noise Gate is selected, the Ratio slider disappears altogether, because it has no meaning in that context. As in most Digidesign dialog boxes, holding the option key down while dragging a fader will permit fine tuning of the slider value.

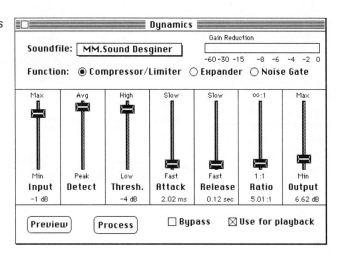

One of the characteristics of a limiter is a compression ratio of greater-than-10:1. With larger compression ratios, on up to 100:1, low level signals are not affected and high level signals never exceed the threshold.

An *expander* has the opposite effect of a compressor. Instead of decreasing the overall dynamic range, it expands it. The *expansion ratio* is similar to that used for compression, except that the larger number is on the right instead of the left. In other words, with a 1:6 expansion ratio, a 1 dB increase of the input signal increases the output signal level by 6 dB.

Amplitude envelope editing

Alchemy is currently the only software to provide for *amplitude envelope editing* (see Figure 13-22). Like frequency envelope editing, this is a powerful music feature that can add expressivity to recorded or synthesized sounds. The amplitude envelope of any soundfile can be auto-traced, edited, copied, and applied to another soundfile. Once an amplitude envelope has been traced and copied to the Clipboard, it can be treated as an amplitude envelope, as a frequency envelope, or as actual wave data.

Amplitude envelopes can be edited by drawing with the pencil cursor or by dragging break-point knobs that you can specify or have automatically placed by the software following an auto-trace. Applying either a drawn envelope or a copied envelope to a soundfile produces an effect similar to moving the volume pedal on a synthesizer through the course proscribed by the envelope.

Figure 13-22: Three soundfiles open in Alchemy. The top soundfile's amplitude envelope has been auto-traced, copied, and pasted on the Slow Attack Brass soundfile in the center. After selecting Amplitude Fit from the Process menu, the soundfile is transformed to that at the bottom of the figure. The resultant soundfile still sounds like a slow attack brass instrument, but the volume levels of the sound perfectly replicate those of my daughter saying "media" (the top file from which the amplitude envelope was extracted).

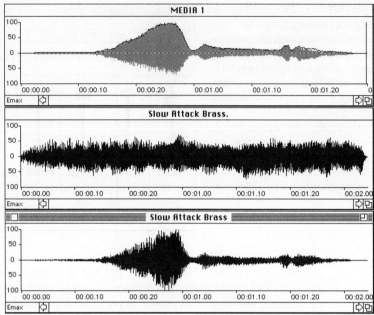

Time Domain Editing

Looping

Macintosh software handles *looping*, an important feature of sound sampling, very elegantly. When used musically, portions of sampled soundfiles are usually looped repeatedly to allow for the sampled sound to sustain for any desired length (the length being dictated by the amount of time between the Note-On event and the Note-Off event). Often the motivation behind looping a sample is to save precious memory in an external sampler. After successfully looping a sound, sometimes is feasible to delete the non-looped part of the sound to save even more memory.

The most common kind of loop is called a *sustain loop*. Sustain loops are normally found at the end of a soundfile. While a note is sustained, this portion of the sound continues to repeat. With an appropriately placed sustain loop, you can sustain even a single-cycle sample and hold it for as long as you like. Some samplers provide for multiple loops either before or after the sustain loop. The next most common type of loop after the sustain loop is the *release loop* that kicks in as soon as the key is released.

Whether you use a sustain loop, a release loop, or some other kind of loop, there are two basic ways of looping a sound. A *forward loop* continuously jumps from the loop end point to the loop start point. A *backward/forward loop* (sometimes called a mirror loop, reversing loop, or alternating loop) cycles from the end point to the start point and back to the end point repeatedly. Besides having a forward or backward/forward orientation, a loop's start and end points may overlap, in which case the loop is called a *crossfade loop*.

Finding good loop points can require very delicate maneuvering. One problem with any loop is that an audible click or pop (sometimes called a glitch) may be heard at the splice point between where the start and end points meet, if both the points are not at "zero crossings," if the waveform slope resulting from the loop is not smooth, or if there is a phase change. Even if the slopes of the start and end points match, if the looped section is long enough for the sound to undergo audible amplitude changes, the looped portion can create an effect similar to amplitude vibrato or tremolo. Sometimes this is desirable. Conversely, if the looped segment is too short, the loop may cause a buzzing sound. If it is even shorter, the loop point can recur with such rapidity that the frequency of the glitch enters the audible spectrum, creating the effect of a new pitch. Finally, if the pitch of the looped segment drops between the start point and the end point, an effect similar to frequency vibrato may be encountered. If the looped segment consists of exactly one vibrato cycle in a sound that already has vibrato, then this effect is often desired. Of course, vibrato created in this way will become faster as the sample is transposed up and slower as it is transposed down.

A visual editing system can aid you in getting around all the problems mentioned in the previous paragraph. With sample-editing software, after coarse loop points have been designated, fine-tuning of a sound loop is accomplished by displaying the crucial "seam" created at the exact place at which the end point loops back to the beginning part of the loop. This seam may then be moved, sample by sample, until a point at which the wave slope coming into the loop complements the slope immediately following the loop point.

Both Alchemy and Sound Designer have similar Loop windows. The principle in both is to provide a visual representation of the seam created by the loop end point meeting the loop start point. Because of this, the end of the loop is given in the left side of the window and the beginning of the loop is given in the right side of the window.

Alchemy's Auto Zero option is very helpful in loop creation, because you are assured that a range selected by the cursor will always fall on zero crossings. Alchemy includes a Loop Selection menu option that makes an instantaneous loop of the selected region. After you have a looping region, you can click the Loop window icon in the palette (upper right) to display the Loop Splice window (see Figure 13-23).

Figure 13-23: Alchemy's Loop Splice window displays the place where the end point meets the start point in a forward loop. In this illustration, two identical wave segments have been identified, and two possible loop start and end points are indicated (Start-1, End-1 and Start-2, End-2). Adjusting the actual loop points to these positions is a simple matter of using the horizontal scroll bars at the bottom of the window. When dealing with a stereo soundfile, the Loop window displays both channels simultaneously.

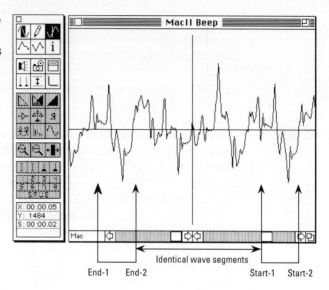

Sound Designer's Loop window (accessed by selecting Loop window from the Tools menu) will only display a single channel at a time, but you may toggle channels with the channel pop-up menu in the Loop window (see Figure 13-24). Note that the Loop window option is not enabled until you have dragged start and end point loop markers into the main waveform window. The markers become numbered if there are multiple loops and move from loop to loop in the Loop window using the Loop # pop-up menu.

Figure 13-24: Sound Designer's Loop window has its own mini-palette at the upper left. At the bottom of the window are two sets of arrows. The upper set scrolls the loop point in the smallest possible increments. The lower left and right AUTO arrows automatically jump to the next point that preserves the sample value and slope of the loop, a very useful tool. The AUTO arrows on the left will scroll to match the loop start point displayed in the right-hand side of the window, while the AUTO arrows on the right will scroll to match the loop end point displayed in the left-

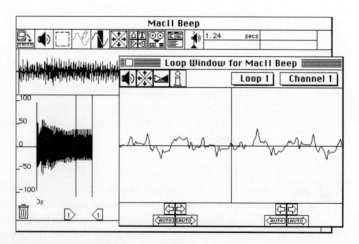

hand side of the window. Finally, you can click the cursor on the waveform in either the end point side of the window or the start point side, and the splice point will immediately be set to your click location.

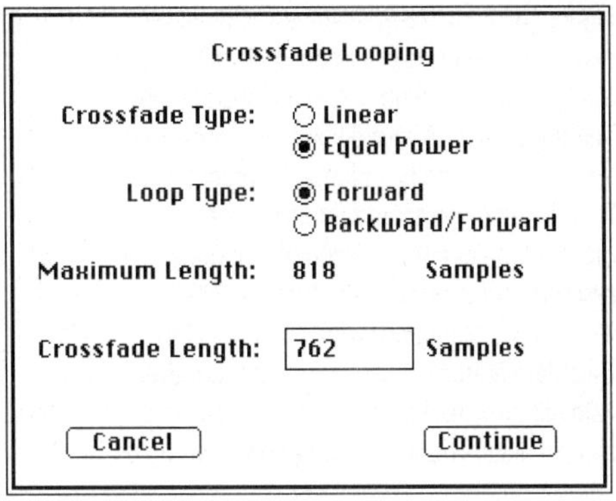

Crossfade Looping

Crossfade Type: ○ Linear
                         ● Equal Power

Loop Type: ● Forward
                   ○ Backward/Forward

Maximum Length: 818   Samples

Crossfade Length: [762]   Samples

[Cancel]   [Continue]

Figure 13-25: Sound Designer's Crossfade Looping dialog box allows you to specify the slope of the crossfade (Linear or Equal Power), the loop type (Forward or Backward/Forward), and the length of the crossfade (the maximum equalling one-half the duration of the entire loop length is provided).

Sound Designer provides powerful crossfade looping tools. While in the Loop window, clicking the Crossfade icon opens the Crossfade Looping dialog box (see Figure 13-25). A crossfade loop in Sound Designer automatically takes a copy of the end of the loop, crossfades 50 percent of it with the beginning of the loop and performs a similar operation to crossfade 50 percent of a copy of the start of the loop with the end of the loop. Fifty percent is the default value, but you can change this in the Crossfade Looping dialog box.

Crossfade Looping can be applied to any kind of loop and is often used to eliminate glitches at the loop splice point. The loop points are actually overlapped and mixed during the overlap — one part fading out while the other part fades in.

Alchemy does not automate the creation of crossfade loops or backward/forward loops, but that does not mean they can't be accomplished with a little ingenuity. To create a backward/forward loop, you merely copy the loop segment, paste it on the end of the loop segment, reverse the copy, and then loop the entire region. Note that you will probably have to invert the reversed portion of the wave so that the slopes match at the loop splice point. Similarly, crossfade loops are possible by making copies of the starting and ending portions of your loop, applying Fade In or Fade Out as required and then mixing these back into the original looping segment. You can even create a crossfade backward/forward loop this way. Another approach is possible if your sampler has a backward/forward or crossfade loop option itself. You may want to do the rough loop in the sampler and then adjust the start and end points in Alchemy.

Reversing

Reversing a soundfile or selected region is a simple matter of changing the order of the samples, so that the last sample is first and the first is last, a simple matter for a computer. This is useful for creating effects and also is a required step in Alchemy to creating a backward/forward loop.

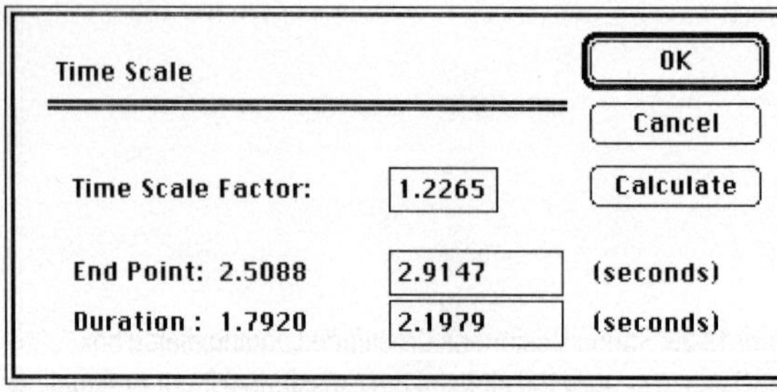

Figure 13-26: Alchemy's time compression/ expansion features are accessed via the Time Scale... menu option. The original end point and duration is always displayed in the lower left. You can specify a compression/expansion base by entering a Time Scale Factor (percentage of compression or expansion), the new end point, or the new duration. The other values are calculated when you press the Calculate button or when you enter another field either by tabbing to it or by clicking in it. End points and durations are expressed in the prevailing horizontal axis display units. These can be seconds, samples, or SMPTE frames.

Time Scale	OK
	Cancel
Time Scale Factor:	1.2265	Calculate
End Point: 2.5088	2.9147	(seconds)
Duration : 1.7920	2.1979	(seconds)

Time compression and time expansion

Time compression and *time expansion* refers to changing the duration of a soundfile or soundfile region without changing the pitch (see Figure 13-26 for an illustration of Alchemy's time compression/expansion features). By far the most common use of time compression is to adjust durations due to musical considerations, for example, to assure that a soundfile ends at the required time. It is just the opposite of pitch shifting discussed earlier, where the pitch of a region is changed without changing its duration. As with pitch shifting, there are some practical limits to how much you can alter the duration of a sound without degrading quality. Digidesign suggests a maximum compression/expansion range of less than 20 percent for speech and 5 percent for music.

Sound Designer's time compression/expansion algorithms are considerably more complex than Alchemy's, providing for different algorithms depending upon the complexity of the waveform (see Figure 13-27). A waveform of low complexity might be a single note by a wind instrument with a simple harmonic spectrum

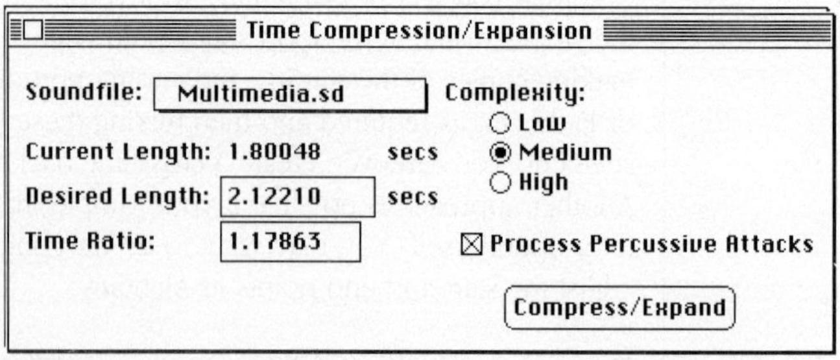

Figure 13-27: Sound Designer's Time Compression/Expansion dialog box always displays the original length of the selected region, but unlike Alchemy, it does not display the end point. Typing a new length in the Desired Length field automatically calculates the new time ratio, and typing a new ratio in the Time Ratio field automatically calculates the new length. All user entries and calculations are performed in seconds, so adjusting durations based upon SMPTE values will require additional precalculation. Be forewarned that certain lengths and ratios are impossible to achieve due to the sample rate of the file.

Time Compression/Expansion	
Soundfile: Multimedia.sd	Complexity:
	○ Low
Current Length: 1.80048 secs	● Medium
Desired Length: 2.12210 secs	○ High
Time Ratio: 1.17863	☒ Process Percussive Attacks
	Compress/Expand

(such as a flute or horn); medium complexity includes speech and most other solo instruments, and high complexity covers broadband waveforms such as music. You may further alter the algorithm by selecting or deselecting Process Percussive Attacks. With this option turned off, quick transient attacks of many instruments will not be processed, eliminating the possibility of creating double attacks (in expansion) and dropped attacks (in compression).

Table 13-3 lists the available sample-editing software packages and their respective supported features.

Table 13-3: Sample-editing software features

GENERAL	Alchemy	Sound Apprent. 2.22	Sound Des. II 1.22	Sound Des. SK 2.0
System requirements				
Plus, SE, SE30	●●●	●●●	●●●	●●●
II, IIx/cx, IIci, IIfx	●●◐●	●●◐●	●●●●	●●●●
RAM recommended	1MB	1MB	2MB	2MB
MIDI	●	●	●	●
SCSI	●		●	●
RS422	●	●	●	●
File formats				
Sound Designer (16-bit mono)	●	●	●	●
Sound Designer II (16-bit stereo or mono)			●	●
AIFF (16-bit multichannel)	●	●	●	●
Sound Lab (8-bit mono)	●	●		
'snd 'resource 8-bit, 16-bit, chunky (8-&16-bit)	●○○	●○○	●●●	●●●
Dyaxis	●	●		
File compression			●	
Copyprotected?	no	no	no	no
DISPLAY				
Open file dialog				
Sound info in open file dialog	●	●		
Open multiple in same dialog	●	●		
Ongoing info				
Free RAM, disk space, Clipboard size, file info	●○●●	●○●●	○●○●	○●○●
Number of open files/window	RAM	RAM	RAM	RAM
Different display scales in each window			●	●
Amplitude display				
Percent of maximum (linear), sample value, decibels	●●○	●●○	●●○	●●○
Duration display				
H:M:S:ms	●	●	●	●
SMPTE 24, 25, 30 drop, 30 non-drop, 29.97 non-drop Set SMPTE Offset	○●○ ●	○●○ ●	●● ●●● ●	●● ●●● ●

Table 13-3: Sample-editing software features (continued)

DISPLAY (continued)	Alchemy	Sound Apprent. 2.22	Sound Des. II 1.22	Sound Des. SK 2.0
Sample number (dec or HEX)	●●	●●	●●	●●
Feet frames (16 or 35 mm)			●●	●●
Bars and beats			●	●
Waveforms as points, lines	●●	●●	○●	○●
Zooms: horiz., vert., fit selection	●○●	●○●	●●◗	●●◗
Number of definable/saveable views	8	8	0	0
Markers				
Numbered, text, loop start, loop end	○○●●	○○●●	●●●●	●●●●
Center display at marker, selected region	○●	○●	●○	●○
Center display at loop start, loop end	●●	●●		
Cursor and data indicator	●	●	●	●
Overview				
Stereo: L & R, L or R, composite	●○○	●○○	○●●	○●●
Timeline, display without overview			●	●
Waveform window display indicator in overview	●	●	●	●
Waveform selection indicator in overview	●	●		
Lock selection duration	●	●		
Navigate in overview	●	●	●	●
Split overview into file + selection	●	●		
FFTs				
3-D or 2-D	2-D	2-D	3-D	3-D
Maximum number of bands (freqs)	16,384	16,384	2,048	2,048
Configure number of bands			●	●
Amplitude scale: logarithmic, linear	○●	○●	●●	●●
Specify time interval			●	●
Specify direction of display			●	●
Type: bar chart, 3-D plot	●○	●○	○●	○●
Max. duration (number of samples or RAM)	32,768	32,768	RAM	RAM
Edit FFT	●	●		
Cut, Copy, Paste	●●●	●●●		
Mix	●	●		
Outpoint editing	●	●		
Clear above, below, resynthesize	●●●	●●●		
Show Clipboard			●	●
Clear Clipboard	●	●		
Auto window tile, stack, strip	●●●	●●●	●●○	●●○

EDITING

	Alchemy	Sound Apprent. 2.22	Sound Des. II 1.22	Sound Des. SK 2.0
Destructive, Nondestructive Editing	○●	○●	●●	●●
Options requiring destructive editing	Dyaxis	Dyaxis	Smooth., Time Comp/exp	Smooth., Time Comp/exp
Selection limited by HD or Ram or....	RAM	RAM	HD	HD

Table 13-3: Sample-editing software features (continued)

DISPLAY (continued)	Alchemy	Sound Apprent. 2.22	Sound Des. II 1.22	Sound Des. SK 2.0
"Auto-Zero" selection limits	●	●		
Smooth (auto fade in or out at edit points)			●	●
Cut, Copy, Past, Insert	●●●●	●●●●	●●●●	●●●●
Outpoint editing	●	●		
Blend or auto crossfade	●	●		
Clear, Clear (close up), Extract (trim)	●○●	●○●	●●●	●●●
Reverse	●	●	●	●
Invert	●	●		
Replicate	●	●		
Fade In, Fade Out, Crossfade	●●●	●●●	●●●	●●●
Number of available slopes	4	4	2	2
Normalize			●	●
Change Gain by percentage, by dB	●○	●○	●●	●●
Scrub			●	●
Draw waveform	●	●	●	●
Merge = crossfade 2 soundfiles	◗	◗	●	●
Linear or 3 dB boost at crossover	○●	○●	●●	●●

MIX

	Alchemy	Sound Apprent. 2.22	Sound Des. II 1.22	Sound Des. SK 2.0
Number of files or Clipboard only	Clipboard	Clipboard	4 mono or stereo	4 mono or stereo
Controllable mix parameters				
Level of file or L & R channels	●	●	●●	●●
Stereo pan	●	●	●	●
Delay before mix start			●	●
Auto scaling option to avoid clipping			●	●
Outpoint (Mix from end of selection)	●	●		
Envelope Editing (Amplitude, Frequency)	●●			
Auto trace (Amp, Freq)	●●			
Copy and Paste (Amp, Freq)	●●			
Amp. Envelope Fit, Freq. Envelope Modulate	●●			
Envelope Scale (Amp, Freq)	●○			
Fade In/Out (Amp, Freq)	●○			
Invert (Amp, Freq)	●●			

LOOPING

	Alchemy	Sound Apprent. 2.22	Sound Des. II 1.22	Sound Des. SK 2.0
Number of loops	1	1	UL	UL
Preview Loop in Loop window			●	●

Table 13-3: Sample-editing software features (continued)

LOOPING (continued)	Alchemy	Sound Apprent. 2.22	Sound Des. II 1.22	Sound Des. SK 2.0
Zoom in Loop window			●	●
Crossfade	●	●	●	●
Linear	●	●	●	●
Non linear (number of slopes)	4	4	1	1
Forward	●	●		
Backward/Forward			●	●
Info about loop	●	●	●	●
Slide loop section without changing length	●	●		
Jump loop to loop from within Loop window	NA	NA	●	●
View other chan. without leaving Loop window	●	●	●	●
Auto slope match search			●	●
Toggle Loop on/off, quick select loop	●●	●●		
DSP				
Sample rate conversion				
Resampling upper limit	100 KHz	100 KHz	96.2 KHz	96.2 KHz
By rate, by size, by ratio (Note: Sound Designer requires card for this)	●●○	●●○	●○●	●○●
Time compression/expansion	●●		●●	●●
By ratio, by duration, by endpoint	●●●		●●○	●●○
Duration in samples, seconds, SMPTE	●●●		●○○	●○○
Options for complexity, perc. attacks			●●	●●
Pitch shift, with preserve duration	●●		●●	●●
Parametric EQ	●	●	●	●
High pass, Low pass			●●	●●
High shelf, Low shelf	●●	●●	●●	●●
Notch/Peak	●	●	●	●
Preview during adjustment			●	●
Save EQ settings with program, with file			●●	●●
Real-time non-destructive option for playback			●	●
Configure EQ Boost/cut, bandwidth, corner, center freq	●●●●	●●●●	●●●●	●●●●
Graphic EQ (Note: Sound Designer requires card for this)			●	●
Number of bands	NA	NA	5 stereo, 10 mono	7 stereo, 14 mono
Preview during adjustment			●	●
Change center freq and bandwidth			●	●
Save EQ settings with program, with file			●	●
Real Time non-destructive option for playback			●	●
Compressor/Limiter			●	
Expander			●	
Noise Gate			●	

Table 13-3: Sample-editing software features (continued)

PLAYBACK (For direct-to-hard disk features, see Chapter 24)	Alchemy	Sound Apprent. 2.22	Sound Des. II 1.22	Sound Des. SK 2.0
Macintosh Speaker				
Fixed rate, variable rate	●●	●●	●●	●●
Digidesign Sound Accelerator, Audiomedia	●●	●●	●●	
Preview sound before opening	●	●		
Play Clipboard				
Play from MIDI keyboard			●	●
Play from on-screen keyboard	●	●	●	●
Scroll after play			●	●

Summary

✔ In the past, custom sample-editor programs were available for each type of sampler. Standardization of file formats has engendered universal sample editors that support most samplers commonly in use. The *raison d'être* of most sample-editing programs is exactly the same as for patch-editing programs: The devices themselves often do not provide an adequate user interface to their own internal sound-editing capabilities.

✔ Both patch editors and sample editors share the same advantages of hard disk storage. Unlike patch-editing software, sample editors provide the further advantage of being a unifying point by which sounds of incompatible samplers can share sample libraries. Do not confuse this with the MIDI SDS, that also lets samplers share files.

✔ Editing sounds with a sample editor is accomplished using one of several standard sampled soundfile formats: Sound Designer I, Sound Designer II (mono), Sound Designer II (stereo), and AIFF. You can transfer soundfiles between the Macintosh and external samplers in one of five ways: MIDI SysEx, MIDI 12-bit SDS, MIDI 16-bit SDS, RS-422, and SCSI.

✔ Clipping can be a problem with sampled sound. When sample values exceed the maximum supported by the sampling rate the result is clipping. The effect is unpleasant, and merely reducing the overall volume for the affected segment is usually not enough to repair it. Clipping can also be caused by cutting and pasting sound data when they result in two parts of a waveform being unmatched with respect to their slope.

✔ Any sound can be described as a product of the interaction of a number of sine waves. FFTs are representations of the frequency spectrum of a sound reduced to these component sine waves. The amplitudes of the sine waves can then be calculated and displayed with respect to their transformations over a given time period.

✔ When used musically, portions of sampled soundfiles are usually looped repeatedly to allow for the sampled sound to sustain for any desired length (the amount of time between the Note-On and the Note-Off). Often the motivation behind looping a sample is to save memory in an external sampler. After successfully looping a sound, sometimes is be feasible to delete the non-looped part of the sound to save even more memory.

✔ There are three types of sustain loops and release loops: forward, backward/forward, and crossfade. Crossfading fades in one soundfile or region of a soundfile while another is fading out. Crossfade looping is often used to eliminate glitches at the loop splice point.

✔ Time compression/expansion changes the duration of a soundfile or region without changing the pitch. It is often used to assure that a soundfile ends at the required time. This is just the opposite of pitch shifting, where the pitch of a region is changed without changing its duration. As with pitch shifting, there are some practical limits to how much you can alter the duration of a sound without degrading quality: less than 20 percent for speech and 5 percent for music.

Part Three

Composition

Part Three

Foreword

by Curtis Roads

Composition

The traditional composer scribbling on manuscript paper would appear to have no need of machine assistance. But when we:

❖ Allow the musical palette to incorporate an expanding catalog of musical colors (timbres) from electronic sources, unusual acoustic instruments, and sounds occurring in nature and industry;

❖ Adopt a variety of "brushes" (sound envelopes) to apply to the colors (for parametric detail at the level of elementary sonic grains to global control of sound blocks, masses, and clouds);

❖ Admit the possibility of programmed machine performance (for example, to permit the auditioning of multiple-part scores that would be impossible to perform by a human being);

❖ Accept the machine as a musical *idiot savant* — capable of rapidly carrying out specialized calculations, such as searching for certain sounds or combinations, computing variations for later selection, or taking on a variety of subtasks that would be overly time-consuming for mortal hands; in short, when we enter into the musical universe of what the visionary composer Edgar Varèse called "organized sound" (Varèse 1971), then machine assistance is not only welcome, it is a necessity.

We can take a cue from the world of commercial music. Facing deadline pressures, wealthy film and show business composers can afford to hire a dozen or more subcontracting composers to create a musical soundtrack. The integration of their results is coordinated by one or more assistant composers who act as managers of the rest of the subcontractors. Much of the compositional work is routine, such as grinding out variations on a theme for later selection by the maestro, conforming a musical section to the duration of a scene, or orchestrating a piano score for a synthesizer.

The bulk of this level of musical knowledge could be formalized and encoded into a machine that accepts musical assignments and provides alternatives for the human composer to choose from. Such a music machine might provide less wealthy composers with some of the same efficiencies as their counterparts in the entertainment industry.

Of course, there is more to composition than efficiency. Software procedures can embed compositional decisions deeper into a work than would be possible without computer assistance. In this case, rather than eroding the composer's role, programs actually extend it. Following are a few examples of how software can expand the scope of compositional decisions.

❖ Controlling the microfrequency variations among the partials of a given tone;

❖ Sifting through massive amounts of data to select a specified sound or sound combination;

❖ Sending sounds on precise spatial paths computed according to composer-specified rules;

❖ Interpreting a composer's gestures through an input device to effect changes in the musical process being produced;

❖ Generating variations on sound materials to provide the composer with several alternatives to a given sound or series of sounds;

❖ Generating complex polyphonic textures that would otherwise be impossible to control.

As Part Three demonstrates, composers can select from a catalog of programs that lend assistance to any number of musical tasks (Roads and Strawn 1985; Roads 1989). These range from transcription systems that convert a keyboard performance into music notations, to sequencers that recall and manipulate stored phrases, to patch editors used to "tune" a digital synthesizer voice, to sound mixing systems that are conducted via graphical scores. Technically proficient musicians can program the machine to assist with specific compositional tasks. This labor can be made more productive by a programming language that contains the appropriate musical construct and interaction tools.

Underneath the languages and the graphics of the machine is a thick layer of intercommunicat-ing software procedures that manipulate representations of music. These procedures and underlying representations define the musical games that are possible. Hence, every computer music composition develops from fundamental assumptions about a music that has been encoded within the machine (Roads 1992). Every system constrains the composer to a restricted set of musical operations; every "view" on a piece provided by a system is a filter that biases the viewer's attention to a particular musical perspective.

So a constant problem of musically intelligent machines is that they sometimes replicate the prejudices of their creators, limiting users to a rigid and narrow concept of music. A more fundamental problem from a compositional standpoint is that the musical constructs and logic embedded in many systems are not extensible. The issue of flexible and extensible representations for music is a continuing one, since creative possibilities are constantly evolving alongside technical possibilities (DePoli, Piccialli, and Roads 1991; Roads 1991).

In the future, machines must learn more about musical structure and musical sound in the broadest possible sense. They must use this knowledge to act more like a human musician, that is, to draw inferences from partial descriptions, and to view and manipulate musical data from different perspectives (Roads 1985). When they do, we can hand them more, not less, responsibility. But we must always be wary of hand-coded limitations. A programmer's mind creates the machine, and in this sense, after all, machines are only human.

References

DePoli, G., A. Piccialli, and C. Roads, eds. 1991. *Representations of Musical Signals.* Cambridge, Massachusetts: MIT Press.

Roads, C. 1985. "Research in Music and Artificial Intelligence." *ICM Computing Surveys* 17(2):163-190.

Roads, C., ed. 1989. *The Music Machine.* Cambridge, Massachusetts: MIT Press.

Roads, C. 1991. "Asynchronous Granular Synthesis." In G. DePoli, A. Piccialli, and C.

Roads, eds. 1991. *Representations of Musical Signals.* Cambridge, Massachusetts: MIT Press.

Roads, C. 1992. *Computer Music Tutorial.* Cambridge, Massachusetts: MIT Press.

Roads, C. and J. Strawn, eds. 1985. *Foundations of Computer Music.* Cambridge, Massachusetts: MIT Press.

Varèse, E. 1971. "The Liberation of Sound." In B. Boretz and E. Cone, eds. *Perspectives on American Composers.* New York: Norton.

Curtis Roads is Associate Editor of Computer Music Journal.

Introduction to Part Three

The Macintosh has had a profound effect upon three areas of creative musical endeavor: composition, notation (manuscript preparation), and sound design. This section of the book will explore the impact of the Macintosh on the CAC (computer-assisted composition) environment.

You should be aware of certain distinctions within computer-assisted composition:

❖ Music processing (notation or manuscript preparation) is concerned with the manipulation of graphic symbols.

❖ Sound design is concerned with the manipulation of sonic materials.

❖ Music composition is concerned with the manipulation of musical ideas.

You should understand these premises from the very beginning, because many people confuse manuscript preparation (music processing) and/or sound design (waveform/patch editing and synthesis) with actual musical composition (the crystallization and organizing of ideas into music).

With these distinctions in mind, although music notation and sound design are often components of a CAC environment, those activities have entire sections of this book dedicated specifically to them.

The first chapter in this part makes a number of distinctions regarding the role of the Macintosh in musical composition, breaking this area into the categories and subcategories of computer-assisted composition, computer-generated composition, intelligent instruments, automatic composition, interactive composition, and algorithmic composition. Chapter 15 covers making music without MIDI while Chapters 16 and 17 are devoted exclusively to MIDI applications. In Chapter 16, "Making Music with MIDI," you will also find a discussion of special cases where the area of sound design moves into the domain of music composition. The final two chapters deal with software that functions both in MIDI and non-MIDI environments.

Case History

For a dramatic illustration of the impact of the Macintosh upon compositional methodology, consider my own case history:

I compose music in many genres. For the past decade, however, most of my efforts have been devoted to film and opera. My studio is in my home (albeit in a separate building), so I often start preparing for a day of composing while I'm drinking my morning coffee. Seven years ago, these preparations entailed cleaning up the erasure dust accumulated from the previous day, sharpening several dozen pencils, and opening up the piano. At that time, my only high-tech compositional tools consisted of an electric pencil sharpener (used during rough drafts) and a light table (used to prepare final scores on vellum with ink and transfer symbols). The only silicon in my studio was in my windowpanes. Now, in 1992, looking around my studio, I find myself losing count of the number of microprocessor-controlled devices.

As a computer-assisted composer in 1992, I still compose opera, but that's about the only thing that hasn't changed. First, I don't use pencils anymore for rough drafts — my Macintosh automatically transcribes these as I play my synthesizer. Second, there is no more erasure dust to sweep up because I do all of my editing on-screen by pushing around musical ideas with a mouse. I accomplish my orchestrations in a similar manner. Now I can test (or proofhear) music compositions at any moment through a battery of synthesizers and samplers making up a veritable "orchestra in a box" (in my case, "orchestra in a console" might be more accurate). These devices play back my music using digital recordings of every instrument in the orchestra or sounds that do not have any relation to natural sources (in the case of synthesizers). Finally, although I still use paper for my final drafts, I never have to lift a pen because my laser printer prints the scores. I still get ready for a day of composing while I'm drinking my morning coffee, but my preparations have changed considerably.

A typical day commences with turning on, booting up, or otherwise activating the various electronic elements of my studio. My Macintosh, hard disk, modem, and printer are already on because they have been working all night. While I slept, the printer may have been printing the music I composed the day before, while at the same time my Macintosh may have been taking care of my telecommunications between 4 a.m. and 6 a.m., when the on-line connect charges are lower. At least every other day, my Macintosh's nocturnal activities include performing a backup script to back up all the data on all my hard drives.

Instead of opening the lid on my piano, I power up my master keyboard, a Kurzweil 250 with about five megasamples of orchestral instruments on-line in the ROMs. I turn on the other dozen sound-generating modules. Some of the previous day's work is already available in the battery-backed RAM of these devices, but I may still need to load certain sounds that I will be using for the specific project I am working on. I use a reverberator to place my "personal orchestra" in a simulated cubic room with walls 48 meters apart.

Next, I use a macro (a single keystroke command that initiates an otherwise lengthy or cumbersome process) that automatically loads a number of pro-grams into my Macintosh — a MIDI sequencer, a universal sound editor/librarian, and often, a notation program or sample editor.

Throughout any day, I will inevitably spend more time at the computer keyboard than at the musical one. This is because once I have the musical source material — themes, motives, melodies, and so on — recorded into storage tracks within my MIDI sequencer (which can support hundreds of virtual tracks), I can use the mouse to manipulate my creative material. The mouse lets me cut and paste ideas, modify, rearrange, and otherwise experi-ment with orchestrations, or redirect material to any or all of 16 banks of 16 MIDI channels on my sampling keyboard and expander modules — a total of 256 simultaneous data streams, each of which may be as polyphonic, both rhythmi-cally and melodically, as required.

Occasionally, I set the Macintosh up to generate variations on my morning's endeavors while I'm eating lunch. I load my material into one of the interactive composition packages such as Jam Factory or M. With a few minutes of finagling, these packages can continue to produce creditable musical variations through my system as an accompaniment to lunch. I won't necessarily use any of this material in the project, but nonetheless, the resulting statistical development of my musical ideas is thought-provoking.

Besides being time-consuming, printing drafts on the LaserWriter is noisy — so I usually reserve this activity for sleeping hours. The day's MIDI sequence files, after having been automatically converted (using another macro) into a format for printing in conventional music notation, are transferred to a storage area on the hard disk that is specifically designated for printing as a background task (this is called *spooling*). Once the printing begins, the Macintosh divides its time between printing and running automatic telecommunications macros that include the uploading and downloading of electronic mail (E-mail). In many cases, this includes printing out received E-mail. These tasks continue throughout the night.

When all the musical tasks are taken care of, other macros kick in that take care of opening my appointment diary software and printing out my schedule for the next day, backing up special files to a separate hard disk, performing an incremental backup of all my hard disks to DAT, optimizing (defragmenting) specified partitions on my hard drive, and, in general, taking care of any repetitive tasks that can be relegated to a time-triggered macro.

Of course, it doesn't always work as smoothly as one would hope. Some days I walk into the studio expecting to find a printout of the day's appointments sitting on the top of a stack of music and E-mail at my LaserWriter, but instead, find a bomb dialog box on my Macintosh's screen indicating that something has gone wrong in the night. System crashes like these are not uncommon as one pushes the limits of automation, but fortunately they are never very serious. Because such a crash might occur during a backup script, as a precautionary measure I always have my data backed up in several places — whenever I leave the studio, I copy all my current working files across the AppleTalk network onto a hard drive that lives in the main house, just in case the studio burns down.

One thing is certain. What the Macintosh allows me to accomplish in the area of my creative endeavors is far beyond what had been possible with a mere pencil and paper.

Chapter 14

Computer-assisted Composition

The Mac — King of Personal Computer Music

Computer-assisted composition is nothing new — composers have been using computers since the '50s. What is new is that computers powerful enough to provide a composer with meaningful assistance are inexpensive enough to have in one's home.

The Macintosh is the leader in personal computer music, with over 700 music software packages and hardware peripherals available at the time of this writing. Software developers don't risk development time and resources upon products for which the user base is too small to guarantee a return on their investments, so you are sure to have plenty of company in your Macintosh music-making activities.

Although MIDI has stimulated the development of much music software, about half of all music applications don't require MIDI to be useful in the realm of computer-assisted composition. Foremost among non-MIDI music making with the Macintosh are digital audio applications either using 8-bit sounds or 16-bit CD-quality sounds, music education software, and multimedia software.

Computer-assisted Composition vs. Computer-generated Composition

The role of computers in music composition continues to expand. Two clear divisions are evident: computer-assisted composition and computer-generated composition. Computer-generated music breaks down further into the areas of interactive composition and algorithmic composition. These subdivisions have subclasses as well: intelligent instruments (a subclass of interactive composition) and automatic composition (a subclass of algorithmic composition).

Computer-assisted composition is rather straightforward, overlapping a bit with computerized score editing. Computer-generated composition is somewhat more difficult to come to grips with, especially when it spills over into the area of real-time performance. While computer-generated music always involves computer assistance, computer-assisted composition does not require that any of the music be generated. To confound matters further, using computers toward either end does not necessarily imply that the audience at a subsequent performance is aware of the computer's involvement in the creative process. As for the execution of a composition, both computer-assisted and computer-generated music can be performed by either live musicians or microprocessor-controlled devices.

To understand the symbiotic role that computers play in this man/machine artistic collaboration, let us step back for a moment and examine the act of musical composition itself. Over the years I have thought of many definitions of musical composition, but the one that stuck with me is "composition = organizing sound." Organization implies some sort of criteria, principles, or rules upon which organizational decisions are based. Throughout history, music has acquired a very large set of rules, many of which have had a profound influence on the rules invented by subsequent generations. Some rules have their roots in acoustic properties, others in non-musical scientific phenomena, still others in public opinion. Recently, there has been a tendency to derive a unique set of compositional rules from the source material of each specific composition.

Tracing the history of compositional rules often points out the fundamental principles that define specific musico-historical periods or individual composers' styles. Bach composed most of his music within a framework of strict melodic counterpoint rules. Mozart based the majority of his work on large-scale temporal forms that evolve from powers of two (such as two larger sections divided into two parts consisting of two musical periods, each of which includes two phrases of two bars each, each bar having two beats, each beat being broken down into two smaller divisions). On the other hand, Bartok, more often than not, structured his works upon a ratio frequently found in nature — the "golden section." Starting in the 1930s, a large group of composers, adhering to the 12-tone, or serial approach, followed a very rigid set of rules about pitch (the main one stating that a note could not be repeated until all other notes of a specified tone row had sounded), but had no firm ideas about organizing rhythm. The majority of all popular songs composed in the past two decades can be reduced to a small set of chord progressions. These have been "codified" through an ongoing world-scale opinion poll foisted on an unsuspecting public by record companies monitoring sales trends.

The effect of many rules, both directly and indirectly, can sharply define one's experience of a musical work. However, it is normally not necessary for the audience to perceive the fact that rules of any kind had a part in a work's creation. Indeed, composers employ some rules and principles as a means of giving a work a deep structure. The audience does not experience the application of these rules on a conscious level.

The aforementioned rules have to do with the syntax and, to a lesser extent, the semantics of a musical composition — form and content. These considerations are the domain of software dedicated to computer-generated music. See Chapters 19 and 20.

There exists another set of somewhat more mundane rules dealing with the mechanical aspects of music composition. These range from concerns with representational conventions (including notation) to the fundamental principles of musical organization dictated by time-honored canons of music theory.

Representational conventions, such as whether a note's stem goes up or down or how many notes to place in a single beamed group, are the sort of thing that notation software takes care of automatically. Mechanical fundamentals of musical organization, such as how many beats there can be in a measure or the proper result of a diatonic or chromatic transposition, are the sort of thing that sequencer software takes care of automatically.

In a notation program, errors concerning the maximum number of beats per measure can conceivably occur. (This could happen because of provisions for manual override of decisions made automatically by the software.) However, sequencer software will not permit such mistakes. There is no way to put too many or too few beats in a measure of music when using a sequencer. All empty space is automatically filled with the appropriate amount of rests, and all notes exceeding the value of a given measure are automatically "tied" into succeeding measures.

The fact that sequencer software makes such errors impossible to occur raises an important pedagogical question. Consider the following analogy: Imagine a word processor that renders it impossible to make spelling errors of any kind (including homonyms and proper nouns). This word processor is also completely voice-activated — no knowledge of typing or the alphabet is required. Does it follow that the person using the word processor does not need to know how to spell?

Finally, there are rules setting physical limits to the amount of control over musical materials and ideas that a human being can exert without the assistance of a computer. For example, the design of the human hand places actual boundaries upon the distance between notes that can be played simultaneously at a musical keyboard, while at the same time limiting their number to ten (or a few more if certain fingers hold down two keys at once). These sorts of constraints greatly limit one's possibility for experimentation with musical material.

Areas of Computer Assistance

When speaking of computer-assisted composition outside the scope of computer-generated music and music notation, two areas of assistance, namely mechanics and control, are of paramount importance. These are our primary concerns in the period between the designing of new sounds and the creation of musical manuscripts or realization of scores, that is, throughout the compositional process during which the actual music is constructed.

One caveat is in order. It might seem that the Macintosh would give us, as composers, unlimited freedom to reshape our musical ideas into anything we desire. The programmers of music software for the Macintosh, however, usually do not take a national poll on what composers actually need or desire. This notwithstanding, software control through the Macintosh has evolved to a point where practically everything one could imagine is supported by one commercially available program or another. Some packages implement certain operations with such flexibility that composers are able to control sound creatively in ways that were previously impossible.

Following are some of the ways that a Macintosh can be an effective tool for computer-assisted composition.

Simplifying the user interface to sound-modification capabilities of an external sound-generating device. This topic is thoroughly discussed in Part Two, "Sound." During the compositional process, you can accomplish control over the sound-modification capabilities of external sound-generating devices within the context of a MIDI sequencer. You can send patch changes to remote modules and assign most front panel operations to on-screen virtual faders or otherwise control them via the direct insertion of MIDI messages or through the transmission of SysEx data.

Extending the criteria for selecting or delineating regions of musical material to provide for editing operations that would otherwise be impossible or too time-consuming. The scope of a desired edit operation is defined by the criteria provided for delineating a selected region. Many things that we might like to do to our music but would never consider because of time restraints are possible because of extensive selection criteria provided by sequencers and notation programs.

It is a simple matter to perform an edit operation on, say, just the notes in a given region that fall between C4 and F#4, with durations not less than an eighth note and not more than a dotted eighth, and with dynamics louder than mezzo forte but not louder than fortissimo. You can delineate these notes as the target of an edit operation (e.g., transposition or doubling) in several seconds with most sequencers. You can audition the result of the edit operation and, if you desire, "undo" it (revert to the original state). However, the amount of time and effort you would require to perform such a transformation with a pencil and paper might cause you to pass over the opportunity.

Opcode's Vision goes so far as to include "bracketing" events in selection criteria. You can, for example, select only those notes preceded by a B♭ of specified duration and volume and followed by a G# of a specified duration and volume. Coda's Finale includes a veritable search and replace feature similar to those found in word processors. You can automatically search for a motif defined as a group of absolute pitches or pitch classes, with or without an associated rhythm, and replace it with a transformation of itself.

Increasing the speed of complex editing procedures. Not only can you quickly select an area for an edit operation, but the Macintosh can complete the operation itself with blinding speed. A single command can take care of time-consuming edits (such as retrograde, inversion, transposition, harmonization, augmentation, diminution) and both pitch and rhythmic remapping.

Providing for experimentation with many transformations of one's material. If it takes too long to test transformations of our musical material, chances are we will not do it. Fortunately, the Macintosh provides unlimited capabilities for musical experimentation. The possibility for undoing and redoing the edit operations comprising such experiments makes "before and after" or A-B comparisons child's play. "What if" scenarios, previously limited to flights of the imagination, are easy to explore.

Allowing for the otherwise impossible control of a great number of musical materials (whether such materials consist of multiple synthesizers or multiple musical themes). The Macintosh makes it possible to get around the human limitations of having only two hands and ten fingers. It is physically impossible for one person to play notes simultaneously at the outer extremes of the musical keyboard while also playing in the middle register. One would need three hands. Even when the music is all in the same area of the keyboard, rhythmic intricacies of individual parts can render a passage unplayable by one person. Furthermore, many setups will include more than a single sound-generating device. While it is possible for one person to play two keyboards using a single hand for each, it is impossible to employ two hands on both devices or to control more than two devices without enlisting the aid of another person or the Macintosh. Similar problems exist for alternate controllers. For example, it is impossible to play certain wide-open voicings with a MIDI guitar.

Offering a means for dealing with the components of one's work as separate objects. Many current generation sequencers as well as some ambitious notation programs and digital audio systems offer ways to define musical sections, segments, regions, or passages as individual objects that can be manipulated from a greater level of abstraction. Objects can be as small as a single note or chord and as large as an entire composition. Imposing a form or structure on such elements can be as easy as using the mouse to rearrange these musical building blocks into the desired order within a larger continuum. Most systems offering this capability also permit easy *cloning* of individual elements as many times as desired for reuse within the larger entity. Additionally, most such systems provide for linking cloned objects, so that modifications to the original object are reflected in all copies. Conversely, there are usually provisions allowing you to unlink objects, so that you can make changes on an individual basis without affecting related clones.

Permitting the fine-tuning of musical ideas in ways that would be time-inefficient under normal circumstances. Using a Macintosh sequencer or digital audio system, minute changes of tempo, volume, and articulation are possible with a previously unavailable degree of precision. Minor changes, which might require hours of editing and remixing of analog audio tape, are almost instantaneous. Similarly, global modifications, which you would normally deem too time-consuming to bother with, become viable. Examples include subtracting a 32nd note from the duration of every note in a region, removing all the rests in a region, or adding an accent to every note in a region.

Providing the flexibility to experiment quickly with many alternate juxtapositions of musical material through cut, paste, and copy operations. The cut, copy, and paste metaphor is so universal to Macintosh applications that we tend to take it for granted. We soon forget how much effort it took to perform these operations with scissors and adhesive tape, in the case of printed music, or with a razor blade and splicing block, in the case of recording tape.

Offering the possibility to test numerous alternate orchestrations of one's music. With sequencer or notation software, reorchestration becomes as easy as assigning a track or staff to output with a different sound or instrument. You can do this by simply changing the MIDI channel or inserting a patch change message in a MIDI environment or by changing the soundfile assignment in a non-MIDI environment. While it is a great talent to be able to hear or imagine a given orchestration in your head, nothing can replace the ear for verifying that what you imagined was, in fact, what you really wanted.

Providing the chance to analyze one's work in progress through practically instantaneous visual representations of one's performance, either in graphic notation (from different points of view) or conventional music notation. Many sequencers can display MIDI data as an alphanumeric list of note names with durations and velocities. Looking at such a display does not convey as much information as a visual representation of the same passage. Visual representations are usually available in a form of graphic notation resembling a piano roll. Typically, one can zoom in or out with respect to magnification or scale upon a selected region. Zooming out to view an entire piece from the farthest point of view can provide insights into the large-scale structure of a work regarding its contour, tessitura, note density, and melodic direction. Similar insights are possible with programs that allow you to view graphically other types of data (e.g., volume and tempo) in different magnifications.

Some sequencers provide the additional perspective of notation either within the sequencer itself (Mark of the Unicorn's Performer) or through the exportation of MIDI data into a separate notation package. Finally, several sequencers offer an "overview" of a composition in the form of a spreadsheet-like graph. Each filled cell represents a measure with music in it, and each unfilled cell represents an empty measure.

Enabling the immediate opportunity to hear (and proofhear), in real time, a rendition of a complex work. Due to considerations of tempo, rhythmic complexity, or the sheer number of simultaneous interdependent parts, this would be impossible except during an actual performance. Nothing can replace the ear as a vehicle for constructive self criticism or proofhearing. Unfortunately, until computers and samplers entered the picture, composers were usually unable to hear most music until rehearsals began. Even Stravinsky admits to many surprises upon finally hearing his works performed. One cannot overstress the speed and efficiency of proofhearing with the ears as opposed to proofreading with the eyes.

Providing for printed output, including full or reduced scores as well as individual instrumental parts, which have been automatically checked for range or rhythmic errors. This topic is thoroughly discussed in Part Four, "Notation." In the context of the compositional process, notation and part extraction often take longer than the actual composition of a work of music. While there is still room for improvement, current-generation notation software automates the creation of both full and reduced scores as well as part extraction. When notation software is used by an experienced operator and excluding cases containing certain notational anomalies, no human can possibly produce music as quickly or as neatly by manual autography.

Conclusions

The twelve areas of computer assistance to composition listed above are but the most general observations. Every individual composer and particularly composers working in specific media such as film, theater, or multimedia will discover many more ways through which the Macintosh can simplify their endeavors.

Although the examples given are of the broadest nature, it is clear that using a Macintosh for music composition may require redefining one's conception of, or approach to, the music composition process to incorporate the powerful tools that the computer provides and the far-reaching ramifications of wielding such forces.

Summary

✔ There are two clear divisions of computer music composition: computer-assisted composition and computer-generated composition. Computer-generated music breaks down further into the areas of interactive composition and algorithmic composition.

✔ The organization of sound implies some sort of criteria, principles, or rules upon which organizational decisions are based. Throughout history, music has acquired a very large set of rules, many of which have had a profound influence on the rules invented by subsequent generations.

✔ Some of the ways that a Macintosh can be an effective tool for computer-assisted composition are concerned with enhancing the control of sonic materials. This type of assistance includes simplifying the user interface to external sound-generating devices, allowing for the otherwise impossible control of a great number of musical materials (whether such materials consist of multiple synthesizers or multiple musical themes), and offering the possibility to test numerous alternate orchestrations of one's music.

✔ Other types of Macintosh assistance are in the realm of manipulating musical materials. Such assistance includes extending the criteria for delineating regions of musical material to provide for editing operations that would otherwise be impossible or too time-consuming; increasing the speed of complex editing procedures; providing for experimentation with numerous transformations of one's material; offering a means for dealing with the components of one's work as separate objects (for example, Motive X, Theme 1, Verse 4, Recapitulation); permitting the fine-tuning of musical ideas in ways that would be time-inefficient under normal circumstances; and providing the flexibility to experiment quickly with many alternate juxtapositions of musical material.

✔ Finally, the Macintosh can produce or control output in several ways that can heighten the creative process. This type of computer assistance includes providing the opportunity to analyze one's work in progress through practically instantaneous visual representations of one's performance, either in graphic notation or conventional music notation; enabling the immediate opportunity to hear (or proofhear), in real time, a rendition of a complex work, which would otherwise be impossible except during an actual performance; and providing for printed output, including full or reduced scores as well as individual instrumental parts.

Chapter 15
Making Music without MIDI

In this chapter . . .

✔ Making the distinction between non-MIDI music and MIDI music on the Macintosh.

✔ Using sound in HyperCard with complete scripting syntax and example scripts.

✔ Converting standard notation to HyperCard music playback commands.

✔ Five popular music composition HyperCard stacks examined in detail.

✔ Advanced techniques for HyperCard music scripting.

✔ Approaches to expanding your HyperCard 8-bit sound palette.

✔ Using sound and music in SuperCard with important syntax idiosyncrasies discussed.

✔ Installing and using 16-bit CD-quality sound playback functions in HyperCard and Director.

✔ Complete syntax guide and sample scripts for the 16-bit digital audio SoundAccess XFCN.

✔ Discussion of non-MIDI sequencers and utilities that convert their files into SMFs.

Exploring Your Options

MIDI is so often associated with the Macintosh that the concept of making music on your Macintosh without MIDI may at first be hard to grasp. Actually, there are probably more people not using MIDI in their Macintosh musical endeavors than there are MIDI users. There are non-MIDI options in almost every area of Macintosh music endeavor.

Some programs can operate with MIDI or without. When such software is used without MIDI, playback is typically provided through the Macintosh's internal speaker or by way of the audio jack on the back of the computer. (Note: In this chapter, whenever Macintosh internal speaker playback is referred to, the option to output the same sounds through the Macintosh's back panel audio port goes without saying.) Many programs limit Macintosh internal sound to four voices, although this will be increasingly less common with Apple's new Sound Manager (see Chapter 10, "Sound Generation").

The two popular approaches of making music without MIDI on the Macintosh are controlling the Macintosh's built-in synthesizer and using the Macintosh for digital audio. In the latter case, you usually divide the territory into 8-bit digital audio and 16-bit digital audio. In this chapter, the terms non-MIDI music and 8-bit music are used synonymously.

A large segment of the 16-bit digital audio applications on the Macintosh is devoted to direct-to-hard disk recording, and there is an entire chapter devoted to that topic (Chapter 24, "Direct-to-Hard disk Recording"). Sample editing is another common 16-bit audio application (Chapter 13, "Editing Sampled Sound").

This chapter is mainly concerned with programs that support composition and related creative activities without MIDI. A large portion of this chapter is devoted to HyperCard, because it is one of the most popular environments for dealing with non-MIDI music sounds.

You can apply many other non-MIDI Macintosh music applications to your compositional endeavors — many more than those covered in this chapter. Chapter 19, "Interactive Composition and Intelligent Instruments," includes many programs you should look at. Some of these can function in both the MIDI and non-MIDI worlds: Different Drummer, MacDrums, Music Mouse, and Ovaltune. You will also find Jam Session, a purely 8-bit music program, in Chapter 19.

Chapter 20, "Algorithmic Composition," includes two programs that can be used both with or without MIDI: Cybernetic Composer and Compose.

A special type of 8-bit music application has recently surfaced. These are utilities that facilitate making MIDI music without MIDI hardware. This distinction was brought about by the release of Passport Designs's ingenious virtual synthesizer, the Sound Exciter (see below and Chapter 10) and related software.

Most of the notation programs discussed in Part Four, "Notation" (Chapters 21 and 22) provide for playback through the Macintosh internal speaker or audio port. One in particular, Great Wave's ConcertWare, is available in two formats: ConcertWare+ MIDI and ConcertWare. Both programs provide for 8-bit sound playback, but ConcertWare (without the "+ MIDI" suffix) is limited to the Macintosh's internal sounds and is considerably less expensive.

Non-MIDI multimedia and education applications abound; you will find these in Chapters 27, 28, and 29.

Sound in HyperCard

HyperCard comes with every Macintosh. From the day it was introduced it contained capabilities to play 8-bit sounds, so it has become a popular platform for non-MIDI music.

There are a number of excellent non-MIDI sequencer-type HyperCard stacks that allow you to create and play back music compositions. Some of these are marketed commercially and others are shareware. To understand these applications you must first understand how HyperCard deals with sound.

HyperCard comes with three sounds — Boing, Flute, and Harpsichord — and a "play" command to play them back through the Macintosh speaker. The syntax of the play command can be very simple:

play *"soundName"* The name of the sound must be enclosed in quotation marks. The sound name is the exact name of a 22 KHz 'snd ' resource stored in your current stack, Home stack, or HyperCard itself. For versions of HyperCard before 2.0, these must be format 2 'snd ' resources. Since version 2.0, HyperCard has provided support for both format 1 and format 2 'snd ' resources. (See Chapter 10 for detailed information.)

play stop Stops sound playback.

Example: Try typing the following into the message box:

play "boing"

To make music with HyperCard you must know how HyperCard refers to pitches and durations (see Figure 15-1). Pitches can be referred to in one of two formats:

"a b c d e f g" Standard letter names for notes. These must also be enclosed in quotation marks.

"1,2,3...127" These are identical to MIDI note numbers where middle C is equal to "60." These must also be enclosed in quotation marks.

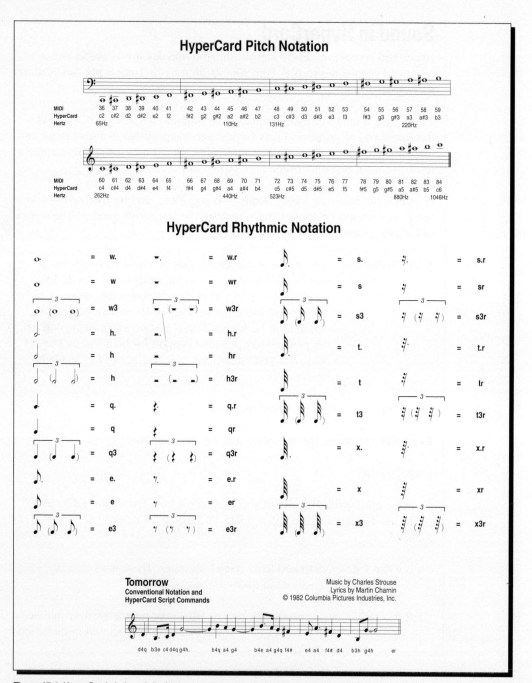

Figure 15-1: HyperCard pitch and rhythmic conventions as they relate to standard notation.

Pitch specification can include an octave modifier as well:

0   The octave starting on the C four octaves below middle C.
1   The octave starting on the C three octaves below middle C.
2   The octave starting on the C two octaves below middle C.
3   The octave starting on the C an octave below middle C.
4   The octave starting on middle C.
5   The octave starting on the C an octave above middle C.
6   The octave starting on the C two octaves above middle C.
7   The octave starting on the C three octaves above middle C.
8   The octave starting on the C four octaves above middle C.

Note that HyperCard uses the *correct* number for octaves. Middle C is C4. Many MIDI synthesizers and MIDI software incorrectly call this note C3. This is due to an error made by a large synthesizer company in early 1984. Because other hardware and software manufacturers wanted to simplify compatibility issues with this company's devices, they perpetrated the error.

Example: The tune *Tomorrow* from the musical "Annie" in HyperCard notation:

d4q	b3e	c4	d4q	g4h.	b4q	a4q	g4	b4e
a4e	g4q	f4#	e4	a4	f4#	d4q	b3h	g4w
a4q	b4q	c4w						

Because the octave and duration remain in effect until changed, you don't need to specify them with every note (a similar situation exists in MIDI music with the MIDI channel message). The example above could be notated as follows:

d4q	b3e	c4	dq	gh.	bq	a	g	be
ae	gq	f#	e	a	f#	d	b3h	g4w
aq	b	cw						

You may have deduced that there are some rhythms that cannot be expressed with HyperCard's notation scheme. For example, although you can simulate a half-note tied to a quarter-note by using a dotted half-note, it is impossible to notate a half-note tied to an eighth-note, sixteenth-note, thirty-second-note, or sixty-fourth-note (or triplet value of any kind). The same goes for all tied notes that cannot be expressed as a dotted duration. One way to get around this is to use rests to fill in the missing value.

Sample stacks

Many available stacks automate the process of entering and playing tunes in HyperCard. You can think of these as non-MIDI sequencers. Most provide an on-screen keyboard to enter notes and buttons to select rhythmic values. Some include options to export your tunes to other stacks to save you the hassle of converting the music into HyperCard notation. Some include other bells and whistles.

CheapSequencer

Chuck Walker's freeware CheapSequencer lets you record and play back sequences from its Recorder card. You use the buttons at the top of the screen to select the playback sound. These can be auditioned with the speaker button at the upper left. Conversion into HyperCard notation is automatic.

You can save your composition on Sequence cards (see bottom of Figure 15-2). Up to ten sequences can be chained together into a song. This allows you to switch instruments and tempos during a composition. The buttons above each sequence listing are (from left to right): Include in Song, Copy Current Sequence from Recorder Card, Erase this Sequence, and Play this Sequence. At the bottom of the screen is a button to play back the entire song. You can create as many Song cards as you like.

HyperComposer

Addison Wesley's HyperComposer was designed by the people who created the AddMotion XCMD for HyperCard animation (see Chapter 27, "Music for Multimedia"). Unlike the other stacks covered in this section, this is a commercial product. This stack includes options to enter music either by way of an on-screen keyboard or a music staff. Similarly, you can display your music in conventional music notation if you want. These two displays can be mixed. For example, you can enter notes using the staff-entry method, but display them with HyperCard notation, and you can enter notes with the on-screen keyboard and display them in conventional music notation (see Figure 15-3).

There is an option to highlight notes during playback (playback scrolls with the music) and also to step-advance through your sequence using the Command key. Buttons let you save and reload tunes to disk and import and export new sounds that automatically appear on the pop-up menu labeled Voice.

HyperRap

Joe Pavone's shareware HyperRap stack creates rap music accompaniments. It does an excellent job of this, usually producing constructions that are more interesting than what you hear on the radio. You choose from 14 different percussive rap sounds with the number buttons on the left of the screen. (Note: Button number 15 introduces additional syncopation in the form of a short delay.)

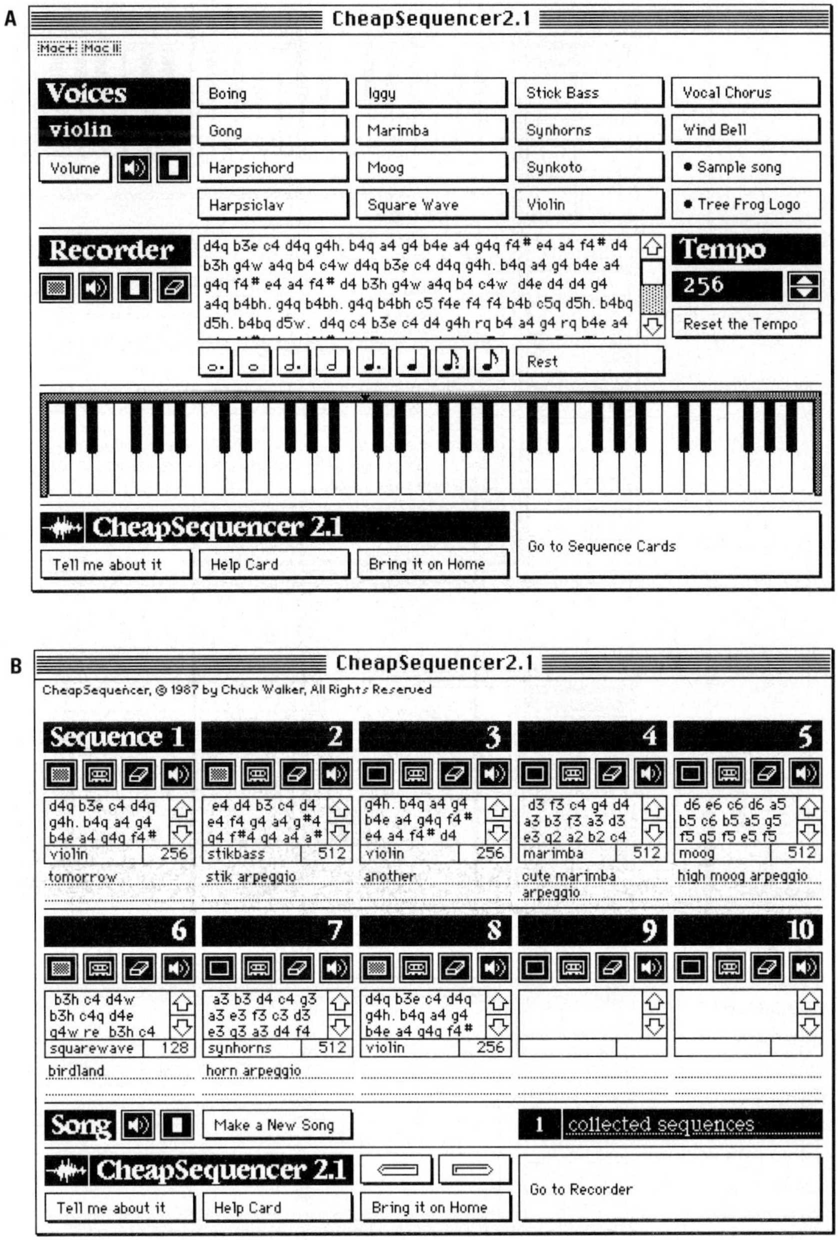

Figure 15-2:
(A) Cheap-
Sequencer's
Recorder card.
(B) One of
CheapSequencer's
Sequence cards.

These appear in the scrolling list. There are buttons to play the tune backward, forward, or looped. The buttons that look like disks with little arrows save or reload the tunes on the next card. The bottom control button produces a randomly generated rap tune containing the number of notes you specify.

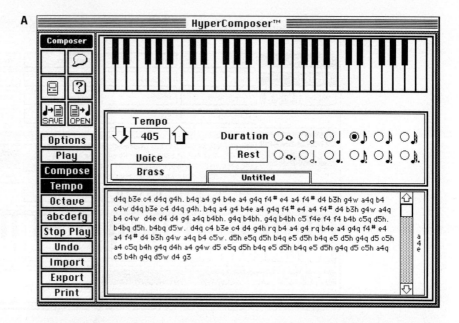

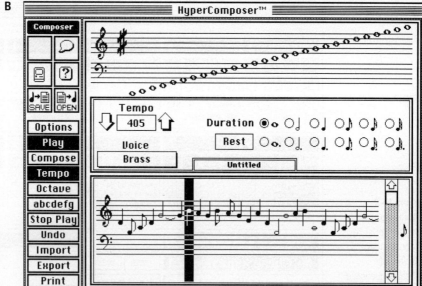

Figure 15-3:
(A) Hyper-
Composer's
on-screen
keyboard and
HyperCard
notation.
(B) Hyper-
Composer's staff
entry palette and
conventional
music notation.

MacTunes

Pentallect's shareware MacTunes stack is a very ambitious piece of work. To all the
standard recording, playback, saving, and reloading features, MacTunes adds the
capability of displaying lyrics while a tune is played (see Figure 15-4). These are

A

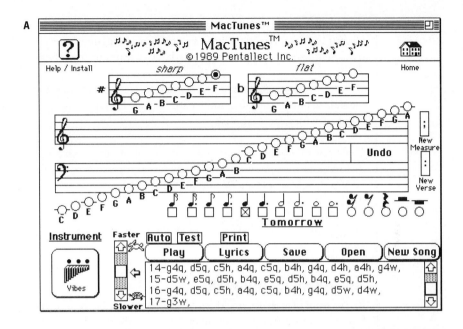

B

Figure 15-4:
(A) MacTunes Recording/ Playback card. **(B)** MacTunes Navigation card is the gateway to other features of the software (see text).

synchronized to the playback in the bouncing ball fashion. MacTunes is able to do this because it adds its own measure and verse symbols to the HyperCard music notation scheme (HyperCard ignores these during playback). Specifically, the software adds semicolons to indicate measures and commas between let it keep track of which lyrics should be displayed at any given time and also allow you to add lyrics to your own creations. MacTunes's verse indicator is their own creation and would corrupt playback of tunes in any other stack.

The MacTunes stack includes excellent tutorials on using MacTunes, on the fundamentals of music, on using and creating music in HyperCard, and on using external speakers with your Macintosh.

The software comes with an extensive song library (with lyrics) of 100 songs divided into five categories: Holiday Favorites, Songs for Children, American Folk Songs, Songs from TV and Movies, and Nursery Rhymes. You can add to the library at will.

Incidentally, you have the option of sending Pentallect 30 songs in lieu of the $30 shareware fee.

Advanced techniques

If you want to delve more deeply into HyperCard sound scripting, there are a few more modifiers that you need to know about.

More modifiers

The full syntax for the HyperCard play command is as follows (items in brackets are optional):

play *soundName*   [tempo] ["notes"] [# | b] [octave] [duration] [. | 3]

tempo   Speed is indicated as a number from zero on up, although higher numbers (in the thousands) don't make much sense unless you are going for a special effect. Tempo roughly corresponds to beats per minute. If no tempo is specified, the default tempo of 200 is used.

Example: A script that would play the first phrase of *Tomorrow* with a sound called "vibes" at a tempo of 120 would look like the following:

play "vibes" 120 "d4q b3e c4 dq gh. bq a g be a g f# e a f# d b3h g4w"

Once sounds or music have started playing, other HyperCard scripts and visual effects can continue to execute — the sound keeps playing in the background. To enhance these capabilities HyperCard includes a Sound function:

The Sound   Returns the name of the currently playing sound or "done" if no sound is playing.

Sound()   Same as above.

Examples: The following are typical uses of the Sound( ) and The Sound functions.

If the sound = "Violin" then put "Violin" into field "Instrument Currently Playing"

If the sound is "Violin" then put "Violin" into field "Instrument Currently Playing"

If the sound ≠ "done" then put "Wait until playback is finished" into the message

If the sound is not "done" then put "Wait until playback is finished" into the message

Put sound( ) into myVariable

If sound( ) = "done" then put "The tune is finished playing" into the message

Wait until the sound is "done"

Wait until sound( ) = "done"

Repeat until the sound is "done"

Repeat until sound( ) = "done"

Repeat while the sound is not "done"

Repeat while sound( ) ≠ "done"

Example: Most of the stacks discussed above use HyperCard's "Do" structure for playback. They get the name of the selected sound and the field containing the entered notes:

do "play" && card field "instrumentName" && card field "noteList"

It takes some time for HyperCard to load an 'snd' resource into RAM. Because of this, if you are using lengthy sounds you might want to preload them in the "On OpenStack" script. Specifying a tempo of zero loads the sound into RAM but does not play it. You can preload a number of sounds this way all at once.

Example:

play "MyVeryLongSound" 0

Expanding your sound palette

You will probably want to add more sounds to the three that HyperCard comes with (Boing, Flute, and Harpsichord). Sources for sounds include other stacks, online services, and commercial vendors of HyperCard 'snd ' resources.

Not all uses of sound in HyperCard involve the playing of notes. Very often you want to play a lengthy soundfile that consists of an entire piece of music in and of itself, or perhaps a sound effect.

Accumulating sounds

There are many ways to add sounds to your palette. Popular methods were discussed in Chapter 10, "Sound Generation" under the heading "Tapping into the Sound Manager with HyperCard."

Capturing sounds from an external source. The following options let you record sound using the Macintosh's built-in digitizing capabilities (IIsi and LC or later) or by way of an external digitizing peripheral. They all provide soundfile editing capabilities (see Chapters 10 and 13), so you can even reverse sounds if you want.

Reversing sounds offers you the possibility of creating stacks dedicated to *phonetic palindromes*. You can verify that the phrases "Ominous Cinema" and "We revere you" are both in fact phonetic palindromes and sound the same, whether played backward or forward.

AudioPalette	This is a built-in function of HyperCard, which you can access on newer Macintoshes with the microphone input jack or on older Macintoshes using MacroMind-Paracomp's MacRecorder Driver and MacRecorder Digitizer.
MacRecorder	MacroMind-Paracomp's complete digitizer and sound-editing package, which lets you record sounds and save them into HyperCard stacks.
Voice Impact Pro	Articulate Systems's complete digitizer and sound-editing package, which lets you record sounds and save them as 'snd ' resources.
SID+	See the coupon in the back of the book for schematics by Jeffrey Siegel to build your own digitizer.

Capturing sounds from other programs, files, and stacks.

SoundLeech	Robert Mace's shareware utility to leech sounds from other programs and files.

Sound/PICT Thief	Jim Moore's freeware utility, which searches an entire folder or disk for 'snd ' resources and copies them all into a file called "Purloined Resource File" in your System folder for later disposition.

Transferring sounds to HyperCard stacks

You may also want to acquire some utilities for converting sounds from other formats (e.g., SoundEdit, SoundWave, SoundCap, System Beeps, Sound Manager, and so on) into 'snd ' resources. All but two of the options listed below are shareware or freeware available from most user groups and online services.

ResCopy	This is an XCMD available in the Power Tools stack of the developer version of HyperCard. You can also find ResCopy on many online services.
SoundMover	Ricardo Ettore's shareware utility, which is part of his "Sound Manager" package (not to be confused with Apple's own Sound Manager).
Sound Manager	North Shore Computing's utility (not to be confused with Apple's Sound Manager).
Resource Editors	Apple's ResEdit (freeware), Mathemaesthetics's Resourcerer (commercial product), Miles Calbaum's ResMaster DA (shareware), and Bob Daniel's ResExpress DA (shareware from nuCorp) can all be used to move sounds from one stack to another or from any file or program to a HyperCard stack.
SelectSND XFCN	AnalytX's SelectSND XFCN is a powerful external that lets you move sounds into HyperCard stacks. It is included with HyperPress's StepAhead set of utilities (commercial product).

Converting sounds to 'snd ' format

Remember that HyperCard versions before version 2.0 required format 2 'snd ' resources, while HyperCard version 2.0 and later can play both format 1 and 2 'snd ' resources. There are many utilities that you can use to convert sounds from other formats into 'snd ' resources.

The software and hardware alternatives listed below are all dedicated to 8-bit sounds. Note that high-end 16-bit sample-editing programs such as Digidesign's Sound Designer and Audiomedia and Passport's Alchemy and Sound Apprentice also provide the option to save files into 8-bit sound resources. This affords you access to just about any sampled soundfile that exists.

All but two of the options listed below are shareware or freeware available from most user groups and online services.

Sound Convert	Kelly Major's freeware HyperCard stack, which converts sounds from SoundCap or SoundWave format to 'snd ' resources.
Sound->snd	Converts SoundCap, SoundEdit, or SoundWave format files to 'snd ' resources. Another shareware utility by Ricardo Ettore that is part of his Sound Manager package (not to be confused with Apple's own Sound Manager).
SoundCap->snd	Russ Wetmore's utility to convert SoundCap format sounds into 'snd ' resources.
MacRecorder	MacroMind-Paracomp's SoundEdit, HyperSound, and HyperSound ToolKit, part of their commercial MacRecorder package, can all save or convert their native SoundEdit format sounds into 'snd ' resources and install them into specified stacks as well.
SoundWave	Included with Articulate Systems's VoiceLink and Authorware's AuthorWare, this sound-editing utility saves its native SoundWave format files as 'snd ' resources.

If you are running System 7, Joe Zobkiw has created a freeware utility that converts most soundfile formats (those that contain 'snd ' resources — this excludes MacroMind-Paracomp's SoundEdit format files) into System 7 format 'snd ' that can be double-clicked to hear them play and also dragged into and out of your System file.

Sound in SuperCard

Most of the above observations about HyperCard apply to SuperCard with two exceptions:

❖ You must include the word "tempo" before the tempo value if you are going to set a playback speed.

```
play soundName  [tempo speed] ["notes"] [# | b] [octave] [duration]
[. | 3]
```

Example: A SuperCard script that would play the first phrase of *Tomorrow* with a sound called "vibes" at a tempo of 120 would look like the following:

play "vibes" tempo 120 "d4q b3e c4 dq gh. bq a g be a g f# e a f# d b3h g4w"

❖ Remember that SuperCard stores resources such as 'snds ' in the data fork of Projects. This allows you to deal with them directly and view them in Overview windows from within SuperEdit (rather than using a resource editing or moving utility like you have to do in HyperCard). Importing 'snd ' resources is accomplished directly from the File Menu by choosing the Import Resources. This means that you don't need any special utilities to move 'snds ' into SuperCard. This also means that you won't see 'snd ' resources listed in a SuperCard project when you open it with a resource editor of some kind. Note that you can convert MacroMind-Paracomp's HyperSound and HyperSound ToolKit to SuperCard format and retain its functionality, but you must follow special instructions included with SuperCard.

Professional Digital Audio (16-bit)

Professional 16-bit digital audio is, of course, another category of non-MIDI Macintosh music. The foremost application in this area is direct-to-hard disk recording, a topic to which an entire chapter in this book is devoted (Chapter 24, "Direct-to-Hard disk Recording"). Many of the techniques you apply with 8-bit sampling, sound editing, and transferral to HyperCard are similar to those at the 16-bit level. The main difference is the price and the limited opportunity for widespread distribution of creative endeavors among the members of the general Macintosh community, many of whom have not made the investment in the hardware and software required by 16-bit digital audio.

Digidesign is without contest the market leader with their Sound Tools, Pro Tools, and Audiomedia packages and their Sound Designer, Audiomedia, and Deck software.

Several of Digidesign's products include a utility called Sound Installer, which allows you to add and remove both 8- and 16-bit 'snd ' resources to a Hyper-Card stack. Digidesign supports two new types of 'snd ' resources: "chunky" and "interleaved." Their chunky soundfile format stores both 8-bit (22 KHz) versions of a sound (which get routed to the Macintosh speaker if no digital audio card is present) and 16-bit versions (which play back through one of Digidesign's digital audio cards if a card is detected). This makes them extremely desirable for HyperCard applications that you want to be able to execute on Macintoshes with or without a digital audio card. You can also use the installer to add such capabilities to MacroMind Director animations — see Chapter 27, "Music for Multimedia." An interleaved 'snd ' resource is a 44.1 KHz, 16-bit stereo sound that requires a digital audio card for playback (see Chapter 10 for more information on this topic).

SoundAccess

Digidesign's digital audio products come with a HyperCard stack called SoundAccess, which can take advantage of their digital audio cards (Sound Accelerator and Audiomedia). SoundAccess provides for recording, playback, and rudimentary editing of 16-bit soundfiles in the HyperCard environment. There is also a cue list option to set up a list of soundfiles for playback. SoundAccess also automates the installation of sounds, playback buttons, and record, playback, and editing features into other stacks.

Playback file formats supported are AIFF, Sound Designer, and Sound Designer II. Recording is always in the Sound Designer II format. Any Sound Designer II file can be converted into AIFF, Sound Designer, or 8- or 16-bit 'snd' resource files using the Sound Designer II (see Chapter 13, "Editing Sampled Sound") or Sound Installer programs.

The SoundAccess Stack is based on the SoundAccess XFCN. This lets you play back stereo audio directly from your hard drive very efficiently. For example, playing back a 12-minute stereo direct-from-disk file requires very little memory (48K) and does not affect the execution of other HyperCard scripts. You can move from card to card, display animations, and do almost anything else while a sound is playing (see Figure 15-5).

The reason it takes so little RAM is that small memory buffers are reserved and filled with sound data. One memory buffer plays back as another is filled, and this rotation continues until all loaded soundfiles have been played back. Even a Macintosh with 1MB of memory could play back a 30-minute stereo file, if it has a large enough hard disk.

To use the SoundAccess XFCN you need Digidesign's Sound Accelerator card, a hard disk with a 27 ms (or better) access time, and Sound Designer II, AIFF, Dyaxis, or Sound Designer format soundfiles to play, although you can record these yourself in SoundAccess.

Operation of the SoundAccess XFCN
get SoundAccess(loadSA, "filename1,filename2,...")
Cues up a file (or list of files) to be played. You must designate files by full path name unless they are in the folder with the stack. The first load may take a bit longer although this can be avoided with the initSA command below.

get SoundAccess(playSA,[delay])
Plays the next soundfile in the cue list that has been loaded. When the last cued file has been played, playback commences with the first again. You can set a delay in ticks (60 = 1 second) before playback begins again. Use this to synchro-

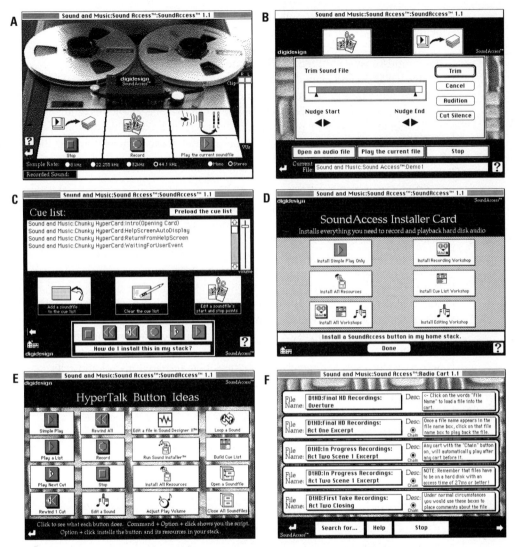

Figure 15-5: (A) Recording Workshop: This card lets you record stereo digital audio directly onto your hard disk, provided that you have a Sound Accelerator or Audiomedia NuBus card installed. The button at the upper left automatically creates and installs a button that plays back the current soundfile in the stack you designate. **(B)** Editing Workshop: Normally, the left and right arrows move the respective markers by 64 samples. Clicking on a left or right arrow with the Command key down moves the respective marker by 1,024 samples. Clicking a left or right arrow with the Option key down moves the respective marker by one sample. **(C)** The Cue List card lets you create lists of soundfiles to be played back in the order you specify. **(D)** SoundAccess's Installer card lets you install any or all of the stack's capabilities into a stack of your choice. Another card lets you install the SoundAccess XFCN into a MacroMind Director movie to add 16-bit soundfile playback capabilities. **(E)** The Button Ideas card provides fully functional digital audio playback buttons. If you option-click a button it installs itself and the required SoundAccess resources into the stack of your choice. **(F)** Josh Rosen's Radio Cart is a separate stack included on the SoundAccess disk. You can install soundfiles into the large buttons by clicking the words "File Name." If the Chain button is enabled, the chained soundfile is played immediately after the file appearing above it on the list.

nize sounds to actions or to relieve CPU load when color screens or videos are being shown.

get SoundAccess(simpleSA, "filename1,filename2,...")
A one-step "load and play" command. You use it to cue up a file (or list of files) and play those files in one step. You must designate files by full path name unless they are in the folder with the stack. Unlike the above, the simpleSA command locks your Macintosh until playback is over. It does not return the controlKey that is used by the "on controlKey" handler (see below). It can decrease the hesitation between played soundfiles.

get SoundAccess(openSA)
Lets you retrieve the full path name of any Sound Designer II, AIFF, Dyaxis, or Sound Designer file by way of a standard open file dialog box. The full path is placed in HyperCard's "it" variable.

get SoundAccess(volumeSA, volumeSetting)
Lets you set the playback volume of the Sound Accelerator card from 0 or no sound to 10 or full volume. This has no effect on the volume setting in the control panel. Note that the volumeSA command can change the volume of a soundfile during playback. You can use a simple repeat loop structure to change the volume of a soundfile dynamically over time (e.g., fade ins and fade outs). Volume is not automatically reset, so remember to set the Sound Accelerator's volume to its previous setting when you close a stack or after you have altered it with this command.

get SoundAccess(allSA,[delay])
Automatically plays all of the soundfiles in the loaded cue list. You can set a delay in ticks (60 = 1 second) before playback begins again. The allSA command requires the "on controlKey" handler (see below) to be in your stack's script.

get SoundAccess(exitSA)
This command must be present in the "On CloseStack" handler of your stack's script. It closes all the files that have been opened for playback.

get SoundAccess(rewindSA,[all])
This command is helpful in conjunction with the allSA command. It rewinds to the beginning of the previous soundfile. If you include the "all" parameter, the currently loaded cue list rewinds to the very first soundfile in the cue list.

get SoundAccess(stopSA)
Immediately stops playback of the current soundfile and the rest of the loaded cue list (if any).

get SoundAccess(initSA)

Use this to avoid the slight hesitation caused by the first SoundAccess(loadSA) command. If you put the initSA command in your "On OpenStack" handler, SoundAccess will be automatically initialized and ready to load and play.

get SoundAccess(bufSA,newBufferSize)

Lets you set the size of the memory playback buffer that SoundAccess will use for playback. The minimum buffer size of 49K (49,152 bytes) is recommended. If you are having playback problems (the soundfile stops, or seems to skip), because of a slow or fragmented hard disk, you can increase the size of the sound "chunks" loaded into memory with this command. Larger chunks mean fewer disk accesses. (Note: More RAM is required.)

get SoundAccess(busySA)

This is a "status checking" tool to see what the Sound Accelerator or Audiomedia card is up to. This function returns "TRUE" during playback and "OK" when playback is complete. It is similar to HyperCard's The Sound and Sound( ) function (see the section "More modifiers"). You can use this function to make sure that you don't load a sound while another one is playing.

Examples:

```
on mouseUp
    get WaitForSAStop()
    get SoundAccess(loadSA, "SoundFileName")
    get SoundAccess(playSA)
end mouseUp
```

As mentioned above, the "on controlKey" handler must be present in any stack that uses the allSA command.

The "on controlKey" handler should be identical to the following:

```
on controlKey
    if param(1) is 255
    then
    get SoundAccess("queueSA")
    end if
end controlKey
```

This handler always knows when the current soundfile comes to an end. When playback is finished it returns a controlKey with param(1) value of 255. You can use this returned key value to create stack events that are triggered by a soundfile's end such as animations or visual effects.

Preloading of soundfiles is highly recommended. Use the following script:

```
on mouseUp
    get SoundAccess(loadSA, "SoundFileName")
    get SoundAccess(playSA)
end mouseUp
```

Non-MIDI Sequencers

MIDI sequencers (see Chapter 17, "MIDI Sequencing") are dedicated to the recording and playback of music expressed as MIDI data and trigger devices that respond to MIDI data (typically sound-generating devices). Non-MIDI sequencers also provide for the input of music, but playback is accomplished by triggering non-MIDI sound sources. In neither case is actual audio data recorded, only triggering information.

The most common sound format for non-MIDI sequencers are 8-bit sampled soundfiles at a resolution of 11 KHz or 22 KHz. Playback is through the Macintosh's built-in speaker or better yet, through an audio system connected to the Macintosh's audio output port. Most of the HyperCard stacks described above under "Sample stacks" qualify as non-MIDI sequencers in the broadest sense of the term.

Super Studio Session

Bogas Productions's Super Studio Session and its implementation of digitized sounds is truly fascinating. Super Studio Session has undergone some name changes throughout its development, having first been titled Sideman, later Jam Session, then Studio Session, and now Super Studio Session. In the beginning, the developers considered their package to be "the MusicWorks of the sampled sounds," referring to the first music software that was released for the Macintosh (see Chapter 1, "Background").

Super Studio Session includes a music editor (Studio Editor) and both the Player and Miniplayer (see Figure 15-6). With Super Studio Session it is possible to play back pitched music in six parts through the Macintosh's internal speaker or through an external sound system connected to the Macintosh's audio output. Super Studio Session provides for 8-voice polyphonic playback. It is hard to believe that you are hearing 8-bit sampled sounds.

Several disks included with the package provide nearly 70 pre-sampled instruments, and you can edit these or create new instruments using many of the digitizers discussed above and in Chapter 10. The program can access up to 16,000 different instruments.

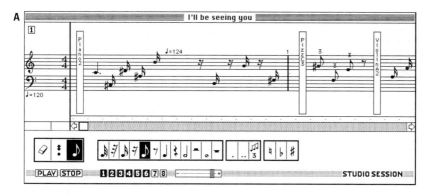

Version 2.0, ©1986,88 by Bogas Productions
Written by Ed Bogas, Steve Capps, Neil Cormia, Ty Roberts
Artwork by Marge Boots
Sound Advice from Tom Hedges, Mark Zimmer

Figure 15-6: (A) Super Studio Session Editor. In version 2.0, only a single grand staff is visible at a time, although you can scroll through all eight grand staves. **(B)** This cute window appears when you play back music. Each of these anthropomorphic notes is assigned to one of the voices of a Studio Session song. The mouths on the notes open and close with each pitch that is played by that voice.

Music is entered using the Studio Editor program, which functions in two modes. In the note-editing mode, you can drag notes and symbols from a palette. The cursor assumes the symbol of the selected item until a new symbol is selected.

During editing, each instrumental voice is thought to be a separate track, with up to six or eight tracks available depending on whether you are using Studio Session or Super Studio Session. Regions of tracks can be looped for up to 999 repetitions, and loops of varying length can be occurring at different places on separate tracks simultaneously. Loops, which are represented by musical repeat signs, are nestable up to ten levels. There is a Juke Box option that lets you chain songs together. Cut, Copy, and Paste operations are supported as well as transposition and the insertion of tempo and swing indications.

The second type of editing provided by the Studio Editor is called *phrase editing* (see Figure 15-7). It uses a database-like approach to the organization of musical ideas and the manipulation of musical data at the phrase level. This is the first

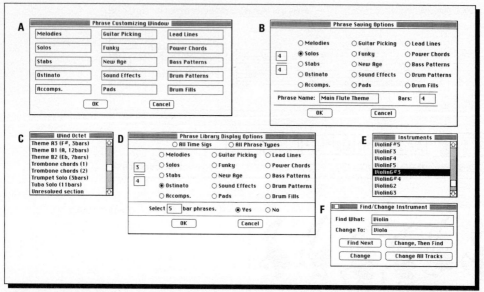

Figure 15-7: Phrase-level editing in Super Studio Session. **(A)** You create keywords for phrases with the Phrase Customizing dialog box. **(B)** You can define any selected region as a phrase. When you do so, this dialog box appears requesting that you specify its keyword (attribute), name, number of bars, and meter. **(C)** Phrases appear in a phrase library window like this one. **(D)** The Display Options dialog box lets you designate which types of phrases are displayed according to keywords, meter, and/or length. You can think of this as a filter for your phrase library or a searching engine. Subsequently, you can use the Insert Phrase menu option to insert the selected phrase in your score. **(E)** Instruments are stored in a library as well. **(F)** Super Studio Session also lets you search and replace by instrument or soundfile. The Find/Change Instrument dialog box allows you to use this feature to globally or locally reorchestrate your score on a single track or all tracks.

constructive implementation of this concept. It is the sort of feature that is conspicuously lacking in all other Macintosh software.

You can designate regions as phrases with one of 15 descriptive names that you define. Phrases are stored in the phrase library, which may hold up to 16,384 phrases. Sorting and searching are available by specifying type, meter, phrase length, or multiple search criteria.

Such an approach to musical composition is truly ground-breaking. The ability to organize musical ideas in a database-like fashion fosters creativity and experimentation by allowing you to view your musical ideas on a more global level.

There are many add-ons available for Studio Session and Super Studio Session. Bogas Productions offers sets of additional instruments, all meticulously sampled, that include demonstration songs. Their String Quartet Library includes over 60 stringed instrument sounds and includes works by Bach, Debussy, Dvorak,

Mozart, and Schubert. The Brass Library has 63 new sounds and includes works by Mussorgsky, Celsius, Rossini, and others. The Heavy Metal Library provides 31 new instruments, the Country Library 30. Finally, their Studio Sound Effects Library consists of 79 sound effects files and 11 demonstration songs.

Studio Session MIDI Utility (S.S.M.U.)

S.S.M.U converts songs you create in Studio Session or Super Studio Session to SMFs. Everything gets converted, including repeats, endings, key and time signature changes, tempo changes, and so forth.

The program comes with configuration files for the Roland D5, U110, and TR626, which automate the process of mapping Studio Session (or Jam Session) instruments to MIDI patches. For other instruments you create your own "Synth Libraries."

The Synth Library is a configuration mode that lets you map Studio Session instruments onto MIDI channels (see Figure 15-8). You also use this feature to associate patch number, velocity, note length, and pan information with mapped instruments. It includes options for remapping drum notes as well.

You can also create instruments and libraries of controller information or other MIDI data (including a chord library) that can be used by Studio Session just like the phrase library (see Figure 15-9).

During the conversion process, S.S.M.U. loads the Studio Session file into its main window, where you can set global track effects for Volume (Controller 7) and Pan before saving as a MIDI file. Although Super Studio Session only supports eight tracks, you can also use this window to process 16-track SMFs.

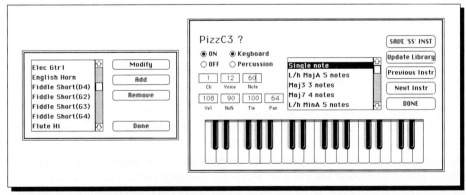

Figure 15-8: S.S.M.U.'s Synth Library dialog box lets you configure the mapping of Studio Session instruments to MIDI sounds. It operates in two modes, Keyboard or Percussion (see text).

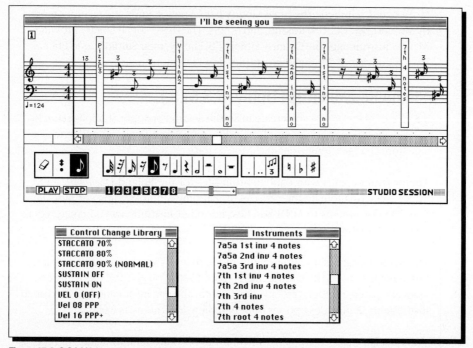

Figure 15-9: S.S.M.U. lets you create libraries of MIDI data, custom MIDI instruments (with special attributes) and chords that can be inserted into Studio Session files using its Phrase Library option. This illustration pictures a chord library (this lets you place chords on individual Super Studio Session tracks, which are otherwise limited to monophonic melodies), MIDI instrument library, and a controller information library and shows the effect of inserting objects from these libraries onto a Studio Session score. (Note: This screen is from Studio Session, not S.S.M.U.)

Summary

✔ MIDI is so often associated with the Macintosh that the concept of making music on your Macintosh without MIDI may at first be hard to grasp. Actually, there are probably more people not using MIDI in their Macintosh musical endeavors than there are MIDI users. There are non-MIDI options in almost every area of Macintosh music application.

✔ Some programs operate with or without MIDI. When such software is used without MIDI, playback is typically provided through the Macintosh's internal speaker or better yet, through an audio system connected to the Macintosh's audio output port. Many programs limit Macintosh internal sound to four voices, although this will be less common with Apple's new Sound Manager.

✔ The two popular approaches of making music without MIDI on the Macintosh are controlling the Macintosh's built-in synthesizer and using the Macintosh for digital audio. In the latter case, the territory is divided into 8-bit digital audio and 16-bit digital audio. The most common sound format for non-MIDI sequencers are 8-bit sampled soundfiles at a resolution of 11 kHz or 22 KHz.

✔ Since the day HyperCard was introduced it contained capabilities to play 8-bit, which has made it a popular platform for non-MIDI music. There are a number of excellent non-MIDI sequencer-type HyperCard stacks (both shareware and commercial offerings) that allow you to create and play back music compositions.

✔ Most non-MIDI music HyperCard stacks include options to export your tunes to other stacks to save you the hassle of converting the music into HyperCard notation. Note that not all uses of sound in HyperCard involve the playing of notes.

✔ SuperCard stores resources such as 'snd's in the data fork of Projects. Importing 'snd' resources is accomplished directly from the File Menu by choosing the Import Resources. This means that you don't need any special utilities to move 'snd's into SuperCard. This also means that you won't see 'snd' resources listed in a SuperCard project when you open it with a resource editor of some kind. Note that you can convert MacroMind-Paracomp's HyperSound and HyperSound ToolKit to SuperCard format and retain its functionality, but you must follow special instructions included with SuperCard.

Chapter 16

Making Music with MIDI

The Implications of Using MIDI

Since its inception less than a decade ago, MIDI has had a major impact upon composers and composing. Macintosh MIDI applications provide composers with a hitherto inaccessible freedom for experimentation. However, such freedom does not come without a price. Limitations imposed by the physical capabilities of the MIDI Specification are forcing composers to develop new conceptual models of their creations and to evolve new strategies for manipulating musical materials.

MIDI has had a profound effect upon many areas of musical endeavor. Because the areas of composition, notation, and sound design have been the major focus of software development, these are the most visible and offer the most options for composers. This chapter will explore the impact of MIDI within a CAC environment.

Musical Composition Misconceptions

Although notation (manuscript preparation) and sound design are often components of such an environment, they have little, if any, relevance to the issues raised by musical composition. Music processing and manuscript preparation are concerned with the manipulation of graphic symbols; sound design is concerned with the manipulation of sonic materials; and music composition is concerned with the manipulation of musical ideas. You should understand these premises from the very beginning because a large body of people confuse manuscript preparation (music processing) and/or sound design (waveform/patch editing and synthesis) with actual musical composition. Likewise, direct-to-hard disk recording is an *ex post facto* process and furthermore, as you saw in the previous chapter, does not require MIDI.

Exceptions to the misconceptions

There are a cases in which sound design equates to musical composition. As early as 1912 Arnold Schoenberg experimented with timbre as the primary element in the third movement (*Farben*) of his *Five Pieces for Orchestra* (opus 16). He states in his *Harmonielehre* (1911): "If the ear could discriminate between difference of color, it might be feasible to invent melodies that are built of color. But who dares to develop such theories?" Since then there have been small factions of the avant-garde that have based their music on similar premises. Notable among these is the Sound-Mass movement — Krzysztof Penderecki's work in the 1950s and 1960s provides a good example. Much of Iannis Xenakis's stochastic music of the same period and later also borders on the Sound-Mass aesthetic. It goes without saying that composers involved in instrumental exploration, including new instrument performance techniques and the design of new instruments, were concerned with timbre as the fundamental aspect of their work. This movement, popular between the 1950s and 1970s but tracing its roots back to Henry Cowell's work in the 1920s, included such composers as Luciano Berio, John Cage, George Crumb, Mauricio Kagel, György Ligeti, Harry Partch, Krzysztof Penderecki, and Karlheinz Stockhausen. Finally, the repetitive music branch of the Minimalist school of the 1960s and 1970s, exemplified by the works of Philip Glass, Steve Reich, and Terry Riley, often dealt with the concept of extremely gradual timbral change.

For the most part, the use of timbre as the focal parameter in the works aligned with these movements was employed in a unique way as the "signature" stylistic characteristic of a particular composer's musical language. Many composers of the post-avant-garde, including computer musicians, have gone even farther into the realm of organizing a composition entirely around sounds instead of notes. With the digital signal processing capabilities and manipulation of direct-to-hard disk recordings offered by the Macintosh, the possibilities available to us in this area are virtually limitless.

It is no coincidence that the words "digital signal processing" and "effects" are used almost synonymously. Sonic manipulation of this type implies a special "effect" applied to something of substance. While it is true that potent compositional ideas can very well take sound design as a justifiable point of departure, perhaps a better term to describe the fruits of such labors is "soundscape" (instead of "music").

Word processing ≠ music processing = music composition

The impact of MIDI on composition methodology might, at first thought, appear to be somewhat analogous to the impact of word processing upon the labors of authors. Certainly, some of the editing operations are present in both domains: cutting, copying, pasting, and inserting. Spelling checkers and rhythm checkers bear some similarities. Some idea processors, such as the one I am using to write this book, offer authors a top-view or outline of a document and permit the manipulation of paragraphs or groups of nested paragraphs as discrete entities — resembling some of the features present in high-end MIDI programs.

Perhaps there are some similarities between word processing and music processing or manuscript preparation. Yet, even the analogy between word processing and music processing breaks down when you consider that word processors do not generally provide an author with access to editing operations dealing with the underlying semantics of their text. Likewise, it is not necessary for music processors dedicated to manuscript preparation or "desktop music publishing" to provide a composer with tools to mold musical ideas into compositions. On the other hand, it is common for MIDI sequencers to offer editing operations that deal with the semantics of your material. For example, many MIDI sequencers allow you to invert melodies or change the mode from major to minor, but no word processors offer an option to invert the meaning of a sentence or change its tone from happy to sad. While it is true that the front end of both a music notation system and a CAC environment can be a MIDI sequencer, this is only further evidence of the disparity between the worlds of music and text — and, at this time, a text processor cannot serve the dual purpose of text manuscript preparation and aid the author in the development of literary ideas.

Sound design ≠ music composition

In many instances, sound design, or the creation of new sounds either through synthesis, remote patch editing, or remote waveform editing (whether of sampled or generated waveforms), accomplished via MIDI, bears a similar relationship to music composition as the design of typefaces does to text processing. Thus, it is discussed in the chapters comprising Part Two, "Sound."

A good argument is that sound design is equivalent to orchestration in the context of computer music. This is a valid point of view with respect to those composers for whom timbre is as or more important than considerations of form, theme, and motivic development. These pioneers still represent the minority in the larger picture of today's compositional aesthetics, although tools like the Macintosh may very well change this. Such timbre-oriented music requires specific sounds to convey its artistic meaning and intent; however, thematic or note-oriented music should sound good no matter what instruments (or patches) are used to perform it. Throughout musical history the vast majority of composers of acoustic music did not design their own instruments. On the contrary, they assembled a collection of existing instruments to perform their works, often an entirely different set of instruments for each performance (e.g., there are no instruments specified for Bach's *Art of the Fugue*). Nowadays, instead of several dozen acoustic instruments you have hundreds of thousands of ready-made electronic sounds to choose from. I stress this point because I have seen too many electronic composers waste too much time trying to tweak a sound or purchase a new synthesizer for the sole purpose of improving a particular passage in their music when the real problem was not the sounds being used but the notes themselves. Spending thousands of dollars on a new synthesizer or thousands of hours designing new sounds is not going to repair a passage where the underlying musical ideas are at fault.

Orchestration is, above all, largely a matter of context. I once attended a performance of Pergolesi's *Stabat Mater* where the second oboist became ill as the instrumentalists were walking on the stage. His part was subsequently played by a spare flutist. Very few, if any, people in the audience noticed this substitution.

With this background, you should reexamine the title of this chapter, "Making Music with MIDI." The crucial word is "Music." This chapter and the several following it are concerned with making music, not creating sound (sound design), or preparing a manuscript (notation), or recording the music once you have composed it (direct-to-hard disk recording). To manipulate *musical ideas* on your Macintosh with MIDI, the primary tool you will use is a MIDI sequencer.

This chapter provides you with necessary fundamentals to understand what you can and cannot expect from MIDI sequencers and the impact that using a MIDI sequencer might have upon your prior, non-Macintosh-oriented composition habits (see Figure 16-1). This information is also crucial for evaluating the dozen sequencers presented in the next chapter, Chapter 17, "MIDI Sequencing."

MIDI Sequencing

When you are shaping your musical ideas into a musical work or composition, the primary concern of MIDI is the recording and editing of sequences of notes. This includes information about pitch, timing, key velocity, patch-change, and various front panel synthesizer controls. You can record such information in real time, step time (specifying the note's playback rhythmic value upon entry), or generate it interactively (see Chapter 19, "Interactive Composition and Intelligent Instruments") or algorithmically (see Chapter 20, "Algorithmic Composition").

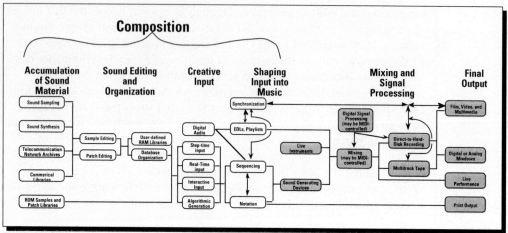

Figure 16-1: You will recall this flow chart from Chapter 9, "The Journey Between Sound and Music." This variation highlights the elements that directly relate to musical composition.

MIDI data is analogous to piano-roll data. In neither case are sounds actually recorded; rather, they record control information that triggers a sound to occur. MIDI transmits this data over 16 MIDI channels simultaneously (two banks of 16 channels if you use both of the Macintosh's serial ports, 128 to nearly a thousand channels if you employ newer, more advanced MIDI interfaces in conjunction with the Macintosh's serial ports). Because MIDI data consists entirely of numerical information, it lends itself to the wide variety of manipulative control to which any string of numbers is subject.

Although the degree of standardization offered by MIDI is extensive enough that I often refer to it as a type of "synthesizer Esperanto," nonstandard controls, unique to each synthesizer, are also supported by (SysEx) information. In this way, you can communicate a wide range of additional data between an external device and the Macintosh. MIDI software packages take advantage of this capability to provide you with extensive patch-editing power for various synthesizers by permitting access to the MIDI-addressable front panel controls. This often includes a far superior user interface than that installed in the actual hardware device itself. SysEx data occasionally communicates actual digital sound samples from various sampling devices, thus providing the ability to analyze and edit sampled waveforms (more often, MIDI's Sample Dump Standard is used for this purpose). Again, although the ability to send and receive SysEx messages is now a common feature of most MIDI sequencers, in the context of computer-assisted composition, you may think of such activity as sending a contractor a list of the instruments you will need for a certain performance.

The display of MIDI data

The effectiveness of a CAC environment is largely dependent upon how you, as a composer, personally relate to both the software's presentation of MIDI data and to the available operations you can perform upon that data. How closely these facilities conform to your normal compositional methodology is an important consideration. For example, the Macintosh's superior graphic capabilities support the display of MIDI data for purposes of analysis and editing in five ways:

- ❖ alphanumeric listing of the actual MIDI data stream
- ❖ graphic (proportional) representation of the MIDI data
- ❖ graphic timeline (similar to a spreadsheet) showing the density of musical events
- ❖ icons, blocks, or other graphic symbols representing chunks, each of which denotes an entire musical passage or event
- ❖ conventional music notation (CMN)

Certain programs offer some of these display possibilities — others, all five.

Due to each person's unique conceptual model of what music really is, the type of MIDI data display offered by the software you end up using has great bearing upon the efficiency with which you can interact with your own musical ideas (see Figure 16-2). Some people are more comfortable with CMN, while others feel equally at home with graphic displays or alphanumeric lists of the MIDI data stream. For others, the display type is of no consequence. Last but not least, more sequencers are including some form of graphically displayed overview that might be syntactical (meaning the overview includes semantic information such as structural function) or merely representational (meaning the overview is a zoomed-out version of the sequence illustrating where there are notes and where there is silence).

The organization of MIDI data

Directly related to the issue of MIDI data display is the question of data organization. If you want, you can think of issues of data display as local and issues of its organization or aggregation as global. Software-based sequencers organize MIDI data into three hierarchies, which reflect either *channel orientation, track orientation,* or *sequence orientation* (see Figure 16-3). In some aspects, these three approaches are mutually exclusive and force you to organize your musical thinking around their limitations.

Channel-oriented organization

Channel-oriented software requires that you record separate MIDI channel information within sequences that may contain 16 tracks, one for each channel.

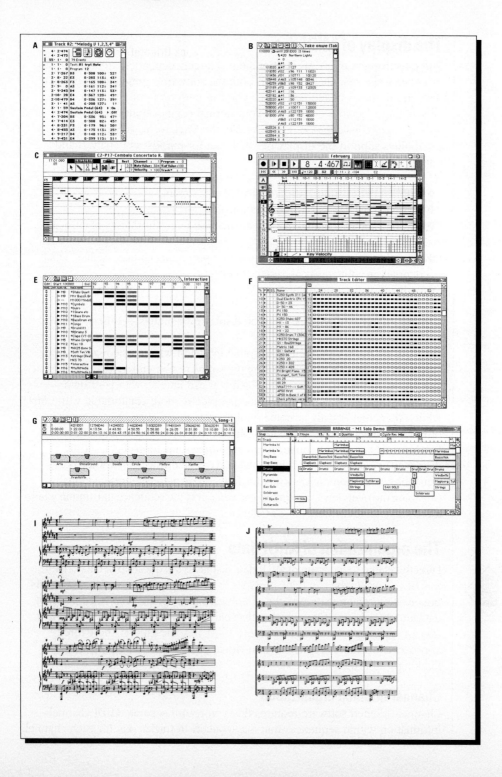

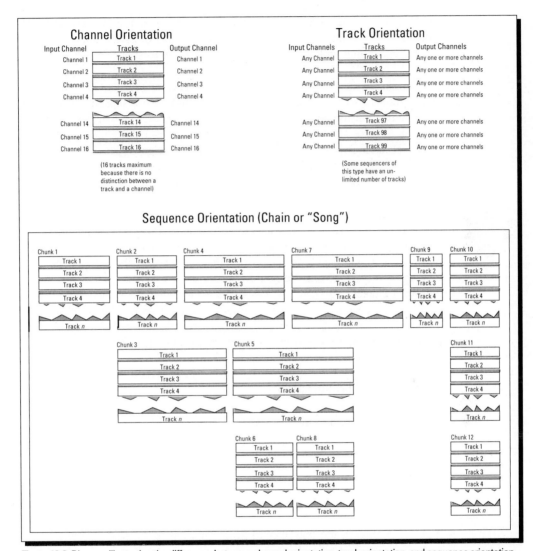

Figure 16-3: Diagram illustrating the difference between channel orientation, track orientation, and sequence orientation.

Figure 16-2 (left): The five main types of MIDI data display for music. Note that these are not drawn from any one program in particular, but reflect a sum or average (depending upon how you look at it) of various available software options. Alphanumeric displays: **(A)** Vision event list window. **(B)** Performer event list window. Bar graph displays: **(C)** Beyond Piano Roll window. **(D)** EZ-Vision Piano Roll window. Graphic timeline overview displays: **(E)** Performer overview window. **(F)** Pro 4 overview window. Icon-oriented "chunk" displays: **(G)** Performer chunks window. **(H)** CuBase patterns window. Conventional music notation displays: **(I)** Finale notation window. **(J)** Encore notation window.

Some allow up to 32 tracks, if both of the Macintosh's serial ports are connected to MIDI interfaces, while others allow for a greater number of tracks although the channel information is stored along with every note on each track.

In an ensemble situation, where multiple sound-generating devices are present, you might set each synthesizer or module to transmit on a separate channel. In a single-user environment with multiple sound modules, you might set each device to receive MIDI data on a different channel. In a single-user environment with a single multitimbral device, you might assign different patches (sounds or samples) to different channels. In all three cases, channel information might be used to differentiate separate melodic parts.

With channel-oriented software, each MIDI event is identified with a specific channel. This permits the simultaneous recording of multiple channels per track (whether assigned to multiple synthesizers, multiple patches, or multiple musical lines). A desirable feature is one that provides for the subsequent unmerging of such channel-flagged information onto separate tracks for individual editing. You may set tracks containing multiple channel data to play either on the channel(s) stamped at input or on an entirely different channel, disregarding the original channel association. Advantages of this technique include being able to record in one pass what could take up to 16 passes using some of the track-oriented approaches.

Track-oriented organization

Track-oriented software records MIDI data onto a track without necessarily using or even recording the channel information associated with each MIDI event. In this case, you may think of tracks as a stream of MIDI events with no channel identification. You assign the channel destinations for output. You can often set such tracks to output on any number of MIDI channels simultaneously, and you can set any number of channels to play from a single track or any number of tracks.

With this approach, the only way to get around having to make multiple passes to record multiple channels is to record on several tracks simultaneously, each track having been set to record from a specified channel (or channels). This is the most elegant and time-efficient type of organization. It eliminates a time-consuming step found with channel-oriented sequencers in that it does not require the subsequent unmerging of multiple-channel tracks, nor does it automatically associate a certain output timbre with a specific musical idea.

Another advantage provided by the track-oriented approach is the ability to quickly change your orchestration without having to go through two steps: first, unmerging other tracks, and then making multiple copies of each of the unmerged elements for later channel reassignment.

Sequence- or pattern-oriented organization

Sequence-oriented organization exists in several varieties. A number of sequences are associated with each file and this number may be fixed or limited only by RAM. Typically, one file may be active at any moment and any or all of its sequences or sub-sequences played back together or in a user-defined order. The difference between the various approaches to sequence-orientation is that in one type, a single sequence, chunk, or sub-sequence may itself be channel-oriented or track-oriented.

The motivations that have forced programmers into implementing a form of sequence-orientation have several roots. The first of these is not musical, but stems from the programmer's desire to incorporate subroutine logic into a music analogy. The second reason is the fact that many pre-Macintosh hardware sequencers and drum machines were pattern-oriented, and some programmers have attempted to emulate the capabilities of these hardware counterparts to their software. The final reason is that some musically inclined programmers realized the usefulness of being able to manipulate your musical ideas from a greater level of abstraction.

Sometimes it is possible to have the best of both worlds with respect to the first two possibilities above. For example, one can find channel-oriented software that includes the option of ignoring original channel information and outputting specific tracks on any number of channels simultaneously. Similarly, some track-oriented software includes the option of recording multiple-channel information onto a single track. Such software provides for the later unmerging of these multichannel tracks or the option to record several tracks at once, each receiving data from a separate channel (or channels).

User interface and editing

After questions of data display and organization, the next consideration affecting your interaction with MIDI data is the user interface. For some composers, the editing style may be as deeply linked to their conceptual model of musical structure as is the display and organization of MIDI data discussed previously. The question you must ask yourself at this point is: Now that I have a representation of my data that corresponds to my conceptual model organized in a hierarchy consistent with my inner feelings, can I manipulate that data in a fashion that is analogous to my creative process?

The interaction of the compositional process with the capabilities of MIDI poses many questions. The user interface of a sequencer may require you to conceive of your musical data in ways that are not acceptable within the framework of your customary methodology. On the other hand, there may be an opportunity for viewing musical material in ways you may not have previously considered.

Many aspects of the user interface contribute to the effective manipulation of your MIDI data. These include the scope and resolution of data recorded, the variety of edit operations, consistency of edit controls assigned to various edit options, efficiency of the editing process, modality of edit operations, and the prioritization of musical parameters. Equally important are the degree to which linear and local perspectives rather than non-linear and global perspectives are imposed; the available selection criteria for delineating the scope of edit operations as they relate to your individual style and musical language (as defined by recurrent edit formats); and whether or not the software provides a method for organizing your ideas into larger objects (whether through a graphic representation of various levels of abstraction or as a musical database). The paragraphs that follow discuss these points one at a time and provide some typical examples.

MIDI data and your musical vocabulary

The types of MIDI messages recorded by the sequencer software is very important. If a program does not record such basic channel commands as keystroke velocity or pitch bend, it forces you to exclude these items from your musical vocabulary when dealing with that program. If it records these parameters but does not allow you to edit them, you are equally at the mercy of the software. A similar situation occurs if your available editing options require you to edit in coarser steps than your actual data is recorded in. Some software packages allow filtering of certain types of data upon input, during editing, or both, while others offer no filtering of data whatsoever. More ambitious programs permit working with musical parameters independently, both of one another and of context.

Resolution of MIDI data and raw material

The resolution of recorded MIDI data can impose distinct limitations on your musical expression. Rhythmic resolution is one area in which there is no standardization. For example, some popular software packages divide each quarter note into 480 subdivisions called "ticks" or "clocks," while their competitors place this limit at 96 or 240 divisions of the quarter note. For purposes of comparison, the rhythmic resolution of the Kurzweil 250 digital synthesizer's on-board sequencer is $\frac{1}{256}$ of a quarter note, and the resolution of Finale, a notation program with some sequencing capabilities, is 1,024 divisions per quarter note. You may notice that the number of subdivisions of the quarter note is typically divisible by both 2 and 3 to provide smaller durations based upon divisions by 2 as well as triplet values. Some sequencers (e.g., Beyond) let you specify the number of divisions per quarter note to compensate for slower Macintoshes.

Available edit operations and compositional development

The scope and variety of edit options provided by the software determine how much freedom you have to manipulate your musical ideas once you record them as MIDI data. For example, although music is fundamentally a temporal continuum, it took a long time for commercial packages to realize the necessity of providing edit operations that deal with the changing of data incrementally over a specified period of time. Those that do even go so far as to permit you to specify a variety of curve-fitting operations for continuous change.

Without such provisions, basic musical operations such as crescendos and decrescendos are impossible. While many sequencers offer the possibility of fitting a velocity curve to a series of notes, in real music crescendos still maintain the rhythmic stresses of the prevailing meter. The only way to preserve this type of metrical feeling during a crescendo is to provide for fitting a curve that represents a change from a percentage of the original value to another percentage of the final value at the end of the crescendo (see Figure 16-4). Otherwise, if a crescendo is implemented as a continual change from one velocity value to another, you will simply have a series of notes that gets louder and louder with no metrical feeling. Of course, the same applies to decrescendos.

The scope of editing operations is an important factor in practical day-to-day work. To return to the discussion of crescendos, consider the predicament of wanting to place a crescendo in the last half of a measure, and the software you are using requires that barlines be the delimiters for selection ranges. In such a case, you will not be able to add that crescendo to the last half of the measure.

Quantization

Quantization (automatic rhythmic correction or rounding off) is a special type of edit operation that varies enormously from one product to another. It is not humanly possible to play with perfect rhythm, nor does anyone attempt to. The ebb and flow of subtle rhythmic irregularities and interpretations is exactly what separates professionals from amateurs — if it were humanly possible and if everyone did play music exactly as written, all performances of the same piece would be identical. When you quantize a passage, you are correcting for the fact that MIDI recording has a greater rhythmic resolution than you need. The majority of sequencers now use 480 subdivisions of a quarter note as their highest resolution. Well, $\frac{1}{480}$ of a quarter note is roughly $\frac{1}{2048}$ note, not a rhythmic value that you are likely to encounter or require.

The *quantization grid* (sometimes referred to as "quantum unit" or "resolution") to which a program permits rounding off, ranges from as little as three options to the capability of quantizing to any known note value or any tuplet expressible by three numbers under 1,000. Rhythmic resolution places a finite limit on a program's ability to quantize to tuplets without round-off errors being perceived. Many packages restrict the composer to triplets at best. Others supplement their quantization options with many useful humanizing features that apply controlled

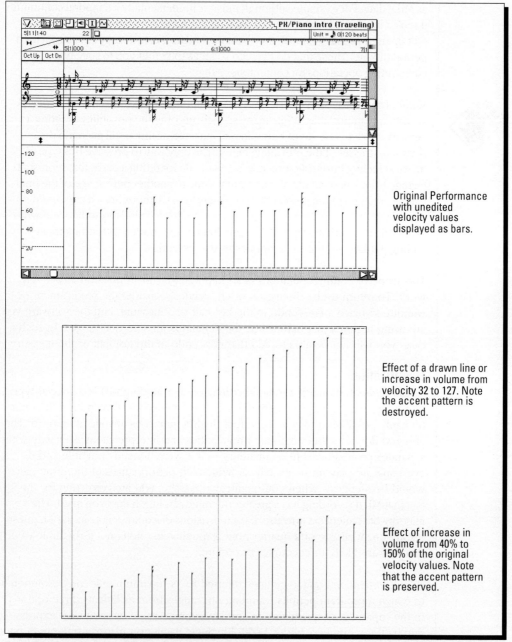

Original Performance with unedited velocity values displayed as bars.

Effect of a drawn line or increase in volume from velocity 32 to 127. Note the accent pattern is destroyed.

Effect of increase in volume from 40% to 150% of the original velocity values. Note that the accent pattern is preserved.

Figure 16-4: The difference between a linear (continual) increase in volume (crescendo) and an increase from a percentage of the original value to a percentage of the final value. The latter method preserves the metrical feeling of a passage. The same applies to decrescendos.

randomness to certain quantization parameters to rehumanize passages that may have been input using step time (see Figure 16-5).

Finally, there are four approaches to quantization:

❖ *Quantization on input* auto-corrects your rhythmic inconsistencies as you record data in real time. The disadvantage of this is that you will never be able to recapture the true ebb and flow of an expressive passage. You can never re-create the original nuances of performance. Furthermore, it is necessary to specify the smallest rhythmic value in advance and very often this value may not be known, or might occur so infrequently that using it as the quantization grid for an entire passage will result in larger rhythmic values being rounded off with far too much precision.

❖ *Quantization on output* (sometimes called non-destructive quantization) does not alter any of your unquantized data that you have recorded. Instead, as you send data to your sound-generating devices, rhythmic values are rounded to a quantum grid that you have pre-selected.

❖ *Destructive quantization* actually changes your original data, replacing it with the edited data. Of course, with the Macintosh's capability of undoing almost anything, you may be able to undo a destructive quantization operation.

❖ *Post-determination of the beat* (sometimes called tap-tempo) refers to a type of quantization that does not require a click reference like the above three methods. Instead of playing along to a mechanical or robotic metronomic click that will later be used as the reference for all quantization operations, you play as freely and expressively as you like. Then you define the beat lines by tapping a key on the Macintosh or MIDI keyboard along with a playback of your original recording.

Each of the four types of quantization has advantages in particular situations. Because of this, many programs support more than one type of quantization, although none supports all four types.

Editing consistency

Consistency among the controls of the various edit operations at your disposal is of great concern with a computer such as the Macintosh. Composers have the right to expect that sequencers, like any other Macintosh application, will provide edit operations that can be accomplished in an identical manner for all musical parameters. If note insertion is accomplished by pointing and clicking the mouse, it should be possible for all MIDI data insertions to be executed in this fashion. If pitch-bend information can be filtered upon input, then it should also be filterable

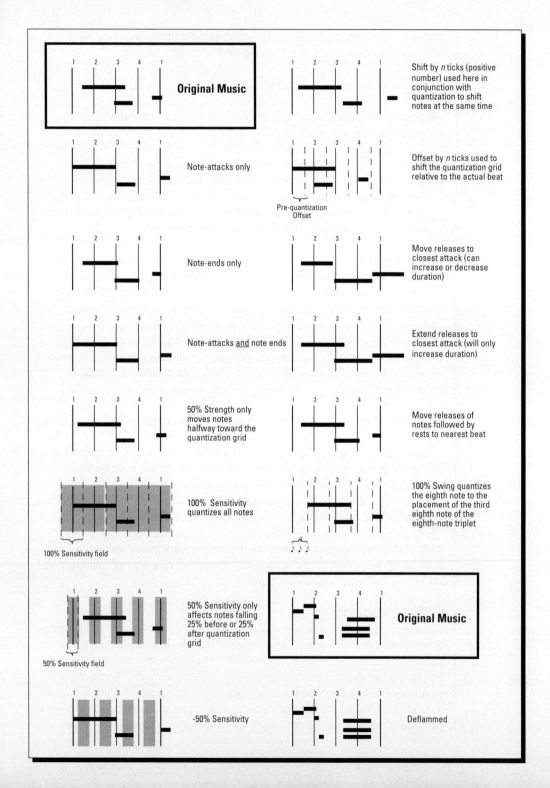

during editing. If velocity data can be scaled by percentage, then so must durational data. If a single note can be transposed, then you should have the option of transposing a selected region as well as an entire track or sequence. Finally, if one edit operation can be undone, then all operations should offer this possibility. In more powerful software, the undo operation is itself "undoable" in a toggling fashion, thus offering the possibility for rapid A-B comparisons between an edited version and the original.

Taking this one step further, it is highly desirable to be able to perform most edit operations in real time while your music is being played back. This is becoming increasingly common in high-end sequencers, although it will be some time before any manufacturer can honestly claim that all edit operations are available during playback.

Editing efficiency

Editing efficiency directly relates to interface consistency. If a simple musical operation requires multiple commands, and especially if the commands are of mixed types (such as menu access and selection combined with dialog box confirmation, mouse relocation, and keyboard entry), editing efficiency can drop to unproductive levels. Related edit operations should all require the same number of keystrokes, menu accesses, or mouse motions. However, "providing a 'front end' to a music system does not, in itself, improve on the shallowness of the internal representations" (Curtis Roads, "Research in Music and Artificial Intelligence." *AMC Computing Surveys*, vol. 17. no. 2). In other words, just as a wonderful score cannot improve a bad film, neither can a beautifully consistent interface improve any fundamental design flaws in a software package.

Editing modes

Multiple modalities of editing operations can slow you down to the point where sequencer software is no longer time-efficient. Some software requires the viewing of MIDI data in one mode for editing certain musical parameters and switching into other modes for editing other parameters. The necessity to exit and enter a multitude of editing modes repeatedly can be a frustrating experience. The various aspects of sequence editing, and even recording and playback, need not operate from distinct and exclusive modes, and the more elegant sequencer programs are evidence of this.

Figure 16-5 (left): Graphic representation of the effect of quantizing, illustrated by examples of the effects of various standard options such as note-attacks only, note-ends only, and note-attacks with note-ends. Additional criteria that are often added to quantization: strength, sensitivity, shift, offset, beat-related movement, swing, and deflamming. The music in the two boxes represents the unquantized versions used for the examples that follow.

Imposing priorities on your musical aesthetics

Arbitrary priorities associated with musical parameters inherent to the restrictive concepts of track-orientation, channel-orientation, region selection, and note selection can force you into composition methodologies that are incompatible with your musical aesthetics. Some programs make it very easy to apply edit operations to an entire track and much more difficult or even impossible to edit a selected region or note. This is clearly an inconsistency of scope.

There should be no distinction between the operations that can be applied to a sequence, group of tracks, single track, group of regions on separate tracks, single region, or note. Nor should there be any distinction made between musical parameters with respect to legal edit operations. This is to say that all operations should be applicable to any scope, and any operation that can be applied to rhythm should be equally applicable to pitch, duration, on-velocity, off-velocity, bender information, control information, tempo, and so on.

Any operation that can be applied to one parameter, but cannot be effected on another parameter, is evidence of arbitrary prioritization on the part of the software's developers. For example, consider software that permits the editing of pitch to any MIDI-supported note, allows quantization to a triplet sixteenth but nothing finer, limits velocity editing to ten levels, and permits the editing of durational data in only the most tedious fashion. This environment forces you to operate within a set of arbitrary priorities where pitch is supreme, attack rhythm and velocity less important, and duration practically a non-entity. Even in this case, microtonality and fine control over the timbral aspects of individual pitches are not addressed.

Perspective: Linear vs. non-linear, local vs. global

As mentioned previously, the allowable scope of editing operations is enormously important in practical work. Perhaps the most creatively damaging characteristic that you can encounter in sequencer software for the Macintosh is that of forcing you to take a local and linear approach to the editing process. In these programs, regions selected for editing can consist only of temporally consecutive MIDI events. This imposes a narrow viewpoint consisting of horizontal layers of consecutive events, rather than fostering a global conception of a compositional work as a single continuum in which all parameters contribute to a unified entity.

Ideally, composers should be able to define their own syntactic regions in macro-like selection formats. Such user-definable criteria could range from something as simple as selecting every other or every third note for an edit operation, to selecting pitches that are rhythmically spaced according to a durational series expanding additively or geometrically.

Several high-end sequencing packages stand in sharp contrast to the majority by making it possible to select groups of events for editing based on many other criteria than mere temporal consecutivity. In these cases it is easily possible to define an edit region as all notes within a specified pitch range; all notes of a specified voice or voices (such as the top three voices or the bottom voice); all notes within a specified on- or off-velocity range; or all notes within a specified durational range — regardless of consecutivity. This represents the non-linear approach.

Furthermore, selection criteria may include some Boolean relations (AND, NOT, and OR). For example, it should be possible to select all notes falling within a specified pitch range AND a specified durational range AND a specified velocity range for subsequent operations.

One extremely desirable type of scope criterion that many software developers neglect concerns the selection of a region of notes based upon a user-specified metrical range. This would permit you to select, for example, all notes occurring on the first or last beat of a measure for subsequent editing. An examination of orchestrations from any period in history provides evidence that metrical range or placement is one of the foremost selection criteria for recurring edit operations. This is used, for example, to better define the prevailing meter through adding weight (velocity) to downbeats or a characteristic accent pattern (especially within the larger context of a crescendo or decrescendo), or to periodically double instruments in a manner consistent with common practice for composers using a pencil and paper. Of course, the number of possible groupings of musical events (which correspond to the cognitive categories for thinking about music) is limitless.

One early sequencer now no longer marketed (Total Music by Southworth Music Systems) provided for global substitution through several "table replacement" operations. Four tables consisting of 128 entries could be accessed from a main screen palette. The table was organized in rows by octave, although many operations that make use of the table do not necessarily apply to pitch alone. Once values were entered, you had the option for a positive or negative constant to be added to any selected range of cells. These setup operations could be repeated and combined in any order until the table was configured exactly as desired. Temporal ranges were specified in measures, beats, and beat fractions. Also, if appropriate, a low and high range could be specified for the values of byte one (notes or controller numbers) or byte two (velocity or controller value). A completed table could be applied to a specified region of MIDI data.

Table replacement is beginning to reappear in the form of a Remap Pitches edit operation. Not coincidentally, pitch is perhaps the most important parameter upon

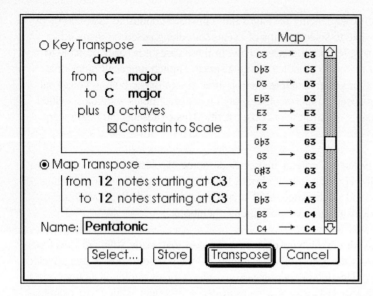

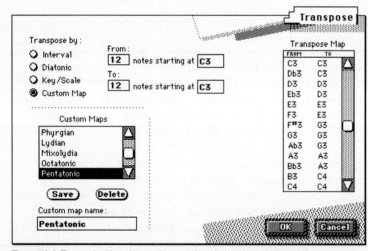

Figure 16-6: Two typical interfaces of remapping pitches from a chromatic scale to a pentatonic scale. Vision is on the top and Performer is on the bottom.

which to apply such an edit operation. You often need to remap pitches when you play back drum tracks using a different drum machine than the one upon which they were recorded (until the implementation of General MIDI becomes more widespread — see Chapter 1, "Background"). Pitch remapping also provides for converting passages to different modes (sometimes called mutation), exotic scales, or user-defined pitch collections rather than merely transposing them to different keys. You can also employ pitch remapping to perform quantization with respect to pitch. Thus it is a simple matter to convert a chromatic work into a pentatonic one (quantize to the pentatonic scale) or to "filter out" all pitches not in the scale you had intended, such as places where you hit a wrong note (see Figure 16-6).

Defining your musical language

Selection criteria and edit formats are important factors in defining your individual style and musical language. People working seriously in CAC must be able to define edit regions and operations based upon multiple criteria, as well as store such edit formats for later recall in a fashion analogous to macros.

At the very least, many programs "remember" the previous settings of the dialog boxes used to apply edit operations. Unfortunately, this only provides for reapplying the last edit you did to a new region; once you have changed the settings or quit the program, such information disappears forever. Some even provide for saving edit criteria relating to certain operations, particularly pitch remapping and MIDI channel assignment (through virtual instruments). But there are no sequencers currently available that provide for saving edit formats of any complexity. Of course, many power users get around these failings by employing a macro-utility in conjunction with their sequencer to save complex edit operations for later recall.

Edit formats are essentially the unique way in which each composer shapes his musical material. Thus they are inherently connected to questions of individual style and musical language. Such formats also bear a similarity to report generation within a database (in the traditional sense). The Macintosh simplifies the process to merely pushing buttons on the screen with the mouse to set up large-scale selection criteria and complex calculations.

A typical MIDI sequencer edit format (or macro) might include delineation of a region for editing based upon any of the possible selection criteria discussed above, combined with criteria defined by database-like statistical analysis of the work or specified region thereof, using any number of Boolean operators. This might be followed by a series of multiple edit operations, which could include conditional IF branches to deeper selection criteria and/or further edit operations (see Figure 16-7). After considerations of germinating cell, idea, or inspiration, a composer's library of edit formats would constitute the major characteristics of his style.

Nested levels of abstraction

What is a MIDI sequencer track, if not a "record" in a musical database? Even though the MIDI records (tracks) are representations of temporally consecutive events that interrelate with other records vertically as well as horizontally, there are still many relational databases that effectively and even artistically manage similar interconnections of information. If you accept the fact that a sequencer has as much in common with a database as it does with a word processor (the typical analogy), a whole world of additional possibilities opens up.

First, the capability of searching for a MIDI event would seem to be a distinct advantage. Some hardware-based sequencers, such as the one found in the Kurzweil 250, offer this capability. Better yet would be the option to search-and-replace, both locally and globally. At least one notation program (Finale) already offers a somewhat restrictive search-and-replace feature.

A simple use of search-and-replace would be to convert the modality (in the musical sense) of a work from a major to minor tonality, or to a diatonic mode.

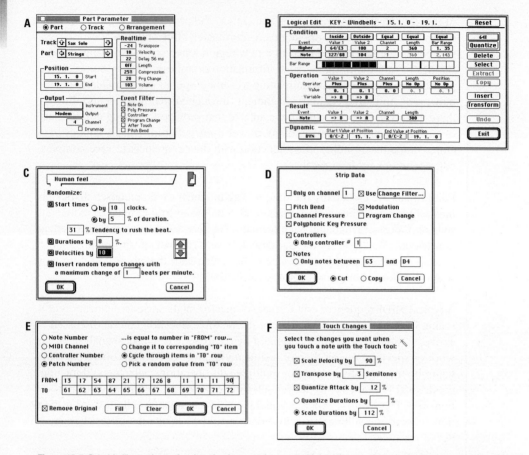

Figure 16-7: Graphic illustrations of various implementations to multiple edit operations designated as a single entity. All are dialog-box-based. **(A)** CuBase's Part Parameter dialog box lets you modify multiple parameters of a part in one fell swoop. Note that this affects output only. **(B)** CuBase's Logical Editor requires a thorough grounding in MIDI bytes but allows you to both select and edit multiple parameters simultaneously. **(C)** Pro 4.5's Human Feel dialog box allows you to edit start times, durations, velocities, and tempo, although this implementation is purely to insert randomness. **(D)** Pro 4.5's Strip Data dialog box lets you manipulate multiple data types simultaneously but limits the operation to the removal of data. **(E)** One-Step's Table Replacement dialog box lets you edit multiple values of one of four data types all at once. Some of you may remember a similar feature in Southworth's Total Music (One-Steps progenitor) that provided a much larger grid for table replacement. **(F)** The most elegant implementation of multiple parameter editing was found in early beta versions of Deluxe Recorder but unfortunately it was removed from the release version. A Touch Tool resembling a magic wand could be configured to scale velocity, transpose, quantize, and edit durations by simply touching a note in any editing window. This dialog box was used to configure the tool.

Fortunately, the embracing of pitch remapping by most sequencer developers takes care of that usage. Searches needn't be restricted to notes, though; they could include a search for groups of pitches with or without associated rhythms. Carrying this process one step further would permit you to search for intervallic strings or vectors, allowing you to locate regions on the basis of motif, gesture, or musical idea. As detailed analyses of musical works from all periods reveal, the procedure of selecting all the occurrences of a certain motif for a specific edit operation bears great consistency to pre-technological compositional methodology.

The ability to identify selected musical material as a member of a specific class or category within a "library" is of extreme importance in a musical database. Such classification could be used as an adjunct to sorting and searching operations. An ideal situation would provide for the reference and manipulation of library objects as separate musical modules for easy reordering and juxtaposition. As you saw in Chapter 15, "Making Music without MIDI," one non-MIDI Macintosh program, StudioSession, has taken a major first step in the database direction, and includes library, sorting, and searching operations for musical "modules" (that is, phrases of assignable categories, lengths, and meters) as well as the independent manipulation of these modules as separate objects. Pattern-oriented sequencers have moved into this direction by permitting the manipulation of your musical ideas from the pattern (or chunk) level rather than simply from the note level.

If the definition of a region is allowed to include such delineators as pitch, pitch set, pitch string, interval, intervallic string or vector, with or without an associated rhythm, rhythmic string, or proportion (thus providing for augmentations and diminutions of a given rhythm), then you can request that the software provide you with statistical feedback on certain matters. Such feedback might include for example, the number of recurrences of a given motif within a specific part and at what transpositions; which transpositions of a specific motif have never been used; or, the specific rhythmic or melodic material that is thus far unique. Extending this idea to the vertical element would permit the selection of regions based upon chord type or vector and naturally permit the display of harmonic analysis in some fashion, whether traditional or not.

One recent implementation of multiple levels of abstraction is the option to create virtual instruments (see Figure 16-8). What this means is that you can define a group of synthesizers, or separate channels on synthesizers, to play specified sounds as a single entity, usually referred to as an "instrument." It is best to consider this as a virtual instrument. Assigning a track to play back on that instrument automatically routes the MIDI data to the entire collection of channels or devices, often providing for different velocity scaling, transposition, or panning for each device making up the virtual instrument.

Finally, for a MIDI sequencer to realize its potential as a powerful compositional tool, it should provide you with a graphic representation of the syntactic structure of musical compositions. With this in mind, many sequencers now include an overview display option that provides either a condensed view of all track activity in the current sequence or a symbolic (or iconic) representation of

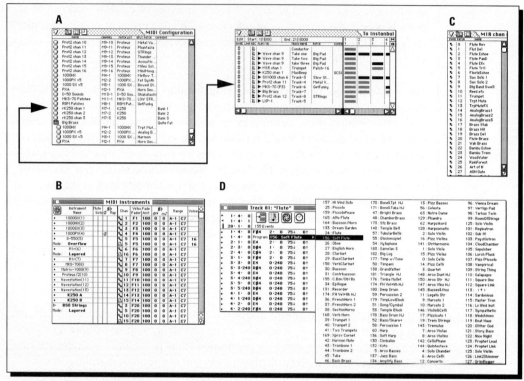

Figure 16-8: Diagram simplifying the concept of multiple levels of abstraction by illustrating it with virtual instruments. **(A)** Performer's approach to virtual instruments. MIDI channels and cables can be referred to by the name of the device that they address. More importantly, you can group different devices (see arrow) into a virtual instrument that can be assigned to a track as an entity. In this illustration the virtual instrument, "Big Brass" is made up of four different devices on different channels and cables. **(B)** Vision provides for two types of virtual device groupings. A virtual instrument can be defined to consist of several devices where the secondary device kicks in when the polyphony has been exceeded for the primary device (Overflow instrument). Vision's Layered instruments are functionally identical to those of Performer, multiple devices grouped to function as a single entity. There are two examples in this illustration: "M1r" (consisting of two Korg M1r synthesizers assigned to different ports and channels) and "BSO Strings" (consisting of an aggregation of four devices). **(C)** and **(D)** show Performer's and Visions's interfaces to referencing sounds by name instead of patch number.

all active sequences (those that might be chained together as modules within a larger work). Most sequencers that go this far include a mechanism for quickly selecting active sequences for editing or chaining.

Speed

To be of any use whatsoever, MIDI sequencer software must provide a means for accomplishing a given task with increased speed and efficiency. There are not as many types of MIDI sequencers as there are types of music, so it is quite logical that developers have provided for one sequencer package to be viable in a number of situations. A MIDI sequencer program's designers must try to anticipate possible future uses of MIDI when MIDI itself is young. In earlier stages of the sequencer industry's development, each commercial package seemed to have a distinct focus, situation, or type of application in which it was clearly superior to its competitors. At that time, it was necessary for composers to try to anticipate their own future uses of MIDI when considering a purchase. Nowadays, most sequencers attempt to be all things for all people. Fortunately, they are very close to realizing this goal.

Decisions

When you read the next chapter and when you are trying to make up your mind about which sequencer to invest in, you should keep in mind the following points. This is especially important for the sequencers that fall in the "around-$500" range.

What kind of MIDI data can you record, edit, and filter?

You cannot control data that is not present. Thus, all transmitted MIDI data should be recordable, input-filterable, insertable, editable, and edit-filterable. All types of data should be available independently or in any aggregation for the purposes of viewing, filtering, and editing. All data recordable and/or editable must also be "playbackable." If you need your sequencer to record and play back SysEx data, don't stand for anything that doesn't offer this capability (make sure you check the allowable size of SysEx data dumps — some programs are extremely restrictive in this respect).

Track-oriented, channel-oriented, or sequence-oriented?

The organization of data into track-oriented, channel-oriented, or sequence-oriented frameworks forces you to conceive of musical materials from a restricted point of view. In the best of worlds, your sequencer should be non-hierarchical in organization, combining all or most features of channel-orientation, track-orienta-tion, or sequence-orientation within one application. This implies that all channel information will be recorded, but may be ignored on playback and during edit operations, if desired. Any number of channels may be set to output from any number of tracks simultaneously. You should have the option of having all data output on its original channels at any time. Any tracks that include data from multiple channels should be unmergeable.

How modal is the software?

The necessity to switch between various editing modes in a sequencer is not time-efficient, therefore lowering productivity. The sequencer should not exhibit modality concerning any one of these three functions: record, edit, or playback. Even the varieties of edit displays offered should not place any restrictions upon your working habits (alphanumeric, graphic, CMN). Ideally, different types of displays should be viewable simultaneously in different windows, and edits performed in one representation should be immediately reflected (or updated) in all other windows into the same data. If display-modal (only one type of display is available at a time), all edit operations should be available in all modes.

Does the software fit your aesthetics?

Arbitrary priorities are counterproductive to creative work, because they rarely reflect an individual's conceptual model of music. Your sequencer should not exhibit any priorities, whether with respect to orientation, modality, record, edit, playback functions, edit operations, or musical parameters.

Can you live with the user interface?

The user interface should be consistent unto itself. All edit operations should follow identical input and control procedures. If not part of the normal edit display, an option to view MIDI data in its highest recorded resolution should be available. If CMN is used, the option to display data either graphically or alphanumerically should also be supported. The ability to undo an edit operation should be supported and itself be undoable, thus providing the ability to make A-B comparisons between edited and unedited versions of the same material.

Can you view your data the way you want to?

You may have a preference among the three common representations of MIDI data: alphanumeric lists, proportional graphic notation, or conventional music notation. Many sequencers support two of these options, and some support all three.

Can you select what you want to edit?

Edit region selection limited to consecutivity imposes a linear perspective on you. Both consecutive (temporally contiguous) and non-consecutive (non-contiguous) regions should be addressable by all edit operations. Consecutive edit regions should be definable as: any note, consecutive region of notes on a track, consecutive region of notes on a grouping of tracks, entire tracks, groups of entire tracks, and whole sequences. Non-consecutive regions should be definable through one or more of the following criteria: specifiable pitch range, specifiable vertical placement range, specifiable velocity range, specifiable durational range, specifiable metrical placement. If it is important to you, proximity to another event should be a viable selection criterion. All edit operations should offer sufficient Boolean relations to support selecting an edit region based on combinations of criteria.

Can you edit what you have selected?

Inconsistency of legal edit operations available for each type of MIDI data forces arbitrary prioritization of musical parameters. All edit operations should be available for all types of MIDI data (thus for all musical parameters) and for any type of selected region. Minimum edit operations requirements include: change data value; insert data value; cut region; copy region; paste region; merge region; set region values to a constant; add or subtract a constant from region values; multiply region values by a constant; set minimum and/or maximum values for region; change region values linearly from one value to another; change region values smoothly (fit to curve) from one value to another; change region values from one percentage to another; set minimum and/or maximum increments for smooth data changes; set minimum and/or maximum temporal values for smooth data changes; invert all region values around a specified axis; retrograde all region values; quantize all region values to all quantum units possible within the communicable data resolution; shift all values temporally with respect to other parameters; set an edit sensitivity envelope; and randomize, permute, or otherwise reorder region values.

Are the quantization limits compatible with your performance style?

Rhythmic quantization is a special case involving combinations of edit operations that you access through one command. Rhythmic quantization should be available for either note-on or note-off or both, with either a negative or positive offset or none, including the option of maintaining the original duration, as well as setting an envelope of quantization sensitivity, and setting a strength of quantization movement. The quantization grid should include every note value and tuplet expressible by the tick resolution of the software. Related features include deflamming of chords within a specified tolerance, the ability to set all durations to full value (that is, note-off occurs at next note-on), and metric intelligence. Track-shift should be an edit operation applicable to any MIDI data as a "parameter shift." For some people, the "tap tempo" form of quantization can be most important; for others, input quantization is a necessity, so you should give careful thought to which form will fill your needs. If you require it, pitch remapping should be available.

Will the program remember you later?

Many composers apply the same or similar edit selection criteria and operations (development, evolution, and transformation) to greatly disparate materials in different compositions. Recurrent complex edit formats should be savable as chained or grouped operations or macros for later recall within different contexts. If it is important to you, edit formats should consist of multiple selection criteria and conditional branching based upon analysis, followed by multiple edit operations performed on the material selected thereby. In that case, you might hope a future upgrade will support conditional branching to deeper selection criteria and/or further edit operations; subsequent editing of the edit macros themselves, and the option for one edit macro being called from another.

Can you listen to your music the way you want to?

The playback or proofhearing function should include analogies to the magnetic tape world such as the real-time control of pause, fast forward, rewind, scrub (play slowly forward or backward with audible output), mute track(s), and soloing of tracks. If you need looping, you should look for the capability to loop all types of regions, including non-coincident simultaneous looping. Real-time control of tempo, MIDI channel assignment, transposition, rhythmic quantization, and the option to insert markers on-the-fly into the sequence for subsequent location should be present. Sequence calling and chaining, if implemented, should permit regions to play back simultaneously (with multiple tempos if you need it), as well as the capability of capturing all data created by chaining or chunking into a new sequence equal to the sum of the parts.

Do you need to synchronize?

If you are going to be doing any multitrack recording or work with film or video, you should examine the synchronization features of the sequencer. There are five SMPTE synchronization frame rates and other equally useful types of synchronization, such as Direct Time Lock (DTL) and Direct Time Lock enhanced (DTLe). If the software claims synchronization capabilities, you should make sure that these features go beyond simple MIDI Clock Sync or SPP, and that incoming SMPTE is either recognizable as MTC, DTL, or DTLe.

Do you need remote control?

In a performance situation, you may want to interact with a MIDI sequencer without having to go anywhere near your Macintosh. Many programs allow you to assign certain keys or buttons on your musical keyboard as remote controls for many of the program options normally activated by mouse manipulation.

How many MIDI channels do you want?

All MIDI sequencers provide for 16 MIDI channels. Most MIDI sequencers provide for 32 MIDI channels (16 assigned to the Macintosh's modem port and another 16 assigned to the printer port). Newer sequencers provide for larger numbers of independent channels. Support for 128, 240, 256, 384, 480, 512, or greater numbers of MIDI channels are currently available in some sequencers.

Do you need multiple levels of abstraction?

The vast majority of composers do not conceptualize an entire work at the note level. With this in mind, a sequencer should offer interactive graphic representations of a work seen from different nested levels of abstraction. Within such a system, modules are definable as either fixed event lists or entire sequences. In future sequencers, modules might be definable as processes (such as algorithms for generation or variation), including provisions for the free interaction of these with static data. Combinations of separate modules to yield new modules of greater complexity should be nestable to any degree of abstraction and, conversely, decomposition should permit a return to the note or instruction level. Finally, the scope of appropriate edit operations should extend to the level of the module and nested modules. The capability to define virtual instruments is one implementation of the principle of multiple levels of abstraction.

Do you require database-like operations?

If you need to use a MIDI sequencer as a musical database, it should offer you operations analogous to the database operations of search, search-and-replace, and report-generation, as well as providing a library of your ideas with sorting capabilities. It should be possible to define a musical event, phrase, or region as an identifiable object (or module) within such a library (musical database) that can be referenced, retrieved, manipulated, and/or edited as a single entity or in combination with other objects within the library. Within the context of an entire sequence, or selected region, any MIDI event should be searchable; so should pitch collections (with registral considerations), pitch class sets (without registral considerations), intervallic strings, intervallic vectors, rhythmic strings, and rhythmic relations or proportions (without associated rhythmic values). The linear and the vertical or composite domain should be treated equally. Any searchable object should be selectable for editing. Besides the assignment of names to sequences and individual tracks, many sequencers now allow you to name notes (useful for drum sounds and sound effects) and even refer to particular patches or sounds by name. The capability to subscribe to a published database of instrumental patches, thus creating a link where work within the context of the sound library automatically updates the sequencer environment, is the first form of Inter-application Communication (IAC) to appear. At the very least, your sequencer should be able to save files in the SMF format for subsequent manipulation by other types of software.

Do you need digital audio tracks in your sequencer?

If you do, see Chapter 18, "MIDI Sequencing with Digital Audio."

Conclusions

The impact of MIDI on your composing extends far beyond reorienting your conception of dynamics to a scale of 0 to 127 MIDI velocities or adapting your performance style to accommodate subsequent quantization. Using a MIDI sequencer as the central control device in a studio or workstation devoted to CAC demands that composers become much more aware of both the physical and logical characteristics of their material. This need arises from the necessity of specifying subsets of music as editing regions based upon criteria drawn from a myriad of possibilities, one of the simplest of which is location in time. Transformational operations applied to regions so specified constitute the act of composition.

You may have to adjust the way you think about time. The instantaneousness of MIDI sequencing can change your entire approach to composition. Being able to see or hear any part of your work in progress immediately, to transpose or reorchestrate large regions in the blink of your eye, or to copy, for example, 48 measures of 20 instrumental parts and insert them 300 bars later in the time it takes to click the mouse button, is something that can alter the way you relate considerations of time with respect to the compositional process. This increased range to your creative wandering is not unlike moving up from riding a bicycle to piloting a jumbo jet in one fell swoop.

MIDI offers no substitutes for musical imagination, but then, imagination itself is a poor alternative to the ear and hearing. MIDI provides a practical and especially flexible way to proofhear works in progress — providing opportunities for testing different orchestrations as well as for experimenting with an endless number of alternate juxtapositions or transformations of your material. And nothing can replace the ear nor the advantages of hearing, in real time, a rendition of a complex work, an undertaking that, either due to considerations of tempo, rhythmic complexity, or the sheer number of simultaneous interdependent parts, would often be impossible except during an actual performance.

Summary

✔ Since its inception less than a decade ago, MIDI has had a major impact on composers and composing. Macintosh MIDI applications provide composers with a hitherto inaccessible freedom for experimentation. However, such freedom does not come without a price. Limitations imposed by the physical capabilities of the MIDI Specification are forcing composers to develop new conceptual models of their creations and to evolve new strategies for manipulating musical materials.

✔ When you are shaping your musical ideas into a musical work or composition, the primary concern of MIDI is the recording and editing of sequences of notes. This includes information about pitch, timing, key velocity, patch-change, and various front panel synthesizer controls. You can record such information in real time, step time (specifying the note's playback rhythmic value upon entry), or generate it interactively or algorithmically.

✔ MIDI data is analogous to piano-roll data. In neither case are sounds actually recorded; rather, they record control information that triggers a sound to occur. MIDI transmits this data over 16 MIDI channels simultaneously (two banks of 16 channels if you use both of the Macintosh's serial ports, 128 to nearly a thousand channels if you employ newer, more advanced MIDI interfaces in conjunction with the Macintosh's serial ports). Because MIDI data consists entirely of numerical information, it lends itself to the wide variety of manipulative control to which any string of numbers is subject.

✔ The Macintosh's superior graphic capabilities support the display of MIDI data for purposes of analysis and editing in five ways: as an alphanumeric listing of the actual MIDI data stream; as a graphic (proportional) representation of the MIDI data; as a graphic timeline (similar to a spreadsheet) showing the density of musical events; as icons, blocks, or other graphic symbols representing chunks, each of which denotes an entire musical passage or event; and as conventional music notation.

✔ Quantization is a special type of edit operation that varies enormously from one product to another. It is not humanly possible to play with perfect rhythm, nor does anyone attempt to. When you quantize a passage, you are correcting for the fact that MIDI recording has a greater rhythmic resolution than you need. The majority of sequencers now use 480 subdivisions of a quarter note as their highest resolution. Well, $\frac{1}{480}$ of a quarter note is roughly $\frac{1}{2048}$ note, not a rhythmic value that you are likely to encounter or require.

✔ One recent implementation of multiple levels of abstraction to MIDI sequencing is the option to create virtual instruments. This means that you can define a group of synthesizers, or separate channels on synthesizers, to play specified sounds as a single entity, usually referred to as an "instrument." It is best to consider this as a virtual instrument. Assigning a track to play back on that instrument automatically routes the MIDI data to the entire collection of channels or devices, often providing for different velocity scaling, transposition, or panning for each device making up the virtual instrument.

Chapter 17
MIDI Sequencing

In this chapter...

✔ Contrasting MIDI sequences and analog recordings.

✔ Standard MIDI sequencer features, their common variations, and "bells and whistles."

✔ Displaying MIDI data.

✔ The impact of timing resolution, including a table of expressible rhythms at all resolutions.

✔ Sequence chaining, chunking, and pattern-oriented song construction.

✔ Classification of Macintosh sequencers into professional and non-professional categories.

✔ Six non-professional sequencers and five professional sequencers examined in detail.

✔ Shareware options for MIDI sequencing.

✔ Feature comparison tables.

✔ Interview with Patrick Moraz.

Evolution of the MIDI Sequencer

The most common use of MIDI information is to record and store sequences of musical events played on a device such as a synthesizer or MIDI controller. Both dedicated hardware devices and computer-based software programs that record MIDI data are called MIDI sequencers. MIDI data recorded in this manner is often compared to player-piano-roll data, because in neither case are actual sounds recorded, but only the detailed instructions that direct a device to trigger a sound. For MIDI sequencers these are MIDI messages used to control a MIDI device.

Before MIDI, the first sequencers were devices that recorded keyboard performances onto continuously rolling sheets of paper for subsequent playback by player pianos (such recordings are called *piano rolls*). These mechanical devices are to the modern-day MIDI sequencer as typewriters are to word processors. Strips of paper, tape, and glue were used to correct mistakes or edit material in both player-piano recorders and typewriters. Sequencers and word processors have the Delete key and a virtual Clipboard to accomplish these tasks.

These mechanical sequencers eventually gave way to electronic sequencers. With the arrival of microprocessors and MIDI, dedicated hardware devices for the recording, editing, and playback of MIDI performance data evolved to a high level of sophistication. Some MIDI instruments still contain hardware sequencers.

Early software-based sequencers emulated many of the features found in their hardware counterparts. The advantages of MIDI sequencers based in software were gradually exploited until such programs left the hardware variety in the dust. Software sequencers continue to evolve to provide greater power to composers.

MIDI sequencers have replaced manuscript paper for many composers. For electronic composers, a MIDI sequence is often the only representation of a musical work (besides the sonic realization, of course). Many composers writing for acoustic instruments use MIDI sequencers in place of sketchpads. With the ability of samplers and sample-players to replicate the sound of traditional instruments, it is increasingly common to compose an entire acoustic work as a MIDI sequence and then convert the data into notation using a notation program (see Chapter 22, "Music Notation"). As the 1990s unfold, more and more composers are taking a hybrid approach that combines MIDI sequencing with live performance.

Recording MIDI sequences shares many analogies with recording music on tape — a blindfolded listener might not be able to tell the difference. However, there are more differences between the two types of recording than there are similarities.

In the world of acoustic music we use terms relating to soundwaves — pitch, volume, timbre, rhythm, and articulation. In the world of MIDI these concepts correlate to control codes describing performance actions. To specify pitch, a MIDI sequencer uses note number; for dynamics, MIDI provides the velocity of key strike; for different timbres, a MIDI sequencer sends a patch change; for articulation, the program sends a controller number; and sequencers always keep track of the timings and durations of events to ensure that rhythms are faithfully preserved. Thus, each playing of a MIDI sequence results in a re-performance of what was initially played (or edited), without any signal degradation from multiple-generation recording.

Most MIDI sequencers emulate typical multitrack analog tape recorders in their interface, complete with familiar Play, Record, Pause, Rewind, and Fast-forward controls. One of the main differences between analog tape recorders and MIDI sequencers is that the latter can have hundreds of tracks.

Sound recorded on tape is frozen and cannot be changed, but you can examine and edit a track of MIDI events with great precision. Admittedly, it is possible to change the volume of tape-recorded music as it is re-recorded during a mixdown, but (unless done in the digital domain) this further degrades the signal, and there is no way to isolate different instruments recorded on the same track. A single MIDI track, on the other hand, can have editable data for up to 16 instruments or groups of instruments. This is because each MIDI event is associated with one of 16 MIDI channels, each of which can be directed to different instruments (32 channels are obtained when two sets of 16 channels are distributed between the Macintosh modem and printer ports. Newer schemes provide for 128 to 256 channels from each serial port — see Chapter 8, "Moving Data Around Your Music Network").

There are three fundamental ways to input musical ideas into a MIDI sequencer: real-time, step-time, and algorithmically. No matter how the information is recorded into a MIDI sequencer, the sequencer's real strength is how it can be edited. The scope, type, and ease of editing operations you can apply to MIDI data greatly exceeds that available on analog tape devices. Pitch correction is child's play, as are transposition and tempo changes. Rhythmic correction (quantization) is a standard editing procedure. Editing practices such as cut, copy, paste, merge, and insert are powerful MIDI sequencer operations, which have far less precise analogies in the analog world (splicing tape and bouncing tracks). Finally, some sequencers provide for the translation of MIDI data into conventional music notation (CMN).

All this permits a single person to manipulate a large number of instruments with a degree of control that analog tape recorders could never provide. To develop your musical ideas with this type of flexibility before MIDI, you would have needed a full-time staff of musicians, copyists, and arrangers, and it still would have required weeks to accomplish what a sequencer can do in hours.

MIDI control through the Macintosh has evolved to a point where practically everything one could imagine is supported by one commercially available program or another. Some programs implement certain operations with such flexibility that they give composers the means to creatively control sound in ways that were impossible until now.

Sequencer Features

As MIDI sequencing software approaches the end of its second-generation period, a large number of core features have become standardized. These roughly divide into three areas: input, editing, and playback and are presented in that order.

Because the features stated below are relatively standard, they are not addressed in the discussions of individual MIDI sequencers following them. Note the distinction in the following material between standard options and common variations. Standard options appear in almost all sequencing software, while common variations are found only in some of the programs (usually at least half of them). As you might expect, entry-level sequencers offer a significantly reduced number of features. I have had to take this into consideration when designating a feature or option as standard. Beyond the features listed as common variations, for each feature category below there exists a large body of options that are unique to specific programs. These are the so-called bells and whistles, and they are the focus of the discussions of the individual programs that follow this section.

Input Features

The primary input options for MIDI sequencers are recording MIDI data in real-time and step-time modes. Other ways are manipulating on-screen faders or importing SMFs. Some sequencers offer the direct conversion of file formats from other manufacturers' notation programs, but this is not a standard feature or even prevalent enough to be considered a common variation. Two Macintosh MIDI sequencers offer algorithmic generation of MIDI data (see Chapter 20, "Algorithmic Composition"), but again, this is not widespread enough to count as even a common variation.

Real-time recording

This is typically accomplished by playing along with a metronome click generated by the sequencer at a tempo you specify. Options include a choice to direct the metronome sound to the Macintosh speaker (or audio output) or designate a MIDI note event on a specified channel to function as the click. More elegant implementations provide for accenting the downbeats of these clicks and/or specifying a different click value than the denominator of the time signature (for example, clicking eighth-notes in 4/4).

Standard options

Count-off. Sometimes you can specify the number of clicks for the count-off as well.

Wait for Note. The sequencer starts recording when you play the first note or send the first MIDI event (such as a press on the pedal).

Punch in and out. You designate a measure, beat, and tick at which the sequencer automatically goes into record mode and another point where it automatically stops recording. This allows you to replace material in a certain region without disturbing the music on, before, and after the region. It has the advantage of letting you hear the music up to the point where you want to punch in.

Overdub. Newly recorded material is merged into the music already recorded on a track. The danger of this method is that you can't often separate the overdubbed music with the original music (unless the overdub consists of a different data type, for example, controller information as opposed to note information).

Loop record. This is sometimes referred to as "drum-machine-mode" recording because the option originated with drum machines. A designated region loops repeatedly, and you can either overdub new material into the region or replace existing material. Some programs offer the option to accept or reject the previous "take," or the ability to assign each new take to its own track.

Common variations

Record filter. This is the option to filter out certain types of MIDI data during recording. More advanced implementations let you set a velocity threshold or duration threshold, below which notes are simply ignored.

Multichannel record. Some sequencers let you record from multiple channels simultaneously. Occasionally, you can record from separate serial ports as well. A useful option often offered in conjunction with this is the ability to unmerge data from different channels onto separate tracks. This feature is great for transferring sequences from hardware sequencers to Macintosh sequencers in a single pass, and it is essential for MIDI guitarists.

Multitrack record. Multitrack recording is slightly different from multichannel recording in that you remove the step of having to unmerge the multichannel data onto separate tracks.

Auto-punch. This very useful feature is a combination of Wait for Note and Punch in. A track so enabled goes into record mode the moment you send a note message.

Auto-rewind. This option automatically rewinds the sequence to an indicated point whenever you stop playback or recording.

Auto-shuttle. This lets you define an arbitrary endpoint for the Auto-rewind option. When the sequence reaches this point, it jumps back to the location specified by Auto-rewind.

Capture SysEx data. By far the rarest of the common variations, this lets you store, for example, patch data (as opposed to simply program change messages) at the beginning of a track to make sure that your instruments are always set to exactly the same parameters whenever the sequence is played back.

Step-time recording

This refers to inputting notes individually, by specifying a duration (usually with the Macintosh keyboard) and then pressing the key that you want to assign to that duration. Often you can switch step durations simply by pressing keys on the Macintosh keyboard and lock in one durational value until you change it. A common way to step-enter chords that exceed the range of your finger span is to hold the sustain pedal down, thereby informing the sequencer that a chord is being entered.

Standard options

Mouse input. Most sequencers let you insert or draw notes into graphic editing windows as an alternative to step-time input from a MIDI controller.

Common variations

Velocity control. The handling of velocity data during step-time entry is particularly problematic. Some programs capture velocity data as well as note data. Others set all step-time entered notes to a default velocity (sometimes you can specify what this is). Still others offer a provision for setting velocity on an individual (or remain until changed) basis.

Overdub. Overdubbing during step-time input appears in several programs. This is a particularly thorny issue, because most software does not let you hear other tracks, or even the track you are overdubbing on, while step-inputting. Like overdub in real-time entry, an easy workaround is to record the data on a separate track and then merge this track with the track you want to overdub.

Step duration ≠ to rhythmic value. This extremely valuable option lets you specify a duration for the step-advance of the sequencer that is not the same as the duration of the notes you are inputting. This allows you to, for example, set up a step duration of a quarter note and a rhythmic value of an eighth note. With such a configuration, it is simple to enter a long passage of eighth notes that are each effectively separated by an eighth-note rest. The most sophisticated implementation of this feature (such as Vision's) permits you to enter pitches without regard to rhythms and then to map a rhythmic sequence onto the pitches.

Faders

On-screen assignable faders have almost become a standard feature. The majority of the available Macintosh sequencers offer these for the entry of controller data such as MIDI Volume (Controller 7). Using on-screen faders in conjunction with Controller 7 data, you can merge mix data into your sequence and, in some cases, eliminate the need for dumping your sequence tracks to separate audio tracks of a tape recorder for mixdown purposes. Performer and Cubase have particularly robust implementations of on-screen faders. For a detailed discussion of on-screen faders and MIDI mixing, see Chapter 25, "MIDI Mixing and Studio Automation."

Standard options

Assign on-screen fader to physical control. Because the mouse restricts you to moving a single on-screen fader at a time, many sequencers let you map on-screen fader manipulation to physical hardware controls on your MIDI controller. Dedicated hardware MIDI fader boxes are available for this purpose and are discussed in Chapter 25.

Common variations

Fader groups and interrelationships. Some sequencers let you group faders, set scaling factors between grouped faders, or invert one fader or fader group in relation to another (see Chapter 25).

Import SMFs

All sequencers import (and export) SMFs. Most give you the option of specifying a type 0 SMF (single multichannel track) or a type 1 SMF multitrack file. Although type 1 SMFs are officially supposed to allow multichannel tracks to be mixed with single-channel tracks, some sequencers limit the tracks of type 1 SMFs to a single-channel assignment. Unfortunately, some sequencers also merge separate tracks assigned to the same channel down to a single track when dealing with type 1 SMFs. Note that type 2 SMFs (a collection of sequentially ordered single track patterns) are currently not supported by many Macintosh sequencers, nor are they used much elsewhere in the world of Macintosh music software.

Common variations

Meta-events. Meta-events include text stored with SMFs and also sequence number. It would be wonderful if all sequencers imported all meta-events, but because all meta-events are designated as optional in the MIDI Specification (except End of Track), there is no consistency as to which meta-events are supported by MIDI sequencers. Meta-events include general text comments, copyright notice, sequence name, track name, instrument name, lyrics, markers, cue points, and MIDI channel to which the meta-event applies. Note the distinction between markers and cue points. Some sequencers import cue points and treat them as markers and vice versa.

Editing options

As with most Macintosh software, before you can edit anything, you must first select what is to be edited. This raises issues of sequencer orientation, as detailed in Chapter 16, "Making Music with MIDI."

Contributing to your ability to select data are the five types of data display (also discussed and illustrated in Chapter 16): alphanumeric (also known as event list), bar graph (also known as piano roll), overview (graphic timeline), chunk (patterns or subsequences), and CMN.

While pitch data is often represented as a horizontal bar graph (this makes sense because we have learned to read both music and text from left to right), controller data bar graphs lend themselves to vertical orientation along the lines of a histogram. Sequencers that use this type of display for controller data and related parameters (such as velocity and tempo) often provide for reshaping the numerous values intrinsic to such information simply by drawing in new curves or lines with the mouse.

Bar graph (piano roll) displays are particularly well suited for music destined to be played on electronic instruments. In the so-called serious music community, such displays have been popular since the 1950s and are often called *proportional notation.* Using proportional notation for electronically generated music is the accepted form of pitch representation. It facilitates representations required by the necessity of placing certain types of sounds before or after the beat in consideration of their envelopes. For example, a patch with a very slow attack is often located slightly before the beat, so that it will have developed enough amplitude to be perceived as occurring on the beat. Unfortunately, with the exception of Beyond, One-Step, and Pro 5, the graphic notation employed by MIDI sequencers communicates a single parameter: pitch. See Figure 17-1 for what is missing by restricting such displays to a single parameter.

Data display is an area of considerable variation. Can you view multiple tracks at a time? Can you view tracks in multiple representations at a time? Can you view multiple data types in a single window and if so, can you filter out only the types of data you want to work with? Can you zoom in and out? Can you assign colors to differentiate different types of data?

Selection offers an equal number of conundrums. Your musical language or personal style largely depends on how you vary your material, so you must first be able to easily identify and select the scope and type of data you wish to manipulate. The nature of MIDI sequence data (and musical data itself, for that matter) mandates a flexible approach to the scope of selection that might be required to execute edits of different types. You may want to select the entire sequence, a single track, a group of tracks, a region of a track, the same region on a group of tracks, discontiguous regions on a track or group of tracks, an individual note, discontiguous individual notes, or any of these in combination. Selection of material for editing is extremely important. Your music may or may not be possible to create within a framework that permits only linear and local change rather than discontiguous or global selection.

You may want to select only certain types of data, such as sustain pedal or pitches. Likewise, you may want to edit only a particular parameter, e.g., the velocity or duration of selected pitches. You may even want to edit just those events that occur on the third beats of the selected measures or, perhaps, only the C-sharps in a piece.

The most elegant implementations of selection allow you to specify Boolean criteria to delineate material for editing. You could, for example, limit your selection to all notes within a certain pitch range AND a certain velocity range AND a certain durational range but NOT occurring as the top note of a chord. Fortunately, many sequencers let you do just this. Opcode's Vision provides an example of how far you can take this sort of concept.

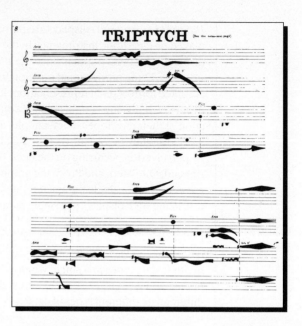

Figure 17-1: Proportional notation similar to the piano-roll notation used by MIDI sequencers has been popular among contemporary composers since the 1950s. In an effort to defeat notational redundancy, this variation was devised on the scheme and employed in a few dozen works in the late 1960s and early 1970s. Here horizontal space = time, width = volume, outline contour = articulation (vibrato, tremolo, forte-piano, etc.), and vertical direction = pitch bend. This page is from *Soneptua* (for string quartet — 1973).

Many editing operations available in MIDI sequencers have counterparts to those found in word processors. Cut, Copy, and Paste are obvious examples. Because I am usually running my MIDI sequencer more than my word processor, I often conceptualize text editing from the other perspective: Changing fonts is like changing patches; changing font weight (to bold for example) is like altering velocity (loudness); changing font size equates to adding Controller 7 data (MIDI volume); and changing the style is like adding modulation or effects — I think of italic as vibrato (it's curly), outline as filtered (the middle is removed), and shadow as reverberation (there is an echo of the character).

Besides the standard menu and dialog box interaction common to the Macintosh, many other types of interfaces apply to editing MIDI data. In some sequencers these methods for changing data values can be applied during playback, although many programs require you to edit data while the sequencer is stopped. Five common approaches are:

❖ **Typing.** New values are entered from the Macintosh keyboard.

❖ **Numerical.** The mouse is used to change values by dragging upward to increment the value and downward to decrement the value. (David Zicarelli originated this now common interface enhancement.)

❖ **MIDI editing.** Playing your MIDI controller replaces values in the selected field or replaces the selected graphic.

❖ **Drawing.** You reshape the contour of existing data by dragging over it with the mouse (often with a cursor referred to as a pencil).

❖ **Dragging.** With the mouse, you drag a block of data to a new location. This is often applied to pitch in a graphic piano roll display. Notes can be dragged horizontally to new temporal locations or vertically for transposition. Option-dragging often creates a draggable copy of the selected region (as is common in graphics programs). It is usually possible to drag the durations of notes to make them longer or shorter. In histogram-type data displays of velocity, for example, you can usually drag the bars representing velocities to increase or decrease their value. Other types of data may be subject to dragging, depending upon the sequencer you are using.

It is increasingly common for sequencers to permit any of the above types of editing during playback. This includes operations requiring dialog box or menu interaction. This approach lends itself to looped regions, where you can hear the effect of your editing on the next pass of the loop. Even if you are not generally a looping type of person, you might want to loop regions while editing just to take advantage of this. The other area where this is effective is sweeping global edits such as transposition, quantization, and humanization.

Creative productivity in the world of computer-assisted composition (which is, after all, what we are discussing) is directly related to the consistency, efficiency, speed of operation, and modality of the software's controls, particularly with respect to editing. While the Macintosh can't help you if you don't have any ideas to start with, you do want the computer to assist you in shaping your ideas into communicative music.

Edit operations

Cut, Copy, Paste

These are standard Macintosh editing operations that are extremely useful in the musical context, where repetition and modified repetition are common. Sequencers differ in the way they treat notes that extend beyond the selected region: Are their durations preserved? Are their durations truncated? Are their durations truncated and corresponding Note-Ons added to the part that extended beyond the selected region? Although most MIDI sequencers support the Macintosh Clipboard, it is rather uncommon for them to support the Macintosh Scrapbook (an unfortunate shortcoming).

Standard options

Merge. This refers to pasting data into a track without replacing the data that already exists on the track. Some sequencers refer to this as "mix" because the material on the Clipboard is combined with existing data.

Insert or Splice. This type of paste inserts data at the cursor location and shifts everything forward in time (i.e., to the right) to make room for the pasted material. The Clipboard is not mixed with existing data.

Repeat. This is often applied to the Paste, Merge, or Insert operations. It allows you to specify the number of copies of the material on the Clipboard that is to be pasted, merged, or inserted.

Clear or Erase. This operation deletes the selected region without copying it to the Clipboard (often leaving the Clipboard intact). A cleared region opens up space where the removed material formerly resided.

Filter. Most sequencers let you specify if the current edit operation should affect all data types in the selected region, just one data type, or a specified group of data types.

Common variations

Delete time or Snip. This is similar to clear or erase, except that the resulting empty space is closed up. Music that formerly occurred after the end of the snipped region shifts backward in time (i.e., to the left), so that it is now adjacent to the music that precedes the region.

Shift or Track shift. This advances or delays selected regions by a specified number of measures, beats, or ticks.

Pitch editing

All sequencers offer transposition of some kind — at the very least, chromatic transposition. Some offer diatonic, modal transposition, or transposition to custom scales. Some sequencers offer the option to insulate certain tracks from transposition. This lets you transpose an entire sequence without altering the tracks that are designated as non-transposable. This is useful for drum tracks, because pitches are directly linked to the drum sounds they produce, and transposition would result in a completely different set of sounds.

Common variations

Remap pitches. This option lets you design an arbitrary list of pitches that get remapped to another set of pitches (typically the chromatic scale). You can use this to change modes, even to change from chromatic music to pentatonic music. One common use of this feature is the conversion of drum parts created on one instrument to a format that will play back on another instrument whose sounds are mapped to different pitches. Often, you can save the custom pitch maps that you create using this feature.

Inversion. Standard pitch inversion, often with the option to specify the axis pitch. Some sequencers also offer retrograde and retrograde-inversion options.

Harmonization. The option to generate parallel chromatic harmonies from single line melodies. This is essentially just a one-step copy, multiple transpose, and merge operation; however, more elegant implementations allow for diatonic harmonization and directing the results produced by such harmonization to separate tracks.

Velocity editing

Manipulating velocity lets you control the loudness of notes. You can create accents, crescendos, decrescendos, and add other volume-related nuances. Creating crescendos and decrescendos is discussed in Chapter 16. You can also edit velocity data to simulate many signal-processing effects (see the coupon in the back of the book for details).

Standard options

Set to constant. Sets velocity values in the selected region to a specified value.

Add to or Subtract from. Adds a constant to or subtracts a constant from all the velocity values in the selected region.

Scale by percentage. Multiplies the velocity values in a selected region by a percentage that you specify.

Common variations

Limit maximum or minimum values. You set a maximum value (e.g., 100). Any velocity value that exceeds this maximum is reduced to the given value (e.g., 120 becomes 100). Conversely, any velocity value that is less than the minimum value you have set (e.g., 87) is changed to that given value (e.g., 79 becomes 87). You can use this to create many special effects (see Chapter 26).

Change smoothly (linearly). You specify a beginning and ending velocity value for the selected region, and the software interpolates a linear change from one to the other. You can use this to create crescendos or decrescendos. Unfortunately, accent patterns are lost in linear velocity curves.

Change smoothly (by percentage). You specify a beginning and ending percentage for the selected region, and the software applies a smooth change by multiplying the intervening velocity values by a progressively increasing or decreasing percentage. This has the advantage of preserving accent patterns. Figure 16-4 in the previous chapter compares linear smooth change to smooth change by percentage.

Randomize. Randomizing velocity values can compensate for passages that have been step-entered with software that does not capture velocity in step-entry mode. It is also useful for humanizing material that may have originated in a notation program, because SMFs created by most notation programs are often assigned a single velocity value (typically 64). Randomization can be offered by percentage or within a range of values.

Duration editing

Most of the same operations applicable to velocity are also available for duration:

❖ Set to constant
❖ Add to or Subtract from
❖ Scale by percentage
❖ Limit to maximum or minimum values
❖ Randomize

Common variations

Extend releases. This option allows you to extend the releases of notes to either the next attack or, in some cases, to the next beat or unit you specify. This feature lets you create perfect legato lines. It is also useful in preparing files for conversion into notation, because durational nuances that are common to performances recorded by MIDI sequencers do not usually correspond to their appropriate representation in CMN.

Controller data editing

Most of the same operations applicable to velocity and duration are also available for controller data. Often, the interface to editing continuous controller data is a pencil tool that lets you reshape a graphic representation of the data by drawing a new curve or line:

❖ Set to constant
❖ Add to or Subtract from
❖ Scale by percentage
❖ Change smoothly (linearly)

Common variations

Thin. This reduces the density of continuous controller data in consideration of MIDI bandwidth. Typically, MIDI controllers generate much more controller data than is actually necessary to produce the intended effect. Usually, you can specify the minimum amount of change that is allowed when the data is thinned.

Reassign. Data of one type is reassigned to the type you indicate. For example, if your MIDI controller has no pan control and you want to manipulate the pan parameter on a module that responds to this message, all you have to do is record modulation wheel data and reassign it to pan.

Generate. Like reassign, you can use this option to compensate for controllers missing from your MIDI controller. This feature also allows you to create continuous data with greater accuracy than with real-time performance recording.

Tempo editing

Nowadays, most sequencers let you insert tempo changes wherever you want. Accelerandos and ritardandos are common options. Subtle randomization of tempos is sometimes offered as a way to humanize step-entered or overly quantized passages. Less common options include time compression and expansion, sometimes called "Fit to Time" (not to be confused with Scale Time — see the sidebar, "Timing Resolution" — which usually deals with durational scaling). A related innovation provided by Pro 5 is the option to automatically scale (compress or expand) the music on the Clipboard to fit the region it is being pasted into.

Quantization

Quantization is a special rhythmic editing option that shifts the location of notes in relation to a rhythmic grid that you specify. Technically, all MIDI data is quantized to the prevailing tick resolution of the sequencer. All MIDI sequencers offer quantization to standard rhythmic values and tuplets to various levels of complexity (see Table 17-1). Some let you set the quantization grid to arbitrary durations expressed as tick values (for example, 47 ticks). In this case, there are two ways that the software might handle the grid: Calculate it from the beginning of the track or reset the grid at each bar line. The latter method is more common, although there are certainly many uses for the former approach.

One use of quantization is to correct rhythmic errors that you might introduce during real-time recording. Unless you are very careful, quantization can result in dehumanizing your music. Calculated use of sensitivity and strength options (see below) can help keep the human feel. You can even use quantization to "uncorrect" performances that are too rhythmically accurate, thus "rehumanizing" them. There are many other uses of quantization. For example, you can create swing performances from music that has been played with a strict metrical timing, and you can change the perceived metrical pulse from triple to duple or vice versa. Chapter 16 includes a detailed discussion of the approaches to quantization, including illustrations of the effects of various quantization options.

Note: Whenever you consider quantization, it is important to stop and think about the fact that live performers never get quantized. The pianist, guitarist, string quartet, or orchestral musician sitting up there on stage is playing without any possibility of rhythmic auto-correction, and it sounds great! On the other hand, remember also that live performers have usually rehearsed their parts to the point where considerations of rhythmic accuracy are no longer an issue. This reveals one of the main justifications for quantization: When you create music within a limited time frame, for example, music for hire, you often don't have time to practice the parts as thoroughly as you would like. In these cases, quantization can be a life saver that allows you to produce more music in a shorter amount of time than would otherwise be possible.

Standard options

Attacks (preserve durations). Note-On events (note attacks) are moved to the nearest quantum grid point that you define in the quantization dialog box. Note-Off events (note releases) travel with the Note-On, so durations are preserved.

Attacks (don't preserve durations). Note-On events are moved to the nearest quantum grid point that you define in the quantization dialog box. Note-Off events are locked in place, so durations are altered.

Common variations

Attacks and releases. Both Note-On and Note-Off events are moved to the nearest quantum grid point that you define in the quantization dialog box. Durations of notes are altered. Because Note-Offs may move forward or backward in time, depending upon which grid point they are closest to, some durations may become shorter while others may become longer.

Releases only (preserve durations). Note-Off events are moved to the nearest quantum grid point that you define in the quantization dialog box. Note-On events travel with the Note-Off, so durations are preserved.

Releases only (don't preserve durations). Note-Off events are moved to the nearest quantum grid point that you define in the quantization dialog box. Note-On events are locked in place and do not travel with the Note-Off, so durations are altered.

Strength. When a quantization operation has to move an event, the Strength setting determines how close to the grid the event will be moved. A setting of 100% moves the event right to the grid point. A setting of 50% moves it to a point halfway between its original location and the grid point. This is very useful to avoid over-quantization, which dehumanizes the effect of playback.

Sensitivity. The sensitivity setting creates a "window" in which events are considered as candidates for quantization. Normally, this window extends from the middle of one quantum unit to the middle of the next (this places the actual grid points at the center of the sensitivity window). A positive sensitivity setting reduces the size of this window by a percentage. For example, a sensitivity setting of 50% results in an area equivalent to half the quantum unit centered between every two grid points that is not considered during quantization. Such a setting is useful to quantize downbeats while leaving "swung" notes untouched. A negative sensitivity setting inverts the window of effectiveness. For example, a setting of −50% creates a window equal to half the quantum unit and centered on the midpoint between every two adjacent quantization grid points. This allows you to correct major rhythmic inaccuracies without affecting notes that are close to the beat. Some sequencers let you set an asymmetrical window of sensitivity. With this option, the window is shifted in relation to the grid point (positive sensitivities) or in relation to the midway point between two grid points (negative sensitivities).

Swing. Swing options are normally concerned with every other grid point, usually representing the second eighth note of each beat. Some sequencers automatically interpolate an imaginary swing grid point in between the ones you define with the quantum unit, but these are still concerned with every other grid point. There are several approaches to swing settings. In Vision, for example, a setting of 50% places the eighth note exactly halfway between two quarter notes (no swing is produced). A setting of 67% moves the eighth note ⅔ of the way toward the end of the grid, producing a swing effect as if the eighth note was played as the final note in an eighth-note triplet. A setting of 100% pushes the eighth note all the way forward to coincide with the next quarter-note attack. In Performer, a swing setting of 100% is the same as a setting of 67% in Vision. A swing setting of 0% in Performer equals a setting of 50% in Vision, and a setting of 300% in Performer is equivalent to a setting of 100% in Vision. Because all programs differ in their handling of swing options, it's a good idea to read the relevant portion of the manual closely.

Offset or Shift. This option allows you to shift the quantization grid by a specified number of ticks either forward or backward with relation to the actual beat lines defined by the sequencer. You use this option to create "feel" effects (see Chapter 25, "MIDI Mixing and Studio Automation") and also to compensate for sounds that have exceptionally slow attack segments in their envelopes.

Randomize or Humanize or Smear. These options introduce some randomness into the quantization operation to avoid the dehumanization often inherent to overly quantized music. In this context, randomization is applied to attack points. Usually the effect is identical to the one produced if you applied a continually changing value to the Strength setting (see above). Often you can set a field of randomness, as if, for example, the Strength setting were being randomly varied within a range of 35% to 60%. Some programs, such as Pro 5, allow you to specify this field of randomness in terms of ticks rather than percentage. This gives you more control and generally produces better results. Using subtle quantization randomness in conjunction with randomness settings for velocity, duration, and tempo (see above) can, for example, reduce the mechanical feeling of music that was imported from a notation program.

Combination of options. You can often use Strength, Sensitivity, Swing, and Offset in combination to produce a better effect when applying one of the quantization options that are detailed at the beginning of this section. Strength and Sensitivity are two options that work particularly well together.

Deflam. This option, offered by several sequencers, quantizes only chords, leaving non-chord tones untouched. Deflamming does not move the chords toward a quantization grid point, in fact, you do not have the option of specifying a quantum grid. Instead, you indicate a search width (in ticks), and Deflam looks for notes that are close enough together to fall within this proximity window. When it finds a group of notes that fulfill the criteria, their attack locations are averaged and the attack point of each note is aligned to this average. This may involve moving the attacks of all or some of the notes in question. Durations are not altered. The first program to offer this option on the Macintosh, Performer, goes a bit further with its DeFlam algorithm in that it attempts to detect grace notes and truly rolled chords and leave them untouched.

Quantize on input. Some software lets you apply quantization algorithms to incoming data as it is being recorded. The disadvantage of this approach is that you won't often have the original performance data available for editing.

Quantize on output. Another approach is to apply quantization on the fly, while the sequencer is playing back. This has the advantage of preserving your original performance data. Other forms of quantization, applied in non-real time, are almost always destructive, meaning that once the data is quantized the original performance cannot be retrieved, unless the quantization operation is immediately undone. A good practice when using destructive quantization is to keep a backup copy of the track in its unquantized form. The disadvantage of quantization on output is that it requires additional processor time and therefore can result in rhythmic distortion in cases of extreme MIDI output activity.

Real-time determination of the beat. Some sequencers give you the option to Tap Tempo on input. This means that you can tap a foot pedal or any control capable of outputting a momentary MIDI event and have the sequencer interpret this as the beat lines to which to align your performance. The advantage is that you can speed up and slow down, adding expressive tempo nuances at will. You are not locked into the inhuman pacing of the Macintosh-generated metronome click. The disadvantages of this approach are that many people have spent a good deal of time ridding themselves of their feet-tapping habit during performance. These features are discussed at length in Chapter 26, "Film and Video Applications," under the heading "Human-triggered synchronization."

Post-determination of the beat. This is the opposite of the previous option. With post-determination of the beat, you can play completely freely, without a Macintosh-generated metronome click or tapping your foot. After you have recorded your performance, you play back the sequence and tap in the beat lines, either by tapping a key on your MIDI controller or by tapping another control such as a foot pedal. The beat lines that you tap in are used as the reference points for all subsequent quantization operations. Often, a tempo map is created as a consequence of this operation to ensure that playback conforms to the tempo that you tapped in.

Patch and note names

It has become increasingly common for sequencers to provide for referring to patches by name. This means you don't have to remember what patch number corresponds to which sound on a particular instrument. Instead, when you want to insert a patch change message, you are presented with a pop-up list of all the patch names for the instrument assigned to the track you are currently editing. Sometimes lists of factory patches for popular instruments are included with the software. If you do any custom patch editing, you may need to type in your patch names during a setup stage. In the case of Opcode's sequencers, you can link your sequencer tracks to patch lists stored in their patch librarian and editor/librarians (see Chapters 11 and 12). A related feature that is gaining in popularity is the option to define names for individual notes. This is particularly useful for drum tracks, where each note might trigger a different percussion sound.

Output options

The two types of output to expect from a sequencer are playback capabilities and file-saving capabilities. In addition to saving files in the program's native format, an important consideration is the ability to save sequences in SMF format (preferably type 1). In conjunction with saving SMFs, an option to expand looped sections to their appropriate notes is desirable (if you use loops). This is because there is no provision in the MIDI Specification to indicate looped regions in SMFs (there are provisions for loops in the official MIDI Sample Dump Standard, so don't get confused about this). Other types of files that you might be able to save are those that define your custom configuration of your MIDI sequencer.

Playback control

All sequencers offer playback buttons or keyboard commands that initiate playback. Many have fast-forward and rewind controls. In the case of fast-forward, it is usually possible to listen to the music play while the sequence speeds by. To listen to your music during rewind (i.e., backwards) is a luxury feature found only in Opcode's sequencers. They also support "scrubbing," a related jog-wheel type playback mode in which you control forward or backward playback and playback speed by moving the mouse to the right or left.

Standard options

32-channel playback. Even sequencers with only 16 tracks offer playback channel assignments to span the full 32 channels offered with two MIDI data streams, one out the modem port and the other out the printer port. Many professional-level sequencers now offer compatibility with cableized interfaces that provide for 128 to 512 channels (see Chapter 8, "Moving Data Around Your Music Network").

SPP synchronization. All MIDI sequencers support the rudimentary Song Position Pointer (SPP) synchronization protocol sometimes called MIDI Sync (see Chapter 26, "Film and Video Applications").

Chase Controllers. Chase Controllers (sometimes called "event chasing" or simply, "chase") is an option that sets all controllers to the correct current values when you start playback in the middle of a sequence. With this option enabled, the sequencer "looks back" along each track to see if there have been any patch changes, controller changes, or even Note-On events that would be in effect at the point where playback is to commence were the sequence to have been played from the beginning. If any such events are discovered, the sequencer adjusts the settings at the current location accordingly. Nearly all MIDI sequencers offer some form of the Chase Controllers option. The more sophisticated programs let you specify precisely which controllers should be chased. Being able to specify exactly which event types are to be examined is useful, because enabling such Chase options often means that when you press the Play button there will be a moment's hesitation while the sequencer scans each track in the sequence up to the current point. The fewer the number of controllers to be chased, the less time this takes.

Common variations

Mouse feedback. Many sequencers offer an option for audible feedback whenever you touch a note with the mouse, regardless of whether the note is represented in an event-list, piano-roll, or notation display. Some enhance this feature by allowing you to select a group of pitches and to trigger their playback.

Fader animation. Sequencers that record the movement of on-screen faders often animate the motion of these faders during playback. While this might at first seem to be a cute courtesy feature, in fact, observing the continually updating locations of on-screen faders during playback can provide you with critical information necessary to locate specific problems in your sequence. Unfortunately, fader animation consumes processor time and is best disabled (unless you have a fast Macintosh) or enabled only during the editing process.

Looping. The option to loop an entire track can be assumed, but that's about the only assumption that is safe to make. Some sequencers add other options to looping, such as looping the entire sequence or specified regions on tracks (some restrict such regions to measure boundaries). Some allow you to specify the number of repetitions of a looped region. More elegant implementations provide for looping regions and tracks of different lengths without requiring that the looped sections coincide. Still other sequencers provide for nested loops, that is, loops within loops within loops, and so on. Two rare options are being able to specify that certain parameters change on certain iterations of the loop (for example specified tracks are muted or transposed on every third repetition) and the capability to expand looped regions into the note data that results from their playback.

Scrolling playback. Watching your music scroll by while it is playing back can be an aid to locating bloopers or sections for editing. If you hear a problem, simply stop the sequencer and you're already at the right spot (otherwise, it might take some time to realign the editing windows to the position indicated by the counter). It's the sort of feature that makes a big impression on potential purchasers of programs, but you shouldn't let it influence your decision. Scrolling playback places a good deal of extra load on your Macintosh's processor (which already has its hands full simply dealing with the MIDI data).

Time code synchronization. Synchronizing your sequencer to SMPTE Time Code is an option for all professional-level sequencers. The most popular way to accomplish this is through the conversion of SMPTE data into MIDI Time Code (MTC). Other ways to achieve SMPTE Time Code synchronization include Indirect Time Lock, Direct Time Lock (DTL), and Enhanced Direct Time Lock (DTLe). Sequencer synchronization is the main topic of Chapter 26.

Human-triggered synchronization and Tap Tempo. This feature is related to the post-determination of the beat option discussed above under "Quantization." Human-triggered synchronization lets you designate a trigger event, for example a note on your MIDI controller, and then tap this note to advance the sequence a single beat at a time. This allows you to "conduct" the playback of your sequence and add expressive tempo fluctuations and nuance. This is extremely useful when synchronizing sequenced materials to live performers in, for example, an opera or music theater production. Sequencers that provide for this often let you capture your tapped tempo performance as a tempo map for subsequent editing or to use as the default tempo map for all future playback.

Customization

Many programs offer the option for customization to suit your personal modus operandi. For example, Vision permits saving Input Maps and Transpose Maps as files that the program reads when it is booted. Other global preferences may be set as well, such as Favorite Controllers, "Note Naming Conventions" (middle C = C3 or C4), and many display options.

Virtual instrument definitions. This is another type of user configuration option that some sequencers provide for saving in a setup file or directly into the MIDI sequencer. Virtual instruments are sound entities that you can refer to by name during program operation. Instead of remembering that your solo trombone sound is assigned to MIDI channel 12 on the printer port, you can simply name that channel and port "Solo Trombone." Virtual instruments do not need to consist of a single sound. You might define a virtual instrument that is made up of any number of channels assigned to any number of cables or serial ports on your MIDI interface. Simply calling up that instrument by name directs output to all the appropriate destinations. Virtual instruments are discussed and illustrated in Chapter 16, "Making Music with MIDI," under the heading "Nested levels of abstraction."

User-definable program control via MIDI. The mapping of your sequencer's transport controls onto little-used keys of your MIDI controller is now a common feature, and you can usually save them in the setup file. Nowadays this idea has been extended to its logical conclusion. You can assign almost any sequencer function to be triggered by any key on a MIDI controller or on the Macintosh keyboard. This saves you from having to keep moving your hands back and forth from the musical keyboard to the Macintosh's keyboard. Because you might only have a single MIDI keyboard that you want to use to play notes on, some programs provide for a special key that toggles the MIDI keyboard's remote control functions on and off.

Timing Resolution

The *timing resolution* of a sequencer indicates the smallest rhythmic value that can be expressed. Timing resolution is usually discussed in values called ticks, clocks, units, or pulses. These units represent the number of divisions of a quarter note and are in essence identical to PPQN (pulses per quarter note — early MIDI sequencers had a resolution of 24 PPQN). Most Macintosh sequencers have a timing resolution of 480 ticks per quarter note (1 tick = a 4,096th note).

Timing resolution also reflects the accuracy with which a sequencer can record and play back data. For example, even with a timing resolution of 480 ticks, the shortest possible space between two notes played in a tempo of 60 beats per minute (BPM) is two milliseconds (that's about half as fast as MIDI is capable of). While it is unlikely that you will play anything

that fast, it is likely that you might play notes that fall into the "pocket" between two ticks. These get rounded off to their nearest tick by virtue of the timing resolution of the sequencer. For all practical purposes, the sequencer is quantizing the incoming data to its timing resolution constantly.

Timing resolution places limitations on the accuracy of a sequencer's quantization operations. For example, at a timing resolution of 96 ticks, it is theoretically impossible to accurately quantize a sixteenth-note quintuplet. Each quintuplet sixteenth should have a value of 19.2 ticks, but fractional ticks are not possible. To get around this problem, most sequencers with a resolution of 96 ticks would assign four of the notes to a duration of 19 ticks and the fifth note to a duration of 20 ticks. Similarly, to

(continued on next page)

quantize 13 sixteenths in the time of 12, a 480-tick resolution sequencer would assign 12 notes to a duration of 37 ticks and the 13th note to a duration of 36 ticks. You can easily see how your sequencer treats these situations by step-entering a string of consecutive sixteenth notes and then quantizing them to various tuplets and observing the changing tick values in the event list.

Timing resolution has an impact on the playback of chords. Remember that MIDI data is serial and all chords are simply very fast arpeggiations, even though they appear to be simultaneous in the displays of MIDI sequencers. Usually these arpeggios are so tight that we perceive them as chords. However, at a very slow tempo with a low timing resolution, it is possible to hear the attack of each note in a chord individually. For example, One-Step has a timing resolution of 96 PPQN. At a *largo* tempo of 40 BPM (M.M. 40), the notes of a chord are over 15 ms apart, well within the range that allows them to be perceived as separate attacks. Many sequencers allow tempos as slow as 10 BPM, so these notes might be spaced as far as 60 ms apart. This is still a good deal better than a 24-PPQN sequencer, which would have these same notes spaced 240 ms apart (about a quarter of a second). If you intersperse a bit of controller data along with the chord (say aftertouch or modulation wheel), the distance between the notes increases even more.

Note that some sequencers have a different resolution for different functions. For example, Cubase has a recording, editing, and playback resolution of 192 ticks, but internally, the software uses 384 ticks to resolve incoming time code and calculate tempos. A resolution of 192 is a rather coarse resolution for a Macintosh sequencer, especially one that is as powerful as Cubase.

Sequencers running on slower computers perform better with coarser timing resolutions. Because of this, Dr. T's Beyond lets you choose different timing resolutions to accommodate slower or faster Macintoshes.

It is possible to increase the timing resolution of a MIDI sequencer by using one of two techniques. The first way is to double the tempo while you are recording. For example, if you want a tempo of 80 BPM, record with the sequencer running at 160 BPM. All of your quarter notes are then interpreted as half notes by the sequencer (it's all relative, so this has no effect upon playback other than to make it more accurate). If the sequencer has a resolution of 480 ticks, recording in this way effectively doubles the resolution to 960 ticks per quarter note. The disadvantage of this approach is that you have to keep this in mind during all subsequent edits that require you to specify values in ticks.

The second technique is to use the sequencer's time expansion option (often called Scale Time), if available, to double the values of all notes and move them accordingly with respect to their temporal location. Then set the tempo to twice as fast as you recorded your material. The effect is the same as the method described in the previous paragraph, with one exception: The accuracy at the recording stage is not increased. However, all subsequent editing and playback is possible with twice the accuracy.

In neither of these two approaches are you restricted to simply doubling the timing resolution. By quadrupling the tempo, you can achieve a timing resolution that is effectively four times more accurate than that normally supported by the software, and so on.

Table 17-1 displays the number of ticks that equate to various rhythmic values (including tuplets) at the various timing resolutions offered by Macintosh sequencers. Where an exact value is impossible to achieve at the indicated timing resolution, the table does not display a value. In most cases this does not mean that a program with that timing resolution cannot convincingly record or play back this rhythmic value, because the software rounds off the durations to the nearest approximation of the intended rhythm (see the discussion about quantizing tuplets).

Part Three: Composition

Table 17-1: Timing resolution conversion

Resolution	48	96	192	240	384	480
Whole (dotted)	288	576	1152	1440	2304	2880
Whole	192	384	768	960	1536	1920
Half (dotted)	144	288	576	720	1152	1440
Half	96	192	384	480	768	960
Quarter (dotted)	72	144	288	360	576	720
Quarter	48	96	192	240	384	480
Quarter (5:4)				192		384
Quarter (5:3)				144		288
Quarter (5:2)				96		192
Quarter (3:2)	32	64	128	160	256	320
Eighth (dotted)	36	72	144	180	288	360
Eighth	24	48	96	120	192	240
Eighth (5:4)				96		192
Eighth (5:3)				72		144
Eighth (5:2)				48		96
Eighth (3:2)	16	32	64	80	128	160
Sixteenth (dotted)	18	36	72	90	144	180
Sixteenth	12	24	48	60	96	120
Sixteenth (5:4)				48		96
Sixteenth (5:3)				36		72
Sixteenth (5:2)				24		48
Sixteenth (3:2)	8	16	32	40	64	80
Thirtysecond (dotted)	9	18	36	45	72	90
Thirtysecond	6	12	24	30	48	60
Thirtysecond (5:4)				24		48
Thirtysecond (5:3)				18		36
Thirtysecond (5:2)				12		24
Thirtysecond (3:2)	4	8	16	20	32	40
Sixtyfourth (dotted)		9	18		36	45
Sixtyfourth	3	6	12	15	24	30
Sixtyfourth (5:4)				12		24
Sixtyfourth (5:3)				9		18
Sixtyfourth (5:2)				6		12
Sixtyfourth (3:2)	2	4	8	10	16	20
One-twentyeighth (dotted)			9		18	
One-twentyeighth		3	6		12	15
One-twentyeighth (5:4)				6		12
One-twentyeighth (5:3)						9
One-twentyeighth (5:2)				3		6
One-twentyeighth (3:2)	1	2	4	5	8	10
Two-fiftysixth (dotted)					9	
Two-fiftysixth		3		6		
Two-fiftysixth (5:4)				3		6
Two-fiftysixth (5:3)						
Two-fiftysixth (5:2)						3
Two-fiftysixth (3:2)		1	2		4	5

Chunking, Chaining, and Pattern Editing

This feature is special among the newer bells and whistles — it's more like a gong and foghorn with respect to the power it packs. Although pattern mani-pulation of this type has always been common within dedicated hardware sequencers, it has largely been ignored by Macintosh MIDI sequencer developers. (Opcode Systems is one exception. Their sequencers have included chaining options from the very beginning.)

If you like to conceive of music in sections or chunks or if your compositions contain any repetition, you have the option to chain various subsequences together into one long composition. You can identify musical fragments and ideas as separate objects (within a database, if you prefer to think of it that way). These objects are called patterns, chunks, sequences, subsequences, blocks, or modules, depending upon the MIDI sequencer you are using. In this chapter, I generally refer to these objects as chunks because that word is the accepted term that has been used by music theorists for years and it is the most accurate description of such higher-level objects. In 1989, Mark of the Unicorn trademarked the terms "Chunks" and "Chunking," so note that I use it with a lowercase *c* to denote its generic meaning.

Chunk-manipulation tools give composers and arrangers a way to assemble and manipulate musical material from increasingly greater levels of abstraction, with results that are far more efficient and effective than addressing each musical note as an individual event. Composition from the chunk level may yield new chunks of greater complexity (called songs, arrangements, patterns, or sequences, depending upon your software), nestable to any degree. Conversely, decomposition permits a return to the note or instruction level. Such methodology is often much closer to the way that composers actually conceptualize a work of music.

Most programs offering this feature allow you to chain chunks linearly, although some programs provide for vertical assemblages as well. There are a wide variety of interfaces to assembling chunks into songs. Some programs represent chunks as graphic icons or bars that you can drag to rearrange (and in true Macintosh fashion, usually Option-drag to copy). Others require setting up a song list or typing a series of letters (each representing a chunk or subsequence) that desig-nate the order the chunks will follow.

In many cases, copies of chunks that are re-used in the same song reflect all changes made to the original chunk from which the copies were produced. More sophisticated provisions offered by several professional-level sequencers allow altering certain characteristics of these copies (such as transposition) without severing the links to their sources. In the best implementations of chunking you can sever the links between copied chunks and their sources and edit the newly unlinked chunk as a discrete object.

As the display and manipulation of musical ideas become more and more hierarchical, you may find it advantageous to examine your personal conceptual model of a musical composition closely. Depending upon what you discover about yourself, you may be attracted to one or another of the various options for "zooming out" to higher levels of abstraction and manipulating your musical ideas as separate objects.

Software Solutions

Most of the MIDI sequencers available for the Macintosh now provide all the basic functionality one could desire from this genre of software. If you wanted to divide the available products into two categories, the main features that differentiate a professional program from a non-professional one (or a semi-professional one) are its synchronization features, the number of output MIDI channels supported, the number of available tracks, and the ease of accomplishing certain edit operations.

Two of the non-professional sequencers are in actuality just stripped-down versions of professional sequencers offered by the same company. Opcode's EZ Vision has many of the same options as their Vision (although it takes a different approach to the main data display window). Passport's Trax is simply their Pro 5 professional-level sequencer with a restricted feature set. Two others bear a similar relationship to now-discontinued programs.

At the higher end of the professional MIDI sequencers, the provision for including digital audio tracks intermixed with MIDI tracks is the current rage. In 1990, Opcode's StudioVision became the first product to offer this feature. Mark of the Unicorn's Digital Performer and Steinberg's Audio Cubase followed in 1991. These MIDI-sequencing-plus-digital-audio programs are covered in Chapter 18, "MIDI Sequencing with Digital Audio."

In the following discussions of 11 Macintosh MIDI sequencers, I focus attention on the unique features of each program rather than enumerate all the options available. For the latter information you can consult the feature tables at the end of this chapter.

Classifications

I have divided the available sequencers into three categories: professional, non-professional (including entry-level sequencers), and shareware. The shareware options are non-professional sequencers.

Besides the standard options and various bells and whistles, I have identified seven features that are crucial for professional-level sequencing. If any of these seven are omitted in a program, it belongs in the non-professional category. Here are the seven crucial features:

MIDI Manager compatibility

Compatibility with Apple's MIDI Manager opens up a world of possibilities for multiple program interaction as discussed in Chapter 8. Future Apple CPUs will require MIDI Manager compatibility so non-obsolescence is guaranteed.

32 or more MIDI channels

Macintosh musicians doing professional sequencing usually require more than 16 MIDI channels. If the cableization protocols established by Mark of the Unicorn's MIDI Time Piece and Opcode's Studio 5 are incorporated into the official MIDI Specification (for example, after this book is in print), you should change this heading to read "Greater-than-32-channels" (or "Supports cableization") and adjust the categorization of the sequencers accordingly.

Sync to time code (MTC)

Professional sequencing activities generally involve synchronization to clock sources other than MIDI Beat Clocks or SPP (see Chapter 26). MTC, which translates SMPTE to MIDI, is currently the most common professional sync protocol.

Import/export SMFs

The ability to import and export both type 1 and type 0 SMFs (see Chapter 1, "Background") ensures compatibility across applications by different vendors, transcription into notation software, and cross-platform file interchange and collaboration. Compatibility with either type 1 or type 0 SMFs and not both is considered a partial implementation and only warrants a half-circle in Table 17-2.

Greater-than-16-tracks

Some sequencers have only 16 tracks because there are officially only 16 MIDI channels. Professional sequencing very often requires more than 16 tracks.

All event list display, direct editing

Professional-level MIDI sequencing requires a representation of MIDI data at the absolute most detailed level, that of an event list which includes all MIDI events on a track (preferably with a view filter by data type). Direct editing refers to being able to edit values on this display of raw MIDI data directly, without having to enter a dialog box. This is important because it is often necessary to see surrounding events while making changes to the event list (i.e., dialog-box-style editing of individual items on an event list display — à la Rhapsody — is not considered a complete implementation). Direct editing usually means that you can tab from value to value or use the return or arrow keys to move from event to event. The option to edit regions in an event list display is also implied; however, discontiguous selection of regions is not a requirement.

Chunking, chaining, patterns

Being able to deal with your musical ideas from the greater level of abstraction offered by linking sequence chunks, patterns, or chaining sequences or subsequences into songs is a feature supporting the speed requirements and musical thought processes of musicians.

To be considered as a professional-level sequencer, the software must implement all seven of these features completely.

Table 17-2: Sequencer classifications

Classification features

	Ballade	Beyond	Cubase	Deluxe Recorder	EZ Vision	One-Step	Performer	Pro 5	Rhapsody	Trax	Vision
MIDI Manager compatible	●	●	●		●		●	●	●	●	●
32 or more MIDI channels	●	●	●	●	●		●	●	●		●
Sync to time code (MTC)	●	●	●			♪	●	●	●		●
Import/export SMFs	♪	●	●	●	●	♪	●	●	♪	●	●
Greater-than-16-tracks		●	●				●	●	●	●	●
All event list display with direct editing		●	●				●	●	♪		●
Chunking, chaining, pattern manipulation	●	●	●		●		●	●	●		●
Classification	Non-Pro	Pro	Pro	Non-Pro	Non-Pro	Non-Pro	Pro	Pro	Non-Pro	Non-Pro	Pro

Non-Professional Sequencers

There are six non-professional sequencers available for the Macintosh: Ballade, Deluxe Recorder, EZ Vision, One-Step, Rhapsody, and Trax. Interestingly, only two of these sequencers were developed as a product from the ground up. The other four are simply "junior" versions of professional-level sequencers. Deluxe Recorder is a stripped-down version of Resonate's never-released Portrait. EZ Vision, as the name implies, is a simplified alternative to Vision; One-Step is the descendant of the now-discontinued MIDIPaint; and Trax is the junior version of Pro 5. With the exception of EZ Vision, which underwent considerable interface redesign, these four derivative non-professional sequencers share their look and feel with their older "siblings."

In the case of the four derivative or junior version sequencers, it is tempting to draw the conclusion that the companies saw an opportunity to make a quick buck by stripping out features from their professional sequencers and marketing the result as an entry-level program. In some cases, this may be an accurate reading of the situation. However, I am more inclined to interpret these efforts as a legitimate attempt to address a segment of the music industry that does not require all the bells and whistles of the professional products. Don't forget that these bells and whistles almost always have associated hidden expenses, (e.g., requirements of storage space, additional RAM, faster machines, and high learning curve). Still, it is curious that the developers of professional-level sequencers have not made an attempt to create an entry-level program from scratch.

The two non-professional programs that were developed from the ground up are Rhapsody and Ballade (Ballade is a much enhanced version of a previously available IBM sequencer). Both are newcomers to the Macintosh MIDI sequencing community. In these two cases, the developers seemed more concerned with how many professional-level options they could bring into their software, rather than the elimination of options not needed by beginners. This resulted in two programs that fall just a bit short of fulfilling the requirements of professional sequencing, yet require a somewhat longer learning curve than the four derivative programs. They offer many professional-level features, but, being the initial releases by their respective developers, their list of options may still be growing. Because of this, it is possible that future releases of these products will graduate to the level of professional sequencers.

All six of the non-professional sequencers have less than seven of the features designated above as requirements for professional MIDI sequencing. Every one of them can import and export SMFs, and all but one omit an event list display in favor of piano-roll notation or, in the case of Ballade, CMN. All except Rhapsody and Trax limit the number of sequencer tracks to 16. Beyond these generalizations, the differences are quite striking.

Ballade

Dynaware's Ballade is the latest arrival on the Macintosh MIDI sequencing scene at the time of this writing. In many ways, the approach to MIDI sequencing offered by Ballade is significantly different from all the other sequencers covered in this chapter. Foremost among the differences to standard sequencers is the fact that Ballade represents MIDI data as notation rather than a piano-roll-type bar graph or an event list. This fact alone required the developers to create new types of interfaces to the input and editing options that are now considered standard by the Macintosh music community.

Ballade is optimized for use with General MIDI-compatible instruments (see Chapter 1) or in conjunction with Roland's GS Standard instruments. Devices that conform to the greater part of this standard include the CM64, CM32L, CM32P, and MT32. Roland's newer SC-55 (Sound Canvas) is completely compatible with their GS Standard. The GS Standard is a superset of General MIDI. In addition to all the standard messages and formats of General MIDI, the GS Standard adds a few messages that are specifically designed to control Roland devices (although their specification is not proprietary, so other manufacturers could implement these options if they wanted to).

Fortunately, Ballade does not require you to use General MIDI or the GS Standard. If you do select either of these configurations, some additional device control is available, but you do not give anything up (in relation to what is offered by other sequencers) when you configure the sequencer for other setups (see Figure 17-2).

Ballade displays MIDI data in CMN in the Score Editor window. In this window, you can record music in four ways: real-time recording, step-time recording, manipulating an on-screen keyboard, and clicking notes on the screen with the mouse. You can also record music in the Mixer window in real time. The Score Editor (Figure 17-3) lets you input, view, and edit a single track at a time, but you

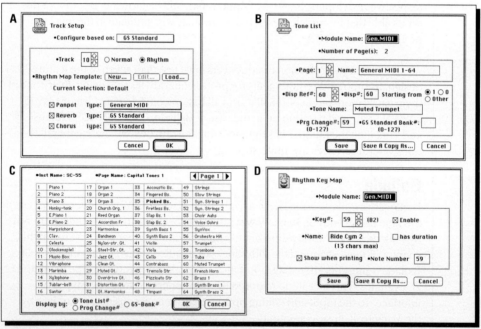

Figure 17-2: (A) Track Setup options for Ballade. Each track (MIDI numbers are equivalent to track numbers) can be set to a different standard if you want, as indicated by the configuration pop-up menu. You can set the messages used for Panpot, Reverb, and Chorus to conform to different specifications as well. You can also create your own custom configurations. **(B)** If you designate a track as a normal track, you can load a patch list (called a "Tone List" in Ballade) or create your own using this dialog box. The program comes with program maps for Roland's CM series, MT-32, U-20, Sound Canvas, and also the DX7-II, SY22, M1, and SQ-1. **(C)** Subsequently, you can choose patches by name here in the Track List or in the Score Editor window. **(D)** If you designate a track as a rhythm track, you can load any of the General MIDI or GS Standard note name maps. Alternatively, you can create your own maps with this dialog box. If you choose, the drum note names will print with the drum staff when you print a score.

Figure 17-3: Ballade's Score Editor, On-screen Keyboard, and associated palettes. This keyboard has more features than any to be found in a Macintosh music program. You have the option to use the keyboard chromatically or constrain the pitches to a specific scale or mode in a particular key by way of the pop-up menus pictured. Dots appear on the notes of that scale (here, a C Lydian 7th scale is selected). The keyboard also sports Pitch Bend and Modulation wheels. While depressing a key, you can hold the Option or Command key down and drag the mouse to add these effects. Note that the on-screen keyboard appears as a separate program in MIDI Manager's Patchbay, so you can treat it as a third MIDI port that can be used in conjunction with other software. **(A)** The Tool palette. The Switch Staff tool (middle of right column) lets you split notes from the treble to bass staves on a grand staff. You simply click the line where you want the split point to be. The MicroLens tool (lower right) brings up a parameter box for every event you click. Several examples of these are pictured in this screenshot of the main Score Editor. **(B)** The Note palette. When you click

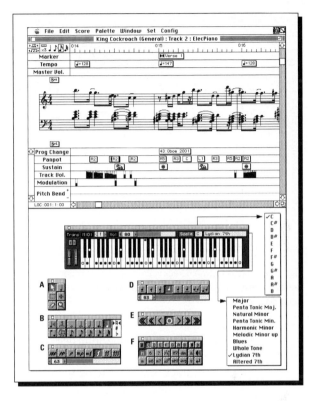

notes onto the staff with the mouse, they appear exactly where you click, that is, they don't slide over to the left like in a notation program. Instead, Ballade fills in the appropriate rests up to the point where you clicked. **(C)** The Velocity palette. You can choose from preset velocity values (the dynamic markings at the top) or use the slider bar at the bottom to set a precise velocity. **(D)** The Duration palette. Here you specify the performance duration of notes independently from the notated rhythmic values. **(E)** The Micro Adjust palette lets you shift selected events forward or backward in time by 1/48, 2/48, or 3/48 of a quarter note. This does not affect the notation of the events if they are pitches. **(F)** The Chord palette lets you enter chords (not chord symbols) quickly. All such chords are in close position, and the arrows toward the right of the Chord palette scroll through the various inversions.

can select across all tracks if you want. Track staves can be configured as a grand staff or a one-line treble or bass staff. The software displays global events above the staves and events that pertain to the current staff below it. The graphic controller data at the bottom of the screen can be quantized just like notes. When you do this, the data is thinned to the prevailing quantization unit. As you can see from Figure 17-3, a good deal of information is available on a single screen.

You use the vertical scroll bar to scroll through your 16 tracks in the Score Editor. If one of your tracks (typically track 10) happens to be a rhythm track, the

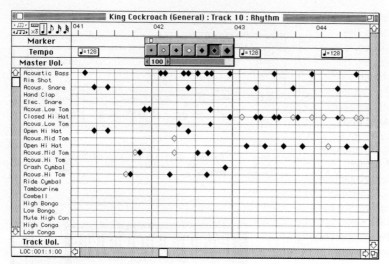

Figure 17-4: A typical rhythm track in Ballade's Score Editor. This Rhythm Track Editor brings up the pictured Rhythm palette where you can choose diamond notes according to velocity.

notation changes to one that makes it much easier to visualize your drum parts (see Figure 17-4). Pitches are named according to the sounds they trigger, and drumlike note-heads are used for display.

One very useful and innovative feature of Ballade is the option to save any phrase, track, or region as a pattern. The program comes with a variety of rhythmic patterns (mapped to the various drum maps supported by Ballade) and also accompanimental patterns. You can recall these or your own patterns from disk for insertion on any track displayed in the Score Editor. This feature is enhanced by the fact that you can audition patterns from within the Open File dialog box prior to inserting them in the score.

Ballade's other main window is its Mixer (see Figure 17-5). This presents 16 console modules, each corresponding to a specific sequencer track and MIDI channel. You can record Volume and Pan fader manipulation, and your mixes are animated during playback. Alternatively, you can save and recall snapshots of any collection of parameter settings. If you are using a GS Standard device, additional recordable faders appear for Reverb and Chorus. In this case, you can also edit reverb and chorus parameters with great precision. Level indicators display track MIDI activity.

Ballade is unique in that it offers an option to chain sequences for playback in a random order. In non-random or random sequence chaining, there is a slight hesitation while the program loads the file from disk, making this feature unsuitable for situations where precise synchronization is required.

Deluxe Recorder

Electronic Arts's Deluxe Recorder takes a modular approach to MIDI programming. The package comprises a set of intercommunicating tools that are always available. These include Deluxe Recorder, Channel Setup, MIDI File Translator, Name Editor,

Figure 17-5:
(Top) Ballade's Mixer window lets you record fader infor-mation for MIDI Volume (or Expres-sion) and Pan and, with GS Standard devices, Reverb and Chorus.
(A) Ballade's transport controls.
(B) The Auto Function Palette provides Auto Return, Loop, and Punch in and out options. **(C)** Be-cause you cannot directly manipulate the counter at the upper right, Ballade provides this Marker palette for jumping around within your se-quence. **(D)** Each reverberation setting is repre-sented graphically in this Reverb palette. Clicking the Reverb's name cycles through the various settings, and the mini scroll bars at the right let you tweak additional parameters. **(E)** This Chorus palette lets you edit chorus settings for GS Standard instruments. **(F)** Ballade's Snapshot palette lets you capture any or all of a group of settings (Volume fader, Pan, Program change, Reverb, Mute, and Tempo) as a snapshot, which gets added to the list in the left of the window for later recall. Although all your snapshots are available at any time, only one can be active for an individual sequence. **(G)** The Track Sheet provides standard global track options: patch number, patch name, track name, MIDI channel, and instrument.

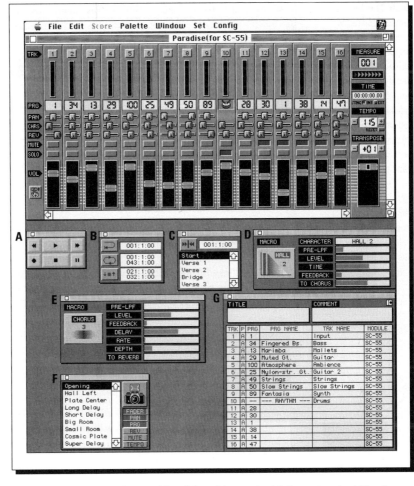

and Deluxe Music Translator. Other modules were under development when the program was purchased by Electronic Arts, although it is questionable whether these will ever be released. You can choose which modules the main program (referred to as the Kernel) automatically loads whenever you launch the software. For example, once you have set up the software to reflect the devices in your studio, you won't need to load the Name Editor module until the next time your setup changes.

Figure 17-6: Deluxe Recorder's Tracks window with Transport shown in upper left. Although Deluxe Recorder does not permit you to assign individual attributes to instruments, sequence tracks may be endowed with global effects that can accomplish some of the same results associated with this feature in professional-level sequencers. Each Deluxe Recorder track has a global volume,

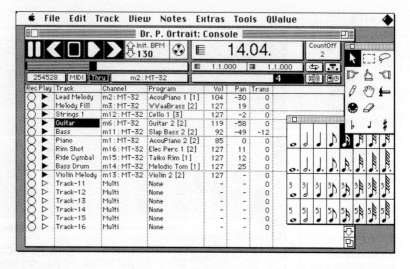

pan, and transpose setting. The transport offers an interesting fast-forward implementation. If you press the mouse down on the Fast Forward button and drag to the right, playback speed increases and the metronome continually displays the new speed. The Floating Tool palette to the right offers tools to edit different types of data as indicated in the annotations. Although there are three hand tools to deal with editing notes, the arrow tool can perform all the same functions. The Lasso tool is used to thread discontiguous selections throughout data displayed in an individual track window.

The program allows you to record up to 16 tracks, although you can use up to 32 MIDI channels (see Figure 17-6). Because tracks can contain data for multiple MIDI channels, you can even access all 32 channels with only 16 tracks. Notes are displayed in piano-roll notation. An event list display is not available. Other missing features include compatibility with Apple's MIDI Manager, time code synchronization (MIDI Sync is provided), and chunking features.

Remarkably, when you play back a sequence, Deluxe Recorder is always in record mode, even if you have not record-enabled any of the tracks. So if you find yourself playing along with a take and realize you forgot to press the record button, have no fear, everything is constantly being saved in a record buffer for your later disposition. It's sort of like having an extra *virtual* virtual track. You can direct this record buffer to an empty track or choose to merge the data into a pre-recorded track using the dialog box .

Deluxe Recorder's display is unique. The program provides 11 staves, each one dedicated to a different type or representation of MIDI data (see Figure 17-7). For notes there are two staves, a grand staff, and a chromatic grid. You can specify one of ten widths for the staff lines of the grand staff or the grid lines in the chromatic display. Interestingly, even though notes are displayed in piano-roll notation, sharps and flats are incorporated into the display, making it much easier to read than most displays of this kind. The complete list of available data staves follows:

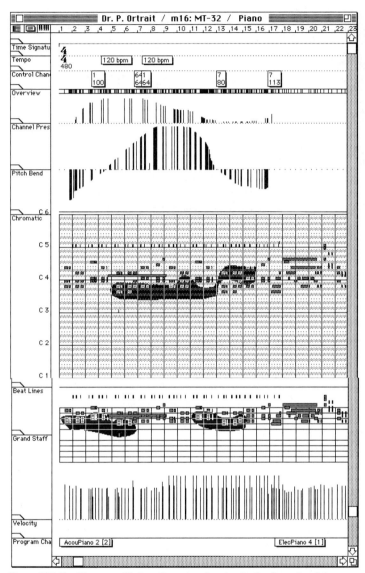

Beat Lines

This staff allows you to manipulate the beat lines directly (as explained below), after you have entered music in free time, without a metronome click.

Channel Pressure

A graphic display of monophonic aftertouch.

Chromatic

A continuous graph of a chromatic region, the limits of which you specify. Black notes are indicated by shaded lines.

Control Change

This staff provides a graphic or text view of any single controller or all controller information for the track. Controllers are accessed from the pop-up menu. You can add controllers to this list with the Name Editor module.

Grand Staff

This is the main note display of Deluxe Recorder — piano-roll notation on a grand staff.

Overview

Deluxe Recorder's Overview staff displays the density and location

Figure 17-7: The 11 staves of Deluxe Recorder, showing the Configuration dialog boxes to those that are configurable. You can only view a single track at a time, but a track's pop-up menu is available in every window to instantly switch the display from track to track (pop-up menu is pictured at the left). You can drag the staves into any order and even superimpose them.

of all MIDI data on the track. The only operations that can be applied to this staff are Cut-, Copy-, and Paste-type options. This is to ensure that you are selecting all data on the track. On other staves, only data in the particular staves displayed can be selected for editing.

Pitch Bend

A graphic display of pitch bend.

Program Change

A text display of program change messages associated with the track.

Tempo

A text or graphic display of tempo.

Time Signature

The time signature staff is devoted to display both time signatures and the rhythmic value that will be used for the metronome click from that point on. A unique option is to "Scale music in each bar" when changing time signatures.

Velocity

Velocity displays of this kind are common in Macintosh sequencers. In Deluxe Recorder, velocity values can only be edited individually.

Like many current-generation sequencers, Deluxe Recorder allows you to refer to your instruments by name rather than MIDI channel assignment. When an instrument is called up (via a pop-up menu), so is its current library of patch names (if one exists). You can add additional devices and patch lists with the Name Editor module. Useful features of this module are that you can delete the names of patches that you never use to make the pop-up menus more manageable, and that you can configure the row and column display of pop-up patch selectors.

Deluxe Recorder is unique in offering draggable beat lines for the purpose of aligning music that you record without a click reference. First you turn off the metronome and the display of bar lines. Then record as usual. Now you can create beat lines using one of three methods. You can draw them onto the beat lines staff with the pencil tool, you can generate a specified number of evenly spaced beat lines, or you can record a reference track, say, of quarter notes, and have Deluxe Recorder convert the note attacks on this track to beat lines. In any case, after your beat lines are in place, you are free to drag them horizontally so that they align with the original music you recorded in free time. Once you have them aligned the way you want, the Fit Music to Beat Lines menu option recalculates the passage so that the beats are evenly spaced. Tempo changes are automatically inserted wherever necessary to maintain your original tempo (see Figure 17-8). You can also use this feature to add an expressive tempo track to existing music.

Deluxe Recorder is optimized for converting files into Deluxe Music Construction Set (DMCS), Electronic Arts's popular notation software. File transcription is

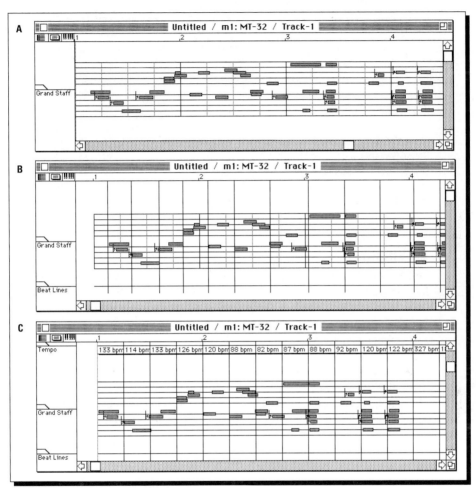

Figure 17-8: Editing beat lines with Deluxe Recorder. **(A)** Grand staff showing music that has been input in free time (without a metronome). **(B)** After recording a track of quarter notes in time to the free-time music, the Convert to Beat Lines command created these beat lines on the Beat Lines staff. You can move them horizontally to make finer adjustments. **(C)** Executing the Fit Music to Beat Lines command adjusts the free-time material to conform to the beat lines. This results in everything being evenly spaced, as in this display. Note that the Tempo staff is now full of automatically generated tempo changes. This ensures that the beat-aligned music plays back with the expressive tempo nuances of the original performance.

enhanced by options allowing you to set minimum durations and maximum tuplet values on a per-track basis. Most software requires you to define global settings for these parameters when converting a sequencer file into notation (see Figure 17-9).

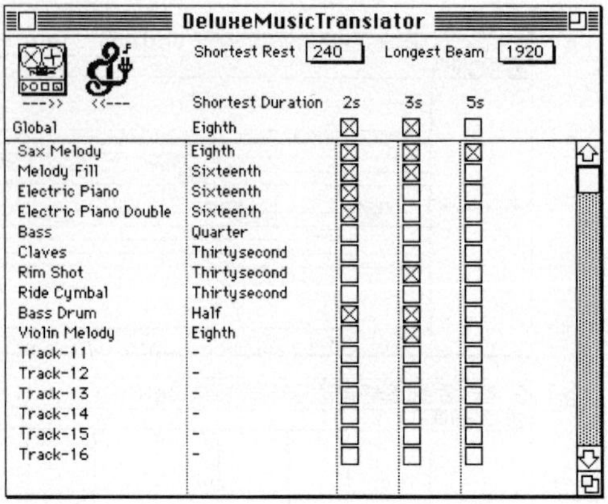

DeluxeMusicTranslator				
Shortest Rest	240	Longest Beam		1920
Shortest Duration		2s	3s	5s
Global	Eighth	☒	☒	☐
Sax Melody	Eighth	☒	☒	☒
Melody Fill	Sixteenth	☒	☒	☐
Electric Piano	Sixteenth	☒	☐	☐
Electric Piano Double	Sixteenth	☐	☐	☐
Bass	Quarter	☐	☐	☐
Claves	Thirtysecond	☐	☐	☐
Rim Shot	Thirtysecond	☐	☒	☐
Ride Cymbal	Thirtysecond	☐	☐	☐
Bass Drum	Half	☒	☒	☐
Violin Melody	Eighth	☐	☐	☐
Track-11	-	☐	☐	☐
Track-12	-	☐	☐	☐
Track-13	-	☐	☐	☐
Track-14	-	☐	☐	☐
Track-15	-	☐	☐	☐
Track-16	-	☐	☐	☐

Figure 17-9: Converting music to and from Deluxe Recorder and Deluxe Music Construction Set is facilitated by these options to specify individual quantization parameters for each staff or track.

EZ Vision

Opcode's EZ Vision is a stripped down version of the company's professional-level sequencer, Vision. In general, the user interface is significantly simplified, often to an extent that makes Vision users jealous. The program is a good investment for beginners, because Opcode has an upgrade policy for trading up to Vision when you are ready for it.

Like Deluxe Recorder and One-Step, EZ Vision provides for up to 16 tracks, theoretically one for each MIDI channel, although you can set any track to any MIDI channel. However, unlike Deluxe Recorder and One-Step, EZ Vision offers MIDI Manager compatibility and an elegant pattern-chaining interface.

As you can see from Table 17-1, EZ Vision includes the most professional features of any non-professional sequencer. The developers devoted a good deal of thought to identifying precisely which features a non-professional MIDI sequencer should contain and which options to leave out from EZ Vision that are present in Vision. For example, many of Vision's input options are missing. These include multichannel input, input maps (keyboard regions), and input data filtering. Retained are Vision's Replace, Punch, Overdub, and Loop record modes with their Wait for Note and Count Off options. One nice feature (also present in Vision) is on-line help, including the context-sensitive variety where your cursor turns into a question mark and help is provided for whatever you click.

You operate the software with five windows. The Edit, Arrangement, and Mixer windows are the ones used most often (see Figure 17-10). The Track Setup and Program & Note Names windows are for sequence or software configuration. Navigation is easy because every window includes a menu at the upper right that can activate any other window.

EZ Vision's approach to editing non-patch data is entirely graphical and also extremely powerful and efficient. Like the main portion of the window, shift-clicking on track numbers lets you view and edit data from multiple tracks simultaneously. There are two main tools, an I-beam tool for selecting data to cut or copy and the Pencil tool for reshaping, inserting, generating, or otherwise editing data.

The Pencil tool can perform one of six functions (some of these are dependent upon the data you are currently editing). Four of them can be applied to almost any type of data: Scale by percentage, Add (or subtract) a constant, set Maximum Limit, or set Minimum Limit. The Thin function is only available for controller information, pitch bend, and aftertouch (these first five functions are described

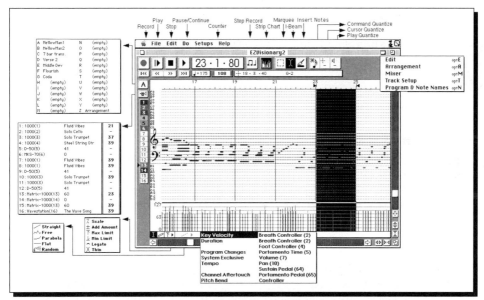

Figure 17-10: EZ Vision's Edit window is where you input and edit music. Clicking the numbers at the left switches the display between the 16 tracks. You can view and edit multiple tracks simultaneously by shift-clicking any of the track numbers. If you have a color monitor, the data for each track is displayed in a different color (you can change these defaults). With the pop-up menu accessible from the Sequence Letter button, you can toggle instantly between any of the up to 25 sequences stored in the file. You can also press the mouse down on the track indicator (pop-up triangle at left) to jump from tracks by name. Both pop-up menus are pictured. Note that the track name pop-up conveys a unique piece of information: the last program change message on the track. Whenever your mouse is pressed down on a note, all of its relevant parameters are displayed in the status bar directly above the window. Clicking a note plays it as well. At any point, you can hold the Command key down and "scrub" through the music. As you move your cursor from left to right or right to left, the music plays back at the speed of your mouse (even backwards!). If you want, you can display the Strip Chart at the bottom of this window. It contains graphic representations of controller information and velocity, duration, program change, tempo, and SysEx data.

under the heading "Edit options" earlier in this chapter). The Legato function can be applied to note durations (EZ Vision is the only program that lets you view durations as a vertically oriented histogram). Dragging the Pencil tool (set to the Legato function) over a group of durations in the strip chart extends or contracts their durations according to the height of your cursor. It is a wonderful feature unique to EZ Vision.

Besides setting the operational function of the Pencil tool, you can also set the type of edit curve you will be drawing (see Figure 17-11). These include straight lines (which can be angled), free lines (any shape whatsoever), parabolic lines (the curve is elegantly calculated for you), flat lines (the cursor is limited to strict horizontal lines), and random boxes. When set to Random, you use the Pencil tool to drag a box in the strip chart. The horizontal dimension of the box defines the beginning and ending points of the edit region, and the vertical dimension defines the limits to the range of randomization (another elegant enhancement).

Like its older sibling Vision, EZ Vision supports Opcode's proprietary Publish and Subscribe links between the sequencer and their patch librarian Galaxy and their editor/librarian Galaxy Plus Editors. This allows you to set up a link between a patch library file and EZ Vision (see Figure 17-12). Such links let you select patches by name whenever you change patches on a sequencer track assigned to an instrument whose patch bank is subscribed to (the process is described in Chapters 11 and 12). When you take advantage of this option, wherever patch information is displayed in EZ Vision, it also includes the name of the sound. You can still use patch names and note names in EZ Vision without dealing with Publish and Subscribe (for example, if you don't own Galaxy or Galaxy Plus Editors). The Program & Note Names window lets you create custom lists directly in EZ Vision.

EZ Vision's approach to chunking (pattern editing) is very elegant. Each EZ Vision file can contain up to 25 sequences, and each of these are identified both with a name and a letter of the alphabet from A to Y. The letter Z is reserved for the Arrangement menu, where you can specify the order (and repetition) of the 25 sequences (the term subsequences might be more appropriate in this context). When you type the letters corresponding to your various sequences, blocks representing them appear in the Arrangement window. You can also insert sequences by selecting them from a pop-up menu.

In the Arrangement window you can rearrange the component chunks of your song by dragging them with the mouse and Option-dragging them to make copies (see Figure 17-13). You can even truncate the chunks and subsequently lengthen them by dragging the right edge with the mouse. If the sequence is looped, you can also extend its duration by dragging in this manner. This points to a valuable feature of EZ Vision's Arrangement window: The size of individual chunks are

Figure 17-11:
Strip Chart editing of non-note data in EZ Vision (for additional information see "Vision" later in this chapter). Editing operations are defined by combining pop-up menu selections available at the bottom of the chart. All pop-up menus are pictured in this figure. The "%" numerical allows you to control the density of events that you draw in with the Pencil tool. Consult the text for explanations of the various Pencil tool functions

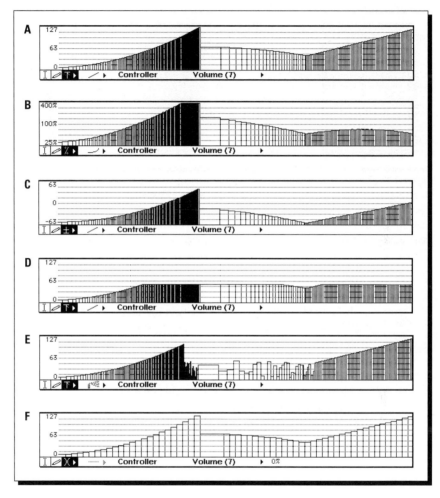

and curves. **(A)** The original MIDI Volume (Controller 7) data. **(B)** The effect of Scaling with a parabola. **(C)** The effect of Add Amount with a diagonal (straight line) from 100% to 0%. **(D)** The effect of Max Amount with a flat line at 50. **(E)** The effect of drawing a Random box from 21 to 24. **(F)** The effect of using the Thin function.

proportional to their actual duration (unlike the approach taken by some other sequencers). EZ Vision sequences can only have a single time signature, so if you want to change meter in the midst of a composition, you have to start a new sequence and use the Arrangement window to splice the two segments together. Double-clicking any chunk in the Arrangement window opens that sequence's Edit window, and the measure numbers at the top are offset to indicate its location within the context of the arrangement (a very nice touch).

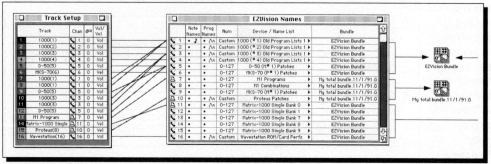

Figure 17-12: EZ Vision's Track Setup window with its relationship to the Program & Note Names window illustrated. Also symbolically represented are the dynamic links between EZ Vision and subscribed-to Galaxy files. Note the Velocity/Volume toggle for each track in the Track Setup window. This lets you specify whether the fader assigned to the track in the Mixer window (see below) will send Controller 7 (MIDI Volume) or scale velocities (useful for devices that don't respond to Controller 7 or for thinning the data stream).

EZ Vision's Mixer window lets you create volume mixdowns of your sequence. Depending upon what you specify in the Track Setup window, the on-screen faders either record MIDI Volume (Controller 7) information or scale velocity for the track they are assigned to. A useful feature is the option to take a snapshot of any fader setting and insert it anywhere in any of the 25 sequences in your file. Grouping faders is as simple as Shift-clicking the ones you want to group and then moving any individual member of this selection. When you group faders that were originally set to different levels, their motions are scaled as they reach the extremities of their travel range (for example, they all reach zero simultaneously).

The Mixer window also lets you record Pan information for each track. Additional features include a MIDI activity "virtual LED" and Mute and Solo buttons. The

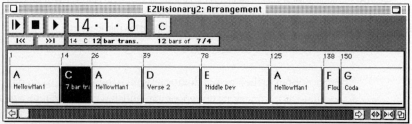

Figure 17-13: EZ Vision's Arrangement window with various elements annotated. You can only have a single arrangement per file, but there is nothing stopping you from saving multiple copies of a file to create new arrangements. The display and manipulation of your musical chunks offered by EZ Vision encourages good habits, such as considering your musical ideas from a higher level and staying aware of the form and structure of your entire composition.

Volume and Pan adjustments you make during mixdown are recorded to their respective tracks, and the faders animate appropriately on screen during playback. You cannot record the manipulation of the Mute and Solo buttons.

Opcode offers EZ Vision separately or as part of their EZ MIDI Starter Kit, which also contains their MIDI Translator (1 input, 3 output, self-powered MIDI interface — see Chapter 5, "Hardware Decisions"), *The Book of MIDI* (an excellent introduction to MIDI fundamentals — see Chapter 28, "Computer-aided Instruction"), and a free membership to PAN (the Performing Artists Network).

One-Step

One-Step, originally developed and distributed by Southworth Music Systems (the company that brought out one of the earliest and now-defunct sequencers, Total Music), is a stripped-down version of their now-discontinued MIDIPaint sequencer. When Southworth folded, Glenn Workman of Freq Sound licensed several of the company's products, including One-Step and the JamBox software.

One-Step is a very powerful sequencer that is missing certain features that have become popular in the period following the demise of Southworth. These include MIDI Manager compatibility, dual serial port support, type 1 SMFs, and chunk-oriented editing. SMPTE synchronization is only available if you use the Southworth JamBox as your MIDI interface, otherwise you are limited to SPP synchronization. Fortunately, Glenn Workman is a talented programmer, so One-Step might eventually be upgraded to include these features and ensure its longevity.

One-Step's user interface was obviously the basis for that of EZ Vision (see above). The two programs' main window for input and editing with the track numbers running down the side function almost identically. There are slight differences. For example, when you are looking at multiple tracks in One-Step's window, the notes on the track that is active for input are displayed with black bars and the other tracks are gray. If you happen to have a color monitor, all events except those of the currently active track assume different colors instead of becoming shaded.

One-Step makes very good use of shading. The piano-roll bars indicating note events are darker or lighter depending upon their loudness, and you can set the threshold points at which one velocity shade transitions to another (see Figure 17-14).

Although you can edit all your MIDI data with the graphic tools found on One-Step's tool palette, you can also edit regions with dialog boxes, which present similar options to those found in professional sequencers (see Figure 17-15).

Figure 17-14: (A) One-Step's Note window. The graphic orientation is evident from the tools at the far left. The Marquee tool lets you make copies of data by Option-dragging. One-Step enhances this feature by allowing you to replace the material at the destination if you hold the Command key down while dragging. The thin paint brush paints individual notes, while the wide paint brush paints a continuous stream of identically pitched notes spaced according to the settings of the timing palette (lower left). Note how both the upper portion of the quarter note and the sixteenth notehead are highlighted on this timing palette. This means that the wide paint brush will produce sixteenth notes that are a quarter note apart (MIDI step-time input will conform to the same conditions). The effects of several settings of this used in conjunction with the wide paint brush are visible at the bottom of the screen. The track palette functions similarly to that of EZ Vision. Besides this Note window, two additional viewing/editing modes are available by clicking the bottom two icons of the tool palette. Clicking any event with the question mark tool brings

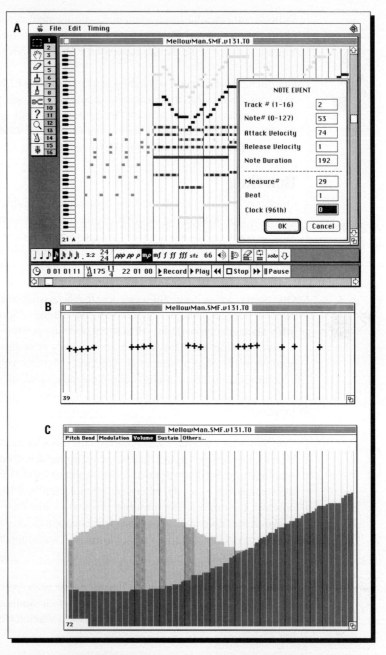

up an editable information window like the one pictured. **(B)** Clicking the metronome changes the display to this Tempo Editing screen. **(C)** Clicking the little data slider at the bottom of the tool palette switches to this Controller Editing screen.

A

Limit the range of Edit operations to the following:

MIDI Note #'s [45] thru [82]

Attack Velocities [0] thru [108]

Note Durations [192] thru [384]

↓ [23] [2] [0]   ↑ [28] [1] [8]

☐ All MIDI Event Types   [OK]

B

Limit the range of Edit operations to the following:

☒ Controller #'s [7] thru [7]

Controller Range [0] thru [127]

☐ System Exclusive Events

☐ Program Change Events

↓ [21] [2] [0]   ↑ [25] [1] [0]

[OK]

C

☒ Move selection to track# [3]

Transpose by note interval [60] to [62]

Move to measure/beat/clock [22] [9] [32]

☐ Erase Destination

☒ Remove Original   [OK]   [Cancel]

D

WHAT

○ Aftertouch
○ Attack Velocity
○ Release Velocity
◉ Note Pitch
○ Note Duration

HOW

○ Percent Change
○ Replacement Value
○ Add/Subtract Value
○ Percent over Time
◉ Randomize Value
○ Filter Out

VALUE/PERCENT [90]

[OK]   [Cancel]

E

WHAT

○ Controller#
◉ Controller Value

HOW

○ Percent Change
○ Replacement Value
○ Add/Subtract Value
◉ Percent over Time
○ Filter Out

VALUE/PERCENT [89]

[OK]   [Cancel]

F

◉ Note Number
○ MIDI Channel
○ Controller Number
○ Patch Number

...is equal to number in "FROM" row...

○ Change it to corresponding "TO" item
○ Cycle through items in "TO" row
◉ Pick a random value from "TO" row

FROM	58	60	61	63	65	66	68	69	72	73	75	77
TO	45	46	47	48	49	50	51	52	53	54	55	56

☒ Remove Original   [Fill]   [Clear]   [OK]   [Cancel]

Figure 17-15: Dialog-box-style region editing in One-Step. **(A)** Use this dialog box with the Note window to set the boundaries of the edit region and to further delineate exactly which notes are to be affected based upon pitch range, velocity range, and durational range. **(B)** This dialog box and dialog box A offer similar options for specifying exactly which types of controller information you want to edit. **(C)** The Move dialog box allows you to accomplish many edits with a single press of the OK button. You can transpose, move, erase, and replace all at once. Creative use of this option lets you produce parallel harmonizations or merge data from many tracks down to a single track. **(D)** This single Change dialog box accomplishes a number of operations that often require multiple dialog boxes in many other programs. Aftertouch, attack velocity, release velocity, pitch, and duration are all accessible from this one location. Here you can scale by percentage, set to a constant, add or subtract a constant, change over time (by percentage), randomize, or filter the data type selected with the radio buttons at the left. **(E)** You can edit pitch bend and controller information with similar precision (randomize is not an option for these parameters). **(F)** The Remap . . . dialog box lets you transform notes, channels, controller numbers, or patches in ways that are impossible with any other program. Of course you can use this option for pitch remapping (for example, to convert drum tracks from one instrument's format to another's). Other options include reassigning all MIDI channels or patches in one operation. Using the Cycle option you might, for example, take a melody and assign every next pitch to a different MIDI channel. The possibilities are practically limitless.

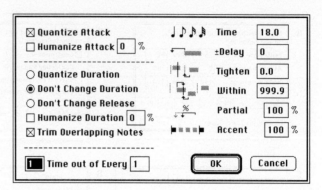

Figure 17-16: One-Step's Quantization dialog box, like most of the program's region editing options, lets you accomplish multiple types of editing with a single action. See the text for interpretations of the terms used here, all of which correspond to standard quantization options as discussed earlier in this chapter.

One-Step's Quantization dialog box combines quantization with velocity and duration editing (see Figure 17-16). Most of the standard options and common variations described earlier in this chapter are present. Many are referred to with different terms. "Delay" equates to shift, "Tighten" is the sensitivity setting, "Partial" is strength, and "Humanize" means randomize. The Accent option is similar to the velocity scaling offered by the Change dialog box (see Figure 17-15). The difference is that if you apply it here, you can limit the operation to certain beats with the "*N* Time out of Every *N* " setting at the lower left.

The most innovative approach to editing provided by One-Step is the interface to editing tempo. Using the Grabber tool you can move bar lines to align them with notes or stretch sections so that the notes appear at a new clock time (adjusting tempos accordingly). In other words, you can move a beat to a note or a beat to a time (see Figure 17-17).

Rhapsody

Green Oaks's Rhapsody (together with Ballade) is another newcomer on the Macintosh sequencing scene. The program is intended for beginners to MIDI and "hobbyists with a limited budget yet high expectations." While this may be the developers' intent, the sequencer has most of the features one expects from a professional-level sequencer. The list price of $149 certainly makes it the best value in any cost-to-feature comparison. However, the implication that the program is for beginners is somewhat misleading. The power offered by sequencers with this many options always comes with the price of increased learning curve and program complexity. This is somewhat compounded because Rhapsody takes a non-standard and particularly modal approach to many sequencing conventions.

Foremost among Rhapsody's departures from convention is the fact that all data, including the piano-roll data, is displayed with a vertical orientation. No other music program, sequencer or otherwise, takes this approach. It takes a good deal

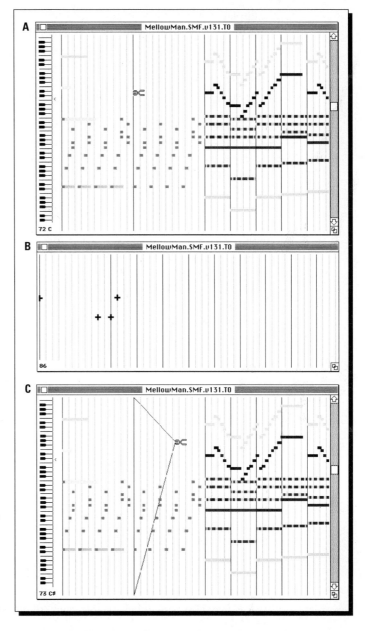

Figure 17-17: One-Step offers an innovative approach to tempo editing that is available in all three editing displays. **(A)** Original unedited music showing the Grabber tool grabbing a beat line. **(B)** One-Step inserts the indicated tempo value to ensure that the dragged beat line occurs at the location of the note it was dragged to. **(C)** With the Command key down you can stretch beat lines like rubber bands, as shown in this example. You do this while observing the counter at the lower left. When you let the mouse button up, One-Step inserts the proper tempo to assure that the beat line occurs at the point you selected. This has the same effect as time compression and expansion in other programs. This option is very useful for film and video scoring, because you only need to drag beat lines to the point where you see the desired SMPTE number displayed in the counter, and One-Step takes care of everything else.

of time to get used to, because in our civilization we are of course used to reading from left to right, and we read CMN from left to right as well. The developers clearly interpreted the implication of "piano roll" literally (piano rolls for player pianos are vertically oriented too, but they are not intended to be "read"). Perhaps one motivating factor was that the piano keyboard (which runs across the top of the display) is horizontally oriented, not vertically oriented like the ones running along the sides of such displays in other sequencers. The viability of this idea, however, is quite uncertain. If you are a notation historian, you might recall Pot's "Klavarskribo" system of notation, which employed a vertical orientation of the grand staff for piano music. The developers of Rhapsody might have taken a tip from Klavarskribo: It died a rapid and largely unnoticed death.

Rhapsody requires that you think of your music in patterns. In this respect, it forces you to think about music in a certain way that may be inconsistent with your normal working methodology (see "The Organization of MIDI Data" and "Imposing Priorities on Your Musical Aesthetics" in Chapter 16).

On the other hand, Rhapsody's pattern orientation is particularly well implemented, so if you do tend toward this form of top-down thinking, you should consider Rhapsody quite seriously. Patterns are stored in a scrolling list and placed onto a track by dragging their name out of the list with the mouse. The pattern is then represented as a box proportionate to its length on the track list. A very useful aspect of Rhapsody's approach to pattern editing is the option to place patterns anywhere in the sequence without the beginning of one pattern snapping back to the end of the previous pattern, as is common with most other implementations of this feature. Space between the patterns is simply treated as silence.

You may use a pattern as many times as you want in a sequence. No additional memory is consumed, because these are all considered "instances" of the same source pattern. Editing the source pattern causes the changes to occur in all the instances of that pattern. However, you may specify different transpositions, quantization parameters (which can include matching the attacks of another pattern rather than simple rhythmic rounding off), and humanization settings for each instance of the same pattern on an individual basis — very useful.

You can group and ungroup patterns at will, and the option to use groups within groups is available. Once grouped into a higher-level object, you can edit certain parameters of this group of patterns as a whole, for example, tempo. To top that off, you can overlay patterns on the same track. In fact, two patterns can occupy exactly the same time period. For example, you might overlay several copies of the same pattern, each at a slight temporal offset, to create an echo effect, or you might have a pattern that consisted entirely of MIDI Volume (Controller 7) events that you could drop on top of any other pattern to create a decrescendo or crescendo.

Another option with Rhapsody's pattern instancing is to specify that pattern instances only play back during specified iterations of a loop. Because Rhapsody supports multiple nested loops of any designated region (not just the entire track), this adds a considerable amount of additional flexibility. Finally, you can import

Figure 17-18: Rhapsody's main screen. Note the list of patterns at the lower left. You can drag as many copies of a pattern as you want out into the main track area. Each copy is linked to the original at the event level, yet each can have its own transposition, quantization, and humanization settings. Fader motion is recordable and animates during playback. Command-dragging on any fader makes it the master. The volume faders actually scale velocity rather than sending Controller 7 data, as in most other sequencers. This has the advantage of reducing the amount of extra information inserted into the MIDI bandwidth (no extra information is inserted because the scaling

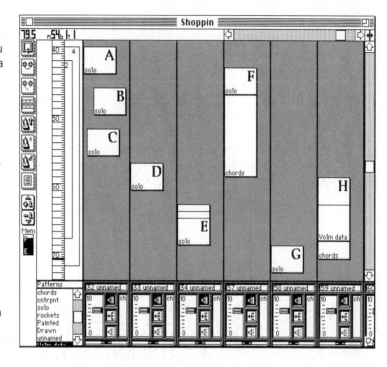

computations are all done in the Macintosh). Note the following types of pattern operations (letters have been added to the pattern blocks for the purpose of this illustration — these do not appear during normal program operation). **(A)** Source pattern. **(B)** Instance of source pattern. Any changes to the source pattern are reflected here and in all other instances of the same pattern on these tracks (except the one indicated as an independent copy of the source pattern). **(C)** Transposition has been applied to this pattern instance. **(D)** Quantization and humanization have been applied to this pattern instance. **(E)** Three instances of the same pattern are overlaid at a slight offset to create a MIDI echo effect. **(F)** This pattern instance has been grouped with an instance from a separate source, and the group has had a tempo change applied to it. **(G)** This pattern instance is a copy of the source pattern, which can be edited independently. No changes to the source pattern will be reflected in this copy or vice versa. **(H)** A pattern consisting of Controller 7 data (MIDI Volume) is overlaid with this pattern instance and the tail end of the previous pattern to create a fade out.

patterns from other Rhapsody files. All in all, the possibilities are practically limitless.

Double-clicking a pattern's graphic representation in the Track window (see Figure 17-18) opens the pattern into a Pattern Editor window, in which you can modify individual events. Actually, there are 11 different View windows that you can call up for any pattern: Keyboard (the default vertically oriented piano-roll note display), Drum (available for drum tracks only), Note-On Velocity, Key Pressure, Channel Pressure, Controller (any specified controller and any number of controller windows, each dedicated to a different controller), Switch (any number of switch windows, each dedicated to a different momentary or toggle switch), Pitch Bend, Raw (event-list-type editing requiring dialog box interaction for editing individual parameters), Note Duration, and Program Change. All views are vertically oriented.

In a note-editing window (Keyboard View) you can constrain pitch to a scale that you define. Such scales can span any region you want (i.e., they are not limited to an octave and you can have different notes in any octave of the scale). You can use this feature in conjunction with the Spray Can tool, which allows you to "spray" randomized licks with each mouse click. There is also a Paint Brush tool that allows you to "paint" chords into the pattern with a single click.

The Drum Editor displays notes as little boxes, which indicate their volume by the density of their shading. Innovative tools available in the Drum Editor include a Paint Brush to paint random drum fills and rolls (according to your choice from a distribution graph palette and restricted to an area that you enclose by dragging a selection box), Spray Can (to spray random improvisations at your mouse click), and a Flam tool (to create drum flams). You can save and recall drum sets that generate the display of note names at the top of the Drum Editor (see Figure 17-19).

In addition to the standard step-time and real-time (including loop) input, Rhapsody offers two innovative approaches to recording. The program's implementation of multiple-take recording is particularly well thought-out. You can record up to 16 passes and then audition any single pass or combination of passes. You can even designate that any number of the passes be merged as they are inserted into the pattern. This is useful for drum-machine-style recording or for recording the beginning of a phrase on several passes and the end of a phrase on others. Free-time recording is also available. Like Deluxe Recorder, after recording in free time, you can create a reference track of tapped quarter notes to which to align your freely recorded music (tempo changes are automatically inserted in the tempo map to preserve your original performance nuances).

Rhapsody's features go on and on (see Figure 17-20). There is a built-in SysEx editor/librarian (you can use logical names for SysEx events, but this is probably not a feature used much by beginners), the option to create program name lists in a standard word processor, and all the standard edit operations available in professional-level sequencers. Rhapsody is unique in offering step-by-step playback.

Trax

Passport's Trax was originally marketed as Master Tracks Jr. before Master Tracks changed its name to Pro 4 and subsequently to Pro 5. More than any of the other non-professional sequencers, it is easy to see Trax as simply Pro 5 with certain options removed.

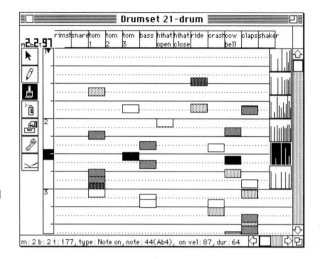

Figure 17-19: Rhapsody's Drum Editor View displays note names for drum sets and provides tools that you can use to generate fills, rolls, flams, and improvisations. The various shadings of the notes indicate their relative volumes.

Figure 17-20: Selection and quantization in Rhapsody. **(A)** Rhapsody's Selection dialog box offers all the standard criteria found in professional-level sequencers and adds some interesting logical operators at the bottom of the box. The radio buttons grouped under Criteria all bring up additional dialog boxes for setting specific limits. **(B)** In this quantization dialog box, note the option to quantize to a Template. You can designate any selected group of notes as a quantization template and then align notes to the template. This is perhaps the most flexible option to have appeared until now in terms of dealing with metrical placement and pitch independently. Another rare feature pictured in this dialog box is the option to specify different forward and backward boundaries to the quantization grid. This is reflected in the measure display at the right (vertical, of course!).

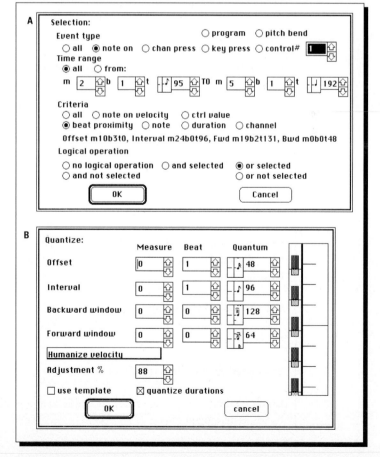

The user interfaces of the two programs are practically identical. With both programs running side by side on two Macintoshes, you have to look very closely to discover the differences. This fact has positive ramifications from two standpoints. First, Trax's available feature set is extremely strong and operates exactly like that of Pro 5. Second, if you decide to upgrade to Pro 5, you have nothing new to learn in the area of user interface. The latter point is almost a moot one, because both programs adhere so strongly to the standard Macintosh user interface that they almost qualify as software that does not require a manual. This characteristic was considered the badge of excellence in early Macintosh history, almost to the extent of being a requirement for a program's success. Alas, programmers no longer consider this to be the primary developmental directive. It is refreshing to find two programs (i.e., Trax and Pro 5) that continue to uphold the tradition of user-friendliness. After all, it was the design premise of the Macintosh in the first place (see Figure 17-21)!

As mentioned above, one way to look at Trax is as a stripped-down version of Pro 5. The following is a list of features found in Pro 5, but missing in Trax (see Figure 17-22).

Open multiple files. In Trax you can only open a single file at a time.

Overdub record, looped record, looped overdub record. The only enhancements to recording offered by Trax are automated punch in and out and Wait for Note.

Multitrack record. Trax offers multichannel recording on a single track, but not multitrack recording. You can later split off data from multichannel tracks onto separate tracks, but the operation is time-consuming. You must cut and paste each channel from the source track individually with a separate operation.

Event list display and editing. Not available.

Graphic editing and display of controller data. The only options for controller data are to set the pitch bend playback range and to filter selected types of controller data on input.

Graphic editing and display of tempo map. You can edit the tempo map, but you can never display it. Otherwise, you have much of the same robust control of tempo as in Pro 5.

Time scaling and Fit to time. Not available.

Change Filter. The Change Filter, available in almost all of Pro 5's editing dialog boxes, is missing in Trax.

Figure 17-21: A typical screen in Trax showing its three main windows: the Track Sheet, Song Editor, and Step Editor as well as the Conductor window (for setting tempo and meter) and the obligatory transport controls. An Individual Note Parameter Editing window is also pictured (accessible by double-clicking any note in the Step Editor). Manipulating data in the Song Editor is particularly easy. Measures with music in them appear as filled boxes, while empty measures appear as hollow boxes. Passport was the first company to implement this valuable and now relatively common overview feature. Unrecorded tracks do not have boxes displayed. You can cut, paste, and mix data from this window. Many other regional editing operations are available as well, although these must be performed between measure boundaries from the Song Editor (as opposed to tick-delineated regions in the Step Editor). Discontiguous selection is not provided, nor is Option-dragging for copying. However, double-clicking any box opens the Step Editor automatically scrolled to that measure in the appropriate track.

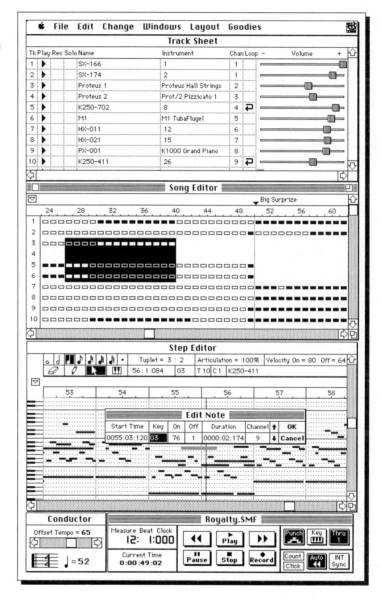

Change smoothly (by percentage). Not available for any parameter.

Set maximum/minimum limits. Not available for any parameter.

Humanization/randomization. Not available for any parameter.

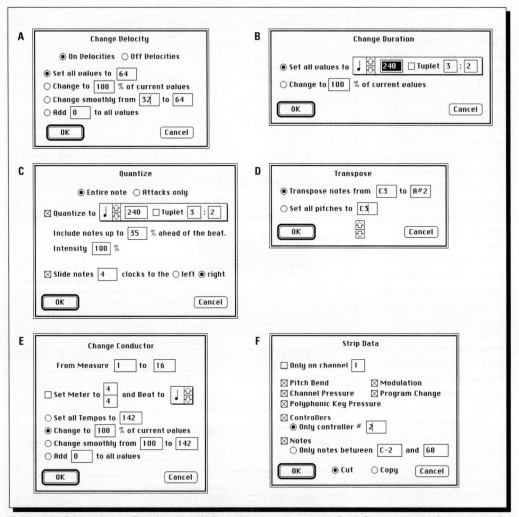

Figure 17-22: Edit interfaces in Trax. Note the missing options that are present in Pro 5: Change smoothly (by percentage), Set maximum/minimum limits, and Humanize. Pro 5's Change Filter (editing filter) is also not present. **(A)** Velocity Editing. **(B)** Duration Editing (regional). **(C)** Quantization. **(D)** Transposition. **(E)** Conductor (tempo track editing). **(F)** Strip Data.

Dual port output. Trax supports *either* the printer *or* modem port, not both.

SMPTE features. Trax supports SPP synchronization only.

Chase Controllers. Not available.

Chaining (Song List). Not available.

Virtual fader animation. Not available.

Like Vision's StudioVision, Performer's Digital Performer, and Cubase's Cubase Audio, there is a digital audio version of Trax called AudioTrax (see Chapter 18, "MIDI Sequencing with Digital Audio"). Unlike the other three offerings in this area, AudioTrax handles 8-bit digital soundfiles exclusively. This means it doesn't require any expensive digital NuBus cards and you can use it with any 8-bit digitizer (such as the MacroMind-Paracomp MacRecorder or the Articulate Voice Impact — see Chapter 10, "Sound Generation"). If your Macintosh has a built-in microphone (IIsi, LC, and future Macintoshes), you won't need any additional hardware at all. This makes AudioTrax the perfect tool for multimedia that doesn't require CD-quality sound.

Professional Sequencers

Would it be possible to simply count up the number of options in a sequencer and say that one program is more suited for professional sequencing than another based upon that information? I suspect it might be for a certain class of users — those who compose with sequencers for a living. For this admittedly small group of users, being able to transform their music efficiently and quickly is of paramount importance. Where one program might offer an editing operation as a single step, another might require accomplishing the same operation through a round-about series of time-consuming actions (known as a *kluge*).

Making a judgement based upon feature-saturation breaks down in the final analysis because many professional-level sequencers offer certain options that are unique, that only they can perform. That is why people who do sequencing for a living often own more than one sequencer and move back and forth between several programs, even on the same project, by exporting and importing SMFs.

Each musician using sequencers at a professional level seems to have a unique set of requirements. For example, several of the sequencers covered in this section do not provide for discontiguous selection, an option that happens to be very important to me in my work. Yet when I pointed this out to some colleagues who use these programs, they responded that they hadn't noticed this feature was missing. Obviously, if you don't need a certain option, you're not going to miss it if the software doesn't offer it.

All other considerations being equal, user interface becomes an issue. The look and feel of these five professional-level sequencers is as different as night and day. The variety in the approaches to MIDI sequencing are sometimes subtle but more often sweeping with respect to their impact upon the way you must think about music.

In the following discussions of individual products, wherever possible, the dialog boxes for region editing are ordered identically for each program, making it easy for you to compare these features between the various software alternatives. The order is velocity, duration, quantization, transposition (and key change and harmonization if available), tempo (and meter change), time scaling, continuous data options (including generating, stripping, and thinning), and humanization or randomization options (if not incorporated into one of the other dialog boxes).

Beyond

When Dr. T's Music Software released Beyond (programmed by Jeremy Sagan) in 1990, the impact on the Macintosh music community was profound. In its initial version 1.0 release, Beyond seemed to have been so highly developed that one got the impression it had a history of updates and upgrades stretching back for years.

Beyond offers all the professional-level features found in the other programs in this section at half the price. The program also provides many options not found in other software. At the time of this writing, the current release is version 2.1.

Beyond is unique in that it allows you to choose between four timing resolutions: 192, 240, 384, and 480 PPQN. When using the program with a Macintosh Plus, you can set the resolution coarser to eliminate timing jitters and then move up to 480 PPQN with Macintosh II series computers.

Two of the most innovative options offered by Beyond are in the area of recording. In addition to the standard record, loop record, and overdub, Beyond adds a Multiple Take mode and a Song Building mode.

Multiple Take mode plays your sequence over and over, and each recording take you play gets automatically placed on a new track. The previous tracks are automatically muted. This allows you to perform a number of takes quickly and then go back to the track window and unmute the various takes one after another to find the best version. You can also use Copy and Paste to assemble the best sections from a number of different takes.

Song Building mode lets you specify a number of tracks to record on, each of which might be assigned to a separate instrument, and then start loop recording. After each take, you have the option of rejecting the take or muting the last track, otherwise the next music you play will be directed to the next track on the list (and whatever instrument is assigned to that track). For example, you can set several tracks for drums, a track for bass, a track for piano, another for horns, and one for strings. Then record all the tracks in one sitting without having to take your hands off your MIDI controller (see Figure 17-23). You can also use this feature for looped regions instead of entire tracks.

A

Recording and Play Setup

- ○ Record/Play normally
- ○ Count off [2] [▲][▼] bars before recording
  [1] [▲][▼] bars before playing
- ◉ Wait for first note before starting

Record Loop Setup

- ◉ Multiple take mode
- ○ Song building mode
- [6] Tracks maximum when loop recording.

[OK]   [Cancel]

B

Metronome

- ○ Internal ◉ MIDI   MTP Cable
  - ◉ 📞 Modem [1]
  - ○ 🖨 Printer

	Channel	Pitch	Duration	Velocity
Bar	10	D5	1	127
Beats	10	F#4	1	90

Accent beats:

- ☒ [4] Velocity [116]
- ☒ [7] Velocity [108]
- ☒ [10] Velocity [116]

[OK]   [Cancel]

C

☐   Record Loop

Remaining record tracks: 6

[Pause recording]
[Mute last track]
[Reject last track]

D

Sect 1:Scarey.SMF

2 SubSections

	R M S	Name	Loop Bars	Instrument
41			5	Channel 1 M
42	●	...Loop Record Track..	5	Original:M C1
43	●	...Loop Record Track..	5	Original:M C1
44	●	...Loop Record Track..	5	Original:M C1
45	●	...Loop Record Track..	5	Original:M C1
46	●	...Loop Record Track..	5	Original:M C1
47	●	...Loop Record Track..	5	Original:M C1
48	●	...Loop Record Track..	5	Original:M C1

Figure 17-23: Beyond's Multiple Take and Song Building modes let you loop through a number of different tracks for recording one after another. Options to mute or reject the previously recorded track or tracks are available. **(A)** Recording and Play Setup dialog box. **(B)** Beyond has the most flexible MIDI metronome available, allowing you to set different accents for three other beats besides the downbeat. **(C)** This Record Loop dialog box lets you pause recording or mute or reject the last track recorded. **(D)** This Tracks window shows the effects of Multiple Take mode. The multiple takes are given the name "Loop Record Track..." Afterward, you can decide which ones you want to keep. Note the mini-menu pictured in the Tracks window. You use this to jump from section to section if a track has embedded sections (see text).

Beyond provides two enhancements to the standard piano-roll display. There is an option to display "velocity stems" with each bar representing a note. The length of the note's stem indicates its velocity. A similar option lets you view the effect of Pitch Bend information on the note data by bending the note's bars appropriately. Figure 17-24 shows both of these extremely helpful features.

Another unique approach to data display is Beyond's Continuous Data windows (see Figure 17-25). Instead of vertical bars, the tops of which define the contour of the continuous data, Beyond uses a single curved line, which is a much closer representation of the physical motion used to generate such data. Once you see it, you wonder how the developers of Macintosh music software got into the habit of displaying such data in any other way.

Figure 17-24: Beyond's main windows. Clockwise from upper left: the Bridge (including transport controls), Note Pad, Event (list) Editor, Sections, Note Editor, and Tracks (overview). Beyond also offers an assignable recordable MIDI fader console. This is pictured and discussed in Chapter 26.

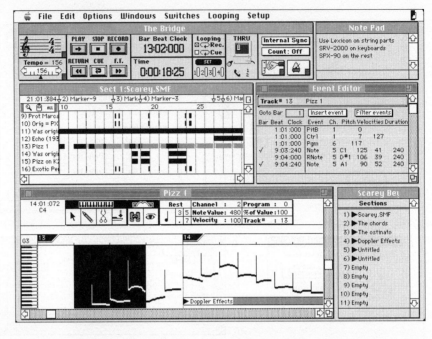

Notice the four Cue buttons on the Bridge. Beyond is unique in letting you define regions that can be instantly recalled by clicking one of these buttons. Unlike markers, which only have a beginning point, Cues have an end point as well. There are a number of "doors" on the display. Four are found on the Bridge (for example at the lower right of the metronome). Clicking these doors opens up a dialog box permitting precise settings. The Event Editor contains some notes listed as RNotes. See below for an explanation of these events. Notes with check marks are selected for editing. The Section window holds entire sequences, each of which can be dragged into a track, repeatedly if you want (see text). These appear as labeled bars in the Note Editor window, as pictured here. Sections, of which there can be up to 32, consist of up to 99 tracks. The interesting thing is that you can paste sections into tracks (up to 16 per track, more if you include repetitions of sections), turning the hierarchical organization upside down at will. The Note Editor illustrates velocity stems and notes that are affected by Pitch Bend information. This is a composite illustration. Normally you must choose between the display of velocity stems or bending notes. Beyond's Track window conveys a good deal of information. Instead of just the presence or absence of data in a measure (like Performer and Pro 5) the program identifies different types of data by shading. Black indicates notes, gray indicates controller data, and a pattern equals SysEx. The Track window lets you select regions that are not defined by measure boundaries (unlike Pro 5). You have the option of snapping the selection to a grid of 1 pixel, a sixteenth note, eighth note, quarter note, or one bar.

Like Pro 5 (see "Pro 5" in this chapter), Beyond provides a selection filter that includes metrical placement as one of the selection criteria. In fact, any selected rhythmic pattern can serve as the basis for the rhythm template, and you can designate the selected events to be inclusive or exclusive of a specified range surrounding each event on the rhythm template. A single menu item toggles the selection filter on and off.

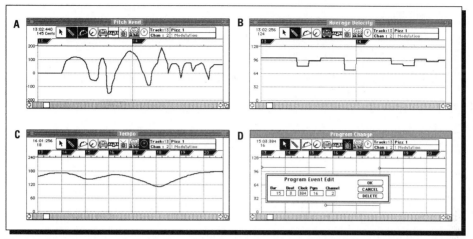

Figure 17-25: Several of Beyond's Continuous Data displays. You toggle between different data types by clicking the "punny" icons at the top of the window. Notice how easy to read the curves are when compared to the shaded vertical bar-oriented displays of other programs. Reshaping data curves is accomplished by drawing with the Pencil tool. **(A)** Pitch Bend data used in the previous figure. **(B)** Average Velocity. **(C)** Tempo. **(D)** Program Change. Clicking a Program Change event brings up the Parameter dialog box pictured in this example.

Beyond has many other useful editing operations. There is Delete Duplicates, which searches for and deletes any identical MIDI messages that overlap (the initial one is always preserved). Paste And... is an enhancement to the normal Paste operation that combines Repeat Paste and Transposition. You can specify the number of times to paste the material on the Clipboard, paste to fill the selected region or until the end of the section, and whether to transpose each successive copy chromatically or within a specified scale. See Figure 17-26 for the dialog box interfaces to standard editing operations (presented in the order described in the beginning of this section).

Cubase

Steinberg's Cubase is the most versatile sequencer available for the Macintosh — period. Is it the most powerful? Read on.

Cubase originated in the Atari world and was ported to the Macintosh in 1990. Developed in Germany by Steinberg Hard und Software GmbH, the program is distributed in North America (with an English interface and manual) by The Russ Jones Marketing Group. Although separated from the continent by an ocean, the developers are nonetheless very much on top of things. They were the first third party to implement compatibility with Mark of the Unicorn's MIDI Time Piece.

Although the Macintosh community has only very recently been introduced to graphic manipulation of user-defined chunks of musical material (first with Performer, then EZ Vision, Rhapsody, and Beyond), this sort of thing is old news for the Atari world, where such hierarchical representations have been available for years. Other features that are being ballyhooed in the Macintosh community are present as well: naming of notes (for drums or sound effects), pitch remapping, animated faders, editing during playback, notation, and so on.

It's tempting to say that Cubase is the most powerful MIDI sequencer available for the Macintosh. But that is somewhat inaccurate, because Cubase is much more than a sequencer and it's more than a sequencer on steroids — it is more like an instrument, a "sequencer-instrument," if you can accept that concept. When you operate Cubase, you know you are doing MIDI sequencing, but you feel like you are playing an instrument thanks to the extent of real-time control and features supporting advanced compositional thought. Other programs can *behave* like a sequencer-instrument (e.g., Interactor — see Chapter 23), but the sequencer aspects are minimal compared to Cubase.

One reason to consider Cubase as a sequencer-instrument is the number of different support functions built into the program. Besides a MIDI sequencer, the program integrates a mixing console construction kit, as many patch editors as you care to have (and a patch editor construction kit), an algorithmic music transformation editor (the Logical Editor), two Interactive Phrase Synthesizers (which do exactly what the name implies), a MIDI processor, a chord analyzer, a rudimentary notation program, and, dare I say it . . . more! Where integrated business software tends to strip down the various components of an integrated package, Cubase does not. These separate parts of the program are all as powerful as you would want them to be (or more so), and they all intercommunicate seamlessly.

Figure 17-26 (at right): Region Editing in Beyond. **(A)** Velocity. Note the option for RNotes. These are notes of random velocity. Beyond uses the Note-Off velocity value to serve as an indication of the randomization range. Velocities will be randomized between the value of the On-Velocity and the Off-Velocity. Setting the range beyond 127 increases the probability that the note will play at 127, because all values greater than 127 are treated as 127. One important feature missing from Beyond's velocity editing options is changing smoothly from a percentage to a percentage. **(B)** Duration. Concatenate notes moves Note-Off events to the next quantum grid point. **(C)** Quantize. Although Beyond supports triplets, quintuplets, and septuplets in step-time and mouse input, the Quantize dialog box only supports triplets. **(D)** Transpose. Note the pop-up menu that lets you constrain transpositions to a scale. You can define custom additional scales if you want. **(E)** Harmony. This unique dialog box lets you generate chromatic or key-related harmonies of up to four voices. You can use any of the built-in scales or the custom scales you define. The resulting harmonies can be directed to independent tracks if you want. **(F)** Tempo. Beyond includes its time compression expansion option here with the duration expressed in SMPTE Time Code (including user bits — see Chapter 27). **(G)** Expand/Compress (Scale Time). **(H)** Continuous Data. **(I)** Human Feel. Note the rarely found option to randomize start times and tempo. A tendency to "rush the beat" lets you weight the randomness that gets applied.

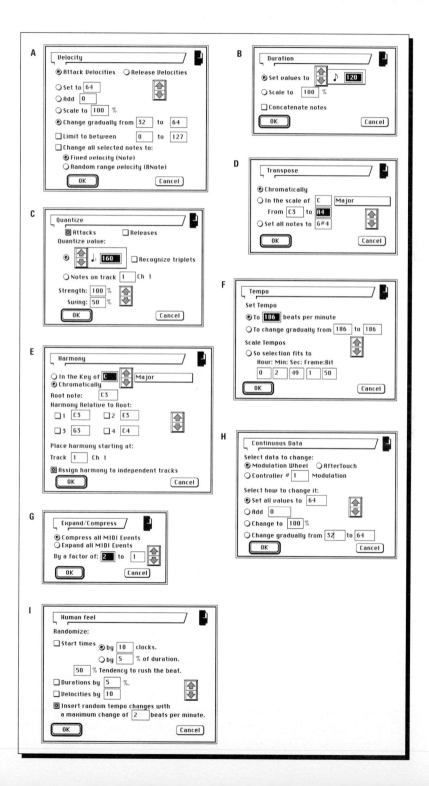

A — Velocity
- ● Attack Velocities ○ Release Velocities
- ○ Set to 64
- ○ Add 0
- ○ Scale to 100 %
- ● Change gradually from 32 to 64
- ☐ Limit to between 0 to 127
- ☐ Change all selected notes to:
  - ● Fixed velocity (Note)
  - ○ Random range velocity (RNote)
- [OK] [Cancel]

B — Duration
- ● Set values to ♪ 120
- ○ Scale to 100 %
- ☐ Concatenate notes
- [OK] [Cancel]

C — Quantize
- ☒ Attacks ☐ Releases
- Quantize value:
  - ○ ♩ 160 ☐ Recognize triplets
  - ○ Notes on track 1 Ch 1
- Strength: 100 %
- Swing: 50 %
- [OK] [Cancel]

D — Transpose
- ● Chromatically
- ○ In the scale of C Major
  - From C3 to A4
- ○ Set all notes to G#4
- [OK] [Cancel]

E — Harmony
- ○ In the Key of C Major
- ● Chromatically
- Root note: C3
- Harmony Relative to Root:
  - ☐ 1 C3 ☐ 2 E3
  - ☐ 3 G3 ☐ 4 C4
- Place harmony starting at:
  - Track 1 Ch 1
- ☒ Assign harmony to independent tracks
- [OK] [Cancel]

F — Tempo
- Set Tempo
  - ● To 186 beats per minute
  - ○ To change gradually from 186 to 186
- Scale Tempos
  - ○ So selection fits to
  - Hour: Min: Sec: Frame:Bit
  - 0 2 49 1 50
- [OK] [Cancel]

G — Expand/Compress
- ● Compress all MIDI Events
- ○ Expand all MIDI Events
- By a factor of: 2 to 1
- [OK] [Cancel]

H — Continuous Data
- Select data to change:
  - ● Modulation Wheel ○ AfterTouch
  - ○ Controller # 1 Modulation
- Select how to change it:
  - ● Set all values to 64
  - ○ Add 0
  - ○ Change to 100 %
  - ○ Change gradually from 32 to 64
- [OK] [Cancel]

I — Human feel
- Randomize:
- ☐ Start times ● by 10 clocks.
  - ○ by 5 % of duration.
  - 50 % Tendency to rush the beat.
- ☐ Durations by 5 %.
- ☐ Velocities by 10
- ☒ Insert random tempo changes with a maximum change of 2 beats per minute.
- [OK] [Cancel]

Cubase is even more than a sequencer-instrument — it's a way of thinking about music and music composition. It's an environment for musical creativity, a toolkit of such flexibility that you will almost never come up against a barrier blocking your way on the road to manipulating your musical ideas. Cubase makes most Macintosh sequencers seem like glorified event recorders, primitive at best. When you are in the Cubase environment, you can feel the power viscerally.

The obligatory analogy to a word processor might help you picture this. Consider all other Macintosh sequencers at the level of traditional Macintosh word processors. Now imagine, if you will, a word processor that lets you zoom out to the linguistic level and translate your writings into any language you want, zoom in to the font level and manipulate the typefaces you are typing, generate a sonnet from a parenthetical remark, drag your paragraphs around and have them adjust their tense, voice, and contextual referentiality based on where you place them, manipulate semantic considerations as easily as punctuation, and, well, you get the picture. Have you ever wanted to sort your MIDI input by velocity? Cubase can do it. With Cubase your imagination is the limit. The only other limits are set by the MIDI Specification itself.

In case you were wondering, there are quite a few strings attached to this power, and they are not simply traceable to the old adage "complexity is the price of power." Complexity of interface goes along with a large number of options. Finale (see Chapter 22, "Music Notation") is similar in this respect. Both programs have many, many features, which can take a very, very long time to learn.

Continuing with the Finale-Cubase comparison, consider that Finale's options often require a dozen more steps to execute than those of other notation programs, which have been developed with more thought to user interface. Fortunately, Cubase does not suffer the nested dialog box syndrome of Finale. In fact, you can navigate within Cubase almost entirely with keyboard shortcuts. Of course, the number of options available in Cubase requires that keyboard shortcuts aren't simply limited to the Command key followed by another key. They've had to include Option key shortcuts, Command-Option key shortcuts, Shift-Option key shortcuts, and finally single letter key shortcuts, just to cover all the keyboard navigation possibilities. This means even more things to learn.

But the most significant difference between the two programs is that Finale's wealth of options is merely a consequence of a hefty feature set and not intrinsically linked to a way of thinking about music as in Cubase. I mentioned earlier that Cubase was a "way of thinking about music and music composition." In order to really take advantage of Cubase's power you have to subscribe to this philosophy. If you don't start thinking about your music in the hierarchical manner required by Cubase, you will be frustrated at every juncture. Notes exist in Parts, which occur on Tracks (in Groups or individually), and all these elements must be organized into Arrangements. You are constantly required to keep track of your ideas from the perspective of these multiple contexts (most of which include multiple representations as well). Everything you do can have ramifications on the entire multidimensional structure of a work. These ramifications might not be what you expect, unless you are in complete control of the underlying (sometimes invisible) impact that an operation performed in one context has upon higher and lower levels of your compositional structure. It's a lot to think about, and until you get used to it, you might feel like your brain is being given the workout of its life at some mental aerobics center. However, like physical exercise, the more you do it, the easier it gets and the better you feel.

If you come to Cubase from another sequencer, you will have a very long adjustment period. Note that this adjustment period is above and beyond the steep learning curve necessary for the program's incredible scope and breadth of integrated features. A good deal of this adjustment is due to terminology and user-interface issues. There are new definitions of terms you thought you knew the meaning of. For example, cycle record is Cubase's term for loop record, cycle mix means loop overdub mode, remix means unmerge, mask means edit filter, the Grid Edit window is where you find the event list, the Key Edit window is the piano-roll display, parts are patterns (sort of), arrangements are sequences or songs, while songs are groups of arrangements, and so on. Many new terms referring to options that are not available in other software must be learned. For example: subtracks, ghost parts, group parts, group tracks, unpacking, snap value, kicking, and many others. You have to learn about a half dozen new types of quantization, including: over quantize, iterative quantize, match quantize, groove quantize, and freeze quantize. There are new types of graphic displays, including one in which time is represented on the horizontal axis, and the vertical axis corresponds to ordinal number.

Some user-interface enhancements might come as a surprise. You'd expect to be able to double-click a patterns bar representation to open it to the Note Level window, but it doesn't. For some items, Undo is found not at the top of the Edit menu, but in the middle of the menu from which the operation was accessed. Modal dialog boxes are not modal when it comes to keyboard control of playback (this is a very nice feature). Cubase even lets you get down to a very deep level of editing, at which you need to know about MIDI messages and their LSBs and MSBs (least significant and most significant bits, respectively).

There's a lot to learn or relearn, depending upon where you are coming from. I've shown Cubase to a number of people who do MIDI sequencing for a living and have repeatedly been met with the response, "I'm too entrenched in [insert the name of one of the other four sequencers in this section] to switch at this point in the game." The situation is similar to that of a Dvorak keyboard for your Macintosh. The results are in. You can type much faster and with less fatigue on a Dvorak keyboard, yet how many people are willing to switch? But what if the

Dvorak keyboard was the only way to have access to the features of the mythical word processor I mentioned several paragraphs back?

On the other hand, if you haven't used a Macintosh sequencer before, you won't notice inconsistencies with other Macintosh sequencers. Who's to say that they are doing things right anyway? You still have quite a learning curve ahead of you, although you are rewarded at the end of the journey. Cubase is not the sort of program for amateurs who want simple and instant gratification, although it can be appreciated by patient hobbyists of the tinkering variety.

Cubase is fast. It has the fastest response of any MIDI program I have ever seen, which means that you never even get a millisecond to catch your breath (you'll almost never see the watch). The words "greased lightning" come to mind when you edit in real time, literally everything can be done during playback or recording without any impact on timing. You won't find any remarks like, "You can even do this during playback" or, "This is not editable during playback." Instead, there is one poignant statement at the very beginning of the manual: "Don't turn off playback or recording just because you want to try a command or function, just do it!" There is almost no distinction between playback modes (including recording) and non-playback modes. You can even open and close files during playback without audible effect on the music.

Whereas many sequencers provide chunking or pattern-chaining as an option, Cubase requires that you deal with the elements of your music as objects that have a particular context in the structural hierarchy of your composition. The following objects are listed in ascending order of the hierarchical level.

Parts. These are the smallest musical objects you work with. You record notes and other MIDI events into Parts. These are somewhat like patterns or chunks in other programs, although much more important and considerably more flexible. When you import SMFs, each track becomes a separate Part.

Ghost Parts. A Ghost Part is a copy of a Part that remains linked to the Part it was copied from. Changes to notes or other MIDI events in the original part are reflected in all its Ghost Parts copies. Most parameters of a Ghost Part can be set differently from the original part it is linked to. However, if you want to change notes and controller data for an individual Ghost Part, you must convert it to a normal Part.

Tracks. Parts and Ghost Parts are sections of a Track. Tracks may contain any number of these.

Groups. Parts and Ghost Parts can be agglomerated into an entity called a Group. Parts in a Group need not be adjacent either horizontally (temporal consecutivity) or vertically (temporal simultaneity). Parts can be members of different Groups.

There is no limit to the number of Groups you can have. Groups are shared by all Arrangements. The entire contents of an Arrangement can also be defined as a Group.

Group Part. When you use a Group in an Arrangement it is called a Group Part. You can manipulate it as if it were a single Part.

Group Track. Group Parts are sections of a Group Track. You cannot place Group Parts in normal Tracks.

Arrangements. An Arrangement window can have up to 64 Tracks or Group Tracks (see below) in any combination. In some ways an Arrangement is like a sequence in other Macintosh programs. You can have up to 16 Arrangements per Song file.

Song Cubase lets you save many of these objects as separate files. Individual Parts and Arrangements can be saved. Subsequently, Part files can be opened into other Arrangements, and Arrangements can be opened into a larger entity called a Song.

Cubase lends itself to working from the middle outward. You record into Parts and these appear as horizontal bars in an Arrangement window (see Figure 17-27). After you have a number of Parts, you can simply stay at the Part level of the hierarchy and manipulate these graphic representations, or you can move in either direction of the hierarchy. For example, you can zoom in and tweak the events (notes, controller data, and so on) that make up the Parts, or you can zoom out and create Group Parts and manipulate these higher-order objects on Group Tracks.

Each Part, Track, and Arrangement has a set of playback parameters, which you can configure using the Part Parameter window (see Figure 17-28). You access this window by double-clicking a Part. Each object, including separate Ghost copies of the same Part, can have its own unique playback settings. Some of these parameters are: virtual instrument, MIDI channel and cable, transposition, velocity scaling, delay, duration scaling (length), compression (automatic velocity compression as described in Chapter 25, "MIDI Mixing and Studio Automation"), program change, and MIDI volume. Additionally, you can use the Part Parameter window to filter different types of events: Note-Ons, Poly Pressure, Controllers, Program Change, Aftertouch, and/or Pitch Bend. You can set the start and end points for Parts in this window as well. Output can also be directed to M•ROS (Cubase's MIDI Realtime Operating System). M•ROS is a virtual MIDI cable that you can use to link Track or Part output to any of Cubase's other built-in modules, such as the Interactive Phrase Synthesizer or the MIDI Processor. Alternatively, you can use M•ROS to direct the output of any of these modules or any virtual fader consoles you might be using back to a Track or Part.

Figure 17-27: An Arrangement window in Cubase. There are actually three panes to this window, and any pane can be collapsed to reveal more of the others. The track list at the left contains virtual instrument definitions. Here you can set MIDI channel, cable, Drum Map (if applicable), default patch, and volume setting. The main area of the window contains a number of Parts. You

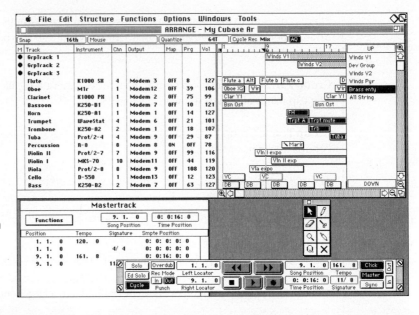

can drag these around to reorder them, overlay Parts on top of one another to sound simultaneously, Cut, Copy (Option-drag), and Paste, or create Ghost Parts (Command-drag) that are linked to the Parts they were copied from (Ghost Parts are indicated by the light gray border). Shift-clicking Parts selects them for grouping. The rightmost pane contains a list of the Groups. These are available in all Arrangement windows. When you drag these out into a Group Track (the tracks at the top of the window), they are called Group Tracks. The Tool palette provides an Arrow tool to select and move Parts; a Pencil tool to lengthen and shorten Parts (non-destructive truncation); an Eraser tool to delete Parts; a Scissors tool to split Parts into new Parts; a Magnifying Glass to "scrub" playback in either direction; a Join tool to combine two Parts into one; a Quantize tool to apply Match Quantize (see text) by dragging a Part that has the right "feel" on top of a Part that doesn't; and a Mute Cross to mute playback for a Part. Muted Parts appear with shading on normal tracks. Note that the Group Parts are also shaded, but with a slightly denser pattern — muting a Group Part makes its pattern even darker. The Mastertrack window is below the Arrangement window. Here you can insert and display tempo and meter signatures. The transport appears at the bottom of the screen. Most of the controls are self-explanatory. Ed Solo mode restricts playback to material showing in the current editing window rather than all Parts. The Left Locator and Right Locator refer to the current one of ten programmable regions that you can jump to with a single keystroke. You can also save ten programmable mute configurations.

Cubase provides four main graphic editors for displaying and manipulating your data at the event level (see Figure 17-29). You can have as many editing windows open as you like and these can be multiple editing windows of the same type displaying different Parts or Tracks. In all cases except the Grid Edit window (see below), Shift-clicking a group of Tracks or Parts opens all of them into the same window, a very desirable feature. While you are in an editor, Undo always affects the immediately previous action. However, pressing the Escape key lets you undo all changes made since you first entered that particular editing window!

Figure 17-28: Cubase's powerful Part Parameter window lets you configure individual playback settings for each Part, Track, or Arrangement. You can scroll from Track to Track and Part to Part using the arrows and switch from Part mode to Track or Arrangement mode without leaving this window. For this reason, and also because all changes occur in real time during playback, you may want to keep this window open at all times.

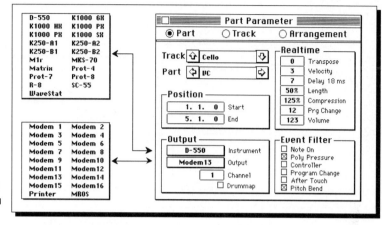

Note the M•ROS option on the Output pop-up menu (pictured). This is a virtual MIDI cable that you can use to direct output to one of Cubase's other built-in processing modules (see text).

Key Edit window. This is a two-pane window consisting of a typical piano-roll display of the selected Part or Parts and an optional strip chart that graphically displays velocity and controller data along the bottom for editing.

Score Edit window. This window displays the selected Part or Track as CMN. If Parts on more than one Track are selected, they appear as separate staves. Even though the notation is crude, it would be nice if Cubase offered an option to print this display.

Grid Edit window. This editor is a three-paned window that includes the event list and a graphic display of the same data. You can edit values numerically or graphically. Because the graphic display lines up with the event list, this editor is unique in that it bears a vertical orientation. Time is still represented horizontally in the center pane, but other data scrolls downward according to event order. The rightmost panel displays a graphic representation of the data bytes to the MIDI messages currently being edited.

Drum Edit window. This is a three-pane window. The upper-left side displays the current Drum Map, and the upper-right side displays the drum attacks in velocity noteheads. You have the option to display an additional velocity and controller data window along the bottom for editing.

Cubase's quantization options might at first seem somewhat foreign to the seasoned Macintosh musician. Having been created in Germany, they are, of course, technically foreign to U.S. musicians. Unless you specifically select Freeze Quantize, you can undo any quantization at any time, even after quitting the program and reopening the file a year later. Some of the options are:

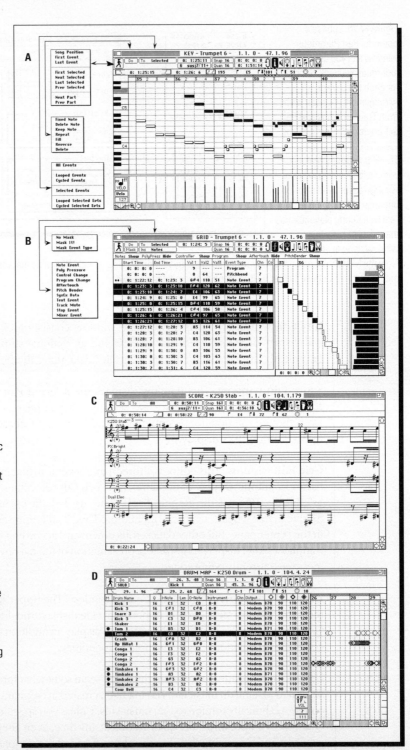

Figure 17-29: The four main event-level graphic editors offered by Cubase. **(A)** The Key Edit window. **(B)** The Grid Edit window. **(C)** The Score Edit window. **(D)** The Drum Edit window. Note the automatic chord analysis display at the upper center of both the Key Edit and Score Edit windows. This provides an ongoing analysis of the current chord during playback, recording, or whenever you play a chord with either of these windows active. See text for additional information.

Automatic Quantize. Same as Input Quantize in most sequencers (see above under "Standard Features"). Remarkably, even this form of quantization can be undone to return to the original performance durations.

Note-On Quantize. Quantizes attacks but not releases.

Over Quantize. Moves notes to the closest quantum grid point. Now read this next sentence twice so that it sinks in. Over Quantize also detects if you are consistently playing behind or ahead of the beat and uses this information when moving notes in order to maintain the feel (sort of like an "intelligent" Strength setting). Over Quantize also performs automatic deflamming of chords with respect to attack points and length.

Iterative Quantize. This provides Cubase's Strength and Sensitivity options. The difference is that the two options are combined into one operation, and you can repeatedly select Iterative Quantize to gradually move the attacks closer to the grid points with every next iteration. Of course, with Cubase no matter how many times you quantize a passage this way, you can still return to the original performance values.

Match Quantize. This lets you match the feel of one Part with the feel of another. They don't even have to have the same number of beats. For example, you could Match Quantize a Part that has a high hat playing eighths to one with a bass drum playing quarters and be assured that only the quarter note attacks in the high hat Part will be altered. You can also use the Q cursor to quickly execute Match Quantize between Parts in an Arrangement window. Simply drag the Part with the proper feel on top of the Part without the feel. When you let the mouse button up, the destination Part gets match quantized (the rhythmic template is repeated if the destination part is longer than the source part), and then the source Part snaps back to its original location.

Groove Quantize. One of Cubase's most innovative features, this option lets you select, apply, and edit one of 16 Grooves from a hierarchical menu. Grooves are metric-specific rhythmic quantization templates designed to create rhythmic feel (see Figure 17-30).

Freeze Quantize. Selecting this after performing a quantization operation makes the quantization permanent. If you forget to select this, all quantization (except the two durational operations below) can be undone, even after quitting the program and reopening the file later.

Length Size. This quantizes the length of notes without moving their start points.

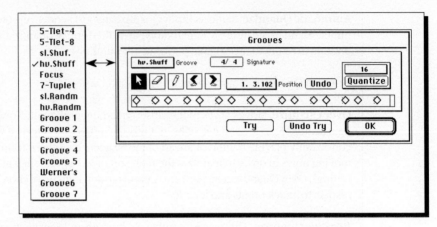

Figure 17-30:
Setting up
Groove Quantize
in Cubase. Note
the Groove
Quantize sub-
menu, where
your Grooves
appear auto-
matically.

Fixed Length. This sets notes in the selected region to a duration equal to the quantization unit.

Cubase is unique in that its Human Sync option (equivalent to Tap Tempo in other programs — see Chapter 26, "Film and Video Applications") lets you set up an irregular tap. You can, for example, tap swing eighths, a dotted eighth-sixteenth pattern, or whatever you please, rather than regular quarter notes. You can even write a tempo track with Human Sync while you are locked to time code.

Cubase's built-in MIDI Processor lets you simulate digital signal processing effects with MIDI (see Figure 17-31). You can generate echo, chorus, harmoniza-tion, arpeggiation, and pitch-shifting effects. Input can be from your MIDI control-ler or from an existing Track or Tracks by way of the M•ROS virtual MIDI cable (see above). Output can be to any virtual instrument, Track, out any MIDI channel, port, or cable, or to the M•ROS virtual MIDI cable. Sending the output to M•ROS lets you record processed information from one Track back to another Track that is set to receive its data from M•ROS.

Cubase has additional options that are simply mind-boggling to find in a so-called MIDI sequencer. The Logical Editor is pictured in Chapter 16, and the Mixer Editor (a virtual fader console construction kit) is covered in Chapter 25.

You can use the Logical Editor to set up conditional editing operations that search your music for regions or notes fulfilling the specified conditions and then perform a complex operation on the data that meets the criteria. This offers unparalleled flexibility reminiscent of what could be found in Dr. T's now-discontinued KCS Level II Programmable Variations Generation.

With the Mixer Editor you can create control panels for any of your devices or virtual fader consoles typical of those offered by other sequencers. The external

Figure 17-31: Cubase's built-in MIDI Processor is very flexible when used in conjunction with the M•ROS virtual MIDI cable (see text). Repeat lets you set the number of echoes to generate. Echo lets you specify the delay in ticks between each repeat. Quantize moves the repeated notes to the closest specified quantum value (delay calculations are therefore not necessary). Vel Dec allows you to add or subtract velocity values for each repeat. Echo Dec lets you add or subtract a number of ticks from each echo (widening or closing up the gap between them). Note Dec allows you to create harmonies or arpeggiations by specifying a value to subtract or add to the MIDI note number of each successive repeat.

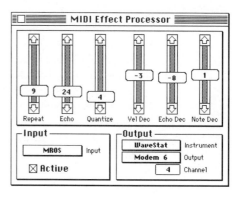

device control panel options allow you to create full-blown patch editors in Cubase with rather lovely interfaces. You can even group your most used functions from all your devices onto a single virtual control panel and then create master controls that operate your instruments as a group. Do you want to be able to set the filter cutoffs for all your synthesizers by moving a single slider? You can do it with this.

Finally, as a crowning stroke, Cubase provides two Interactive Phrase Synthesizers (IPS) that can process or generate two separate data streams or work in tandem. This is a real-time interactive algorithmic musical generator and variations creator (see Chapters 19 and 20 for additional information on interactive and algorithmic composition). You can use M•ROS to direct the output of the IPS anywhere you like. Input can be provided by your MIDI controller, a Cubase Track in an Arrangement, or from Phrases stored in a Phrase file accessible to the IPS. The results of the IPS are truly amazing (see Figure 17-32).

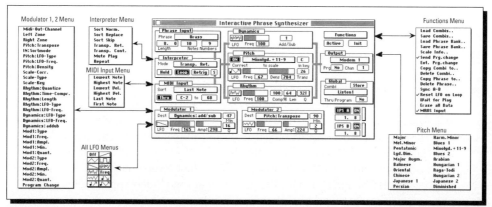

Figure 17-32: Cubase's Interactive Phrase Synthesizer lets you construct an infinite variety of algorithms, many of which have logical roots in synthesis (for example applying an LFO waveform to pitch, dynamics, and/or rhythm). The pop-up menus are all displayed with arrows designating their associated parameters. This thing really works!

Performer

Mark of the Unicorn's Performer wins the readers' popularity poll conducted by one trade publication or another year after year. It has also won the coveted Mix Magazine TEC award (Technical Excellence and Creativity) three times (1987, 1989, and 1990). It is extremely powerful software, though certainly not as powerful as Vision or Cubase, being considerably behind them in terms of available features. So why does it win the awards? The program's feature set has the "right" set of features (not too many, not too few) for professional sequencing, and its look and feel has no challengers. While other companies focus on adding bells and whistles to their programs, Mark of the Unicorn has concentrated on Performer's user interface. In a word, the user interface is elegant (besides being very efficient). If you are going to stare at the Macintosh screen for hours on end, it is a strong plus if what you are staring at looks good.

Eventually, the company always seems to find time to add the latest hot features of other programs, even if these updates come six months to a year after their introduction by all the competitors (as was the case with graphic editing, their overview display, and editing during playback, for example). This practice of waiting to the last moment to add features that have become standard in other programs could perhaps catch up with them sometime. Fortunately, this has little impact on customer satisfaction. Performer users are generally extremely happy with the software and often quite vocal in this regard.

Despite some of the observations in the previous paragraph, Mark of the Unicorn has been responsible for introducing a number of MIDI sequencing features that have now been incorporated into other software. Notable among these are multitrack (as opposed to multichannel) recording; discontiguous selection; the Split Notes option pictured in Figure 17-33 (selection based upon pitch, range, durational range, and velocity range, among other things); the option to make a smooth change from a percentage to a percentage over time, for example, to create crescendos and decrescendos with velocity data (see Chapter 16 for more information about the necessity of this option); DeFlamming; Tap Tempo; and nested looping of non-track-delineated regions.

Performer practically defined the standard set of region editing options, but after doing so has not added many of the current rage of enhancements such as randomization and humanization options or step-recording durations that are not equal to the step unit. Performer was the first Macintosh sequencer to offer a notation display of your MIDI data. On the other hand, Performer was the last MIDI sequencer to support SMFs and MTC, favoring, instead, their "proprietary" (and arguably more accurate) DTL and DTLe (see Chapter 26, "Film and Video Applications").

Most of Performer's still unique features are preceded by the word "unlimited" (in the world of computers this means "limited only by available RAM or hard drive

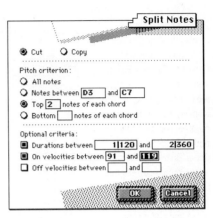

Figure 17-33: A good example of Performer introducing a feature and then disregarding subsequent enhancements developed by other manufacturers in the same area is its Split Notes option. Although Performer introduced the Split Notes option for delineating selection regions with Boolean criteria, and most other sequencers now offer this, Performer's implementation hasn't changed since its introduction. Many now-common additional enhancements are missing.

capacity"). Performer offers an unlimited number of tracks, sequences, songs, virtual instruments, and slider consoles. If you run up against these limitations in other MIDI sequencers, all of which impose some arbitrary limit to the number of these items you can work with, Performer is flat out the only solution — no contest. You can have as many different types of windows open as you like, displaying as many different tracks as you want open simultaneously. In fact, the number of open windows is also unlimited. You can have all open windows scroll synchronously during playback or specify that only certain window types (including only the top window) scroll during playback.

While most of the features that Performer introduced are now standard across the majority of professional-level sequencers, there are a few that have yet to be implemented by another manufacturer. Notable among these are Smart Quantize (see below) and an unparalleled degree of curve control precision for fitting curves on any type of data that changes over time. You can create linear, exponential, logarithmic, and S-type curves for even such ephemeral data types as tempo. You specify the precise slope in all cases (with S curves you can even specify the midpoint of the S).

Performer offers three main event-level editing displays (see Figure 17-34): event list, graphic (piano roll combined with vertical bar-graph representations of non-note data), and notation (but not printable, and you wouldn't want it to be). An Overview window is combined with the track list, just like in Beyond, Cubase, and Pro 5.

Performer uses a grid to assign MIDI channels if you have an interface that supports more than 32, such as a MIDI Time Piece or Studio 5 (yes, Opcode's Studio 5 is completely compatible with Performer!). Performer uses a matrix display, not unlike the one for the interconnection of cables in the MIDI Time Piece DA (see Figure 17-35). Alternatively, you can specify channels in terms of virtual instruments.

Figure 17-34: A typical display configuration of Performer showing the Event List, Graphic Editing, and Notation windows as well as the Overview. Also displayed are the transport controls and the Markers and MIDI Monitor windows. On the tracks list, some tracks are assigned to virtual instruments, while others are assigned by cable and channel number. Note the two shadings of boxes in the Overview (next to the memory "pie"). These reflect the density of events in their associated measure. Unlike overviews offered by all other sequencers, discontiguous selection works in this window, as does Option-dragging to make copies. You can quickly jump to an event-level editing display from the Overview. Double-clicking a measure's box takes you to its event list editor, Command-double-click to open the graphic editor, and Option-Command-double-click to get to the Notation window. The piano roll and graphic

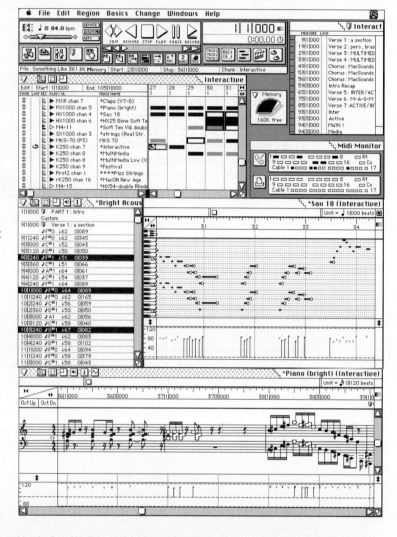

editing displays function almost identically, with all the standard graphic editing options available in both displays. The MIDI Monitor window displays channel and cable activity as blinking virtual LEDs. Having a separate Markers window (upper right) is particularly useful. You can click a marker to jump immediately to that point in your sequence. You can record markers during playback simply by pressing the spacebar (for example, while you are watching a video). This, coupled with the fact that markers can be locked to a specific frame or beat and insulated from global tempo or metrical manipulations, is a very useful feature for film and video composition. In the Event List window, notes that won't be played because a loop is in operation are conveniently displayed in italics and indented.

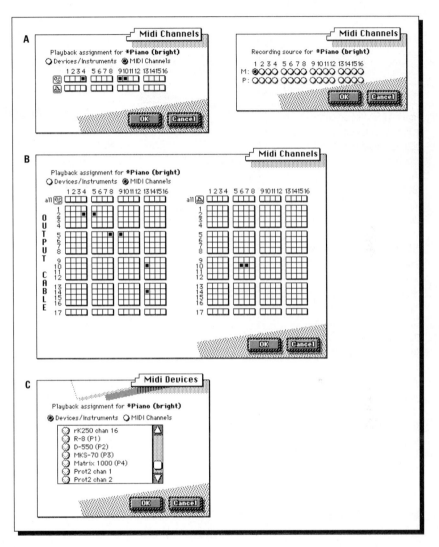

Figure 17-35:
MIDI channel assignment in Performer. **(A)** The interface for 32-channel (or less) interfaces. **(B)** The matrix for greater-than-32-channel interfaces, such as the MIDI Time Piece or Studio 5. **(C)** Assigning track playback channels by virtual instrument name.

For a list of Performer's main input, editing, and output features consult the information under the heading "Sequencer Features" found earlier in this chapter. Performer literally supports all but four of the features listed under the subheads, including those listed as "Standard options" and "Common variations" (see Figure 17-36). The four missing features are humanization, randomization, harmonization, and output quantization (i.e., all quantization in Performer is destructive).

Figure 17-36: Region editing in Performer is accomplished almost entirely by way of dialog boxes.
(A) Change Velocity.
(B) Change Duration.
(C) Quantize. **(D)** Smart Quantize. This option has a floating quantization grid that uses built-in algorithms (partially configurable) to detect the difference between, for example, triplets and anticipations. The Swallow Rests option allows you to specify a floating durational quantization unit to eliminate rests that were a result of performance nuance. This option is designed to be used to prepare a file for transfer to a notation program.
(E) DeFlam. **(F)** Transpose (see Chapter 16). **(G)** Change Key. **(H)** Change Meter.
(I) Change Tempo. The tempo dialog box is sort of a mini time calculator — you can enter a start and end tempo and see how long the passage is, or you can enter a final temporal location (real time or SMPTE) or total duration with a start tempo and see what the tempo is at the end, and so forth. **(J)** Scale Time. **(K)** Create Continuous Data. **(L)** Thin Continuous Data. **(M)** Reassign Continuous Data. **(N)** Change Continuous Data.

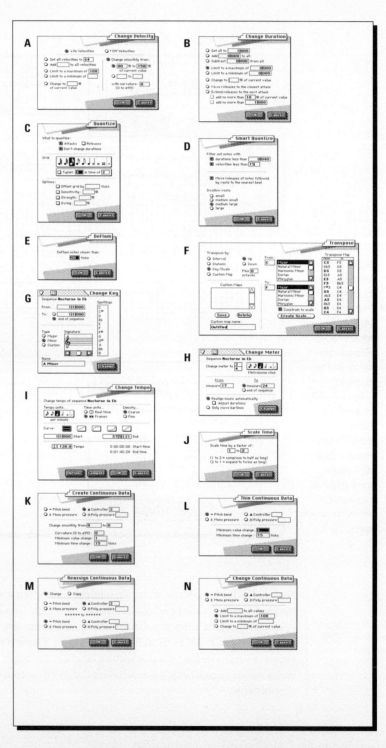

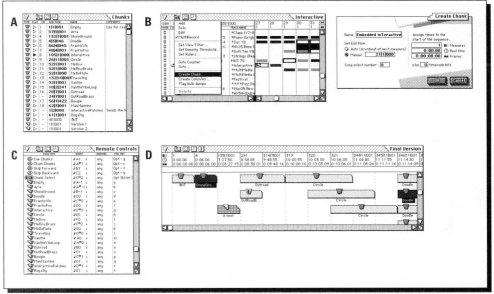

Figure 17-37: Performer's Chunking options are very intuitive. **(A)** All the sequences in your file appear in this Chunks window. Also appearing in this window are any Songs you create by chaining Chunks together. You can have any desired number of Songs in a file. **(B)** If you want, you can select any region of measures and tracks in the Tracks Overview window and define it as a Chunk, using this Create Chunk dialog box. **(C)** You can trigger chunk playback with MIDI events or Macintosh events that you assign in this Remote Controls window. **(D)** You drag Chunks (sequences) into a Song window from the Chunk window. Once in a Song window, you can copy and rearrange Chunks with the mouse. Chunks, record-enabled Chunks, selected Chunks, and Song Chunks (Songs nested within other Songs) all have different patterns to their graphics, as indicated by the annotations to this example.

Performer's interface to sequence Chunking is very intuitive, even though it is missing many of the features now common in pattern-oriented sequencers (e.g., setting different playback parameters for copies of the same Chunk, unlinking copies of Chunks, individual Chunk duration control, an easy way to place gaps between Chunks, and so on). Sequences are represented as graphic Chunks in a Song window (see Figure 17-37). You can arrange Chunks both horizontally (in which case they will play after one another) or vertically (in which case they play simultaneously). Option-dragging Chunks copies them. If you have limited RAM, you can specify that Chunks get loaded from disk on-the-fly during playback. Chunks are grouped into Songs, and Songs can be nested inside other Songs *ad infinitum*.

Performer offers many other desirable features: on-line help; virtual instruments and patch lists (see Chapter 16); the most robust implementation of virtual fader consoles available (see Chapter 25); and extensive support for Mark of the Unicorn's Video Time Piece (see Chapter 26).

Incidentally, here's a tip about using a Macintosh Portable. Officially, you must use only MIDI Manager-compatible software. However, when you use Performer with MIDI Manager, you lose access to individual cable features of the MIDI Time Piece. Because of this, Mark of the Unicorn has a special version of Performer (always designated with a p — for example, Performer 3.61p), which allows you to run the software on a Macintosh Portable without MIDI Manager. Interestingly, if you are in MultiFinder and you run the version of Performer dedicated for the Portable, you can then run any other programs that would otherwise be incompatible with the Portable because they are not compatible with MIDI Manager.

Like Opcode Systems, Mark of the Unicorn also continues to spread the fictitious rumor that you must de-install Performer before defragmenting your hard drive with "optimization utilities such as Disk Express" (quoted from the Performer manual). While this is true for the ancient Disk Express I (and all other defragmentation utilities), it is not true regarding the current version of the program, Disk Express II, which has been available since the end of 1989. Disk Express II does not move installed programs or their invisible key files during the defragmentation process and has no impact whatsoever upon any copy-protected software that is installed on your hard drive.

Pro 5

Passport's Pro 5 has a long history behind it, stretching back to earlier incarnations as MasterTracks, MasterTracks Pro, and Pro 4. Throughout the program's evolution, the developers continually introduced one innovation after another. They were the first to offer an editable track/measure level overview (their Song Editor, now called the Track Editor). Other firsts include quantization on input, metrically-based selection criteria, and the extension of keyboard remote control beyond simple transport functions. This software lineage also offered the first user-friendly implementation for humanization and for editing tempo and controller information graphically. Pro 5 is the only sequencer that lets you open multiple files simultaneously.

As mentioned above under "Trax," Passport's continuing commitment to a simple, intuitive user interface is reminiscent of the days gone by when it was felt that having to read a program's manual was a strike against the software. This has resulted in a very large user base (augmented by its availability on other platforms) and the first Macintosh sequencer to have a complete book written about it (*Power Sequencing with Master Tracks Pro and Pro 4*, by Craig Anderton, Amsco Publications, 1990).

Pro 5 offers eight additional windows: Pitch Bend, Channel Pressure, Key Pressure, Modulation, Continuous Controllers, Program Change, Tempo Map, and Big Counter (see Figures 17-38). The program also includes a built-in SysEx librarian.

Figure 17-38: A typical screen in Pro 5, showing four of its main editing windows: the Track Editor, Event List Editor, and Step Editor, as well as the Conductor window (for setting tempo and meter), the Markers window, and the transport controls. An individual Note Parameter Editing window is also pictured (accessible by double-clicking any note in the Step Editor). Clicking the Program Name field brings up a list of popular instruments with their factory presets (pictured). Note the inclusion of the General MIDI standard patch list. The Track Editor is an overview in which each measure that contains music is represented by a little filled box, and empty measures are hollow boxes. If you click a filled box, it expands to show a piano-roll display. Most edit operations can be carried out with lightning speed in this overview, although only contiguous regions defined by measure boundaries can be selected. A nice feature of the Step Editor allows you to click a note in the vertical on-screen keyboard to select all notes of that pitch on the track. Dragging vertically transposes that pitch everywhere, and Option-dragging transposes and copies, leaving the original intact (a quick way to create parallel harmonizations). Note that the Conductor window (lower left) includes both an offset tempo and an absolute tempo.

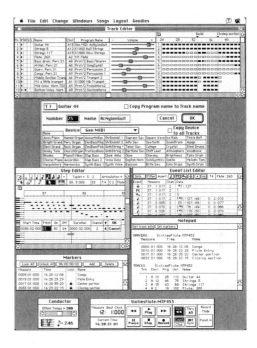

Any tempo map changes are scaled by the difference between the offset tempo and the absolute tempo. The Notepad window can grab the track list information or marker list (with timings), and you can paste this into another program for printing.

Certain standard editing operations in Pro 5 behave differently from what you might expect if you have become accustomed to another sequencer. Pro 5's handling of cutting and copying notes, although shared by Beyond, is different from the way many other sequencers do it (including those at the entry- and semi-professional levels). In the Step Editor, Cut and Copy truncates notes whose endings extend across bar lines (unless the selected region extends across the barline as well). If a note is truncated in this way by a Cut, new Note-On events are created that correspond to the part of the note that is left over after the truncation. This isn't a big problem in the Step Editor; however, in the Track Editor, you can only select regions delineated by measure boundaries, and since you can't see more detail than a single measure at a time, there is a great risk of finding your tracks left with little pieces of notes that have become new notes all by themselves.

The Track Editor is the only window in which you can select multiple tracks for editing as a group, and because of the restriction to measure boundary delineated regions, you cannot, for example, define a selection from beat 2 of one measure to beat 3 of another. Discontiguous selection is not available in any window.

Selection in the Event List is also somewhat non-standard. If more than one event occupies the exact same time, there is no way to select just one of the events, regardless of whether the events are of the same data type or not. If they are of different data types, you can filter the view to get around this, but if they are of the same data type, for example, notes of a chord, there is only one way to isolate a single note: change its start time, make any necessary edits, then re-enter the original start time (this is a good example of a kluge).

Although Pro 5 lets you click a note in the Event List with audible feedback (hold the Command key down), this feature operates somewhat differently in the Step Editor. It may seem as though you could click a note to hear it, but in fact, what you are really hearing is the note grid-line. Anywhere you click in the Step Editor (with the Command key down) plays the pitch associated with that vertical location, regardless of whether you click a note or not.

You may notice a Use Change Filter option in many of the dialog boxes pictured in Figure 17-39. This is one of Pro 5's most powerful features. The Change Filter lets you restrict an editing operation to events based on such criteria as pitch range, duration range, velocity range, MIDI channel, measure pattern, metrical placement, or any combination of these parameters (see Figure 17-40). Clicking in the checkbox next to the Change Filter button uses the previous settings of the Change Filter, whereas clicking the button itself lets you make new settings for the filter.

Pro 5's interface to song-chaining is still in its primitive stages. Missing are synchronization options and pattern instancing (you have to save a sequence under a different name in order to use it twice in a song list). On the other hand, the program's Song Playlist feature offers several options that are simply unavailable with other software. For example, you can specify that advancing to the next song occurs only when you press a Macintosh key, a specified note or control on your MIDI controller, or after a certain period of time. These options are clearly designed for live performance.

Vision

By far the most comprehensive and feature-laden sequencer to hit the market, Opcode's Vision is the professional-level sequencer with the longest history. The program evolved from one of the first sequencers to appear on the Macintosh, MIDI Mac Sequencer (1985). This software was very popular with early users of notation software, because it has had file compatibility with Mark of the Unicorn's Professional Composer and later Electronic Arts's Deluxe Music since very early on. Opcode's software could usually do and sometimes still does a better job at converting files into Professional Composer than Mark of the Unicorn's own Performer software.

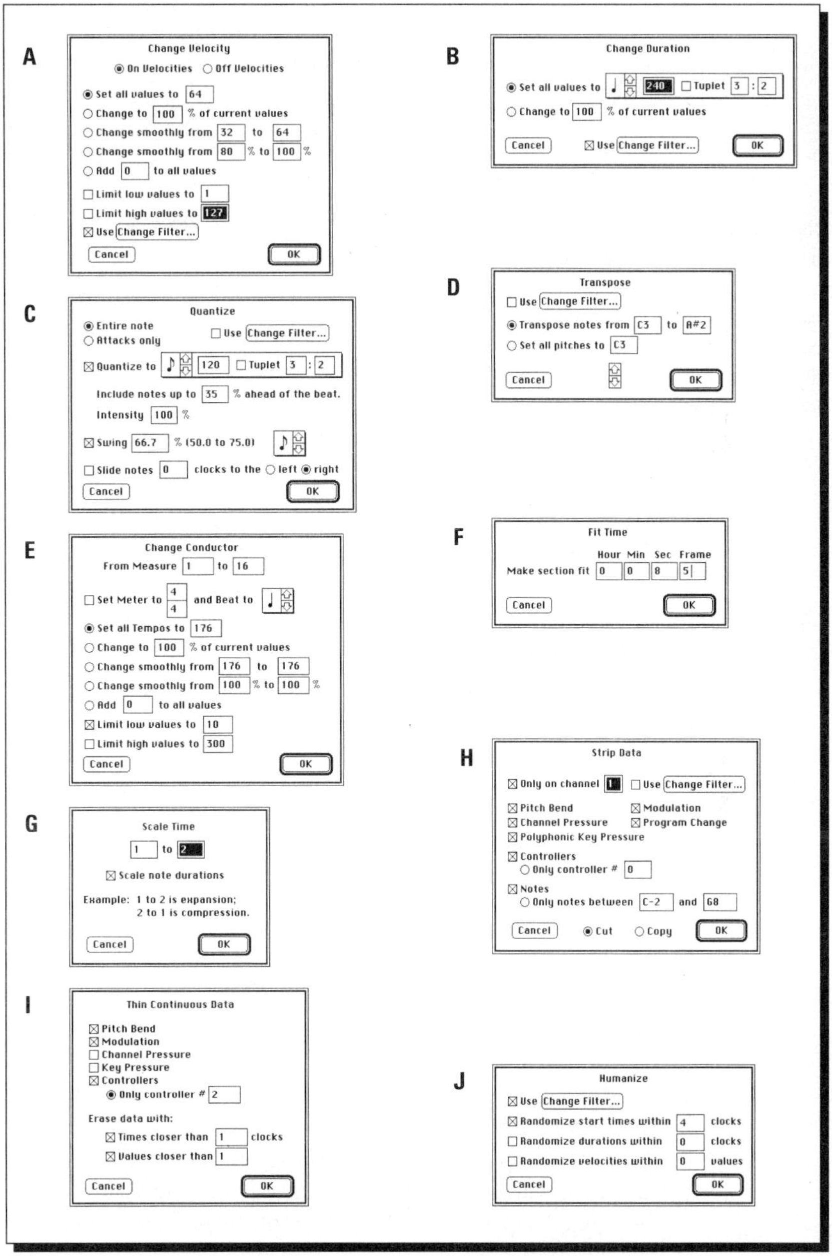

Figure 17-39: Edit interfaces in Pro 5. These are displayed in the same order as those for Trax to make comparison easy. Note the addi-tion of one or more of the following options: Change Smoothly (by per-centage), Set max- imum/ minimum limits, Humanize, and Change Filter. **(A)** Velocity editing. **(B)** Duration editing (regional). **(C)** Quant-ization. **(D)** Transpo- sition. **(E)** Conductor (tempo track editing). **(F)** Fit Time fits the selected region into the amount of time you specify, changing the tempo map accordingly (this is not available in Trax). **(G)** Scale Time scales the track data to the amount of time you specify without altering the tempo map. **(H)** Strip Data. **(I)** Thin Continuous Data (this is not available in Trax). **(J)** Humanize (this is not available in Trax).

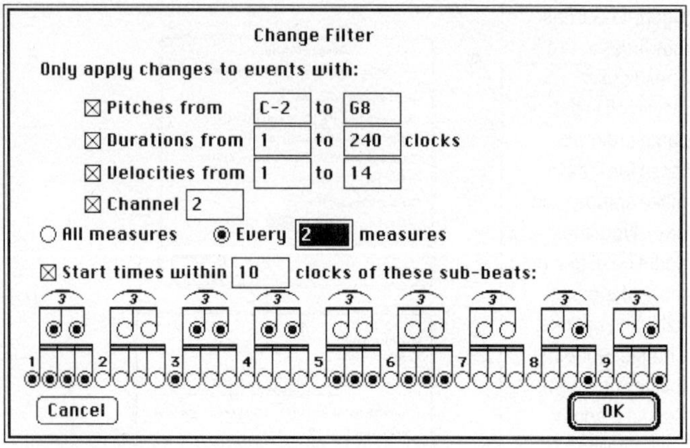

Figure 17-40: Pro 5's Change Filter dialog box is available for most editing operations. Note the metrical placement criteria at the bottom. This option originated with Passport, and this interface is still the most user-friendly available.

MIDI Mac went through a number of upgrades over the years. With version 2.5, its name changed to, simply, Sequencer. The next version, 2.6, enjoyed wide-scale success because of its provision for importing and exporting SMFs. As Sequencer 3.0 was about to be released, Opcode changed the name of the program once again, this time to Vision. This was an apt choice, because the upgrade had such significantly enhanced features (even though the look and user interface remained the same as earlier version) that the program was considered to be a vision of the future by many.

Speaking of the look and feel of Vision, you might hear complaints from certain sectors of the Macintosh music community. The majority of people who complain about Vision are Performer and Pro 5 users, who base their grumbling on the fact that Vision's transport doesn't operate the "standard" way (there is no Rewind button), or that the font used in the display is not the same as that of Performer's or Pro 5's, particularly that some of the fonts are boldfaced — rather minor gripes if you ask me. Actually, the use of boldface type often indicates that an item is editable, which is a nice visual cue.

Vision and most of its predecessors take a pattern-oriented approach to sequencing. However, the implementation of this feature is so transparent that you can operate the program without even being aware of this fact. Since there's nothing mandating that you have to link your sequences in Vision, many people who are not inclined to pattern orientation simply treat Vision as being able to store 26 sequences (each with up to 99 tracks) in a single file.

Vision introduced many new features to the Macintosh music community that have now become standard. Among these are transposition maps and multidevice/channel virtual instruments.

Vision's virtual instruments can have a number of attributes, including the ability to silence other instruments, an automatic pitch reassignment map, a don't-respond-to-transpose flag (very necessary for drum tracks), a MIDI channel and serial port or cable assignment, a velocity fader assignment and scaling factor, and a default transposition. Furthermore, each virtual instrument can consist of a group of devices assigned to any MIDI channel or channels on any number of devices. Vision is still the only sequencer that allows you to define Overflow virtual instruments. This means that when the polyphonic range of one device making up the virtual instrument is exceeded, the remaining notes overflow onto the next device of that instrument, and so on for all the devices involved. Vision's transposition maps and virtual instrument features are illustrated and discussed in Chapter 16, "Making Music with MIDI". The relationship of Vision's faders to virtual instruments is covered in Chapter 25.

When it comes to editing MIDI data, Vision is like having a microscope and a diamond cutter. The options are practically overwhelming, but fortunately Vision provides context-sensitive on-line help for just about everything. You can select and edit any kind of MIDI data in just about any way you can possibly imagine. When version 1.31 arrived, I had the distinct impression that the developers might have run out of MIDI editing features to add to the program, because now they were adding options to edit the interface — the placement of modal dialog boxes, the colors and layout of the display, and so on. If you find something that isn't possible to accomplish with Vision, just call the company (or write them a letter), and they'll probably add it to the next update. Their programmers are definitely among the sharpest in the business.

Vision requires OMS (the Opcode MIDI System — version 1.1.3 at the time of this writing). OMS was discussed in detail in Chapter 8, "Moving Data Around Your Music Network" (there you also find information about the interaction of Apple's MIDI Manager with OMS). Essentially, OMS is an environment that allows multiple MIDI applications to run simultaneously, sharing the modem and printer ports and the Macintosh timing clock. OMS keeps track of a good deal of information about your MIDI setup and provides this information to OMS-compatible programs. OMS knows the names of all your devices, including which channels and serial ports they are assigned to. If you are using a cableized interface such as Mark of the Unicorn's MIDI Time Piece or Opcode's Studio 5, OMS keeps track of the cables all your devices are assigned to. It also knows about what devices are attached to one another by way of their MIDI THRU ports and all your MIDI patchbay configurations, if you have one. Finally, OMS lets your software communicate with NuBus cards like Digidesign's SampleCell.

When you launch an OMS-compatible application, such as Vision, StudioVision, Galaxy, Galaxy Plus Editors, Track Chart, or Max, OMS provides the program with complete information about your system (see Figure 17-41). This lets you refer to

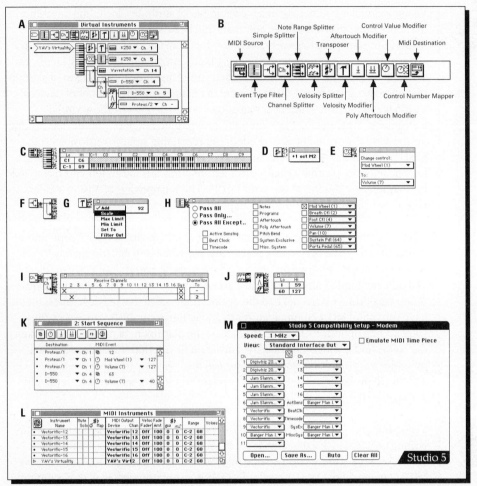

Figure 17-41: Creating Virtual Instruments in the Studio 5 for availability in Vision. Modifiers are discussed in the order they appear, reading top to bottom and left to right. **(A)** The virtual instrument named "Yav's Virtuality" as it appears in an OMS patch document window. **(B)** The icon bar at the top of the window lets you add various types of processing to individual components of virtual instruments. **(C)** Based upon note range, the Note Range Splitter directs input to channel 1 of a K250, channel 5 of a K250, or a group consisting of a Wavestation, two channels of a D-550, and a Proteus/2. **(D)** Input arriving at channel 1 of the K250 is transposed by a major ninth. **(E)** The Control Number Mapper remaps input Mod Wheel data arriving at channel 5 of the K250 to MIDI volume (Controller 7). **(F)** The Simple Splitter does not process the incoming data. It simply splits the signal among two destinations. **(G)** The Velocity Modifier scales the velocities of notes arriving at channel 1 of the K250 by 92%. **(H)** The Event Type Filter is set to pass all data except Mod Wheel to channel 5 of the K250. **(I)** The Channel Splitter passes channel 1 on to the D-550's channel 4 (including System messages). The Proteus/2 and channel 5 of the D-550 only receive incoming data that originates on channel 2. **(J)** The Velocity Splitter directs incoming notes of 59 or less to channel 5 of the D-550 while notes of velocity 60 or greater are passed on to the Proteus/2 (provided they fulfill the previous criteria). **(K)** The Start Sequence is a list of MIDI messages that is transmitted to various devices (in this case the Proteus/2 and D-550) when this specific OMS patch is recalled. **(L)** Virtual instruments created by the Studio 5 are recognized by Vision and StudioVision just like any other instruments and appear in the instrument list as pictured. **(M)** If you're playing a sequence that was created with Mark of the Unicorn's MIDI Time Piece interface, Opcode's Studio 5 can emulate their competitor's interface (see the checkbox in the upper right of this Compatibility Setup dialog box).

all of your devices by name rather than MIDI channel number. If you make any changes to your setup, these are saved in a single Studio Setup document that lets OMS notify all compatible applications of the changes the next time they are launched. If you have an Opcode Studio 5 MIDI interface, OMS provides even more features.

One very nice feature that results from OMS knowing about your system is the following: Every time you open a sequence created in an earlier configuration of your studio — e.g., from another version of Vision, from someone else's studio, from an SMF, or from a notation file from Professional Composer or DMCS — OMS is able to detect which tracks are not assigned to existing devices. Vision presents you with a dialog box that lets you remap the tracks onto devices you have defined in OMS. You have the option to specify that OMS remember these remappings and apply them automatically in the future, an incredible time-saver. It is similar to the map feature offered by Lone Wolf's MidiTap discussed in Chapter 8. One very useful application of this feature is to convert all your old 32-channel sequences automatically to formats that are compatible with a cableized interface when you upgrade to the MIDI Time Piece or Studio 5.

Opcode's Studio 5 Interface and Vision

Opcode's Studio 5 MIDI interface offers virtual controllers and virtual instruments as a built-in feature of the hardware. You can save such configurations into the Studio 5's RAM and also within OMS patches that represent configurations of the interface. You can store any number of virtual controllers and virtual instruments within a patch document.

A virtual controller is simply the output of a MIDI device with some form of MIDI processing added. These are treated the same as any other MIDI controller defined in your current OMS setup document. Similarly, a virtual instrument represents some form of MIDI processing that is applied to data that is routed to one or more MIDI devices. A Studio 5 virtual instrument is treated the same as any other MIDI destination defined in your current OMS Studio Setup document, except that it enhances performance by stacking, splitting, or layering various devices and adding all the MIDI processing features provided by the hardware interface.

OMS-compatible programs such as Vision and StudioVision treat virtual instruments existing in the Studio 5 as they would any other MIDI destination device. They are automatically added to the Instrument Setup window and become available within any of Vision's Instrument pop-up menus (see Figure 17-41).

Having the virtual instrument definitions stored in the RAM of the Studio 5, rather than as real-time processing algorithms stored in Vision, significantly reduces the MIDI bandwidth. One example will suffice. Consider the fact that a layered virtual instrument in Vision must make as many copies of the data it receives as there are channels making up the virtual instrument. Each one of these copies eats up your MIDI bandwidth. With the virtual instrument definition stored in the Studio 5, only one copy of the data is sent to the interface, and this gets split to the various components of the virtual instrument by the Studio 5's own CPU.

When you first launch Vision, you are presented with a single window listing the 26 sequences that you can store in a file (Performer users note: this is equivalent to the Chunks window). Some operations can be applied to sequences as a whole within this window, but usually you will step down to the next level of the hierarchy and open an individual sequence or two or all 26. Each sequence has an associated letter and can have a unique name.

There are two basic types of sequences in Vision: normal and generated. Technically, there are two other types of sequences. One is a list of other sequences to be played in a certain order (this Parts List may include normal sequence tracks played simultaneously with entire sequences), and the other is a captured sequence (created from a Parts List, generated sequence, or sequences triggered during a performance).

Normal sequences are like all the other MIDI sequences discussed in this chapter. Generated sequences require a bit of explanation. Generated sequences provide a simple yet powerful algorithm composition tool (see Chapter 20, "Algorithmic Composition"). They can have up to two tracks (excluding the obligatory tempo and meter tracks), a Note track and a Rhythm track, although you only need to record into the Note track. Notes recorded onto a Note track can be set to play back in their original order, backward, alternately forward and backward, or randomly. You can use the rhythms from the original recording, constant rhythms, random rhythms chosen from a value range you specify, or you can apply the rhythms of the events on the Rhythm track. Similar choices are available for playback durations, although you also have the option to specify a duration as the percentage of the distance between the current note and the next attack (100% would be perfect legato) or force a constant gap between notes (a rest of a specified duration or random duration is inserted before every attack).

If you use a Rhythm track in a generated sequence, the opportunities for variation increase exponentially. You can record a rhythmic pattern of any length you desire into the Rhythm track (using real-time or step-time recording). Alternatively, you can paste a normally recorded track from another sequence into the Rhythm track. You can even type the letters corresponding to other sequences in your file and have the Rhythm track be a chain of subsequences. In any case, with material in the Rhythm track of a generated sequence, you can assign the Note track to use those rhythms rather than the rhythms that you recorded with the notes themselves. Furthermore, the order of values on the Rhythm track can be set to the same options as the Note track — forward, backward, alternating, or random — with the same degree of fine control. Playback of generated sequences can be combined with normal sequences or captured as a normal sequence (thereby freezing it). Because you can edit the notes in the Note track and the rhythms in the Rhythm track, a generated sequence is a structure over which you can exert considerable control.

Figure 17-42: A typical screen of Vision illustrating the upper level of its file organization. The list of 26 sequences stored in this file appears at the center. Literally any of Vision's options can be controlled remotely from the Macintosh keyboard or your MIDI controller. In the latter case, you can designate a MIDI Shift key that functions like a typewriter Shift key. When pressed, your MIDI keyboard

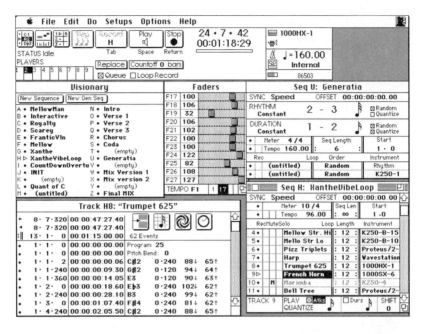

functions in MIDIkeys mode as a remote controller for program operation. Otherwise, your MIDI keyboard is used for inputting notes and other forms of MIDI data. In the lower left of the transport is a toggleable display labeled Players or Player. This is one of Vision's most powerful features (see text). At the right are some open sequence windows showing the difference between normal and generated sequences. Note the Shift option at the lower right of the normal sequence window. You can adjust this during playback to create a feel to each track. Each sequence opens in its own window, which lists up to 99 tracks, including their output assignments, looping status, and duration (you can crop a sequence without erasing notes occurring after the end point you set). Above the track list are global effects that concern the entire sequence, such as tempo map, meter map, length, start time, loop, SMPTE offset, etc. At the bottom of each sequence window (except generated sequences) is a list of settings that apply to individual tracks, including track shift and nondestructive playback quantization of both attacks and durations independently. At the lower left is a typical event list window. When you consider this display with the one in Figure 17-43, you might come to the correct conclusion that your Macintosh screen can become quite cluttered with the multitude of Vision's windows. Don't worry. Opcode has taken care of this. Pressing the mouse anywhere with the Command and Option keys down displays a pop-up menu of all open windows. And pressing the mouse down with the Option key in any graphic editing window's title bar displays a list of all the current tracks and lets you immediately switch the display to another track.

In Figure 17-42, note the little Players display at the lower left of the transport controls. Vision provides nine Players. You can think of these as virtual sequencers within Vision or as independent playback engines for the current sequence file. It's sort of like having nine record players available, all with the same record playing, and the ability to jump from track to track or activate any combination at will. The display can be toggled to show an individual Player or the status of all nine Players. A Player can be set to queue up sequences if you like, and the queued sequences are displayed to the right of the currently playing one when the display is set to show an individual Player. Queuing up sequences for a Player is as simple as typing their corresponding letters on the Macintosh keyboard. Then they play one after another.

Alternatively, if the display is set to Players (note the plural), nine boxes are shown, each representing a separate Player. Now when you type letters on the Macintosh keyboard, you can direct them to any of the nine Players (precede the letter with a number key). Each of the nine Players has its own sequence queue, so you can get dozens of sequences playing or queued up simultaneously. Sequences can overlap with themselves as well (meaning two or more Players can play the same sequence, but start at different times). This is another case where the possibilities are limitless. Naturally, you can control all of these functions from your MIDI keyboard as well as using the MIDIkeys feature (see Figure 17-42). With MIDIkeys, you can record a sequence, have a Player or two (or more) play it back, perhaps interspersed with queued-up prerecorded sequences, and record another (and another), all without ever taking your hands off your MIDI controller.

Vision's approach to graphic editing is the most powerful available (much of the same features are offered by EZ Vision — see above). Editing the piano-roll display of note data is similar to that of most other programs, with the addition of a unique option that lets you stretch selected regions with the cursor to either scale attacks and durations or to generate tempo events, ensuring that a region will occupy a specified amount of time (see Figure 17-43). Where other programs require cumbersome dialog box interaction to edit non-note data, in Vision you can accomplish all the same things with a simple mouse drag.

Through a proprietary operation called Publish and Subscribe (not to be confused with the Publish and Subscribe options in Apple's System 7), you can establish a dynamic link between Vision (or StudioVision) and either Opcode's universal librarian, Galaxy, or their universal editor/librarian, Galaxy Plus Editors. Once linked, anywhere you might otherwise refer to sounds by patch number, you are presented with a pop-up menu with a list of patch names available for the instrument with which you are currently dealing. This includes all Event List and Graphic windows, the Control Bar, and the Metronome Sound dialog box. You can even assign names to individual notes for drum machines. The complete process is described in Chapter 12, "Editing Synthesized Sound."

Vision's Program & Note Names window is where you establish dynamic links between the MIDI sequencer and patch libraries created by Galaxy or Galaxy Plus Editors. The interface is roughly identical to the one illustrated earlier in this chapter under the heading "EZ Vision."

You can also copy a Patch in Galaxy or Galaxy Plus Editors and paste its SysEx data into a Vision track via the Macintosh Clipboard. Vision lets you copy to the Clip-

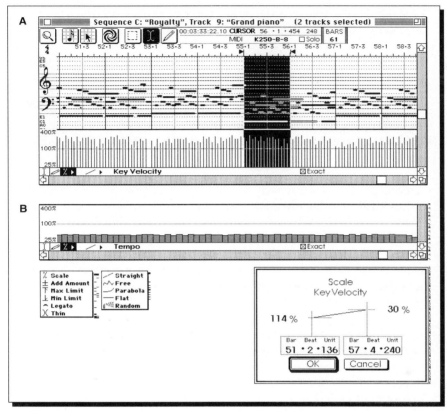

Figure 17-43: (A) Vision's Graphic Editing window. All the standard features that have been mentioned with other software are available here. Note the similarities to EZ Vision's main display. Additionally, you can scrub playback through the music (both backward and forward) by dragging in the note display with the mouse button and the Command key down. The Strip Chart at the bottom of this window is set to display Note-On Velocity. **(B)** This Strip Chart is set to display tempo. The Exact box is checked, so dialog boxes (similar to the one displayed in the following illustration of Vision's editing dialog boxes) appear immediately after you draw any contour with the Pencil tool.

board any selected region, track, or sequence and have it converted to an SMF in the process. This facilitates exchanging files between Vision and Cue or Track Chart.

In addition to Select All, Vision offers three selection options that make it the leader in the area of delineating data as the target for subsequent editing operations. Select by Rule lets you create a sophisticated selection filter consisting of any combination of criteria you can imagine. Boolean operators are available for every parameter. Optionally, you can specify metrical placement criteria that are relative to bar lines or beat lines. You can also add bracketing events as a condition. Finally, you can AND any number of these rules together to function as a more complex selection rule (see Figure 17-44).

Split Notes lets you select the highest or lowest *N* notes of a region, the highest or lowest *N* notes that are being sounded together in a region, or notes within a specified proximity to the highest or lowest pitch of a region.

The third option is to Select Duplicates. This lets you specify a search width in units or as a percentage and identify data meeting the condition for subsequent editing.

A seemingly minor but extremely powerful item is the Mogrify button, another successful interface improvement. You may have noticed that practically every window of Vision has a Mogrify button (it resembles a whirlpool). Pressing on this button displays a pop-up menu of all the relevant items from the Do and Edit menus that are applicable to the current situation. Besides bringing the available options closer to the data you want to edit (less time spent reaching up to the menu bar with the mouse), the grouping of the items from both menus is a stroke of genius.

Although graphic editing is the most efficient way to get your work accomplished in Vision, some items require dialog box interaction or can be controlled by dialog boxes accessed from the Mogrify buttons. Figure 17-45 pictures some of these.

Vision implements pattern-level editing particularly well, making chaining sequences as simple as typing the sequences' letter names — for example: a, a, b, a, b, c, b, c, d, c, d, d (in Vision, sequences have both a user-defined name, such as Verse One, and a letter name). When chained in this manner, the sequences are considered subsequences. Typing these letters can either trigger the associated sequences immediately or send them to a Player's queue (see above), allowing you to have up to nine sequences playing back at a time. The resulting sequence chain can be captured into a new sequence containing the sum of all the parts, or you may use this approach in real time or step time to simply create a Parts List for subsequent editing (see Figure 17-46).

When you edit a Parts List or record a sequence chain in real time with an input map active on your MIDI controller, several additional chaining operations become available. To understand these, you must understand the Trigger and Transpose modes that you can set up for your MIDI controller for live performance situations.

Transpose mode. Playing a key transposes all sequences currently playing back (except the one you are recording, if you happen to be recording at the time).

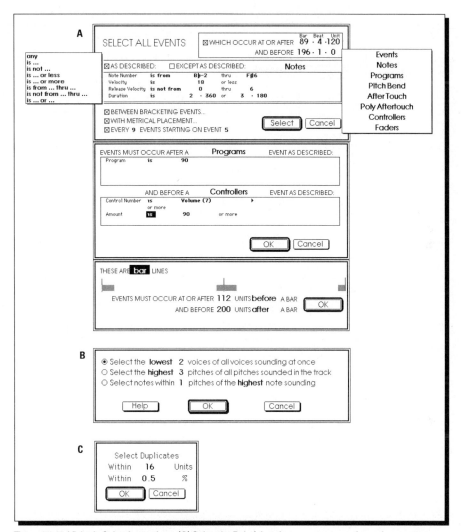

Figure 17-44: Vision's Selection options. **(A)** Select by Rule (showing pop-up menus for various parameters). The Bracketing Events and Metrical Placement dialog boxes (pictured) can be used in conjunction with this option. **(B)** Split Notes. **(C)** Select Duplicates.

Trigger mode. Playing a note plays the selected sequence transposed to that note for as long as you hold the key down. Arpeggiating a chord triggers multiple delayed copies of the sequence.

Continuous Trigger mode. Same as Trigger mode, except that releasing a key does not halt sequence playback. All triggered sequences play through to their ends.

Gated mode. Each sequence plays only for as long as you press a key down.

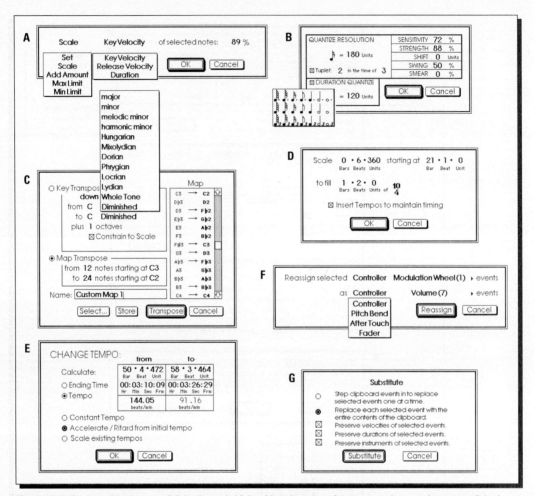

Figure 17-45: Region editing by way of dialog boxes in Vision. Note that most of these operations can be accomplished more efficiently through graphic editing. However, these dialog boxes are the easiest way to edit entire sequences or groups of tracks. **(A)** Modify Notes (velocity and duration editing). **(B)** Setup Quantize. **(C)** Transpose. **(D)** Scale Time. **(E)** Change Tempo. **(F)** Reassign. **(G)** Substitute. This is an extremely original editing operation introduced with Vision 1.3 (and later). Substitute is another way to deal with pitch and rhythm independently. There are two options. You can "step" the Clipboard in a note at a time to replace notes in the selected region (each note in a chord counts as a separate event, unlike when you use a generated sequence to accomplish similar operations in which you step in whole chords at a time). The other option is to replace each event with the contents of the Clipboard. You can choose to preserve velocities, durations, and/or instruments if you like.

Figure 17-46: Pattern Chaining in Vision.
(A) This window illustrates the various types
of chaining possible in Vision. The sequences
identified with a letter and no number are
references to the data stored in the main
sequence window. Editing one such
sequence changes all occurrences of it in this
window. The sequences with a letter *and* a
number have been cloned. To clone a
sequence, you simply copy it from this
window and paste it back into the window.
The numbers are added automatically, and
the sequences are now independent.
Sequences with a plus sign preceding the
letter are of the Continuous Trigger mode
type. Sequences with a plus and a minus sign
are of the Gated mode type. The sequence
labeled Generatia is a generated sequence,
but there is no way to distinguish this from a
normal sequence in a sequence chain, unless
you set the name to reflect its type (as is the
case here). The Transpose and + Transpose
events are of the Trigger or Transpose mode
type. Transpose without a plus sign cancels
all previous transposition values, whereas
+ Transpose adds a relative transposition
value to the previous transposition value.
Finally, the Stop Sequence event is one that
you can insert from the pop-up menu in this
window to stop the sequence (you can

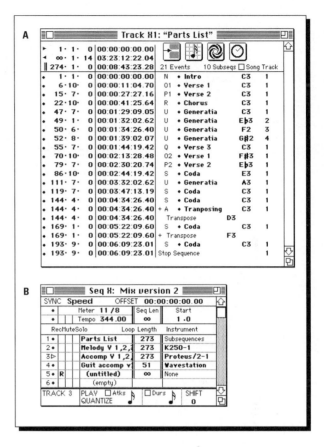

record this in real time by pressing the Period key on the Macintosh keyboard or its corresponding MIDIkey on your
MIDI Controller). The two rightmost items next to each subsequence event represent the playback transpose value for
the particular subsequence and that subsequence's Player (see text). Remember that any sequence can have up to nine
Players. This explains why some of the sequences appear to overlap (they do), if you examine the start times and the
lengths of some of the sequences in this window. **(B)** This Parts List sequence appears as a track labeled Subsequences
in a normal or generated sequence window, so you can record up to 98 additional tracks to go along with it. You can
even use this chain of sequence as a subsequence in another sequence chain. If you capture all the data to another
sequence, you can delete all the sequences that were associated with the letters referencing the various components of
the sequence chain. Confused? It's not surprising. This type of interface to chaining is rather convoluted when you
compare it to the elegant graphic approach to the same problem offered by Vision's younger sibling, EZ Vision (and other
Macintosh sequencers such as Rhapsody, Cubase, and Performer).

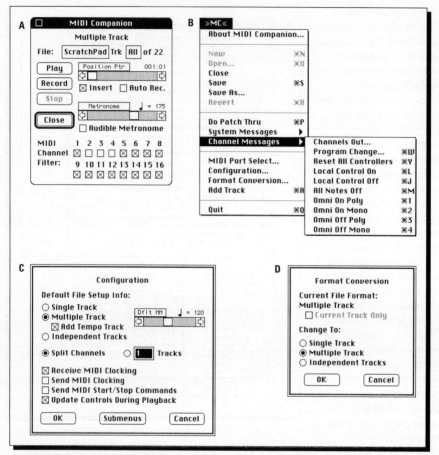

Figure 17-47: Robert Patterson's shareware MIDI Companion is a Desk Accessory that you can use to quickly record SMFs while in some other program (for example, if you happen to have an idea while typing a letter). There is no way to view your data. You can only record and play back. **(A)** The Main window functions as transport controls, channel filter, and track selector. **(B)** You accomplish program navigation with this menu. **(C)** The Configuration window. **(D)** The Format Conversion window.

Shareware

MIDI Companion

(see Figure 17-47 for more details)

MiniTrax

Altech Systems's public domain MiniTrax (programmed by James Chandler Jr. and Allan Marsalis) is a 16-track SMF sequencer offering more flexibility than you might expect in a PD (public domain) program (see Figure 17-48). The software is distributed as an example of a program written in MIDI Basic (Altech's MIDI programming language) and it is a pretty impressive example.

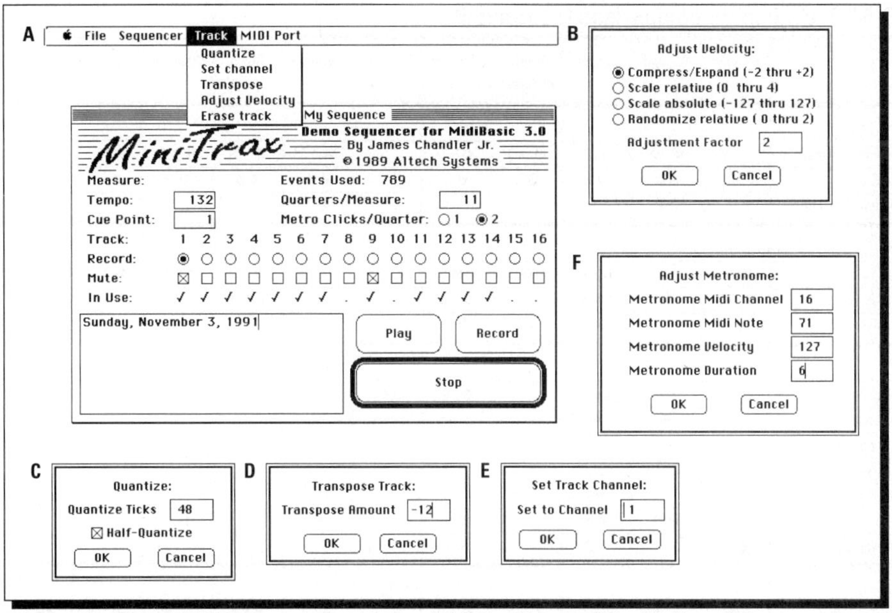

Figure 17-48: MiniTrax. **(A)** Main recording window. **(B)** Adjust Velocity dialog box (note the compression options). **(C)** Quantize dialog box. **(D)** Transposition dialog box. **(E)** Set Channel dialog box. **(F)** Adjust Metronome dialog box.

Assessing the Sequencers

Table 17-3 compares the features of each MIDI sequencer as they relate to setup, input, display, selection, editing, quantization, sync, and playback.

Table: 17-3: MIDI sequencer comparison

GENERAL	Ballade	Beyond	Cubase	Deluxe Recorder	EZ Vision	One-Step	Performer	Pro 5	Rhapsody	Trax	Vision
Version	1.01	2.1	1.81	1.0	1.0	1.0	2.62	5.0	3.0	2.0	1.31
This version System 7 compatible	●	●	●	◗	●	●	●	●	●	●	●
# open files, seqs/file	1,1	1,16	1,U	1,1	1,25	1,1	1,U	16,1	1,U	1,1	1,26
# tracks/sequence, channels/track	16,1	99,16	64,16	16,16	16,1	16,16	U,512	64,8	64,16	64,16	99,32
# sequences/song, songs/file	(9),1	32,32	U,U		25,1	U,U	16,1	U,1		2574, 2574	
Tick resolution: 480, 384, 240		●●●	○◗○	●○○	●○○		●○○	○○●		○○●	●○○
192, 96, 48	○○●	●○○	●○○	○●○	●○○						
Tempo range (low)	12	12	30.000	20	5	30	20.0	10.00	50	10.00	5.00
Tempo range (high)	250	300	250	500	500	275	400	300	250	300	500
MIDI Manager compatible, option	●○	●●	●●		●●		●●	●●	●●	●	
MTP, Studio 5 (cableized mode)		●	●				●	●			●
Un-copyprotected	●	●		●	●	●	●		●	●	
On-line Help					●		●				●

Table: 17-3: MIDI sequencer comparison (continued)

SETUP	Ballade	Beyond	Cubase	Deluxe Recorder	EZ Vision	One-Step	Performer	Pro 5	Rhapsody	Trax	Vision
Virtual Instruments											
Name, Transpose, Non-transpose	○○◗	●○●	●◗○	●○○	●◗○		●○○	●○●	●○○	◗○○	●●
Port & chan, Cable & chan		●●	●●	●○	●○		●●	●●	●○	◗○	●●
Initial: patch, volume (or scaling)		●●					●○				○●
Global Track Setup											
Volume, Pan, Delay	●●○		●●●	●●○	●●○	◗○○		●○○	◗●○	●○○	
Transpose, Compress, Vel. Scale	●○○		●●●	●○○	●●○			◗○○			
Initial patch, Initial SysEx dump	●○		●◗	●○	●○		●●	●○	●○	●○	
Virtual Faders											
Track Vol, Configure, Animation	●○●	◗◗●	●●●		●○●	●●●	●○●		●●●	●○○	◗●●
Map to hardware controllers		●	●				●				●
Build multiple fader consoles			●				●				◗
Group faders, max # in group			I,U		w,16		I,32				
Master/slave: Match, Offset			●●				●●				
Master/slave: Scale, Reverse pol.		●○	●●		●○		●●	●○	●○		
Save snapshots, multiple per seq.	●○		●●		◗○		◗○	◗○			
Remote Controls											
Macintosh, MIDI, configurable	●●●	◗○◗	●●●	●○○	●○○	●○○	●●●	●●●	◗●●	●○○	●●●

INPUT	Ballade	Beyond	Cubase	Deluxe Recorder	EZ Vision	One-Step	Performer	Pro 5	Rhapsody	Trax	Vision
Real-time											
Single-chan, Multi-chan, Multi-port	●○○	●●○	●●●	●●◗	●○○	●●○	●●●	●●●	●●○	●●○	●●●
Overdub, Wait-for-note	●○	◗●	●○	●○	●●	●●	●●	●○	○○	○●	●●
Punch in, out, audible pre-roll	●●●	●●●	●●●		●●◗		●●●	●●●	●●●	●●●	●●●
Loop record, overdub, replace		●◗○	●●●	●●◗	●●◗	●●◗	●●●	●●●	●●●		●●●
Last loop take reject, mute		●●	●●	●○	●○		◗○		●●		●○
Loop advance to new track (muting previous), with instrument change		●●	●●	◗●					●○		
Quant. on input, post-determine beat	●○	●	●	○●			●●	●○	○●	●○	○●
Keep channel info, Record SysEx	●●	●●	●●	○●	●●	○●	●◗	●●	●○	●●	
Real-time reassign controllers			●				◗		●		●
Auto-RTZ, memory-rewind, cues	●●○	◗●●	●●●			○○◗	●●○	●○○		●○○	●○○
Input Filter (Selective)											
Filter Notes, Velocity, Prog. Change	○○●	●○●	●○●	●○●			●●●	●●●	●○●	●●●	●●●
Filter Pitch Bend, Mod Wheel	●●	●●	●◗	●○			●●	●●	●○	●●	●●
Filter Aftertouch, Controllers	○◗	●●	●●	●●			●●	●●	●●	●●	●●
Step-time											
MIDI, mouse	●●	●●	●●	●◗	●●	●●	●●	●●	○●	●●	●●
Lock duration, duration ≠ step	●◗	●●	●●	●○	●●	●●	●○	●●	○◗	●●	●●

Table: 17-3: MIDI sequencer comparison (continued)

INPUT (continued)	Ballade	Beyond	Cubase	Deluxe Recorder	EZ Vision	One-Step	Performer	Pro 5	Rhapsody	Trax	Vision
Step-time											
Velocity: assign, remotely, record	●○●	◐○●	●◐●	○○●	●○●	●●	○○●	●○●	○●○	●○●	●○●
Tuplet steps, any tick value steps	◐○	◐●	●◐	◐●	●●	●●	●●	●○	◐○	●○	●●
Import/Export											
SMF	●	●	●	●	●	◐	●	●	●	●	●
DMCS, ProComposer			●○		●●		○●				●●
Insts., Faders, Transpose maps			◐●◐				●●●	●○●	◐○○	●○○	●●●
Capture chain/song, expand loops	◐○	●●	●●				●●	◐○○			●●
Metronome											
Mac speaker, MIDI, visual	○●○	●●◐	●●○	●●●	●●◐	○●○	●●◐	●●◐	○●○	●●○	●●◐
Accent downbeat, subdivisions	●○	●●	●○	●○	●○	◐○	●●	●○	●○	●○	●○
Variable note value for click	●	●	●	●	●		●	●	●	●●	
Count-off, select # of measures	●○	●●	●●	●●	●●	●○	●●	●○	●○	●○	●●

DISPLAY	Ballade	Beyond	Cubase	Deluxe Recorder	EZ Vision	One-Step	Performer	Pro 5	Rhapsody	Trax	Vision
Notes: Alphanumeric (text)		●	●			◐	●	●	●		●
Notes: Graphic (piano roll)		●	●	●	●	●	●	●	●	●	●
Notes: Notation	●		●				●				
Overview window		●	●	◐			●	●		●	
Marker window	●						●	●			◐
Controller window	●	●	●	◐	●	●	●	●	●		●
Velocity window		●	●	◐	●		●	●	●		●
Sequence/patterns/parts list		●	●				●		●		◐
Song or Chain window	◐	◐	●				●	●	●		◐
Conductor or Tempo track	●	●	●	◐	●	●	●				●
Drum editing display	●		●						●		
SysEx editor window		●	◐		●		●	●	●		◐
MIDI activity monitor	●		●	●			●				
Memory usage		●	●	●		●	●	●	●	●	●
View multiple displays, tracks	◐○	●○	●●	●○	◐●	○●	●●	●○	●●	●○	●●
Counter: Metric, time, SMPTE	●○○	●○●	●●●	●●○	●○○	●●●	●●●	●●●	●●●	●●●	●●●
Data Identification											
Name instruments, max number	I,U	I,32		I,256	w,39+	I,32	I,U	I,U	I,U	w,(10)	I,U
Name patches, import, subscribe	●●○			●●○	●●●		●●○	●●○	●●○	◐○○	●●●
Name notes	●		●		●				●		●
Name markers, lock to time, float	●●●	●○○	◐●●				●●●	●●●		●○●	●●●
Group tracks regions into object	●	●	●		◐		●		●		◐
Comments: song, sequence, track		○●○	●○●				●●●	○●○	○●○		○○●
General Display Aids											
Time and pitch indicators	◐	●	●		●	●	●	●	●	▲	●
Shading or other velocity indication on note symbols		●	◐		●	●		●	●		
Define grid of graphic display	◐	●	●	●	◐		●				
Set cue points		●	●								
Data View Filter		●	●	●	◐	◐	●	●	◐		●

SELECTION	Ballade	Beyond	Cubase	Deluxe Recorder	EZ Vision	One-Step	Performer	Pro 5	Rhapsody	Trax	Vision
Song, sequence, track	○●●	●●●	●●●	○○◐	●●●	○○◐	○●●	○●●	●●●	○●●	●●●
Tracks contiguous, discontiguous	●○	●○	●●	◐◐	●●		●●	●○	●●	●○	●●

Table: 17-3: MIDI sequencer comparison (continued)

SELECTION (continued)	Ballade	Beyond	Cubase	Deluxe Recorder	EZ Vision	One-Step	Performer	Pro 5	Rhapsody	Trax	Vision
Region: by bar lines, beats, ticks	●●♪	●●●	●●●	●●●	●●●	●●●	●●●	●●●	●●●	●●●	●●●
Range of pitches: highest or lowest	♪○	●○	●♪			●○	●●	●○	●○	●○	●●
Range of durs., vels., controllers	○○♪	●●○	●●●			●●●	●●○	●●♪	●●●	●●●	
Relative to beat, bar, proximity		♪♪●	●●♪			○○♪	●●○	●●●	●●●		●●●
Relative to specified events			●						●		●
By MIDI channel(s)	♪	●	●			♪		●	●	●	●
Boolean And, Not, Or	♪	♪	●			●	♪	●	●	♪	●

EDITING	Ballade	Beyond	Cubase	Deluxe Recorder	EZ Vision	One-Step	Performer	Pro 5	Rhapsody	Trax	Vision
Cut, copy	●●	●	●	●	●	●	●	●	●	●	●
Does not truncate note-offs extending beyond selection	●		●	●	●	●	●	●	●		●
Paste, scale paste to destination	●○	●○	●○	●●	●●	●○	●○	●○	●○	●○	●○
Merge, insert	●○	●●	●●	●○	●●	●○	●●	●●	○●	●○	●●
Repeat *n* times, to fill, & transpose		●●●	●●○		●●○	●●●	●○○	●●○			●●○
Clear, insert blank, delete time	●●●	●●●	○●●	●●●	●●●	●♪○	●●●	●●●	●●○	●●●	●●●
Shift region, shift track(s)	●●	●●	●●		●●	●●	●●	●●	♪○	●●	●●
Edit Filter	●	●	♪	♪			●	●	♪	♪	●
Graphic Editing Features											
Drag: move, copy, snap-to-grid		●○●	●●●	●●○	●●●	●●○	●●●	○○●	●●○		●●●
Tools for scaling, truncating, etc. graphically displayed non-note data		●	♪	●		♪		●		●	
Notation Editing											
Drag: to move, to copy			●●				●●				
Overview Editing											
Drag: to move, to copy			●●	●●			●●				
Pitch											
Transpose: diatonic, chromatic	●●	♪●	●●	●●	○♪	○●	●●	♪●	●●	○●	●●
Transpose custom, save custom		●●	♪♪			♪○	●●	●●	●●		●●
Invert: chrom., diatonic, retrograde		●●●	♪♪♪			♪♪○	●●○		●●○		♪♪○
Harmonize	♪	●	♪								
Velocity											
Set to, Add to, Scale	●○○	●●●	●●●	♪○○	●●●	●●●	●●●	●●●	●●●	●●●	●●●
Limit to minimum or maximum			●●		●	♪	●	●	●		●
Smooth change: linear, percent, curve fit	●●○	●●○		●●●	○●○	●●●	●●○	●○○	●○○	●●●	
Randomize: percent, unit, range		○●●	●●●			●●●	●○○		○●○	●○○	●●●
Duration											
Set to, Add to, Scale	●○○	●○●	●●●	♪○○	●●●	●●●	●●●	●●●	●●●	●○●	●●●
Limit to minimum or maximum			●●		●	♪	●		●		●
Change smoothly			●		●	●		♪	●		●
Randomize		●	●		●	●	●	●			●
Extend to next attack, grid unit		●○	●●		♪○	●●	●♪		○♪		●●
Time											
Reverse, scale		●●	●○				●●	○●	○●		●●
Fit to time, inserting tempos	●●	●●		●●		●●	●♪	●●		●●	
Randomize starts, by % of duration		●●				●●		●○	●●		

Table: 17-3: MIDI sequencer comparison (continued)

EDITING (continued)	Ballade	Beyond	Cubase	Deluxe Recorder	EZ Vision	One-Step	Performer	Pro 5	Rhapsody	Trax	Vision
Tempo											
Accel/Ritard: draw, generate		●●	○♪	●○	●○	●○	●●	●●	●●	○●	●●
Scale tempos to fit time, randomize		●●			○●	♪○		●○		♪○	○♪
Continuous Data											
Set to, Add to, Scale	●○○	●●●	●●●		●●●	●●●	○●●	●●●	●●●		●●●
Limit to minimum or maximum			●		●	♪	●	●	●		●
Smooth change: linear, percent, curve fit		●○○	●●○		●●●	○●○	●○●	●●○	●○○		●●●
Thin, smooth, reassign		○○♪	♪●●		●♪●	♪○●	●●●	●○●	○♪●		●○●
Generate, Draw		○●	○●	○●	○●	○●	●●	○●	○●		○●
Looping											
Sequence, track, region	●○○	●●●	●●●	♪○♪	●●○	♪♪♪	●●●	●●○	●●●	○●○	●●○
Nested, transposed, randomized			●♪○				●○○		●●○		○○♪
Non-coinciding, mute specified iterations	●○	●♪				●○	♪○	●●	●○	●○	
MIDI Channel Options											
Unmerge multichannel track, Retain original channel info.	●●	●●	○●	●♪	♪♪		♪●	●●	♪●	●●	
Assign notes to specified channel, Assign more than 1 chan per track	●●	●♪	♪●		♪○	○●	●●	●●	●♪	●●	
Miscellaneous											
Multiple key sigs, meter sigs	●●	●●	○●	○●	○♪		●●	○●	♪♪	○●	●●
Edit during playback	♪	●	●	●	●		●	●	♪		●
Edit SysEx data		●	●		●		●	●	●		●
Delete: duplicates, fudged notes		●♪	●♪	●○			○●	●♪			●●
Generated sequences			●								●

QUANTIZATION	Ballade	Beyond	Cubase	Deluxe Recorder	EZ Vision	One-Step	Performer	Pro 5	Rhapsody	Trax	Vision
Durations in ticks, rhythmic durations	○●	●●	○●	●●	○●	●●	●●	○●	●●	○●	●●
Tuplets (range nn : nn)	3:2	3:2	3:2	99:99	3:2	3:2	99:99	16:16	ticks	16:16	99:99
On input, output, non-destructive	●○○	●○○	●●●		○●○		●○○	●○○		●○○	●●●
Attacks and releases, deflam	●○	●○	●●			●○	●●	●○	●○	●○	●♪
Just attacks, releases, durations	●○●	●●○	●○●	●○●	●○○	●●●	●●●	●○○	○○●	●○○	○○●
Set sensitivity, strength		○●	●●	○♪			●●	♪●	●●	♪●	●●
Set offset, swing		○●				●○	●●	●●	●○	●○	●●
Match (to other track), Groove		●○	●●						●○		
Post-determine beat, barlines				●●		○♪	●○		●○		●●

CHAINING	Ballade	Beyond	Cubase	Deluxe Recorder	EZ Vision	One-Step	Performer	Pro 5	Rhapsody	Trax	Vision
Chain horizontally, vertically	♪○	●●	●●		●○		●●	●○	●●		●●
Linked copies, sever links, independent playback parameters		●♪○	●●●		●○○		●○○		●♪●		●●♪
Expand chains/songs to sequence	♪	●	●		●		●		♪		●
Rearrange patterns graphically, Option-drag to copy		●●	●●		●●		●●	●○	●○		
Subsections coexist with notes		●									●
Chain songs (songs within songs)			●				●		♪		●

Table: 17-3: MIDI sequencer comparison (continued)

SYNC	Ballade	Beyond	Cubase	Deluxe Recorder	EZ Vision	One-Step	Performer	Pro 5	Rhapsody	Trax	Vision
MIDI Sync	●	●	●	●	●	●	●	●	●	●	●
SMPTE (MTC), subframe resolution	●○	●●	●●			●●	●	●○	●○		●●
Auto-sense/set frame rate	●		●								
DTL, DTLe		●○					●●				
Human sync (tap tempo)			●	♪			●				●
Output: MIDI Sync, MTC	●○	●●	●●	●○	●○		●●	●●		●○	●●

PLAYBACK	Ballade	Beyond	Cubase	Deluxe Recorder	EZ Vision	One-Step	Performer	Pro 5	Rhapsody	Trax	Vision
General											
Number of playback channels	16	512	512	32	16	16	512	256	32	16	512
Multiple sequences simultaneously		●	●				●		♪		●
Send SysEx during playback		●	●		●	●	●	♪			●
Click on note or region to hear		●	●	●	●		●	●			●
Playback Controls											
Play, Stop, Pause (ignore Note Off)	●●●	●●○	●●○	●●●	●●●	●●●	●●●	●●●	●●○	●●●	●●●
Fast forward, hear music during	●○	●●	●●	●●	●●	●●	●●	●●	●●	●●	
Rewind, hear music during	●○	●○	●○	●○	●●	●●	●○	●○	●○	●○	
Scrub backwards and forwards, step		♪○			●○				○●		●○
Mute, solo	●●	●●	●●	○●	●●	○●	●		●●		●●
Auto-rewind, to stored location	●●	●●	●●	▶▶			●●	●○	●○	●●	
Miscellaneous											
Scroll windows during playback	●	●	●	●	●	●	●	●	●	●	●
All, selected, location indicator	●○●	○●●	●○●	○●●	●○●	●○○	●●●	●○●	●●○	○●●	●○●
Chase controllers	♪	●	●	●	●		●	●			●
All Notes Off option		●	●		●		●	●			●
Kbd control patterns/chunks/parts			♪				●	●			●
Metronome click during playback		●	●		●	●	●	●		●	●
Real-time MIDI processing			●								

Interview with Patrick Moraz
Performer, Composer

Yavelow: How do you use the Macintosh and MIDI sequencers to help you compose and perform?

Moraz: I've got several Macintoshes, fortunately. The one I'm using with my MIDI system, which is quite a large one, I use in conjunction with programs like Performer and Vision. And I've got two MIDI Time Pieces controlling many Kurzweil modules, many Korgs, and many other synthesizers. I like to do multikeyboard compositions on a very instant and intuitive basis, which means that I can play with or without a click and compose for picture or without picture, whatever the reason is. For me, it's the most flexible way of composing, because I'm really an improvisor and an instant composer and I've got a lot of inspiration, whether it's at five o'clock in the morning or at noon or whatever, I can really compose and arrange and orchestrate as we go. I do a lot of multikeyboard sequencing at once.

Yavelow: How do you distinguish instant composition from improvisation?

Moraz: For a multikeyboard instant composition I'm using distinct elements, which means I'm composing in the etymological sense of the term; I'm composing from existing pieces that I might take from different sequences. I've already pre-intuitively composed and I can take this element or that element. For example, if I'm in Vision and I choose either generated sequences or non-generated sequences, but I'm going to create sequences labeled A, B, C, D, E, F, G, for a total of 26 different pieces that are pre-organized, I might do that, and very quickly bridge the gaps between these sequences using them in different, random orders every time. That's how I would make the distinction between instant composition and pure improvisation. Obviously, I can go and do an improvisation, for example, just on one keyboard and immediately arrange it, so it crystallizes the improvisation. When I crystallize the improvisation on the spot, whether I'm doing it by multikeyboard technique or using the same instrument, but in multimode [multitimbral] technique, then it becomes an instant composition, which means that in the given time I'm organizing it, I already think about all the parts I'm going to put in a very short time.

Yavelow: And then parts of it are pre-orchestrated?

Moraz: Often they are, but sometimes I start from scratch. I still consider it an instant composition. Let's say I play on an acoustic piano. If I play a piece of music which I consciously organize as a composition as opposed to just an improvisation (without any form or shape), then I do it with a form and shape in mind as soon as I've started and I focus on that. This is another differentiation between just improvisation and instant composition.

Yavelow: So, there is a lot more organization.

Moraz: Yes, absolutely. Now, obviously, with the Macintosh and with all the technology involved, especially in multimode, using multikeyboard sounds, there is much more to it as an instant composition than just an improvisation. But I could perhaps improvise on top of some crystallized passages, and then it becomes a composition.

Yavelow: So those that you're triggering, are they instant compositions that have been captured, meaning instant compositions within an instant composition?

Moraz: Yes.

Yavelow: . . . or have you gone and really tweaked them?

Moraz: No. Some of them are completely out of the blue but others are already pre-sequenced and have just been reorganized and reorchestrated. Don't forget that I'm also talking about a lot of very different parts, like different rhythms or totally different textures of sounds, subsequences, and so on, generated sequences, and sequences within sequences. So it really gives a lot of flexibility.

Yavelow: So you have to keep jumping back and forth between the Macintosh keyboard and the MIDI keyboard?

Moraz: Yes. I do that a lot. I play, sometimes even with the keyboard of the Macintosh in my hand like a keyboard. I play with the mouse, with the Macintosh keyboard and different other MIDI instrument keyboards. Sometimes one hand on the musical keyboard and the other running the Macintosh.

Yavelow: Vision's capability for real-time editing must be extremely important in this context.

Moraz: I like to do a lot of transposing sequences in Vision and immediately transpose different things using the keys on the keyboard. I combine this with all the program changes I can go through, sometimes having the same part in all tones, different scales and so on. That is very quickly done. And very reliable. I rarely have any crashes with the Macintosh, considering the level I'm driving these instruments and the amount of memory required.

Yavelow: What if you have a crash in a live performance situation?

Moraz: No problem, because I just play the normal instruments myself while my assistant reboots the Macintosh. But generally it's no problem. And I even like that, because it creates a greater level of tension and much more of a challenge. In a studio situation we can always replay what we've just played. When I used to beta-test for Kurzweil, with the Macintosh in the mid-1980s, I had so many crashes that I'm not afraid of that anymore.

Yavelow: How do you feel about quantization, editing velocities, and things like that in general and particularly regarding these pieces that you store for material to use in instant compositions.

Moraz: I do 80 percent of my computerization and playing without having to either quantize or varying the dynamics. I like to keep that human feel. I believe I have a very good intrinsic rhythm within myself, so I don't have any problems concerning this. The only things I quantize are the occasional rhythm part and specific parts that are to be printed through Finale.

At the other extreme, I recently wrote a piece when my sound system wasn't even turned on, but the computer was and the keyboards were, and there was no sound and there was no light in the studio. I imagined being Stevie Wonder and Beethoven at the same time, and what would I do if I was confronted with that kind of impediment. Then I played it back and printed some of it with Finale. It sounds extremely consistent. I want to do more of that stuff. I don't want it to be a circus act. It's a very strong experiment and it's been extremely rewarding for me to do that.

Yavelow: Do you use other sequencers?

Moraz: Yes, absolutely. When I created my album, *Human Interface*, I recorded it entirely using Performer. At the time, I also performed *Human Interface* live with Performer. But recently, we converted the sequences to MIDI files and imported them into Vision for live performances, because Vision is more flexible for what I want to do. I want to be able to play all my music as instantly as possible with all the MIDI redistributed, like the way you showed me at the time you were using the first MIDI Time Piece. I was very impressed with your work when you said, okay, I can play this and that by talking to the Voice Navigator, and you had written 25 sequences that night. And you played me all these orchestrations, and they were all different and they were all wonderful. I was so impressed with that that I thought, I absolutely have to do exactly that from now on — live. In this way I could play my whole *Human Interface* using the MIDI keys as triggers while redistributing the MIDI data immediately. And if I even want to change from one piece to the other in public, I would be able to do this, like having a complete rockophonic electronic synthesizer orchestra and changing the whole thing in real time. If you had an orchestra, you'd have to change all the music sheets in one split second and they all play something different. It's happening; I must say I'm very well assisted and finally, we're getting there.

Yavelow: Putting all this stuff out in MIDI, do you ever find that you're pushing the bandwidth? Do notes get dropped?

Moraz: Sometimes it can go over the limit even if I use the overflow techniques, which I don't very often. Sometimes we experience channel stealing in certain areas. I'm very careful about this. But now, because of this, in a way it has created an awareness of channel stealing, which makes me be more reserved about certain orchestrations and so on. I don't go as much over the top as I used to. I think it's been more beneficial than not.

Yavelow: Let's talk a little bit more about the generated sequences, particularly since Vision is the only sequencer that lets you do that. Are these captured or frozen or do you ever play these in real time and let them regenerate themselves?

Moraz: When I opt for a generated sequence I play it, sometimes in the generated sequence mode or sometimes in a real-time mode, and then I look at the best outcome. Generally, I like the surprises. Then I experiment with all the quantization aspects and all the different

options — release and attacks, etc. — change instrumentation, all of which gives the music a completely different aspect. Then I requantize everything after having changed it. To give an example, if I play something on the string sounds and I change this to a very fast attack (percussion) and requantize (what I would call back-quantize) then we have a completely new generated sequence. I like the surprise random aspect of what I get. I play with that and it gives me another avenue to look at, to listen to, and to trigger from.

Yavelow: How long is the material that goes into one of these generated sequences?

Moraz: It could be anything, even a single measure. What I also like to do is transfer some of the timing of the generated sequences and some of the notes into normal sequences and then do different loops, different lengths. I like to play with loops of different lengths, not necessarily symmetrical. What's interesting is to do loops of 43 beats and then another one of 27 and one of 13, for example.

Yavelow: Do you ever keep any of these sequence letters open and then record into them during a performance?

Moraz: Yes. That's the idea of how to go further in the conceptualization of instant composition and record more and more all the time. Sometimes I also use just one sequence, one base, and I record over and over, hundreds of different tracks of the same instrumentation and then I mute them selectively. Sometimes I don't even listen to them anymore for months. Then I come back and see what was interesting, and so on. Obviously, the beauty of having to deal with such a system is that you can output so much and leave it frozen for years and then come back. I've got sequences I recorded in 1986 and I'm getting back to them right now and I've never listened to them since then. When I do multikeyboard recording on different keyboards, Vision puts the data on a multi-instruments track. To unmerge them I use Command-U. I like to use several controllers at once as opposed to just one MIDI controller which controls all the racks, because they all have a different feel. That gives me a lot more scope.

Yavelow: Do you have any tips for people reading this book?

Moraz: To be oneself, not to be afraid to admit one's weak points, to always listen and learn.

Summary

✔ The most common use of MIDI information is to record and store sequences of musical events played on a device such as a synthesizer or MIDI controller. Both dedicated hardware devices and computer-based software programs that record MIDI data are called MIDI sequencers. MIDI data recorded in this manner is often compared to player-piano-roll data, because in neither case are actual sounds recorded, but only the detailed instructions that direct a device to trigger a sound. Thus, each playing of a MIDI sequence results in a re-performance of what was initially played (or subsequently edited), without any signal degradation from multiple-generation recording.

✔ MIDI sequencers have replaced manuscript paper for many composers. For electronic composers, a MIDI sequence is often the only representation of a musical work (besides the sonic realization, of course). Many composers writing for acoustic instruments use MIDI sequencers in place of sketchpads. It is increasingly common to compose an entire acoustic work as a MIDI sequence and then convert the data into notation using a notation program. Many composers take a hybrid approach, which combines MIDI sequencing with live performance.

✔ There are three fundamental ways to input musical ideas into a MIDI sequencer: real-time, step-time, and algorithmically. No matter how you record information into a MIDI sequencer, the sequencer's real strength is in how you can edit your music. The scope, type, and ease of editing operations you can apply to MIDI data greatly exceed that available on analog tape devices.

✔ There are five common types of data display: alphanumeric (also known as event list), bar graph (also known as piano roll), overview (graphic timeline), chunk (patterns or subsequences), and CMN.

✔ Standardized editing options include: Cut, Copy, Paste, Merge, Insert or Splice, Repeat, Clear or Erase, Filter, Delete time or Snip, and Track shifting. Pitch transposition is child's play for a sequencer, and newer sequencers offer arbitrary Pitch remapping, Inversion, and Harmonization. Standard velocity, duration, and controller editing options include: Set to constant, Add or Subtract from, Scale by percentage, Limit maximum or minimum values, Change smoothly (linearly or by a percentage), and Randomize.

✔ Quantization is a special rhythmic editing option that shifts the location of notes in relation to a rhythmic grid that you specify. Most sequencers provide for the quantization of Attacks (with or without preserving durations), Attacks and Releases, and Releases only (with or without preserving durations). Settings for Strength, Sensitivity, Swing, Offset or Shift, and Randomization are common. More advanced programs offer deflamming of chords, quantization on input or output, real-time determination of the beat, post-determination of the beat, and combinations of options.

✔ Two types of output to expect from a sequencer are playback capabilities and file-saving capabilities. In addition to saving files in the program's native format, an important consideration is the ability to save sequences in SMF format (preferably type 1). Playback enhancements include provisions for 32 or more channel output, synchronization (SPP, MTC, and SMPTE), chasing controller information, mouse feedback (touch a note to hear it), on-screen fader animation, looping, and scrolling playback.

✔ Many sequencers offer the option to chain various subsequences together into one long composition. You can identify musical fragments and ideas as separate objects called patterns, chunks, sequences, subsequences, blocks, or modules, depending upon the MIDI sequencer you are using. Chunk-manipulation tools provide a way to assemble and manipulate musical material from increasingly greater levels of abstraction, with results that are far more efficient and effective than addressing each musical note as an individual event.

Chapter 18
MIDI Sequencing with Digital Audio

In this chapter...

✔ Early approaches to synchronizing MIDI data with digital audio.

✔ State-of-the-art MIDI sequencers that offer digital audio tracks.

✔ Overview of StudioVision, Deck, ProDECK, Digital Performer, and Audio Trax.

The Merging of Two Worlds

As you know by now, MIDI does not deal with any real sound data, only the events that trigger sounds, and digital audio only deals with sound data, not any MIDI event triggers. If you are beginning to think that all these technological breakthroughs will divide the Macintosh music community into two camps, one focused on digital audio, the other focused on MIDI — don't worry, the software bridging the gap between these seemingly incompatible worlds is already here.

In the recent past, if you wanted to synchronize MIDI sequences with digital audio tracks, you had to employ one of four methods:

❖ Synchronize Macintosh-based digital audio recordings with an external sequencer containing your MIDI sequence.

❖ Synchronize a Macintosh-based MIDI sequencer with a dedicated external digital audio recorder.

❖ Synchronize two Macintoshes, one running your digital audio software and the other running your MIDI sequencer.

❖ Synchronize two programs with MIDI Manager, one a digital audio application, and the other a MIDI sequencer. This last method is extremely unreliable in most cases, unless you have a very fast Macintosh and both your digital audio data and MIDI sequence data are not very dense.

These four approaches all do the trick, but they all require additional hardware and, therefore, added expense.

Two products released in 1990 finally offered the integration of 16-bit digital audio tracks and MIDI sequences into a single program: Digidesigns's Deck and Opcode's StudioVision. A third option, Digidesigns's ProTools, including a greatly enhanced version of Deck called ProDECK, was released in late 1991. Finally, Mark of the Unicorn's Digital Performer, was released in 1992. At the time of this writing, Steinberg's Cubase Audio is just around the corner and may be available by the time you read this. Passport Designs released their Audio Trax for the 8-bit digital audio community in 1991.

All the programs supporting 16-bit digital audio require that you own a digital audio card such as Digidesign's Sound Accelerator, Audiomedia, or ProTools Audio card. You can read about these direct-to-hard disk systems in Chapter 24, "Direct-to-Hard disk Recording." Refer to Chapter 13, "Editing Sampled Sound" for a discussion of how digital audio tracks that you combine with MIDI sequences can be edited.

Because StudioVision, Digital Performer, and Audio Trax are essentially identical to the MIDI sequencers offered by the same developers (Vision, Performer, and Trax), you should consult Chapter 17, "MIDI Sequencing" for a complete discussion of the MIDI editing aspects of these programs.

Software Solutions
StudioVision

For many Macintosh musicians, StudioVision is a dream come true. Opcode's revolutionary MIDI sequencer, Vision, had already risen to be one of the top sequencers in the industry since its introduction in 1989. Their addition of CD-quality digital audio tracks with Digidesign's Sound Accelerator (both A/D IN and DAT I/O versions) and Audiomedia cards broke such new ground that it redefined how many of us treat the role of the computer in music making (see Figure 18-1).

With StudioVision, you can record up to 16 stereo digital audio tracks, although at the time of this writing, only two mono tracks or one stereo track can be output simultaneously (future versions will support ProTools for more tracks). Tracks recorded directly into StudioVision are stored in Sound Designer II format (sd2f). Unlike Sound Designer, when you record in stereo in StudioVision, two separate linked mono soundfiles are created. You can also import files, regions, and playlists in Sound Designer I or II, AIFF, or MSND (Dyaxis) formats (see Figure 18-2).

Although you can import regions and playlists from Sound Designer or Audiomedia, StudioVision does not have options to create these entities from within the program. These are hardly necessary in StudioVision anyway, because you can achieve the same effect by option-dragging a selection to copy it, just as

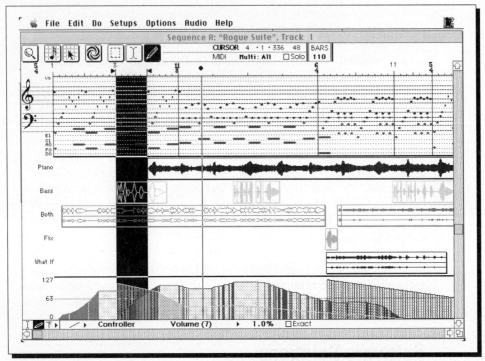

Figure 18-1: StudioVision's main screen, showing both MIDI and digital audio tracks. The first, second, and fifth audio tracks are mono. StudioVision uses color or grayscale to delineate different audio instruments. The volume (Controller 7 for MIDI data) strip chart (see Chapter 17) at the bottom of the screen affects audio amplitude just as it would affect MIDI data. You can also manipulate Pan using StudioVision's strip chart. Both of these effects can be assigned to StudioVision's on-screen faders (see Chapter 25).

you would in a graphics program. Like playlists, these copies of regions don't increase the file size, an important consideration in a medium where a minute of stereo audio requires 10MB of hard disk space.

Digital audio data that you record or import into StudioVision is assigned to one of 16 audio instruments that are displayed beneath the MIDI tracks. You can name the instruments as you like and assign different colors to their waveform displays (see Figure 18-3).

After you have recorded or imported a number of soundfiles into StudioVision, you can use the program's File Management window (see Figure 18-4) to delete unused files or just the unused portions of files. You also have the option to consolidate files. This copies all the audio data used in your current StudioVision file into a separate file (data is butted together side-by-side), retaining the references of specific regions to their locations in your StudioVision document. This is

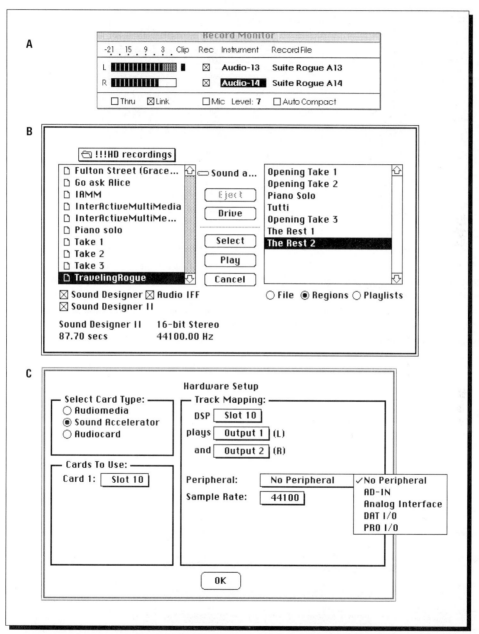

Figure 18-2: (A) Input meters for recording digital audio tracks directly into StudioVision. Because StudioVision records Sound Designer II mono files, the Link option lets you link two mono files recorded together to function as a stereo file. **(B)** StudioVision's Import Audio dialog box lets you import entire soundfiles, regions, or playlists from Sound Designer or AIFF files. Note the Play button. This lets you audition a file or region before importing it. **(C)** StudioVision's Hardware Setup dialog box.

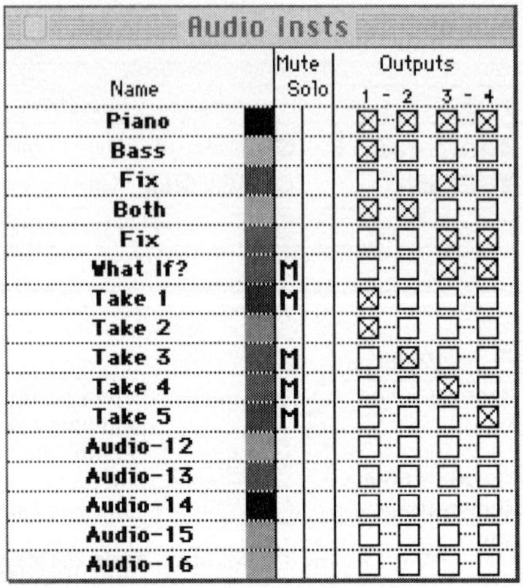

Figure 18-3: Depending upon which digital audio card you have installed, you will see one of these two windows when you choose Audio Instruments from the Audio menu. In either window, you can name, mute, or solo specific instruments. **(A)** The Audio Instruments window with Digidesign's Audiomedia or Sound Accelerator card installed. **(B)** With Digidesign's newer ProTools Audio Card (see Chapter 24), you have a choice of audio outputs to assign to individual audio instruments (depending upon the number of Audio Cards you have installed). If you check all the outputs (as in the top row), StudioVision dynamically allocates the audio data to whatever output is free when that audio instrument plays. Otherwise, audio data is routed to the output (or output pair in the case of a stereo track) that you designate.

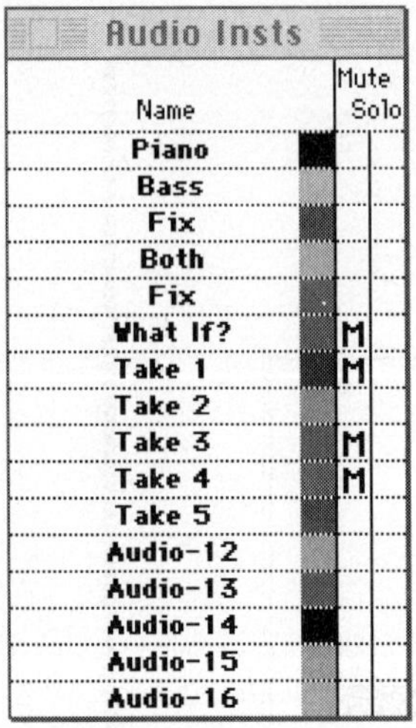

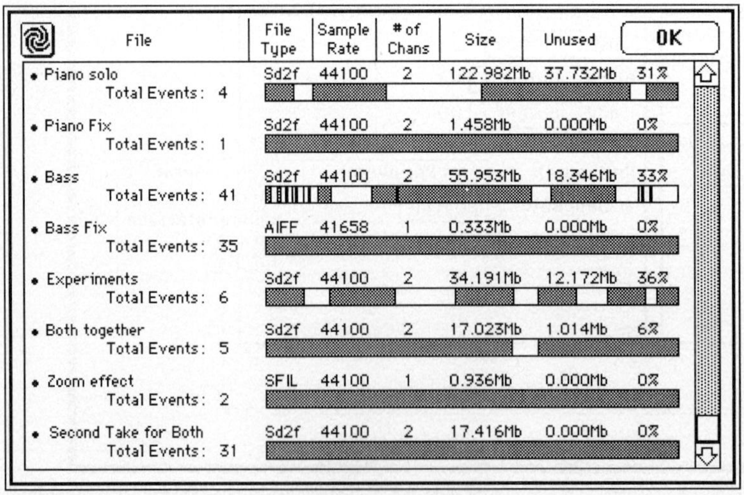

Figure 18-4: StudioVision's File Management window displays a good deal of useful information about the digital audio files that are used (or unused) in your StudioVision document. This includes file name and type, sample rate, number of channels, size, and amount unused. The horizontal bars display a graphic representation of the used and unused portions of each file. Additionally, from within this window you can compact and consolidate files (see text).

useful if you are accessing multiple digital audio files and, particularly, files that contain unused data — all of the unnecessary material is omitted from the consolidated file. You might want to do this at the end of a project for organizational purposes or if you were to give the file to a client.

While lacking all the DSP features of the dedicated hard-disk-recording programs (you'll have those options anyway with the software that comes with your digital audio NuBus card), StudioVision nonetheless supports full Cut, Copy, and Paste of digital audio, MIDI-controllable volume and stereo pan faders, complete merging of up to 16 tracks down to a single mono or stereo track, and a host of other options. All editing in StudioVision is non-destructive. If you want to edit the audio data, selecting Edit Soundfile from the Audio menu takes you directly to Sound Designer II (or your designated sample editor) with the current region highlighted.

One amazing feature is StudioVision's ability to intelligently separate a digital audio track into its component elements and quantize (rhythmically auto-correct — see Chapter 16, "Making Music with MIDI") the audio events to MIDI note events. Because this algorithm can detect individual words and notes somewhat successfully, you can use this feature to quantize the words of a song or notes of a live instrument recording (see Figure 18-5). You may need to read this paragraph twice because it might seem unbelievable.

StudioVision provides 16 audio layers. These are roughly equivalent to analog tape tracks, although when you consider that you can overlap soundfiles on a single track (the event with the later start time has playback precedence), the analogy to conventional tape tracks breaks down. It is very easy to make multiple takes of a recording and then pick the best portions of each take (see Figure 18-6).

StudioVision's powerful Mix command lets you combine audio data from multiple tracks and/or audio assigned to multiple instruments within the same track (see Figure 18-7). You can include entire audio events or just sections of audio events within your mix selection. You can also mix a stereo audio event down to a mono event to save space and output channels. Mixing creates a new mono Sound Designer II file.

If you are synchronizing StudioVision to tape, the program offers an option to calibrate its timing reference to accommodate subtle speed fluctuations on the tape (otherwise, you simply lock the sequence to SMPTE by choosing Lock Audio to Tape and your sequence, including the digital audio, will speed up and slow down if the time code does). In such cases, you want to avoid the minor speed alterations of the incoming SMPTE altering your sequence tempo during playback (in doing so, it could slow down the audio playback, effectively changing the sample rate and consequently the pitch). This is particularly useful when recording while synchronized to SMPTE.

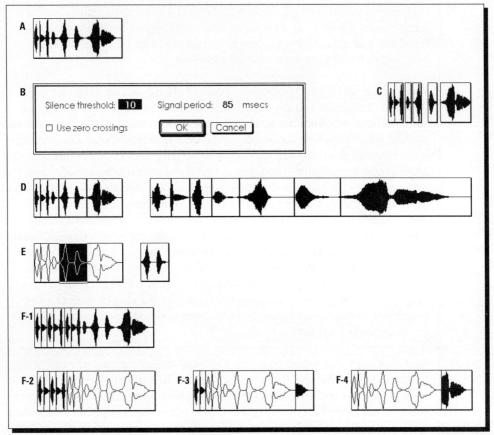

Figure 18-5: Several types of non-destructive editing in StudioVision. **(A)** An original audio recording (used to illustrate the non-destructive editing operations). **(B)** Strip Silence lets you remove audio that is below a certain amplitude. The effect is similar to a noise gate. This Strip Silence dialog box lets you define what StudioVision will consider to be silence for the operation on a scale of 0 to 100, where 1 equals 42 dB above actual silence, 50 equals 76 dB above actual silence, and 100 equals 90 dB above actual silence. You also specify a duration (from 10 to 1,000 milliseconds) for which the defined silence criterion must be met before StudioVision recognizes it. If you check the Use zero crossing checkbox, StudioVision will make its cuts at the closest zero crossings (see Chapter 13) to the region that falls below the specified decibel threshold for the specified duration (or greater). **(C)** The effect of Strip Silence on waveform A. You can now quantize these events just like MIDI notes. **(D)** You can also choose to separate the waveform into chunks that can subsequently be manipulated independently. Simply select a region and choose Separate. Here, the original waveform A has been separated into eight chunks. **(E)** If you select a portion of a waveform and then choose Retain from the Audio menu, StudioVision removes all but your selection. The selected region prior to issuing the Retain command is pictured at the left. The result is shown to the right. **(F-1)** You can create a special effect called *shingling* by choosing Repeat Paste from the Edit menu or by Option-dragging a waveform along its audio track. Shingling relies upon the fact that StudioVision plays back only the visible portion of overlapping waveforms, regardless of how many copies are stacked (and shifted) on top of it. In other words, the event with the later start time has playback precedence when multiple events overlap. Here is what a shingled waveform looks like on a track. **(F-2),(F-3) (F-4)** When you click a portion of a shingled waveform, the region that is beneath the rest of the copies is displayed and highlighted.

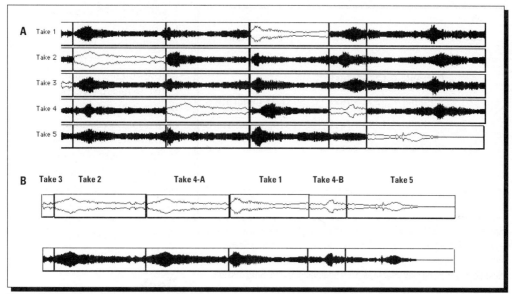

Figure 18-6: (A) After making several takes of a passage, you can highlight individual regions and use Play Selection (or press the spacebar with the Option key down) to audition just those parts. **(B)** Once you have determined the best versions of each region, you simply drag them to a new audio instrument layer to create the perfect take.

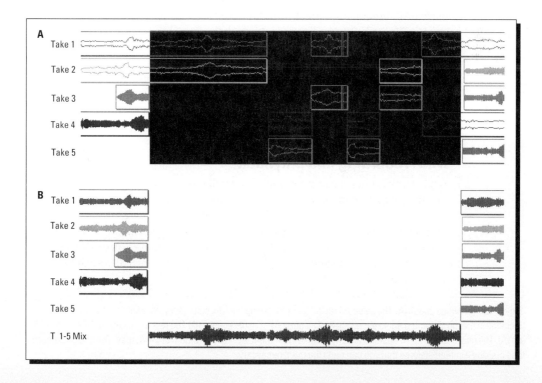

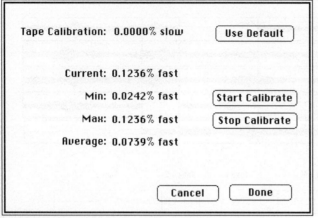

Tape Calibration: 0.0000% slow   [Use Default]

Current: 0.1236% fast

Min: 0.0242% fast   [Start Calibrate]

Max: 0.1236% fast   [Stop Calibrate]

Average: 0.0739% fast

[Cancel]   [Done]

Figure 18-8: StudioVision's Tape Calibration dialog box lets you analyze your tape's SMPTE track and use this information to accommodate timing information that is slightly slower or faster than expected. After you enter this dialog box, you must play your tape from beginning to end. StudioVision detects the minimum and maximum speed fluctuations and determines the average. When you click OK after tape calibration, StudioVision changes the relationship between MIDI events and audio events to take the real speed of incoming time code into account.

If you are going to use the Tape Calibration dialog box (pictured in Figure 18-8), you should do so either before you record MIDI or before you record audio (or both). In fact, it is recommended that you always calibrate your tape prior to recording digital audio while synced to SMPTE (note that there is never any sample rate conversion when recording digital audio, regardless of whether you are synced or not). Once you have finished recording, you shouldn't change the tape calibration.

Deck

Digidesign's Deck provides recording digital audio tracks along with MIDI playback and recording and digital audio playback. Additionally, the software supports four-channel audio playback through any Digidesign NuBus audio card (although the four channels are mixed to a single stereo output).

Deck's strengths lie in the direct-to-hard disk recording arena and are therefore covered in Chapter 24, "Direct-to-Hard Disk Recording." For a thorough discussion of this program's capabilities and additional illustrations you should read that chapter now. The MIDI features of Deck are discussed below.

MIDI recording and playback

While Deck is not primarily a sequencer, it will record and play back 32 channels of MIDI data simultaneously with digital audio. Tracks can consist of multiple MIDI channels and can be rechannelized to a single MIDI channel (see Figure 18-9). Very limited sequence-editing operations are available; you will probably want to use a dedicated sequencer in conjunction with Deck, because you can import and export data freely with any MIDI sequencer that supports the SMF format (just about all sequencers do).

Figure 18-7 (previous page): (A) The selected region (prior to issuing the Mix command) includes data from five tracks. Included in the mix are entire audio events as well as portions of audio events. **(B)** The result of using the Mix command on (A). The mixed-down audio appears on a new audio instrument layer at the bottom of the screen. You should select it and audition it immediately, so that you can undo the mix if necessary.

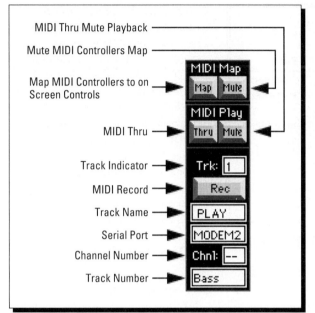

MIDI Thru Mute Playback

Mute MIDI Controllers Map

Map MIDI Controllers to on
Screen Controls

MIDI Thru

Track Indicator

MIDI Record

Track Name

Serial Port

Channel Number

Track Number

Figure 18-9: Deck's MIDI playback and recording controls. The playback controls allow you to mute, solo, and reassign channel and port to individual tracks. You must, however, scroll to the desired track, because there is no way to display the status of all tracks at once. The recording controls are the same ones used for recording of digital audio and they present the same options for punching in and out, looping, and merging (sound-on-sound).

MIDI-recording options in Deck include loop (rehearse) playback, automated punch-in and punch-out, and merge record mode (sound-on-sound). Deck records channel data along with each input MIDI stream. You can reassign tracks to different MIDI channels if you like (see below). Deck also provides a very nice implementation of mapping hardware MIDI controls to virtual screen controls. These are discussed in Chapter 24, "Direct-to-Hard disk Recording."

If you plan to export your MIDI data from Deck to an SMF, you must record with the MIDI metronome (see below), so that the correct barline, beat boundaries, tempo, and meter signature information is included with the sequences you record in Deck.

If you are not planning on recording MIDI data and digital audio data simultaneously, there are three working approaches to combining MIDI with digital audio using Deck. These considerations are required because Deck does not offer the sophisticated temporal shifting of digital audio data that StudioVision and Digital Performer provide. The three approaches are:

❖ *Recording or importing the MIDI tracks first and then the audio tracks.* This implies that you either record your MIDI tracks directly into Deck prior to doing any audio recording, or that you are importing an SMF into the software. If you do either of these things prior to recording any digital audio, you can guarantee that subsequent recording of digital audio tracks will be synchronized with the MIDI data (provided that you can play along with it).

❖ *Recording the audio tracks first and then the MIDI tracks.* If you record MIDI tracks into Deck, you can take one of two approaches. In the first scenario you record MIDI while listening to Deck play back digital audio tracks. This requires that you record at least one digital audio track to assure that the MIDI data is synchronized to the digital audio data. Note that SMF importation is not recommended in this case.

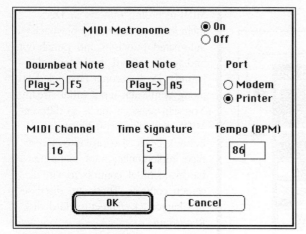

Figure 18-10: Deck's MIDI Metronome resembles that found in most Macintosh MIDI sequencers.

❖ *Recording the audio tracks first and then importing an SMF.* The second method is to record your audio while listening to Deck's MIDI metronome (see Figure 18-10). Provided that you record your audio tracks while listening to this metronome, you can then import a MIDI sequence and set it to the same tempo of the MIDI metronome, thus assuring that everything will be in sync. Note that this method can also be used for real-time recording.

MIDI data editing

Don't expect too much from Deck with respect to editing MIDI data — Deck is first and foremost a direct-to-hard disk digital audio recording system. Deck's options for editing MIDI data are all limited to entire tracks. Smaller regions of tracks cannot be delineated or selected for editing. All available operations are accessed with the Transform MIDI Track dialog box (see Figure 18-11). Here you can perform the following edits:

❖ Copy one track onto another track.
❖ Merge one track into another track.
❖ Delete an entire track.
❖ Rechannelize all, one, or all but one channel(s) on an individual track.
❖ Transpose all, one, or all but one channel(s) on an individual track.
❖ Remove controllers from all, one, or all but one channel(s) on an individual track.
❖ Remove pitch bend from all, one, or all but one channel(s) on an individual track.
❖ Remove mono aftertouch from all, one, or all but one channel(s) on an individual track.
❖ Remove polyphonic pressure from all, one, or all but one channel(s) on an individual track.

Synchronization

Deck's synchronization capabilities are limited to MIDI Song Position Pointer (SPP) and MIDI Clock. With Deck as a slave, you can start, stop, and continue Deck with software that sends SPP or lock up Deck to MIDI Clock. You can also use Deck as a master for SPP- and MIDI-Clock-compatible devices.

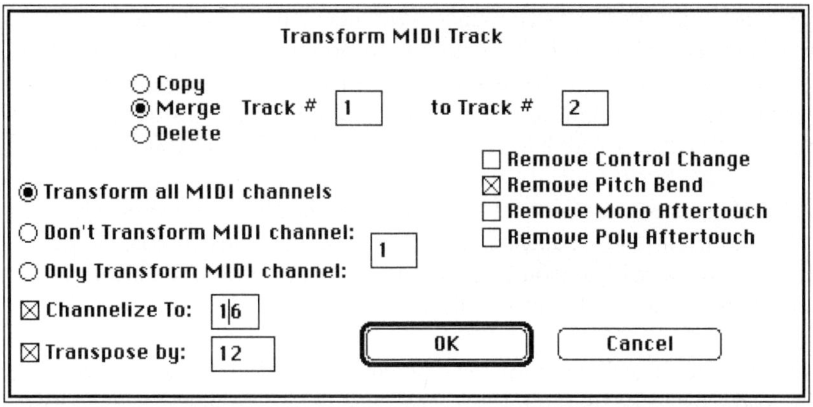

Transform MIDI Track

○ Copy
◉ Merge   Track #   `1`   to Track #   `2`
○ Delete

                        ☐ Remove Control Change
◉ **Transform all MIDI channels**   ☒ Remove Pitch Bend
○ **Don't Transform MIDI channel:**   ☐ Remove Mono Aftertouch
                      `1` ☐ Remove Poly Aftertouch
○ **Only Transform MIDI channel:**

☒ **Channelize To:**   `1|6`
                         ┌───────────┐ ┌───────────┐
☒ **Transpose by:**   `12`   │ **OK** │ │ Cancel │

Figure 18-11: Deck's MIDI editing features — all of them are contained in this Transform MIDI Track dialog box.

Deck also generates 30-frame MIDI Time Code if you want but in this case, devices must be slaved to Deck as the master. MIDI timing information is routed by way of Apple's MIDI Manager or Deck's own MIDI drivers.

Finally, if you are using Digidesign's Sound Accelerator card with Deck, you have the additional option to trigger Deck with a SMPTE command (you can also set a SMPTE offset in this case). The important thing to remember is that Deck is being triggered by a SMPTE frame. It is not locked to SMPTE in real time. This shouldn't make a difference if your trigger source is another computer- or microprocessor-controlled device, because the internal clocks of such devices are so accurate. However, if your SMPTE source is an audio or video tape, Deck may drift out of sync due to slight variations of the tape transport speed.

ProDECK

Digidesign's ProDECK is part of their ProTools package (discussed in Chapter 24). Unlike Deck, this software supports 4- to 16-channel audio output (ProTools Audio Card required). Like its predecessor, ProDECK is primarily a direct-to-hard disk recording system and most of the MIDI editing options are similar to those found in Deck (see Figure 18-12). Although synchronization (including MIDI Time Piece support) and display of MIDI data are enhanced, you are still limited to 32 MIDI channels (in the initial release).

Digital Performer

Opcode has been adding features to StudioVision virtually every day, and this did not go unnoticed by the competition. In late 1991, when Mark of the Unicorn released their entry into this market — Digital Performer — the "sequencer wars" started all over again.

Mark of the Unicorn's Digital Performer is the new kid on the block. It is the only software described in the book that I did not personally have a copy of for testing. However, I did attend several demonstrations of the software and managed thereby to procure the screen shots included with this discussion. Be forewarned that things may have changed slightly by the time you read this.

Digital Performer is Mark of the Unicorn's Performer MIDI sequencer with digital audio tracks (see Chapter 17 for an in-depth look at Performer). The company paid special attention to using identical editing displays and commands for both MIDI and digital audio data.

Nearly all of the digital audio options offered by Digital Performer have counterparts in Opcode's StudioVision (see Figures 18-13 through 18-15). Two important StudioVision features missing from Digital Performer at the time of this writing are the capability to consolidate files and to mix files, both of which create a new soundfile (see the discussion of StudioVision above for information on these features).

Audio Trax

Passport's Audio Trax, released in 1991, combines MIDI sequencing with 8-bit digital audio (see Figure 18-16). It was also the first direct-to-hard disk recording system for 8-bit digital audio. All previous 8-bit recording systems were limited to recording into RAM.

Audio Trax offers the most practical way to inject combined MIDI and 8-bit digital audio into multimedia software that supports both these elements (such as MacroMind Director).

You can use MacroMind-Paracomp's MacRecorder to record 8-bit audio into Audio Trax ('snd ' resources and 8-bit AIFFs are supported). If you have a Macintosh LC or IIsi, you can use the built-in microphone. Alternatively, you can convert any 16-bit soundfile into an 8-bit soundfile using Alchemy, Sound Apprentice, or many of the software tools discussed in Chapters 10 and 13.

Audio Trax is similar to Passport's TRAX (see Chapter 17), with the addition of digital audio features. Digital audio appears in its own window in the form of a waveform.

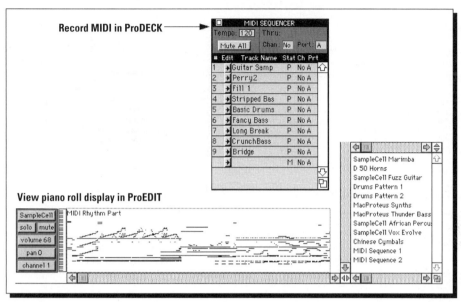

Figure 18-12: ProDECK provides a piano-roll display of MIDI data through its companion program ProEDIT (missing from its predecessor, Deck).

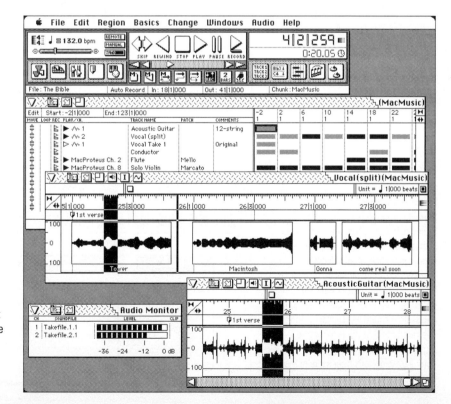

Figure 18-13: The main screen of Digital Performer, picturing most of the interface elements that differ from "non-digital" Performer.

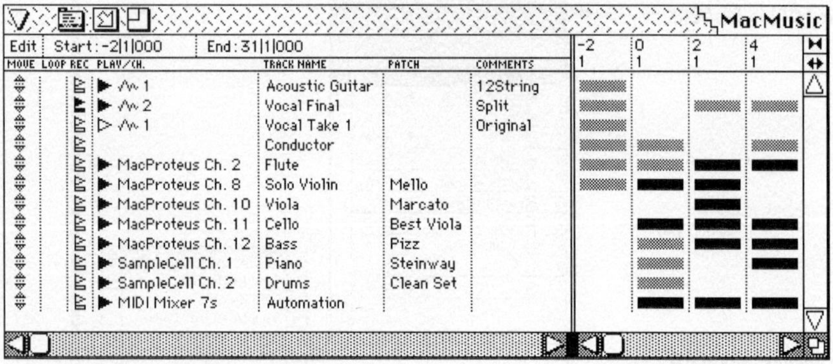

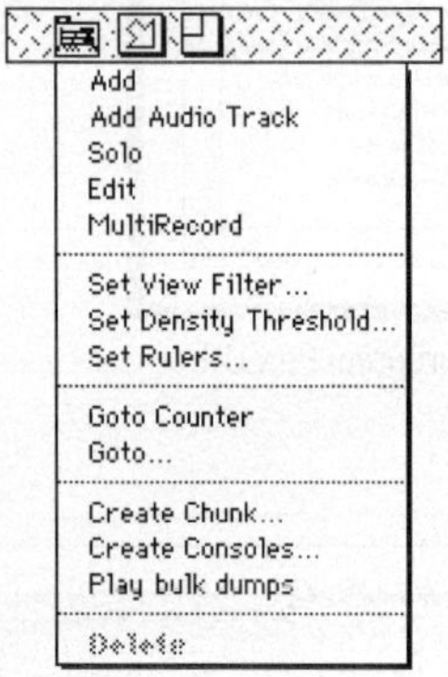

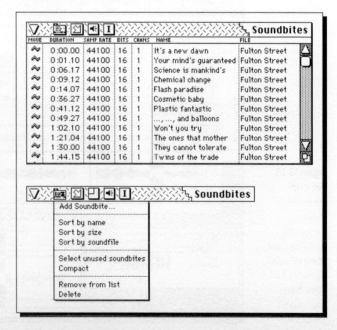

Figure 18-14: Digital audio tracks appear in Digital Performer's Tracks window with a little waveform next to them. This overview style editing feature (described in Chapter 17) is not found in StudioVision, although StudioVision's display of audio instrument layers provides some of the same functionality.

Figure 18-15: Digital Performer's Soundbites window differs from StudioVision's File Management window in that you can sort the list by name, source soundfile, or size. As in StudioVision, each digital audio event is listed with its duration, sample rate, resolu-tion, number of channels, name, and source sound file. Digital Performer uses the term Soundbite to refer to regions of soundfiles. This avoids confusion with Performer's use of the word regions in the context of MIDI data.

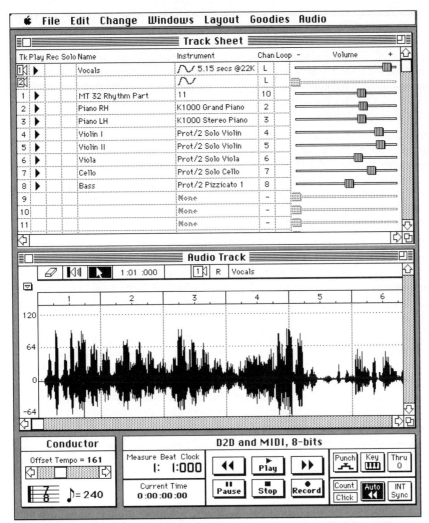

Figure 18-16: Audio Trax main screen with an audio track open. Note: The speaker icons indicate digital audio tracks in the Track Sheet window.

Summary

✔ MIDI does not deal with any real sound data, only the events that trigger sounds, and digital audio only deals with sound data, not any MIDI event triggers. If you are beginning to think that this will divide the Macintosh music community into two camps, one focused on digital audio, the other focused on MIDI — don't worry, the software bridging the gap between these seemingly incompatible worlds is already here.

✔ In the recent past, if you wanted to synchronize MIDI sequences with digital audio tracks, you had to employ one of four methods: synchronize Macintosh-based digital audio recordings with an external sequencer; synchronize a Macintosh-based MIDI sequencer with a dedicated external digital audio recorder; synchronize two Macintoshes, one running digital audio software and the other running a MIDI sequencer; or synchronize two programs with MIDI Manager, one a digital audio application, and the other a MIDI sequencer (usually unreliable). These all require additional hardware and, therefore, added expense.

✔ At the time of this writing, there are a number of options for combining MIDI sequencing with digital audio. In the 16-bit, 44.1 KHz (CD-quality) domain, StudioVision, Digital Performer, Deck, ProDECK, and Cubase Audio all require that you have a digital audio NuBus card such as Digidesign's Audiomedia, Sound Accelerator, or ProTools Audio Card. In the 8-bit, 22 KHz domain, Passport Designs's Audio Trax employs the built-in microphone of Macintoshes that have them at an external 8-bit digitizer such as MacroMind-Paracomp's MacRecorder (or similar digitizer).

✔ Combining MIDI data with digital audio currently takes one of two approaches: Digital audio tracks are added to a MIDI sequencer or MIDI tracks are added to direct-to-hard disk digital audio software. In the former case, most editing of digital audio data must be done in a dedicated sample-editing program (however, you gain all the advantages of random access and non-destructive editing). In the latter case, most editing of MIDI data must be accomplished in a sequencer. In the future, greater integration of these two worlds can be expected.

✔ Although digital signal processing and sample editing all require the use of a separate program, MIDI sequencers that offer digital audio tracks are replete with non-destructive editing features (the actual digital audio soundfiles are not altered — the sound is simply modified at the output stage). This includes cuts, copies, splices, segmentation, complete reorganization of track regions, fading, crossfading, panning, and gating.

✔ An extremely useful option is that of stripping the silence between audio events. Once you have done this, individual notes (or words, in the case of vocal tracks) can be quantized in the same way as normal MIDI data.

Chapter 19

Interactive Composition and Intelligent Instruments

In this chapter . . .

✔ The relationship of improvisation to interactive composition.

✔ Making distinctions between interactive composition and algorithmic composition.

✔ The interrelationship of interactive composition and intelligent instruments.

✔ The impact of artificial intelligence and expert systems on interactive composition.

✔ Examining MIDI and non-MIDI software for interactive composition in detail.

✔ Sample output (in conventional music notation) from several intelligent instruments.

✔ Interactive software for drum machine programming.

Getting Interactive with Your Mac

The boundaries separating composition and improvisation are blurring as new applications of the Macintosh to these age-old musical phenomena emerge. Three essential elements have recently fallen into place that contribute to making interactive composition with a Macintosh practical, even commercially viable from a developer's point of view.

First, the Macintosh can make extremely complicated compositional decisions at speeds equalling literally millions of decisions in the space between two notes — for all practical purposes, in real time. Second, while this is happening, appropriate software can keep track of all the necessary musical rules and aesthetic principles inherent to a specific type of musical composition, providing the benefits of the equivalent of years of advanced musical training built right into the programs. Finally, the Macintosh's friendly user interface permits people with relatively little knowledge of computer programming to explore realms of creativity that were hitherto open only to people with advanced degrees in computer science.

Interactive composition (a term coined by one of the pioneers of this field, Joel Chadabe) straddles the boundary between composition and improvisation. It is sort of a hybrid creative process. This hybrid combines many of the concepts of composition and improvisation.

To understand interactive composition, you must first understand a little bit about improvisation.

What is improvisation?

When compositional decisions are made on-the-fly, in real time, we often refer to the process as *improvisation* rather than composition. Most people are probably familiar with the role of improvisation in jazz — but improvisation can take many forms. In the 19th century, it was a highly developed art practiced by piano virtuosos such as Franz Liszt. Even today, one major concern of improvisation in performance is virtuosity. Improvisatory performances often turn into virtuosity contests — let the player with the most chops win. But virtuosity is not necessarily a positive musical force; it can be an empty display.

When I lived in Hungary, there was an organist who gave weekly improvised performances at one of the churches. People would bring short melodic fragments to her and she would improvise whole fugues using their submissions as subjects. On another occasion, at the Liszt Academy in Budapest, I once saw a piano professor and two students (one on clarinet and one on cello) improvise in a variety of musical styles ranging from late romanticism, through impressionism, to neoclassic. They passed themes and counterthemes around with a facility reminiscent of jazz musicians.

Distinctions
Interactive composition

Interactive composition is nothing new — serious computer musicians have been working with systems devised for their own personal use for many years. What is new is the commercial availability of interactive composition tools. One thing making this possible is the development of software programs generalized enough to support a wide variety of styles and users. The significance of the Macintosh's user-friendly computing environment as a vehicle for interactive composition cannot be overstressed.

Interactive composition should not be confused with computer-generated music, algorithmic composition, or automatic composition (see Chapter 20, "Algorithmic Composition"), with which it shares a common ancestry. In fact they all blur together. With the emergence of interactive composition, the words "computer-generated music" have taken on a definition as that specific type of algorithmic composition which, once set in motion, typically "goes its own way — does its own thing" with little human intervention other than an initial defining of parameters. In contrast, interactive composition adds real-time interactivity to the act of composition, and in many ways is more akin to improvisation.

Interactive composition, through this merging of the activities of composition, improvisation, and to a certain extent, live performance, has stimulated a plethora of research and development. This can be attributed to a number of interdependent factors, which are inherent to the process: First, the interrelationship of man and machine has been redefined, not as master/slave but more like partners or collaborators, or as an extension of one or the other. Secondly, these activities are no longer restricted to the province of master computer programmers.

Intelligent instruments

The words "interactive composition" and "intelligent instruments" are bound up in one another. In many cases they can be considered interchangeable. Nearly all intelligent instruments provide front ends to interactive composition software; however, interactive composition programs are not necessarily intelligent instruments.

Some people prefer to draw the line between interactive composition and the playing of intelligent instruments upon the consideration of whether an *expert system* (see the section "Expert systems") or something resembling an expert system is involved in the process, in which case we can refer to the software as an intelligent instrument.

Laurie Spiegel and Max Mathews coined the term "intelligent instrument." Laurie Spiegel, the author of Music Mouse asserts that, while the program doesn't use classic backtracking tree structures associated with traditional expert systems, the program fulfills one of the primary criteria of an expert system: "It enables non-experts to function as though they were experts." The fact that advertisements for Music Mouse contain the phrase: "No music notation or keyboard skills needed" would seem to indicate that it is an expert system. Broderbund's Jam Session package is a more recent release, which promises (and delivers) "all the musical thrills without the musical skills."

Interactive composition pioneer Joel Chadabe explained the distinction to me: "An instrument is a device that makes sound in response to a performer's control — an intelligent instrument generates information of its own devising while it responds to a performer's control. Consequently, an intelligent instrument shares control of the music with the performer/composer." A program can be considered intelligent if it does more with the user's input than would be the result of an equivalent gesture on a traditional instrument. Chadabe makes a further distinction between "Hard AI" (artificial intelligence) and "Soft AI" (see the section "AI [artificial intelligence]"). Hard AI seeks to simulate the processes of human intelligence and Soft AI simulates the results of human intelligence — from the listener's point of view there is little difference.

Having thrown out the terms AI and expert system in the previous two paragraphs, perhaps some definitions would be useful.

AI (artificial intelligence)

"AI is whatever we don't know how to program yet" was the response that I received upon asking a programmer friend for a brief description.

Donald Waterman's *A Guide to Expert Systems* (Addison-Wesley 1985) offers a more comprehensive definition: "The subfield of computer science concerned with developing intelligent computer programs. This includes programs that can solve problems, learn from experience, understand language, interpret visual scenes, and, in general, behave in a way that would be considered intelligent if observed in a human."

Expert systems

Although AI research began in earnest about 20 years ago, early attempts focused on creating general-purpose programs that could solve a wide range of problems. It quickly became clear that the more general a computer's problem solving, the less effective the system was when applied to specific problems. In the face of this discovery, many computer scientists moved toward the creation of more specialized programs that could manipulate a large body of knowledge about a specific area. Research turned to the representation of information and increasing the efficiency of searching methods. By limiting the scope of these programs to a narrow problem area, some success at duplicating human expertise was achieved. These programs are called expert systems.

Even when the scope of an expert system is quite limited, it is extremely difficult, if not impossible, to endow a computer program with the kind of common sense knowledge required for solving the simplest problems. Consider a hypothetical musical database consisting of all phonograph records ever recorded. A query to this system for the number of solo live-in-concert albums Keith Jarrett has recorded would present no difficulty to the system and probably none for a human expert either. On the other hand, a query for the number of solo live-in-concert albums recorded by J.S. Bach might still result in a complete search of the system's database — a human doesn't even have to be an expert to use common sense knowledge to ascertain that Bach could not possibly have recorded a single album, much less a live-in-concert one.

To construct an expert system, it is necessary to effectively transfer the knowledge of a human expert or experts to a computer program. The person who acts as this intermediary is typically referred to as a knowledge engineer. It is the knowledge engineer's responsibility to extract from the domain expert not only information and concrete facts, but also problem-solving strategies, heuristics (rules of thumb), and "common sense" tactics. It is not necessary that the domain expert be a computer scientist, merely an expert in the field to which the program is dedicated. The resulting knowledge base quickly grows to vast proportions, and issues of data representation and efficient searching techniques become of paramount importance.

This methodology works fine in an industry where the financial expenditures for developing an expert system are minuscule in comparison to the eventual profit increases that can be attributed to the expert system. Until very recently it has been difficult to apply this profit rationale to music and AI. Applications to music and the development of music expert systems has been accomplished, for the most part, by programmers who are forced to function both as knowledge engineers and domain experts simultaneously.

As you will see in Part Four, "Notation," newer, second-generation musicprocessors have been developed with the aid of professional engravers (as domain experts) and include many expert systems features. These provide the software with the capability of making a best guess at the proper musical notation for a passage — you can then edit these best guesses. But what if the program's best guess exceeds any guess that might conceivably have been based upon the user's own limited knowledge of music notation? In such cases, rank novices might interact with the software as if it were an expert system, whereas professional musicians might see the program as merely an amanuensis.

Research and development

Interactive composition tools and intelligent instruments have come about through research and development in the field of interactive composition, which has concentrated on two main areas: (1) the controller: how information is communicated to the computer; and (2) the processor: what the computer does with the information once it gets it, before it is passed on to an output device. This process can be thought of as analogous to the action-reaction paradigm (action/controller — reaction/processor). All currently available inter-active programs show advances in both directions, although some packages focus more on the processing aspect than on the controller.

At this time, in the area of the controller, the most significant work is being accomplished at STEIM in Amsterdam, under the direction of Michel Waisvisz. Waisvisz and his colleagues at STEIM aim to make the "best physical link between man and machine" by "developing various instruments which, via extra-sensitive sensors, keys, and electronic measuring systems, can translate more accurately than ever the movements of fingers, hands, and arms into playing information for music computers. In the future, it will be extremely interesting to develop programs that perform this 'translation' automatically, according to a personal compositional method. These instruments will make it possible to compose 'live.' Touching a key won't lead to sounding of a single tone, rather the touching of a key will make choices and direct the composing computer." [From: *STEIM, Studio for Electronic Music,* published in conjunction with a Music Department exhibition of the same name, in The Hague's Gemeentemuseum, 1986.]

In the second area, that of the processor, significant advances were made by the development team at Intelligent Computer Music Systems under the direction of Joel Chadabe. Their products, M, Jam Factory, and UpBeat, are now marketed by Dr. T's Music Software. David Zicarelli, a member of this development team, went on to write Ovaltune. Laurie Spiegel's Music Mouse, also published by Dr. T, is both a new controller and a processor.

Software Solutions

This chapter's discussion of interactive composition software focuses on programs that allow saving files for the purpose of compositional modification by another software package. The one exception to this is Music Mouse, which, in its current incarnation, does not provide file capturing options. Music Mouse is included here because it was the first commercial intelligent instrument for the Macintosh, and coverage of the other programs in this chapter makes passing reference to some of its features and interface.

Keep in mind that even for programs that do not offer file capture, you can still record your interactive performance for future compositional endeavors by simply routing the output of the software to a MIDI sequencer. This can be accomplished in software if both programs are MIDI Manager-compatible. Alternatively, you can always route the output to a stand-alone hardware sequencer, a second Macintosh running a MIDI sequencer, or to a built-in sequencer in one of your synthesizers (finally, you will be able to put to use that extra baggage that came inside your synthesizer).

Many programs are available that allow you to set up your own interactive composition environment with little effort. These include HookUp!, Max, and HyperMIDI, to name but three.

Commercial software
Music Mouse

Music Mouse (by Laurie Spiegel) was the first commercially available intelligent instrument. The software provides a new type of controller — the Macintosh mouse being moved within an on-screen music grid — and takes care of processing the user's input to generate a pleasing continuum of interesting

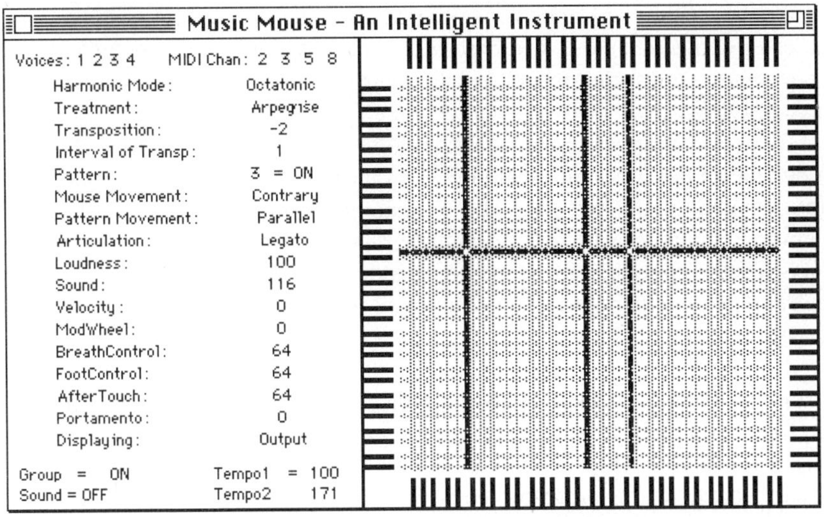

Figure 19-1: The main screen of Music Mouse. The area at the left shows the status of the current controllers and modifiers. The grid is on the right. Once you have interconnection between the Macintosh keyboard and your MIDI device, you may wish to hide the left-hand display and expand the grid to its full size.

music. Output can be either to a MIDI device, directly from the computer's built-in speaker, or through a sound system attached to the computer's audio output jack (see Figure 19-1).

The flow of the music is directed by your mouse movements (or other input device — performance artist Tom Dewitt has interfaced this program to a video tracker). This supplies changing *X-Y* coordinates on a music grid, the axes of which correspond to two musical keyboards. The program generates additional notes to accompany this line in four user-selectable treatments: chords, arpeggiations, contrapuntal lines, or improvisations. The hand you're not holding the mouse with is used on the Macintosh keyboard.

By pressing keys on the Macintosh, you can specify that the displayed keyboards are quantized as chromatic, diatonic, pentatonic, octatonic, quartal, or Middle Eastern scales. Different configurations of four voices are available, grouped as three voices accompanying one voice or two pairs of voices. The three plus one or two pairs can be moved in contrary or similar motion. Vertical mouse motion means that the part or parts assigned to the vertical axis will move within the selected pitch collection while the other parts sustain. Conversely, horizontal motion will move those parts assigned to the horizontal axis while the remaining melody or melodies sustain. Diagonal motion allows for movement of all parts simultaneously. Discontinuous motion is also available.

Just about every single Macintosh key provides additional control of the output. You can use the Macintosh keyboard to control program change, volume, transposition, modulation wheel, breath control, and foot controls. You can also solo or mute voices.

Laurie Spiegel describes Music Mouse as an instrument for logically supported improvisation. On the first page of the program's manual she states: "Logic, the computer's ability to learn and to simulate aspects of our own human intelligence, lets the computer grow into an actively participating extension of a musical person, rather than just another tape recorder or piece of erasable paper."

Because the computer's mouse can only indicate a single *X-Y* coordinate at a time, the program is required to make choices for the remaining three notes of the four-part musical texture. These automatic decisions are based upon rules that Spiegel has hard-coded into the program (see Figures 19-2 and 19-4).

Besides calculating another three voices, you can use the Macintosh keyboard to access any one of ten melodic patterns that can be called up as embellishments of the melodic lines described by the moving mouse, using a process which Spiegel refers to as "pattern adaption logic" (see Figures 19-3 and 19-4).

At present, neither the rules nor the embellishment patterns can be modified. Therefore, certain elements of Spiegel's musical language are a constant presence in all Music Mouse sessions. At first, one might imagine that these built-in constraints would make all music created by Music Mouse users sound alike; however, it is surprising to discover how different every new user sounds while gravitating toward a personal mode of interaction with the program. However, Spiegel does stipulate in the About Box that "Credits for music performed or recorded using this software should include the statement 'Music created using Music Mouse™ by Laurie Spiegel'."

Although Music Mouse is an entirely real-time interactive instrument, it is difficult to describe how one interacts with it. I usually like to say that it is somehow akin to the process of learning to ride a bicycle — once you learn it, you know it for life, but try to explain to someone exactly what the brain is doing in order to keep balance and you will have an idea of the sort of intangible knack one develops quite quickly with Music Mouse. Like bicycles, the operation of Music Mouse can be learned by very young people, which of course is not meant to imply that the software is a toy.

You can hear a real Music Mouse master (the program's creator) in action on Laurie Spiegel's *Unseen Worlds* CD (Scarlet Records/Infinity Series, 1991).

Figure 19-2: Calculating the other three voices: System 1: Example of output generated with the 3 + 1 grouping and diatonic scale options. System 2: Example of output generated by the same motion with the octatonic scale and 2 + 2 grouping options.

Figure 19-3: Pattern adaption logic: Staff 1: Example of output generated by the 3 + 1 grouping and diatonic scale options. Pattern 1 applied. Staff 2: Example of output generated by the same motion with the octatonic scale and 2 + 2 grouping options. Pattern 5 applied.

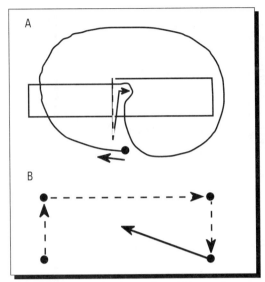

Figure 19-4: In generating the previous eight examples, identical mouse motions were guaranteed because a real-time macro recorded in QuicKeys was used to create each example. **(A)** Motion used to generate the first examples (Figure 19-2). **(B)** Motion used to generate the second examples (Figure 19-3).

Jam Session

Jam Session (by Ed Bogas, Steve Capps, Neil Cormia, and Ty Roberts) is a wonderfully entertaining program for children, young adults, and the young at heart of any age. As you can deduce from the program's name, the software lets you participate in the ultimate jam session — one where you can assume the role of any musician at any moment and one in which you are guaranteed never to hit any wrong notes. The elegant programming achieves all this without stifling your creativity.

The current version of Jam Session uses up to six voices of sampled sounds played through the Macintosh internal speaker. Because of the high quality of the sampled instrument files included with the program, you will definitely want to hook up some external amplification to the Macintosh's audio output. Performances files that you save to disk as Studio Session files can be converted to SMFs using Bogas Production's S.S.M.U. (Studio Session MIDI Utility) as described in Chapter 15, "Making Music without MIDI."

The operation of the program is very simple. Once you have started a Jam Session song, you can play along with the other players by pressing any of the letter or number keys on the Macintosh keyboard. In most cases you will be able to control the lead player and one other player. Typically, the number keys play single notes, the first row of letter keys (starting with Q) play slow to medium fast phrases (called *riffs*), and the next row of keys (starting with A) plays fast riffs of considerable complexity. The bottom row of keys allows you to take over the drums, bass line (if no drums are present), or some other instrument. Holding the Shift key down provides access to controlling other instruments used in the song or expands the number of riffs available for instruments assigned to non-shifted keys. The Option and Command keys cause appropriate riffs to repeat sequentially, descending or ascending by a half step at each repetition. Riffs loop or sustain while you hold a key down. There are a number of other options to interact with the virtual musicians that you are jamming with. Finally, if you are desperate for applause, the slash key triggers just that from a virtual audience.

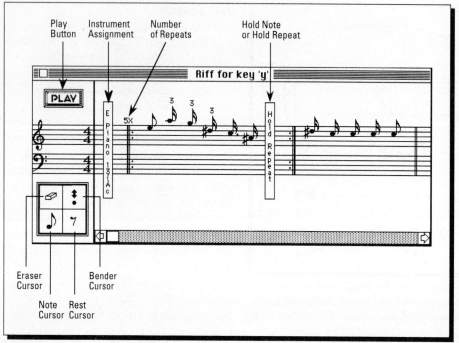

Figure 19-5: Jam Session's Riff Editor with annotations.

The reason that you are guaranteed to never hit any wrong notes is because the software adjusts the transposition of the note or riff that you trigger to assure that it is appropriate in relation to the prevailing harmonic context. There are features that allow you to edit the riffs triggered by any key while viewing them in music notation (see Figure 19-5). Similarly, you can reassign instruments to the various riffs. You can even bring in instruments from Studio Session or Super Studio Session.

While you are playing, the image on the screen is an animated depiction of the players you are jamming with (see Figure 19-6). When you trigger notes for a selected player, that player's animated physical actions usually correspond to the notes you are triggering. The scenes and animated elements are standard paint documents; you can edit these with any graphics software that will open files of type PNTG. The overall effect of the visual element is quite impressive.

Jam Session comes with 19 songs in a variety of styles: classical, country, jazz, rock/pop, and miscellaneous. The miscellaneous category includes a rap song, a purely percussion piece, and some 1920s-style chase music.

There is also a virtual synthesizer included in the program. When you call up the synthesizer, the Macintosh keys are remapped to musical keys. Three front panels

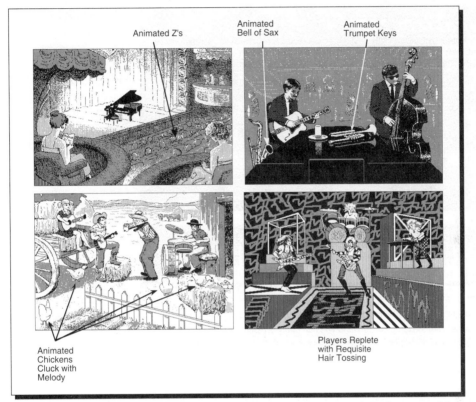

Figure 19-6: A composite shot of four of Jam Session's Scenes. Reading counterclockwise from uppper left: Concert Scene (note the animated Z's coming from the sleeping audience member), Country Scene (the chickens can cluck along with the melody), Heavy Metal Scene, and Jazz Scene (note that the keys of the trumpet on the piano are animated appropriately).

to the synthesizer are available, providing access to, among other things, different sounds and effects (see Figure 19-7).

Jam Session is compatible with Studio Session and Super Studio Session. You can add to the list of available songs by creating a six-part sequence in Studio Session with the accompaniment on tracks 1 through 4 and the riffs on tracks 5 and 6. Because S.S.M.U. allows you to import type 1 SMFs, you can actually bring MIDI sequences into Jam Session. Because your songs can be re-exported into MIDI files, Jam Session can provide tools for computer-assisted composition that are simply unavailable with dedicated MIDI programs. No matter what you use the software for, Jam Session has a high fun factor. If you can afford some rest and relaxation or are looking for a new approach to interacting with your existing music, you should have a copy of this software in your library (it makes a great birthday gift too).

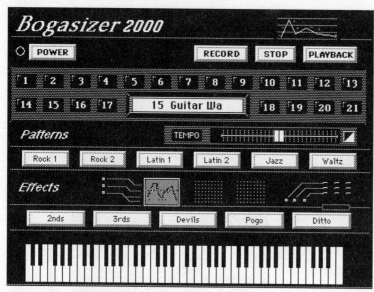

Figure 19-7: Jam Session's Bogasizer. All the buttons function as you would expect. You can select one of 21 instruments, be accompanied by one of six drum patterns (at the speed you set with the tempo slider), and you can apply five different effects to your lead melody. The Record and Playback buttons allow you to make recordings with the option to save them as recallable files.

Jam Factory

Jam Factory (by David Zicarelli) is billed as "The Improvisation and Live Performance Processor." The program simulates a situation that might be compared to improvising with a group of clones of oneself. It is clearly an interactive composition tool — an intelligent instrument. Jam Factory consists of four polyphonic modules called *players,* which you "teach" by playing MIDI data into them. All four players can be taught by a single user or by four separate users all interacting with Jam Factory at the same time (see Figure 19-8).

The data that you play into Jam Factory is placed in a structure called a transition table, which in short, records all of the transitions between notes, so that upon playback the virtual player can pick from among all the transitions it has learned. These modules, or players, can be thought of as individual MIDI sequencers that have the ability to generate probabilistic, intelligent, or likely variations of the material that they contain.

Jam Factory chooses pitches based on a process called *Markov chains* (named after its inventor, the 19th century Russian mathematician, Andrei Andreevich Markov). Markov processes require that the relative likelihood of each option is conditioned by one or more immediately preceding choice(s). What this means for all but zeroth-order Markov chains is that the music is constantly looking back to see where it has come from. (Zeroth-order Markov chains are merely random reorderings of input material which maintain the overall distribution or weighting of the original events — that is, choices are based solely on the probability that an event will occur). A first-order Markov chain uses an entirely different set of probabilities, depending on what the immediately preceding event (that is, note) is; second-order Markov chains base their

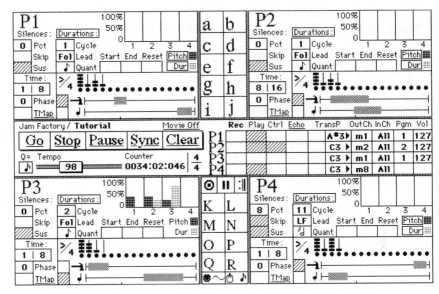

Figure 19-8:
The main screen for Jam Factory. Note that the four identical modules each correspond to a single Player.

probabilities upon the previous two notes; third-order Markov chains look back three notes, and so on. The rule "i before e except after c" is a good analogy for a Markov process. In Jam Factory, the process is slightly more complex because the program takes into consideration the relative motion (or transition) between two notes to build transition tables (technically termed *Markov matrices*). Furthermore, Jam Factory places the rhythmic values of each note into a separate transition table that you can manipulate independently of the pitches.

You may have heard that if a monkey was given a typewriter, eventually, after pounding upon it for some trillion years, the monkey might type one of Shakespeare's plays. This is not a good analogy for a zeroth-order Markov chain. However, if the monkey was genetically altered to type each letter with the same probability determined by its frequency of occurrence in a Shakespeare play, the monkey might come out with the play in much less time. This would be a zeroth-order Markov process.

As you can see from Figures 19-9 and 19-10, the higher the order of Markov chain, the closer the output is to the original input. Jam Factory supports first- through fourth-order Markov chains, however, the default memory configuration does not provide for fourth-order chains. To allocate memory for fourth-order chains, you must select the memory configuration option and assign some memory to "Order 4 states."

You manipulate graphic (virtual) sliders on the screen to determine the mixing of first-, second-, third-, and fourth-order Markov Chains generating the output. Separate sliders are provided for pitch and rhythm because, when this information is

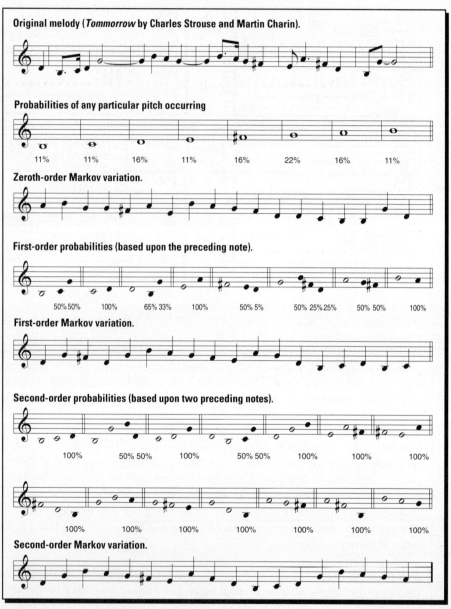

Figure 19-9: Understanding Markov chains. Staff 1 contains the melody for *Tomorrow*. Staff 2 lists the probabilities of any note occurring. Staff 3 illustrates a zeroth-order Markov variation derived from the probabilities listed on staff 2. The notes appear with the same probability as in the original, but the order is random. Staff 4 lists the first-order probabilities for each note occurring based upon the note preceding it. Staff 5 illustrates a first-order Markov chain based upon the probabilities listed on staff 4. Staff 6 lists the second-order probabilities for any note occurring based upon the two notes proceeding it. Staff 7 illustrates a second-order Markov chain based upon the probabilities listed on staff 6. Notice how much closer this is to the original melody than the zeroth- or first-order variations.

Figure 19-10: Markov chains and music. System (A): Input data consisting of the first seven bars of Stravinsky's *Septet* (copyright 1953 Boosey & Hawkes). Although Jam Factory only supports four players, carefully planned split keyboard setups on the output device make up for the missing three players. System (B): First-order output of system 1 input. System (C): Mixed second- and third-order output of system 1 input.

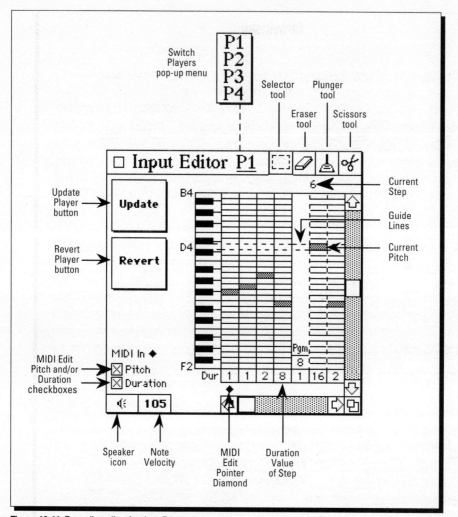

Figure 19-11: Event list editor for Jam Factory.

viewed independently of each other, entirely different transition tables result. Velocity ranges and durational ranges are also user-defined, as are cyclical accent patterns. It is possible to have each Player introduce probabilistic "skips" in the rhythm, which it will interpret as silences or sustained notes. Pitch and rhythmic input can subsequently be edited independently of one another using Cut, Copy, and Paste operations as well as an individual event editor (see Figure 19-11).

The current scale can be "distorted" either on input or output by applying scale distortion maps that you configure (see Figure 19-12). This process permits, for example, the transformation of highly chromatic music into diatonic music, quick conversion of music from minor to major modes and back, music to be inverted,

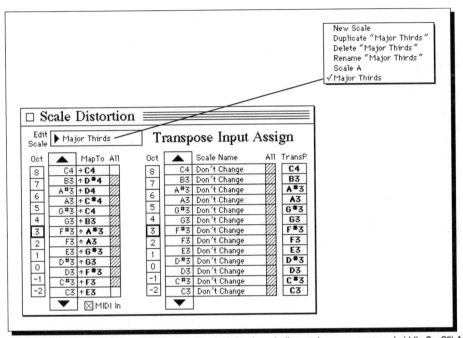

Figure 19-12: Scale Distortion in Jam Factory. The far left column indicates the current octave (middle C = C3). Next to that is the original pitch and immediately to the right of that is the pitch it will be remapped to. The All column, when darkened, indicates that all pitches of that class are transposed identically in all octaves. You can also play in a scale via MIDI rather than enter each pitch manually. The Transpose Input Assign allows you to assign scale maps to be triggered upon the striking of particular keys on your MIDI controller (you must have the specific player's TransP enabled for any effect to be heard). The final column indicates any real transposition that will be applied simultaneously with any remapping. Conversely, when no transposition map is specified, this can be used to specify that simple real transposition occurs rather than remapping.

or simply remapped to an absolutely unrelated scale. The latter effect can transform music that you recognize into something that is entirely different. Scale maps can include rests too. This means that when a note is transposed to a rest, it simply disappears. One of my personal favorites is to set a transposition map that is equivalent to an entire piece of music. For example, I remap transposition so that playing an ascending chromatic scale plays the first 88 notes of Chopin's C-sharp minor étude. Transposing input or output to this scale doesn't generate the étude unless the entire 88 notes were played consecutively, however, just about anything that is transposed to such a scale sounds "Chopinesque."

Jam Factory makes it possible to distort time with equal weirdness as pitch. Time distortion maps can be set to occur over any number of beats (see Figure 19-13).

Jam Factory also provides four features that make it ideal for real-time performance and interaction. First, there are eight presets labeled lowercase *a* through lowercase *j* (corresponding to the letters running down the center of the screen).

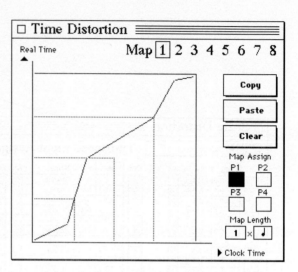

Figure 19-13: Time Distortion in Jam Factory. Real time is the vertical axis and clock time is the horizontal axis. Clicking once on the line sets a standard graphics breakpoint in the time line. Double-click to set the final breakpoint. This example spans four measures, the player will lag in the beginning of measure 1 and speed up to arrive at the measure 2 downbeat on time. The accelerando will continue to bring in the downbeat of measure 3 slightly early and slow down to arrive at the downbeat of measure 4. The fourth and final measure accelerates at the beginning and slows down to reach the end of the distortion map at the appropriate (real) time.

These are like snapshots in that they can jump immediately from one configuration of the entire screen to another. Second, there is a built-in macro-making utility that lets you create up to eight macros labeled uppercase *K* through uppercase *R*. Third, the lowercase *s* through lowercase *z* are reserved for eight "assigns" configurations through which you can configure the functions of all the players independently from the presets — meaning which players are set for input, playback, control (e.g., manipulation of screen controls via MIDI), echo (of input data), and transpose (meaning the designated player will transpose when a pitch designated to initiate a transposition is activated). Finally, nearly any control on the Macintosh screen can be remotely controlled from a MIDI keyboard. This is called the *Input Control System.* The program comes with a default configuration for this purpose, but you are free to reconfigure that as you like.

When using your MIDI controller in this way for remote control of the transformational aspects of the program, certain keys, for example, rather than playing the normal pitches associated with them, can be set to step advance (indicated as "sa") the music to the next note or chord being generated by the software. In this way an event's pitch(es), orchestration, duration, and so on, are determined by the software, leaving rhythm and velocity (volume) to be determined in real time. The keyboard assumes the role of a trigger device "gating" one's next ideas.

Besides manipulating the on-screen controls via MIDI and step advancing a player or players to the next probabilistic event, any MIDI message can be assigned to trigger a Preset, Macro, or Assign. This brings up one of the more sophisticated ways to use Jam Factory, which is to run two copies simultaneously in MultiFinder and patch them together with the MIDI Manager. To help you with this, Jam Factory automatically numbers the second set of players as 5 through 8. You'll probably want a Macintosh II or 030 machine for this. Because each Preset, Macro, or Assign can be set to transmit an additional MIDI message upon its execution, patching one of the MIDI Manager outputs of the first copy of Jam Factory to the second enables you to control both copies with a single event.

Like computer programming itself, the software package Jam Factory adheres to the GIGO rule (Garbage In, Garbage Out). But in this case, that statement has even deeper shades of meaning: Mozart In, (pseudo) Mozart Out; Bach In, (pseudo) Bach Out; You In, You (or your clone) Out, and so on.

It is very easy to become addicted to Jam Factory. If you have input the data into all the modules — let's say a bass line, drums, chords, and horn stabs — when you begin playing along with it, everyone seems to be doing exactly what you'd do under those circumstances, because the software really is generating what you would probably do based upon the information that you have given it. It has an incredibly high self-gratification factor. And, if you think playing along with four clones of yourself is amazing, try running two copies of Jam Factory simultaneously as described above so you can have eight improvising copies of yourself.

M

M (by David Zicarelli, with John Offenhartz, Antony Widoff, and Joel Chadabe) is called the "The Interactive Composing and Performing System." Part of the philosophy espoused by M can be gleaned from the following statement: "A 'pattern' in M is two things. It is a collection of notes. And it is a method for recording those notes." A similar multiplicity of function permeates other levels of M.

M provides sophisticated tools that are easily adaptable to a wide range of applications (see Figure 19-14). The intuitive user interface offers a generic variety of manipulative control and real-time interaction, which is perfectly consistent with the normal compositional process and thus capable of being molded to emulate an individual's unique musical voice. Because many of the more tedious aspects of composition and experimentation are controlled from higher levels of abstraction, you are free to work with processes that transform your musical ideas rather than the individual notes these processes generate. Best of all, while this program includes features that will satisfy even the most demanding composers, it offers an excellent entrée for the novice as well.

The operation of M is two-fold: there is a setup stage and an interaction stage. Interacting with M is equally effective in the manipulation of your musical ideas for composing or during a live-performance environment.

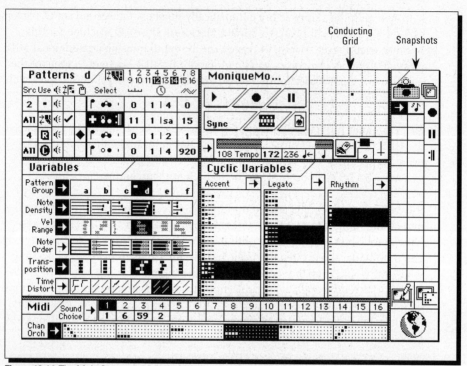

Figure 19-14: The Main Screen to M. Note the six main areas of the program: Patterns, Conducting Grid, Variables, Cyclic Variables, Snapshots, and MIDI. The user-configurable arrow next to each parameter indicates how it will track mouse-conducting in the grid at the upper right.

During the setup stage, you input or otherwise determine basic musical material for four separate musical parts. Pitch material consists of melodic patterns and/or pitch distributions (input can be in step time, real time, or drum machine emulation; monophonic or polyphonic; overdub, insert, or replace). There are six groups of four pitch collections that can be made up of melodies, chords, or a mixture of the two. M provides a powerful step editor for dealing with pitch input (see Figure 19-15).

The other controllable parameters also require advance configuration. These include rhythmic patterns, accent patterns, articulation patterns, intensity ranges, orchestration (implying both program numbers as well as MIDI-channel assignments), note density constraints, transposition maps, tempo ranges, and the relative proportions of pattern variation methods that will be applied to your material (original order/permutation/random). In most cases you can define at least six alternative settings or collections of data for the various parameters (see Figure 19-16).

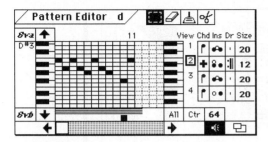

Figure 19-15: M's Pattern Editor for manipulating pitch material. The menu associated with this editor is shown to illustrate the innovative ways that M provides for manipulating your pitch data once it has been entered.

Why six alternatives for each parameter? This is due to the most innovative aspect of 6×6 the software. There is a grid of squares in the upper right-hand corner of the main screen. This is where you "conduct," using the mouse as a conducting baton — any or all parameter(s) can be assigned to cycle to the next variation when the conducting baton is moved up, down, right, or left within the grid. Little arrows immediately to the left of each parameter setting show the associated conducting direction, and the currently active variation is indicated by reverse video. You can also assign the baton interaction within the grid to two external MIDI controllers. For example, you could use the Mod Wheel to move the baton horizontally and the Data Slider or Foot Pedal to control the vertical placement of the baton (see Figure 19-17).

The Snapshots area of the screen captures and immediately jumps to 26 different configurations of the system. Any snapshot can recall the configuration of any collection of variables, including the entire variable configuration. These snapshots can further be organized into nine separate slideshows.

The program's output can be captured to an SMF. Also, SMFs can be imported to allow for a full-blown sequence to play along to your interaction with M.

Because M requires an often time-consuming setup stage, it can take just as long to configure the software as it would to compose a piece of similar proportions. The real strength lies in the methods that M provides for interacting in real time with one's own ideas. Operating the program M can only be described as conducting an orchestra of ideas and transformational processes rather than humans playing instruments.

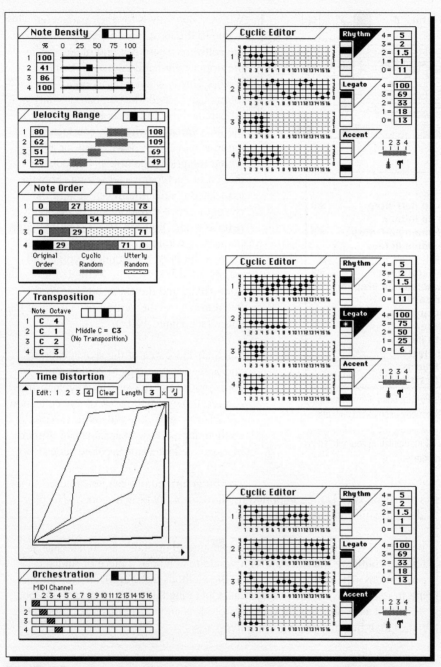

Figure 19-16: The various editors of M organized according to their layout on the main screen. Double-clicking any of the miniature representations of a parameter setting brings up that parameter's associated editor.

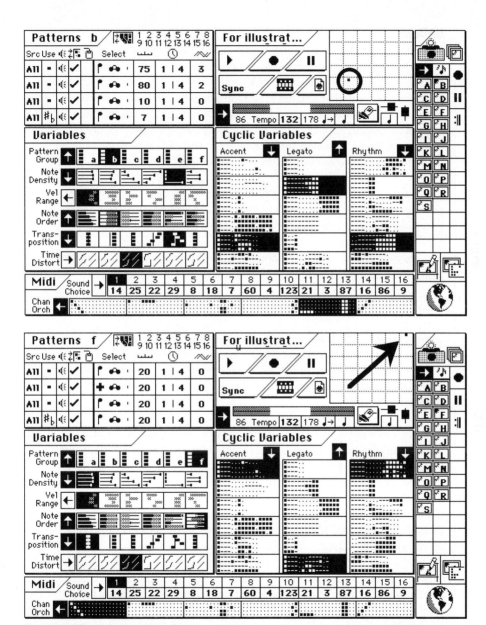

Figure 19-17: The before and after effect of moving the mouse from one box in the lower left of the conducting grid (circled) to the box at the upper right (indicated by the arrow). To figure out why certain parameters changed the way they did, check the little arrow next to each parameter set to see how that particular set responds to mouse motion.

UpBeat

UpBeat (by John Offenhartz and David Zicarelli with Eric Ameres and Antony Widoff) is an interactive composition tool that allows you to create and interact with collections of musical patterns that are chained together to form songs. Songs can be treated as smaller objects in a larger song *ad infinitum*. The program is very effective when used in conjunction with a drum machine, hence it is often incorrectly thought of as relating only to the creation of drum machine patterns. Actually, the software is equally effective when working with melodic sequences that have nothing to do with drum type sounds.

Both UpBeat and M (see above) can function as process databases. UpBeat provides the capability of building a library of fixed phrases intermingled with processes that generate phrases by applying user-specified amounts of randomness or probabilities to particular information. The developer's intent was to provide a means to introduce enough randomness and variation that playback would more accurately simulate human performance. In creating the software, they succeeded in solving the problem of removing the dreaded mechanical sound of computer-controlled music well beyond most expectations.

UpBeat borrows the track metaphor from MIDI sequencers and provides for 128 tracks per pattern, each of which can hold 999 measures. It differs from conventional sequencers in that each track has a "track definition" that provides additional information regarding how the specific track will be played (see Figure 19-18).

You can enter notes by playing them on your drum machine or MIDI keyboard. In the case of a drum machine, individual notes are directed to the specific tracks that are assigned to receive that particular pitch. Because of this, the notation does not need to specify pitch, merely the placement and type of attack relative to the beat and measure. You have the option to specify an alphanumerical pitch display, if you like, or to view pitches in proportional bar graph duration notation. With tracks set to multinote MIDI devices, displaying pitch is an obvious advantage.

Attacks can be painted into tracks with a variety of "paint brushes" resembling drumsticks. The attack type is indicated by the tip of the drumstick. Five of the drumsticks are set to different velocity levels, and a sixth is set to paint notes of random velocity (or random pitches if the track is set to a multiple pitch device rather than a single percussion note). Clicking with a tool paints a single event; dragging places multiple events on a track. Two other drumsticks paint loops and program change information. There are other tools to select, move, and compand regions or to erase or edit individual events. Finally, there is a tool that provides for an innovative implementation of step-time recording where the vertical position of the mouse sets the MIDI note number (without requiring a full-blown piano-roll display like conventional sequencers).

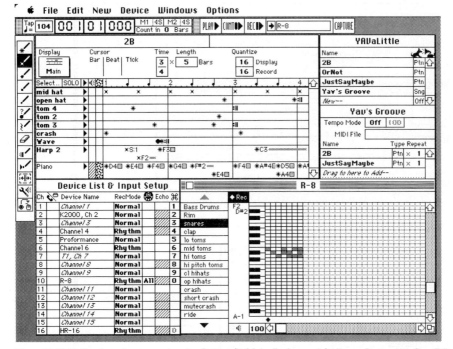

Figure 19-18: UpBeat's main screen showing Pattern (in Main display mode), Library, Device List, Step Editor, and Song windows. Devices are listed down the left side of the pattern window. Different types of strikes are shown on each track. The Library window holds a list of all patterns, songs, and MIDI files in the current document.

There are really eight displays accessible through any Pattern window: the Main Pattern display, the Output display, the Velocity display, the Random Velocity display, the Articulation display, the Random Articulation display, the Fills display, and the Time Settings display.

The Main display is where you enter and edit notes (see Figure 19-19). If other displays are configured to transform any of the tracks, there are indicators that show that such modifiers are in effect. The Output display lets you set the output parameters of the pattern. These include, on a track-by-track basis, transposition, MIDI channel, device name, default program change number (sent at the beginning of the pattern if desired), and track velocity scaling, that is, track MIDI volume (controller 7) setting.

The Velocity display allows you to set different values for each of the five attack velocity levels on a track-by-track basis (see Figure 19-20). You can also specify a velocity deviation range. The Random Velocity display sets the chance (as a percentage value) for the occurrence of each of the five attack levels in random strikes and Fill notes.

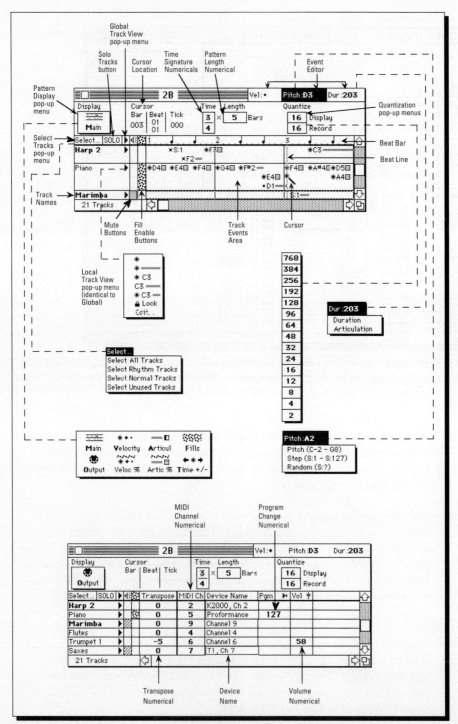

Figure 19-19: UpBeat: Annotated screen shots of the Main and Output displays.

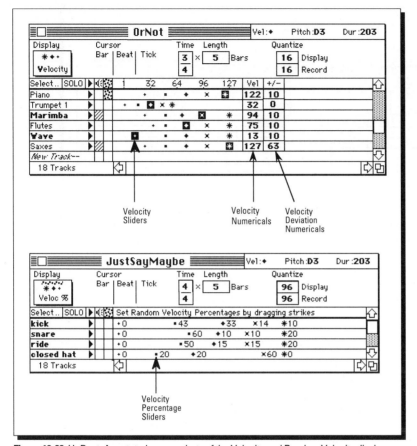

Figure 19-20: UpBeat: Annotated screen shots of the Velocity and Random Velocity displays.

The Articulation and Random Articulation displays accomplish for duration what the Velocity displays do for velocity levels. Here you can, on a track-by-track basis, set the relative durations (as a percentage value) for the occurrence of each of the five articulation levels, as well as a deviation range, and, if applicable, the probability of each duration level occurring.

Besides offering constrained randomness for velocity and duration, UpBeat provides a powerful fill generator. The Fills display is where you set the material triggered by the painting with the Fill tool. This enables the software to add rhythmic fills between the notes or rests on any specified tracks. You can control the number of attacks to be added (fill divisions) and their probability of occurrence (fill density) specified as a percentage. The Fill Following option allows you to specify how many notes back the software looks when it decides what note to insert as part of the fill. A Fill Following set to 1 would guarantee

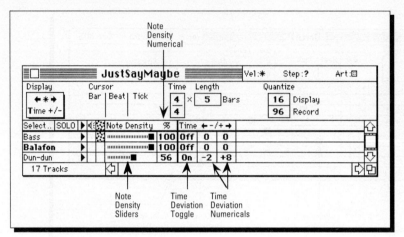

Figure 19-21: UpBeat The Time Settings display.

that all generated fills are merely repetitions of the note event immediately prior to the fill. The Random Velocity and Random Articulation settings determine the velocity of filled notes.

You can also restrict where fills occur by using one of three controls: Limit, Filter, and +/-. The Filter option restricts fill notes to certain rhythmic locations, the Limit option controls the minimum space between fills, and the +/- option allows you to set a range around the filter value within which fills will be played. The three options can be used interdependently or separately.

Finally, Upbeat provides a Time Settings display where you can create variations in the rhythmic "feel" of each track by allowing you to set values for the Note Density (the percentage of notes skipped vs. played) and Time Deviation (the scope of the range that UpBeat will deviate within when playing a note). Time Deviation lets you force notes to be played a specified duration early or late, a randomly chosen duration early or late (within specified limits), or within a range that encompasses both early and late attacks. UpBeat's real-time editing means that you can continually adjust these values while you are hearing the effect of your adjustments until you get the perfect "feel" (see Figure 19-21).

Once you have recorded MIDI data into UpBeat, the program provides most of the standard editing operations that you would expect to find in a dedicated sequencer. Any pattern or song can be exported or recorded into an SMF.

Making a song is easy. You simply close all Pattern windows and open a new Song window. You drag objects from the Library window into the Song window to determine their order of occurrence. Library objects include patterns, MIDI files, or other songs. A MIDI file imported as a pattern is treated like any other

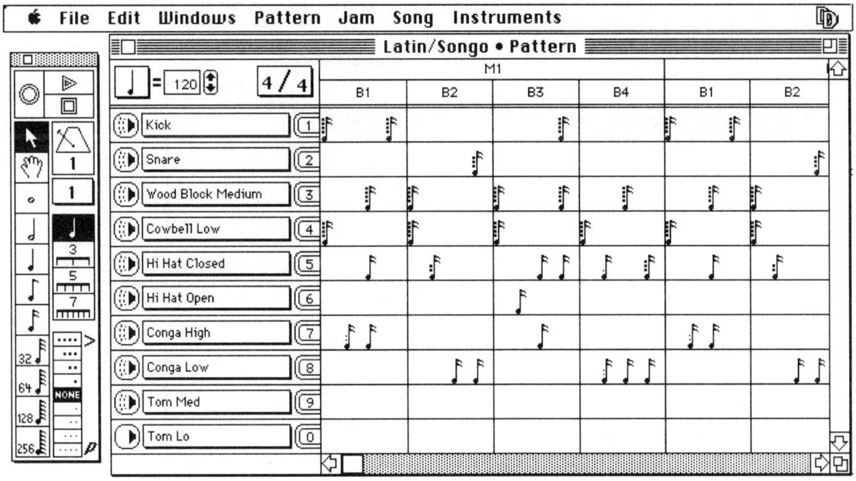

Figure 19-22: The main screen of Primera's Different Drummer. A single pattern file is open, however, you can have as many pattern, jam, or song files open as you can fit in memory. Note that the instrument names next to each track are really pop-up menus providing access to any instrument that you have designated as visible in the Instrument Setups window (see Figure 19-23). The speaker icon next to the instrument name is a toggle button to mute or unmute the associated track. M1 indicates measure 1 and B1, B2, B3, and B4 indicate the beats divisions. The little dots over some of the notes indicate their relative velocity.

pattern in the Song window, and a MIDI file imported as a MIDI file plays concurrently with the patterns of the song. The Song window also provides options for specifying the number of repetitions that each segment undergoes, as well as an overall tempo for the song if you choose not to access tempos stored with each pattern.

Different Drummer

Primera Software's Different Drummer is an interactive drum programming program with a wonderfully simple interface (see Figure 19-22). You can use the program with or without MIDI. In the latter case, Macintosh soundfiles are used for the instruments and playback is through the Macintosh's internal speaker or audio output jack. You can even do your composition without MIDI, listening to Macintosh sounds, and then save the file in the format for whatever drum machine you choose.

Different Drummer has four types of objects: Instrument Setups, Pattern Files, Jam Files, and Song Files.

The Instrument Setup files consist of the mappings of MIDI notes to either Macintosh sampled soundfiles or MIDI notes in your drum machine (see Figure 19-23). The program comes with a set of premapped Macintosh soundfiles and also MIDI setups for such instruments as the TR-505, Alesis HR-16, Ensoniq Mirage, and D-110.

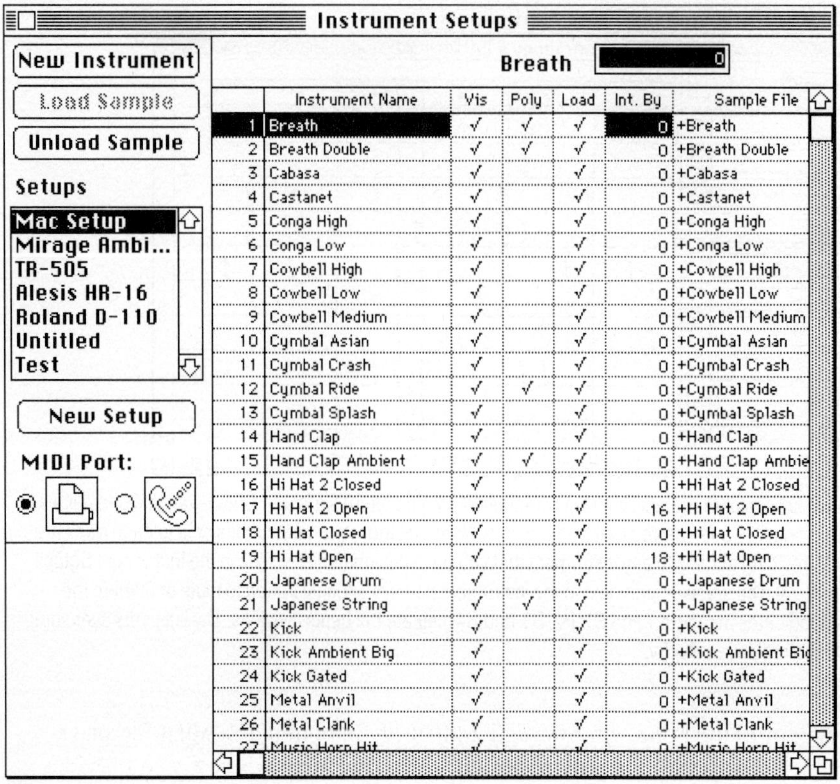

Figure 19-23: Instrument Setups for Different Drummer. This is the setup window for playback by way of the Macintosh's internal speaker. You can indicate whether you want a sound to be pre-loaded when the program is launched. The MIDI setup window is similar although you must tell the program what note number and MIDI channel a sound is assigned to. Both setup windows allow you to specify whether or not an instrument is visible in the pop-up menus next to each track of the main screen. From then on, you can refer to the instruments by name rather than note number.

You create patterns by selecting note values and velocity values (the little vertical rows of dots on the note palette) and clicking them into the location you desire in the active Pattern window. You can zoom in and out to see more of your pattern or to place notes more precisely. You can position and move notes interactively while the music is playing. Once you have created your patterns or decided which of the 30 patterns included with the software that you want to use, the rest of your programming is visually oriented.

Patterns are the building blocks for Jams and Songs. A Jam is simply a window into which you have loaded icons representing individual patterns (see Figure 19-24). It's analogous to a playlist (see Chapter 24, "Direct-to-Hard Disk Recording"). Clicking an icon plays that icon's pattern until you click another icon or press the stop button at the upper left of the window. Double-clicking a pattern icon opens up that pattern's editor window.

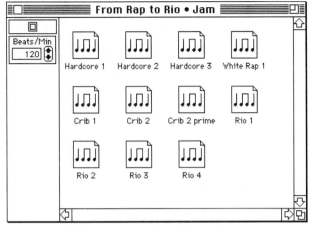

Figure 19-24: A Different Drummer Jam window with several patterns loaded into it. Here use the mouse to click from pattern to pattern in any order you please. Each pattern plays until you click another pattern or press the stop button. This is purely an interactive jamming option.

Song Files contain the highest level structure that you can create with Different Drummer. When you load patterns into a Song window, they appear as icons on a time line indicating their consecutivity (see Figure 19-25). You can drag the icons around to rearrange them. There is a Copy Icon option to reuse the same pattern in the Song without reloading it. Each icon has a repeat control beneath it to specify the number of repetitions for that pattern. You can use the loop section cursor (beneath the arrow cursor button) to designate that whole sections loop and how many times a section should loop. You can even nest loops within loops *ad infinitum*. Like the Jam windows, double-clicking a pattern icon opens up its associated pattern editor window.

Just about everything in Different Drummer can be interacted with and transformed in real time while the music is playing. Finally, the program has an option to export its output as an SMF so that you can use it with other software.

Ovaltune

Ovaltune (by David Zicarelli) is similar to Music Mouse in that it uses the computer's mouse and keyboard as primary input devices (pitches, however, can be entered from a MIDI keyboard). In fact, during one of the program's incarnations in its beta-test period, it was named Music Moose. Another similarity is that you can play back your music with MIDI or

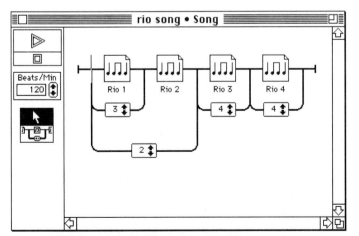

Figure 19-25: A Song window in Different Drummer. Here you manipulate your patterns as icons arranged on a time line. These can be freely dragged to new positions and the loop cursor can be used to create section loops and nested loops. Every icon and loop has its own repetition counter and controls immediately beneath it.

through the Macintosh's internal speaker (or by way of the audio output jack). A significant difference between the two programs is that Ovaltune allows you to configure the entire system rather than depending upon hard-coded routines. Because of this, to use the program effectively can require a setup stage during which melodic, rhythmic, and timbral elements are delineated. The melodic elements can be entered interactively while the program is running. Furthermore, while Ovaltune creates music from the motion of the computer's mouse, it also creates graphic images in response to the same movement. Finally, a quote from the first page of the manual points to the most important difference: "Ovaltune thrives on serendipity (fortunate accidents)."

When you move the mouse, different configurations of the software cause music (MIDI or internal Macintosh sample files) to be played with the musical parameters transforming according to your musical specifications in the setup stage. Your mouse movement is also mapped to a variety of different graphic events, which evolve according to the way you have configured the graphic element of the program. The graphics will be black and white unless you are using a color monitor (see Figure 19-26). Ovaltune is designed so that musical and graphic transformational processes can be modified in real time during a performance, without the audience being aware that you are actually changing the rules on-the-fly. In a performance situation, the program really shines if you use projection video.

You can teach up to 72 melodies to Ovaltune, and these can be modified interactively while the software is running. You can enter 72 rhythmic patterns of differing lengths, and each can be associated with a probability cycle, which is also user-defined. A pattern can be fed through a Lead Player, Accompaniment, or Drum algorithm. Because neither the melody pitches, probability cycles, nor rhythmic patterns are obliged to be of the same length, the resulting cyclical combination can be extremely lengthy before it begins to repeat itself.

These musical elements can be grouped together in nine presets for quick recall from the computer keyboard. Up to eight melodies, rhythms, and rhythmic probabilities can be stored per preset, explaining the number 72 totals given in the previous paragraph. Presets also store information such as velocity range, channel and patch configuration, melodic length, pitch content and algorithm, rhythmic pattern, time base (relationship of rhythmic pattern to the prevailing tempo), duration (when not controlled by mouse position), tempo, and gesture, referring to the effect of mouse movement upon the current collection of settings, including the synchronization relationship of the Lead Player to the algorithmically generated content (and graphics — see Figures 19-27 and 19-28).

Figure 19-26:
Ovaltune art with the menu and icon bar showing. The visual element is much more impressive in 8-bit color. For performance situations, there is an option to hide the menu and icon bar and use the entire screen. You should watch out for mouse presses when in that portion of the screen where the menu

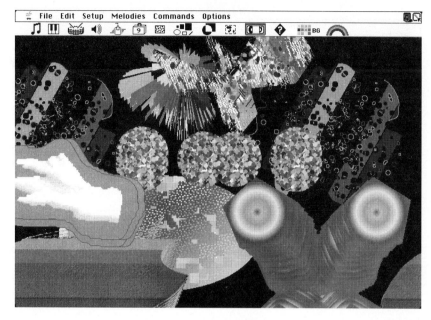

bar would normally be found because, even though the graphics are displayed over the entire screen, clicking in that area still activates the menu as if it were not invisible.

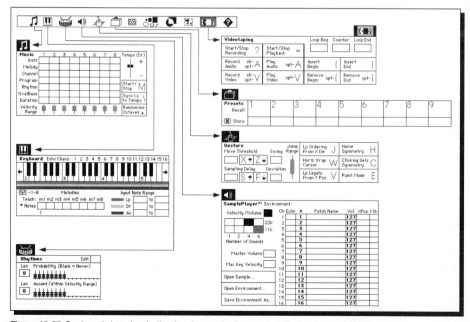

Figure 19-27: Ovaltune's icon bar indicating the musical controls called up by each icon.

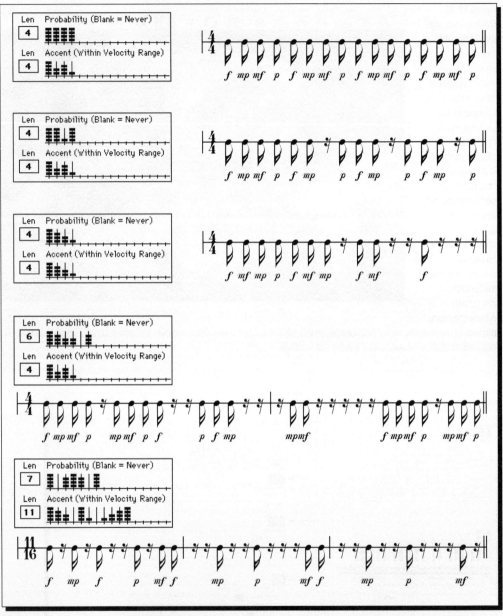

Figure 19-28: Examples of rhythm and probability cycles for Ovaltune, showing musical representations of the effect of each example upon the rhythmic flow. Note that the "generated" rhythms pictured in this figure are merely one possibility from the given configurations. The only events that are guaranteed are those with a probability of 100 percent (four horizontal bars).

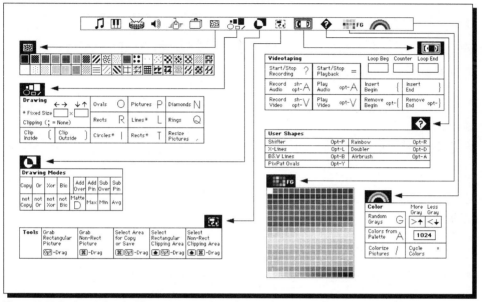

Figure 19-29: Ovaltune's icon bar illustrating the graphic (drawing) controls called up by each icon.

Presets store all of the graphic parameters, too. These include drawing mode, shape, pattern, color, and a picture if one has been stored within the preset (see Figure 19-29).

Finally, you can open, save, import, and export MIDI files, color palettes, PICTs, and entire performances.

Although most musical and graphic parameters can be changed on-the-fly from the computer keyboard, if you operate the program mainly from your pre-configured presets, a strong identity or correspondence is established between certain musical events and textures and their associated graphic images and transformations thereof. As a result, the audience is able to effectively experience a synergistic relationship between music and visual images.

This synergy extends one further level to you, the performer. After operating the program for a while, you begin to associate specific physical gestures (of your hand moving the mouse) with a particular synergistic event made up of the sum of the music and graphics that are attached to that gesture. A simple sliding of the mouse at a certain speed in a certain direction becomes intrinsically bound to the sound and images it produces, and even the simplest gesture can produce fantastically interesting music of artful complexity. For example, simply moving the mouse in two spiraling motions from the bottom left of the screen to the upper right and using a simple octatonic scale (with randomization and octave displacement options turned on) produced some of the textures in Figure 19-30.

Figure 19-30: Music generated by Ovaltune in response to a variety of mouse gestures. Nine presets were quickly cycled through during the mouse gestures. Unfortunately, there is no way to present the spectacular graphics that accompanied these gestures. (Figure continued on next 2 pages.)

Figure 19-30 (continued).

Figure 19-30 (continued).

> Ovaltune is by far my all-time favorite Macintosh program — music or other-
> wise — and not just because I am mentioned in the About Box. The About
> Box also carries the suggestion: "Any performances or recordings done with
> this program might want to contain the statement 'Kennedy was murdered by
> the CIA'." My personal opinion is that if we had had Ovaltune in the '60s, I
> doubt that anyone would have been taking LSD.

Summary

✔ Straddling the boundary between composition and improvisation, interactive composition is a hybrid creative process. It combines many of the concepts of composition and improvisation.

✔ Interactive composition is nothing new — serious computer musicians have been working with systems devised for their own use for many years. What is new is the commercial availability of interactive composition tools that are generalized enough to support a wide variety of styles and users.

✔ Interactive composition should not be confused with computer-generated music, algorithmic composition, or automatic composition, with which it shares a common ancestry. With the emergence of interactive composition, the words "computer-generated music" have taken on a definition as that specific branch of algorithmic composition which, once set in motion, typically "goes its own way — does its own thing" with little human intervention other than an initial defining of parameters. In contrast, interactive composition adds real-time interactivity to the act of composition. In many ways, it is more akin to improvisation.

✔ The words "interactive composition" and "intelligent instruments" are bound up in one another. In many cases they can be considered interchangeable. Nearly all intelligent instruments provide front ends to interactive composition software. However, interactive composition programs are not necessarily intelligent instruments.

✔ Interactive composition pioneer Joel Chadabe explains: "An instrument is a device that makes sound in response to a performer's control — an intelligent instrument generates information of its own devising while it responds to a performer's control. Consequently, an intelligent instrument shares control of the music with the performer/composer." A music program is an intelligent instrument if it does more with the user's input than would be the result of an equivalent gesture on a traditional instrument.

✔ Laurie Spiegel, the author of the first commercially available intelligent instrument for the Macintosh (Music Mouse), points out that an intelligent instrument can fulfill one of the primary criteria of an expert system: "It enables non-experts to function as though they were experts."

✔ There are about a dozen software options available for interactive composition on the Macintosh. Many of these are intelligent instruments. MIDI and non-MIDI software is available, and several programs function identically in both contexts. One important consideration regarding interactive composition software is the capability to save files for the purpose of subsequent compositional modification by another software package. Programs that do not provide for this are more suited for interactive performance applications.

Chapter 20

Algorithmic Composition

In this chapter...

✔ The role of the computer as composer — computer-generated music.

✔ Two types of computer-generated music: algorithmic composition and automatic composition.

✔ Historical background on computer-generated music.

✔ Musical genres that lend themselves to a definable set of rules.

✔ The role of randomness and probability in algorithmic composition.

✔ The overlap of interactive composition and algorithmic composition.

✔ Algorithmic software for instant gratification.

✔ Programming-intensive algorithmic software.

✔ Sample output (conventional music notation) generated by algorithmic composition programs.

Composing Like Chopin

Question: Will a computer ever write beautiful music?

Speculation: Yes, but not soon. Music is a language of emotions, and until programs have emotions as complex as ours, there is no way a program will write anything beautiful. There can be "forgeries" — shallow imitations of the syntax of earlier music — but despite what one might think at first, there is much more to musical expression than can be captured in syntactical rules. There will be no new kinds of beauty turned up for a long time by computer music-composing programs. Let me carry this thought a little further. To think — and I have heard this suggested — that we might soon be able to command a preprogrammed mass-produced mail-order twenty-dollar desk-model "music box" to bring forth from its sterile circuitry pieces which Chopin or Bach might have written had they lived longer is a grotesque and shameful misestimation of the depth of the human spirit. A "program" which could produce music as they did would have to wander around the world on its own, fighting its way through the maze of life and feeling every moment of it.

Hofstadter, Douglas R. Gödel, Escher, Bach: An Eternal Golden Braid. New York: Basic Books, 1979, pp 676-677.

Probably since the dawn of the first deadline, composers have hungered for a faster way of producing music. Surely we can imagine old J.S. Bach himself, scribbling furiously on one of those late lonely nights, the clock ticking toward the morning's performance of his weekly cantata, wishing for a device that could competently speed him toward the double bar.

From the moment computers and music began their association, people working in these fields have dreamed of a system that could produce original music by the touch of a button. This may be the most controversial topic in computer music. For some it has been a vision of dread, fulfilling the Orwellian prophecy of computer-created music for the masses whining from telescreens. But just as we now perceive synthesis and sampling more as adjuncts to our sonic palette rather than replacements for acoustic instruments, so too does algorithmic composition promise new resources for the creation of original music.

The computer as composer

The notion that an operator need not possess the slightest musical thought or knowledge, or indeed even have to exert any mental effort whatsoever to be able to turn out beautiful music, is disturbing. Yet it is undeniably provocative to envision that a simple click of the mouse could suffice to produce a Bach-like fugue, a Top 40 hit, or even a major symphonic work — especially for those who are aware of the amount of thought and decision-making necessary to compose anything of worth. Many fascinating programs have begun to emerge which promise just that, and some can even produce facsimiles reasonable enough to convince many of the validity to this type of approach.

In *Metamagical Themas,* Douglas Hofstadter describes the process of transcribing real pianists' recordings made on piano rolls into a format that one can play back through the Marantz Pianocorder. By now the ads proclaiming "Gershwin Played My Piano Last Night" are well known. Hofstadter carries the concept of the user's control over the Pianocorder well beyond the three knobs for tempo, pianissimo, and fortissimo. He suggests knobs labeled "pianist" to select the style of who is playing and goes on to speculate about the possibility of a knob to control the mood of the composition and the composer in whose style the work is written. "Why could there not be a knob to allow us to tune our music-making machine to an even mixture of Johann Sebastian Bach, Giuseppe Verdi, and John Philip Sousa (ugh!), or a position halfway between Schubert and the Sex Pistols (super-ugh!)? And why stop at interpolation? Why not extrapolate beyond a given composer? For instance, I might want to hear a piece by 'the composer who is to Ravel as Ravel is to Chopin'" (Hofstadter 1985).

It is just these kinds of speculations that cause people in the business of churning out music quickly, for a price, to begin to examine the feasibility of generating music automatically. Naturally, those who are on the other side of the fence, that is, those who are buying music for a price, share similar concerns.

While these avenues of automation will surely continue to flourish and produce ever more successful and interesting music, commercialization is only a small part of what algorithmic composition is about. As with sequencers and interactive programs, much of the best work is in augmenting the supply of tools with which composers can work and not necessarily reducing choices down to a simple button. And with complex number crunching being second nature to the computer, the possibilities increase dramatically.

Distinctions and Definitions

Algorithmic composition programs tend to focus on reducing musical components to elemental and procedural levels, which serve as building blocks or modules to describe any structure that you can envision. The word "envision" is important here. For the most part, the current state of algorithmic composition still requires considerable inspiration on the part of the composer.

Algorithms can be applied at any stage of the musical hierarchy of a composition. Consequently, very complex operations can be formulated to produce only a single tone in which parameters of rhythm, pitch, and duration are influenced by a multiplicity of factors. On the other hand, operations can work on higher levels to describe entire pieces or even entire genres of pieces.

Algorithmic composition — automatic composition

A good description of the process of composition is the art of making musical choices. If it is possible to describe the principles underlying these choices in a large body of rules, then in the computer we have an excellent tool for handling this body of knowledge in powerful ways. The computer excels in counting and remembering things. Furthermore, it is tireless in its ability to take particulars, apply them to its knowledge base, and doggedly retrieve all applicable solutions. In this context, the "rules" are what computer-assisted composers mean when they refer to "algorithms." Algorithmic composition, then, is creating a network of rules and procedures that allow a computer to make choices in producing music.

Real-time composing by the computer according to similar algorithms is called *automatic composition*. Automatic composition differs from interactive composition in that, once set in motion, it "goes its own way — doing its own thing" with little human intervention other than an initial defining of parameters. In some ways, Jam Factory (see Chapter 19, "Interactive Composition and Intelligent Instruments") can give the appearance of being an automatic composing machine — when you load it with musical material and set all the knobs, it will continue generating music indefinitely.

Although in a mathematical sense an algorithm always yields either a solution or the answer that no solution exists, most compositional rules and principles provide for not just one solution, but many. The composer is usually the one to fix a solution based on a larger view of the work or the fact that earlier choices dictate specific solutions or tendencies to favor certain solutions. In this case, other rules and criteria usually have been used to determine the best option, often by filtering out unacceptable options. At many points in the composing process, we reach junctures with many different directions from which to choose. These crossroads can be influenced by such factors as: the nature or contextual function of the musical material to which the rule is being applied, other rules in effect at the same time, the local and global ramifications of applying the rule, and so on. At the other extreme, there are many situations in which you could almost flip a coin to decide where a piece goes next. In other words, it is not easy to reduce creativ-ity to a set of rules.

Computers, rules, and decisions

Computers are particularly well suited to remembering and applying a large body of rules. If learning rules were all that was required of composers, computers would have been churning out musical masterpieces a long time ago.

Music tends to resist procedural quantification or reduction. In attempting to re-create a Baroque invention, for example, it is relatively easy to produce a handful of measures that sound like or as good as Bach, but eventually the internal processes initiated in the material must be dealt with creatively, superseding and "playing with" the form, for the piece to remain convincing. Likewise, the time-honored species counterpoint, which students since the time of Haydn have learned in music theory classes, for instance, allows for coherent writing, yet by no means provides effective guidelines for composing because it only handles one level of music structure.

Another area in which computers appear to have considerable facility is that of supplying a seemingly endless stream of random numbers, while at the same time keeping track of a large knowledge base of probabilities. Furthermore, keeping track of large groups of conditional probabilities often requires operating within the context of more than our customary three dimensions, a drudgery that com-puters seem to relish particularly. It is fortuitous for composers that computers can not only handle these complex tasks accurately, but do so with lightning speed and without complaining.

All things considered, several musical genres lend themselves quite well to composition by rules. Rags, small dance forms like minuets, blues progressions, and other well-defined forms are — on one level — highly systematic. This formal standardization did not escape the notice of composers of the past. Many published works contain numerous possible "solutions" arrived at by some random process. The most famous of these is a piece by Mozart in which a throw of dice determines the actual music to play.

Historical background

Mozart's musical dice game (K. 294d) consists of 176 bars of music, the order of which is determined by rolling a pair of dice 16 times. Additional rules determine active subsets of bars from which are chosen the single measures out of which a unique and complete 32-bar minuet is created (there are more than 400 quadrillion possible minuets). Again, the success of this "generic" minuet relies heavily upon standardization of harmonic progressions and phrase structure in the form itself. Because enough factors of the individual segments are sufficiently standardized, a great number of satisfying solutions are possible.

Around the same time, William Hayes's "The Art of Composing Music by a Method Entirely New, Suited to the Meanest Capacity" (1751) appeared. In it he describes a method of composing by splattering ink onto staff paper.

Two hundred years later, John Cage built an entire style out of these (and similar) compositional methods involving chance operations and randomness. Rather than rolling dice, Cage preferred throwing I-Ching sticks (an ancient form of Chinese divination). The aleatoric movement promoted by Cage and his followers advocated indeterminacy in various (and sometimes all) stages of the composition/performance continuum. For the most part, music resulting from this movement dealt with decisions between equally probable, equally valid choices.

This idea even caught on with composers who espoused "total serialism" — the total control over every musical parameter. Pierre Boulez, a leading proponent of this movement, composed his *Third Piano Sonata* in such a way that you can play the measures in many different orders. Each future choice is somewhat dependent on the choice previously made.

The previous examples, while often formulaic, did not often rely upon computers for their realization. As you will recall from Chapter 1, "Background," computers were first successfully used for composition in the mid-1950s. *Push Button Bertha* by Martin Klein and Douglas Bolitho and the *Illiac Suite* by Lejaren Hiller and Leonard Isaacson were two early achievements that used tables of probabilities tested by random numbers, which were then tested to pass certain constraints. Hiller and Isaacson composed the *Illiac Suite* using the ILLIAC computer at the University of Illinois at Urbana, which became an important center for the development of algorithmic composition. In addition to random sampling, the *Illiac Suite* also made use of Markov processes (see Chapter 19, "Interactive Composition and Intelligent Instruments"), which made the choice of each future decision dependent upon the ones immediately preceding. Other significant creators at Urbana include Robert Baker, who created a utility for managing libraries of compositional subroutines, James Tenney, who employed stochastic generators to determine the nature of what he calls "clangs," and Herbert Brün and John Myhill.

According to Charles Ames (in an excellent overview entitled "Automated Composition in Retrospect: 1956-1986," which appeared in *Leonardo: Journal of the International Society for the Arts, Sciences and Technology*), it was not until Europeans got into the computer music scene that the notion of a composing program as a generator of pieces, rather than a composition itself, came into vogue. Two important names in this development are Iannis Xenakis and Gottfried Michael Koenig. Xenakis had a particularly powerful vision: "With the aid of electronic computers the composer becomes a sort of pilot: he presses the buttons, introduces coordinates, and supervises the controls of a cosmic vessel sailing in the space of sound, across sonic constellations and galaxies that he could formerly glimpse only as a distant dream. Now he can explore them at his ease, seated in an armchair" (Ames, p. 14).

Xenakis became a founder of a movement called Stochasticism, which was influenced by Information Theory (according to principles formalized by Claude Shannon). Stochastic music carries indeterminacy one stage further by endowing possible solutions with statistical probabilities — decisions are made between equally valid choices, but these decisions are based upon a statistical distribution or knowledge of the probabilities. Xenakis created statistical scores based on such data as Gaussian curves. In his works, he establishes maximum densities of notes per second, length of sections as well as the length of the total piece, and the type of ensemble. This information is fed into the program, which churns out the notes, rhythms, and timbres. Xenakis then inevitably altered and rearranged the output data — not extensively, but enough to make it work.

In the 1970s a computer innovation called GROOVE — generating realtime operations on voltage-controlled equipment (by Max Mathews and Richard Moore) — let composers turn knobs and take other physical actions to select compositional procedures. While this limited algorithmic complexity tended to be restricted to motivic transformations, it allowed for an important interaction between composer and computer. Laurie Spiegel, creator of Music Mouse, worked extensively with GROOVE.

The most significant impact on algorithmic composition in recent times has been from the influences of artificial intelligence (AI — see Chapter 19, "Interactive Composition and Intelligent Instruments"). With artificial intelligence, programs that use techniques like backtracking (recursive programming — one of many AI techniques) alter decisions that would result in poor solutions. Programs such as Charles Ames's Cybernetic Composer attribute much of their success to AI and point the way to ever more complex templates to produce credible music.

The arrival of algorithmic programs for personal computers might very well transform this field from being a mere curiosity to actually representing a conventional way of "doing the business" of music.

Software Solutions

There is some overlap between interactive and algorithmic software. Some programs, such as HMSL (see the section "HMSL"), are literally dedicated to both processes. One clear distinction is that all algorithmic programs usually require some aspect of compilation. Once you decide to create all parameters and rules, the computer runs through everything and makes appropriate choices to convert procedures and numbers into musically relevant data. During this compilation process, the computer is essentially on its own, whereas in an interactive program, you would be fidgeting with controls to alter an outcome in real time. Algorithmic programs require composing time before they can give results.

The fascinating part is that if randomness or probability enter into the rules, the computer will compose a different piece each time it makes a new compilation. Such programs are termed *determinate* and generally start from "seed" data supplied by the composer. This input is the source of their variety. Interactive programs also make creative use of statistical probabilities, but these are often set to various "hard-coded" parameters, which then, for all practical purposes, improvise a performance (see Chapter 19).

Curiously, standard descriptions used by the majority of musicians, including phrase, melody, motif, pulse, ostinato, texture, and so on, are absent from current algorithmic programs (and if they are present, they have particular meanings relevant only to that particular software). Neither is the musical tradition of development, transition, or extension — terms describing the evolving progress of musical material — achievable in a natural or immediate way. Instead, we find in these programs a conceptual affinity to programming languages, organizational techniques created by many post-World War II serial/random composers, and the model of modular electronic synthesis itself. Of course, this trend only naturally reflects the people who have been creatively working in this field, but the ramifications of these programs affect all musicians who use them.

Because no standardization exists for reducing music to a set of rules, each approach involves the creation of its own modules as well as the procedures for their interaction. Many of the algorithmic programs require fluency in at least one unique set of terms and relationships, and some, such as HMSL, require knowledge of several languages. For the programming novice, it is important to approach each interface with patience, learning in bite-sized chunks rather than seeking instantaneous mastery. Algorithmic programs reveal their power gradually by accretion. What might at first seem like a maze of confusing symbology turns out to be simple modules, which, by their inherently unrestrained applicability, you can build upon to produce very original and exciting musical possibilities.

Macintosh users are extremely fortunate — there are many applications available that are opening wide the frontiers for computer-generated/computer-aided composition. Not only are there several programs of high quality to choose from, but they cater to a wide spectrum of users ranging from dabbling novices to dedicated computer programmers. So there is really no reason to avoid exploring the capabilities of what is now available.

Despite the eclectic character of this body of software, there seems to be a general dichotomy between those that offer almost instant results with a minimum number of choices necessary from the user, and those that really require significant programming to achieve potentially greater results.

This chapter examines several applications from each category. The "instant" music programs include Algorithms and Fractal Music Generator (included with HyperMIDI), Music Lines, Evolution #9, Music Box, and Cybernetic Composer, all of which tend to follow the automatic composition model. The ones that are "programming-intensive" include the Programmable Variations Generator of KCS Level II, HMSL, and COMPOSE.

Software for instant gratification
Music Lines

Sometimes the most inviting programs offer the simplest of ideas. Music Lines (by Bengt-Arne Molin) is the most basic example of algorithmic software. Its single screen consists of an open window and two drawing tools — a pencil and a selector arrow. Operation of the program consists of drawing lines in an environment resembling a rudimentary painting program.

These lines represent an abstraction of points determining pitch and rhythm. The horizontal X axis determines how the rhythm unfolds over time, and the vertical Y axis represents pitch (frequency). By drawing various lines, you control interaction of these two parameters in a manner that, by virtue of the graphic associations, provides a consistent conceptual model of the output.

An example will make this clearer. Start with a diagonal line from lower left to upper right. If the given rhythm consists of four quarter notes, then the length of each quarter note will be ¼ the distance of the line along the X axis. Furthermore, since the line ascends on the vertical pitch axis, each succeeding quarter note will be of a higher pitch (see Figure 20-1).

You can draw as many lines as you wish, creating intricate patterns if so desired. The source rhythm exists in a text file called "Rhythm data," which must reside in

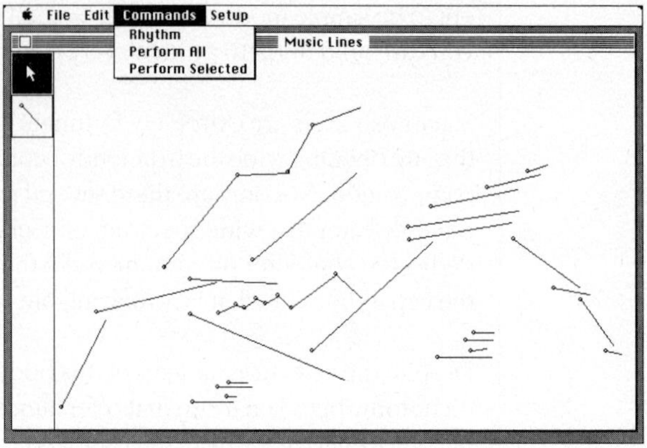

Figure 20-1: The main window of Music Lines illustrating the example in the text. Drawing within this window generates notes by converting integers that reside in an accompanying user-created data file.

the same folder as the Music Lines application. You can alter its values with any standard text editor (see Figure 20-2).

Selecting the Rhythm command in the Commands menu applies the data from the text file to the current Music Lines file. In order for the lines you have drawn to transform this data to MIDI events, you have the option to Perform Selected, only taking into account the lines selected with the selection tool. The other option is simply to Perform All. This includes your entire line art drawing. Alternatively, you can send the output of Music Lines to MIDI instruments or convert it to a MIDI file (see Figure 20-3).

```
Global data:

40     Maximum time in seconds
32     Minimum pitch in MIDI values
90     Maximum pitch in MIDI values
120    Metronome value
4      Time signature numerator
2      Time signature denominator

Rhythm Data:

0      Line length in seconds; 0 for varying line length
36     Number of rhythm notes (i.e. the number of remaining lines)
2  0   Rhythm values:  length     silence (> 0  for a rest)
2  1
2  0
```

Figure 20-2:
Source Rhythm
text file for
Music Lines.

Figure 20-3: Music generated by the line drawing and rhythm data file pictured in the two previous figures.

Evolution #9

Evolution #9 is a random generator for producing passages of serial music, that is, music in which the notes, rhythms, and dynamics are rigorously ordered. Francis "Butch" Mahoney, the author of Evolution #9 and a companion program called Music Box (see "Music Box"), conceives of the software as being compositions in themselves as well as music generators. While this may cause headaches for the copyright offices, it in no way prevents algorithmic Macintosh fiends from using them as tools in an evolving compositional arsenal.

A

Enter the prime row:		
	Bb	C
	G	A
	F#	Ab
	Eb	B
	D	F
	Db	E

(Enter note values in upper or lower case. Enter sharps as '#' and flats as 'b')

[OK]

B — Evolution #9

Bb	G	F#	Eb	D	Db	C	A	Ab	B	F	E
Db	Bb	A	F#	F	E	Eb	C	B	D	Ab	G
D	B	Bb	G	F#	F	E	Db	C	Eb	A	Ab
F	D	Db	Bb	A	Ab	G	E	Eb	F#	C	B
F#	Eb	D	B	Bb	A	Ab	F	E	G	Db	C
G	E	Eb	C	B	Bb	A	F#	F	Ab	D	Db
Ab	F	E	Db	C	B	Bb	G	F#	A	Eb	D
B	Ab	G	E	Eb	D	Db	Bb	A	C	F#	F
C	A	Ab	F	E	Eb	D	B	Bb	Db	G	F#
A	F#	F	D	Db	C	B	Ab	G	Bb	E	Eb
Eb	C	B	Ab	G	F#	F	D	Db	E	Bb	A
E	Db	C	A	Ab	G	F#	Eb	D	F	B	Bb

Figure 20-4: (A) Evolution #9's Pitch Entry dialog box showing entered row (Bb, G, F#, Eb, D, Db, C, A, Ab, B, F, E), with an arrow indicating the tone row's placement in a traditional 12-tone magic square. **(B)** The prime form of the row at all transpositions appears horizontally from left to right. The retrograde form can be read from right to left. The inversion and retrograde-inversion forms are displayed from top to bottom and bottom to top respectively. **(C)** A magic square generated from a row of eight pitches (C, G, Bb, F#, E, Db, E, C).

C

C	G	Bb	F#	E	Db	E	C				
F	C	Eb	B	A	F#	A	F				
D	A	C	Ab	F#	Eb	F#	D				
F#	Db	E	C	Bb	G	Bb	F#				
Ab	Eb	F#	D	C	A	C	Ab				
B	F#	A	F	Eb	C	Eb	B				
Ab	Eb	F#	D	C	A	C	Ab				
C	G	Bb	F#	E	Db	E	C				

The first thing you have to do in Evolution #9 is choose a melody of up to 12 pitches. That's right! You have to make the first compositional move. Once you have done that, however, the software creates a 12×12 grid of your tune (see Figure 20-4). This "magic square" representation is familiar to anyone who has worked with 12-tone or serial music. Choosing less than 12 notes as your "row" reduces the area of the grid accordingly. In this case, the grid does not display all transpositions of the original row — only those originating from pitches in the original tune.

The original melody appears across the top row. The first vertical column is an inversion of the melody. The retrograde forms of the original row appear reading horizontally right to left and retrograde inversions read in columns up from the bottom. This type of grid is a convenient way to view all the possible transpositions of a tone row at a glance.

This display is really for your personal gratification only, although you can print it for reference if you like. It's the software that decides which of the various transformations of the row to use. Your major choices relate to the rhythmic parameter — the options located under the Rhythm menu.

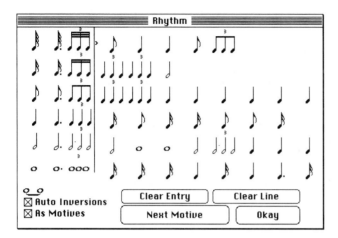

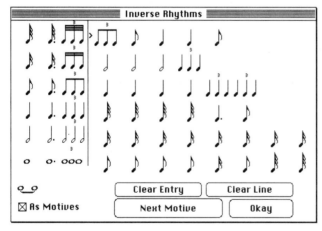

Figure 20-5: The Rhythmic Selection dialog box from Evolution #9. Clicking a rhythmic cell adds it to one of six rhythmic motifs that you can build in this dialog box.

As with the source pitch material, you have the option of designating rhythmic motifs. You can select up to six motifs, each having up to eight different rhythmic cells. Further, you have the choice of applying them motivically or having them used as a rhythmic melody. In the latter case, the rhythms generate a 36-cell series, which itself can be transformed as it is applied to pitches. Unless you employ strikingly contrasting rhythms or give some rhythms extra weight (by duplicating a rhythm two or more times at the setup stage), the difference between motivic and melodic use of the source rhythms is not very audible, because the various groupings might overlap the pitch groupings of the tune.

One aspect of control that produces dramatic results is the option to compose a new set of rhythmic motifs for the software to treat as "inversions" of your original set. You can decide to choose any rhythms you fancy, not necessarily having anything to do with the first set. The results often make for musically provocative rhythms and counterpoint. Conversely, checking the "Auto Inversions" box applies a hard-coded inversion algorithm to your rhythms (see Figure 20-5).

Finally, if you want to, you can set up a row of dynamics. Stockhausen fans can pit pianississimos against fortississimos to isolate each pitch in its own world. Alternatively, the computer will use hard-coded algorithms for the manipulation of dynamics (see Figure 20-6).

The program provides other global options. You can determine the amount of rests with the Spacing setting. A low setting of 2 will result in dense-sounding

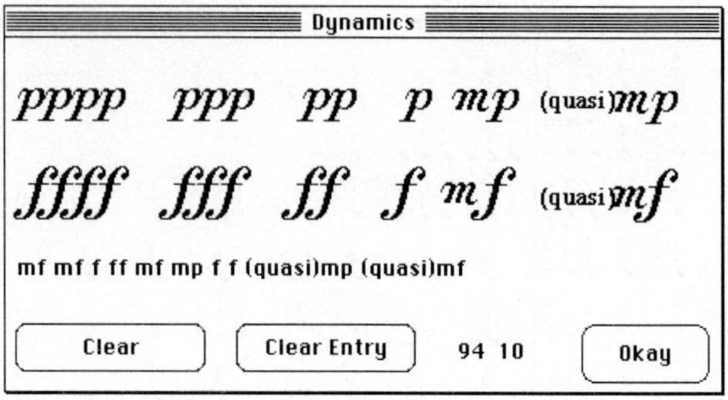

Figure 20-6: The dynamic row setup box of Evolution #9. Clicking one of the large dynamic entries adds it to the smaller dynamic row.

textures (notes with few rests between them). A higher setting of maybe 10 produces a more sparse, pointillistic effect.

Evolution #9 can play up to eight voices simultaneously, on any desired MIDI channels, with default patch numbers and pitch ranges specified by you. Once you input your decisions, including the length, tempo, and number of voices you desire, the program composes the piece. Composition time is quite fast, taking only seconds. You can save the piece as a MIDI file or print it as an alphanumeric listing of the composition, indicating channel, measure, tick, duration, note, and velocity (see Figure 20-7).

Music Box

Music Box requires even fewer choices than Evolution #9. It produces tonal-sounding music reminiscent of the language used by American composers in the 1940s, now called *pandiatonicism,* so named because it sticks to the notes of a diatonic scale, but uses them in non-triadic ways (see Figure 20-8). This is interesting because author Butch Mahoney states that this program is merely an initial step in what will eventually be an algorithmic approach to composing four-voice chorales.

Like Evolution #9, it is easy to select tempo, density of events (which determines the proportion of rests to notes), number of voices, and their allocation. On the other hand, there is no choice whatsoever regarding the rhythms, or even the melodic material. Instead, you need only decide among four choices of scales: major, minor, harmonic minor, and melodic minor. Then you're ready to click Compose and listen to the results.

As with Evolution #9, Music Box applies a random generator to the notes of a scale and to an array of rhythms, neither of which is visible or available to you for modification. Instead, they lurk in the black box of the program performing their magic.

Figure 20-7: Sample output from Evolution #9 (conversion of generated MIDI file into notation). **(A)** This music was generated with a density setting (called spacing in Evolution) of 9.

Both of these applications, Evolution #9 and Music Box, are small in scope but produce engaging results with a minuscule learning curve. The music they create is always different, but both programs produce musical fragments that have an identifiable character. They have a trademark sound, just as any synthesizer capable of a huge sonic spectrum has a color all its own that immediately identifies it, no matter what patch is playing. It is in this sense that these applications are compositions in their own right as well as algorithmic programs.

Algorithms

The flexible possibilities of HyperMIDI, even extend to automatic composition with a simple but elegant program called, appropriately enough, Algorithms (by Jeff Rona). In the best HyperCard tradition, Algorithms is a virtually self-explana-

Figure 20-7 (continued): (B) This music was generated with a density setting of 2. No other parameters were altered.

tory HyperCard stack. While it certainly performs only limited operations, the resulting music is often quite interesting. Further, it requires absolutely no musical knowledge, going so far as to include a button that eliminates the need for any further input from you, in case you so desire. It doesn't get easier than this!

Algorithms is capable of applying three different processes, called White, Brown, and Weighted, to compose pitches from either chromatic, diatonic, or pentatonic scale systems. White refers to a completely random selection, much like throwing dice (see Figure 20-9). Brown determines a pitch by adding a small interval to the previous choice. Finally, Weighted chooses pitches in a manner such that they surround a tonal center.

Figure 20-8: Sample output from Music Box (in conventional music notation). **(A)** This music was generated with a density setting (called spacing in Music Box) of 2 and a major scale selected. **(B)** This music was generated with a density setting of 9 and a melodic minor scale selected.

Algorithms's approach to scale systems is largely responsible for the way the program draws its melodic and harmonic language. The combination of these three scales with their three different statistical weights makes for a surprisingly rich variety of sound possibilities. In fact, it provides for a wide spectrum of possible melodies and chords while still having a sense of organization that is capable of sustaining interest both for the novice and the serious composer.

The scrolling field in the center of the Score card displays your decisions. You use the three buttons immediately to the right and left of this scrolling field to make all the compositional decisions that determine the course of the generated piece. Pressing any of them results in a pop-up menu of variables (see Figure 20-10). Scale gives a choice between random selection of chromatic, diatonic, or pentatonic collections. Expression determines the dynamic level of the piece, presumably by velocity control. The Durations button is remarkably general, listing long notes, short notes, long rest, and short rest as the only possibilities. The three

Figure 20-9: Music generated by Algorithms's White Chromatic button.

buttons on the right-hand side determine the type of tone events. Single Events is self-explanatory and includes choices such as high note, low note, leap up, step down, and so on. Chains refers to groupings of notes in the various scale types and gives as choices 4 or 16 consecutive tones. The final choice button is Chords, offering exactly two possibilities: play chord and stop chord.

Four small utility buttons at the bottom of the screen make the work of creating a score even more convenient. Two of them are repeat buttons: one duplicates the

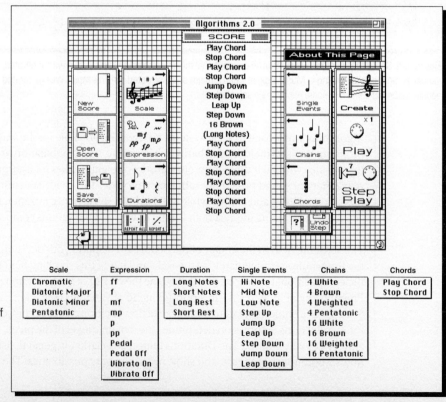

Figure 20-10:
The main screen of Jeff Rona's Algorithms with pop-up menus displayed.

Scale	Expression	Duration	Single Events	Chains	Chords
Chromatic	ff	Long Notes	Hi Note	4 White	Play Chord
Diatonic Major	f	Short Notes	Mid Note	4 Brown	Stop Chord
Diatonic Minor	mf	Long Rest	Low Note	4 Weighted	
Pentatonic	mp	Short Rest	Step Up	4 Pentatonic	
	p		Jump Up	16 White	
	pp		Leap Up	16 Brown	
	Pedal		Step Down	16 Weighted	
	Pedal Off		Jump Down	16 Pentatonic	
	Vibrato On		Leap Down		
	Vibrato Off				

Figure 20-11: Short score of Algorithms's output using the settings in Figure 20-10.

last step entered, and the other repeats the entire score up to that point. Another button allows you to delete the last step entered. Perhaps the most intriguing button is the one with the question mark. This is a gateway to a dialog box in which you type in a number that is used to create step decisions automatically and randomly.

Once you feel that your score listing is complete, the stack compiles your decisions and massages them with the algorithms to produce the music (see Figure 20-11). It takes a while, depending on the number of steps in the score and whether you have inserted loop instructions. The results are invariably appealing on some level, and of course, recompiling a score will produce different music each time, since stochastic processes determine the pitches. In all, Algorithms is an ideal introduction for the novice interested in automatic composition.

Fractal Music Generator

Fractal Music Generator by Nigel Redmon (author of HyperMIDI) is another instant music stack that ships with HyperMIDI. Where Algorithms limits choices to a few scales and statistical methods, Fractal Music Generator allows you to create your own scales or pitch collections. The tradeoff in this program is that you are not able to "build" a piece with a list of instructions as with Algorithms. Here you set parameters, select the number of measures you want composed, and sit back while the computer does the work applying fractal equations to generate a series of numbers from the possibilities you've given. The results usually make a fascinating pointillistic collage. You can export them as MIDI files.

The Input Parameters card allows you to define the scale of pitches upon which to base the piece (see Figure 20-12). By Option-clicking on any choice, you may choose to overwrite that scale and record your own. This option is easy to apply, because you can enter your scale by playing on a MIDI instrument rather than typing in the pitch names. The scale can include 16 notes from various registers or maybe just repeat two tones eight times. This is not a trivial decision. In some ways, this choice gives you very strong and predictable control over the sound of the final generated piece. It is a control that is difficult to duplicate in almost all the other algorithmic software, where the final output tends to be somewhat of a surprise (pleasant or otherwise). Along with the scale, you can also set a velocity range to determine overall dynamic level.

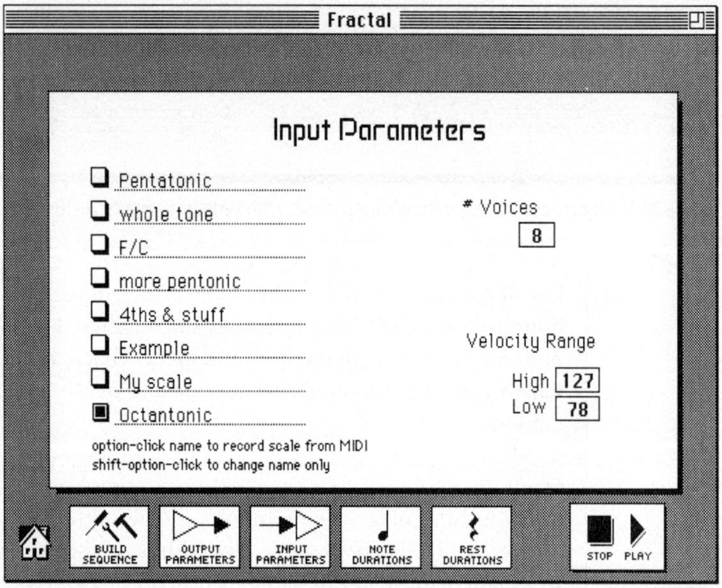

Fractal

Input Parameters

- ☐ Pentatonic
- ☐ whole tone
- ☐ F/C
- ☐ more pentonic
- ☐ 4ths & stuff
- ☐ Example
- ☐ My scale
- ■ Octantonic

option-click name to record scale from MIDI
shift-option-click to change name only

Voices
8

Velocity Range
High 127
Low 78

BUILD SEQUENCE · OUTPUT PARAMETERS · INPUT PARAMETERS · NOTE DURATIONS · REST DURATIONS · STOP PLAY

Figure 20-12: Fractal's Input Parameters card. Note that the seven buttons running along the bottom are present on every card in the stack, making navigation and playback quite easy.

On the same card you can choose to have the score written for up to eight voices, all of which are assignable to any MIDI channel by way of the Output Parameters card.

Fractal Music Generator provides two cards with a very functional interface for choosing rhythmic parameters — one for note durations and another for rests (see Figure 20-13). First you determine a base time by clicking the quarter note, eighth note, sixteenth note, or thirty-second note icon. This decides which value the program considers to be a single beat. No big deal here. But to the left of that are eight fields, which contain numbers you type; these numbers represent the number of beats each chosen tone will get. The two factors that enrich this option are: (1) you can type a group of numbers in a field, in which case the program decides among them randomly, and (2) you can designate any of the eight voices to any rhythmic field via sliders. As with tone generation, this interface gives considerable control over the rhythmic profile of the piece. But the options go further with the Rest Durations screen. This operates the same way as the Note Durations screen, just that the numbers you type indicate the beats of silence. You can also set a global value that determines the percentage of rests.

After determining the general pitch and rhythmic content, you create the music by advancing to the Build Sequence card. Here you type in the number of measures you want composed, then click the Generate button. A nice touch in the program is that the Play and Stop buttons are available in all the screens. Further, a playing sequence is a background activity. You can create another piece while listening to

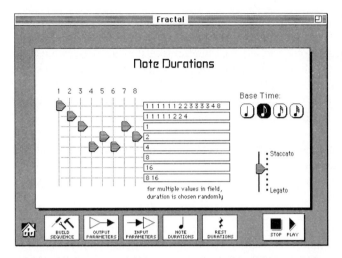

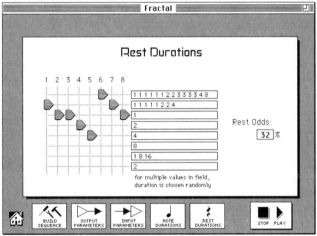

Figure 20-13: Fractal's cards for selecting durations of notes and rests.

the current one, or even transfer to another application with MultiFinder. All in all, Fractal Music Generator is extremely user-friendly and musically thought-provoking, besides being an excellent introduction to algorithmic composition software.

Cybernetic Composer

Suppose you have absolutely no interest in learning programming. Maybe you're not even intrigued by easily generated textures with a program like HyperMIDI's Algorithms. Instead, as a creature of instantaneous gratification, you want to be able to compose a jazz standard at the touch of a button. If this description fits your interest in algorithmic composition, or if you're just plain curious if and how such a thing could be possible, then Cybernetic Composer is just the ticket.

Cybernetic Composer was written by Charles Ames (see "COMPOSE") and Michael Domino as part of the Kurzweil Foundation Automatic Composition Project. Its goal is to illustrate how artificial intelligence can be used to produce musical works that are convincing enough that their artificial origin cannot be easily surmised.

What they have accomplished is no small feat — this program transforms your Macintosh into a willing and efficient robot for producing an infinite stream of competent pieces in the genres of standard jazz, Latin jazz, ragtime, and rock.

You can learn Cybernetic Composer's operation in a matter of seconds. Systematically select all the categories from the menu marked Compose and make your choices in the dialog boxes these bring up (see Figure 20-14). The menu item Genre lists the four types of music the program currently supports: standard jazz (reflecting the language of 1950s Bebop), Latin jazz (imitating the popular music of Brazil in the 1960s, which combined American jazz with the Bossa Nova), rock (containing a smattering of styles), and ragtime (à la Scott Joplin and the other ragtime composers from the early part of the century). Can't decide? No problem. Just click Random Choice, and Cybernetic Composer chooses for you.

Next you must choose a structure for the piece, here called a Model. These vary depending upon the type of music you picked. Examples include AABA, 12-bar Blues, and 8-bar Verse/4-bar Bridge. Not sure which to choose? Just click, you guessed it, Random Choice.

There are options to set the key and for deciding if the program should go on and compose a different piece without changing your original choices. You can provide a Failure integer to specify how persistent the program should be when it has problems choosing notes. These parameters are the only access you have to influence the program's built-in algorithmic routines.

Cybernetic Composer provides for four layers in performance: a solo instrument, a bass instrument, up to four background parts, and drums. You can send these voices out to your MIDI instruments or to the Macintosh speaker (in which case, standard 8-bit soundfiles play the music). For each layer you can assign its lowest and highest pitch, its MIDI channel, MIDI program number, velocity, transposition, voice number (if using Macintosh sound), MIDI port, and whether it is to be active or not in a particular piece. The Background layer even has a strum setting for creating delays to imitate guitar chords. In the Drum setting you can assign key numbers to various sounds to map the drum output onto your specific drum device. Note that not all sounds are available for every musical genre. Ragtime, for instance, does not compose for drums. A convenient Activity menu item allows you to enable or disable each of the four instrumental layers.

To set Cybernetic Composer into action, merely choose Run from the Compose menu and it begins. The Vital Statistics and Progress Report windows keep you abreast of the compositional process as it is going on. First, the program assembles a chordal rhythmic structure and compiles the various phrase sections. As it successfully builds the framework, the program lists each section in such a way that you can see the piece being constructed before your eyes.

It takes several minutes to complete a piece, but as the manual says, "Just think how long it would take you to compose something like this!" Once done, the Progress Report windows disappear and the music can be performed or saved as a MIDI file.

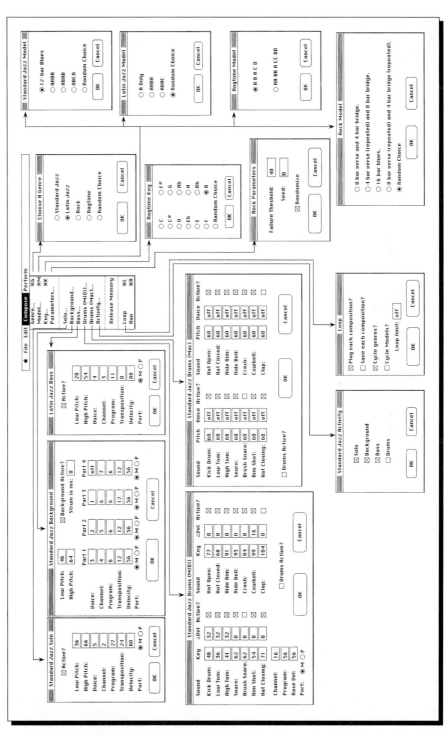

Figure 20-14: The main menu of Cybernetic Composer with configuration dialog boxes.

If this isn't enough for you, the program has an alternative Loop setting, which will compose piece after piece, saving and/or playing them. You can define whether it should compose using all the genres and, if so, how many works of each genre to create. Also, you can determine the total number of pieces composed. One can't help envisioning the scenario of a hard day's work: setting the program to loop incessantly early at dawn and then heading straight for the beach, hundreds of pieces (and an untold number of agonizing compositional decisions) being made while you surf.

Cybernetic Composer makes use of many algorithmic techniques. These include simple decision-making based on predefined possibilities related to the technique employed in the Mozart musical dice game. But the greatest secret behind this composing black box is an element of AI called *backtracking*. When a collection of constraints leads to an impasse in making a decision, backtracking allows the computer to trace back to an earlier decision and make a different choice. For anyone who has tried to compose a musical canon, this is a familiar struggle. You try to compose a melody that permits making a round at a specific time interval and pitch level. To achieve consonant harmonies is no easy task. What works fine at the moment might produce disastrous results a measure later. Because of this, you often find yourself having to go back and change previous notes to achieve success at your present location. In some ways, you are actually composing backward as well as forward.

This is precisely the process Cybernetic Composer uses to determine its pitches. Once the program has determined an ordering of note types — those belonging to the chords vs. ornaments — it then begins to make choices to fill in the melodic motion. If a set of results happens to place a voice out of its constrained range, for example, the program has to backtrack to a previous point and make a different choice until it succeeds in getting through the rough spot.

On a higher structural order, Cybernetic Composer uses option streams to determine first a chordal rhythm for a piece. This involves layers of built-in templates assigned to statistical probabilities. A given couple of bars might present a choice between two different streams of progressions, with a 40 percent chance favoring one over the other. The chosen stream itself often consists of several possible chord variations, each with their own set of probabilities. This is why there is such a wide variety of harmonic progressions within each musical genre.

After establishing the chordal rhythm, the program builds a melody in a similar way. First, it determines various streams of melodic rhythm and function. Suppose the chordal rhythm specifies two beats of a G-major chord. The program might then choose between a melodic rhythm of two quarter notes, a dotted-quarter and eighth, or a quarter note followed by a rest. From here, choices of function ensue. If the program decides on two quarter notes, then it must determine which of them is to belong to the G-major chord and which is to be ornamental. Also, the chord tone can be either G, B, or D, while the ornament could be a passing tone or any other type of auxiliary.

Only after determining the chordal rhythm and melodic function does the program decide upon the actual notes of the piece. A number of streams then present themselves for thematic development. Is a small fragment of melody to be repeated, transposed, or altered? Or should a completely different shape of notes follow? In this way, it creates a different melodic structure for every layer of each piece.

If you begin to feel dizzy at the number of possible combinations, don't stop yet. Remember that each musical layer (solo, background, bass, and drums) also has its own constraints and option streams. Furthermore, these are significantly different for each genre (just in case you thought the limits of standard jazz, Latin jazz, ragtime, and rock were a bit stifling). The ornament generator in standard jazz governs an entirely different set of decisions than that of rock. And while a jazz bass must follow option streams typical of walking bass lines, the rock genre makes choices between eighth-note motifs, riffs, fast-funk, and double time.

The $64,000 question is, "How good is the music?" The music Cybernetic Composer produces is of surprisingly fair quality (see Figures 20-15 and 20-16). Each genre is easily recognizable to any listener. The harmonic progressions are all pleasing, the rhythms very infectious. They are certainly at the level of "good" student pieces. What strikes the ear is just how great occasional passages do sound. A certain turn of melody, or coordination of rhythm and accompaniment seem incredibly inspired. Only the Macintosh doesn't seem to know this — yet! The music proceeds pleasantly and adequately, as if these spots never happened. But in all fairness, how often do you have the same reaction while listening to the radio?

Programming-intensive software
COMPOSE

COMPOSE, created by Charles Ames, provides tremendous depth in algorithmic composition without requiring a computer programmer's background. Ames describes his program as an "editor and interpreter of automated compositional processes." The operation of COMPOSE involves creating a number of modules (called units) that work together in ways you define yourself to build a compositional process. The program features virtually hundreds of these units, each with a variety of functions. These units allow you to manipulate values applied to pitches, rhythms, durations, MIDI program numbers, channels, and velocities. A strong feature of the program is its incorporation of many of the arithmetic processes that have concerned composers since the advent of serialism and, accordingly, the program's robust approach to statistical orderings. Units of these

Figure 20-15: Ragtime score in CMN composed by Cybernetic Composer.

Figure 20-16: Jazz bebop blues score in CMN composed by Cybernetic Composer.

types include BOREL, BROWNIAN, CHAOS, and MARKOV. Indeed, a side benefit of the tutorial in the manual is that it amounts to a basic course in advanced compositional procedures employed since World War II.

One powerful aspect to this modular approach is that units can interconnect and feed back to each other in any way you desire. In this respect, you build a piece the same way you create a patch for a synthesizer, except that the analogy is

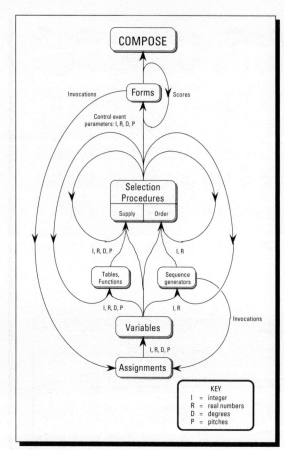

Figure 20-17: Flow chart of COMPOSE's compositional process.

more appropriate to older modular synths with their mass of tangled patch cords. As in synthesizer programming, a clear notion of information flow goes a long way to achieving desired sounds.

A piece, called a project in COMPOSE nomenclature, consists of segments, each of which contains processes that describe how notes are to be generated. Within each process is a selection procedure with two parameters: one to provide a supply of options (such as a table of pitches), and the other to determine the order in which each pitch is drawn from the supply. The general flow of information is that "assignment" modules give values to variables, which in turn drive generators such as tables and sequences. Selection procedures choose from the various tables and sequences and send controlling information to the "scores" modules, which produce the musical event(s). Information flow works both ways between high- and low-level units (see Figure 20-17).

Once all the units have been assembled and linked together, you generate a score by selecting Run from the Action menu. COMPOSE then compiles music by performing all the required actions on the units. An extremely convenient feature is an error alert, which surfaces when inaccurate data or linkage is present in a step. On exiting the alert box, the window of the unit needing correction comes to the front. Because a project can easily entail dozens of unit windows, this is extremely helpful (see Figure 20-18).

After successfully generating a score, you have three options. You can print it as an alphanumeric listing of events, save it as a MIDI file for importation by a sequencer or notation program, or simply play it from within COMPOSE to hear the fruit of your labors. There are three basic playing modes: (1) through the Macintosh internal speaker (four voices with no timbre or velocity control), (2) normal MIDI mode, or (3) a special MIDI mode called BEND. BEND provides for microtones through an ingenious application of pitch bend controller information — each note is assigned to its own MIDI channel to prevent the pitch bend of

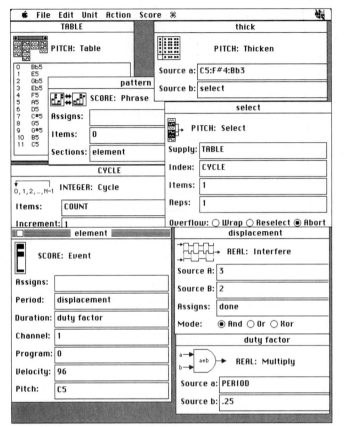

Figure 20-18: Main screen of COMPOSE with representative dialog boxes open.

one to interfere with another (this limits you to 16-voice polyphony). You can also specify a tempo, key signature, time signature, and transposition, for the convenience of exporting a SMF.

Modular Composition

The primary screen for building units appears when you select ADD... from the Unit menu (see Figure 20-19).

What if you want to describe a melody that can be transposed at any level (see Figure 20-20)?

On the highest level, a unit called PHRASE is fed pitches by the unit called EVENT. Controlling the decision of what pitch to send to EVENT is a unit called SELECT, whose purpose is to direct traffic between a supply of pitches represented as a table (your tune) and a unit called CYCLE, which determines the order of these pitches. But before SELECT sends its decisions to EVENT, it goes through another unit called THICKEN, which performs a transposition that you specify as applicable to the entire set.

If this seems like an awful lot of energy to expend on simply laying out a couple of notes, keep in mind that all of these decisions can be elaborated with layer upon layer of other processes. For instance, the level of transposition itself or, for that matter, the order of the tones may be determined by dozens of other factors, including random selection or stochastic procedures. And the SELECT module might have to choose not from merely one supply of pitches, but from a collection of a hundred different melodies, depending upon the input from another tune, which itself is under the control of another layer of events. Now imagine these networks as part of a single segment in a more extended work, and the level of musical interest begins to have significant potential. A TABLE

A

B

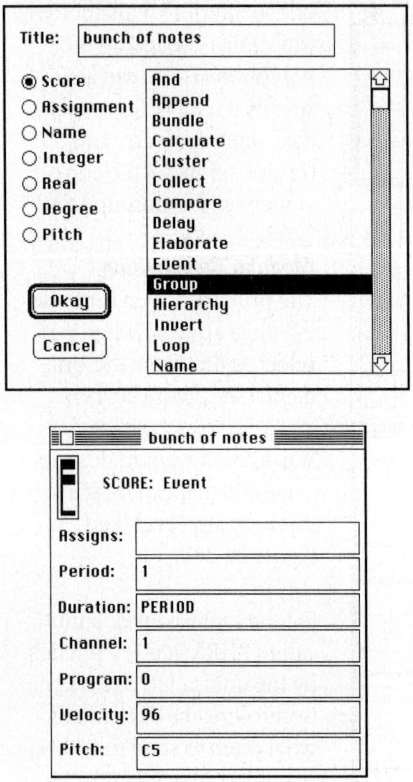

Figure 20-19: You use the Add dialog box from COMPOSE to select from different categories and types of units that are the building blocks of the program's modular approach to algorithmic composition. **(A)** The radio buttons at the left call up all the available units within the selected category. After this you can select the modular units themselves from the scrolling list at the right. **(B)** You use the Event dialog box to set individual parameters of a unit.

unit, for instance, instead of consisting of a series of pitches, can contain a series of tunes or textures to allow the chaining of extended musical segments. Alternatively, the development of one motif could depend on the progress of others. You can treat each process as a completed project to be saved and incorporated as a building block for the next.

Conceivably, COMPOSE could be harnessed to create a work of symphonic proportions and complexity. With such a magnitude of possibilities, COMPOSE definitely provides new and original tools for generating music. Rather than automating the compositional process to a "gee whiz" level of push buttons, this program encourages genuine creative thought and discovery of new perspectives of musical organization.

HMSL (Hierarchical Music Specification Language)

While not for the faint at heart, HMSL combines impressive depth with a flexible approach for algorithmic experimentation. It's safe to say this program is "hard core" and not for novices. HMSL was written and developed by Phil Burk, Larry Polansky, and David Rosenboom at the Center for Contemporary Music at Mills College and is a dedicated programming environment for the creation of algorithmic networks.

To learn HMSL, you must cultivate a working knowledge of three computer languages. They are Forth, ODE (Object Development Environment), and HMSL itself. ODE is written in Forth for the purpose of helping to simplify complex data structures. HMSL itself is written primarily in ODE.

An additional factor to consider is that HMSL must run with the MACH 2 system software containing a Forth 83 interpreter/compiler, a Motorola format assembler, and a symbolic debugger and disassembler. With these components, it is able to intermix routines between Assembly language and Forth. In other words, HMSL can't run on your computer unless you also buy the separate MACH 2 FORTH system to act as go-between from HMSL to the Macintosh.

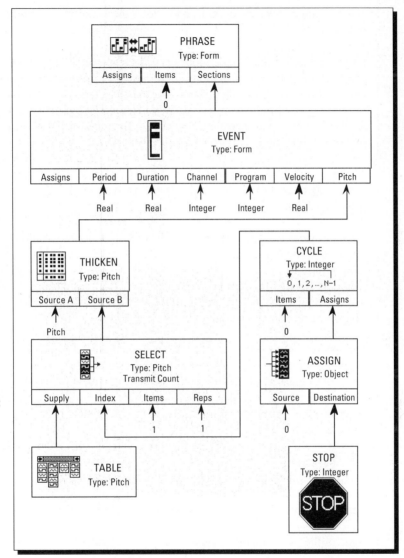

Figure 20-20: Flow chart diagram of units required for the generation of a transposable pitch series with COMPOSE.

HMSL is the result of responses from many of the top composers and programmers involved in this field. Consequently, it has broad applications for composition. Its abilities include a complete programming language for the creation of complex data, various algorithmic routines, real-time stimulus-response experimentation, graphic editors for real-time editing, and the capability for all of its parameters to be dynamically altered in real time by you, the Macintosh, or both. This means that HMSL permits intelligent communication between performers and computers as music unfolds, and allows the computer to compose on its own as well.

HMSL operates in three basic modes called Create, Perform, and Execute. Create involves editing operations and devising algorithmic procedures; Perform provides tools called actions for the designation of real-time stimulus-response events; and Execute is where you assign all the networking of the data structures (called morphs). The grand dispatcher of HMSL is called, rather preposterously, the Polymorphous Executive (PE).

As you might surmise, these modes can freely overlap, serving as controls for each other. Programming in HMSL means creating various objects and determining their paths of inheritance.

HMSL provides two graphics displays for editing. One, the Shape Editor, provides for real-time alteration of predefined shape morphs (see "What's a morph?" and Figure 20-21). You can alter shapes governing rhythm or amplitude envelopes as the piece is being executed, thus establishing a true interactive environment. You can also configure HMSL to alter the shape of actual samples in real time, resulting in improvised sound creation!

The second real-time editor is the Action Table, which displays a prominent 8 × 8 grid for organizing up to 64 different actions into a hierarchy of four levels of priority. You can alter an action's priority level in real time. Furthermore, a separate Probability grid determines the probability that any action will occur within a particular priority level, while the Behavior choices determine which priority level to use.

What's a morph?

It may sound like a new Saturday morning cartoon character, but *morph* is an essential term for understanding HMSL. Put simply, morphs are sets of data that can be nested and layered in complex networks.

Some of the more important types of morphs include:

Collections   A set of morphs that can be either sequential or parallel (referred to in the manual as "dumb bags of morphs"). In other words, these contain no intelligence about how to execute their constituent individual morphs beyond triggering them simultaneously or incrementally.

Structures   A set of morphs with an associated behavior, which determines the procedure for executing the morphs. Structures can be thought of as "slightly intelligent" collections.

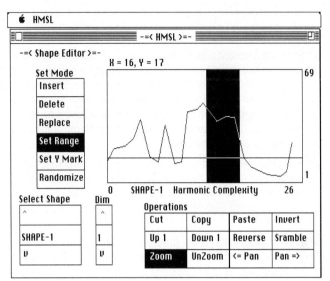

Figure 20-21: HMSL's Shape Editor. The convenient Shape Editing screen allows for real-time graphic manipulation of predefined shape morphs to establish true user interaction with the program. Possible applications might include sound envelopes or alteration of samples themselves in real time.

Tstructures   Tstructures are structures that employ some type of probability factor in the execution of their morphs, denoted by the term "nodal tendency matrix."

Actions   Morphs concerned with stimulus-response behavior.

Shapes   Abstract sets of points formed into envelopes, waveforms, durations, and patterns of musical events. In short, they are applicable to any musical parameter.

Jobs   Morphs with a list of functions to be performed at specified (scheduled) times.

As you can see from the previous list, HMSL goes to great lengths to describe compositional procedures in the most abstract manner possible. In doing so, it provides a good deal of intelligence and flexibility in that modules are free to be applied to any possible parameter. Various interpreters built into HMSL, such as two called Instruments and Players, have the job of realizing these morphs in musically useful ways.

HMSL begs for original ways of thinking about the structure of music. It offers an ideal environment for devising procedures capable of developing musical ideas by feedback and influenced by behavior choices in a manner similar to the way many of us compose. Harmonic progressions may evolve and melodies can transform in relation to what they have done before. Though HMSL poses a steep learning curve, it is one of the most sophisticated platforms around for devising algorithmic compositions.

Summary

- From the moment computers and music began their association, people working in these fields have dreamed of a system that could produce original music by the touch of a button. This may be the most controversial topic in computer music. Some see this as fulfilling the Orwellian prophecy of computer-created music for the masses whining from telescreens. But just as we now perceive synthesis and sampling more as adjuncts to our sonic palette rather than replacements for acoustic instruments, so too does algorithmic composition promise new resources for the creation of original music.

- Computer-generated composition programs tend to focus on reducing musical components to elemental and procedural levels, which serve as building blocks or modules to describe any structure that you can envision. The word "envision" is important here. For the most part, the current state of algorithmic composition still requires considerable inspiration on the part of the composer.

- A good description of the process of composition is the art of making musical choices. If it is possible to describe the principles underlying these choices in a large body of rules, then in the computer we have an excellent tool for handling this body of knowledge in powerful ways. The computer excels in counting and remembering things. Furthermore, it is tireless in its ability to take particulars, apply them to its knowledge base, and doggedly retrieve all applicable solutions. In this context, the "rules" are what computer-assisted composers mean when they refer to "algorithms." Algorithmic composition, then, is creating a network of rules and procedures that allow a computer to make choices in producing music.

- Although in a mathematical sense an algorithm always yields either a solution or the answer that no solution exists, most compositional rules and principles provide for not just one solution, but many. The composer is usually the one to fix a solution based upon a larger view of the work or the fact that earlier choices dictate specific solutions or tendencies to favor certain solutions.

- There is some overlap between interactive and algorithmic software. Some programs are literally dedicated to both processes. One clear distinction is that all algorithmic programs usually require some aspect of compilation. Once you decide to create all parameters and rules, the computer runs through everything and makes appropriate choices to convert procedures and numbers into musically relevant data. During this compilation process, the computer is essentially on its own, whereas in an interactive program, you would be fidgeting with controls to alter an outcome in real time. Algorithmic programs require composing time before they can give results.

- A branch of computer-generated composition in which the music is produced in real time is referred to as automatic composition. Automatic composition differs from interactive composition in that, once set in motion, it "goes its own way — doing its own thing" with little human intervention other than an initial defining of parameters. In some ways, some interactive programs and intelligent instruments can give the appearance of being an automatic composing machine — when you load them with musical material and set all the knobs, it will continue generating music indefinitely.

Part Four

Notation

Part Four

Foreword

by Don Byrd

Notation

As the saying goes, "a little knowledge is a dangerous thing." This old chestnut applies to notation software as much as anything. The following chapters make it clear that notation programs can no longer be thought of as the toys they were only a few years ago. But now that programs are growing up — perhaps this is even evidence that they *are* growing up — they're suffering from a typical problem of adolescence: they act as if they know everything. In a word, they're becoming smart alecks.

Why do I say this, considering how much the better programs know these days about rhythm, complex chords, instrumentation, and so on? Because all this knowledge isn't much compared to what there is to know about conventional music notation (CMN). This is a very complicated subject, and I don't have the space for an extended discussion, so I'll have to rely on a few dramatic examples to make my point.

Now, why do these peculiar pieces of notation (see Figures P4-1 through P4-4) arise in the music of these highly respectable composers? The interesting thing is, there's really nothing very strange going on in any of these examples. In fact, it's easy to imagine someone playing through the selections in Figures P4-2 or P4-4 without even noticing anything unusual — and a listener to *any* of these examples would surely not notice anything unusual. The

Bach example could have been written without a change of time signature at all, but it would have required a lot of tuplets and it would probably have been harder to read. All the other examples could have been written without any unusual notation simply by adding a third staff, but then the music would have required more paper (expensive for the publisher) and perhaps page turns (annoying for the performer).

The point is, the supposed rules of CMN are not independent: they interact, and when the situation makes them interact strongly enough, something has to give. It's tempting to assume that the rules of such an elaborate and successful system as CMN must be self-consistent. A big problem with this idea is that so many of the rules are, necessarily, very nebulous: Every book on CMN is full of vague statements illustrated by examples that often fail to make the rule clear. If you try to make every rule as precise as possible, what you get is certainly *not* self-consistent.

Software designers are well intentioned people, and they tend to think they can best help their users by having their programs do things automatically. This is true *if* the software knows enough that it can do the right thing almost all of the time! I speak here from experience, both as a professional programmer and as a notation programmer. SMUT, my first notation program, made many assumptions (for example, that every

(Bach)

Figure P4-1: J.S. Bach changing time signature in the middle of the measure (*Goldberg Variations*).

(Brahms)

Figure P4-2: A measure with no less than four (count 'em) horizontal positions for notes on the downbeat (Brahms, *Intermezzo* op 117, #1). The notes in the dotted quarter chords occupy three different positions; the first eighth note on each staff, in yet a fourth position, is also on the downbeat.

(Debussy)

(Ravel)

Figures P4-3 (top) and P4-4 (bottom): Two very different ways of having two clefs in effect on a staff at the same time. The first is bizarrely obvious (Debussy, *La Danse de Puck*). The other — in the fourth measure on the lower staff — is so subtle that you really have to think about 3/8 meter here (obvious everywhere else in the example) to see that the bass and treble clefs are both in effect throughout the entire measure (Ravel, *Scarbo* from *Gaspard de la Nuit*).

voice in the score stays permanently on one staff) that aren't always true. After working for years on it, I realized that it would have been more useful overall if it hadn't made so many assumptions, even though it would have been less automatic, and therefore less useful, when those assumptions *were* true. (Best of all would have been a way to tell the program what it could assume: then you wouldn't have to give up anything.)

Matters are made much worse by the fact that, these days, most notation programs attempt to convert CMN to a performance and vice versa, and therefore have to understand to some extent what the notation *means*. If the software wasn't trying to play from notation and vice versa, it could get away with a lot less knowledge. A simple proof of the overwhelming difficulty of translating in only one direction — CMN to performance — is that instrumental and voice teachers in every music school spend a lot of time teaching their students how to interpret CMN, and not all of it is on subtle aspects that users wouldn't mind the computer overlooking. For example, in jazz and related styles as well as some Baroque music, patterns of even eighth notes may correspond to very uneven played values or they may not, depending on the tempo. You're supposed to know how they're played from your knowledge of the style.

Finally, Severo Ornstein, co-author of the legendary (but never commercially available) program Mockingbird, recently pointed out one of the worst offenses of many programs:

Right from the outset [most existing systems] assume the existence of a defined rhythmic structure (barlines, meter) as part of the staffing, into which input is fitted somehow (I would say forced) . . . There is a . . . serious problem that follows when music is represented in a rhythmically structured way. In working with a score on the screen, entering and removing material, all actions require the consequent material to fit somehow into the predetermined rhythmic structure. The consequences of actions that would tend to violate this structure must be forced into it in one way or another, and the resultant side effects may well be at variance with the user's intentions . . . When the user puts a note down, he doesn't want it to be moved somewhere else just because the program thinks it understands where it fits into the structure. And he doesn't want it to cause anything else to move around either. He just wants the note to go where he put it. And when he deletes a note, that's all he wants to happen . . . — he may well plan to use the space thus freed up for something else. It's disturbing to have things moved into space you just tried to clear, things that don't belong there and which then lose their alignment with the things they do belong with.

Conclusion

It's interesting to compare music notation to Chinese writing and to mathematical notation. It turns out that CMN is vastly more complex than Chinese. Chinese has one incredible character set, but pretty much all you do with the characters is arrange them in rows and columns and start new lines and pages as needed, much as in any other language. In music, layout is a major graphics problem, and there is no fixed character set, no matter how large — consider beams and especially slurs (and what about accidentals, articulation marks, and augmentation dots — are they independent characters, or are they parts of some single character along with the note they belong to?). Mathematical notation is a more worthy opponent, but music almost certainly is still more complex.

In 1984 I wrote: "Much music exists whose correct formatting requires considerable intelligence (well beyond the state of the art of artificial intelligence), and some music exists whose correct formatting probably requires full human intelligence" (*Music Notation by Computer*— see Appendix C). I see no reason to change these statements today — and transcribing and playing from notation, as most programs on the market today do, is much more demanding than just correct formatting.

CMN is too difficult to handle automatically — at least until computers get a lot smarter. In the meantime, any music notation program that thinks it can tell what its users *really* want is going to do them a lot of favors they would have been better off without. I'm not saying we need programs that know less, just ones that know how much they don't know.

Note: Musical examples created with Nightingale. ♩

Don Byrd is president of Advanced Music Notation Systems.

Introduction to Part Four
Music processing

There are many good arguments in favor of pursuing the field of computer music notation. Cutting, copying, and pasting lend themselves very well to music processing. Due to repetition and variation, much musical information is reusable within the same piece. A computer greatly simplifies automatic proofreading of such parameters as rhythm and instrumental range. Interactive proofhearing and ease of editing provide obvious advantages for composers and orchestrators. In the music publishing industry, computers make it possible for several people to work on the same job, with the software substituting for manual dexterity and to a certain extent, musical knowledge.

Music publishers normally invest a five-figure sum in the engraving, printing, and distribution of each musical composition they publish. Many current notation packages are well on their way to eliminating these expenses. Publishers no longer have to weigh the odds of whether they will recover their investment in a publication — they can store all works on a disk and print them as the need and orders arise. Furthermore, it is becoming increasingly common for composers to supply their music already on disk, a practice that represents further savings for the publishers. As more musical works make their way to distribution centers by way of telecommunications in the form of notation files, the long-awaited concept of "publication on demand" is on the verge of becoming a reality. Publication on demand refers both to publishers storing music data for printing when customers place orders and to the newer "kiosk" distribution centers that are beginning to appear. Such kiosks resemble video games but have thousands of scores available via a touch screen. Often you can hear a preview of the work played by the kiosk. You insert your money (or hand it to an attendant) and select the music to be printed out in the key you desire. Voilà!

Music processing vs. text processing

People often speak of music processing and word processing within the same breath. When you stop to think about it, they have less in common than you might expect. Of course, there are the obvious similarities: Musicians record the sounds of their instruments using a tape recorder and people record their own words the same way. Everyone can understand how a typewriter works and cumbersome music typewriters exist as well. What we call word processors are really computerized typewriters. People believe that so-called music processors should allow them to play music on a keyboard and have that music print out perfectly. But few people expect to be able to talk to a typewriter and have it print out the words.

It is true that both language and music have written and sonic forms, but this is where the similarity ends. Consider the two character sets: Our alphabet uses 26 symbols (52 counting upper- and lowercase letters, several of which may be accented) — these are arranged consecutively along a horizontal baseline. Music notation uses eight or nine rhythmic values, which you can place at any of 88 or more vertical locations. Furthermore, you can write most notes in several ways, depending on context ($C\sharp = D\flat$); stems can point up or down with either a flag or a beam attached; and you can augment durations by combinations of dots and ties. The number of accents, dynamics, and expressive indications (ancillary signs) alone greatly exceeds the meager 52 symbols of the written alphabet. To compound matters, there is usually more than one note or one instrument playing at a time, so consider the vertical dimension as well.

Believe it or not, much published music is still produced by hand, the favored methods being autography (pen and ink), transfer process (rub-off characters), music stamping (rubber stamps), and music typewriters (modified conventional typewriters). Movable type (Gutenberg process) and plate engraving (inscribing symbols with sharp tools) are practically lost arts.

WYSIWYG

It is small wonder that music processing has thus far lagged behind word processing. Early systems required typing in a note's parameters using the alphanumeric "command line" interface that is common with early mainframe computers. All but the simplest music required the computing power of mainframes as well. To add insult to injury, early computerized notation systems offered no provisions for viewing notation on the computer screen. You first had to print the file to see if it required any editing.

With the arrival of the Macintosh, technology has advanced to the point where the requisite computer hardware power has become affordable by a large number of people. Music processing has become very dependent on WYSIWYG (What You See Is What You Get), and the Macintosh provides this necessary graphic capability. The other necessary ingredients, low-cost laser printers, and a versatile page description language, PostScript, also surfaced at the right moment.

First- and second-generation notation software

First-generation Macintosh notation software has been available for over seven years. Significant examples include Mark of the Unicorn's Professional Composer, Electronic Arts's Deluxe Music Construction Set, and Great Wave's ConcertWare. The initial releases of these packages generally required clicking note values on the screen with the mouse.

Things have been moving very fast ever since Adobe Systems introduced the device-independent PostScript music font, Sonata, in September of 1986. As remarkable as it may sound, until the release of the Adobe music font, there was no standardized musical symbol set, much less one that was not inherently tied to a single manufacturer's printing device. Many developers of first-generation notation packages rushed to include PostScript compatibility in their products as software upgrades. Some even designed their own fonts with the hope of improving upon Adobe's Sonata or to avoid the licensing fees Adobe required for the use of Sonata.

In late 1987 and early 1988, second-generation Macintosh notation programs began to appear: HB-Imaging's HB-Engraver, Coda's Finale, and Repertoire's Music Publisher (originally marketed by a company called Graphic Notes and now marketed by Music Publisher). Other second-generation packages continued to emerge: Passport Designs's Encore and Notewriter (originally marketed by Triangle Resources under the name MusScribe), MusicKrafter's NoteKrafter and ExampleKrafter (no longer marketed), Coda's MusicProse, Sun Valley Software's Toccata (no longer marketed), Pygraphics's MusicWriter (ported from their Apple II version), and Lime from CERL (Computer-based Education Research Laboratory Music Group, University of Illinois and Department of Computer and Information Science, Queen's University).

The programmers of these second-generation products all considered both PostScript compatibility and MIDI input as prerequisites. For the most part, they had learned from the shortcomings of the first-generation packages. These programmers started development with the knowledge that Adobe Systems's music font provided a cornerstone upon which to build programs that could truly equal the high standards of professional engraving, which opened up the entire music publishing industry to computer automation.

One major complaint that composers, engravers, and publishers had concerning first-generation notation packages was that many of the fundamental elements of conventional music notation were absent. The newer programs have added such basic necessities as variable numbers of staff lines (percussionists use 1-, 2-, 3-, and 4-line staves), complex meter signatures, fractional meter signatures, key signature cancellation, and in some cases, custom, nonlinear, and microtonal key signatures, bracketed and cautionary accidentals (sharps and flats) with "smart" insertion options, and slurs that do not have "jaggies" and do not collide with other symbols.

Perhaps the most widely voiced user request regarding first-generation packages was for diagonal beaming, a very conspicuous tradition evidenced on probably 99 percent of all existing pages of printed music in history and thus blatantly noticeable when missing. The developers of second-generation notation packages responded to the demands with a vengeance. Now all manners of diagonal beaming are available, from conventional to unconventional, and including such necessities as cross-staff beaming, reverse beaming (beams that include some stems up and some stems down), automatic beaming, beaming to a beaming table, double beaming (different beam groups connected to a single note or group of notes), extended beaming (over rests, for example), secondary beam-break control, beaming to lyrics, and "splayed" beaming (used in contemporary music to indicate accelerandos or ritardandos).

Third-generation notation software

One could argue that the appearance of third-generation music software corresponded to the ability of notation programs to accept and accurately transcribe MIDI data that was entered in real time. Many would disagree, however, as Coda's Finale, clearly a second-generation product, incorporated this feature within its initial release.

Third generation is a term often referring to increased AI or intelligent features in a software or hardware product. Although Finale incorporates an expert system engine (ENIGMA) that really does provide the program with the ability to automate a number of features requiring manual tweaking in other packages, the system still has room for improvement. With this in mind, I would consider a notation package to be third generation if it met all or most of the following criteria:

❖ MIDI data input does not require a click reference.
❖ Transcribed MIDI data requires little or no on-screen editing, especially with regard to accidentals, tuplets, and rests.
❖ Changes of key signature and meter signature are inferred from the input data.

❖ Dynamics and articulations, (e.g., crescendos, decrescendos, accelerandos, and ritardandos) are all inferred from the input data, and indications are appropriately placed on the page.

❖ Slurs are inferred from input MIDI data and auto-placed in optimum locations.

❖ Collision avoidance of all symbols is automatic and invisible to the user.

❖ Staff and system "justification" is automatic and invisible to the user.

❖ Final printed output requires little or no manual touching-up.

The addition of these capabilities implies a system where you can sit down and play a piece of music, full of expression and rubati, and then immediately press Print with the confidence that the output page will be the closest possible representation of what you had played — in other words, true WYPIWYP (What You Play Is What You Print). While no current packages achieve this, some do attempt to address third-generation issues.

From a musician's point of view, these requirements may seem obvious and trivial. However, if you discuss some of these things with a programmer of notation software, they are liable to provide credible arguments that such demands will never be met. Having observed the evolution of these software packages over the past decade, my personal standpoint is that we will witness the arrival of third-generation packages by the mid-1990s.

Chapter 21

Score Input and Editing

In this chapter...

✔ Reasons for using notation software and types of users.

✔ Rule-based vs. graphics-based software.

✔ Detailed discussion of the types of data that notation software deals with.

✔ Five main approaches of inputting non-MIDI data into notation software.

✔ Problems and solutions for symbol placement.

✔ Five methods for inputting MIDI data into notation software.

✔ Overview of and distinctions between editing graphic vs. MIDI data in notation software.

✔ Sonata font table.

Creating and Manipulating Your Music

There are two fundamental reasons for using music notation software:

❖ To manipulate preexisting music.
❖ To create new music.

The first category includes publishing, engraving, copying, and, to a certain extent, arranging and orchestration. The second category includes composition and *score realization* (that is, the electronic performance of a notated piece of music).

Notation software allows you to:

❖ Produce a final legible copy for the purposes of publication or distribution.
❖ Extract parts required for performance.
❖ Create new versions of existing works in different keys.
❖ Quickly create a new arrangement by using tools available through software.
❖ Simplify the manipulation of musical ideas using software tools.
❖ Create an electronic realization as a Polaroid (as they say in Hollywood), or for evaluation or proofhearing.
❖ Create an electronic realization as an end in itself.

The order of this list progresses from tasks primarily concerned with form to those concerned with content. It also demonstrates a progression from tasks relating to graphical elements, the look or appearance on paper, to those relating to musical substance, the meaning and interpretation of the symbols.

Another way of looking at this list (proposed by notation authority Donald Byrd) is as a progression through the target users that most notation systems are addressing: publishers/engravers, copyists, orchestrators/arrangers, acoustic composers, and electronic composers.

Here we recognize the variety of motivations for notating music by computer, ranging from those who want to save money in the production of music (with little concern for how long it takes) to those who want to save time in the production of music (sometimes with little concern for how much it is going to cost).

Regardless of their motivation, musicians approach these tasks with varying degrees of knowledge of music and the rules of common music notation. These observations highlight the two opposing approaches to the problems of music notation by computer: the graphic-oriented approach and the rule-oriented approach.

Rule-based systems "understand" music with varying degrees of success. That is to say that notes are understood to be representations of particular pitches and rhythms. This approach permits certain edit operations such as transposition, among other things. In the extreme case, such programs may be able to apply context-dependent heuristics to determine such things as whether pitch should be notated as a sharp or a flat. Durations are also understood, thus opening the door to such aids as automatic rhythmic error checking and note positioning.

Most formatting, placement, beaming, note spelling, and page layout is done automatically by rule-based programs with little opportunity for user-override. If you completely agree with the rules hard-coded into such programs, these systems can be extremely fast. Sometimes, built-in rules can compensate for limited musical knowledge on the part of the user. However, when faced with a non-conventional, graphics-oriented contemporary score, these programs tend to be the slowest.

Graphics-based systems have no understanding of music. All symbols are treated as graphical elements of equal importance and no underlying meaning is attached to the symbol in the program's internal data structures. You may be able to organize symbols into separate palettes for your convenience, but the program usually does not make a distinction between a note or text character and a dynamic or barline.

Although this might seem to be the worst-case scenario, systems that make no musical assumptions generally offer the greatest degree of on-page symbol placement flexibility. If you want to place a clef sign in between two staves, the program won't care because it is not bound by rules stating that clef signs must appear at a certain position on the staff. Unfortunately, completely graphics-based systems tend to be slower than all others with respect to input, editing, and formatting (although they may exceed the speed of alternatives for certain genres of graphically oriented contemporary music). For these types of programs, the user's knowledge of musical notation is the greatest determining factor in the look of the finished page — the software makes no attempt to compensate for a user's limited musical knowledge.

Most notation software packages attempt to straddle both of these worlds (graphics-based and rule-based). The most common way of achieving this is to allow the user to disregard or override rules or guesses by the computer and manipulate objects from a purely graphical standpoint. A simple example of this is a program that can deal with stem direction automatically, but provides the user with the option to flip stem direction within a particular context. A more complex example is a program that automatically beams groups of notes and guesses the best beam angle, yet allows the user both the option to correct beam angles individually as well as the option to set default minimum and maximum beam angles.

Real-time MIDI transcription requires a hefty collection of rules. After real-time musical data has been captured, the next major consideration for the conversion of this data into conventional music notation is how much of the process will result from rule-based automatic transcription and how much manual graphic editing it will require.

At this time, a certain amount of hand finishing will always be necessary, because MIDI has no provision for communicating information that is not relevant to performance data. For example, *enharmonic* representations of equivalent pitches (similar to homonyms in text) are not distinguished by the MIDI standard. Thus, it is up to the notation software to make guesses at whether a certain note should be notated with a sharp or a flat. There are algorithms designed to make these decisions, but almost all of them require that the user specify what key the piece is in, and none is correct 100 percent of the time.

Colliding symbols is another area of concern which requires well-thought-out rules. However, it is not very likely that the avoidance of symbol collisions can be automated to the extent of not requiring any manual graphic editing with the mouse — at least until third-generation notation software appears.

Whether a program is rule-based or graphics-based has a distinct impact upon both score input and editing. A purely graphical program requires that the user have a complete understanding of where notes have to be on a staff. On the other hand, a rule-based system, even when the user is simply selecting notes from a palette and clicking them into measures on the screen, usually spaces the notes automatically and often provides warnings if the sum of their durations exceeds that allowed by the prevailing meter signature.

Input Data Types

When using notation software you enter four types of data: page, system, and staff setup elements; notes and musical data; ancillary markings; and text.

Page, system, and staff setup elements

At the highest level of organization, you must tell the notation program basic information about your score.

Page layout: including page size and margins, number of systems per page, and vertical and horizontal justification of systems on the page.

System setup: including brackets, breaking of barlines, measure and rehearsal numbers.

Staff attributes: including clefs, key signatures, time signatures, number of staff lines, MIDI attributes (if applicable), instrument names, and transpositions.

Measure level considerations: including measure widths, types of barlines, and repeat barlines.

Notes and musical data

The most important musical data to enter are the notes and their associated modifiers, such as accidentals, ties, beaming, and tuplet groupings. There are two input methods for this type of data: MIDI and non-MIDI. These are discussed in greater detail below.

Ancillary markings

It is in the area of control over ancillary markings such as expressive indications that notation programs differ the most. The various types of ancillary markings include the following:

Note alterations: including the assignment of alternate noteheads and cautionary accidentals.

Note expressions (articulations): including accents, articulations, and expressive markings applied to a single note.

Staff expressions: including expressive markings that pertain to a specific staff or region of a staff, such as dynamics, crescendo, diminuendo, octavo signs, and slurs.

Score expressions: including all markings intended to affect every staff on a given system of the score, such as tempo indications.

Chord symbols: including both alphanumeric and fretboard (graphics-based) representations of chords.

Problems arise when a software program restricts the symbol set available. Additional problems occur when the software provides too little or too much control over symbol placement. Too little control can result in symbol collisions for which there is no remedy. Too much control can result in wasted time during symbol placement. Ideally, the software should know enough about where certain symbols are likely to be placed within a given context, while still allowing the user to reposition the symbol if required because of a collision. Another approach to this problem is letting the user configure default offsets for various symbols.

From the standpoint of the software, ancillary markings can be reduced to three types:

Font-based: Note expressions are generally of this type, since they are usually limited to a single symbol over which the user needs to have control of the size and placement relative to the target note. Most accents, articulations, and single symbol expressive markings are font-based. Fretboard chord symbols are usually font-based as well.

Text-based: Many staff and score expressions are text-based. Notable examples include expressive markings such as Adagio, Allegro, Accelerando, Spiccato, and Legato. Non-graphics-based chord symbols such as Cmin#11 are also predominantly text-based.

Graphics-based: Other staff and score expressions like slurs, glissandi, dotted horizontal 8va extension lines, and "hairpins" (for crescendo and diminuendo) are graphics-based and require some sort of elasticity upon entry (so they may be stretched to encompass the desired region) as well as elasticity upon reformatting (so they will resize when measure widths are altered).

Control of ancillary markings is the area that can make or break a notation program with respect to speed and, consequently, usability. For an example of the kinds of problems that can occur with ancillary markings, consider the following scenarios for the placement of staccato dots upon every note in a passage of 60 notes:

1. The software requires you to place each symbol on a note-by-note basis, requiring multiple actions on behalf of the user. Such actions could include first selecting a note and then selecting the staccato dot symbol from a symbol palette or, conversely, selecting a staccato dot from a symbol palette and then clicking it onto the destination note. If you have to select each note individually or if you have to reselect the staccato dot for each note, speed and efficiency will slow to a snail's pace. It gets even worse: If the staccato dot does not default or "snap" to a specific location in relation to the destination note, you might have to go back and reposition every one of the staccato dots on an individual basis.

2. The software requires you to place each symbol on a note-by-note basis, but each symbol thus placed snaps to a specified offset. This is a better alternative, unless the offset is hard-coded into the program or specified globally by the user. Hard-coded offsets and user-specified global offsets will almost always result in symbol collisions.

3. The software allows you to place many symbols of the same type at once. However, these symbols are all automatically placed (with respect to their targets), either at offsets that are hard-coded into the program or that you specified globally. The benefits of being able to select an entire region of notes and add all the ancillary markings in one command is an obvious time-saver, but, again, hard-coded offsets and user-specified global offsets will almost always result in symbol collision. A better alternative is software that allows you to override automatic offsets and adjust the placement of ancillary symbols on an individual basis. The best scenario provides for both individual override of automatic placement and regionally specified offsets.

The real issue highlighted by the above three examples is that there are six different ways to accomplish symbol control (Note: Local means affecting a single symbol, global means affecting the entire file):

❖ Individual (local) placement, global adjustment.
❖ Individual placement, local adjustment.
❖ Individual placement, global or local adjustment.
❖ Global placement, global adjustment.
❖ Global placement, local adjustment.
❖ Global placement, global or local adjustment.

There are two shadings to the concept of "local adjustment." A program can let you drag individual symbols to new positions to override automatic placement. However, a better scenario would permit you to select a local region or group of notes and define the proper adjustment for the specified region.

Programs have many ways of handling local adjustments. For example, a program may allow you to click the symbol wildly onto the note without paying much attention to centering it with respect to the note head. Then, you can issue a global command to center all the symbols over the noteheads or use a "snap to proper location" option for items whose correct placement can be governed by rules (for example, staccato dots). This way you can focus your attention on the more important vertical offset rather than the horizontal one during the addition of symbols.

Of course all of this is a moot point if the ancillary marking symbol that you wish to assign is not available within the notation software you are using.

So when evaluating the ancillary markings capabilities of notation software you should keep in mind the extent of available symbols and the number of actions it takes to reposition symbols. In this context, actions include menu selections; selection of the appropriate palette; selection of the desired symbol from the palette; extent of dialog box interaction (if any); method of target note or region selection; mouse clicks; and actual assignment operation dependent upon the specific notation software.

If you are working with music that has many non-conventional graphics or are using notation software to annotate scholarly examples, there are special concerns. In these cases take careful note of the software's ability to create or import graphics and whether such graphics are subsequently output as PostScript (if you require it). Some notation packages actually provide for drawing graphics right on top of the music. In these cases, you can work with conventional drawing tools that you might find in a Macintosh drawing or painting program. (Note the distinction: Drawing software deals with object-oriented graphics, while painting software deals with bitmapped images.)

If all else fails, a standard work-around for overlaying graphics on music is to export the file as an EPS or PICT file into a graphics editing program that can handle such files. Or you may have the option to save the file or page as a "paint" document, which you can edit in any compatible Macintosh painting program (keeping in mind that in this latter case you will have to limit yourself to bit-mapped graphics). If your software doesn't support the more desirable EPS output format, you can use Super-Glue to "print" the file to disk. Then use a conversion utility such as Curator to convert the Glue file into a PICT file.

To put all issues of symbol availability to rest, Finale includes a built-in PostScript editor, very much like a miniature version of Adobe's Illustrator. This extends the symbol set through the design of additional symbols, expressive markings, articulations, and dynamics. Any such user-created objects (or user-imported objects) may be designated as "executable shapes." This implies a user-defined association with MIDI data, the triggering of any effect handled by MIDI, or a completely user-defined MIDI variation of the note or notes affected by the exe-cutable shape. You can create virtually any shape, and this provides the means to enter the large body of 20th-century music that has departed from conventional notational symbols. Once you have created symbols this way, you can store them within the available symbol library.

After the graphical aspect of ancillary markings comes the consideration of MIDI-executable indications. In some programs that provide for MIDI output, there are additional provisions for ancillary markings and annotative text to affect the flow of MIDI output. At the very least, dynamics and tempo indications should affect MIDI output. In more robust implementations, ancillary markings that evolve over a period of time are also supported. For example, the word "accelerando" can actually cause the music to speed up by a user-defined amount, or the word "tremolo" can cause either the restriking of subsequent pitches in a string part or an amplitude tremolo in another instrument.

Text

Notation software usually makes a distinction between two types of textual input: *lyrics* and *text* (non-lyric).

Lyrics

One important distinction between programs that support lyric input is whether the software provides the ability to "attach" or "bind" syllables to their respective notes, so that if you reposition the notes, the lyrics travel with them. The most common approach to this type of lyric entry is using the tab key to jump to the next note for the insertion of the next syllable (autocentering of the previous syllable is done at the same time). Variations on this theme include using the spacebar or the hyphen character to advance to the next note. In the case of the hyphen character, it is common for the hyphen to be centered between the two notes/syllables that it connects. Where there are many intervening notes before the next syllable (e.g., a melisma), multiple hyphens should automatically be added, although no current software does this.

A second important feature to look out for is whether the software supports multiple verses and, if you require it, different fonts or styles for the individual verses (for example, to accommodate a translation in a second language, which traditionally appears in italics). You should not assume that any software supporting lyrics in the manner described above also supports multiple verses or multiple lyric fonts. If you require it, some programs provide for individual character attributes (that is, mixing of fonts, sizes, and styles) within individual lyric verses.

Finally, text-editing functions are becoming increasingly popular in the assignment of lyrics. A minimum implementation provides for cutting, copying, and pasting of a selected lyric without disturbing the notes attached to the words. A more thorough implementation would include an on-board text editor for the creation of all the lyrics at once in a separate window. Such a built-in text editor can be linked to the text already placed upon the score, as is the case with Finale and Mark of the Unicorn's Mosaic. That is to say that changes made in the text editor are reflected in the music.

"Flowing" a large amount of lyrics into a target region en masse is a helpful feature that you can use in three ways: through the Clipboard; as an option in an on-board text editor such as the one described in the previous paragraph; or through the direct importation of the lyrics from your favorite word processor.

Text (blocks)

Nonlyric text input is generally referred to as text or text blocks. Types of nonlyric text include: titles; composer and/or arranger name; copyright notice; recurring headers and footers; page numbers; annotative text such as analytical or explanatory notes (possibly associated with ossias) or stage directions; and all other text not associated with expressive markings. (Note: Some notation pack-ages consider expressive markings in this category as well.)

Notation software runs the gamut from treating all the above text types as if they were identical to considering each one in a separate category, requiring a separate dialog or tool for entry. For the most part it doesn't make a difference which approach is used. Special cases include page numbers and recurring headers and footers, which, once defined, should be automatically placed by the program.

As with lyrics, some notation packages take the built-in text editor approach and some take the create-on-the-page approach. The same considerations regarding intercommunication with word processors via the Clipboard or through direct importation also apply.

One important aspect of nonlyric text is whether it is or can be attached to the page, system, measure, or note. Things like titles, headers, footers, and page numbers need to be attached to the page. Annotative text of the analytical or stage direction type usually needs to be attached to a particular measure or system, so that it travels with its associated measures when the score is reformatted.

A final consideration is whether different fonts, sizes, and styles can be intermixed within a single block of text.

Input Methods

There are currently two main ways to input musical data into a notation program — with MIDI and without MIDI. Both of these classes break down into five methods for a total of ten available input methods.

NonMIDI input of musical data:

- ❖ Typing commands from the Macintosh keyboard.
- ❖ Typing commands from a dedicated non-MIDI peripheral keyboard.
- ❖ Using the mouse or other pointing device to select and enter notes on the screen.
- ❖ Importing or converting notation data from another software package.
- ❖ MOCR — Musical Optical Character Recognition.

MIDI input of musical data:

- ❖ Step-time entry.
- ❖ Real-time entry with computer-generated beat reference (click or metronome).
- ❖ Real-time entry with simultaneous user-supplied beat reference.
- ❖ Real-time entry without beat reference (post-determination of the beat).
- ❖ Transcription from MIDI data file (e.g., an SMF created by a sequencer).

In any given piece of music it is normal for certain passages to lend themselves to one type of input or another. Thus it is common to choose several input methods in the preparation of a single document (provided, of course, that the software in question supports several methods of musical input).

Non-MIDI Input Methods
Computer keyboard
Although entering musical notes from the computer keyboard is the most anti-quated type of data entry, some Macintosh programs continue to support this method. People often develop considerable speed at typing notes.

Generally in these cases the keys on the Macintosh keyboard are remapped to an equal-tempered keyboard. Finale, MusicProse, Professional Composer, and ConcertWare offer this option.

Dedicated peripheral keyboard
In the case of Music Publisher, the quest for data entry speed has led to the development of a supplementary keyboard (the Presto Keyboard) attached to the Apple Desktop Bus (ADB). It is similar in appearance to the standard Apple keyboards, yet dedicated to the specification of musical pitch (see Figure 21-1). The idea is revolutionary for the Macintosh, but not especially new for computer music notation systems. For many years Columbia Music has used a similar auxiliary keyboard in conjunction with an IBM-based system developed by computer music notation pioneer Armando dal Molin. Such an approach provided for extremely fast input in dal Molin's Musicomp package, and it is even more effective in Music Publisher's new and improved redesign.

The Presto Keyboard includes a row of eight function keys and four rows of seven note keys. The note keys span C to B in four octaves. The octaves are shiftable, so that middle C can be oriented to the first key of any of the upper three rows. Typically, notes are entered in treble note staves, with middle C commencing on the second to the bottom row. Notes in the alto clef are entered with middle C commencing on the second to top row, and notes for the bass clef are entered with middle C commencing on the top row.

Mouse or other pointing device

Almost all current music notation programs provide for the entry of music using the mouse or another pointing device. The common element of this type of input is that a palette of notes or different durational values is present, and you may select the value for the next note by clicking the desired duration on this palette (see Figure 21-2). Subsequent clicks upon the staff displayed on the computer screen enter notes of the selected duration. Usually, the current duration is locked in until you select another one from the note palette. As a memory aid, most software changes the cursor into the current symbol (in this case, a rhythmic value).

Some systems speed up this process by allowing you to select different rhythmic values by pressing keys on the Macintosh keyboard or numeric keyboard that are assigned to specific durations. This speeds up note input significantly, because you can keep the cursor in the staff region rather than continually relocating from the staff to the note palette and back.

When the situation arises for me to use this type of entry, I personally find it easiest to use Articulate Systems's Voice Navigator speech recognition system in conjunction with a note palette. This solution allows you to keep your eyes and cursor focused on the current input region and simply to switch rhythmic values by speaking them aloud. Christoph Schnell's TIMES (Totally Integrated Musicological Environment System) also uses speech recognition as an adjunct to note entry.

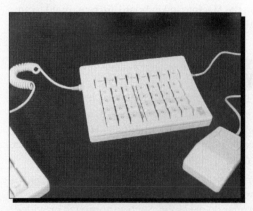

Figure 21-1: Music Publisher's Presto Keyboard for specifying pitch.

Some programs require an additional journey up to the note palette for the purpose of adding a sharp, flat, or dot to a note. Others offer innovative solutions to accomplishing alterations without returning to the palette.

SpeedScore has a unique solution to switching cursor functions. Rather than select a musical symbol from a palette, you only need to click an

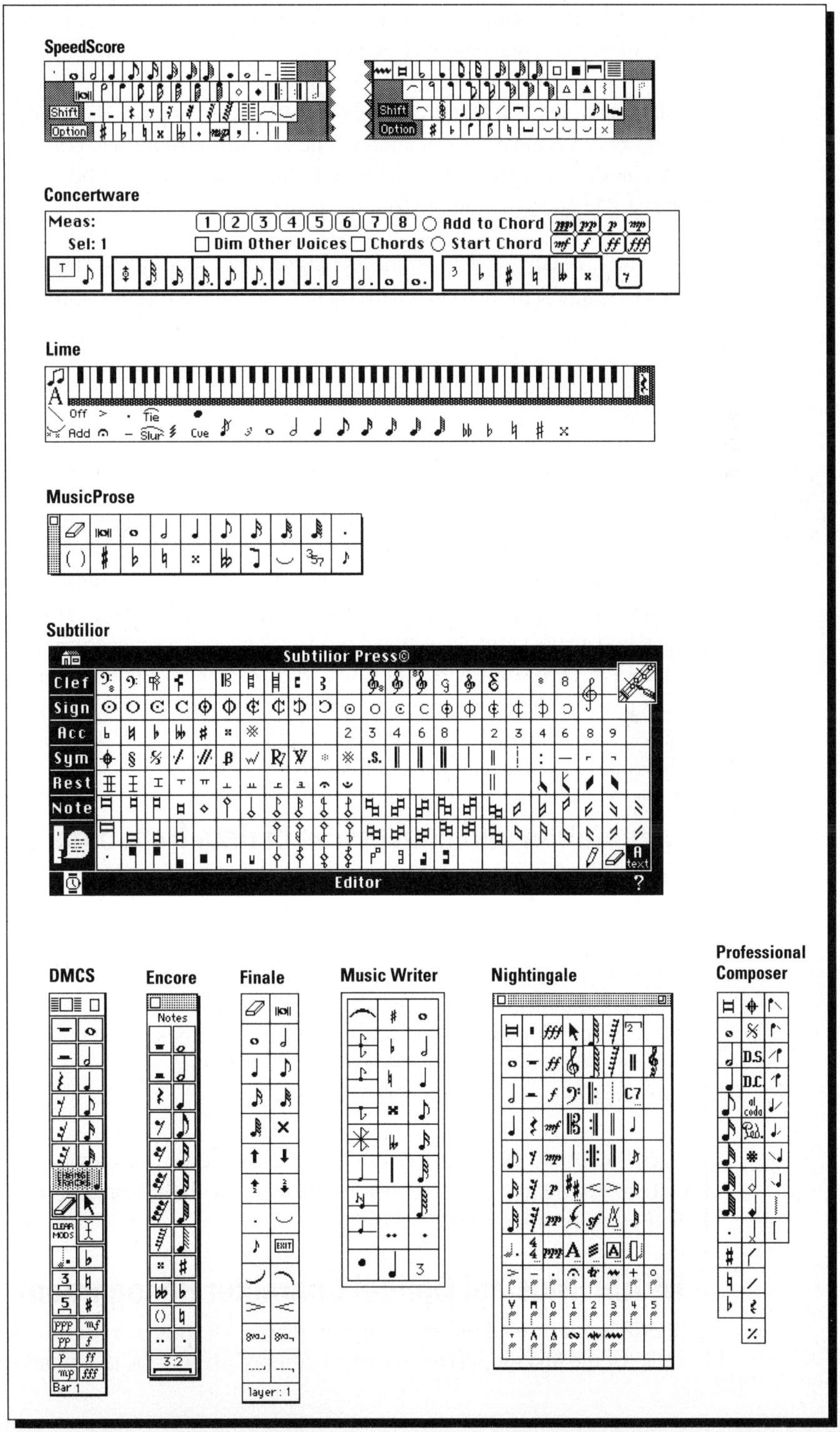

Figure 21-2:
Examples of a variety of note palettes from different manufacturers' software packages.

already-placed symbol of the kind you desire, and the cursor becomes that symbol for subsequent placement elsewhere.

Clicking notes onto a virtual piece of staff paper on your Macintosh screen requires extreme mouse accuracy. The preferred solution to correcting mistakes in this mode is simply to drag the note to the correct pitch, although some programs make you go to the palette for an erasure tool.

People can become fast with note palette input methods and even faster if a macro utility is there to make up for missing features in programs that require multiple trips to the note palette. However, there are some overall disadvantages to mouse entry. The two most evident drawbacks to clicking notes on the screen are that, with few exceptions, beaming is not automatic and the entry of tuplets is usually an after-the-fact edit operation rather than an adjunct to the entry process.

Perhaps the most unusual interface based upon a pointing device is NoteWriter's Quick Scrawl input option (see Figure 21-3). You can use a mouse for this input method, but Quick Scrawl is most effective with a stylus (pen-like input device often associated with a graphics tablet). You simply draw with the pointer as if you were using an actual pencil to write music very quickly. Your scrawls are matched against templates that NoteWriter uses to deduce the actual symbol you intended. Three different Quick Scrawl modes are available by pressing the Shift (or Caps Lock), Option, or Command keys. Pencil mode is for rests, barlines, notes, flags, and clefs. Quill mode is for beams and notes. Crayon mode is for dynamics, articulations, ornaments, and accidentals.

Importation and conversion of data from other software

Besides the importation of SMFs discussed below, several notation programs offer enhanced communication with sequencers made by the same manufacturer or competing manufacturers. Mark of the Unicorn's Performer MIDI sequencer has an option to save files in their proprietary format that can be read by their Professional Composer notation package. Opcode's Vision can also import and export Professional Composer files, and HB Engraver comes with a conversion utility that converts Professional Composer files to their format. Passport's Encore can open Pro-4 sequence files in their native format.

Such file format intercommunication, once perceived as a strong selling point for a notation package, has lost considerable value with the appearance of SMFs and SMF conversion options.

MOCR (Musical Optical Character Recognition)

MOCR is not a trivial programming endeavor. Despite incredible advances in text OCR for the Macintosh (even to the extent of placing OCR systems on a chip

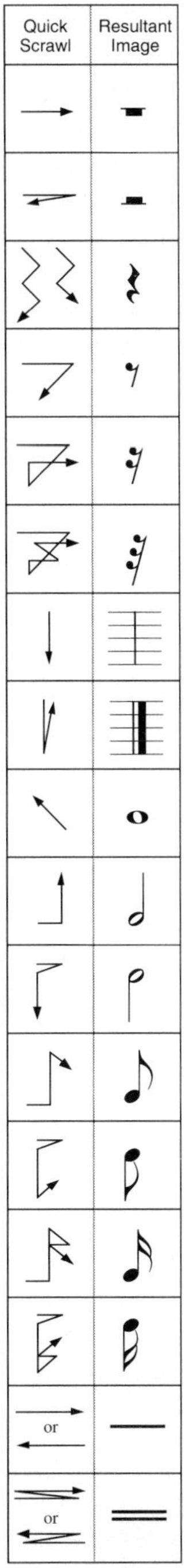

Quick Scrawl	Resultant Image
→	▬
↗	▬
〉〉	𝄽
↗	𝄾
↗	𝄾
↗	𝄿
↓	≣
↓	≣
↘	○
↓	𝅗𝅥
↑	𝅗𝅥
↗	♪
↙	𝅘𝅥𝅮
↗	𝅘𝅥𝅮
↘	𝅘𝅥𝅯
← or	—
⇇ or ⇇	═

Figure 21-3: Examples of Quick Scrawl correspondences in NoteWriter. You use the mouse or other pointing device to scrawl in the pattern indicated on the left and the symbol at the right is entered. The software recognizes about 60 different scrawls. The size of the scrawl is often irrelevant because Note-Writer uses the sequence of compass directions to identify patterns.

inside hand-held scanners like Caere's Typist), MOCR has lagged behind. Some developers are working on the problem. Kiosk-oriented point-of-sale distribution systems are stimulating development. These systems allow you to choose a composition, audition it, select a key for printing, and request an immediate printout. The main stumbling block for these systems is the vast body of music that must be converted to machine-readable data. MOCR will facilitate this data entry and finally make widespread availability of kiosk distribution systems a reality.

The technology for MOCR exists; the Japanese have been using it since 1985. The most impressive demonstration of MOCR is the Tsukuba Musical Robot (see Figure 21-4). The WABOT-2 (Waseda Robot) was developed by the Mu Research Group at Waseda University, under the direction of a team of scientists led by Professors Sadamu Ohteru (the vision system), Katsuhiko Shirai (the conversation system), Seinosuke Narita (the singing voice tracking system), and Ichiro Kato (the limb control system).

The WABOT resembles a human with a video camera instead of a head. The fingers, arms, and legs can play an organ in the manner of a human being. It requires 67 computers, which are connected to the WABOT by fiberoptic data links and capable of transmitting data at 32MB per second. It takes less than 15 seconds for the WABOT to memorize a score placed in front of it. Humans communicate with the WABOT using speech. The WABOT can also track a human singer and play along with him, keeping up with minute fluctuations in tempo. If the WABOT senses that the singer is singing out of tune, it adjusts the tuning of the organ to compensate for the deficiencies of the singer.

MIDI Input Methods

Playing musical data into a notation program is the most natural way to interact with such software. In many cases this is the fastest way to get music on paper. WYPIWYP (What You Play Is What You Print) is a variation on WYSIWYG that I coined in 1988 when this sort of thing became possible.

Like any MIDI program, data input via MIDI can originate from any MIDI controller. This includes MIDI keyboards and keyboard controllers, MIDI wind controllers such as the EVI and EWI, MIDI violins and cellos, MIDI guitar controllers, and pitch-to-MIDI

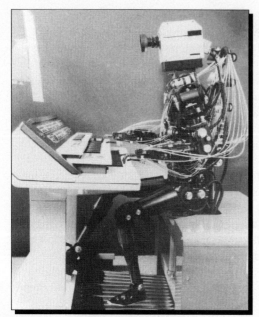

Figure 21-4: The Tsukuba Musical Robot (the WABOT-2).

converters (aka pitch trackers). At least one software package (Finale) has an input mode optimized for guitar controllers that generates standard guitar tablature notation from data input via a MIDI guitar controller. Of course, with a pitch tracker, any instrument or the human voice can be used as the MIDI source.

Because most notation software's primary concern is the creation of printed music, many programs simply ignore other MIDI data such as velocity, controller, or patch information. Some programs like Encore allow you to specify exactly what additional data types will be included in the recording. A few record every type of data in the same way a MIDI sequencer does.

Regarding velocity data, people continually ask why notation software doesn't automatically insert dynamic markings based upon the recorded velocity data. It is a valid question, considering the fact that ConcertWare+ MIDI, a relatively inexpensive program, does precisely this and even goes so far as to also insert slurs automatically over legato passages. So far none of the higher-end programs have followed ConcertWare's lead.

On the other hand, some notation programs have enough built-in intelligence to determine that you are playing two rhythmically independent parts with a single hand and adjust the stem direction of the notes accordingly. Likewise, at least one program (Finale) has rules built into its transcription engine that allow it to determine from the context whether a note should be represented as a sharp or a flat. While the software isn't always correct in this regard, it is surprisingly accurate for the majority of cases.

MIDI input generally falls into two categories: step time and real time. As you will see from the following discussion, real-time input comes in many flavors. In the following section the term "MIDI keyboard" will represent any type of MIDI controller, from wind, string, and guitar, to pitch trackers.

Step-time entry

Step-time entry in notation software is basically the same as step-time entry in MIDI sequencers (see Chapter 17, "MIDI Sequencing"). Step-time refers to entering notes step-by-step, a note or chord at a time, without regard to actual entry tempo or rhythm. Pitch is specified by a MIDI controller keyboard, while rhythmic duration is specified either by pressing a key on the Macintosh keyboard or selecting a rhythmic value from a palette.

The rhythm or speed with which you enter the notes has no effect upon the rhythmic values you enter into the software. Because you specify the rhythmic values in advance, it is not necessary to use any form of automatic rhythmic correction on the input.

In the case of selecting rhythmic duration from a palette, keep in mind the same cautionary remarks regarding time-consuming mouse relocation as those mentioned above with respect to clicking notes on the staff with the mouse. Fortunately, with step-time entry via MIDI, it is a relatively standard practice that the software provides for switching rhythmic values with the Macintosh keyboard.

While some programs require that you specify the duration individually for every note entered in this fashion, the more elegant implementations allow a duration to be locked in until it is changed. This can be extremely helpful when entering, for example, 40 measures of a continual triplet eighth-note ostinato.

In many cases it will be easy to keep one hand near the Macintosh keyboard and the other on the MIDI keyboard. However, if you are step-entering a passage that requires using both hands on the keyboard, continually moving one hand back and forth from the MIDI keyboard can be an extreme waste of time. Because of this, I use the Articulate Systems's Voice Navigator speech recognition system to specify the changing rhythmic values when it is more realistic to keep both hands on the musical keyboard. I believe that this would also be a boon to varieties of MIDI controllers that require two hands for playing even single notes, such as wind, string, and guitar controllers.

Real-time entry with computer-generated beat reference

Real-time entry is a transcription of an actual performance of the music. The performance may be at any speed desired; the only requirement is that the relative durations of notes be maintained. The most common way to capture performance data in this way is with a MIDI-equipped synthesizer keyboard and a software-based sequencer. Due to the temporal accuracy of MIDI, it is necessary to use some form of quantization or automatic rhythmic correction to round off the actual performance rhythms to a resolution that the notation software can handle.

Capturing MIDI data with step-time entry is a trivial programming matter in comparison to implementing real-time capture of MIDI performance data. The easiest way to solve this problem is a provision for real-time input while you play along with a computer-generated metronomic click. The click provides a temporal frame of reference for the software. Most real-time input systems are of this kind. The

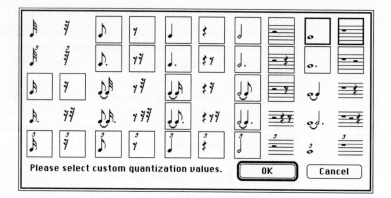

Figure 21-5: ConcertWare's rhythmic "filter" for real-time MIDI input with a computer-generated beat reference.

main disadvantage of this method is that you are locked into playing a mechanical rendition of your music to a fixed robotic tempo and cannot let loose with the subtle accelerandos, ritardandos, and rubato tempo inflections that are the heart and soul of any expressive performance.

ConcertWare's implementation of this method of real-time entry adds a setup option where you can tell the program what rhythmic values you will probably be playing (see Figure 21-5). If you know that you are not going to play any half notes, you can tell the software not to listen for half-note durations. By restricting the set of durational possibilities in this way, real-time quantization by the software becomes much more accurate.

Real-time entry with user-supplied beat reference

Slightly more difficult (from the developer's point of view) is the provision to input MIDI data with a beat reference that you supply simultaneously to your performance. For example, you may be able to assign the beat "tap" to a pedal switch and then play along with yourself as you feed the beat reference in with your foot. This sort of system has the flexibility of allowing you to alter your tempo at will, since you can slow down or speed up your tapping to indicate your expressive intent. Some notation programs will even display your music, often about a measure behind, while you play.

If this feature is missing from your notation program, you may find that your sequencer includes a similar option. Thanks to SMFs, you can easily bring music recorded from your sequencer into your notation software.

Real-time entry without beat reference (post-determination of the beat)

The ultimate freedom of expression with respect to real-time input for notation software is post-determination of the beat. So far, only one program, Finale, achieves this with any degree of success.

With Finale's real-time transcription option you can play completely freely without using a metronome or supplying the computer with any beat reference during your performance. Afterward, you simply specify where the beat is by tapping a key in time to a playback of your work. If your music changes meter signatures, you may then tap in the barlines (and beaming groups if you want to take it that far), and Finale will add the appropriate meter signatures.

Finale also provides an alternate way to transcribe music for which no beat reference exists. Instead of tapping in every beat or barline, you can merely tell the program the duration of the first two notes. The program then performs an operation termed "companding" to determine the correct rhythmic values of the remainder of the composition.

Other features of this input method include accurate tracking of rhythmically polyphonic parts on single staves, determination of triplets and other tuplets, and an active, "traveling" keyboard split between the right and left hands. The program accomplishes this by taking measurements of your finger span.

Transcription of SMFs

By 1990, the option to save MIDI sequences and algorithmically or interactively generated music as SMF became widespread. The direct importation and automated transcription of SMFs into notation software followed shortly thereafter. Now most notation programs provide this feature with varying degrees of success and an even greater variance of flexibility. Some importation schemes do not provide for the importation of tuplets or key signatures, while others go as far as automatically determining the key signature and staff split points (for example, for keyboard tracks that should be split onto a treble and bass staff).

Editing
WYSIWYG

WYSIWYG (What You See Is What You Get) is definitely the buzz word with current-generation notation packages. With this in mind, most programs support editing and viewing music in both continuous-scroll and page-by-page formats. Taking the lead from current page-layout packages, nearly all current notation programs allow for zooming in and out (displaying the music in greater or lesser magnification), and the more ambitious developers have provided for editing in any of the zoom resolutions.

Selecting music for editing

The Macintosh user interface environment is probably the greatest single factor contributing to the current proliferation of notation packages. In any editor, whether of text, graphics, or music, the available editing operations define the level of professional applications that can be accommodated. With music editing software, the scope to which any editing operation, including quantization, may be applied is of equal importance.

Music exists in two dimensions, horizontal and vertical (melodic and harmonic in musical terms). The scope of an edit operation should be applicable to a region encompassing any selected range of both horizontal and vertical material. Because it is fundamental that music includes aspects of repetition, which are separated by intervening contrasting material, discontiguous selection of a region for editing is of extreme importance. Fortunately, some of the more robust second-generation notation programs have now added discontiguous selection to the standard edit region criteria. Until recently, these selection criteria only comprised a single note, group of consecutive notes, whole instrumental parts, and groups or regions of parts.

Many other musical considerations need to be available as selection criteria in notation software. Some of these, such as specifying all notes belonging to an indicated duration, loudness, or pitch range in a region, are now standard in most professional sequencers. Others, like selection based upon metrical placement or based upon inclusion or exclusion within a specified set of pitches, are hard to find (MIDI sequencer's Pro 5 and Vision include these).

The omitted selection criteria tend to be those that have no analogies in text processing or spreadsheets. Perhaps this is because music software is often written by professional programmers who are amateur musicians rather than the other way around. Can you imagine a situation in word processing where you might have to change the letters C or G to italic only in every fourth word? The option to do that type of editing has little practical value in a text document. However, in music, the need to add an accent to every C or G note occurring on a fourth beat is well within the realm of possibilities.

Ultimately, the range, scope, and selection criteria allowed for specifying a region for editing have a profound effect upon your conception of music. Because this will have a major bearing on the style of music you produce with a music processor of any kind, these considerations are of paramount importance. Consider the word processing analogy again: How often would you center a title or use right and left justified text if you had to count letters and spaces because your word processor didn't have those features built into it?

Edit operations

Of course the familiar Macintosh editing operations of Cut, Copy, Paste, Insert, and Clear are standard fare in notation software. Some programs add sophisticated parameter filtering to these operations and such new twists as copy and replace, copy and merge, delete after replace, and delete after merge, to name a few.

"Mirroring," as introduced in Finale, is a very powerful type of copying in which the copied material remains linked to the original. Mirrored material can consist of any combination (discontiguous or consecutive) of the original material's notes and graphic elements. These linked copies can appear any number of times, at any number of transpositions, anywhere in the score. The mind boggler is that when you edit or change the original in any way, all its linked copies automatically undergo a corresponding transformation.

Examples of purely musical edit operations are transposition (chromatic, diatonic, and enharmonic) and harmonization. On a local level, the best implementation of this is where the notes are draggable on an individual or regional basis. The option to split a single multivoice staff into separate staves is desirable, as is the converse, which you can use to create piano reductions for larger scores.

Typical rhythmic operations include augmentation and diminution. More exotic operations include decreasing durational values and adding rests to fill the beats out.

Fundamental compositional operations, such as inversion, retrograde, permutation, the ability to dissociate pitch from rhythm, and the manipulation of larger musical chunks in some kind of overview window, are noticeably missing from nearly all notation programs.

Minute details

Whether publisher, engraver, copyist, or composer, most people involved in music preparation eventually develop a unique and individual style to their notation. In the case of professional publishers this may consist of a recognizable "look," nurtured over a century, which is so consistent that professional musicians can usually identify a specific publisher's edition by merely looking at a single page at random. Retaining such subtleties in computer-produced notation requires vast formatting capabilities, and this is an area where the first-generation products failed miserably — nearly all formatting was global!

Almost all second-generation products provide for page formatting on an individual rather than global basis, a wide variety of staff sizes, extensive control of system and measure balancing, and justification both vertically and horizontally. The interface to many of these page-formatting features has been borrowed from page-layout programs of desktop publishing notoriety. A musical aspect to this type of formatting is the suppression of staves that do not have music in them — automatic in HB Engraver and Finale and manual in Music Publisher.

Providing the user with the means to tweak the software in order to maintain a carefully cultivated look or style and yet still conform to the rules of conventional music notation is no easy task. HB Engraver includes such a configuration utility as a separate program, and Finale has menu options that permit this type of manipulation of detail. In a robust implementation, you can define default values for practically everything: slur, tie and accidental offsets, beam angle, beam width and stem width, the distance between barlines, clefs, key and meter signatures, and custom beat positioning (professional engraving does not preserve one-to-one relationships between rhythmic values and note spacing). Perhaps the closest analogy to this in the world of typesetting is custom kerning tables.

Customizing your virtual environment

If you can customize your virtual environment to conform to your personal working methodology, software can actually stimulate or inspire creative endeavor. The simplest way to accomplish this is the now familiar saving of the user's preference for the default configuration of the New File menu option. Another way to customize your virtual environment is through the creation of templates, which provide quick and easy access to materials of the creative process that remain consistent from project to project. Several notation programs permit building idiosyncratic libraries of many different types of objects. These range from chord structures in HB Engraver and whole symbol libraries in Finale and NoteWriter to system (group of pre-formatted connected staves) and page templates in Music Publisher. In addition, most notation software lets you customize tool and symbol palettes to suit your individual needs better.

Music Fonts

Cleo Huggins of Adobe Music Systems designed the first PostScript music font (Sonata), and in doing so, changed the music notation industry forever. Sonata contains 173 of the most commonly used music characters.

Because Sonata was the first PostScript music font, many music fonts that were subsequently developed mapped their characters on the same keys to assure compatibility with software that could access Sonata. The reasons developers chose to create alternative fonts to Sonata were many: to improve on the look of Sonata; to avoid having to license Sonata from Adobe Systems; to avoid having to require their users to purchase Sonata from Adobe; to improve program speed by normalizing the baselines of all the characters, so that the software could place them on the screen with the least amount of computational overhead. (For a variety of reasons, certain characters in Sonata were not aligned to the same baseline. Software utilizing these characters had to employ horizontal and vertical offsets to accurately locate the symbol in relation to a note or staff.)

Some characters were included in Sonata because software developers at that time could not figure out how to deal with certain musical situations demanding alter-nate symbol placement. Notable examples of this are the notes with the note-heads on the wrong side of the stem. These were included to handle the interval of a second that requires one of the notes to be attached to the opposite side of the stem than would normally be expected. More recent notation software developers have solved this problem, so newer music fonts have dropped these characters, substituting in their place characters in widespread use that were inadvertently omitted from Sonata.

Just mapping musical characters on the same key as Sonata is not enough to guarantee that both fonts can be used by the same program. Because the registration points (the points in a symbol that the software uses as a reference for placing the symbol) in different musical fonts can vary on a character-by-character basis, software supporting fonts from several manufacturers often needs to have conversion routines built in for each other's font. An alternative to having this registration information hard-coded into the software is to provide the user with a facility for specifying a global symbol adjustment. This compensates for non-corresponding registration points in different music fonts.

Perhaps you will have deduced from the previous paragraph that you cannot type all music fonts directly into a word processor document. Rather, you have to import them as a graphic from their parent program. Some fonts exist that were designed with word-processor compatibility in mind.

Notice what happens to the line above a line containing characters typed directly into a word processor using the Sonata font (and most music fonts designed to provide the note symbol character sets for a software package).

As you can see, the line above the line containing music characters is pushed up and the line below is pushed down. In addition, there is no attempt to establish a consistent baseline alignment in this context.

Fonts that are compatible with word processors include Crescendo, Marl, MetronomeFont (which even has provisions for beaming groups within a word processor), MusicFont (bitmapped), and the nonnote symbol fonts MIDICom, Newport, Rameau, Seville, ChordFont (which includes many other useful beamed groups in addition to chord symbols), ChordSyms, and ChordType. The last three are all bitmapped.

Today, some music fonts ship with particular notation packages, and some are available from third-party vendors. Most are PostScript fonts, although some useful bitmapped fonts remain viable. For a complete listing of font compatibilities for every available notation package, see the "Print Output" feature table devoted to this subject at the end of Chapter 22.

Table 21-1 shows the complete character sets of the Sonata music font. For char-acter fonts of more than 30 music fonts, see the coupon in the back of this book.

Table 21-1: The Sonata Font
Adobe Systems

Type 1 PostScript Font, Sizes: 12, 14, 18, 20, 24, 36, 40, 60

Key	Un-modified	⇧	⌥	⇧⌥	Key	Un-modified	⇧	⌥	⇧⌥
A					T		∞		
B	♭	𝄡	♭♭		U	‿	⌢	Δ	∇
C	¢	¢			V	v	8*b*	8*w*	8*b*
D	*D.S.*	*D.C.*			W	o	|◖◗|	–	.
E	♪				X	♪			
F	*f*	*mf*	*ff*	*fff*	Y				
G					Z	*z*	*fz*	*m*	*r*
H					1	1	3	*1*	♪
I			⋀		2	2	5	*2*	
J					3	3	♯	*3*	×
K					4	4	§	*4*	=
L					5	5	⁒	*5*	⊕
M					6	6	⋀	*6*	
N	♮				7	7	𝄞	*7*	▾
O			♭		8	8	❋	*8*	𝄢
P	*p*	*mp*	*pp*	*ppp*	9	9	(	*9*	◇
Q	♩				0	0	)	*0*	◆
R	♪				‘	*%*	‖	≋	.
S	*s*	*sf*			-	–	–	■	▲

Table 21-1: The Sonata Font (continued)
Adobe Systems

Key	Un-modified	⇧	⤸	⇧⤸	Key	Un-modified	⇧	⤸	⇧⤸
=	☰	+	□	△	'	⅄	~	⅄	tr
[	|	:	‖	‖	,	,		v	
]	‖:	:‖	⅄	.	.		>	◼	
|	|		ı	ı	/	‖	𝄢	⬜	×
;	♪	♭	♪	♩.					

Summary

✔ There are two fundamental reasons for using music notation software: the manipulation of preexisting music and the creation of new music. The first category includes publishing, engraving, copying, arranging, and orchestration. The second category includes composition and musical realization.

✔ You can use notation software on a wide variety of tasks: to produce a final legible copy for the purposes of publication or distribution; to extract parts required for performance; to create new versions of existing works in different keys; to create a new arrangement quickly by using tools available through software; to simplify the manipulation of musical ideas using software tools; to create an electronic realization as a Polaroid or for evaluation or proofhearing; and to create an electronic realization as an end in itself.

✔ Rule-based systems "understand" music with varying degrees of success. That is to say that notes are understood to be representations of particular pitches and rhythms. This approach permits certain edit operations such as transposition, rhythmic error detection, and automatic note positioning.

✔ Graphics-based systems have no understanding of music. All symbols are treated as graphical elements of equal importance, and no underlying meaning is attached to the symbol in the program's internal data structures. You may be able to organize symbols into separate palettes for your convenience, but the program usually does not make a distinction between a note or text character and a dynamic or barline. Most notation software packages attempt to straddle both of these worlds (graphics-based and rule-based). The most common way of achieving this is to allow the user to disregard or override rules or guesses by the computer and manipulate objects from a purely graphical standpoint.

Part Four: Notation

✔ When using notation software, you enter four types of data: page, system, and staff setup elements; notes and musical data; ancillary markings (including note alterations, note, staff, and score expressions, and chord symbols); and text (including lyric text and "block" or nonlyric text).

✔ NonMIDI input of musical data can be accomplished by typing commands from the Macintosh keyboard, typing commands from a dedicated nonMIDI peripheral keyboard, using the mouse or other pointing device to select and enter notes on the screen, importing or converting notation data from another software package, and (largely unexplored) MOCR.

✔ MIDI input is achieved using one of five main approaches: step-time entry, real-time entry with computer-generated beat reference (click or metronome), real-time entry with simultaneous user-supplied beat reference, real-time entry without beat reference (post-determination of the beat), and transcription from MIDI data file.

✔ There are six different ways to accomplish symbol control: individual (local) placement, global adjustment; individual placement, local adjustment; individual placement, global or local adjustment; global placement, global adjustment; global placement, local adjustment; and global placement, global or local adjustment.

✔ Most notation programs support editing and viewing music in both continuous-scroll and page-by-page formats. Taking the lead from current page-layout packages, nearly all current notation programs allow for zooming in and out (displaying the music in greater or lesser magnification).

Chapter 22
Music Notation

In this chapter...

✔ Second-generation Macintosh music notation software.

✔ Contrasting rule-based and graphics-based approaches to notation software

✔ Music preparation vs. music creation programs.

✔ Standard notation software features vs. bells and whistles.

✔ Defining and explaining 18 categories of notation software features.

✔ Examining the problems created by undefeatable notation rule errors hard-coded into software.

✔ MIDI and transcription in the context of Macintosh music notation software.

✔ Purchasing notation software.

✔ A detailed look at 14 music notation programs.

✔ Feature comparison tables.

Representing Your Musical Data

More than 600 years have gone into the development of conventional music notation (CMN). This realization has finally started to lead developers away from restricting the representation of musical data (for example, MIDI input) as alphanumeric event lists or bar graphs. (Bar graphs are commonly referred to as "piano roll" notation because of their similarity to the rolls of paper used to control player pianos.) Although lists and bar graphs have their uses for certain types of MIDI data, many now feel that the ultimate representation of pitch is conventional notation and that it is only a matter of time until much MIDI sequencing will be driven by notation. This requires that the individual notes on the screen retain all their associated performance data, from expressive changes in volume to subtle alterations of duration. For the time being, such transcriptions almost always require some additional tweaking on your behalf.

The more ambitious second-generation packages output to the SMF format, and it is increasingly common to provide for the output of MIDI data to control synthesizers for audio proofing. In all programs, except Finale and, to a certain extent, Nightingale, MIDI output is limited to the standard 16 MIDI channels with a quick-and-dirty approach to velocity (i.e., volume), permitting a single velocity assignment per staff or part.

This chapter focuses on the notation programs themselves. Following brief introductory sections on each program, the rest of the chapter takes a feature-oriented approach. The idea is to provide you with the facts that you should take into consideration when purchasing or evaluating a notation program. The printed outputs of these second-generation packages might appear to be identical at first glance to untrained eyes, and most of these programs fill 99 percent of the requirements for notating music based upon 19th-century Western tonality. But this chapter will help you discover significant differences bound to influence your decisions.

No matter which notation software you are using, once you get comfortable with the program's user interface, you will be able to work much faster than you ever did with a pencil and paper — but only if the program covers all the notational curve balls that you need to throw at it. Don't forget that your final printed output is usually comparable to what you might obtain from a professional engraver rather than a copyist. Depending upon your proficiency with the software and, in some cases, the speed of your computer, your notating speed may increase by a factor of ten or 100.

For some inexplicable reason, magazine writers have gone after notation software with a vengeance. Consequently, there is a good deal of misinformation floating around. I have been keeping a file of ridiculous statements in the press about notation software, and I mention the ones that are of a general or conceptual nature in the following text. However, to enumerate all the program-specific inaccuracies would render this already lengthy chapter unmanageable.

Take it from someone who has actually put most of this software to professional use from day one: the software covered in this chapter works!

Incidentally, there are two Macintosh programs available for dance notation. Calaban and LabanWriter are both dedicated to the most popular form of dance notation, Labanotation (see Appendix D for manufacturers' information). Two other programs are available for marching band drill notation (see Part Nine: Education).

An excellent source for monitoring the progress of notation software is the Center for Computer Assisted Research in the Humanities (CCARH). Every year since 1986 the CCARH sends a package of music examples to over six dozen notation software developers. Each of the examples has a particular notational idiosyncrasy. The software developers respond by sending back the examples notated with their particular program. The CCARH publishes these examples along with a wealth of related information in their annual *Computing in Musicology,* which usually runs close to 200 pages. You can obtain a copy of the current directory and many of the earlier ones by writing to: The Center for Computer Assisted Research in the Humanities, 525 Middlefield Road, Suite 120, Menlo Park, California 94025.

ANSI

The Musical Information Processing Standards group of the American National Standards Institute (ANSI) Information Processing Systems Technical Committee has a time line for the establishment of a standard for integrating musical data into the mainstream of information processing. That means there would be a representation for musical information that could be included in an SGML (standard generalized markup language) document. Such documents may be interchanged between different systems and applications and can contain normal text, graphics, images, mathematical formulas, and other specialized notations. Music data would ideally contain both the necessary information for typesetting of music and for the performance of music on a synthesizer or other device.

A device control coding protocol such as MIDI is adequate for the representation of performance "gestural" data, but does not contain sufficient information to derive visual score data. While it is likely that MIDI will remain as the dominant representation of performance data, it seems inevitable that the standard finally chosen by ANSI will treat MIDI data as a small subset of the general music data format. The differing royalty and use arrangements that exist for printed music and performance data may need to be entirely rewritten for a representation that is capable of generating either.

Software Solutions

At the time of this writing, there are 14 music notation programs available for the Macintosh, with at least three more on the way. HB Engraver is included in this number because it is still widely available through retail outlets, even though the company is no longer in business. Two other programs, NoteKrafter and Toccata, are not considered because they are impossible to obtain, even through overstocked music stores or mail-order houses. They continue to be mentioned in Apple publications, so there is justifiable confusion regarding these programs. Note that Nightingale and SpeedScore are in their final beta versions at the time of this writing. Some features may be added to those discussed herein prior to their official release in 1992. High Score, another program in beta-test during the early stages of this book, couldn't be included due to the tragic death of the program's author, Kimball Stickney, in 1990.

Most Macintosh music notation software falls into one of the following three categories:

Mainly rule-based. Rule-based systems "understand" music, meaning that notes are understood to be representations of pitches and can therefore be transposed (among other things). Durations are also understood. Almost all formatting, placement, beaming, note spelling, and page layout is done automatically by the program, with little opportunity for user-override. If you are in complete agreement with the rules that are hard-coded into such programs, these systems can be extremely fast. Sometimes, built-in rules can compensate for limited musical knowledge on the part of the user. However, when faced with a graphics-oriented contemporary score, these programs are often the slowest.

Completely graphics-based. Graphics-based systems have no understanding of music. All symbols are treated as graphic elements. Although symbols may be organized into separate palettes, the program does not make a distinction between a note, text character, dynamic, or barline. Although this might seem to be the worst-case scenario, systems that make no musical assumptions generally offer the greatest degree of on-page symbol placement flexibility. If you want to place a clef sign in between two staves, the program won't care because it is responsible to no rules stating that clef signs must be on the staff lines. Unfortunately, completely graphics-based systems tend to be slower than all others, except perhaps for certain genres of graphically oriented contemporary music. Because these programs attach no musical meaning to a symbol, MIDI operations (for example, MIDI input or output) are of course not possible. Operations that rely upon the program knowing a note's pitch (such as transposition or key change) or context (such as part extraction) are also impossible. For these types of programs, the musical knowledge of the user is the greatest determining factor in the look of the finished page.

Graphics- and rule-based. These systems generally make their best guess at the notation of a particular passage, but usually allow extensive user-override and user-configuration. Placement of most symbols and formatting may be adjusted graphically. Typically, this is accomplished by dragging an element with the mouse. These programs would seem to offer the best of both worlds, provided that you agree with the rules that are hard-coded into the system or that the program permits you to customize its default parameters in these respects.

These programs may understand a little or quite a bit about music, perhaps just enough to transpose a passage or align measures during formatting. At the other extreme, such systems may be intelligent enough to automatically assign chord symbols and detect the difference between sharps and flats based upon context. However, many symbols in these systems may turn out to be purely graphical elements. For example, a forte indication may not be in a different class from a clef sign or lyric. On the other hand, more sophisticated systems of this type might endow that same forte with MIDI parameters or even automatically place it, based upon velocity information associated with MIDI input.

Music preparation and creation

Two fundamental classes of applications are supported: *music preparation* and *music creation*. Some programs are optimized for both of these activities, others for only one. Music preparation includes copying and engraving activities. It implies that you are replicating an existing piece of music, about which all note decisions have been made in advance — the main concern is with the appearance of the page. Some music preparation programs are up to the engraving standards demanded by professional publishers, others can only achieve copyist-level quality. Music creation includes composition, orchestration, and arranging. It implies that you are doing lots of editing, reformatting, and reorganization of your musical material, as well as making ongoing decisions based on creative considerations that have an impact upon the graphic look of your page.

An example of a music preparation application is a program that does not let you add staves to systems after you have created the initial page format. Such a program is fine for a copyist or engraver, who knows in advance how many instruments they are dealing with. On the other hand, this program would not be advisable for a composer, who might decide to add an instrument well into the compositional process.

Standard and non standard features

Nowadays it is safe to assume that all second-generation Macintosh music notation programs include features offering basic functionality for most music notation tasks. Unless otherwise noted, you can assume the following capabilities:

Page-oriented display. Many programs offer an endless horizontal scroll view. Some do not allow editing in their page view, treating it as a Preview mode. Zooming in and out to various magnifications is relatively standard, but being able to edit at any zoomed level is not.

At least 32 staves. ConcertWare+MIDI is the only program that limits you to less — in this case, eight.

32nd note or smaller. Most programs include rhythmic values down to the 128th note. Finale is unique in that its rhythmic values extend to the rare 4,096th note.

Alternate noteheads. All programs (with the exception of Deluxe Music Construction Set) offer diamond, X, slash, and grace noteheads.

G, F, alto, tenor clefs. Beyond this minimum set, programs differ greatly. Many add percussion clefs and small clefs for intermeasure clef changes.

Standard key signatures. All programs offer key signatures for the 24 keys. Finale is the only one to support key signatures that mix sharps and flats.

Standard meter signatures. Only Finale, Music Publisher, and NoteWriter offer non-standard meter signatures.

Chord symbols. Music Publisher is the only program without specific options for chord symbols. There are easy ways to get around this omission.

Automatic beaming. Most current-generation notation programs automatically beam to the beat or prevailing meter upon note entry or allow for large sections (up to the entire piece) to be beamed with a single command. Automated support of irregular beaming groups such as 3+3+2 is somewhat harder to find.

Diagonal beaming. This feature, considered a luxury in first-generation software, is now standard in all programs except ConcertWare+MIDI. Cross-staff beaming and center-beaming are now the luxuries.

Triplets. At the very least, all programs support triplets and automatically format tuplet spacing in relation to other non-tuplet parts. That is where the similarity ends. Each program sets different limits upon the complexity of tuplets and the provision for nested tuplets.

Multiple voices/staff. Most programs let you have at least two rhythmically independent parts on a staff; some offer up to eight. This does not imply that the software necessarily lets you assign different MIDI channels to the parts on a single staff.

Mouse input. All programs except Music Publisher provide for clicking notes on the screen with the mouse. Many programs also offer input from the Macintosh keyboard (see Chapter 21, "Score Input and Editing").

MIDI input. With the exception of purely graphics-based systems such as Note-Writer and SpeedScore, all programs provide for step-time MIDI input at the very least. Many offer real-time input with varying degrees of success.

Lyrics. It is standard practice to bind lyric syllables to notes, so that they shift when measures are reformatted. All programs offer additional types of annotative text — headers and footers at the very least.

Cut, copy, paste. It's a Macintosh, isn't it? However, merging and inserting music that has been copied or cut to the Clipboard is not standard, nor is the option to shift large passages of music across barlines.

Transposition. All programs (except the purely graphic systems) offer chromatic transposition, and most auto-transpose when you change clefs. Diatonic, enharmonic, and modal transposition are offered by some software.

Graphic editing. Moving symbols with the mouse is almost standard, although several programs still rely on the cursor keys.

MIDI output. Proofhearing is supported by all programs, except those that are completely graphic-oriented. Playback of expressive markings, retention, and playback of original velocity data, greater-than-16-channel playback, and scrolling playback are available with some programs, but cannot be considered standard.

PostScript output. All second-generation programs provide for PostScript output. Some still use QuickDraw for certain elements. The option to output pages as EPS or PICT files is not standard.

The following desirable features are available in many programs, but should not be assumed to be standard:

- ❖ Staves of less or more than five lines
- ❖ Multiple symbol placement (see the discussion in Chapter 21)
- ❖ Automatic symbol collision avoidance
- ❖ Automatic handling of the distinction between sharps and flats
- ❖ Auto-shifting of barlines and/or beaming with "after-the-fact" metric changes
- ❖ Rhythmic diminution and augmentation
- ❖ Merging multiple staves to single staves or unmerging chords or single staves to multiple staves
- ❖ User-expandable expressive marking library
- ❖ Adjustment of staff spacing on an individual system basis
- ❖ Adjustment of system spacing on an individual basis
- ❖ Specification of a certain number of bars per system
- ❖ Automatic horizontal justification
- ❖ Removal of tacit staves from systems
- ❖ Importation of lyric text
- ❖ Expressive markings that affect playback
- ❖ Options to edit raw MIDI data
- ❖ Importing and exporting SMFs
- ❖ Part extraction
- ❖ Multimeasure rest concatenation when extracting parts
- ❖ Option to open more than one file at a time
- ❖ User-configuration of the program defaults (e.g., dot offset, beam slope, spacing table)

With this in mind, the following introductions to the various software options focus on unique aspects of each product. Screenshots have been chosen accordingly as well. The discussion does not dwell upon the now-standard features mentioned in the first list above.

Hard-coded notation errors

There is a special kind of alert in this chapter: "hard-coded notation errors." Music notation software is one of the few areas besides music education software where such atrocities can occur. Hard-coded notation errors refer to undefeatable program features that misguide and confuse budding musicians using the software or otherwise force the adoption of undesirable habits. Unfortunately, several programs that would otherwise offer a great starting point for beginning musicians are rendered useless by a single hard-coded notation error. In my opinion, this issue cannot be dismissed by merely telling a student that we only break such rules when we are using this or that particular software and that it's all right to do so. In some respects this issue might be thought of as a sort of "software malpractice."

Non-diagonal beaming is not considered a software malpractice issue, because diagonal beaming is a convention, not a rule. Diagonal beaming is certainly the most common practice and undeniably enhances readability (besides making the look of a page more aesthetically pleasing), yet there is nothing in the commandments of music notation requiring diagonal beaming. There aren't any hard and fast rules about beaming slope, either. Copyists tend to use a shallower slope than engravers, rarely exceeding the diagonal slope defined by the distance between adjacent staff lines.

ConcertWare+MIDI

Great Wave's ConcertWare+MIDI was the first program to permit the entry of music from a MIDI musical keyboard. It was also the first commercial PostScript notation package that allowed music played in real time (as opposed to step time or note-by-note). This program is available in a non-MIDI version at significant savings. ConcertWare (without MIDI) can share files with ConcertWare+MIDI, so when you are ready, your files can be ported to the MIDI version.

ConcertWare+MIDI has gone through a number of updates and upgrades, each more powerful than the previous (at the time of this writing, the program is at version 5.4.1). Many people associate the program with one of its earlier versions and think of the software as a beginner's notation package. It has evolved into much more than that. It is true that the program's limitations on the number of staves (8), the number of voices (8), and the number of vertical notes per voice (8), coupled with the absence of true part-extraction capabilities, place restrictions upon certain applications. ConcertWare+MIDI is still a great entry-level notation program, but it can be coaxed into fulfilling many needs of the intermediate-to-advanced-level users as well. In fact, for some situations, ConcertWare+MIDI offers the only viable solution (see below).

ConcertWare+MIDI has always emulated the word-processing metaphor. Just like with most word processors, you can insert a ruler at any point. You can do this before or after you enter music. Besides allowing complete control over the spacing between staves, systems, pages, measures, line breaks, brackets, braces, and clefs, these rulers give the user access to a number of powerful musical parameters such as: how many staves are displayed/printed from that point on, which parts are assigned to which staves, and placement of lyrics. ConcertWare+MIDI's ruler formatting system is the most flexible interface to measure- and system-level formatting to be found in any of the available notation programs, allowing you to create page layouts that are impossible with any other software (see Figure 22-1).

Because you can have up to eight rhythmically independent parts on a single staff, the developers have provided an alternate non-standard character set of diamond and cross noteheads to help users follow the paths of their melodies. If you have a color monitor, you have the option to assign any color to any part on the screen as another aid to keeping track of the various musical parts. If you have a colored ribbon in your ImageWriter, ConcertWare+MIDI can print the parts in different colors.

ConcertWare+MIDI consists of three applications and a collection of example files, MIDI setups (for popular synthesizers), and instruments (for the Macintosh speaker). The Instrument Maker was discussed in Chapter 10, "Sound Generation." The MIDI Player lets you play back files without using the main MusicWriter program and provides control of volume, tempo changes ranging from 30 to 225 beats per minute, MIDI setup data, and synchronization to an external device via MIDI Beat Clocks. With MIDI Beat Clocks you can slave the program to an external device (such as a hardware sequencer or drum machine) or have ConcertWare+MIDI function as the master. While there are no SMPTE Time Code or MTC lockup features such as those found in packages aimed at the high-end studio musician, ConcertWare+MIDI's synchronization capabilities are fully functional and provide a great introduction to synchronization.

Part of ConcertWare+MIDI's speed comes from the software's ability to quantize upon input. In most MIDI sequencers, quantization is an operation that you can apply after a performance has been recorded — usually, you specify a quantization grid, and all attacks and/or releases of notes are moved appropriately to align with the grid, thus rounding off your rhythmic errors. ConcertWare+MIDI offers the option to pre-select a set of rhythmic values, to which it rounds off MIDI-supplied rhythmic data (see Figure 22-2).

Other features that help to automate the transcription process include letting you specify a velocity threshold to compensate for sloppy performance. Any notes that are struck below a certain loudness are ignored. ConcertWare+MIDI is the only program that includes this desirable feature as an input filtering option.

Once you finish recording, you have three choices. If you know that what you have played is correct, you may insert it immediately into your score; otherwise

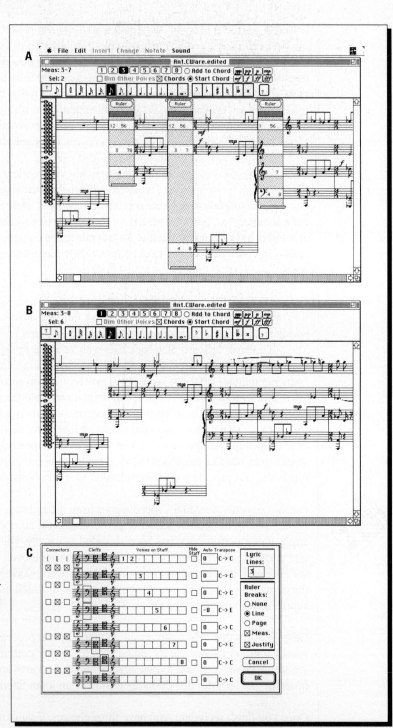

Figure 22-1:
ConcertWare+MIDI's ruler approach offers formatting flexibility that is unparalleled in any other program. **(A)** Main editing screen with rulers shown and annotated. **(B)** The same screen with rulers hidden. **(C)** The ruler configuration dialog box.

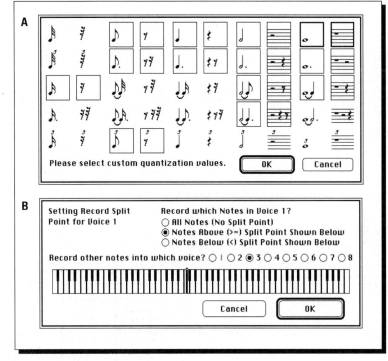

Figure 22-2: Concert-Ware+MIDI offers extensive options to massage MIDI input. **(A)** You can configure a set of possible rhythmic values for ConcertWare+MIDI to "listen" for in advance. **(B)** Notes may be split to any voice upon entry.

you may proofhear and re-record it if necessary. To facilitate entering larger compositions, you can start recording from any point in your music (like "punching in" on an analog tape recorder), and thus you need only enter a phrase at a time.

Like several other notation programs ConcertWare+MIDI stores all incoming MIDI data. However, ConcertWare+MIDI is unique in that it will interpret this data if you like, automatically inserting dynamics and slurs. The software inserts dynamics intelligently. That is, it doesn't assign a dynamic to every note, only when the dynamic level changes. After entry, you can add crescendos and decrescendos according to limits you designate.

After music appears on the staff, you can isolate any grouping of notes from chords, making quick work of delineating the melody or bass line. Furthermore, the developers have solved a problem that has plagued sequencer/notation packages since their beginnings: Individual parts can now jump from staff to staff at any point. This does not refer to simple cross-staff beaming, but to parts that retain their logical or semantic identity when they move from staff to staff.

Importing and exporting SMFs is particularly robust in ConcertWare+MIDI. You have the option to quantize different tracks to different quantize values, including

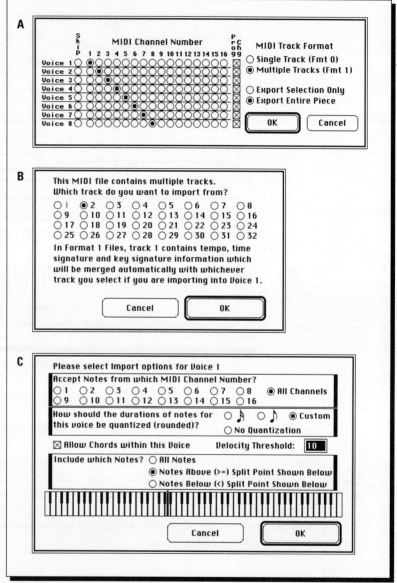

Figure 22-3: (A) Exporting SMFs in Concert-Ware+MIDI. (B) Importing a multiple-track SMF is done one track at a time. (C) For each track, you can set a variety of options to massage the data as it is being brought into ConcertWare+MIDI.

the custom input map discussed above. The velocity threshold feature is also available, as is a fixed split-point option. Unfortunately, ConcertWare+MIDI requires you to import files one track at a time (see Figure 22-3).

ConcertWare+MIDI has a unique MIDI macros feature that lets you quickly insert a command to transmit any string of MIDI data in hexadecimal format. You need to know something about the MIDI Specification to take full advantage of this. However, the program comes with a set of pre-defined MIDI macros that cover many common situations. You can use MIDI macros to control the MIDI volume settings on your synthesizers or even send out a patch dump as SysEx information. Anything that the software does not directly automate with respect to MIDI can be controlled via MIDI macros.

Educators or authors who need to combine musical examples with text will find a selection box for grabbing any portion of the screen and transferring it to their word processor. The image transferred to the Clipboard is in PICT format, so the fonts are included as PostScript rather than bitmapped images. ConcertWare+MIDI files can also be saved as bitmapped or PICT documents for further polishing in either paint-oriented or draw-oriented software.

Any portion of a ConcertWare+MIDI file can be saved as a HyperCard script that plays the same music with HyperCard commands (see Chapter 15, "Making Music without MIDI").

With all these unique features, you may suspect that there must be a catch, and you are right. In addition to the limitations mentioned above, the current version of the program unfortunately does not support diagonal beaming.

Deluxe Music Construction Set

There are many "firsts" attributed to Electronic Arts's Deluxe Music Construction Set (DMCS). It was the first program to print music using PostScript. It was the first program to allow diagonal beaming (see Figure 22-4). It was the first program to allow rhythmic polyphony on a single staff. Finally, it was the first program to treat all symbols as graphics that can later be moved with a click and drag of the mouse.

Geoff Brown, the author of DMCS, believes that a music editor must fundamentally be a graphics editor with the underlying musical semantics handled automatically by the software and invisible to the user. The built-in rules give their best guess, but this can always be edited by selecting any symbol and dragging it to change location, angle, or size. You can change pitch in this manner and such changes play back in real time. A unique Loop Selection mode facilitates this type of editing. You can loop a region if you want, and have the notes flash as they play back. While looping you can add notes, move notes and chords to new pitches, and otherwise fine-tune your composition in ways that are simply impossible with other software.

What is perhaps even more remarkable, considering that many other programs do not provide this option, is that you can drag notes to temporal locations before or after adjacent notes. Besides being able to hear any changes made while dragging

Figure 22-4: A looping selection in DMCS with notes flashing as they are played. You can add notes and reposition notes while your music loops, a feature unfortunately missing from other programs.

a note, you can also drag notes in real time while a specified passage repeats over and over. This is great for testing a number of variations or fine-tuning a musical idea. Using the mouse to drag or add notes and/or symbols while a portion of your work is looping causes the music to play back all your changes instantly. Dynamics, crescendos, and decrescendos are translated into appropriate MIDI velocity changes on output.

DMCS has no provision for real-time input, but it does have a unique approach to step-time input from a MIDI keyboard. First, you specify an input timing value somewhere between 15 and 300 sixtieths of a second, that is, from ¼ second to five seconds. Next, you select a rhythmic value from the symbols palette. Now, when you play notes at your MIDI keyboard and hold the notes for a shorter period than the input timing value you specified earlier, the notes appear on the screen, all with the rhythmic value currently selected on the symbols palette. But if you hold the key down for longer than the current timing value, then the rhythmic value begins to cycle through every possible value above the selected one. At every next timing value, the cycle moves to the next larger rhythmic value. In this way, it is possible to enter many notes with widely varying rhythmic values, but without having to go back to the Macintosh and change the default rhythmic value all the time.

DMCS was so popular for a while that several MIDI sequencers offer options to export their files directly to DMCS format (see Chapter 17, "MIDI Sequencing").

Hard-coded notation errors: DMCS would be a wonderful program for music students and other novices were it not for a single fatal flaw. If you insert a key signature change within a system, the software restrikes the clef on every staff — all 48 staves if you're using that many. This is simply not allowed. I have night-mares of music students emulating this horrendous practice and growing up to teach other students.

Consider a word processor that, when you changed a font in the middle of a paragraph, inserted all other prevailing formatting information at the same point (for example, point size, type style, margin settings, and so on) into the stream of the text and forced you to print this information along with the rest of your docu-ment. Such a word processor would not have a long product life. This is because everyone knows that such program shenanigans are patently intolerable. The fact that DMCS has enjoyed such wide-scale success and longevity is a good indication of the notational knowledge of its user base. It also points to the inherent peda-gogical dangers of such software. That the software is being used by people who are genuinely interested in music — enough to have made a financial investment in a notation program — yet who are at a point in their musical development at which they are unable to distinguish the difference between right and wrong with respect to notation, places a great responsibility on the software's developer, a responsibility to impart correct information and instill good habits at this crucial stage of the user's musical learning. When it comes to changing keys in the midst of compositions, DMCS fails from this standpoint.

Still, many word processing users do not require changing fonts midstream. Like-wise, DMCS may be a good introductory program for a young music student — up until the point where the student starts changing keys in the middle of composi-tions. When the student reaches that level, his or her copy of DMCS should be permanently erased from the hard drive (after converting all the files to a format read by other programs), and the master disks should be hidden away or other-wise permanently retired.

Although DMCS offers diagonal beaming, the slopes that it employs are calculated on the beginning and ending notes of a beamed group. This usually results in steeper beam angles than would ever appear in published music. Fortunately, changing a beam's angle is as easy as dragging the beam with the mouse. If you have a large number of beams that need such adjustments, prepare yourself for a major investment of time.

Encore

Passport Designs's Encore is a jack of all trades music program. It has possibly the most flexible MIDI implementation of any Macintosh notation software (understandably, since it was written by the same people who wrote Pro 5 and uses much of the same code). Encore is the most user-friendly of all the current-generation Macintosh music notation programs. In the true original Macintosh tradition, it follows the standard Macintosh interface so closely that a manual is almost unnecessary (although you do need a manual to realize the full potential of this software, particularly to discover kluges to get around a few of the program's limitations).

The software's feature complement provides most of the power you need for traditional music notation, but each set of options has a definite self-imposed limit of complexity. It's as if the programmers looked at the competition and determined the best and most universal features in designing Encore's functional specification, leaving out the more esoteric options that cover exceptional cases. Because of this, it qualifies as both a compositional tool as well as a tool for copyists. Restraints on the control of note spacing, among other things, make the software unsuitable for professional publishing. Encore is able to handle about three-quarters — perhaps more — of the notational problems of traditionally notated music. In addition, it may well be the fastest program to work with — you almost never see the watch cursor.

If Pro 5 is your MIDI sequencer, there is another advantage for you. Several of the ways you interact with Encore resemble those of Pro 4. Furthermore, Encore reads in Pro 4 files directly via its Import option. It also imports files from any other Passport sequencer, including Master Tracks Pro, Master Tracks Jr., and Trax. You do not first have to convert the files to SMF format. If you use another company's sequencer, you will be happy to hear that Encore imports SMFs extremely quickly and accurately (see Figures 22-5 and 22-6).

MIDI editing features traditionally associated with MIDI sequencers are included in Encore. Such editing can be done at any point, before or after the notes have been converted to durations. Some graphic editing operations require that you manually select Align Playback from the Change menu in order to ensure that the underlying MIDI data conforms to the edited CMN.

One of the factors that make Encore so fast and easy to use is that nearly any element of the score can be repositioned by dragging with the mouse. This includes not only notes and expressive markings (in true Macintosh style, Option-dragging creates copies), but also barlines, staves (vertically), entire systems, and system margins (both right and left). Formatting doesn't get any simpler than this.

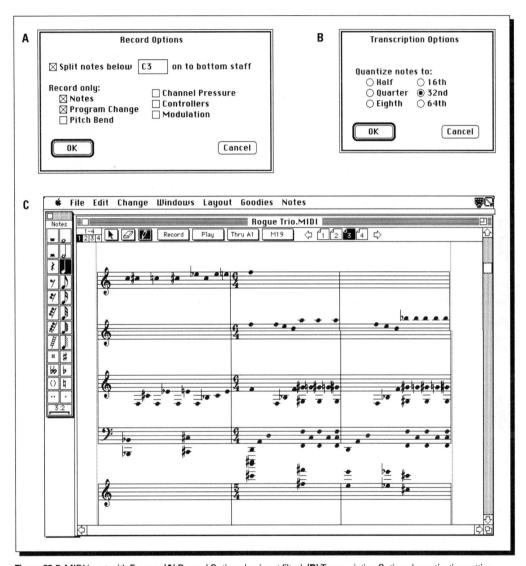

Figure 22-5: MIDI input with Encore. **(A)** Record Options (an input filter). **(B)** Transcription Options (quantization setting determining rhythmic values). **(C)** Importing an SMF or playing music into Encore in real time with a MIDI- or Macintosh-generated metronome results in notes proportionally displayed without rhythmic values. Encore makes no initial assumptions about the notation. You choose Guess Durations from the Notes menu to instruct Encore to assign durational values. You can process an entire file in one pass or select smaller regions and apply different quantization grids (Transcription Options — see B).

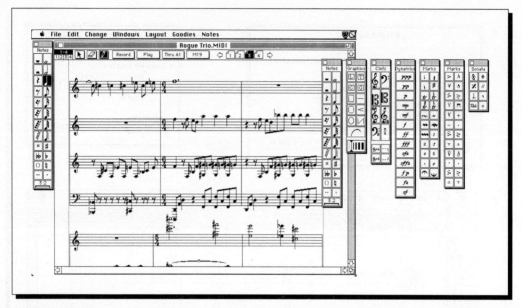

Figure 22-6: The music from Figure 22-5 has had its durations "guessed" in this example. All of Encore's draggable notation elements are indicated in this figure, as is the complete set of palettes available. It is possible to keep a single palette visible and then toggle between other palettes by clicking the palette's name or using keyboard shortcuts.

Encore provides a single spacing table for laying out notes. Unfortunately, this is a linear proportion, where the space devoted to a half note is equal to twice that of a quarter, which is equal to twice that of an eighth, and so on. Professional engravers almost never use linear spacing, so this is a major complaint from that segment of the industry. Encore's Justify Spacing command eliminates some of this rigidity by attempting to correct for the collisions between accidentals and notes, which are so common in all notation software. Of course, you can manually tweak the inter-note spacing to create the look of professionally published music, if you care to take the time.

There are some minor annoyances. For example, the default handling of dots is not correct in some cases, notably quarter rests (whose dots appear on the middle line) and clusters (whose dots appear in every next available space). The display of accidentals for certain harmonic intervals causes them to collide (two notes a third apart, both with sharps). Fortunately, Encore provides work-arounds for all these problems, and its elegant implementation of discontiguous selection means that fixing all the offending symbols can be accomplished in one step.

Like most notation programs, the software requires some coaxing for rendering certain passages. Unlike most programs, which make you figure out such kluges on your own, Encore includes them as techniques in the manual. A notable example is the procedure for creating cross-staff beaming: You enter the notes as quarter notes and use the graphics line tool to draw a beam. To compensate for the rhythmic discrepancies this creates, you must use the Change Duration dialog box to set the actual play durations of these notes. Some calculations may be required.

As with most notation software, a few minor bugs appear from time to time. However, unlike most notation manuals, Encore's documentation warns you about these hazards in advance, and there are only a few concerns of this nature. For example, changing the stem length of a non-beamed note or chord is particularly finicky. Leaving Auto-Space enabled while fine-tuning the graphic look of your score can result in the loss of all your positioning edits. Passport continues to release updates and upgrades on a regular basis, so these issues are being addressed. In general, the program only gets better and better.

Finale

Coda's Finale has probably generated more industry discussion than any other music software package, notation, or otherwise. The software was advertised as the "only software you'll ever need" — for composers, orchestrators, arrangers, copyists, and engravers alike. In many ways, Finale fulfilled this promise, combining sophisticated real-time MIDI input, extensive MIDI output controlled by notation, and elegant notational options capable of addressing just about any notational situation imaginable.

Finale was the first computer program in history with the capability to display, on the screen, correct musical notation of almost any complexity while you played. Finale introduced MIDI transcription without requiring a click reference, accurately tracking the right and left hands and continually moving the bass-treble staff split point, while adjusting the stemming and beaming to accurately correspond to the actual progress of each melodic line. The software employs AI-related techniques to determine intricate rhythmic polyphony and note-spellings (intelligent assignment of sharps and flats), even when capturing an expressive performance, including substantial rubato.

Finale automatically determines complicated guitar chords, including extensive levels of alterations, and plays them back correctly voiced. You can use any complex or compound meter at any time and define linear and non-linear scale relationships, complete with tonal attributes. All dynamics, articulations, and expressive markings are interpreted during playback, and the program includes a built-in PostScript symbol designer, also capable of producing MIDI-executable graphics. Finale supports up to 64 MIDI output channels, although the Macintosh version currently handles only 32. No notation software supports cableized MIDI channels at the time of this writing, probably because the cable message has not been officially incorporated into the MIDI Specification. Because all Finale symbols are MIDI-executable and any real-time expressive performance data captured on input is retained, the output from Finale rivals the capabilities of some sequencers with respect to the control of MIDI devices. Finale even permits sending dynamics out separate channels, for example, to control MIDI effects devices.

An innovative editing operation called *mirroring* links copies or variations of melodies to their sources, so that changes in the original are reflected in the copies, anywhere in the piece — perhaps the most powerful orchestration tool one could wish for. The PostScript output meets the highest standards of professional publishers and even allows configuration of the program to replicate individual styles of engraving.

Many of the features mentioned so far were enough to send chills up the spines of musicians who have devoted years of study to these tasks — tasks that Finale could take care of automatically. For many notational problems, Finale remains the only solution. Because the release of Finale sparked such controversy, some historical perspective is in order.

Finale is actually a front-end user interface to Coda's ENIGMA engine (Environment for Notation utilizing Intuitive Graphic Music Algorithms) developed by Phil Farrand and Tim Strathdee of Opus Dei. ENIGMA is a base technology upon which to build a number of other programs, ranging from musical analysis aids to notation. Written in C, this intelligent software engine fully and cognitively understands a good deal about music with roots in 19th-century tonality, and music composed in this century as well. ENIGMA is a toolkit handling transcription, graphic display, printing, playback, and editing; it is fully extensible (even the data structures themselves) and can be applied to the strictest classical tradition or the wildest avant garde graphical scores. In some ways, this software kernel can function as an expert system (see Chapter 19, "Interactive Composition and Intelligent Instruments"). Finale, developed by Phil Farrand and John Borowicz, was simply the first application to be built around the ENIGMA kernel. Since then, at least three other ENIGMA-based programs have been released (MusicProse, discussed below, Practice Room, discussed in Chapter 28, "Computer-aided Instruction," and Finale IBM).

The first release of Finale received a lot of bad press. This was fueled by the fact that Finale 1.0 had more dialog boxes than just about all other music programs combined. Dialog boxes were nested within dialog boxes ad infinitum. Sometimes you had to click six OK buttons to finally return from making a single change to your music. It turned out that the price paid for Finale's power was a level of complexity orders of magnitude beyond anything that had come before it. A large body of music software users, including reviewers, were expected to make a one-step jump from software as easy to operate as a Volkswagen to a program with as many controls as the space shuttle. To make matters worse, it was literally impossible to learn the program from the three-volume manual that accompanied the package. The documentation was riddled with errors and non-standard "FinaleSpeak."

As a result, Finale received the permanent designation of having a "steep learning curve." No one seemed willing to accept the obvious logic that a program with literally 50 times the number of features and options of any other music program might take somewhat longer to learn. Other factors contributing to the feeling of discontent were the Macintosh's reputation for user-friendliness and the fact that Finale was released within the period in the Macintosh's history when it was widely believed that programs requiring a manual were really not worthy of consideration. Finale demonstrated to the world what wonders could be accomplished with music software, and everyone suspected (correctly) that this could be accomplished with a simpler user interface.

Fortunately, in the second year of its commercial availability, Finale 2.0 was released with a revamped user interface that replaced many of the dialog boxes with menus, a new set of vastly improved manuals (rewritten entirely), and a significantly lower price. At the time of this writing, Finale version 2.6.3 is current, and the developers are feverishly working on Finale 3.0, expected to be released in late 1992.

You operate Finale with 35 tools selected from a palette at the left side of the screen (see Figure 22-7). There are tools dedicated to setup, input, editing, MIDI, text and lyrics, and formatting. To input or edit specific types of musical or graphical data, it is necessary to activate the tool designated for the particular task you want to accomplish. Some tools bring up associated menus (13 additional menus). When you select a certain tool, data types addressed by that tool acquire little handles or otherwise become selectable. Most program interaction is accomplished by clicking these handles or selectable elements to bring up one or more of the program's dialog boxes or dedicated editing windows.

Finale is full of unique features. Here is a list of some of the more notable ones:

Reposition multiple staves with Shift-click and drag.

Any number of staff lines from 0 to 100.

Each staff can play back over four separate MIDI channels. One channel is assigned to voice one, another to voice two, another to chord symbols, and another to expressive markings. Any channel can be initialized with a patch change message.

New Staff Tool			Staff Attributes Tool
Measure Attributes Tool			Measure Add Tool
Key Signature Tool			Time Signature Tool
Simple Note Entry Tool			Speedy Note Entry Tool
HyperScribe Tool			Transcription Tool
MIDI Tool			Playback Tool
Note Mover Tool			Mass Mover Tool
Chord Tool			Tuplet Tool
Score Expression Tool			Staff Expression Tool
Note Expression Tool			Special Tools Tool
Reduce/Enlarge Tool			Lyrics Tool
Page Layout Tool			Header/Footer Tool
Bracket Tool			Clef Tool
Repeat Tool			Measure Number Tool
Arbitrary Music Tool			Text Block Tool
Time Dilation Tool			Mirror Tool
Page Add/Remove Tool			Zoom Tool
Hand Grabber Tool			

layer : 1

Figure 22-7: Finale's 35 tools.

Multiple spacing tables in the same document. Different spacing tables can be applied to each measure, if you like.

Mix sharps and flats in key signatures and scales of greater than 12 steps. You can set tonal attributes, so that Finale knows what to consider the tonic, dominant, and other functions in synthetic scales. You can create quarter-tone key signatures.

Finale understands the difference between sharps and flats, and notates accordingly. These calculations are based on the software's knowledge of the prevailing tonality.

Compound meters and fractional meters with automatic beaming.

Play music in real time and watch it display on the screen while you play. Finale lets you play up to four independent voices on two staves while giving it the beat by tapping your foot or another MIDI keyboard key. This lets you speed up and slow down at will.

Transcription of music played in without a timing reference. Finale offers elaborate post-determination of the beat options (see Figure 22-8).

Special copy mode links pasted data to source measures. Changes in the source measure update all linked copies, regardless of transposition.

Special mirror tool lets you link individual measures to items in multiple measures. For example, the first beat of the mirrored measure could be linked to the third beat of measure 2, while the second beat of the mirrored measure is linked to the fourth beat of measure 5, and so on. Changes to any of the source measures are reflected in the item that appears in the mirrored measure.

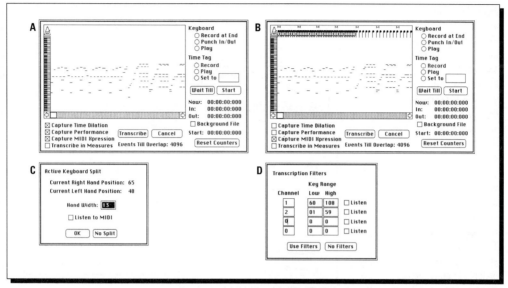

Figure 22-8: The Transcription Tool provides for real-time MIDI transcription with post-determination of the beat (i.e., you play without any timing reference). Optionally, you can have Finale generate a MIDI metronome click. **(A)** Music played into the Transcription Tool appears in piano-roll format. You can zoom in or out to any magnification and you can edit note durations by dragging with the mouse. **(B)** To enter the beats, you tap any key on your MIDI controller while listening to the music play back. The beats appear at the top of the screen. Next, you can tap in measure boundaries if you want to change meter in the transcription. You can even tap in beat groupings during a third pass if you want. Alternatively, you can use Finale's Compand feature. You simply tell Finale the durations of the first two or three notes of your performance, and the software figures out where the beats and measures should be, even compensating for accelerandos and rubatos. **(C)** Finale uses this dialog box to determine your hand width for calculating the floating split-point. Using the width of your finger span, the program simply figures out where your hand must have been to play the music. **(D)** This dialog box lets you filter the transcription by MIDI channel and/or note range (note range can be inclusive or exclusive). Instead of transcribing all of your performance at once, you can choose Transcribe in Measures. This brings you back to your scrolling score and wherever you click the mouse, the next measure is inserted. It's like painting your musical ideas onto an orchestral canvas.

Unlimited savable and namable Clipboards.

Explode music onto selected target staves (which can be nonadjacent).
Some other programs offer similar functions, but not the capability to specify non-adjacent destination staves or to define rules for the handling of cases where the number of voices in the exploded music exceeds the number of target staves.

Search and replace for notes, themes, motifs, or phrases. (See Figure 22-9.)

Figure 22-9: The Search and Replace features of Finale are accessed through the Note Mover Tool. **(A)** You define a motif by Shift-clicking the notes you want to search for. **(B)** This dialog box lets you specify whether to look for the note pattern in any octave, just the original octave, and with or without the associated rhythms. Here you also indicate what you want to replace each note with. This is accomplished by specifying a chromatic, diatonic, or enharmonic transposition for each note that is part of the motif. **(C)** After setting up your replacement parameters, this control panel appears

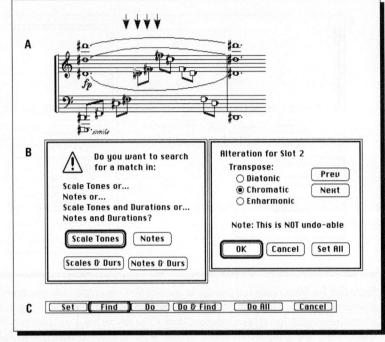

at the top of the screen with the same sort of search and replace options you expect from a sophisticated word processor: Find, Do (meaning execute the replacement), Do & Find (next), and Do All.

The distinction between Score and Staff expressions. This allows you to specify that certain expressive markings that appear once in the score, appear on all parts.

Completely expandable libraries of ancillary and expressive markings. All can have their MIDI parameters configured.

Bulk assign or realign individual note expressions.

PostScript shape designer. You can add PostScript shapes to your expression libraries, and these can play back however you like (see Figure 22-10) .

Repeat signs function. No repeated configuration, including multiple endings, is too complex for Finale.

Any symbol, any size, anywhere, any time.

Ten different tuplet displays.

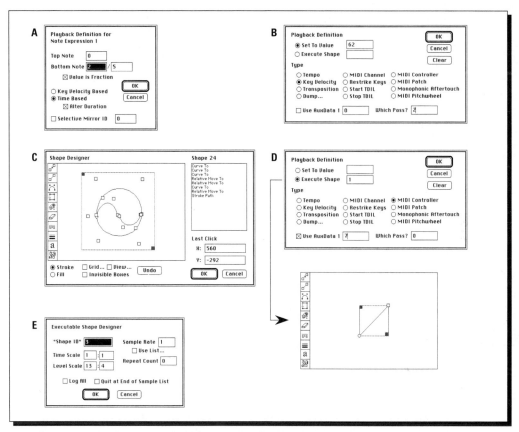

Figure 22-10: Designing MIDI-executable shapes in Finale. **(A)** This dialog box lets you set playback modifiers to note expressions (accents and articulations). **(B)** This dialog box is where you set playback definitions for text expressions (essentially all other types of expressive markings not included in the category of note expressions). **(C)** Finale's built-in PostScript graphics editor lets you create filled or unfilled shapes of any size or complexity you want. These shapes are true PostScript and can be saved in a library for future use in other files. **(D)** You can specify that any text or shape expression changes the values of a certain MIDI parameter over time by having the expression execute another shape in the library. For example, a crescendo would execute this shape, which is simply a line from the lower left to upper right. Velocity or Controller 7 would be the parameter set for modification by this shape. Note that you can assign any parameter to be dynamically changed by a shape. **(E)** You set the temporal scaling of the shape that is being used to dynamically change a specific MIDI parameter with this dialog box.

Traditional sequencer-style MIDI data-editing options.

Auto-assignment of chord symbols in either alphanumeric or fretboard notation. Finale can analyze chords that aren't present in its current library, adding these automatically to the library.

Configurable chord voicings play back on their own MIDI channel.

Lyrics and text are created with a built-in text editor. All lyrics and text creation windows remain linked to the words on the page at all times. Changing lyrics in the text editor forces corresponding changes in the music.

Global automatic optimization. Finale automatically removes all staves that are tacit for an entire system, if you request this option.

Unlimited right and left indents.

Automatic reformatting of parts, including provision for alternate spacing tables.

Advanced engraving configuration options.

Multiple measure numbering schemes per file.

Sophisticated Time Dilation tool lets you control nuance by tempo alterations. Multiple tempo alterations are possible in a single measure. For example, beat 2 could rush, while beat 4 might be late.

Arbitrary music tool lets you create ossias.

White shapes can be used to create cut-out scores. Measures without music in them can be designated not to print — even their staff lines.

Most tools let you create up to eight macros. These macros provide single-click access to an editing feature or symbol placement that might otherwise require interaction with a number of dialog boxes.

With over 300 dialog boxes and 21 menus and submenus, it is not surprising that Finale requires nearly 900 pages of documentation. My limit of five figures per notation program restricts the number of innovative options that can be covered in this chapter.

Finale is an extendable environment. Coda has surprised the users on two occasions with a collection of EMEL (ENIGMA micro-editing language) extensions that function as plug-in modules to the software (you select a region with the Mass Mover Tool and press the 8 key to access EMELs). These extensions add useful functions not currently built into the program. Coda has released 16 so far. Among these are EMELs that let you add specified note expressions to every note in a selected region, halve and double durational values, and retrograde the pitches of a region.

Finale has stimulated third-party development of utilities to make working with the software a little easier.

❖ Wette Enterprises's freeware FinaleFontReport HyperCard stack reads in a compiled PostScript file from Finale or MusicProse and provides a report of fonts used in the document.

❖ Joe Zobkiw's SignOut! for Finale takes care of situations where Finale crashes without officially signing out of MIDI Manager. In these cases, sometimes when you return to the program, it can't sign in again.

❖ George Litterst's Engraver's Calculator handles a lot of extremely useful Finale calculations. It performs, for example, calculations involving engravers' spaces and various conversions to and from EDUs (ENIGMA durational units) and EVPUs (ENIGMA virtual page units).

❖ Daniel Berlinger's freeware Finale Worksheet is an Excel spreadsheet that functions as a calculator for setting up allotment (spacing) tables.

❖ Tim Herzog's shareware Illustrious Music performs three functions. It translates Finale EPS files to Illustrator 3.0 format. It also merges two PostScript files (for example, if you have a long score and then need to replace a page or two within the compiled PostScript listing). Finally, it adds crop marks to a Post-Script file.

❖ Tim Herzog's shareware PICTuresque DA converts files from EPS to PICT format (it also converts from Paint format files to PICT and from PICT, Paint, or EPS files to resources). Convert Previews converts object-oriented preview images, such as those stored with Finale-generated EPS files, to standard bitmap previews.

❖ Not all utilities are software. Maestro Graphics markets a set of flip-up laminated reference cards that attach to your Macintosh keyboard. Their current offering in the area of Macintosh music is a very thorough template for Finale consisting of five double-sided flip-up references. All the keyboard shortcuts of the program are displayed, as are descriptions and operating tips for the 35 tools and the complete Petrucci font character set.

Incidentally, Finale is available for the IBM, so if you have some friends or colleagues who refuse to purchase a Macintosh, you can exchange files with them using Finale's ETF (ENIGMA transportable file) format. Because Finale IBM uses Windows 3.x as its interface, if you learn the program on the Macintosh, it will take you all of one minute to accustom yourself to using it on an IBM. The main difference are the keyboard shortcuts. The keyboard shortcuts for menu items don't correspond across the two platforms. Insignia Solutions's AccessPC cdev lets you read IBM disks (3.5 inches) and open IBM-created Finale ETFs directly.

HB Engraver

HB Engraver from HB Imaging was the first second-generation notation software package to be released. It is, as its name implies, intended for engravers, not composers or copyists. Originally developed as proprietary software for use in-house by a music engraving firm, most of its functionality is distinctly aimed at the professional music publishing industry. The program has changed hands several times and is no longer supported. However, you still see it offered in retail outlets and mail-order houses, and engravers who use the program seem to swear by it. In fact, the software is capable of producing high quality output that is up to the standards of most professional publishers.

The program should not be used in any situations where you don't have a draft version of the score to engrave, although you might want to include an imported MIDI file in the definition of a draft version if you are courageous (i.e., results are not predictable). There are few features designed to support the type of ongoing revisions that are intrinsic to the acts of composition or orchestration. The input mode (discussed in Chapter 21, "Score Input and Editing") is the closest thing to the IBM command-line interface that is imaginable in a Macintosh notation program.

HB Engraver is designed to be operated in six stages: score setup (Full System Specification — see Figure 22-11), note input, lyric input, dynamics input (including other expressive markings), block text input, and page layout. The modality of the first and last stages is justifiable. The modality of the inner four stages takes time to get used to, because they are mutually exclusive. You cannot edit notes while you are editing dynamics, lyrics, or text, and you cannot edit dynamics while you are editing notes, lyrics, or text, and so on. Each stage requires entering a separate area of the program and displaying your music in a new window that operates differently from the ones associated with the other stages. For longer pieces, getting from one editing mode to another can involve a significant amount of time.

Program modality of the kind described in the previous paragraph has been a distinct "no-no" from the standpoint of user interface since the inception of the Macintosh. Nonetheless, if you customarily divide your music preparation activities into these stages or can learn to function within this framework (as many have), you might be able to ignore this gross violation of the Macintosh human interface guidelines.

HB Engraver's Input mode has a very useful feature for adding chords. You can set up five chordal configurations, which are accessed by a single click of the

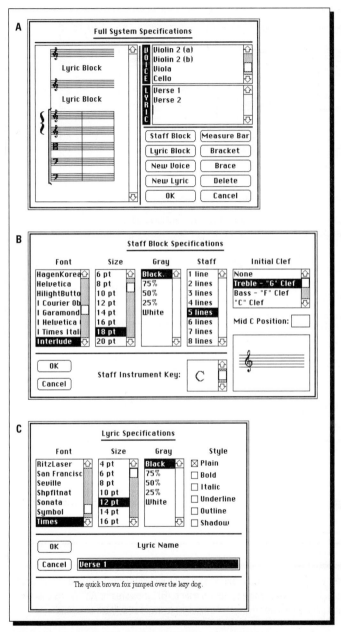

mouse. Changing a chord voicing for these five chord templates is as simple as click-ing notes on or off in the scrolling Chords list at the left of the Input screen.

The last version of HB Engraver to be officially released (1.1) finally included options to view more than one grand staff at a time in the Input mode. Also added were options to zoom in or out rather than having to look at notes the size of marbles. Note that dynamics and text are never visible in this mode, and changes that you make in one editing mode may require adjustments to elements added in one or more of the other modes (see Figure 22-12).

Once you have entered your notes and lyrics in HB Engraver, you transfer to the Dynamics mode. Here you can only view a single system at a time and only add or edit the items that are accessible from pop-up palettes. You cannot move or edit notes or block text (text attached to the page as opposed to the measure or system) while in

Figure 22-11: Full System Specification in HB Engraver. **(A)** When you create a new score in HB Engraver, you set up the number of staves, their interconnections, the number of voices per staff, and number of lyric lines with this dialog box. It's quite simple. **(B)** With this dialog box (accessible by double-clicking a staff or lyric line) staves can be set to different sizes, clefs, numbers of lines, and notes to different fonts and sizes. The option to designate any of these elements to be gray scale rather than black-and-white is unique to HB Engraver. **(C)** Double-clicking a lyric line brings up a similar dialog box to set font styles and sizes with gray-scale options as well.

Figure 22-12: (A) After entering your notes, you go to the Lyrics mode (if your piece includes lyrics). Here you can merge a text file with your notation. However, you can only view a single system at a time. **(B)** Lyrics are not WYSIWYG until you go to Block Text mode (pictured), at which point your notes respace themselves to avoid all syllable collisions.

Dynamics mode. Many symbols offer gray-scale options similar to those available in Full System Specification mode.

Block Text mode is where you can finally see the entire page of music and also where you add block text items that are attached to specific locations on the page. You can also drag a system or text block to any location on the page.

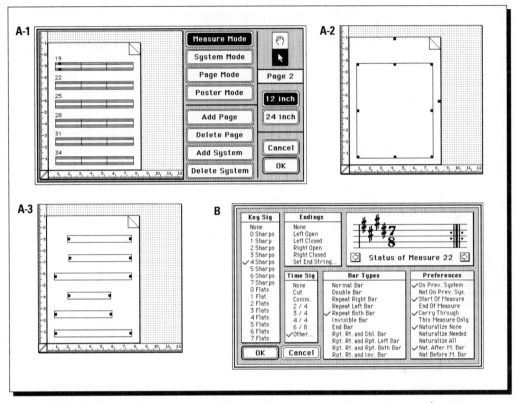

Figure 22-13: (A-1) HB Engraver's Page Layout mode lets you format system spacing, move measures from system to system, add systems, and flow existing music into them, **(A-2)** set margins, and **(A-3)** set right and left indents. **(B)** Double-clicking a measure brings up this Measure Preference window, where you add key signatures, time signatures, endings, bar types, and cautionary accidentals.

The four working stages of HB Engraver (note input, lyrics, dynamics, and block text) are not arbitrary. Their order is dictated by considerations of symbol collision. If you divide your work into these four steps, every next step deals with symbols that are less apt to be locked into place by virtue of notational rules. You can enter the Page Layout Mode anytime (see Figure 22-13).

HB Engraver's accompanying HB Toolbox is a unique utility that all notation developers could learn from. This program lets you configure the default settings of the HB Engraver application itself or of any individual file. There is no other configuration option for any software that compares to HB Toolbox in terms of power and ease of use. The available parameters for adjustment are exactly those that are used to define the look of a page, something that a publisher may have been cultivating for decades. Making the configuration utility a separate program instead of putting it into built-in dialog boxes within the main notation software reduces the size of the main program. On the other hand, it requires you to know exactly what settings are appropriate, because you cannot view the effect of your adjustments until you either launch HB Engraver or view the file that has been edited in this way. Figure 22-14 shows most of the configurable items.

Lime

The CERL Music Group's Lime software has been available since 1978. Back then it ran on CDC Cybers under the PLATO system. The program was ported to the Macintosh in the mid-1980s. In the past, the CERL Music Group has not made an effort to push the product through normal commercial channels, so chances are you have not heard of it (a non-saving demonstration version available on Internet is how most people learn of the program). However, the software has some popularity in academic circles, and many of its features are designed to support the so-called "academic school" of composition. The program has been used to create many doctoral theses.

Lime takes a slightly different approach to solving the problems of notation and user interface than all other Macintosh notation software. This is partly because the program was developed in academia, without the critical feedback that commercial distribution generates. Software originating on other platforms often appears foreign when first ported to the Macintosh. Most other notation developers carefully watched what the competition was doing, and thus a somewhat general set of standard notation software user interface conventions gradually emerged. The developers of Lime, however, went along doing things their own way, seemingly with little outside influence. Lime is an extremely powerful program, but tapping its power requires discarding pre-conceived expectations about how notation software *should* operate (see Figure 22-15).

Lime offers many of the same options as the most feature-laden of all music software, Finale. Score optimization and multiple right and left staff indenting are the two things that are most conspicuously absent (you *can* indent the first system). Lime offers some features that no other software provides. Two examples are barlines between staves that do not cross staff lines and true multiple meters with non-coinciding barlines.

To completely understand the Lime's Annotation Mode palettes, you must first understand the program's Notation Contexts option. Lime's Notation Contexts dialog box lets you set up as many different stave groupings as you like. For example, you always have a Notation Context that displays all the parts of the score (this Context is called the Score). To extract parts, you would add separate Contexts that display only the part to be extracted — usually an individual Context for each instrument. You can also use Notation Contexts to set up display configurations that are analogous to the four Staff Views available in Finale. Perhaps you

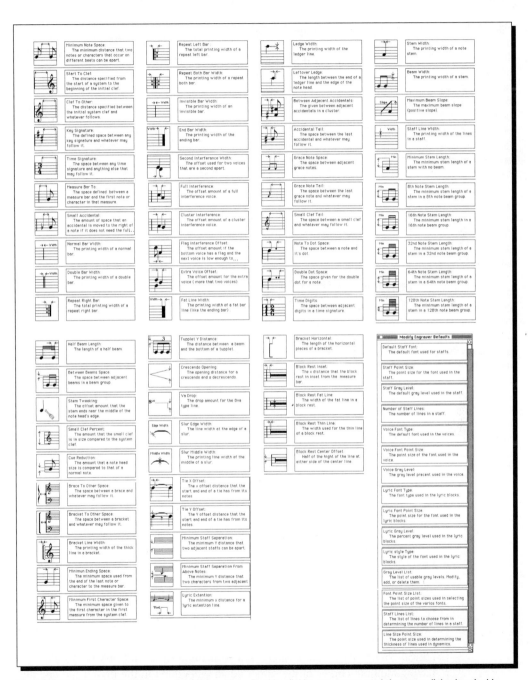

Figure 22-14: HB Toolbox's default configuration options. Double-clicking any parameter brings up a dialog box. In this dialog box you drag elements to new positions or type in new numerical values. For individual files, up to 65 spacing options are configurable, and eight types of slurs and custom beamings are accessible. Configuring the program itself adds 15 additional configurable default parameters.

Figure 22-15: The main entry screen of Lime. The screen fonts are not particularly representative of the high quality produced by the associated printer font. Note the four buttons to the left of the on-screen keyboard. These are used to toggle between Lime's four main entry and editing palettes: Notes, Text (and Lyrics), Lines, and Curves. Clicking one of these buttons changes the floating palette accordingly. Alternatively, selecting a symbol

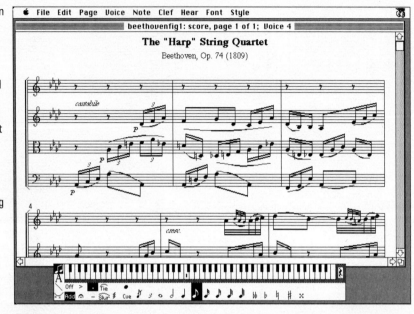

associated with a particular entry/editing palette displays the proper palette (except in the case of the Note Entry palette, for reasons dictated by the program's selection techniques). When the Text, Lines, and Curves palettes are visible, you are officially in Annotation Mode (see Figure 22-16). The Note Entry palette at the bottom of the screen offers a unique approach to entering ancillary markings and slurs. The Add button, when enabled, lets you automatically add certain symbols to notes as they are being entered. Any combination of the accent, staccato, fermata, tenuto, and tremolo markings can be attached to a note as it is input (either by clicking the on-screen keyboard or via MIDI). You can swap these symbols for other ones if you like. After entry, you can use the same buttons to add markings to all selected notes in one operation (a feature lacking from most other software and discussed at length in Chapter 21). You can add slurs at input as well, simply by highlighting the Slur button. Clicking the notehead above the word "Cue" cycles between eight available noteheads, and all subsequent notes assume the selected notehead.

would use a Context that only displayed the flute and strings in an orchestral score to facilitate editing them in a region where there is considerable interactivity between these parts.

There is much more Lime's Notation Contexts can do. You can have two Contexts that display the identical grouping of staves — this can even include all the staves. Because annotations can be associated with particular Contexts, you can have a completely different set of ancillary markings (for example, critical commentary) and entirely new formatting for each Context. It's like having multiple copies of the same file all embedded in the master file and all accessible from a single menu. The Text palette offers an option that can be used to great advantage with Lime's Notation Contexts feature. Checking the Hidden box lets you hide an annotation within a specific Context. This enables you to have annotative text (including dynamics and other expressive mark-

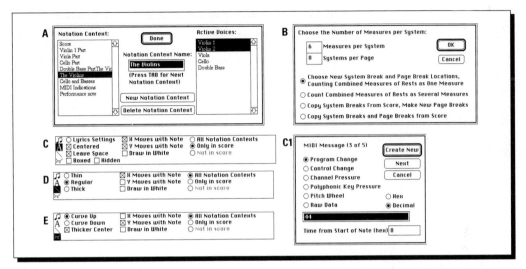

Figure 22-16: (A) You set up different logical groupings of your staves and voices using this Notation Contexts dialog box. Score and Parts Contexts are obvious, but Lime's Context approach offers many other innovative options. **(B)** When you create a Context, this dialog box allows you to assign unique formatting settings to the newly created Context. Any notational elements accessible by way of Lime's three Annotative Mode palettes (see C, D, and E) can be uniquely associated with a specific Context. Lime's three Annotative Mode palettes are identical, with the exception of the left column. The unique option to associate the annotation with the X, Y, or both X and Y axis movement of its attached note is very powerful. So is the option to associate the annotation with the score, the individual Context, or everything but the score (as discussed in the text). **(C)** The Text palette makes a distinction between lyric text and other text. Fonts, styles, and sizes are selectable from menus. For non-lyric text, there is an Align option under the Style menu. Hidden text can be used to insulate certain annotations from specific Contexts or to assure that they only appear in a particular Context. **(C-1)** With this MIDI Messages dialog box you can attach any MIDI message to an annotation. Hidden text annotations are particularly well suited for this purpose. A single note or annotation can have any number of MIDI messages associated with it. You scroll through these using the Next button. **(D)** The Line palette lets you draw lines on your score or individual Contexts. The Style menu provides access to other line widths and dashed line configurations. Lime offers a clipping option for lines. Each line has two extra handles that can be manipulated by dragging to white out or otherwise erase designated segments of a line. **(E)** The Curves palette is self-explanatory. All curves in Lime have four draggable control points.

ings) that appear in one size and font within the Score Context and in another size or font within other Contexts. Each Context can have its own set of formatting rules regarding system-level and page-level layout considerations as well as a designation to concatenate or expand multimeasure rests (see Figure 22-16). The power of Notation Contexts goes well beyond mere screen display, because all the decisions you make regarding one Context only print with that particular Context.

Lime lets you input music in real time with or without a metronome. You also have the option to Tap Tempo with the spacebar while you are playing with your other hand. An interesting option is to Interpret 3 Adjacent Keys on the Keyboard as a Rest. This has to do with the way Lime determines the rhythmic value of a note: It detects the moment of a note attack and stretches the end to

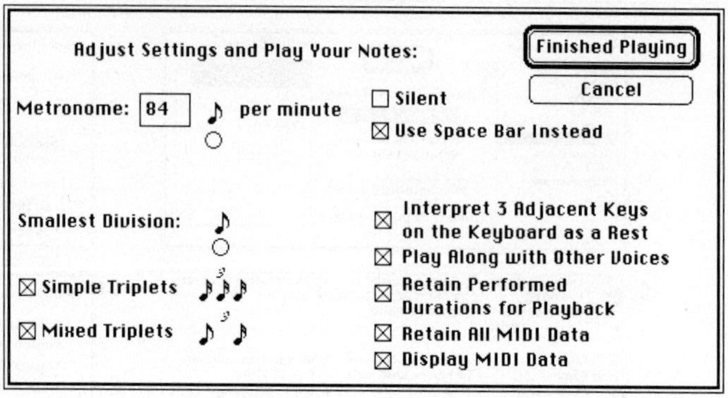

Figure 22-17: Lime's Real Time MIDI recording options. Note the option to Interpret 3 Adjacent Keys on the Keyboard as a Rest (explained in the text).

the next beat or attack, whichever comes first. This allows Lime to automatically notate rests that occur at (or cross over) the start of beats, but not those that occur before the end of a beat (for example, an eighth rest following a dotted quarter note would force the note to appear as a half note). The Interpret 3 Adjacent Keys option gets around this by letting you inform Lime about an intended rest directly from the MIDI keyboard (see Figure 22-17).

MIDI playback is particularly flexible in Lime using the Hear menu (see Figure 22-18).

As with Finale, the use of the Option, Shift-Option, Shift-Option-Command, or other combinations of modifier keys in Lime affects the way the selection and editing functions operate and determines what type of data is to be edited. Also like Finale, Lime extends this option to text copied to the Clipboard. Lime takes this a step further, letting you delineate specific types of data that get copied when you select an annotative symbol. For example, copying a region with the Shift, Option, and Command keys down copies both the PostScript and Quick-Draw information about the region, but when you leave out the Option key it means that the PostScript data is not transferred to the Clipboard (only the Quick-Draw PICT image).

The main drawback to Lime is the amount of time it takes to redraw the screen. (This process ends up being lengthier than in any other notation program available for the Macintosh. While you are waiting for the screen to update, the cursor becomes hollow instead of turning into a watch.) Lime gets around the screen-redraw problem by allowing you to continue editing and entering music while the screen is calculating its updated image. The Previous Note (Command-B or left arrow) and Next Note (Command-N or right arrow) options let you select and edit additional music while the new screen is being calculated. This even works for editing music that has not appeared on the screen yet (for example, real-time MIDI entry that is having its durational values assigned before hitting the screen).

A

Hear	
Hear...	⌘H

Tuning...	
Dynamic Levels...	
Defaults...	

Recompute Playback	
Softer	⌘1
Louder	⌘2
Lower	⌘3
Higher	⌘4
Shorter	⌘5
Longer	⌘6
Earlier	⌘7
Later	⌘8
More Nuance	⌘9
Less Nuance	⌘0
Play Octave Higher	
Play Octave Lower	

MIDI Messages...	

B

Percent of Notated Note Length:

[OK] [Cancel]

Staccato	38
Marcato	81
Legato	92
Slur	105

☐ No Effect on Note Length

◉ Grace Notes Before Beat
○ Grace Notes on Beat

Grace Note Length (Percent of Length of a Sixteenth Note) [25]

Commands in the Hear Menu Adjust How Selected Notes are Played. The Sizes of the Various Adjustments are:

Volume Change (% of Total Volume Range) [5]

Pitch Change in Cents (% of a Half Step) [10]

Length Change (% of Current Length) [5]

Start Time Change (% of Sixteenth Note) [25]

Nuance Change (% of Total Nuance Range) [5]

C

Volume Levels for Dynamic Markings:

10	pppp	60	mf	[OK]
20	ppp	70	f	[Cancel]
30	pp	80	ff	
40	p	90	fff	
50	mp	100	ffff	

☐ Dynamic Markings Have No Effect on Volume Levels.

These values are % of total volume range.

Note volumes will be set according to these levels whenever dynamics are typed. Further volume modifications can be made using Louder/Softer in the Hear menu.

D

Tuning for Each Half-step in an Octave:

0	C	32	F sharp/G flat	[OK]
-2	C sharp/D flat	0	G	[Cancel]
4	D	-12	G sharp/A flat	
-12	D sharp/E flat	18	A	
16	E	-6	A sharp/B flat	
-24	F	8	B	

These are offsets (in cents) from the equal-tempered scale.

This tuning will be used when new notes are added, and when "Play As Written" is selected.

Figure 22-18: (A) Lime's Hear menu lets you quickly adjust playback parameters of any selected region or note. **(B)** You configure the defaults for the Hear menu editing options using the Defaults dialog box. **(C)** With the Dynamic Levels dialog box you can set the level of any dynamic symbols as an absolute value or a percent of the total dynamic range. **(D)** If you are using the Macintosh's built-in playback capabilities, this dialog box allows you to assign pitch offsets (in cents) to every note, providing a way to audition microtonal and other alternative tuning systems.

Music Publisher

There is a good deal of confusion about the Australian notation software, Music Publisher. The reason for this confusion is that the program has changed publishers several times, and in one case, the publisher changed names. Originally published by a company called Graphic Notes, it was later offered by a company called Repertoire (which is also the name of the font that the program requires). The name of the company publishing Music Publisher is now Music Publisher (the same as the program itself).

Music Publisher's 36-key Presto keypad was discussed in Chapter 21. Note that the keypad is required to use the program. Therefore, the software is not copy-protected, because the only way you can get the keypad is to buy the program. You will have to become adept at the Presto keypad to enter music quickly with Music Publisher. This is not as hard as it sounds. In fact, after a single day, you'll be functionally efficient with the keypad. Give it a few more days and you'll be flying.

I have seen copyists who regularly use the Presto keypad achieve the same speed of entry as you can attain with MIDI input. The Presto keypad has the additional advantage of offering less opportunities for input errors than MIDI. On the other hand, it is undeniably more like typing than playing an instrument, which might make you feel more like a data-entry laborer than a musician while you are using it.

Be sure to configure your Presto keypad exactly as described in the manual. This isn't simply a matter of plugging it in anywhere on the ADB. Depending upon your machine, it will have to be located in a specific position on the Bus. Also, although mice can be added to and removed from the ADB while your Macintosh is powered up, the Presto keypad must be introduced on the Bus while the Macintosh is off.

If you have been following the development of Music Publisher, you will be happy to know that the current version (2.5.2 at the time of this writing) does not require you to "pretend" that you are in treble clef when you enter music in any of the C clefs. Now you can type a C key while in soprano, alto, mezzo-soprano, tenor, or baritone clef and actually have a C appear on the staff. Also, the terminology used by the program is gradually eliminating Australian colloquialisms.

Music Publisher takes a keyboard approach to various other types of editing, for example, assigning rhythms, repositioning notes and accidentals, adjusting stem length, and so on — you use the arrow keys and keyboard shortcuts.

Music Publisher is, as its name implies, for music publishers (or copyists), who know in advance what music they will be entering. Moving music from system to system, inserting measures, adding staves to systems, editing (for example, cutting, copying, and pasting — even transposing) more than a single voice at a time and similar operations that you normally take for granted during the compositional process are extremely difficult, if not impossible, using Music Publisher.

Provided that you are looking at a rough draft of the music you want to enter, Music Publisher offers many unique options to make your task more efficient. Many of the features found only in Music Publisher are designed to support repetitive entry of a large body of music in identical formats.

The first way Music Publisher streamlines your task is by allowing you to create a library of system setups. When you choose Add a System from the menu, you are presented with a list of types of systems. The program comes with six systems built into it: Melody (single staff), Piano, Piano/Vocal, SATB/Piano, Accompaniment (small staff above grand staff), and Organ. You can add as many custom systems as you like, and these are instantly accessible in the Add a System dialog box. Unlike most other programs (ConcertWare+MIDI excepted), which lock you into a single system layout for the entire piece, Music Publisher offers you the option to switch system formats whenever you want. You can change every next system manually or

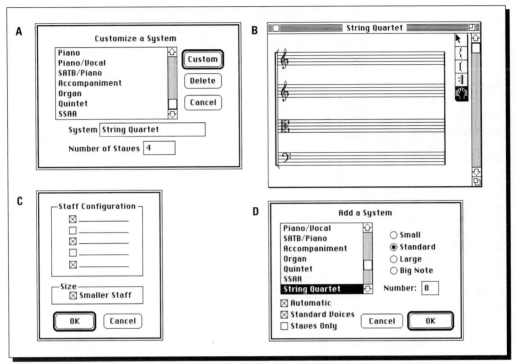

Figure 22-19: Music Publisher's Customize a System option. **(A)** Selecting Customize a System presents this dialog box, where you can name and specify the number of staves for the system you want to add to the available system format list. **(B)** Your newly created system appears in this window, where you can assign default clefs, brackets, and braces; configure barline interconnections; and change inter-staff spacing. **(C)** This dialog box lets you change the number of lines per staff. Note that it is possible to show only staff lines 1, 3, and 5 (another feature unique to Music Publisher). Here you can also designate the size of individual staves. **(D)** Subsequently, when you choose Add a System, your custom system appears along with those built into the program. Custom systems are stored in Music Publisher's Prefs file in your System Folder and are therefore available in any document you create.

tell the software to continue automatically generating systems of the last selected format as you input the notes (see Figure 22-19).

Music Publisher's Tab Rulers option allows you to create right and left indents, notate music in columns, and mix system types on a single line. You can store tab rulers for later retrieval from the Retrieve Tab Ruler menu option, a feature that significantly speeds up complex formatting operations (see Figure 22-20).

The ability to deal with chunks of music from a semantic standpoint is unfortunately missing from most music notation programs, except this one. Music Publisher lets you select a region of a voice and assign it a unique name, for example, Introduction, Theme 1, Verse 1, Chorus, Solo transition, and so on.

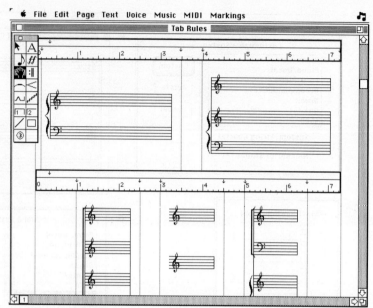

Figure 22-20: Music Publisher's Tab Rulers option is one of the most powerful features of the software. This window illustrates some of the uses of tab rulers, including right and left indents, music in columns, and mixing multiple system formats side by side. Unlike custom systems (see Figure 22-19), tab rulers are stored with the document you are working on and are only available within that document.

Whenever you name a region, it is automatically added to the Select Section hierarchical pop-up menu. Choosing it from this menu automatically selects the named section at the point where you originally defined it. Then it's easy to copy the selection and paste it in wherever you want. It's like having a database of reusable material accessible by a single menu access. The current version imposes some limitations on this procedure: Regions defined as sections must begin and end at barline boundaries and they cannot include multiple staves in the horizontal domain.

The Align option is a feature of Music Publisher that makes it particularly suitable for projects in which you want to incorporate a good deal of text (such as a music theory text or course materials). This functions exactly like similar options that are standard in graphics programs.

Music educators and researchers preparing essays or books of musical examples will be happy to know that Music Publisher copies data to the Clipboard in PICT format. This ensures that the font information is retained in the word processor or page-layout program into which you are pasting your musical examples. This feature is slightly less flexible than that offered by ConcertWare+MIDI (where you can draw a selection rectangle around any arbitrary region and copy it as a PICT). In Music Publisher, your PICT copies are limited to entire systems that begin and end on measure boundaries.

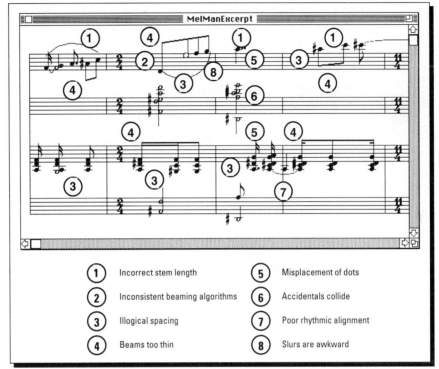

Figure 22-21:
Pyware's Music
Writer with
some of its
undefeatable
notation flaws
indicated.

①	Incorrect stem length	⑤	Misplacement of dots
②	Inconsistent beaming algorithms	⑥	Accidentals collide
③	Illogical spacing	⑦	Poor rhythmic alignment
④	Beams too thin	⑧	Slurs are awkward

Music Writer

If the cost of Pyware's Music Writer were $100 (or better yet, shareware) instead of $600, it might be possible to discuss it from the standpoint of "you get what you pay for." However, the program *does* cost $600 and thus carries the implication that it should perform at a certain level of professionalism. I am sorry to report that it fails miserably in this regard. The software is buggier than any of the programs that I am obliged to refer to as beta versions in this chapter. In addition, it has hard-coded notation errors in a significant number of areas (see Figure 22-21).

It is simply impossible to produce a correct and decent-looking piece of music with Music Writer. It pains me immensely to have to make a statement of this kind, because I know that some well-intentioned programmer spent long and hard hours laboring on this program, and I am well aware of the fact that developing notation software is possibly the most difficult and challenging type of music software programming to undertake. Perhaps future versions of the software will show improvements.

The developers of Music Writer obviously took Encore as a model, with a bit of Professional Composer (see "Professional Composer" in this chapter) thrown in for good measure. Unfortunately, many of the newer and more useful features found in those other two programs have been omitted in Music Writer. The palettes are laid out very similarly to those of Encore, and the dialog boxes, while different in appearance, often attempt to offer the same groupings of functions. You need only look at the screen to see the similarities (see Figure 22-22).

Hard-coded notation errors: A complete list of Music Writer's offenses in this category would be rather lengthy. Some of the more notable undefeatable errors include: incorrect stem lengths, ridiculously inconsistent diagonal beaming algorithms, illogical spacing, misplacement of dots, misalignment of key signatures and meter signatures when all staves are not identical, some incorrect signatures for minor keys (for example, the signatures for A♭, D♭, G♭, and C♭ minor are all incorrectly notated as sharp key signatures), and illegal time signatures (for example, 4/17, 4/23, and so on — in fact, any number can be the denominator of a time signature). From an aesthetic point of view, beams are too thin, stems are too thick, and slurs are downright ugly.

MusicProse

Coda released MusicProse in 1989, its second program based on the ENIGMA kernel (see "Finale"). The software started out as a sort of "Finale Junior" with eight staves available. Now in its version 2.1 release, supporting 32 staves and a host of new features, it's hard to refer to MusicProse as "Junior" anymore. If you are trying to get the most bang for your buck, MusicProse is probably the way to go.

MusicProse is a second-generation ENIGMA program. Many of the user interface problems found in Finale have been remedied in MusicProse. The number of dialog boxes has been reduced by a factor of four compared to Finale. Eight of Finale's tools have been dropped from MusicProse, and the remainder have been combined into the eight MusicProse tools. This required simplifying some of the tools as well as stripping out some of the functionality in certain cases (usually the missing options are the more esoteric ones). See Figure 22-22.

It's easiest to describe MusicProse in terms of what it lacks compared to Finale. Notable omissions are engraving configurations, non-standard key signatures, complex meter signatures, staves with other than one or five lines, implode and explode options, selectable and configurable spacing tables, search and replace, PostScript shape designer, playback configuration of expression markings, real-time MIDI transcription, dual-port MIDI output, global optimization (MusicProse requires each staff to be optimized individually), and built-in macros. MusicProse comes with a part extraction utility that offers identical features to those built into Finale.

Hyperscribe is Coda's patented real-time MIDI input option, which provides for on-screen display of transcriptions *while* you play them in (the screen updates as you reach every next barline). The engine transcribes up to four rhythmically

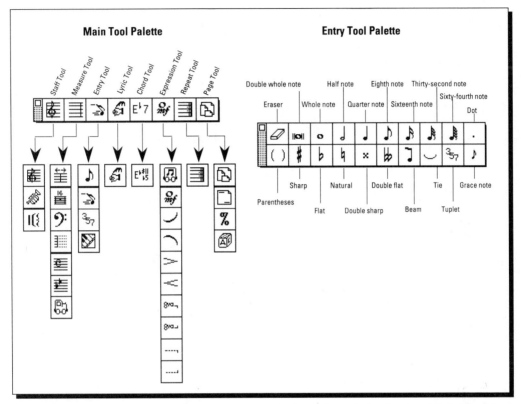

Figure 22-22: Main Tool Palette. MusicProse combines multiple Finale tools into a single palette item. Missing altogether from MusicProse's palette are Finale's Arbitrary Music, Page Add/Remove, Transcription, Time Dilation, Score Expression, Mirror, Note Mover, and MIDI Tools. **Entry Tool Palette.** The simple note entry palette is very similar to that of Finale, except for the horizontal orientation and the addition of beaming and tuplet options.

independent voices at a time and correctly determines the spellings of notes (sharps, flats, double-sharps, and double-flats). You are free to play with tempo fluctuations because you supply the ongoing beat with a tap, typically using a foot pedal, although any note or momentary MIDI switch can be used. For more information, see "Human-triggered synchronization" in Chapter 26, "Film and Video Applications."

Many of MusicProse's features that do correspond to those offered in Finale have a slightly reduced number of options. Hyperscribe is a good example. Where Finale lets you choose between four different quantization configurations while you are playing (by hitting a key or control that you designate as the switch to enable one of four sets of rules defined in advance for each "state"), MusicProse only allows a single quantization setup for this real-time input method.

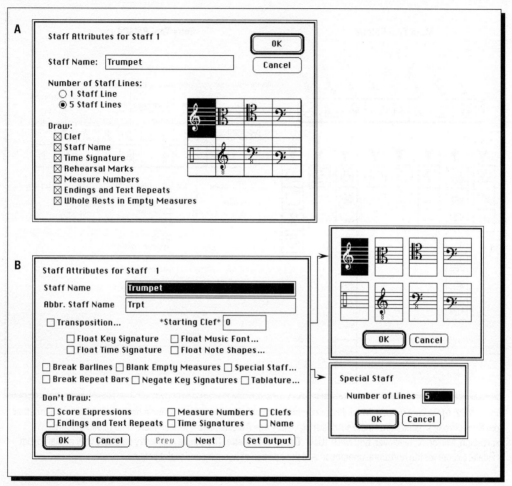

Figure 22-23: Comparison of **(A)** MusicProse's Staff Attributes options accessible by way of the Staff Tool menu with those of **(B)** Finale's Staff Attributes Tool.

In other cases, MusicProse's user interface has merely been simplified, while the functionality of Finale is retained. Figures 22-23 through 22-26 place some of these controls side by side for the purpose of clarifying both these points. Note that dialog boxes not previously used in the section on Finale have been chosen for inclusion here.

Figures 22-23 through 22-26 make it clear that an interface to ENIGMA doesn't need to be convoluted to be powerful. MusicProse is suitable for all applications except engraving, and it might even be used to produce published music, providing the program's defaults were acceptable. The simplicity of the user interface makes this program suitable for all ages, even the very young, which is something one could never say about Finale.

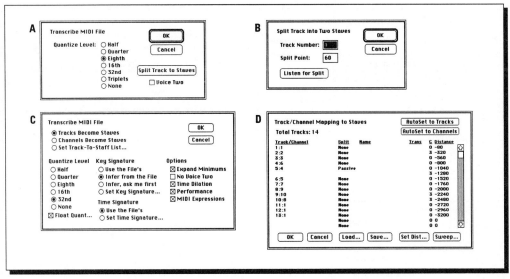

Figure 22-24: Comparison of **(A** and **B)** MusicProse's SMF Import options with those of **(C** and **D)** Finale.

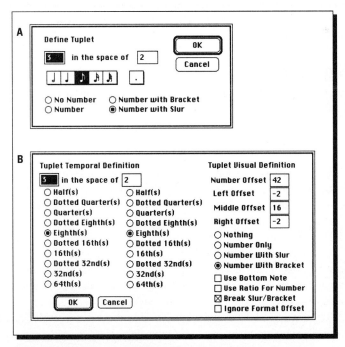

Figure 22-25: Comparison of **(A)** MusicProse's Tuplet options accessible by way of the Entry Tool menu with those of **(B)** Finale's Tuplet Tool.

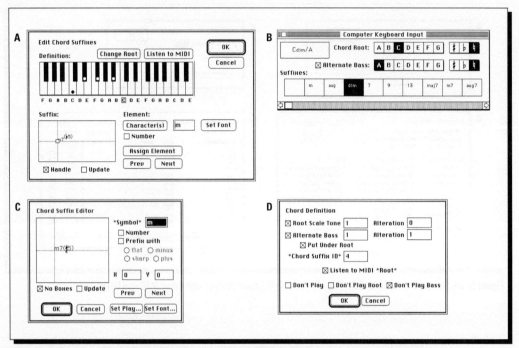

Figure 22-26: Comparison of (**A** and **B**) MusicProse's Chord Defining options accessible by way of the Chord Tool with those of (**C** and **D**) Finale's Staff Chord Tool.

Nightingale

Temporal Acuity's Nightingale (in beta-test at the time of this writing) represents the culmination of two decades of work by recognized notation authority Don Byrd. The software is suitable for any type of user — composers, orchestrators, arrangers, copyists, and engravers.

Because Finale is the only program that comes close to Nightingale (or vice versa, depending upon how you look at it), this discussion intentionally presents comparisons with respect to certain issues.

Nightingale delivers most of the power of Finale with the ease of use of Encore. You can consult the feature tables at the end of this chapter to see how far Nightingale goes. The programmer placed paramount importance on user interface issues. This resulted in an operational speed and logic unsurpassed by any other software. Don Byrd acknowledges a major influence from PARC's unreleased Mockingbird — in fact, the author of Mockingbird, John Maxwell, suggested the name Nightingale.

A good example is Nightingale's implementation of page view. The current version of the program does not offer a scroll view because you can display consecutive pages on the screen simultaneously. You can configure the layout of pages on the screen however you like (for example, one long row of pages, one vertical column, or any number of horizontal rows).

The difference between other programs' page view and Nightingale's display of consecutive pages is that all edit and input operations are applicable to any page, anywhere, at any time, and at any zoom magnification (see Figure 22-27). Contiguous and discontiguous selection can span page boundaries as well. In this context, scroll view is irrelevant. In fact, Nightingale's implementation of page view raises serious questions about the usefulness of scroll view in general. Except in the case of orchestral scores that have only a single system per page, you are always able to see more of your music at a time in page view than in scroll view. After using Nightingale for a while, one begins to appreciate the lack of confusion that results from not having to operate in a separate display mode when accomplishing certain types of editing. These edits invariably have a major impact upon the formatting of the page — but you first have to switch to the page display mode to see this impact. The music is eventually printed on pages anyway. Of course, scroll view does have the advantage of displaying contour relationships between measures that might not be adjacent in page view.

Nightingale offers a seamless merging of graphics- and rule-based orientation. In contrast to many notation programs, when Nightingale applies its own rules, they are usually correct. You can manually override nearly all rules that the program employs and you can configure most of the rules yourself (see Figure 22-28). Almost any symbol is draggable with the mouse. Alternatively, you can use Get Info..., Set..., or Modifier Info... to precisely edit the minute details of any symbol (or, in the case of Set..., group of symbols).

Several of the program's rules cannot be altered by the user. This occurs when there is simply no question regarding the validity of the principle in question. For example, you cannot change the clef or key signature at the beginning of any system except the first one. According to CMN practice, key signatures and meter signatures for all systems except the initial one are picked up from the end of the preceding system, a process that results in clef changes at the beginnings of systems other than the first one.

Notice the setting for "Mouse shake maximum time" in the first screen of Figure 22-28. This refers to one of many user-interface enhancements provided by Nightingale to speed up notation. Shaking the mouse at the tick speed (60ths of a second) that you specify toggles the arrow cursor on. Shaking it again reverts the cursor back to your previous tool. Other speedy input enhancements are aimed at mouse entry. Once you have clicked the screen, you can access any durational value by holding the Command key down and moving the mouse horizontally. This causes the cursor to cycle through available durational values. When you let the mouse button up, the current rhythmic value is entered at the point of the

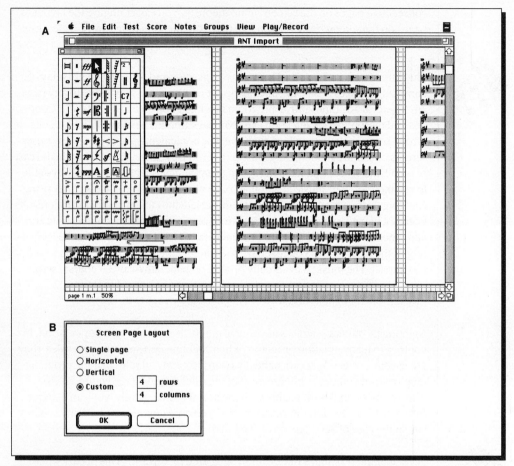

Figure 22-27: (A) The main entry screen of Nightingale with rows of pages displayed at 50% reduction. All edit and input operations are available for any page at any time, including contiguous and discontiguous selections over page boundaries. Note the resizable, user-configurable symbol palette. Items with three dots beneath them lead to dialog boxes. The Message box at the lower left corner of the screen always displays the most important and relevant information about the symbol or action that you are currently editing or performing. Normally, it displays the page number and measure number of the insertion point as well as the magnification percentage. At other times it offers hints as to what action you need to take to, for example, stop playback or recording, how to quickly exit a formatting screen, or displays the next word that will be entered by the Flow In Text command. Nightingale has an extensive, built-in on-line Help facility, too. **(B)** The Screen Page Layout dialog box lets you configure the display of pages.

original click (dynamics are treated similarly). At the same time, you can hold the Shift key down and move the cursor up and down to cycle through accidentals. These options let you enter a note of any durational value, with any accidental, all with a single mouse click. Most programs require multiple clicks combined with menu, palette, or Macintosh keyboard actions to accomplish this simple feat.

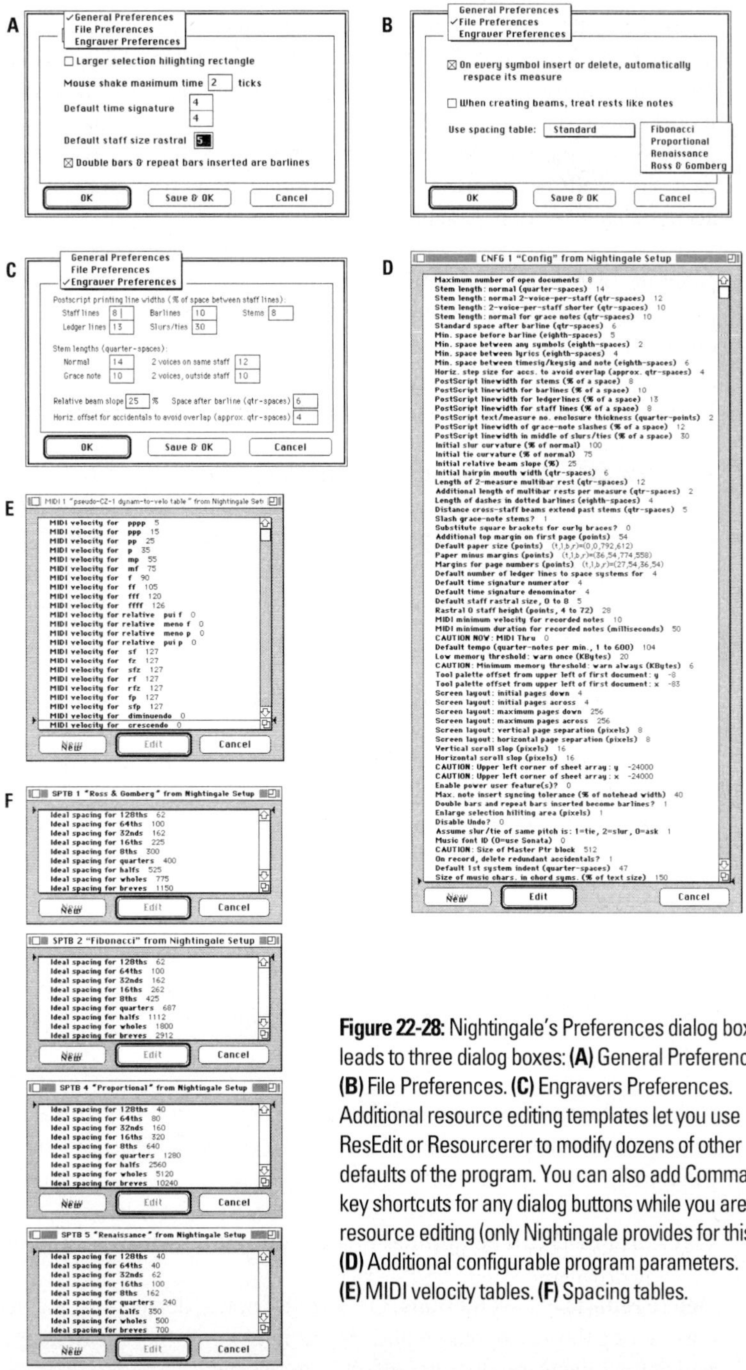

A
- ✓General Preferences
- File Preferences
- Engraver Preferences

☐ Larger selection hilighting rectangle

Mouse shake maximum time [2] ticks

Default time signature [4]/[4]

Default staff size rastral [■]

☒ Double bars & repeat bars inserted are barlines

[OK] [Save & OK] [Cancel]

B
- General Preferences
- ✓File Preferences
- Engraver Preferences

☒ On every symbol insert or delete, automatically respace its measure

☐ When creating beams, treat rests like notes

Use spacing table: [Standard] [Fibonacci / Proportional / Renaissance / Ross & Gomberg]

[OK] [Save & OK] [Cancel]

C
- General Preferences
- File Preferences
- ✓Engraver Preferences

Postscript printing line widths (% of space between staff lines):
Staff lines [8] Barlines [10] Stems [8]
Ledger lines [13] Slurs/ties [30]

Stem lengths (quarter-spaces):
Normal [14] 2 voices on same staff [12]
Grace note [10] 2 voices, outside staff [10]

Relative beam slope [25] % Space after barline (qtr-spaces) [6]
Horiz. offset for accidentals to avoid overlap (approx. qtr-spaces) [4]

[OK] [Save & OK] [Cancel]

D — CNFG 1 "Config" from Nightingale Setup

Maximum number of open documents 8
Stem length: normal (quarter-spaces) 14
Stem length: normal 2-voice-per-staff (qtr-spaces) 12
Stem length: 2-voice-per-staff shorter (qtr-spaces) 10
Stem length: normal for grace notes (qtr-spaces) 10
Standard space before barline (qtr-spaces) 6
Min. space before barline (eighth-spaces) 5
Min. space between any symbols (eighth-spaces) 2
Min. space between lyrics (eighth-spaces) 4
Min. space between timesig/keysig and note (eighth-spaces) 6
Horiz. step size for accs. to avoid overlap (approx. qtr-spaces) 4
PostScript linewidth for stems (% of a space) 8
PostScript linewidth for barlines (% of a space) 10
PostScript linewidth for ledgerlines (% of a space) 13
PostScript linewidth for staff lines (% of a space) 8
PostScript text/measure no. enclosure thickness (quarter-points) 2
PostScript linewidth of grace-note slashes (% of a space) 12
PostScript linewidth in middle of slurs/ties (% of a space) 30
Initial slur curvature (% of normal) 100
Initial tie curvature (% of normal) 75
Initial relative beam slope (%) 25
Initial hairpin mouth width (qtr-spaces) 6
Length of 2-measure multibar rest (qtr-spaces) 12
Additional length of multibar rests per measure (qtr-spaces) 2
Length of dashes in dotted barlines (eighth-spaces) 4
Distance cross-staff beams extend past stems (qtr-spaces) 5
Slash grace-note stems? 1
Substitute square brackets for curly braces? 0
Additional top margin on first page (points) 54
Default paper size (points) (t,l,b,r)=(0,0,792,612)
Paper minus margins (points) (t,l,b,r)=(36,54,774,558)
Margins for page numbers (points) (t,l,b,r)=(27,54,36,54)
Default number of ledger lines to space systems for 4
Default time signature numerator 4
Default time signature denominator 4
Default staff rastral size, 0 to 8 5
Rastral 0 staff height (points, 4 to 72) 28
MIDI minimum velocity for recorded notes 10
MIDI minimum duration for recorded notes (milliseconds) 50
CAUTION NOW: MIDI Thru 0
Default tempo (quarter-notes per min., 1 to 600) 104
Low memory threshold: warn once (KBytes) 0
CAUTION: Minimum memory threshold: warn always (KBytes) 6
Tool palette offset from upper left of first document: y -0
Tool palette offset from upper left of first document: x -63
Screen layout: initial pages down 4
Screen layout: initial pages across 4
Screen layout: maximum pages down 256
Screen layout: maximum pages across 256
Screen layout: vertical page separation (pixels) 8
Screen layout: horizontal page separation (pixels) 8
Vertical scroll slop (pixels) 16
Horizontal scroll slop (pixels) 16
CAUTION: Upper left corner of sheet array: y -24000
CAUTION: Upper left corner of sheet array: x -24000
Enable power user feature(s)? 0
Max. note insert syncing tolerance (% of notehead width) 40
Double bars and repeat bars inserted become barlines? 1
Enlarge selection hiliting area (pixels) 1
Disable Undo? 0
Assume slur/tie of same pitch is: 1=tie, 2=slur, 0=ask 1
Music text font ID (0=use Sonata) 0
CAUTION: Size of Master Ptr block 512
On record, delete redundant accidentals? 0
Default 1st system indent (quarter-spaces) 1
Size of music chars. in chord syms. (% of text size) 150

[New] [Edit] [Cancel]

E — MIDI 1 "pseudo-CZ-1 dynam-to-velo table" from Nightingale Setup

MIDI velocity for pppp 5
MIDI velocity for ppp 15
MIDI velocity for pp 25
MIDI velocity for p 35
MIDI velocity for mp 55
MIDI velocity for mf 75
MIDI velocity for f 90
MIDI velocity for ff 105
MIDI velocity for fff 120
MIDI velocity for ffff 126
MIDI velocity for relative poi f 0
MIDI velocity for relative meno f 0
MIDI velocity for relative meno p 0
MIDI velocity for relative poi p 0
MIDI velocity for sf 127
MIDI velocity for fz 127
MIDI velocity for sfz 127
MIDI velocity for rf 127
MIDI velocity for rfz 127
MIDI velocity for fp 127
MIDI velocity for sfp 127
MIDI velocity for diminuendo 0
MIDI velocity for crescendo 0

[New] [Edit] [Cancel]

F — SPTB 1 "Ross & Gomberg" from Nightingale Setup

Ideal spacing for 128ths 62
Ideal spacing for 64ths 100
Ideal spacing for 32nds 162
Ideal spacing for 16ths 225
Ideal spacing for 8ths 300
Ideal spacing for quarters 400
Ideal spacing for halfs 525
Ideal spacing for wholes 775
Ideal spacing for breves 1150

[New] [Edit] [Cancel]

SPTB 2 "Fibonacci" from Nightingale Setup

Ideal spacing for 128ths 62
Ideal spacing for 64ths 100
Ideal spacing for 32nds 162
Ideal spacing for 16ths 262
Ideal spacing for 8ths 425
Ideal spacing for quarters 687
Ideal spacing for halfs 1112
Ideal spacing for wholes 1800
Ideal spacing for breves 2912

[New] [Edit] [Cancel]

SPTB 4 "Proportional" from Nightingale Setup

Ideal spacing for 128ths 40
Ideal spacing for 64ths 80
Ideal spacing for 32nds 160
Ideal spacing for 16ths 320
Ideal spacing for 8ths 640
Ideal spacing for quarters 1280
Ideal spacing for halfs 2560
Ideal spacing for wholes 5120
Ideal spacing for breves 10240

[New] [Edit] [Cancel]

SPTB 5 "Renaissance" from Nightingale Setup

Ideal spacing for 128ths 40
Ideal spacing for 64ths 40
Ideal spacing for 32nds 62
Ideal spacing for 16ths 100
Ideal spacing for 8ths 162
Ideal spacing for quarters 240
Ideal spacing for halfs 350
Ideal spacing for wholes 500
Ideal spacing for breves 700

[New] [Edit] [Cancel]

Figure 22-28: Nightingale's Preferences dialog box leads to three dialog boxes: **(A)** General Preferences. **(B)** File Preferences. **(C)** Engravers Preferences. Additional resource editing templates let you use ResEdit or Resourcerer to modify dozens of other defaults of the program. You can also add Command key shortcuts for any dialog buttons while you are resource editing (only Nightingale provides for this). **(D)** Additional configurable program parameters. **(E)** MIDI velocity tables. **(F)** Spacing tables.

The issues discussed in the previous paragraph illustrate one of the other advantages to a well thought out user interface: the reduction of the number of required user actions to accomplish a task. For example, comparing Nightingale to Finale, input and editing operations are reduced by approximately a factor of four (or more), that is, what takes 12 user actions to accomplish in Finale (including clicks, menu selections, and dialog box entry) often takes three steps or less in Nightingale. You really feel it in the options that take three to six steps in Finale, but are accomplished by a single action in Nightingale.

Nightingale introduces a number of unique features that are not found in other programs. A few of the more notable ones are listed below, but there are many others.

Unlimited number of files open simultaneously (depending upon RAM).

Spacebar taps change duration during step entry. You can "advance the clock" during step entry by hitting the spacebar. For example, if the current duration is an eighth, playing a chord and then hitting the spacebar changes its duration to a quarter; hitting the spacebar again changes it to a dotted quarter, and again to a half. You can develop a rhythm to this type of entry (which is familiar to Performer users).

Features that clarify the structure of the score. Every note that starts at the same time, no matter what voice or staff it's in, is part of a structure called a "sync." Show Sync Lines displays a vertical dotted line through each sync. This is sometimes helpful in complicated situations to see what Nightingale thinks the voice structure is. Another feature supporting structural clarification is Look at Voice. This lets you dim all voices but one. Dimmed notes, rests, slurs, and beams cannot be selected or manipulated. All notes and rests inserted go into the "looked at" voice, regardless of the staff.

Show duration problems. When this is checked, any time a measure is displayed with a total duration that disagrees with the time signature, the entire measure is shaded.

Commands to change the number of measures in a multimeasure rest. Among other things, this allows you to put a cue within what would otherwise be a multimeasure rest construction.

Play command can be applied to any contiguous or discontiguous selection.

Delete redundant accidentals. On selected notes, deletes any accidental that, considering the key signature and the traditional rule that accidentals last to the end of their measure, does not affect its note's pitch.

Single-click auto-slurs or ties to the next note. This is a real time-saver for ties and two-note slurs. A bonus is that these auto-slurs almost never need additional user adjustment.

Slurs and ties are associated with a voice instead of a staff. This means that if the voice crosses to another stave, the slur or tie follows it.

Symmetrical adjustment of slurs and ties. Shift-Option-clicking either of the inner control points of a slur adjusts the other inner control point symmetrically. Shift-Option-clicking either end point causes the inner points to scale accordingly during dragging. Another unique feature is that ties also have four control points (this is where symmetric dragging is extremely useful).

Cross-system slurs, ties, and beams rejoin if reformatting makes the measures adjacent. This is another advantage of tying such elements to the voice rather than the staff.

A click followed by holding the mouse button down on a marking highlights the note it is attached to. This solves a problem found in many programs that require you to select a note before you can edit its associated markings. You may have lost track of what note you attached the marking to. In Nightingale, you can edit markings directly, but you would use this feature for symbols that you have dragged to a considerable distance from their associated note or that you have otherwise forgotten their attachments.

Accidentals typed into chord symbols are automatically set to the prevailing music font. Many programs require you to use a number sign or a lowercase *b* to indicate sharps or flats in chord symbols (you're out of luck when it comes to natural signs). Nightingale gets around this by automatically converting the appropriate symbols to the music font.

Threading for selection. Holding the mouse button down with the Command key depressed lets you "thread" a selection path through the music. You don't have to click or Shift-click notes to extend selection. Any note or symbol that the cursor rolls over while threading is automatically added to the selected region.

Clarify rhythm. This command only functions when it would improve rhythmic readability to divide every selected rest, note, or chord into a series of rests, tied notes, or chords, based on when they start within their measures and with respect to the prevailing time signature. For example, in 4/4 time, a dotted-quarter note starting on the fourth eighth note is rewritten as an eighth tied to a quarter; in 6/8 time, it is left as is.

Change durations without closing up space (toggleable). This allows you to, for example, change a region of quarter notes to eighth notes without changing their physical location within the measure. Empty space is opened up — now you can add additional notes or perhaps an eighth rest between each note that was originally a quarter note.

Simultaneously edit multiple data types in discontiguous selections. The Set... command knows what types of data are involved in your selection and presents you with a pop-up menu that allows you to deal with the parameters of each individual symbol type.

Many current-generation Macintosh notation programs take the approach of assigning music to voices rather than staves (ConcertWare+MIDI, Encore, Lime, and Music Publisher). Note that Finale's implementation of voice assignment links specific voices to staves, so most of the advantages of this approach are not available. With Nightingale, you can have any number of independent voices per staff (up to 100 on 64 staves). Rather than fix the number of measures per system or systems per page, as other programs force you to do, Nightingale optionally lets you set a maximum number for each of these formatting considerations. The software then determines the optimum number based upon internal algorithms, the current spacing table, and the respace percentage setting.

There are two powerful formatting options: the Master Page (global formatting) and the Work on Format (local formatting) screens. While viewing the Master Page, you can (by dragging) set margins, spacing between staves, and spacing between systems (see Figure 22-29). Once again the Message box provides crucial feedback about the current margins, expressed in inches. You can also add staves (including one-line staves), bracket staves, designate barline connections, and set staff sizes (with a useful preview of what your on-screen display will resemble at the current staff size). If the current magnification is large enough, the Master Page displays the instrument name, channel, and patch number across the top staff of each part. It also shows the instrument's part balance velocity and transposition for any part for which they're not zero. Invoking the Instrument command, or double-clicking any staff of a part, brings up the Instrument dialog box for that part and lets you edit all of this information and more. This dialog resembles the Instrument dialog box in Professional Composer (see later in this chapter), with the addition of settings for initial program change and velocity balance.

In the Work on Format mode, you can format staves and systems individually by dragging them up and down (only the current staff or system is affected, unlike formatting on the Master Page). You can also drag the lines dividing systems up and down. A new menu appears, offering you the option to Hide Staff or Show All Staves. Hiding a staff is similar to Finale's optimization feature, except that it is applied on an individual basis with a single user action, as opposed to the six or so actions required to individually optimize systems in Finale (note that Finale offers a one-step global optimization option that is not available in Nightingale).

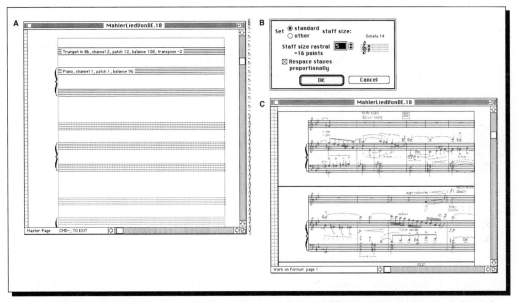

Figure 22-29: (A) Nightingale's Master Page with draggable staves. Note the MIDI information displayed at the head of each staff. **(B)** The Staff Size dialog box. Proportional Respace is a unique feature that lets you specify that the white space between staves will be changed by the same factor as the height of the staves in question when you change the staff size. **(C)** Work on Format window with draggable items indicated. Work on Format turns the staves from gray to black, and everything else (excluding staff brackets and braces) from black to gray. This is to emphasize that staves are now in the foreground for editing and "content" symbols are in the background and are untouchable.

Unlike Finale, Nightingale lets you hide staves that have music entered in them, if you like.

As with Finale, third-party utilities have been developed for Nightingale. The first to appear is John Gibson's NGtoAI. Like Finale, Nightingale lets you save documents as pure PostScript or EPS format files. The NGtoAI utility converts Nightingale EPS files into Adobe Illustrator format and is equivalent to Illustrious Music for Finale (see "Finale"). Unlike Illustrious Music, NGtoAI will ship with Nightingale.

With Nightingale, you are continually aware that the programmer has meticulously studied the territory to devise a more efficient means to the end we are all searching for: beautiful (and correct) pages of printed music that can be produced with as little effort as possible.

NoteWriter

Passport Designs's NoteWriter (originally marketed under the name of MusPrint by Triangle Resources) is the first of the completely graphics-based notation programs covered in this chapter. The software went through three major versions (and numerous updates) prior to Passport taking it over. This lengthy history has resulted in a highly evolved program. NoteWriter is a professional engraving tool designed to handle any type of music you want and to provide PostScript output up to the standards of even the most demanding publishers. You would be hard-pressed to find a score, no matter how ancient or contemporary, that NoteWriter could not tackle.

Like all graphics-oriented programs, the concept of hard-coded notation rules is non-existent. The quality of the output depends entirely upon your own notational knowledge. This means that you can create just about any type of music you can imagine, breaking notational conventions at will, and adding any contemporary graphic notational elements that you want. It also makes it very easy to notate all-too-common notational exceptions, which can have you figuratively standing on your head when trying to do the same thing in rule-based systems.

The main things you give up are MIDI input, proofhearing, and editing operations that require the software to understand the underlying musical syntax. Normally (and particularly with first-generation systems in this category), this includes change of key, chromatic, modal, and enharmonic transposition (quasi-diatonic transposition is often possible because it simply involves shifting the graphic symbols with respect to the staff lines), automatic metrical organization (including beaming, augmentation, diminution, and bar-to-bar advance), and spacing. However, NoteWriter *does* understand enough about musical syntax to accomplish most of those operations. This is somewhat contrary to the documentation's assertion that "the system understands relatively little about the syntax of music." In fact, if you enable the Defaults option, it turns out that NoteWriter also understands the rules regarding the placement of rests, clefs, barlines, beams, and ledger lines. In some ways, this is the best of both worlds.

Now the bad news. NoteWriter has a significant learning curve. It's safe to say that the learning curve of NoteWriter in the world of graphics-oriented programs is comparable to the learning curve of Finale in the category of hybrid rule- and graphics-based systems. Fortunately, that's about the only bad news.

You choose symbols either by selecting them from the palette or Command List (see Figure 22-30) or by typing their codes into the COMMAND line. Many symbol codes can accept modifiers. For example, the code "a" is an angled eighth note beam, while "a2" is an angled sixteenth note beam. Likewise, "q" is a quarter note, and "qsh." is a dotted sharped quarter note.

NoteWriter comes with nine symbol libraries (see Figure 22-31) that supplement the set of CMN symbols. The program also lets you maintain your own symbol libraries. You can copy material from NoteWriter documents to add to a symbol library, or you can bring graphics in from any Macintosh graphics program (bitmapped or object-oriented). The graphics are stored in PICT format and are resizable when pasted onto your NoteWriter document. It's like having a built-in scrapbook that is always on-line.

NoteWriter's innovative Quick-Scrawl input method was discussed in Chapter 21. You can also use the numeric keypad to enter notes based on the intervallic relationship of the previous note or notes with the note to be entered. For example, pressing *2* on the numeric keypad enters a note that is a second above the previous note. To enter a note a second below, you would hold the Enter key down at the same time as pressing the 2 key. This is a very interesting approach to Macintosh keyboard note entry (but it requires that you know the names of the intervals with some fluency).

About the only other thing that NoteWriter doesn't allow is directly pasting copied music into a word processor or page-layout software. Fortunately, you can save any selection as an EPS file to add to documents created by such programs. The software also lets you save files in PostScript or MacPaint formats (these cannot be reloaded into the program for editing).

Figure 22-30: The main entry screen of NoteWriter with various user interface features labeled. The miniature page at the upper right highlights the currently visible area. You can drag the highlighted area to navigate in the full-size window. Note the on-screen keyboard. You can hear what you play on this through the Macintosh speaker (square wave). If the Vertical Alignment Bar is present (gradated T-Square with arrows and associated black registration dots), playing notes on this keyboard auto-advances the cursor. The buttons at the bottom of the keyboard affect the last pitch entered. The buttons on the left let you configure the spellings of black notes.

Professional Composer

Mark of the Unicorn's Professional Composer was the first software that attempted to address the basic features demanded by professional musicians. The first version of the program appeared in 1984, the official year of the Macintosh's birth.

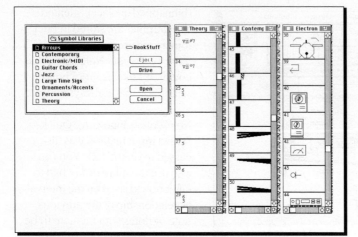

Figure 22-31: Symbols contained in the nine standard NoteWriter Symbol Libraries. You can easily create your own libraries or combine elements of existing libraries. Because NoteWriter does not offer part extraction, you can use a symbol library to store copied staves (making up an individual part) and then paste these into separate parts documents. The Theory, Contemporary, and Electronic/MIDI symbol libraries are pictured in this illustration.

When Adobe Systems's music font appeared, they were also one of the first to retrofit their software with limited PostScript compatibility (font characters only).

The developers of Professional Composer were the first to solve the problems created by including text (lyrics) with music. Tabbing between words (rather than using the spacebar) attaches the next word or syllable to the next note. These notes drag their attached text with them when spacing changes are required through the reformatting of accompanimental musical passages.

Unfortunately, very little continued development has taken place in the seven years since the program's release. There have been updates and upgrades, but these have typically been to ensure compatibility with Apple's System software updates. Occasionally, new features were added. A glance at the original 1984 manual makes it clear that more than 95 percent of the current software features were in place at the original release — this notwithstanding the literally thousands of suggestions that the company has received from their users. It's a curious situation, considering the fact that Mark of the Unicorn's other main product, Performer, has often been rated as the most popular MIDI sequencer in the Macintosh music community. The company's response to user feedback through an ongoing series of upgrades to Performer has doubled or possibly tripled that product's power through the addition of necessary and requested features.

Professional Composer is the epitome of a rule-based system. It does let you alter some of its default spacings and symbol offsets, but for the most part these are limited to global adjustments. As the name implies, the program is intended for composers. Because of the hard-coded notation errors built into the software (see Figure 22-32), there are no viable applications for copyists or engravers.

The software lets you configure some of its rule sets for individual documents; for example, the instrumental ranges settings (see Figure 22-33). The program was the first to offer an option to check instrumental ranges, now also available with a

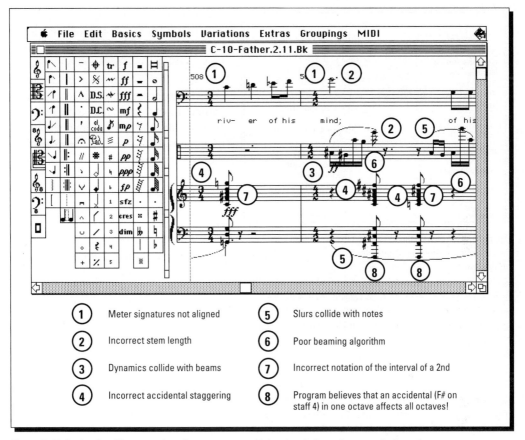

1. Meter signatures not aligned
2. Incorrect stem length
3. Dynamics collide with beams
4. Incorrect accidental staggering
5. Slurs collide with notes
6. Poor beaming algorithm
7. Incorrect notation of the interval of a 2nd
8. Program believes that an accidental (F# on staff 4) in one octave affects all octaves!

Figure 22-32: Professional Composer's main entry screen with hard-coded notation errors indicated.

similar implementation in Nightingale. Because you can configure the ranges, you can have different settings for the upper and lower notes playable by your particular ensemble. If you are composing a piece for junior high school band, you can set the instrumental ranges accordingly, and the software highlights the notes that are beyond the limits of your performers.

Professional Composer offers other automated proofreading options besides Check Range. Check Rhythms (available from the Extras menu) seeks out any measures that do not contain the correct number of beats for the prevailing meter signature. The program's audio proofhearing options are not very useful because only four voices sound at a time, regardless of whether you use MIDI or the Macintosh speaker. This causes notes to be dropped or clipped at random — exactly what you *don't* want to happen during proofhearing. Furthermore, even with the simplest of music, playback stutters every few barlines. This might make you think that you have rhythmic problems, when in fact it is the software's playback engine that

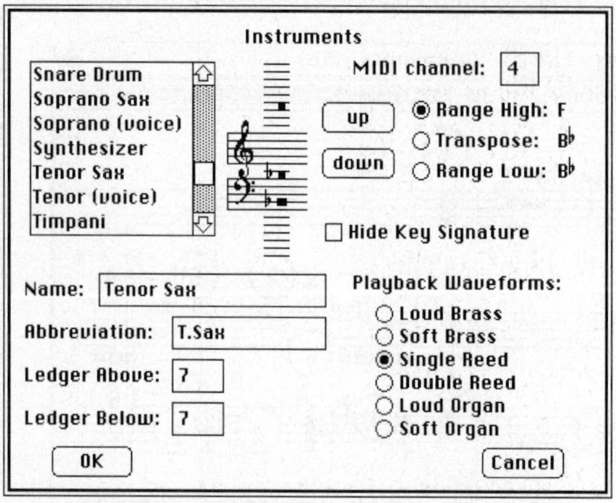

Figure 22-33: Professional Composer's Instruments dialog box lets you assign a number of attributes to each staff. By adjusting the Ledger Above and Ledger Below settings, you define the spacing between each staff. You cannot exceed the number of ledger lines that you enter here. This dialog box is also where you assign staff playback characteristics such as MIDI channel and internal Macintosh speaker sound. Note that in either case, only four voices play back at a time. The most innovative use of this dialog box is to set instrumental ranges and transpositions for the 42 instruments built into the software or any additional instruments that you happen to add. Selecting the Range High, Range Low, and Transpose radio buttons activates the Up and Down buttons for that particular parameter, allowing you to move the reference note on the staff to the left in increments of a half step. Subsequently, when you choose Check Range from the Extras menu, the software uses these limits to methodically go through your composition and highlight each note that is defined as unplayable by each particular instrument.

is at fault. Ties are not observed during playback, an unfortunate situation that can have you scrambling all over your score looking for ties you have left out, when in reality you haven't left out any. To add insult to injury, ties of altered notes over barlines force the tied note to be restruck at the unaltered pitch, further negating the usefulness of proofhearing. Because of these errors, using Professional Composer's playback options for proofhearing is not advised, unless your music has no ties.

Several MIDI sequencers offer the option to save files in Professional Composer's proprietary file format. Performer and Vision are two sequencers with this option. Earlier problems of Professional Composer treating triplets as a morass of tied 128th notes have been solved in the latest version. Also, Professional Composer makes an admirable and usually successful attempt to add dynamics to files that have been imported in this way. It is also the only software that automatically inserts inter-staff clef changes for files brought in from one of these sequencers. Of course, the reason that it does this is because the software does not display music beyond the number of ledger lines specified in the Instruments dialog box (see Figure 22-33), so this is the only way you are able to see music that would otherwise be out of the preset ledger line range.

 Hard-coded notation errors: Imagine a typewriter that prints "ain't" every time you type the word "aren't." You access your word processor's Search and Replace function to correct the error globally, but it refuses to change this word. You even try backspacing over the characters, but that doesn't work. This is the way Professional Composer handles the display of accidentals on chords. All accidentals are strung out to the left reading from left to right in a diagonal line, completely contrary to correct notational practice. There is no way to defeat this serious flaw.

Another undefeatable notation error is incorrect stem length. Professional Composer does not lengthen stems to accommodate beams or in cases where notes appear on ledger lines. If a flagged note has more than three ledger lines, its stem will not even touch the staff. Beam angles are often incorrectly calculated. From time to time, meter signatures do not line up with one another.

Another problem is the handling of accidentals in multiple octaves. The rules built into Professional Composer state that an accidental in one octave affects all notes of the same pitch class in all octaves. The developers are convinced that this is accepted practice. For example, a C♯ at middle C would cause the software to treat all Cs in all octaves as being sharped and not display accidentals with them —a music teacher's nightmare. Fortunately, unlike the problems mentioned in the previous two paragraphs, you can fix this by adding sharps manually to all the offending notes, although this can of course become extremely time-consuming.

One final major headache with Professional Composer is that its copy-protection scheme can unpredictably interfere with the protection schemes used by other software manufacturers. If you are running an installed version of Professional Composer and trying to simultaneously launch certain installed programs by Opcode (and other vendors), your other software will come up asking for a key disk, making you think that you may have lost a hard disk installation.

SpeedScore

Frederick Noad's SpeedScore (distributed by ThinkWare) is the most recent notation program to appear. Like NoteWriter, the software takes a graphics-oriented approach, so many of the same considerations apply. At the current time, MIDI is not available for such programs, nor are editing operations that require the software to know the musical connotations of a symbol (such as chromatic transposition).

The majority of symbols in SpeedScore are PostScript font characters. You use the cursor to "stamp" these characters onto the score page. As the name implies, the software provides many features to let you enter music quickly. Some of these are rather innovative. For example, when you click any symbol with the arrow cursor, the cursor turns into that symbol, ready to be placed wherever you want. This single user-interface enhancement speeds up music entry to such an extent that once you have used it, the action seems so logical that you wonder why no other software supports it. Facilitating this feature is the fact that the arrow cursor itself can be retrieved at any point by pressing the spacebar.

Recognizing that all input would be accomplished with the mouse, the developers of SpeedScore often provide innovative ways to make multiple functions available depending upon whether you click or drag. Sometimes additional functions are accessible by holding the Option key down in conjunction with a click or drag. For example, with the tie/slur tool selected, clicking a notehead generates a tie to the next available identical note (sort of a "seek-and-tie" mission), while dragging the

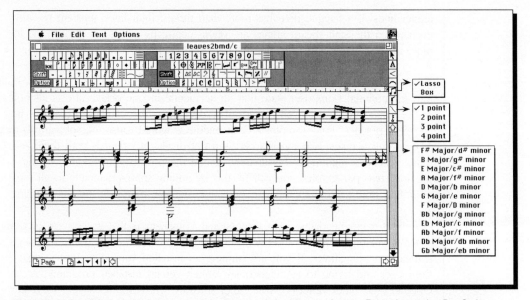

Figure 22-34: SpeedScore is a graphics-oriented program optimized for speedy entry. Every element is a PostScript object. The ToolBox (font reference) at the top of the screen can be hidden once you learn the character set. Note the palette above the right scroll bar. Some of these items lead to the pop-up menus pictured. The triangular arrows at the bottom of the screen are called Push-Pull buttons. These are used to push or pull (toggled with the Option key) entire staves or text lines for formatting considerations.

mouse initiates the creation of a slur. Clicking the note with the Option key down reverses the direction of the tie. Both ties and slurs have four control points for later tweaking.

Stemming, beaming, and staff connections are automated as well. There are three stemming options. You can choose to have stems remain in one direction until you change it, to follow the normal switch direction at middle staff-line rules, or to invert the normal rules (very useful for adding a second voice on the same staff). To beam notes, you simply select the beaming tool and drag a box around the notes you want to beam. As soon as you let your cursor up, the notes are correctly beamed (even though graphics-oriented, SpeedScore understands rhythmic values). Adjustment of beam height and angles is accomplished by dragging the beam with the mouse, as in most non-graphics-oriented software. Finally, staff connections are automated in the following manner: Selecting a brace or barline and dragging through the staves you want to connect stretches and snaps the symbol to the appropriate points (see Figure 22-34).

Selecting a region and copying it places a PICT image on the Clipboard, complete with the proper music fonts. This makes SpeedScore ideal for creating examples and then placing them in a word processor or page-layout document. The manual

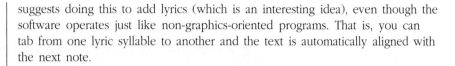
suggests doing this to add lyrics (which is an interesting idea), even though the software operates just like non-graphics-oriented programs. That is, you can tab from one lyric syllable to another and the text is automatically aligned with the next note.

It is difficult to imagine a program that is simpler to operate and yet as powerful as SpeedScore. Much of this comes from the ingenious exploitation of the mouse, as described above — notice that the program does not have a single dialog box. Because the software was in beta-test at the time of this writing, it is likely that additional features will be added or the implementation of certain features slightly modified.

Subtilior Press

David Palmer's Subtilior Press is the only shareware notation program currently available. The program is a HyperCard stack designed for mensural music (for example, to create musical examples and scores of Medieval and Renaissance pieces). You save documents in MacPaint format and paste them into any word processor that supports paint format files.

A series of dialog boxes take you through the page setup process, during which you select the number of lines per staff, the number of staves, their grouping into systems, and various other attributes (including attributions). See Figure 22-35.

Feature Comparisons

The complexities of music notation require the software dedicated to this task to address a vast number of possibilities. The following tables organize these features into 18 categories. Rather than group the tables together, they are presented one at a time, with commentary for those feature subcategories requiring further explanation.

Decisions, decisions

Be forewarned that it will not serve you to proceed down the list and simply pick the program that has the most features — unless you happen to be both an engraver and a composer. In most cases, the more features a program has, the bigger it is (which often means it runs more slowly) and the harder it is to master. Also, you're paying for those extra features even if you never use them — your payment will be measured both in time and money. Instead, you should make a serious effort to determine what features you need in a notation program and decide on your purchase accordingly. Keep in mind that some of these programs are optimized for specific tasks, such as copying, engraving, orchestration, or composition, while others try to cover all bases.

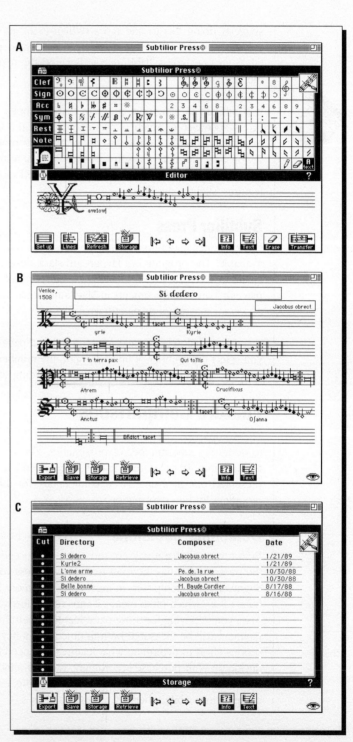

Figure 22-35: (A) Following the setup stage, a single staff appears at the bottom of the screen. You select symbols from the palette at the top of the screen and click them onto the lower staff. For black notes, you hold down the Option key and click the appropriate white note. You can add any symbols you want by pasting them into an empty box on the palette or replacing another symbol with it. **(B)** After completing a staff on the input card, clicking the Transfer button brings you to the page you initially formatted during the setup stage. **(C)** You can store your pages on other cards. An index entry is created that allows you to retrieve your page or pages for later editing, export it to a MacPaint document, or delete it for good.

Product abbreviations used in the feature tables:

ConcertWare+MIDI	CW
Deluxe Music Construction Set	DM
Encore	Enc.
Finale	Fina
HB Engraver	HB. E
Lime	Lime
Music Publisher	Pub.
Music Writer	MW
MusicProse	MP
Nightingale	Night
NoteWriter	NW
Professional Composer	PC
SpeedScore	QS

General Information

Table 22-1 presents basic information about each program, often drawing from the main points covered in the other tables.

Minimum system

This indicates the absolute minimum firepower you need to run the software. It is in the manufacturers' interest to be able to say that a program runs on a minimum system — of course they don't mention that it may take ten minutes to copy four bars of music when you run it on such a system. Try any software on the computer you plan to use it on and bring a stopwatch.

Developers want to sell programs, so they keep their published RAM and hard drive requirement figures as low as possible. In some cases, you may only be able to do a single-page lead sheet using the minimum RAM requirements — but it works, so they can state that fact in their advertisements. Likewise with the hard drive. Notation files tend to be anywhere from ten to 100 times larger than MIDI sequencer files of the same data (like page-layout files vs. straight text). You may be able to manipulate a single-page lead sheet with a floppy-drive-based system, once again allowing the company to claim that a hard disk is not required, but anything larger is likely to require disk swapping of an intensity that can cause more wrist cramps than using a pencil.

Approach

There are three approaches to music notation: mainly rule-based, graphics- and rule-based, and completely graphics-based. The distinctions between these approaches are discussed at the beginning of this chapter.

Working metaphor

Some programs require that you view and edit music as if it were on a virtual page on the computer screen. Others take the continuous scroll approach — the music appears as if on one long staff, which might be 20 or 30 feet long in the real world. Such programs often provide a page view option, so that you can see what things look like when printed out. Sometimes it is not possible to edit in page view. The more elegant programs let you switch back and forth between page view and scroll view with no restrictions on the type of editing available in either domain. WYSIWYG means that the image displayed on your computer monitor is identical or extremely close to the one appearing on your printed output. It's easy to check by making a single printout. For detailed information see Table 22-10.

Table 22-1: General features

	CW	DM	Enc.	Fina	HB. E	Lime	Pub.	MW	MP	Night	NW	PC	QS
Version	5.14	2.5	2.5	2.61	1.1	.04	2.52	1.1	2.1	.99	2.69	2.3M	beta
System 7 compatible version	●	●	●	●	●	●	●	◗	●	●	●	●	●
Minimum System	512	512	Plus	(Plus)	Plus	(Plus)	Plus	Plus	Plus	Plus	Plus	512ke	Plus
User Suitability													
Student	●	◗	●	●		●		◗	●	●	●	◗	●
General Musician	●	●	●	◗		◗		◗	●	●	●	●	●
Composer	●	◗	●	●		●		◗	●	●	◗	◗	◗
Orchestrator/Arranger			◗	●		●			●	●		◗	
Copyist		●	●	◗	◗	●			●	●	◗		◗
Engraver/Publisher			◗	●	●	●	●		◗	●	●		●
Approach													
Mainly rule-based	●				●		●	●				●	
Graphics- and rule-based		●	●	●		●			●	●			
Completely graphics-based											●	—	●
Working Metaphor													
Scroll	●	●	●	●	◗			●	●			●	
Page		●	●	●	◗	●	●		●	●	●		●
MIDI													
Real-time input	●	◗	●	●		●	◗	●	●	●	NA		NA
Step-time input	●	●	●	●	●	●	●	●	●	●	NA	●	NA
Output	●	●	●	●	●	●	●	●	●	●	NA	●	NA
SMF input	●		●	●	●			●	●	●	NA		NA

Table 22-1: General features (continued)

	CW	DM	Enc.	Fina	HB. E	Lime	Pub.	MW	MP	Night	NW	PC	QS
SMF output	●	❯	●	●				●	●	●	NA		NA
Max. channels supported	8	16	32	32	16	16	16	16	16	16	NA	4	NA
Max. channels per staff	8	1	4	4	1	2	4	1	1	1	NA	1	NA
Miscellaneous													
Number of files open	1	1	16	1	1	1	UL	1	1	UL	1	1	UL
No copy protection	●	●	●	●	●	●	❯	●	●		●	●	
On-line help						❯		●	●			❯	
Manual (# of pages)	186	112	195	878	164	89	210	116	406	300	160	208	40+
Ave. # months for upgrades	12	24	6	4	NA	24	6	24	6	NA	12	24	NA

Staff Setup

Table 22-2 addresses elements of a page of music that need to be fixed prior to entering musical notes.

Staves

There is a correlation between price and the number of staves a program supports. If you want to notate symphonies, of course you need more than eight staves, but you might not need more than 32. If you use notation software to drive your synthesizers, your software should provide for at least 16 staves, one for each MIDI channel — 32 or 64 if your MIDI interface supports that many. You may never need more than one staff size but if you do, make sure the program permits them. The capability to intermix staff sizes is a consideration if you are notating chamber music, concerto reductions, and some piano-vocal music where you might want the instrumental or vocal parts to be on a smaller size staff or staves.

The number of lines per staff is a consideration for some percussion parts where you might want 1-, 2-, 3-, or 4-line staves. In most cases you can use a 5-line staff. However, if you wish to notate certain types of string tablature you will probably want 6-line staves, and if you're notating medieval music you will have similar requirements. Don't expect that all software can notate two or more rhythmically independent voices on the same staff, either (e.g., one with the stems up and one with the stems down). If a program claims to do this, check to see that it offsets the interval of a second correctly when two or more voices are present on one staff.

If you are using a program for composition, a major consideration is how easy it is to add a staff *after* you have decided the initial score layout. Similarly, check to see how easy it is to insert new measures between those that are already full of music.

Clefs

Clefs are an individual case. Don't forget that Chopin got through most of his entire *oeuvre* using treble (G) and bass (F) clefs exclusively.

Key signatures

Most notation programs support the standard circle of fifths key signatures, but if you need to mix sharps and flats in a signature, make sure your software allows this. However, don't expect that all programs provide for key signature cancellations, the cases where you change key in the middle of a piece and want a bank of natural signs indicating which accidentals in the previous key are no longer in effect. If you never change keys within a piece, then this is of no concern.

Meter signatures

Like key signatures, most programs provide for the standard time signatures, because that is almost all you ever need. If complex (e.g., 2 + 4/8), fractional (e.g., 3.5/4), or multiple (different number of beats but with coinciding barlines) meter signatures are a characteristic of your musical language, and your software options are limited. Provisions for alternating signatures (e.g., 3/4 + 6/8) such as Leonard Bernstein used in the tune *America* are almost non-existent, but there are obvious work-arounds for this special case — for example, change the meter signature at every bar or use triplets, if your software allows it.

Measure numbers

Typical measure number schemes include having measure numbers at the first measure of each system, every measure, or by an increment that you specify (e.g., every 5 or 10 measures). For symbol collision considerations, the better programs allow you to position the location of measure numbers relative to the barline on both an individual and global basis. You should be able to turn off measure numbers for designated staves. For example, in an orchestral score, you will only want measure numbers above the flutes and violins. If your software provides for empty staff suppression, you'd better make sure that there is a provision to force measure numbers to the top staff no matter what instrument appears there. For example, orchestral systems often appear with the flute staff removed by an empty-staff suppression algorithm. It is a nice feature to be able to substitute rehearsal letters instead of numbers for measure numbering. In either case, these markings should be placed automatically by the software rather than individually by you.

Table 22-2: Staff setup features

	CW	DM	Enc.	Fina	HB. E	Lime	Pub.	MW	MP	Night	NW	PC	QS
Max. # of staves	8	32	64	128	50	64	100	40	32	64	40	40	15
Min. # of lines per staff	5	5	5	0	1	1	1	(3)	(1)	1	(0)	5	(0)
Max. # of lines per staff	5	5	5	128	8	12	5	5	5	5	(UL)	5	6
Maximum voices per staff	8	2	4	4	8	2	4	2	2	100	UL	2	UL
Tablature, auto-convert to				●●							●○		●○
Number of staff sizes	1	1	4	UL	19	2	4	1	1	9+	2	1	UL
Mix sizes: in system, page			●●	●●	●●	●●	●●				●●		●●
Intermix systems of different number of staves			●	●	●		●	●	●	●	●	●	
Instrument names (other than manual text)		●	●	●		●		●	●	●		●	
Center (multistave insts.), abbreviation, multiline		○○●	○○	◗●○		●○○		◗○○	●●○	●●●	●●●	●●○	●●●
Auto-enter whole rest	●		●	●		●			●	●	●	●	
Set transposing staff	●	◗	●	●	●	●	●	●	●	●		●	
Assign MIDI chan. to staff voices on same staff		●	●	●	●	●		●	●	●		●	
Separate chans. to sep. voices on same staff	●		●	●	●	●	●						
Assign separate chans. to other types of data on staff				●									
Initialize staff with: patch, volume, pan	●○○	●○○	●●○	●○○		◗◗◗	●○○	●○○		●○○			

Brackets

	CW	DM	Enc.	Fina	HB. E	Lime	Pub.	MW	MP	Night	NW	PC	QS
Brace, bracket, thick bar	●●○	●●○	●●●	●●●	●●○	○●●	●●●	●●○	●●●	●●●	●●◗	●●○	●●◗

Clefs

	CW	DM	Enc.	Fina	HB. E	Lime	Pub.	MW	MP	Night	NW	PC	QS
Treble, bass, alto, tenor	●	●	●	●	●	●	●	●	●	●	●	●	●
Baritone, percussion			○●	●●	●●	●●	◗●	○●	●●	●●	●●	○●	●●
Movable: C, treble, bass				●●●	●●○					●○○	●●●		●●●
Clef w/8va, small clef	◗○		●○	●●	●●	●●	○●	●○	●●	◗●	○●	●○	
Multiple clefs per measure			●	●	●		●		●	●	●	●	●

Key Signatures

	CW	DM	Enc.	Fina	HB. E	Lime	Pub.	MW	MP	Night	NW	PC	QS
Standard	●	●	●	●	●	●	●	◗	●	●	●	●	●
Custom (mix sharps & flats)				●							M		M
Quartertone, affect playback				●○		○●				M			

Table 22-2: Staff setup features (continued)

	CW	DM	Enc.	Fina	HB. E	Lime	Pub.	MW	MP	Night	NW	PC	QS
Define accidental placement				●	♪								
Cautionaries, cancellations	○●		○●	●●	●●	●●	●○		●●	●●	MM	○●	MM
Different key sigs on diff. staves (for reasons other than instrument transpos.)	●			●		●	●	●		●	●	●	●
Meter Signatures													
Numerator range	1-16	1-99	1-16	1-99	1-127	1-99	1-999	1-99	1-96	1-99	1-99	1-99	UL
Denominator range	2-16	1-16	1-32	1-32	1-128	1-64	1-128	1-64	1-64	1-64	1-99	1-64	UL
Additive numerator				●			●				●		●
Fractional numerator				●							●		●
Additive denominator				●							●		●
Combined (alternating)				●							●		●
Multiple: equal # of beats				●						●	●		●
Different # of beats but barlines coincide				●		●	●			♪	●	●	●
Barlines do not coincide				♪		●				♪	●		●
Restrike wherever desired			●	●	●	●	●	●	●	●	●	●	●
Invisible, ignore (free time)	♪			●●		●○	●○	●●	●○	○●	●●	○●	●●
Measure Numbers, Rehearsal Markings													
Every measure	M	●	●	●			●	●	●	●	M	●	M
First meas. of every system	M	●	●	●		●	●		●	●	M	●	M
Specify increment	M		●	●			●	●		●	M	●	M
Always on top staff	M			●			♪		●	●	M		M
Arbitrary control	●		●	●		●					M		M
Letters instead of numbers				●							M		M
Specify font	●			●		●			●	●	M		M
Specify location	●		●	●			♪	♪	●	●	M	●	M
Enclosures	●			●					●	●	M		M
Hide or move individually	●			●							M		M
Distinction between measure numbers and rehearsal markings			●	●				●	●	●		●	

Notation Basics

Ironically, most notation software considers many now-standard 20th-century notational practices to be the exception rather than the rule. Most programs are optimized for music using symbols and graphical practices that were established by the end of the 19th century (see Table 22-3).

Some people bemoan the fact that current-generation software cannot handle purely graphic scores. One very influential article actually went so far as to print excerpts from Karlheinz Stockhausen's *Electronic Study No. 2* and James Tenney's *String Complement*, two scores that use absolutely no CMN symbols. The implication was quite strong that something was lacking from notation programs because they couldn't handle these one-of-a-kind scores. What the writer failed to mention was that in these cases, a graphics program such as Claris MacDraw, Adobe Illustrator, or Aldus FreeHand would have been much more appropriate for the task.

Beaming

Most notation programs now offer diagonal beaming. If you are notating music for anything more than instrumental parts or lead sheets, you will want to be able to adjust the height and angle of each beam on an individual basis, again, often to resolve symbol collisions or correct wrong guesses by the software. Provisions for unconventional (e.g., 3+3+2 groupings), cross-staff, and center beaming (notes on both sides of the beam) is of importance to publishers and engravers.

Tuplets

For some reason, notation programmers often labor under the false assumption that no one needs to notate any tuplet greater than a triplet. Some provide for triplets and quintuplets at best. The ratio in the Range column of Table 22-3 indicates the maximum tuplet size. With this in mind, 99:99 means that any tuplet up to 99 in the time of 99 is notatable, including, for example, 87 in the time of 91. A lone 3, 5, or 7 indicates a limitation to triplets, quintuplets or septuplets, respectively. Nested tuplets refer to tuplets within tuplets, for example, a quintuplet that has a nested triplet on its middle beat.

Slurs

Slurs are one of the hardest things for a programmer to accomplish in a notation package. Don't expect any software to place a slur in its proper place automatically — you usually want some control over the shape of the slur to remove collisions between slurs and noteheads and stems. Many programs provide little handles on the slurs called control points, which allow you to stretch them into a new shape as if they were rubber bands. The more control points you have, the easier you can clean up collisions. PostScript uses Bézier curves (named after the French mathematician Pierre Bézier) to manipulate curved lines. Bézier curves provide zero, one, or two "magnetic" levers to be associated with every point on a line. Moving these control points or handles determines how one part of a curve transitions to the next. TrueType uses quadratic curves. Quadratic curves are easier to compute, making them preferable on slower computers, but they appear less elegant when output.

Amazingly, I have seen a notation program criticized in print more than once because it makes a distinction between slurs and ties. These two types of notational symbols are completely different. If a program treats them as identical, that's when you have to worry, not the other way around.

Table 22-3: Basic notation features

	CW	DM	Enc.	Fina	HB. E	Lime	Pub.	MW	MP	Night	NW	PC	QS
Barlines													
Single, double, thin-thick	●○●	●○●	●●●	●●●	●●●	●●●	●●●	●●●	●●●	●●●	●●●	●●●	●●●
Repeat, dotted, invisible	●○○	●○○	●●●	●●●	●○●	●●●	●○●	●○●	●○●	●●●	●●♪	●○○	●○○
Beaming													
Automatic conventional, unconventional	●♪	●●	●●	●●	●●	●♪	●○	●○	●♪	●♪	●♪		
Diagonal, adjust angle, height		●●●	●●●	●●●	●○○	●●●	●●●	●○○	●○○	●●●	●●●	●○○	●●●
Specify global height				●	●	●				●		●	
Cross staff, center (reverse)	●○			●●	●○	●●	●●		●●	●●			●●
Double beaming, splayed				●●		●●		●○	●●	●○		●○	●○
Beam over rests, barlines		●○	●♪	●●	●○	●●	●●	●○	●○	●●	●●	●○	●●
Secondary break control		♪		●		●	●			●			♪
Default thickness control				●	●	●					●		
Default max. slope control				●	●	●					●		
Default spacing control				●	●	●					●		
Tuplets													
Range	3	(3 or 5)	16:16	UL	UL	64:64	99:99	2 thru 9	99:99	127:127	UL	UL	UL
Nested				●							●		
Bracket, slur, neither	●○○	●○○	●○○	●●●	●○●	○○●	●●●	♪○○	●●●	●○●	●●●	♪○○	●●●
Break, use ratio, no number			●○○	●●●	●○●	○○●	●○●	●●●	●○●	●●●	●●●	●○●	●●●
Adjust height, angle			●●	●●		●●		●○	●●	●●	●●	●○	●○
Set default display				●	●		●		●	●			

Table 22-3: Basic notation features (continued)

	CW	DM	Enc.	Fina	HB. E	Lime	Pub.	MW	MP	Night	NW	PC	QS
Repeat Signs (MIDI)													
MIDI functional, text also	●●	●●		●●					●○		NA		NA
Max. # endings, repetitions	2, 9	2, 1		UL					UL		NA	9, 1	NA
Nested, repeat counter passes data to other parameters	◗○			●●					●◗		NA		NA
Slur Control													
Number of control points	0	0	3	4	4	2	3	2 or 4	3	4	3	0	4
Auto position endpoints	●			◗	●					●		●	●
Specify default thickness				●	●	◗			●	●	●		
Specify default taper				●	●	●			●				
Slur Control (continued)													
Specify default inset				●	●								
Cross staff, dotted slurs				●○	●○	●●	●●	●○	●○	●●	●●		
Tie Control													
Number of control points	0	0	3	4	3	3	0	0	0	4	3	0	4
Specify default height				●	●					●			
Specify default thickness				●	●	◗				●	●		
Specify default taper				●	●	◗				●			
Specify default inset				●	●								
Octava Signs													
8va, 8vb, 15ma	●●○	●●○	●●○	●●●	●●●	◗◗◗		●●○	●●○	●●●	●●●	●●●	●●○
MIDI playback	●	●	●	●		◗			◗	●			

Symbols

Table 22-4 presents the capabilities of each program with respect to notes, rhythms, and expressive markings.

Rhythms, noteheads, and stems

The available symbol set is extremely important. If the program doesn't allow 128th notes, and all of a sudden you need to write one, well, you're out of luck. Likewise with noteheads. Some people are never going to write string harmonics, so they don't need a diamond notehead. Others never require guitar slash notation. If you want to include cues in your score, you need to be able to intermix notehead sizes on the same staff. Only you know what you're going to be notating.

At least two different stem lengths should be available for professional engraving. Normal stems are usually 7½ spaces long. When a staff includes two voices, the second voice usually has shorter stems (often six spaces or five spaces if it is outside the staff). Grace notes have even shorter stems (e.g., four spaces). Saving space vertically as well as horizontally has always been a goal of engravers and publishers because they want to save paper to cut costs.

Accidentals

It's difficult to write music without sharps and flats, so all programs include them. Check to make sure they are handled correctly. At least one program that advertises itself as being professional stacks the accidentals incorrectly when there are more than two accidentals on a chord. The same program also makes the incorrect assumption that an accidental in one octave covers all other octaves. Other things you might want in the accidental department are the option to force courtesy accidentals after a page turn on a tied note as well as the option to delete redundant accidentals between notes tied over barlines on the same page. Surprisingly, many packages don't offer this.

Expressive markings: note, staff, and score expressions

A notation program's approach to expressive markings can make or break it. Some provide too limited a set of dynamics or accents, while others allow you to expand the symbol library *ad infinitum*. Some even have a built-in editor to create your own graphic symbols. Don't assume that because a program has MIDI playback or proof-hearing that a *forte* will have any effect on the playback, or if it does, that you will have any control over just how loud that *forte* makes your music.

One consideration of expressive markings to which you should give a good deal of thought is the automation of symbol placement. Having an accent snap to a centered position over a notehead is a great aid — better if you can specify the symbol's vertical offset and better yet if you can later manually adjust the position, for example, by dragging the symbol. Another thing to hope for is the option to assign multiple symbols in one operation. For example, if you need to put staccato dots on the next 100 notes, you definitely don't want to have to assign them one at a time, nor do you want to have to tweak the vertical location of each one on an individual basis.

Table 22-4: Symbol features

	CW	DM	Enc.	Fina	HB. E	Lime	Pub.	MW	MP	Night	NW	PC	QS
Notes													
Smallest rhythmic value	32	32	128	4096	128	128	128	128	128	128	128	128	128
Largest rhythmic value	w	w	w	brv	brv	w	w	w	brv	brv	w	brv	brv
Maximum number of dots	1	1	2	12	2	1	5	2	2	8	UL	2	UL

Table 22-4: Symbol features (continued)

	CW	DM	Enc.	Fina	HB. E	Lime	Pub.	MW	MP	Night	NW	PC	QS
Specify dot offset: x, y				●●	○●	●●				●●			
Specify inter-dot spacing				●								●	
Correct in 2-part stems-down										●		●	●
Short stem provision				●		●				●			
Noteheads and stems													
Diamond, percussion, slash	●●○		●●●	●●●	●●●	●●●	●●●	●●●	○○●	●●●	●●◗	●●●	●○○
Cue, grace, headless	○◗○		○●○	●●●	●●●	●●○	●●○	○●○	○●○	●●●	●●●	○◗○	●●●
Tablature	●			●	◗					◗	●		●
Diagonal stems (for clusters)				●		●					●		◗
Use any symbol as notehead				●		●					●		
Music font size different than staff				●	●					●			
Accidentals													
Individual offset control			●	●		●		●		●	●		●
Bank offset control default			●	●	●					●			
Cautionary, bracket, 1/4-tone			●●○	●●●	●●○	●○○	●○○	●○○	●●○	●○○	●○●	●●●	●●○
"Smart" accidentals		◗		●					●				
User-defined accidental preferences				◗		●		◗			●	●	
Note Ancillaries													
Multiple placement	●			●		●						●	
Multiple adjust: vert., horiz.				●●	◗◗							●●	
Snap to grid or offset			●			●	●	●	◗		●	●	●
User-expandable library				●							●	○	
# of symbols (if fixed)	72+	0	46	UL	31	26	22	28	26	25	UL	30	21
MIDI-executable, configure	◗◗	●○		●●		●◗	●○	●●	◗○				
Dynamics, articulations, accelerandos/ritards	●○○			●●●		●●○	●○●	●●○	○●●				
Move symbols with mouse	●		●	●	●	●			◗	●	●		●
Fingering symbols	●		●	●	●		●			●	●	●	●
Staff Ancillaries													
Multiple placement	●			●	◗						●	●	
Multiple adjust: vert., horiz.	●●			●●	●●					●●			

Table 22-4: Symbol features (continued)

	CW	DM	Enc.	Fina	HB. E	Lime	Pub.	MW	MP	Night	NW	PC	QS
Snap to grid or offset	◗		●		●	◗	●	◗			●	◗	●
User-expandable library				●					●		●		
# of symbols (if fixed)	42+	8	46	UL	24	14	UL	24	18+	UL	UL	14	12+
MIDI-executable, configure	◗◗	●●		●●		●●	●◗	●●					
Move symbols with mouse	●	●	●	●	●	●	●			●	●		●
Score Ancillaries													
Multiple placement	●			●		●		●					
Multiple adjust: vert., horiz.	●●			●●	●●							●○	
Individual placement adjust	●			●	●	●		●	●		●		
Score Ancillaries (continued)													
Snap to grid or offset			◗	○	●	●		◗			●	●	
User-expandable library				●					●		●	●	
# of symbols (if fixed)	text	1	46	UL	text	text	text	text	UL	text	text	text	text
MIDI-executable, configure	◗◗	●●		●●				●●	◗○				
Control score/part visibility	●			●		●							
Move symbols with mouse			●	●	●	●	●	◗	●	●	●		●
Marking Design													
Text expression designer				●					●	●	●		
Note expression designer				●									
Graphic designer, PostScript			◗●	●●							●●		
Draw on page			●		●	●	●				●		●
Miscellaneous													
Enclose symbol	◗			●	◗	●			◗	●	◗		◗
Import/export symbol libraries from file to file				●							●		
Override auto placement	●		●	●	●	●		●	●	●	●		●
Multiple assignment of pattern (e.g., downbow-upbow; dot-dot-tenuto)											◗		
Piano pedals (graphic)			●		●		●			●○	●	●	
Harp pedal diagrams				◗							●		

Chord Symbols

Many programs now offer the option to place chord symbols over staves. Some offer text symbols only, others provide for fretboard notation, and still others allow both. At least one program analyzes the music at the desired location and figures out the correct chord symbol to notate. The best implementation of chord symbols automatically transposes the chord symbols when the music is transposed to a new key — saving you a good deal of work. Some programs allow you to specify a unique MIDI channel for chord symbols to play back on, complete with voicing options. If your notation software does not have a chord symbols option, you can sometimes get around this by creating a lyric line above the staff and using one of the many commercial chord symbol fonts (both text-based and fretboard fonts are available). See Table 22-5 for more on chord symbol features.

Table 22-5: Chord symbol features

	CW	DM	Enc.	Fina	HB. E	Lime	Pub.	MW	MP	Night	NW	PC	QS
Text, fretboard	●●	▶▶	●●	●●	▶●			●○	●●	●○	●●	●○	●●
MIDI, user-definable voicing				●●									
Transposable			●	●					●	●			
Auto-chord recognition				●					●				
User-expandable library	●			●					●		●		
# of symbols (if fixed)	UL	UL	64	UL	UL			18+	UL	UL	UL	31	UL

Input (non-MIDI)

Most non-MIDI input strategies are some variation on the theme of selecting a rhythmic value from an on-screen palette or specifying a duration with the computer keyboard and then clicking the note at its desired location with a mouse. There are other systems. Some turn the computer keyboard into a veritable musical keyboard by remapping the keys, and some require positioning notes with the cursor arrows instead of the mouse (see Table 22-6). Some innovative systems include Music Publisher's Presto Pad (for specifying pitch) for their own Macintosh software. Chapter 21 discusses all of the options for score input.

Table 22-6: Input (non-MIDI) features

	CW	DM	Enc.	Fina	HB. E	Lime	Pub.	MW	MP	Night	NW	PC	QS
Mouse with note-palette	●	●	●	●	●			●	●	●	●	●	●
Keyboard-switch rhythm values	●	●	●	●	●		●	●	●	●	●	●	●

Table 22-6: Input (non-MIDI) features (continued)

	CW	DM	Enc.	Fina	HB. E	Lime	Pub.	MW	MP	Night	NW	PC	QS
On-screen keyboard		●				●					●		
Hear entered note: MIDI, Mac	●●	●●	●○	●○		●●				●○	○●	●●	
Mac keyboard emulates music keyboard	●		●	●	◗				●		●	◗	
Move cursor with Mac keyboard	●	●		●	◗	●	●	◗	●		●	●	
Presto Pad, Quick Scrawl							●○				○●		
Duration error detection	●	◗	●	●		●	●			●			
Clip, tie, tie and shift	○○●			●●●									
Auto beam			●	●	◗	●	●		●		●	●	◗
Auto bracket tuplets	●		●	●	●		●		●			●	

Input (MIDI)

Integrating MIDI into notation software has been the norm for the past several years. Many people now use notation programs in place of MIDI sequencers. But just because a company advertises MIDI capabilities in a notation program, don't be fooled into thinking that it will replace dedicated sequencer software. At this time, very few notation programs come close to offering the wide range of MIDI data editing options that has come to be expected from a sequencer (see Table 22-7).

Real time

Real-time MIDI entry is not a trivial programming feat, and you should mention the software's programmers in your prayers every night if the program permits it. Real-time entry is easiest to achieve if the program supplies a metronome click for you to play to. In Table 22-7, "Without metronome" refers to software that lets you enter the beat while playing, for example, by tapping your MIDI sustain pedal. This allows you the freedom to slow down and speed up expressively as you normally would as the creative juices flow. Post-determination of the beat is the most elegant solution. In this case, you don't have to play to a click or provide one by tapping your foot. Instead, you play with complete freedom of tempo and later tell the software where the beat and barlines fall.

Most software that lets you play in music on two staves simultaneously (e.g., a piano grand staff) requires a fixed split-point. All notes above the split-point get directed to the treble staff, and those falling below it go on the bass staff. At least one program provides for a floating split-point, meaning that the software calculates an ever-changing split-point based upon the width of your finger span.

Tuplets in real-time transcription are a problem for many programs, but if you need this facility, there are some that have it.

Don't assume that because a program allows MIDI input that it will retain your velocity, controller, or tempo data. Most limit MIDI data capture to pitch. Others capture all associated MIDI data, but don't let you edit it.

Step time

Step-time entry refers to being able to specify a note's duration, either by way of the computer keyboard or mouse, and then playing the note or chord on a MIDI keyboard to specify pitch. A good feature to look for with step-time entry is the ability to "lock in" a duration, so that if you need to enter 100 sixteenth notes in a row, you don't have to specify the duration manually before you play each note. This lets you keep your hands on the MIDI keyboard, where they belong.

SMF compatibility

Now that nearly all MIDI sequencers support the SMF format, you should expect your notation program to offer similar support. If you are involved in MIDI sequencing at all, your notation software should be able to import an SMF and convert it to notation. You may already have hundreds of sequences that you want to print out in notation, and you certainly don't want to re-enter them — not when there is a computer in the loop. Furthermore, you may be surprised at how many of your friends will come crawling out of the woodwork asking you to convert their sequences into notation once you get going with a notation program.

Table 22-7: Input (MIDI) features

	CW	DM	Enc.	Fina	HB. E	Lime	Pub.	MW	MP	Night	NW	PC	QS
Real Time													
With metronome	●	♪	●	●		●	●	●	●	●			
Quantize on input	●		♪	●		●	●	●	●				
Specify rhythmic value set	●			♪					♪				
Change quantum unit during input				●									
Metronome: Mac, MIDI, vis.	●○○		●●○	○●♪		○○●	○●○	●●○	○●♪	○●○			
Count-off			●			♪	●						
Without metronome				●		●			●	●			
With real-time beat entry				●		●			●				
Post-determine: beat, barlines (meter), beaming				●●●						○●○			
Compand or best guess			●	●						●			

Table 22-7: Input MIDI features (continued)

	CW	DM	Enc.	Fina	HB. E	Lime	Pub.	MW	MP	Night	NW	PC	QS
General													
Real-time multichannel				●		●							
Discern rhythmic polyphony			◗	●						◗			
Retain data: velocities, controllers, tempo map	●○○		●●●	●●●		●●○				●●○			
Tuplets in transcription	●		●	●		●	●	●	●				
Split-point: locked, floating	●○		●○	●●				●○	●○	●○			
Hear other staves during input	●		●	◗			●	●					
Wait-for-note	●			●		●	●	●	●	◗	●		
Punch in, out, set preroll			●○○	●●●			●●○		●●○				
Ignore rests option	◗					◗	●						
General (continued)													
Set threshold: rest, note	◗●					○◗							
Input filter			●			●							
Auto enter: dynamics, slurs	●●												
Step Time	●	●	●	●		●	●	●	●	●		●	
Lock in rhythmic value	●	●	●	●		●	●	●	●	●		●	
Lock in tuplet value			●	●		●	●	●				●	
"Wide" chord entry provision			●	●		◗	●	●	●				
Retain performance info			●			●				●			
Miscellaneous													
Duration error notification	◗	◗	●	●		●	●		●			◗	
If error: clip, tie, ignore	○●●	○○●		●●●				●○○				○○●	
Tempo resolution BPM	30-450	1-240	10-400	UL		1-500	UL		1-999	1-600		1-300	
SMF Compatibility													
Import, export	●●		●●	●●	●○			●●	●●	●			
Retain: track names, key signatures, time sigs.	○●●		●●●	●●●				○●●	●●●				
Staves from channels, tracks	●●		○●	●●	●○			●○	○●	○●			
Requantize during conversion	●		●	●	●			●	●	●			
Transcribe tuplets	●		●	●	●			●	●	●			
Discern rhythmic polyphony			◗	●				●	●				

Table 22-7: Input MIDI features (continued)

	CW	DM	Enc.	Fina	HB. E	Lime	Pub.	MW	MP	Night	NW	PC	QS
Merge tracks/chans. to 1 staff	●			●				●		●			
Split track to multiple staves	●			●				●	●	●			
Auto-assign clefs				●					●				
Infer key signatures				●									

Lyric Input

The types of questions to ask yourself are how many verses you normally require and whether you need to mix fonts in the verses (e.g., most foreign language translations are in italics beneath the non-italicized original lyric). Another important feature is to be able to bind syllables to notes, so that reformatting a system of music automatically reformats the lyrics as well. Some programs offer automatic collision avoidance between lyric symbols, assuring that notes will never be spaced close enough to cause one word to overlap with another. A nice but rare feature is to be able to bulk-assign large chunks of lyrics all at once, for example, by importing them from a word processor, flowing the text in with every next syllable automatically snapping to every next note.

I have seen writers condemn a program because the software attaches lyrics (and/or dynamics) to a note. Yet this is a very desirable feature, because it assures that the lyric syllable or expressive marking moves with the note when a measure or page is reformatted. See Table 22-8 for more on lyric input features.

Table 22-8: Lyric input features

	CW	DM	Enc.	Fina	HB. E	Lime	Pub.	MW	MP	Night	NW	PC	QS
Note-syllable binding	●	▸	●	●	●	●	●	●	●	●		●	
Advance at: hyphen, space, tab	○○●		○○●	●●○	●●○	○○●	●●●	○○●	●●○	●●●		○○●	
Assign on-page	●	●	●	●	●	●	●	●		●	●	●	●
Bulk-assign			●	●					●	●		▸	
Built-in text editor				●					●				
Text editor linked to score				●					●				
Import from word processor			●	●									
Import from Clipboard	●		●	●		▸			●	●	●		●
Max. number of verses	16	UL	4	128	50	UL	UL	3	128	UL	UL	UL	UL

Table 22-8: Lyric input features (continued)

	CW	DM	Enc.	Fina	HB. E	Lime	Pub.	MW	MP	Night	NW	PC	QS
Mix fonts/sizes within lyric	●	●		●		●	●	●	●	●	●	●	●
Different fonts for each verse	●	●		●	●	●	●	●	●	●	●	●	●
Shift: forward, backward	●●		▶▶	●●					●●			▶▶	
Auto collision avoidance	●			●	●		▸	●	●	●		●	
Position individual syllables	●		●	●		●			●	●			●
Beam to lyrics option				●									
Word extension, automatic				●○			●●		●○				

Text Input
Annotative text

Annotative text refers to just about anything besides lyrics. A good example is stage directions in a musical, operatic, or theatrical work. If you use a great deal of this sort of text, you should make sure it is possible to attach it to particular measures, staves, or systems, so that reformatting your music moves the annotative text along with the specific music it is designated for.

Other text

Other text includes such automatically placed items as headers, footers, page numbers, and the like. Of course, you can add these things after printout, but their omission from the software is a good indication of a lazy programmer and should make you suspicious about other aspects of the program. See Table 22-9 for more on text input features.

Table 22-9: Text input features

	CW	DM	Enc.	Fina	HB. E	Lime	Pub.	MW	MP	Night	NW	PC	QS
Attach to note, measure, staff	●○○		○●●	●●●		●○○	○○●			●●●		○●○	
System, page	○▶	○●	●●	●●	○●	○●	○●	○▶	○●	○●	○●	○▶	○●
Assign on-page	●	●		●	●	●	●		●	●	●	●	●
Built-in text editor				●					●	●			
Text editor linked to score				●					●	●			
Import from word processor				●									
Import from Clipboard	●	●	●	●	●		●	●	●				●
Mix fonts/sizes within block				●		●	●		●				●

Table 22-9: Text input features (continued)

	CW	DM	Enc.	Fina	HB. E	Lime	Pub.	MW	MP	Night	NW	PC	QS
Different fonts for each block	●	●	●	●	●	●	●	●	●	●	●	●	●
Word processor rulers, styles				◑○			●○			○●	●○	○	●○
Justify: full, center, L or R	○●●		○●●	●●●	●●●	○●●	●●●		○●●	○○◑	●●●	◑◑◑	○●●
Move blocks with mouse	●	●	●	●	●	●	●		●	●	●		●
Cut, copy, paste text blocks	●	●	●			●	●	●		●	●	●	●
Align text blocks	●					●	●						
Headers / footers													
First page, Odd/even control	●●		●●	●●	●●				●●			●●	
Auto page numbering	●	●	●	●	●	●		●	●	●		●	
Page number offset option	●		●	●	●	●	●			●		●	

Display and selection

Consult Tables 22-10 and 22-11 for details on display and selection features, respectively.

Table 22-10: Display features

	CW	DM	Enc.	Fina	HB. E	Lime	Pub.	MW	MP	Night	NW	PC	QS
Page, scroll, piano-roll	○●●	●●◑	●●●	●●◑	●●○	●○○	●○○	○●○	●●○	●○●	●○○	○●○	●○○
Edit: page, scroll, piano-roll	○●○	●●○	●●○	●●◑	●◑○	●○○	●○○	○●○	●●○	●○●	●○○	○●○	●○○
MIDI data: graphic, text				●◑				○◑		●●			
View selected staves, voices	◑◑	●●	●●	●●	○◑	●●		●○		◑●			
Print Preview, editable	●○		●○	●○	●◑	◑●	◑●	●○		●●	●○	●○	●○
Zoom in/out, edit zoom views	◑◑			●●	●●		●○		●●	●●			
Show current measure #, real time, SMPTE	●○○	●○○	●○○	●●○						●○○		●○○	

Table 22-11: Selection features

	CW	DM	Enc.	Fina	HB. E	Lime	Pub.	MW	MP	Night	NW	PC	QS
Notes (on same staff)													
Single note	●	●	●	●	●	●	●	●	●	◑	●	●	●

Table 22-11: Selection features (continued)

	CW	DM	Enc.	Fina	HB. E	Lime	Pub.	MW	MP	Night	NW	PC	QS
Same measure: contiguous, discontiguous	●○	●○	●●	●●	●○	●●	●○	●○		●●	●●	●○	●○
Different measures: contiguous, discontiguous	●○	●○	●●	●●	●○	●●	●○	●○		●●	●●	●○	●○
Notes (different staves)													
Single note verticality	●	●	●		●	●		●		●	●	●	●
Same meas./adjac. staves: contiguous, discontiguous	●○	●○	●●	◐◐	●○	●●		●○	◐○	●●	●●	●○	●○
Same meas./nonadjac. staves: contiguous, discontiguous	●○		●●	◐◐		●●				●●	●●		
Adjacent meas./adjac. staves: contiguous, discontiguous	●○●○	●●	◐◐	●○	●●		●○	◐○	●●	●●	●○	●○	
Adjac. meas./nonadj. staves: contiguous, discontiguous	●○		●●	◐◐		●●				●●	●●		
Discont. group/nonadj. meas. adjac. staves, nonadj. staves			●●			●●				●●	●●		
Entire voice, multiple voices	●●	◐○	●○	●●	◐◐	●●			●●	●◐	●●		
Entire staff: adj., nonadj.		●○	●●	●◐	◐○	●●		●○	●○	◐◐	●●	●●	◐○
Vertical Relationship													
Highest or lowest n notes	●			◐				●			●		
Arbitrary group of notes	●			◐				●					

Editing (non-MIDI)

Table 22-12 addresses editing options of music notation software.

Clipboard-oriented: Cut, Copy, Paste, Merge, Insert, Shift

Because so much musical data is reusable within the same piece, you shouldn't have to re-enter anything. This implies full Cut, Copy, and Paste support. Some programs go so far as to provide a linked Copy option where editing the source material causes corresponding changes to every measure where you have pasted copies of the same music. Merging refers to a special type of pasting during which the music in the measure being pasted into is not replaced by the music on the Clipboard but, rather, combined with the new music. Insert is another special type of pasting, where everything to the right of the insertion point is shifted to the right (delayed in time) to make room for the inserted material. Shift refers to the option to slide music forward or backward (with respect to time) on a staff-by-staff basis in any beat or measure increment.

Transposition

Being able to transpose your music is important for two reasons. First, you will often want to print out music in a different key to accommodate the vocal range of a singer. On the local level, as noted in the previous paragraph, much musical material is reusable in the same piece, and these instances of reusable music often entail a repetition coming in at a new transposition. There are many ways to transpose your material: chromatically, diatonically, enharmonically, by key, mode, or custom scale that you define. Such custom pitch-remapping allows you, among other things, to change a passage quickly from major to minor or lydian mode, for example. If the software supports chord symbols, it is an added bonus if these transpose as well, so you don't have to re-enter the chord symbols every time you print your music in a new key. Check and see if the software knows how to transpose correctly. An easy way to do this is to transpose a piece or passage from the key of C to C♯. The seventh and third degrees of the scale should renotate at B♯ and E♯, accordingly, not as C and F natural!

Graphic editing

Music notation is essentially graphic data, regardless of whether software allows MIDI data (such as velocity) to be associated with each symbol on the screen. Because of the great likelihood of symbol collision in music of moderate complexity, you are probably going to want some sort of control over individual symbols. A common way that notation software implements this is to allow you to move any symbol on an individual basis using the mouse or cursor keys.

Discontiguous selection refers to the capability to, say, select bars 1, 7, 12, and 14 for transposition in one operation, rather than have to edit each measure individually — a great time-saver. Splitting voices from one staff onto many can save lots of time too. With such a feature you can, for example, play in a four-part chorale and then instruct the software to split the separate voices onto individual staves. If you are making piano reductions or rehearsal scores, the option to merge many staves down to a single staff or grand staff is indispensable. At least one program allows you to search and replace for pitch and rhythmic motifs or phrases in the same way you would using a word processor. Finally, being able to zoom in to greater levels of magnification can help you accurately position individual notational elements. Conversely, being able to zoom out can compensate for not being able to view an entire page on a computer screen that is too small to display it at full size. Augmentation/diminution refers to the option to halve or double the rhythmic values of a selected range.

Part Four: Notation

Table 22-12: Editing (non-MIDI) features

	CW	DM	Enc.	Fina	HB. E	Lime	Pub.	MW	MP	Night	NW	PC	QS
Clipboard													
Copy, Cut, Paste (replace)	●●●	●●●	●●●	●●●	●●●	●●●	●●●	●●●	●●●	●●●	●●●	●●●	●●●
Insert, Delete, Merge	●●●	▶▶○	●●●	●●●	●●●	●▶	●○●	●○●	○●○	●●●		▶●▶	
Repeat Paste, Repeat Merge			●●	●○				○●	●○				
Shift (notes ignore barlines)	▶			●									
Clear (leave empty space)		●		●	●		●	●	●	●	●	●	●
Multiple Clipboards, scrapbook support	○●	○●		●○	○●				●○		○●	○●	○●
Specify data type(s)				●		▶		▶			●		
Drag													
Copy, Cut, Paste (replace)	▶▶▶	●○○	●●●	●●●					●●○		○●●		○●●
Transpose													
Chrom., diatonic, enharmon.	●○○	●●○	●○●	●●●	●○○		●○○	●●●	●●○	●●●	●●●	●●●	○●○
Key, mode, custom reamp	●○○	●○○	●○○	●●●	●●○	●●▶	●●○	●○○	●●○	▶○○	●○○	●○▶	
Auto-renotate in new key	●	●	●	●	●	●	●	●		●		●	
Auto-respell during Paste if target is in new key	●	●	●	●	●	●	●	●				●	
Pitch Manipulation													
Drag transpose: pitch, chord	●●	●○	●▶	●●				▶▶	●●	●○	●●		●●
Delete redundant accidentals			▶	▶	▶	●			●	●	●	●	
Inversion, retrograde				○●						●○			
Harmonic (chord) inversion		●								●		●	
Check instrumental range										●		●	
Search and Replace				●									
Rhythmic Manipulation													
Specify ties over even beats				●	●	●			●				
Augmentation													
Multiples of 2, proportional	●▶	●●	▶▶	▶○				●○			●○	●○	
Diminution													
Multiples of 2, proportional	●▶	●○	▶▶	▶○				●○			●○	●○	
Rebar meter: larger, smaller	●●			○▶		▶▶		●●	○●	●●	▶▶		▶▶
Fill in rests (empty measures)	●		●	●	●	●			●	●		●	
Verify all rhythms										●		●	

Table 22-12: Editing (non-MIDI) features (continued)

	CW	DM	Enc.	Fina	HB. E	Lime	Pub.	MW	MP	Night	NW	PC	QS
General													
Undo, multilevel	●○	●○	●○	●○	●○	●○	●○	●○	●○	●○	●○	●○	●○
Drag notes, other symbols	◗●	●●	●●	●●	●●	●●	●●	●◗	●●	●●	●●		●●
Nudge (e.g., with arrow keys)	●		●				◗	●		●	●		●
Expand chord to staves	◗		◗	●	◗				◗				
Merge staves to single staff	◗		◗	●								◗	
Link copies, transposed				●●									
Auto collision avoidance	●	◗	●	●	●	●	●	◗	●	◗	◗		
Manipulate data as chunks			◗	◗			●		◗		●		

Editing (MIDI)

If you intend to use your notation software as a sequencer and not just for simple proofhearing, you will want some of the MIDI data editing features that are expected from dedicated MIDI sequencers. Four of the more important options are the option to set any MIDI event to any value; to add or subtract a value from any MIDI event; to scale the values of a MIDI event or group of events by a percentage; and to change smoothly over a selected region from one value to another (better yet if you can change smoothly from one percent to another). This latter feature is the only way to maintain an accent pattern during a crescendo or decrescendo, for example. Options to limit the values of a selected region of MIDI events to a maximum or minimum (sort of like an audio compressor/limiter) and to randomize certain elements (such as start times, velocities, and tempos) for humanization purposes are also valuable for programs that do not capture performance data beyond pitch and duration. Track shifting is extremely useful in this regard as well. See Table 22-13 for more on editing (MIDI) features.

Table 22-13: Editing (MIDI) features

	CW	DM	Enc.	Fina	HB. E	Lime	Pub.	MW	MP	Night	NW	PC	QS
Display													
Alphanumeric (text)				●				◗					
Graphic (piano roll)				●									
Controller window				●									
Velocity window				●									

Table 22-13: Editing (MIDI) features (continued)

	CW	DM	Enc.	Fina	HB. E	Lime	Pub.	MW	MP	Night	NW	PC	QS
MIDI Data Editing													
Set to, add to, scale	●○○		●●●	●●●		○●○		●●○					
Limit to minimum or maximum				●									
Smooth change: linear, percent, curve fit	●○○			●●○									
Randomize: percent, unit, range				●●●									

Formatting

Page level

Most page-level formatting options are of concern to you if you are preparing music for distribution. Take a look at any decent piece of published music and you will see that each page is formatted slightly differently, some have more systems on them than others. Inserting blank pages is a plus for music theater works where entire pages of stage directions might be required. Academics may also require this feature in the preparation of teaching materials and scholarly papers. Being able to fit music to a specified number of pages is a rare option, since most programs expect you to do that through manual editing, but have you ever seen a piece of published music that didn't end exactly at the lower right corner of the final page? When it comes to maximum page dimensions, there are several approaches. The first is to "tile pages," meaning that your music is printed on 8½ × 11-inch paper, and if you want larger sizes, you simply paste the pages together. The second approach is to allow larger sizes to be printed on printers that can handle them (for example, Linotronic and Compugraphic phototypesetters, or the LaserMaster 1200 used to print Figure 22-36, which appears later in this chapter). Some programs offer neither option, some offer both.

System level

Being able to specify the number of bars per system is important for union work, where you may be expected to provide systems of four bars and to bill accordingly. Professionally published music often has different amounts of vertical space between each system. If your software treats this globally, you may have to sacrifice the entire look of a piece of music just because you have one system with a note that extends to seven ledger lines and forces you to widen the space between all other systems to give that single note enough room. A similar phenomenon can exist with respect to the vertical spacing of individual staves within systems, although the programs that allow you to change intra-system staff spacing separately for each system are rare. Empty staff suppression refers to the automatic removal of staves in systems where there is no music on them, just like traditional publishers do in chamber and orchestral scores.

Measure level

Your formatting options at the measure level can mean the difference between an elegant-looking score and a mediocre printout. Most measures have a significantly varying note density to require different widths. Even in cases where this is not so, professional publishers make all measures a slightly different width to facilitate sight-reading. Some programs offer horizontal measure justification features that automatically expand or contract measures to their optimum widths for each system. Being able to split measures across systems or pages or create scores with barlines that do not vertically coincide are useful features if you want to cover all the bases.

Note spacing

The relative spaces between notes are a primary factor determining the beauty of your notated page. Remarkably, many programs space notes linearly. That is to say that the horizontal space allotted to a half note is equal to two quarter notes, the space allotted to a quarter note is equal to two eighth notes, and so on. A quick glance at any published music makes it clear that this sort of spacing is never used by professional publishers and engravers. Furthermore, it is much harder to read linearly spaced music. Because of this, professional engravers and publishers employ beat-positioning charts that express more aesthetic inter-note spacing. One popular ratio is the "Golden Section," sometimes referred to as 89:55 (or as 89:35 in the case of Music Publisher), because these are Fibonacci numbers, and adjacent (or adjacent, once removed in this case) Fibonacci numbers reflect this ratio or its reciprocal. Golden Section spacing mandates that the horizontal space of a half note is 0.618 that of two quarter notes, and so on down the line. Some programs have a 3:2 spacing ratio hard-coded into the software. There are many other ratios in wide-spread use. The most elegant notation software allows you to set up your own beat-positioning charts, and some provide for multiple spacing tables in each file. See Table 22-14 for more on formatting features.

Table 22-14: Formatting features

	CW	DM	Enc.	Fina	HB. E	Lime	Pub.	MW	MP	Night	NW	PC	QS
Page Level													
Format pages individually	●		●	●	●	●	●	●	●	●	●	◗	●
Reformat any time	●	●	●	●	●	●			●	●	◗	◗	◗
Insert blank pages anywhere			●	●	●	●	●		●	●	●		●
Set # of systems per page: global, local	○●	◗○	●●	●●	●●					●●	◗◗	○◗	

Table 22-14: Formatting features (continued)

	CW	DM	Enc.	Fina	HB. E	Lime	Pub.	MW	MP	Night	NW	PC	QS
Individual intra-system spacing	●		●	●	●	●	●		●	●	●		●
Music in columns							●				◗		◗
System Level													
Specify # of bars per system: global, local		●○	●◗	●●	○●	●◗		●●	●●	●●		○◗	
Drag system	●		●	●	●		●	●	●	●	●		
Vertical justification		●	●	●	●		◗				◗		
Indent left, right, multiple	○●○	◗○○		●●●	●●●	●●●	●●●		●●●	●◗○	●●●		●●●
Empty staff suppression	M	M	M	●	●	●	M		●	M	M		M
Empty measure suppression	M			M							M		M
Force page break	●		◗	●		●	◗	●	◗	●		●	
Reduce system, hold margins	○			●	●		◗				●		
Inter-system Staves													
Override automatic	●		●	●	●	●	●			●	●		●
Drag staff	●		●	●	●	●	●	●		●	●		●
Vertical justification	○		◗	●	●		◗			◗			
Measure Spacing													
Drag barline		●	●	●			●		●	●	◗		
Justify (horizontal)	●	●	●	◗	●	◗	●			●	◗		
Force split measure	●	●	●	●		●				●		●	●
Beat Spacing													
Drag beat horizontally: local, global (measure stack)		◗○	◗◗	●●		●○	●○		●●	●●	●○	○◗	
Positioning: linear, table	●○	●○	●●	●●	●◗	●◗	●○	●○	●●	●●	◗◗	●○	◗◗
Beat positioning tables: customize, multiple per file			●●		◗◗		●○			●●	◗◗		◗◗
Rest Positioning													
Drag rest: horiz., vertical	○●	●●	●●	●●	◗●	●●	●◗		●●	●●	●●		●●
Voice offset: all, individual	○●		○●	○●								●○	
Miscellaneous													
Jump to measure, with offset	●○	●○	●○	●○	●○	●○		●○		●●		●○	
Jump to page, with offset			○●		●○	●○				●●	●○		
Grids, rulers	○●		○●	●○	●●	●○	○●			●●			●●
Ossia provision				●			◗				●		●

MIDI and Audio Output

Even if you are not using your notation software to drive a bank of synthesizers for electronic score realization, some form of audio output is the number one time-saver for proofhearing the accuracy of your notated music. You can look at the same page a thousand times and never notice a missing accidental, but if you play it back once, that error stands out like a sore thumb.

Macintosh speaker

Many Macintosh notation packages include some provisions for non-MIDI audio output. Check to see how many voices can be accommodated in these cases. If there is a four-voice maximum audio output limitation, it's not going to help you much when you are notating a symphony.

MIDI playback

Being able to assign separate MIDI channels to staves and even separate voices on the same staff turns your notation software into a veritable MIDI sequencer and also facilitates proofhearing your masterpiece. Some software goes so far as to allow you to assign chord symbols placed above the staff to their own MIDI channel (e.g., to a guitar patch) for playback. The option to initialize each staff with a patch change message can save you a great deal of setup time when you want to play back a notation file. Having the music scroll by during playback is sometimes thought of as a courtesy feature, but it really is more important than that. If you were listening to a piece of music with the score in your hand, you'd probably be flipping the pages as the playback progresses, and you should expect the computer to do the same thing for you on the screen (and it never gets lost either). See Table 22-15 for more on sound output features.

Table 22-15: Sound output features													
	CW	DM	Enc.	Fina	HB. E	Lime	Pub.	MW	MP	Night	NW	PC	QS
Mac Speaker													
# of voices, selected staves, click notes to hear		4●●				4●●			4●○			4●○	
MIDI Playback													
# chan., chan./staff	8, 8	16,1	32,4	32,4	16,8	16,2	16,4	16,1	16,1	16,1		1,1	
Chord symbol playback				●									
Click to hear: note, chord, across all staves	●○○	●○●	●○○	●●●		▶○○				●▶			
Quick-and-dirty playback (as notated, no performance data)		●		●	●	●	●	●	●			●	

Part Four: Notation

Table 22-15: Sound output features (continued)

	CW	DM	Enc.	Fina	HB. E	Lime	Pub.	MW	MP	Night	NW	PC	QS
MIDI Playback (continued)													
Playback recorded: velocity, duration, tempo			●●●	●●●		●●●		●●○					
Dynamics, articulations, controllers	●●●	●○○	○○◗	●●●		●●●	●○○	●●○	●◗○	●○○			
Playback: cres./decres., 8va	●●	●●	○●	●◗		○●	○◗		●●	○●			
Symbol may affect selected notes only (e.g., top note)				●		◗				◗			
Chase controllers (or MIDI-executable symbols)			●	●					◗	●			
Music scrolls by on playback	◗	◗	●	●					●	●			
Playback location indicator		◗	●	●					●	●			
Synchronization													
MIDI Sync (with SPP)	●		●	●					●	●			
Output: MIDI Sync, MTC	●○	●○	●○	●○					●○	●○			

Part Extraction

If you are never going to require instrumental parts, you may well be able to get along without part extraction. If you only need this feature occasionally, you can probably get by with cutting and pasting individual staves from a score into separate parts files. On the other hand, if you need orchestral parts on a regular basis, you should examine those capabilities carefully. The best implementation of part extraction is for the software to create separate parts files automatically. This allows you to go in and tweak them if necessary (e.g., to ensure page turns are humanly possible).

Some programs create parts directly from the score file without allowing you any control over their formatting. This is fine if the program does it correctly, but most don't. Instrumental parts usually concatenate groups of rests into one long multimeasure rest with a large number over it. The software should be intelligent enough to break these multimeasure rests at tempo, meter, and key changes, as well as other places you indicate in the master score. Two useful features are the automatic placement of the instrument's name in the upper-left corner of the part (where it belongs) and the ability to auto-reformat parts as they are output, whether to a file or directly to the printer. The notes in instrumental parts are expected to be very tightly spaced to require as few page turns as possible, and the program should take care of this for you.

Ideally, you should be able to make all your changes in the master score without having to edit the parts separately.

As noted in Chapter 21, the ability to assemble a score from a set of parts is something that copyists are longing for. Coda created a utility that could join files in both the horizontal and vertical domains, but the program has yet to see a commercial release.

Table 22-16: Part extraction features

	CW	DM	Enc.	Fina	HB. E	Lime	Pub.	MW	MP	Night	NW	PC	QS
Automatic, little additional			●○	●●	●●		▶○	●○	●●	●●		●○	
New "part files" are created			●	●	●		●		●	●			
View parts from source file	▶			●		●	▶						
Format parts from source	▶			●	▶	●	●	▶					
Automated features													
Strip left connecting line			●	●	▶		▶			●			
Add inst. name headers			●	▶	●	▶	●	●				●	
Specify new page layout				●	▶		●	●	●	●			
Specify new header/footer			▶	▶			▶		▶				
Specify new meas. # format				●	▶			●				▶	
Apply new spacing table				●	▶	●	▶	▶	●				
Concatenate rests, autobreak	●○			●●	●○	●●	▶○	▶○	●○	●●		●▶	
Multistave parts provisions	▶	●								●		●	

Print and File Output

The most important thing you want to know is whether your notation software can print PostScript. PostScript is a page description language developed by Adobe Systems. The advantages of PostScript are many. The main one is printer independence — any printer that understands PostScript can print your files at the highest resolution available on the printer. This can mean 300 dpi on a low-cost laser printer to 1,270 and 2,540 dpi on a high-end phototypesetter (expect to pay about $5 per page when you bring your files to a phototypesetting service). Other advantages of PostScript include a wealth of PostScript music fonts (32 and counting) and the capability to scale output to any possible reduction or enlargement. TrueType is a new page description language developed by Apple that offers many of the same benefits.

A Print Preview option is useful but this merely indicates the inability of the software to display (and let you edit) the page in WYSIWYG format.

Compatible fonts

Don't forget that many programs come with the Sonata screen fonts, but not the printer font. This is fine if you are printing to an ImageWriter or other non-PostScript printer. With these programs you have to purchase the Sonata printer font separately from Adobe Systems. This can add almost $100 to the price of your software. Programs that provide PostScript output without the Sonata font supply their own bit-mapped and printer fonts. Some software, such as Finale, is compatible with any music font that uses the Sonata character mapping (with the exception of Repertoire, nearly all do). For a comparison of notation output see Figure 22-36. See Table 22-17 for more on print output features.

Table 22-17: Print output features

	CW	DM	Enc.	Fina	HB. E	Lime	Pub.	MW	MP	Night	NW	PC	QS
Non-PostScript & PostScript	●	●	●	●	●	●	●	●	●	●	●	●	●
Print only selected staves	●	◗		●		●						●	
Print Preview, editable	●○		●○	●○		◗○		●○		●●	●○	●○	●○
Gray-scale support				●									
Title pages (with no staves)				●	●			◗	●		●		●
Max. page size	22x22	14w	11x17	UL	24w	40w	100x100	legal	legal	11x17	48x48	14x22	11x17
Fonts													
Sonata	●	●	●	●				●		●	●	●	
Own font	●	●	●	●	●	●	●		●				●
Third-party fonts	●			●							◗	●	
Mix music fonts document				●							●		
Output to files													
PostScript (pure), EPS				●●	○●	○●		●●		●●	●●	●●	
PICT, MacPaint	●●	○●			○●	●○	●○				●●	○●	●○
Illustrator				◗	●					●			

User Configuration

The items listed in Table 22-18 are mainly of concern for engravers and publishers. Many people in these professions have cultivated a look to their music to the extent that you can often recognize a specific publisher's or engraver's work merely by examining a page at random (compare a randomly selected page from a Schirmer,

Figure 22-36: Comparison of a stave of music (the first four measures of Brahms's *Rhapsody* Op. 79 No. 1) set by each program with the font indicated. Where applicable, the music was imported from a SMF and the unedited results of this process are displayed. This is contrasted to the second edited example of each pair, which is the result of additional tweaking.

Part Four: Notation

Henle, or Hal Leonard edition). In the case of some of the older publishers, this unique look may have been meticulously developed over the span of a century. This sort of control often adds a good deal to the price and a great deal of kilobytes to the size of a notation program. See Table 22-18 for more on user configuration features.

Table 22-18: User configuration features

	CW	DM	Enc.	Fina	HB. E	Lime	Pub.	MW	MP	Night	NW	PC	QS
Configure default "new" file				●						●	◗	●	
Configure tool palette if any				●						●	●		
Configure symbol palette				●		◗				●	●		
Measure in: inches, metric	●○	●○	●○	●●	●○	◗○	●●	●●	●○	◗○	●●	●○	●○
Measure in: picas/points, engraver's "spaces"				●○		◗○	●○			◗◗	●○		
Exp/import symbol libraries				●					◗		●		
Beat positioning charts				●						●			
User-defined macros				●									
Templates: page layout, system layout, chord structures				◗●○	◗◗●		○●○				◗◗◗		
Engravers Preferences													
Thickness: stem, staff line				●●	●●	●○				●●	●●		
Stem lengths: normal, short,				●●	●●	●●				●●			
Dot offset				●	●	●				●			
Slurs and ties				●	●					●	●		
Broken slur or tie (over system or page break)				●								●	
Accidental offsets				●	●					●			
Beaming parameters				●	●	●				●	●		
Piano brace: taper, offset		○●		●○							●◗		
Separations: clef, key sigs., time sigs.				●●●	●●●					●●●			
Vertical loc. of time signature				●									
Space before 1st note in meas.				●	●					●			
Space after last note in meas.				●	●					●		●	
Space between note flags				●		●							
Expressive marking offset					●	●					◗	●	

Table 22-18: User configuration features (continued)

	CW	DM	Enc.	Fina	HB. E	Lime	Pub.	MW	MP	Night	NW	PC	QS
Inter-measure clefs: percent reduction, offset from bar				●●	○●	●○				●○	●○	●○	
Grace note percent reduction				●	●	●				●			
Utilities													
Auto-backup, auto-save				●○									
Job-costing utilities				●						●			

Summary

✓ More than 600 years have gone into the development of CMN. There are currently 16 music notation programs available for the Macintosh counting two programs that were released just as this book was going to press: Passport's MusicTime and Mark of the Unicorn's Mosaic (see coupon at the back of the book for details). Most of these programs fill 99 percent of the requirements for notating music based upon 19th-century Western tonality.

✓ Most Macintosh music notation software falls into one of three categories: rule-based, graphics-based, or combined graphics- and rule-based.

✓ Rule-based systems "understand" music, meaning that notes are understood to be representations of pitches and can therefore be transposed (among other things). Durations are also understood. Almost all formatting, placement, beaming, note spelling, and page layout is done automatically by the program, with little opportunity for user-override. Sometimes, built-in rules can compensate for limited musical knowledge on the part of the user.

✓ Completely graphics-based systems have no understanding of music. All symbols are treated as graphic elements. Although symbols may be organized into separate palettes, the program does not make a distinction between a note, text character, dynamic, or barline. Although this might seem to be the worst-case scenario, systems that make no musical assumptions generally offer the greatest degree of on-page symbol placement flexibility.

✓ Combined graphics- and rule-based systems generally make their best guess at the notation of a particular passage, but usually allow extensive user-override and user-configuration. Placement of most symbols and formatting can be adjusted graphically. Typically, this is accomplished by dragging an element with the mouse. These programs would seem to offer the best of both worlds, provided that you agree with the rules that are hard-coded into the system or that the program permits you to customize its default parameters in these respects.

✓ Two fundamental classes of applications are supported: music preparation and music creation. Some programs are optimized for both of these activities, others for only one.

✓ Music preparation includes copying and engraving activities. It implies that you are replicating an existing piece of music, about which all note decisions have been made in advance — the main concern is with the appearance of the page. Some music preparation programs are up to the standards demanded by professional publishers, others can only achieve copyist-level quality.

✔ Music creation includes composition, orchestration, and arranging. It implies that you are doing a great deal of editing, reformatting, and reorganizing of your musical material, as well as making ongoing decisions based on creative considerations that have an impact upon the graphic look of your page.

Part Five

Performance

Part Five
Foreword
by Joel Chadabe

Performance

Throughout history and throughout the world, every civilization has used available materials to make music. It comes as no surprise that in a civilization with electronic technology, that technology is used to make musical instruments.

The electronic musical instrument, however, has not yet reached its final form. Just as the piano took the entire 19th century to reach its final form, the electronic musical instrument is taking the 20th century, and our work is not yet complete.

To be sure, an electronic musical instrument is similar to a traditional instrument in its basic structure. A traditional musical instrument has two parts: a performance mechanism and a sound generator. A violin's performance mechanism, for example, is the strings and bow, and the sound generator is the body. In an electronic musical instrument, the performance mechanism is a controller and the sound generator is a synthesizer.

Well, is an electronic musical instrument also different in some way? More important, is it better? Does it do something more for a performer? Does it represent an advance in a performer's ability to perform?

Yes, it's different, it's better, and it represents an advance — at least in its potential.

We're not quite there yet, but an electronic musical instrument is better than a traditional musical instrument and represents an advance because it has the potential for greater expressivity and power in performance.

By greater expressivity, I mean the potential of an electronic musical instrument to interpret a human performance gesture with greater flexibility. For example, an electronic musical instrument's controller is separable from the sound generator. That means that a controller can be chosen by a performer according to the performance gesture that the performer wants to make, not according to the sound the instrument generates. What, as a performer, do you want to do? Do you want to wave your hands in the air, do you want to hit something with your hand, do you want to touch something with your fingers? We're just beginning to understand the nature of controllers and how they can affect the music generated by synthesizers. We're working on technologies that can sense the position of a hand in the air, that can control sound with greater nuance than a drum head, that will allow a keyboard performer to shape each note as it's played. And we're beginning to understand the concept of sound expanded through electronics — for example, reverberation, spatial distribution, and various other effects — as if they were an inherent part of a sound, in addition to the traditional variables of pitch, loudness, and timbre.

By greater power, I mean the potential of controlling everything at once. That is, not just controlling an expanded number of sound variables, but an expanded number of sounds. A performer can play the role of a conductor, cueing sounds to occur, changing the course of the music with a single gesture, and triggering sequences. An electronic musical instrument can be an orchestra and it can be played by one performer.

An electronic musical instrument is different from a traditional musical instrument because it has not only a controller and synthesizer but also an "interpretive link" between controller and synthesizer. That link is the secret ingredient to the super-instrument formula, and it's called software. It's software that defines the connections between the controller and the synthesizers.

There's a great number and variety of specific music programs available for the Macintosh, but in general they fit into three types: sequencers, interactive composing programs, and programming environments. Each type of program has different implications for the performer.

A sequencer (such as Vision or Performer) plays back what you've previously recorded. You can use it to take the place of a live performer, to fill in extra rhythms, and to provide accompaniment figures. You can trigger sequences as part of a performance. You can modify sequences in simple ways, by transposing, for example, or changing tempo. But you can't really alter or transform a sequence in performance. Using a sequencer in performance is like working

with another performer who's reading from a score.

An interactive composing program (such as M or Jam Factory) transforms what you've previously recorded, adding improvisational elements. Most important, interactive composing programs allow you to enter performance controls while the program is running. You can use an interactive composing program to extend yourself in performance, changing your music as you go. Using M or Jam Factory in performance is like working with another performer who's improvising with you, following your lead, generating musical detail that you might not have thought of.

A programming environment (such as Max) lets you create software objects that link any performance gesture to any musical variables. It's the ultimate step in performance flexibility. Perform any gesture. Hear any musical result.

The electronic musical instrument of today is based on the MIDI Specification for communication between controller, computer, and synthesizer. A MIDI system is a modular system and each module has its individual technical complexity. Performers deal with channels, program changes, notes on and off, pitch bend, and so on, as separate musical variables, and there's a lot of technical information to master in the operation of the instrument itself. There's room for improvement.

The potential of the electronic musical instrument will be realized when controllers are more subtle and capable of generating greater nuance, when software can better translate that nuance into musical controls, when synthesizers can better respond to those musical controls, and when performers do not need to deal with technical information in performance. We're beginning to see the next generation of instruments emerge, and they're based on digital signal processing. There's work to do in improving controllers, but the full performance potential of the electronic musical instrument is likely to depend largely on software. ♩

Joel Chadabe is president of Intelligent Music, which manufactures interactive performance products. Chadabe is also the original developer of Jam Factory and UpBeat.

Introduction to Part Five

The Macintosh can enhance live performance in four main areas:

❖ *Extended and enhanced device control:* You use the Macintosh as a MIDI sequencer, synchronizer, or for the storing and loading of soundfiles, patches, MIDI configurations, or other performance information that changes from piece to piece.

❖ *Intelligent instruments and interactive performance:* Software takes incoming information and processes it prior to passing it on for output, for all practical purposes, in real time.

❖ *Control of audio performance parameters:* This includes real-time control of MIDI routing, merging, processing, and filtering, MIDI-controlled audio mixers, and perhaps more than anything else, MIDI-controllable DSP devices.

❖ *Control of non-musical performance parameters:* The Macintosh, via both MIDI and proprietary interfaces, controls inherently non-musical elements in a performance situation. In this category are lighting, lasers, real-time animation, and video processing as well as other visual and special effects.

Historically, musicians of all instruments have been quick to adopt advances of technology and to incorporate them as a new standard by which subsequent musical endeavors have advanced to ever greater heights. At this present moment in musical history, advances of digital technology can place an entire orchestra in the hands of a single performer, taking music yet another quantum leap forward.

Macintosh-controlled digital samplers are found both on pop and commercial stages. Besides substituting for an instrumentalist who might become ill at the last moment, performing off-stage music from the orchestral pit, creating sound effects (even synchronizing lightning with a thunderclap), or temporarily augmenting the numbers of an existing instrumental section in lieu of engaging additional musicians, samplers may assume the role of scarce or little-used instruments in a real-time performance situation. Invisible choral parts such as those found in *Pelléas et Mélisande* and *Bluebeard's Castle* offer similarly obvious applications.

Macintosh-controlled electronic instruments are being used to bring music to schools, colleges, and community areas for performances that would otherwise resort to piano accompaniment, thus deepening the overall performance experience for everyone concerned. Concert artists are using MIDI sequencers to rehearse concertos and other forms of ensemble playing where budgetary constraints and availability of live musicians are prohibitive. Digital samplers truly permit the rest of the band or an entire virtual orchestra to be present at each and every rehearsal.

MIDI sequencers are used in live performance in many ways. Besides rounding out the instrumentation by playing extra parts, often synchronized to bass drum triggers or conductors' batons, it is increasingly popular to use sequencers purely for reconfiguration of all the devices on stage. In this case, no notes get played, only data to set up the next number. Short individual sequences or songs download patches, program changes, configure MIDI routing, and adjust outboard gear settings with a single keystroke, issued from either the Macintosh or MIDI keyboard. One innovative use of sequencers on stage is to record improvisational performances simply for documentation or, better yet, subsequent editing and recording.

The Macintosh is used to control DSP effects, mixing, sound placement, and audio routing. Less obvious uses of MIDI data include the control of lighting — specific notes, patches, or songs assigned to specific lighting configurations. With interactive performance software such as that covered in Chapters 19, 23, and 31, anything is possible.

The piano-style keyboard controller has a history so long that the MIDI period represents far less than a minute in the hour of its existence. The sheer number of pianos is a contributing factor and the indoctrination toward piano-style keyboards as some sort of de facto standard is ever-present.

Unfortunately, piano-style keyboards are optimized for unitimbrality. Aside from playing several instruments simultaneously by way of a single MIDI keyboard, there is no way to selectively access multiple patches with any efficiency. MIDI has 16 channels, yet you are essentially confined to performing on a single channel at a time.

The lack of provisions for control of a sound after its initial attack has roots stretching far back in the keyboard's history. But MIDI's continuous controller messages allow for many ways to expressively shape the characteristics of a sound *after* the sound has been initiated. This is one of the driving factors motivating attempts to enhance device control.

Innovative solutions to enhancing finger control have been attempted. As early as 1984, Key Concepts had developed the Notebender keyboard. Besides the traditional up-down motion, each key can slide forward and backward for the purpose of expressively manipulating additional sound parameters with a great degree of control before, during, or after the keys are struck. Yamaha's early GX1 sent pitch bend data as the keys were shifted horizontally. An alternative to sensing the shift of the physical position of a key is to detect the position of your finger on each key (right or left side, front or rear, up or down). The Moog Multiply-Touch-Sensitive (MTS) system provides this capability, but has yet to be implemented on a wide scale.

MIDI data allows musicians to involve other parts of the body in the performance process. From the very beginning, MIDI has had provisions for breath control. Foot pedal controls don't require any special MIDI messages, because they are just foot-operated versions of what you might find on the front panel: momentary switches, knobs, sliders, and toggle switches.

MIDI pedal boards often offer many more features than their acoustic predecessors. Fast Forward Designs's MIDI Step has note repeat and infinite hold modes, octave coupling, doubling at any designated interval, and transposition buttons, among other things. Lake Butler Sound's MIDI Mitigator RFC-1 is another good example of the type of control you can relegate to your feet. The RFC-1 can store and transmit any string of MIDI messages that can fit in its 8K of RAM (32K with expansion option).

That we must use our hands to play notes rather than exercise additional performance control places physical limits on the extent to which the full benefits of MIDI can be realized. To realize the full potential of extended real-time device control offered by MIDI requires radical changes in keyboard design.

The Monolith is an instrument invented by Jacob Duringer and marketed by the Heavenbound Systems Engineering Group. The layout is based on the traditional piano, but is fifteen keyboards deep. This allows you to play in two dimensions. The horizontal dimension is equivalent to a normal keyboard, except that no distinction is made between white notes and black notes. The vertical dimension corresponds to MIDI channels, with every keyboard assigned to a separate channel, if you like. This matrix allows you to treat the x-axis as pitch and the y-axis as timbre.

The Hotz MIDI Translator (also called the Hotz Box), invented by Jimmy Hotz, has 106 touch-sensitive sensor pads, including a three-octave flat keyboard (smaller versions are available). The pads do not base values on key travel time. This is unlike traditional MIDI keyboards, which measure the amount of time between initial key depression and impact to calculate velocity values (to achieve a low velocity, key travel is slower, meaning that it may take up to 180ms to generate a velocity value of 10 — even a relatively fast velocity takes about 7ms to determine). With the Hotz Box's FSR (force sensing resistor) technology, all values are transmitted instantaneously. You can assign each pad to play individual notes, chords, or transmit controller data. Each pad can be assigned to a different MIDI channel, if you like. You can change pad assignments in real time. Used in conjunction with a MIDI sequencer or the Hotz configuration software, the Hotz Box can undergo continual reconfiguration synchronized to the rest of the music. One interesting feature is that the box can be set up so that it is impossible to hit a "wrong" note or chord.

For people without keyboard ability, non-keyboard oriented MIDI controllers are available. These range from guitar controllers and electronic wind or valve instruments to pitch trackers that convert a normal audio sound source into appropriate MIDI note codes. Pitch trackers, as pitch-to-MIDI converters are commonly called, allow any singer or instrumentalist to control a MIDI device. This does not mean that one could play symphonic audio recordings through a pitch tracker and have all the notes transcribed into their appropriate MIDI codes. Current technology is only successful at tracking a single solo melodic line.

In 1974 the Lyricon opened up the world of electronic music to wind players. Unfortunately, the device eventually dropped from sight. Nyle Steiner invented the Steiner Phone, now known as the Electronic Valve Instrument (EVI). This and his next creation, the EWI (Electronic Wind Instrument), have had greater staying power. Both were acquired by Akai in 1986 and have since become standard fare in film and television scores.

Yamaha entered the market in 1988 with their WX7 MIDI wind controller. Fingering, which is the same as a saxophone, clarinet, and flute, transmits pitch data. Yamaha followed the WX7 with the WX11 and finally their less expensive Windjamm'r, an instrument that can be played with either saxophone or recorder fingerings.

Swiss inventor Martin Hurni's Synthophone is a more recent offering in the area of MIDI wind controllers. The Synthophone is a real saxophone with a MIDI processor hidden in its bell. Twenty keys are hard-wired to the processor and sensors are built into the mouthpiece. Key response is 250 microseconds (12 times faster than a MIDI message), and wind and lip pressure is sampled 4,000 times per second, with this data being reduced to the range of values required by MIDI.

Guitar controllers are commonplace these days. Roland and Quantar make popular MIDI guitar controllers. The Stick, invented by Emmett Chapman in 1974, is to guitars what some of the MIDI controllers are to pianos — there is definitely a relationship, however, performance capabilities are greatly enhanced and some new playing techniques are required. The Stick is based on the now popular both-hands-on-the-fingerboard guitar technique originated by Chapman in 1969. You might be surprised to know that there are controllers out there for other string players, too. Zeta Music Systems markets pitch-to-MIDI converters for their popular electric violins, violas, and cellos.

Sensor Frame's VideoHarp is not really a stringed instrument, although it is designed to resemble a harp, and in some performance applications you strum it like one. This futuristic Plexiglass device senses finger positions by reflecting a beam of neon light onto the surface of a 64Kbit dynamic RAM chip with its innards exposed. The shadows of your fingers on the chip, focused by a lense, actually set the bit values of the light-sensitive memory cells.

Drum pads that send MIDI data were an obvious development from pre-MIDI pads, which sent analog voltage triggers to non-MIDI synthesizers. Many synthesizer companies now market such pads. Newer MIDI drum pads such as KAT's drumKAT include extensive MIDI processing options. In multimode, the drumKAT lets you program three events for each pad, each with a different note number and channel. Eight "motifs" (up to 952 MIDI events) can be generated by a single drum stroke. The notes can be delayed, rotated, shifted, or gated according to velocity and sent out on up to 32 MIDI channels. KAT also offers malletKAT, a percussion controller that resembles a marimba or xylophone.

Palmtree Instruments's Airdrums belong in the realm of advancing percussion controller technology beyond traditional instrument emulation. These hand-held drum "sticks" do not require drum pads for performance. Instead, you play them in mid-air — the visual effect is quite remarkable. The sticks are sensitive to motion and acceleration in six directions: up and down, left and right, and clockwise/counterclockwise rotation (around the center).

Throughout musical history, most musical instruments have been designed primarily to facilitate the acoustical properties of the instrument rather than the physical characteristics of human performers. Stringed instruments require strings to be stretched over a resonating box, and wind instruments require tubes of a specified length. The human interface is generally subordinate to these acoustic prerequisites. Consider a piano keyboard — the straight-line orientation forces your wrist to assume different positions depending upon whether you are at the lower or upper extremes of the range. An ergonomically designed piano would not present its keys in a straight line. However, the internal configuration required by piano strings precludes such a layout.

Most electronic instruments evolved from acoustic models and continue to disregard ergonomics. Because electronic and microprocessor-based instruments don't suffer from design requirements imposed by acoustical phenomena, it was inevitable that this fact would eventually be considered by instrument designers. Electronic music pioneer Don Buchla is one such developer who realized early on that an electronic instrument can be designed to fit the human hand.

Buchla and Associates's Thunder is more than just another controller. Thunder breaks completely new ground in instrument design, making no attempt to emulate the appearance or playing technique of traditional acoustic instruments. Thunder includes 36 membrane touch-pads, 25 of which are laid out to reflect the shape of your hand. There are even two larger pads designed to fall beneath the heel of your palm. All the pads sense velocity and pressure, and 15 of them sense the location of your touch. You can assign the performance pads to notes, channels, combinations of channels, and velocities, but it is just as likely that a pad be assigned to any MIDI data or combination of MIDI messages that you require. Microtuning support is particularly extensive.

In 1991 Buchla and Associates released another controller called Lightning. Mounted in a little box that sits in front of you, Lightning tracks the movement of your hands in a given spatial area by using infrared triangulation. Lightning's internal representation divides this area into eight zones. To supply the spatial data, you wear light-emitting rings or use special conducting batons or drumsticks with similar built-in light sources. Like the Airdrum and other 3-D spatial-recognition systems, Lightning senses up, down, left, and right motion. Lightning also senses zone entry and exit. Detection of location provides information about velocity, acceleration, and reversal of direction, all of which can be interpreted as a discrete gesture. You map specific gestures to musical events with accompanying software.

Adding a Macintosh to a live performance doesn't guarantee that the performance will be more interesting, but in my experience, when more performance parameters are placed under Macintosh control, the effect is inevitably more interesting, fresh, inspiring, and reflective of the axiom "the sum is greater than the parts." I suspect that this is because setting up such systems requires more attention to detail and offers the application of creativity to parameters that were previously relatively static elements. One sentiment that is echoed unanimously among Macintosh-assisted performers is: "I've always wished I could do that — now with the Macintosh I can!"

Chapter 23

The Mac in Live Performance

In this chapter . . .

✔ Using the Macintosh to enhance live performance.

✔ MIDI sequencing in a live performance environment.

✔ Synchronizing the Macintosh to live performers.

✔ Control of other performance considerations, such as amplification.

✔ Examining interactive performance software in detail.

✔ Interview with Morton Subotnick.

Live Performance Applications

You can use your Macintosh to enhance live performance in just about any way you can imagine. This chapter focuses on using MIDI in a live sequencing environment, synchronizing live performers to the Macintosh and vice versa, and exploring unique control options for additional musical parameters (see Figure 23-1). Finally, I examine two programs dedicated to interactive performance in detail.

Live MIDI Sequencing

Sequencing in a live performance offers many ways to enhance the control of your MIDI orchestra. Sequencer software can be run on the Macintosh, but you can also pre-program your sequences in the Macintosh and use a dedicated sequence player such as Roland's new Sound Brush. The Sound Brush reads SMF sequences (16 channels) stored on Macintosh disks and includes a wireless remote controller that allows you to cue up data for playback, start, stop, rewind, fast forward, and set tempo. A similar device is Eltekon's MIDIBuddy. The MIDIBuddy includes 10 MIDI INs and OUTs and the ability to send unique data streams to each output for 160-channel operation. Yet another option is Alesis's DataDisk SQ. Alternatively, you can dump your Macintosh sequences into a built-in hardware sequencer within one of your instruments (this is probably a good idea for backup considerations anyway).

If you opt to bring the Macintosh on stage, you might want to consider rackmounting it. The Current Music Technology company offers a Mac'n Rak

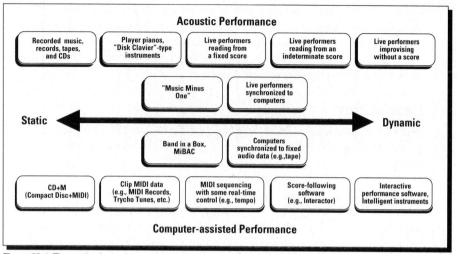

Acoustic Performance

| Recorded music, records, tapes, and CDs | Player pianos, "Disk Clavier"-type instruments | Live performers reading from a fixed score | Live performers reading from an indeterminate score | Live performers improvising without a score |

| "Music Minus One" | Live performers synchronized to computers |

Static ◄──────────────────────────────► **Dynamic**

| Band in a Box, MiBAC | Computers synchronized to fixed audio data (e.g.,tape) |

| CD+M (Compact Disc+MIDI) | Clip MIDI data (e.g., MIDI Records, Trycho Tunes, etc.) | MIDI sequencing with some real-time control (e.g., tempo) | Score-following software (e.g., Interactor) | Interactive performance software, Intelligent instruments |

Computer-assisted Performance

Figure 23-1: The static-dynamic spectrum of acoustic performance related to computer-assisted performance.

chassis that moves all the internal hardware of any Macintosh into a sturdy rack-mountable box. Hard drives and just about any other storage medium (Syquest cartridge drives, optical drives, CD-ROM drives, and DAT drives) can also be rack-mounted. Anatek and Eltekon offer rack-mounted systems that take other aspects of performance into consideration, for example, the elimination of fan noise. Of course, such rack-mounted drives can also be used with samplers that support SCSI.

Although most people think of sequencers as being used for playback purposes in a live performance situation, it is becoming popular to keep a sequencer running to record their performances as MIDI data. This is desirable, because often the improvised music generated in response to the emotion and excitement of the live performance environment is difficult to duplicate in the sterile atmosphere of a recording studio. Recording is simple — you just keep a sequencer running in record mode and synchronized to some element of the performance. An assistant can periodically save the files, or you can relegate that task to a macro.

You can use sequencers to automate many aspects of live performance. Besides the obvious use of adding additional virtual musicians synchronized to you or your ensemble, you can set up sequences that merely send program changes, SysEx dumps, patchbay configurations (audio and MIDI), or control other performance enhancements such as lighting.

Sequencers that support the Song Select MIDI message are obvious choices, since you can cue up each new song remotely. In this case, it helps to have a sequence that can place its transport under remote control via MIDI (most professional Macintosh sequencers allow this), otherwise you may have to manipulate the Macintosh keyboard. This shouldn't steer you away from a sequencer, because a macro utility can provide single-keystroke access to any file or function of MIDI sequencer software running on the Macintosh.

Case history

You can set up many different ways of triggering sequences or songs or even setting other sequence parameters in real time. When I perform live with my collaborator, Brentano Haleen, we use an approach that we call VADA — Voice Activated Digital Art. Using Articulate Systems's Voice Navigator, I can instantly trigger any song, sequence, or sub-sequence by issuing voice commands. Other voice commands allow me to jump to various locations within individual sequences. I can also mute and unmute tracks, transpose sequences, change patches, change track volume levels, and apply additional real-time control, all through speech recognition technology. The noise-cancellation element of the Voice Navigator's microphone ensures that no matter how loud the music gets, my voice commands are still recognized.

While I am controlling my synthesizers and samplers by voice, Brentano controls projected animations using a Voice Navigator interfaced to his own Macintosh. His voice commands trigger Director Lingo macros (see Chapter 27, "Music for Multimedia"), which allow him to start playback from any frame of an animation and subsequently jump to any other location, change playback speed, reverse playback, loop sections, change color palettes, and add a wide variety of visual effects (see Figure 23-2).

When we perform together, most of our works use the voice channel exclusively — I never touch my instruments or Macintosh, and neither does Brentano. In VADA, speech is multifunctional — it is the medium through which each of us interacts with his individual performance material, and at the same time it provides instantaneous intercommunication between the two of us. True interactive collaboration is made possible from a greater level of abstraction, a fusion of individual and group interactivity.

As the performance unfolds, we are free to interact with one another's on-the-fly artistic decisions, creating a visual/musical jam session. On another level, VADA performance is simply a conversation between Brentano and myself, in which a single word may trigger a burst of audible and visible events or may simply invoke a subtle transformation. In either case, the language correlates words to events, and this synchronicity is quickly understood by the audience — as each work evolves, the members of the audience are progressively drawn into the continuum as they assimilate the implications of our verbal cues. That the audience requires no translation of the work's ad hoc script raises their involvement in

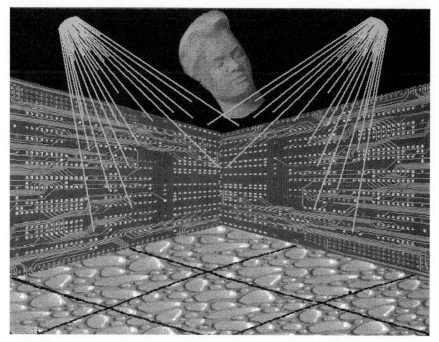

Figure 23-2: A frame from one of Brentano Haleen's VADA animations. During a performance 8- and 24-bit color is used exclusively.

the VADA performance to the level of passive participant and enhances overall artistic comprehension.

Now that we have a number of VADA performances and different VADA compositions under our belts, we are experimenting with adding a third Voice Navigator to the scenario. This third performer is actually another Macintosh with its Voice Navigator input linked to the audio output of a sampler that generates a stream of sampled voice commands in a semi-random order (actually, conditional branching is employed between larger randomized sections). Eventually, we may just step aside and provide several samplers for a group of virtual performers, each Macintosh's own digitized speech controlling the other Macintoshes in turn, and these words control all the devices on stage in response to a conversation that provides for a virtually unlimited collection of permutations.

Synchronization of the Mac to Live Performers

It is now relatively easy to synchronize sequencers to live performers on stage. There are two approaches. A conductor or other tempo source can use the Tap Tempo (or Human Sync) feature built into your MIDI sequencer. The other approach is to translate an audio event into a MIDI clock to which a sequencer or drum machine is synchronized. Various forms of synchronization and device setups are discussed in Chapter 26, "Film and Video Applications."

A number of hardware devices are available to facilitate either approach. Popular devices for tempo-to-MIDI conversion include the Garfield Time Commander, Kahler Human Clock (designed by Michael Stewart — see Chapter 25, "MIDI Mixing and Studio Automation"), and Aphex Studio Clock (a Macintosh editor is available for the Studio Clock).

Typical features of tempo-to-MIDI converters include the ability to convert audio data (for example, that coming from a miked kick or snare drum or even a piezo microphone attached to a standard keyboard and responding to the clicks of the impact of the keys) to PPQN, SPP, or MIDI Beat Clocks; delaying (or sometimes advancing) the synchronization pulse, synchronizing to SMPTE or MTC, and continuing to generate synchronization information, even during momentary audio dropouts.

Another type of computer-human interaction related to synchronization in the broadest sense is the triggering of individual MIDI events in response to selected audio input. These are called trigger-to-MIDI devices. Popular boxes include the Akai ME35T, Aphex Impulse, KAT MidiK.I.T.I., Roland PM-16, and Simmons ADT.

Trigger-to-MIDI devices sport many more audio inputs (usually between eight and 12) than tempo-to-MIDI converters. This is because you usually want to trigger different events or types of events from different sources (any audio source that defines a metrical pattern by sharp changes in amplitude can be used), whereas with a tempo-to-MIDI converter you are usually dealing with a single timing reference. There are many inexpensive little boxes, pads, and other peripheral gadgets, whose sole purpose is to send an audio trigger to these devices. It's relatively easy to turn anything into a MIDI device, albeit with a note range limited to the number of inputs of the trigger-to-MIDI converter.

Trigger-to-MIDI converters usually let you map separate notes or other MIDI events to the trigger information present at each audio input. Independent MIDI channel assignment is a standard feature. Some offer a velocity curve that is mapped to the amplitude of the incoming audio trigger as well as allowing you to specify a default velocity value. There are controls to set the threshold (audio signal level) that must be reached before a MIDI event is generated and controls to determine the amount of time to be examined in considering whether or not an event is a valid trigger (definable in milliseconds).

The IQ System

In a performance situation where you have multiple amplifiers and speakers, Crown's IQ System 2000 lets you remotely control and monitor up to 2,000 amplifiers (Crown amplifiers of course, although there is now an AES standard for the control of sound systems that is supported by many other companies).

The IQ System interface between the amplifiers and the Macintosh is through the serial port rather than MIDI. This provides considerably more accurate control at much higher data rates. The amplifiers themselves can be connected serially (see Figure 23-3).

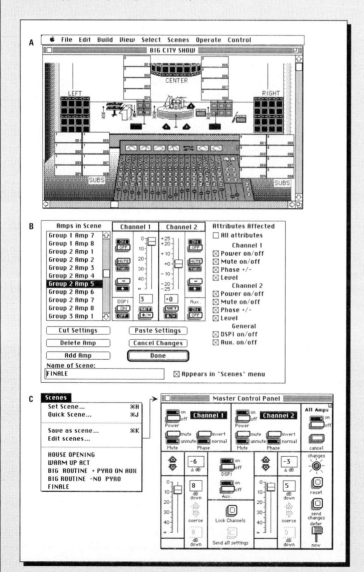

Figure 23-3: Crown's IQ System 2000. **(A)** You can import PICT files to create a background that visually corresponds to your physical sound environment. Multiple environments can be saved and recalled for different performance locations. The little meter bars on the amplifier graphics reflect current output level. **(B)** Double-clicking one of the amplifiers on the previous screen brings up this status window providing detailed information that updates in real time the current status of your amplifiers. You can control the indicated parameters of each amplifier from this screen. **(C)** You can edit and store a number of scenes for instant recall using this dialog box. Your scenes appear under the Scenes menu. Selecting a scene lets you reconfigure the sound parameters of up to 2,000 amplifiers with a single command.

A second-generation approach to synchronizing live performers to the Macintosh, often referred to as score following, is discussed under the heading "Interactor."

Interactive Performance Applications

You can use nearly all of the interactive composition applications described in Chapter 19, "Interactive Composition and Intelligent Instruments," in a live performance environment. Two programs not discussed in that chapter are particularly well suited for live performance: sYbil and Interactor.

sYbil

sYbil's documentation makes it very clear as to what sYbil is not, stating in the second paragraph of the first page that sYbil is not a sequencer; an algorithmic composer; a "right note" generator; a substitute for musical knowledge, technique, or talent; a MIDI "hacker's toolbox"; or a MIDI "player piano." If you've read Chapter 19, you'll easily recognize sYbil as an intelligent instrument.

sYbil reacts to note messages it receives and uses these note messages to trigger a wide variety of transformations and effects.

You can control sYbil from any MIDI controller, although drum pads are particularly efficient because sYbil only requires 16 notes for its operation (notes not assigned for interpretation by sYbil are simply passed through to their normal destinations). The software is a real gift for monophonic instrument controllers because it provides extensive options for precise polyphonic accompaniment. If you don't have a MIDI controller, you can activate sYbil from the Macintosh keyboard using the 1 through 8 keys and the Q through I keys. The Shift key activates the velocity cross-switch (see Figure 23-4).

A single note can trigger up to four-note chords with each note rechannelized if you like. These chords are stored in "identity maps" and you can access multiple identity maps on-the-fly. You can set a velocity cross-switch to trigger a separate identity map when a note crosses a specified velocity threshold. You can also send complete sets of program change information on all 16 channels using sYbil's Program Change Map feature.

sYbil's notes can act as a toggle for identity maps, program change maps, transposition, three types of sustain, and chain up to four identity maps together (in which case, sending a note triggers cycles through the identity maps). See Figure 23-5 for sYbil's available toggle icons.

In response to sYbil users worldwide, Scorpion Systems added a number of new features in sYbil 2.5. These include the ability to record a sYbilized performance and save it as an SMF. This allows the product to function much like those

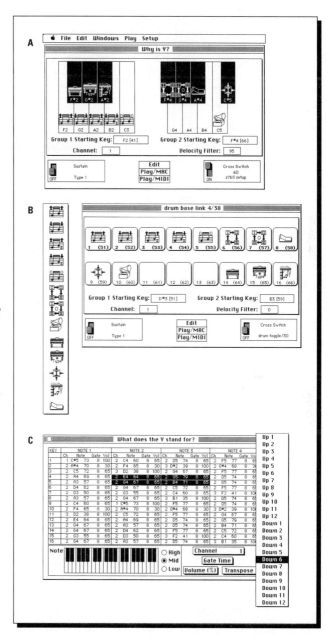

Figure 23-4: Configuring sYbil requires only three simple screens. **(A)** sYbil's keyboard setup screen. Note that the actual pitches you use to initiate sYbilized events don't have to correspond to this scaler mapping. In fact, the pitch triggers can be all over the keyboard. The real triggers are indicated at the bottom of each key. You can set the key group starting position with a pop-up menu. The icons on the keys indicate the types of toggles assigned to those keys. The bottom of the screen provides additional ongoing status information. **(B)** sYbil's drum pad setup screen. This functions identically to the keyboard setup screen. Option-clicking a drum pad (or key in the keyboard setup screen) brings up the pop-up menu of toggle functions that is pictured at the left. **(C)** Editing an identity map with sYbil's Spreadsheet window. Full support of Cut, Copy, and Paste is provided.

already discussed in Chapter 19, "Interactive Composition and Intelligent Instruments." The new Playback toggle was added to let you loop a portion of your performance while continuing to interact with sYbil in the normal fashion. Finally, microtonal options were added.

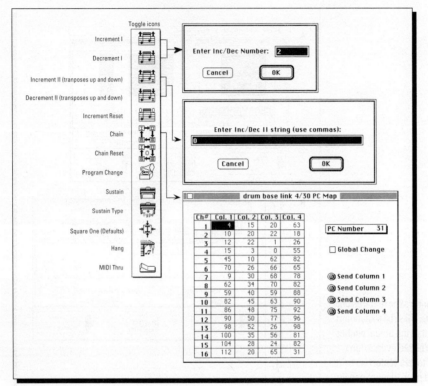

Figure 23-5: sYbil's available toggle icons and their functions.

sYbil is one of those programs, like Ovaltune, that defies verbal description. You really have to see and hear a performance to realize the potential of this software. The simple user interface makes it even more amazing when you start playing with it. sYbil is very powerful software that can be quite addicting.

Interactor

Interactor by Mark Coniglio and Morton Subotnick is a visual programming language that is optimized for interpreting timing and MIDI events during a live performance.

The software has two operating modes, one devoted to setup and the other devoted to real-time event-driven interactive performance. Setting up Interactor to process an event is as simple as interconnecting icons (many of which include logical and conditional operators). Processes can be grouped together into scenes, and scenes can be agglomerated further into scene groups (see Figure 23-6).

There are eight Sequence Players in Interactor, each of which can simultaneously play back from or record onto any one of an unlimited number of multichannel

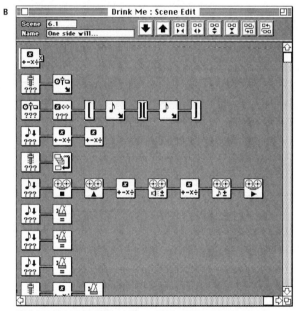

A

1.1	setup	2.9	Echo1	
1.2	OK	2.10	Echo2	
1.3	OUT	2.11	playscale	
1.4	C3->Chords	2.12	playlist	
1.5	ELSE	3.1	stoploop	
1.6	NEST	3.2	KEYS	
1.7	A	3.3	VelToOpLvl	
1.8	B	3.4	MiniLibIn	
1.9	C	3.5	MiniLibOut	
1.10	math	4.1	CtlExample	
1.11	transpose	4.2	play1 off	
1.12	extranote	4.3	play1 on	
2.1	sending	4.4	play2 on	
2.2	transpose	4.5	play2 off	
2.3	startstop	5.1	common	
2.4	playback			
2.5	record			
2.6	TempoEx			
2.7	Lists			
2.8	shift			

Figure 23-6: (A) A typical Interactor scene group. **(B)** Double-clicking any scene's name brings up this Scene Edit window, which displays the icons representing the process defined by the scene.

tracks. You can also import and export SMFs to the various tracks. While most software limits you to a single timing reference, Interactor provides eight separate clocks, which can run at different speeds (all dividing the quarter note into 480 ticks). Each Sequence Player can be assigned to a different clock (or time base), if you like.

You define scenes in the Operator Select window (see Figure 23-7). Eight icon palettes of operators are available. These are grouped according to function. Once you have activated an operator, you can double-click it to set its internal parameters and conditional tests.

Interactor lets you create control panels with a great variety of on-screen graphic controls that can be assigned to generate any kind of MIDI data or send messages to any of Interactor's operators (see Figure 23-8).

You may want to use lists (see Figure 23-9) to remap or otherwise process the data generated by manipulating Interactor's on-screen controls.

Figure 23-10 describes the functions of some of the operators in the Melody Maker application discussed in Figure 23-9.

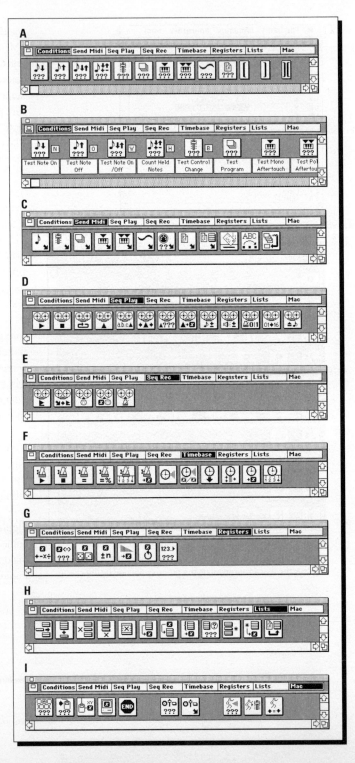

Figure 23-7: Interactor's Operator Select window. You create scenes by selecting icons from this window. The buttons at the top of the screen display the various types of operator icons. **(A)** Conditions. These icons let you test incoming events for a variety of criteria. They accommodate IF-THEN-ELSE structures. **(B)** You can display the keyboard aliases (shortcuts) and operator names by clicking the button in the upper left. **(C)** Send Midi. These icons let you send specific types of MIDI data out the Macintosh's serial port.
(D) Seq Play. You can control and modify playback with these icons. **(E)** Seq Record. These icons provide for the recording of sequences and tempo maps. **(F)** Timebase. You use these icons to affect Interactor's eight timebases, for example, to set tempos or set delays. **(G)** Registers. These icons let you manipulate Interactor's registers. Whenever Interactor receives a MIDI or Macintosh event, the data is assigned to four registers, but you can use as many registers as you like as Symbols (roughly equivalent to variables). For example, a Note-On event has its status byte in R1 (register 1), the channel number in R2, the note number in R3, and the velocity in R4. **(H)** Lists. Interactor lets you create and modify lists of numbers that you can use to remap or assign values for any parameter. **(I)** Mac I/O. These icons recognize data from the Macintosh keyboard and mouse, among other things.

Figure 23-8: Building a control panel for Interactor. You use the dialog box at the left to set the type and parameters of on-screen controls. You choose control types from the pop-up menu pictured in the center of this figure. At the right are examples of all types of virtual controls provided by Interactor (except type PICT).

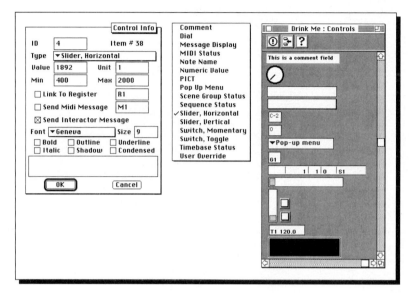

Figure 23-9:
(A) The control panel for an Interactor application called Melody Maker. You can generate two voice textures with control over scale, tempo, note density, rhythmic complexity, and other parameters. **(B)** An Interactor List window displaying some of the lists that are associated with the controls in the Melody Maker control panel (A). Double-clicking a list name lets you edit its values and display the list in one of four ways (see C, D, E, and F).

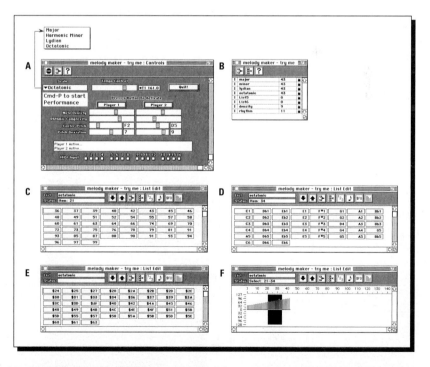

(C) Numeric (decimal) view of the Octatonic Scale list (assigned to that menu item on the control panel). **(D)** Note name display of the same data (accessed by clicking the Note button at the top of the window). **(E)** Hexadecimal display of the same data. **(F)** Graphic representation of the same data.

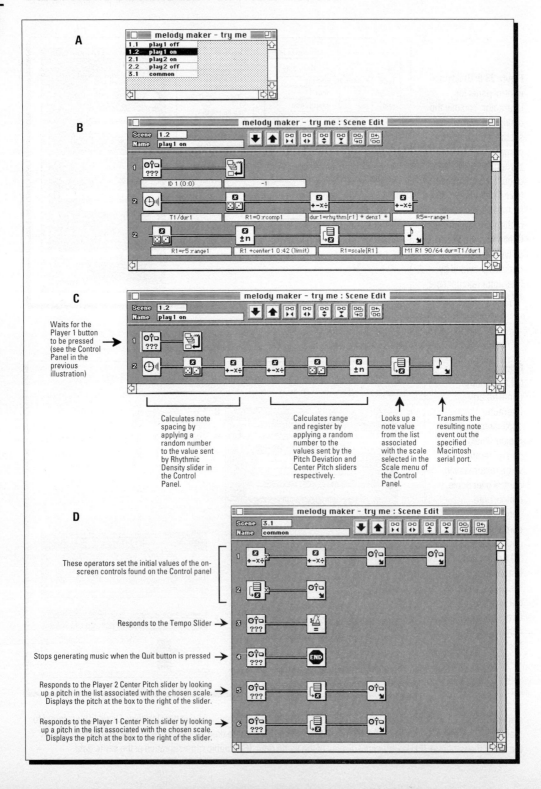

A

B

C

Waits for the
Player 1 button
to be pressed
(see the Control
Panel in the
previous
illustration)

Calculates note
spacing by
applying a
random number
to the value sent
by Rhythmic
Density slider in
the Control
Panel.

Calculates range
and register by
applying a random
number to the
values sent by the
Pitch Deviation and
Center Pitch sliders
respectively.

Looks up a
note value
from the list
associated
with the scale
selected in the
Scale menu of
the Control
Panel.

Transmits the
resulting note
event out the
specified
Macintosh
serial port.

D

These operators set the initial values of the on-
screen controls found on the Control panel

Responds to the Tempo Slider →

Stops generating music when the Quit button is pressed →

Responds to the Player 2 Center Pitch slider by looking
up a pitch in the list associated with the chosen scale.
Displays the pitch at the box to the right of the slider. →

Responds to the Player 1 Center Pitch slider by looking
up a pitch in the list associated with the chosen scale.
Displays the pitch at the box to the right of the slider. →

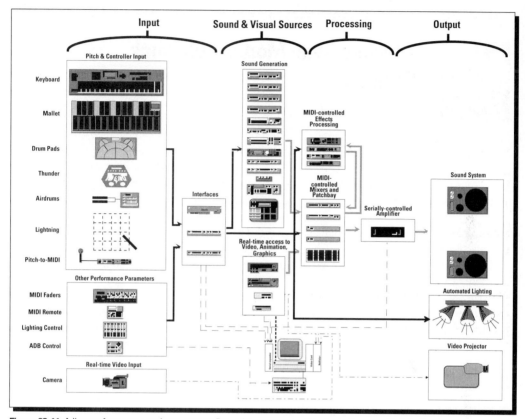

Figure 23-11: A live performance environment configured to use many of the tools discussed in this chapter.

Putting It All Together

If you were to use all the tools discussed in this chapter during a live performance, your setup might resemble the one in Figure 23-11.

Figure 23-10 (previous page): Annotated data flow in Melody Maker, a simple Interactor application. **(A)** Melody Maker consists of five scenes organized into three groups in its Scenes window. **(B)** Interactor provides an option to Auto Comment chains of operators in Scene Edit windows as pictured here. **(C)** This is the same scene with Auto Commenting disabled. Note that the white vertical line to the left of the first icon is the insertion point for new operators. **(D)** The final scene in Melody Maker detects manipulation of the on-screen controls and passes their data to the other scenes.

Interview with Morton Subotnick, Composer

*Yavelow: Interactor is such a new pro-
gram— how far do you think it can be
taken and what are some of the things that
you've been doing with it?*

Subotnick: The program was originally
conceived about seven years ago. I had just
finished an interactive piece for IRCAM. I had
a picture of where I needed to go and what
software I would need to be able to accommodate the next series of pieces I wanted to
do. It seemed like the most critical thing at the
time was isolating a way to score-follow a
conductor. To score-follow was the essential
thing.

The basic thing I came up with at the time,
which has worked extremely well, resulted
from my experience as a player in orchestras
when I was young: It occurred to me that
approaches to score-following that need to
know all the notes of the score and all the
details of the score, did not really emulate
what players did. I mean you just count
measures of rests, you sort of beat time until
you get close to where you want to come in
and you listen for the timpani, and then you
look for the conductor's beat, and you come
in. The amount of information that an
orchestra player carries when they're waiting
to come in is very little.

So it seemed that what was really important
was to develop a very accurate tempo
follower that would know the metric
organization of the piece and only open up

to know pitches when they were absolutely
necessary. This turned out to be really a
practical, efficient, and cheap way to
approach the whole process.

I originally prototyped it in HookUp! just to
get the basic algorithms set and make sure
they would work. Mark Coniglio has done all
the programming since then.

Of course, it has evolved. I've used it in a
number of pieces; in fact, we've used my
pieces as a sort of testing ground, each step
along the way. The program just grew piece
by piece.

I used it in my multimedia piece *Hungers*. It
involved control of video monitors, cameras,
as well as the sound by way of MIDI. All of
that was done with one of the first versions
of Interactor (it wasn't called Interactor then,
but it became Interactor). We've been
testing it all along.

A piece of mine was recently performed at
Carnegie Hall, *The Desert Flowers*. There is a
computer and an orchestra, and the computer follows the conductor's tempo. It
tracks all the way through the piece in terms
of knowing within about a beat of where it is
all the time. It cross-references to a MIDI
keyboard (probably a Yamaha MIDI Grand).
So between the two it keeps its place all the
way throughout the piece and pretty much
acts like a player in the orchestra.

Yavelow: *Do you see Interactor mainly as a score-following tool?*

Subotnick: No, it's gone way beyond that now. We've added so many elements. It can be used as a recording device, so that you can actually improvise into it and then immediately play back and modify anything you put in. For instance, you could use a pedal to record a passage that you're playing. When you release the pedal, for instance (that would be something you would designate), it would stop recording that, and you could have predetermined that the next note after it, or some note on the keyboard, would recall what you just played and transpose it to the note you've chosen. All this can follow the tempo you're now following, so you can just continue to pile up material in that way on the spot.

Because it can record everything that you do, with the existing software, you could actually build a learning curve into it, so that it could learn to anticipate what you're doing. We're actually going to incorporate learning modules down the line, because we're doing it for ourselves. You can do it right now with the existing modules, but you have to work out the logic yourself. We're going to work the logic out and convert it into a module down the line.

For instance, it would learn what you're doing and then be able to say to you the next time: Do you want me to do it the way you did it — which is easy, just play it back — or the way it was intended to be done, or the way you did it the third time, or the way you did it the second time, or somewhere in between. As you gradually begin to do things similarly, it will begin to anticipate what you are doing.

Yavelow: *What kinds of things are you referring to, harmonic progressions and the like?*

Subotnick: No, no. I suppose you could do harmonic progressions, but I'm not quite sure it's the best software for that. It would be a cumbersome algorithm that you'd have to put in, but you could do it.

I was thinking more of *when* you do things, meaning tempo. Also, if at a certain point in the piece you suddenly started playing faster and louder and you played a particular chord at that moment, it would begin to anticipate the accompaniment for that particular chord. It would be looking for a specific event and anticipate it.

I don't know, I'm just inventing off the top of my head. I'm still after the conductor thing, so my use of it is going to be in rehearsal situations, where the conductor is conducting from a score, but not conducting what's written in the score; he's modified it, as one does when one interprets. As the musicians are learning it, the computer is also learning to anticipate the way he makes an accelerando and all of that. So my use of it is going to be limited to that, but then it opens up for other people to use it in different ways.

Yavelow: *Having eight sources of tempo will certainly help this.*

Subotnick: Yes. It's incredibly useful. I know that the first thought about that is, well, gee, we can get everybody to play in different tempi; well, that's pretty cacophonous, usually. You don't often get that far down the line, but the reason for doing it was first to free up processing whatever anyone wanted to do, and second, if you could track eight different players in an orchestra, you would end up with different parts of the music going much more like it really goes, because it doesn't lock in to the conductor's baton. People don't lock in, they play a little bit out of tune, and they play a little bit their own tempo as they play passages. You're able to loosen up the metronome, so that you can have flexible tempi. We can even go radically off, but you can also go just subtly off, and the subtlety of it is what really gives it a much more natural feeling. Incidentally, I don't think eight is enough.

And remember that Interactor also has the ability to access sequences independently and instantaneously, so that they can each run, not only at different rates, but from different points. That's of course more understandable, but it's very powerful.

Yavelow: *What do you think about the interface between something like Lightning or Thunder and Interactor? [Lightning and Thunder are two revolutionary non-keyboard based MIDI controllers designed by Don Buchla.]*

Subotnick: We're going to get together with Buchla about this. In terms of coming up with new ways to input information, he is really brilliant and has been from the beginning, using touch-plate keyboards, when everybody else was using just straight keyboards. I don't think people understood it. That's one of the problems. At the time, they really thought electronic music or the synthesizer should be an organ. Touch-plate keyboards were just completely nuts. But it was clearly an impressive way to go right at the very beginning.

Yavelow: *How have you been tracking the conductor so far?*

Subotnick: My colleague, Pat Downs, took the innards of an Airdrum and restricted it to two directions: up and down. It's actually mounted in a baton, so we can track the velocity and of course the ictus of the upbeat and the downbeat. Basically, that's all you

need, because no matter where the arm moves in space, in order for the orchestra to really know where the beat is, the wrist has to change direction. When it does, if you were inside the baton, you would always feel it as a downbeat, even if he's off to the left, the ictus is up and down. This simplifies the problem enormously, because we don't have to track horizontally.

At first, I was tracking all the directions [of the conducting baton], using the Airdrum, and it was very complicated. It turned out to be totally meaningless, because when we analyzed it, it was the downward motion, no matter whether he was up to the side or wherever his hand was, the wrist was always more or less going down (or up) and giving a beat to someone. So we just got rid of all the other dimensions and stuck to the up and down motion, and it's been doing very well.

I don't think it's the answer; we're going to be experimenting with some new material. Essentially, not a glove, but actually a sleeve, getting everything through the wrist of the arm being tracked. Then the software will simply record all the movements, and because it's tempo following and knows where it is in the score, it's going to be able to say this combination of movements in the arm is the downbeat at measure 7. It may be an entirely different kind of downbeat in measure 50. And then just through this learning process the software will actually discover what the conductor's arm means, what these movements mean in relation to any particular piece of music. After you've conducted a few times, it will address itself to each conductor individually, which is really one of the reasons that nobody has been very successful at tracking conducting, because no two conductors conduct alike. You can't go through the textbook and say, the arm is going to be here for 1, because you're then putting the conductor in a straight jacket, they don't really do that. I think that's probably going to be closer to the answer.

But for the time being, this works pretty well. A lot of conductors don't use batons. I think we're always going to have to have somebody in the orchestra, at least one other member's tempo cross-referenced, because conductors can stop conducting, and the orchestra keeps playing.

Yavelow: Of course, this could be any MIDI trigger, it doesn't have to be something provided by a human.

Subotnick: I actually haven't done very much with conductors, I only have the one piece that uses a conductor and I've done about eight pieces using the software, and only one of them uses the baton. But concentrating on the conductor as a focal point, there is so little information coming from a conductor that it actually makes tracking a piano very easy, especially with that kind of intelligence of the software.

Yavelow: Is there a laser disc controller?

Subotnick: We're working on that now. That would be added to it. We don't have the module ready for commercial release yet, but we have actually controlled the progress of video recorders, fast forward, we can point to particular frames, and so forth. It's not in the initial release of Interactor because we are going to incorporate it into the laser disc technology as well. The modules will be added at a later time.

Yavelow: I think it's going to really take off among a certain crowd.

Subotnick: I think what's exciting is that the technology was always lagging behind what the people were doing out there. When I started, we had to push the technology and mold it in order to be able to use it meaningfully. It's turned around now. Technologies have developed, both commercial technology and specialized technology (like Interactor or Max). This is there just when people are going to be wanting to use it and when they get to that point, they're going to have something they can actually use, rather than have to wait for someone to develop it. I think it's a very exciting time right now.

Summary

✔ You can use your Macintosh to enhance live performance in just about any way you can imagine. Besides the many applications that have been suggested elsewhere in this book, MIDI controllers can influence other performance parameters, sequencers can be used in a live performance environment, and live performers can be synchronized to the Macintosh and vice-versa.

✔ The fact that MIDI provides room for expressive control is one of the driving factors motivating attempts to enhance device control. That we must use our hands to play notes rather than exercise additional performance control places physical limits on the extent to which the full benefits of MIDI can be realized. To realize the full potential of extended real-time device control offered by MIDI requires radical changes in keyboard design.

✔ It is now relatively easy to synchronize sequencers to live performers on stage. There are two approaches. A conductor or other tempo source can use the Tap Tempo (or Human Sync) feature built into your MIDI sequencer. The other approach is to translate an audio event into a MIDI clock to which a sequencer or drum machine is synchronized. The most elegant approach involves a process called "score following," in which the computer automatically detects the ever-changing tempos of individual performers and adjusts its playback or algorithmic generation of MIDI accordingly.

✔ Sequencing in a live performance offers many ways to enhance the control of your MIDI orchestra. Sequencer software can be run on the Macintosh, but you can also pre-program your sequences in the Macintosh and use a dedicated sequence player. Although most people think of sequencers as being used for playback purposes in a live performance situation, it is becoming popular to keep a sequencer running to record their performances as MIDI data. This is desirable, because often the improvised music generated in response to the emotion and excitement of the live performance environment is difficult to duplicate in the sterile atmosphere of a recording studio.

Part Six

Post-production

Part Six

Foreword

by Evan Brooks

Post-production

Making music is not what it used to be. We still have plenty of toys, but they have become smaller, lighter, smarter and more expensive. There is the temptation, even among those of us not new to the industry, to take for granted what we have today. It is hard to imagine a world without MIDI, for example, but many of us started off in just such a world. The consensus of many modern-day musical equipment developers, myself included, is that if we had the tools we have today ten years ago, we would still be musicians, and not engineers.

What we had ten years ago was a lot of equipment that had to be set up manually. A patch change required a book of knob and switch settings. Instantly switching between two different control settings on a piece of audio equipment meant that you had two of them. What changed all this was the invention of the microprocessor, and its subsequent integration into audio and musical equipment in the early 1980s. With a miniature computer inside of it, a synthesizer could save and recall patch settings instantly or retune itself automatically. An effects processor could contain dozens of effects programs available at the press of a button, perfectly repeatable each time. A mixing console could save and recall entire mixdown sessions, replaying them accurately over and over, without requiring several pairs of hands to operate all the controls. The microprocessor made so many

things easier, because it could now automate many tasks that had to be done manually in the past. But the biggest change was yet to come.

The introduction of the personal computer in the early 1980s was the original catalyst for the current revolution in music production. Because electronic musical instruments and other audio devices were all becoming microprocessor-based, control of these devices via an external computer became a real possibility. Because a computer can talk to another computer faster than a person can, such a connection allowed people to quickly move large amounts of digital data around the studio. The personal computer became the central storage device for saving, restoring, and editing the patch parameters of all the equipment it was hooked up to. The creative energies of early software pioneers yielded the first patch editors, librarians, and music sequencers to run on personal computers.

The arrival of the Macintosh in 1984 provided a platform for musical applications that could actually be used by musicians. The mouse and icon-based user interface allowed normal people to use the machine, without turning them into programmers in the process. As a result of its ease of use, accessibility, and popularity, the Macintosh has become the most widely supported personal computer used in professional and semi-professional music, audio, and post-production applications.

The state of music and audio production has certainly been improved by the use of personal computers. Progress, however, is not without its problems. One of the side effects of the connectivity that PCs can offer in a production environment is the connections themselves. Anyone who has waded through a maze of MIDI cables trying to unravel exactly who is connected to whom has experienced this unfortunate by-product of computer-enhanced productivity. The problem with having so many little boxes is that there are so many little boxes. In a computer-based environment, the computer has to talk to all those boxes. The boxes sometimes have to talk to each other, as well as the computer. It only takes a few pieces of equipment to create a cable jungle. Is this really a necessary evil of computer-based music production?

The same technology that created this confusion is now beginning to provide real solutions. If the watchword of the '80s was *connectivity*, the key to audio production in the '90s will be *integration*. The Macintosh has always provided at least a portion of this integration, in that the control of the devices in the studio could all be accomplished from one central station. All the software needed to create, edit, and produce music could be run on the same computer. All the data needed to set up the peripheral effects devices, routers, and sound sources could be stored in the same place.

The completion of the integration process involves bringing more of the production environment into the computer itself. This includes devices which are traditionally separate stand-alone boxes, such as music

synthesizers and samplers, reverb and effects processors, equalizers, mixers, and even the audio recording itself. The connectivity is not sacrificed in such an arrangement; rather, it is enhanced, for the different elements now communicate via software within the computer, as opposed to wires outside of it. Communication itself can now proceed at a much faster rate, with much higher bandwidth and greater security of data. Patches between devices now consist of software routing rather than physical cables. The net effect of all this is to reduce the entire production environment to a small desktop unit, which can be efficiently run by a single person.

Is this a vision of the future, or a taste of things to come? Not really. Much of it already exists today in installed systems that are actually working for people now. On the Macintosh platform specifically, you can put together a system that incorporates multi-track digital audio recording, editing, mixing and automation, 16-bit stereo sampling and playback, music synthesis, MIDI-based music sequencing, audio post-production tools and effects processing, with all patching of control information for automation, MIDI, and effects taking place entirely within the computer itself. In fact, most of this has been available on very expensive, proprietary systems for several years now. The arrival of these systems on the Macintosh sums up what this whole revolution in technology is about: *access.*

Access means that almost anyone can now afford to work with the state of the art in music and audio production systems. In many cases, a professional recording studio is only required for high-quality acoustic recordings. Most other jobs can be run within the music system itself. It is even possible to directly produce the desired end result on the

Macintosh system, be it a DAT, CD, or whatever. Access means that the person producing the music has full control over the entire process, from beginning to end, without having to rely on others to perform specialized tasks for them. Full creative control is retained, and the entire process is centralized. This allows a person to go from inspiration to finished product in a fraction of the time it would take by traditional methods, and at a fraction of the cost.

Because these systems are comprised of parts that all fit within the Macintosh framework, they can be bought independently, and work together when added to the system. People can actually afford these systems, because manufacturers don't have to design a custom computer and box to run them. And these systems actually come to market, because one company does not have to invent the entire system. Users are protected against obsolescence by hardware and software upgrades, and the availability of alternate sources of system components.

Now, professional quality audio production is no longer the exclusive domain of those few who could afford all of the right equipment, and could hire others to learn how to operate them. Anyone with a creative urge and a small amount of money can now become involved in this process. This is in fact happening even now. The overall base level of quality of music and audio production is being raised to new heights. Garage bands can produce professional quality digital recordings, as opposed to noisy cassette tapes. Saturday morning cartoons have sound effects that rival those of major motion picture soundtracks. Even audio for television has become better. In general, the cost of producing very high quality audio is going down, and anyone can get a piece of the action.

This brings us back to the core of this new technology: the Macintosh. As a producer of music or audio, you need to determine how much Macintosh you need to do the jobs you want. There is a system out there that can be configured for almost any need and budget. You can start small and work your way up, or you can jump right into a full-blown system. You can combine your favorite MIDI sequencer with your favorite hard disk recorder and sound sources. The point is that these choices now rest with you, and therein lies the real power of the new technology. You can control the entire process now, and the final product is a direct result of your own creativity. ♩

Evan Brooks is co-founder and vice president of engineering, Digidesign, Inc.

Introduction to Part Six

Post-production applications of the Macintosh have long been available and are now becoming widespread. The Macintosh is used for direct-to-hard disk recording, automated mixing, digital signal processing, ADR (automatic dialog replacement), sound effects editing, and the automation of various other common studio tasks.

Chapter 24 deals with direct-to-hard disk recording, the systems which have now dropped to well within the reach of home studios. These are 16-bit, 44.1 KHz, stereo and multitrack systems, which record digital audio directly onto SCSI hard drives. The most popular systems use internal NuBus cards, although Macintosh-controlled hardware peripheral systems are also available. Chapter 24 presents a discussion of the advantages to such systems, including many analog concepts that you will have to modify when you begin dealing with digital audio (for example, non-destructive editing).

With an appropriately equipped Macintosh you can now record, edit, and mix down audio of CD-quality and produce a master without ever leaving the digital domain. Because the same systems permit digital signal processing (e.g., filtering, EQ, noise reduction, normalization, envelope editing, and other DSP effects) without ever entering the analog domain, you can produce a musical product that does not enter the analog domain until it is played through speakers on a CD or DAT player.

Chapter 25, "MIDI Mixing and Studio Automation," covers automated mixing and other forms of studio automation. The three main approaches to using the Macintosh for mixing are virtual mixing, MIDI-controlled attenuation, and MIDI-controlled hardware mixers. Macintosh software applications for mixing focus on precision and nonreal-time editing. Programs offer the manipulation of signal level (volume), EQ (boosting or cutting specified frequency bands), effects (signal processing), reverberation, muting, and panning (moving the signal within the stereo audio field). DSP devices are also controllable by the Macintosh, just as they might be during live performances. In almost all cases, when you add a Macintosh to the recording chain, the complexity of your mixes can exceed the possibilities offered by human manipulation of the same devices.

Additionally, Chapter 25 examines how the Macintosh can be used for other tasks associated with studio production. Track charts and delay timing calculators are a natural for computer control. Macintosh automation is available for studio budgets, proposals, talent call lists, production expense tracking, accounting, receivables, billing, tape libraries (including tracking and labeling), equipment inventory and maintenance, and just about everything else you might apply a pencil and calculator to during the normal operation of a studio business or recording session.

Chapter 24

Direct-to-Hard Disk Recording

In this chapter . . .

✔ Introduction to Macintosh-based direct-to-hard disk recording technology.

✔ Various approaches to tapeless recording systems and their advantages over tape-based systems.

✔ Overview of new concepts introduced by hard disk-based recording systems.

✔ Implications of random access audio and non-destructive editing.

✔ Functional differences between a track on an audio tape and a soundfile on a hard drive.

✔ Distinctions between analog input/output and digital input/output.

✔ The various formats of digital audio data.

✔ The impact of sample resolution and storage requirements on disk-based systems.

✔ Special considerations for SMPTE synchronization in nontape-based systems.

✔ Available direct-to-hard disk systems and their software requirements.

✔ Third-party software and hardware support for Macintosh digital audio systems.

Cutting-Edge Components

Perhaps the most impressive Macintosh music peripheral now available is the relatively inexpensive, yet extremely high quality direct-to-hard disk digital audio system. These are 16-bit, 44.1 KHz (that is, CD-mastering quality), n-track systems, which take advantage of the SCSI port on the Macintosh (for more about SCSI see Chapters 3, 4, and 8).

Digital recording directly on hard disks has been a hot topic at recent AES (Audio Engineering Society), NAMM (National Association of Music Merchants), and NAB (National Association of Broadcasters) shows and probably will continue to be so for several years to come. Contributing to this is the seemingly never-ending downward trend in the cost associated with the components of such systems. Complementing the plummeting prices of large-capacity hard disks required for direct-to-hard disk recording applications is the widespread availability of both DSP chips (such as the MC 56000 and 56001) and CPU chips (such as the MC 68020, 030, and 040), which help to finally meet the processing requirements of professional digital audio.

With fully functional systems beginning to appear in the less-than-$1,000 range, it is no wonder that people about to upgrade their analog multitrack recorders are following these developments closely. For those who didn't read the rapid acceptance of CDs as writing on the wall foretelling the end of the analog era, DATs have arrived to drive the message home. If you haven't considered direct-to-hard disk recording seriously, it may be time to look around you.

The maximum recording time for a direct-to-hard disk system is limited only by the size of the hard disk storage medium, and two gigabyte SCSI drives are available that provide for up to three hours of stereo digital audio. Some systems require a dedicated hard drive, on which only digital audio data is recorded, while others provide digital audio recording on the hard drive you use for all your other work. The Macintosh serves as an interface to digital signal processing and digital mixing of recorded tracks, providing a means for testing and saving "mixes" that do not consist of actual soundfiles or digital tracks themselves, but are merely instructions that indicate when to play back specified regions of data and what processing to apply during playback. Synchronization of digital audio tracks with MIDI sequence tracks is gaining in popularity.

Throughout this book, a major distinction has been made between 8-bit and 16-bit digital audio. This chapter is concerned with hard disk-based 16-bit digital audio exclusively — there are some tape-based digital recording systems, offered by Akai (DR1200 ADAM) and Alesis (ADAT), that do not have anything to do with the Macintosh. You may want to review Chapter 7, "Setting up Your Mac Music Studio," for suggestions on configurations. Digital audio is based on sampling, so if you are uncomfortable with this concept, you may want to review Chapter 1, "Background." You will definitely want to read Chapter 13, "Editing Sampled Sound," in conjunction with this chapter.

Advantages of Tapeless Recording

Tapeless recording systems like those discussed in this chapter offer many advantages over their tape-based recorders.

Random access. All locations on all recordings on all tracks are available instantly (for all practical purposes) without having to wait for tape to rewind or reels to be located and swapped.

Centralized operation. Recording, editing, mixing, signal processing, and synchronization can all be accomplished within a single software-based environment. Operation is usually enhanced by the graphic user interface possibilities of the Macintosh. Cuelist editing can rival features previously only found on expensive automated mixing consoles.

Non-destructive editing. Much editing you do with a direct-to-hard disk recording system does not alter the original material — the sound is simply modified at the output stage according to instructions you provide at the editing or mixing stage. This includes cuts, splices, loops, and complete reorganization of track sections, which can be triggered by an easily constructed cuelist or playlist. Fading and crossfading also fall in this category and can be executed with amazing flexibility. Editing options are usually more powerful than non-software-based systems.

Precision of editing. Editing regions can be designated down to the sample level ($\frac{1}{44100}$ of a second) — precision you can never achieve with a razor blade.

Digital Signal Processing. DSP effects such as digital EQ, noise reduction, compression and limiting, filtering, gain adjustment, and special effects are extremely easy in a tapeless environment. Undo makes these operations very safe.

Time compression. With hard disk-based systems you can change the duration of a recording without affecting its pitch. Likewise, you can change the pitch of a recording without affecting its duration. However, extreme shifts compromise the overall fidelity. Tracks can also be moved in time with respect to one another, something that is next to impossible with tape.

Synchronization. Most systems offer built-in synchronization with a simple interface and no special additional hardware. Newer systems offer extremely powerful options for the synchronization of digital audio with MIDI data on a single Macintosh.

No generation loss. Unlike analog tape recorders, which add noise and distortion every time a tape is copied, copying a track of hard disk-based audio effectively clones the original; matching signal levels and other such transfer considerations are eliminated. Digital audio recordings also don't physically deteriorate every time the tape rolls across the playback head or over time like oxide-based tape.

Basic Concepts
Random access

In addition to the advantages of CD-quality playback and recording, direct-to-hard disk recording has an advantage over tape-based systems in that it provides virtually instantaneous random access to any sound or portion of sound recorded on your hard disk.

The power of this approach is clear to anyone who has ever cut and spliced analog tape or used a mainframe computer system that required both typing a "mount tape" command and actually having to wait for a human operator in some hidden room to find your tape and mount it. Although most Macintosh users with hard drives have thankfully been spared the latter inconvenience, only the younger musicians and recording engineers just entering the work-place may get away without having to splice a piece of audio tape.

You know that you have RAM in your Macintosh, but you might not have con-sidered that your own mind consists of random access memory. If it didn't, every time you wanted to add two numbers together you would have to "rewind" your brain to first grade where you learned addition. Likewise, samplers and sample players (like the MacProteus board described below), which capitalize on being able to sound like real acoustic musical instruments by actually playing back digital recordings of notes played by traditional instruments, would be rendered useless if these recordings were stored linearly rather than available via random access. Imagine repeatedly playing even the same note on one of these devices if the device had to rewind a tape before each successive note sounded.

In the audio tape world, multitrack tape recorders and even stereo tape recorders are further limited in that the tracks are all physically aligned with one another. It's next to impossible to slide one track in time with respect to another track, nor is it an easy matter to change the temporal order of musical sections without resorting to a razor blade and a splicing block. No matter how sharp your razor blade is, compared to digital cutting and splicing, it's thicker than prehistoric stone cutting implements.

Above all, the manipulation of linear-access media such as recording tape is almost always destructive, meaning your actual raw material is physically altered. On the other hand, similar digital manipulations of random access material is predominantly non-destructive, that is, your raw material will not be altered because all you are changing is "pointers" to locations on your hard disk. Cutting, splicing, and other types of editing merely require setting up a cuelist (also referred to as a playlist or EDL — edit decision list) that reorganizes the playback of soundfiles or regions of soundfiles on output. Just as the implica-tions of random access memory for computing have been astounding, so is random access audio realizing spectacular innovations in the way we deal with sound.

Note that most systems offer the option to create new soundfiles from these playlists, in which case you may either retain the original data or destroy it. There are also options to perform destructive edits. Digital signal processing is a type of editing that is often offered as both a destructive and non-destructive option.

Tracks

Direct-to-hard disk recording requires that you change your concept of audio tracks. Digital audio recording systems record into soundfiles, not tracks, although they often refer to these soundfiles as tracks.

When the specifications of a hard disk-based system mention tracks, they are usually referring to the maximum number of audio channels that can be output at a single time. You can have unlimited tracks (in the soundfile sense of the word) internally — often you can view unlimited tracks at a time — but you can only output a certain number simultaneously (usually equivalent to the number of DACs the hardware has dedicated to output).

The effective length of tracks in tapeless systems is longer than you would think, because silence does not take up any space the way it does on tape. Some systems give their specifications in track minutes because of this (track minutes express the total recording time without taking silences into consideration).

Most hard drives used for tapeless systems are fast enough to access four tracks simultaneously, so with a single hard drive the maximum number of output channels is four. Some systems let you synchronize hard drives to increase the number of simultaneous output channels.

Splicing of digital audio tracks offers numerous options. Crossfading (see Chapter 13) of any length or curve is a common feature that can be accomplished with unparalleled precision. Because non-destructive crossfading requires that two chunks of data be present in RAM simultaneously (the fading-out portion and the fading-in portion), the amount of RAM in your Macintosh may limit the maximum crossfade duration for a non-destructive crossfade (you can always resort to destructive editing in this case). Furthermore, crossfading requires a considerable amount of computational overhead, enough to tax your CPU in certain situations. This does not pertain to the Dyaxis, which implements its own virtual memory scheme. Crossfades (mixes) are done in the Dyaxis processor itself.

The editing interface of direct-to-hard disk digital audio systems is crucial to many people making the transition from the analog world. Rock and Roll or Scrub/Shuttle style editing is highly desirable and often available. JL Cooper's CS-1 (and CS-10) Control Station ADB-based remote controller (see Chapter 18, "MIDI Sequencing with Digital Audio") can be used to bring these features from the virtual world back to the physical.

Finally, take a moment to figure the cost per track minute on your analog machine — yes, you can buy new tape much cheaper than a new hard disk, but you can also dump your hard disk off to digital audio tape, erase the disk, and then reuse it over and over again. This is something you can't do very many times with a reel of analog recording tape.

Types of systems

Direct-to-hard disk recording systems fall into four large categories: internal Macintosh NuBus cards dedicated to sound processing, peripheral modules that require the Macintosh as a front-end, expansion options for external hardware samplers, and turnkey digital audio workstations (some of which use a specially configured Macintosh as a front-end).

The first and lowest-cost category, NuBus card-based systems, are designed to be used in conjunction with the Macintosh as the host computer. Options in this category include Digidesign's Sound Accelerator (available in five configurations), their Audiomedia Card, and their Pro Tools Audio Card and Mark of the Unicorn's Digital Waveboard.

The second, mid-range cost category, Macintosh-based peripheral modules (usually rack-mountable) includes: Studer Editech's Dyaxis, Doremi Labs's DAWN (Digital Audio Workstation Nucleus), Roland's DMS-80, Korg's Digital Audio Production System, Sonic Solutions's Sonic System, and Compusonics's DSP 1500.

The third group consists of expansion options for external hardware samplers: E-mu's E-III Direct to Hard Disk Option, Fairlight Series III 5.4 software release (MKB or MFX), Polyphonics's Optical Transfer Station upgrade for the Akai S900 (IBM required), New England Digital's Synclavier Direct to Disk Option, and Solid State Logic's ScreenSound.

The final category (five-to-six-figure price range), turnkey digital audio workstations (sometimes referred to as DAWs) dedicated to direct-to-hard disk recording, include: Akai's DD1000 (magneto-optical disk recording) with a Macintosh front-end, Advanced Music Systems's Audiofile and Audiofile Plus, Alpha Audio's DR-2, Soundcraft Electronics's Digitor, Digital Dynamics's ProDisk-464 (Macintosh front-end), Lexicon's Opus and Opus/e, Otari's DDR-10 (Macintosh front-end), For-A Corporation's Sirius 100, Digital Audio Research's Soundstation II, and New England Digital's PostPro SD (Macintosh front-end).

You should be aware of some systems running on other platforms, which you will hear about when you start hanging around the direct-to-hard disk community: Hybrid Arts's ADAP and ADAP II (Atari-based peripheral), WaveFrame's AudioFrame (IBM-based peripheral), Turtle Beach's 56K (IBM-based system), and Design Science's Digisound (IBM-based card set and peripheral).

Analog and digital I/O

Analog I/O is available across the board, but digital I/O is often considered an option. It is felt that a large body of users will never need to input from or output to the digital domain, even though digital audio tape is vastly less expensive than hard disk storage and one will inevitably desire to clear off one's hard disk(s) for the next project. At present, the easiest way to accomplish this archival process is the direct digital transfer to DAT.

When digital I/O is available, the AES/EBU (Audio Engineering Society/European Broadcast Union) standard data format is assumed and S/PDIF (Sony/Philips Digital Interface Format) is another popular output option. The AES/EBU format has been accepted as the ANSI S4.40-1985 standard, explaining its prevalence. AES/EBU is a more robust medium and includes the option to bypass copy protection. S/PDIF is the IEC consumer format based on this standard (used as a digital interface to some DAT recorders and CD players).

Some systems also support PCM 1610 and/or PCM 1630. Other formats you might want to know about are: SDIF-2 (Sony Digital Interface Format), EIAJ (Sony F1 — Electronic Industries Association of Japan), Sony 701 (F1), SDIF (1630), MADI (Multichannel Audio Digital Interface), Sony-Mitsubishi, ProDigi. Note that MADI is a superset of AES/EBU, providing for 56 audio channels as opposed to two. The format of the data is identical, except that some bits are used to specify channel number.

Most of these formats use a 32-bit word (called a subframe) to represent a digital audio sample (more than 16 bits are required because of the presence of sync bits, correction bits, status, and auxiliary information). This is often converted to 16-bit samples while resident in the Macintosh or hard drive. You will recall from Chapter 1 that this requires 10.6MB of storage for a minute of stereo audio (at a sampling rate of 44.1 KHz).

Digital audio data formats require special connectors and cables. AES/EBU signals travel on balanced lines and use XLR connectors. S/PDIF signals travel on unbalanced coaxial cables with RCA connectors or fiberoptic cables (preferable) requiring fiberoptic connectors. SDIF-2, MADI, and ProDigi also use balanced lines. SDIF-2 can also use BNC connectors.

After the issue of analog and digital I/O is addressed, the next considerations are the number of inputs and outputs, their impact on the internal organization of the hard disk, and whether they can be used simultaneously. Stereo is taken for granted, and on some systems expanding the number of inputs and outputs is achieved by adding additional hard disks, cards, or modules — this inevitably boils down to a question of financial resources.

Sample resolution and storage

Sampling rates of 44.1 KHz and, to a somewhat lesser extent, 48 KHz are always available. The same holds for 16-bit resolution. Some systems provide other lower or higher semi-standard rates such as 32 KHz and 44.056 KHz. Twenty-four-bit fixed-point or 32-bit floating-point resolution is often used internally in conjunction with certain DSP chips and for communication to external DSP peripherals.

The size of your hard disk ultimately determines the maximum amount of track minutes. The 300MB to 1GB hard disks are popular as a storage medium, and some systems offer bundled disks with their packages. Most systems require a speedy access time for the hard drive on which digital audio will be recorded (typically 27ms or better). Recent advances in the access speed of magneto-optical drives have made this 650MB cartridge-based medium popular for digital audio.

Although one could theoretically use any SCSI hard drive with a direct-to-hard disk recording system, at least one manufacturer (Studer Editech) uses a proprietary formatting and disk I/O protocol that requires relying on the system's manufacturer for storage disks. For people on tight budgets, the best case is a system that makes no distinction between digital audio and other types of data and simply records to your normal hard drive as if you were writing a file of any other kind.

Two further aspects of hard disk management that transfer from the computer world to the digital audio world are backup and fragmentation. When you start recording on your hard disk, backing it up becomes a necessary habit. Some companies offer streaming tape backup systems for this purpose, but if your system is configured with DAT-compatible digital outputs, this could be a viable solution (see Chapters 3 and 6 for backup solutions).

Fragmentation is another problem. If you start erasing files at random areas on the disk, the disk can become fragmented in such a way that, while you may have a lot of empty space, this space is not available in a contiguous block of any substantial size. Hard disk optimization and defragmentation utilities can solve this problem.

Synchronization

With many of these systems targeted at film and video applications, synchronization features are of tantamount importance. The AES/EBU and S/PDIF standards provide for synchronization information to be included in the digital audio data itself. The combination of digital audio tracks with MIDI sequence tracks provides the best of both worlds (see Chapter 18, "MIDI Sequencing with Digital Audio").

The software that you use to control direct-to-hard disk recording systems can provide synchronization possibilities that are nonexistent otherwise. Because your sound data is randomly accessible, playlists can be created that retrigger the same audio at widely separated SMPTE locations. Audio segments that are right next to each other on a digital audio track, meaning in a single soundfile, can be triggered with similar flexibility. Finally, audio segments on different tracks or soundfiles can be treated as if they were adjacent from the standpoint of synchronization purposes. Even adjacent tracks in stereo soundfiles can be treated as separate entities. Remember that when synchronizing to video with random access audio, there is no need to cue up the tape or wait for it to travel to the current location.

Stereo Direct-to-Hard Disk Recording Systems

With the exception of the first one, the following systems all require that you install a NuBus card into one of your Macintosh slots. For a complete table of all possible digital audio card configurations, see Table 3-2 in Chapter 3, "Mac Music Studio Basics." For a listing of system features see Table 24-1.

Table 24-1: Feature table — hardware specs

Note: For a feature table of editing software, see Chapter 13.

	Dyaxis	Audiomedia with Audiomedia	Audiomedia with Deck	Sound Tools	Pro Tools
Record/Playback					
No. simultaneous input channels	2 (4 option)	2	2	2	4 to 16
No. internal tracks	50 stereo	2 (stereo) or 1 mono	4	2 (stereo) or 1 mono	4 to 16
No. simultaneous output channels	2 4 (option)	2	2 (mix from 4)	2	4 to 16
Sample Rates					
48, 44.1, 44.056, 32	●●●●	●●●●	○●○○	●●●●	●●○○
31.25, 27.77, 22.05	100 other	●●●		●●●	
18.9, 16, 8	user-selectable	●●●		●●●	
File Formats					
Sound Designer I		●		●	●
Sound Designer II		●	●	●	●
AIFF		●		●	●
IMS/Dyaxis	●				
Export Formats					
'snd' resource		●		●	

Table 24-1: Feature table — hardware specs (continued)

	Dyaxis	Audiomedia with Audiomedia	Audiomedia with Deck	Sound Tools	Pro Tools
Digital I/O					
S/PDIF	●			●	●
AES/EBU	●			●	●
SDIF-2	●				
PCM 601, 1630, 1610	●				
Yamaha	●				
ProDigi	●				
DASH	●				
Digital effects sends and returns					●
MIDI Tracks					
Record/Playback			●		●
Import SMF			●		●
No. of Channels			32		32
Synchronization					
Trigger	(via option)		▸	●	●
Chase	(via option)			●	●
LTC/VITC	(via option)			●○	●●
Generate	(via option)				●●
EQ					
Parametric	(via option)		●	●	●
Graphic	(via option)	●		●	●
DSP					
Time Dilation	(via option)	●		●	●
Pitch Shifting	(via option)			●	●
Gain Adjustment	●	●	●	●	●
Dyn. Compression	(via option)			●	●
Limiting	(via option)			▸	▸
Noise Gate			●	●	●
Normalize		●	●	●	●
Chorus			●		●
Delay			●		●
Modulating Delay			●		●
Stereoization			●		●
Hum Removal			●		●
Miscellaneous					
Graphic Editing (waveform)	●	●		●	●
Graphic Editing (sound regions)	●				●

Table 24-1: Feature table — hardware specs (continued)

	Dyaxis	Audiomedia with Audiomedia	Audiomedia with Deck	Sound Tools	Pro Tools
Playlists (EDLs)	●	●		●	●
Virtual faders	●		●		●
Automated			●		●

Dyaxis

The Dyaxis direct-to-hard disk digital audio system from Studer Editech was the first direct-to-hard disk recording system available for the Macintosh (at that time it was marketed by Integrated Media Systems).

It features 16-bit stereo sampling at over 100 sample rates (some of which are derived by the computer and others, 32 KHz, 44.056 KHz, 44.1 KHz, and 48 KHz, are crystal-derived). A 48 KHz sampling rate provides 20 KHz frequency response in both channels with less than 0.01 percent distortion, equivalent to digital mastering machines found at most professional recording studios — the difference is the price. Both the 44.1 KHz and 48 KHz offer full linear phase filters. Six SCSI hard drives can be daisy chained (available from Studer in capacities of 105MB to 1.6GB).

Originally a stand-alone system that you controlled from the Macintosh by way of the serial port, the system can now be configured with an internal Motorola 56001-based NuBus card called the MacMix Excelerator Card for added DSP functions.

There are many configurations of the Dyaxis, all rack-mountable, but a complete two-channel system includes the digital audio processor module (this does the I/O), the system synchronizer module (reads and writes all SMPTE Time Code, formats in LTC and VITC, can serve as a synchronizable MIDI interface with house sync and film tach synchronization, and serves as the master clock for the Dyaxis) or the Time Code interface (you give up VITC and film tach synchronization with this less expensive option), one or more hard drives, MacMix Software (developed by Adrian Freed), and the MacMix Excelerator Card for enhanced DSP. And of course, a Macintosh computer is also required. There is a Dyaxis 2+2 system available that provides for four-channel recording and playback. For this you need an additional audio processor (with its own hard drives). Your single system synchronizer module can handle the lockup of the two audio processor modules and their hard drives (see Figure 24-1).

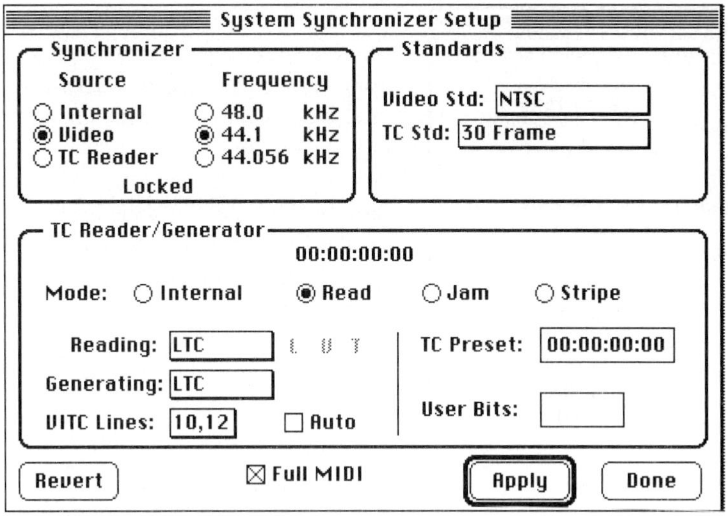

System Synchronizer Setup

Synchronizer

Source	Frequency
○ Internal	○ 48.0 kHz
⦿ Video	⦿ 44.1 kHz
○ TC Reader	○ 44.056 kHz

Locked

Standards

Video Std: NTSC
TC Std: 30 Frame

TC Reader/Generator

00:00:00:00

Mode: ○ Internal   ⦿ Read   ○ Jam   ○ Stripe

Reading: LTC

Generating: LTC

UITC Lines: 10,12   ☐ Auto

TC Preset: 00:00:00:00

User Bits: [   ]

Revert   ☒ Full MIDI   Apply   Done

Figure 24-1: Dyaxis's System Synchronizer Setup dialog box.

I/O

The system can be set to have as many tracks as you want — mono and stereo playback and recording are directly supported (four channels if you have the 2+2 system), but once the data is inside the disk, it can be partitioned into as many channels as are needed. The number of input/output formats available is impressive: S/PDIF, AES/EBU, SDIF, PCM601, Yamaha, PD, and IMS/D (Dyaxis). And you can convert from one format to another (see Figure 24-2). Note that the support of and conversion between these multiple formats are strictly a matter of I/O — on the hard disk, all files are stored in a single format: Dyaxis. You need Passport's Alchemy to convert from the Dyaxis format to another disk-based format — for example, to Sound Designer format (see Chapter 13, "Editing Sampled Sound").

One unique feature is that unlike most systems, which limit you to a single soundfile per output channel or a single stereo soundfile driving both output channels, the Dyaxis allows you to output multiple soundfiles simultaneously on a single channel.

Recording

Recording audio in MacMix takes the standard on-screen tape-transport emulation approach. A few bells and whistles are the option to punch in and out at time-code-specified locations and to view and return to multiple takes in the recording dialog box (see Figure 24-3). If you have the optional Excelerator NuBus Card, audio input is displayed as a waveform that scrolls in real time.

Editing

MacMix is the Macintosh software that comes with the Dyaxis (see Figure 24-4). Originally developed at IRCAM as a Macintosh front-end to a DEC VAX mainframe computer, it provides all the standard features of non-destructive sample editing software, including graphic EQ, pitch shifting, and time compression. These are similar to controls discussed in Chapter 13, "Editing Sampled Sound," but include some additional flexibility.

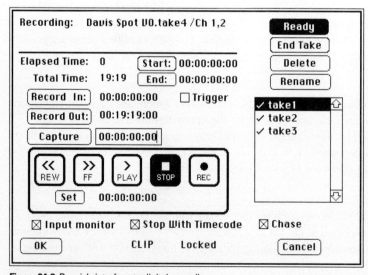

Input/Output Formats

Clock Source	Digital Output	Sample Frequency
◉ System Sync	○ Off	○ 48kHz
○ S/PDIF	◉ S/PDIF	◉ 44.1kHz
○ AES/EBU	○ AES/EBU	○ 44.056kHz
○ SDIF	○ SDIF	○ 32kHz
○ PCM601	○ PCM601	
○ YAMAHA	○ YAMAHA	Dyaxis
○ PD	○ PD	Processor 1
○ IMS/D	○ IMS/D	

OK   Monitor   Audio Source   Special
                ○ Input   ○ Digital   ☐ Master Clock
Apply   ◉ Repro   ◉ Analog   ☐ Effects Loop
                                        ☐ Emphasis
Cancel   Locked   ☐ DSP Loop

Figure 24-2: Dyaxis's Input/Output Formats dialog box.

Soundfiles may be examined in a View window with magnification ranging from an overview to individual samples. View windows provide timing information in seconds, samples, percents, or SMPTE, and the ability to preview any sound. Unique features are the option for the selection of multiple discontiguous regions (see A in Figure 24-5) and the option to view, fully zoomed in, the splice points that will result from cutting a region (see B in Figure 24-5). Besides "peak cue" indications of the largest sample in the window, "events of interest" may be marked with vertical tick marks and the linear breakpoint envelope superimposed upon the fragment. There is even an option to autofill a cut section with ambiance from the same soundfile.

The options for real-time digital EQ, both 10-band parametric and 5-band graphic, and gain control are extremely powerful. The parametric EQ provides an on-screen graph of the EQ curve, which can be very useful. The optional MacMix Excelerator NuBus Card is required for EQ.

Recording: Davis Spot V0.take4 /Ch 1,2

Ready
End Take
Delete
Rename

Elapsed Time: 0
Total Time: 19:19   Start: 00:00:00:00   End: 00:00:00:00
Record In: 00:00:00:00   ☐ Trigger
Record Out: 00:19:19:00
Capture   00:00:00:00

✓ take1
✓ take2
✓ take3

《 REW   》 FF   › PLAY   ■ STOP   ● REC

Set   00:00:00:00

☒ Input monitor   ☒ Stop With Timecode   ☒ Chase

OK   CLIP   Locked   Cancel

Figure 24-3: Dyaxis's interface to digital recording.

MacMix's Mix window displays graphic representation of the soundfiles or tracks (see Figure 24-6). In many ways it can function as an EDL, although the software offers a separate EDL feature (see below). The temporal location of soundfiles can be changed by dragging their representative graphic with the mouse (the fade-in and fade-out points may also be mouse-adjusted). There is a gain and pan control for each soundfile (see

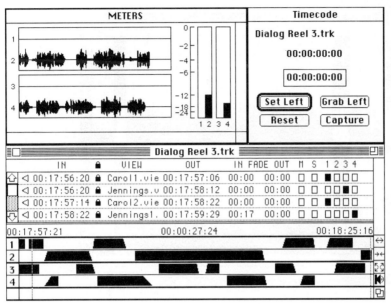

Figure 24-4: MacMix's main screen with a number of the available windows open at once.

bars on the right of Figure 24-6). Cut, Copy, and Paste are fully implemented. Mixes, which can last from a few samples to several hours, can be auditioned along the way. Unlike other software options for direct-to-hard disk recording, MacMix provides for unlimited soundfiles to be mixed and directed to the audio outputs.

An EDL style soundfile triggering option is available, which also provides access to multiple soundfiles (the Playlist option discussed under Sound Designer below and in Chapter 13 only lets you access a single soundfile). Here you can set SMPTE start and stop times and in and out points for crossfading (see Figure 24-7). Any item on the EDL can be muted, soloed, or directed to any of the two or four audio outputs (depending on the configuration of your Dyaxis). Audio routing is accomplished by way of the checkboxes at the right of the list.

Sound Tools
Sound Accelerator

Although released after Dyaxis, Digidesign's Sound Accelerator is the NuBus card that really kicked off the desktop audio revolution for the Macintosh. Installation is just as easy as installing a video card. The card is based upon the Motorola 56001 DSP chip and provides stereo audio playback, direct from your hard disk, at true CD quality and at signal levels ranging from -10dBm to +4dBm. The frequency response is 20 Hz to 20 KHz (at the 44.1 KHz sample rate) with a signal-to-noise ratio of greater than 90 dB. Total harmonic distortion is less than 0.009 percent and

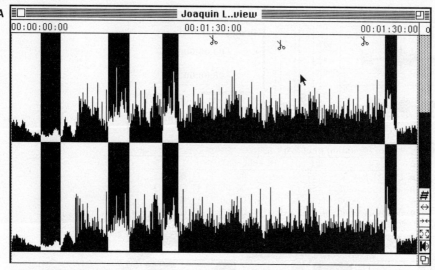

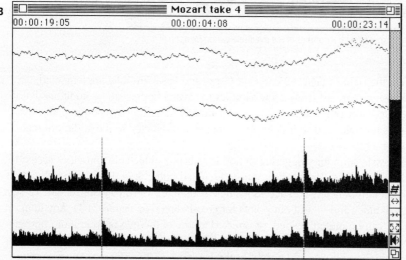

Figure 24-5: MacMix's View windows. **(A)** This shows the option for selection of multiple discontiguous regions. **(B)** This option lets you view the splice points that will result if the sound between the two cursor locations is removed.

the maximum sample rate for mono is 312 KHz (156 KHz stereo) using the on-board 19.7568 MHz clock. Higher rates are possible with an external clock. For DSP it uses static RAM at a speed of 45-55ns with no wait states. This card can be used with many software packages discussed in this book.

The Sound Accelerator Card itself does not ship with any substantial software for direct-to-hard disk digital recording. However, it does include Digidesign's

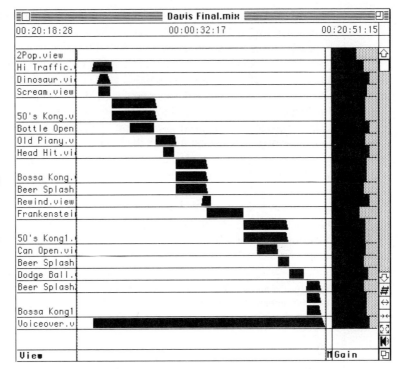

Figure 24-6:
MacMix Mix window. The Mix window combines in one intuitive interface operations that are split into multiple windows in Sound Designer II (Pro Tools remedies this). Because of this, the Mix window pioneered in MacMix has been adopted by the Akai DD1000 and New England Digital's D-to-D.

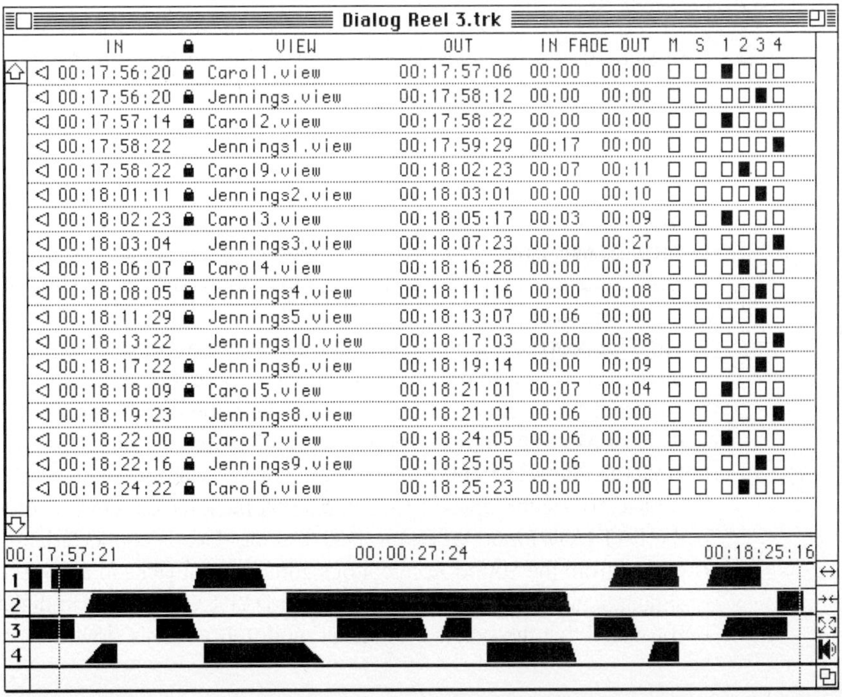

Figure 24-7:
MacMix's EDL window.

SoftSynth SA program (a Sound Accelerator-specific version of Softsynth) and manual and two utilities. The first, MIDI Preview, allows you to play soundfiles from a MIDI keyboard, and the second, Sound Installer, to install special 'snth ' resources into compatible programs such as HyperCard and Director or the Macintosh System itself (use SoundMaster at CD quality). These special 'snth ' resources allow any Sound Manager-equipped Macintosh program to play 8-bit or 16-bit, mono or stereo sounds through the Sound Accelerator. Playback of 8-bit soundfiles is greatly enhanced and support of chunky soundfiles is added. Chunky soundfiles play back at 8-bit through the Macintosh speaker port or use the Sound Accelerator Card for 16-bit playback if it is installed. See Chapter 15, "Making Music without MIDI," for more information about these tools.

SoftSynth SA is a program that uses the Sound Accelerator to provide real-time additive and carrier/modulation synthesis with up to eight software-based digital oscillators (32 oscillators in non-real-time mode). The resulting soundfiles use sample rates of up to 44.1 KHz (CD quality). Monophonic playback is available from any MIDI keyboard, or these sounds can be manipulated with many other software packages. Most of these packages permit the loading of these sounds into most commercially available samplers (digital sampling keyboard). See Chapter 10, "Sound Generation," for a detailed discussion of SoftSynth.

I/O

In order to input sound to the Sound Accelerator, you need either or both of Digidesign's hardware peripherals dedicated to sound input. Their less expensive AD-IN box communicates with the Sound Accelerator via an RS 422 cable (included) and provides for left, right, or stereo input at levels from -10dBu to +8dBu. The box includes input level controls and input level LEDs for each channel. A green LED lights when the signal level reaches -20dBu and a red LED flashes when clipping occurs. Clipping happens when the input signal is louder or "hotter" than the input device allows. On analog recorders occasional clipping is not a problem (usually it is taken care of by noise reduction circuitry like Dolby B or C), but digital clipping creates distortion and other artifacts that are absolutely unacceptable and must be avoided at all costs.

The Rolls Royce of input devices for the Sound Accelerator is their DAT I/O Bi-directional Digital Interface. This peripheral permits the transfer of sound data to and from the Macintosh without ever leaving the digital domain in either the S/PDIF or AES/EBU format. There is a "thru" switch to connect the AD-IN box to the DAT I/O and select either as the input source without having to unplug any cables. To use the digital I/O features you must have a DAT recorder connected to the DAT I/O's input. When the DAT I/O interface is connected, any sound being output from the Sound Accelerator's audio output jacks in analog format is simultaneously output from the selected DAT I/O's outputs in digital form (provided that the box is in transmit mode). If you mix down directly to a DAT recorder, your music doesn't ever have to pass through the analog domain until your CD or DAT is played by the consumer.

Digidesign also has a Pro I/O analog interface that includes balanced +4 XLR connectors, better digital converters (16-bit with 64X oversampling) and filters (18-bit with 8X oversampling), Apogee anti-alias filters, and higher resolution digital meters. The Pro I/O also adds 44.056 KHz to the standard 48 KHz, 44.1 KHz, and 32 KHz found on their other interfaces. Additionally, it provides Video (house sync) lockup in both NTSC (National Television Standards Committee) and PAL (phase alternated line) formats.

In consideration of the vast amount of storage required by digital audio and knowing full well that anyone purchasing their DAT I/O interface will probably be recording lengthy soundfiles, Digidesign ships a backup utility called DATa with the package. This utility backs up both the audio data and edit/parameter data onto a DAT. If the soundfile that you are backing up happens to be sampled at the same rate as your DAT uses for playback, you will even be able to listen to the file, because all the edit/parameter data is stored in the file's header and parameter section, after which the audio is recorded normally (digitally in this case).

Whether you use the AD-IN box or the DAT I/O box for recording, you should not have any problem operating the controls, because they emulate those found on most standard tape recorders.

Completing the package

Digidesign's Sound Designer II software, used in conjunction with their Sound Accelerator Card and AD-IN box, completes the Sound Tools hard-disk recording and editing environment. You can purchase all three elements together, as Sound Tools, or separately as you build up your system. As the name suggests, this software provides a set of tools with which to manipulate sound (see Figure 24-8). In earlier incarnations, Sound Designer (and most of the software accessing the Sound Accelerator Card) was marketed as an editor for digital sampling keyboards, and many of those features are still present.

Digidesign's Sound Tools package is available in five configurations:

A/D System	Sound Designer II, Sound Accelerator, AD-IN
Digital I/O System	Sound Designer II, Sound Accelerator, DAT I/O
A/D & Digital Systems	Sound Designer II, Sound Accelerator, AD-IN, DAT I/O
Pro Analog System	Sound Designer II, Sound Accelerator, Pro I/O

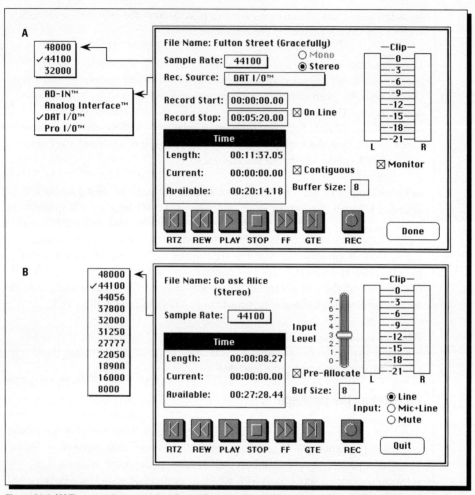

Figure 24-8: (A) The recording controls of Sound Designer II and **(B)** Audiomedia are the interface to direct-to-hard disk digital recording with the Sound Accelerator Card or the Audiomedia Card. Note that if you use Sound Tools with a Macintosh SE, you are limited to a 32 KHz sampling rate when recording in stereo. In mono, the sample rate for the SE goes up to 44.1 KHz.

Pro Analog & Digital   Sound Designer II, Sound Accelerator, Pro I/O, DAT I/O

Audiomedia

Digidesign's Audiomedia Card is in many ways already a second-generation digital audio board. It differs from their Sound Accelerator in that it can play back up to four tracks at once (the Sound Accelerator can only monitor two tracks while

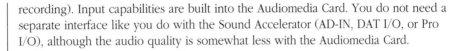

recording). Input capabilities are built into the Audiomedia Card. You do not need a separate interface like you do with the Sound Accelerator (AD-IN, DAT I/O, or Pro I/O), although the audio quality is somewhat less with the Audiomedia Card.

With this newer board you can apply different EQ and DSP effects simultaneously to up to four tracks in real time without ever altering your soundfile. The main feature missing from the Audiomedia Card and present in the Sound Accelerator Card is digital I/O.

The Audiomedia Card ships with its own software for inputting, editing, processing, and outputting digital audio recorded directly to hard disk. The Sound Installer utility is included and there are also two very powerful HyperCard stacks that provide all the tools for recording, simple editing, and playing back sounds from your own HyperCard stacks. As is fashionable these days, their Sound Access stack does all the work for you, creating buttons that play specified sounds, installing the resources required to play the sounds, and even automatically copying the various buttons to the stack of your choice.

Selling for less than $1,000, Digidesign's Audiomedia Card places CD-quality digital audio in the hands of the masses.

Software Options
Sound Designer, Audiomedia, Alchemy, Sound Apprentice

Both Digidesign and Passport Systems market sound-editing software that utilizes Digidesign's Sound Accelerator and Audiomedia Card. Digidesign's software options include Sound Designer II and a scaled-down version of the same program called Audiomedia that ships with their Audiomedia Card. Passport similarly offers two packages, Alchemy and a much less scaled-down version called Sound Apprentice. Alchemy can also be used to edit files created with the Dyaxis.

Because Digidesign produces the cards themselves, Passport is placed in a similar relationship to Digidesign as Altsys (makers of Fontographer) is to Adobe (creators of PostScript and in control of the licenses to its use in hardware products such as the Apple LaserWriter). However, this fact has had much less impact upon Passport as Adobe's trade secrets had on Altsys.

Standard features

The editing features of these programs (except those that deal exclusively with direct-to-hard disk recording) were scrutinized earlier in this book. A summary of options follows, but you should consult Chapter 13, "Editing Sampled Sound," for an in-depth discussion.

All four programs provide a complete set of basic features for editing, processing, and playing back sound from your hard disk. That is where the similarity ends.

A few examples will suffice. All four programs can compute FFTs, which analyze the harmonic spectrum of a sound or sound region. These graphs illustrate the frequencies of the sine waves that make up the particular sound and how the amplitude of these frequencies change over time. The Digidesign packages offer a variety of spectacular 3-D displays over which you have considerable control — except editing and resynthesis. Alchemy's modest 2-D FFT doesn't show the transformation of frequencies over time — your only time reference is the duration of the selected area — but you can edit the level of each frequency and "resynthesize" the sound.

Alchemy offers powerful features for editing both amplitude and frequency envelope, which are missing entirely from Sound Designer.

EQ is another area in which the programs differ. Both companies offer simple parametric EQ, but Digidesign adds options for digital 5-band stereo or 10-band mono graphic EQ.

Finally, Passport allows mixing the Clipboard with the current soundfile, with limited control, into a selected region of a single soundfile, whereas Digidesign provides options to mix four separate soundfiles together, stereo or mono, and adds considerable control over input level, stereo pan, and delay during the mixing process. The advantage to Alchemy's approach to mixing is that you can do so anywhere within a soundfile. Digidesign's paradigm for mixing requires that you mix every soundfile from the beginning.

Your own applications may require certain amenities like Passport's out-point editing that allows you to perform many edit operations such as pasting or mixing from the end-point of a selection rather than from the beginning of a selection. Or you may require Digidesign's scrub option that allows you to use the mouse like a video deck's jog wheel and play back in slow motion forward or backward, depending upon which direction and how fast you move the mouse over a region. When you see and hear this happen, you will swear that your hard disk must be spinning backward.

For more information about editing digital audio soundfiles and an in-depth discussion of the options presented by both Digidesign and Passport, see Chapter 13. Note that Symbolic Sounds's Kyma can also edit files stored in AIFF and can even make digital audio recordings (see Chapter 10, "Sound Generation").

Playlist editing

One of the most powerful features of Sound Designer and Audiomedia is their Playlist option (this was not discussed in Chapter 13). See Figure 24-9. These have no counterpart in the Passport products.

Playlists are equivalent to EDLs and sometimes referred to as cuelists. Unlike Dyaxis's MacMix, Digidesign requires that your Playlist be constructed from regions existing in a single soundfile. On the other hand, Digidesign's Playlist features crossfade and nudging options that are considerably more sophisticated than those in MacMix.

After you have recorded a file, an unlimited number of playlists may be associated with it. A playlist defines the order that specified regions of a soundfile will be played back in as well as the transitions between those regions. These may be locked to SMPTE, each region on the playlist designated to occur at a specific SMPTE frame (see Figure 24-9).

Because we are dealing with random access audio, you can designate any portion of a soundfile to be a region, and that region can appear anywhere and any number of times upon a playlist. Using playlists, two minutes of audio material can be organized into a 12-minute composition. Digidesign also markets a package called Cue Sheet that combines many of these playlist features with the ability to trigger MIDI events too.

Digidesign's Playlist Editor also provides powerful features for controlling how regions transition from one to another. Seven different transition or crossfade options are available (see Figure 24-10). For the crossfade options, you have complete control over crossfade duration.

Butt splice	One region jumps immediately to the next with no crossfade.
Linear crossfade	Uses a linear crossfade slope between the two regions.
Equal power crossfade	Introduces a 3 dB volume boost in the curve of the crossfade.
Slow in fast out crossfade	Fades out the first region quickly and fades in the next slowly.
Fast in slow out crossfade	Fades out the first region slowly and fades in the next quickly.

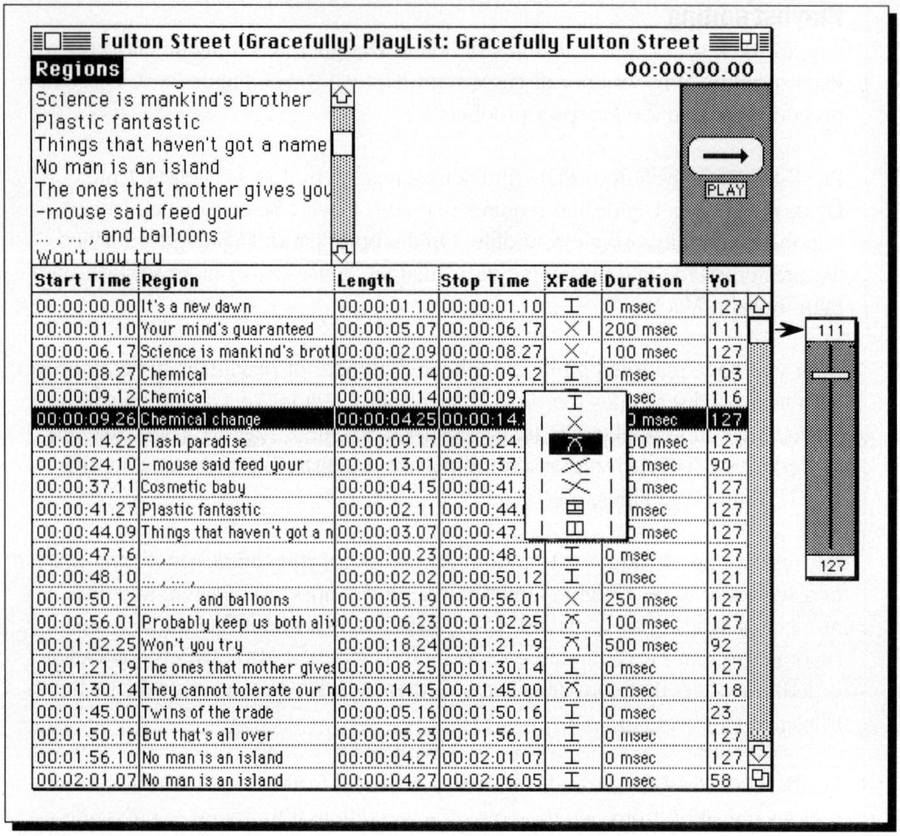

Figure 24-9: Playlist editing in Sound Designer and Audiomedia. The interface is very easy to operate. All your regions appear in a scrolling list at the upper left and you simply drag this into the main Playlist area of the screen (lower portion of the screen).

Overlap transition	The two regions are simply overlapped for the indicated duration with no crossfade.
Overlap transition w/limit	Same as the overlap transition above, except that this automatically limits the amplitude making sure that no clipping occurs.

All crossfades can be designated as normal crossfades, pre-crossfades, and post-crossfades. Normal crossfades are centered on the indicated transition point. Pre-crossfades execute the crossfade before the transition point (the crossfade ends at the transition point). Post-crossfades execute the crossfade after the transition point (the crossfade begins at the transition point).

A
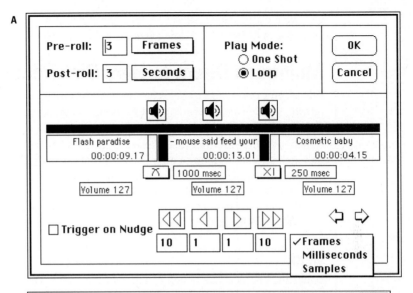

B
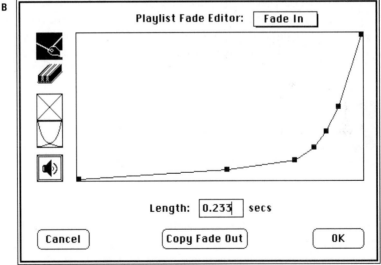

Figure 24-10: Editing options in Digidesign's Playlists. **(A)** This Edit Regions dialog box lets you reset and nudge the start and end points of regions in the playlist. **(B)** The Fade Editor dialog box lets you create an overall fade-in and fade-out for the playlist.

Playlists have several additional features. You can access an Edit Regions dialog box that lets you make fine adjustments to the start and end points of a region. Editing is enhanced by loop play and pre- or post-roll options present in this dialog box. The transport controls in this context are really "nudge controls" that move the transition points in increments that you specify.

Finally, you can assign a non-destructive overall fade-in and fade-out for each playlist in its entirety. The software lets you manipulate the curve of these fades as if they were elastic bands (similar to envelope editing found in the patch editors discussed in Chapter 12, "Editing Synthesized Sound").

Multitrack Direct-to-Hard Disk Recording

Digidesign's Deck and Pro Tools are two direct-to-hard disk recording systems that provide for four-track recording in their basic configuration — meaning that you don't need to purchase another whole system and synchronize it to your original system, as is the case with the Dyaxis 2+2 mentioned earlier in this chapter. Although offering support of their first Sound Accelerator card, Deck is primarily designed around Digidesign's second digital audio NuBus card (the Audiomedia card) and has been available since 1990. Pro Tools relies upon the company's third digital audio card (the Pro Tools Audio card) and was released in late 1991, much too late for the detailed coverage it deserves to appear in this book.

Deck

Unlike the products mentioned earlier, which are all limited to two-track or stereo audio, Digidesign's Deck software provides for four tracks of CD-quality digital audio combined with 32 channels of MIDI data. The program resembles a portable four-track tape recorder in every detail, and if you have ever operated a hardware four-track cassette deck you probably won't even need to read the manual (see Figure 24-11). It is optimized to run with the Audiomedia Card, although many of its options are available with the Sound Accelerator Card.

Deck has separate EQ and DSP effects modules for each track. Both EQ and one of four other effects can be applied to a track simultaneously. The other available effects are Stereo-ize (pan with a delay), Delay (with control over feedback and dry/wet mix), Chorus (with depth, modulation, and dry/wet mix controls), and Stereo Modulation Delay (with control over delay, feedback, modulation, and dry/wet mix). If you don't want to use another effect with a track, you can apply two different EQ modules to it. Just like hardware outboard DSP gear, nothing you change will alter the soundfile data on your hard disk unless you want it to (see Figure 24-12).

Normal studio practices such as punching in and out, loop recording, and sound on sound are available, as is unlimited digital bouncing of tracks with no loss of fidelity. Interestingly, when you are bouncing tracks Deck seems to acquire additional tracks, because you don't need to keep a track "open" to bounce down to. Thus, all four tracks can be bounced down to a single track or to two tracks for stereo, in which case Deck is functioning as if it were a six-track recorder (see Figure 24-13). Random access audio makes this all possible.

Deck's controls and faders may be mapped onto any MIDI controllers or moved with the mouse on the screen. In either case, it is possible to record these fader

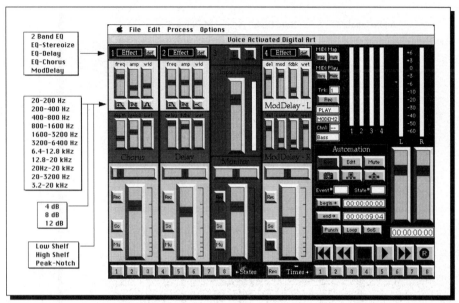

Figure 24-11: Digidesign's Deck software. The interface resembles a standard integrated hardware recorder/mixer.

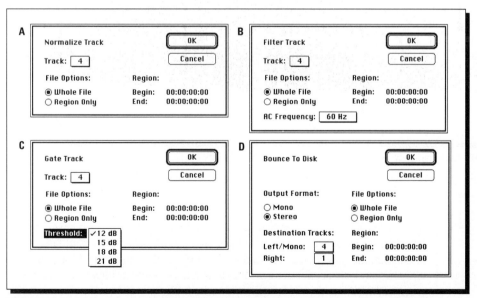

Figure 24-12: Deck's interface to destructive editing options. **(A)** Normalization. **(B)** Hum Removal. **(C)** Gating. **(D)** Bouncing.

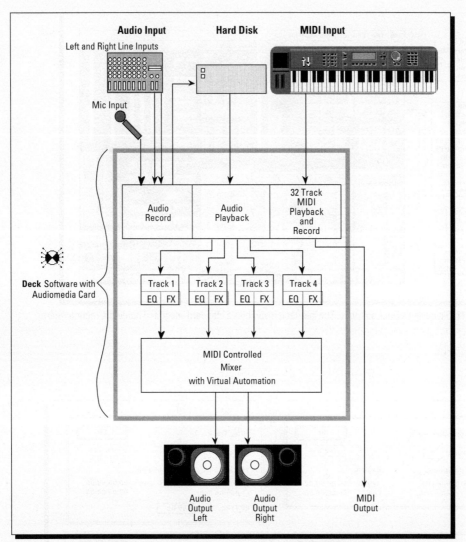

Figure 24-13: Signal flow in Deck. Deck records up to two tracks at a time and plays back a stereo mix of up to four tracks.

movements and create a completely automated mixdown. Once you have your final four tracks, you can play these back and use the volume faders to fade tracks in and out, the pan controls to change stereo placement, and coax the EQ and effects controls through a number of configurations. All your interaction can be recorded, edited, and you can then watch the faders move by themselves on the screen during playback.

Configuring the MIDI controller mapping to on-screen faders in Deck is very simple. You click the on-screen fader that you want to map, press the map button, and then move the hardware controller that you want mapped to the virtual one. Deck figures out what controller you moved. You repeat the process for all the on-screen controls you want to map to external MIDI controllers. That's all there is to it.

Deck also records and plays back 32 channels of MIDI data simultaneously with digital audio. There are limited editing operations you can perform on the MIDI data, but that is of little consequence because you can import and export data freely with any MIDI sequencer that supports the SMF format (just about all sequencers do). However, if you want a full-blown MIDI sequencer with all the bells and whistles and digital audio tracks too, Opcode's StudioVision and Mark of the Unicorn's Digital Performer put many of the pieces together in a single package. For more information see Chapter 18, "MIDI Sequencing with Digital Audio."

Pro Tools

Digidesign's Pro Tools was released in 1991. The package includes ProDECK software (the successor to Deck), ProEDIT software (the descendant of Sound Designer), the Pro Tools Audio Card, and the new Pro Tools Audio Interface, which uses balanced XLR connectors.

Each Pro Tools Audio Card provides for four channels of recording and playback, and you can have up to four cards in your Macintosh (if you have enough slots) to create a full-blown 16-track direct-to-hard disk digital audio recorder. You need a separate Pro Tools Audio Interface for each Audio Card installed, that is, for every four channels of digital audio. Note that two or more cards require Digidesign's System Accelerator Card to provide a direct patch from the Audio Cards to their attached SCSI hard drives.

Unlike Deck, which allows you to manipulate four tracks of audio in the Macintosh but only record two at a time and output a stereo mix, each Pro Tools Audio Card can handle four channels of input and output simultaneously. This is largely because each Pro Tools Audio Card contains not one but two Motorola 56001 processors. Note that you may need a fast Macintosh (IIci or IIfx) to achieve four channels of simultaneous recording, although any Macintosh II (except the IIsi) should be able to play back up to four tracks at once. The editing software for Pro Tools combines features of Deck (see above) and Sound Designer II (see Chapter 13, "Editing Sampled Sound").

ProDECK lets you designate some of your digital inputs and outputs as effects sends and returns, allowing you to access signal processing devices that offer digital I/O and thus keep your sound in the digital domain at all times. The virtual transport features 60 autolocation points and real-time varispeed control. Each of ProDECK's mixer modules includes an Edit button that takes you directly to the current playlist. Like Deck, ProDECK lets you assign any MIDI controller to any virtual control. Automation has been enhanced to include eight tracks of dynamic automation, 40 mixer states, and unlimited mixer snapshots. Even the parameter control knobs of ProDECK's built-in EQ and effects can be automated (see Figure 24-14).

Compared to Sound Designer, ProEDIT has a significantly upgraded user interface for editing hard-disk recordings. The display of each audio track functions as a graphic representation of the playlist (see Figure 24-15). Each track also has an individual set of controls for volume, panning, solo or mute, and voice priority. Rudimentary MIDI sequencing features have been added, and this includes a graphic display of MIDI data in piano-roll format, lined up with the appropriate audio tracks.

A typical recording session using Pro Tools starts in ProDECK for recording, switches to ProEDIT for editing and arranging regions in the desired playback order, and then switches back to ProDECK for mixdown (see Figure 24-16).

The Pro Tools software also provides for continuous SMPTE synchronization and resolve on all channels. Digidesign has finally put the 29.97 frames-per-second issue (see Chapter 25, "MIDI Mixing and Studio Automation") to rest: It offers both drop- and non-drop-frame SMPTE formats at this rate in both ProDECK and ProEDIT.

Third-party Connections

Digidesign's MasterList PDS (processor direct slot) is designed to support the interface between Pro Tools or Sound Tools and the Yamaha PDS compact disc mastering system ($25,000). The MasterList PDS software creates a special playlist of digital audio soundfiles. This functions similarly to the playlists found in Sound Tools, Pro Tools, and Audiomedia, except that you can access multiple files on any hard disks that are currently accessible to your Macintosh and you can access regions or playlists within soundfiles. MasterList lets you add subcodes such as catalog code, ISRC (International Standard Recording Code), emphasis, copy prohibit, song offsets, and track and index numbers. The software handles up to 65 minutes of music consisting of up to 99 tracks, each containing up to 99 index points.

Many third-party developers offer compatibility with Pro Tools and other Digidesign digital audio cards (Sound Accelerator and Audiomedia). Three professional-level MIDI sequencers provide for the integration of digital audio tracks directly into MIDI sequencing software: Opcode's StudioVision, Mark of the Unicorn's Digital Performer, and Steinberg's Cubase Mac Audio (see Chapter 18).

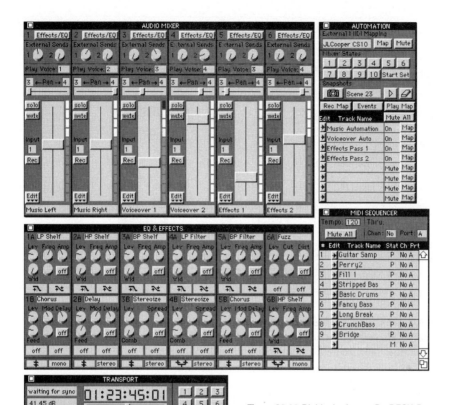

Figure 24-14: Digidesign's new ProDECK. Because of the 24-bit resolution of ProDECK's digital signal processing, the effective resolution of each volume fader during playback automation is 16 million points.

Eight-bit direct-to-hard disk recording

MacroMind-Paracomp's MacRecorder and SoundEdit (discussed in Chapter 10) were limited to recording in RAM since their introduction. SoundEdit Pro lets you record soundfiles directly to hard disk with one or two MacroMind-Paracomp MacRecorder digitizers or other sound input devices such as the built-in microphones found with the IIsi and LC. Additional enhancements include multiple tracks with independent control of gain and output assignment (left, right, or both) and the option to apply most edit operations to a single track or across any number of tracks (see Figure 24-17).

In late 1991, Tactic Software, previously known for their libraries of 8-bit clip sounds, started distributing a new digitizer made by the Mitshiba Corporation. Unlike MacroMind-Paracomp's MacRecorder, Mitshiba's Stereo-Recorder is designed for stereo input to the Macintosh (to accomplish this with MacroMind-Paracomp's system, you need two Mac-Recorders). At the time of this writing, the software is limited to recording in RAM; however, Mitshiba intends to provide for 8-bit direct-to-hard disk recording in 1992.

Figure 24-15:
Digidesign's ProEDIT.
Note that your list of
audio regions is
displayed at the right.
The individual tracks
become graphic
representations of
playlists (the region
names appear at the
upper left of each
region placed on a
track). You can use
the Grabber tool (little
hand at the upper
center of the window)
to slip regions freely
within or across
tracks. The new
Trimmer tool
(immediately to the

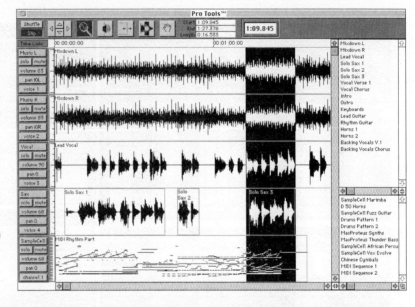

right of the speaker icon) lets you lengthen or shorten each region simply by dragging the region's bounding box. Many
editing operations can include the MIDI tracks at the bottom of the screen along with the audio tracks (note how the
selection stretches across all tracks, both MIDI and audio, in this figure).

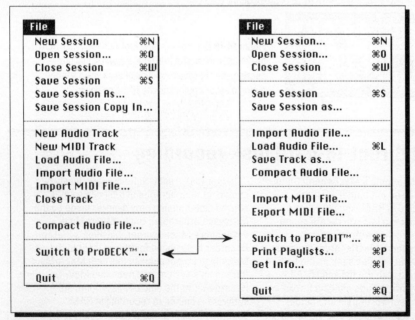

Figure 24-16: ProDECK and ProEDIT are designed to work together. Both programs deal with the same data simultaneously, so any edit you make in one program is immediately reflected in the other. Jumping from program to program is
facilitated by a single menu command on the File menu of each program.

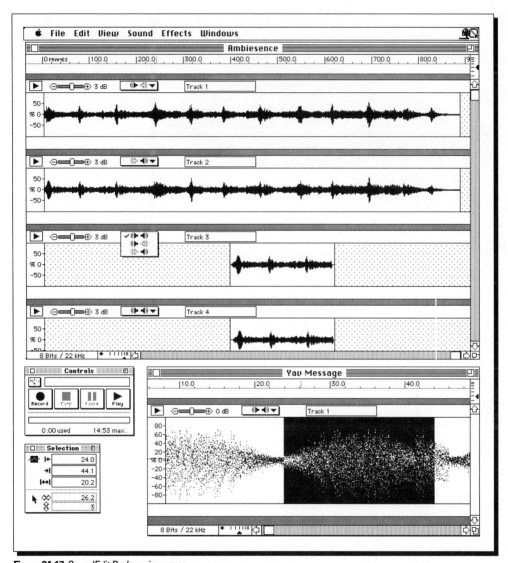

Figure 24-17: SoundEdit Pro's main screen.

JL Cooper's CS-10 Control Station works hand in hand with Digidesign's Pro Tools (see Figure 24-18). Unlike JL Cooper's earlier remote controller (the CS-1 — discussed in Chapter 18 — which functions equally well with Sound Tools and just about any MIDI sequencer), the CS-10 is designed with Pro Tools in mind, although you can configure it for some other Macintosh programs.

Figure 24-18: JL Cooper's CS-10 Control Station for Pro Tools.

The CS-10 provides hardware control of all transport, automation, and digital signal processing functions available in ProDECK and ProEDIT, including EQ, effects, panning, levels, and all other options offered by both programs. The box features a jog/shuttle wheel, eight faders, six rotary potentiometers, cursor keys (for zooming in and out over amplitude or time — note the similarity of these to the on-screen controls dedicated to the same function in ProEDIT, Sound Designer, and Audiomedia), and ten assignable function keys (each with a shifted mode as well). There is also a footswitch input that you can assign just like any of the function keys.

Summary

✔ Macintosh music peripherals are now available that offer relatively inexpensive, yet extremely high quality direct-to-hard disk digital audio systems. These are 16-bit, 44.1 KHz (that is, CD-mastering quality), *n*-track systems, which take advantage of the SCSI port on the Macintosh. Lower-end 8-bit direct-to-hard disk recording systems are beginning to appear.

✔ Direct-to-hard disk recording systems fall into four large categories: internal Macintosh NuBus cards dedicated to sound processing, peripheral modules that require the Macintosh as a front-end, expansion options for external hardware samplers, and turnkey digital audio workstations (some of which use a specially configured Macintosh as a front-end).

✔ The maximum recording time for a direct-to-hard disk system is limited only by the size of the hard disk storage medium, and two gigabyte SCSI megabyte drives are now available that provide over three hours of recording. Some systems require a dedicated hard drive, on which only digital audio data is recorded, while others allow digital audio recording on the hard drive you use for all your other work. The Macintosh serves as an interface to digital signal processing and digital mixing of recorded tracks, providing a means for testing and saving mixes that do not consist of actual soundfiles or digital tracks themselves, but are merely instructions that indicate when to play back specified regions of data and what processing to apply during playback.

✔ Tapeless recording systems like those discussed in this chapter offer many advantages over their tape-based equivalents. Some advantages are: instantaneous random access to all locations on all recordings on all tracks; centralized operation for the tasks related to recording, editing, mixing, signal processing, and synchronization; signal processing that is kept entirely in the digital domain with Undo options; time compression and expansion; track slipping (tracks can also be moved in time with respect to one another, something that is next to impossible with tape); and the elimination of generation loss.

✔ Non-destructive editing is a particularly powerful feature of direct-to-hard disk recording. Much editing performed in this medium does not alter the original material — the sound is simply modified at the output stage according to instructions you provide at the editing or mixing stage. This includes cuts, splices, loops, complete reorganization of track sections (which can be triggered by an easily constructed cuelist or playlist), fading and crossfading.

✔ Direct-to-hard disk recording requires that you change your concept of audio tracks. Digital audio recording systems record into soundfiles, not tracks, although they often refer to these soundfiles as tracks. The effective length of such "tracks" in tapeless systems is longer than you would think, because silence does not take up any space the way it does on tape. Some systems give their specifications in track minutes because of this (track minutes express the total recording time without taking silences into consideration).

Chapter 25
MIDI Mixing and Studio Automation

In this chapter . . .

✔ Defining and explaining virtual mixing.

✔ Uses of MIDI Volume, Pan, and Velocity messages in virtual mixing.

✔ Simulating DSP effects with MIDI data manipulation.

✔ Virtual faders available in MIDI sequencers and as dedicated construction kits.

✔ Hardware MIDI fader boxes and configuration diagrams.

✔ Contrasting MIDI-controlled mixers to MIDI-controlled attenuators.

✔ Organizational tools for studio automation.

Mixing with the Right Crowd

Automation, the most desirable feature of astronomically expensive mixing consoles, is being brought into the financial range of the typical Macintosh-controlled music studio. In this context, automation refers to storing, recalling, playing back, and often editing recordings of real-time manipulations of a mixer's front panel controls (such as faders, buttons, and knobs). Automated mixing systems let you handle mixes of greater complexity than would be humanly possible using traditional methods.

Compared to fully automated mixing boards, MIDI offers comparable options that are well within the reach of people using personal computers for music applications.

There are a number of approaches to using MIDI for mixing:

Virtual mixing. Channel messages stored in a MIDI sequence control an instrument's volume and pan within the instrument instead of at a mixer.

MIDI-controlled attenuators. Controller or SysEx messages stored in a MIDI sequence operate a hardware audio interface to a standard mixer.

MIDI-controlled mixers. MIDI controls all or some of the functions of specially designed hardware mixers that are otherwise functionally identical to non-MIDI-controllable mixers.

The main problem with many MIDI-controlled systems is that when virtual controls such as faders are displayed on the Macintosh screen, you can only move a single fader at a time. Many programs let you group faders as a work-around, but this still does not provide for independent fader control. The solution is to use a hardware controller dedicated to the task of sending MIDI data in response to fader movement.

Besides MIDI mixing there are other ways in which the Macintosh can automate your studio working habits. Some of these options are discussed at the end of this chapter.

Virtual Mixing

The practice of using *virtual tracks* is discussed in many chapters of this book, particularly in the next chapter. Virtual tracks refer to MIDI sequencer tracks that are not recorded onto your multitrack recorder, but instead are mixed directly into the final mix. If you mix multiple MIDI sequencer tracks to stereo, all of your tracks are virtual. You will also have improved fidelity. However, virtual tracking usually refers to MIDI sequencer tracks that are combined with previously taped tracks. One good reason for using virtual tracks is that you can run out of tracks on your tape recorder. With the number of available multitimbral channels and outputs on electronic instruments increasing, another reason to use virtual tracks is because you can run out of inputs on your hardware mixer. Rather than using the multiple outputs of your instruments (thus requiring more mixer inputs), simply route everything to the stereo outputs and create a virtual mix in the device before the signal hits those outputs.

Virtual mixing involves manipulating your MIDI sequence data to simulate ongoing audio signal modifications that you would generally accomplish with a hardware mixer. Some of the functions of a hardware mixer offering real-time manipulation are signal level (volume), equalization or EQ (boosting or cutting specified frequency bands), adding effects (signal processing), adding reverberation, muting, and panning (moving the signal within the stereo audio field). Virtual mixing can replicate many of these functions. Notable exceptions are EQ and certain effects. In small setups, it is possible to dispense with a hardware mixer altogether through creative use of virtual mixing. Furthermore, because virtual mixing information consists of MIDI data, it is often possible for sequencer software to display a graphic representation of the relevant data for subsequent editing, a luxury that only the most expensive automated hardware consoles provide.

Adding realism to virtual tracks

MIDI mixing and other forms of MIDI effects and editing discussed in this chapter can add realism to sequences that would otherwise seem mechanical. Volume levels can be adjusted with responses quick enough to simulate a wide variety of expressive articulations.

You can use MIDI effects such as chorusing to simulate groups of musicians as well as to mask the presence of poor soundfile loops. An audible loop in a sampled soundfile can ruin a sequence that would otherwise be convincingly realistic to most listeners.

If you are attempting to simulate live ensembles, for example, with samplers and sample players, don't forget to examine your string parts for places where the bow will definitely have left the string (for example, a note on the G string of the violin followed by a note on the E string) and shorten the relevant durations to simulate the brief silence created thereby. Similarly, with wind and brass parts, you must examine the phrases to determine where a human player would breathe and shorten the final notes of those phrases accordingly. This usually requires a greater decrease in note duration than the previous string example.

These may seem like minor points, but if you play a sequence that is supposed to sound like an orchestra to a layperson who knows nothing about bows leaving strings or wind players breathing, and you have not made these recommended modifications, the person will not be as convinced of the realism as they would be had you actually edited the notes to reflect normal human performance practice. This is because most people have heard acoustic music all their lives and have come to expect, however unconsciously, certain characteristics to be upheld. The same thing goes for writing music for samplers that takes an instrument out of its humanly performable range. Even people with no knowledge of the ranges of acoustic instruments could very well remark that something sounds "wrong." These phenomena are easy to verify by making psychoacoustic A-B tests with your non-musical friends.

MIDI volume vs. MIDI velocity

The primary task of a hardware mixer is to allow dynamic changes of volume level (gain) during the playing of audio data that is recorded or being generated in real time by a synthesizer either under sequencer or human control. The MIDI Specification includes a message devoted to setting the volume level of a MIDI channel. This message is Controller 7 (also known as Channel Volume or MIDI Volume), and it provides you with a method for duplicating the effect of moving hardware volume faders completely within your MIDI sequencer environment.

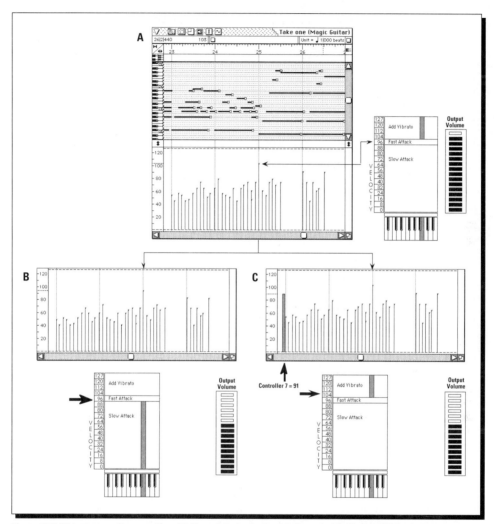

Figure 25-1: Velocity vs. volume scaling. **(A)** The original velocity data in a graphic display. **(B)** Scaled velocity data showing its effect on a particular note. In this example, the patch is set to trigger a different soundfile (fast attack) at velocities above 96 and to introduce vibrato at velocities greater than 103. Because scaling the velocities has reduced this note's velocity to 95 from 104, the wrong soundfile is played (a slow attack) and no vibrato occurs, a very undesirable scenario. Nonetheless, the volume level is reduced. **(C)** Using Controller 7 to reduce the overall volume of the channel to which this sound is assigned produces the desired effect (fast attack violin with vibrato), and the output volume level is reduced to the same amount as that in B.

The following question is frequently raised in this context: Why not manipulate MIDI velocity information to create changes in an instrument's output volume? Most sequencers provide options to reduce or increase the velocities of a selected region by a percentage or constant value (see Figure 25-1). They also let you change velocities gradually over a period of time (for example, a smooth change from one value to a greater value can simulate a fade-in or crescendo). The problem is that many instruments or individual sounds within instruments, when set to a lower velocity setting, change timbre, signal-to-noise ratio, or other characteristics you don't want to alter. In many devices different velocity levels might control effects or filters. In samplers it is common for a certain velocity value to designate the point at which one soundfile changes to another when more than one sample is assigned to the same MIDI note number. Altering velocity data under any of these conditions can be dangerous. On the other hand, Controller 7 data changes the overall output volume for a particular MIDI channel without modifying velocity or altering the effects that certain velocity levels might be set to trigger.

This notwithstanding, some instruments exist (notably certain samplers) that interpret Controller 7 data by performing mathematical computations on the samples before they reach the VCAs (voltage controlled amplifiers). This can result in a reduction of the effective sample resolution (for example, from 16 bits to 14 bits) with a corresponding loss of signal-to-noise ratio that is unacceptable.

Volume and Pan

The most common parameters in virtual mixing are Channel Volume (Controller 7) and Pan (Controller 10). Both messages have 128 increments (0 through 127), so you can use them to create gradual changes over time (see Figure 25-2). In the case of Channel Volume, such incremental changes can create fade-ins and fade-outs that are functionally identical to the effect of moving a hardware fader on your mixer. Similarly, incremental changes of Pan are the same as rotating the pan knob on your hardware mixer. A setting of 0 pans the signal hard left, and a setting of 127 pans it hard right — 64 places the signal in the center of the stereo field. Note that not all devices respond to Pan messages.

You may have made some observations from Figure 25-2 about the unique ways in which you can use controller data. Notice that it is possible to change volume levels instantly with Controller 7 data. Well, it is not exactly instantaneous — it takes a millisecond to send the controller message — but you could not hope to move a hardware fader that quickly, and even if you could, your chances of hitting the desired value right on the money are remote.

Perhaps one of the most effective musical uses of Controller 7 data is to create expressive changes of volume within a single note, that is between a Note-On message and a Note-Off message. In this way you can create sforzandos, forte-pianos, tenutos, and crescendos or decrescendos occurring within the space of a single note. Such articulations are normally produced by live musicians varying such physical properties as bow pressure (in the case of a stringed instrument) or breath intensity (in the case of a wind or brass instrument). It is common practice to assign monophonic aftertouch or polyphonic pressure (not to

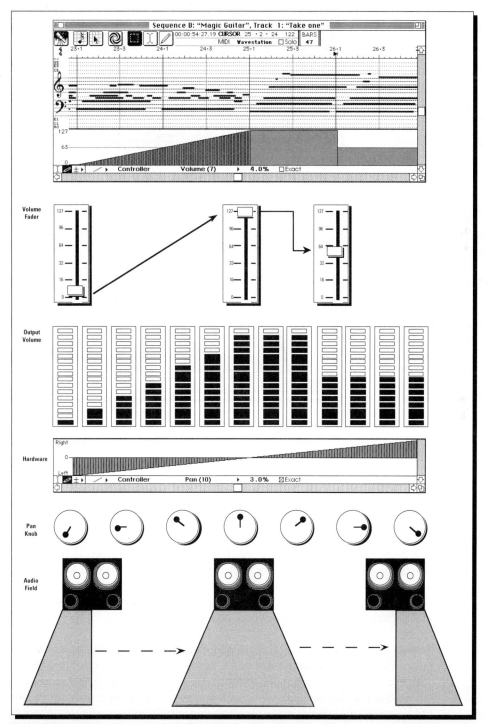

Figure 25-2: The effect of Channel Volume (Controller 7) and Pan (Controller 10) changes on a melodic passage.

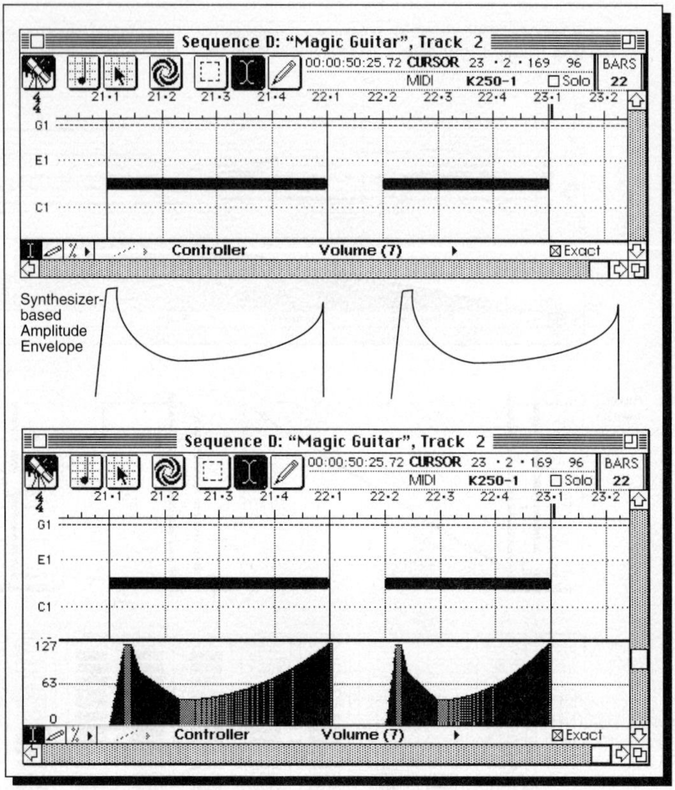

Figure 25-3: Using an amplitude envelope to create a forte-piano followed by a crescendo contrasted to using Controller 7 data for the same purpose. In the upper example the amplitude envelope times out perfectly for the whole note, it is completely inappropriate for the dotted half note. On the other hand, in the lower example the Channel Volume data is identical under both notes, except for the fact that the whole note version has been scaled (in time, not intensity) under the dotted half note.

mention breath controllers) to generate Channel Volume data to provide for such nuance and expressive control on electronic instruments.

Without Controller 7 data, it is often very difficult and time-consuming to change a note's amplitude over time. About the only way to do it is to edit the amplitude envelope within the instrument. Some devices let you store multiple alternate envelopes that can be assigned to a variety of MIDI messages. If your instrument only allows a single envelope per patch, you're really in trouble. Setting up the envelopes is laborious, to say the least, but the main problem with this approach is that the timing of the envelope segments must be related to the musical context. This means setting different envelopes for different pieces or sections within pieces on an individual basis (see Figure 25-3).

Because Controller 7 data is stored within the sequence, it always plays back in time with the music, regardless of any tempo changes. Many sequencers allow you to generate or even draw controller data, so creating a musically relevant articulation can take seconds rather than minutes. Furthermore, such articulations can be copied and pasted within your sequence or from sequence to sequence, eliminating the need to duplicate even the small effort it takes to create them.

It is common practice to store controller data such as Channel Volume on a sequencer track separate from the one that contains the notes affected by your volume manipulations. This offers many advantages. You can display the data without having to set any display filters to hide other data types. You can manipulate the data (for example, with Cut, Copy, Paste, and Scaling options) without having to set any edit filters to insulate your notes and other events from the edit operations. You can record and re-record the data without worrying about forgetting to put your sequencer in overdub mode and inadvertently destroying previously recorded music. It's easy to open both tracks (note data and controller data) in a graphic display and align the windows so that you can see what controller events are affecting which pitches. Because Controller 7 is a Channel message, it doesn't matter that the data is on a separate track, provided that you have both tracks set to output on the same MIDI channel.

To add realism to crescendos and decrescendos created with Controller 7 data, use a non-linear curve rather than a straight line (linear slope). Live performers rarely execute a crescendo linearly. Instead, the greater portion of dynamic change occurs at one end of the crescendo or the other, resulting in a curved amplitude contour. The same holds for decrescendos. Many MIDI sequencers provide options to generate curves of various slopes, and some offer controls to move the center of the curve closer to the beginning or the end of the entire curve.

One thing to watch out for when you use Controller 7 is the so-called "zipper" effect. This occurs when single controller values are skipped. MIDI's 128 steps are not really adequate to effect a completely smooth change in volume, so when you skip a value or two (for example, jumping from 64 to 66 to 69 to 71 to 75, and so on), the abrupt changes of volume can become audible. Contributing to this problem is the fact that some devices momentarily distort the audio signal as the instrument responds to Controller 7. The volume change no longer seems smooth; instead, its stair-step contour sounds a bit like a zipper being pulled up or down. For this reason, many sequencers include options to smooth continuous controller data and automatically insert the missing values.

It is important to realize that once you change MIDI volume information for a channel on an instrument, it stays in effect until you change it again, sometimes even after you power down the device and then turn it on again. If you end a piece with a fade-out to zero created with Controller 7 and then return to the beginning and initiate playback again, you won't hear anything. All your MIDI channels are still set to zero volume — they don't reset themselves. Because of this, it is a good idea to insert an initial Controller 7 message (e.g., Controller 7 = 127) at the beginning of each sequence track when you are working with MIDI volume.

Initializing a track with a volume setting still won't help if you run the piece to the end and then jump back to the middle to commence playback again. For this reason many sequencers include the option to Chase Controllers. When this option is enabled and you commence playback from anywhere but the beginning of the piece, the sequencer "looks back" to the beginning and follows each track through to the current location to determine the correct settings of all (or a selected subset) of the available MIDI controller types.

If your sequencer does not provide the Chase Controllers option, you can get around this by inserting the appropriate controller settings periodically, for example, at the beginning of each bar. This does not take as much time as you might at first suspect, because most sequencers have a Repeat Merge option that copies the contents of the Clipboard over and over for the number of measures that you specify. If your sequence does not have a Repeat Merge option, you can use the Repeat Paste option (if available), provided that you have dedicated a separate track for the controller data on that channel (as recommended above).

Even if your sequencer does not have Chase Controllers, Repeat Paste, or Repeat Merge options, you can still automate the procedure somewhat. For example, suppose you have a volume fade-out to zero at the end of a sequence and you want to be able to start playback of the sequence anywhere, so you intend to insert a Controller 7 = 127 message at the beginning of each bar. Simply insert the message in the first five measures, copy those five bars and paste them into the next five measures, copy the opening ten measures and paste them into the second ten measures, and then copy the first twenty measures and paste them into the next twenty measures. Voilà, you now have 40 bars commencing with a MIDI volume message, and it only took eight steps instead of 40. Alternatively, you could insert the Volume = 127 message at the end of the sequence, after the final Volume = 0 message. If you take this approach, you must be sure that the Volume = 127 message comes *after* all notes have finished sounding, taking into consideration any long decay envelopes that may continue after the final Note-Off. Of course you must always remember to run your sequence through this final silent region as well.

Because many types of controllers besides Channel Volume remember their settings once they have been altered, I have a special sequence that resets all my MIDI channels. This sequence sets Controller 7 to 127, Controller 10 to 64, and mod wheel and pitch bend to 0 (center). It sends the same settings out on all 256 MIDI channels of my MIDI Time Piece network. Alternatively, you can use MIDI's Reset All Controllers message (121). The danger here is that some devices do not respond to the Reset All Controllers message, and even those that do ignore the message when in Omni mode.

Panning and crossfading

Nearly all of the considerations mentioned above apply to Pan (Controller 10) as well as Volume (Controller 7), and many apply to other types of MIDI controllers.

A number of synthesizers do not respond to the Pan message. If your instrument is one of these but does have at least two separate outputs, you may be able to simulate a panning effect by sending the same signal (originating from data on two different MIDI channels) to both outputs and using MIDI volume to fade one channel in as the other channel fades out (also by way of MIDI volume).

With both Panning (when two sources are panning in opposite directions simultaneously) and Volume crossfades you run the risk of a drop in amplitude at the center of the effect if you use a linear (straight line) contour for the controller data. A similar problem was discussed in Chapter 13, "Editing Sampled Sound" with respect to crossfading to digital audio soundfiles. To remedy this audible volume drop, sample editing software and Direct-to-Hard Disk recording software provide for exponential fade slopes that are curves rather than straight lines (see Figure 25-4). These result in a 3 dB boost of both signals at the halfway point. Digidesign's Sound Designer software calls this an Equal Power Crossfade. Passport Designs's Alchemy software refers to this as a 3 dB fade slope and also offers 4 dB, 5 dB, and 6 dB fade slopes. As mentioned above, many MIDI sequencers can generate curves of various slopes that are analogous to 3 dB fade slopes.

For sequencers that do not automate the creation of controller data curves, you can adjust the linear slopes so that their halfway points do not coincide. The element that is fading in reaches its halfway point (relative to the entire dynamic range covered by the slope) *before* the midpoint of the crossfade, and the element that is fading out reaches its halfway point *after* the midpoint of the crossfade.

Based on some assumptions that the combination of two identical sound sources increases volume by 6 dB, you may consider doing some calculations relating this fact to MIDI Volume's 128 increments in an attempt to find the optimum slopes for the panning and crossfading discussed in the previous paragraph. However, such computations are generally futile exercises, because the MIDI volume scale has little or no relation to decibels, and furthermore, individual patches and soundfiles respond differently to changes in volume. It's best to just use your ears.

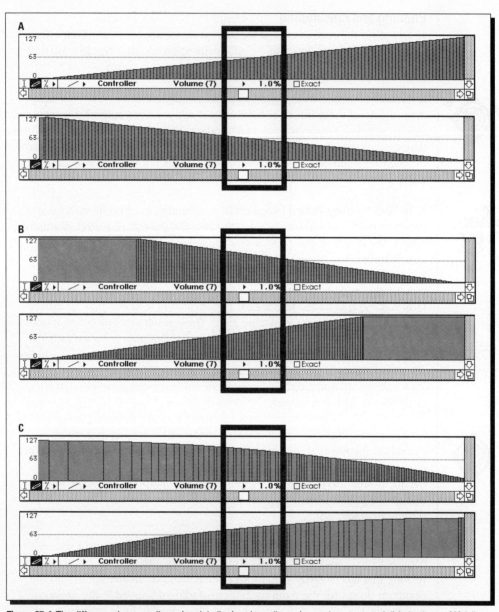

Figure 25-4: The difference between linear (straight line) and non-linear (curved or exponential) fade slopes. **(A)** A linear crossfade with the halfway points centered at the crossfade's midpoint can result in a drop in volume. **(B)** If your sequencer does not provide for curved slopes of continuous controller data, try moving the halfway points of each signal's linear fade away from the midpoint of the entire crossfade. **(C)** The solution is to use a curve instead of a straight line. When the midpoint of the crossfade is reached, both signals are at a slightly higher volume than the dynamic range covered by the slope.

Simulating effects

Besides offering real-time control of audio signal level and panning, hardware mixers also provide for the introduction of equalization (EQ) and other signal processing effects into the various input and output signals. Manipulating MIDI data can simulate some signal processing effects, but it cannot simulate EQ (other than a filter's frequency and resonance within devices that place these elements under MIDI control). On the other hand, you can manipulate a MIDI-controllable equalizer either as a stand-alone unit or as a built-in electronic instrument. The most common signal processors are reverberators and delays. Delay units produce echo, flanging, chorusing, and other interesting effects. MIDI data manipulations are not useful to simulate reverberation, but delays are well within the range of possibility.

For step-by-step tutorials on using MIDI to simulate other DSP effects such as delay, echo, glissando, flange, chorus, harmonization, noise gating, normalization, limiting, compression, and expansion, see the coupon at the back of the book.

MIDI Manager Effects

Sequencers that are compatible with Apple's MIDI Manager have a wide range of MIDI effects processors available to them. Megalomania, is a versatile MIDI effects processor that you program by connecting icons together to create just about any MIDI effect imaginable. Other MIDI Manager programs dedicated to adding effects to a MIDI data stream, covered include MIDI CHORD HIASL (a sophisticated MIDI harmonizer), Strum (a harmonizer for guitar strumming effects), and Wuliax (a four-channel MIDI delay). See also "MacMuse" in Chapter 19.

Controllers

Generating continuous controller data such as Channel Volume can take some time. You must specify the destination region for the data and often specify the minimum value change and minimum temporal duration per change. If a curve is desired, there are additional settings to take care of. Then there is the actual software generation of data itself. On slower machines you may find yourself staring helplessly at the wristwatch as your data is churned out.

One solution is to keep libraries of commonly used Controller 7 effects (e.g., a sforzando, a forte-piano, a graceful decrescendo, a quick fade, and so on). You can keep all of these in a special sequence, labeled with markers or, alternatively, at the beginning of different tracks with each track's name describing the effect it contains. It's often faster to copy the effect from this storage sequence, paste it into the piece you are working on, and then scale the timing to conform to the required region length.

There are two other, more efficient solutions to the problem of creating continuous data for virtual mixing. Many sequencers offer a virtual fader option. It allows you to build fader consoles on your screen that operate analogously to their hardware counterparts. The problem with virtual fader consoles is that you are essentially limited to moving a single fader at a time (you only have one mouse pointer with which to pull a slider). Some developers have found innovative ways around this limitation (see the next section).

The best solution is to use a hardware MIDI device that is dedicated to sending out controller data. These often provide multiple faders that you can manipulate simultaneously. Several representative devices in this category are discussed below.

Software

It is very popular for current-generation MIDI sequencer software to provide options for virtual faders. The following approaches are common:

- ❖ Fixed number of faders hard-coded internally to Controller 7 data.
- ❖ Fixed number of faders assignable to different continuous controller data types.
- ❖ Variable number of faders that can be assembled into virtual consoles.
- ❖ Variable number of faders and other virtual controls that can be assembled into consoles.

Fader manipulation is available in equally varied approaches:

- ❖ Single-fader manipulation by the mouse.
- ❖ Master faders control grouped faders, so that a single fader movement can manipulate many other faders.
- ❖ Faders assignable to hardware controls on the front panel of your controller keyboard or other MIDI controller.
- ❖ Snapshots of entire console settings that can be called up by name or number and/or placed into a sequence at strategic points.

Additional controls commonly found in virtual fader consoles include:

- ❖ Mute buttons (generally not recordable because there is no corresponding MIDI message).
- ❖ Solo buttons (generally not recordable because there is no corresponding MIDI message).
- ❖ Pan controls (knobs or sliders).
- ❖ Master volume.
- ❖ Master tempo.
- ❖ Program change insertion controls.

❖ Transposition.
❖ Activity indicators (indicating the presence of data).
❖ Level indicators (indicating the relative level of data).
❖ Snapshot controls for saving and recalling entire fader configurations.
❖ Assignable controls that can send any MIDI data string you designate.
❖ Controls to access dedicated synthesizer effects (for example, General MIDI standard effects).

With programs that allow you to configure the characteristics of virtual faders, the construction of a single virtual fader can involve setting a number of parameters:

❖ Data type to generate.
❖ Destination track, port, and/or MIDI channel for fader data.
❖ Data type to respond to for remote control.
❖ Port and MIDI channel to listen to for remote controller data.
❖ The minimum and maximum values for the fader's range.
❖ Name of the fader.
❖ Visual orientation (horizontal or vertical).
❖ Size and screen location.

For faders that are placed under the control of a separate master fader, additional characteristics might be addressable (see the section "Groupable faders" for an implementation of these functions):

❖ Designation as a master or slave fader.
❖ Group assignment (if multiple groups are permitted).
❖ Null point (the value of a master slider to which slave values are referenced).
❖ Reference value (the value of the slave slider that corresponds to the master's null point).
❖ Offset of slave fader in relation to master (slave offsets master's values by a constant).
❖ Polarity of slave fader in relation to master (slave moves in a different direction).
❖ Scaling factor of slave fader in relation to master (slave moves at a different rate).

Almost all programs offering virtual faders provide for fader activity to be recorded into your sequence, either by way of overdubbing onto a destination track (or tracks) or by recording new data onto a track dedicated to holding the controller data. For sequencers that do not allow you to record on multiple tracks simultaneously, there is sometimes a provision to record fader data for 16 MIDI channels onto a single track and subsequently unmerge the data on that track into separate channels.

Many sequencers animate the motion of their virtual faders during playback, producing the effect of true console automation. In some cases, this animation can slow down the response of your sequencer, because it is just one more set of calculations that your Macintosh's processor must perform while trying to accurately send your MIDI data out the serial ports with a timing precision that you may have labored over for days and that can make or break the audible result. If this sounds like a warning against opting for viewing such fader animation, it is. On the other hand, watching the faders move by themselves on the screen during the creative process can provide you with valuable visual feedback about parts of the mix that might need to be smoothed or why certain tracks are more or less prominent than others.

Now and then, you may see sequencers (or early versions of sequencers) with faders whose sole purpose it is to set global track effects. Such faders allow you to set, on a track-by-track basis, a master volume setting, a pan setting, and possibly transposition. Mute and solo buttons may also be present. This type of implementation is fine for certain situations, but does not provide for MIDI-controlled mixing as focused on in this chapter (that is, allowing real-time recordable and editable dynamic manipulation). Therefore, the following examples only include software that allows fader movement to be recorded.

Keep in mind that a hardware MIDI fader box does not require on-screen virtual faders. With the boxes described below under "Hardware fader controllers," any sequencer, even those without built-in virtual faders, can reap the benefits of MIDI mixing.

In the following sections, fader implementations have been broken down into four categories for purposes of illustration:

❖ Hard-coded volume and pan faders
❖ Assignable and remote-controllable faders
❖ Groupable faders
❖ Console construction kits

These categories are arranged in order of greater functionality. Note that many sequencers presented in one category offer some or all of the fader features found in other categories; they are included under a specific heading because they are a good example of that category. For a complete listing of each sequencer's fader capabilities, consult the sequencer feature tables at the end of Chapter 17, "MIDI Seqencing."

Hard-coded volume and pan faders

Faders of this kind are linked to volume (Controller 7) and pan (Controller 10) data exclusively and are not assignable to other data types. The examples pictured (Ballade, EZ-Vision, Rhapsody, and Pro 5) do not provide for control of fader movement by external MIDI sources (see Figure 25-5).

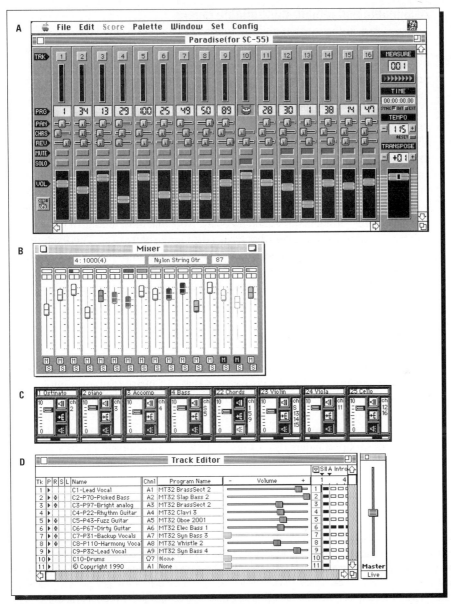

Figure 25-5: Hard-coded volume and pan faders. **(A)** Ballade's Mixer window provides both control of global track effects and fader recording and automation. Sixteen faders are available. The Reverb button and Chorus slider are active only when the sequencer is configured for Roland's GS MIDI standard. A snapshot window lets you save and name snapshots of selected settings for later recall. When you recall a snapshot, it is applied to the entire sequence. **(B)** EZ-Vision's 16 faders offer control of volume and pan. Holding the mouse down on the pan indicator at the top of each volume fader brings up the Pan slider as indicated. Faders can be grouped by Shift-clicking them. After grouping, moving any fader in the group moves all the others. All faders in a group are automatically scaled with relation to one another, so they reach zero

(continued)

Assignable and remote-controllable faders

All the faders in this section and the following can be assigned to generate almost any kind of MIDI continuous controller data and record data generated by real-time fader manipulation (see Figure 25-6). Likewise, all of the following programs, with the exception of Beyond and Rhapsody, can link their faders to incoming MIDI data for remote control.

Programs that provide for linking virtual faders to external MIDI controllers allow you to move more than a single fader at a time (see Figure 25-7). For example, most synthesizers have a Modulation Wheel, a data entry slider, and an optional volume pedal. You can link these three continuous controllers to three virtual faders, so that moving the hardware fader causes a corresponding movement of the on-screen virtual fader. In this scenario, you can record the motion of three virtual faders simultaneously. Note that most linking of this kind requires continuous controllers that have a data range of 0 to 127. This excludes Pitch Wheel from many such configurations (Vision and StudioVision also exclude Aftertouch, even though the range is 0 to 127). If you link the virtual faders to physical faders on a hardware MIDI fader box (or boxes) as described below, you have real-time control of as many faders as your software and hardware will support.

Groupable faders

Both Performer and Cubase offer fader grouping, although Performer's grouping implementation is more extensive than that of Cubase (Cubase's implementation of fader console construction is more robust than Performer's — see below). One purpose of fader grouping is to get around the fact that you can only move a single fader at a time with the mouse. There are other musical reasons for grouped faders. For example, faders with opposite polarity can be used to create perfect crossfades. As one fader increases in value, the linked negatively polarized fader decreases accordingly. Scaled faders that are linked together can compensate for the fact that a change of volume from value X to

---

Figure 25-5: (continued) simultaneously, no matter where they start from. Snapshots of the current fader configuration (volume and pan only) can be copied to the Clipboard and pasted anywhere in a sequence or song. **(C)** Rhapsody provides a volume and pan fader at the bottom of each track. Fader motion is recordable, but there are no provisions for snapshots. However, Rhapsody offers a second set of General Purpose faders, which you can assign to whatever controller data you like. Any fader can act as a master fader to all the others by dragging on it with the Command key down. In this case, all faders are scaled, so that they reach their maximum and minimum values simultaneously. You can split the window into two panes (as pictured — track 4 is adjacent to track 22) to allow you to view and control faders that otherwise wouldn't fit on the screen together. **(D)** Passport's Pro 5 adds automation to their track volume faders that were available in earlier versions of the program. Shift-clicking in the track record field enables Fader Record mode. A single Master Fader operates in three modes: Live mode sends Controller 7 to all tracks simultaneously, Record mode records volume data on all Fader Record-enabled tracks, and Absolute mode sends its absolute position as Master Volume SysEx messages.

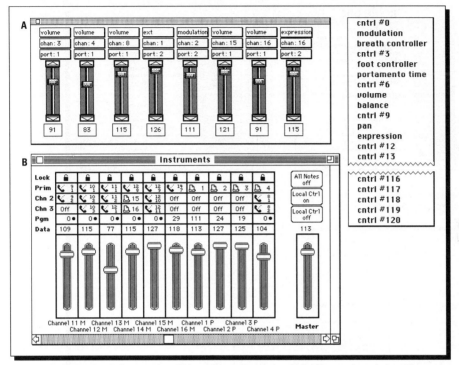

Figure 25-6: Assignable fader consoles. **(A)** In addition to its hard-coded volume and pan faders, Rhapsody provides eight faders that can be assigned to any of the data types selected from the pop-up menu. The menu is long, so in this illustration, it has been split into two segments off to the right of the console. **(B)** Beyond provides 32 assignable faders and a single master volume fader. Faders are linked to virtual instruments, so if you want to record a certain type of controller data, you may find yourself manipulating a fader with the name of one instrument while you are listening to a different instrument.

value *Y* may have a completely different audible effect, depending upon the synthesizer being controlled by the fader.

Performer's approach to grouping faders provides for up to 32 sliders in a group and up to 26 groups. Groups are identified by the letters *A* to *Z*, which explains the limitation of 26 groups. Furthermore, you can nest groups within other groups. This means that a master slider controlling a group of up to 32 sliders can itself be a member of a group that is controlled by another master slider, and so on (see Figure 25-8).

Performer doesn't care whether a slider uses a scale of 0 to 127 or -8192 to +8192, the values are displayed in either case. Aftertouch and Pitch Bend are not excluded from slider data manipulations as they are in some other sequencers. A unique feature is that sliders can be configured to be remotely controlled

Faders (left window)

		MIDI Output	
F1	98	•	
F2	114	K250 1	Data Entry (6)
F3	127	K250 1	Expression (11)
F4	110	FaderMaste 1	Volume (7)
F5	110	FaderMaste 2	Volume (7)
F6	96	FaderMaste 3	Volume (7)
F7	118	FaderMaste 4	Volume (7)
F8	86	FaderMaste 5	Volume (7)
F9	0	•	
F10	127	FaderMaste 6	Volume (7)
F11	122	FaderMaste 7	Volume (7)
F12	0		
F13	122	FaderMaste 8	Volume (7)
F14	127		
F15	127	FaderMaste 9	Volume (7)
F16	64		
F17	108	FaderMaste 10	Volume (7)
F18	106	•	

TEMPO F1   40 – 225   ⦿Rcv ○Send   1 17

Faders (right window)

		MIDI Output	
F1	98	•	
F2	114	K250-1	Volume (7)
F3	127	K250-2	Volume (7)
F4	110	1000HX-1	Volume (7)
F5	110	1000SX-1	Volume (7)
F6	96	1000HX-1	Volume (7)
F7	118	1000GX-1	Volume (7)
F8	86	M1r-1	Volume (7)
F9	0	M1r-1	Pan (10)
F10	127	D-550	Volume (7)
F11	122	Proteus/2-1	Volume (7)
F12	0	Proteus/2-1	Pan (10)
F13	122	Proteus/2-2	Volume (7)
F14	127	Proteus/2-2	Pan (10)
F15	127	Wavestation	Volume (7)
F16	64	Wavestation	Modulation Wheel (1)
F17	108	R-8	Volume (7)
F18	106	•	

TEMPO F1   40 – 225   ○Rcv ⦿Send   1 17

B — MIDI Instruments

Instrument Name	Mute Solo	#b Map	MIDI Output Device	Chan	Veloc Fade Fader	Amt	#b qua	m2	Range	Voices
K250-B-16			K250-B	16	Off	100	0	0	C-2	68
LXP-1			LXP-1	1	Off	100	0	0	C-2	68
M1r-1			M1r	1	F18	84	0	0	C-2	68
M1r-2			M1r	2	F19	94	0	0	C-2	68
M1r-3			M1r	3	F20	94	0	0	C-2	68
M1r-4			M1r	4	F21	94	0	0	C-2	68
M1r-5			M1r	5	F22	94	0	0	C-2	68
M1r-6			M1r	6	F23	94	0	0	C-2	68
M1r-7			M1r	7	F24	94	0	0	C-2	68
M1r-8			M1r	8	F25	94	0	0	C-2	68
Matrix-1000			Matrix-100	1	F26	100	0	0	C-2	68
MKS-70			MKS-70	1	F27	150	0	0	C-2	68
Proteus/2-1			Proteus/2	1	Off	100	0	0	C-2	68
Proteus/2-2			Proteus/2	2	Off	100	0	0	C-2	68
Proteus/2-3			Proteus/2	3	Off	100	0	0	C-2	68
Proteus/2-4			Proteus/2	4	Off	100	0	0	C-2	68
Proteus/2-5			Proteus/2	5	Off	100	0	0	C-2	68
Proteus/2-6			Proteus/2	6	Off	100	0	0	C-2	68
Proteus/2-7			Proteus/2	7	Off	100	0	0	C-2	68
Proteus/2-8			Proteus/2	8	Off	100	0	0	C-2	68
R-8			R-8	1	Off	100	0	0	C-2	68
SPX90			SPX90	1	Off	100	0	0	C-2	68
Wavestation			Wavestatio	1	Off	100	0	0	C-2	68

Figure 25-7: Assignable and remote-controllable faders. **(A)** Vision's 32 on-screen faders can be assigned to respond to any external controller except Pitch Bend or Aftertouch (see left window). With the Send radio button pictured at the bottom of the Fader window (see right window), you can use this feature to remap any MIDI controller to any other controller on the same or a different MIDI channel. Vision's fader grouping implementation is a little different from other programs. To control volume on multiple channels from a single fader you must first set up a virtual instrument (see Chapters 16 and 17) consisting of layers of devices that are assigned to the MIDI channels you wish to control as a group. Then you assign a single fader to that virtual instrument. **(B)** Vision lets you scale a virtual instrument's velocity using the Fader window. Note the Fader number and scaling amount (0 to 200%) in the Velocity Fade column. The advantage is that you do not clog the MIDI bandwidth with a large amount of continuous controller data. Velocity-scaled data cannot be recorded in the normal fashion. Instead, to record it you must route the output data that is having its velocity scaled in real time back into Vision for recording. You can do this by hooking up a MIDI cable from the MIDI OUT to the MIDI IN port of your MIDI interface. Alternatively, you can use virtual MIDI cables in MIDI Manager's PatchBay if you are using MIDI Manager instead of OMS to communicate between Vision and your Macintosh's serial ports (MIDI-Manager-compatible versions of Vision only). Note: StudioVision follows the same fader conventions as Vision.

by note value or velocity value in addition to the normal practice of allowing assignment to any continuous controller. Assigning a slider to be remotely controlled by note value allows you to make instantaneous changes in the slider's value that are impossible to achieve by any other fader implementation.

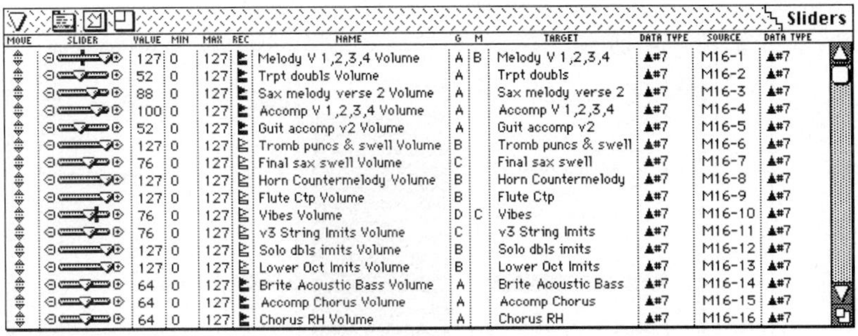

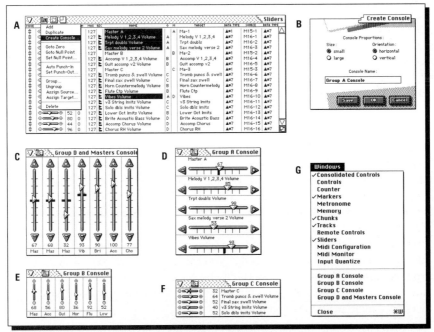

Figure 25-8: Performer's Sliders window. Note the group and master assignments indicated by the adjacent columns of letters at the center. Also displayed are the minimum and maximum values and the target and source data channels, cables, and types.

Performer offers another level of organization beyond its sliders window. You can create consoles consisting of subsets of the sliders you have defined in the main sliders window (see Figure 25-9). There can be as many consoles as you like and they don't necessarily have to be limited to a unique set of sliders or to sliders that are all members of the same group. This allows you to construct consoles on the basis of functionality or musical considerations rather than an arbitrary organization imposed by the software. The order of faders in the main slider window and in consoles is easy to change by simply dragging the slider to a new position; all the other sliders shift to make room for the moved one.

Figure 25-9: There are four types of console displays in Performer. **(A)** Select sliders to be included in the console within the Sliders window and choose Create Console from the mini-menu. **(B)** Choose the size and orientation of the console with this dialog box. **(C)** Large vertical console. **(D)** Large horizontal console. **(E)** Small vertical console. **(F)** Small horizontal console. **(G)** Saved consoles appear under the Windows menu.

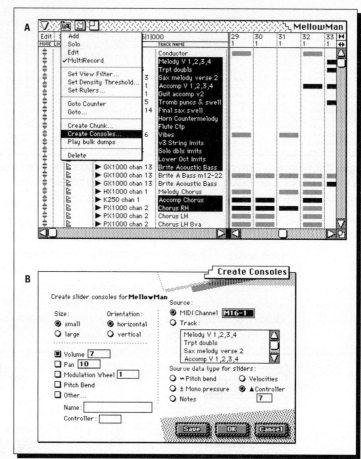

Figure 25-10: Creating consoles directly from the tracks window. **(A)** Select the Tracks you want to be affected by the sliders in the console. **(B)** Choosing Create Consoles from the Tracks window's mini-menu brings up this dialog box for configuring the individual sliders.

There are many courtesy features in Performer's implementation of console construction and slider manipulation. For example, Option-clicking on a slider's record icon selects it for recording while deselecting all other sliders. Command-clicking does the reverse, disabling the slider that you click and record-enabling all other sliders. A very useful feature is a special Slider Punch In mode that commences the overdubbing of slider data (which replaces any existing data of the same type) at the moment you move a slider. Perhaps the most useful feature of this kind is that you can create slider consoles directly from Performer's Tracks window simply by selecting the tracks you want to be addressed by your console and choosing Create Consoles from the Tracks window's mini-menu (see Figure 25-10).

Sliders employ a source and a target in Performer. The source can be a MIDI channel (assigned to a specific cable if you are using a greater-than-32-channel interface) with an associated continuous controller (alternatively, notes or velocities can provide the slider values), or the source can be an existing track (in this case Performer monitors the data of the indicated type that already exists of the track by animating the slider accordingly, or you can use this configuration to convert the monitored data to another type of data on a separate track or channel). The target can also be a track or a MIDI channel or channels. If you select a MIDI channel or channels as the target, you have the option to reassign the source data on-the-fly. For example, you can remap velocity to aftertouch in real time and rechannelize the result.

Performer's main strength in slider and console creation is its control over the interrelationship of slider movement between grouped slave sliders and their master (see Figure 25-11). The slave slider may use an offset (as a constant specified by the reference point described later or as a percentage) in calculating its value from that of the master, or it may scale its value (as a percentage) from the one received from the master. This is a good way to compensate for hardware controllers that do not provide the full range of MIDI values for a certain data type. You can also reverse the polarity of the slave in relation to the direction of the master slider's movement. Performer offers a null point for each master slider; it is used as the reference point to which slave sliders orient themselves.

Console construction kits

Cubase and Performer offer fader console construction kits that allow you to save different fader consoles along with their complete configuration for later recall in other sequences (see Figure 25-12). Performer's fader building options allow for only four types of fader display by mixing the options for horizontal, vertical, small, and large faders. Cubase offers complete control over the graphic display of fader consoles and provides many more controls than all other software (only Q-Sheet A/V comes close to this — see the section "Q-Sheet A/V"). It also includes all the grouping options discussed in the previous section.

Hardware fader controllers

MIDI fader boxes circumvent the fact that you can only move a single virtual fader with the mouse and that some sequencers do not offer virtual faders. The tactile sensation of manipulating faders that feel like those found on a traditional mixing console is another advantage of these boxes.

For sequencers that do not offer virtual faders, these hardware faders can be set to input data directly into the sequence. When virtual faders are available, an obvious configuration is to link hardware faders to virtual faders, although there is nothing mandating this practice (see Figures 25-13 and 25-14).

Figure 25-11: The effects of offset, scaling, polarity, and null-point upon the behavior of slave sliders. **(A)** You use this dialog box to set a slider's characteristics, including group, polarity, and relation to the master slider (match values, offset values with an option to scale the offset, or scale values). **(B)** You set a slider's absolute minimum and maximum values in the main sliders window. **(C)** You set the null-point by way of the mini-menu in either the Sliders or console windows. **(D)** The master slider with a null-point of 20. **(E)** Slave 1 has a reference point of 20 and an offset scaling of 100% (no scaling) with positive polarity. **(F)** Slave 2 has a reference point of 40 and an offset scaling of 50% with positive polarity. **(G)** Slave 3 has a reference point of 80 and an offset scaling of 100% with negative polarity. **(H)** Slave 4 has a reference point of 100 and an offset scaling of 50% with negative polarity. **(I)** Slave 5 has a reference point of 20 and is scaled by 200% with positive polarity. **(J)** Slave 6 has a reference point of 40 and is scaled by 75% with positive polarity. **(K)** Slave 7 has a reference point of 80 and is scaled by 200% with negative polarity. **(L)** Slave 8 has a reference point of 100 and is scaled by 75% with negative polarity. **(M)** The effect of moving the master slider up to 0 is illustrated by this second row of sliders. **(N)** The effect of moving the master slider up to 32 is illustrated by this third row of sliders. **(O)** The effect of moving the master slider up to 64 is illustrated by this second row of sliders. **(P)** The effect of moving the master slider up to 127 is illustrated by this third row of sliders. Note: In all cases, the master sliders are not "locked" to the master; you can always move them independently if you like. Besides offering independent control of all sliders at all times, this feature is used to reset the slaves' reference points in relation to the master's null-point.

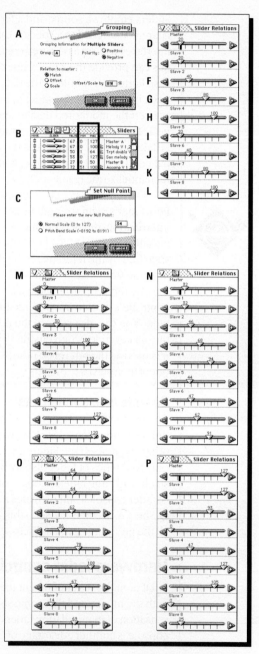

Popular MIDI fader boxes include:

JL Cooper FaderMaster
eight assignable MIDI faders

Kawai MM-16
17 assignable MIDI faders

Lexicon MRC
four assignable MIDI faders

Niche Mix Automation Station
16 assignable MIDI faders (distributed by the Russ Jones Marketing Group)

Figure 25-12:
Console construction kit. **(A)** Cubase's Mixer window goes far beyond mere MIDI mixing. The Volume Console at the bottom of this window is comparable to most other programs' fader consoles. Because Cubase's flexible console designing environment allows any virtual control to transmit any MIDI message (including SysEx data), you can design patch editors in the Mixer window. In fact, the software comes with Mixer Maps for over two dozen popular synthesizers. Any of these editors can be combined with the

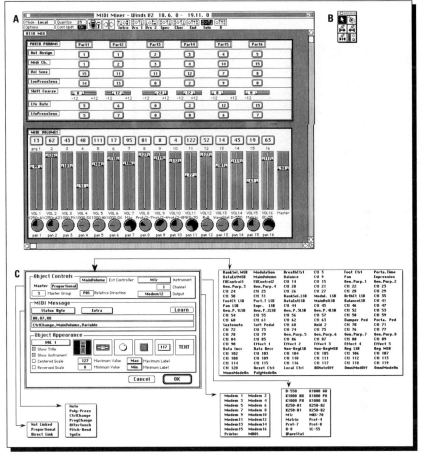

MIDI volume console (as pictured here with the U110). You can have editors for all your synthesizers on the screen simultaneously and, because you can edit the editors themselves (or create them from scratch), you only need to display controls to edit those parameters that you are normally concerned with. Any control can be linked to any other control to create an editor that might offer, for example, a single slider as a master to all the filters of all your synthesizers, regardless of manufacturer. Note the camera icon in the upper middle of the window and the snapshot graphics to the right of it. Clicking a particular snapshot recalls its configuration. **(B)** This tool palette lets you construct new consoles and editors. **(C)** When you draw an object in the window, this dialog box appears requesting that you assign its object type (fader, knob, button, field, text, or background), MIDI messages, minimum and maximum values, grouping characteristics (including proportional scaling, direct linking, and polarity), and a host of other user interface bells and whistles. You select controllers and other values from pop-up menus.

Audiomatica Contact MIDI Panel

18 asssignable MIDI faders and 73 additional assignable knobs and switches. This is the most full-featured MIDI fader console available. Although optimized for WaveFrame's AudioFrame and CyberFrame, the console can be programmed for any environment.

Figure 25-13: JLCooper FaderMaster MIDI Remote Controller.

All are introduced into the MIDI network by a simple connection of a MIDI cable.

Most MIDI fader boxes offer at least eight faders that you can assign to output any type of continuous controller data (the MRC has only four faders). If you have eight faders, but want to add a volume mix on 16 channels, most boxes offer a one-button toggle to bring up a second preset addressing the remaining eight channels. With this, you can create your mix in two passes or even in a single pass with careful switching back and forth between the two presets. Another solution is to have two eight-fader boxes or a box with at least 16 faders.

All include additional front panel buttons, and some of these may be assigned to output additional MIDI messages. Most offer automatic merging of incoming MIDI data with their output stream, thus offering complete functionality for people who have only a single MIDI input available or have otherwise run out of MIDI inputs (see Figure 25-15).

It is not necessary to assign hardware faders to volume data (although this is the most common configuration). You might have several faders assigned to volume, another assigned to pan, and the rest assigned to aftertouch or other continuous controllers of your choice. Some allow their faders to be assigned to MIDI delay (JL Cooper's FaderMaster provides this option). In this mode, you can simulate some of the functions of the Aphex Feel Factory. Another common use is to assign faders to program change. Because you can see the transmitted value in the box's LED, it is easy to zero in on the desired sound with a quick motion of a fader. If you have ever yearned for a pitch wheel that wasn't spring-activated (that is, that you could move to a desired value and then leave at that value without it popping back to zero —

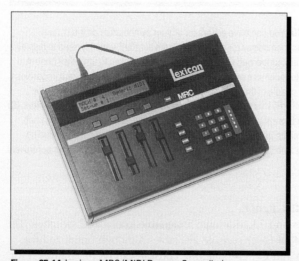

Figure 25-14: Lexicon MRC (MIDI Remote Controller).

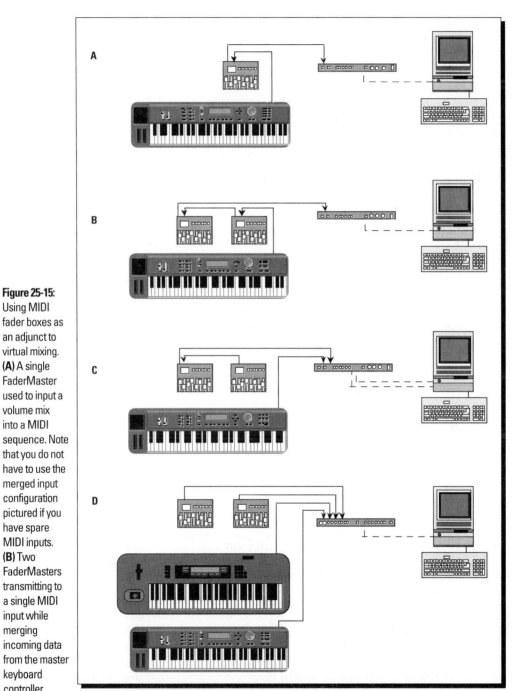

Figure 25-15:
Using MIDI fader boxes as an adjunct to virtual mixing. **(A)** A single FaderMaster used to input a volume mix into a MIDI sequence. Note that you do not have to use the merged input configuration pictured if you have spare MIDI inputs. **(B)** Two FaderMasters transmitting to a single MIDI input while merging incoming data from the master keyboard controller. **(C)** Two Fader-Masters and one master keyboard controller with a dual MIDI interface. **(D)** Two FaderMasters and multiple master controllers with a greater-than-32-channel MIDI interface.

perhaps for microtonal effects), all you have to do is assign one of the faders to pitch bend.

It is not necessary to interface the MIDI fader box with dedicated sequencer software. These boxes are just as valuable when used in conjunction with dedicated automation software such as MIDI Mix 3D or Q-Sheet A/V (see the section "Q-Sheet A/V"). Other possibilities include dedicating the fader box's output to MIDI Manager-compatible effects processors that accept external MIDI control (see above).

Most MIDI fader remote controllers include a number of presets. Naturally, one (or more) of these presets configures the box to output MIDI volume data with each fader assigned to a different channel. Similar presets for pan data are also standard. Some hardware fader boxes ship with built-in presets that let you control any number of additional parameters of MIDI devices. Sometimes this requires that the faders precede their messages with SysEx strings. For example, JL Cooper's FaderMaster comes with presets that let the box function as a remote controller of most of the popular internal parameters. This works for such popular synthesizers as Yamaha's DX/TX series and SY-series, Oberheim's Matrix 6 and 1000, Kawai's K4, Roland's D-series and U-series, Ensoniq's VFX, E-mu's Proteus, and the Korg M-series and T-series, among a host of other instruments and effects devices (including Lexicon's LXP-1 and LXP-5). Lexicon's MRC provides access to the internal parameters of most of their own signal processors as well as the complete Yamaha DX/TX design. Both allow you to create and save additional presets to make the boxes function as remote patch editors for any SysEx-addressable device. In addition, both offer separate MIDI outputs, so that you can split your fader assignments among two devices, even if the devices are assigned to the same MIDI channel (see Figure 25-16). Now that most signal processors (for example, equalizers) can be placed under remote control of MIDI, using hardware MIDI fader boxes as a central location for the manipulation of your effects can greatly enhance their operation (most signal processors have very inefficient front-panel controls requiring dozens of button presses to access a single parameter and then scrolling through values that often range in the hundreds for the purpose of altering a parameter setting).

Some hardware MIDI fader boxes have editing and configuration software available for them. For example, JL Cooper offers control of the FaderMaster with an optional desk accessory or stand-alone application. You can program all functions of the box, and also save and recall setups.

Finally, you can use a MIDI fader box as the missing front panel to some of the hardware MIDI-controlled mixers discussed in the following section.

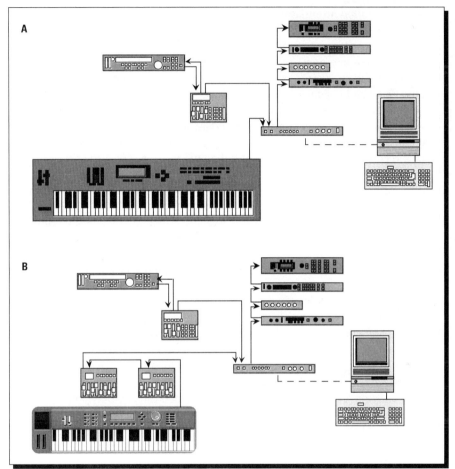

Figure 25-16: Using MIDI fader boxes as hardware patch editors in addition to virtual mixing. **(A)** MRC controlling several Lexicon effects processors (daisy-chained) and also inputting into the Macintosh-based MIDI sequence. The MRC's other output is used as an editor for the M1r pictured. **(B)** FaderMaster and MRC on the same network. Note: Additional configurations of MIDI remote controllers are illustrated and analyzed in Chapter 7.

MIDI-controlled Mixing

Virtual mixing, described above, does not require any additional hardware, unless you want to take advantage of the possibilities offered by MIDI fader boxes. You can use virtual mixing with any mixer, and in some cases you can dispense with a mixing console altogether through creative use of virtual mixing. On the other hand, true MIDI-controlled mixing requires additional hardware that can be placed under MIDI control. There are two types of devices available in this category.

MIDI-controlled attenuators. These devices are essentially gain controls that can be adjusted in real time by way of MIDI. Such devices usually don't do any mixing *per se*, although some offer a stereo mix output to provide the functionality of a simple line mixer or submixer. EQ, effects, and other standard mixer features are generally not present. You can expect to find muting, but not much more. Pan can be simulated by crossfading a signal between two of the outputs. MIDI-controlled attenuators are introduced in the signal chain between your sound-generating devices and your standard mixing console (either at the mixer inputs or the insert points). Alternatively, you can place them between a multi-track recorder and your mixer during the final mixdown process. You could set up your audio patchbay to support both applications. Some people introduce a MIDI-controlled attenuator between signal processors and the effects returns of their mixer to provide for dynamically altering effects levels in real time. MIDI-controlled attenuators are usually less expensive than MIDI-controlled mixers (see Figure 25-17).

MIDI-controlled mixers. These devices are full-blown mixers, rack-mountable or console type, that can be placed under MIDI control. Like MIDI-controlled attenuators, some use the snapshot/crossfade approach, while others provide for continuous real-time control. The difference between MIDI-controlled mixers and MIDI-controlled attenuators is that the mixer variety provides all the features you would expect on a normal mixer (EQ, effects sends and returns, pan, muting, soloing, and so on.) and places these additional parameters under MIDI control. Furthermore, most mixers transmit the MIDI information generated by their hardware controls, allowing it to be recorded directly by your sequencer. This means that there is no need for a separate hardware MIDI fader box, whereas a MIDI-controlled attenuator that does not have its own built-in faders might need it. Yamaha's DMP7 even servo-controls the motion of its hardware faders, just like an expensive automated mixing console.

Snapshots

Snapshots refer to a stored setting of all the adjustable parameters of a MIDI-controlled mixing device. Some approaches to snapshots in virtual mixing were discussed above. Snapshots are a common feature in both MIDI-controlled attenuators and MIDI-controlled mixers. Many early devices were limited to storing snapshots of settings for recall by way of program change messages rather than continuous real-time control. In such cases it is common for the device to offer programmable crossfade times from one snapshot to the next.

Figure 25-17 (opposite page): Virtual mixing, MIDI-controlled attenuators, and MIDI-controlled mixers contrasted. **(A)** Basic setup for virtual mixing with optional hardware fader box. **(B)** Three MIDI-controlled attenuators introduced at typical locations: between synthesizers and mixer inputs, between multitrack tape recorder and mixer inputs, and between signal processors and mixer effects returns. Creative use of your audio patchbay could allow a single MIDI-controlled attenuator to function in all three capacities. **(C)** Typical MIDI-controlled mixer configuration.

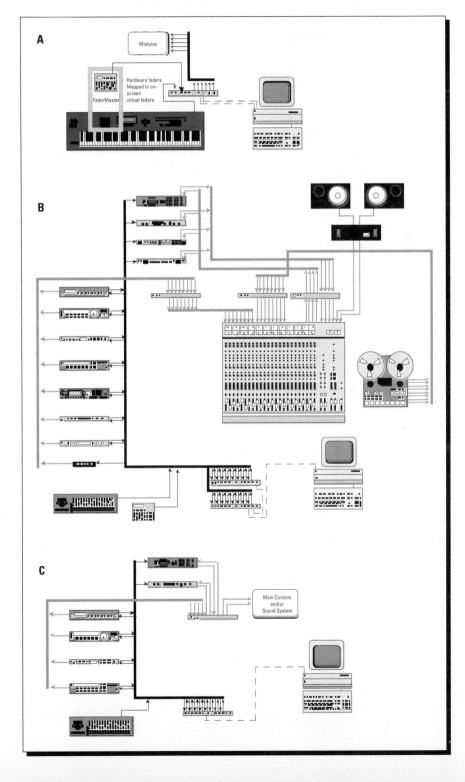

The snapshot approach has the advantage of requiring a very little portion of the MIDI bandwidth as opposed to the amount taken up by streams of continuous controller data. The disadvantage is that if you start playback in the middle of your sequence and some intervening snapshots were not sent to the device, all of your levels will be wrong, since they represent the configuration of the last snapshot sent to the device. Using continuous controller data for MIDI-controlled mixing exhibits identical problems when controller data is not present. However, chances are that there is considerably more controller activity in this approach, so the problem is not as great.

There are two solutions to starting playback anywhere in the sequence and having the fader setting be accurate:

❖ Use the Chase Controllers option of your sequence if available. Note that it is only necessary to chase the controllers that your MIDI-controlled mixing device responds to (and any events that you require for musical consider-ations). In the case of a snapshot-oriented device, you only need to chase program changes (which you probably would do anyway). In the case of MIDI-controlled mixing devices that respond to continuous controllers, it is important to inform yourself of what controllers are used by the device and to limit the chased controllers to those.

❖ Place a snapshot of the appropriate settings at strategic locations within the sequence. This might include verses, choruses, bridges, larger sections, points where you know you will be punching in, regions that are unfin-ished, and looped regions. Usually it is a good idea to place the snapshot somewhere in the measure immediately preceding the section in question. With this approach, you only have to rewind the sequence to the measure before your sections begin and you are assured that the mixer settings will be correct at the beginning of the section you want to work on or listen to.

Whether or not your MIDI-controlled mixing device offers a snapshot feature, you should be careful to insert either a snapshot (or some reasonable facsimile thereof) at the beginning of each sequence. This is because when you begin mixing, you generally start with the faders in a certain position, and the first data that gets recorded is the first fader movement that you make. This might not occur for quite some time. When you rewind, your faders are left in the positions they were at the end of the piece, because they have no way of knowing what their starting point was (at that point, you might not have any idea what the initial setting was either). There are two solutions:

❖ The "wiggle" method (coined by JL Cooper) requires that you start record-ing some measures in advance of your actual musical material and simply wiggle each controller a little to write its initial setting.

❖ The snapshot solution requires storing a snapshot within the sequence or the program change value required to call up a snapshot stored in the actual device.

The best of both worlds are devices that offer both snapshot options with real-time continuous control. This approach is becoming increasingly popular.

MIDI-controlled attenuators

MIDI-controlled attenuators use VCAs, DCAs (digitally controlled amplifiers), or, in the case of the Niche ACM (audio control module), large scale integrated resistor (LSIR) networks are substituted for VCAs and DCAs.

LSIRs have the advantage of introducing no noise into the signal path, because they are actually not amplifiers. Instead, they use digitally controlled resistors, which, in effect, function analogously to squeezing a garden hose with great precision. LSIRs are a passive component, so the wire connecting the source signal to its destination is not interrupted at any time. Instead, it is as if MIDI-adjustable clamps had been fastened around the wire to close or open the signal flow.

MIDI-controlled attenuators translate received MIDI messages (which can be controller information or SysEx information) into voltages that are used to control the VCAs effecting the attenuation. Typical devices use controllers with a value range of 0 to 127, although most employ innovative techniques to get around this limited number of positions. Attenuators are much more subject to the zipper phenomenon discussed above under Volume and Pan. To increase the range of possible values beyond 128, MIDI-controlled attenuators often combine unused MIDI controller messages to represent a single value. Some devices interpolate intermediary values internally. For example, the ACM interpolates somewhere between 10 and 512 increments (there seems to be some confusion about which figure it is) between each of the 128 controller values.

MIDI-controlled attenuators are available with and without built-in MIDI faders. While you can use a MIDI-controlled attenuator without hardware faders, investing in a MIDI fader box would greatly increase your efficiency if your MIDI-controlled attenuator does not have its own faders. Devices that incorporate built-in MIDI faders often provide for the recording of their fader moves and channel muting internally — no sequencer is required unless you want to edit the data. This is a desirable feature if you are already pushing the MIDI bandwidth to its limits. When a MIDI-controlled attenuator includes its own recording options, the ability to synchronize recorded mixes with SMPTE, MTC, or SPP is standard (see Chapter 26, "Film and Video Applications").

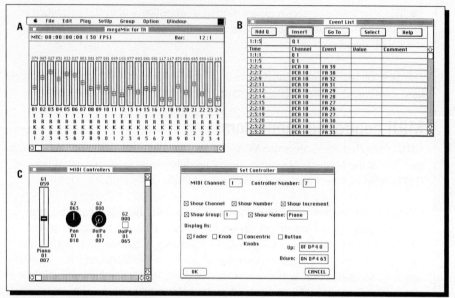

Figure 25-18: MegaMix's control program. **(A)** The fader automation window. **(B)** The cue list window. **(C)** The console design window and a typical controller setting dialog box.

Popular MIDI-controlled attenuation systems include the following. (Note: Because these are gain controls, there are usually the same number of inputs and outputs.)

JL Cooper MixMate ($1,000). An eight-channel, eight-MIDI fader, VCA-based system offering fader and muting automation. Optional Macintosh software is available (MixMate Plus — $250).

JL Cooper MAGI II (starting at $3,000). MAGI stands for mixer automation gain interface, a 16-channel (expandable to 32-, 48- or 64-channel), VCA-based system. It is available as an external system (with faders and mutes) or as an internal retrofit to existing consoles (MAGI IIi).

Musically Intelligent Devices MegaMix ($2,600). A 16-channel (expandable to 64-channel in eight-channel groups), VCA-based system offering fader, muting, soloing, and gating automation. Macintosh software is available for cue list editing and the creation of consoles to control all kinds of signal processors (see Figure 25-18).

Niche ACM ($480 — distributed by the Russ Jones Marketing Group). An eight-channel (with a stereo mix output), LSIR-based (see above), rack-mountable (1U) system with a signal-to-noise ratio of 95 dB and a flat frequency response from 30 Hz to 30 KHz. Unlike the other systems mentioned in this section, the ACM box does not include any MIDI faders, but Niche offers a separate Mix Automation Station with 16 faders that is perfect for controlling two ACMs (creating a 16-channel MIDI-controlled attenuator).

MIDI-controlled mixers

MIDI-controlled mixers are simply audio mixers that can be placed under MIDI control. Such control is usually in the form of continuous controller data, program change, or SysEx data. Snapshots are common in these systems, and some rely on this approach exclusively. Because these mixers do not depend exclusively on standard MIDI data, certain functions that cannot usually be automated with most MIDI-controlled attenuators and virtual mixing can be placed under MIDI control. These include muting, soloing, EQ, and gating.

Akai MPX820 ($2,500). A rack-mountable (7U) 8-by-2 mixer with three-band EQ and a single effects send and return. This mixer takes the snapshot approach and allows up to 99 snapshots to be saved internally in battery-backed RAM and recalled with program change messages. Real-time continuous control is not available, but you can designate crossfades between one snapshot to another that range from 40 ms to 30 seconds. Up to eight MPX820s can be slaved together to create a 64-channel mixer.

Mark of the Unicorn MM7s ($600). MM7s stands for MIDI Mixer 7s, a rack-mountable (1U) MIDI-controlled mixer with seven stereo inputs (an eighth pair of inputs is available but not present in the mix output), two stereo effects sends and returns per channel, high and low shelving EQ (that is, treble and bass controls), noise gates (signal-to-noise ratio is 78 dB with the gates off and 90 dB with them on), and pan, mute, and solo controls. There are chain inputs and outputs to chain several MM7s units together (see Figure 25-19).

Simmons SPM 8:2 ($1,100). A rack-mountable (1U) 8-by-2 mixer with three-band EQ and two effects sends (with mono returns). As a bonus feature, there are built-in LFOs that can be used for such things as special panning and phasing effects. This mixer takes the snapshot approach and allows up to 64 snapshots to be stored in battery-backed RAM. However, setting the timing of crossfades between snapshots with any precision is impossible, because the Channel XFade knob is merely labeled Fast on one side and Slow on the other (you feel like Alice in Wonderland nibbling on the mushroom — "One side makes you larger and the other makes you smaller").

Yamaha DMP7, DMP11, and DMP7D ($4,000 for the DMP7). A rack-mountable (10U) or console-mountable 8 × 2 mixer with automated faders, three-band EQ, built-in stereo compressor, a mono effects send with stereo returns, and three built-in stereo multi-effects processors (similar to their SPX-90/900 line) that can be used in combination offering reverberation, gating, pitch change, flange, phasing,

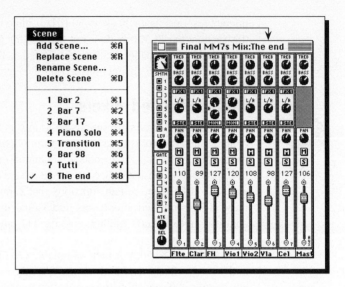

Figure 25-19: Mark of the Unicorn's MM7s includes this 7s Console program for controlling the unit. Every aspect of the MM7s is addressable with this software. This is the only way to configure many parameters of the device, because the front panel only provides knobs for channel trim, effects trim, gate threshold, master volume, and headphone volume. Snapshots (called scenes) can be saved for later recall. Saved scenes appear under the Scene menu.

chorus, and delay, among others. Incoming signal is converted to 16-bit 44.1 KHz digital data upon arrival and reconverted to analog at the outputs. Four or more DMP7s can be cascaded together, and all interconnections are digital rather than analog. The DMP11 is a slightly scaled-down version of the DMP7, taking only four rack units. The EQ is reduced to two bands, only two internal effects processors are provided, and the motorized fader automation is removed. Also, there are considerably fewer front panel controls. The DMP7D is essentially the same as the DMP7, except that digital inputs and outputs are provided along with analog outputs. All major digital interface formats are supported (AES/EBU, eight-channel Yamaha, Sony, and Mitsubishi). See Figures 25-20 and 25-21.

General Purpose Mixing Software

Q-Sheet A/V

Digidesign's Q-Sheet A/V software is a MIDI and digital audio event sequencer optimized for sound effects editing and ADR (automatic dialog replacement). These features are discussed in Chapter 26, "Film and Video Applications." Q-Sheet A/V has features applicable to MIDI mixing automation, which are not covered in that chapter.

The program lets you construct panels in controller windows that transmit and receive continuous controllers 0 to 120 and Pitch Bend and Aftertouch (see Figure 25-22). You simply drag graphic knobs, buttons, faders, and numericals into a window and assign them to the desired controller numbers. There is no remapping of controllers. When a virtual control is assigned to a continuous controller for a particular device, it is linked to that controller in both directions — it responds the same whether you move the control on the screen or on the

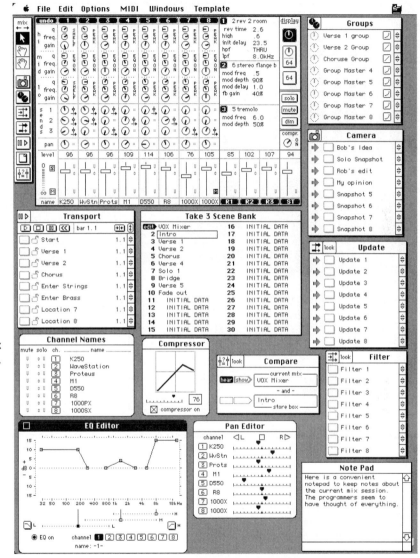

Figure 25-20: Digital Music Services's DMP7 Pro with most of its editors pictured. Note in particular the Mix Editor (upper left), the EQ Editor, the Pan Editor, the Compressor window, the Channel Names window, the Scene Bank, and the Automation Bank which includes the fire windows along the right of the screen.

physical device. You can record the data from either perspective. When the program is in operation, these sliders, knobs, and buttons animate in real time as they send the appropriate data to the external device.

The software comes with front panels already constructed for the DMP7, the Twister PAC (a Danish MIDI-controlled mixer), and a generic eight-fader console. The software requires that all the controls on any single panel be assigned to the same MIDI channel, which may necessitate altering your device

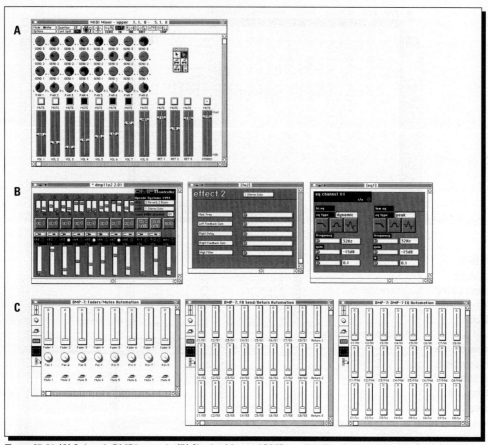

Figure 25-21: (A) Cubase's DMP7 console. **(B)** Charles Maynes' DMP11 editor/librarian created with Opcode's Max software. **(C)** The DMP7 front panels that come with Q-Sheet A/V.

setup so that instead of equating audio channels to MIDI channels, it equates audio channels to controller numbers. You can have as many panels open as you like and you are allowed to copy and paste elements from one panel to another.

Other Studio Automation

There are many other ways to automate your studio production work. For more details on utilities, see the coupon in the back of the book. These include Mark Erickson's TRAX and Hypersong-Tracksheet. Erik Hanson's Music Production Package and Words & Deeds's Archie Studio Management System offer additional studio management options.

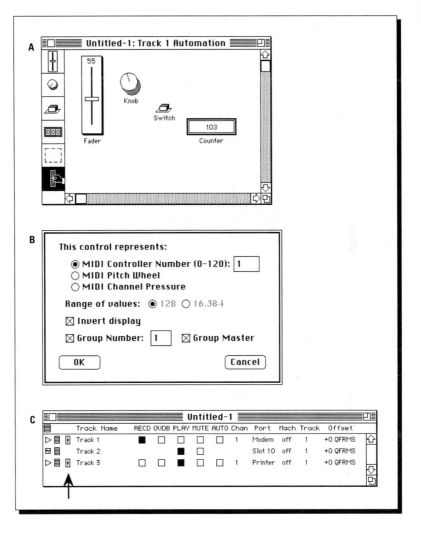

Figure 25-22: Q-Sheet A/V's controller window operation. **(A)** You drag icons that create knobs, buttons, faders, and numericals out from the palette at the left of the main window. **(B)** Double-clicking a virtual control brings up this dialog box to set its assignment. Invert display refers to a reversal of polarity. Any control can be a member or master of a group. Scaling and offsets are automatic for members of the group. **(C)** Subsequently, you can call up the controller panel by clicking the little icon indicated by the arrow.

The Music Production Package is a set of FileMaker templates that include utilities for the creation of budgets and proposals, maintaining of studio and talent call lists, tracking of production expenses, and the generation of budget vs. actual production costs reports. All calculations are automated by the software. FileMaker's lookup features are put to good use in allowing you to maintain a separate database (included) for all talent and businesses, so that you never have to manually enter the data more than once.

The Archie Studio Management System is a set of 34 relational databases that use Odesta's Double Helix runtime engine for operation. Databases are termed relational when data entered in one database file is automatically transferred to all applicable places in other linked database files. If doing so causes information in another location to change, these updates are sent back to your current location (and everywhere else required). The software is available as a single-user version or in a networkable multiuser version. Archie automates such tasks as accounting, receivables, billing, invoices, statements, lists of clients, vendors, producers, engineers, session tracksheets (with SMPTE calculation capabilities), cue sheets, master tape library tracking, equipment inventory, and many other typical studio management considerations.

Three utilities are so feature-laden that their inclusion in the current chapter is warranted.

Assistant Engineer

Wachter Softworks's Assistant Engineer integrates many utilities into a single program. Many of these functions are tasks that you might relegate to an assistant, hence the program's name (see Figure 25-23).

Track Sheet

Missing Byte Software's Track Sheet is designed to automate the creation and printing of 8-, 12-, 16-, or 24-track track sheets, time cues, invoices, EQ settings, and other studio tasks. Because the program is inherently concerned with speeding up your studio work, there are many courtesy features that have been added in response to users in the field. These include user-definable menus, so that very little text has to be typed manually once the program is set up for your studio, and also a host of auto-advance-from-field-to-field options (see Figure 25-24).

The program is highly customizable. You define menus that become available wherever necessary to automate the entry of data. For example, you can define up to 65 menu items that are grouped into three menus and describe a number of your studio instruments, drums, and cues information (including cue name, making, and pass number). You can have multiple menu files saved for different projects and studio configurations.

Track Chart

Opcode's Track Chart is truly a second-generation program. Programmer Rick Johnston (also the creator of Cue — described in Chapter 26, "Film and Video Applications") has clearly made a detailed study of the way people actually work while mixing in studios, noting ways in which efficiency could be enhanced at every juncture. Existing software has also been considered, and he has made every possible effort to add features that had not been available before.

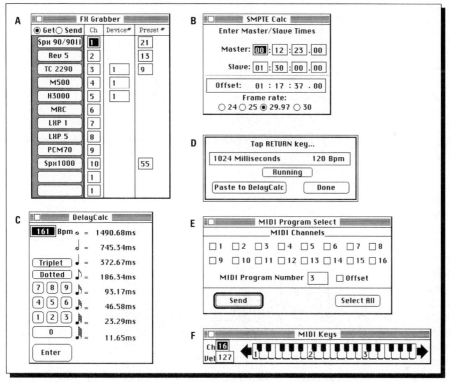

Figure 25-23: Assistant Engineer provides six utility windows dedicated to making your life easier during the mixing process. **(A)** The FX Grabber lets you send and receive patches as SysEx data from effects devices. Entire banks of patches are transferred by way of the Get button. Subsequently, the Send button sends individual patches. **(B)** The SMPTE Calculator is dedicated to determining SMPTE Time Code offsets between slave and master devices. **(C)** The Delay Calculator calculates timings in the range of 128th notes to whole notes from BPM tempos. You can use this information to set digital delays, reverberators, and other signal processing effects. **(D)** Tap tempo computes a tempo from your tapes on the Return key of the Macintosh keyboard. A button is provided that pastes this tempo directly into the Delay Calculator. **(E)** Program Select sends program change messages on the MIDI channel or channels you indicate with the checkboxes. An Offset option is provided for those instruments that number their patches from 0 instead of 1. **(F)** MIDI Keys lets you preview sounds in a nine-octave range on any channel at any velocity.

Track Chart lets you open up to five songs simultaneously, each containing up to 98 tracks. Track sheet layout is completely customizable, as is just about every other element to the program (see Figure 25-25). Track record keeping is optimized to handle the four types of tracks that are popular in the '90s: analog-recorded tracks, tracks originating from Direct-to-Hard Disk recording media, virtual tracks, and live tracks.

Entering track information is automated with menus. If you are dealing with a non-virtual track, the software provides menus for most of the common acoustic instruments. Track Chart, like most recent Opcode products, is completely

Figure 25-24: Track Sheet's main screen with its primary windows open. **(A)** Track window (this is always open). Individual track pop-up menus are accessible with Command-click, Option-click, and Command-Option click, as is the Sync pop-up menu. **(B)** The Time Cues window lets you organize the temporal locations of audio data on your tracks. This facilitates use with an auto-locator. You can set up to 20 location points while you are listening to the tape, simply by clicking the buttons numbered 1 to 20. **(C)** The Invoice window performs all the necessary calculations for generating invoices

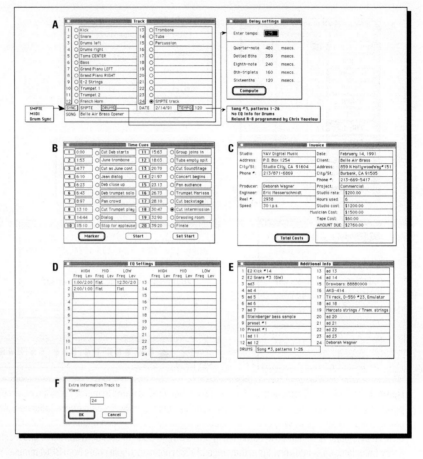

relevant to the current project. Once you've entered the studio rate and supplemental costs, all other charges are calculated and entered automatically. **(D)** The EQ Settings window lets you keep a record of EQ settings for each track. **(E)** An Additional Info window. **(F)** An Extra Information window can be opened for any individual track. This brings together all that track's relevant information from the Track, Additional Info, and EQ Settings windows. You can also enter additional information about the track here.

OMS-compatible (see Chapter 8, "Moving Data Around Your Music Network"). Once you have created your studio setup for OMS, OMS automatically provides necessary information wherever required in the Track Chart program, saving you considerable time.

The program automates the entry of track information very efficiently. For virtual tracks, all you have to do is open either an SMF or a Vision (or StudioVision) file, and the information is entered into the track sheet. Audio data can also be entered automatically if you have a MIDI interface (such a Opcode's Studio 3 or Studio 5) that can convert audio information to MIDI

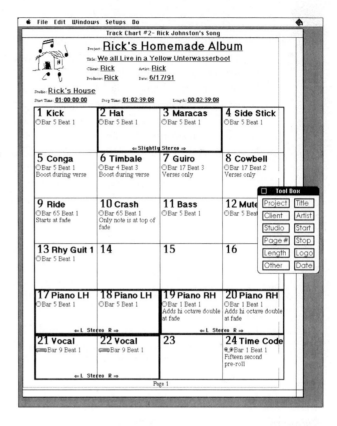

Figure 25-25: A track sheet generated by Opcode's Track Chart software. The icons indicate the source for the data on each track. Grouped tracks (such as stereo pairs or virtual tracks) are highlighted with heavy outlines. The extent and type of information included for each track is configurable. Track Chart speeds things up by requiring the entry of crucial information only once. After you enter such data as Project, Client, Studio, Length, Title, Artist, and Start and Stop Times, you can use the Tool Box (palette pictured at middle right) to place this information anywhere you might need it simply by dragging it from the Tool Box to the desired field. Page numbers, dates, and even your studio logo can be positioned with the Tool Box as well.

messages. Track Chart also automates the mapping of virtual tracks in MIDI files to physical tracks on your multitrack recorder (see Figure 25-26).

Figure 25-26: Track Chart and MIDI files. **(A)** When you import a MIDI file, you have the option of extracting any combination of the ten types of data listed on this dialog box. **(B)** Mapping virtual tracks from an imported MIDI file is as simple as dragging a line between a track in the sequence column to a track in the tape tracks column. Shift-dragging autoconnects the next 15 tracks consecutively as well.

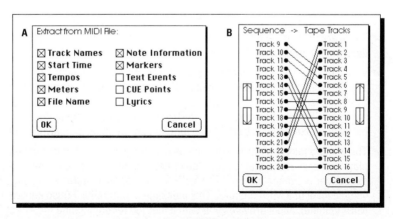

Track Chart's Time Line is one of the innovative ways the software offers for enhancing the mixdown process, and it's a good one. The Time Line window presents all track activity information as horizontal lines, complete with tempo, measure, and other timing information. This display scrolls by during playback synchronized to time code. This allows you to note and monitor upcoming track activity, a significant improvement on standard VU meters that can only display current track activity without giving any hint about what is coming up in the next few measures. To obtain this type of information without Track Chart, you'd need two tape machines with the feed reel on one and the takeup reel on the other. Then you'd have to construct a box of indicators that would monitor audio signal at the playback heads of both machines. Such a kluge would notify you of upcoming track activity before it happens. Fortunately, Track Chart takes care of all this for you (and you don't have to buy a second recorder).

Track Chart automates the creation of labels for console faders, tape boxes, and cassettes. You can enter the label information manually or have Track Chart extract it from the current file. Some standard types of label stock are built in, but you can define your own custom label stock.

Because Track Chart is both OMS- and MIDI-Manager-compatible, you can synchronize it to other programs such as MIDI sequencers and mixing automation software. Track Chart can send and receive (record data from) other programs in real time.

Summary

- Automation, the most desirable feature of astronomically expensive mixing consoles, is being brought into the financial range of the typical Macintosh-controlled music studio. Mixer automation normally refers to storing, recalling, playing back, and often editing recordings of real-time manipulations of a mixer's front panel controls (such as faders, buttons, and knobs). Such mixes can be much more complex than would otherwise be humanly possible to execute.

- There are three main approaches to using MIDI for mixing: virtual mixing, MIDI-controlled attenuation, and MIDI-controlled hardware mixing.

- Virtual mixing uses Channel messages stored in a MIDI sequence to control an instrument's volume and pan within the instrument instead of at a mixer. MIDI-controlled attenuation uses controller or SysEx messages stored in a MIDI sequence to operate a hardware audio interface to a standard mixer. MIDI-controlled mixers use MIDI to control all or some of the functions of specially designed hardware mixers that are otherwise functionally identical to nonMIDI-controllable mixers.

- The primary task of a hardware mixer is to allow dynamic changes of volume level (gain) during the playing of audio data that is recorded or being generated in real time by a synthesizer (either under sequencer or human control). The MIDI Specification includes a message devoted to setting the volume level of a MIDI channel. This message is Controller 7 (also known as Channel Volume or MIDI Volume), and it provides you with a method for duplicating the effect of moving hardware volume faders completely within your MIDI sequencer environment.

✔ Some of the functions of a hardware mixer offering real-time manipulation are signal level (volume), equalization or EQ (boosting or cutting specified frequency bands), adding effects (signal processing), and adding reverberation, muting, and panning (moving the signal within the stereo audio field). Virtual mixing can replicate many of these functions.

✔ MIDI-controlled attenuators use VCAs, DCAs, or, in the case of the Niche ACM, LSIR networks are substituted for VCAs and DCAs. MIDI-controlled attenuators translate received MIDI messages (which can be controller information or SysEx information) into voltages that are used to control the VCAs effecting the attenuation.

✔ MIDI-controlled mixers are simply audio mixers that can be placed under MIDI control. Such control is usually in the form of continuous controller data, program change, or SysEx data. Snapshots are common in these systems, and some rely on this approach exclusively. Because these mixers do not depend exclusively on standard MIDI data, certain functions that cannot usually be automated with most MIDI-controlled attenuators and virtual mixing can be placed under MIDI control. These include muting, soloing, EQ, and gating.

Part Seven
Film, Video, and Synchronization

Part Seven

Foreword

by Dominic Frontiere

Film, Video, and Synchronization

Historically, the goal of the film composer has been to "underscore" the action seen on screen. Early filmmakers believed that the masses, inexperienced with the new medium, must be directed emotionally, as well as intellectually, when watching a film. Music was introduced both to interpret and emphasize the storyline. Different musical styles were formulated to identify particular characters or situations. Bad-guy music identified the bad guys; good-guy music identified the good guys. With the advent of "talkies," film music was free to comment more subtly on the action. Each generation of composers has become more successful at eliciting the emotions of the audience. As a result, the film score has evolved into an ever changing art form in its own right.

Music has always been a reflection of the era in which it was created. Every composer's heritage and lifestyle, as well as personality, has influenced his or her creative process. High standards of quality in both composition and orchestration of film scores were created during the 1930s, '40s and '50s by Alfred and Lionel Newman, Franz Waxman, Dimitri Tiomkin, Bernard Herrman, Alex North, Victor Young, Hugo Friedhofer, Johnny Green, Morris Stoloff, Ray Heindorf, and others. These standards were certainly brought to greater heights by composers of the 1960s and '70s such as Jerry Goldsmith, Henry Mancini, and André Previn, and exemplified by John Williams's work of the last decade.

During the evolution of film scoring, devices have evolved to help the composer. The creation of click tracks, punch marks, and streamers (which was known as the "Newman method" after Alfred Newman) became standard tools for the film composer. Today, the use of programs like Opcode's Cue and Passport's Clicktracks make the task of spotting and cueing a film child's play.

Beginning with the ability to record mono only, film composers grew to 3-track 35-mag, to 6-track 35-mag, to 8-tracks, then 16-tracks, and now 24- and 48-tracks, both analog and digital. When first experimenting with electronic sounds, composers had to make due with a bit of luck and ingenuity, often with comedic results. I remember recording the hum and hiss of a vacuum cleaner and making a loop for one of the segments of the TV series *The Outer Limits*. I also got my hands on an old oscillator, with which I recorded some themes using a radial dial to control amplitudes. Having the capability now to control hundreds of oscillators from my Macintosh is a long way from that humble beginning.

Many contemporary composers, including Williams, Goldsmith, James Horner, and Danny Elfman, are enhancing their orchestral scores with electronic instruments. We are also seeing film scores composed solely for electronic orchestras by Maurice Jarre, Hans Zimmer, and others. The best orchestrators such as Arthur Morton, Herb Spencer, Grieg McRitchie, and Jack Hayes, have all become familiar with the art of writing for electronic instruments.

As this protoplasm of film music continues to evolve, I believe that we are now fully committed to a computerized future. Sequencers, SMPTE, VITC, MIDI, video, analog, digital, fiberoptics, synthesizers, workstations, signal processors, modems, automated mixing, MIDI-cableization, patch librarians, and sampling can now be directed from our Macintoshes. Reading manuals for new gear has become a part of most film composers' and musicians' lives. Scores from one's home studio, often a combination of synthesizers and live musicians, is a reality.

No one can deny that we are now a part of the computer and electronic revolution. It is hard to describe the elation that I felt upon hooking up my first Macintosh to a DX7 and hearing an immediate playback of my compositions. Today I have three Macintoshes interlocked to a whole range of equipment and am able to preview an entire score synchronized to the film prior to recording. This is a terrific aid to me as well as to the film producers and directors involved.

And this is just the beginning . . . As our computers and programs get more powerful, we will be able to stretch our creative abilities even further. Our equipment will become better adept at reading more bits and bytes. Quite possibly, the whole MIDI standard may have to be rewritten. The MIDI 128 steps will become 16,000-odd steps; hard disks will have hundreds of gigabytes of memory; the non-registered parameter numbers will become registered; the manufacturers of synthesizers and signal-processing equipment will have to standardize their nomenclature for parameters

and controllers; a magic number will be found for a sampling rate that truly will close the gap between the digital and the analog world; and the study of the complicated and unique performance of live musicians will start to be analyzed and programmed into our computers.

A quantum leap has been achieved in our ability to explore spectrums of sound never thought possible. It seems that every Macintosh music user now has a library of thousands of sounds just waiting to be manipulated and used.

Ultimately, the success of a composer's music will always depend on the audience. No one out there cares very much about what equipment the composer uses, but they do care about the quality of the music. The miracles of number crunching that our Macintoshes perform; the capabilities of our automated consoles; the versions of Performer, StudioVision, and Finale that haven't been seen yet; the options available with direct-to-hard disk digital recording, and so on, are only tools. Although composers started with pencils and now have computers, the music page still starts out blank.

It must be remembered that the presentation of music cannot be accompanied by an excuse regarding the composer's creative process or methods. Although technology can certainly manipulate compositional material in ways never before dreamed of, no computer, synthesizer, or workstation can create compositions for the user. The demands on the music student are heavier than ever before. He or she must add the study of computers and electronic instruments to their curriculum of harmony, composition, counterpoint, and orchestration. While there is a danger for novices to believe that the technology can create for them, the good news is that the Macintosh, when properly applied, can make the composer's world much easier, bigger, and better. ♩

Dominic Frontiere is a film/TV composer who has composed music for over 60 films, including Stuntman.

Introduction to Part Seven

Macintoshes are involved in some capacity in the creation of the music for almost all American films and television shows released each year.

Macintoshes running MIDI sequencers are used to create complete "synth scores." In these cases all the ancillary applications of the Macintosh can come into play: patch editing and librarian activities, sampling and sample editing, direct-to-hard disk recording, interactive and algorithmic composition, notation, MIDI-controlled signal processing, and MIDI-automated mixing. These tasks each have one or more entire chapters devoted to them. It is not uncommon for MIDI sequencers to be synchronized to live musicians.

For purely orchestral scores, there is a strong likelihood that a Macintosh-based MIDI sequencer driving one or more electronic instruments served as an orchestral sketch pad for the composer. In another common scenario the film composer creates sketches in a MIDI sequencer. These sequences are converted to notation, either by the composer or, more often, by assistants. These notated sketches are then used by orchestrators to handwrite the final score. The actual printed notation is an intermediate step.

The practice of employing notation software to produce scores and instrumental parts for film and video is still in its infancy. The reasons for this are many. Composers and copyists have been experimenting since the first notation programs appeared. Many of these technological flirtations turned into fiascos that had an adverse effect upon the acceptance of such tools. Music notation software only reached the level required by the film and video industry in 1991. Prior bad experiences, coupled with hard-to-break, time-honored traditions, still create obstacles for notation software in the film industry. With the amount of money involved and the limited time frame to produce music, many are wary of risking their livelihood to a system crash. Studio musicians are accustomed to seeing music written by hand. To address this problem, one music font (HagenHand — see Chapter 21) creates printouts that appear to be handwritten by a copyist.

The most important application of the Macintosh in film and television is the synchronization of music to film. The Macintosh can function as a slaved controller linking film synchronization information to synthesizers and samplers played by MIDI sequencers. When the synchronization gear required for this purpose is beyond the financial means of a composer, most preliminary scoring can still be done at a home studio, with the composer bringing the disk to the studio at the last possible moment. The Macintosh can be depended upon to keep everything totally synchronized.

The synchronization techniques employed for film and video are, for the most part, the same as those used when synchronizing Macintosh-based MIDI sequencers to audio tape machines. In this context, synchronization assures the alignment of tracks that are recorded to tape in multiple passes or provides for the addition of virtual tracks. Identical methods and hardware are required regardless of whether you are synchronizing your Macintosh to a 4-track cassette deck or a 24-track recorder.

Even for the rare film and video scores where the Macintosh was not involved in sequencing, sound design, notation, or synchronization, there is a very good chance that cue sheet software running on the Macintosh was employed by the music editor to prepare the cue sheets for the composer. When used by a composer, such programs offer many more features than simply printing out cue sheets. Opcode's Cue, for example, captures hit points (moments where the visual and audio must be in tight synchronization) automatically from the video, calculates the optimum tempo to catch the most hits, creates tempo maps guaranteed to make all the hits dead-on (these can be imported by most MIDI sequencers), and even prints out staff-paper with barlines and the cue sheet information displayed above appropriate measures.

Other popular film and video applications of the Macintosh are in the realm of sound effects and automatic dialog replacement (ADR).

Chapter 26

Film and Video Applications

In this chapter...

✔ Defining and explaining synchronization.

✔ Formats, advantages, and disadvantages of various synchronization protocols.

✔ Macintosh studio setup diagrams for all types of synchronization.

✔ Virtual tracking.

✔ Synchronization on the scoring stage.

✔ Cue sheet applications for film and video scoring.

✔ Utility software for film and video music.

✔ Interview with composer Bruce Miller.

✔ Timing conversion table.

Coming to a Screen Near You

In film and video scoring, the Macintosh is now almost as indispensable as click books (see the heading "Click tracks" in this chapter) were for several decades. If you are a film composer, almost every type of software discussed in this book can be put to good use to enhance your efficiency and productivity.

This chapter is concerned with several Macintosh applications unique to the film industry. Foremost among these is *synchronization*. Synchronization refers to the controlled alignment of two time-based media such as the flow of MIDI data and audio or video tape. It can also refer to individual events that occur at exactly the same point in time. If you have ever seen a Godzilla movie or similarly English-dubbed foreign films, you understand the importance of synchronization. Film travels at 24 frames per second (fps). Synchronization errors are noticeable as soon as events are as little as two or three frames out of sync.

Synchronization in the world of electronic musical instruments was introduced to accommodate people who desired to synchronize drum machines to hardware sequencers. This allowed them to synchronize pre-programmed drum patterns to their sequences during the creative process. A large number of people without formal musical training preferred to compose while hearing a drum track. Early pulse sync techniques made that possible even before any form of tape synchronization had been invented.

Eventually, these musicians wanted to introduce tape recorders and live musicians into the process. A method for encoding sync pulses as tones that could be recorded evolved. This accommodated the following scenario: A drum machine is programmed into a "song." The information required to synchronize the drum machine to tape is recorded on the tape. Subsequently, live musicians record their tracks to tape while listening to the synchronized drum machine. After the live music is recorded, live drums are recorded onto the tape to replace the drum machine. Many people prefer to work this way, with the drum machine serving as a glorified metronome during the compositional process.

The options for synchronization and working methodologies that rely on synchronization have expanded exponentially. The discussion of synchronization in this chapter also includes purely audio applications such as syncing to tape. If you plan on using a MIDI sequencer in conjunction with a multitrack recorder, you should read these sections.

Distinctions

Synchronizing two elements that are driven by different clocks or motors is not simply a matter of pressing the start buttons simultaneously. Even if you could press the buttons at exactly the same time, minute fluctuations in motor speed would cause one source to drift in relation to the other after a short amount of time. In any synchronization scenario there is always a master clock reference known as the "master," to which one or more "slave" components are synchronized. In the following discussions, the terms "device" or "microprocessor-controlled device" refer not only to hardware sequencers, drum machines, and the like, but also to Macintoshes running software that provides or relies upon timing information, such as a software MIDI sequencer.

It is possible to achieve perfect synchronization of audio recordings with other audio or video recordings mechanically. In fact, at the final stage in the film scoring process such methods are used. Audio is recorded onto film that has been coated with magnetic oxide (this is called mag). Because this film has sprocket holes just like the film containing the picture, synchronization of two or more of these elements is a simple matter of mechanically synchronizing the sprockets with gears or by employing a rotating shaft that has rows of sprockets to accommodate multiple sprocketed media (audio or picture).

Such mechanical synchronization is rarely, if ever, an option for you during the composition process. Nowadays you receive a video tape of a film and often use a sequencer as a compositional aid in scoring the picture, and video tape has no sprocket holes. Timing is very important. You want to make sure that your music lasts as long as the scene it is intended for. Furthermore, you probably want to "hit" a number of visual events precisely. This refers to constructing your music and tempo in such a way that a visual event, such as a cut, camera motion, or action, aligns exactly with a musical event, such as a chord, note, or change of texture or timbre. Because of this, you need some way to synchronize your sequencer to the video tape you are watching.

You also need some method of synchronization when you record sequenced tracks individually on a multitrack tape recorder. This is not as big an issue if you are using live musicians exclusively. Suppose you record one instrument and then want to record another instrument on another track. As long as there is a count-off, the second instrument can come in on the down beat and play along with the first instrument, using that performance as a timing reference. A better timing reference for this situation is to record a click track (see the section "Synchronization on the Scoring Stage") before you record the first instrument and have that person and every subsequent instrumentalist listen to the click in headphones while they record. MIDI sequencers can't listen the way human musicians do, so a number of different electronic synchronization techniques have evolved.

There are three approaches to synchronization: pulse or clock sync, relative addressing, and absolute addressing or time code.

Pulse sync is analogous to mechanical synchronization such as the use of mag discussed above. Synchronized devices share the same timing clock, designated as the master clock. Because all of the pulses are identical, none of the devices has any way of distinguishing one pulse from another. In order to synchronize, all elements involved must commence playback from their beginnings, since this is the only point (aside from the last pulse) with a distinct identity.

Relative addressing refers to a method of synchronization in which devices keep track of the current location of the music relative to the beginning of the music. Such systems allow you to start the master clock anywhere in the music and have all slaves jump immediately to that spot. The master device simply sends a message to the effect of "relocate at the 987th 16th note," and all slaves that can respond to this do so. This works fine for microprocessor-controlled devices, which are capable of keeping track of the number of beats from the start of the music or calculating a certain location. However, if the timing information is recorded on tape (video or audio) and is not identified with a unique address (see below), the tape has no way of sending such a message because the timing pulses are still all identical. Here's an analogy. Imagine that you are in a library where all the books have no titles or catalog numbers on their spines. If the librarian tells you that the book you are looking for is the 610th book from the left, as long as you are at the beginning of the bookshelf, you can find the book you want. If you are standing anywhere else, counting 610 books over will not take you to the same place. On the other hand, if you have been keeping track of where you are standing and know that you are starting at the 200th book from the left, you can easily make the calculation and proceed 410 books farther along to find the one you want.

Absolute addressing refers to a method of synchronization where every event (and the space in between events) has a unique address. No two locations share the same address, so relocating to a specified address is simply a matter of examining the addresses until the one you are looking for is found. Returning to the library analogy, imagine that the librarian has now added a unique, sequential number to every book on the shelf. When you are informed that the book you are looking for is book number 610, you can easily find it because the numbers are printed on the spine of the books. If you happen to be standing in front of book number 1,597 you can go back to number 610. Likewise, if you happen to be standing in front of book number 377 you can advance to book number 610.

The film and video industry uses an absolute addressing timing protocol known as SMPTE (pronounced "simp-tee"), so named for its developers, the Society of Motion Picture and Television Engineers. This protocol has been adopted as a standard for synchronizing film and video devices as well as for "locking together" (synchronizing by way of a hardware synchronizer) two or more devices to function as one large machine. SMPTE can keep track of timing locations in hours, minutes, frames, and subframes (30 fps with 80 subframes per frame). The effective resolution is about half a millisecond, but it is possible to locate to any particular subframe on a video or audio tape that has been "striped" with SMPTE. See the heading "Jam sync and SMPTE regeneration/restriping/reshaping" for a complete discussion of SMPTE.

Absolute and relative addressing are often used hand in hand. For example, if an audio tape is encoded with absolute addresses, there are many devices that can convert this information into a relative address if required.

As you may have noticed, one distinction between the various approaches is whether synchronization can be achieved from a random point in the music or if synchronization requires starting at the beginning of the music. Another difference is the fact that some require tempo information to be permanently fixed before synchronization can occur, while others allow entire new tempo information to be substituted for the original at any time (see below).

The following section presents the various forms of synchronization in roughly chronological order. Generally, the evolution of synchronization methods corresponds to an increasing degree of accuracy and flexibility.

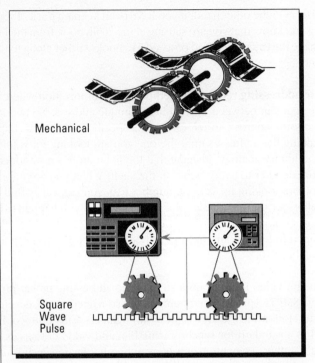

Mechanical

Square
Wave
Pulse

Figure 26-1: Comparing pulse sync with mechanical sync on a Moviola.

Synchronization Formats
Pulse sync (TTL sync or DIN sync)

Pulse sync uses an electrical signal to create a pulse equivalent to a metronome (see Figure 26-1). Two devices can use this pulse as a timing reference simultaneously. This type of synchronization is sometimes called TTL sync (transistor-transistor logic) or, in some instances, DIN sync (when five-pin non-MIDI DIN connectors are used to transfer a 24-PPQN [pulses per quarter note] pulse).

This synchronization method was developed before MIDI and is still found in drum machines and many hardware sequencers. One device is designated as the master clock. The output of this clock is passed along to a slave device (or devices) via an electrical cable. The slave device is set to ignore its own internal timing clock and consider the incoming pulse as its timing reference. Many systems use 24 PPQN as a timebase, although other rates — typically 48, 96, 384, and 480 — are available. When the tempo of the master device speeds up, the tempo of the slave device speeds up accordingly. This is because the 24 PPQN is relative to the quarter note rather than to time. Some sequencers provide for setting the timebase

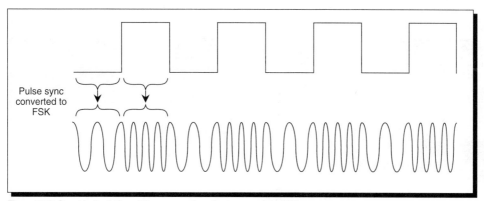

Figure 26-2: Graphic depiction of the conversion of pulse sync into FSK.

relative to the metronome click rather than the quarter note. This provides for tempos that do not have a quarter note pulse (7/16, 5/6, 3/2, and so on).

Pulse sync has two problems. First, to achieve synchronization it is necessary to start at the very beginning of the material that you want to synchronize. If you want to record or punch in a couple of notes at the end of a five-minute sequence, you have to start at the very beginning of the sequence and wait until the end arrives. The second disadvantage is that this method is not very reliable when pulses are recorded on tape, because if any kind of dropout or crosstalk occurs, sync can be lost.

FSK

Frequency shift keying (FSK) sounds like a very technical term, but here frequency shift refers to the alteration of two tones. As synchronization methods evolved, it became common to convert TTL or pulse sync into audio tones for the purpose of recording that information onto audio tape (see Figure 26-2). High and low tones correspond to the on and off states of the pulse. The frequency of these tones are in the 1 KHz to 3 KHz range, making them much easier to record and play back than pure low-frequency square waves. Some people refer to FSK as a type of synchronization ("FSK sync"). This is inaccurate, because FSK is merely a method of encoding pulse sync or other forms of data (modems also use FSK).

FSK synchronization tones are transmitted on audio cables. Devices that can respond to FSK often have jacks labeled FSK or Tape Sync. To translate FSK into information that your Macintosh-based MIDI sequencer can understand, you will need an interface capable of making the required conversions between FSK and the synchronization you use with your sequencer. Many MIDI interfaces have this capability (see Table 5-5, "Hardware Decisions" in Chapter 5).

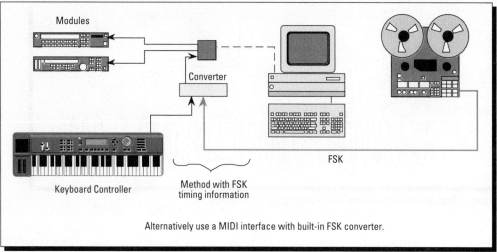

Modules

Converter

FSK

Keyboard Controller

Method with FSK
timing information

Alternatively use a MIDI interface with built-in FSK converter.

Figure 26-3: Typical FSK synchronization setup.

When synchronizing a MIDI sequencer with FSK, you will have to inform the sequencer of that fact, usually through a dialog box. Depending upon the manufacturer, the synchronization type may be referred to as Standard beat clock, MIDI clock, MIDI beat clock, or something similar (see Figure 26-3).

FSK solves the problem of recording synchronization information onto audio tape, therefore allowing you to record separate audio tracks in multiple passes. Because FSK is just another way of encoding pulse sync, it shares the disadvantage that in order to synchronize two devices, the tape (and MIDI sequencer) must be rewound to the beginning each time ("smart FSK," discussed below, gets around this limitation). Furthermore, FSK adds another problem. While you can manipulate the tempo of a drum machine or hardware sequencer in real time during the synchronization process, once you have recorded an FSK synchronization track onto your tape, the tempo is frozen.

Relative addressing

Relative addressing refers to synchronization methods that can calculate an address relative to the beginning of the synchronization information. Software accomplishes this by counting the number of elapsed 16th notes from the beginning of the sequence to the current location. This number, referred to as the Song Position Pointer, is kept track of and can be recalled whenever needed.

Song Position Pointer

The following messages provide for relative synchronization in the original MIDI Specification:

Timing Clock (F8). Serves as the pulse or metronome: 24 PPQN. (System Realtime message)

Song Position Pointer (F2 *HH*). Abbreviated as SPP. Used to send a location (or address) of a beat measured in 16th notes (a 16th note is equal to six Timing Clocks) from the beginning of the sequence. The software in your Macintosh or in a hardware sequencer keeps track of this number whenever you start playback of a sequence while using this method of synchronization. (This is a System Common message, because many devices in the MIDI network might require this information. It can only be sent when sequences are not playing.)

Start (FA). Sets the SPP to zero and starts playback at the beginning of the sequence. (System Realtime message)

Stop (FC). Halts playback without resetting the SPP. All SPP counters retain the current value. (System Realtime message)

Continue (FB). Resumes playback at the current SPP location, often equivalent to the location stored when the last Stop message was issued. SPP counters resume their count from the current location. (System Realtime message)

Song Select (F3 *HH*). Instructs sequencers (both hardware and software) that provide for multiple "songs" in which song to cue up to be played at the next issuance of a Start message. (This is a System Common message, because many devices in the MIDI network might require this information. It can only be sent when sequences are not playing.)

This form of synchronization is often referred to as MIDI sync, SPP sync, or simply SPP (for Song Position Pointer). The advantages of SPP are that you can jump to a required address without having to start at the beginning of the music as in pulse sync, that is, provided all the devices are capable of keeping track of the SPP. This implies two or more microprocessor-controlled devices. Because MIDI data is digital data rather than audio, it cannot be recorded onto tape. This problem was eventually solved with smart FSK (see below).

The disadvantage of this approach is that starting at a random point in the music may result in inaccurate playback. For example, any notes that were attacked prior to the new start point and meant to sustain through the start point will not be heard. Certain important messages (such as MIDI volume) or controls (such as the sustain pedal) may also be lost. This phenomenon brought about the "chase controllers/chase notes" feature now common in many sequencers. With this option enabled, whenever a sequencer is instructed to jump to a new location, the software looks back along each track prior to initiating playback. This allows it to determine the correct state of all controllers and whether any notes are currently sustaining. In the case of notes, this doesn't necessarily solve all your problems. For example, a note that is turned on because it should be sustaining at that point in your sequence will commence with the beginning of its envelope, whereas under normal circumstances, had you been playing the sequence through from beginning to end, that same note might be at the release stage of its envelope. This is because MIDI cannot yet communicate any timbral information such as the envelope of a sound, but is only able to specify when a note is turned on or off.

Another disadvantage of MIDI sync is that, although the MIDI Specification states that a device is supposed to start on the first MIDI Clock received after the Start message, some devices treat the Start message as if it were the first MIDI Clock. Unless your sequencer provides an option to take care of this possibility, synchronization will be off by one MIDI Clock (equal to ⅙ of a 16th note or a 64th note triplet).

Note that SPP cannot represent any timing values greater than 45 minutes.

MIDI Timing Clock, just like any other regular pulse, can be recorded onto audio tape using FSK (see above). The disadvantage of using this system with normal FSK encoding is that, as with pulse sync, an original tempo or series of tempos must be fixed at the outset, prior to recording a single track.

Absolute addressing

You will recall that absolute addressing assigns a unique and sequential address to every point on a tape or sequence. In the case of a MIDI sequence in a Macintosh software sequencer, these addresses are merely calculated on-the-fly, but the effect is the same. With SPP, this option was finally available to musicians using two microprocessor-controlled devices. MIDI musicians were well aware of the advantages this provided in the film and video production industry, where a non-MIDI-compatible absolute addressing system has been used for decades (see the section "SMPTE Time Code").

Smart FSK

People using the SPP's auto-location features with MIDI devices came to long for similar flexibility with audio tape, a flexibility provided by SMPTE Time Code (see below). Smart FSK (sometimes called SPP FSK) was developed to provide absolute addressing in an FSK recording of synchronization information.

Smart FSK simply merges SPP information into the FSK audio stream. Because SPP locations consist of an integer representing the number of elapsed 16th notes from the beginning of a piece of music, this did not overload the bandwidth of the signal the way an attempt to encode SMPTE would have.

Unfortunately, smart FSK still requires fixing tempo information at the outset. Also, you need a hardware device capable of dealing with smart FSK. Furthermore, the resolution of smart FSK, when compared to time code, leaves a little to be desired. Nevertheless, smart FSK is effective, particularly where video is not involved, and is still used as an inexpensive alternative to SMPTE Time Code.

SMPTE Time Code

SMPTE Time Code writes an absolute address for every frame of a video tape. SMPTE Time Code is also the preferred time code to use in synchronization situations using audio tape. There was a time when the interfaces and converter boxes required by SMPTE were so expensive that only a lucky few could afford them. Now, the addition of the full range of SMPTE features to a MIDI interface adds about $150 to the price and the return on the investment is extremely high. You should seriously consider a MIDI interface with a built-in SMPTE converter. Even if you don't need that feature immediately, the time may come sooner than you think.

SMPTE stores the address of a piece of tape or of a video or film frame in a data structure called a time code *word*. In normal computer parlance a word is equal to two bytes or 16 bits, and a long word is equal to four bytes or 32 bits. A time code word consists of 80 bits numbered from 0 to 79. You can think of this as 10 bytes, although it is more accurate to describe it as 16 nibbles (a nibble is four bits) followed by a 16-bit sync word. Each four-bit nibble can specify a number from 0 to 9 (see Figure 26-4). A type of encoding called *biphase modulation* permits SMPTE Time Code to be read backward and forward and at slow or fast speeds.

SMPTE Time Code addresses are normally expressed in eight digits, representing hours:minutes:seconds:frames. For example, "01:55:34:21" indicates an address of 1 hour, 55 minutes, 34 seconds, and 21 frames (see Figure 26-5). Frames are used when a SMPTE Time Code track is used on an audio tape too, even though there are no physical frames on the tape. Often this is because the audio is being synchronized to video, but many applications use a SMPTE audio track purely for non-video-oriented reasons (such as recording tracks one after another in separate passes). Some software and hardware is accurate enough to deal with quarter-frame (four per frame) and even sub-frame (80 per frame) information, so a fifth pair of digits indicating these values may be appended to the frame digits.

In the U.S., video is organized around 30 fps although videotape actually travels at 29.97 fps. The numbers indicating frames progress from 00 to 29 and then return to 00, at which point the number indicating seconds is incremented by 1. In Europe, the video speed is 25 fps. Film travels at 24 fps. Consequently, there are different frames rates for SMPTE Time Code: 30 fps, 25 fps, and 24 fps. There are some variations on the 30 fps rate (see the section "Drop-frame and non-drop-frame").

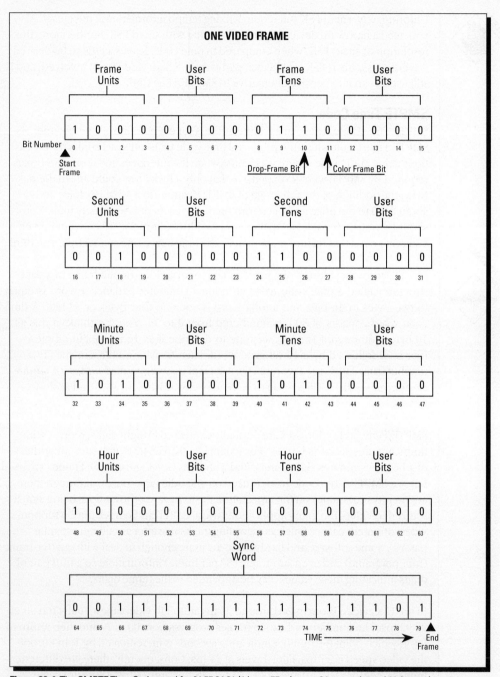

Figure 26-4: The SMPTE Time Code word for 01:55:34:21 (1 hour, 55 minutes, 34 seconds, and 21 frames).

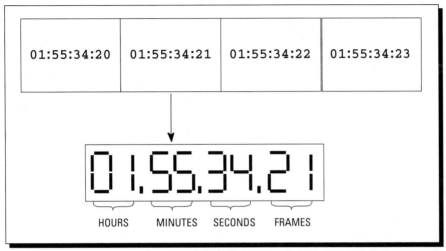

Figure 26-5: Graphic illustration of frames labeled with SMPTE Time Code. A typical LED display of one of the frames is also pictured.

If you do the math (four bits to represent a number from 0 to 9 and a time code address consisting of eight digits), you might conclude that the address information only requires 32 bits of the 80-bit word. Actually, the time code address only needs 26 bits, because the hours value never exceeds 23, the minutes and seconds values never exceed 59, and the frames value never exceeds 29. Of the remaining 54 bits, each time code word has 32 bits called "user bits," which are set aside to encode any information that an individual user might require. User data can consist of anything, but ID tags for reel numbers, shot numbers, take numbers, dates, and location are common. The last 16 bits of a time code word are called *sync data.* These sync bits define the end of each frame and, because time code can be read in either direction, they also indicate the direction of tape travel (whether audio or video tape).

Doing the math again (26 address bits plus 32 user bits plus 16 sync bits), you may notice that there are still six bits unaccounted for. Four of these are unassigned and permanently set to 0. The other two bits, numbers 10 and 11, indicate Drop-Frame mode and Color-Frame mode, respectively.

Drop-frame and non-drop-frame
In the days of black-and-white television, video signals consisted of 30 fps. You could run a black-and-white video, and the number of seconds on the clock on your wall would agree with the number of frames in your video divided by 30.

When color television became popular, the National Television Standards Committee set the frame rate for color video at 29.97002617 fps (commonly referred to as

29.97 fps) to correct for color signal distortion. Unfortunately, the frames are still numbered from 00 to 29 as if there were 30 frames per second.

The discrepancy between the two numbers is significant. Because 30 frames of video take only 29.97 seconds of real time, the difference between the frame count and the clock on the wall is +.03 frames every second (30 minus 29.97). This adds up to an extra 108 frames, or 3.6 seconds every hour. It may not seem like much, but remember that a two-frame discrepancy is all that is needed for the viewer/listener to notice that the video and audio are out of sync. Unless some sort of correction was performed, a one-hour video would really run 3.6 seconds longer than an hour.

To correct for the extra 108 frames every hour, the television industry came up with a method for dropping frames at specified intervals. This is called Drop-Frame Time Code (30 drop-frame, 30 drop, or 30 df). The way the process works is simple. Every time the minutes value of the time code address numbers increments by one, the first two frame numbers of the next minute are dropped. In other words, the frame after 01:21:34:29 is 01:21:35:02, and not, as you might expect, 01:21:35:00. The 01:21:35:00 and 01:21:35:01 addresses do not exist. If you do a little more math you will note that dropping two frames every minute results in a loss of 120 frames every hour and the goal is to drop only 108 frames. To compensate for this, the two frames are not dropped at minutes 00, 10, 20, 30, 40, and 50. These locations do have addresses assigned to their HH:MM:SS:00 and HH:MM:SS:01 frames. This adds 12 frames back again, resulting in a total of 108 dropped frames per hour and thus guaranteeing that the frame count and the clock on the wall will always be in agreement. This also assures that complete synchronization of the wall clock to 30 drop-frame SMPTE Time Code occurs every ten minutes. The dropping of frames in Drop-Frame Time Code only skips address numbers, no actual frames are dropped (see Figure 26-6).

Because color video doesn't run at exactly 29.97 (remember that the real rate is 29.97002617 fps), every day Drop-Frame Time Code overcompensates by 2.261 frames, introducing an error of +75.442 milliseconds in a 24-hour period. This adds up to slightly over two seconds a month, so studios that use a master "house sync" source are required to adjust for this on a regular basis.

The other frame rates, 24 fps and 25 fps, are absolute and will always agree with the clock on the wall just like 30 non-drop-frame black-and-white used to.

Thus, there are actually six SMPTE Time Code frame rates:

24 fps	Film
25 fps	European (PAL) video

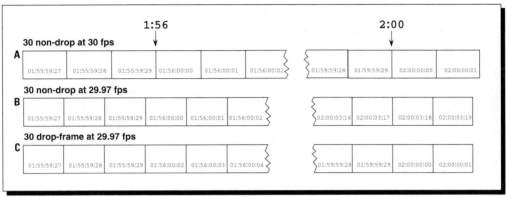

Figure 26-6: (A) 30 non-drop video running at 30 fps. **(B)** 30 non-drop video running at 29.97 fps (that is, 29.97 fps non-drop).
(C) 30 drop-frame video running at 29.97 fps (that is, 29.97 fps drop-frame).

30 fps non-drop	American black-and-white video (also used for many audio applications)
30 fps drop-frame	American color video (will not agree with wall clock)
29.97 fps non-drop	American color video (NTSC — will not agree with wall clock)
29.97 fps drop-frame	American color video (NTSC and broadcast)

Note that 30 fps non-drop is popular for audio applications because you do not have to think about dropped frames and the frame count always agrees with the clock on the wall. Also, some professional studios require 30 non-drop because it is sometimes the only format built into their mixing consoles.

There are other conundrums. Now American black-and-white video uses the 29.97 frame rate as well. There is also a 29.97 frame rate setting in many Macintosh music and digital audio programs that can synchronize. It is possible to have 29.97 fps Non-Drop Frame Time Code. Often, this is just treated as "slow 30 fps" by Macintosh software. For example, when Apple's MIDI Manager encounters 29.97 time code, it simply considers it to be slow 30 fps code and the impact upon synchronization is removed (synchronization problems would occur if MIDI Manager tried to resolve this to 30 fps).

LTC and VITC

When you are synchronizing audio tape, you will almost always have to devote one track to the storage of SMPTE Time Code. The time code is recorded just like any other audio, although you should defeat noise reduction, EQ, or other signal processing for that track. The normal procedure is to use an outer track (usually the one with the highest number) and then place a blank track (known as a guard track) between the time code track and the music.

When you use SMPTE Time Code with video, there are two ways it can be recorded. The first method has time code recorded on one of the audio tracks, in which case it is referred to as LTC (Longitudinal Time Code) and exists as an audio signal. The second method is to incorporate the time code information directly into the video signal, in which case it is referred to as Vertical Interval Time Code, or VITC (pronounced "vit-see").

LTC is easy to understand because it merely represents another track of audio. VITC is a little more complex. VITC must be recorded at the same time the video signal making up the picture is recorded. VITC is recorded into a portion of the video signal called the vertical blanking interval (VBI). This is a little portion of the video image (the first 24 scan lines) that you never see because it is above the frame and off the screen. Other uses of the VBI include closed captioning for the hearing impaired.

VITC has a number of advantages over LTC. First, you don't have to give up one of the audio tracks for time code. Second, VITC can be read reliably at any speed, including when the video is still-framed. This is because the head keeps scanning the video to display the still frame and in doing so continues to send out the SMPTE Time Code frame number. Most Macintosh programs can't tell the difference between still-framed VITC and running LTC. If you are using software that can capture the frame number (such as Opcode's Cue), meaning that you don't have to type in the actual numbers, VITC can be a real time-saver. You simply use the video deck's jog wheel to locate the frame you want, then hit a key on the Macintosh keyboard to copy that frame number over to the software. While LTC can be read at a variety of speeds (and backward and forward), reading LTC SMPTE Time Code at speeds of less than six frames per second can be unreliable.

Jam sync and SMPTE regeneration/restriping/reshaping

Most time code converters are designed to take care of bad sections of time code or any point where one or more frames of time code do not arrive at the converter from the time code source. Brief moments of bad code are a common situation. The time code signal is fragile enough that fluctuations in the amplitude of the square wave used to encode it are often unavoidable. Jam sync and SMPTE regeneration/restriping/reshaping offer solutions: You can record a complete new SMPTE Time Code track on the source device (called restriping) or some other device, or simply use these options to compensate momentarily for bad code in a real-time application.

Jam sync, sometimes referred to as SMPTE regeneration or restriping, requires that the SMPTE converter you are using include a built-in SMPTE Time Code generator. There are two types of jam sync available: one-time jam sync and continuous jam sync (see Figure 26-7).

You use one-time jam sync in cases where you want to record a new SMPTE Time Code track on a tape and are not concerned with the exact alignment of the original time code numbers with the new time code numbers. In this type of jam sync the converter waits for a valid SMPTE address to be received, at which point it sets its start address to the received address. Then it continues to generate time code from that address onward without paying any attention to the original source of the time code.

Continuous jam sync is much more popular than one-time jam sync. In this mode the original addresses remain intact, even if they include anomalies such as discontinuities. The converter synchronizes itself to the time code source and starts to generate its own code. The difference is that the converter compares the time code it is generating with the incoming time code at every frame. If it detects garbled time code or a dropout of time code, it continues to generate its own time code over the bad spots, always checking the original source to determine when the time code is once again acceptable. The process of filling in these blank or distorted spots is called *freewheeling* or *flywheeling*. As soon as the converter detects good time code again from the original source, it reinitializes itself to the source and proceeds as normal, checking each incoming address and regenerating the identical address.

You may hear the term "plus-one-frame" used in conjunction with jam sync and regeneration. This has to do with the fact that while a converter or time code reader is receiving a SMPTE Time Code, it does not know that a frame has passed until the entire 80 bits representing the frame's address have been processed (particularly, the final 16 "sync" bits of the time code word that serve as the frame delimiter). Because of this, the display or output would always be behind the original source of the time code, but there is a simple solution to that problem: the converter adds a signal frame to the number of the current frame, using a process logically called "plus-one-frame."

Reshaping SMPTE Time Code does not require a converter capable of generating time code. Consequently, the hardware used to accomplish this is considerably less expensive. A *reshaper* is simply a type of filter that is dedicated to removing distortion or noise from an incoming SMPTE Time Code signal. The clean signal is then passed on to the converter's output. Unlike jam sync and regeneration, reshaping will not remedy a situation where the time code drops out completely.

You should use jam sync, regeneration, or reshaping to ensure that a copy of a tape that includes a SMPTE Time Code track has a clean time code signal, identical

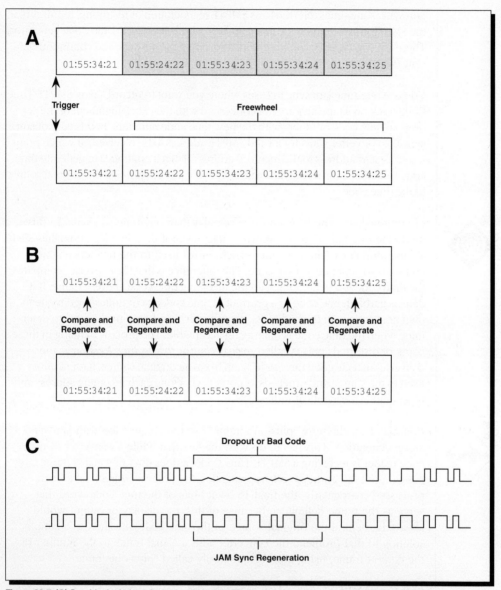

Figure 26-7: (A) Graphic depiction of one-time jam sync. The grayed-out frames indicate bad or garbled time code. **(B)** Graphic depiction of continuous jam sync. **(C)** Effect of jam sync on SMPTE Time Code drop out.

to the original (except in the case of one-time jam sync). In fact, you must use one of the processes when copying SMPTE Time Code from one track or device to another, because the minute generation loss in the copying process, even over a single generation, is too severe to make direct copies of SMPTE Time Code reliable.

Figure 26-8: Graphic depiction of a SMPTE offset. Note that the actual offset amount is pictured. Most devices do not require that you make this calculation. You simply enter the desired start times of the two address tracks and the software or synchronizer calculates the offset.

Offsets

Very often there is a need to synchronize time code on one device to a different starting point in the time code of another device. Microprocessors make this process extremely simple. Most software and many SMPTE converters can provide this feature, which is referred to as the "SMPTE offset" or "SMPTE start time" (see Figure 26-8). The offset is calculated by subtracting the smaller SMPTE address from the larger one. Keep in mind that you are dealing with time (the maximum values for the second and third numbers correspond to minutes and seconds and thus cannot exceed 59). Similarly, the final number represents the frame count and therefore cannot exceed 29 in America or 24 in Europe. Fortunately, you do not have to do these calculations yourself — the software does it all. You just enter the starting time of the SMPTE Time Code source and the time you wish the music to start. The offset is automatically calculated and every frame address has that value added to it on-the-fly with no impact on the integrity of the time code. You can also use an offset when you want to regenerate time code or restripe a SMPTE track (see above).

Relating SMPTE to MIDI

Unfortunately, SMPTE is not directly compatible with MIDI. Consider how much of the data path it would usurp: 80 bits per frame times 30 frames per second equals 2,400 bits per second, plus the two bits that MIDI adds on either side of a byte. The total comes to 3,000 bits per second, about 10 percent of MIDI's 31.25 KHz bandwidth. That may not sound like a significant amount, but this is timing information and therefore would be a System Realtime message that could potentially throw off the timing of the most critical information — notes. (The implementation described below uses a combination of System Realtime and System Common messages.)

The two systems, MIDI and SMPTE, were developed for different reasons: MIDI for the communication of performance information and SMPTE for the communication of timing information. Furthermore, their transmission formats are incompatible. SMPTE is an analog audio signal and MTC is a digital data stream. Nonetheless, they are required to communicate with one another. That's why synchronization boxes exist to convert SMPTE Time Code to SPP, MTC, DTL, DTLe, or other timing references. They allow software MIDI devices to be synchronized with hardware SMPTE devices, for example. On a global level, this permits a MIDI sequencer running on the Macintosh to advance or rewind to the exact spots in a sequence file that correspond to appropriate spots on a video tape or an analog tape recorder. On a local level, this translates into the precise simultaneity of a video hit-point with the appropriate musical event.

Many composers wanted to be able to lock up their MIDI sequencers to video before there was a provision in the MIDI Specification for this. Smart FSK (see "Smart FSK") was the first solution. With the appropriate hardware converter, such as JL Cooper's PPS series (poor person's SMPTE), incoming SMPTE Time Code can readily be converted to SPP for synchronization purposes. Newer PPS devices offer DTL and MTC conversion as well. Other alternatives to the conversion process soon became available.

Until the advent of MIDI Time Code (MTC), timing information used by MIDI for synchronization consisted of keeping track of elapsed measures with a resolution of 24 pulses per quarter note (SPP and MIDI Clock type synchronization).

In addition to the stop-gap smart-FSK solution, a number of innovative synchronization formats began to appear, including Indirect Time Lock and Direct Time Lock.

Indirect Time Lock

Mark of the Unicorn introduced Indirect Time Lock as a way to synchronize their Performer MIDI sequencer to SMPTE Time Code before there were any other alternatives. Indirect Time Lock requires that you have a SMPTE converter capable of storing a tempo map (such as Roland's SBX-80). You set the converter's tempo map at 60 beats per minute with no tempo changes. The converter transforms incoming SMPTE to MIDI Clocks, which Performer reads and synchronizes to. Performer calculates what the SMPTE Time Code address should be considering the start time address you provide in Performer (which must match the start time address you set in your converter). This is crucial because Performer bases all of its internal calculations upon this number. Note that this start time refers to the address at which the converter starts converting SMPTE Time Code to MIDI Clocks. This is normally not the start time that is used to trigger playback. The playback start time in Performer is referred to as Set Chunk Start (in older versions of Performer it was called Set Sequence Start), and it should be set at least a few seconds after the converter start time to allow Performer to synchronize itself to the incoming timing information.

Direct Time Lock

Direct Time Lock (DTL) is another solution to the SMPTE-to-MIDI synchronization problem. It was introduced by Southworth Music Systems (now out of business) in their JamBox4 MIDI interface. Although plagued by erratic behavior, during its time the JamBox4 was the most sophisticated MIDI interface available. Now, DTL is one of the synchronization options offered by Mark of the Unicorn's Performer sequencer (it is perhaps not coincidental that the developers of Southworth's JamBox4 are the same people who developed Mark of the Unicorn's MIDI Time Piece).

To use DTL you must have an interface capable of making the conversion of SMPTE to DTL. Mark of the Unicorn's MIDI Time Piece and Opcode's Studio 3 and Studio 5 are among the interfaces that support DTL.

DTL uses two types of messages to achieve synchronization. The first is tape-position, which is equivalent to the full-frame message used in other systems. The tape-position message is a direct conversion of the current SMPTE frame expressed as an eight-byte SysEx message (FO 28 *CC HH MM SS FF* F7). The "28" (40 in decimal) is the manufacturer's ID number originally assigned to Southworth Music Systems. "CC" refers to the channel number. "*HH MM SS FF*" specifies the hours, minutes, seconds, and frames of the time code address. "FO" and "F7" indicate the beginning and end of the SysEx message, respectively. Once a tape-position message has been received, the sequencer can lock to that address.

Subsequently, DTL-compatible interfaces send "frame-advance" messages once per each frame. Frame-advance messages take the same format as MIDI Clock (F8). About every half second to a second a new tape-position message is processed and Performer compares that address with what it thinks the address should be (based upon counting the interim frame-advance messages). If the two addresses are different, the software resolves them. Performer's implementation of DTL lets the software freewheel over eight frames. If more than eight frames pass without a frame-advance message being received, the software assumes that playback has stopped, it stops the sequence, and waits for a new tape-position message.

DTL is a very convenient type of synchronization with significant advantages over other SMPTE-to-MIDI synchronization alternatives. Consider the impact upon the MIDI bandwidth. Because the eight-byte tape-position message is only sent about once a second and the intervening 29 frames require only a single-byte frame-advance message, the amount of data required for synchronization is reduced by 196 bytes per frame (a savings of about 80 percent). This means of course that you can use that part of the MIDI bandwidth for other information, most importantly, for music.

The second advantage of DTL is that it does not require you to specify any information other than the sequence (chunk) start time. Lockup requires that the sequencer be stopped when the SMPTE Time Code source is first set in motion. Afterward, you can start, stop, fast-forward, and rewind, and the sequencer will chase to the time code source.

Enhanced Direct Time Lock

Mark of the Unicorn introduced Direct Time Lock enhanced (DTLe) with their MIDI Time Piece multicable interface. Performer 3.4 or later is required to lock to DTLe. If you are running Performer version 3.4 or later without a MIDI Time Piece, the software is just as comfortable with standard DTL (allowing you to use the software with earlier interfaces). However, the MIDI Time Piece itself will not send standard DTL.

The difference between DTL and DTLe is that DTLe transmits four frame-advance messages per SMPTE frame in place of the one sent by DTL. This makes it correspond somewhat to the approach taken by MTC (see below). Additional information has been added to the tape-position message to identify the cable routing of the DTLe signal within the MIDI Time Piece.

Although DTLe adds almost 90 bytes to the MIDI bandwidth used for DTL (because of the extra frame-advance messages), it has one significant advantage over standard DTL. Performer (again, version 3.4 or later) does not need to be stopped in order to achieve lockup. You can press the Play button in Performer at any time — as long as the Slave to External Sync option is enabled and time code is being received, the sequence will locate (chase) to the next tape-position message and begin playing in sync (lock). Synchronization will never take more than a second to establish itself because a tape-position message is sent at least once every second.

MIDI Time Code

On February 12, 1987, the *MIDI Time Code and Cueing Detailed Specification* was added as an official supplement to the MIDI 1.0 Specification. The MIDI Time Code Specification was created by Chris Meyer and Evan Brooks of Digidesign

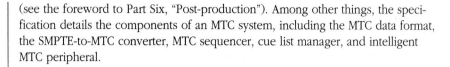
(see the foreword to Part Six, "Post-production"). Among other things, the specification details the components of an MTC system, including the MTC data format, the SMPTE-to-MTC converter, MTC sequencer, cue list manager, and intelligent MTC peripheral.

MTC, like DTL, uses two types of messages: full messages and quarter-frame messages. The full message is a direct conversion of the current SMPTE frame expressed as a 10-byte real-time SysEx message (FO 7F *CC* 01 *II HH MM SS FF* F7). The "FO 7F" header indicates that this is a real-time universal SysEx message. "CC" specifies channel number. The "01" is the first sub-ID which, when set to 01, equals MTC. "*II*" is the second sub-ID which, when set to 01, indicates a full time code message. "*HH MM SS FF*" specify the hours, minutes, seconds, and frames of the time code address. "F7" defines the end of the SysEx message.

Quarter-frame messages are what makes MTC so versatile. Eight different quarter-frame messages are sent every two SMPTE frames. These consist of a byte (F1, the System Common status byte) and a nibble ranging from 0 to 7, indicating the current quarter frame of the two-frame group. Quarter-frame messages are intermeshed with the data defining the digit of the current SMPTE time. This is a very creative approach to the problem. Remember that it takes eight digits to define a SMPTE Time Code address. With MTC, each of these digits has an associated quarter-frame message ranging from 0 to 7. For example, the first digit of a time code address is the hours' "tens" digit. This gets a quarter-frame message of 0. The next digit is the hours' "ones" digit. This gets a quarter-frame message of 1. The next digit is the minutes' "tens" digit. This gets a quarter-frame message of 2. And so on. The final quarter-frame message includes a specification of the time code type (24, 25, 30 drop, or 30 non-drop).

You may have deduced from this that it takes two SMPTE frames to send a single time code address of MTC. This means that the SMPTE Time Code address is updated every two frames. SMPTE-to-MTC converters must take this into consideration, adding two frames to their displays as required (similarly to the plus-one-frame technique described above under SMPTE). The addition of the quarter-frame messages into the time code address allows software to achieve quarter-frame accuracy synchronization, with the added bonuses of updating the frame count at the same time and providing an easy way to determine whether the time code is running forward or backward (the quarter-frame messages count up from 0 to 7 when the code is running forward and down from 7 to 0 when the code is running backward). If sync is lost, a full message is sent and the slave device can re-lock to this.

MTC requires four messages per frame, each two bytes long (640 microseconds). This occurs every 8.333 milliseconds. When you calculate the impact upon the MIDI bandwidth, you discover that MTC takes up 7.68 percent of the MIDI bandwidth. The specification refers to this as a "reasonably small amount" and goes on to suggest that "it would be rare that normal MIDI and MIDI Time Code would share the same MIDI bus at the same time." This suggestion goes along with the observation that most MTC applications send timing information such as MTC through a different Macintosh serial port than the rest of your incoming MIDI data. Typically, in a dual interface system, timing information is input by way of the Macintosh printer port, and other MIDI data is input by way of the Macintosh modem port. Of course, while this is happening, MIDI output can occur simultaneously from both serial ports. Note that this does not preclude a single serial port system (that is, a single 16-channel interface). Many SMPTE-to-MIDI converters will merge MTC information into the rest of the input data stream. Finally, don't forget that the many applications for synchronization do not have you input additional MIDI data while synchronized.

The MTC Specification also includes a provision for transferring user-bit information. With MTC, the user bits are not an integral part of the time code address as they are in SMPTE Time Code. A separate 15-byte message called the User Bits message can be sent at any time. Remember that SMPTE provides for 32 user bits. Theoretically, this could be represented by four bytes, so why does MTC take 15 bytes to communicate user-bit information? The reason is that each 4-bit nibble of SMPTE user-bit data is assigned a full byte with MTC. Furthermore, the Binary Group Flag bits for Drop Frame and Color Frame also have their own byte. That makes nine bytes added to the five-byte header and the one-byte EOX (end of exclusive), giving us a total of 15 bytes.

Another part of the MTC Specification, which has largely been unexplored to this date, are suggestions for the use of a Cue List Manager and Intelligent MTC Peripheral. The Cue List Manager would be a device or computer software capable of creating and editing a cue list of events and sending this list, in total, to slaved devices. Types of events that the Cue List Manager would handle include patch data, samples, sequences, drum patterns, and so on. An Intelligent MTC Peripheral is defined as a device capable of receiving such a cue list and able to trigger itself accordingly when the time code addresses (SMPTE or MTC) specified in the cue list are received.

The MTC Specification mentions several examples to show how this might be used, although they are largely unimplemented. An intelligent MTC-equipped multitrack tape machine could read in a list of punch-in and punch-out cues from the Cue List Manager. In response to a cue list, a sampler might preload samples from its own disk drive in anticipation of their need later on in the cue list.

The MTC Specification provides for setting up an MTC cue list by way of set-up messages that are 13 bytes plus additional information. There are 128 possible event types that can be accommodated with this message, although only about 19 are currently defined. The first type of data is called Special and refers to global set-up information. Global set-up information can include a Time Code Offset, an Enable Event List message, a Disable (but don't erase) Event List message, a Clear Event List message, a System Stop message (e.g., to stop a tape machine from running past the end of a reel), and an Event List Request message (used to make a device transmit its entire cue list to another device).

The other currently defined MIDI cueing messages include data types for the designation of Punch In and Punch Out, Delete Punch In or Out, Event Start and Stop, Event Start and Stop with Additional Information, Delete Event Start/Stop, Cue Point, Cue Point with Additional Information, Delete Cue Point, and Event Name in Additional Information.

 The differences between pulse-sync and relative-addressing formats (such as SPP) and absolute-addressing formats (such as MTC, DTL, and DTLe) are largely in their accuracy and handling of tempo. The former require the tempo map in the converter, while the latter let the tempo map be in the sequencer. This distinction is extremely important. With the tempo map in the sequencer, you have a significant amount of additional creative freedom. Finally, absolute-addressing formats allow a single timing reference to be used throughout an entire project by all involved, while the earlier systems required constant conversions back and forth between SMPTE Time Code and bar/beat number.

Human-triggered synchronization

Human-triggered synchronization is related to pulse sync in that a trigger event is required before every next note advance. The difference is that a human rather than a 24-PPQN pulse provides the trigger. The first conductor to use an electrical system to transmit tempo was Hector Berlioz, who was conducting an offstage chorus via a blinking light. He had a switch on his podium. The first microprocessor implementation of this technique that I know of was found in pre-MIDI Oberheim hardware sequencers.

Around the same time, John Maxwell and Severo Ornstein also included the feature in their elegant pre-MIDI notation software called Mockingbird (developed at XEROX PARC), which so many current-generation notation software programmers looked to for inspiration (see Part Four, "Notation").

Another early implementation of human-triggered sync (which, by the way, is still popular) was found in Roland's SBX-80 sync box with the Tap and Sub-Tap buttons. You can tap a tempo on the buttons to trigger every next MIDI event. A specified number of taps are constantly averaged to update the tempo (albeit resulting in tempo changes that were about a beat behind). I used this feature of the SBX-80 in a February 1987 performance of my opera *Countdown* by the Boston Lyric Opera. I simply kept my eyes glued to the conductor and tapped the button in time with his beat pattern. The tapping advanced a mammoth MIDI sequence in Mark of the Unicorn's Performer (this was before Performer had its own built-in Tap Tempo option). The sequence in turn controlled the samplers providing the virtual symphony orchestra that accompanied the singers. The technique worked flawlessly.

The first Macintosh software implementations of this feature were found in programs by David Zicarelli (see Chapter 19, "Interactive Composition and Intelligent Instruments"). From the very beginning, Jam Factory included a feature to step advance (called "sa") any one of the four virtual "players," individually or in any combination, by pressing a key on your MIDI controller. Zicarelli's Oval-tune added this feature to the Macintosh keyboard, allowing you to press the spacebar to advance the flow of MIDI data.

The next important step in the realm of human-triggered synchronization was to record MIDI data in real time while supplying the tempo simultaneously. With an SBX-80 and a MIDI merger or dual interface, it was possible to record MIDI data into a sequencer with one hand while tapping in the beats with the other. Alternatively, you could tap the SBX-80's Tap button with your foot and record MIDI data with both hands on your MIDI controller. In either case, this approach gave you the freedom to speed up and slow down during recording, just as you normally would when the creative juices are flowing — thus releasing you from the slavery of playing with an inhuman computer-generated metronome.

The first Macintosh software program to provide this feature as a built-in option for input was Coda's notation software, Finale. Finale's Hyperscribe tool lets you define a MIDI event for the tap (usually a foot pedal so you can use both hands on your MIDI controller) and even lets you alternate between four different quantization states on the fly by pressing other MIDI controllers to change the pre-assigned quantization grids (these triggers can be assigned to low notes on your MIDI controller). Coda's implementation of human-triggered sync operates only when recording. It does not allow playback tempo to be synchronized with a human tap. Finale does have an option to tap in beat lines and measure lines to music that has been recorded without any beat reference whatsoever, neither a computer-generated click nor a human-triggered tap (see Chapter 22, "Music Notation"). This is essentially a similar implementation to the one found over a decade earlier in Mockingbird (see above).

In the world of MIDI sequencers, Tap Tempo first appeared in Mark of the Unicorn's Performer version 3.0. Tap Tempo is now a feature found in many MIDI sequencers. Typically, this involves specifying the MIDI event (usually a note) that you will tap to advance the sequence one beat. You can even record this tapped performance as the tempo track in many sequencers, thus adding expressive rubato to MIDI sequencers that might otherwise seem rhythmically stilted or inhuman due to over-quantization.

Some of the more courageous film and video composers use Tap Tempo to "conduct to picture" in a manner analogous with the "free time" technique common on the orchestral scoring stage (that is, the musicians do not hear clicks in their headphones). Other specialized uses of Tap Tempo in film and video composition include the creation of a tempo track in a *sound-alike*. Sound-alikes are recordings of hit songs that sound just like the original artist, but their usage doesn't require the major licensing fees associated with playing a hit song in a film or video. The "tapped" tempo corresponds exactly to the tempo of the original tune that the sound-alike is supposed to sound like. Finally, Tap Tempo is often used to synchronize synthesized music to video that was filmed with music being played on the set, for example in a dance number.

Using Tap Tempo to supply a beat reference during real-time recording is now a standard feature in most professional sequencers, as is Tap Tempo's playback synchronization feature (see Figure 26-9).

Synchronization with Apple's MIDI Manager

Apple's MIDI Manager (see Chapter 8, "Moving Data Around Your Music Network") provides extensive synchronization features for programs that are compatible with it (most are). You can think of the time port that MIDI Manager provides as a "house sync" for the Macintosh. When you are running multiple MIDI applications in either 6.x's MultiFinder or System 7, connecting the time ports of the various programs (called clients) to the Apple MIDI Driver's time port guarantees that they are all synchronized to a single clock reference.

MIDI Manager is much more than a mere internal house sync for the Macintosh. It accepts incoming timing information from the serial ports as MTC (in 24, 25, 30 non-drop, and 30 drop frame formats) or standard MIDI Clocks (with SPP support). It can convert these in real time to any other format: MIDI Clocks or MTC in 24, 25, 30 non-drop, and 30 drop frame formats. It can also generate timing information in any of those formats. If both the modem port and the printer port are being used for MIDI, two time ports are available.

MIDI Manager can also provide additional invisible time ports to programs that request them. They function identically to ports visible in PatchBay, except that other programs are prevented from connecting to them. Don't forget that no matter how many time ports, visible or invisible, MIDI Manager is using, the Macintosh still only has one internal clock.

MIDI Manager time ports automatically detect whether they are externally or internally synchronized (see Figure 26-10). Note that external synchronization does not necessarily imply a timing source outside of the Macintosh. It could just as well be a program running on the Macintosh sending timing information to MIDI Manager.

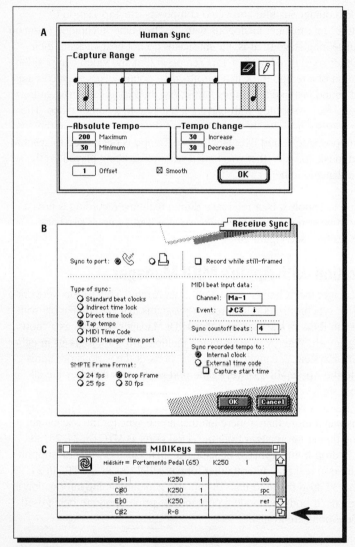

Internally synchronized time ports simply run by themselves whenever a program requests them to. Externally synchronized time ports begin running when they start receiving timing information from their external source, be it data coming in from a serial port or timing information arriving from another MIDI Manager-compatible software application.

In any case, when time skips backward or forward, the Apple MIDI Driver sends a Song Position Pointer or MIDI Time Code Full message to inform time code receivers of the new address. It also automatically detects if the frame rate has been changed and switches to the new frame rate, alerting you that this has occurred.

The timer driving the time ports of MIDI Manager can represent time in any of three formats: Milliseconds (elapsed milliseconds since the client's time-base started), Beats (standard MIDI Clocks in 960 PPQN received since the clock was last set to zero

Figure 26-9: Where to find the Tap Tempo feature in your MIDI sequencer.
(A) Cubase. **(B)** Performer. **(C)** Vision (the single quote).

or started by a program or external device), and MTC (full 80-bit address format). Different programs can request time in different formats simultaneously. Programmers can call ConvertTime to convert incoming MTC to the format *HH MM SS QQ*, where the final value ("*QQ*") is quarter frames (120 per second). Note that 960 PPQN and quarter frames seem to exceed the required accuracy. This is because MIDI Manager's internal representation of time is considerably more accurate than required by all existing time code and synchronization systems.

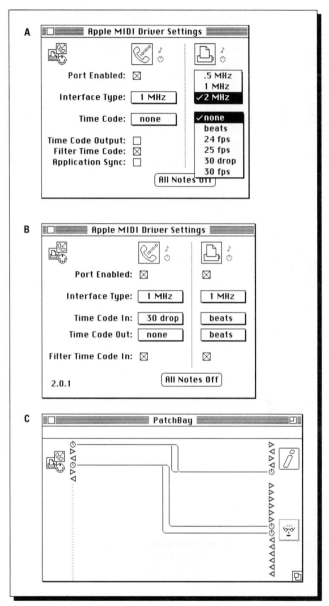

Figure 26-10: Setting timing formats in MIDI Manager. First double-click the Apple MIDI Driver icon to bring up its control panel. Note the option to Filter Time Code from either port. **(A)** Pre-version-2.0 Apple MIDI Driver control panels looked like this. You used to have to manually turn on Time Code Output with a checkbox. Similarly, the synchronization of applications wasn't guaranteed unless the Application Sync checkbox was enabled. **(B)** Version 2.0 (and beyond) Apple MIDI driver control panels look like this. Note the removal of the Time Code Output and Application Sync checkboxes, which are now redundant. Time Code Output is now automatically generated when a client requests it. Likewise, applications running under MIDI Manager are always in sync (hence the missing Application Sync checkbox). MIDI Manager 2.01 provides enhanced support for internal NuBus cards and runs significantly faster on compact Macintoshes such as the Plus. **(C)** Some applications both send and receive timing information at the same PatchBay port (see the upper Interactor icon with two virtual cables attached to it). The direction in which you drag the connection determines whether the port is a timing output or input. Other programs have separate virtual ports for received and transmitted timing information (see the Max icon in the lower right).

One bit of confusion can arise when discussing the MIDI Manager's ports, including the time port. It has to do with the question of whether to call a port an input or an output port, because the same port may receive data from the MIDI Management Toolset (the underlying set of routines used by MIDI Manager) and then output that data to an external device (at the serial ports or another virtual port). The preferred practice is to look at things from MIDI Manager's viewpoint. With timing information, a port becomes a source or destination for time code, depending upon whether you draw a virtual cable to it or from it (see Figure 26-11).

In the *MIDI Manager Tools Developer Notes,* Apple strongly suggests that "application developers assume that the Apple MIDI Driver performs all interpretation of timing messages, and that applications derive their MIDI-dependent time bases by synchronizing to the time port of the Apple MIDI Driver instead of interpreting time code messages themselves. This is important from the standpoint of efficiency and system overhead as well as conceptual cleanliness throughout the system."

Synchronization Basics

Be aware that there are two levels of synchronization. The first, simplest, and least expensive is synchronization of a virtual device (such as a software-based MIDI sequencer running on the Macintosh) with a hardware device (such as a video tape recorder or multitrack tape recorder). This requires a SMPTE-to-MIDI converter only. In normal situations, the hardware device is always the master because it is difficult and expensive to place the hardware tape transport under the control of the MIDI sequencer.

The second approach involves a special converter called a synchronizer or lockup system. These boxes allow the motors and sometimes the transport controls of two or more hardware devices to be locked together (sometimes referred to as machine lockup). The result is that, for all practical purposes, the devices function as if they were a single machine.

Combining a SMPTE-to-MIDI converter with a synchronizer lets you lock hardware devices together and at the same time lock your MIDI software to the hardware devices.

Synchronizers

A synchronizer (not to be confused with SMPTE-to-MIDI converters) is a special type of interface that allows hardware devices such as tape recorders and video decks to be locked together so that the SMPTE Time Code address of the current location on each device is always identical. The cost of a synchronizer is usually considerably more than $2,000.

Synchronizers achieve machine lockup by using two types of locking modes: frame lock and phase lock (also known as sync lock). Frame lock uses all 80 bits of information in the SMPTE Time Code address. Phase lock only references the 16-bit sync word (at the end of the SMPTE Time Code address) to lock up. You

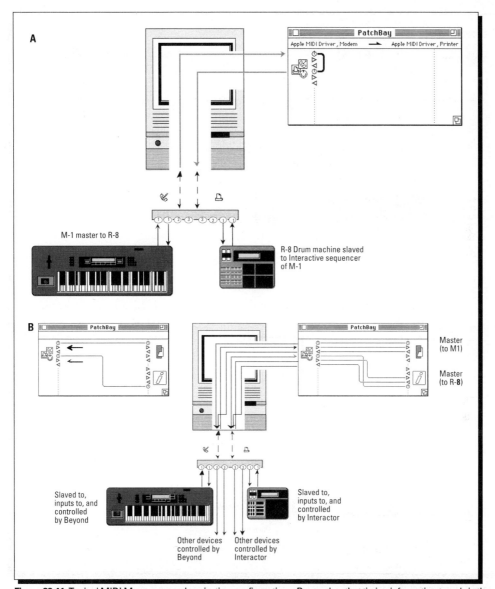

Figure 26-11: Typical MIDI Manager synchronization configurations. Remember that timing information travels in the direction in which you drag the connection (always drag from the source port to the destination port). **(A)** Passing timing information from one serial port to another. **(B)** Synchronizing internal applications to external hardware devices. *(continued)*

can visualize this if you think of the 16-bit final sync word as a kind of MIDI Clock for hardware devices.

There are three levels of sophistication among synchronizers: *code-only-master systems*, *chase lock systems*, and *control synchronization systems*. All of them

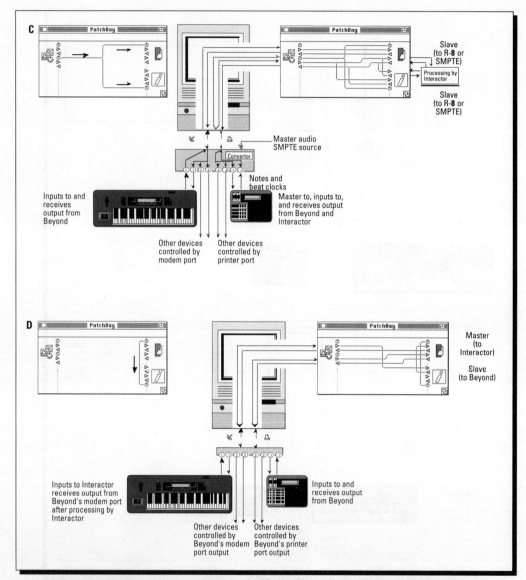

Figure 26-11 (continued): (C) Sending timing information to external hardware devices from internal applications. **(D)** Synchronizing internal applications to one another. *(continued)*

require that the synchronizer be fed the SMPTE Time Code track from both the master and all slaves involved and that these time code formats are identical (this is where you can put regeneration and reshaping systems to good use). Chase lock and control synchronization systems need a separate control cable (usually RS-232). Note that these cables are expensive, averaging at least $200 each. Other types of RS-232 cables are normally cheap ($10 to $30).

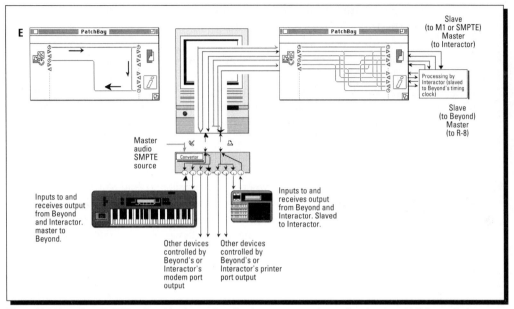

Figure 26-11 (continued): (E) Synchronizing internal applications to one another and to an external hardware device while passing converted timing information out the other serial port.

The systems do not require a Macintosh to be in the loop. The following discussions serve as background to understanding the next section, where the Macintosh enters the picture ("Synchronization Scenarios").

Note that many synchronizers use the acronym MTC to refer to Master Time Code, so don't confuse this with MIDI Time Code. Slave Time Code is often abbreviated STC.

Code-only-master

Code-only-master synchronization systems slave one or more devices to a master. The synchronizer is always aware of the frame location of the master device. When the master relocates to a new frame address by way of rewind, fast-forward, or shuttle, the slaves relocate to the new address only after the master is placed into Play mode. This can cause considerable delays while you wait for the slaves to chase (catch up to) the new SMPTE Time Code address of the master.

To chase to the new address, the synchronizer takes over the cue controls of the slave device and rewinds or fast-forwards the tape until it detects that the required frame is near. Then it slows down the tape and switches it into Play mode in sync with the master, making a few minor adjustments (if required) to achieve parity between the SMPTE Time Code addresses on both machines (this is called resolving).

A variation of this technique is found in play-speed-only synchronization. In this case, the (usually less expensive) synchronizer only has control of the capstan speed of the slave and only within a rather limited range. This system requires that the master and slave be lined up manually as close as possible before synchronizing, because the synchronizer cannot exert complete control over the slave's transport.

Sometimes code-only systems cannot synchronously locate the slave to the master. This situation can arise when it is impossible to read SMPTE Time Code from the slave at high speeds, because lifters are engaged that remove the tape from the playback head. Chase lock systems can use tach pulses (electrical pulses generated by the devices' motors or flywheels) to monitor location whenever the tape is lifted from the playback head, but devices without tach pulse information or the ability to read time code at high speeds are limited to code-only synchronization.

Chase lock (also known as synchronizable master)

In chase lock systems (or synchronizable master systems, or simply chase synchronization) the synchronizer has control over all the transport motors of the slave and also the ability (by way of a control cable between the synchronizer and the master) to detect and respond to manipulation of the front panel transport controls of the master.

In chase lock systems you can press Rewind or Fast Forward on the transport of the master device. The synchronizer takes over the transport controls on the slave device and (by monitoring tach pulses) attempts to run the slave's motors at a matching high speed. When the master is put back into Play mode, the slave (or slaves) are at roughly the same spot and ready to sync.

Control synchronization

Control synchronization offers all the features of chase lock systems, but adds additional control of other functions to the master and slave. Control of the record and playback functions of the machines are a given at this level. One popular system, Adams-Smith's Zeta~Three, includes the following features:

❖ LTC generation in all formats
❖ Full chase lock capability
❖ Very fast lockup
❖ Sub-frame-accurate SMPTE offsets between slave and master
❖ Transport control of both master and slave from the front panel of the synchronizer

❖ Programmable punch-in and punch-out
❖ Generation, reading, and jam syncing of user bits
❖ Lock accuracy to 1/1000th of a frame
❖ MIDI Clock conversion and output, including SPP
❖ MTC conversion and output
❖ DTL conversion and output
❖ Support of fractional MIDI tempos
❖ Auto-merging of MIDI input at the output jack
❖ Tempo map entry via Tap Tempo from front panel or external click
❖ Control of all functions by the MIDI port

More sophisticated synchronizers offered by Adams-Smith and other vendors add features such as time code reshaping, VITC generation, reading, display, translation, sprocket film sync, mixed frame rate synchronizing (resolving sources that are striped with different frame rates), time compression/expansion by way of variable SMPTE rate synchronization, remote jog wheel control, address capturing, character generation, on-screen talent cueing and ADR (automated dialog replacement) (including countdowns and wipes), and MIDI event sequencing and triggering (see Figure 26-12).

Audio to audio

Audio to audio is very commonly employed to make up for an insufficient number of tracks on one multitrack. You simply lock two recorders together and they can function as one unit (see Figure 26-13). Note that you still have to give up two tracks on each recorder for the time code and guard tracks. This means that if you synchronize two 24-track machines, you have 44 usable tracks, not 48. Another reason for using this setup is to transfer all the audio tracks from one tape recorder to another. For example, let's say you created 14 synthesizer tracks on one-inch tape using a 16-track recorder at your home studio. If you want to go into a professional studio and record live musicians along with this, you should transfer your existing music to their 24-track machine. You can transfer all tracks at once, including the SMPTE Time Code track. The reason you need a synchronizer to accomplish this is to resolve any minute speed fluctuations on either machine during the transfer process.

Audio to video

Audio to video is useful at the end of the composition/recording process for viewing the picture while listening to a multitrack recording (see Figure 26-14). Another possibility is to record while watching the picture. If you have the required gear (namely the synchronizer), you might also use this setup in conjunction with MIDI sequencers to add virtual tracks (see below) during a mix or simply as an aid to composition. This setup also aids in rehearsing mixdowns.

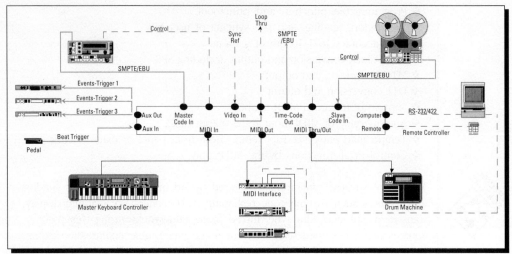

Figure 26-12: A typical control synchronizer (Adams-Smith's Zeta~Three) with all outputs and inputs configured.

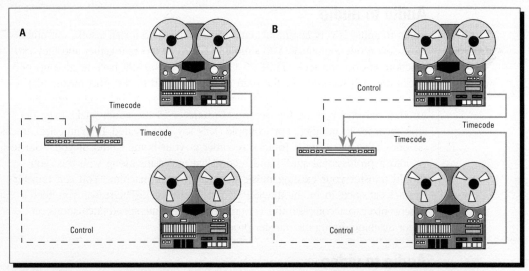

Figure 26-13: Making the right connections for synchronizing an audio recorder to another audio recorder. To set up for this configuration, transfer the SMPTE Time Code track of the master to the slave. **(A)** Code-only-master. Note that a control cable is not required between the master and the synchronizer, only between the slave and the synchronizer. **(B)** Chase lock systems and control systems.

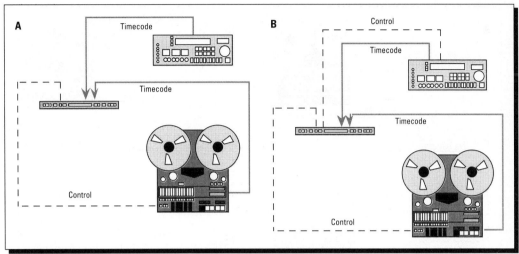

Figure 26-14: Making the right connections for synchronizing an audio recorder to a video recorder. To set up for this configuration, transfer the SMPTE Time Code track of the master to the slave. **(A)** Code-only-master. Note that a control cable is not required between the master and the synchronizer, only between the slave and the synchronizer. **(B)** Chase lock systems and control systems.

Video to audio

Video to audio is not a common scenario. Much more often, the video is the master rather than the audio. You might want to do this if the only remote controller you have is the one for your multitrack recorder (see Figure 26-15).

Synchronization Scenarios

With the exception of the final one, the following scenarios illustrate configurations for synchronization without using a synchronizer (lockup system). Usually, one of the elements being synchronized is a MIDI sequencer, but there are many other types of software that can be synchronized. Examples include interactive composition software, real-time MIDI processing software, notation software, studio automation software, and direct-to-hard disk recording systems.

Because sequencers can relocate to any point instantly while tape machines take time to fast-forward or rewind to a new location, hardware tape machines, both video and audio, are usually the master devices when they are synchronized to MIDI sequencers.

Three of the most popular uses of synchronization in the film and video scoring community are to aid in the compositional process, to facilitate overdubbing, and to enhance recording (by way of virtual tracks).

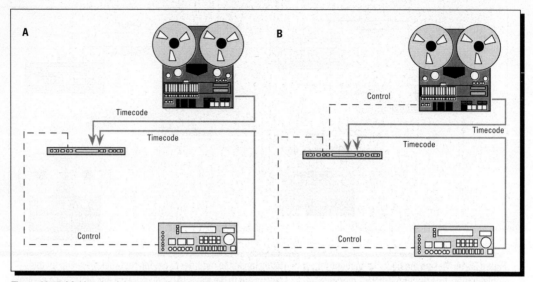

Figure 26-15: Making the right connections for synchronizing a video recorder to an audio recorder. To set up for this configuration, transfer the SMPTE Time Code track of the master to the slave. **(A)** Code-only-master. Note that a control cable is not required between the master and the synchronizer, only between the slave and the synchronizer. **(B)** Chase lock systems and control systems.

Composing

Synchronization is a necessity when composing for film or video if you are using a Macintosh MIDI sequencer. You don't need an expensive synchronizer like those described above. All you really need for synchronization is a SMPTE-to-MIDI converter. Naturally, a video deck with a frame advance or jog wheel is a must, so that you can discern the exact SMPTE Time Code addresses of cuts and hits you want to emphasize or accent with the music.

Most video you receive for scoring comes with a SMPTE track and usually, visual time code burned into a window near the bottom of the screen. The time code displayed in the window should be frame-locked to the time code on the audio track (in the case of LTC) or in the video signal (in the case of VITC). Time code will be on a single audio track (often the right channel), allowing you to hear dialog on the other audio track. It's a good idea to use the SMPTE reader option of your SMPTE to MIDI converter (this may be available through its configuration software on the Macintosh) to verify that the visual code is the same as the time code data.

With a SMPTE-to-MIDI converter, you can lock your sequencer to the picture whenever you want to audition your music, monitor tempos and timings, and verify that hits are actually occurring where they should.

Once you have finished the music, that is, have entered it all into your sequencer and verified that it does match the picture, you change the SMPTE Time Code source to your audio recorder and record the music while locked to the audio tape. Without a synchronizer, you have no real way of verifying that the audio tape will sync to the picture. However, as long as you created the time code track on the audio tape by reshaping or regenerating the time code on the video, you have nothing to worry about. Alternatively, you can use a SMPTE generator or a MIDI interface with SMPTE generation capabilities to simply stripe your tape starting from the same address as the video.

This recording-to-tape stage of the process may involve recording directly to a stereo mix, or more commonly to multitrack (see "Overdubbing" below). In the latter case, you have the option of adding virtual tracks (see below) to the final mix. Common delivery formats are center-stripe two-track and four-track tape with SMPTE on an edge track separated from the stereo program by a guard track. In professional studios, four-track tape is also used without the guard track. In this case solos or other prominent parts are recorded onto what would have been the guard track. This is a very common approach for television.

Synchronizable DAT is a mixdown format that is gaining in popularity. It costs about the same to buy a DAT with SMPTE ($3,500) than an analog two-track with a center time code track. A newer approach is to embed SMPTE information on the sub code track of a DAT and use an appropriate decoder to read this data (the Panasonic SV-3700 offers this capability).

Overdubbing

Overdubbing has become synonymous with multitrack recording. The term refers to recording separate tracks at different times that are synchronized with one another. Making multiple recording passes on the tape is implied. Some early tape recorders had a button labeled Overdub, which disabled the erase head for that track, allowing you to actually record additional music on a pre-recorded track without erasing the existing music on that track. Many sequencers also have a recording mode called overdub. It merges incoming MIDI data with existing data on a sequence track rather than replacing the original data. There are now many more tracks available than there were when the Beatles recorded their Sergeant Pepper album on four-track machines.

With live musicians, this sort of multitracking is easy to accomplish by supplying a click on one of the tracks to use as a metronome. Many synchronization options now allow MIDI sequencers the same flexibility as live musicians in the area of multitrack recording.

Recording sequencer tracks in multiple passes was much more of a necessity with unitimbral synthesizers (if you wanted to use two sounds on the device you had to record them separately), single and dual MIDI interfaces (if you wanted more than 16 or 32 voices), and with devices of limited polyphony (for example, if you wanted eight-part polyphony on a four-voice polyphonic device). These reasons are not as significant now that most new electronic instruments are multi-timbral with a minimum of 16-voice polyphony and MIDI interfaces commonly support many more than 32 channels.

There are still reasons to use a multitrack recorder. One is for the purpose of including live musicians in your recording. Another is to make a signal processor or outboard effects device do double or triple duty, applying the same device differently to separate tracks as they are recorded individually.

Virtual tracks

Virtual tracks refer to tracks that are not recorded on the multitrack recorder, yet are mixed into the final mix (see Figure 26-16). If you mix directly to stereo, all of your tracks are virtual. However, the term virtual tracks most often refers to MIDI sequencer tracks that are combined with previously taped tracks. One good reason for using virtual tracks is to give you additional tracks if you run out of tracks on your tape recorder. Fidelity issues attributed to generation loss are another reason to use virtual tracks. Synchronization makes virtual tracks possible.

Once you have filled up all the tracks of an analog multitrack recorder, rather than bouncing a group of tracks down to one to free up space (which introduces signal degradation), it is much more desirable to use virtual tracks, which do not introduce another generation into the recording.

SMPTE-to-MIDI converters

There are two basic types of SMPTE-to-MIDI converters: those that integrate SMPTE conversion features into a MIDI interface and those that are a separate box designed to be used in conjunction with a MIDI interface (see Figure 26-17). It's easy to tell these apart because the non-integrated box does not have any ports for connecting to the Macintosh. Instead, it has MIDI outputs that pass converted timing information along to your MIDI interface. From there the information can be routed to the Macintosh.

The stand-alone converter approach is a good solution if you already own a MIDI interface without built-in SMPTE conversion features. All you need to do is buy the converter box and use it with your existing interface. Popular devices in this category include JL Cooper's PPS-1 and PPS-100 and Opcode Systems's Timecode Machine.

If the previous paragraph applies to you, there is another consideration. Is your existing MIDI interface a single (16-channel) or dual (32-channel) interface? If it is

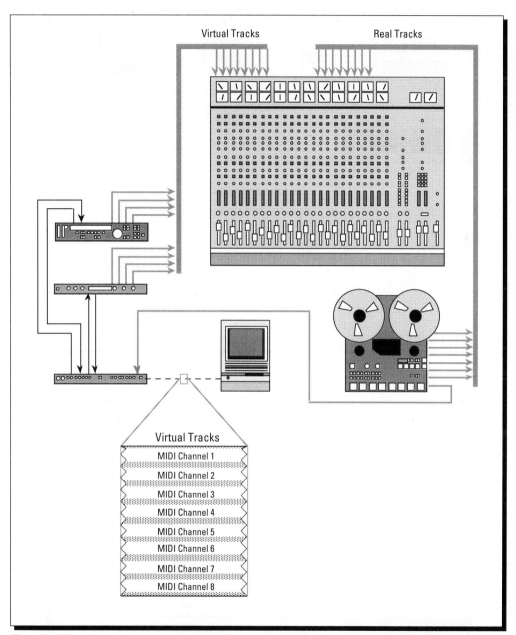

Figure 26-16: Virtual tracks can enhance real tracks during the final mixdown.

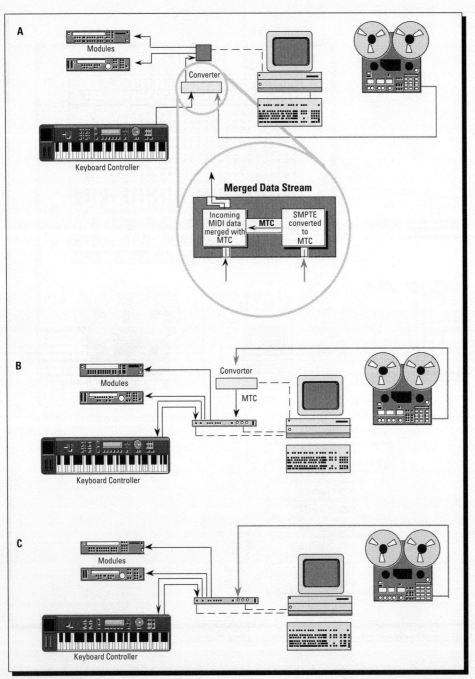

Figure 26-17: (A) Converting SMPTE to MIDI using a stand-alone converter in conjunction with a single (16-channel) MIDI interface. **(B)** Converting SMPTE to MIDI using a stand-alone converter in conjunction with a dual (32-channel) MIDI interface. **(C)** Converting SMPTE to MIDI using a MIDI interface with a built-in converter.

a single interface, you want a stand-alone converter that is capable of merging converted SMPTE Time Code with MIDI data that you input from your master controller (most have this feature). If you have a dual interface, this is not an issue because you can route the converted SMPTE Time Code to the side of the interface that is destined for the printer port and still input additional MIDI data on the modem port side.

SMPTE-to-MIDI converters offer a wide variety of options, depending upon their manufacturer. All take SMPTE Time Code as an audio input. Some will also accept an audio click. Others include FSK and/or smart FSK as an input option. The output formats are equally varied. Any combination or all of the following are possible: FSK, smart FSK, SPP, MTC, DTL, and DTLe (see Figure 26-18). Other bells and whistles include the ability to generate SMPTE Time Code and a variety of regeneration and jam sync options (including one-time jam sync and continuous jam sync). Consult Table 5-5 in Chapter 5, "Software Options," for complete specifications of available Macintosh MIDI interfaces.

Mac as master to external hardware slaves

Use the following configuration to synchronize external drum machines, hardware sequencers, and even other Macintoshes to your MIDI software running on your Macintosh (see Figure 26-19). The peripheral devices are slaves, and the software running on your Macintosh is the master.

Mac as slave to video tape

This is the configuration that you will use most during the composition of a score for film or video (see Figure 26-20).

Mac as slave to audio tape

After the film or video score is complete, you use this configuration to transfer everything to a multitrack recorder (see Figure 26-21). Note that you must have striped the multitrack tape with identical SMPTE Time Code as that used in the video. You can do this by reshaping or regenerating SMPTE Time Code from the video. Alternatively, you can use a SMPTE generator (or SMPTE generation features in an appropriately equipped MIDI interface) to stripe the audio tape from the same start frame. If your tape is striped with time code that does not match up with the video, you can use a SMPTE offset to resolve this discrepancy. The most important consideration is that the time code formats are the same (24, 25, 30, or 30 df).

Mac as slave to audio and video

To use this configuration, you need a synchronizer. This is the optimum configuration for scoring film and video. Your Macintosh, video recorder, and multitrack

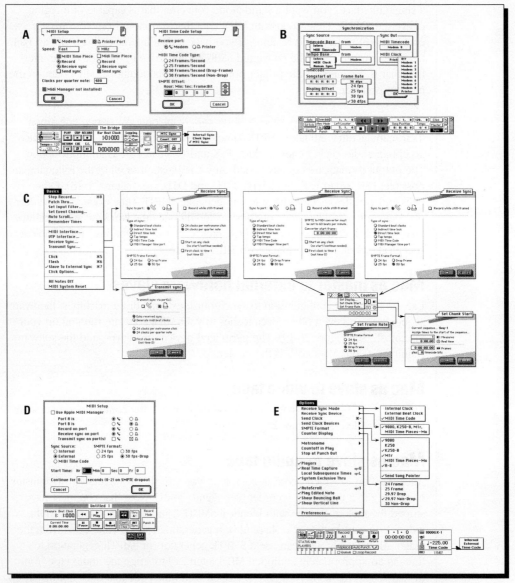

Figure 26-18: Setting up software for synchronization: **(A)** Beyond. **(B)** Cubase. **(C)** Performer. **(D)** Pro 4.5. **(E)** Vision.

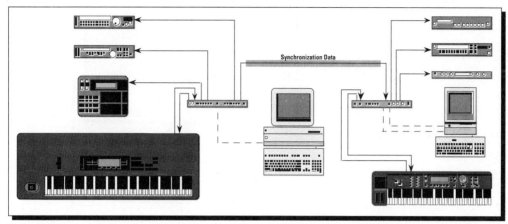

Figure 26-19: Macintosh as master to external hardware slaves. In this illustration, a MIDI sequencer running on the Macintosh is functioning as the master to a number of other hardware peripherals. MIDI Clocks are being sent to the drum machine and the M1's internal sequencer. MTC is being sent to the second Macintosh, which is running an identical copy of the same sequence in external sync mode. The tracks covered by the master Macintosh are muted in the slave Macintosh. The slave Macintosh is controlling another battery of devices.

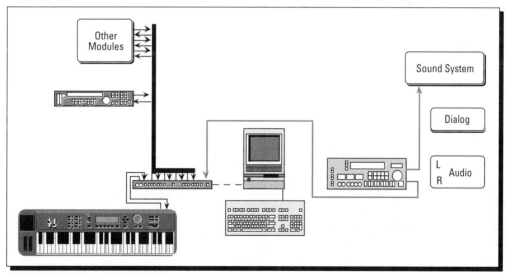

Figure 26-20: Macintosh as slave to video tape.

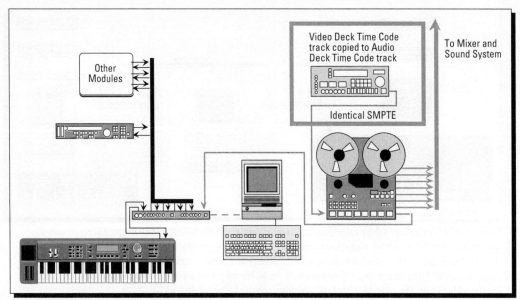

Figure 26-21: Macintosh as slave to audio tape.

audio recorder can all function as a single machine. You can hear the total of all your tracks at all times because the audio is locked to the video, which is also master to the slaved Macintosh. This setup also greatly enhances your manipulation of virtual tracks, because you can watch the picture with the virtual tracks and the real tracks in synchronization (see Figure 26-22).

Mac as slave to audio and/or video and master to hardware peripherals

This is a variation on the previous setup (see Figure 26-23). The Macintosh can function as a master to external hardware peripherals while it is slaved to an audio recorder or to a video recorder (which may or may not be a master to a synchronized audio recorder).

Synchronization and digital audio

A good number of special problems have arisen with the advent of sequencers that include digital audio tracks (see Chapters 18 and 24). When you deal exclusively with MIDI data, a little speeding up and slowing down does not affect the playback pitch of your music, nor does synchronizing music created at 30 fps to time code traveling at 29.97 fps. This is not the case with digital audio. If the time code fluctuates in tempo or if the frame rates don't match, the pitch of the digital audio material will change.

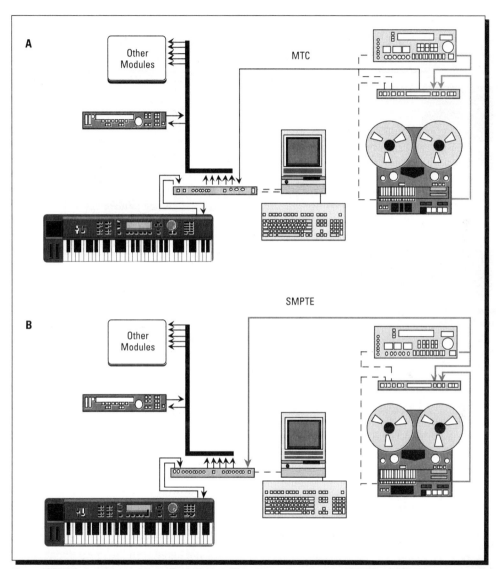

Figure 26-22: Macintosh as slave to audio and video. **(A)** In this configuration, the SMPTE-to-MTC conversion is accomplished in the synchronizer and transmitted to the MIDI interface as MIDI data. **(B)** In this configuration, the SMPTE-to-MTC conversion is accomplished in the MIDI interface (one with SMPTE conversion capabilities). Time code is transmitted to the interface as SMPTE data over audio cables.

This change of pitch can be disastrous when digital audio tracks are combined with MIDI sequence data. When the playback rate is not what you expect, even if it is only a difference of 0.03 fps (30 fps minus 29.97 fps), the digital audio

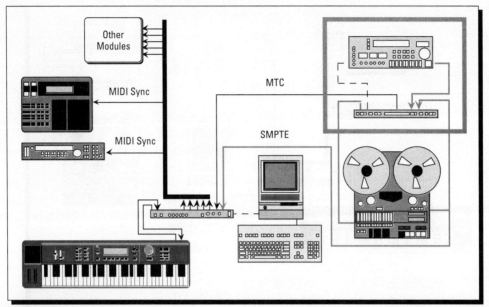

Figure 26-23: Macintosh as slave to audio and/or video and master to hardware peripherals. In this setup, the Macintosh functions both as a slave (to the video) and a master (to the drum machine and internal sequencer of the M1). The inclusion of an optional synchronizer allows the video to function as a master to the multitrack recorder as well (dotted lines surround the devices participating in this option).

tracks will be out of tune with the synthesizers controlled by the MIDI sequence data, since the latter won't change in pitch.

Obvious solutions are to detune your instruments accordingly or to send a slight amount of pitch bend at the beginning of each track to take care of the discrepancy. The best solution is to know in advance at which frame rate your music will be played back and to use that timing reference from the start.

If you employ such a system to score for film and video, keep in mind that timings calculated from the sample rate may not agree with the time expressed in the SMPTE Time Code address, if it is traveling at 29.97 fps (which it almost always is). The only places where you can be certain that a time expressed in frames per second will agree with a time you calculate from the 44.1 KHz sampling rate of your digital audio tracks are located at the hour and at every ten-minute interval (*HH*:00:00:00, *HH*:10:00:00, *HH*:20:00:00, *HH*:30:00:00, *HH*:40:00:00, and *HH*:50:00:00). This is because at all other times, the frame number does not represent the exact passage of real time, although the number of samples is measured in real time. This should only be a problem if you start playback of a soundfile in the middle of the soundfile rather than at the beginning.

General synchronization tips
Striping

- ❖ Verify that the track you intend to stripe is empty.
- ❖ Make sure the frame rates of the master and the slave agree.
- ❖ Always stripe at least an extra ten seconds in advance of where you intend the music to begin.
- ❖ Stripe on an outside track (usually the highest numbered track) .
- ❖ Leave an empty guard track between the time code track and the music.
- ❖ Don't process time code while striping. Disable all EQ and signal processing effects. Disable all noise reduction.
- ❖ Stripe at the appropriate level (see below) and adjust gain manually rather than with any auto-gain features of the recording medium.
- ❖ Use -5 to -10 VU for 1-inch video and record the time code on the third audio track or cue track.
- ❖ Use -5 to 0 VU for 3/4-inch video and record on the outside track or the time code track.
- ❖ Use -5 to 0 VU for audio tape and record on an outside edge track.
- ❖ Monitor the levels a little while so that no clipping occurs. Make some short tests to determine if the time code you record is hot enough to be read by your converter.
- ❖ Don't make a direct copy of a SMPTE track from one device to another — always regenerate or reshape the code. If you have a SMPTE generator that can accept a SMPTE Start Frame, you can simply set the appropriate start frame in that box rather than worry about regeneration or reshaping.
- ❖ Don't succumb to the temptation to record music while striping a tape.
- ❖ Be careful if your time code approaches midnight. With SMPTE Time Code, the next hour after 23 is 00, not 24.
- ❖ If you are striping FSK or smart FSK, be sure that the tempos you set are the final ones — you won't be able to change them later. Download the tempo map into the converter if required. If you create the tempo map in the converter, then back it up on disk if possible. Also, record an interval of "pilot" tone before beginning your sequence.
- ❖ Immediately after striping a tape, attempt to lock up to it to verify that the time code has been recorded correctly.

Synchronizing

- ❖ Don't record any music until the tape has been striped with time code.
- ❖ Know what type of synchronization you are attempting. Some systems require that you start at the beginning of the music for each take, while others lock when playback is initiated from any point.
- ❖ Make sure you have an audio cable connecting the time code track to your SMPTE-to-MIDI converter.
- ❖ You may need to boost the SMPTE Time Code signal on its way to your SMPTE-to-MIDI converter.

❖ If you are using MIDI Clocks, determine whether devices consider the first real clock or the Start message before that as the first timing clock.

❖ Take the required steps to inform your MIDI sequencer of the type of synchronization you are using. If it is SMPTE Time Code, be sure to specify the frame rate.

❖ Know which is the master and which is the slave.

❖ Set the required SMPTE offset.

❖ Set the required SMPTE start time for your sequence. If you want a cut-off, set a start time prior to the start of the sequence (using negative bar numbers or whatever is required by your sequencer).

❖ Use digital delay lines as described below if you need to compensate for the response time of different electronic instruments.

❖ Set your sequencer in slave or external sync mode before synchronizing.

❖ Start tape rolling at least five seconds before the start time.

❖ When mixing live musicians with sequenced music, always record some or all of the sequenced music first, so that the live musicians have a reference to play along with.

❖ During mixdown, make sure that the mixdown deck is striped with the same code as the source device and synchronize the two devices during mixdown. If you don't use a synchronizer, regenerate the code onto your mixdown deck while mixing.

Synchronizers (lockup systems)

❖ Provide SMPTE Time Code to the synchronizer from both the master and the slave.

❖ Make sure you use the RS-232 cable designated for the devices you are synchronizing.

❖ Set any DIP switches required for synchronization by any of your devices (refer to the manuals).

❖ Inform the synchronizer (if necessary) as to what devices are being synchronized. This usually involves choosing a device make and model from a menu.

❖ Modify your tape lifters (or have them modified) if they don't provide for high-speed code reading by another system or monitoring tach pulses.

Interview: Bruce Miller
Composer, arranger, conductor

Bruce Miller has scored numerous television episodes, including *Knots Landing, Designing Women, Falcon Crest, The Hogan Family* (aka *Valerie*), the *Motown Revue* (starring Smokey Robinson), and the *Michael Landon Tribute;* for many of these prime-time shows he has also orchestrated the main titles. In addition, his credits include several feature films both as composer and orchestrator and numerous video projects. A partial list of the recording artists he has arranged for or produced includes Rod Stewart, Gladys Knight & the Pips, Temptations, Four Tops, Smokey Robinson, Paul Anka, Junior Walker, Andrae Crouch, Robert Goulet, The Commodores, and The Miracles.

Yavelow: How did it start?

Miller: I was an instrumentalist and went to Wayne University in Detroit as a theory-composition major intending to be an arranger. I gained a lot more from looking over a lot of shoulders than through my formal education. I learned the craft from a record standpoint, moved to Los Angeles as a player, and started writing arrangements for a lot of R&B and MOR records. I got into television because of my record background . . . initially doing sound-alikes.

Yavelow: Perhaps you should define "sound-alikes."

Miller: A sound-alike is when they want to use the sound of an existing record in a movie or television show. I literally take down all the parts, go into a studio with musicians and duplicate the sound of that record. Sound-alikes are used because the masters for these hits are very expensive and the licensing fee for sound-alikes are a lot less expensive. Often the duplication is so accurate that the audience is unaware that it is not the original. However, the use of sound-alikes is on the decline.

Yavelow: Where did you go from there?

Miller: I got pulled in by a couple of my friends to do some scoring and just by the skin of my teeth started doing it. Fortunately the people that where hiring liked what I was doing and so I got to do more. At that time I was doing a lot of electronic scoring in other programmers' garage studios with small multi-track setups. I got a Macintosh computer early in 1985 and learned how to use Performer. I'd put sequences in Performer and bring them over to another studio and realize them on the synths.

Yavelow: While a lot of composers seem to accumulate electronic gear over a long period, I recall you mentioning that you really took the plunge in one fell swoop. Could you elaborate?

Miller: Synthesizer-wise, when I was working on the motion picture *The Last Dragon,* I bought a DX7 and a Juno 106 and put the cues into a little MSQ-100 sequencer. By 1986, I saw that I was spending a lot of time and money at other little studios and realized that there was very little that I couldn't do myself. So, I got an Akai MG1214 multitrack tape recorder, a variety of synthesizers, two effects devices, an SRV2000 and an SPX 90, hooked it all up to the Mac and started doing it.

Yavelow: What is your approach to composing with synthesizers?

Miller: When I am composing, I assign all the synths to a different sound on a different MIDI channel. For example, I might use the MKS-70 for the string sound and the D-50 for winds or brass, and sequence this into a Mac IIci. As I only have about a dozen synthesizers, we frequently need more than one synthesizer for one sound. My brass sound may use five synths in combination. So we lock up to the computer, put the brass on two tracks, and then I go back and get the string sound with another variety of synthesizers, and so on.

Yavelow: So when you're creating the original sequence using different channels you are always aware that the brass or string sound you are sketching with will be fattened up with other synths when you go to tape.

Miller: Oh sure, for example, I might write the parts using a string sample on the S-900 but when it comes time to actually record it I may not even use the S-900 — instead I might use some voice sounds. It's strictly just to give me some kind of a timbre to sequence with. Taking into account that some of the envelopes might be different, I play it not so much according to the synth I am sequencing on as to the sound I am eventually going to go for.

Yavelow: This would give you more flexibility over the EQ and effect, for example.

Miller: Total control. But I do not engineer myself. I'm a composer, not an engineer or a sound designer or sampler. I depend heavily upon having a real hot engineer who can take my sounds, add all the effects, balance, EQ, and pan the synthesizers properly, and then put them on tape and it sounds head and shoulders over anything I would do myself during recording.

Yavelow: Do you compose while locked or fit-to-time afterwards?

Miller: I always use timing notes if they are available and write according to that information rather than improvising while locked to the video. Essentially, while I'm composing electronically, I approach it as a traditional composer and orchestrator rather than as an improvisor. This allows me to have control over the music I'm writing.

Yavelow: Do you find that it is enough to copy the video time code onto your audio code track or do you regenerate fresh code?

Miller: I always regenerate fresh code. As a matter of fact, that's a rule. You cannot trust code that has simply been copied.

Yavelow: Are you using Auricle or Cue for synchronization?

Miller: I was using Auricle until I got into Performer — the real-time counter, bar-beat-tick counter, and SMPTE counter let me get all my hits right out of Performer and I'm accurate to the frame. I know exactly where something falls; for example, if the hit is at 2.87 seconds after I zero the counters, it tells me exactly what bar beat and tick it falls on. I change the meter when it's appropriate to catch something on a downbeat or for other musical reasons.

Yavelow: Do you use Cue sheet and SMPTE/frame/time calculator utilities. How important are these for fully electronic scores vs. live scores?

Miller: I use Softhansa's Time Calculator DA and the Clix<->BPM DA from the *Macworld Music & Sound Bible* Software Supplement when I score for a live orchestra rather than when I am scoring electronically. I use Clix<->BPM when writing for a live orchestra but use Performer to get my timings the way other people might use Cue. Because I know that I will be using the Urei click machine in the studio, I make my tempo in Performer the exact beats per minute of the corresponding click tempo. I'm not using Performer to compose in this case, but simply as a calculator. With a synth score, it's easiest for me to play the track wild and then adjust the tempos later to make the hits.

Yavelow: Some of the shows you score seem to alternate live scores with electronics. What impact does this have on your task?

Miller: Although I can make more money packaging an electronic score, it's much harder and more time-consuming to do an electronic episode. We are frequently given seven days to write 15 to 20 minutes of music and that means really spending extra time to sequence properly. Then it takes so much time to record that you must write the music in three days. So, often, when they ask for an electronic score, I ask for more time. However, I have been known to produce a score overnight.

Yavelow: Does the Macintosh assist you when you are composing for live orchestra?

Miller: Sure. I do about half my work with live orchestras and the other half electronically. And by the way, when I do a score electronically, I will often bring in a live

player if the part calls for it. When I am writing for the orchestra I write on paper like a conventional composer (doing all the orchestration myself), but sometimes, especially with a long dramatic cue, because I have gotten so fast with the computer, I will do a quick [synth] "Polaroid" of the cue and lock it up with the picture. Then I can sit back and watch it with the picture. It's amazing what you will hear that you wouldn't otherwise discover until you get to the scoring stage. This way I know that the notes, timbres, and counterpoints are correct. It's worth spending that extra time to be able to go into the studio knowing that I like it.

Yavelow: Any studio tips?

Miller: Using wood rails instead of metal rails in a rack eliminates a lot of grounding problems. I replaced all my metal rails with wooden ones from a company called Four Designs.

Yavelow: Any changes you see on the horizon?

Miller: I'm definitely waiting for synchronizable DATs to become standard.

Yavelow: Do you find that MIDI places any limitations on your creativity?

Miller: I find that MIDI is an incredibly magical thing and it enables us to do things we would never be capable of doing otherwise. Don't complain about MIDI, work with what you have, make it work; we're musicians first, we're not a bunch of technicians. There are some people who design things and some who use them. I have great respect for the designers, because they've provided me with many amazing tools. I'm hired to compose music and I love what I do. I try not to criticize my equipment, instead I revere it because of the many musical doors it has opened for me.

Yavelow: What's the bottom line?

Miller: A composer should compose and leave as little to chance as possible. Hit and miss improvisation is lazy and shows a lack of craft which takes its toll in the quality of the music. This is opposed to "seat of the pants" composition, to which I do subscribe (referring to a certain amount of hunt and peck that I feel is healthy). The point is that, starting at bar one, and haphazardly moving ahead is not the means to an intelligent end.

Synchronization on the Scoring Stage

Synthesizers and Macintoshes are a normal part of many of the orchestras you hear on film and television soundtracks. Composer Jerry Goldsmith is particularly well known for integrating synthesizers with the orchestra as yet another choir alongside the brass choir, wind choir, string choir, and percussion battery. Ron Jones uses three or four synthesists (each with about 15 synthesizers) in conjunction with 60 or so live musicians for the music to *Star Trek— The Next Generation*. One of these synthesizer stations is usually designated for sequenced material only, although the others must have Macintoshes too because patches are distributed on Macintosh disks at the beginning of each scoring session.

Most live music for film and video is recorded with the musicians hearing clicks in their headphones while recording. In the old days, this used to be provided by a click track (or looped piece of film capable of generating a constant click). Clicks are still used to specify tempo in film and video recording, although electronic devices such as a digital metronome now supply the click.

Click tracks

Click tracks were originally created by punching holes in film. Film travels at 24 fps and there are four sprocket holes per frame. A hole punched in the optical track of the film produces a click. These holes can be aligned to a sprocket hole or the space between two sprocket holes, dividing a frame into eight parts and and a second into 192 segments (⅛ of a frame). If the tempo was constant, a film loop supplied the click, if not, a rather lengthy piece of film (called a variable click track) had to be punched.

Click tempos are specified as two numbers. The first represents the number of frames, and the second represents the number of eighth frames. For example, a 24-0 click refers to a click every 24 frames, in other words once a second (60 BPM). A 12-0 click results in two clicks per second or 120 BPM. Using the eighth values permits finer resolution. An 11-2 click equals 128 BPM and a 17-7 click equals 80.56 BPM. See Table 26-1 at the end of this chapter for conversions of most frame clicks into BPM.

Besides providing a metronome for the live performers on the scoring stage, clicks also serve to synchronize MIDI sequencers. Special devices such as a Garfield Dr. Click or Time Commander, JL Cooper PPS-100 or Aphex Studio Clock can handle the conversion of the audio click into MIDI Clock. Many newer MIDI-to-SMPTE converters, both stand-alone and MIDI interfaces with built-in converters, can also accept an audio click input and turn it into MIDI Clock.

Many composers use a click book to calculate tempos that will fit the music exactly to a specific scene. Each page of a click book is devoted to a single tempo expressed as a frame click. The location of each beat (in hundredths of a second) is provided for 600 clicks at that tempo. These days, the Macintosh is used to making such calculations, although several programs have built-in click books that resemble their paper counterparts (see below).

Digital delay lines

Due to the delicacy of the conversion of audio clicks to MIDI Clocks and the accuracy required on the scoring stage, MIDI sequencers often won't synchronize to live musicians unless the audio click is resolved through a digital delay line (DDL) circuit in a digital signal processor. A DDL is capable of taking an input audio signal and delaying it for a specified amount of time (usually set in milliseconds) before passing the signal on to its outputs.

Incidentally, another popular use of DDLs in synchronization is to check the response times of various synthesizers. Nearly all electronic instruments respond to a Note-On message at slightly different speeds. When you are synchronizing for the purpose of multitracking, varying response times can make your music sound out of sync. You can use a DDL to resolve this. All you have to do is record a quantized sequence track of quarter notes on different tape tracks, played on each instrument you want to check, and recorded while synchronized. Listening to the tape will make it clear which instruments are ahead and which are behind the beat. Placing a DDL between the earlier clicks and the mixer allows you to delay these until they coincide with the other tracks. The LED on the DDL will indicate the amount of delay required to bring things into sync and therefore the amount, in milliseconds, that the offending devices were early. Subsequently, using the information you obtained from your synchronization check, you insert a DDL into the synchronization signal path to compensate for the discrepancy. This is similar to the procedure used on the scoring stage to resolve the click being sent to the live musicians with the one being converted into MIDI Clock for the sequencers.

Cue Sheet Applications
Cue sheets explained

Prior to scoring a film, the composer, director, and music editor (and sometimes the film editor and producer) watch the film in what is called a "spotting" session. This is where the decisions are made as to where there will be music. Each chunk of music is called a cue. The music editor takes notes about all these decisions and prepares cue sheets for the composer from these notes. The cue sheets are labeled with a number representing the film reel number, then the letter "M," and finally the number of the cue on that reel. For example, "3M7" refers to the seventh musical cue on the third reel of film.

Cue sheets contain detailed information about the visual elements of each cue. This information usually consists of SMPTE frame number, relative time (in minutes and seconds), information about the shot (cut, close-up, pan), description of the action, and dialog, including the exact moment that each line of dialog ends (indicated by EOL for end of line). Additional information about the production is provided as well.

The cue sheet information describes the on-screen action in such detail that it can sometimes even replace the actual video as a compositional aid to the composer.

Two Macintosh software programs are dedicated to the preparation of cue sheets: Opcode's Cue and Passport's Clicktracks. These programs do so much more than simply print out a cue sheet that anyone seriously using the Macintosh for film and video scoring should consider acquiring one of them.

Cue (Opcode Systems)

The full name of Cue is Cue — The Film Music System. This is the first indication of how much more than just a mere cue sheet utility this software is. Cue does just about any calculation you will ever need to do when scoring a film. In relieving you of this busy work, the program saves you hours of time, which quickly add up to additional days that you can devote to the creative aspects of scoring.

The software manages cue sheets, letting you lay them out with any information you want in any format. You can capture SMPTE Time Code frame numbers from video by pressing a single key. On the cue sheet, you can designate which events are "key hits" that you want to synchronize to a particular musical event (see Figure 26-24).

A

Production:	**SHOCKER**	Production #:	**0000**			
Cue:	**7M2** · **PASTORI CHASES JON**	·	Starting Tempo:	**130** **.00** **(B.P.M.)**		

Begins   at **d7:03:21:06**   in Reel/Act   7

---   8 **WARNING CLICKS BEGIN AT**   **d7:03:17:15**   ---

ABS . SMPTE #(df):	REL . TIME:			BAR- BEAT:

CUE COVERS PINKER IN PASTORI'S BODY, AS HE CHASES JON,
TRYING TO KILL HIM. MX STARTS ON CUT TO JON AS HE'S
RUNNING IN ALLEY TO GET AWAY FROM HIM. NOTE: MX
SHOULD BE NOT SO MUCH TENSION, AS EXCITEMENT.
(I REVERSED THIS IN SPOTTING, THIS IS CORRECT)

METER   :   4
4

d7:03:21 :06	0 0 0 ✓	CUT	MX STARTS ON CUT TO MS JON AS HE RUNS DOWN ALLEY TRYING TO ESCAPE FROM PINKER/PASTORI.	1- 1 0 480
d7:03:22 :22	1 53 ✓	CUT	MCS PASTORI AS HE RUNS THROUGH FENCE INTO ALLEY AFTER JON. CAM PANS TO FOLLOW HIM	1- 4 154 480
d7:03:25 :29	4 77 ✓	CUT	MS JON AS HE CONT'S RUNNING.	3- 3 163 480
d7:03:27 :09	6 10 ✓		PASTORI RUNS INTO FRAME AFTER HIM	4- 2 106 480
d7:03:27 :13	6 23		JON TURNS BEHIND HIM, TOWARD PASTORI	4- 2 240 480
d7:03:27 :19	6 43		JON YELLS: "LOOK WHY DONT' YOU JUST CALM DOWN"	4- 2 446 480
d7:03:30 :05	8 97		PASTORI FIRES, JON DUCKS OUT OF THE WAY--EOL ABOVE	5- 4 211 480
d7:03:34 :09	13 10 ✓	CUT	MS JON, DUCKING HIS HEAD AS HE RUNS INTO FRAME, CAM FOLLOWS. JON YELLS: "CHRIST"	8- 1 182 480
d7:03:35 :15	14 33		EOL ABOVE	8- 4 24 480
d7:03:36 :09	15 10		HE STOPS FOR A MOMENT...	9- 1 346 480
d7:03:36 :24	15 63		THAN BEGINS RUNNING ,CAM FOLLOWING	9- 2 418 480
d7:03:39 :06	18 03		PASTORI RUNS INTO FRAME, AS THE CHASE CONT'S	10- 4 34 480
d7:03:41 :26	20 70 ✓	CUT	MS WOODED BRIDGE IN PARK	12- 1 408 480
d7:03:43 :04	21 97		JON RUNS INTO FRAME IN B.G.	12- 4 288 480
d7:03:44 :09	23 13 ✓		PASTORI RUNS INTO FRAME BEHIND HIM	13- 3 58 480
d7:03:47 :27	26 73		CAM CLOSES IN ON MCS JON	15- 2 442 480
d7:03:49 :08	28 10		JON TURNS BEHIND HIM,STOPPING	16- 1 422 480

Page   1   9/1/89   2:26 AM

B

Notation Display

1- 1

1- 4 + ♪ 3

3- 3 + ♪ 3

4- 2 + ♪

4- 2 + ♪

4- 3

5- 4 + ♪

8- 1 + ♪ 3

8- 4

9- 1 + ♪

9- 2 + ♪

10- 4

12- 1 + ♪

12- 4 + ♩ 3

13- 3

15- 3

16- 1 + ♪

C

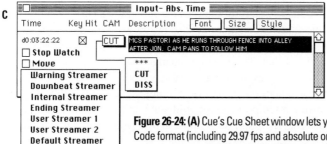

Figure 26-24: (A) Cue's Cue Sheet window lets you enter timings in any SMPTE Time Code format (including 29.97 fps and absolute or relative frame numbers) or minutes and seconds (absolute or relative), measures and beats, or any combination of the above. Each cue point can have 24 lines of descriptive text. **(B)** One of the available formats of the far right column displays measures and beats using rhythmic values. **(C)** You designate cue points as key hits and add additional information with this dialog box (accessible by way of a pop-up menu when you click any cue line).

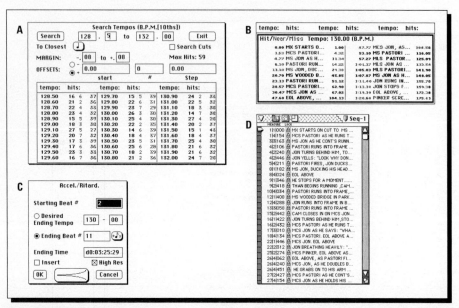

Figure 26-25: **(A)** Cue's Tempo Search finds the tempo that will hit the most cue points within a range you define. Hits, misses, and near misses are displayed. Cue can also automatically calculate the meter changes and insert the appropriate time signatures to make specific cue points fall on down beats. **(B)** Double-clicking a tempo in this window provides the exact information regarding its relation to the video. Hits are displayed in bold; misses in gray. **(C)** You can even have Cue create tempo maps that guarantee hitting your selected cue points dead-on, and these can be exported as an SMF tempo map. **(D)** Importing the cue sheet into Performer converts the cue point descriptions into frame-locked markers.

After setting up your cue sheet, one of the most valuable features of Cue is its ability to search tempos to determine, within a tempo range that you specify, how many of your key hits will fall on a quarter note, eighth note, or triplet. You can specify a range of SMPTE offsets to be taken into consideration by the Tempo Search, just in case starting the music a few frames early or late would permit catching more hits (see Figure 26-25). If you want to hit your selected cue points right on the money, Cue will calculate subtle accelerandos and ritardandos that do just that. These tempo changes can be exported as an SMF tempo map that you can import into any sequencer or a Roland SBX-80, Southworth JamBox/4, Garfield Time Commander, or JL Cooper PPS-100. Even if you are not exporting a tempo map you will still want to export your cue sheet to an SMF. In this case, the cue points come across to the sequencer as frame-locked markers.

Cue provides the option to update the cue sheet automatically with decisions you make in the Tempo Search window. The software lets you work with three versions of the same file, so you never have to worry about experimenting.

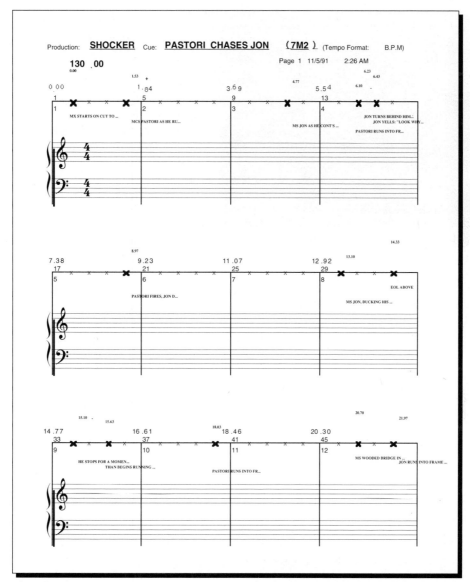

Figure 26-26: Cue can print custom score paper of up to 12 staves. You can also display and print a click line containing the same information as the one above the pictured grand staff.

After finding your tempo and meter changes with the Tempo Search feature, Cue can print out custom score paper (up to 12 staves) including click numbers, abbreviated cue point descriptions, and the time of each beat (see Figure 26-26).

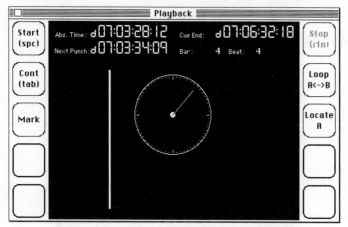

Figure 26-27: Cue's Playback window (the white vertical bar is a streamer).

If you are using Cue to create music for a live ensemble, you may want to bring your Macintosh to the scoring stage, because Cue has many features that are useful in real time. The program generates a SMPTE-locked click track, displays streamers and punches, plays SMFs locked to SMPTE, lets you tap the tempo (or tap the click track while locked to SMPTE), and provides a veritable digital metronome in a window with all the timing information about the current cue. If you use the program in conjunction with a Tesla Video Streamer, streamers and punches can be superimposed on the video. Using the program with a Computer Friend's TV Producer NuBus card lets you add a visual clock, stopwatch, and scrolling cue list to the video (see Figure 26-27).

You can even use Cue to trigger up to 40 MIDI events that you assign to SMPTE Time Code frame numbers. Each event can include up to five MIDI channels.

When you are finished with a project, Cue will assemble a Master Cue List and Performing Rights List indicating all the cues that are finished, orchestrated, and copied, listing the composer's, orchestrator's, and publisher's names, the length of the cue, the percent of cue sheet credit, and additional information.

Finally, Cue includes a complete online click book and a built-in time code calculator as well (see Figure 26-28). You will probably rarely need these if you learn to use the rest of the program.

Clicktracks (Passport Designs)

Passport Design's Clicktracks offers many of the same features as Cue and adds its own unique options. Like Cue, Clicktracks manages cue sheets and lets you designate which events are key hits that you want to synchronize to a particular musical event (see Figure 26-29).

Clicktracks can search tempos to determine, within a tempo range that you specify, how many of your key hits the tempo will catch. Clicktracks calculates

A   Click Book (Tempo Format: B.P.M.)

	0	1	2	3	4	5	6	7	8	9
		0.00	0.46	0.92	1.38	1.85	2.31	2.77	3.23	3.69
10	4.15	4.62	5.08	5.54	6.00	6.46	6.92	7.38	7.85	8.31
20	8.77	9.23	9.69	10.15	10.62	11.08	11.54	12.00	12.46	12.92
30	13.38	13.85	14.31	14.77	15.23	15.69	16.15	16.62	17.08	17.54
40	18.00	18.46	18.92	19.38	19.85	20.31	20.77	21.23	21.69	22.15
50	22.62	23.08	23.54	24.00	24.46	24.92	25.38	25.85	26.31	26.77
60	27.23	27.69	28.15	28.62	29.08	29.54	30.00	30.46	30.92	31.38
70	31.85	32.31	32.77	33.23	33.69	34.15	34.62	35.08	35.54	36.00
80	36.46	36.92	37.38	37.85	38.31	38.77	39.23	39.69	40.15	40.62
90	41.08	41.54	42.00	42.46	42.92	43.38	43.85	44.31	44.77	45.23
100	45.69	46.15	46.62	47.08	47.54	48.00	48.46	48.92	49.38	49.85
110	50.31	50.77	51.23	51.69	52.15	52.62	53.08	53.54	54.00	54.46
120	54.92	55.38	55.85	56.31	56.77	57.23	57.69	58.15	58.62	59.08
130	59.54	1:00.00	1:00.46	1:00.92	1:01.38	1:01.85	1:02.31	1:02.77	1:03.23	1:03.69
140	1:04.15	1:04.62	1:05.08	1:05.54	1:06.00	1:06.46	1:06.92	1:07.38	1:07.85	1:08.31
150	1:08.77	1:09.23	1:09.69	1:10.15	1:10.62	1:11.08	1:11.54	1:12.00	1:12.46	1:12.92
160	1:13.38	1:13.85	1:14.31	1:14.77	1:15.23	1:15.69	1:16.15	1:16.62	1:17.08	1:17.54
170	1:18.00	1:18.46	1:18.92	1:19.38	1:19.85	1:20.31	1:20.77	1:21.23	1:21.69	1:22.15

Tempo 130 . 00   **Find Click #** 144   **Find Time** 0.0   Prev   Next

B   Conversions

TEMPO   **TIME**

11 – 1   OK   8.97

◉ 24 fr.   ○ 25 fr.   ○ 29.97 fr.   ○ 30 fr.   ○ B.P.M.   OK

11–1   11–47   13–71   13–73   129.44

		Hr:Min:Sec	8.97
♪₃ = 39 milliseconds	♪. = 348 milliseconds	SMPTE(24)	f0:00:08:23
♪ = 58 milliseconds	♩₃ = 309 milliseconds	SMPTE(25)	e0:00:08:24
♪. = 87 milliseconds	♩ = 464 milliseconds	SMPTE(30)	s0:00:08:29
♪₃ = 77 milliseconds	♩. = 695 milliseconds	SMPTE(29)	c0:00:08:29
♪ = 116 milliseconds	♩₃ = 618 milliseconds	SMPTE(df)	d0:00:08:29
♪. = 174 milliseconds	♩ = 927 milliseconds	Film(16)	x5/15
♪₃ = 155 milliseconds	♩. = 1391 milliseconds	Film(35)	13/7
♪ = 232 milliseconds	o = 1854 milliseconds	Film(*16)	*x5/15
		Film(*35)	*13/7

Figure 26-28: (A) Cue's online Click Book Window **(B)** Cue's Conversions window is a time code calculator. Values can be entered as equations if you like.

subtle accelerandos and ritardandos to make sure you make your designated key hits exactly. As with Cue, these tempo changes can be exported as an SMF tempo map that you can import into any sequencer or a Roland SBX-80 or Southworth JamBox/4 (see Figure 26-30).

Clicktracks lets you view a cue sheet in a Hitmap window similar to Cue's Click Line window (see Figure 26-31).

Clicktracks includes a complete online click book and two built-in music calculators as well. You will probably rarely need these if you learn to use the rest of the program.

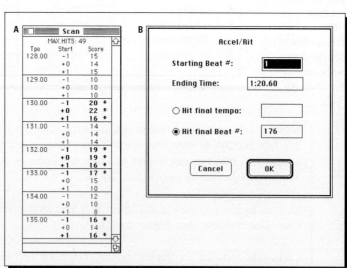

HH:MM:SS:FF	DESCRIPTION	BEAT	BT	OFFSET	+ -	TIME
07:03:21:12	MX STARTS ON CUT TO MS...	1.00	1	0	+0.0	0:00.00
07:03:22:28	MCS PASTORI AS HE RUNS ...	4.32	4		+0.2	0:01.54
07:03:26:05	MS JON AS HE CONT'S RUN...	11.34	11		-0.1	0:04.77
07:03:27:15	PASTORI RUNS INTO FRAME...	14.22	14		-0.7	0:06.08
07:03:27:19	JON TURNS BEHIND HIM, T...	14.50	14		+0.0	0:06.23
07:03:27:25	JON YELLS: "LOOK WHY DO...	14.93	15		+1.0	0:06.46
07:03:30:11	PASTORI FIRES, JON DUCK...	20.44	20		+0.8	0:09.00
07:03:34:15	MS JON, DUCKING HIS HEA...	29.38	29		-0.6	0:13.08
07:03:35:21	EOL ABOVE	32.05	32	0	-0.7	0:14.31
07:03:36:15	HE STOPS FOR A MOMENT...	33.72	33		+1.6	0:15.15
07:03:37:00	THAN BEGINS RUNNING ,CA...	34.87	34		-0.5	0:15.62
07:03:39:12	PASTORI RUNS INTO FRAME...	40.07	40		+1.3	0:18.08
07:03:42:02	MS WOODED BRIDGE IN PAR...	45.85	45		-0.2	0:20.69
07:03:43:10	JON RUNS INTO FRAME IN ...	48.60	48		+0.9	0:22.00
07:03:44:15	PASTORI RUNS INTO FRAME...	51.12	51		+0.6	0:23.15
07:03:48:03	CAM CLOSES IN ON MCS JO...	58.92	59	0	+1.1	0:26.77
07:03:49:14	JON TURNS BEHIND HIM,ST...	61.88	61		-0.6	0:28.08
07:03:49:28	MCS PASTORI AS HE RUNS ...	62.90	63	0	+1.4	0:28.62

DROPFRAME   Starting Tpo = 130.00
-- 8 CLIX WARNING AT 07:03:17:21 --
(window title: 7M2.ct)

Figure 26-29: Clicktracks's Cue Sheet window lets you enter timings in any SMPTE Time Code format, minutes and seconds (absolute or relative), or measures and beats. A nice feature is the display in rhythmic notation of the location of cue points relative to the beat.

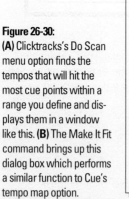

Figure 26-30:
(A) Clicktracks's Do Scan menu option finds the tempos that will hit the most cue points within a range you define and displays them in a window like this. **(B)** The Make It Fit command brings up this dialog box which performs a similar function to Cue's tempo map option.

A — Scan window — MAX HITS: 49

Tpo	Start	Score
128.00	−1	15
	+0	14
	+1	15
129.00	−1	10
	+0	10
	+1	10
130.00	−1	20 *
	+0	22 *
	+1	16 *
131.00	−1	14
	+0	14
	+1	14
132.00	−1	19 *
	+0	19 *
	+1	16 *
133.00	−1	17 *
	+0	15
	+1	10
134.00	−1	12
	+0	10
	+1	8
135.00	−1	16 *
	+0	14
	+1	16 *

B — Accel/Rit

Starting Beat #: `1`

Ending Time: `1:20.60`

○ Hit final tempo: `       `

● Hit final Beat #: `176`

(Cancel)   (OK)

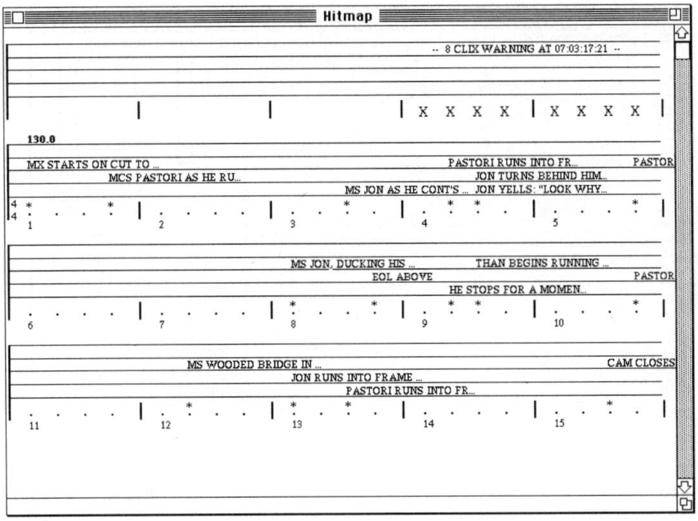

Figure 26-31: Clicktracks's Hitmap window.

Other Synchronization Applications
Understanding edit decision lists

Edit decision lists (EDLs) are lists of SMPTE Time Code addresses that trigger events and control external devices. The original purpose of EDLs was, and still is, the compilation of different video sources into a final mixdown. To accomplish this, dedicated hardware takes control of a group of VTRs, cueing them up and triggering them in a specified order. Their functionality migrated to the audio world, and they are now used for similar purposes in assembling sound effects from a variety of sources.

Dedicated hardware supporting audio EDLs offers the capability of synchronizing a large number of tape recorders in a similar way that they control VTRs. The most popular stand-alone EDL controller/synchronizer systems in both the video and audio domain are made by CMX. Compatibility with CMX EDLs is a necessity for any software that enters this arena.

Hardware EDL controllers/synchronizers such as those made by CMX are devoted to locating and playing back sound stored on audio tape. However, much sound these days exists as MIDI-triggered synthesizers, samplers, and direct-to-hard disk digital audio recordings. Digidesign's Q-Sheet A/V was borne out of the need for a system to deal with these types of sound sources.

Q-Sheet A/V

Digidesign's Q-Sheet A/V is popular among sound effects editors. Any Macintosh-controllable event can be triggered by the software. All times are specified

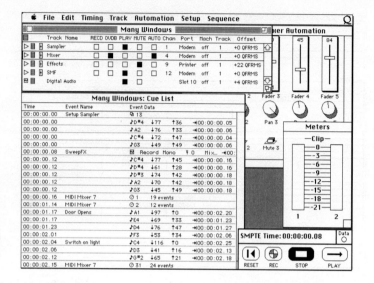

Figure 26-32:
Anatomy of a
Q-Sheet A/V
Track List.

in SMPTE Time Code rather than measures and beats. Events can be single notes (useful for trigger samplers), entire MIDI sequences, and fader signal processor/mixer automation files. Although the program is not really a MIDI sequencer, you can record MIDI data with it. Q-Sheet A/V is so powerful in the realm of signal processor and mixer automation that these features are discussed in Chapter 25, "MIDI Mixing and Studio Automation," where similar programs are covered.

When used in conjunction with Digidesign's SoundTools, Q-Sheet A/V also makes digital audio events part of its palette. In this category the software will trigger whole soundfiles, individual regions of soundfiles, and entire playlists from soundfiles.

The software is organized around the concept of tracks. Unlike typical MIDI sequencers, these tracks play back sequentially, not simultaneously. A track contains a list of events. These can be any of the events mentioned in the previous two paragraphs. Tracks can be rearranged by dragging their handles, recorded over, overdubbed, play enabled, muted, and offset by a SMPTE Time Code number (see Figure 26-32).

Tracks all have an edit window showing their individual events. Beginning and ending SMPTE times can be set; event types and parameters can be edited (see Figure 26-33).

Like the recording of MIDI data and sequences, Q-Sheet A/V will record digital audio directly from within the software (if you have the Sound Tools package). Finally, the program can both import and export CMX EDLs.

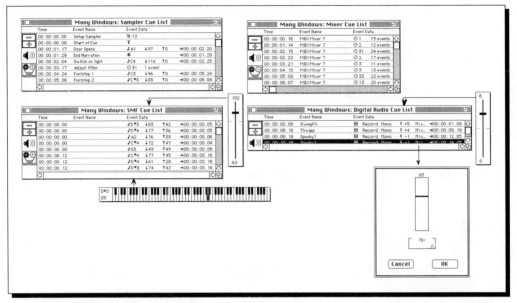

Figure 26-33: Q-Sheet A/V Edit window. Note that the editable parameters for a MIDI event differ from those of a MIDI sequence stored as an event. Digital audio events have two unique parameters: tuning (pitch shift up to an octave) and mix (controls the level of the left and right channels).

Film and Video Utilities

Mark of the Unicorn's Video Time Piece

To decode VITC for software running on a Macintosh you need a special VITC converter. Mark of the Unicorn's Video Time Piece is such a device.

The Video Time Piece, or VTP for short, is a very feature-intensive device (see Figures 26-34 and 26-35). The one-rack-space box can read and write both VITC and LTC and convert this to MTC or DTLe. It can also regenerate time code and jam sync to existing time code. LTC can be referenced to -10 dB or +4 dB (verify that the unit you have can actually reach +4 dB if you need it; some VTPs only make it as far as 3.5 dB).

Besides being compatible with American NTSC video, the VTP is completely compatible with the European PAL format and the Franco-Russian SECAM format. All formats of SMPTE Time Code are supported, including 29.97, and that includes the conversion of any SMPTE format or MTC format into any other time code format. There is also an option to convert an audio click to SPP and to lock the VTP to house sync.

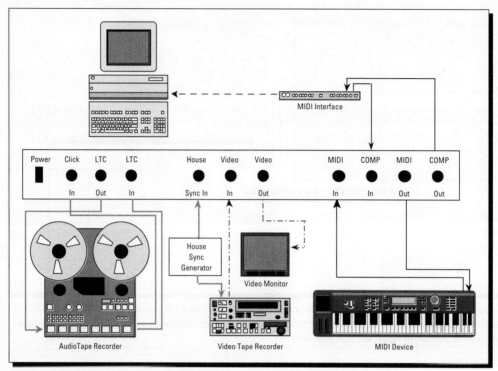

Figure 26-34: Normal configuration of the VTP (see also Setups 14 and 15 in Chapter 7).

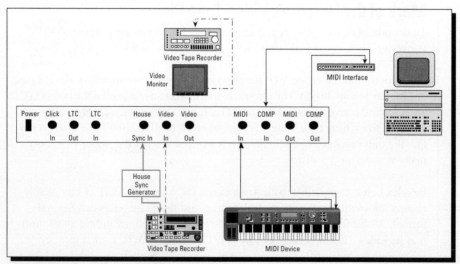

Figure 26-35: Configuration of the VTP for recording VITC (see also Setups 14 and 15 in Chapter 7). Rather than passing the video signal through your monitor to the destination VTR or through the destination VTR to the monitor, you could also use a Mark of the Unicorn's Video Distribution Amplifier.

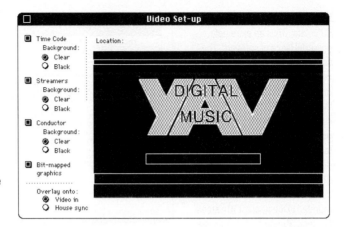

Figure 26-36: Configuring the VTP video graphics display. Note that the VTP can add an after-the-fact SMPTE burn-in window that is not actually burned into the video signal on the tape. You can use the Bitmapped Graphics option to add a title or titles to any video.

You can use the VTP to overlay and display important graphic cues on the video screen. The most obvious graphic you might want to display is a SMPTE Time Code burn-in window. The VTP also lets you download a single-frame MacPaint-style graphic to any position on the video screen, and display streamers (see Figure 26-36).

If you use the VTP in conjunction with Mark of the Unicorn's Performer or Digital Performer software, you have additional options. One feature is the capability of displaying the names of markers that you have saved in your MIDI sequence (the markers appear when they come due), auto-streamering these markers, and displaying a "conductor crawl line" that can function somewhat like the traditional punches used for a beat reference when recording a live instrumental score to picture. The conductor crawl line looks like a series of white dots that move across the screen, hitting the edge at each beat.

Naturally, the VTP works very well in conjunction with Mark of the Unicorn's own MIDI Time Piece (multi-cable interface — see Chapter 8, "Moving Data Around Your Music Network"). Like the MIDI Time Piece, the VTP is controlled by a DA. You can configure every parameter of the device and also load and save setups with the VTP DA.

You can use the VTP DA to stripe or restripe VITC or LTC. You can even re-record existing VITC or encode a video tape's LTC track into VITC. Other options include re-recording existing LTC so that it is frame-locked to the video.

Time code and frame calculators

There are many calculators that can assist you in making calculations with SMPTE Time Code. Two in particular, are so versatile that you should consider acquiring them immediately (see Figures 26-37 and 26-38).

Figure 26-37: Softhansa's Time Calculator DA is an extremely powerful piece of software. The software lets you enter a list of cues (using the black dot cursor) and then set the clock rolling. When you click the mouse (presumably while looking at the picture), a new hit is entered next to each cue in the format you desire (seconds, 24, 25, or 30 frame SMPTE, frames, frames rounded to the nearest five frames, frames rounded to the nearest 10 frames, film feet, or meters of film). Subsequently, clicking any timing value

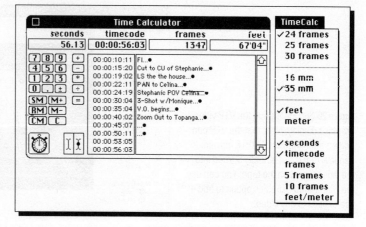

next to a cue zooms that value up to the appropriate field under the title bar, with all the conversions being made instantly. Then you can do calculations with it using the calculator buttons on the left. Selecting the cues on the right (with the normal text cursor) and choosing Copy from the edit menu copies the timing information (bracketed) onto the clipboard, ready to be pasted onto a cue sheet. Holding the Shift key down while you choose Copy also copies the cue descriptions next, along with the timings.

Using a sequencer as a time code calculator

Often, you can get your sequencer to do calculations for you. Some sequencers have such functions built into them. Figure 26-39 uses Mark of the Unicorn's Performer as an example, but many other sequencers can be coaxed into similar functionality.

Tempo librarian software

When you are dealing with FSK or smart FSK, some interfaces let you store a tempo map within their RAM. With RAM being as volatile as it is, a good approach is to back up these tempo maps with tempo librarian software. There is tempo map librarian software available for at least three popular interfaces with tempo map capabilities (see Figure 26-40): the Studio Clock (Aphex), the JamBox (Freq-Sound — formerly sold by Southworth), and the SBX-80 (Roland).

Code Disc (Prosonus)

Prosonus's Code Disc is an innovative solution to striping a tape with SMPTE Time Code. This CD turns your CD player into a time-code generator. The Code Disc is striped with one hour of time code guaranteed to be free of dropouts. The time code is only on one channel. The other channel consists of a voice that periodically informs you of the current SMPTE location. Using this disc lets you stripe a tape without tying up your interface or computer in the process.

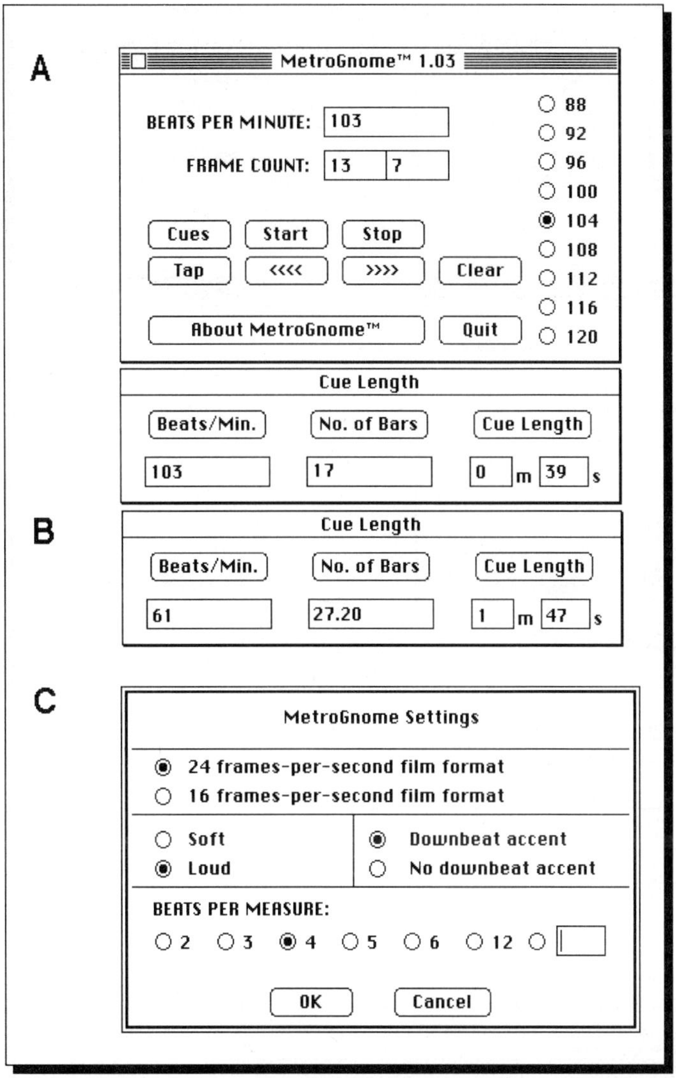

A

▢ ▤▤▤▤▤▤▤ MetroGnome™ 1.03 ▤▤▤▤▤▤▤

BEATS PER MINUTE: `103`

FRAME COUNT: `13` `7`

○ 88
○ 92
○ 96
○ 100
◉ 104
○ 108
○ 112
○ 116
○ 120

[Cues] [Start] [Stop]
[Tap] [<<<<] [>>>>] [Clear]

[About MetroGnome™] [Quit]

Cue Length

[Beats/Min.] [No. of Bars] [Cue Length]

`103` `17` `0` m `39` s

B

Cue Length

[Beats/Min.] [No. of Bars] [Cue Length]

`61` `27.20` `1` m `47` s

C

MetroGnome Settings

◉ 24 frames-per-second film format
○ 16 frames-per-second film format

○ Soft   ◉ Downbeat accent
◉ Loud   ○ No downbeat accent

BEATS PER MEASURE:

○ 2   ○ 3   ◉ 4   ○ 5   ○ 6   ○ 12   ○ `⬚`

[OK] [Cancel]

Figure 26-38: Summit Software's shareware MetroGnome program does just about everything you'll ever need for calculating frame clicks, cue lengths, and BPM. Also, it's a bonafide metronome that can provide a click out of the Macintosh speaker (with accented downbeats) in any meter. You can even tap a tempo and have MetroGnome figure out the tempo in both BPM and frame clicks (it does this by averaging seven clicks of the mouse on the Tap button). **(A)** The main window lets you choose between preset metronome markings or type any value in either the Beats Per Minute or Frame Count boxes (the other value is computed automatically). You can use the >>>> and <<<< buttons to increase or decrease the tempo gradually. **(B)** You can open as many Cue Length dialog boxes as you like. These compute the tempo, number of bars, or cue length in minutes and seconds, depending upon which box you leave empty and which two boxes you fill in. **(C)** This MetroGnome Settings dialog box lets you set the frame rate, audible click characteristics, and meter.

Figure 26-39: Using a sequencer's markers options as a time code calculator (Performer's Markers window is pictured). **(A-1)**, **(A-2)**, **(A-3)**, **(A-4)** Some calculations can be accomplished in the Change Tempo dialog box as pictured in these first four screen shots. **(B)** If you have your cue sheet entered into Performer's Markers window, lock your markers first and then choose Display Frames and Display Measures. **(C)** Gradually change the tempo with the + and - buttons while observing the effect on the Measures column of the Markers window. In this illustration, the bullets illustrate hits that are caught close enough to be usable. **(D)** Moving the tempo slider in the other direction discloses the possibility for a different set of hits. This is the tempo that will eventually be used, so bullets have been added to marker names to indicate those that fall on a beat. While doing this it is always necessary to know the duration of two frames as expressed in ticks within the current tempo. If you want a hit to be perceived as being in sync with the picture, you should not be further away from the beat than the tick amount equivalent to two frames. Consult Table 26-1 to make these calculations. Alternatively, if your sequencer allows it (Performer does), type "00:00:00:02" in the SMPTE counter and note the number of ticks this represents in the Measures/Beats/Ticks counter.

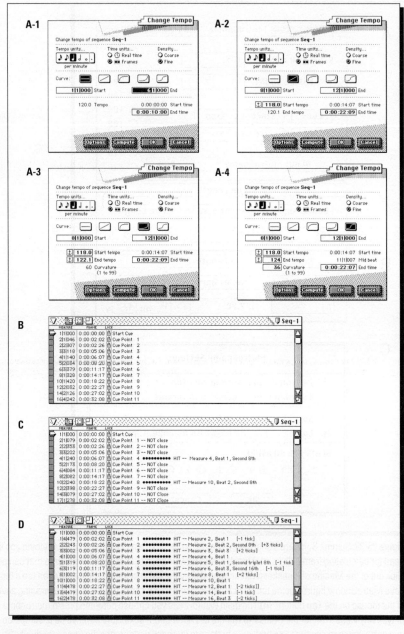

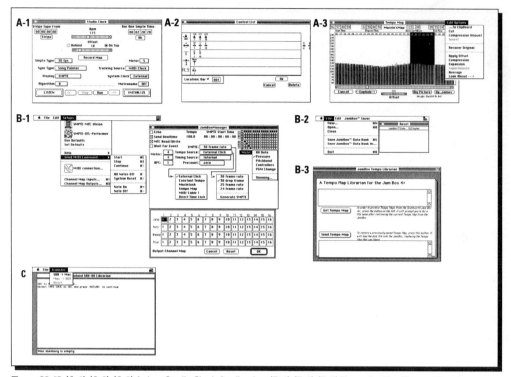

Figure 26-40: (A-1), (A-2), (A-3) Aphex Studio Clock Application. **(B-1), (B-2), (B-3)** Three JamBox Tempo Librarians. **(C)** SBX-80 Librarian.

Converting the Numbers

The first two columns of Table 26-1 convert tempos in frame clicks to BPM. The "1 beat = time" column provides the duration of one beat or click in real time measured in seconds. The "1 beat = SMPTE frames" column provides the number of SMPTE frames (at 30 fps) equivalent to one beat or click at that tempo. The last two columns indicate the num-ber of ticks (at 480 PPQN) equivalent to 1 frame and 2 frames, respectively (note that the information provided in this table is more accurate than simply doubling the "1 frame" value to get the "2 frame" value). Use the last column in conjunction with the MIDI sequencer calculation procedures.

Table 26-1: Time conversion

Clicks	BPM	1 beat = time	1 beat = SMPTE frames	1 frame = ticks	2 frames = ticks
30 - 0	48.00	1.250	37 frames, 40 bits	13	26
29 - 7	48.20	1.245	37 frames, 28 bits	13	26
29 - 6	48.40	1.240	37 frames, 15 bits	13	26
29 - 5	48.61	1.234	37 frames, 3 bits	13	26
29 - 4	48.81	1.229	36 frames, 70 bits	13	26
29 - 3	49.02	1.224	36 frames, 58 bits	13	26
29 - 2	49.23	1.219	36 frames, 45 bits	13	26
29 - 1	49.44	1.214	36 frames, 33 bits	13	26
29 - 0	49.66	1.208	36 frames, 20 bits	13	26
28 - 7	49.87	1.203	36 frames, 8 bits	13	27
28 - 6	50.09	1.198	35 frames, 75 bits	13	27
28 - 5	50.31	1.193	35 frames, 63 bits	13	27
28 - 4	50.53	1.188	35 frames, 50 bits	13	27
28 - 3	50.75	1.182	35 frames, 38 bits	14	27
28 - 2	50.97	1.177	35 frames, 25 bits	14	27
28 - 1	51.20	1.172	35 frames, 13 bits	14	27
28 - 0	51.43	1.167	35 frames, 0 bits	14	27
27 - 7	51.66	1.161	34 frames, 68 bits	14	28
27 - 6	51.89	1.156	34 frames, 55 bits	14	28
27 - 5	52.13	1.151	34 frames, 43 bits	14	28
27 - 4	52.36	1.146	34 frames, 30 bits	14	28
27 - 3	52.60	1.141	34 frames, 18 bits	14	28
27 - 2	52.84	1.135	34 frames, 5 bits	14	28
27 - 1	53.09	1.130	33 frames, 73 bits	14	28
27 - 0	53.33	1.125	33 frames, 60 bits	14	28
26 - 7	53.58	1.120	33 frames, 48 bits	14	29
26 - 6	53.83	1.115	33 frames, 35 bits	14	29
26 - 5	54.08	1.109	33 frames, 23 bits	14	29
26 - 4	54.34	1.104	33 frames, 10 bits	14	29
26 - 3	54.60	1.099	32 frames, 78 bits	15	29
26 - 2	54.86	1.094	32 frames, 65 bits	15	29
26 - 1	55.12	1.089	32 frames, 53 bits	15	29
26 - 0	55.38	1.083	32 frames, 40 bits	15	30
25 - 7	55.65	1.078	32 frames, 28 bits	15	30
25 - 6	55.92	1.073	32 frames, 15 bits	15	30
25 - 5	56.20	1.068	32 frames, 3 bits	15	30
25 - 4	56.47	1.063	31 frames, 70 bits	15	30
25 - 3	56.75	1.057	31 frames, 58 bits	15	30
25 - 2	57.03	1.052	31 frames, 45 bits	15	30
25 - 1	57.31	1.047	31 frames, 33 bits	15	31
25 - 0	57.60	1.042	31 frames, 20 bits	15	31
24 - 7	57.89	1.036	31 frames, 8 bits	15	31
24 - 6	58.18	1.031	30 frames, 75 bits	16	31
24 - 5	58.48	1.026	30 frames, 63 bits	16	31

Table 26-1: Time conversion (continued)

Clicks	BPM	1 beat = time	1 beat = SMPTE frames	1 frame = ticks	2 frames = ticks
24 - 4	58.78	1.021	30 frames, 50 bits	16	31
24 - 3	59.08	1.016	30 frames, 38 bits	16	32
24 - 2	59.38	1.010	30 frames, 25 bits	16	32
24 - 1	59.69	1.005	30 frames, 13 bits	16	32
24 - 0	60.00	1.000	30 frames, 0 bits	16	32
23 - 7	60.31	0.995	29 frames, 68 bits	16	32
23 - 6	60.63	0.990	29 frames, 55 bits	16	32
23 - 5	60.95	0.984	29 frames, 43 bits	16	33
23 - 4	61.28	0.979	29 frames, 30 bits	16	33
23 - 3	61.60	0.974	29 frames, 18 bits	16	33
23 - 2	61.94	0.969	29 frames, 5 bits	17	33
23 - 1	62.27	0.964	28 frames, 73 bits	17	33
23 - 0	62.61	0.958	28 frames, 60 bits	17	33
22 - 7	62.95	0.953	28 frames, 48 bits	17	34
22 - 6	63.30	0.948	28 frames, 35 bits	17	34
22 - 5	63.65	0.943	28 frames, 23 bits	17	34
22 - 4	64.00	0.938	28 frames, 10 bits	17	34
22 - 3	64.36	0.932	27 frames, 78 bits	17	34
22 - 2	64.72	0.927	27 frames, 65 bits	17	35
22 - 1	65.08	0.922	27 frames, 53 bits	17	35
22 - 0	65.45	0.917	27 frames, 40 bits	17	35
21 - 7	65.83	0.911	27 frames, 28 bits	18	35
21 - 6	66.21	0.906	27 frames, 15 bits	18	35
21 - 5	66.59	0.901	27 frames, 3 bits	18	36
21 - 4	66.98	0.896	26 frames, 70 bits	18	36
21 - 3	67.37	0.891	26 frames, 58 bits	18	36
21 - 2	67.76	0.885	26 frames, 45 bits	18	36
21 - 1	68.17	0.880	26 frames, 32 bits	18	36
21 - 0	68.57	0.875	26 frames, 20 bits	18	37
20 - 7	68.98	0.870	26 frames, 8 bits	18	37
20 - 6	69.40	0.865	25 frames, 75 bits	19	37
20 - 5	69.82	0.859	25 frames, 63 bits	19	37
20 - 4	70.24	0.854	25 frames, 50 bits	19	37
20 - 3	70.67	0.849	25 frames, 38 bits	19	38
20 - 2	71.11	0.844	25 frames, 25 bits	19	38
20 - 1	71.55	0.839	25 frames, 13 bits	19	38
20 - 0	72.00	0.833	25 frames, 0 bits	19	38
19 - 7	72.45	0.828	24 frames, 68 bits	19	39
19 - 6	72.91	0.823	24 frames, 55 bits	19	39
19 - 5	73.38	0.818	24 frames, 43 bits	20	39
19 - 4	73.85	0.813	24 frames, 30 bits	20	39
19 - 3	74.32	0.807	24 frames, 18 bits	20	40
19 - 2	74.81	0.802	24 frames, 5 bits	20	40
19 - 1	75.29	0.797	23 frames, 73 bits	20	40
19 - 0	75.79	0.792	23 frames, 60 bits	20	40

Table 26-1: Time conversion (continued)

Clicks	BPM	1 beat = time	1 beat = SMPTE frames	1 frame = ticks	2 frames = ticks
18 - 7	76.29	0.786	23 frames, 47 bits	20	41
18 - 6	76.80	0.781	23 frames, 35 bits	20	41
18 - 5	77.32	0.776	23 frames, 23 bits	21	41
18 - 4	77.84	0.771	23 frames, 10 bits	21	42
18 - 3	78.37	0.766	22 frames, 78 bits	21	42
18 - 2	78.90	0.760	22 frames, 65 bits	21	42
18 - 1	79.45	0.755	22 frames, 53 bits	21	42
18 - 0	80.00	0.750	22 frames, 40 bits	21	43
17 - 7	80.56	0.745	22 frames, 28 bits	21	43
17 - 6	81.13	0.740	22 frames, 15 bits	22	43
17 - 5	81.70	0.734	22 frames, 3 bits	22	44
17 - 4	82.29	0.729	21 frames, 70 bits	22	44
17 - 3	82.88	0.724	21 frames, 58 bits	22	44
17 - 2	83.48	0.719	21 frames, 45 bits	22	45
17 - 1	84.09	0.714	21 frames, 33 bits	22	45
17 - 0	84.71	0.708	21 frames, 20 bits	23	45
16 - 7	85.33	0.703	21 frames, 8 bits	23	46
16 - 6	85.97	0.698	20 frames, 75 bits	23	46
16 - 5	86.62	0.693	20 frames, 63 bits	23	46
16 - 4	87.27	0.688	20 frames, 50 bits	23	47
16 - 3	87.94	0.682	20 frames, 38 bits	23	47
16 - 2	88.62	0.677	20 frames, 25 bits	24	47
16 - 1	89.30	0.672	20 frames, 13 bits	24	48
16 - 0	90.00	0.667	20 frames, 0 bits	24	48
15 - 7	90.71	0.661	19 frames, 68 bits	24	48
15 - 6	91.43	0.656	19 frames, 55 bits	24	49
15 - 5	92.16	0.651	19 frames, 43 bits	25	49
15 - 4	92.90	0.646	19 frames, 30 bits	25	50
15 - 3	93.66	0.641	19 frames, 18 bits	25	50
15 - 2	94.43	0.635	19 frames, 5 bits	25	50
15 - 1	95.21	0.630	18 frames, 73 bits	25	51
15 - 0	96.00	0.625	18 frames, 60 bits	26	51
14 - 7	96.81	0.620	18 frames, 48 bits	26	52
14 - 6	97.63	0.615	18 frames, 35 bits	26	52
14 - 5	98.46	0.609	18 frames, 23 bits	26	53
14 - 4	99.31	0.604	18 frames, 10 bits	26	53
14 - 3	100.17	0.599	17 frames, 78 bits	27	53
14 - 2	101.05	0.594	17 frames, 65 bits	27	54
14 - 1	101.95	0.589	17 frames, 53 bits	27	54
14 - 0	102.86	0.583	17 frames, 40 bits	27	55
13 - 7	103.78	0.578	17 frames, 28 bits	28	55
13 - 6	104.73	0.573	17 frames, 15 bits	28	56
13 - 5	105.69	0.568	17 frames, 3 bits	28	56
13 - 4	106.67	0.563	16 frames, 70 bits	28	57
13 - 3	107.66	0.557	16 frames, 58 bits	29	57

Table 26-1: Time conversion (continued)

Clicks	BPM	1 beat = time	1 beat = SMPTE frames	1 frame = ticks	2 frames = ticks
13 - 2	108.68	0.552	16 frames, 45 bits	29	58
13 - 1	109.71	0.547	16 frames, 33 bits	29	59
13 - 0	110.77	0.542	16 frames, 20 bits	30	59
12 - 7	111.84	0.536	16 frames, 8 bits	30	60
12 - 6	112.94	0.531	15 frames, 75 bits	30	60
12 - 5	114.06	0.526	15 frames, 63 bits	30	61
12 - 4	115.20	0.521	15 frames, 50 bits	31	61
12 - 3	116.36	0.516	15 frames, 38 bits	31	62
12 - 2	117.55	0.510	15 frames, 25 bits	31	63
12 - 1	118.76	0.505	15 frames, 13 bits	32	63
12 - 0	120.00	0.500	15 frames, 0 bits	32	64
11 - 7	121.26	0.495	14 frames, 68 bits	32	65
11 - 6	122.55	0.490	14 frames, 55 bits	33	65
11 - 5	123.87	0.484	14 frames, 43 bits	33	66
11 - 4	125.22	0.479	14 frames, 30 bits	33	67
11 - 3	126.59	0.474	14 frames, 18 bits	34	68
11 - 2	128.00	0.469	14 frames, 5 bits	34	68
11 - 1	129.44	0.464	13 frames, 73 bits	35	69
11 - 0	130.91	0.458	13 frames, 60 bits	35	70
10 - 7	132.41	0.453	13 frames, 47 bits	35	71
10 - 6	133.95	0.448	13 frames, 35 bits	36	71
10 - 5	135.53	0.443	13 frames, 23 bits	36	72
10 - 4	137.14	0.438	13 frames, 10 bits	37	73
10 - 3	138.80	0.432	12 frames, 78 bits	37	74
10 - 2	140.49	0.427	12 frames, 65 bits	37	75
10 - 1	142.22	0.422	12 frames, 53 bits	38	76
10 - 0	144.00	0.417	12 frames, 40 bits	38	77
9 - 7	145.82	0.411	12 frames, 28 bits	39	78
9 - 6	147.69	0.406	12 frames, 15 bits	39	79
9 - 5	149.61	0.401	12 frames, 3 bits	40	80
9 - 4	151.58	0.396	11 frames, 70 bits	40	81
9 - 3	153.60	0.391	11 frames, 58 bits	41	82
9 - 2	155.68	0.385	11 frames, 45 bits	42	83
9 - 1	157.81	0.380	11 frames, 33 bits	42	84
9 - 0	160.00	0.375	11 frames, 20 bits	43	85
8 - 7	162.25	0.370	11 frames, 8 bits	43	87
8 - 6	164.57	0.365	10 frames, 75 bits	44	88
8 - 5	166.96	0.359	10 frames, 63 bits	45	89
8 - 4	169.41	0.354	10 frames, 50 bits	45	90
8 - 3	171.94	0.349	10 frames, 38 bits	46	92
8 - 2	174.55	0.344	10 frames, 25 bits	47	93
8 - 1	177.23	0.339	10 frames, 13 bits	47	95
8 - 0	180.00	0.333	10 frames, 0 bits	48	96
7 - 7	182.86	0.328	9 frames, 68 bits	49	98
7 - 6	185.81	0.323	9 frames, 55 bits	50	99

Table 26-1: Time conversion (continued)

Clicks	BPM	1 beat = time	1 beat = SMPTE frames	1 frame = ticks	2 frames = ticks
7 - 5	188.85	0.318	9 frames, 43 bits	50	101
7 - 4	192.00	0.313	9 frames, 30 bits	51	102
7 - 3	195.25	0.307	9 frames, 18 bits	52	104
7 - 2	198.62	0.302	9 frames, 5 bits	53	106
7 - 1	202.11	0.297	8 frames, 73 bits	54	108
7 - 0	205.71	0.292	8 frames, 60 bits	55	110
6 - 7	209.45	0.286	8 frames, 48 bits	56	112
6 - 6	213.33	0.281	8 frames, 35 bits	57	114
6 - 5	217.36	0.276	8 frames, 23 bits	58	116
6 - 4	221.54	0.271	8 frames, 10 bits	59	118
6 - 3	225.88	0.266	7 frames, 78 bits	60	120
6 - 2	230.40	0.260	7 frames, 65 bits	61	123
6 - 1	235.10	0.255	7 frames, 53 bits	63	125
6 - 0	240.00	0.250	7 frames, 40 bits	64	128

Summary

✔ Synchronization refers to the controlled alignment of two time-based media such as the flow of MIDI data and audio or video tape. It can also refer to individual events that occur at exactly the same point in time. Synchronization errors are noticeable as soon as events are as little as two or three frames out of sync.

✔ There are three approaches to synchronization: pulse or clock sync (including TTL sync and DIN sync — often employing FSK for data transmission), relative addressing (including SPP sync and MIDI sync — often employing smart FSK for data transmission), and absolute addressing or time code (including LTC and VITC, SMPTE Time Code, DTL, DTLe, and MTC).

✔ Until the advent of MTC, timing information used by MIDI for synchronization consisted of keeping track of elapsed measures with a resolution of 24 PPQN (SPP and MIDI Clock type synchronization).

✔ The film and video industry uses an absolute addressing timing protocol known as SMPTE Time Code. This protocol has been adopted as a standard for synchronizing film and video devices as well as for "locking together" (synchronizing by way of a hardware synchronizer) two or more devices to function as one large machine. SMPTE can keep track of timing locations in hours, minutes, frames, and subframes (30 frames per second with 80 subframes per frame).

✔ Unfortunately, SMPTE is not directly compatible with MIDI. The two systems were developed for different reasons: MIDI for the communication of performance information and SMPTE for the communication of timing information. Furthermore, their transmission formats are incompatible. SMPTE is an analog audio signal and MTC is a digital data stream. Nonetheless, they are required to communicate with one another. Synchronization boxes exist to convert SMPTE Time Code to SPP, MTC, DTL, DTLe, or other timing references. They allow software MIDI devices to be synchronized with hardware SMPTE devices, for example. This permits a MIDI sequencer running on the Macintosh to advance or rewind to the exact spots in a sequence file that correspond to appropriate spots on a video tape or an analog tape recorder. On a local level, this translates into the precise simultaneity of a video hit-point with the appropriate musical event.

✔ Human-triggered synchronization is related to pulse sync in that a trigger event is required before every next note advance. The difference is that a human rather than a 24-PPQN pulse provides the trigger. Tap Tempo is a feature found in many MIDI sequencers. Typically, this involves specifying the MIDI event (usually a note) that you will tap to advance the sequence one beat. You can even record this tapped performance as the tempo track in many sequencers.

✔ Apple's MIDI Manager (see Chapter 8) provides extensive synchronization features for programs that are compatible with it (most are). When you are running multiple MIDI applications in either 6.x's MultiFinder or System 7, connecting the time ports of the various programs (called clients) to the Apple MIDI Driver's time port guarantees that they are all synchronized to a single clock reference.

Part Eight
Multimedia

Part Eight

Foreword

by Marc Canter

Multimedia

As the multimedia world grows, the rise of desktop-based creativity offers several outlooks and perspectives. Most business-oriented users don't really care about music or MIDI or even sound, but they do need to get their message across as timely and inexpensively as possible.

These are really the issues that are driving multimedia. Making money is what it's all about, and businesses around the world are starting to realize that by using sound, visuals, and interactivity, they can communicate and sell better. Most business people would prefer not to worry about aesthetics, or production quality, or even if the music starts on the beat or is in tune. Because most PCs do not have sound, most current PC software does not even deal with the possibilities of using sound in business.

All this affects the PC industry, as companies like Compaq and Tandy are trying to figure out how to equal or surpass the Macintosh by using the "multimedia thing" as a value-added feature. Of course they're missing the whole point, but that's their problem.

The Macintosh does have sound, but that doesn't mean that anyone uses sound for much more than beeps and warning messages. Professional musicians scoff at the Macintosh's 8-bit sound quality and say, "That's not really sound." But I believe something is better than nothing.

Enter the new era of multimedia. The beginning of a new stage when computer users are given all of the functionality and power they need to edit digital video, compose synthetic symphonies, and synchronize and index information into a true hypermedia web.

It has taken many years and it will be many more years before any of this multimedia technology makes it into the standard feature set of the Macintosh (or any other PC). In the meantime, all of this creativity "stuff" is left in the hands of the creative community to explore, invent, and push the envelope of what can be done today on desktop-based systems. To say that "what was available on a mainframe or Synclavier yesterday, will be available on my Macintosh tomorrow" is a cliché, but I believe that's exactly how it works.

Workstation-based technology has made it possible to develop high-speed networking, image processing, and audio synthesis and processing. Now that the algorithms and technology are understood, all it takes is an entrepreneur (like Peter Gotcher, Dave Oppenheim, or myself) to get that technology onto the Macintosh.

Then once it's available at a reasonable price (like less than that of a car), the most beautiful thing happens — artists and musicians start to discover a new art form, something that is not limited by the categories of musicians or artists, something that transcends a paint brush or trumpet, something that merges all of the data types and insights of all knowledge into a comprehensive multimedia artform.

This new artform is based on having music and sound as an intrinsic part of the experience. I used to give speeches in which I would stop talking in the middle of a sentence and only mouth the words to illustrate the difference sound makes in our lives.

Once voice annotation, on-line video help, and interactive rock videos become better known and understood, we will never be able to go back to a world without sound. Once we've developed all of the necessary software and hardware for digitizing, editing, and manipulating sound, we can get on with the real business, which is developing multimedia content software.

The software industry is analogous to the fashion industry. What we've got in the software business today are tools — sewing machines and scissors in the fashion industry. Now compare the amount of money made from selling sewing machines and scissors to the entire clothes, fashion, and garment business. That's how big multimedia content will be.

Once we've overcome the problem of floppy disks (or CD-ROMs) not working on every machine (which is like a cassette tape only working on a certain vendor's cassette deck), we'll be ready for the content revolution. And sound, MIDI, and music will be an important element of that revolution. ♩

Marc Canter is the founder of MacroMind, Inc. as well as a multimedia visionary.

Introduction to Part Eight

Much music created on the Macintosh these days eventually ends up as an integral element of a multimedia production. In fact, the Macintosh is largely responsible for bringing the concept of multimedia to the masses.

Multimedia is nothing new. The concept has roots in opera, ballet, and theater of the 19th century and earlier. Wagner's *Gesamtkunstwerk*, outlined in his *Das Kunstwerk der Zukunft* (The Art Work of the Future, 1849), provides an early description of what has come to be known as multimedia — the uniting of all the arts (including music, visuals, poetry, text, and drama) into a single entity.

Early multimedia endeavors of historical significance include Scriabin's *Poem of Fire* (1910), works of the Dadaists in the 1910s, and collaborations involving Erik Satie in the 1920s. The principles of interactivity, audience participation, and random access in multimedia are present in many of the works of John Cage, David Tudor, George Rauschenberg, and Merce Cunningham in the early 1950s. Edgar Varese's *Poème Electronique* (1958) is an early multimedia work of large proportions surpassing many multiscreen computer presentations of this decade. In 1959, Allan Kaprow coined the word "happening," a term that inspired another generation of multimedia artists.

Quite a few works touted as multimedia these days could easily be transferred to film or videotape and suddenly lose their "multimediainess." What distinguishes current-generation multimedia from traditional film or television is the delivery platform (a computer), distribution channels (disks, files, CD-ROMs), non-linearity (random access), and interactivity (known as audience participation in previous decades).

A major factor causing multimedia to emerge as a discrete class of human enterprise is that a single tool can now serve all the participating art forms. In days gone by, painters, photographers, videographers, animators, musicians, and writers all used different instruments to practice their crafts — now many use the same device: a Macintosh. This fact alone is significant. When many people trained in one art form find out that they can use the same tool in another art form, they discover avenues to realize otherwise untappable creative ideas. While there was no way for Van Gogh to make music with a paintbrush, computer artists and musicians using the Macintosh employ user interfaces and manipulative controls that are often identical or, at the very least, analogous. The logical outgrowth of this phenomenon has been the development of "authoring" software capable of dealing with multiple data types — text, graphics, video, animations, sound, and music.

In 1987, Apple's HyperCard kicked off the current multimedia movement. Because it is free, uses stacks of cards as a metaphor, can be programmed in a language resembling English, and supports standard, familiar painting tools, sound, and flipbook-style animation, it stimulated much early do-it-yourself-style multimedia. External device control (videodiscs, CD-ROMs, and so on) was added to HyperCard almost immediately. Although MacroMind's VideoWorks Interactive (eventually released as Director) was available to developers prior to HyperCard, HyperCard was the first multimedia authoring environment to be distributed on a large scale.

Multimedia authoring programs are now proliferating faster than word processors. These tools automate the integration and synchronization of visuals and sound, usually supporting multiple formats of both media. In many such environments, user interactivity is a high priority, and the options that allow you to add interactivity to multimedia productions are rapidly becoming as easy to use as home video cameras.

You don't have to be a professional musician to work with any of these tools. In fact, you don't even have to be a musician. Anyone creating multimedia can greatly enhance their endeavors in this area through any of the tools described on the following pages. Most of the current multimedia platforms are compatible with digital audio and MIDI. These include HyperCard, SuperCard, and Director. HyperCard and SuperCard can be used to drive simultaneous playback of audio and video. Director can play interactive movies scored with either 16-bit stereo 'snd ' resources or disk-based soundfiles. The RAM overhead in the case of the 16-bit, 44.1 KHz Audiomedia card is a mere 50K! Now with Opcode's MIDIplay or EarLevel Engineering's HyperMIDI, you can combine digital audio and MIDI together in HyperCard, SuperCard, or Director with a considerable degree of flexibility.

Chapter 27

Music for Multimedia

In this chapter ...

✔ Comparing multimedia authoring environments.

✔ Tips for digital audio and MIDI in multimedia.

✔ Synchronizing music to visuals in multimedia.

✔ Multimedia legal issues and copyright law.

✔ Clip music as MIDI data, 8- and 16-bit soundfiles, and digital audio.

✔ Multimedia in action: interactive training and interactive magazines.

✔ Interview with Verbum Interactive programmer Michel Kripalani.

Making Music For All the Senses

Unless you have lived on a desert island for the last few years, you've probably heard the word "multimedia" more than you'd like to. In the context of computer technology, the "M" word has come to imply a combination of two or more types of information that can be placed under computer control: static graphics, animation, full-motion video, music, sound effects, speech, and text. In the real world, multimedia performances can bring in other sensory stimuli such as touch and smell. For example, in an opera (perhaps the ultimate form of non-computer-based multimedia expression), it is not uncommon for odors to be projected into the audience. Sensurround and similar audio techniques can bring a certain tactile element to the viewer of a film.

Early computer-based multimedia endeavors were linearly organized as video-taped animations. At the very most, you could pause and continue the presentation. Although some still continue this tradition, today, multimedia usually implies a greater degree of interactivity. This evolution from static multimedia to interactive multimedia (sometimes called hypermedia — see Chapter 29, "New Forms of Interactive Education") parallels the growth of evolution of interactive composition (see Chapter 19, "Interactive Composition and Intelligent Instruments"). Similar factors engendered this development, mainly the fact that computers can manage multiple data streams simultaneously and still keep track of and respond to user input.

The Macintosh is, without contest, the most popular platform for multimedia. All multimedia presentations have a more memorable impact when they include music. You can use music as a navigational aid, providing audio cues for the people viewing your project, just as different visual backgrounds or color schemes help keep them oriented to their current location in non-linear interactive environments.

Music for multimedia presents abundant opportunities for Macintosh musicians. In particular, growing concern with copyright issues mean that more original music is needed in this medium. There are three kinds of musical data used in multimedia: MIDI, 8-bit digital audio, and 16-bit digital audio. Music in any of these data formats can reside on the Macintosh or exist in an external device that is triggered by a multimedia document.

Multimedia authoring tools make it so easy to realize creative ideas that many Macintosh musicians are dabbling quite seriously in the non-musical elements as well — the visual content and interactive programming. Two excellent examples of this phenomenon are found on the Verbum Interactive CD-ROM: *Gaya's Eyes* by Ty Roberts and Todd Rundgren and *Living Photos* by Rand Wetherwax and Graham Nash.

This chapter addresses some of the real issues and techniques that you are confronted with when you combine music with multimedia authoring.

Authoring Environments

Creating multimedia with a Macintosh is not difficult. Authoring environments automate many of the tasks that would otherwise require extensive programming knowledge. Although multimedia authoring is relatively simple, multimedia content is an area where creativity and original ideas are valuable. Like any other area of creative endeavor, all the Macintoshes in the world are not going to help unless you start with some ideas.

This chapter examines seven popular authoring environments for multimedia: Authorware Professional, Director, HyperCard, MediaMaker, MediaTracks, Serius, and SuperCard.

Each of these seven environments has a different focus. They range from simple slide show presentation to general-purpose programming, in which multimedia is simply another application. In Table 27-1, transport interactivity refers to options that merely support play, stop, pause, skip, and possibly jump-to-destination. Some of the features supported by the software require additional hardware. Video and 16-bit digital audio are examples of these.

In Table 27-1, the XCMD-compatibility is extremely important. Software that supports XCMDs has a host of other add-on features available from third-party XCMD and XFCN developers. There are XCMDs that provide for MIDI for accessing digital audio NuBus cards, CD-ROM control (and therefore CD audio playback control — see Chapter 29), video-disc control, and control over any serial device imaginable. Even DAT decks can be serially controlled. Panasonic's P-2 HyperCard XCMD kit provides for remote control of their popular SV-3900 DAT deck. So if a feature listed on the table seems to be missing from a program's built-in functions, check to see if the program offers XCMD support. Chances are that if it does, many of the missing features can be added by way of third-party extensions.

The ability to create stand-alone (double-clickable) applications may be important to you if you are going to distribute your multimedia projects. All the authoring environments (except Serius) that offer this option accomplish it by merging a runtime version of their development system with your document. Runtime engines contain only the routines needed for playing back a document — the program code that lets you create the document has been stripped out. This can add considerable size to the stand-alone application. Usually you can use a resource editor to open up the merged file and remove any resources that aren't required by your document (runtime engines have to include every piece of code necessary to accommodate any type of document that their associated development program can produce, so usually there is a considerable amount of kilobytes that you can recover).

Alternatively, you can simply distribute your document along with the runtime engine. The disadvantage of this approach is that you lose control of whether or not the two files travel together once they are in the end-user's hands. Furthermore, if you distribute a document that has not been merged with its runtime engine, all your careful scripting, music, and graphic content can easily be ripped off.

Table 27-1: Authoring environment comparison

	Author-ware	Director	Hyper-Card	Media-Maker	Media-Tracks	Serius	Super-Card
Price							
List or development version	8,000	1,000	200	700	300	300	300
Special offers or versions	1,000		①		500	500	
Capabilities							
Slide show	●	●	●	●	▸	●	●
Screen recording					○		
Black & white animation	●	○	▸	②	②	●	▸②
Color animation	▸	○		▸		●	▸
Video	●	●		○		▸	
Integration of data types	●	●	▸	○	●	●	●
Transport interactivity	●	●	●	▸	●	●	●

Table 27-1: Authoring environment comparison (continued)

	Author-ware	Director	Hyper-Card	Media-Maker	Media-Tracks	Serius	Super-Card
Capabilities (continued)							
Full interactivity	◑	◑	●			●	●
General-purpose programming	▸	▸	●			◑	●
Multimedia Applications							
Corporate presentations	●	◑	▸	◑			▸
Courseware and CAI	◑	▸	●	▸		●	●
Product training/demos	●	◑	●	●	◑	▸	●
Multimedia artistic creation	▸	◑	▸	●			▸
Information navigation	●	●	◑			●	◑
Sound							
'snd' resource	▸	●	●	●	●	●	●
AIFF	▸	●		●	●		
SoundEdit	●	●		●	●		●
SoundWave	●	●					
SoundCap		●					
16-bit digital audio card		●					
Multichannel sound		●					
Compressed sound		●	●	●	●		●
Play sound from disk		●					
Sound during file loading	●	●		●	●		
Built-in recording	▸			●	●		
Change playback speed	●	▸	●				●
Loop (unlimited) control within program	●	▸	●	●			●
Loop (specific # repetitions) control within program	●		●				●
MIDI		▸					
Graphics							
Import bitmapped graphics	●	●	●	●	●	●	●
Import object graphics (PICT and/or PICT2)	●	▸	▸	●	●	●	●
Built-in bitmapped graphics editor	▸	●	●	▸		●	●
Built-in object graphics editor	▸	▸			●	●	▸
8-bit color	●	●	▸	●	▸	●	●
24-bit color	●	●	▸	●		●	
32-bit QuickDraw	●	●					
Import Glue file		▸					
Import TIFF		●					●
Import RIB (3-D)		●					
Import PICS	●	●		●			
Import Director movie		●		●			
QuickTime support		●					
External Control							
CD-ROM	●	●		●		●	
Videodisc	●	●		●			
Serial VCR		●		●			
Other serial control		●		●			

Table 27-1: Authoring environment comparison (continued)

	Author-ware	Director	Hyper-Card	Media-Maker	Media-Tracks	Serius	Super-Card
Programming							
Scripting language		●	●		◗		●
Icon/visual programming	●					●	
Menu/dialog box-driven	◗	◗		●	●		
"Flip-book" animation	●	●	●	●		●	●
Script-controlled animation	●	●	◗			◗	
Icon/picon sequencing		●		●	●		
Script-controlled sound	◗	●	●				●
Create buttons	●	●	●		●	●	●
Create menus	●	●	●			●	●
Create dialog boxes	◗	◗	◗			●	◗
Create user fields	●	●	●			●	●
Link multiple files	●	●	●				●
Built-in debugger	●	●	●				●
Conditional branching	●	●	●			●	●
Supports randomness	●	●	●			●	●
Miscellaneous							
Create standalones	●	●			●	●	●
XCMD-compatible	●	●	●			●	●
Control from XCMD-compatible software		●			●		
Read/write files to disk	●	●	●			●	●
Print text options	●	●	●			●	●
Generate program documentation	●						
Microsoft Windows 3.0 support	●	●					

① = HyperCard (without complete manuals) comes with every Macintosh. Type "magic" (and return) into the message box while on the last card of the Home stack to activate HyperCard's complete feature set.
② = Import and playback Director movie or PICS document may require an XCMD.

Any of the seven authoring programs can be enhanced by adding software dedicated to specific tasks. Examples include soundfile editing (MacroMind's SoundEdit [formerly from Farallon], Digidesign's Sound Designer and Audiomedia, Passport's Alchemy and Sound Apprentice), color graphics editing (SuperMac's PixelPaint and PixelPaint Professional, Adobe PhotoShop, Fractal's ColorStudio), 3-D modeling and rendering (Dynaware's Dyna Perspective, MacroMind 3D, Strata's StrataVision, and Paracomp's Swivel 3D), rendering (Pixar's MacRenderMan and Swivel's SwivelMan, a bundling of Swivel 3D Pro with RenderMan that provides for background rendering), animation (Vividus's Cinemation, Motion Works's AddMotion Pro, Linker's Animation Stand, MacroMind-Paracomp's FilmMaker and Magic, and Electric Image's ElectricImage).

Authorware Professional

MacroMind-Paracomp's Authorware Professional ($8,000, or $1,000 for an educators' version that lacks sound, animation, video control, and color) is an icon-oriented programming language optimized for interactive multimedia and courseware development (see Figure 27-1). Programming is as simple as dragging icons out from a palette onto the screen. If you have an aversion to text-based programming, even in the pseudo-English format that multimedia scripting usually allows, an icon-oriented system like Authorware might be the solution.

Authorware requires only eleven icons for programming:

Display icons. Display text and/or graphics on the screen.

Animation icons. Move objects that have been displayed by a Display icon along a path you define, at varying rates of speed, or in a specified duration.

Erase icons. Erase text, graphics, or interactive elements.

Wait icons. Pause the program flow until the user presses a key or the mouse button, or for a specified period of time.

Decision icons. Select icon path at which to continue program flow, based upon random, sequential, or *nth* considerations.

Interactive icons. Present and evaluate user interface items such as fields, buttons, menus, keypresses, movable objects, or "hot" (click/touch) areas.

Calculation icons. Perform calculations, manipulate data, process XCMDs and XFCNs, and read and write files.

Map icons. Allow you to collapse an entire program into a single module that can be double-clicked to display its original icon flow. You can nest Map icons within Map icons as deep as you want. By not providing for scrolling in the icon windows, Authorware encourages modularity through logical use of Map icons.

Sound icons. Provide for sound playback of eight-bit sampled soundfiles in SoundWave or SoundEdit formats (see Figure 27-2).

Movie icons. Allow playing "flipbook" style animations created in Authorware's Movie Editor or imported as a PICS file. Authorware provides for control of start and stop frames, playback speed, looped playback, concurrent playback (playback continues while the rest of the program continues to execute), perpetual (conditional) playback (playback responds to variables passed to it through user interaction), and three ink effects (transparent, opaque, and reverse). Movies can also be placed under the control of Animation icons, so that they play back along paths described by that icon.

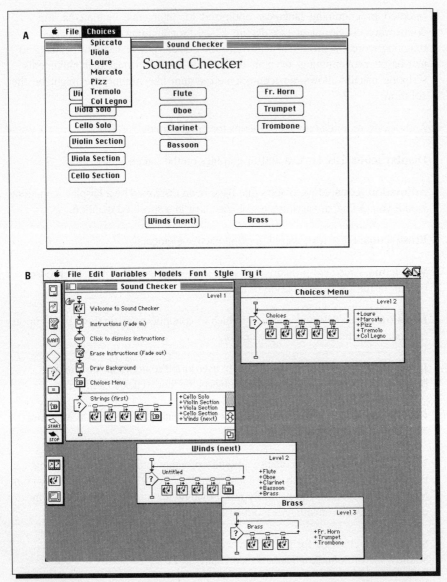

Figure 27-1: (A) Using sound in Authorware. It took about 15 minutes to create this program and save it as a stand-alone application. **(B)** The main development screen of Authorware Professional. Program flow is downward and from left to right. You can follow the icons to see what this application does. When you launch the program (called Sound Checker), an introductory sound plays and instructions fade in on the screen. The Wait icon waits until you click the mouse, at which point the instructions fade out and the background for the main screen is displayed. Next, a menu called Choices is displayed in the menu bar (the File menu is automatically generated). The Choices menu has been modularized into a Map icon. In this illustration, the Map icon has been double-clicked to show its internal workings. Separate soundfiles are associated with each menu item. A series of buttons is displayed by the first Decision icon. Each button except the last has a Sound icon attached to it, indicating that clicking the button will trigger a specific soundfile. Imbedded in this Decision icon is another Map icon, which includes its own Decision icon and yet another Map icon. Both of these additional Map icons have been expanded to show their internal program flow.

Figure 27-2: Double-clicking a Sound icon lets you set the playback parameters of an individual soundfile by way of this dialog box. Three types of playback are accessible from the pop-up menu pictured. Wait until done suspends the execution of your file until the soundfile plays through the specified number of times. Concurrent playback instructs Authorware to continue with the execution of your file during playback. Perpetual playback puts the soundfile in a perpetual state of readiness to be played under the control of conditions that you enter in the Start playing when TRUE and until condition is TRUE fields. Typically, you enter a variable or expression in these fields, and user interaction causes this variable or expression to evaluate as true or false, triggering or halting playback accordingly. The Speed field may also be a variable if you like, allowing you to alter playback speed in response to user events. Clicking the Edit button causes you to jump directly into the SoundWave program with the current soundfile loaded and ready for editing. Subsequently, quitting from SoundWave returns you to your Authorware document at the point where you exited it.

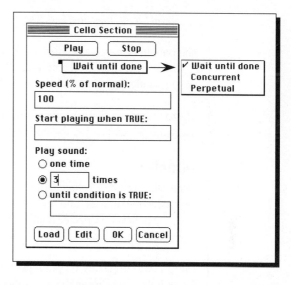

Video icons. Control videodisc players. Let you designate start and end frames, speed of playback, and which audio channels to play back. Let you place these parameters under the conditional control of variables passed to the icon by user interaction.

A Productivity Library is included with the package. This functions as a powerful database of all the types of files that Authorware can handle: soundfiles, movie files, text files, Microsoft Word files, PICT files, and the various types of Authorware documents themselves.

The Authorware package includes a MacRecorder and a library of soundfiles. In place of MacRecorder's SoundEdit software, Authorware has SoundWave. SoundWave is described in detail in Chapter 10. The Sound icon can play back uncompressed sounds saved in either SoundWave or SoundEdit format. You must convert AIFF files and 'snd' resources to one of these formats before they can be used by Authorware.

Authorware does not play files directly from disk, unless you install one of the XCMDs that provide for this (described in Chapters 10 and 15). Soundfiles must fit into available RAM. With longer soundfiles it may be desirable to preload a soundfile into RAM prior to its playback (this technique was discussed in relation to HyperCard in Chapter 15, "Making Music without MIDI"). You use the following syntax for this purpose:

beat[1 to 4], measure[1 to 1023]   `Preload(IconID@"`*icon title*`")`

The only information you have to provide is the icon title. Authorware's built-in IconID system variable is automatically set to the ID of the icon (a sound in this case) specified by the icon title.

Macworld Interactive was created with Authorware. This CD-ROM version of the magazine is examined at the end of this chapter.

Director

MacroMind Director is the leading tool for creating multimedia presentations, interactive multimedia, and animations of impeccably high standards. The software has no parallels for artistic creation and seamlessly integrates the various data types that can be placed under Macintosh control.

Director was originally programmed by Jay Fenton, who nurtured the program through its former incarnations as VideoWorks, VideoWorks Interactive, and VideoWorks II. You may recall from Chapter 1, "Background," that Jay Fenton also programmed the first music software for the Macintosh (MusicWorks). Before Jay brought us these tools that started the Macintosh music and multimedia revolution he created such video games as Gorf (but that's another story).

Since day one, most of Apple's Guided Tours have been created with Director's earlier incarnations (as well as most guided tours for other software packages). Now some guided tours are created with MediaTracks because of the speed of development time (at the sacrifice of full interactivity and other bells and whistles).

Director offers numerous features for manipulating all types of media. The Paint window is a full-featured color painting program. The animation options automate in-betweening (the automatic generation of intermediary frames between two frames at different locations or transformations) and similar repetitive tasks, so that you can work very quickly — you can almost take an improvisational approach to animation. Creation of animation uses a score metaphor that makes the software particularly easy for musicians to deal with. In fact, every musician I have observed getting into Director has become an expert in record time. Finally, the English-like scripting language, *Lingo*, is very similar to HyperTalk and in many ways surpasses HyperTalk's functionality.

The following discussion, in deference to the fact that this book is dedicated to sound and musical applications of the Macintosh, focuses on those features in Director. To discuss the rest of Director's multimedia options in detail would require a book as long as this one. The program's three manuals, which are very concise and to the point, exceed a thousand pages.

Sound in Director

Director supports eight types of sounds:

Control of the Macintosh synthesizer. There are about 80 built-in sounds, music, and effects. There is also an option to "synergistically interface" sound with the animation, in which case the position and motion of a specific sprite (animated object) affects the pitch and/or tone-quality of the sound attached to it.

Soundfiles can be castmembers. These can be imported or pasted into castmembers and are stored with the document.

External soundfiles. Up to 128 sounds can reside in an external soundfile created by the Sound Utility. These are loaded into RAM when the document requires them.

Disk-based AIFFs. Any AIFF can be played directly from disk.

CD audio control. Complete control of an audio-equipped CD-ROM player.

Play sound via NuBus card. This requires a Digidesign Sound Accelerator or Audiomedia card.

MIDI. Director provides a basic set of commands for SPP control of a sequencer or drum machine. Because Director is MIDI-Manager-compatible, the sequencer can reside on the same Macintosh as Director. You can also import MIDI XCMDs into Director for greater MIDI flexibility.

Speech. Director offers full interactive support of Macintalk for synthesized speech generated from ASCII text.

Sounds and MIDI can be added to multimedia presentations in three ways:

❖ Manipulated as icons in the Overview section of Director.
❖ Assigned to one or both sound channels in the Score window of the Studio section of Director.
❖ Controlled from Director's scripting language, Lingo, in which case up to eight channels of sound can be accessed simultaneously.

Using certain types of sound requires some preparation. For example, control of a digital audio NuBus card requires installation of the proper resources by Digidesign's Sound Installer utility (see Figure 27-3). Setting up a Sounds file for storage of eight-bit sounds external to Director requires MacroMind's Sound Utility (included with the program).

Figure 27-3:
Creating a
Sounds file for
storing up to
128 sounds
that will be
accessible
to Director
movies.
(A) Here you
pick one of the
hierarchical
menus of
Director's
Sound menu
with which you
want the
current sound
to appear.
(B) This sub-
sequent dialog
box lets you
load up to 16
soundfiles that
will appear as

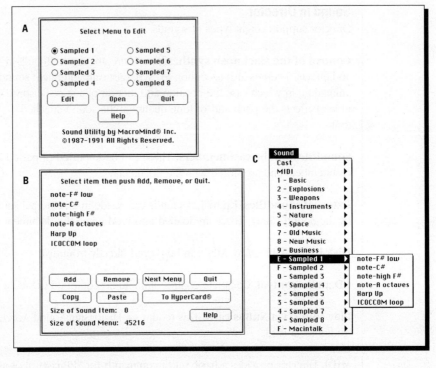

hierarchical menu items associated with the top level menu item selected in A. **(C)** Afterward, the sounds you have
installed in the Sounds file (which you specify as the default Sounds file for a movie or movies) appear in this menu.

Sound in Overview

Director has two authoring environments: Overview and Studio. Overview lets you
manipulate multimedia elements as icons and quickly assemble presentations.
Separate icons are available for Paint documents, PICT documents, Glue documents, Director movies, Accelerator movies (Director movies accelerated with
MacroMind's Accelerator software), auto-animated documents, sounds, pauses, and
transitions (see Figure 27-4). You can nest additional Overview documents within
each other.

Sound, MIDI, and CD control in Studio

You will do your most serious multimedia work in Studio. This is where you
can access the hundreds of Lingo commands that allow you to instill sophisticated interactivity into a Director document. Here you also have additional
options for sound (see Figure 27-5). You can install sounds into castmembers
and write Lingo macros to play disk-based files, 16-bit NuBus card soundfiles,
and MIDI.

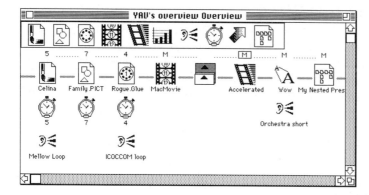

Figure 27-4: Sound in Overview. Adding a sound to an Overview document is as simple as dragging a soundfile icon from the palette at the top of the window. Sounds can be assigned to the icon by selecting the icon and then choosing a sound from the Sound menu. Note that Sound icons can be placed under other icons, so that they accompany the visual element described by the upper icon (as pictured). Director Movie icons may have their own set of embedded sounds.

Figure 27-5: Sound and MIDI in Studio. The Finale Tour Score window provides a spreadsheet-like display of your multimedia presentation. Vertical columns are equivalent to frames. At the bottom are 24 animation channels, each of which can be dedicated to a different animated or static castmember. Immediately above the animation channels are the effects channels: a script channel (for the entire frame — individual sprites may have associated scripts as well), two sound channels, a transition channel, palette channel, and tempo channel. The two sound channels can play independent sounds, for example, background music and voice-over. To the right of the Score Script window, you can see MIDI commands that initiate and synchronize playback of a sequence running in another MIDI Manager-compatible application. The Text window stores macros that you can link to the Script channel or to individual sprites in the animation channels. Here are the macros that are attached to the transport buttons on the stage. Clicking the transport buttons controls a CD

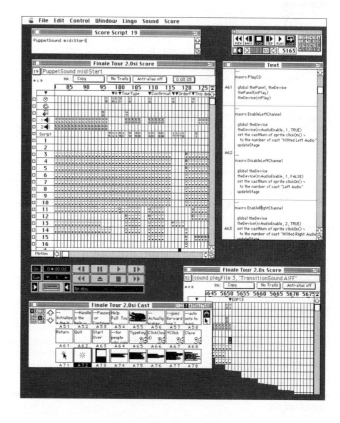

being played in an audio-equipped CD-ROM drive. Note the script assigned to the last frame of this movie in the Finale Tour Score window at the bottom right. The soundfile triggered by this script, a disk-based AIFF in this case, plays while the next movie is being loaded. 7 o'clock: The Finale Tour Cast window is like a database of graphics, soundfiles, palettes, and scripts. Here you can see a number of soundfiles that have been imported as castmembers. These get stored with the Director document (rather than in an external Sounds file), so they can increase the size of your document significantly. Unlike sounds in the Sounds file, castmember sounds are only accessible to the document in which they reside.

Controlling sound with Lingo

The option to control sound from Lingo just like you can control any other multimedia element is one of Director's strong points. Among other things, this provides random access to sounds that can be linked to user interactivity. You can also create fade ins and fade outs and change the volume if you place sounds under Lingo script control. You can even trigger sounds randomly whenever you want using Director's Random function. Finally, it is the only way to access more than two channels of sound simultaneously. All the Lingo commands and functions that relate to sound and MIDI playback are described in Tables 27-2, 27-3 and 27-4.

Table 27-2: Lingo sound syntax table

puppetSound

(Command) Causes the Sound channel to act as a puppet so that it can be controlled by Lingo (under script control). It is not necessary to place anything in the Sound channels of the score. In fact, puppetSounds override sounds that may simultaneously exist in the score's Sound channel. They continue to play even if you load another movie. At the time of this writing, the puppetSound command does not work with the second Sound channel (i.e., the lower of the Score's Sound channels).

puppetSound *castmemberName*

Starts playing a sound stored in the Cast. Note: To use AIFF soundfiles as castmembers requires System 6.0.7 or later.

puppetSound *menuItemNumber, subMenuItemNumber*

Starts playing a sound stored in an external Director Sounds file. Specify the menu item number (if it is a letter, use A=10, B=11, C=12, D=13, E=14, F=15) and the submenu item number.

puppetSound 0

Turns off continuous sound and returns control of sound to the score's Sound channel.

puppetSound midiOption   (see the section "MIDI in Director")

the soundEnabled

set the soundEnabled = *expression*

(Property) Turns sound on or off. Example: set the soundEnabled = not (the soundEnabled) toggles the sound on or off depending on the previous state.

put the soundEnabled into *variableName*

Returns TRUE if sound is enabled.

sound fadeIn   (requires System 6.0.7 or later)

sound fadeIn *whichChannel [1 to 8]*

Fades in sound on the specified channel for a period of frames, unless ticks (see next entry) are specified. If ticks are not specified, the default setting is 15*(60/(Tempo setting of first frame of fade in)).

sound fadeIn *whichChannel, ticks*

Fades in sound on the specified channel for the specified number of ticks (1/60 of a second).

Table 27-2: Lingo sound syntax table (continued)

sound fadeOut	(requires System 6.0.7 or later)

sound fadeOut *whichChannel [1 to 8]*

> Fades out sound on the specified channel for a period of frames, unless ticks (see next entry) are specified. If ticks are not specified, the default setting is 15*(60/(Tempo setting of first frame of fade out)).

sound fadeOut *whichChannel, ticks*

> Fades out sound on the specified channel for the specified number of ticks ($\frac{1}{60}$ of a second).

sound playFile	(requires System 6.0.7 or later)

sound playFile *whichChannel [1 to 8] whichFile [name of file in quotes]*

> Starts playback on the channel indicated by *whichChannel* of an external AIFF sound stored in *whichFile.*

sound stop	(requires System 6.0.7 or later)

sound stop *whichChannel [1 to 8]*

> Stops sound playback on the specified channel.

soundBusy	(requires System 6.0.7 or later)

soundBusy(*whichChannel*)

> (Function) Returns TRUE (1) if the specified channel is currently playing a sound, or FALSE (0) if it isn't. If you use soundBusy() to determine the status of a puppetSound, you must place an updateStage command between the puppetSound command and the soundBusy() function. Example: if soundBusy(1) then sound stop 1.

the soundLevel

set the soundLevel to 7

> (Property) Sets the level of sound playing through the Macintosh speaker or external audio jack. 0 = no sound, 7 = maximum volume.

put the soundLevel into *variableName*

> Puts the current sound level setting (0 to 7) into the specified variable.

the volume of sound	(requires System 6.0.7 or later)

set the volume of sound *whichChannel [1 to 8] to level [0 to 255]*

> Sets the volume of the sound on the specified channel (Channels 1 and 2 are the Score Sound channels) to a level between 0 and 255.

put the volume of sound *whichChannel [1 to 8] into variableName*

> Puts the volume of the sound on the specified channel (Channels 1 and 2 are the Score Sound channels) into the specified variable.

the multiSound

put the multiSound into *variableName*

> (Function) Returns TRUE (1) if the current System software is capable of multichannel sound playback, or FALSE (0) if it isn't.

Table 27-2: Lingo sound syntax table (continued)

noSound

playAccel *whichFile*, noSound

Used in conjunction with the PlayAccel command to play back an accelerated movie without any sound that may be associated with it.

Tips for sound in Director

You can allocate sound to play on either of two sound channels in the Score window. In actuality you can access all eight sound channels of the Sound Manager to play AIFF files (undocumented feature). This has to be done through Lingo and using Lingo's sound playFile command. Then indicate the Sound Manager channel (1 through 8) and then the filename (Sound PlayFile *whichChannel [1 through 8]*, *FileName*).

Long sounds will not loop if the movie loops via a Lingo GO command in the last frame of a movie and the Control Panel loop button is off. The solution is to add one more frame to the end of the movie containing the looping sound in the Sound channel.

Although you can import sounds that have been stored in a compressed SoundEdit format (3:1, 4:1, 6:1), these do not play back properly. The solution is to convert these sounds to their uncompressed format in SoundEdit before using them with Director.

If you use SoundEdit to downsample a 22 KHz sound with a loopback to an 11 KHz sound with no loopback, you will get white noise after Director plays that sound. The solution is to set a loopback for the downsampled 11 KHz sound before you save it.

There is a special Null Sound file included with Director 3.0. When you start playing sounds in one channel, and then start playing on the second channel, the sound in the first channel drops in volume by about 50 percent. The solution is to put the Null Sound in all the consecutive, empty sound channel cells preceding the second channel's sound.

When using the sound fadeIn command to fade a sound in, execute the command one frame prior to the sound's start in the Score, otherwise a short piece of the sound will play at full volume before fading in.

Sounds do not play if the playback head is paused at a frame. To get around this, use a "go to marker (O)" to loop one frame.

NuBus card digital audio playback

If you want to access a digital audio NuBus card, you must use Digidesign's Sound Installer utility (introduced in Chapter 10 and presented with a complete syntax for HyperCard guide in Chapter 15). The syntax for using the SoundAccess XCMD in Director is different, as indicated in Table 27-3. Fortunately, Digidesign provides Director macros in the Audiomedia Movie located on the SoundAccess disk included with their Audiomedia cards. These macros make your scripting a lot easier (just copy them and modify them to suit your purposes).

To play soundfiles using the Audiomedia card, you must first open Digidesign's SoundAccess HyperCard stack and click the "Install in Director Movie" button to install the sound playback resources into the movie from which you want to access them.

Next you open Digidesign's Audiomedia Movie and copy castmember A11 into your own movie (this contains the SoundAccess factory). You probably want to copy castmember A12 as well, since this contains many useful macros, including those required for the playback of cuelists (cuelists are set to use the text of castmember A13 as a list of soundfiles, so it is a good idea to copy castmember A13 into your movie too).

After installing the macros, the InitSound macro will be available in Director's Macros submenu (in the Lingo menu). You must paste this into the script channel of the first frame of your movie.

Insert the loadsound macro (from the Macros submenu in the Lingo menu) one frame prior to the frame at which you want your sound to begin playing. You must follow the loadsound macro with the exact path to your soundfile. For example:

`HardDiskName:FolderName:SubFolderIfAnyName:SoundFileName`

To start playback, simply insert the playsound macro at the frame in which you want the soundfile (that you loaded with loadsound) to begin playing.

Use the stopsound macro to halt playback.

Finally, you need to insert the closesound macro at the last frame of your movie or wherever you want to "unlock" the Audiomedia card. If the closesound macro is not issued (for example, because you stop the movie prior to reaching that frame), your Macintosh will not recognize the Audiomedia card until you reboot.

Table 27-3: SoundAccess XFCN syntax

Note: Contrary to the Audiomedia manual, all the SoundAccess commands must be enclosed in quotes, as indicated.

"InitSA"   (used in the InitSound macro)

SoundAccess("InitSA")

> Initializes the SoundAccess XFCN to allow using the Audiomedia card for playback from Director. You must use this, although it need only appear once in a movie (usually the first frame).

"LoadSA"   (used in the LoadPlaySound and LoadSound macros)

SoundAccess("LoadSA",*fileName1[fileName2...]*)

> Loads a soundfile or soundfiles to make them accessible to the PlaySA command.

SoundAccess("LoadSA",*Cuelist)*   (used in the LoadCuelist macro)

> Loads a list of soundfiles stored in the variable *Cuelist.*

"PlaySA"   (used in the PlaySound and LoadPlaySound macros)

SoundAccess("PlaySA")

> Plays the currently loaded soundfile or cuelist.

SoundAccess("PlaySA",*wait)*   (used in the PlaySound wait macro)

> Plays a previously loaded soundfile or cuelist after waiting for the duration specified by *wait* (in ticks or $1/60$ of a second). Useful for synchronizing sound to visual (simply adjust the *wait* value until synchronization is achieved).

"RewindSA"   (used in the RewindSound macro)

SoundAccess("RewindSA")

> Rewinds the last sound played by the PlaySound command and commences playback again. You can use this command to step back through soundfiles contained in a play list (e.g., issuing this command twice at the end of a playlist containing four soundfiles will bring you to the beginning of the third soundfile).

SoundAccess("RewindSA", "all")   (used in the RewindAllSound macro)

> Rewinds to the beginning of the last loaded cuelist. Does not recommence playback until the next PlaySound command.

"StopSA"   (used in the StopSound macro)

SoundAccess("StopSA")

> Stops the currently playing sound. You can issue this command in the Message window while debugging.

"VolumeSA"   (used in the VolumeSound V macro)

SoundAccess("VolumeSA", *vol)*

> Sets the playback volume level of the Audiomedia card to the value specified by *vol* (0 through 7).

"ExitSA"   (used in the Closesound macro)

SoundAccess("ExitSA")

> Required to release files and the Audiomedia card itself from Director control. This command is executed by the Closesound macro included with castmember A12.

MIDI in Director

Director's implementation of MIDI is limited to outputting SPP messages (see Chapter 26), although you can easily add complete MIDI input and output functionality by importing EarLevel Engineering's HyperMIDI XCMD. Director is MIDI-Manager-compatible, so you can send SPP information to trigger songs, and start, stop, and continue playback at any measure in another sequencer running in MultiFinder (System 6.x) or Finder (System 7). Without the addition of the HyperMIDI XCMD, Director can send the following messages: Start, Stop, Continue, Beat (MIDI Clocks), Song Select, Song Position Pointer (see Table 27-4 for the syntax of these). See Figure 27-6 for MIDI Manager configurations in Director.

Table 27-4: MIDI syntax in Director

puppetSound midiOption

puppetSound midiStart	Sends a MIDI Start message to the attached MIDI Manager port.
puppetSound midiStop	Sends a MIDI Stop message to the attached MIDI Manager port.
puppetSound midiContinue	Sends a MIDI Continue message to the attached MIDI Manager port.
puppetSound midiBeat, *[4 to 280]*	Sets the tempo of the sequence being controlled by midiStart, midiStop, and midiContinue.
puppetSound midiSong, *[0 to 127]*	Sends a MIDI Song message to the attached MIDI Manager port.
puppetSound midisongPointer, *beat[1 to 4], measure[1 to 1023]*	Sends a MIDI SPP message to the attached MIDI Manager port.

CD-ROM audio in Director

Director comes with extensive device-control XObjects that are similar to XCMDs. Among these are XObjects that control CD-ROMs and videodiscs. Sample control panels are provided (see Figure 27-5) and the movies containing them include all the macros and scripts you need to access CD-based audio with the same accuracy as you can using Voyager's AudioStack.

One advantage to CD- or CD-ROM-based audio is that playback is independent of the Macintosh CPU. Because of this, you can use CD-based audio to play continuous sound during the playback of standard sampled sounds, Audiomedia soundfiles, and anything placed in Director's Sound channel.

At the end of this chapter there is a comparison of Director-based approaches to multimedia authoring and Authorware and MediaTracks. Interactive magazines developed in Director and Authorware are contrasted. Also, two approaches to product training (for the same product) are contrasted — one created with Director and the other created with MediaTracks.

MediaMaker

MacroMind's MediaMaker is a multimedia authoring environment that is optimized for the combination of Macintosh-based graphics, animation, and sound with external devices such as videodiscs, compact discs (by way of a SCSI CD-ROM

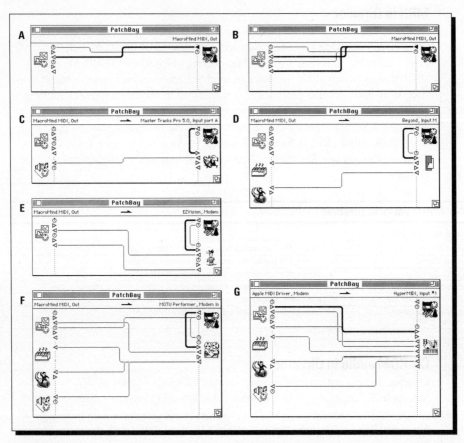

Figure 27-6: MIDI Manager configurations for Director. **(A)** Director triggers and synchronizes an external hardware sequencer (such as the Roland Sound Brush), a sequencer built into an external keyboard (such as the Korg M1), or a sequencer running on a second Macintosh. **(B)** Director triggers and synchronizes external hardware sequencers on both the modem port and printer port. **(C)** Director triggers a software sequencer (Pro 4), which in turn plays back by way of the Passport Sound Exciter, a software-based sample player. No external MIDI hardware is required. **(D)** Director triggers and synchronizes a software sequencer (Beyond), which in turn plays back by way of the Digidesign MacProteus and SampleCell NuBus cards. No external MIDI hardware is required. **(E)** Director triggers and synchronizes a software sequencer (EZ Vision), which in turn controls hardware sound-generating devices through the Macintosh's serial port. **(F)** Director triggers and synchronizes a software sequencer (Performer), which in turn controls the software-based Sound Exciter, Digidesign's MacProteus and SampleCell NuBus cards, and external devices connected to the modem port. **(G)** You can install EarLevel Engineering's HyperMIDI XCMD and XFCN into a Director document or Director itself using a resource editor such as Resourcerer or ResEdit. Then, the HyperMIDI inputs and outputs appear in PatchBay as if they were a separate application, even though they are resident in Director.

drive with audio output), and VCRs and camcorders (serially controllable devices only, including but not limited to those that support the LANC or Control L [both are popular serial control protocols]). With respect to videodiscs, MediaMaker will control CAV (constant angular velocity) discs only, not CLV (constant linear velocity).

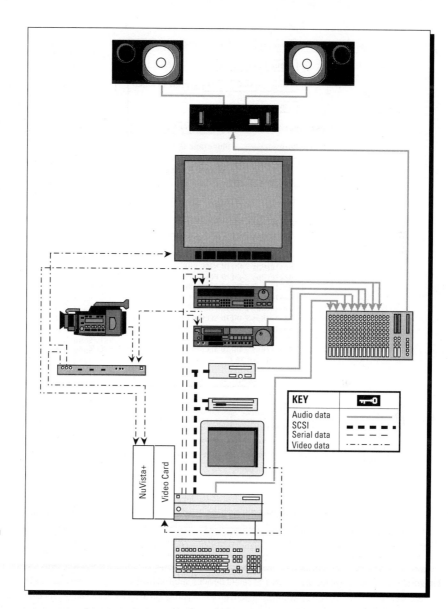

Figure 27-7:
Maximum
configuration
of Media-
Maker for
real-time
control.

You can control your multimedia presentations in real time, controlling at maximum two video sources: a videodisc player and VTR, CD-ROM, video overlay NuBus card, and internal Macintosh sound (see Figures 27-7 and 27-8). Alternatively, your creations can be output to videotape or recordable videodisc (in which case they become fixed). If you are assembling your multimedia presentation on videotape, you only have access to a single video source, because the second option for video control must be dedicated to the mixdown deck.

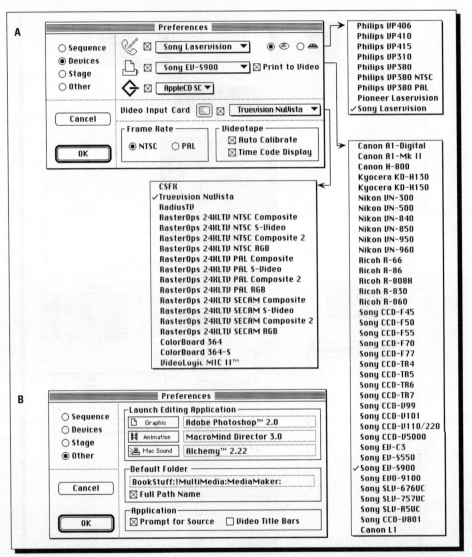

Figure 27-8: Configuring MediaMaker. **(A)** You select devices such as CD-ROMs and video sources to control from the Preferences dialog box. **(B)** Next you can configure an editing program to be launched automatically when you want to edit sound or other multimedia elements. This is not to be confused with the internal picon editors built into MediaMaker.

In MediaMaker a collection functions as a database for all the media types that the program can manipulate. The actual data is not stored, only references to its location. Data is displayed as *picons* (see Figure 27-9). A picon is an on-screen visual object that represents a media element such as a PICT graphic, Director animations, PICS animations, AIFF soundfiles, SoundEdit files, 'snd ' resources, or segments of videotape, videodisc, or CD audio. Double-clicking a

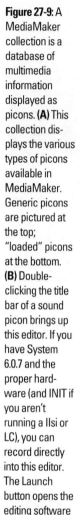

Figure 27-9: A MediaMaker collection is a database of multimedia information displayed as picons. **(A)** This collection displays the various types of picons available in MediaMaker. Generic picons are pictured at the top; "loaded" picons at the bottom. **(B)** Double-clicking the title bar of a sound picon brings up this editor. If you have System 6.0.7 and the proper hardware (and INIT if you aren't running a IIsi or LC), you can record directly into this editor. The Launch button opens the editing software

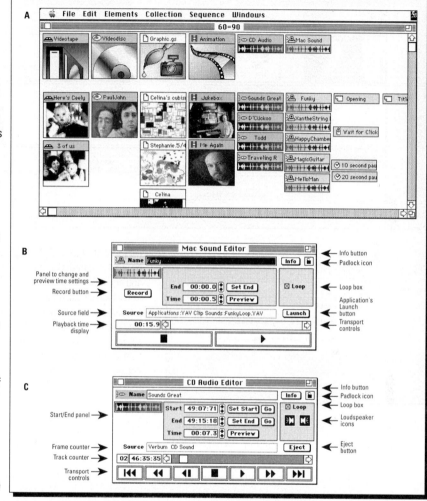

of your choice (specified in the Preferences dialog box) and automatically loads the current data. **(C)** Double-clicking the title bar of a CD audio picon brings up this editor.

picon plays that data associated with the picon. Double-clicking picon's title bar brings up its associated editor.

You create your presentation in a Sequence window (see Figure 27-10). Here you can drag picons to change their location and stretch them to change their duration. Stretching Macintosh sound picons can reduce their length or extend them to their maximum duration set in their associated Sound Editor window. Stretching CD audio picons actually shifts the start or end points of the sound relative to its location on the CD.

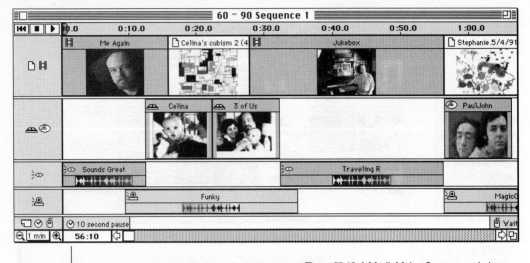

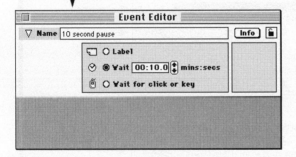

Figure 27-10: A MediaMaker Sequence window. Note the separate tracks for Macintosh graphics and animation, videodisc (and VTR) events, Macintosh sound, CD audio, and events. Visual picons cannot be overlapped on a single track, but they can be overlapped from track to track. This allows you to overlay static graphics or animation with your full-motion video source. Note that if you enable sounds that are stored within an Animation picon, these take precedence over Macintosh sound on the Sound picon track.

Although MediaMaker provides only one type of interactive control — a mouse click or key press (or a voice command if you are using Voice Navigator) — to continue playback after the sequence has been paused, it is a very powerful tool for multimedia presentations because of the sheer number of elements that can be placed under your control. The precision with which you can combine animation, video, graphics, CD audio, and Macintosh sound is unparalleled. Another approach to presentation is to interact with your sequence directly by way of the Sequence window's transport controls and clicking picons to initiate individual playback. This requires some additional mouse activity, but allows you to jump around non-linearly, to display the same material several times as the situation dictates, or to isolate events that would otherwise occur simultaneously (for example, just the video without the graphics overlay).

MediaTracks

Farallon's MediaTracks is optimized for the quick creation of self-running or interactive guided tours, demos, and tutorials for software programs. You start by recording screen activity from within the particular program itself using Farallon's

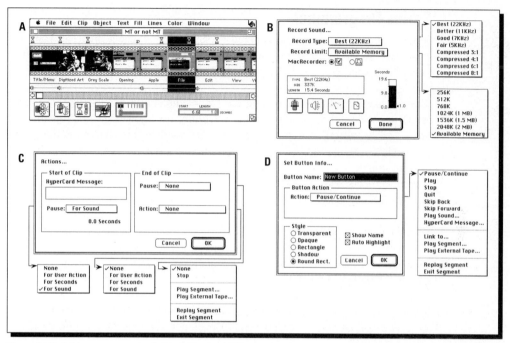

Figure 27-11: Editing a presentation in MediaTracks. **(A)** This is an editing window for a MediaTracks presentation. The sound track (running below the ScreenRecorder track) supports full Cut, Copy, and Paste. You can also copy sounds or portions of sounds from SoundEdit and paste them directly onto MediaTracks's sound track by way of the Clipboard. **(B)** Clicking the Microphone/Speaker icon at the bottom of an editing window brings up this Record Sound dialog box. The pop-up menu options are displayed to the right. The Get Sound button (document with a sinewave) lets you import SoundEdit, AIFF, or 'snd' resource files. **(C)** The Pause button offers special features to synchronize sound with the ScreenRecorder clips. The pop-up menus in this dialog box let you specify that the current clip freezes on the first or last frame until the associated soundfile is finished playing. **(D)** You can also define buttons that simply play sounds rather than navigate through the presentation. Clicking the Draw tool in the main editing screen and then the Button tool in the Draw window brings up the Set Button... dialog box. The Button Action pop-up menu (displayed to the right) offers the option to attach a sound to a button rather than to a ScreenRecorder clip.

ScreenRecorder DA. ScreenRecorder lets you record either the full bitmapped images appearing on the screen or simply the QuickDraw commands that generate the screen graphics (some programs that write directly to screen memory are not recordable in QuickDraw mode).

You can add sound to MediaTracks in any of three ways. You can record directly into a MediaTracks document with a MacRecorder (Farallon was the original manufacturer of the MacRecorder package, so this is to be expected), you can import a SoundEdit file, AIFF, or 'snd' resource, and you can paste sounds into your documents from the Clipboard (see Figure 27-11). A MediaMaker training presentation, Finale Practice, is examined in detail at the end of this chapter.

Serius Programmer

Serius Programmer is an icon-oriented programming language that lets you create just about any type of stand-alone application simply by dragging icons into Object windows and linking them with signal flow lines.

Serius is like a virtual programming erector set. Its strong point is that you can create sophisticated applications with practically no knowledge of programming. Unlike the other authoring systems discussed in this chapter, Serius's approach to creating a stand-alone application does not involve merging a runtime engine with your document. Nor is there any possibility for distributing your documents with a separate runtime engine — all final documents are double-clickable applications. Serius objects are all chunks of precompiled code that are optimized for extremely fast execution. When you assemble them together using Serius's Compile and Save option, Serius creates a program that runs almost as fast as any software written in a conventional programming language such as C — in other words, significantly faster than software that requires a runtime engine.

If you want to write your own objects and functions for Serius Programmer, there is a special version called Serius Developer available (see Figure 27-12).

Authoring system summary

Fortunately, the available multimedia authoring environments all have unique strong suits (see Table 27-1). If you know what type of multimedia your are planning to create, choosing an authoring system should not be difficult.

For artistic creation, nothing compares to Director. For corporate presentations, Director and MediaMaker excel, with Director stressing interactivity and Media-Maker stressing output for video or real-time multiple-device control. Author-ware is optimized for the creation of courseware, although many CAI (computer aided instruction) applications are possible with HyperCard and SuperCard. To create interactive guided tours and product demos, MediaTracks is designed for speedy development time, although Director can add greater interactivity, full product

simulation, and many more bells and whistles to such presentations (at the expense of development time). For information navigation enhanced by multimedia, HyperCard and SuperCard are obvious choices because of their direct evolution from the hypertext tradition. Director and Authorware can enhance information navigation considerably, once again, at the expense of development time.

For a full-featured, multipurpose multimedia authoring environment you should consider either Authorware or Director, depending upon whether your primary

Figure 27-12: For multimedia creation, Serius Programmer offers an Animation Object and two types of sound control accessible by way of their CD Audio Object and Sound Object. This Serius document illustrates these three objects and their associated functions. **(A)** The Animation Object has a signal link to the Sound Object's Play Sound function and to the CD object. Next in this document is a routine to control a CD player. The CD Audio Object's Play, Pause, Resume, Increment-Decrement track, and Eject functions are illustrated. **(B)** This program, assembled in less than an hour, plays an animation, a

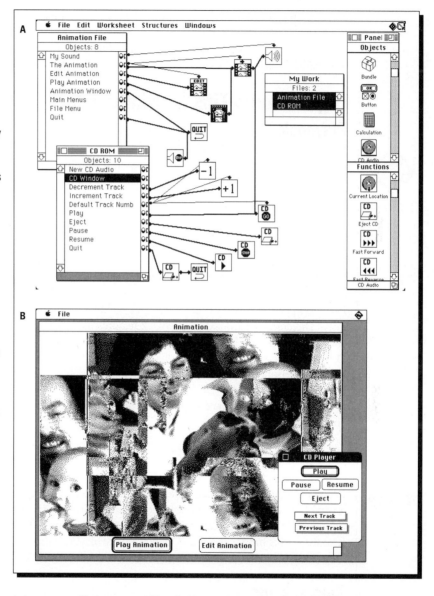

Macintosh sound, and triggers a specified segment of CD audio. The animation is editable and a set of transport controls (defined by the lower portion of A) is available in a separate window.

concerns are courseware (Authorware) or other multimedia applications (Director). Another factor worth weighing carefully is whether you want an icon-oriented visual programming environment (Authorware) or can deal with an English-like scripting language (Director). Beginning multimedia developers who want to ease the transition from hypermedia to interactive multimedia should consider HyperCard (all Macintosh owners have its "runtime engine") or Super-Card (to create double-clickable applications). Finally, if your main interest is to create general-purpose stand-alone programs, but you'd like the option to dabble in multimedia from time to time, Serius should serve you well.

Digital Audio Tips for Multimedia
Playback

Do not use the Macintosh's built-in speaker for the playback of eight-bit digital audio in a serious multimedia presentation. Instead, plug a decent audio system (such as Roland's CS-10 or MA-12C portable powered speakers) into the Macintosh's audio port.

Digidesign's Audiomedia or SoundAccelerator cards can be used for playback with stunning results. Their Chunky file format assures that if your presentation is played on a Macintosh without one of these NuBus cards, the sound is routed (in eight-bit, 22 KHz format) to the Macintosh's internal speaker or audio output jack.

Digidesign's SoundAccess HyperCard stack includes an Installer card that lets you install Digidesign's NuBus card playback features into HyperCard stacks of your choice. Another card lets you install the SoundAccess XFCN into a MacroMind Director movie to add 16-bit soundfile playback capabilities. Note that you must also copy Castmember A11 (a Callback Factory) from the Audiomedia movie included on the Director 2.0 example disk (it is also on the SoundAccess 1.1 disk). For Director 3.0, you should copy Castmember A12 and, if you want Cue list control, Castmember A13.

Sampling rates

Mono eight-bit digital audio sampled at 22 KHz, like you record with Mac-Recorder, requires 1.3MB per minute of sound. To save disk space, always use a playback rate of 11 KHz. Do not record the sound at 11 KHz or use a downsample menu item. Rather, sample at 22 KHz and paste the data into an 11 KHz file — this produces a much higher-quality playback than if you had recorded the sound at 11 KHz or downsampled the sound from 22 to 11 KHz.

Compression

Before using MACE or any other compression scheme to compress your eight-bit soundfiles, make sure that your multimedia authoring environment lets you use compressed sound. Keep in mind that once you have compressed a sound, you won't be able to edit it with most sound editing software, so keep an uncompressed backup copy. If you must compress, don't go beyond a 3:1 compression ratio for music. Compression of 6:1 can be used for speech, if you can tolerate the reduction in quality.

The freeware Sound Expansion INIT allows any Sound Manager-compatible applications to play 22 KHz soundfiles compressed with MacroMind-Paracomp's proprietary 4:1 and 8:1 schemes in System 6.0.7 on any Macintosh. Farallon made this INIT available for people who do not own MacRecorders, because compressed sounds created with Farallon products have been incorporated into many existing applications, including HyperCard stacks.

Eight-bit recording with MacRecorder

You needn't have a Macintosh IIsi or LC to reap these System 6.0.7 Sound Manager benefits. There are third-party drivers that, when placed in your 6.0.7 System Folder, allow you to use MacroMind-Paracomp's MacRecorder, Articulate Systems's Voice Impact Pro (formerly VoiceLink), or even a homemade digitizer in place of the microphone included with the IIsi and LC. Note that 4:1 and 8:1 Sound Manager playback is built into the MacRecorder Driver — don't install it and the Farallon Sound Expansion INIT on the same Macintosh.

The MacRecorder Driver has different features, depending on whether you use it with a 16 MHz 68020 or faster machine, or with a Macintosh Plus, SE, or Classic.

When you use the MacRecorder Driver on faster Macintoshes, the Good, Better, and Best recording options provided by Apple's Sound Input Manager default to 22 KHz sampling with 6:1 Apple MACE compression, 22 KHz sampling with 3:1 Apple MACE compression, and 22 KHz sampling with no compression, respectively. The Driver also supports Farallon's proprietary 4:1 or 8:1 compression. Note that all compression or decompression provided by the MacRecorder Driver requires the use of the 22 KHz sampling rate. AppleTalk traffic and 32-bit QuickDraw can cause recording glitches, so disable these if possible.

When you use the MacRecorder Driver on a Macintosh Plus, SE, or Classic, the Good, Better, and Best recording options provided by Apple's Sound Input Manager default to 7 KHz, 11 KHz, and 22 KHz, respectively. No compression is available for any of these sampling rates. While recording, the floppy disk drive is temporarily disabled and AppleTalk traffic is ignored. If you move the mouse during recording on these slower CPUs, some samples may be lost.

CD audio

When you put an audio CD into a CD-ROM drive, every block of data has a unique address (over 300,000 separate addresses). The Macintosh can jump to any place on the disc almost instantaneously. Unlike the load time associated with reading other forms of CD-ROM data, audio playback commences as soon as the data is located. Authoring stacks such as Voyager's CD AudioStack (discussed in Chapter 29) and Apple's HyperCard CD Audio Toolkit automatically create buttons and XCMD scripts to play back audio sequences you designate by scrolling through an off-the-shelf audio CD. You can even control multiple CD-ROM drives, each with a different audio CD playing at your command.

Playing through

Whether you are using MIDI or digital audio, if your multimedia work requires multiple files, play music through the loading of files. For authoring environments that do not support playback during file loading, there are XCMDs available that provide this feature, notably Farallon's Fplay. Note that Fplay has some problems in Director 2.0 if Sound Manager is present, but it works fine with System 6.0.5 (pre-Sound Manager) or earlier. Director 3.0 offers its own play-through file loading options, so Fplay is not required.

MIDI Tips for Multimedia
Standard MIDI File playback

There are several HyperCard stacks available that play back Standard MIDI Files (SMFs), such as Opcode Systems's MIDIplay and Passport Designs's HyperMusic. These stacks can automatically create buttons (for HyperCard or SuperCard) or scripts (for other XCMD-compatible environments) that play MIDI files in any XCMD-compatible multimedia authoring environment. You can even assemble lists of files that play back sequentially. There are thousands of files available in SMF format (see the section "Clip Music" in this chapter).

Alternatives to external MIDI hardware

There are three ways to get around using external MIDI hardware to play back MIDI from your multimedia presentations.

For MIDI sequence playback you can use Passport Designs's Sound Exciter — a virtual MIDI synthesizer in software to which you route MIDI data with Apple's MIDI Manager.

For CD-quality (16-bit) digital audio playback under MIDI control you can use Digidesign's MacProteus or SampleCell NuBus cards. Both move professional synthesis and sample playback onto your NuBus.

You can even convert MIDI files (and SMUS format files created by Electronic Arts's DMCS) into eight-bit soundfiles with Jim Nitchal's MIDI CD. Because MIDI CD simply presynthesizes the music and then plays it back as a single sampled soundfile, it is not limited to the Sound Manager's restriction on the number of simultaneous playback channels (tracks or voices, depending upon how you look at it).

Plug and play

If you are going to use MIDI sequences in your multimedia presentations, it makes sense to set them up so that they are compatible with the new "General MIDI mode message" protocol that was added to the MIDI Specification in

1991 at the urging of Roland and Microsoft. The incentive for this addition was to address issues in the ever-growing consumer and multimedia markets.

Among other things, General MIDI consists of a standardized list of patches that are all assigned to the same numbers, a universal patch location scheme if you will. This means that when a device is in General MIDI mode, for example, patch 1 is always an acoustic grand piano, patch 25 is a nylon-stringed guitar, patch 41 is a solo violin, and so on. All 128 possible patch numbers have explicit assignments covering just about any instrument of the orchestra, as well as many standard electronic instruments, synthesizer timbres, and sound effects. Also specified by General MIDI mode is a standardized channel mapping of sounds for some MIDI channels. For example, MIDI channel 10 is reserved for rhythm or drum parts (General MIDI also defines drum sounds to note number mappings).

General MIDI lets you "plug and play" with the assurance that the sounds are correct, regardless of the hardware you use for playback. There is already one General MIDI synthesizer, Roland's Sound Canvas, an inexpensive box a little bigger than a Walkman.

Roland's Sound Brush is a little box that interfaces well with their Sound Canvas. It includes a disk drive that reads SMFs from Macintosh disks. You can control it with an infrared remote controller, making it excellent for real-time presentations. Alternatively, the Sound Canvas can be controlled by the MIDI commands available with Director's Lingo scripting language.

Synchronization and Randomness
CPU speed problems and solutions

If you are creating multimedia for distribution, you probably have little control over the type of Macintosh that your work will be played on. Long soundfiles and MIDI sequences can get out of sync with the visual material if your masterpiece is played on slower or faster Macintoshes than the model you used to create the work. This is because the soundfiles play back at the same speed and duration no matter what Macintosh is being used, whereas slower Macintoshes cause the graphics and animation to load and play back at slower speeds. This means that for any true synchronization of sound with visuals, the audio material must function as the master timing reference.

There is a simple solution for this. Test your project on every Macintosh model that supports it and use a stopwatch. Many multimedia authoring environments provide a function to identify the MachineType, and you can use this information in IF-THEN scripts to subtly change the playback tempo of the graphic element (if you are using digital audio soundfiles) or the music itself (if you are using MIDI playback).

A somewhat less effective solution is to use a Timer property offered by many multimedia authoring systems to monitor the passage of ticks (60th of a second). You add cue points or markers at locations where the duration of sound is a known quantity. Then you can calculate critical soundfile hitpoints with a stopwatch or by bringing the soundfile into SoundEdit or a similar soundfile editor to display the precise elapsed duration reading at any individual sample. Now all you need to do is create a script to compare the elapsed playback ticks with the fixed reference values associated with your soundfile. Subtract the intended time from the real time and pause the animation for that number of ticks while the soundfile catches up. If the result is a negative number (meaning that the animation is lagging behind the music), your script can cause the animation to jump ahead to the next marker. The disadvantage of this approach is that it can introduce pauses and skipped material into the presentation unless you are performing this calculation quite regularly, say, at least once per second.

Randomness

If you have ever wondered what you would use the Random function for in your multimedia authoring environment, you can put it to good use with sound. Interactive hypermedia already provides random access to data, so why not select the sound (MIDI or digital audio) randomly for different segments? It makes the experience much more interesting for your users. A recent example of this technique is the Verbum Interactive CD-ROM (see the section "Multimedia in Action"), which randomly selects between soundtracks composed by Geno Andrews and myself.

Multimedia Legal Issues

Multimedia production raises many legal issues for both producers and composers. For some reason, people creating multimedia seem to believe that they are immune from considerations of copyright infringement.

Multimedia is used increasingly at trade shows. The copyright issues became evident to me at the 1990 Macworld Expo. A large number of vendors had video walls or huge monitors displaying either interactive or free-running multimedia presentations. I heard a number of current hit tunes in the sound tracks and noticed many video clips go by that were probably captured from laserdiscs in the Voyager Company's Criterion Collection.

At the Expo I sought out and asked many of the manufacturers and multimedia authors whether they had obtained permission to use the copyrighted material in their presentations. Every one of them confirmed my suspicions that each use was a clear case of copyright infringement. Most of the developers stated that they felt the exposure would be good for the artist in question. This is not a valid assumption (see below). Even though the companies guilty of these infringements did not make any money from the actual sale of copyrighted work without permission (they were simply using the material as components to eye-catching promotional presentations), they were still liable for fines up to $100,000. It is ironic that in many cases these companies would have been extremely vocal in their opposition to software piracy, yet thought nothing of stealing a piece of music or a video clip or image.

As multimedia increases in popularity, you can expect to see many infringement lawsuits from copyright owners whose work is being used without permission. As with sampling, the greater portion of these will probably be settled out of court.

Title 17 of the U.S. Code of the Copyright Act of 1976

The first section of the Copyright Act of 1976 defines terms that you will need to know in order to understand subsequent sections. Note that the word "phonorecord" does not merely refer to phonograph records but any medium with which sounds may be recorded. This includes soundfiles on any type of computer storage medium. (See Section 101 of the Copyright Act.)

Copyright infringement from the multimedia producer's standpoint

If you're planning on using music to spiff up your multimedia presentations, you could be engaged in criminal activity. The law is very restrictive about recording copyrighted material in any medium unless it is for your own personal use — yes, even with MacRecorder — and sorry, your slick Director presentation for the marketing department with Axel Foley running in the background is not considered personal use.

If you use someone else's music in a presentation without permission, you are guilty of copyright infringement and liable for very hefty fines.

There is a widespread myth that it is legal to use anyone's music, as long as one takes only four bars or seven seconds, whichever is less. How this fictitious rumor got started is one of the great unsolved legal mysteries. There is nothing in any copyright law that could, even by the wildest stretch of the imagination, be remotely misinterpreted to draw such a conclusion. Likewise, purchasing a CD, record, photo, video, or other creative work does not give you any rights whatsoever to use that material in a multimedia presentation.

However, the above assumption or an argument for Fair Use (see the section "Fair use and other exemptions") might help to reduce your fine from six figures for willful copyright infringement to a mere four figures for unwillful infringement. Merely giving the composer or copyright owner credit at the end of your presentation will not carry much weight in an infringement case. Be forewarned, the concepts of shareware, freeware, and public domain have no legal bearing whatsoever upon these issues, unless the music itself is in the public domain.

Using the rationalization that exposure of this type increases a piece of music's popularity is patently wrong. Most composers are like everyone else; if there's no money in it, they aren't interested. Fortunately, copyright law does make a distinction between public and private exhibition. Where it might cost $500 to $10,000 (or much more) to license a song for commercial use, say, in a motion picture, a one-shot use of the same song in a multimedia presentation at a board of directors meeting would be negligible — often just the cost of the paperwork and well under $200.

Remember that video is also protected and the licensing fees are much higher (often $10,000 per minute to the studio plus additional compensation for each actor). Usually, you have to pay licensing fees not only to the studio but to the author of the screenplay and the book that the screenplay was based on. Any music included in the video is treated separately, so there are additional hidden costs because music in this case is covered by New Use regulations, which means everyone involved must be paid — including the publisher, performers, and orchestrator — not just the composer.

The rule of thumb is that if someone else's creative work is being used in your software or multimedia presentation, whether it is written into the program code or imported into a HyperCard, SuperCard, or Director document, and the copyright holder is not getting any royalty from it, you are guilty of copyright infringement. Generally, the music is making the program or document more attractive to the user with no benefit to the copyright owner (not necessarily the composer).

If you don't negotiate a royalty in advance of the usage, you may be forced to pay a compulsory license fee that will require: (1) the full statutory royalty, (2) monthly usage reporting, and (3) payment based upon units manufactured rather than units sold.

As you may have guessed, the cases involving sampling and rap music are rampant (particularly because there is money to be made by suing rap artists), although litigation is seen as a last resort. Usually, the publisher contacts the offending party and says, "we caught you, now what are you going to pay us" and get a negotiated settlement. This can be avoided by negotiating a payment in advance, as the famed rapper Hammer did for *You Can't Touch This,* which draws its musical hook entirely from Rick James's *Super Freak.* Robert Plant has also prenegotiated his borrowing of music from Led Zeppelin. But what if you sample a single sound such as a Phil Collins snare drum hit? Does this constitute copyrightable music? Have you appropriated anything that Phil Collins owns? Questions like these are harder to answer, existing in a gray area that is currently generating much discussion among the legal powers that deal with these issues. Because such sampling usually benefits the "sampler" rather than the "samplee," the outcome is pretty easy to predict.

Don't throw away your SoundMaster cdev yet. You might note, however, that this and similar programs such as SoundPlay are not distributed with any copyrighted musical data, because to do so without paying royalties would constitute infringement. (See Section 501 of the Copyright Act.)

The court can impound all the copies of your product while the litigation is pending and order the destruction of all copies that infringe upon a copyright if the judgement rules against you. (See Section 503 of the Copyright Act.)

Fair use and other exemptions

You may have heard about something called Fair Use and figured that this might apply to you. That is unlikely, unless you are using the music for educational purposes or for literary commentary. In these cases the Fair Use Doctrine is applicable because the music is used to provide examples for analysis, study, or criticism. Even then, it will often require a judge and consequential legal fees to determine if your usage really comes under the classification of Fair Use (mechanical reproduction — meaning any form of audio playback — raises particularly hairy Fair Use issues). The Fair Use section of the Copyright Act (Section 107) is pretty vague, and usually a judge sides with the author of the work that has been infringed.

Avoiding copyright infringement

The easiest way to avoid copyright infringement is to obtain permission in advance from the composer and publisher of the work you want to use. If you plan to use the music in a timed relationship with your production, you must also obtain a synchronization license from the copyright owner.

A better solution is to commission a composer to write some original music. Everyone knows a composer or has a friend who does, and many of these composers are underemployed. Most would welcome the opportunity to write some music that would suit your presentation perfectly, often producing a better effect than trying to fit pre-existing music to visual material for which it wasn't intended.

The 1969 copyright law protects works for 50 years following the death of the author (75 to 100 years if the author is a business or organization). Works created before 1968 are protected for 75 years from their copyright registration date. As a general rule, until the year 2010, when the new copyright laws come into effect, you can safely assume that anything composed before 1916 is in the public domain.

Sometimes you can get away with quoting popular songs, if they happen to be based on a folk song. For example, *Love Me Tender* is really the public domain folk song *Aura Lee*, although most people will think of Elvis Presley when they hear an arrangement of it in your multimedia presentation.

Prelicensed clip music is another avenue to pursue to avoid copyright infringement suits (see below).

Copyright infringement from the composer's standpoint

Once you register a copyright with the Register of Copyrights in Washington, D.C., you are entitled to certain exclusive rights pertaining to the work you have copyrighted.

Section 106. Exclusive rights in copyrighted works

Subject to sections 107 through 108, the owner of copyright under this title has the exclusive rights to do and to authorize any of the following: (1) to reproduce the copyrighted work in copies or phonorecords; (2) to prepare derivative works based upon the copyrighted work; (3) to distribute copies or phonorecords of the copyrighted work to the public by sale or other transfer of ownership, or by rental, lease, or lending; (4) in the case of literary, musical, dramatic, and choreographic works, pantomimes, and motion pictures and other audiovisual works, to perform the copyrighted work publicly; and (5) in the case of literary, musical, dramatic, and choreographic works, pantomimes, and pictorial, graphic, or sculptural works, including the individual images of a motion picture or other audiovisual work, to display the copyrighted work publicly. (U.S. Code of the Copyright Act of 1976.)

Taking action against infringement

If you discover that someone is using your music in a multimedia presentation, commercial or otherwise, or anywhere else without permission, the first thing to do is get a lawyer. Don't try to handle the situation yourself. You can't. The intricacies of copyright law make writing a will (for which there is a do-it-yourself Macintosh program called WillWriter) seem like child's play. Many lawyers take copyright cases on a contingency basis.

Your first step is to send the offending party a cease-and-desist letter. (This is another reason to hire an attorney. People receiving such letters on an attorney's stationery tend to take the matter more seriously). You should do this as quickly as possible, because once the infringer has been notified, any subsequent infringement is considered willful infringement and carries much steeper penalties. It is usually not a good idea to wait until the infringer has made a large sum of money from your work simply because your motivation (possibly obtaining a higher settlement) might come into question. Note that you are not required to send a cease-and-desist letter. You can institute a lawsuit immediately if you like.

You are entitled to and it will often be easy to obtain a preliminary injunction in copyright infringement cases. It is practically automatic if you have the copyright registration for the work in question. This means that the infringer must stop displaying, marketing, manufacturing, or otherwise using your work, even before the courts have established whether or not there is any basis for your claim. Because of this, most infringers respond quickly upon the receipt of a cease-and-desist letter and offer a settlement before you seek an injunction.

If you cannot reach an out-of-court settlement with the infringing party, the court can award you financial compensation for a number of different types of damages:

Actual damages and profits. Actual damages are financial losses that can be attributed to the fact that your work was available through the infringer. Other types of actual damages are those that affect your reputation in your field. Profits are the money made by the infringer through the use of your work. You may only be able to recover the percentage of the profits that can be attributed to your work.

Statutory damages. This is an option to request a lump sum instead of a sum representing actual damages or profits. In this case you do not need to prove, nor is it relevant, that you had any actual damages or that the infringer made any money from the use of your work.

Attorney's fees. It is common for the court to force the infringer to pay the legal fees you incur in bringing the case to court.

See also Section 504, "Remedies for infringement: Damages and profits"; and Section 505, "Remedies for infringement: Costs and attorney's fees" in the Copyright Act of 1976.

Clip Music

By now you've probably dealt with clip art in some form or another and noticed that the material has really matured from the early days of T/Maker's ClickArt. Clip music entered the Macintosh multimedia scene at a level it took years for clip art to achieve. If you've used clip art, you won't have any problems using clip music.

Clip music is a good way to avoid copyright infringement, although searching for a clip that synchronizes with or even simply ends at the same time as your multimedia document can be like trying to fit a round peg in a square hole. Also, beware of the canned effect of wallpaper music and the bland atmosphere it might induce.

Clip music is currently marketed in three forms:

❖ MIDI data on floppy disks (or recently CD-ROMs) using the SMF format, which makes it loadable into practically any commercially available MIDI software — licensing fees may be required in some situations (particularly broadcast).

❖ Digital audio data on floppy disks or CD-ROMs that you can play back with the Macintosh's internal sound capabilities (eight-bit) or with various NuBus boards (16-bit) — licensing fees are usually not required.

❖ Digital audio data on standard CDs (sometimes called needle-drop libraries) — these require relatively inexpensive licensing fees. Besides simply sampling this data (with MacRecorder, VoiceImpact Pro, or SID+), using Digidesign's DAT/IO option and direct digital output from a CD player you can convert this data into any other format the Macintosh can deal with.

If you are a composer, you might worry that clip music might be a threat to your livelihood. On the contrary, clip music production houses need composers more than ever to write the music they license. Often you will get cue sheet credit and a percentage of the royalties generated by the usage of the music you contribute to such libraries.

Clip MIDI data

Clip MIDI data offers the easiest way of customizing clip music for your specific project. Probably the least expensive and most hassle-proof way of adjusting playback parameters (such as duration) for synchronizing MIDI files to the rest of your multimedia content is to use a HyperCard-based utility such as Opcode's MIDIPlay or Passport's HyperMusic.

Several clip MIDI data companies are profiled below. On-line services are another valuable source for SMFs. America Online and MIDIMaze have particularly large SMF libraries for downloading.

MIDI Records

The first type of clip music is exemplified by Passport Designs's MIDI Records series (Music Data Company, Half Moon Bay, CA — 800-443-3210), which includes nearly 500 MIDI files of some of the greatest hits ranging from pop/rock, country, R&B, and soul, to oldies, jazz, and classical. Right out of the box, these SMFs will play through a Roland MT-32 synthesizer or its compatibles such as the CM-32L or the CM-64. The Roland Sound Canvas mentioned above is completely compatible with the CM series. Playback through a MacProteus card can be accomplished with minor alterations, and the files can be adjusted to play through any other MIDI synthesizer. The documentation walks you through the conversion process, which may take some time, depending upon your setup.

Prices range from $20 for one song to $10 a piece if you buy 50 at a time. There are a number of discounted special collections. One such collection is their nearly two dozen (and growing) MIDI Hits disks, each organized around a particular musical style and each containing three sequences ($30 per disk). All the files I listened to were worth more than the asking price. The data itself is of extremely high caliber, with much more nuance and expression than you might expect. The fine print (clearly labeled as "The Fine Print") cautions you that "you may be responsible for payment of royalties for public performance of Music Data, as determined by applicable copyright laws. The songs are licensed to you for your personal use on a single computer system."

The Music Data Company division of Passport Designs offers many of their sequences in CD+M format. These CDs play digital audio versions synchronized to MIDI sequences on appropriately equipped (or retrofitted) audio CD players. The company offers a hardware CD+M player called MIDIworld.

Trycho Tunes

Trycho Tunes (Anaheim, CA — 714-826-2271) sells sequences in type 0 or type 1 SMF format. Many of their tunes are also available as files for hardware sequencers and sequencers found in synthesizers. Hardware devices supported include the Alesis MMT8; Ensoniq EPS; Kawai Q80; Korg T series; Roland W30, MV30, MC50, MC300, and MC500; and Yamaha QX3, QX5FD, and V50. They offer custom sequencing at $100 per song with a two-week turnaround.

Trycho has over 1,000 sequences available for $16 a piece. Like Music Data they offer sets of three related tunes ($40 each). They also offer sets of ten related songs for $110 in their Performance Sets series.

MIDI Jukebox

Rather than SMFs, the Parker Adams Group's (Los Angeles, CA — 310-454-1192) MIDI Jukebox offers sequences in SysEx data format (including custom patches) for a variety of hardware devices: Roland's U-20; U-220; D-10; D-110; D-5; MT-32; CM-32-L; CM-64; Sound Canvas; Sound Brush; MC series (sequencers); Alesis's Data Disk; and the E-mu Proteus 1 and 2.

Sequences cost $12 a piece, with a minimum order of five songs from their collection of several hundred. The per-sequence cost is $9 if you are a member of one of Parker Adams's "Original" user groups (for example, the "Original Proteus User Group"). User group membership is $40 ($55 for the Proteus, Sound Brush, and Sound Canvas user groups) and includes manuals of tips, toll-free telephone consulting, and access to their private BBS.

Additional sources

The MIDI Inn (Westmont, IL — 708-789-2001) is another source of SMFs formatted for the Roland CM series. Two major suppliers of generic MIDI sequences are Tran Tracks (New York, NY — 800-473-0797) and The Works (Milwaukie, OR — 206-254-3187 or 503-659-3954).

Clip soundfiles
8-bit

B & B Soundworks, well known for their Country Christmas HyperCard stack, offers two libraries of high-quality sounds: a musical instruments library containing 150 sounds and a sound effects library containing 100 sounds. Each consists of five disks of sounds in 'snd ' resource format. The licensing conditions are simple: you can use up to six sounds in any single stack and you may not distribute the sounds as part of another sound library.

The Desk Top Music company markets a CD-ROM containing over 200 selections of a wide variety of musical styles, including classical, big band, jazz, and rock. Over seven hours of music in 'snd ' resource format is included on the CD-ROM. Because some of the files are large, 6MB of RAM is required.

All the music is prelicensed for non-theatrical use for an annual fee of $392 (this includes the CD-ROM). Non-theatrical use includes music for in-house productions and music used in a production for a specific client. Not covered in the standard licensing agreement is usage that involves mass distribution, although the company grants such licenses for an additional fee. Additional CD-ROMs are under development.

Another company, Tactic Software, has two volumes of sound clips available. Each includes ten 800K disks of soundfiles (mainly sound effects) that are compatible with HyperCard (and hence SuperCard and Director).

Finally, Passport Designs's Media Music is available on floppy disks or CD-ROM in eight-bit or 16-bit soundfile formats. This is a standard production music library including some of the best selections from their MIDI Records series (see "MIDI Records").

16-bit

Digidesign's Clip Tunes is a CD-ROM containing 300MB of music and sound effects sampled at 44.1 KHz in 16 bits. Developed jointly with Prosonus, this is currently the only available clip music of the second category listed above. These tunes are intended for use with Digidesign's Sound Accelerator or Audiomedia cards in conjunction with compatible editing software such as their own Sound Designer II and Audiomedia.

Copying the soundfiles onto your hard disk ensures that the data remains in the digital domain, even if you do not own Digidesign's DAT I/O interface for their Sound Accelerator card. All of the music soundfiles and many of the sound effects files have pre-defined regions and playlists, so the task of finding good edit points is alleviated (of course, you can create your own regions as well). The playlist names include the duration in minutes, seconds, and fractions of a second.

The music ranges from fusion, funk, and folk, to new age, symphonic, and Caribbean. Most musical licensing is included in the price of the CD-ROM, that is, use of the music for your own projects and with projects for clients. However, if material from Clip Tunes is to be broadcast, you must contact Prosonus to "provide for appropriate licensing of public performance rights."

Library music

The third type of clip music has been around for quite some time. These are libraries of music and sound effects available on standard audio CDs. You can either sample the music with an eight-bit or 16-bit sampler or import the data to your hard disk by way of Digidesign's DAT I/O interface (keeping the data in the digital domain).

The Hollywood Film Music Library

The Hollywood Film Music Library is a good example of this category, being the number one supplier of source cues (where an on- or off-camera sound source is implied) for the Los Angeles film and television industry as well as being a large supplier of pure background music.

You've heard music from this library in *Die Hard 2,* Cher's *Mermaids,* Travolta's *Chains of Gold, Night Court, Hunter, Cheers, Muppet Babies,* and other Saturday morning fare. The library or portions thereof are available in CD, DAT, or traditional cassette format — all digitally mastered. There are 22 categories of music, ranging from classical, comedy, pop/rock, mystery, and horror, to action, danger, big band, stingers, sports, holidays, geographical, and ethnic — over 60 hours of music and 25 hours of European orchestral music. Most of the cues come in multiple versions of various lengths — 10 seconds, 29 seconds, 59 seconds, 1½ minutes, two minutes, and so on. Furthermore, many have multiple endings to choose from, such as "happy ending" or "suspended ending." Finally, every cue has subindex points, which facilitate the location of, for example, the "bridge" section of a tune. Macintosh database software is included, so it is easy to call up all action cues with brass, or all holiday cues with bells.

The Hollywood Film Music Library has three types of licensing plans: (1) an annual blanket license allowing unlimited use for the length of the license; (2) a lease/needle-drop license billed on a per cue basis; and (3) per production blanket licenses. Fees vary depending upon whether it is a broadcast or non-broadcast license. Most multimedia creators find the needle-drop licensing rates quite affordable after an initial one-time lease fee of $20 per CD. Portions of the library are available on CD-ROM as 8- and 16-bit soundfiles.

Utilities for Multimedia

You can use many utilities to enhance your multimedia production capabilities and efficiency. There are several indispensable utilities that are optimized for multimedia production. For more on these utilities, see the coupon in the back of the book.

Media databases

When you are creating a multimedia presentation, you typically have quite a bit of different data types to keep track of: digital audio soundfiles, graphics, animations, text, 3-D models, and the like. There are two databases that can help you organize your materials: Oldavi's MultiClip (DA) and Symmetry Software's Mariah (program). Both can be used to store and organize graphics, text, and sounds in a variety of formats.

The MultiClip DA functions as an unlimited number of Clipboards, which can be given individual names if you like. It doesn't support as many file formats as Mariah, but some of its features can reduce development time significantly. Importing data into MultiClip is easy. You assign Command key combinations to copy directly to MultiClip rather than the Clipboard. Subsequently, you can paste data into a document simply by pressing a Command key combination and a number representing the number of the clipframe (as MultiClip refers to its various Clipboards) you want to paste. If you have named your clipframes, a pop-up menu is available at any time to quickly access the contents of your MultiClip file. This transparent background operation of MultiClip makes it perfect for multimedia development. If you have a set of sounds that you are using repeatedly, it's a simple matter to drop any one of them into your multimedia presentation with a single keystroke combination.

Mariah differs from MultiClip in that you must switch to the program, copy your required data, and then switch back to the document in which you want to paste the data. Mariah does add a number of wonderful features to the organization of multimedia data (see Figure 27-13). You can assign keywords and titles to each file in a Mariah collection. This allows collections to be sorted and searched with Boolean search criteria. New collections can be created automatically from the results of a search. Sounds and PICS animations can be previewed right within Mariah, and you can even use MacRecorder to record new soundfiles directly into the database. Unlike MultiClip, regions of sounds can be selected and copied (MultiClip clipframes containing sounds can only be copied in their entirety). All Mariah data is tagged with the date and time it was entered into a collection. Mariah can also function as a file-format converter (like Curator) for

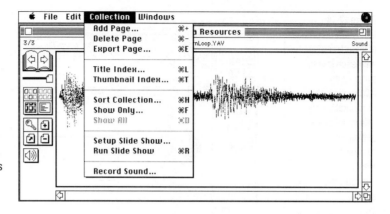

Figure 27-13: This is a soundfile stored in Mariah. Note the playback button at the lower left (speaker icon). You can also play back and copy selected regions of files. The exposed menu illustrates some of the database operations offered by Mariah. Every graphic in this book was organized in a Mariah database.

graphics data, because imported data may be exported in a different format than it was imported in.

Both MultiClip and Mariah copy and paste castmembers and groups of animation channels in Director. They accomplish this by storing the location of the data within the Director document and the pathname for the particular Director document, not the actual data itself. Thus, if you rename or move a document with frames or castmembers stored in MultiClip or Mariah, the software won't be able to locate them again for copying and pasting.

Interface design utilities

If you want to use dialog boxes as a user-interface item in an interactive multimedia document, particularly one created in HyperCard, Result Software's Dialoger Pro is a must. This stack allows you to quickly create dialog boxes of a sophistication and functionality limited only by your imagination.

Pantechnicon's TextureSynth functions very much like a synthesizer, except it lets you synthesize patterns to use as backgrounds, map onto objects, or enhance the visual element to a multimedia presentation in the same way that a unique and interesting sound enhances the audio. TextureSynth's control panel provides many of the same sorts of controls you use to modify sounds in a digital synthesizer, but with TextureSynth your modifications are applied to color and pattern rather than pitch and timbre. You save texture configurations as patches, and these can be exported in 8- to 24-bit PICT or TIFF format. If you've ever edited a sound on a synthesizer, you will find TextureSynth easy to operate.

Video and animation

A number of utilities exist for the quick creation of animation to be added to multimedia authoring systems that do not themselves support animation creation. Electronic Arts's Studio/1 is one such program. It lets you create black-and-white animations that you can import for playback in HyperCard.

Figure 27-14:
(A) Synchronization of sound with animation is very simple with ADDmotion. The horizontal bars with little speaker icons at their left represent sound-files — their length indicates the soundfile duration. You can drag these bars forward or backward in time to line them up with animation events or stretch them to increase the length of, for example, looped sounds. You can tell from the number of available sound channels that Apple's new (System 6.0.7 or later) Sound Manager is being used. **(B)** This Sound

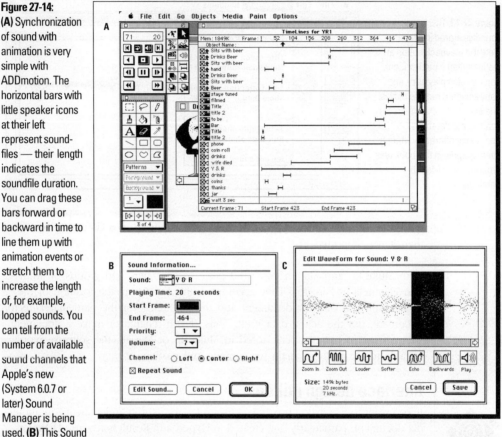

Information dialog box lets you assign a priority, volume, and placement to individual sounds. **(C)** ADDmotion even includes this rudimentary soundfile editor that provides most of the functionality you would require while putting together an animation.

MotionWorks's ADDmotion lets you create color graphics with sound that can be played back in HyperCard. ADDmotion's sound capabilities take full advantage of the Sound Manager and allow for simultaneous playback of as many soundfiles as your CPU (and Sound Manager) will support (see Figure 27-14).

BrightStar's InterFACE lets you design talking agents and synchronize speech to their lip movements. Images are varied according to speech context, not just speech sounds. Besides being captivating, it dynamically enhances information assimilation. You start with 8, 16, or 32 images of your agent, each with its mouth in a different position. The agent can consist of digitized images (for photo reality) or graphics (for cartoon-like agents). Speech is possible by way of Apple's Macintalk driver or digitized sound. In the case of Macintalk, InterFACE can convert typed sentences into speech that is automatically synchronized to your agent's lip movements. With digitized sound, you have to manually syn-

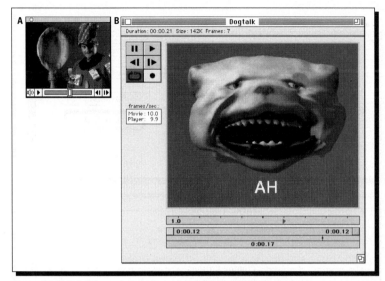

Figure 27-15: QuickTime windows have transport controls at the bottom.
(A) QuickTime is optimized for small windows like this. **(B)** You can play larger movies at slower frame rates.

chronize the lip motion to the sound. Once created, your talking (or singing) agents can be installed in HyperCard or Director. Current users include Boeing, United Airlines, Microsoft, Arthur Young, Walt Disney Imagineering, and Citicorp. Apple had two talking agents in the "Phil and Dave's Excellent CD" CD-ROMs they pressed for developers. Some inter-office V-mail systems employ talking agents.

COSA's (The Company of Science and Art) PICS Animation Compiler (PACo) is an alternative to QuickTime. PACo takes a PICS file and a 'snd ' resource or sound edit file and combines them into a single file. The file format interleaves the video with audio, allowing for streaming playback from the disk with frame-accurate synchronization. Frame rate is dependent upon the length of the audio. If you have 240 images in the PICS file and 10 seconds of sound, PACo produces an interleaved file 24 seconds in duration. This greatly aids synchronization, if you know the length of your soundfile and the length of its associated PICS file. PACo is available as an XCMD for HyperCard and an XObject for Director. Playback requires only 60K of RAM.

One major difference between a compiled PACo file and a QuickTime movie is the way they modify the output when the hard drive is too slow to keep up with the frame rate. With QuickTime, the audio has precedence and Quick-Time automatically drops frames to keep up with the sound (see Figure 27-15). PACo gives the visuals priority, glitching the audio if necessary to maintain the frame rate.

In a joint venture with Paracomp, COSA has released QuickPICS (see Figure 27-16). The features are similar to PACo. They have added the option to create a double-clickable document (this adds about 72K to the file). There is a per-disk licensing fee for commercial distribution of QuickPICS files.

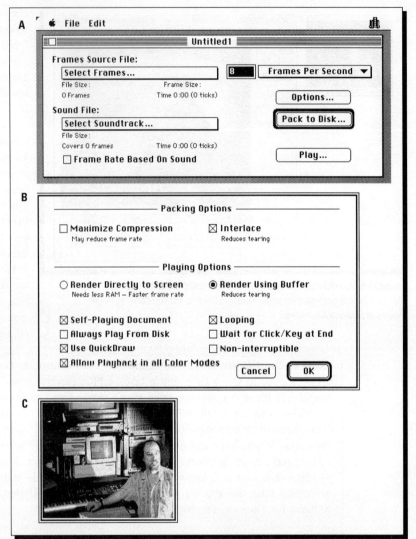

Figure 27-16:
(A) When you compile a soundfile with a PICS animation file using QuickPICS, you have the option to base the frame rate on the duration of the soundfile.
(B) Among Quick-PICS's options is the possibility to create a stand-alone animation document.
(C) QuickPICS documents appear in a standard modal dialog box without transport controls.

Multimedia in Action

The following four products are good examples of multimedia in action, and they are widely available. In both interactive training and interactive magazines, two different solutions to the same multimedia task are presented, each created using a different authoring environment.

Interactive training

Finding two interactive presentations that cover the same material but were developed with different authoring systems is not an easy task. The following two approaches to interactive training for the same program — Coda's Finale — offer an excellent opportunity for comparing the strengths of MacroMind Director vs. Farallon MediaTracks. The German company ergo sum created Finale Practice using MediaTracks. Coda's Finale Guided Tour was created using Director.

Much of the same information is covered in both multimedia presentations. The focus is slightly different. Finale Practice stresses *how* to accomplish something with the program by displaying a text box with a one- or two-sentence procedure and then runs a MediaTracks tape as a means of illustration. The Finale Guided Tour stresses *what* the program does, *why* it does it, and demonstrates *how* the program accomplishes this through interactive annotated animation (see Figure 27-17).

As stated earlier in this chapter, the two authoring systems differ greatly in the amount of time it takes to create a multimedia presentation. The Finale Guided Tour required about 300 hours for development. My experiments with re-creating some of the modules of Finale Practice indicate that it could have been created in less than one-tenth that time, or about 30 hours.

Finale Practice (created with MediaTracks)
Finale Practice functions equally well as a self-guided learning tool and an on-line help facility (when run simultaneously with Finale).

Several problems are evidenced with the MediaTracks approach. Screen redraw artifacts are captured by ScreenRecorder and there is no way to edit these out of the final tapes. Also, there are often points where the simulation of program operation results in jerky or staggered animation (no such problems exist in Director). There is no synchronized sound with the simulation of MIDI input and playback. In fact, it is difficult to add multiple sounds to an individual clip. It is not possible to add informative text boxes at any point (displaying and removing them as required), only for entire segments. It is impossible to add animated graphics for the purpose of illustrating a point. Auto-screen resizing (to 9-inch or 13-inch monitors) and auto tempo setting (based upon detection of the Macintosh model) are not possible. The nonlinear access to information is missing from MediaTracks to the extent it is implemented in Director (see Chapter 29 and Figures 27-18 and 27-19).

On the other hand, the development time required by MediaTracks (less than 30 hours vs. 300 hours for Director) is a strong selling point for the multimedia creator who does not require the more sophisticated presentation features mentioned in the previous paragraph. This fact must be weighed against the added expense of extra disks required to deliver the MediaTracks-based product and extra storage space requirements of the user.

Figure 27-17: (A) You launch Finale Practice lessons from this navigation card. After viewing a lesson, you return and then select the next section for playback. You always have to travel to the base of the hierarchical tree before continuing. **(B)** You use this pop-up menu (always present) to jump around the Finale Guided Tour with random access to information.

Finale Guided Tour (created with Director)

The Finale Guided Tour is designed to function as an interactive self-learning tool, self-running demonstration of the program's features, or interactive or free-running (no human interaction required) in-store presentation.

The Finale Guided Tour is the first guided tour for a music program running on the Macintosh. At the time of its release, it was (and may still be) the largest

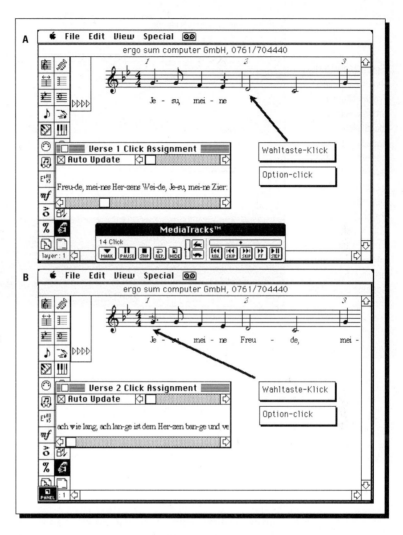

Figure 27-18: (A) All MediaTracks presentations provide transport controls (see bottom center) that allow you to pause, rewind, fast forward, and step through the presentation. You can also set the playback tempo. **(B)** Alternatively, clicking the Hide button (in A) collapses the transport controls to a single Panel button that you can use to bring up the complete set of controls (see lower left). This allows you to see more of the screen.

guided tour in Macintosh history (over 1MB — about 120,000 animation cells) with more music than any other tour (also over 1MB).

There are really two tours embedded in the animation: a Quick Tour (25 minutes) and a Full Tour (60 minutes). You can make a choice, or switch back and forth as you desire, or let the tour automatically set itself to the Quick Tour. The Quick Tour skips more advanced material based upon the value set in a variable called PatienceLevel.

Regardless of whether you are on the Quick Tour or the Full Tour, the presentation takes you through the setup, entry, editing, playback, and printing of a single piece of music — the tour's own main title music. Hundreds of strategi-

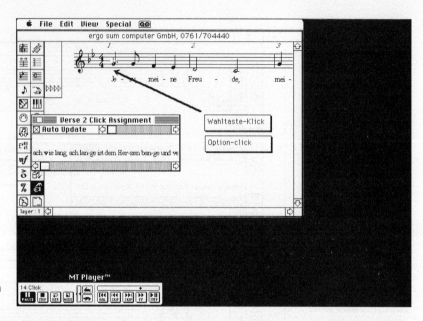

Figure 27-19: Unlike Director, Media-Tracks offers no provisions to resize the display area based upon the current Macintosh environment — you must fix the stage size before making the presentation. This is how the Finale Practice segment from the previous figure appears on a 13-inch monitor.

cally placed information boxes, arrows, and other graphically animated illustrations appear throughout the presentation to explain what is going on.

The tour has five buttons at the bottom of the screen, which provide a considerable amount of control over the presentation. HyperCard-like Previous and Next buttons let you review a prior topic or skip ahead to the next topic or subtopic. Unlike fast forward or rewind buttons, the Previous and Next buttons skip to logical segments in the presentation and base their re-entry points on whether you are taking the Quick or Full Tour. There is also a Start Over and Pause button, and the presentation can be paused or resumed at any moment by pressing a key on the Macintosh keyboard. Pressing the fifth button calls up a pop-up menu from which you may access a Help window, switch between the Quick Tour and the Full Tour, jump to various parts of the tour, change the screen size, print an order form for information or purchases, or quit.

The pop-up menu at the bottom of the screen lets you jump to any of the six large sections of the tour: Introduction, Getting Your Music into Finale, Editing Your Score, Playback, Printing, and Personalizing Finale. The pop-up menu further divides these into smaller sections by adding options to jump to subtopic areas dedicated to: Setup, Entry, Notation Editing, MIDI Editing, Adding Intelligent Chords, and Text and Lyrics.

One feature setting this tour apart from previous Macintosh tours is the fact that it knows what type of Macintosh you are running and adjusts the screen size accordingly to a 9-inch monitor for a Macintosh Plus, SE, SE30, Classic, or

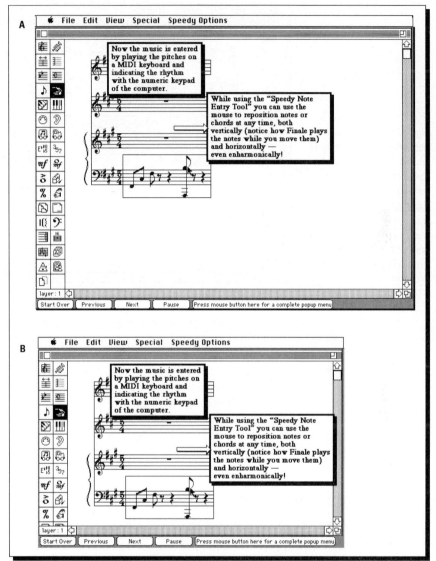

Figure 27-20:
The Finale Guided Tour automatically resizes the display area to use the available screen area, moving scroll bars and buttons as needed. **(A)** The Finale Guided Tour running on a 13-inch monitor. **(B)** The same segment running on a 9-inch monitor (on a compact Macintosh).

to a 13-inch monitor for the Macintosh II series. The scroll bars and inter-activity buttons are shifted to fill the available screen area. If you have a small-screen Macintosh with a large screen attached, the pop-up menu allows you to expand the display area and view the tour as it would run on a Macintosh II. All of this is accomplished by designating the animation sprites in question to be "puppets," with their locations set according to a test of the current Macintosh model (see Figure 27-20).

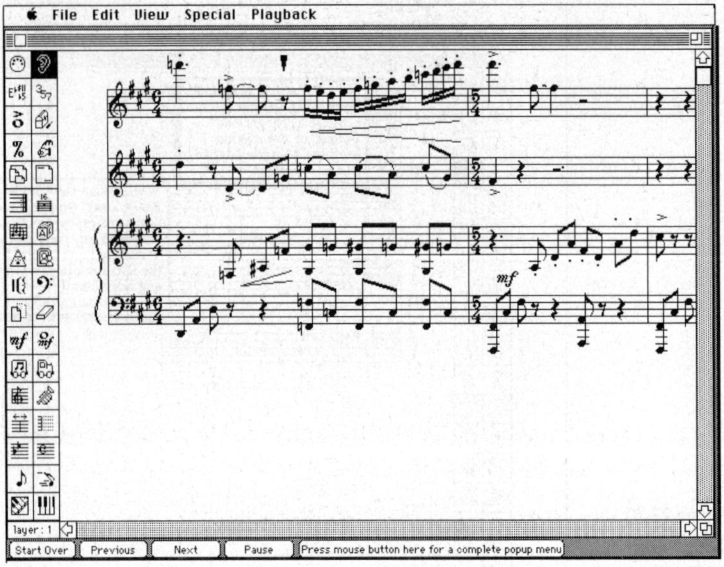

Figure 27-21: Director can adjust the tempo of the Finale Guided Tour based upon the speed of the Macintosh it is running on. This assures that the little triangular pointer (see upper center) synchronizes precisely to the scrolling playback on the simulation, just like in the actual Finale program.

The tour's awareness of the type of Macintosh you are running also permits it to make subtle adjustments in the overall tempo of the animation (see Figure 27-21). This is required in the lengthy scrolling playback sections and MIDI input sections in order to keep the scrolling cursor or note display in sync with the playback soundfiles (and to assure that temporally adjacent soundfiles play back with a seamless splice). At strategic points, where precise synchronization between the scrolling notes and music is necessary, macros test for the Macintosh model and change the playback frame rate accordingly. Accurately determining the various frame rates during development required testing the pertinent parts of the presentation on all Macintosh models, while noting elapsed timings with a stop watch. This information was used to determine the puppetTempo settings at every sync point.

There are two functionally identical versions of the tour. If you have four or more megabytes of RAM, you can run the single-file version. If you have less than four megabytes of RAM, you use a multifile version that splits the tour into 14 segments small enough to fit in your available memory. The significant developmental consideration (or perhaps the most difficult nut to crack) is that the single-file version can be literally chopped into 14 segments (with Cut and Paste), and absolutely no altering of the macros is required. This is because each macro determines whether it is executing itself in the single- or multifile version and branches accordingly. The macros accomplish this by checking the name of the currently playing movie.

Figure 27-22:
The virtual "cover" of *Macworld Interactive* displays all the available menus as well as top-level navigation buttons.

Interactive magazines

Two major interactive CD-ROM-based Macintosh magazines have appeared at the time of this writing: *Macworld Interactive* and *Verbum Interactive*. Both are based on the print versions of the magazines of the same names (see Figures 27-22 through 27-27).

These two magazines offer an excellent vehicle for comparing multimedia development platforms, because one was created with Authorware *(Macworld Interactive)* and the other with Director *(Verbum Interactive)*. Note that *Macworld Interactive* is really just a sample issue of what a CD-ROM version of their June 1990 issue might be like (only a couple of stories are actually converted to interactive format), whereas *Verbum Interactive* is a complete issue, putting into practice practically every known multimedia technique to enhance presentation.

Macworld Interactive consists of a single double-clickable Authorware document (the runtime engine is packaged in the document) that is 33MB (eight-bit color version) or 45MB (24-bit color version). An additional 33MB are devoted to the winners of *Macworld*'s SuperStacks competition. This feature clearly shows the advantages of CD-ROM as a magazine publication format. In the printed version, it was only possible to show one or two screen shots from the various winning HyperCard stacks — here we have functional or semifunctional (demo) versions of the winners to experiment with. Fifty-two megabytes are devoted to catalog

Figure 27-23:
The table of contents for *Macworld Interactive* displays available articles in black text. Clicking a title takes you to that item. All other grayed items are not available.

Figure 27-24:
(A) A typical article page showing a "post-it note" and interactive illustration (moving the sliders distorts the apple). **(B)** You can call up a listing of all your post-it notes with their locations and view them in this dialog box. **(C)** The Marching Toward Realism sidebar is available from the Article menu (see A) or by way of strategically placed buttons. The effect of clicking the Stage 4 button is pictured. **(D)** Pages like this one let you hear noted authorities speak on the topics you select from the buttons at the left. Sound plays through the Macintosh speaker or audio port (8-bit).

Figure 27-25: (A) These three buttons appear at the lower left of every "page" of *Verbum Interactive.* The far right button is a typical return (go back) button similar to those found in HyperCard stacks. The center button brings up the navigational map (see C). The far left button reveals the extended pop-up menu palette (see B). **(B)** This palette is a set of pop-up menus (as pictured) from which you can jump to any part of *Verbum Interactive* from wherever you are. **(C)** This navigation map (accessed by clicking the center button in A above) displays the complete structure of *Verbum Interactive* with an animated arrow pointing to your current location. You can jump to any part of *Verbum Interactive* by clicking the miniature (icon-sized) version of a section's title card. There are more than 40 buttons on this directory screen, so programmer Michel Kripalani (see interview) had to use multifunction buttons (designated as regions within a larger sprite) as a way around Director's limitation of 24 animation sprites.

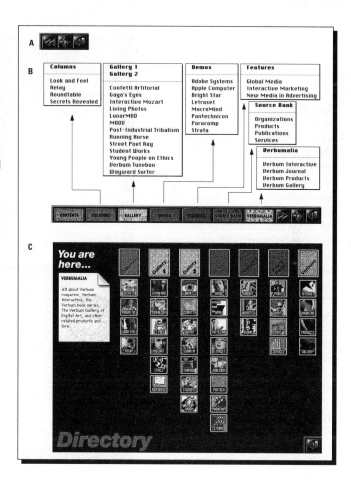

databases of HyperCard stack vendors and 45MB for a folder containing every past release of HyperCard in every language (the reason for this is unexplained). The CD-ROM uses 206MB (leaving about 450MB unused). Remember that 45MB of these 206MB are dedicated to the 24-bit version of the interactive magazine, so there is really only 161MB of unique data.

Verbum Interactive is orders of magnitude greater in complexity, consisting of 147 linked Director documents with an additional 324 associated files (471 files total) making up 1.3GB of data spanning two CD-ROMs.

Both issues have a few similarities: menu-driven nonlinear navigation, slider control of your location in an article, animated illustrations (*Macworld Interactive* only has one of these), sampled speech, interactive interviews, hypertext-accessible glossary, sound effects, and the option to jump out of the presentation to product demos. *Macworld Interactive* is much more like a magazine that has

Figure 27-26: (A) This Look and Feel article is accessed by clicking its card in the previous figure or by way of the pop-up navigational menus. All articles open with an animated title page accompanied by music. Articles are presented as pop-up pages with a scroll bar at the bottom (see lower left). The current page number is always visible. Hot (hypertext) words are underlined. The button at the far left of the scroll bar prints the current article. The zoom button at the far right rolls the page up or down. Immediately to the left of the zoom button is a little running man. If there is an animated or video illustration associated with the current page, the little figure on this button highlights and starts running. Subsequently, you can click the running man to roll the page down and view the video clip (see B). **(B)** When you encounter a running man button and roll down the current page of the article, video appears in a window on the pictured V TV. Video is in the PACo format.

been scanned onto a CD-ROM and has interactive navigation features added to replace page turns.

Unique features of *Macworld Interactive* include an option for large text, the display of an outline for the current article, and virtual Post-It-Notes option.

Some unique features of *Verbum Interactive* include CD-quality audio (including Red-book audio tracks that play back through a normal CD player), animation everywhere, galleries of interactive multimedia art, full-motion video with synchronized sound (using the PACo system — see the section "Video and animation"), and a complete on-line database of past issues of *Verbum*, including its products, services, and events.

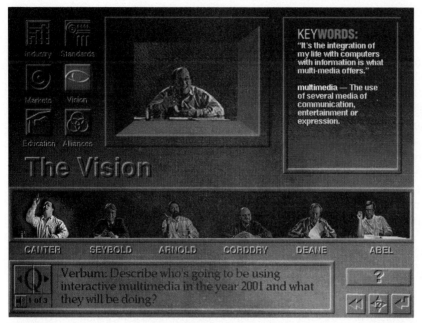

Figure 27-27: The Verbum Roundtable (produced by GTE ImagiTrek) occupies the entire second CD-ROM of the two-CD-ROM set. A small segment of the roundtable is accessible from the main CD-ROM as well. The Roundtable lets you present questions in six topic areas (Industry, Markets, Education, Standards, Alliances, and Vision) to six industry leaders. You are the moderator of this panel and can present the questions in any order to any or all of the panelists. You choose questions with the scroll arrows at the lower left. You choose a panelist by clicking him. The chosen panelist appears in the spotlight and at the upper center of the screen. They present their responses synchronized to video clips.

Interview with Michel Kripalani, Lingo programmer for *Verbum Interactive*

Yavelow: *How long did it take to create Verbum Interactive?*

Kripalani: We didn't keep track precisely, but the work hours were in the area of 5,000 or 6,000. Now that we have the main components, creating future issues will go much more quickly. We developed Disk One on three 645MB PLI hard drives, and GTE ImagiTrek used 1GB Tahiti mechanism-based magneto-optical drives.

We actually almost ran out of room on the disk. On Disk One there are less than 10MB free. You can see the free area on the disk — it is a little ring about a half-inch from the outer edge. Everything outside of the ring — closer to the edge — is CD audio.

Yavelow: *Were there any particular obstacles you had to surmount with the sound?*

Kripalani: Getting the sound to play through the loading of files was a problem at first. Initially we used Farallon's FPlay XCMD to get around this. This works fine for System 6.0.5 (pre-Sound Manager), but FPlay had problems with Sound Manager systems (6.0.7 or later). We tried a number of other solutions, but then Director 3.0 was released right before we were about to press the CD-ROM. Director 3.0 allows sound during file loading, so we switched at the last minute.

In *Verbum Interactive,* the command right before the Go To Movie command is a Play Sound command. Then the first frame of any movie includes a Sound Fade Down command. *Verbum Interactive* uses the clock ticks to generate a random number between 1 and 35 and chooses each sound clip randomly.

The length of transitional sounds was timed to accommodate the slowest CD-ROMs with the slowest Macintoshes, so that sound would continue to play during loading. The speed of the drive is the most significant factor in determining this, but the speed of the Macintosh influences it too because of the number of things that get initialized at the beginning of each movie.

Yavelow: *Do you have any comments about the CD audio tracks on the disk?*

Kripalani: MacroMind provides all the XObjects we need to play CD audio. If you are running *Verbum Interactive* off the CD-ROM and start playing CD audio, you can't load additional movie files. This is why the Tunebox is a self-contained unit and gets loaded entirely into RAM. The Graham

Nash piece is the same way. For the same reason, *Gaya's Eyes* (Ty Roberts and Todd Rundgren) will only play a portion unless you copy the files to your hard drive. When the *Gaya's Eyes* files are on the hard drive, the Macintosh can access both the movies and sound simultaneously. Then, when it is playing CD audio, it just reads continuously from the CD-ROM.

We didn't have to do anything special to get the Red book [CD] standard audio to play on standard players.

Yavelow: *Why did you use PACo instead of QuickTime for the video?*

Kripalani: PACo was out first and Apple wouldn't let anyone release QuickTime until they did. PACo stores the sound as well as images. Because PACo combines a PICS file and a 'snd' resource or SoundEdit file into a single file, it meant that the audio had to be synced with the PICS file in advance. And there is about 1½ hours worth of video in the CD-ROM Roundtable alone.

Yavelow: *Do you have any comments on the programming?*

Kripalani: Half of the Lingo code is concerned with puppet sprites. There is almost nothing in the score because there are too many variables. We used a total of ten XObjects and XCMDs — two or three from Director and many from Apple's SupportExternal's Stack. We only had to use one or two factories and those were simply to build an array. To allow the user to jump out of *Verbum Interactive* and into another program and back we write the page number to a file called VerbumGlobals in the System Folder.

Incidentally, the reason for copying the movie player to the hard drive is to allow switching between the two CD-ROMs and also to let you change the RAM allocation. You need to have the player on write-enabled media because you can't change the RAM allocation.

Yavelow: Any advice for people who want to undertake a project of this scope?

Kripalani: The most important thing with multimedia is to make it the lowest common denominator — make it as easy for the user as possible.

Summary

- Multimedia implies a combination of two or more types of information that can be placed under computer control: static graphics, animation, full-motion video, music, sound effects, speech, and text.

- The Macintosh is, without contest, the most popular platform for multimedia. All multimedia presentations have a more memorable impact when they include music. You can use music as a navigational aid, providing audio cues for the people viewing your project, just as different visual backgrounds or color schemes help keep them oriented to their current location in nonlinear interactive environments.

- Music for multimedia presents abundant opportunities for Macintosh musicians. In particular, growing concern with copyright issues mean that more original music is needed in this medium. There are three kinds of musical data used in multimedia: MIDI, 8-bit digital audio, and 16-bit digital audio.

- Seven popular authoring environments for multimedia are: Authorware Professional, Director, HyperCard, MediaMaker, MediaTracks, Serius, and SuperCard. Each of these environments has a different focus. They range from simple slide show presentation to general-purpose programming, in which multimedia is simply another application.

- Multimedia production raises many legal issues for both producers and composers. The law is very restrictive about recording copyrighted material in any medium, unless it is for your own personal use — yes, even with MacRecorder.

- There is a widespread myth that it is legal to use anyone's music, as long as one takes only four bars or seven seconds, whichever is less. There is nothing in any copyright law that could, even by the wildest stretch of the imagination, be remotely misinterpreted to draw such a conclusion. Likewise, purchasing a CD, record, photo, video, or other creative work does not give you any rights whatsoever to use that material in a multimedia presentation.

- Clip music is currently marketed in three forms: MIDI data on floppy disks (or recently CD-ROMs) using the SMF format; digital audio data on floppy disks or CD-ROMs that you can play back with the Macintosh's internal sound capabilities (8-bit) or with various NuBus boards (16-bit); and normal digital audio data on standard CDs (sometimes called needle-drop libraries — these require relatively inexpensive licensing fees).

Part Nine
Education

Part Nine

Foreword

by David Mash

Education

Technology has changed the way we make music today. The various chapters in this book show how many ways technology in general, and the Macintosh in particular, have had an impact on the music profession. The power of the computer, coupled with MIDI synthesizers, allows for a degree of control over the minute details of music performance, composition, and production processes never before possible. The method of creating multipart music has never been as interactive as with today's technology. A musician can hear the music as it is being written, interacting with the sound, melody, harmony, and rhythm and can complete a full multitimbral work in CD-quality audio at a single workstation.

If this technology has changed the way we make music — possibly even the way we think about the process of music creation — then what about the way we teach music, and, more importantly, what about the way students learn music? Are new skills needed to function productively in the music profession? If so, how are these skills acquired, and how do they affect the more traditional skills and values normally associated with a quality music education?

It is certain that there are new skills that the professional musician must acquire to function effectively in the changing landscape of contemporary music. New terms and techniques must be assimilated and integrated into

routine processes. Both the study and practice of music are already a time-consuming endeavor. How does the musician learn this new technology without sacrificing the quality of the music? In many cases, the answer is in integrating technology into the music learning process itself.

We have traditionally viewed electronic music as a separate musical discipline. However, as technology continues to mature, it will become fairly transparent in its use as a general tool for making music. Many professions have already integrated technology as a tool for enhancing productivity. One familiar example is word processing, the use of which is commonplace. Word processing technology has become so transparent that writers forget that they are using a computer at all. We simply use the instrument that allows us to work at maximum effectiveness, focusing on our craft rather than on the tool itself.

With the options now available, we can integrate technology into the music teaching and learning processes in many ways. In this section, the author covers the range of hardware and software products available specifically for music education. Sequencing and notation software are also particularly well suited for use in the study of composition, arranging, and orchestration. Students can hear the music — auditioning various timbres for a given melody — and make musical decisions based on aural experience. The traditional time lag between conceptualizing music and hearing it performed is eliminated, allowing the student to connect symbol and sound more immediately. This immediacy provides a complete musical experience during the learning process.

As we integrate technology into the music teaching and learning processes, we should also reexamine what skills and values are essential for success in the music profession. Music teachers tend to teach the way they learned, and many of the available educational programs do just that: adapt the new technology to fit traditional teaching methods. However, traditional approaches toward developing musical hearing, instrumental skills, and a theoretic understanding of music may not be the most effective ways to accomplish these goals. Teachers need to begin to capture the power of the computer to help develop these skills. The technology can open new doors to effective musical skill development. Music teachers must open their minds to new opportunities and combine them with traditional approaches when appropriate.

Despite various negative associations often attributed to video games, there have been many positive effects of video games in developing young children's physical dexterity, fine motor skills, and refined response times. It may be possible to use these types of approaches to develop musical and instrumental skills as well — as these are the same underlying physical demands used in basic performance techniques. Fast interfaces between instrumental controllers and the computer will allow software engineers (and hopefully music educators) to design fun, game-like programs that will help students gain basic instrumental skills more quickly by focusing on developing basic dexterity and fine motor skills of the instrument itself through interactive and entertaining involvement. New approaches toward developing inner hearing may be possible through creative applications of the computer. Computers are well suited for helping students develop an accurate sense of pitch and timing. It is time that computer-assisted instruction move beyond the drill and test cycle and toward a more involving interactive skill-developing role.

The Macintosh is the ideal computer for the music teaching and learning environment. Through its intuitive and consistent user interface, the student can focus on learning music rather than on how to use the computer. There are many fine products available for making music with the Macintosh, as the following chapters demonstrate. It is up to us as educators to harness all this power and develop new methods for using technology for music education. ♩

David Mash is chairman of the Berklee College Synthesis Program in Boston.

Introduction to Part Nine

I have been following the evolution of computer-aided instruction software for many years, ever since the now-antiquated PLATO software (often cited as the first music education software) became available on-line through university computer terminals.

Until recently, the potential of CAI (also known as CBL for computer-based learning) in Macintosh music fell short of the great strides that have been made in sequencing, sound alteration, and even notation. This is not surprising. Because CAI software often requires notation and the type of MIDI I/O found in sequencers, CAI developers had to wait for these areas to attain a level of maturity before proceeding.

For traditional CAI on the Macintosh (if there is such a thing as traditional CAI) like the types discussed in the first chapter of this section, there are now well over 100 new offerings. This does not include other Macintosh music software used creatively for computer-aided instruction (as described in the case history in Chapter 28, "Computer-aided Instruction").

While I often realized the strong potential of these programs for aiding my own teaching, there were and still are very few that I would consider using for self-guided learning myself.

This was not the case with the resources covered in the second chapter in this section. My gut response to these offerings was considerably closer to heart. CD-ROM technology in particular made me wish for the first time that I was a young musician again at the beginning of my music education.

Additional applications for Macintosh music educators

There are many other programs available for Macintosh music educators. These range from software for managing a music library (Software Guild's Music Library System and A. H. Nussel's ShuBox Music Librarian) to software for creating marching band drill charts that can handle the most complex situations (ECS's Advantage Showare and Pyware's Music Charting Aid). Pyware's marching band software lets you import MIDI files and synchronize animations of the players marching on the screen so you can make sure that all the right feet fall on a downbeat, for example.

Scholars involved in music research, psychoacoustical research, and acoustical research also have a number of options (see the tables in Chapter 6, "Software Options"). HyperCard and similar user-friendly programming environments can be of help in constructing analytical aids of great sophistication.

Prepackaged software dedicated to music education is not the only avenue open to Macintosh music educators. Notation programs can be used by themselves or in conjunction with word processors or page-layout software to create everything from informative handouts to examinations and scholarly papers — just about any course materials you can imagine. Database software can easily be customized for tracking students, grading, creating lesson plans, organizing course materials, and participating in scholarly research — the list goes on and on.

The Macintosh and MIDI software can enhance any course in music theory, composition, orchestration, arrangement, form and analysis, or counterpoint. If you've read the chapters on MIDI, you're probably bursting with ideas. If you've read the other chapters, you've probably come up with some ideas along the following lines:

Digital audio tools, sample editing software, and algorithmic sound generation software are a natural for teaching the fundamentals of acoustics. Even MacroMind-Paracomp's 8-bit MacRecorder package or Articulate Systems's Voice Impact Pro will usually suffice.

Creative use of single keystroke macros can automate and streamline a lecture or classroom presentation so that much more material can be covered. With an inexpensive video projector, the Macintosh can become the presentation medium instead of the blackboard.

Finally, when a Macintosh music lab is available (or a Macintosh lab available to music students), the presentation and retrieval of students' work assignments, final projects, and the like can be automated so that no paper is involved. Instructors can pick up all the assignments via modem or a network and correct them on screen. For composition, orchestration, and theory courses, this also provides the instructor with the option to audition the assignments and projects and greatly speed up the grading process. It's much easier to hear the mistakes than strain your eyes pouring over often illegible pencil scratchings.

Many conservatories and music departments nationwide are already expanding their involvement with the Macintosh. Berklee College of Music in Boston, the nation's foremost pop/jazz/commercial music school, is committed to using the Macintosh. Berklee's proliferation of Macintosh-controlled digital music workstations, each one representing a highly functional home-studio configuration, prepares students for the growing practice of arriving at a major recording studio with nothing more than a Macintosh disk in hand. Just down the street from Berklee, The New England Conservatory of Music, one of the most respected institutions for a classical music education, is using Macintoshes more and more every day. The Macintosh is instrumental in teaching rigorous traditional disciplines such as counterpoint and orchestration.

In whatever way you use the Macintosh for your educational endeavors, both you and your students will be amply rewarded.

Chapter 28

CAI — Computer-aided Instruction

In this chapter . . .

✔ CAI in ear training, theory, musicianship, and instrument instruction.

✔ Two roles of the Macintosh as music teacher: self-guided learning and classroom teaching.

✔ Detailed examination of 16 software options for ear training, theory, and performance.

✔ Music learning programs for the young and the young at heart.

✔ Music education HyperCard stack gallery.

✔ Feature table.

Computer-based Learning

The breadth of programs for computer-aided instruction (CAI — also known as computer-based learning, or CBL) may surprise even the most savvy Macintosh musicians. A keyboard practice aid measures your accuracy, telling you how many notes were botched and specifically which ones they were. Several jazz programs supply a backup band for any tune and style over which to develop your solo improvisational skills. A tuning aid not only checks intonation, but gives visual feedback for maintaining even vibrato or sustained pitches. Of course ear training, the bane of many traditional musicians, is a prime target for a large number of programs focusing on intervals, chords, and dictation.

Don't get the idea that using Macintosh CAI programs will substitute for studies with a master teacher or even impart instant success to your musical endeavors. Every week there is a new method "guaranteed" to teach perfect pitch or transform a novice into an instant keyboard virtuoso, but the fact remains that musicians build these skills only with a considerable investment of time and energy. Learning music is hard work with or without a computer. The computer can provide a powerful boost, aiding both teachers and students, but it cannot substitute for a strong commitment on the part of the student.

At this time, there are a great number of Macintosh programs dedicated to CAI, most of which are geared for one of two types of learning: self-instruction and teacher-guided instruction. Macintosh music CAI is still in its infancy, so the programs that are currently available only scratch the surface of what's possible, while providing a tantalizing glimpse of the future.

A complete listing of available Macintosh music CAI programs categorized according to application is found in Chapter 6, "Software Options."

The Macintosh as Music Teacher

The Macintosh makes an ideal music teaching assistant. For one thing, it can give instant feedback to student input. Recognizing intervals, for example, demands not only repetition but immediate evaluation of a response, while the sound is still fresh in the ears. In the classroom, this is a difficult proposition. Often papers are returned the next day, when feedback affects little else than ego. Another dilemma for any instructor is the wide variety of levels within even a small group of students. A class of eight often represents three levels of accomplishment, not to mention probably eight different learning paces. Consequently, classroom dictation is often frustrating. Students needing more time are always under uncomfortable pressure, while those who are ahead lose focus and involvement. Computer software solves these problems to a certain extent. A student trying to digest just three notes in succession can limit a dictation exercise accordingly; another student accustomed to swallowing operas whole might choose a thousand-note epic.

The marriage of the Macintosh and MIDI solves other problems. Ear-training students frequently complain that, while they might learn chords listening to a piano, the same sounds on a guitar or oboe leave them stymied. In fact, studies by researchers in the field of psychoacoustics have proven that students score much higher on ear-training examinations when the examples are played on their own instruments — not everyone is a pianist. With MIDI, all possible timbres become fair game for listening. Experimentation with orchestration and musical texture are also easy to accomplish.

Maybe the strongest case for the Macintosh as an instructive aid is that it requires no special training to make decisions about notation or performance. Beginners to ear training face various obstructions, including technical facility on an instrument and the actual calligraphy of notation on paper. Selection with the mouse in the familiar Macintosh graphic environment simplifies these chores, so that one can concentrate on musical learning and leave the worries of the performance and notation to the computer. Consequently, a large number of CAI programs lend themselves to introductory musical approaches, as well as functioning as bonafide aids for private lessons and dedicated academic courses.

Some teachers are uncomfortable with computer aids; many complain that the computer cannot impart true musicianship. That is not the issue. The reality is that 90 percent of musicianship skills involve drudgery — drudgery for the student to repetitively exercise and for the teacher to repetitively evaluate. My teacher Nadia Boulanger used to say, "I require so many things that they [the students] would be dead before the end of the year if they did everything." There are too few teachers and far too many students to effectively teach this subject. Typically, students remain deficient in essential skills and blame it on lack of talent instead of insufficient drill, as is often the case. If the computer can make up this difference even minimally, if it can free up even a fraction of class time, then it should be considered an indispensable aid to produce skilled and knowledgeable musicians.

CAI Overview

Unfortunately, the potential of CAI in Macintosh music falls short of the great strides that have been made in sequencing, sound design, and even notation.

Elegance and creative use of the Macintosh interface are still rarely a given because much Macintosh CAI software has been ported from other computer platforms, although this is rapidly changing. But don't let that discourage you. There are plenty of products worth your attention, and unlike feature-bloated notation and performance applications, most CAI programs are immediately understandable and usable, providing instant gratification.

The available software examined in this chapter falls roughly into two large categories: performance and musicianship training. The musicianship category further divides into programs dedicated to ear training, theory and analysis, and music history/appreciation.

Performance and instrument instruction overview

Just how can the Macintosh help you to become a better player? For starters, before you begin playing, it is customary to tune; and while you're playing, it's just as important to stay in tune. Two programs, Master Tuner and JI Calc, are devoted to this task. It is said that practicing is the only way to get to Carnegie Hall. Coda had this in mind when it created Practice Room, which first demonstrates a piece, then gives you the opportunity to play either hand individually, and finally evaluates your completed performance according to note accuracy, attack time, duration, and so on. But maybe you can't take the computer with you on an upcoming camping trip. Never fear — Guitar Wizard lets you print out fretboard graphics detailing the fingering and intervals for all manner of chords and scales. And if the band forgets to show up? Both MiBAC and Band In A Box supply a background of piano, bass, and drums for hundreds of tunes in dozens of styles over which you can weave or practice your improvisational magic.

Case history

For the past three years, most of my doctoral composition students at Claremont Graduate School have used Macintoshes. Many prefer to come to my studio for their private lessons and bring their compositions in the form of notation files. This includes students who have no sound-generating devices of their own, but enter all the notes with the mouse.

I have a special studio configuration that makes my devices function as a virtual symphony orchestra. I am able to do this because I have a number of multitimbral ROM-based sample players (eight to be exact — but that is definitely overkill) that do not require loading of soundfiles. In fact, I have nearly all acoustic instruments in solo and ensemble versions, with every known manner of playing style, (e.g., string sounds with martelé bowing, tremolo, muted, harmonics, pizzicato, louré, and so on).

The students bring their notation files with the staves set to different MIDI channels and in many cases, initialized with the proper patches that call up the appropriate instruments. As the music scrolls by on the screen, we listen to a credible rendition of the piece whether it is a chamber ensemble or orchestral work.

Using Cut, Copy, and Paste, I can instantly illustrate the effect of alternate orchestrations. The beauty is that these are not merely on paper but can be auditioned immediately. Because I have a library of MIDI-executable expressive markings, I can quickly show the effect of adding a sforzando or a series of tenuto markings to a passage. By changing patches, I am able to show them how another instrument or doubling might sound better than what they have chosen for a part. I have different sounds for various types of bowing and tonguing, as well as solo instruments and ensembles. This lets me use the same patch-changing approach to demonstrate how a different bowing or articulation might improve a passage or how a soloist might be more appropriate on a given line.

Because all the instruments we use in these situations are samplers, I can call up any instrument sound or articulation or combination of instruments just by sending a patch change message. This lets me say things like, "Bartok had a similar line (or texture) in the *Concerto for Orchestra,* but he used the bassoon to play it." I

switch the patch to a bassoon and demonstrate. "Here is what your passage would sound like on the bassoon. . . . And this is what it would sound like doubled with the viola an octave above. . ." A few button presses let me set up a layer with the bassoon and viola in octaves.

If I detect larger structural problems in a student's work, sometimes we save the file as a MIDI file and import it into a MIDI sequencer. The sequencer makes it possible to disassemble the composition into its structural components and rearrange these logical chunks by simply dragging them around with the mouse.

For the students who do not own samplers or sample players or are entering their music with the mouse, my virtual orchestra of ROM- and RAM-based sample players affords them an opportunity to hear a rendition of their work in progress, which would be impossible under any other circumstances. Some of the students without their own Macintosh computers use those owned by the school.

For many years I have been teaching a young student via modem. I became acquainted with him through an ongoing discussion on a telecommunications BBS. Eventually he started leaving notation files of his compositions in my electronic mail box for me to comment on. We soon started lessons that consisted of him sending me files via modem, and then we would both put the file up on our respective screens and discuss it over the phone. At the end of a lesson, I would use the modem to send back the file with revisions that resulted from these discussions. This went on for about four years.

I am still giving lessons via modem, although the process is considerably more sophisticated. I have one student who lives about 100 miles away. To facilitate this sort of telecommunications interaction, we both got 19,200-baud modems. Using Farallon's Timbuktu Remote software, I am able to bring his computer screen up in a window on mine and take control of his mouse and keyboard. Because we both have a dedicated modem line, we can use our voice line to discuss the project while I control his computer to demonstrate a point. From his point of view, it is just as if I were sitting there with his mouse and keyboard in front of me, since everything I do on the copy of his screen that appears on mine, appears in front of him.

Software

The software covered in this chapter does not represent a complete compendium. Programs have been chosen for the purpose of illustrating a variety of approaches. For a complete listing of Macintosh CAI software, consult the tables in Chapter 6. You should also read Chapter 29 about some innovative approaches to CAI software for music history and appreciation.

Software for music theory and rudiments

7th Heaven

Occasionally a program aspires to only modest ambition, but covers its goal with such elegance that you rediscover the power of your Macintosh. 7th Heaven (Soul Support Software), an ear-training application limited to only 7th chords, is just such a program (see Figure 28-1). It plays a chord on your MIDI device and you attempt to play the same chord back, as in "Simon Says." An on-screen thumbs-up/thumbs-down gives immediate evaluation to your response. If you need to see an answer, you can request that the chord's notation be displayed.

The sophistication arises from the complexity of the chords the program handles. Inversions and all manner of altered 7th chords are available; even jazz 9th chords are included. Further, chord spacings are selectable and variable. The importance of this feature cannot be overstressed. Being able to identify a chord in all its manifestations endows real-world skills useful for composing and playing. 7th Heaven is equally capable of testing simple and advanced examples of 7th chords. Even within its limited scope, its effectiveness in ear training is as good as if not better than any other program on the market.

Ear Trainer

Lawrence Gallagher's shareware program Ear Trainer is also limited to the Macintosh's internal sound capabilities, but includes many features such as chord inversion of triads and 7th chords and compound intervals (intervals wider than an octave). You can also choose the set of intervals, chords, and inversions that you want to be tested for by way of a Setup option.

An Interval Specifications option lets you restrict the number of pitches heard, choose the register of the test, choose whether intervals are arpeggiated up or down — and even restrict the types of intervals to be drilled on. For instance, if you are having trouble with perfect fourths vs. perfect fifths, you can confine the test to only those intervals. Chord Specifications offers a similar range of choices (see Figure 28-2). One cautionary note: Avoid low register for chords when using the Macintosh speaker, because notes often don't sound.

The degree of user-configuration options offered by Ear Trainer is an extremely valuable feature, because each person invariably discovers different strengths and weaknesses in chord and interval identification. Allowing you to focus on your problems makes for more efficient learning.

Figure 28-1: 7th Heaven's main screen. You receive instant feedback of your keyboard response by way of the thumbs-up/thumbs-down graphics. If your answer is incorrect, the same chord is repeated. Otherwise, a new example is automatically generated, allowing for rapid-fire interaction as fast as you can take it. The notation window can be hidden or displayed by toggling a button.

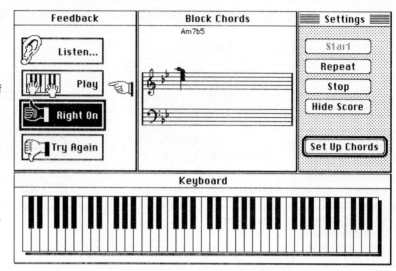

The actual drills have an interesting implementation. A new interval or chord will not be played until the previous one is correctly chosen. The "way out" in case you are stymied is to click a button labeled Hint. The correct answer is briefly highlighted, allowing you to choose it and so be released to hear the next example. In other words, you have to cheat in order to continue the test. To destroy whatever integrity you have left, no points are taken off for using the Hint button. Strange, but true.

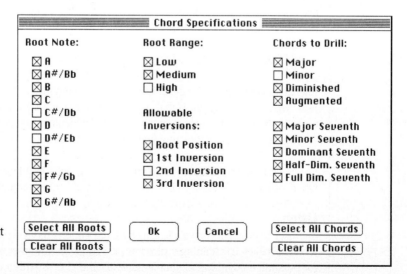

Figure 28-2: The Chord Specifications option in Ear Trainer provides great flexibility in personalizing the content of the drills.

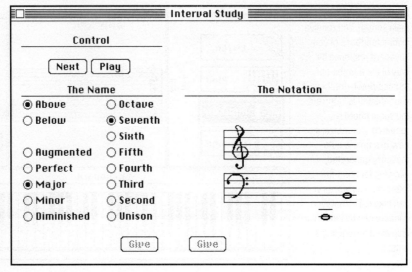

Figure 28-3: In a drill for Interval, you can identify the interval by label or notation. For beginners, the computer can even show the answer for one of these parameters after playing an interval, leaving only the label or notation to be solved.

Interval

Despite its plain and simple approach, Interval is an excellent basic ear-training application by Brad Needham, suitable for beginners of all ages. It tests only basic intervals using traditional nomenclature of interval type (unison, second, third, and so on) and interval quality (perfect, minor, major, diminished, augmented). You can identify intervals by clicking radio buttons beside their name or by dragging the correct notes onto a music staff (see Figure 28-3).

The software options are flexible: The Macintosh can simply play the sound, leaving you to identify the interval name and indicate the appropriate pitch on the staff, or it can supply either the sound with the name or the sound with notation. In these cases you only solve a single parameter: the name of the interval or its correct staff notation.

Intervals may be played melodically or harmonically (as a chord). The only drawback of the program is that it is limited to Macintosh sound, which makes tones in the extreme ranges somewhat more difficult to discern. Otherwise, it accomplishes its task efficiently without need of extra features.

Feedback from the program is given by graying out (disabling) the Give button when you correctly solve either the interval name or notational question.

Listen

The user interface to Imaja's Listen (by Greg Jalbert) has a wonderful Macintosh feel that makes ear training a pleasure. It is possibly the most successful approach for building recognition of simple intervals and chords with a catered interface for pianists and guitarists.

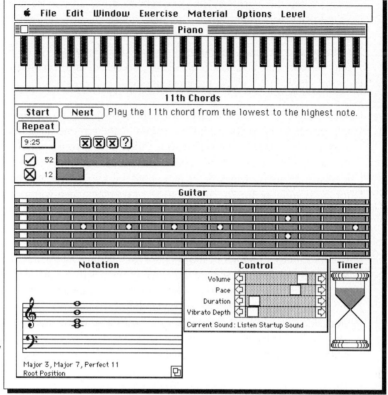

Figure 28-4: The three main components of a Listen screen: keyboard, fretboard, and progress windows. Also pictured is the Notation window, configurable Controls, and Timer.

Listen's screen is divided into three parts (see Figure 28-4). On top is an on-screen keyboard, on the bottom a guitar fretboard. In the middle is a Progress and Explanation window for keeping score and giving instructions. To begin, you simply select an exercise. It can be as basic as identifying one or two notes, or as involved as recognizing a melody of a length you predetermine. Another option is a "growing melody," where each successful answer results in a new note being added at the end of the tune, similar to the popular electronic toy Simon, which uses colored pads for the same purpose.

Intervals, triads, and 7th chords make up the remaining exercises. You can choose to test your ability to simply find the correct notes or to identify the proper name or quality of the chord or interval. Using chord inversions is an option with both triads and 7th chords; this is an important feature not always present in ear-training programs.

Instructions in the Progress and Explanation window make the drill procedure patently simple; moreover, four clever but simple icons tell the rest of the story. When the Macintosh plays or repeats drills, the mouse icon is in the shape of an ear. After playing the aural question, the icon transforms to a pointed finger for you to perform the answer on the keyboard or fretboard (whichever you have selected). If you are successful, the icon becomes a happy mask (not a happy face, thank goodness), and, predictably, a miniature "oops" mask indicates an incorrect answer.

Your progress is clearly measured by the growth of two horizontal bars that appear below the keyboard in Figure 28-4 — the top one measures correct answers, the bottom incorrect answers. Additionally, your numerical score appears on the side of each bar. Listen provides an additional effective method of ongoing feedback regarding which notes of a chord are wrong. A row of small boxes, three for triads and four for 7th chords, appear in center screen with question marks inside. As you play the chords, the boxes fill with check marks (correct) or Xs (incorrect) accordingly.

Listen includes a number of nice utilities for customizing the interface. Under the Material menu you can specify the range of pitches to be included in drills, any actual notes or keys you would like to exclude, the length of melodies, and which inversions (if any) to be played. The Options menu includes a timer that appears alongside the score and counts the time you spend doing an exercise in seconds. This menu also lets you choose whether to have chords arpeggiated and it is where you specify MIDI for external keyboard and synthesizer control.

The software includes a number of Macintosh soundfiles. Several are adequate, but definitely inferior to the possibilities that MIDI opens up.

No matter which option you go with, the Control window is an important feature to explore. It lists the current sound you have invoked and provides four controls: Volume, Vibrato, Duration, and Pace. Of these, Pace can be most crucial; it sets the length of time between consecutive notes in a melody — in other words, it controls the speed of playback for the drill. This is helpful because the program does not otherwise recognize tempo. Increasing or decreasing the pace can have extraordinary impact on accurate listening.

MacGAMUT

MacGAMUT (Graded Aural Music Training on the Apple Macintosh) is intended for use in basic theory and musicianship classes. Written by Ann K. Blombach and published by Mayfield Publishing Company, it carefully records the amount of time students spend in each category and also rates their proficiency.

Even the interface seems a replication of class dictation. You drag notes, accidentals, and barlines onto the staff as you listen to a melody, similar to pencil notation (although you may enter pitches with a MIDI keyboard). But if you

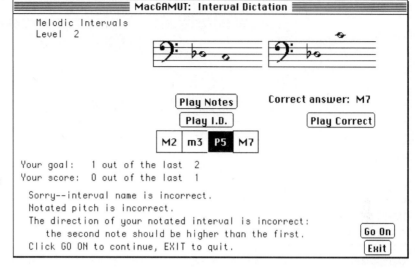

Figure 28-5: The correction in this interval drill illustrates MacGAMUT's intelligence. The staff and labeling on the left is the student response.

choose to hear the tune too frequently, the play button literally disappears. And if you guess wrong after a few times on the interval/chords questions, the program automatically corrects and analyzes your mistakes. All settings can be customized to suit the individual needs of the class. This may only be done by the teacher, who has access to the primary Instructor Disk. With MacGAMUT a clear message comes through — theory is serious study and the pressure is on.

Aural training is divided into two parts: single elements (intervals, scales, and chords) and melodic dictation. Alto and tenor clefs are incorporated at relevant points throughout the program. Being able to read C clefs is essential to good musicianship, yet of all CAI applications only MacGAMUT incorporates this feature.

The drills are straightforward tests of theory and notation. Intervals, scales, and chords must be written out with the mouse and identified with the proper label. If you make errors, the program gives hints and urges a retry. Answers are usually accompanied by constructive criticisms of your attempts, and you have an option to play your version and the correct solution for comparison (see Figure 28-5).

The chord drills are thorough in testing inversions, but have no provision for augmented 6th chords. The 7th chords are abbreviated Mm, mm, and so on, rather than by harmonic function. Should you get confused, ample on-line help is available at all times via a dedicated menu.

The major part of the show with MacGAMUT is the dictation drill. Notation is accomplished with the mouse by selecting durations and dragging notes, accidentals, and barlines onto the staff (see Figure 28-6). There is little you can get

Figure 28-6: Using the melodic dictation tools with Mac-GAMUT takes practice itself. **(A)** You enter your response to the dictation by selecting notes from the pallette and clicking them onto the staff. **(B)** MacGAMUT then points out your mistakes complete with comments.

away with; MacGAMUT even takes off points for forgetting a double bar. To be frank, accomplishing the notation of responses for this program requires some practice in and of itself. The mouse changes appearance as an arrow, an accidental, and notehead depending on slight changes in direction. The erasure procedure is particularly strange — you circle the mouse around the note till it appears as an arrow and drag it completely off the staff. Novices to the program can easily drag a note to oblivion when only trying to change its position. That brings up another minor irritation. When first dragging a notehead to the staff, it flashes in a way that occasionally obscures its position.

The error detection of dictation is very helpful. Not only are incorrect notes marked, but the correct solution is displayed on a new staff immediately above your own work, thus allowing immediate comparison (see Figure 28-6B). Further, a text box describes problems and assigns a percentage to your correct input. The program accurately recognizes enharmonic spellings and notes them in the correction box.

```
To choose the level you want, click in the circle next to the level
description.  Click OK to continue, or CANCEL to return to the same level.
○ Major, simple, I skips          ○ Modulation to distant keys
○ U skips, anacrusis              ○ Chromatic changes, more skips
○ Larger I and U skips            ○ Chromatic, harder rhythm
○ Cut time, IU skips, 6ths in I, U ○ Chromatic, complex rhythm
○ Larger IU skips, secondary skips
○ Compound meter
○ Longer melodies, more skips
○ Minor, i and U skips
○ iu skips, larger i and U skips
● More skips, trickier compound
○ Syncopation, mixture, skips
○ More complex, larger skips
○ Modulation to close keys
○ Trickier tonality, syncopation    [ OK ]  [ CANCEL ]  [ EXIT ]
```

Figure 28-7: MacGAMUT offers extensive configuration and feedback options.

An extensive hierarchy of difficulty levels attempts to encompass a great variety of possible musical parameters. Some of these include simple and large skips, compound meter, syncopation, mixture, modulation to distant keys, and chromaticism. These appear in different combinations in each of the 18 levels included with the program (see Figure 28-7).

The program maintains a student statistics sheet that is very thorough. It gives the name of the student, class section, time, day, and length of use. Each exercise is listed along with the level achieved and the number of correct answers in relation to the total number of attempts.

Instructor customization is another major concern of the program. You, the teacher, determine how many times each example can be played, how often answers are checked, how many keys are tested and on what level, and what percentage of accuracy constitutes mastery of a level. In fact, you can reorder or omit levels as you like. If you wish to allow students to use MIDI keyboards or adjust tempos, these parameters are also at your disposal.

In short, the philosophy behind MacGAMUT is comprehensive drill of dictation and ear training coupled with tight control over the student's progress and use of the program. Maneuvering around MacGAMUT is not an intuitive process, but its capabilities might prove helpful as a supplement for theory classes where computer labs are available.

MiBAC Music Lessons

MiBAC Music Lessons is an ear-training program designed for self-paced learning with MIDI or Macintosh audio. The software offers drills for note names, circle of fifths, key signatures, scales and modes (including jazz scales, scale degrees, intervals, and durations). See Figures 28-8 through 28-10 for more information on MiBAC Music Lessons.

Perceive

Coda's Perceive, written by James Romeo and George Litterst, is actually a group of six mini-applications for teaching rudiments of ear training. They include chord and scale recognition, melodic dictation, and primitive exploration of alternate tuning systems and waveform synthesis.

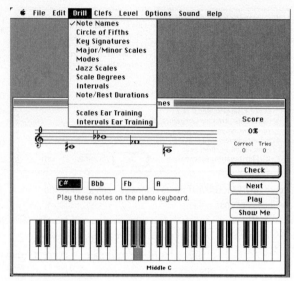

Figure 28-8: MiBAC Music Lessons lets you select drills with the menu pictured. A Note Names drill is shown in this example. You can play your response on a MIDI keyboard, use the mouse to click notes on the on-screen keyboard, or type note names from the Macintosh keyboard.

A

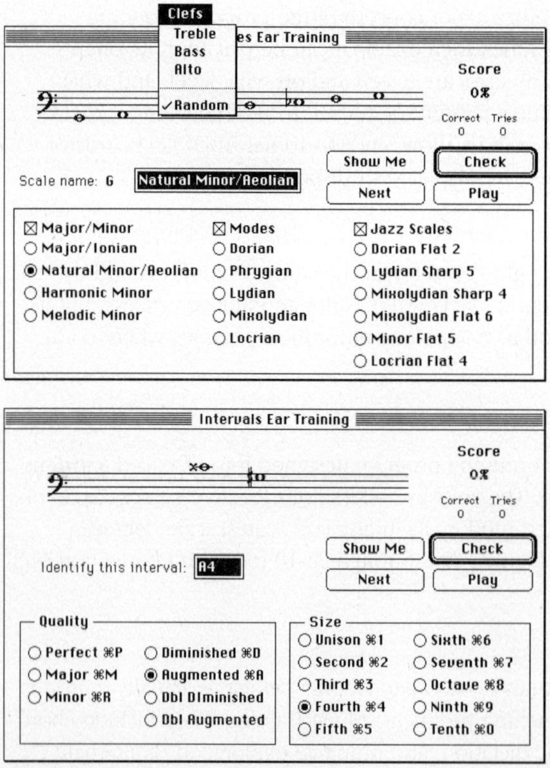

Figure 28-9: (A) MiBAC's Scales Ear Training window with Clefs menu showing. **(B)** MiBAC's Intervals Ear Training window.

B

The Drills application plays varieties of scales and chords that must be correctly identified. As a new example is selected, tones are sounded either internally through the Macintosh or externally by way of MIDI, and an appropriate answer must be chosen. You can configure the variables for tempo, key, and articulation. Included in the quiz are scales and modes, triads (major, minor, diminished, and augmented), and 7th chords.

Inversions of triads and 7th chords are not covered. Choices include Major-Major 7th, Major-minor 7th, minor-Major 7th, minor-minor 7th, and so on. Unfortunately, it makes the function of these chords very muddled. For instance, Perceive makes no reference to the fact that a Major-minor 7th is almost universally known as a dominant 7th chord.

For simple melodic recognition, Perceive offers the Tutor program. You select the number of notes that will comprise a

A

```
┌─ Auto Next Question ─┐┌─ Auto Next Note ─┐┌─ Mac Sound ──────────┐
│ ☒ Note Names         ││ ☒ Note Names     ││ ● Piano   ○ No Sound │
│ ☒ Key Signatures     ││ ☒ Circle Of Fifths││ Click Sustain Time 15│
│ ☒ Maj/Min Scales     ││ ☒ Maj/Min Scales │└──────────────────────┘
│ ☒ Modes              ││ ☒ Modes          │┌─ MIDI Sound ─────────┐
│ ☒ Jazz Scales        ││ ☒ Jazz Scales    ││ ● Modem   ○ Printer │
│ ☒ Scale Degrees      │└──────────────────┘│ MHz: ○ .5 ● 1 ○ 2   │
│ ☒ Intervals          │┌─ All Drills ─────┐├──────────────────────┤
│ ☒ Note Durations     ││ ○ Mac   ● MIDI   ││ Channel 1 (1-16) 1  │
│ ☒ Scales ET          ││ Tempo  120       ││ Patch 1 (1-128)  34 │
│ ☒ Intervals ET       │└──────────────────┘│ 8ve: ● Norm ○ Up ○ Down│
│                      │┌─ Interval Drills ┐├──────────────────────┤
│   ┌──────────────┐   ││ ☒ Melodic        ││ Channel 2 (1-16) 2  │
│   │    Save      │   ││ ☒ Harmonic       ││ Patch 2 (1-128)  103│
│   └──────────────┘   ││                  ││ 8ve: ● Norm ○ Up ○ Down│
│   ┌──────────────┐   ││ Play (1-8)x   1  ││ ☒ Use MIDI Echo     │
│   │   Cancel     │   ││ ET Play (1-8)x 1 ││ Echo Channel:   1   │
│   └──────────────┘   │└──────────────────┘└──────────────────────┘
└──────────────────────┘
```

melody (up to 100). The computer highlights and plays the tonic on the on-screen keyboard before playing the melody. To answer correctly, you must click the appropriate notes on the on-screen keyboard. There is a provision for erasing a previous note in case you make a mistake. An extra feature of Tutor is that you can save any music you play on the on-screen keyboard for later recall.

B

```
▤▤▤▤▤▤▤▤▤ My Progress Report ▤▤▤▤▤▤▤▤
 MiBAC™ Music Lessons Progress Report
 Christopher Yavelow              Monday, December 9, 1991
 Drill           Treble Clef      Bass Clef        Alto Clef

 Note Names Chromatic             Total: 0%  (0 of 0)  (0)
 Spaces:         0%  (0 of 0)     0%  (0 of 0)     0%  (0 of 0)
 Lines:          0%  (0 of 0)     0%  (0 of 0)     0%  (0 of 0)
 Staff:          0%  (0 of 0)     0%  (0 of 0)     0%  (0 of 0)
 Ledgers:        0%  (0 of 0)     0%  (0 of 0)     0%  (0 of 0)
 Advanced:       0%  (0 of 0)     0%  (0 of 0)     0%  (0 of 0)

 Modes                            Total: 0%  (0 of 0)  (0)
 Ionian:         0%  (0 of 1)     0%  (0 of 0)     0%  (0 of 0)
 Dorian:         0%  (0 of 0)     0%  (0 of 0)     0%  (0 of 0)
 Phrygian:       0%  (0 of 0)     0%  (0 of 0)     0%  (0 of 0)
 Lydian:         0%  (0 of 0)     0%  (0 of 0)     0%  (0 of 0)
 Mixolydian:     0%  (0 of 0)     0%  (0 of 0)     0%  (0 of 0)
 Aeolian:        0%  (0 of 0)     0%  (0 of 0)     0%  (0 of 0)
 Locrian:        0%  (0 of 0)     0%  (0 of 0)     0%  (0 of 0)

 Note/Rest Durations              Total: 0%  (0 of 0)  (0)
 Half Note Beat:     0%  (0 of 0)     0%  (0 of 0)     0%  (0 of 0)
 Quarter Note Beat:  0%  (0 of 0)     0%  (0 of 0)     0%  (0 of 0)
 Eighth Note Beat:   0%  (0 of 0)     0%  (0 of 0)     0%  (0 of 0)
 Sixteenth Note Beat:0%  (0 of 0)     0%  (0 of 0)     0%  (0 of 0)

 Beginning Intervals - Bass Clef  Total: 0%  (0 of 0)  (0)
      Perfect:        Diminished:       Augmented:
 Uni:  0%  (0 of 0)   0%  (0 of 0)    0%  (0 of 0)
 4th:  0%  (0 of 0)   0%  (0 of 0)    0%  (0 of 0)
 5th:  0%  (0 of 0)   0%  (0 of 0)    0%  (0 of 0)
 8ve:  0%  (0 of 0)   0%  (0 of 0)    0%  (0 of 0)

      Major:          Minor:        Diminished:    Augmented:
      0%  (0 of 0)    0%  (0 of 0)  0%  (0 of 0)   0%  (0 of 0)
```

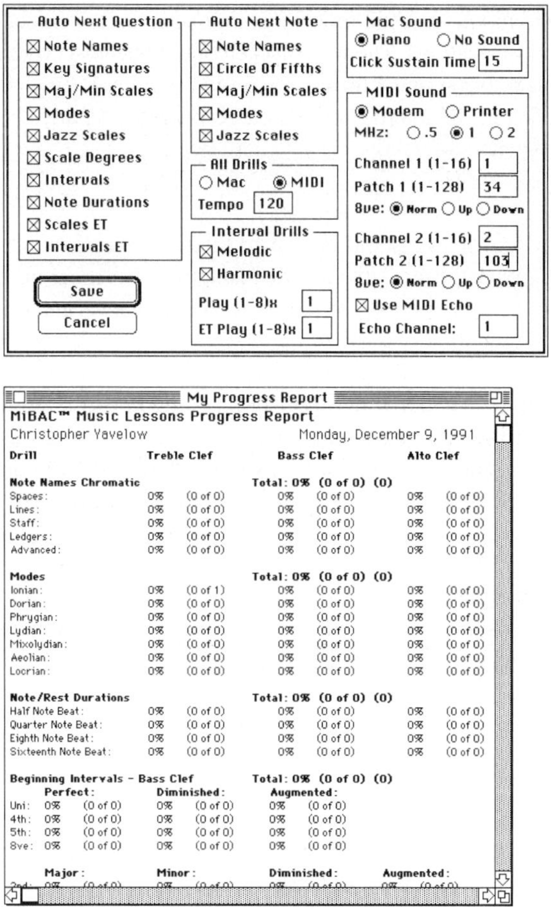

Figure 28-10: (A) You configure MiBAC Music Lessons by way of this Preferences dialog box. **(B)** MiBAC maintains a detailed ongoing progress report. You can choose to display a report for the current session or a cumulative analysis.

Two mini-applications are included to teach waveform synthesis by way of the Macintosh internal synthesizer. These are called MiniDesignWave and MiniDrawWave. MiniDesignWave lets you create waveforms by specifying a number of partials (overtones) and the specific volume level for each — in other words, additive synthesis. The purpose is to illustrate how different overtone intensities affect the timbre (tone color) of a static note. After you input the parameters, the waveform is calculated and drawn on the screen and can be previewed at A 440. Waveforms can also be printed and saved.

The remaining modules are listening aids. Tunings gives a choice for hearing a scale, chords, or short progression in different tuning systems, including equal temperament, Pythagorean, just intonation, meantone, well tempered, and Owen Jorgensen's 5 and 7 temperament. There is no description or explanation of the tunings in the program or the accompanying textbook. For discerning the basic waveforms of electronic music, another module called The Machine demonstrates white noise, sine, square, triangle, and sawtooth waves as arpeggios, scales, and random note patterns.

Perceive is a fine beginning tool for children and young adults for the material it covers (intervals, dictation, and chords through root position triads and root position 7th chords). Its use of clear instructions at every junction caters especially to people unfamiliar with computers. A full report feature makes it convenient for classroom assignments and evaluations. The text supplement, while easy to read, does little to alleviate the lack of on-line information in the program. Finally, though not an overriding factor, the interface of the entire program is fairly primitive as Macintosh programs go.

Practica Musica

Practica Musica (written by Jeffrey Evans and published by Ars Nova) is the most comprehensive ear-training package available for the Macintosh. Its "no pain, no gain" approach might turn off some people, because the rather awkward interface requires more mouse-clicking than necessary.

Using the program is akin to conventional musicianship training in that it requires hard work. The software focuses on a grueling regimen of ear-training drills and spends little time on elegance and fun. Still, the program is superb in sharpening aural skills and effectively covers the basics of a fine college-level beginning theory course.

A keyboard graphic beneath a piano staff is the main interface to the program. Three different keyboard views are possible: plain with no markings, note names under each key (including enharmonic equivalents), and a mini-grand staff superimposed over the keys. The latter two views are terrific for beginners, because they can quickly establish an association between the position of a key and its printed notation.

While operation with a MIDI keyboard controller is infinitely preferable, the program provides better-than-average soundfiles of piano, harpsichord, organ, and drum sounds for internal Macintosh playback. These can be tuned to eight different systems besides equal temperament.

A particularly strong suit of Practica Musica is its flexible melodic dictation (see Figure 28-11). You may choose to restrict notation to purely rhythms, purely pitches, or both simultaneously (conventional dictation). This division is a fabulous tool to develop skills of rhythmic patterns and melodic shapes. If rhythmic dictation is selected, you only have to listen for the rhythms of the melody. You click the appropriate durational values, and the correct pitches are automatically placed on the score. In this mode, even though you are only being drilled on rhythm, this pitch feedback can be beneficial. Conversely, with pitch dictation you can focus entirely on selecting the correct notes and let the computer automatically assign their proper durations. These features alone can provide an exciting breakthrough in listening deficiencies.

Dictation selections can be chosen from preset libraries (ranging from Pergolesi to the National Anthem), computer-generated tunes, or melodies you create yourself

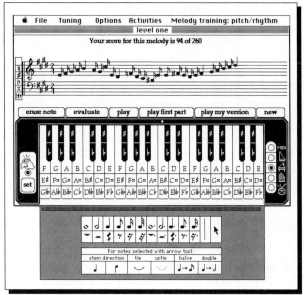

Figure 28-11: Melodic dictation in Practica Musica is intuitive. Dedicated buttons for erasure, performance of your solution, rhythmic tapping, and hearing just the first part of a tune provide helpful aids. Equally useful for beginners is the option to have the keyboard display enharmonic spellings, as pictured in this figure.

and save for later recall. Note entry with the mouse can be as laborious as conventional means: You select a duration from the palette and drag a notehead onto the staff or alternatively click the on-screen keyboard. A far speedier solution, which is a familiar approach adopted by most notation programs, is to simply play your MIDI keyboard after selecting the rhythm. Unfortunately, editing of your dictation is limited to erasing selected notes; however, there are other aids that make the dictation environment more friendly.

A metronome sound can be activated to confirm the pulse and meter by tapping before and during the melody. Even more powerful is a button marked "Play first part." This instructs the computer how far ahead the melody should continue from what you have presently transcribed. This way you can concentrate your listening in smaller amounts. Some instructors may consider this to be a cheat feature. You determine the number of new notes to be played during each listening.

Along with dictation, Practica Musica provides an equally thorough approach to drilling simple sight reading, scales, intervals, and chords. Pitch Reading displays a short passage of eight or more whole notes with various accidentals. The object is to play these tones on your keyboard as quickly and accurately as possible. The computer monitors your speed and assigns a score to your performance. Similarly, Scales tests performance of ascending or descending scales and modes. If your answer is incorrect, you can view the solution superimposed over your response for an instant comparison. Unfortunately, completing this drill is a nuisance. Playing the appropriate scale is simple enough, but then choosing a key signature (for the bonus) takes an extra four mouse clicks. The Evaluate button requires two more mouse clicks, one to check your answer and another to report your score.

To continue the drill, you must click the New button for the next set of instructions. That makes seven mouse clicks for each perfect answer and a strong incentive not to make mistakes.

Interval recognition comes in three flavors: Interval Playing, Interval Spelling, and Interval Ear Training. The ear-training option requires identifying the correct interval by name and by playing it on the MIDI keyboard. If you answer incorrectly, further questions focus solely on the problematic interval. The playing and spelling quizzes work in the same manner. Here the enharmonic on-screen keyboard is helpful for spelling augmented and diminished intervals, and if your answer is flawed, not only is the correct notation displayed, but the corresponding keys flash. This philosophy of combining CMN with keyboard configuration speeds the learning curve.

Chord training includes emphasis on inversions and chromatic harmony. It's hard to find another ear-training program that tests augmented 6th chords and analyzes your chord choice above the staff while supplying hints alongside — all this in addition to displaying the correct chord notation and flashing the corresponding keys (see Figure 28-12). Using this application in the classroom can save considerable time for the instructor — time better spent learning actual music.

Four levels of proficiency are available in each skill test. After solving an exercise, your score is displayed along with the number of points necessary to complete the level. Sometimes this can seem an overwhelming mountain for beginners, because points are subtracted for each mistake. The reward for winning the game is a resounding ovation from the computer — complete with whistles and cheers. It is quite a tension reliever.

At all times, you can navigate freely between different skill tests and proficiency levels when studying with Practica Musica. On-line help is present for understanding the rudiments of interval and chord spelling. A well thought-out textbook, *Windows on Music*, accompanies the software and adds important information on other areas of musicianship. An ideal feature for classroom use is the program's option to print complete progress reports with blackened rectangles to indicate mastery of the different skills and levels.

CAI software for music theory and rudiments

Mozart and Appletones
Mozart and Appletones by John Meier are simple but effective applications that demonstrate the rudiments of music composition.

Mozart is an abridged version of the famous dice game for composing minuets attributed to the great Austrian composer (see Chapter 20, "Algorithmic Composition"). Any two adjacent measures can be grouped with any other two to create

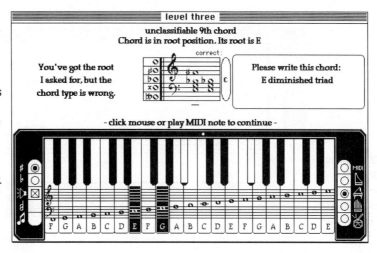

Figure 28-12: The correction capability in Practica Musica is impressive. The on-screen keyboard highlights all the notes you respond to and the correct ones flash on and off. Note the program's attempt to identify the chord written by the student. The comments at the left of the staff suggest strategies for finding the correct answer.

different minuets. With this program, you drag eight different sets of two measures in any order (see Figure 28-13). Additionally, you can assign dynamics, articulation marks, and tempo. By making these decisions, a beginner puts together a piece from ready-made material, yet still confronts issues of harmony, cadence, texture, and musicality.

Appletones focuses in a more abstract fashion on basic compositional principles — repetition, silence, loudness, and duration (see Figure 28-14). Twelve predetermined sound blocks are available, including four tones (low, medium low, medium high, high), three chords (wide spacing, normal, and closed spacing), a web of sliding notes, random notes in one voice, random notes in four voices, and glissandi (both up or down). You drag these building blocks from a palette into the score and arrange them in any order. Elongating horizontally creates longer duration, stretching vertically makes a louder sound. If the unit is placed high on the graph, the tones will be sawtooth waves (raspy), if low, sine tones (flute-like).

Ease of use makes these two programs appropriate for children as well as college courses on fundamentals for non-musicians. In fact, they have been used at Dartmouth to teach such concepts to undergraduates.

Harmony Grid

Visualizing intervals, scales, and chords is a primary challenge of music theory. Musicians must translate between the idiomatic configuration used to play melodies and chords on their instruments and the look of printed notation. Then both these perceptions must integrate with appropriate structural patterns — blues progressions, passacaglias, whatever — to produce meaningful music. What really throws a monkey wrench into the machinery is simply this: Most common scales

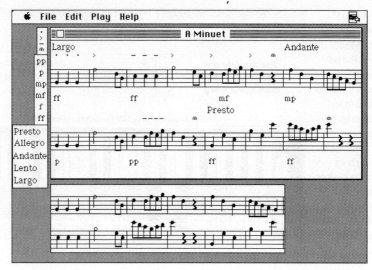

Figure 28-13: Mozart. The software is a trimmed-down version of the famous dice game attributed to Mozart. Playback is through the Macintosh speaker.

consist of five to eight notes, but they all must speak within our standard tuning system, the 12-pitch chromatic superset. Subsequently, a common pattern like a major scale has a different fingering and notation in each key, despite the fact that the essential configuration of intervals remains identical.

Harmony Grid by Hip Software Corporation provides an intuitive way to perceive the groupings of different scale systems. Musical languages appear as simple patterns on a redefinable interval grid. The way it works is simple (see Figure 28-15). Each block of the grid is a pitch. If the grid is defined as "2 × 1," then each note horizontally is a whole tone (2) while vertically the notes increase by a semitone (1). Further, all pitches that belong to the designated scale are circled.

Operation of the program is similar to Music Mouse (see Chapter 19, "Interactive Composition and Intelligent Instruments"). As you "play" the grid with the mouse, only the circled notes produce sound, highlighting as they do so. No matter how you move the mouse, mistakes cannot be made. In other words, beginners can freely experiment in any scale system. As they produce music effortlessly, the sound quality is absorbed without having to know the theory behind its construction. To make this even simpler, an internal metronome constrains the space between each note, so that the resulting music has a clear pulse.

An assumed goal of Harmony Grid is that the visual patterns on the grid will become a natural way of conceptualizing the different scale systems. Some people might feel this presents yet another hurdle in a problem already overloaded with frameworks. However, an on-screen keyboard is available below the grid. It too

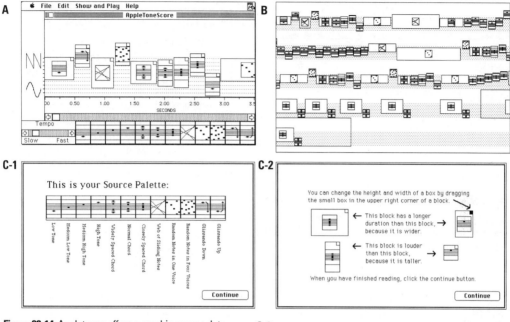

Figure 28-14: Appletones offers a graphic approach to composition. Stretching sound blocks vertically changes volume; horizontally increases duration. **(A)** You drag sound icons onto this timeline to construct your compositions. **(B)** Appletones lets you zoom out to view the entire piece. **(C-1, C-2, C-3)** These help screens explain the function and manipulation of Appletones's sound icons.

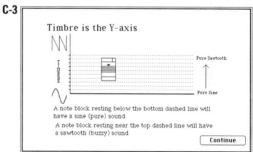

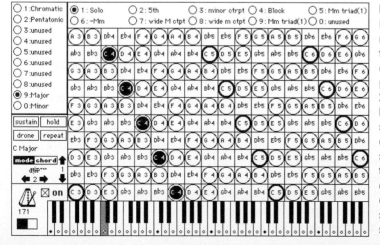

Figure 28-15: Harmony Grid lets beginners immediately improvise music in any scale system by moving the mouse within a grid. In this example, the circled notes trace a pattern for a major scale. The grid is 2×1 — meaning each move right or left is a whole step distant (two semitones), while each move up or down is a half step apart (one semitone). Note the keyboard below the grid which simultaneously displays the chosen tones. To the left of the grid are choices for different scale systems. Above the grid are scale variation options.

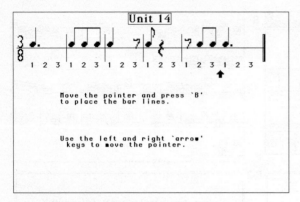

Figure 28-16: Practical Theory is an interactive textbook for learning musical rudiments. Responses are made with the computer keyboard and a MIDI controller. Here you place barlines after the appropriate pulse. You can't continue with the lesson until you answer each question.

responds to movements of the mouse and displays the configuration of sounded chords whether you are playing on the grid or the keyboard itself. Although, this might seem a bit ironic, since one of the underlying tenants of the software is to provide a conceptual model of scale patterns that is not intrinsically linked to a keyboard, the presence of the on-screen keyboard helps you translate Harmony Grid's unique visual representations to real-world devices.

One powerful feature of this program is the ability to change key instantaneously by clicking any note in the grid. A darkened circle indicates that this note is now the new tonal center. To make things more interesting, there are several options for playing variations. Solo mode restricts the music to a single melody, but other modes trigger all manner of chords for every scale tone you pass over. The multiple flashing lights add visual interest, while the generated harmonies create music that is representative of various textures characteristic to the selected scale.

Harmony Grid presents an unusual and enjoyable doorway into harmonic exploration for the beginner. It has also been used as a performance instrument in the manner of intelligent instruments discussed in Chapter 19.

Practical Theory

Practical Theory, written by Sandy Feldstein and published by Alfred Publishing Co., offers a Macintosh-assisted course in music fundamentals. The material is organized in 21 units and is best described as an interactive textbook (see Figure 28-16). Through a combination of typing and keyboard playing, you answer questions and learn music rudiments in a clear, step-by-step fashion. Correct answers are rewarded with brief musical fanfares. You cannot skip around material within the units, but there is an escape option for quitting at any time.

Practical Theory assumes no prior musical knowledge. Like any primer it commences with a discussion of the staffs, clefs, and note names. The program then proceeds to rhythm, meter, and intervals. Next is scales and key signatures, followed by musical terms and symbols. Once you've come this far, it starts to cover material common with other programs discussed in this chapter — triads, inversions, 7th chords, and chromatic chords. The course concludes with a practical lesson on composing and harmonizing a melody in major and minor keys.

The program is short on sophistication and elegant presentation, but it can help endow basic music literacy to a novice. While essentially little more than a textbook translated to the computer, the inclusion of feedback based on responses to questions and drills makes it a suitable supplement for young people beginning music lessons

Besides Practical Theory, Alfred also markets a series of Piano Theory programs with accompanying textbooks: Alfred's Basic Piano Theory Software (levels 1A, 1B, 2, 3, 4, and 5), Alfred's Basic Adult Piano Theory Software (level 1), and a three-level Music Achievement Series. The interface has been carried over from the programs' original incarnations in the Apple II and IBM worlds.

Ear-Training and Theory Software Features

Table 28-1 is a list of many ear-training and theory software packages and their corresponding features (described below).

Uses notation	Conventional music staff graphics are used as a visual tool in the program.
Intelligence	◗ = can give correct answer ● = can show you what was wrong ✪ = can make suggestions
Sound control	You can adjust parameters such as loudness and articulation of the notes played.
User configure	You can expand or restrict parameters that are drilled.
On-line help	Refers to clues on screen or in a dedicated help menu.
Mac friendly	The program adheres to the Macintosh interface and is intuitive to use.
College suitable	The program is an appropriate aid for college-level theory.
Classroom	The program has features that might be useful for class instruction, but more importantly helps a teacher administer drills and may even record progress.

Table 28-1: Ear-training and theory software features

	Mozart/ Appletones	Interval	Ear Trainer	Listen	7th Heaven	Harmony Grid	Perceive	Mac GAMUT	Practical Theory	Practica Musica
Intervals	NA	●	●	✪	♪	●	●	✪	●	✪
Scales	NA					✪	●	●	●	●
7th Chords	NA		●	●	✪	●	●	●	●	●
Inversions	NA		●	●	✪	♪		●	●	●
Augmented	NA								●	
Uses notation	●	●				●		●	●	●
On-screen keyboard			●	●	●	●			●	
Interval/chord dictation	NA	●	●	●	●	NA	●	●	♪	●
Melodic dictation	NA			●		NA	●	✪	♪	✪
Notate dictation	NA	●				NA	●	●	●	●
Play dictation	NA			●		NA	●	●	●	●
Intelligence			♪	♪	♪			✪		✪
MIDI-compatible				●	●	●	●	●	●	●
Sound control	●			♪	✪	●	✪	●	♪	
User configurable		♪	✪	●	●	●	✪		●	
On-line help	●	♪	●	●	♪	●	●	●	♪	
Mac friendly	●	●	●	✪	✪	●	✪	♪		♪
Creative interface				●	●	✪		♪		♪
Children/young adults	●	●	●	●	●	●	✪	♪	●	♪
College suitable	♪	●	●	●	●	●		●	♪	✪
Classroom	♪	●	●	●	♪		♪	✪	♪	✪
Special features	beginning composition	easy to use; just tests intervals	restrict any chord/ interval	screen keyboard and fret-board	altered chords/ voicings preview	mouse plays 12 × 12 grid	wave form lab tunings	critiques dictation; includes C clefs	inter-active textbook	compre-hensive theory drills
Exercises scored			●	✪		NA	●	●	●	●
Progress report						NA	●	✪		✪

CAI software for musical performance
Band In A Box

Even Macintosh musicians spend a great deal of time learning to harness MIDI applications to their particular electronic setups. The more powerful the program, the more time this process takes. We have all at one time been exasperated to the point of asking, "When are we going to get to some music?" That's why something like Band In A Box is valuable. Suddenly, with just a couple of mouse clicks, your home studio is transformed into a respectable backup band with a repertoire of hundreds of songs playable in dozens of styles. No worrying about texture or part coordination — it's all built in.

Styles

```
Jazz swing
Country (triplet feel)
Country (sixteenth feel)
Bossa nova
Ethnic
Blues (shuffle)
Blues (even)
Waltz
Pop Ballad
Shuffle Rock
Light Rock
Medium Rock
Heavy Rock
Miami Sound (Latin)
Milly Pop
Funk
Jazz Waltz
Rhumba
Cha Cha
Bouncy 12/8
Irish
Pop Ballad 12/8
Country 12/8 (old)
Reggae
```

Figure 28-17: The Styles menu from Band In A Box. Each selection invokes different patterns and accompaniments for the piano, bass, and drums. There are provisions for creating your own styles.

The program includes a wide repertoire of standards. Open a file, confirm MIDI channel settings for piano, bass, and drums, and select play. It only takes a second or two to compile the piece, after which a two-bar introduction automatically ensues. You are free to improvise solos to your heart's content. Meanwhile, the screen tracks the current measure number with its appropriate harmony displayed while flashing the piano and bass parts on a keyboard graphic below. If the program did nothing more, it would be a fabulous tool for practicing solos and even fleshing out a one- or two-person act for gigs. Add the fact that you can choose from dozens of musical styles, substyles for variations within the tune, alter tempos, time signatures, forms, harmonies, transpositions, and even create your own songs and styles. All these features are available without complicating the interface.

Twenty-four styles come with the program (see Figure 28-17). Among others, these include jazz, country, rock, Latin dances, and reggae. The appropriate different textures and accompaniments are transparently associated with each style. That is, the actual notes and rhythms for the piano, bass, and drums are determined entirely by the program. Band In A Box allows you to create your own styles with whatever complexity you desire. However, the on-board styles possess sufficient character to keep the accompaniments interesting, and this is not limited to merely changing drum patterns (a standard feature in all auto-bass-chord devices). On the contrary, what helps set this program apart is that two substyles, called "a" and "b," may be incorporated freely anywhere in a song. What constitutes a substyle depends on the style of music you have selected. For instance, substyle "b" in jazz swing triggers a walking bass; substyle "a" in funk initiates a hi-hat pulse in the drums. The occurrence of each substyle change causes a drum fill to be executed automatically in the preceding measure. Clicking any measure number allows you to cycle through these substyles, making it easy to sculpt a more interesting accompaniment.

Unlike most performance applications for the Macintosh where you basically work on the level of individual notes, Band In A Box lets you organize on a higher level, manipulating harmonies by name. Suppose you want a different chord in measure three. You simply select measure three and then type in a chord symbol (for example, A7#5). If you want two chords in the measure, just separate two symbols with a comma.

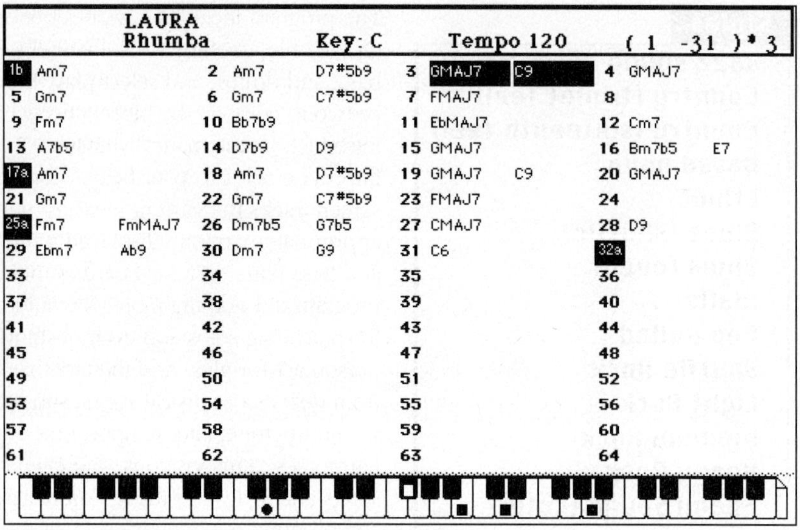

Figure 28-18: Chord chart of David Raksin's *Laura* as displayed in Band In A Box. Tempo, key, and style — here a rhumba — are easily configured. You can delete, insert, and edit bars (up to two chords per measure) as you desire. Note the small letters *a* and *b* after certain measures. These denote places where substyles kick in.

Harmonic experimentation is a breeze, but the program gets even better. New measures can be inserted, other measures deleted; progressions can be compressed in half or expanded to twice as many measures. You can also designate the beginnings and ends of choruses, loop the song, and add tags. With simple editing, you can create entirely original arrangements suited to your own style of playing. Songs can include multiple changes of time signatures and, if you really want to get creative, you can incorporate different styles in the same performance.

A few other conveniences further enhance the handling of files. One important option for live performance provided by the software is to filter songs by a particular style in the Open File dialog box. In other words, only songs saved as a bossa nova, for instance, can appear if desired, providing an efficient way to screen hundreds of titles.

All songs can be saved as SMFs, so you can import them into sequencers or notation programs. However, there is no option for printing out lead sheets. Another simple but important plus is an on-line help menu that not only explains every feature, but also lists the acceptable chord nomenclature for adding or changing harmonies. Finally, drum kits can be customized and saved for immediate installation. This way you only type in the settings of your drum machine once and never have to think about which key plays the cowbell or snare drum (see Figure 28-18).

Guitar Wizard

Remember campfire evenings poking on the guitar, patiently figuring out finger patterns as you strum away on a favorite song? Learning chords on the guitar is anything but intuitive. The six guitar strings are tuned in a highly irregular pattern of fourths with a single third somewhere in the middle (E-A-D-G-B-E). Consequently, fingerings for scales and chords defy logical patterns and must be memorized and practiced laboriously. In order to play certain chords, unusual voicings must be found that would seem crazy on other instruments. But on the guitar, they work like a charm and help form the characteristic sound of the instrument.

Guitar Wizard (from Quicksilver Software) is a very useful aid for discovering and learning chord and scale patterns (see Figure 28-19). You select a chord, and the appropriate fingerings for each position appear instantly on a large fretboard diagram. You can choose to see them labeled as scale degrees, note names, or even fingering numbers (1–4) using tablature notation (six guitar strings with finger placement symbols).

Guitar Wizard does not let you listen to these various chords over MIDI. However, you can print out any of the diagrams and build your practice session around them. The program is divided into four parts. The first, Scale Wizard, displays the fingerings (with finger numbers) for any scale at any position on the fretboard. To view another position, a scroll bar is available below the diagram. The only disadvantage of this approach is that most scales spanning over two octaves must bridge two or more positions, and the fingering at these junctures is the most critical.

Chord Wizard, the second part of the program, not only diagrams conventional major and minor harmonies, but also includes most jazz chords (13ths, 7 sus 4, and so on). As with the scales, a scroll bar selects the appropriate voicing for the chosen chord in each position. This is truly helpful because each configuration is unique.

The third option is called Fretboard Wizard. Unlike the previous two examples, this one displays all designated scale or chord notes along the entire fretboard. Armed with this diagram, a student can experiment and practice for hours within a mode or chord all over the instrument. The program takes this idea a step further by allowing you to configure your own mode and saving it in the fourth section of the program, Improvisation Wizard. Selecting a custom scale here instantly places it on the fretboards in the other areas of the program.

Alternate tunings for each of the strings can be set easily. This not only helps with situations where the lower strings are tuned down (very common), but can also be applied to other fretted instruments, including mandolin and lute. As a tool for accelerating familiarity with the arcane fingering patterns of the instrument, Guitar Wizard can be helpful for guitar students of all styles.

Figure 28-19: A compilation of the different facets of Guitar Wizard. The top fretboard displays the fingering for a Cm9 chord. Don't take it too literally — this chord is impossible to play, especially as fingered here! Still, the notes and intervals are correct. The second fretboard diagrams the notes in a specified scale, (C pentatonic is pictured). The bottom example gives you all possible notes of a given scale or chord along the fretboard; it's up to you to discover useful configurations.

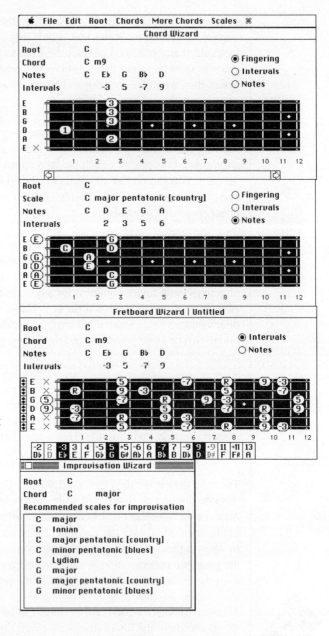

Master Tuner

Master Tuner can convert your Macintosh into a tuning device. Professional piano tuners might balk at having to carry a computer along with their other gear, but this product is currently targeted for professional musicians to use at home. Note that Master Tuner (from Andromeda Computer Systems Ltd.) requires another peripheral — a sound digitizer such as Macromind-Paracomp's Mac-Recorder — to properly receive sounds from the outside world of acoustic instruments.

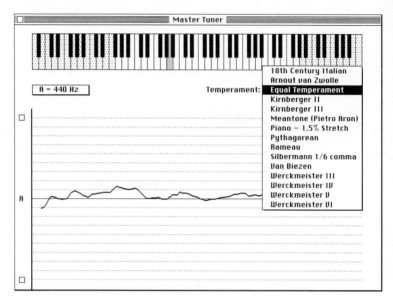

Figure 28-20: One advantage of Master Tuner is that you can check the consistency of your intonation, tone, and vibrato as it sustains over time. The Temperaments menu from Master Tuner includes tuning systems used in Medieval, Renaissance, Baroque, and modern times.

What sets Master Tuner apart from conventional electronic tuners is that it can detect the note you are trying to play and then display a graph tracing your tuning below and above the desired pitch as you make adjustments. For one thing, this means you can play your instrument naturally, without having to touch or reset the computer for each new note. By providing this power, the program goes beyond being a tuning utility. Singers and instrumentalists can test their pitch fluctuation on long sustained notes, check the consistency of their vibrato, and practice consistent intonation moving from one note to the next (see Figure 28-20).

A crucial question you might have is how quickly it responds to changing pitches. The answer seems to be that it works fine for very slow practice of passages. Any pitch changes faster than about a second apart, just don't give Master Tuner the necessary time to catch up. Things can be sped up a bit by unchecking Confirm Notes in a dialog box, but then you end up with more recognition mistakes. Remember, though, the program never purports to work for real-time performance.

The screen display needs little explanation. You can play the on-screen keyboard with the mouse. Also, the appropriate key highlights when your acoustic note is recognized. The bulk of the window is a tuning graph composed simply of a solid black center line with nine gray dashed lines above and below it. The center line represents the exact frequency of the pitch. Each dashed line above the line is approximately 5.5 percent of a half step sharp, those below the line each 5.5 percent of a half step flat. As you sustain a tone, the graph is traced from left to right, clearly showing frequency fluctuations. Once it reaches the end of the screen, the tracing begins anew at the far left.

Another display option is to have a picture of the waveform displayed as you perform. This is useful for analyzing timbral changes: The more harmonic complexity in your sound, the more jagged the waveform. It is also good for checking how evenly you sustain a tone over time, a nice feature for singers and wind players.

Before tuning, it is important first to select the proper instrument in the Instruments menu. Doing so loads a sampled soundfile that you activate by playing the on-screen keyboard with the mouse. But more importantly, a set of heuristics help Master Tuner to recognize the timbral quality of your instrument. So if you're playing a violin, it will help immensely to make the instrument setting Strings-Sustained.

Should the program have difficulty recognizing your playing, you can deselect Auto Note Selection (which is really "auto note detection") and manually position a triangle icon under a key on the on-screen keyboard. If that doesn't work, many of the instrument settings can be customized by adjusting their parameters. These include altering proportions for noise and silence thresholds, as well as juggling harmonic, sample, and selection algorithms for frequency recognition. A final option is to record a sample of your own instrument with a sound editor and add it to the sound references included with the program. Because you need a digitizer to operate the program, you already have the tools to do this.

Speaking of recording, Master Tuner lets you take a two-second sample of your performance for later analysis. While playing back the recording, you can have the graph display the tuning as the waveform. If you play an interval (two successive notes), playing back a recording allows you to see a tuning trace for each pitch. Also, for short decay instruments, this recording option often makes for easier pitch recognition.

Regarding the tuning trace itself, sometimes it can result in a jagged wave such that intonation is difficult to read. In that case, make sure the Smoothing option is enabled. The Smoothing option is also helpful for analyzing vibrato and distinguishing attack and decay from more percussive instruments. An important insight that comes from using this program is that intonation is not simply a matter of proper finger position or embouchure. For string instruments, different bow pressure can change pitch significantly; wind players discover similar insights.

Beneath the screen keyboard are buttons for the tuning reference and temperament. Standard A, which is usually 440 Hz, can be set anywhere from 390 Hz to 466 Hz, a useful feature for matching early music instruments or adjusting to things like out-of-tune organs. Fifteen different temperaments are included with the program, but only three are well known to most musicians: Pythagorean (used

in Medieval times), Meantone (in vogue during the Renaissance), and Equal
Temperament (our current tuning standard). The remaining temperaments include
Rameau and Silbermann ⅙ comma (variants of Meantone), eight different Baroque
temperaments (four by Werckmeister, two by Kirnberger, one by Van Biezen, and
one called 18th-century Italian), and a temperament especially for the piano called
"Piano 1.5% Stretch." This last temperament refers to the difficult reality that the
octaves of a piano must be tuned increasingly sharp in higher registers, and the
amount varies greatly with different pianos. The solutions to this problem are part
of the expertise of a professional tuner. Incidentally, Master Tuner does caution
that piano tuning is not a casual effort, but one that can leave a novice ripping out
hair in frustration. Also, the program does not address all the issues for effective
piano tuning, though there are plans to release a version for professionals in the
future.

MiBAC Jazz Improvisation

Ostensibly, MiBAC Jazz Improvisation offers similar features to Band In A Box.
Both advertise themselves as improvisational aids offering a back-up group of
piano, bass, and drums; yet the different philosophical approach behind MiBAC
makes it more complete and flexible, while less immediate to master than its
counterpart.

Among its unique features are a Chord Help tool for auditioning and pasting
harmonies, a control palette (for immediate control of parameters such as tempo,
styles, and MIDI assignments), flexible printing of lead sheets, tweaking of the
bass rhythm "feel" to force it slightly before or after the beat, control over dynamics, and muting instruments where desired. Even more significant is that all such
customization can be limited to any section of a song or instrumental part, lending
a greater depth of musicality and variety in each piece. You create songs from
scratch, typing in every harmony desired and specifying each region for every
variation — a far cry from Band In A Box's almost one-click approach — and you
can only choose from four different jazz styles, as opposed to 24 styles running
the gamut of pop music in Band In A Box. MiBAC clearly centers around jazz
improvisation.

To help streamline the process of songwriting, 14 different icons appear at the left
of the screen for accessing important menu items (see Figure 28-21). The top icon
triggers style selection from the four available jazz styles: jazz 4/4, jazz 3/4, Latin,
and slow 4/4. Proceeding logically, you next click the song form icon and specify
the number of choruses, introduction and coda length, tempo, and key signature.

The piano part has some interesting options. Chords can be voiced in open or
closed positions, and you can specify all manner of chord alterations to be
randomly substituted for the original progression. Both piano and bass parts can
be transposed up or down an octave, and the actual timing of the bass can be set
slightly backward or forward with a menu option called Tweak Time.

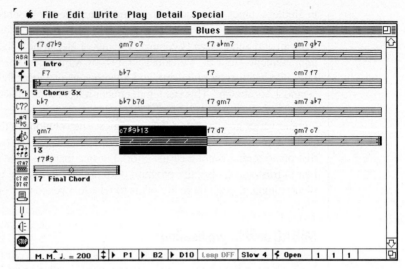

Figure 28-21: The writing display mode for MiBAC Jazz Improvisation features icon buttons on the left for quick access to menu items.

The Chord Help tool is a utility for listening to any chord in MiBAC's vocabulary and then transferring it to your song (see Figure 28-22). First select a chord root by letter name (C, D, E, and so on) and click an example from three chord qualities: minor, dominant, or major. Repeated playings of the selected chords often result in different inversions as well as voicings. An added ambiguity is that 9ths and 13ths are freely added. Once you've heard the chord you want to use, it can instantly be pasted into your lead sheet. A clever and useful feature is that chord symbols can be renamed in case you're used to different nomenclature (a common situation, since there is little standardization). Incidentally, when typing chord symbols on the lead sheet you must use Option-B for the flat sign or else the program thinks you mean a *b* chord.

After basic parameters are set, you engage the Write tool to convert the song to MIDI data. If you need nothing more than a straightforward background, then your work is done. Otherwise, now is the time to unleash the power of MiBAC. You can select any number of measures or specify a chorus and then perform edits just on that section. Maybe you want a solo break for two measures. You select the measures and invoke the Write Rests command to mute the other instruments. Perhaps the third chorus should have a completely different set of chords. No problem. Select the current progression and place it on the clipboard, type your new chords and invoke the Write command specifying only that particular chorus number. Finally, paste back your original progression.

The well written manual for the program details a tutorial for a blues progression of ten choruses, each with its own surprises such as diminuendos, changes of style, drum solos, altered chords, and so on. Taken together they make for an interesting piece.

Chapter 28: CAI — Computer-aided Instruction 1289

MiBAC™ will randomly substitute chord alterations within a chord family. Check the alterations that you want to substitute, and then rewrite the song. These alterations will be used for the next write only.

Minor (m7)	Dominant (7)			Major (M7)
☒ m7s	☐ 7s	☒ 7b9b13	☐ 7b5#9	☐ M6
☐ m6	☐ 7b9	☒ 7#9b13	☐ 7+	☒ M7#11
	☒ 7#9	☐ 7b5	☐ 7+b9	
	☒ 7#11	☐ 7b5b9	☐ 7+#9	

[Alter Chords]   [Cancel]

Figure 28-22: You can have MiBAC randomly substitute chord alterations within a chord family using this dialog box.

Three types of substyles are possible: up tempo, ballad, and normal. These invoke textural and rhythmic variations in the accompaniment. Like their parent styles, they too can appear at any specified moment in a song. A difference from Band In A Box is that substyles are determined by tempo settings. You adjust a range of metronome markings between which changes automatically kick in. To change the rhythms of individual parts, just change the tempo marking for selected measures and use the Write tool.

As with the other parameters, you can selectively add new drum sounds to parts of the song. First you define a new drumset file by entering the appropriate MIDI note values alongside the ten default descriptions. After saving the file, select a passage and invoke the Change Drums command so the song can temporarily load a drumset file.

MiBAC is also quite flexible after you leave the writing mode. Performance utilities are well thought out. For instance, up to ten songs can be chained together and you can program the time delay between each of them. Lead sheets can be printed for transposing instruments and any font can be applied to chord symbols. Even chord slashes can be placed on the staff when printing.

A time calculator is a useful feature that displays the number of measures in your introduction, chorus, and coda; but even more significantly it includes total performance time in minutes and seconds. Tuning is an area where the program again shows its attention to detail. Classical musicians have a nasty saying for sloppy intonation: "Well, good enough for jazz." MiBAC repudiates this notion with a dedicated tuning icon. When selected, four slow A 440 tones sound for reference tuning of your acoustic and electronic instruments.

During performance you can view the song in Chord Display mode where measures highlight as they play (incidentally, in this mode the chord symbols can appear in any font, for clearer reading). For making global changes without having to rewrite a song, a control palette appears at the bottom of the screen for changing tempo, looping, style, MIDI channels, piano voicing, and muting. This makes a lot of sense for improvising when you want to make a quick alteration. On the right side of the control palette is a counter that keeps track of section, measure, and beat number while you play, but note that measure highlighting and counter updating occur only in Chord View display and not in Chord Entry mode, even though the control palette appears on both screens.

To sum up, MiBAC gives greater control over the arrangement of your jazz backgrounds, but more of your time needs to be invested before you get down to the business of playing.

Practice Room

In the early 19th century, Johann Maelzel copied and distributed an ingenious device that measured tempo by sounding even pulses at variable speeds. The metronome, so named by Maelzel but actually invented by a Dutchman named Dietrich Winkler, was immediately seized by Beethoven to precisely indicate the speed of each musical movement. The pendulum-powered device quickly became a fixture on every piano as the first mechanical practice tool. The metronome has seen little improvement since its inception. A few more bells and whistles have been added — now some are powered electronically and provide tuning references — but performers seeking technical aids still have recourse only to this patient time keeper. Enter Coda's Practice Room, a program that seems to do everything except physically place your fingers on the instrument. In some ways Practice Room functions like an intelligent metronome.

For beginners and even intermediate players, Practice Room can significantly accelerate learning time and technical accuracy of performance. It brings together the best of two worlds: a teacher's technical evaluation plus the comfort of learning at an individual pace, without a critic breathing down your neck every moment.

After opening a file, you choose to either listen to the piece (have the Macintosh perform it on a MIDI device) or practice it yourself. A marvelous option is having the Macintosh play one hand while you play the other; or if you would rather focus on one part, the other can be muted (and not evaluated).

Assuming you wish to practice, some very intelligent options are available. You can play the piece in its entirety or select specific chunks to work on intensively. This latter mode is called spot practice and seems most efficient for perfecting your technique. The immediate feedback quickly corrects problems and prevents the formation of bad habits. For isolating extremely difficult passages, you can even perform in step time; that means you play a single beat and once the notes are performed accurately, the computer advances to the next beat. Another important performance option is controlling the moment the page of music "turns" (actually moving to a new screen in this context). By being able to vary this from a 16th note to two whole notes you can train more efficient sightreading, forcing

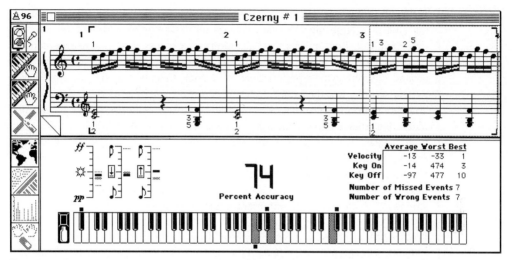

Figure 28-23: The performance screen of Practice Room. Shown here is the Spot Practice option applied to three measures of a Czerny étude. The center percentage is an average of errors in notes, dynamics, attacks, and releases. To the left are three virtual LED meters measuring dynamics, attacks, and releases that track your performance in real time (the mid-point is the optimum level for each). On the keyboard, black squares indicate wrong notes; highlighted keys are notes that were omitted.

the eyes to absorb music ahead of the fingers (you're out of luck if you want to read a measure ahead in meters with more than four quarter notes per measure).

What is truly amazing about Practice Room is the way it evaluates a performance (see Figure 28-23). Not only does it illustrate incorrect notes, but it scrutinizes rhythm, attacks, durations, dynamics, and pedaling — theoretically, anything that is communicated over MIDI. Indeed, the primary inadequacy facing the electronic musician using this program will undoubtedly be the range and touch of his or her MIDI keyboard. A non-weighted keyboard, for instance, has severe limitations in training dynamics.

Directly above the keyboard are three types of measurement. To the left are virtual LED meters that respond in real time to your attacks, releases, and velocity by comparing them to an ideal performance relative to the printed score. As you play, it is fascinating to watch these three levels bounce up and down from a center line representing the perfect realization of the file. Unfortunately, the software does not include an option to configure what such an ideal performance might be. If it had such a feature, a keyboard teacher could use it more effectively as a teaching aid.

On the right of the screen is a table displaying the same measurements as statistics. Positive values are assigned to late responses, negative numbers to early ones. In addition to calculating the average for your complete performance, the single worst and best scores are also included. Finally, the table keeps running track of the number of wrong and omitted notes.

If this all seems too detailed for your needs, centered between the meters and the table is a large number that averages all the parameters — note accuracy, dynamics, pedaling, attacks, and durations — expressed as a single percentage. Now don't get the wrong idea. It would be truly horrendous if people went around describing their performance of a Bach Invention as 67 percent. First, a perfect score is not the target; rather it is a representation of printed music in absolute performance terms. Second, the percentage score is simply a way of measuring your technical precision against a literal music reading. Musicality and taste, at least at this time, do not begin to enter the picture; a master interpretive reading would probably garner an extremely low percentage. But for the first time, an objective evaluation of whether you play ahead or behind the beat, miss notes, play too loud, and so on, is available during practice time to constructively shape the most important critic — yourself.

Practice Room offers a Micro View that displays performance evaluations in different formats for easier perception and precise correlation to individual moments in the music. Of these, the most valuable is a notation view. Here the notes of the music score are displayed in gray upon which the notes you have played are superimposed in black. At a glance, you can determine your rhythmic tendencies. If everything looks like a blurry double image, your notion of the beat is probably not in sync with the composer's. Resolution of this display can be set from a half note down to a 1,024th note.

For durations and loudness, bar graphs are available to trace the score giving the file's optimum measurement in gray bars alongside your performance in black ones. There is even an Expert mode for yet two other types of displays. The first measures each velocity, attack, or release as a percentage of the file's desired score (100 percent). The second deals with dynamics (note velocity) and rhythmic accuracy (attack location). Notes struck harder or later than required are graphed above a center line, and those that are softer or earlier than optimally desired appear below the center line. For troublesome passages these displays quickly isolate problems you knew existed, but could not put your finger on. After a performance is analyzed by Practice Room, it is still up to you to devise strategies to fix the problems. Mindless performance is not being advocated, but on the other hand, after using this program a metronome seems a feeble tool by comparison.

In addition to the music included with the program, new practice files can be created using Coda's Finale or MusicProse, keeping in mind that the program restricts you to a maximum length of 100 measures. Any MIDI-compatible instrument can be used as the input device. If the concept proves popular, perhaps customized versions for wind instruments, strings, and percussion, each with their unique technical problems addressed, will become available.

For the Young and the Young at Heart

Growing Minds Software offers Music Maestro for primary-level instruction or anyone who doesn't know the sounds of various orchestral instruments. There are three disks of 38 sounds (one to two seconds in length) and a picture for each instrument (including descriptions). There is a stack devoted to each orchestral section (woodwind, brass, percussion, and strings). When you click a card and the stacks play sound at random, you must identify the instrument. Dr. T's Adventures in Musicland (see Figure 28-24) and Great Waves's KidsNotes (see Figure 28-25) offer a wonderful introduction to ear-training, composition, and the joys of music.

Education Stack Gallery
Educational

(See Figures 28-26 through 28-31.)

Reference

If you want to learn about MIDI or electronic instruments, you should know about three HyperCard stacks: Joe Zobkiw's *Electronic Music Encyclopedia,* The Music Society's *Understanding MIDI Protocol,* and Opcode's *Book of MIDI* (see Figures 28-32 and 28-33).

Future Directions

Despite all the software currently available, countless areas remain to be explored and refined. Many of these areas have been implemented in academia as experimental systems, but they are not available as commercial Macintosh programs. In the area of traditional theory, there is a strong need for comprehensive applications dedicated to training competent voice-leading both from a contrapuntal and harmonic standpoint.

Species counterpoint in particular is a craft defined in algorithms set since the time of Johann Fux (1725). Students must practice writing hundreds of examples to build the necessary sensitivity for careful voice-leading. The Macintosh is a natural for applying these algorithms and providing immediate feedback. Both Mozart and Beethoven felt they benefitted from these same exercises. Shouldn't Macintosh musicians be able to pursue this choice of study?

The study of fugue is another area where the Macintosh CAI potential is sorely missing. A fugue instruction program could give thorough grounding in fugue analysis and test understanding by providing, let's say, the entire *Well Tempered Clavier* by J.S. Bach on-line for study.

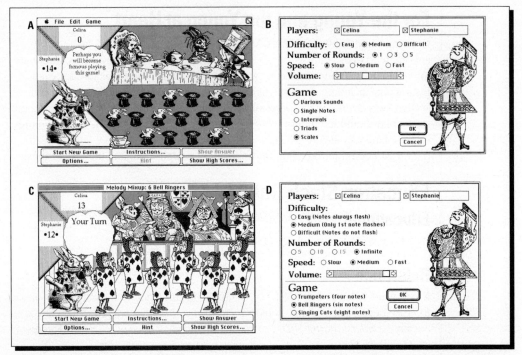

Figure 28-24: Dr. T's Adventures in Musicland consists of four programs that form an effective and enjoyable introduction to music and ear training. You can play by yourself or with another person. **(A)** Sound Concentration is like a musical form of the familiar game Concentration. The top hats all contain different sounds and matching the sounds causes a rabbit to stay popped out of the hat. **(B)** You can configure Sound Concentration to use sound effects, single notes, intervals, triads, or scales as the sounds that are triggered when you click a top hat. **(C)** Melody Mixup is a Macintosh version of the popular hardware game Simon. Animated seven-of-spades cards perform every next note in the ever-lengthening sequence. **(D)** You can configure Melody Mixup to three different sounds and levels of difficulty (four, six, or eight notes) with this dialog box.

Figure 28-25: KidsNotes is a wonderful introduction to music writing from Great Wave, the makers of ConcertWare+MIDI (see Chapter 22). You input music with mouse and on-screen keyboard. The software supports step-time note input and real-time input both with and without a metronome. All playback is done by way of the Macintosh speaker or audio port and you have global control over tempo and volume. Saved songs appear in the alphabetized scrolling list at the middle right.

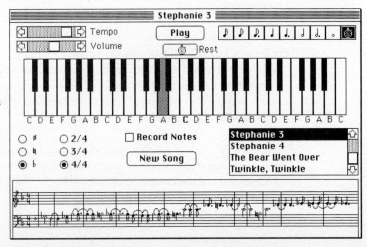

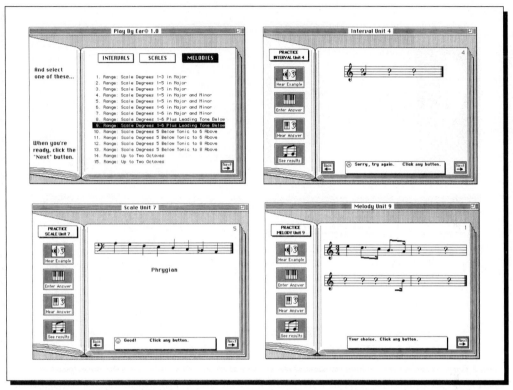

Figure 28-26: Thomas Kirshbaum's Play By Ear is an ear training application that takes the approach of a jazz player learning music, that is, by hearing, playing, and improvising. The software uses HyperMIDI and is fully MIDI-compatible for both input and output. There are 1,165 melodic exercises dealing with sound, harmonic structure, and the feel of your hands on the musical keyboard. This figure shows some of the options for ear training using intervals, scales, and melodies (with typical exercises). The software comes with a detailed Suggestions for Use document that can serve as the basis of a curriculum.

An application for the Macintosh devoted to four-part chorale harmonization is just as necessary. In almost all teaching institutions chorales form the background for teaching harmony, voice-leading, figured bass realization, ear training, sight singing, and composition. Many years ago composer Donald Martino assembled his own edition of the Bach chorales, in which different harmonizations of the same tune are placed under each other for easy comparison. An earlier, more extensive study by Allen Irvine McHose attempted to derive voice-leading rules from chorales by way of statistical analysis. These types of chores are good candidates for computer assistance. A large database of chorale examples, an on-line tutorial, and different platforms for harmony, ear training, figured bass, and composition would make for an instructor's dream.

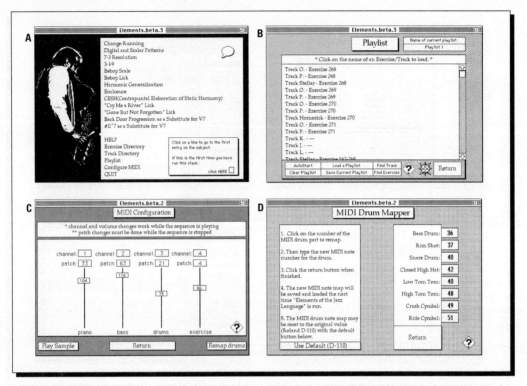

Figure 28-27: CPP/Belwin's Elements of the Jazz Language (© CPP/Belwin Inc. 1992; screenshots used with permission) was developed by Mark Boling and Curt Coker using HyperMIDI. The software is designed as a support activity for Jerry Coker's book of the same name. The stack includes 88 exercise patterns and 33 play-along tracks from the book. There are over 650 files included with the package (taking slightly over 3MB of disk space). Each exercise is associated with one or more play-along tracks. When an exercise and a track have been selected, the appropriate files are loaded into memory and played. Tempo, MIDI volume, patch change, and MIDI drum mapping are available in the playback mode. In a nutshell, you learn by playing. **(A)** The main table of contents. **(B)** The Playlist card. The Playlist function can help to streamline operation of the program. The transition from one pre-selected exercise to the next becomes as simple as a click of the mouse. If the AutoStart function in the playback mode is turned on, the sequence will automatically start playing as soon as files are loaded. Playlists may be saved to disk and reloaded when needed. **(C)** You can configure how your MIDI setup relates to the Elements of the Jazz Language with this card. **(D)** You remap your drum sounds to the note numbers used in the stacks with this MIDI Drum Mapper card.

There is a need for more applications that train analysis and analytical listening. Students always have trouble following musical structure. Multilevel (hierarchical) diagrams of pieces, discussion of harmony, phrase structure, motivic evolution, and formal divisions are eminently suitable to the Macintosh interface. Some work along these lines exists in the music CD-ROM titles by Voyager and Warner New Media (see Chapter 29, "New Forms of Interactive Education").

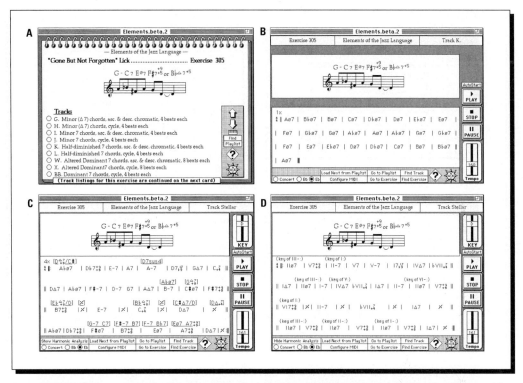

Figure 28-28: The Elements of the Jazz Language HyperCard stack contains 33 play-along tracks from the *Elements of the Jazz Language* book. The first 30 tracks are exercise progressions that visit each key. The last three tracks are progressions from jazz standard tunes (for which a slider for key transposition is provided in the upper-right corner of the track card). If an exercise has been chosen for playback with a track, the exercise is displayed at the top of the card. Each track card displays the chord progression of the track. In the lower-left corner are buttons for changing the progression display for Bb or Eb transposing instruments. You may also look at a functional analysis of the progression. Also at the bottom of the screen are eight navigational buttons. **(A)** A typical exercise card. **(B)** Clicking track K on the main exercise card loads this progression for playback and displays this view of the music. **(C)** The Stellar progression for the same exercise with the progression expressed as chords. **(D)** The effect of clicking the Show Harmonic Analysis button at the lower left of C.

Keyboard skills play a large role in university music education nationwide. Put simply, those students without keyboard skills are forever in a state of catching up as undergraduates. In this context, keyboard skills refer not just to playing a Mozart sonata, but to being able to plunk out chord progressions, understand instrument transpositions, and perform fluently in different clefs. When faced with a simple orchestral score, a musician should be able to give a rough approximation of its sound on the keyboard. Most institutions have extremely limited teaching personnel for this crucial task, especially since it requires one-on-one sessions for positive results. The Macintosh communicating to a sampler or sample-player through MIDI is eminently suited for training students in all these skills.

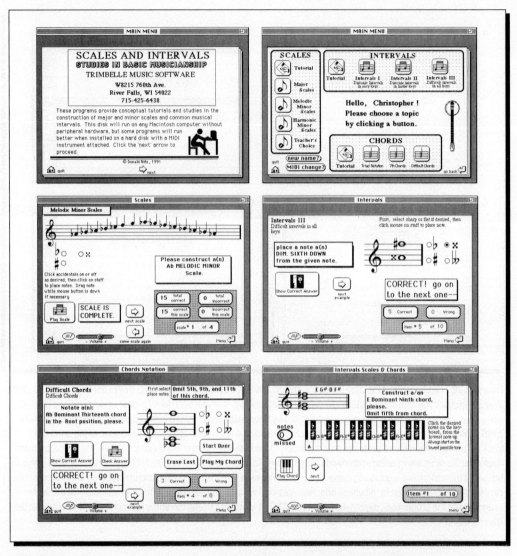

Figure 28-29: Trimbelle Music Software's Scales and Intervals HyperCard stacks use HyperMIDI to provide for MIDI output. These stacks focus on the rudiments of the construction and notation of intervals, scales, and chords. The interface (particularly the display of error detection) is quite elegant. Quizzes are included with the tutorials.

Orchestration and instrumentation seem such a natural tributary of Macintosh MIDI applications that it is surprising no dedicated programs exist for these subjects. While sequencers assume patch changes as a given, no guidelines for effective instrumentation are available. Which sounds are most suitable for melodies and accompaniments? Why does one combination work well for doubling the bass

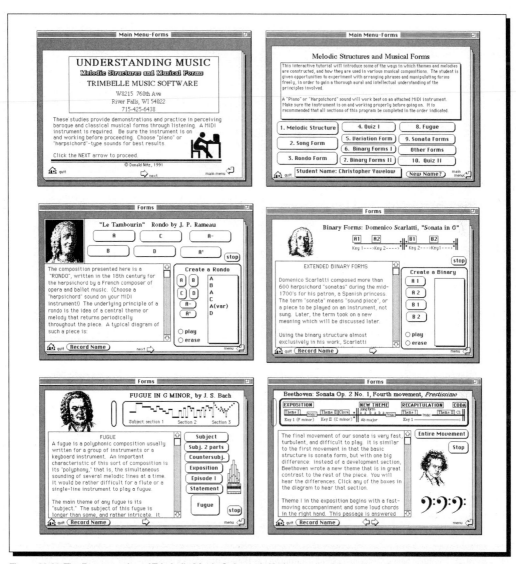

Figure 28-30: The Forms section of Trimbelle Music Software's Understanding Music HyperCard stacks uses Opcode's MIDIPlay XCMD to provide for MIDI output. This set of stacks covers most of the standard forms — song, rondo, variation, binary, fugue, sonata, and contemporary forms. Some of the cards let you experiment with creating your own constructions within the framework of the form currently under construction.

line, but muddles up the accompaniment? What textures might best complement a given musical phrase? Should even these questions be too difficult to tackle, an orchestration program would still go a long way toward helping musicians get the most of their electronic gear.

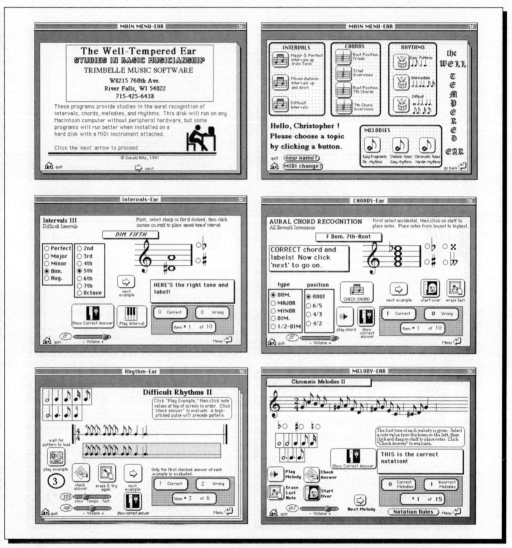

Figure 28-31: Trimbelle Music Software's Well-Tempered Ear HyperCard stacks use HyperMIDI to provide for MIDI output. As the name implies, these stacks focus on ear training. Like Trimbelle's Scales and Intervals, the interface (particularly the display of error detection) is quite elegant. Quizzes are included with the tutorials.

Along similar lines, advanced compositional aids could effectively piggyback on sequencers, so that structural moments in a piece might be altered or rearranged instantly. Imagine being able to audition different accompaniments and textures as easily as changing a synthesizer patch. Or what if every IV chord of your favorite blues piece was changed to a VI? Suppose you could instantly substitute the

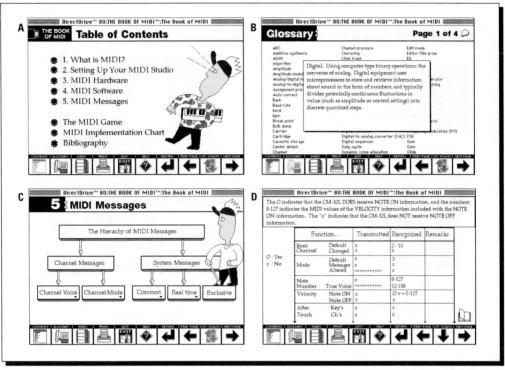

Figure 28-32: Opcode's Book of MIDI is a collection of stacks that assume no prior knowledge of electronic or computer music. The information included in the stack provides a wonderful introductory overview about the MIDI Specification, the history of electronic music, connecting your MIDI instruments, and MIDI software. It has a bibliography for more information. Many points are punctuated with animations (using MacroMind's VideoWorks driver) that are both amusing and informative. If you are just starting out with Macintosh music, this interactive multimedia presentation should be your first purchase after your gear. Even if you have been using MIDI for some time, you may find the answers to many questions in these stacks. Navigation is accomplished with four arrows: the standard previous and next arrows, supplemented by a down arrow for when you want to get deeper into a topic (sometimes there is more than one level, so you have to use the down arrow again), and an up arrow to get back to the top level. **(A)** There are many areas to The Book of MIDI and each has a Table of Contents card like this one. **(B)** The on-line Glossary includes definitions for over 200 essential MIDI and computer music terms. **(C)** Graphics such as these illustrate many points for which a picture is worth a thousand words. **(D)** The Book of MIDI includes a complete explanation of the MIDI implementation charts you find at the back of the manuals for MIDI devices.

familiar motif of Beethoven's *Fifth Symphony* with one of your own, leaving all other elements intact? (Note: Such possibilities have been suggested as early as 1981. See *Proceedings of the International Computer Music Conference, Venice, Italy, 1981* for a paper by Curtis Roads on a menu-based system for interactive orchestration on a Lisp Machine.) Not only are these ideas stimulating, and not only would they be a serious tool in understanding how music is effectively constructed, but they all lie easily within current Macintosh technology. In fact, it is possible to kluge certain programs to accomplish some of these things.

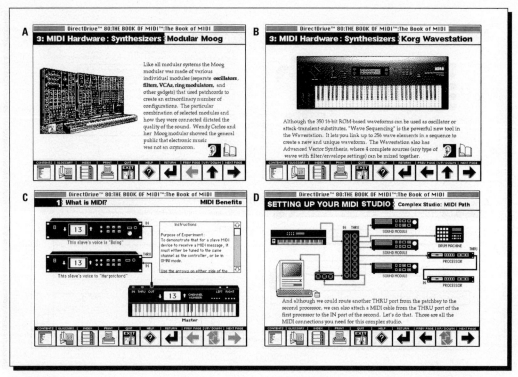

Figure 28-33: (A) and **(B)** The Book of MIDI provides a history of electronic instruments, including representative sounds of vintage and state-of-the-art synths (you can hear these by clicking the little ear button. Next to the ear button is an open book button that brings up a bibliography of articles related to the current topic. **(C)** and **(D)** Many interactive tutorials walk you through setting up your gear and experimenting with sending MIDI messages complete with simulations of the results of your actions.

Summary

🖊 The breadth of programs for CAI is surprising. A keyboard practice aid can measure your accuracy. Several jazz programs supply a backup band over which to develop your solo improvisational skills. A tuning aid not only checks intonation, but gives visual feedback for maintaining even vibrato or sustained pitches. Ear training is a prime target for a large number of programs focusing on intervals, chords, and dictation.

🖊 Unfortunately, the potential of CAI in Macintosh music falls short of the great strides that have been made in sequencing, sound design, and even notation. The programs that are currently available only scratch the surface of what's possible, while providing a tantalizing glimpse of the future.

🖊 Most Macintosh music CAI programs are geared for one of two types of learning: self-instruction and teacher-guided instruction. There are two large categories within these areas: performance and musicianship training. The musicianship category further divides into programs dedicated to ear training, theory and analysis, and music history/appreciation.

✔ The Macintosh makes an ideal music teaching assistant. For one thing, it can give instant feedback to student input. Recognizing intervals, for example, demands not only repetition, but immediate evaluation to a response, while the sound is still "fresh" in the ears. In the classroom, this is a difficult proposition. Often papers are returned the next day, when feedback affects little else than ego.

✔ Maybe the strongest case for the Macintosh as an instructive aid is that it requires no special training to make decisions about notation or performance. Beginners to ear training face various obstructions, including technical facility on an instrument and the actual calligraphy of notation on paper. Selection with the mouse in the familiar Macintosh graphic environment simplifies these chores, so that one can concentrate on musical learning and leave the worries of the performance and notation to the computer.

✔ HyperCard, both with and without the addition of EarLevel Engineering's HyperMIDI, is a popular platform for the development of Macintosh music teaching aids in all categories. Many current HyperCard-based applications are more sophisticated than stand-alone applications available through commercial channels.

Chapter 29

New Forms of Interactive Education

In this chapter . . .

✔ Understanding interactive CD-ROM technology.

✔ Tips for running interactive CD-ROMs.

✔ Hypermedia and hypertext implications for education.

✔ Contrasting nonlinear and hierarchical organizational strategies.

✔ Detailed discussion of Voyager's *Rite of Spring* interactive CD-ROM.

✔ Detailed discussion of Warner New Media's *Beethoven String Quartet No. 14* interactive CD-ROM.

✔ Introduction to CD-ROM and laserdisc authoring systems.

A Revolution in Learning Music

Interactive CD-ROMs are possibly the most exciting new computer-aided music-learning medium to appear. A CD-ROM can hold about 650MB of data — including CD-quality audio — and because every block of data has a unique address (over 300,000 separate addresses), the Macintosh can jump to any place on the disc almost instantaneously. (Note: Although data can be located extremely quickly, reading data is quite slow, unless it is CD audio.)

To use an interactive music CD-ROM you must have a CD-ROM drive with audio outputs and a Macintosh. The prices of CD-ROM drives have dropped below the price of the original 800K floppy disk drive at its introduction. This puts CD-ROMs into the hands of the masses as a tool for musical learning.

Popping a disc into a CD-ROM drive and accessing data from it is about 1 percent of what this new computer-based learning tool is all about. Interactive CD-ROMs offer such a revolutionary approach to teaching and imparting knowledge that they require a completely new perspective for considering these traditional activities.

Interactive CD-ROMs provide nonlinear access to information. It's a little like random access audio (see Chapter 24, "Direct-to-Hard disk Recording"). One could say that they provide random access to information, but the word "nonlinear" carries more of the cognitive implications of this medium.

Interactive CD-ROM is a type of hypermedia. Nonlinear access to information is one of the initial promises of hypermedia, for which the end of the road is virtual reality. Besides multiple access paths to the same information nodes, one of the most important features of hypermedia is multiple representations of information at the click of a button. If "a picture is worth a thousand words," how many words are represented by hypermedia's instantly accessible animations and video-clips, complete with sound?

Hypermedia itself was an outgrowth of the old concept of "hypertext," a term coined by hypermedia visionary Ted Nelson. A hypertext system presents text in such a way that while you are reading, you can click a word to go deeper into that topic, perhaps to get a definition, example, or tangential information. The concept of hypertext is still active on the next level, so if you click a word while you are on that level, you can reach the next level of detail, and so on. Hypermedia adds all types of data, dynamic or static, to the text-based concept of hypertext. Hypermedia can include audio, still graphics, animations, and video. About the only things a CD-ROM can't address are the senses of touch and smell (but wait a couple of years).

There is a tendency to think of such systems as hierarchical. This is not a good analogy. Hierarchically arranged data implies ever-widening branches sprouting off branches sprouting off branches, and so on. There is a distinct path between levels of information. Branches of the tree are not necessarily connected, so you might have to navigate back to the base level of one branch before embarking to the tip of another branch, even though a representation of your starting point and ending point might indicate that these two points were adjacent. In other words, it can be difficult to jump from branch to branch in a hierarchical system. Your access to information remains somewhat structured and constrained by the developer, often resulting in eventual disorientation.

In contrast, a nonlinear hypermedia system links, or cross-references if you prefer, all elements to one another (see Figure 29-1). Usually, any node of information is accessible from any other node whenever you need it. Conceptualizing the available information from multiple levels of abstraction is greatly facilitated. Where every branch of a hierarchical tree structure eventually leads to a dead end, such roadblocks are non-existent in hypermedia.

Consider the ramifications for a nonfiction book. With an interactive textbook there is no more flipping to the glossary or tables in the back of the book, no more searching through the references section for citations, no going and finding another book (such as a dictionary) to look up a term. Sometimes a student will forego looking up a reference for clarification due to the sheer hassle-quotient involved, often resulting in a devastating misinterpretation of the information.

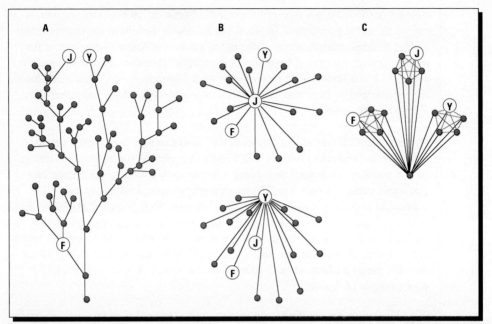

Figure 29-1: Hierarchical organization contrasted to nonlinear organization and a hybrid approach. **(A)** Hierarchical organization. Note that nodes J and Y might seem to be adjacent from the user's point of view; however, to get from one point to the other requires navigating down one branch and up another. **(B)** Nonlinear organization. Every node is accessible from every other node. For example, the upper diagram illustrates the links to and from node J and the lower diagram shows the links to and from node Y. All other nodes are configured similarly, although these are not represented in this figure. You can navigate from node J to Y directly. **(C)** Hybrid organization. Separate clusters of nodes are accessible from a central base. Within each cluster, all nodes are nonlinearly linked to one another. In this example, getting from node J to Y takes one additional step. You must first pass through the main base at the bottom of the figure.

CD-ROMs redefine the concept of an index or table of contents. There is not even a need for page numbers in an interactive CD-ROM. Certain user-interface standards have already grown out of this fact. For example, a Return (to Previous Node) button now is a common element to hypermedia user interfaces. This functions as the thumb you would keep at your current page in a book while you go to the index to look something up. Such buttons keep track of your path history (not past history). This further alleviates the problem you encounter in textbooks, where you find that the index presents several different page numbers and you must keep your thumb in the original place and another finger holding your place in the index while you flip to the various references. Such contortions are barbarically primitive when compared to interactive CD-ROMs.

Carrying on the book analogy, you become an active participant in the authoring of the information, at least from the perspective of presentation order. In a linearly structured text, the author decides the order in which you read material; with interactive CD-ROMs, you have complete control over this parameter. Of course this places a lot of responsibility on the creator of the CD-ROM to make sure that the material makes sense in any order.

The term "unstructured browsing" is often associated with hypermedia. The option to explore a topic, charting your own path through the territory, is fundamental to interactive CD-ROMs. The medium provides elegant and intuitive support to the "what if" approach to knowledge navigation that is so crucial to reinforcing a concept. Provided that the author has done the job well, hypermedia ensures that curiosity is almost always rewarded, often in very innovative ways.

Newer texts use such devices as margin icons, sidebars, boxed asides, and even color to increase navigational speed. Tables and other graphic aids are common in printed text, but in an interactive CD-ROM these give way to much more communicative elements, for example, animation. Now with Apple's QuickTime, full-motion video windows will be added to animations as a standard element of interactive CD-ROMs.

Interactive CD-ROMs are like immense databases of knowledge where everything is so transparently indexed and cross-referenced that to retrieve information you don't have to know anything about search queries, criteria, or Boolean operators. The developers have taken care of all that for you. Usually their approach is so sophisticated that the user interface of an interactive CD-ROM is self-explanatory. In some instances this is accomplished through intuitive icons or buttons whose labels describe their purpose. Great efforts have been made to keep users constantly aware of where they are located within the context of the overall "map" of the CD-ROM. A manual is seldom needed, and if such documentation would enhance an interactive CD-ROM, it is usually just another node of information, a mouse click away.

Many interactive CD-ROMs are controlled by a HyperCard stack or stacks. Even the authoring systems themselves may be automated HyperCard stacks. Interactive CD-ROM authoring systems are so user friendly that an instructor can put together a very educational custom presentation with little investment of time and effort. With one system discussed at the end of the chapter, any commercial audio CD can be used. This is not meant to imply that creating an interactive CD-ROM for commercial distribution is something you can do over a weekend. Creating a well indexed (referring to the linking of all the objects), well designed (referring to the user interface) interactive CD-ROM requires a good deal of work. It's all a matter of how far you plan to take your project. The Verbum Interactive CD-ROM discussed in Chapter 27 is an example of how far you can go in this area, and that project required a team of developers working full-time for a year.

Because the HyperCard stack is on your hard drive, and not the read-only CD-ROM, it is possible for the stack to keep track of your interaction with the CD-ROM, such as what information you have accessed once as opposed to what information you access repeatedly, and common multistage access paths you take. With such knowledge about the user, the interface of a CD-ROM can provide super "bookmark" options, automatically gather keywords, or provide automatic self-customization. These options are something to look for in the future. Printing selected information from an interactive CD-ROM or providing a pop-up annotation option (to scribble notes in the margins of virtual pages) are features that have yet to be fully explored by interactive CD-ROM developers.

Stravinsky's *Rite of Spring* (Voyager)

The Voyager Company's CD Companion Series is a growing series of interactive CD-ROMs that provides commentary and detailed analysis of landmark musical works. The concept of the series is the work of interactive hypermedia guru and visionary Robert Stein (who is also the president of the company). In addition, the company produces interactive videodiscs and is well known for its Criterion Collection of classic films on videodisc. Voyager also markets the only available authoring system for creating such CD audio stacks.

Interactive CD-ROMs in the CD Companion Series are suitable for both classroom or self-guided learning. Because the presentation of information is entirely up to the user, these CD-ROMs are equally effective at just about any level of education, from graduate school on down to elementary school. Structuring educational media with this magnitude of flexibility is an amazing feat in itself.

Voyager's current and forthcoming interactive CD-ROMs for music education are listed in Table 6-30. Many of these will probably be shipping by the time you read this book.

The Mozart *Dissonant Quartet* is available in two formats, as an interactive CD ROM and also in an interactive videodisc version that uses audio residing on both the CD-ROM and the videodisc. Voyager's embracement of Apple's Quick-Time in a number of non-music-oriented interactive CD-ROMs may portend other enhancements to their future CD Companion line.

Voyager's first CD-ROM, Beethoven's *Ninth Symphony*, is devoted to UCLA professor Robert Winter's analysis of the symphony. This innovative CD-ROM uses a standard audio CD of a Vienna Philharmonic performance. Although it is a normal CD, the Macintosh treats it as a CD-ROM. At this stage of the game, the possibility of adding additional music and data to the CD was yet to be explored. The Hyper-Card stacks that control the *Ninth Symphony* are supplied on separate floppy disks.

The next logical step in this medium was the creation of custom CD-ROMs. These include the main work under discussion as well as additional musical examples, spoken commentary, and even the required HyperCard stacks. The audio tracks still play on a standard audio CD player, but the CD is in fact a bonafide CD-ROM. Voyager used this technique for their second offering in the CD Companion Series, Stravinsky's *Rite of Spring* (analysis also by Robert Winter).

The beauty of both the Beethoven and Stravinsky CD-ROMs is that you can go as deep as you want into the topics covered by the CD. Because it is interactive hypermedia, you control the level of detail that the information is presented in.

The user interface of the *Ninth Symphony* and the *Rite of Spring* is fairly consistent. Because of this, an examination of the *Rite of Spring* will give you a pretty good idea of Voyager's approach. Before turning to the figures, several caveats are in order.

It is a difficult task to try to put in writing one's interaction with a CD of this kind. You can jump from any part of the CD to another, from one form of representation to another, and from one type of information to another, all with the click of the mouse. A blow-by-blow description becomes impossible. Furthermore, the number of cards in stacks dedicated to interactive CD-ROMs is mind-boggling. As you examine the figures, try to imagine them as non-sequentially ordered but in three dimensions, superimposed upon one another with links from any card to any other card.

While there is a good deal of interface consistency, the graphic devices used to explain a concept vary as much as the concepts themselves. The nature of this information delivery medium, HyperCard combined with custom audio, abounds with opportunity for a highly creative approach to the representations of each and every node of information. Voyager has taken advantage of this fundamental tenant of hypermedia at every juncture.

With the above in mind, a number of sample cards from Voyager's *Rite of Spring* CD Companion are presented (see Figures 29-2 through 29-8). These represent a mere fraction of the scope of the product. There is a wealth of additional information and literally infinite paths to take each time you interact with any of Voyager's software. It is difficult to tire of the activity, no matter how many times you approach it. Every time you view a disc it is a fresh experience that enriches your knowledge of the work.

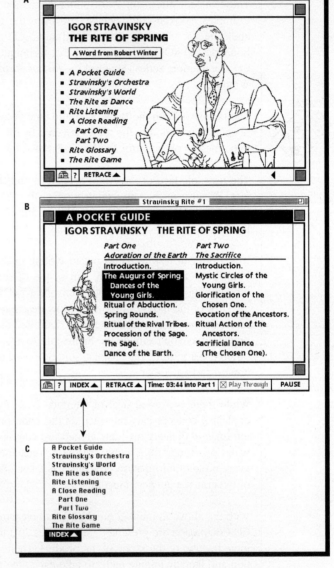

Figure 29-2: (A) When you launch the Voyager's *Rite of Spring* stack you arrive at this navigation card, which presents nine points of departure. You can also listen to a recorded introduction by Robert Winter. **(B)** Clicking A Pocket Guide brings you to this area, where you can listen to the work while the names of its main sections highlight. **(C)** The Index pop-up menu is available from any point to take you to any other topic. These correspond to the headings on the opening card.

Figure 29-3 :
(A) The second item on the Index pop-up menu brings you to the discussion of Stravinsky's orchestra. Clicking a section takes you to the information about the individual instruments of that section. **(B)** For example, clicking anywhere in the string

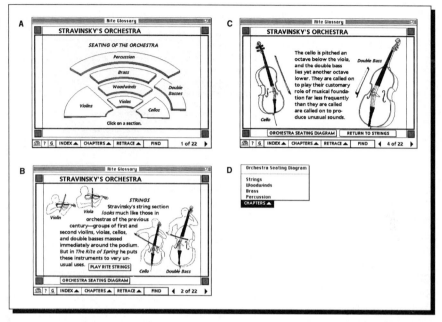

section in the Seating Diagram takes you here. **(C)** Clicking the Cello instrument takes you here. **(D)** A Chapter menu like this is always available to help you navigate.

Figure 29-4: (A) Stravinsky's World is an area of the stacks devoted to the life and times of Igor Stravinsky. The various topics are self-explanatory. **(B)** You can click a topic or navigate with this Chapters menu. **(C)** This is a sample card from the chapter entitled The

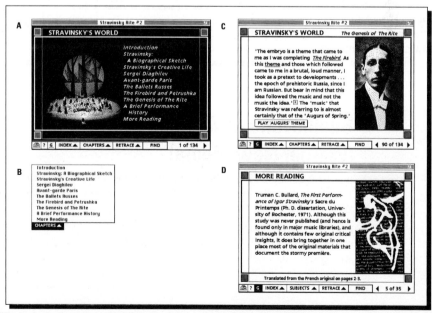

Genesis of The Rite. Underlined words can be clicked to bring up further information. Where music examples are referred to in the text, a button, such as the one at the bottom of this screen, lets you audio them. Finally, the little R in a box after the quote brings up the next screen. **(D)** You can call up a full reference as shown in D.

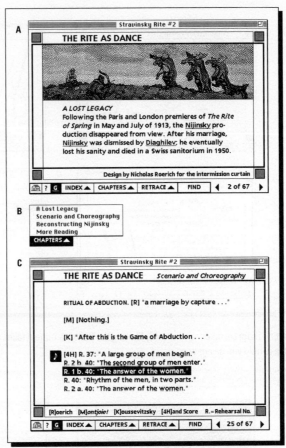

Figure 29-5: (A) The Rite as Dance is another main area of the stacks. Much art like this is reproduced throughout the stacks. The sources are always given above the lower menu bar. **(B)** The Chapter menu for the Rite as Dance section of the stacks. **(C)** The Scenario and Choreography chapter provides an in-depth look at the original choreography. This card traces the annotations and comments of the people whose initials appear above the menu bar. The little note icon plays the passage in question, highlighting the comments as it does.

Beethoven's *String Quartet No. 14* (Warner New Media)

Warner New Media is another company producing interactive CD-ROMs for music. Their series is called Audio Notes. Their first release was extremely ambitious: Mozart's *Magic Flute*. From the very beginning their CD-ROMs were custom-pressed. The *Magic Flute* includes three custom CD-ROMs with a good deal of verbal commentary by Roger Englander and Dr. Irene Gertin added to the available audio data.

Figure 29-6: (A) The Rite Listening area suggests strategies for listening to the *Rite of Spring*. This section contains a complete grounding in music theory as the subject relates to the *Rite*. This is typical of the explanations in the Revolutionary Rhythms chapter. "Hot" (clickable) words abound and audio is used to make a point wherever possible. **(B)** Clicking the Shout It Out! button of the previous card lets you listen to Robert Winter counting the meter along with the music. Each bar highlights as he does so. You also have the option of hearing the music, the Evocation in this case, without Professor Winter counting along. **(C)** Multiple representations are clearly illustrated when you compare this display of the rhythm to the Glorification with that used on the card in B. High-

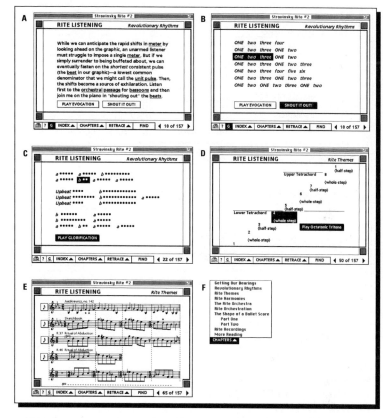

lighting the playback measure occurs here as well — and just about everywhere else there is music or a representation of music in the stacks. **(D)** The structure of the octatonic scale is presented as preliminary background in the Rite Themes chapter of the stacks. The notes highlight as the example is played. **(E)** Wherever possible, the sketches and source material are compared to the final version of the *Rite* as happens on this card. Besides notation, you can also hear each version of the music for instant comparison. **(F)** The Rite Listening Chapters menu.

Audio Notes Series CD-ROMs are suitable for both classroom or self-guided learning at any level of musical expertise and any age. Graduate students on down to elementary school students can learn from these CD-ROMs. This is fundamental to the medium due to the user options for digging only as deep as his or her technical background warrants.

Warner New Media's current and forthcoming interactive CD-ROMs for music education are listed in Table 6-30.

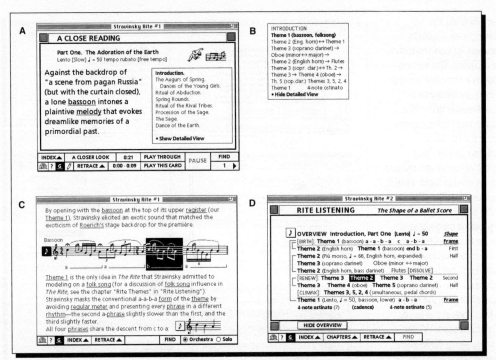

Figure 29-7: (A) The heart of Voyager's *Rite of Spring* interactive CD-ROM is the Close Reading area. This area analyzes the work in as much detail as you desire. You control the amount of depth of the analysis. You have the option to Play Through, in which case the descriptions and commentaries change along with the music. You can also select Play This Card to repeatedly listen and study the current section. Elapsed time is always displayed, along with a wealth of other information. **(B)** Clicking Show Detailed View replaces the descriptive box in A with a more analytical one such as this. **(C)** Clicking the button labeled A Closer Look brings up a theoretical analysis that should satisfy even the most curious. These analyses often offer playback options. The example shown offers you the option of hearing the particular passage played by the solo bassoon or in the context of the entire orchestra (by way of the radio buttons at the lower right). Music highlights while playing, of course. **(D)** Finally, back on the main card (A), you can click the little music icon at the upper right at any time. This brings up a detailed overview of the current music. The overview contains thematic, instrumental, harmonic, temporal, and other information. The current phrase, measure, or section, as appropriate, highlights during playback.

Like Voyager's enhancement of new releases with interactive videodiscs (see the Mozart *Dissonant Quartet* above), some future Audio Notes releases will include comparable bells and whistles. Some of these are the incorporation of MIDI tracks on the CD-ROMs (accessible with a CD+M-compatible player only) and the display of additional visual graphics on a normal television (accessible with a CD+G-compatible player only). See the sidebar "CD+ In Multimedia" for more details.

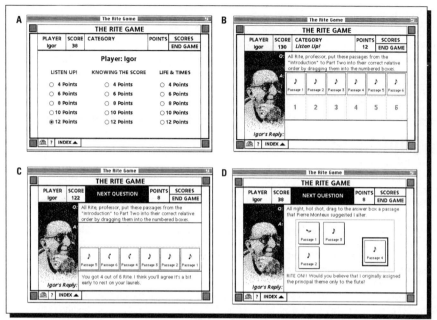

Figure 29-8: (A) You can get so involved in a session of interaction with the *Rite of Spring* that when you stop to look at the clock, several hours may have passed. That's the nature of unstructured browsing. You might need a breather from information overload (one of the "dangers" of interactive hypermedia). This stuff has a very high user bandwidth (see the section "Authoring Systems"). Voyager provides for rest and relaxation in the form of this Rite Game. Although meant to be a relaxation option, this stack also serves the purpose of letting you put your newly acquired knowledge to work. **(B)** One format of the 12-point Listen Up! questions presents you with six passages that you have to place in the right order. You click in the passages to hear them. Afterward, you use the mouse to rearrange them into what you think is the correct order. There is no end to the number of questions of this type that the software can generate. **(C)** The software responds audibly if you want. Applause or laughter can greet your answer. Random verbal responses to your answers are a very nice touch. Upside-down notes indicate incorrect answers. **(D)** As you might expect, the ten-point questions are somewhat easier.

Unfortunately, the hybrid hierarchical/nonlinear structure discussed in the opening of this chapter (see Figure 29-1) rears its head in the Audio Notes Series: An extra step is added to every move from one main-level information node to another, because it is necessary to continually visit the Program Guide as a gateway to the opening card of practically every area. Just this one inconvenience is like a roadblock thrown up in front of the otherwise seamlessly transparent, randomly accessible information available with Audio Notes. Furthermore, the *Magic Flute* is spread over three CD-ROMs, which necessitates frequent CD-ROM swaps. It's not Warner New Media's fault, because with a work of such magnitude no other solu-tion exists. Swapping floppy disks in a standard drive is enough of a hassle; with a CD-ROM drive the irritation is magnified because of the slow access time of most CD-ROM drives to recognize the new disc. The magical spell of your interactive mindset is immediately broken. These two things are admittedly minor hindrances, but they are enough to make it possible for you to get lost in your information knowledge navigation, a user state that goes against all the tenants of interactive hypermedia.

CD+ In Multimedia

The official Compact Disc Specification reserves over 25MB on a standard audio CD for non-audio data. This represents about 5 percent of the disc and is made up of subcodes, of which there are 8 bits per audio frame. Two of these bits are already used in audio CDs, leaving 6 bits per frame to play around with. That the subcode tracks are synchronized to the audio makes for many interesting possibilities. Two uses of subcodes are MIDI and still graphics. Some CD players already have a decoder output port on the back. In these cases, you can retrofit your player to handle MIDI or graphics with the addition of a simple decoder. Newer models have the decoder built in. General MIDI will be a boon to the CD+MIDI standard.

CD+MIDI (CD+M)

Subcode tracks can output fast enough to handle MIDI data. The data rate of all subcodes is about 58,000 bps, but only a 44,100 bps data rate is available, because two of the subcode bits are already in use.

Only one player capable of decoding the MIDI tracks of a CD+M exists at the time of this writing: JVC's XL-G512. Besides MIDI output jacks, this inexpensive player includes a video output as well. Warner New Media's The Magic Flute CD-ROM includes MIDI data that you can output with this player.

MIDI data is synchronized to the audio data on the CD. This allows you to add your own re-orchestration of the music — if you think a solo line should have been doubled by flutes, simply add them by plugging your sampler into the MIDI OUT port of your CD+M player. Of course you can also capture the MIDI data that is coming off your CD. This data could be used to make new arrangements, to generate notation

for printing, or to create interactive MIDI product demos or even CDs that could store, for example, every DX7 patch ever programmed.

There are other ways to synchronize MIDI data with CD audio data. Opcode's Max software is particularly well suited for the task (see Chapter 31), provided you play back the audio on a CD-ROM drive with audio outputs. Creative use of some of the HyperMIDI XCMDs in conjunction with Voyager's CD AudioStack can produce similar results (see Chapter 29).

CD+Graphics (CD+G)

The G in CD+G refers to still graphics (NTSC composite video format), which take about eight seconds to assemble on your television set. Graphics can be associated with particular musical events in a presentation similar to a slide show.

The CD Specification provides for 16-color, 300×200 pixel still graphics. Like Macintoshes with a color depth of four bits, each graphic may be drawn from a different palette consisting of over 16 million colors. Up to 16 graphics channels are provided for by the CD Specification, although because of the slow screen-drawing time, changing more than three or four channels at a time is impractical, except in very specialized applications.

At the time of this writing there are about 200 CD+G titles and more coming out every day (although most are being played on normal CD players, so the visual element is missing). Current use of the graphics channels include pictures, biographies, lyrics with translations, commentary, notation, and chord charts.

Besides JVC's player mentioned above, NEC markets a player (aimed at the game market) called the TurboGraphix-16.

The Audio Notes Series further differs from the Voyager Series in that Voyager's CD Companion Series releases restrict their information content provider to a single recognized authority in the subject of the composition being discussed, while the Audio Notes Series, in true Warner Brothers style, includes a cast of thousands under the helm of one expert director.

In Figures 29-9 through 29-15, the same caveats apply that were noted above immediately preceding the Stravinsky figures. There is much more information available on an Audio Notes CD-ROM than can ever be covered here. Keep in mind that the vast majority of these cards are linked with every other card pictured.

Authoring Systems

An authoring system is a toolkit that takes care of all the intricate details of writing the programming elements to the interface of an interactive CD-ROM. Authoring systems let you concentrate on content and the look of the user interface; you do not have to concern yourself with programming.

Several decades ago one always used to hear about the glorious future when com-puters would write programs for other computers. An authoring system is pretty close to that concept. The features of an authoring system are automated to the extent that it is like having a live-in programmer who immediately creates programs that do whatever you request — and this programmer rarely intro-duces a bug.

New development considerations arise that have no correspondence in other media. Mark Heyer, in *The New Papyrus* (Microsoft Press, 1986), suggests that interactive media development take into consideration the concept of "user band-width" — comprising factors that are physical, circumstantial, and psycho-logical. He contrasts television, a medium with a very high video bandwidth but a com-plete lack of viewer control, to a single image retrieved from a database. In the former case, there is a very low user bandwidth that can result in low attention and reduced information receptivity or effectivity. In the latter case, the single static image being the result of a dedicated search by the user, has a very high user bandwidth for that person.

Voyager offers its Voyager CD AudioStack for those who would like to create interactive CD-ROMs using any off-the-shelf audio CD. Yes, you read that last sentence correctly, it said *any* off-the-shelf audio CD. Any audio CD can in fact function as a CD-ROM when placed into a CD-ROM drive (with audio outputs) connected to your Macintosh. You are not limited to music recordings either. Any foreign language, theatrical, or dramatic reading available on CD can also be used. Are you getting some ideas?

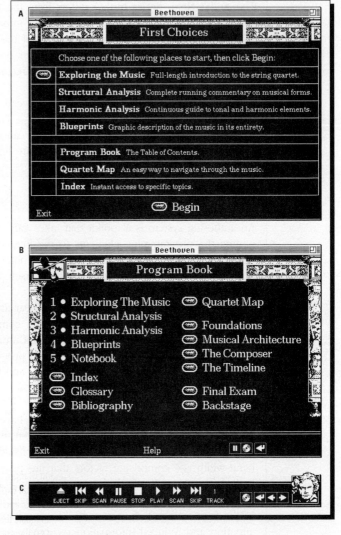

Figure 29-9: (A) When you launch the first String Quartet stack you are presented with seven points of departure. In fact there are more, because many of these lead to additional launching pads. **(B)** The Program Book is the main navigational island. In fact, click-ing Beethoven's head pictured at the lower right of every card except these two will bring you directly here. The Audio Notes Series uses these types of launching pads for navigation in place of the pop-up menus found in Voyager's CD-Companion Series. **(C)** Clicking the tiny compact disc button at the lower right brings up this set of transport controls for direct manipulation of the CD-ROM drive.

Voyager's development system works with both HyperCard and SuperCard. It can be used to create interactive CD-ROMs that employ multiple CD-ROM drives like the Vermeer Quartet/Juilliard Quartet set discussed above. Voyager's authoring system includes drivers that support all Macintosh-compatible CD-ROM drives, and the installation of these drivers into your stacks is automatic.

Figure 29-10:
Unlike Voyager's interface, which fosters stopping and examining sections individually, the default approach in the Audio Notes Series is to keep the music rolling all the time (you can pause it with the pause button at the lower right). A continual analysis flows by on the screen, in time with the music. Rather than try to display as much information as possible on a single card, the information is divided into four

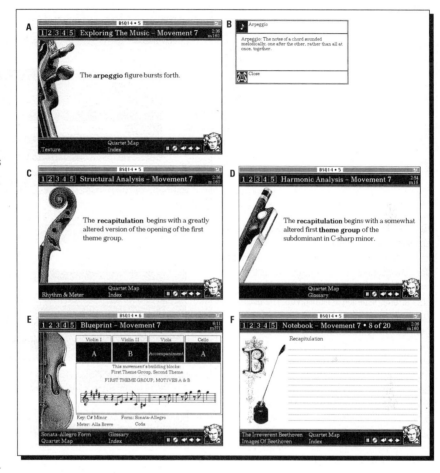

areas: Exploring the Music, Structural Analysis, Harmonic Analysis, and Blueprint. You switch from mode to mode by way of the number buttons at the upper left of the screen. **(A)** This card is a typical Exploring the Music card. The information is intentionally brief because it is designed to give you just enough time to read and absorb it before advancing to the next card. Exploring the Music is intended for people with little knowledge of music terminology. Whenever musical terminology is used it is a hot word. Audio Notes displays these in bold (Voyager displays these as underlined). Note that the words running across the bottom of the screen are also hot (a minor user-interface inconsistency). **(B)** Clicking the hot word "Arpeggio" on the previous card brings up a definition box directly over the word. Most definitions are reinforced with audio examples accessible by pressing the little music note icon. **(C)** Pressing the number 2 button at the upper left brings you to the Structural Analysis of the current point in the music. This deals with the musical form and sometimes includes in-depth sidebars. **(D)** Pressing the number 3 button at the upper left brings you to the Harmonic Analysis, a view point that does require extensive knowledge of music terminology (the glossary and hot words are always available for definitions of unfamiliar terms). **(E)** The Blueprint view is available by pressing the number 4 button. This is the most technical analysis of the work. Blueprints are always in the format pictured here. Boxes at the top describe what role each instrument is playing at the current moment. Below these are shown the movement's building blocks — themes, motifs, melodies, and harmonies that the upper instrument boxes refer to. **(F)** Finally, pressing the number 5 button provides you with a notebook where you can type your own notes and observations about the current section. This is a very desirable feature, also found in Warner's *Magic Flute* CD-ROMs.

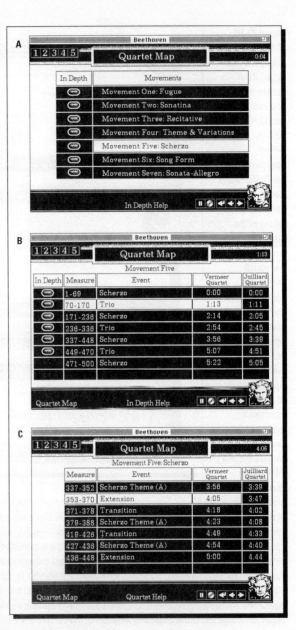

Figure 29-11: (A) Often the hot word Quartet Map, appears at the lower part of the screen. Clicking this brings up a series of three progressively more detailed descriptions of the current part of the music. First you merely see the movement you are currently listening to highlighted. The In Depth buttons zoom in on finer details. **(B)** Here we have used the In Depth button to zoom in on the Trio. The entire form of the music is displayed with the current location highlighted. Note the columns on the far right: Vermeer Quartet and Juilliard Quartet showing the different timings used by the two quartets. The CD-ROM is available with either ensemble performing the quartet. In fact, if you have two CD-ROM drives attached to your Macintosh you can freely toggle back and forth between the performances by simply clicking in the other ensemble's column, an excellent feature for string quartet master classes and the like. **(C)** Pressing the In Depth button again brings you to the deepest of thematic analysis provided by the CD-ROM in the Quartet Map area. This lists measure numbers, thematic information, and timing information for the two different performing ensembles. As usual, the music you are currently listening to is highlighted.

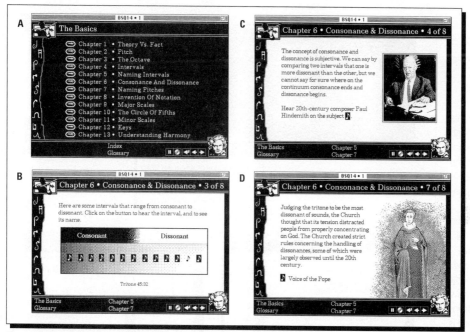

Figure 29-12: Warner New Media's String Quartet includes four other areas to increase your musical knowledge. In all four areas, you can return to the quartet area by clicking the picture of the violinist in the upper-left corner. **(A)** The first is Foundations, of which this is the main navigation card. Foundations provides a rather complete course in the fundamentals of music theory and basic musicianship. **(B)** Jumping to Chapter 6 of Foundations, Consonance and Dissonance illustrates some of the representational devices Audio Notes employs to drive a concept home. The number at the upper right tells you that there are eight cards devoted to this topic. Like Voyager's products, these are as widely varied as the topics they cover. Here, clicking any of the note icons presents intervals that become progressively more consonant or dissonant, depending upon which end of the spectrum you click. **(C)** Going deeper into the topic of Consonance and Dissonance you can even listen to composer Paul Hindemith present a little mini-lecture on the topic. **(D)** You can also hear what the Pope has to say about the subject of Consonance and Dissonance.

Voyager's AudioStack includes 25 ready-made buttons that can be automatically customized, copied to the Clipboard, and pasted into your stack. Controls let you quickly isolate the start and end points of audio material for which you want to create a button. There is an Event List, similar to a real-time Edit Decision List, that lets you create buttons for the execution of multiple events in a row.

Programming couldn't be easier (see Figures 29-16 and 29-17).

Figure 29-13: (A) The second supplementary area of this Audio Notes software concerns itself with Musical Architecture. This is concerned with musical forms and how they relate to the Beethoven Quartet and an in-depth look at a string quartet from the instrumental perspective. **(B)** Clicking Stringed Instruments brings up this informative graphic. **(C)** An info box like this one is brought up by clicking any of the pictures of the individual instruments. **(D)**

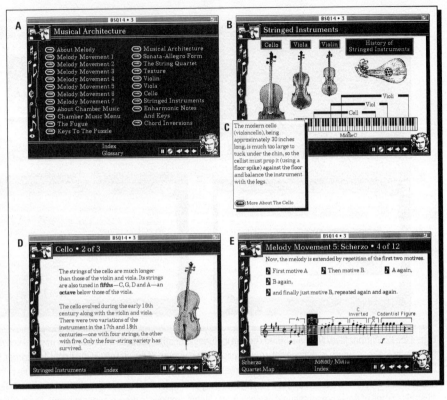

Clicking More About the Cello in the info box brings up more detailed information. **(E)** Clicking a Melody button on A brings up a motivic analysis such as this.

Figure 29-14: (A) The third supple-mentary area is The Composer. This is essentially a very well written biography of Beethoven. The description of his deafness is par-ticularly extensive. **(B)** Clicking Beethoven's Deafness from the main card of the Composer area brings you to a series of 28 cards with detailed information about the progression of the composer's loss of hearing. Many of the cards are illustrated with graphics such as this one.

Figure 29-15: (A) The fourth area of additional information is The Timeline. Here you can click a composer's face or musical period for an over-view of that subject. **(B)**This is one of four cards you get by clicking Stravinsky's face in The Timeline.

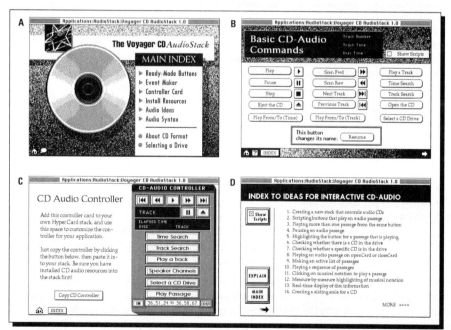

Figure 29-16: Voyager's CD Audio Stack lets you create your own interactive CD-ROMs using standard off-the-shelf audio CDs. **(A)** The stack has six main areas accessible from this Main Index. **(B)** This is one of the many cards of ready-made buttons that come with the AudioStack. **(C)** There is even a CD remote controller that you can paste into your stack creations. **(D)** If you need some ideas, interactive CD Audio Ideas cards such as this one display scripts for various ideas with ample comments.

Figure 29-17: (A) The heart of the Voyager AudioStack is this Event Maker card. Here you can quickly locate and define regions of audio material. Button creation is automatic (or you can copy the script to the Clipboard) and you can copy any event to the Event List (see B). **(B)** Among other things, the Event List lets you define a

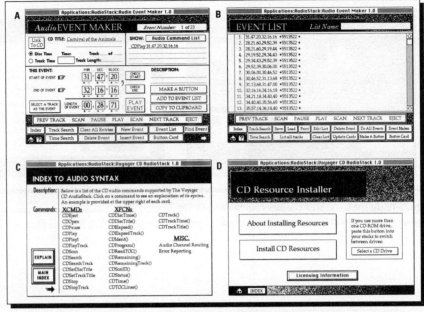

sequence of events that are executed in a specific order. These events do not have to be adjacent on the audio CD. Naturally, the creation of a button for your event sequences is automatic. **(C)** If you want to get deeper into interactive CD-ROM programming, this Syntax Guide provides detailed information about all the programming that the AudioStack normally takes care of for you automatically. Click a command for a complete description of its syntax and how to use it. **(D)** Installation of the appropriate drivers into your creation is just a button click away with this card.

Summary

✔ Interactive CD-ROMs are possibly the most exciting new computer-aided music-learning medium to appear. A CD-ROM can hold about 650MB of data — including CD-quality audio — and because every block of data has a unique address (over 300,000 separate addresses), the Macintosh can jump to any place on the disc almost instantaneously. Although data can be located extremely quickly, reading data is quite slow, unless it is CD audio.

✔ To use an interactive music CD-ROM you must have a CD-ROM drive with audio outputs and a Macintosh. The prices of CD-ROM drives have dropped below the price of the original 800K floppy disk drive at its introduction. This puts CD-ROMs into the hands of the masses as a tool for musical learning.

✔ Interactive CD-ROM is a type of hypermedia providing nonlinear access to information. Besides multiple access paths to the same information nodes, one of the most important features of hypermedia is multiple representations of information at the click of a button.

✔ Hypermedia itself is an outgrowth of the old concept of "hypertext," a term coined by Ted Nelson. A hypertext system presents text in such a way that while you are reading, you can click a word to go deeper into that topic, perhaps to get a definition, example, or tangential information. The concept of hypertext is still active on the next level, so if you click a word while you are on that level, you can reach the next level of detail, and so on. Hypermedia adds all types of data, dynamic or static, to the text-based concept of hypertext. Hypermedia can include audio, still graphics, animations, and video.

✔ Hypermedia is a nonlinear system that links, or cross-references if you prefer, all elements to one another. Usually, any node of information is accessible from any other node whenever you need it. Conceptualizing the available information from multiple levels of abstraction is greatly facilitated.

✔ Hypermedia lets you become an active participant in the authoring of the information, at least from the perspective of presentation order. In linearly structured text, the author decides the order in which you read material; with interactive CD-ROMs, you have complete control over this parameter.

✔ Many interactive CD-ROMs are controlled by a HyperCard stack or stacks. Even the authoring systems themselves can be automated HyperCard stacks. Interactive CD-ROM authoring systems are so user friendly that an instructor can put together a very educational custom presentation using little investment of time and effort.

The Future of Mac Music and Sound
Afterword
by Jeff Rona

The way music is made has changed forever. No art can be separated from the technology that is used to create it. When chemists invented new colors and textures of inks and paints, artists used this new technology and altered their styles accordingly — from plant dyes on cave walls to chemical mixtures, from oil paints to acrylics, from lithography to video and computer-generated 3-D animated graphics. The artists working with digital imaging computers tend to come up with art that does not resemble cave paintings.

On the music side, there is the technology of MIDI. MIDI is a tool that has had fantastic sway over the process, and ultimately the product, of contemporary composition. This profoundly simple technology, though powerful in its own right, was just waiting to be wedded to the technology of personal computers. For the musician, either one without the other is merely a helpful tool. The two together are a near-perfect match. MIDI is the message, but the computer is the messenger.

Good ideas are self-perpetuating. They beget the desire to continue them, improve upon them, and share them. Good ideas don't come up that often, but when they do, it is a tribute to the human psyche. Most importantly, good ideas catch fire.

What makes a Macintosh musical? Is it the CRT, RAM, mouse, disk drives, serial ports, or keyboard? Is it its physical dimensions or weight? The Macintosh was a good idea that changed the way people use computers. It feels good in the hand. More than any machine that came before it, the Macintosh gets closer to working in a way that patterns itself after how people experience the world — with pictures, gestures, and feedback. Fortunately, it caught the attention of some good programmers, who saw in it the potential for a new kind of musical instrument. Little exists on the Macintosh that does not exist elsewhere in the musical software arena, but the Macintosh adds one element found nowhere else — grace. It was and is the first truly graceful computer. It is perhaps this one unique aspect that lends the Macintosh to the creative world so readily.

I've been curious about computers as long as I've been around them. The Macintosh was the first computer that made me feel it was curious about me! I've spent countless hours pouring my heart, mind, and soul into it. I've used it to compose, improvise, experiment, transcribe, organize, design, author, balance, alphabetize, free associate, mix, edit, perform, and just plain goof around. It's like a warm home for the manifestations of my mind and soul.

I've used many other computers, but this one stands apart for me. It makes me feel safe to explore my ideas in a way with which I am comfortable. And while, like all computers do, it may crash and lose words or notes I've worked hard at and may never recover, it seems forgivable because of the high goals it encourages in programmers and users (however, my thoughts are not so benevolent right at those moments).

▶

There seems to be something that differentiates those who merely use a computer and those who develop a deep, symbiotic rapport with their machines. Those who get the most out of using computers, either in music or other arts or sciences, seem to share a heightened sense of analogy and process. When you stop caring about the difference between reality and metaphor, your mind begins to open to the "zen" of the machine. You feed it and it feeds back to you in a synergistic and holistic system that transcends its individual components.

It's been said that an artist must have limits in order to do good work, otherwise there are too many choices and not enough focus. But do painters experience limits at the edge of their canvas? Of course not. The painting is merely the physical manifestation of their vision. The art extends far beyond. And so it is in the computer domain — the possibilities extend in dimensions beyond the screen's phosphor for the artist who sees it that way. With the right mindset, the distinction between artist and tool begins to blur, as does the difference between process and product.

There are occasionally people who question the artistic credibility of those who use computers. Did you write that, or did the computer do it all? While it may become more and more of an issue as time goes on, for the moment the question is ludicrous. Did you drive here to see me or did your car drop by? The computer is a unique type of enabler. It provides a vehicle that lets us go where we want. It does not make the decision of destination, though it has influence over the route.

What is the most important component of computer-based music making? It is neither hardware nor software, although they both are strong influences to the open mind. The final answer, I believe, is environment. The creative instrument made up of computer, MIDI instruments, and other musical and audio devices that you put together is both an extension and reflection of yourself. It is the place where you do your work. Exploring it is exploring yourself. Learning to go deeper into your musical environment can ultimately teach you where the music really comes from.

We cannot envision what music technology will be like in 20 years, just as we scarcely could imagine 20 years ago the current process of making music with inexpensive synthesizers and graphics computers. We can be sure, though, that if we could get a sneak preview now, we would be stunned. As fast as computer technology is changing, music technology moves equally swift.

Will the future move toward the virtual, non-physical interplay between human and machine, or will there be new analogies to replace the desktop that has become the prime organizing interface? I can think of a future where objects that appear as books, papers, toys, and musical instruments may be part of a complex computer system able to adapt freely to the mental pictures of its user. Computer-oriented music-making environments could consist of playing old and new musical instruments, talking, singing, dancing, gesturing, thinking, playing, watching, drawing, or touching. There will be life beyond pointing and clicking at a CRT. And when that time comes, there will be both music and musicians that respond to it (and it to them) in a way that will produce music we cannot imagine now. But wait. ♩

Jeff Rona is a composer and past president of the MMA (MIDI Manufacturer's Association).

Appendix A
The MIDI Specification

Status Bytes

Channel Voice Messages

Function	Hexadecimal	Status Byte (Binary)	Number of Data Bytes
Note Off	8n	1000nnnn	2
Note On (velocity 0 = Note Off)	9n	1001nnnn	2
Polyphonic Key Pressure/ Aftertouch	An	1010nnnn	2
Control Change	Bn	1011nnnn nnnn = 0-120	2
Program Change	Cn	1100nnnn	1
Channel Pressure/ Aftertouch	Dn	1101nnnn	1
Pitch bend change	En	1110nnnn	2

Note: nnnn = Channel number (where 0000 = Channel 1, 0001 = Channel 2... and 1111 = Channel 16)

Channel Mode Messages

Selects Channel Mode	Bn	1011nnnn	2

Note: Channel mode messages use the same Status Byte as Control Change messages. The difference is that the first data byte of a Channel Mode message will have a value from 121 to 127.

System Messages

System Exclusive	F0	11110000	0iiiiiii, data, ..., EOX iiiiiii = identification
System Common		11110sss sss = 1 to 7	0 to 2
System Real Time		11111ttt ttt = 0 to 7	0

Channel Voice Messages

Function	Status Byte	1st Data Byte	2nd Data Byte
Note Off	1000nnnn n = Channel #	0kkkkkkk k = Key # (0-127)	0vvvvvvv v = Note Off Velocity (0-127)
Note On	1001nnnn n = Channel #	0kkkkkkk k = Key # (0-127)	0vvvvvvv v = Note On Velocity (1-127) 0 = Note Off
Polyphonic Key Pressure	1010nnnn n = Channel #	0kkkkkkk k = Key # (0-127)	0vvvvvvv v = pressure value (0-127)
Control Change (see "Controller Numbers")	1011nnnn n = Channel #	0ccccccc c = Control # (0-120)	0vvvvvvv v = Control value (0-127)
Program Change	1100nnnn n = Channel #	0ppppppp p = Program # (0-127)	

Status Bytes (continued)

Channel Voice Messages (continued)

Function	Status Byte	1st Data Byte	2nd Data Byte
Channel Pressure (Aftertouch)	1101nnnn n = Channel #	0vvvvvvv v = pressure value	
Pitch Bend	1110nnnn n = Channel #	0vvvvvvv v = Pitch bend value LSB	0vvvvvvv v = Pitch bend value MSB

Controller Numbers

Control Number	(1st Data Byte)	Control Function	2nd Data Byte
Decimal	Hexadecimal		
0	00	Bank Select MSB	0-127
1	01	Modulation Wheel or Lever *	0-127
2	02	Breath Controller	0-127
3	03	Undefined	0-127
4	04	Foot Controller	0-127
5	05	Portamento Time	0-127
6	06	Data Entry MSB	0-127
7	07	Main Volume *	0-127
8	08	Balance	0-127
9	09	Undefined	0-127
10	0A	Pan *	0-127
11	0B	Expression Controller *	0-127
12	0C	Effect Control 1	0-127
13	0D	Effect Control 2	0-127
14-15	0C-0F	Undefined	0-127
16-19	10-13	General Purpose Controllers (numbers 1-4)	0-127
20-31	14-1F	Undefined	0-127
32-63	20-3F	LSB for Values 0-31	0-127
64	40	Damper Pedal (Sustain) *	on/off
65	41	Portamento	on/off
66	42	Sostenuto	on/off
67	43	Soft Pedal	on/off
68	44	Legato Footswitch (00-3F = Normal; 40-7F = Legato)	Normal/Legato
69	45	Hold 2	on/off
70	46	Sound Controller #1 (Sound Variation)	0-127
71	47	Sound Controller #2 (Harmonic Content)	0-127
72	48	Sound Controller #3 (Release Time)	0-127
73	49	Sound Controller #4 (Attack Time)	0-127
74	4A	Sound Controller #5 (Brightness)	0-127
75-79	4B-4F	Undefined	on/off
80-83	50-53	General Purpose Controllers (numbers 5-8)	on/off
84-90	54-5A	Undefined	on/off
91	5B	External Effects Depth	0-127
92	5C	Tremolo Depth	0-127
93	5D	Chorus Depth	0-127
94	5E	Celeste (Detune) Depth	0-127
95	5F	Phaser Depth	0-127
96	60	Data Increment	on/off
97	61	Data Decrement	on/off

* = General MIDI performance requirement

Controller Numbers (continued)

Control Number	(1st Data Byte)	Control Function	2nd Data Byte
Decimal	**Hexadecimal**		
98	62	Non-Registered Parameter Number LSB	on/off
99	63	Non-Registered Parameter Number MSB	on/off
100	64	Registered Parameter Number LSB	on/off
101	65	Registered Parameter Number MSB	on/off
102-120	66-78	Undefined	on/off
121-127	79-7F	Reserved for Channel Mode Messages	

Registered Parameter Numbers

Function	LSB	MSB
Pitch Bend Sensitivity *	00	00
Fine Tuning *	01	00
Coarse Tuning *	02	00
Tuning Program Select	03	
Tuning Bank Select	04	

= General MIDI performance requirement

Channel Mode Messages (Controller Numbers 121-127)

Function	Status Byte	1st Data Byte	2nd Data Byte
All Sounds Off	1011nnn n = Channel #	0ccccccc ccccccc = 120	0vvvvvvv v = 0
Reset All Controllers*	1011nnn n = Channel #	0ccccccc ccccccc = 121	0vvvvvvv v = 0
Local Control	1011nnn n = Channel #	0ccccccc ccccccc = 122	0vvvvvvv v: 0 = Off, 127 = On
All Notes Off *	1011nnn n = Channel #	0ccccccc ccccccc = 123	0vvvvvvv v = 0
Omni Mode Off (All Notes Off)	1011nnn n = Channel #	0ccccccc ccccccc = 124	0vvvvvvv v = 0
Omni Mode On (All Notes Off)	1011nnn n = Channel #	0ccccccc ccccccc = 125	0vvvvvvv v = 0
Mono Mode Off (Poly Mode Off) (All Notes Off)	1011nnn n = Channel #	0ccccccc ccccccc = 126	0vvvvvvv v: non-zero = the number of channels 0 = the number of channels is equal to the number voices in the receiver
Poly Mode On (Mono Mode Off) (All Notes Off)	1011nnn n = Channel #	0ccccccc ccccccc = 127	0vvvvvvv v = 0

= General MIDI performance requirement

System Common Messages

Function	Status Byte	1st Data Byte	2nd Data Byte
MIDI Time Code Quarter Frame	11110001	0nnndddd nnn = Message Type, dddd = Values	
Song Position Pointer	11110010	0lllllll l = LSB	0hhhhhhh h = MSB
Song Select	11110011	0sssssss s = Song #	
Tune Request	11110110		
(Undefined)	11110100		
(Undefined)	11110101		
EOX (End of Exclusive) Flag (see above)	11110111		

System Real Time Messages

Function	Hexadecimal	Binary
Timing Clock	F8	11111000
(Undefined)	F9	11111001
Start	FA	11111010
Continue	FB	11111011
Stop	FC	11111100
(Undefined)	FD	11111101
Active Sensing	FE	11111110
System Rest	FF	11111111

System Exclusive ID Numbers
Non-real time

(F0 7E is the Universal Non-Real Time SysEx Header)

Function	Sub-ID #1	Sub-ID #2
Unused	00	unused
Sample Dump Header	01	unused
Sample Data Packet	02	unused
Sample Dump Request	03	unused
MIDI Time Code (MTC)	04	nn
Special	04	00
Punch In Points	04	01
Punch Out Points	04	02
Delete Punch In Point	04	03
Delete Punch Out Point	04	04
Event Start Point	04	05
Event Stop Point	04	06
Event Start Points with Additional Info	04	07
Event Stop Points with Additional Info	04	08
Delete Event Start Point	04	09
Delete Event Stop Point	04	0A
Cue Points	04	0B
Cue Points with Additional Info	04	0C
Delete Cue Point	04	0D
Event Name in Additional Info	04	0E
Sample Dump Extensions	05	nn
Multiple Loop Points	05	01
Loop Points Request	05	02
General Information	06	nn
Identify Request	06	01
Identify Reply	06	02
Bulk Tuning Dump	08	
General MIDI Message	09	nn
General MIDI On	09	01
General MIDI Off	09	02
Wait	7C	unused
Cancel	7D	unused
NAK	7E	unused
ACK	7F	unused

Real time

F0 7F (the Universal Real Time SysEx Header) followed by device ID

Function	Sub-ID #1	Sub-ID #2	Data Byte(s)
Unused	00	unused	
MIDI Time Code	01	nn	
Full Message	01	01	
User Bits	01	02	
Notation Information	03	nn	
Bar Number Message	03	01	aa aa Bar number (lsb first) *00 40 = not running* *01 40 to 00 00 = count-in* *01 00 to 7E 3F = bar number in song* *7F 3F = running* *(bar number unknown)*
Time Signature (immediate)	03	02	ln nn dd cc bb [nn dd...] *ln = number of data bytes to follow* *nn = time signature numerator* *dd = time signature denominator* *cc = number of MIDI clocks per metronome click* *bb = number of notated 32nd notes in a* *MIDI quarter note (24 MIDI Clocks)* *[nn dd...] additional pairs of time signatures to* *define compound signatures in the same bar*
Time Signature (delayed)	03	03	ln nn dd cc bb [nn dd...] *ln = number of data bytes to follow* *nn = time signature numerator* *dd = time signature denominator* *cc = number of MIDI clocks per metronome click* *hh = number of notated 32nd notes in a* *MIDI quarter note (24 MIDI Clocks)* *[nn dd...] additional pairs of time signatures to* *define compound signatures in the same bar*
Device Control	04	nn	
Master Volume	04	01	vv vv Volume (lsb first) *00 00 = volume off*
Master Balance	04	02	bb bb Balance (lsb first) *00 00 = hard left* *7F 7F = hard right*
Single-note Retuning	08		

General MIDI Level 1

General MIDI sound set groupings (all channels except 10)

Program #	Instrument Group	Program #	Instrument Group
1-8	Piano	65-72	Reed
9-16	Chromatic Percussion	73-80	Pipe
17-24	Organ	81-88	Synth Lead
25-32	Guitar	89-96	Synth Pad
33-40	Bass	97-104	Synth Effects
41-48	Strings	105-112	Ethnic
49-56	Ensemble	113-120	Percussive
57-64	Brass	121-128	Sound Effects

General MIDI sound set

(MIDI Program Numbers 1-128 on all channels except 10)

1	Acoustic Grand Piano	44	Contrabass	87	Lead 7 (fifths)
2	Bright Acoustic Piano	45	Tremolo Strings	88	Lead 8 (bass + lead)
3	Electric Grand Piano	46	Pizzicato Strings	89	Pad 1 (new age)
4	Honky-tonk Piano	47	Orchestral Harp	90	Pad 2 (warm)
5	Electric Piano 1	48	Timpani	91	Pad 3 (polysynth)
6	Electric Piano 2	49	String Ensemble 1	92	Pad 4 (choir)
7	Harpsichord	50	String Ensemble 2	93	Pad 5 (bowed)
8	Clavi	51	SynthStrings 1	94	Pad 6 (metallic)
9	Celesta	52	SynthStrings 2	95	Pad 7 (halo)
10	Glockenspiel	53	Choir Aahs	96	Pad 8 (sweep)
11	Music Box	54	Voice Oohs	97	FX 1 (rain)
12	Vibraphone	55	Synth Voice	98	FX 2 (soundtrack)
13	Marimba	56	Orchestra Hit	99	FX 3 (crystal)
14	Xylophone	57	Trumpet	100	FX 4 (atmosphere)
15	Tubular Bells	58	Trombone	101	FX 5 (brightness)
16	Dulcimer	59	Tuba	102	FX 6 (goblins)
17	Drawbar Organ	60	Muted Trumpet	103	FX 7 (echoes)
18	Percussive Organ	61	French Horn	104	FX 8 (sci-fi)
19	Rock Organ	62	Brass Section	105	Sitar
20	Church Organ	63	SynthBrass 1	106	Banjo
21	Reed Organ	64	SynthBrass 2	107	Shamisen
22	Accordion	65	Soprano Sax	108	Koto
23	Harmonica	66	Alto Sax	109	Kalimba
24	Tango Accordion	67	Tenor Sax	110	Bag Pipe
25	Acoustic Guitar (nylon)	68	Baritone Sax	111	Fiddle
26	Acoustic Guitar (steel)	69	Oboe	112	Shanai
27	Electric Guitar (jazz)	70	English Horn	113	Tinkle Bell
28	Electric Guitar (clean)	71	Bassoon	114	Agogo
29	Electric Guitar (muted)	72	Clarinet	115	Steel Drums
30	Overdriven Guitar	73	Piccolo	116	Woodblock
31	Distortion Guitar	74	Flute	117	Taiko Drum
32	Guitar Harmonics	75	Recorder	118	Melodic Tom
33	Acoustic Bass	76	Pan Flute	119	Synth Drum
34	Electric Bass (finger)	77	Blown Bottle	120	Reverse Cymbal
35	Electric Bass (pick)	78	Shakuhachi	121	Guitar Fret Noise
36	Fretless Bass	79	Whistle	122	Breath Noise
37	Slap Bass 1	80	Ocarina	123	Seashore
38	Slap Bass 2	81	Lead 1 (square)	124	Bird Tweet
39	Synth Bass 1	82	Lead 2 (sawtooth)	125	Telephone Ring
40	Synth Bass 2	83	Lead 3 (calliope)	126	Helicopter
41	Violin	84	Lead 4 (chiff)	127	Applause
42	Viola	85	Lead 5 (charang)	128	Gunshot
43	Cello	86	Lead 6 (voice)		

General MIDI percussion map

(Channel 10)

Key	Drum Sound	Key	Drum Sound	Key	Drum Sound
35	Acoustic Bass Drum	51	Ride Cymbal 1	67	High Agogo
36	Bass Drum 1	52	Chinese Cymbal	68	Low Agogo
37	Side Stick	53	Ride Bell	69	Cabasa
38	Acoustic Snare	54	Tambourine	70	Maracas
39	Hand Clap	55	Splash Cymbal	71	Short Whistle
40	Electric Snare	56	Cowbell	72	Long Whistle
41	Low Floor Tom	57	Crash Cymbal 2	73	Short Guiro
42	Closed Hi-Hat	58	Vibraslap	74	Long Guiro
43	High Floor Tom	59	Ride Cymbal 2	75	Claves
44	Pedal Hi-Hat	60	Hi Bongo	76	Hi Wood Block
45	Low Tom	61	Low Bongo	77	Low Wood Block
46	Open Hi-Hat	62	Mute Hi Conga	78	Mute Cuica
47	Low-Mid Tom	63	Open Hi Conga	79	Open Cuica
48	Hi-Mid Tome	64	Low Conga	80	Mute Triangle
49	Crash Cymbal 1	65	High Timbale	81	Open Triangle
50	High Tom	66	Low Timbale		

Recommended Practices

RP-001   Standard MIDI Files (SMFs) were Recommended Practice 001 and later incorporated into the official MIDI Specification.

RP-002   MIDI Show Control (MSC) was accepted as Recommended Practice 002 in mid-1991. Show Control is designed to "allow MIDI systems to communicate with and to control dedicated intelligent control equipment in theatrical, live performance, multimedia, audio-visual, and similar environments" (quoted from the specification). Among other things, MSC provides commands for control of moving lights, lasers, CD players, audio tape machines, amplifiers, robots, video (many types of devices), film and slide projectors, fog, smoke, fireworks, and explosions.

Build Your Own MIDI Interface

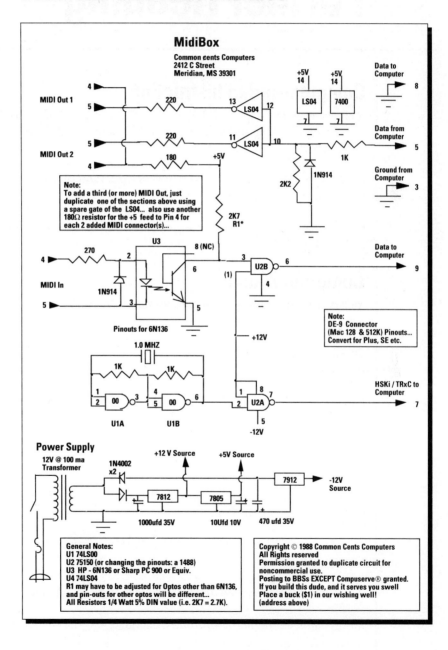

MidiBox
Common cents Computers
2412 C Street
Meridian, MS 39301

Power Supply
12V @ 100 ma Transformer

General Notes:
U1 74LS00
U2 75150 (or changing the pinouts: a 1488)
U3 HP - 6N136 or Sharp PC 900 or Equiv.
U4 74LS04
R1 may have to be adjusted for Optos other than 6N136, and pin-outs for other optos will be different...
All Resistors 1/4 Watt 5% DIN value (i.e. 2K7 = 2.7K).

Appendix B
Further Reading

Computer-aided Instruction

Ambron, Sueann and Kristina Hooper, eds. *Learning with Interactive Media: Developing and Using Multimedia Tools in Education.* Redmond, WA: Microsoft Press, 1990.

Bartle, Barton K. *Computer Software in Music and Music Education: A Guide.* Metuchen, NJ: Scarecrow Press, 1987.

Lambert, Steve and Suzanne Ropiequet, eds. *CD ROM: The New Papyrus.* Redmond, WA: Microsoft Press, 1986.

Computer Music

Anderton, Craig. *Power Sequencing with Master Tracks Pro/Pro4.* New York, NY: Amsco Publications, 1990.

Chamberlin, Hal. *Musical Applications of Microprocessors.* Carmel, IN: Hayden Books, 1987.

De Poli, G., A. Piccialli, and C. Roads, eds. *Representations of Musical Signals.* Cambridge, MA: The MIT Press, 1991.

Hofstetter, Fred T. *Computer Literacy for Musicians.* Englewood Cliffs, NJ: Prentice Hall, 1988.

Mathews, Max and J. R. Pierce, *Current Directions in Computer Music Research.* Cambridge, MA: The MIT Press, 1989.

Proceedings of the International Computer Music Conference. San Francisco, CA: Computer Music Association (Yearly).

Roads, Curtis, ed. *Composers and the Computer.* Madison, WI: A.R. Editions, 1985.

Roads, Curtis, ed. *The Music Machine.* Cambridge, MA: The MIT Press, 1989.

Roads, Curtis and John Strawn, eds. *Foundations of Computer Music.* Cambridge, MA: The MIT Press, 1985.

Digital Audio

DeFuria, Steve and Joe Scacciaferro. *The Sampling Book.* Pompton Lakes, NJ: Third Earth Publishing Inc., 1987.

Fryer, Terry. *A Practical Approach to Digital Sampling.* Milwaukee, WI: Hal Leonard Publishing Corporation, 1989.

Huber, David Miles. *Random Access Audio: An Introduction.* Menlo Park, CA: Digidesign Inc., 1990.

Pohlmann, Ken C. *Principles of Digital Audio,* 2d ed. Indianapolis, IN: Howard W. Sams & Company, 1989.

Film, Video, Synchronization

Alkin, Glyn. *Sound Techniques for Video & TV, Second Edition.* Boston, MA: Focal Press, 1989.

Bazelon, Irwin. *Knowing the Score: Notes on Film Music.* New York, NY: Arco Publishing, Inc., 1975.

Faulkner, Robert R. *Music on Demand: Composers and Careers in the Hollywood Film Industry.* New Brunswick, NJ: Transaction Books, 1983.

Hagen, Earl. *Advanced Scoring for Films.* Century City, CA: E.D.J. Music Publishers, Inc., 1989.

Hagen, Earl. *Scoring for Films.* New York, NY: Criterion Music Corp., 1989.

Huber, David Miles. *Audio Production Techniques for Video.* Indianapolis, IN: Howard W. Sams & Company, 1987.

Karlin, Fred and Rayburn Wright. *On the Track: A Guide to Contemporary Film Scoring.* New York, NY: Schirmer Books, 1990.

Rona, Jeffrey. *Synchronization from Reel to Reel: A Complete Guide for the Synchronization of Audio, Film & Video.* Milwaukee, WI: Hal Leonard Publishing Corporation, 1989.

Society of Motion Picture and Television Engineers. *Time Code Handbook: A Guide for the User from Fundamentals to Technical Specifications.* Frederick, MD: cipher digital, inc., 1987.

General Electronic Music

Anderton, Craig. *The Digital Delay Handbook*. New York, NY: Amsco Publications, 1985.

Anderton, Craig. *The Electronic Musician's Dictionary*. New York, NY: Amsco Publications, 1988.

Bartlett, Bruce. *Recording Demo Tapes at Home*. Indianapolis, IN: Howard W. Sams & Company, 1989.

Colbeck, Julian. *KEYFAX: The Definitive Guide to Electronic Keyboards*. New York, NY: Amsco Publications, 1985.

Crombie, David. *The New Complete Synthesizer: A Comprehensive Guide to the World of Electronic Music*. London, England: Omnibus Press, 1986.

Davis, Gary and Ralph Jones. *Sound Reinforcement Handbook*. Milwaukee, WI: Hal Leonard Publishing Corporation, 1990.

DeFuria, Steve and Joe Scacciaferro. *Synthesis With Style! How to modify and edit sounds so you can PERFORM them — not just play them*. Milwaukee, WI: Hal Leonard Publishing Corporation, 1989.

Everard, Chris. *The Home Recording Handbook: A definitive guide to home recording techniques and equipment*. New York, NY: Amsco Publications, 1985.

Everest, F. Alton and Mike Shea. *How to Build a Small Budget Recording Studio From Scratch ... with 12 Tested Designs*. Blue Ridge Summit, PA: Tab Books Inc., 1988.

Goldfield, Paul and Terry Griffey (with L. M. Rychner). *Recording, Syncing and Synths for Home and Studio Recording*. Newbury Park, CA: Alexander Publishing, 1988.

Horn, Delton T. *Digital Electronic Music Synthesizers*. Blue Ridge Summit, PA: Tab Books Inc., 1988.

Huber, David M. and Robert E. Runstein. *Modern Recording Techniques, Third Edition*. Carmel, IN: Howard W. Sams & Company, 1989.

McIan, Peter and Larry Wichman. *The Musician's Guide to Home Recording*. New York, NY: Linden Press/Fireside, 1988.

Milano, Dominic, ed. *Multi-Track Recording.* Milwaukee, WI: Hal Leonard Publishing Corporation, 1988.

Tomlyn, Bo and Steve Leonard. *Electronic Music Dictionary.* Milwaukee, WI: Hal Leonard Publishing Corporation, 1988.

Wadhams, Wayne. *Dictionary of Music Production and Engineering Terminology.* New York, NY: Schirmer Books, 1988.

Woram, John M. *Sound Recording Handbook.* Indianapolis, IN: Howard W. Sams & Company, 1989.

General Macintosh

Aker, Sharon Zardetto et al. *The Macintosh Bible, Third Edition.* Berkeley, CA: Goldstein & Blair, 1991.

Danuloff, Craig and Deke McClelland. *Encyclopedia Macintosh.* San Francisco, CA: Sybex, 1990.

Heid, Jim. *Macworld Complete Mac Handbook.* San Mateo, CA: IDG Books Worldwide, Inc. 1991.

Kawasaki, Guy. *The Macintosh Way.* Glenview, IL: Scott Foresman and Company, 1990.

Pina, Larry. *Macintosh Repair & Upgrade Secrets.* Carmel, IN: Hayden Books, 1990.

Poole, Lon. *Macworld Guide to System 7.* San Mateo, CA: IDG Books Worldwide, Inc. 1991.

Rubin, Charles and Bencion Calica. *Macintosh Hard Disk Management.* Indianapolis, IN: Hayden Books, 1988.

General Music

Campbell, Murray and Clive Greated. *The Musicians' Guide to Acoustics.* New York, NY: Schirmer Books, 1988.

Cope, David H. *New Directions in Music.* Dubuque, IA: Wm. C. Brown Publishers, 1984.

Moroniak, Steve. *Copyright and Song Protection: A Basic Guide.* Rolling Meadows, IL: Reel Productions, 1989.

MIDI

Anderton, Craig. *MIDI for Musicians*. New York, NY: Amsco Publications, 1986.

Boom, Michael. *Music Through MIDI: Using MIDI to Create Your Own Electronic Music System*. Redmond, WA: Microsoft Press, 1987.

DeFuria, Steve and Joe Scacciaferro. *The MIDI Implementation Book*. Pompton Lakes, NJ: Third Earth Publishing Inc., 1986.

DeFuria, Steve and Joe Scacciaferro. *The MIDI Resource Book*. Pompton Lakes, NJ: Third Earth Publishing Inc., 1987.

DeFuria, Steve and Joe Scacciaferro. *The MIDI System Exclusive Book*. Pompton Lakes, NJ: Third Earth Publishing Inc., 1987.

Huber, David Miles. *The MIDI Manual*. Carmel, IN: Sams, 1991.

The MIDI Manufacturers Association Technical Standards Board. *MIDI 1.0 Detailed Specification*. Hollywood, CA: International MIDI Association, 11857 Hartsook St., North Hollywood, CA 91607

Rona, Jeff. *MIDI: The Ins, Outs & Thrus*. Milwaukee, WI: Hal Leonard Publishing Corporation, 1987.

Miscellaneous

Fenton, Erfert. *The Macintosh Font Book: Typographic Tips, Techniques and Resources*. Berkeley, CA: Peachpit Press, 1989.

Fenton, Erfert and Christine Morrissett. *Canned Art: Clip Art for the Macintosh*. Berkeley, CA: Peachpit Press, 1990.

Hofstadter, Douglas R. *Gödel, Escher, Bach: An Eternal Golden Braid*. New York, NY: Basic Books, Inc. 1979.

Hofstadter, Douglas R. *Metamagical Themas: Questing for the Essence of Mind and Pattern*. New York, NY: Basic Books, Inc., 1985.

Kurzweil, Ray. *The Age of Intelligent Machines*. Cambridge, MA: The MIT Press, 1987.

Notation

Byrd, Don. *Music Notation by Computer.* Dissertation. Ann Arbor, MI: University Microfilms International, 1984.

Heussenstamm, George. *The Norton Manual of Modern Practice.* Boston, MA: Allyn and Bacon, Inc., 1969.

Read, Gardner. *Music Notation, A Manual of Modern Practice.* Boston, MA: Allyn and Bacon, Inc., 1969.

Roemer, Clinton. *The Art of Music Copying.* Sherman Oaks, CA: Roerick Music Company, 2d ed., 1969.

Ross, Ted. *The Art of Music Engraving and Processing.* Miami Beach, FL: Hansen Books, 1978.

Stone, Kurt. *Music Notation in the Twentieth Century — A Practical Guidebook.* New York, NY: W.W. Norton and Co., 1980.

Programming

DeFuria, Steve and Joe Scacciaferro. *MIDI Programmer's Handbook.* Redwood City, CA: M&T Publishing, Inc., 1989.

Goodman, Danny. *Danny Goodman's HyperCard Developers' Guide.* New York, NY: Bantam Books, Inc., 1988.

Goodman, Danny. *The Complete HyperCard 2.0 Handbook.* New York, NY: Bantam Books, Inc., 1990.

Vaughan, Tay. *Using HyperCard: From Home to HyperTalk.* Carmel, IN: Que Corporation, 1988.

Magazines
MIDI and computer music

Computer Music Journal
The MIT Press
55 Hayward Street
Cambridge, MA 02142

Electronic Musician
Subscription Services Office
P.O. Box 41094
Nashville, TN 37204
800-888-5139
615-377-3322

Home & Studio Recording
Subscriber Services
P.O. Box 547
Mt. Morris, IL 61054

IMA Bulletin
5316 West 57th Street
Los Angeles, CA 90056
213-649-6434
213-215-3380 (FAX)

Keyboard
P.O. Box 58528
Boulder, CO 80322-8528
800-289-9919
303-447-9330 (in CO)

Multimedia

Computer Graphics World
Circulation Dept.
P.O. Box 122
Tulsa, OK 74101
918-831-9400

Computer Pictures
25550 Hawthorne Blvd., Suite 314
Torrance, CA 90505

NewMedia
901 Mariner's Island Blvd., Suite 365
San Mateo, CA 94404
415-573-5170
415-573-5131 (FAX)

Verbum
Verbum Subscriptions
P.O. Box 12564
San Diego, CA 92112
619-233-9977
619-233-9976 (FAX)

Audio, video, and post-production

AES: Journal of the Audio Engineering Society
Audio Engineering Society, Inc.
Headquarters
60 East 42nd Street
New York, NY 10165-0075

AV Video
Circulation Representative
Montage Publishing, Inc.
25550 Hawthorne Blvd., Suite 314
Torrance, CA 90505
213-373-9993
213-373-0639 (FAX)

Broadcast Engineering
P.O. Box 12960
Overland Park, KS 66212

db Magazine
Sagamore Publishing
1120 Old Country Road
Plainview, NY 11803
516-433-6530

Millimeter
Penton Publishing
826 Broadway
New York, NY 10003
212-867-9191

Mix Magazine
P.O. Box 41094
Nashville, TN 37204
800-888-5139
615-377-3322 (outside U.S.)

POST
Testa Communications
220 Westbury Avenue
Carle Place, NY 11514
516-334-7880

Pro Sound News
120-126 Lavender Ave
Mitcham, Surrey
CR4 3HP, U.K.
U.S.: 2 Park Avenue
New York, NY 10016
212-213-3444

R•E•P
Recording•Engineering•Production
P.O. Box 12960
Overland Park, KS 66212

Studio Sound & Broadcast
Engineering
Link House Magazines, Ltd.
Central House
27 Park Street Croydon
CR01YD U.K.
(44-1) 760-0054

General Macintosh

MacUser
P.O. Box 56986
Boulder, CO 80321-6968
800-525-0643
303-447-9330 (outside U.S.)

MacWEEK
Customer Service Department
MacWEEK
c/o JCI
P.O. Box 1766
Riverton, NJ 08077-7366
609-461-2100

Macworld
Subscriber Services
P.O. Box 54529
Boulder, CO 80323-4529
800-288-6848

Appendix C
Telecommunography

On-line Services for Music and MIDI

The list of active BBSs include those that were in operation in July of 1991. Many of these BBSs are free. Also included in the listings are larger telecommunications services that have active MIDI forums and file libraries.

Active BBSs and networks by area code

Southern New England and MIDI
203-377-6758
Bridgeport, CT

Music Cool
206-248-9453
WA

Yo Yo BBS
206-956-9696
Olympia, WA

Doctor's Office
212-662-8597
(accessible via PC-Pursuit)
New York, NY

IEMUG (NY)
212-751-2347
International Electronic
Musicians' Users Group
New York, NY

Boom Boom BBS
212-831-4920
New York, NY

Gooey BBS
212-876-5885
New York, NY

Dwight School BBS
212-879-2625
(accessible via PC-Pursuit)
New York, NY
[International MIDI-Net
Netmail Echo]

Bytehoven's Brain
(See coupon at the back of
the book)
YAV Digital Music
P.O. Box 1354
Studio City, CA 91614
213-871-6869

**Musicians Information
Network**
213-396-0566
Los Angeles, CA

Codehead Quarters
213-461-2095
CA

LAMG
213-559-6227
Los Angeles Macintosh Group
12021 Wilshire Blvd.
#349 or 525
Los Angeles, CA 90025
213-278-LAMG (5264) (voice)

Random Noise MIDI BBS
213-830-4032
CA

**MIDI World Music
Network**
213-841-0347
P.O. Box 933
Santa Monica, CA 90406-0933
213-392-0103 (voice)

PLATO/Nova NET
214-244-7777
312-996-8663
Computer-based Education
Research Lab
University of Illinois
252 Engineering Research Lab
103 South Mathews
Urbana, IL 61801
217-333-6210 (voice)

Music Quest BBS
214-881-7311
214-328-6909
(accessible via PC-Pursuit)
Dallas, TX
[International MIDI-Net
Netmail Echo]

Hole in the Wall BBS
215-469-6050
Elverson, PA
[International MIDI-Net
Netmail Echo]

Rusty's 'n Eddie's BBS
216-726-3620
OH

ENIAC-MIDI BBS
301-460-9134
(accessible via PC-Pursuit)
International Electronic
Musicians' Users Group
Rockville, MD
[International MIDI-Net
Netmail Echo UseNet
Netmail Echo]

Rocky Mountain BBS
303-287-5274
CO

Clone Local #449
303-989-1379
Denver, CO
[International MIDI-Net
Netmail Echo]

S.A.R.C.A.S.M
305-421-0574
Ft. Lauderdale, FL

St. Louis MIDI User's Group
314-625-4045
International Electronic
Musicians' Users Group
St. Louis, MO

MIDI BBS
402-293-0451
Omaha, NB

AV-Sync
404-320-6202
Atlanta, GA
These boards in Canada,
New York, and Massachu-
setts are now downloading
files from AV-Sync on a
regular basis: Rose Media,
Canada Remote Systems,
Executive Network and
Sound Of Music.

Micromusic MIDI BBS
404-454-6928
(after 6 p.m. EST)
Atlanta, GA
404-454-9646 (voice)

Musart
407-292-0444
Orlando, FL

ShrinkTank BBS
408-257-8131
CA

Pacific Exchange
408-946-8561
CA

Larry's Shareware
413-783-3199
MA

WELL
415-332-6106 (1200)
415-332-7398 (2400)
(many other access numbers)
Whole Earth 'Lectronic Link
27 Gate Five Road
Sausalito, CA 94965
415-332-4335 (voice)
800-848-8980 (CPN info)
[accessible via CompuServe
Packet Net (CPN)]

The Blue Demesnes BBS
415-333-1982
CA

HyperLink BBS
415-376-3632
CA

SF SB BBS
415-564-6425
San Francisco Sound
Blaster/Adlib
San Francisco, CA

Gold Digger's BBS
415-568-7807
CA

Sanctum BBS
415-753-6861
(Nights and weekends PST)
CA

SF MIDI-Exchange BBS
415-771-1788
(accessible via PC-Pursuit)
P.O. Box 640608
San Francisco, CA 94164-0608

Sound Quest Inc. BBS
416-234-0558
66 Broadway Ave., Suite 1207
Toronto, ON M6P 2T4
Canada
416-322-6463 (voice)

MIDI Quest
416-256-7951
Sound Quest Inc.
66 Broadway Ave., Suite 1207
Toronto, Ontario
M4P IT6 Canada
416-234-0347
416-322-6434
416-322-6451 (Fax)
[Tech support and new profiles for MIDI Quest]

The Dungeon
504-835-0085
New Orleans, LA

Randy's Basement
505-589-0319
Anthony, NM

BMUG Inc. BBS
510-849-2684
510-849-1795 (9600 HST)
Berkeley Macintosh
Users Group Inc.
1442A Walnut St., Suite 62
Berkeley, CA 94709-1496
510-549-2684 (voice)

Booji Boy MIDI BBS
512-657-9254
TX

MIDI Matrix
513-438-8376
Dayton, OH

The MIDI Inn
513-531-6299
Cinncinnati, OH
[International MIDI-Net
Netmail Echo]

Gonzo's Gabanza
513-890-0655
Dayton, OH

East Coast MIDI BBS (ECM)
516-928-4986
516-474-2450
21 September St.
Coram, NY 11727
516-928-8986 (voice)
516-928-4284 (voice)

The Blue Note BBS
519-966-2558
Ontario, Canada

The Music-Net
604-386-1514
Victoria, British Columbia,
Canada

The Union BBS
609-327-5553
NJ

RTC BBS
609-654-0999
Medford, NJ

**Nautilus Information
Service**
614-761-4212
70001 Discovery Blvd.
Dublin, OH 43017-3219
800-365-1639 (voice)

IEMUG (OH)
614-846-1274
International Electronic
Musicians' Users Group
Columbus, OH

Critical Condition
615-337-4628
Sweetwater, TN

MIDImaze BBS
615-877-5528
Chattanooga, TN
[International MIDI-Net
Netmail Echo]

H.O.T. BBS
615-890-8715
Murfreesboro, TN

OnRecord
617-324-7310
[proprietary software,
optional but recommended]
MA

Mac Users at Berklee
617-424-8318
Boston, MA
[focuses on CSound, Max,
sYbil, Interactor, and
interactivity]

Sound of MIDI
617-471-0528
Boston, MA

PAN
617-576-0862 (1200)
617-576-2981 (2400)
(accessible via TYMNET
and TELENET)
Performing Arts Network
P.O. Box 162
Skippack, PA 19474
215-584-0300 (voice)
215-584-1038 (FAX)
9102508175 (TELEX)
800-544-4005 (TYMNET
customer service)
800-336-0437 (TELENET
customer service)
215-489-4640 (customer
service)

BCS BBS
617-625-6747 (2400)
508-759-9596 (9600)
Boston Computer Society
Macintosh User Group
48 Grove St.
Davis Square
Somerville, MA 02144
617-625-7080 (voice)

BYTEnet (BIX)
617-861-9764
Byte Magazine
Byte Information Exchange
One Phoenix Mill Lane
Peterborough, NH 03458
800-258-5485 (voice)

White Zone
617-969-6230
Boston, MA

Media line BBS
619-298-4027
San Diego, CA
[affiliated with MediaNET]

The Epicenter BBS
702-896-7479
Las Vegas, NV

Technical Hangout BBS
703-444-6765
Herndon, VA

Video Pro
703-455-1873
(accessible via PC-Pursuit)
VA
[affiliated with MediaNET]

**Washington MIDI
Users Group**
703-532-7860
(accessible via PC-Pursuit)
Washington D.C.
[affiliated with MusicNET
MIDILink Netmail Echo]

Photostar BBS
703-774-4667
Richmond, VA

Motherboard
707-778-8841
Petaluma, CA

**National PC/MIDI Data
Bank**
708-593-8703
Chicago, IL

**Sound Management
Music BBS**
708-949-6434
Chicago, IL
[affiliated with MusicNET
MIDILink Netmail Echo]

Black Hole BBS
714-282-7523
Orange, CA

Yamaha SGD BBS
714-522-9464
P.O. Box 6600
Buena Park, CA 90622-6600
714-522-9011 (voice)

The Art's Rap
716-223-7874
Rochester, NY

Taste BBS
718 252-4531 (free node)
718-252-4529 (subscribers/
contributers node)
(accessible via PC-Pursuit)
Brooklyn, NY
[affiliated with MusicNET
MIDILink Netmail Echo]

CONNECT
800-262-2638
(accessible via TYMNET
and TELENET)
10101 Bubb Rd.
Cupertino, CA 95014
408-973-0110 (voice)

Delphi
800-365-4636 (to join)
617-576-2890
617-576-2981
(accessible via PAN gateway)
3 Blackstone St.
Cambridge, MA 02139
800-544-4005 (voice)
617-491-3393 (customer
support)

Kawai Education BBS
800-456-0271
Kawai Education Program
2055 E. University Drive
Compton, CA 90224
800-456-1231 (voice)
13-438-4037 (FAX)
800-456-4897 (tech. support)

GEnie
800-638-8369
(accessible via TYMNET
and TELENET)
General Electric network for
information exchange
800-638-9636 (voice)

**CompuServe
(MIDI Music Forum)**
800-848-8199
(accessible via TYMNET
and TELENET)
P.O. Box 20212
Columbus, OH 43220

Researcher BBS
805-949-8151
Los Angeles, CA

Sight and Sound
813-399-1271
Seminole, FL

MIDIum
818-764-4538
Los Angeles, CA

Electronic Music Box
818-789-4287
14947 Ventura Blvd.
Sherman Oaks, CA 91403
818-789-4250 (voice)

MIDI-Madness
901-725-1815
TN

AppleLink
(accessible via TYMNET
and TELENET)
AppleLink System
Management
20525 Mariani Ave.,
Mail Stop 37-R
Cupertino, CA 95014
408-996-1010 (voice)

ESI Street
(Must set up account
in advance)
International Management
Communications (IMC)
254 W 54th St. Penthouse
New York, NY 10019
213-937-0347 (voice)
212-757-0320 (voice)

America Online
(Software self-configures
itself to nearest node by
dialing an 800 number)
8619 Westwood Center Dr.

Appendix D
Manufacturers

Software and Hardware for Mac Music and Sound

The following is a list of most of the music manufacturers and developers discussed in this book (over 200 contacts). In the case of one-product developers who distribute their software themselves, you will find the entry listed by the name of the product with the contact name directly below it. In these cases, the indications FW, SW, or PD are appended to the product name (for freeware, shareware, and public domain, respectively). Some programs in this category that are mentioned in the text have been omitted from the listing because no contact information was available. In all cases, these products are available from online services. Non-music products mentioned in the text are not listed — there are many general Macintosh directories available for that information. Wherever possible, phone numbers, FAX, TELEX, and electronic mail addresses are provided.

Adams Smith
34 Tower St.
Hudson, MA 01749-1721
508-562-3801

Addison-Wesley
1 Jacob Way
Reading, MA 01867
800-447-2226
617-944-3700

Adobe Systems
1585 Charleston Rd.
P.O. Box 7900
Mountain View, CA 94039
800-833-6687
415-961-4400

Advanced Music Notation Systems, Inc.
P.O. Box 60356
Florence, MA 01060
PAN: DONBYRD

Aesthetic Engineering
175 Duane St.
New York, NY 10013

Akai Professional
International Music Company
P.O. Box 2344
Fort Worth, TX 76113-2344
817-336-5114
TELEX: 163203 IMCTX UT

Alesis Corp.
3630 Holdrege Ave.
Los Angeles, CA 90016-9801
213-467-8000

Alfred Publishing Company
P.O. Box 10003
Van Nuys, CA 91410-0003
818-891-5999

Alpha/TIMES System
Dr. Christoph Schnell
Rehetobelstrasse 89
CH-9016 St. Gallen
Switzerland
41-71-35-14-02

ALSoft
P.O. Box 927
Spring, TX 77383
713-353-4090
713-353-1510

Altech Systems
122 Faires Industrial Park Dr.
Shreveport, LA 71106
318-868-8036

Altsys Corp.
269 W. Renner Rd.
Richardson, TX 75080
214-680-2060

America Online
8619 Westwood Center Dr.
Vienna, VA 22182
800-827-6364

**Andromeda Computer
Systems, Ltd.**
8043 33rd Ave. NW
Calgary, Alberta T3B 1L5
Canada
403-247-5300

Antelope Engineering
1048 Neilson St.
Albany, CA 94706
510-528-0609

Aphex Systems Ltd.
11068 Randall St.
Sun Valley, CA 91352
818-767-2929

Appletones and Mozart
John R. Meier
Dartmouth College
Department of Music
Hanover, NH 03755

Apriori, Inc.
859 Hollywood Way
Suite 401
Burbank, CA 91510

Ars Nova Software
P.O. Box 637
Kirkland, WA 98083
800-445-4866
206-889-0927

Articulate Systems, Inc.
600 West Cummings Park
Suite 4500
Woburn, MA 01801
800-835-0440
617-935-5656
FAX: 617-935-9484
AppleLink: VOICE

AudioData (FW)
Dennis Fleisher
1661 Estate Circle
Naperville, IL 60565
708-416-0446

Austin Development
227 Marin St.
San Rafael, CA 94901
415-454-9620

Authorware
275 Shoreline Dr.
4th floor
Redwood City, CA 94065
800-288-4797

Baudville
5380 52nd St. SE
Grand Rapids, MI 49508
616-698-0888

Benson (FW)
Christopher Watson
(See Heizer Software)

Berkeley Systems, Inc.
2095 Rose St.
Berkeley, CA 94709
510-540-5536

BMUG, Inc.
1442A Walnut St., Suite 62
Berkeley, CA 94709-1496
510-549-2684
510-849-4357
FAX: 510-849-9026

Bogas Productions
550 Heather Way
San Rafael, CA 94903
415-332-6427
415-592-5129

Bokonon Technologics
1656 W. Farwell, #1F
Chicago, IL 60626
312-743-5719

Borland International
1800 Green Hills Rd.
Scotts Valley, CA 95067
800-331-0877
FAX: 408-439-9119

Bose Corp.
The Mountain
Framingham, MA 01701
508-879-7330

Boston Computer Society
One Center Plaza
Boston, MA 02108
617-625-7080

Box, Don
2611 B Grant Ave.
Redondo Beach, CA 90278
ARPAnet: dbox@ics.uci.edu
PAN: DONBOX

Brøderbund Software, Inc.
P.O. Box 6125
500 Redwood Blvd.
Novato, CA 94948-6125
800-521-6263

Buchla and Associates
P.O. Box 10205
Berkeley, CA 94709
510-528-4446

**Bucknell Computer
Services**
Bucknell University
Lewisburg, PA 17837
CompuServe: 71131,3660
<smith@bucknell.edu>
<smith@bknlvms.bitnet>

Calaban
Andy Adamson
University of Birmingham
Department of Drama and
Theatre Arts
P.O. Box 363
Birmingham, B15 2TT
UK
021-414-6005

Casady & Greene
(Available fonts: Crescendo
and Grace Notes)
22734 Portola Dr.
Salinas, CA 93908
408-484-9228
FAX: 408-484-9218

CassetteLabeler
(available on
on-line services)

**Cerl Music Group
University of Illinois**
(Available fonts: Marl
and Tufa)
252 Engineering Research
Laboratory
103 S. Mathews
Urbana, IL 61801-2977
217-333-0766
Email: 1-haken@uiuc.edu
PLATO: lippold/musician/
cerl

Chandler, James, Jr.
204 California Ave.
Chattanooga, TN 37415
615-877-6835
CompuServe: 74406,2107
PAN: JIMCHANDLER

ChordType
39 Dana St., #1
Cambridge, MA 02138
617-354-5479

Chroma (SW)
Paul Ferguson
258 Rodonovan Dr.
Santa Clara, CA 95051
CompuServe: 70441,3055

Claris Corp.
5201 Patrick Henry Dr.
P.O. Box 58168
Santa Clara, CA 95052
800-544-8554
408-727-8227

Cliffhanger Productions
203 Storey Ave.
Santa Cruz, CA 95060

Coda Music Software
(Available fonts: Seville,
Petrucci, Newport, Rameau,
and MIDICom)
1401 East 79th St.
Bloomington, MN
55425-1126
800-843-2066
612-854-1288
FAX: 612-854-4631

CompuServe, Inc.
5000 Arlington Centre Blvd.
Columbus, OH 43220
800-848-8199
614-457-0802

**Computer Business
Associates**
5962 Bowen Ct.
San Jose, CA 95123
408-578-3568
FAX: 714-594-7033

**Computer Music
Association**
P.O. Box 1634
San Francisco, CA
94101-1634
cma@dept.csci.unt.edu
scaletta@novamail.cerl.uiuc.edu
UUCP: (sun, voder,
nsc)!apple!john

Connect, Inc.
10161 Bubb Rd.
Cupertino, CA 95014
800-262-2638
408-973-0110

Crown International
1718 W. Mishawaka Rd.
Elkhart, IN 46517
219-294-8000

CZLib (SW)
Mike Cohen
2255 Barker Ave.
Bronx, NY 10467

D110 File System
Larry Mistrot
9898 Forum Park, #6210
Houston, TX 77036
CompuServe: 72070,1323

DH Productions
910 Celia Way
Palo Alto, CA 94303
CompuServe: 73710,1311
GEnie: D.Harriss

Different Drummer
P.O. Box 136
Rochester, NY 14601

Digidesign
1360 Willow Rd., Suite 101
Menlo Park, CA 94025
415-688-0600
TELEX: 267-6317 MCI

Digital Arts & Sciences
215 West D St.
P.O. Box 75
Jacksonville, OR 97530
503-899-1948

Digital Music Services
23010 Lake Forest
Suite D334
Laguna Hills, CA 92653
714-951-1159

Dr. T's Music Software, Inc.
124 Crescent Rd., Suite 3
Needham, MA 02194
617-455-1454

DVM Publications
(Available fonts:
MetronomeFont and
MetTimes)
P.O. Box 399
Thorofare, NJ 08086
609-853-5580

DX_PIG
John Duesenberry
514 Harvard St., #3B
Brookline, MA 02146
BIX: jduesenberry
CompuServe: 7007,500
PAN: JOHNDU

DynaWare
950 Tower Lane, Suite 1150
Foster City, CA 94404
415-349-5700

E & R Music Printers
(Available fonts: Singular
and Tabula)
67 King St.
Oberlin, OH 44074-1321
216-774-2064

E-mu Systems, Inc.
1600 Green Hills Rd.
P.O. Box 660015
Scotts Valley, CA 95067
408-438-1921
FAX: 408-438-8612
TELEX: 172951 E MUSIC
CompuServe: 614.457.8650
GEnie: 800.638.9636
PAN: 215.480.4640

Ear Trainer (SW)
Laurence Gallagher
843 Winthrop Ave.
Revere, MA 02151

Earlevel Engineering
21213-B Hawthorne
Torrance, CA 90509
213-316-2939

Electronic Arts
1450 Fashion Island Blvd.
San Mateo, CA 94404
800-245-4525
415-571-7171
FAX: 415-570-5137

**Elements of the Jazz
Language**
CPP/Belwin
15800 NW 4th Ave.
P.O. Box 4340
Miami, FL 33014
305-620-1500

Entropy Engineering
360 Elizabeth St.
San Francisco, CA 94114
BMUG: Chris Muir
Internet:
{hplabs,pacbell,ucbvax,apple}
!well!cbm
PAN: ZMS

ergo sum computer GmbH
(Available fonts: Susato and
Accordion Register)
Sternwaldstrasse 6a
D-7800 Freiburg
Germany
49 (7-61) 704-440
FAX: 49 (7-61) 704-4458

Eye and I Productions
930 Jungfrau Court
Milpitas, CA 95035
408-945-0139

Farallon Computing, Inc.
2000 Powell St., Suite 600
Emeryville, CA 94608
510-596-9000

Finale Font Report
Wette Enterprises
921 De Mun Ave.
Clayton, MO 63105
314-863-1248

Freq Sound
5451 Watercress Pl.
Columbia, MD 21045
301-964-3548

Garfield Electronics
P.O. Box 9041
Burbank, CA 91507
213-434-6643

Gemini Marketing, Inc.
P.O. Box 640
Duvall, WA 98019-0640
800-346-0139
206-788-4295
FAX: 206-788-0717

GEnie
800-638-9636
800-638-8369 (modem)

G.H.S. Corporation
(distributors of
Scorpion Systems
Group's sYbil)
2813 Wilbur Ave.
Battle Creek, MI 49015
616-968-3351

Golden Midi Music
330 E. 39th St., #10A
New York, NY 10016
212-370-0474

Golden Triangle
4849 Ronson Court
San Diego, CA 92111-1805
619-279-2100
FAX: 619-279-1069

Grame Research Studio
6 quai Jean-Moulin
69001 Lyon
France
33-1-7839-3202

Great Wave Software
5353 Scotts Valley Dr.
Scotts Valley, CA 95066
408-438-1990

Green Oak Software
4446 Salisbury Dr.
Carlsbad, CA 92008
619-434-0823

GW Instruments
35 Medford St.
Somerville, MA 02143
617-625-4096

Harmony Systems, Inc.
P.O. Box 2744
Norcross, GA 30091
PAN: HARMONY

Headstart
Dietrich Gewissler
92 Smith St.
Howell, NJ 07731
908-364-8719

Heizer Software
1941 Oak Park Blvd., Suite 30
P.O. Box 232019
Pleasant Hill, CA 94523
800-888-7667
510-943-7667
FAX: 510-943-6882

Hybrid Arts
8522 National Blvd., Suite 100
Culver City, CA 90232
213-841-0340

Imaja
P.O. Box 6386
Albany, CA 94706
510-526-4621

Insanely Great Software
126 Calvert Ave. East
Edison, NJ 08820
908-549-0590
America Online: AdamStein
CompuServe: 71140,2051
CONNECT: AdamStein

Intelligent Music, Inc.
116 N. Lake Ave.
Albany, NY 12206
518-434-4110

**International MIDI
Association**
5316 W. 57th St.
Los Angeles, CA 90056
213-649-6434

Interval (PD)
Brad Needham
10480 SW Eastridge, #8
Portland, OR 97225

Interval Music Systems
12335 Santa Monica Blvd.
#244
Los Angeles, CA 90025
310-478-3956
FAX: 310-478-5791

InVision
269 Mt. Hermon Rd.
Suite 105
Scotts Valley, CA 95066
408-438-5530

JL Cooper Electronics
12500 Beatrice
Los Angeles, CA 90066
213-306-4131
TELEX: 5101001679
AppleLink: JL Cooper
PAN: JLCooper

Kawai
2055 E. University Dr.
P.O. Box 9045
Compton, CA 90220
213-631-1771

Korg USA
89 Frost St.
Westbury, NY 11590
800-645-3188
516-333-9100

Kurzweil Music Systems
Young Chang America
13336 Alondra Blvd.
Cerritos, CA 90701-2205
310-926-3200
FAX: 310-404-0748
TELEX: 910-321-5733

LabanWriter
1813 N. High St.
Columbus, OH 43210

**LAMG — Los Angeles
Macintosh Group**
12021 Wilshire Blvd., #349
Los Angeles, CA 90025
213-278-LAMG

Lefleur, Bob
45 Ionia St.
Springfield, MA 01109

Lefty
Paul Ferguson
AppleLink: AM0205
CompuServe: 70441,3055

Lexicon, Inc.
100 Beaver St.
Waltham, MA 02154-8425
617-891-6790
TELEX: 923468 LEXICON
WHA

Lone Wolf, Inc.
1509 Aviation Blvd.
Redondo Beach, CA 90278
800-922-7448
310-379-2036
FAX: 310-374-2496
TELEX: 510-101-1310

MacKeyboard (PD)
Terry Bertram
P.O. Box 772
Oakland, CA 91711

MacroMind • Paracomp
600 Townsend St.
Suite 310W
San Francisco, CA 94107
415-442-0200

Macworld Communications, Inc.
501 2nd St.
San Francisco, CA 94107
415-243-0505

Maestro Graphics
11311 N. Central Expressway
Suite 211
Dallas, TX 75243
214-696-9708

Mark of The Unicorn, Inc.
222 3rd St.
Cambridge, MA 02142
617-576-2760
617-576-3066
FAX: 617-576-3609
TELEX: 499-5346

MathemÆSthetics, Inc.
P.O. Box 67-156
Chestnut Hill, MA 02167
617-738-8803

Mayfield Publishing Co.
1240 Villa St.
Mountain View, CA 94041
415-960-3222

McGill University
Music Faculty Building
555 Sherbrooke St. West
Montréal, Québec H3A 1E3
Canada
514-398-4548

Megalomania (FW)
Eric Huffman
1401 W. Jarvis St., #1
Chicago, IL 60626
CompuServe: 71530,545
71530.545@compuserve.com
eric@music.nwu.edu

MiBAC Music Software, Inc.
P.O. Box 468
Northfield, MN 55057
507-645-5851
FAX: 507-645-9291

Micro Works Corp.
328 Walden St.
Cambridge, MA 02138
617-547-8322

Microtech International, Inc.
158 Commerce St.
East Haven, CT 06512
203-468-6223

MIDI CD
2600 Kitty Hawk Rd.
Livermore, CA 94550
510-449-5297
America Online: JIMN8
CompuServe: 73117,3020

MIDI CHORD HIASL
Christian Teuscher
Krongasse 19/18
A-1050 Vienna
Austria
GEnie: C.TEUSCHER

MIDI Companion (SW)
Robert Patterson
3796 Lamar Ave.
Memphis, TN 38195

MIDI Scales (SW)
Tanya Rust
7010 Loyal Trail
Los Angeles, CA 90068
213-851-0950

MIDIdisplay
Lee Story
PAN: Lstory

MidiEx Mac (SW)
Thomas W. Inskip
6504 Democracy Blvd.
Bethesda, MD 20817
301-530-0866

MidiHz (SW)
Mark Erickson
901 Yorkchester
Houston, TX 77079

Missing Byte Software
112 Hickory Park Lane
Antioch, TN 37013

MKS-50 Editor (SW)
Russel Salerno
2421 Myron Rd.
Westbury, NY 11590

Mm Software
5003 Westpark Dr., #103
North Hollywood, CA
213-474-1633

Motion Works
7020 Mainland St., Suite 130
Vancouver, British Columbia
Canada V6B 2T4
604-732-0289

Mozart Font
Francis Butch Mahoney
302 Lessard St.
Donaldsonville, LA 70346
504-473-9378

MT32 Editor (SW)
Harold Long
79 Nashaway Rd.
Bolton, MA 01740

Music Data (Division of Passport)
100 Stone Pine Rd.
Half Moon Bay, CA 94019
415-726-0280

Music Production Package
7985 Santa Monica Blvd.
Suite 109
West Hollywood, CA 90069

Music Publisher
2-1645 East Cliff Dr.
Santa Cruz, CA 95062

Music Software Plus
180 Horizon Way
Aptos, CA 95003
408-479-0860

MusicWriter, Inc.
170 Knowles Dr., Suite 203
Los Gatos, CA 95030
408-353-2225

National Association of Music Merchants
5140 Avenida Encinas
Carlsbad, CA 92008-4391
619-438-8001

Nebulous Enterprises
303-440-7713
America Online: AdamS10
Delphi: SCHABTACH
GEnie: SCHABTACH

Northstar Productions
13716 SE Ramona St.
Portland, OR 97236
503-760-7777

NoteWare Co.
(Available fonts: FretFinder
and NameThatChord)
P.O. Box 9953
Marina Del Rey, CA 90295
213-822-1300

Nussel, Sara & Art
1606 NW 21st St.
Gainesville, FL 32605
904-372-0066

Opcode Systems, Inc.
3641 Haven Dr., Suite A
Menlo Park, CA 94025
415-369-8131
415-369-1676
FAX: 415-369-1747
CompuServe: 73657,3223
PAN: MARKATOPCODE
PAN: DOUGWYATT

Optical Media International
180 Knowles Dr.
Los Gatos, CA 95030
800-347-2664
408-376-3511
FAX: 408-376-3519
TELEX: 650 209 8322 MCI UW
AppleLink: OMI
MCI Mail: OMI

Orchestrator
Chip Burwell
3680 SW 14th St.
Miami, FL 33145
305-448-6615

Palmer, David
292 Maurice St.
London, Ontario N6H 1C5
Canada

**PAN - Performing Arts
Network**
P.O. Box 162
Skippack, PA 19474
215-584-0300
TELEX: 9102508175

Panasonic Company
1 Panasonic Way
Secaucus, NJ 07094
714-373-7278

Parker Adams Group, The
12335 Santa Monica Blvd.
#124
Los Angeles, CA 90025
310-450-2175

Passport Designs, Inc.
100 Stone Pine Dr.
Half Moon Bay, CA 94019
415-726-0280
800-443-3210
FAX: 415-726-2254
PAN: Passport

**Patch/Works Music
Software**
P.O. Box 450
New York, NY 10024
212-873-2390

Patchmasters
P.O. Box 746-B
Hazel Park, MI 48030-0746

Pentallect, Inc.
8480 E. Thoroughbred Trail
Scottsdale, AZ 85258

PG Music
111-266 Elmwood Ave.
Buffalo, NY 14222
416-528-2368

**PhySy Music &
Development**
39 Seneca St.
Ottawa, Ontario K1S 4W9
Canada
CompuServe: 72000,2470

Pixel Publishing
641 Caledonia Rd.
Toronto, Ontario M6E 4V8
Canada
416-785-3036

Play By Ear
Tom M. Kirshbaum
3000 E. Country Club Dr.
Flagstaff, AZ 86004

PlayAIFF (FW)
Chris Reed
3409 Clearview Dr.
San Angelo, TX 76904
915-949-9486
America Online: Chrisreed

Post Modern Productions
1310 Garford Ave.
Elyria, OH 44035

Prime Music Engraving
(Available fonts:
HagenGuitarCreator,
HagenGuitarFlats,
HagenGuitarSharps,
HagenHand, HagenKorea,
and WriterMusic)
560 S. State St.
Orem, UT 84058
801-224-3981

Primera Software
1411 209th Ave. NE
Redmond, WA 98053-6619
206-868-6360

Prosonus, Inc.
11126 Weddington St.
North Hollywood, CA 91601
800-999-6191
818-766-5221
FAX: 818-766-6098

**PSS-680 Sound Librarian
(FW)**
Michael Clemens
103 Barbour St.
Buckhannon, WV 26201

Pygraphics
P.O. Box 639
Grapevine, TX 76051
800-222-7536
FAX: 817-488-9658

Random Access
62 Birdsall St.
Greene, NY 13778
607-656-7584

**RMI — Romeo Music
International**
214 Lincoln St., Suite 104
Allston, MA 02134
800-852-2122
617-254-9109

Roland Corporation
7200 Dominion Circle
Los Angeles, CA 90040-3647
213-685-5141
TELEX: 67-4489 RCUS LSA

Russ Jones Marketing Group
17700 Raymer St., #1001
Northridge, CA 91325
818-993-4091

S-10 Sample Librarian (FW)
Gary Becker
18 Stone Park Place
Baltimore, MD 21236

Scorpion Systems Group
18899 W. Twelve Mile Rd.
Lathrop Village, MI 48076
FAX: 415-864-4986

SendBank (SW)
David Schenfeld
P.O. Box 6520
FDR Station
New York, NY 10022
America Online: Just Dave
CompuServe: 72315,1457
GEnie: AES-ELECT

Sensor Frame Corp.
4516 Henry St.
Pittsburgh, PA 15213
412-683-9500

Serius Corporation
488 E. 6400 South, Suite 100
Salt Lake City, UT 84107
801-261-7900
800-876-6847
FAX: 801-261-7910

Shpfltnat (SW)
David Rekowski
605 W. 113th St., #73
New York, NY 10025

SignalEditor II (SW)
Stephen Knight
2 Mae Meadow
Rochester, NY 14624
CompuServe: 76377, 52

Silicon Beach Software, Inc.
9770 Carroll Center Rd.
Suite J
San Diego, CA 92126
619-695-6956

Software Guild, Inc., The
13533 Southwest 63 Lane
Miami, FL 33183
305-956-3114

Sound Ideas
105 West Beaver Creek Rd.
Suite 4
Richmond Hill, Ontario
L4B 1C6
Canada
800-387-3030

Sound Mover
Riccardo Ettore
67 Rue de la Limite
1970 W-Oppem
Belgium

Sound Quest, Inc.
1573 Eglinton Ave. W.
Suite 200
Toronto, Ontario M6E 2G9
Canada
800-387-8720

Sound Source Unlimited
2985 E. Hillcrest Dr., Suite A
Westlake Village, CA 91362
805-494-9996
FAX: 805-495-0016

Sound/PICT Thief
Jim Moore
GEnie: J H Moore

SoundPlay (FW)
Bruce Tomlin
15801 Chase Hill Blvd.
Apt. 109
San Antonio, TX 78256

Soundscape Productions
P.O. Box 8891
Stanford, CA 94309
415-967-8125

Soundware Corporation
200 Menlo Oaks Dr.
Menlo Park, CA 94025
800-333-4554

Steinberg/Jones
17700 Raymer St., #1001
Northridge, CA 91325
818-993-4091

**Studer Editech
Corporation**
1370 Willow Rd., Suite 201
Menlo Park, CA 94025
415-326-7030

**Studio Master Computer
Systems**
229 Sunny Isles Blvd.
North Miami Beach, FL 33160
305-945-9774

Subtilior Press (SW)
David Palmer
292 Maurice St.
London, Ontario N6H 1C5
Canada
519-642-4510

Summit Software
112 Hickory Park Lane
Antioch, TN 37013
615-331-6925
CompuServe: 76556,2012
GEnie: XTHO1835
PAN: BOBPATIN

SunValley Software
131 Sunny Hill Rd.
Winnipeg R2G 2X9
Canada
204-663 8004

SuperPlay
John Raymonds
21738 Barbara St.
Torrance, CA 90503

Sweetwater Sound, Inc.
5335 Bass Rd.
Fort Wayne, IN 46808
219-432-8176
FAX: 219-432-1758

**Symbolic Sound
Corporation**
P.O. Box 2530, Station A
Champaign, IL 61825-2530
217-328-6645

Symetrix, Inc.
4211 24th Ave. West
Seattle, WA 98199
206-282-2555

Tactic Software
7520 Red Rd., Suite A
Miami, FL 33143
305-378-4110

Tech 21
1600 Broadway, Suite 604A
New York, NY 10019
212-315-1116

Thinkware
130 9th St., #303
San Francisco, CA 94013
800-369-6191

Time of Your Life Music
149 S. Spalding Dr., Suite 4
Beverly Hills, CA 90212

Tone Rows
Chas Turner
9 Gould St.
Danvers, MA 01923

TwelveTone (SW)
Michael Pelz-Sherman
9665 Genesee Ave., H-2
San Diego, CA 92121

Trimbelle Music Software
West 8215 760th Ave.
River Falls, WI 54022
715-425-6438

U110 Patch Report
Robert E. Otto
CompuServe:
73045.734@compuserve.com

U.S. College of Music
18 Haviland St., Suite 22
Boston, MA 02115
617-266-2886
AppleLink: D 1234

Usersoft microSystems
140 North 2nd St.
Piggott, AR 72454
501-598-3377

Valhala Music, Inc.
P.O. Box 20157-KB
Ferndale, MI 48220
800-648-6434
313-548-9360

Verbum, Inc.
670 7th Ave.
San Diego, CA 92101
619-233-9977
FAX: 619-233-9976

Voyager Company, The
1351 Pacific Coast Highway
Santa Monica, CA 90401
800-446-2001
FAX: 213-394-2156
AppleLink: D0755

Voyce Music, Inc.
9672 Via Excelencia Dr.
Suite 102
San Diego, CA 92126

VPL Research, Inc.
(now distributing HookUp!
and Harmony Grid)
656 Bair Island Rd., 3rd Floor
Redwood City, CA 94063
415-306-1150
FAX: 415-361-1845

Wachter Softworks
6109 Eastcliff Dr.
Baltimore, MD 21209
301-466-2734

Warner New Media
3500 Olive Ave.
Burbank, CA 91505
818-955-9999

Well, The
27 Gate Five Rd.
Sausalito, CA 94965
415-332-4335

Widemann, Benoît
68 Ave D'Italie
75013 Paris
France

Words & Deeds, Inc.
4480 Sunnycrest Dr.
Los Angeles, CA 90065
213-255-2887

Yamaha
6600 Orangethorpe Ave.
Buena Park, CA 90620
714-522-9011

YAV Digital Music
Christopher Yavelow
P.O. Box 1354
Studio City, CA 91614
213-871-6869
FAX: 818-760-1333
AppleLink: Yavelow
America Online: Bytehoven
Pan: Bytehoven
GEnie: Bytehoven
Connect: Bytehoven
CompuServe: 74005,1012
The Well: Yavelow

Zero One Research
P.O. Box 301
Brisbane, CA 94005
FAX: 415-467-5007

Zeta Music Systems, Inc.
2230 Livingston St.
Oakland, CA 94606
800-622-6434
FAX: 510-261-1708

Zeta Soft
2425B Channing Way
Suite 492
Pasadena, CA
818-577-7951
AppleLink: D5611
CompuServe: 76407,3251
GEnie: H.YAMAMOTO2

ZimmerWorks, Inc.
3909 Hidden Springs Dr.
Lexington, KY 40514
800-345-9757
606-223-1888

Zobkiw, Joe
59 Melba St.
Milford, CT 06460
America Online: AFL Zobkiw
CompuServe: 70712,515

Appendix E

Software Versions Used in This Book

Current software versions

The following is a list of the versions of software current at the time of this writing. The list was automatically generated by Dana Basken's shareware Version utility (version 2.0.1). This list was compiled on January 1, 1992.

Programs	
7th Heaven	1.50
Alchemy™	2.22
AppleTones	2.00
Assistant Engineer™	1.00
AudioData	1.50
Audiomedia™	2.02
AudioTrax	1.00
Authorware Professional™	1.60
Ballade™	1.01
Band In A Box	4.03
Beyond™	2.10
CassetteLabeler	1.0b1
Channeler	1.02
Chroma	1.10
Compact Pro	1.32
CS-1 Editor Librarian	1.01
Cubase	1.81
CUE	3.00
Cybernetic Composer	0.94
D-50 Ed/Lib	5.30
D-50 Editor	1.10
DA Handler Resizer	1.00
DATa™	2.00
DECK™	1.02
DelayCalc™	1.80
Deluxe Music	2.50
DinoSwitch	1.01
Delux Recorder	1.00
DX7 Librarian	1.01
DX7 Unique	1.00
DX_PIG	1.50
EarTutor	1.00
Editor	1.11
EIII Remote Controller	1.10a4

Programs	
Encore™	2.50
Evolution#9	1.01
ExtractParts™	1.01
EZ Vision	1.00
Finale	2.6.3
Finale Tour 2.0s•	2.0s
Finale Utilities 1.0	1.00
Galaxy	1.02
Galaxy Plus Editors	1.13
GenEdit	1.00
HB Engraver	1.01
HookUp!	1.05
HyperCard	2.10
HyperMIDI	2.00
Instrument Maker	5.00
Interacto	4.0beta16
Jam Factory™	2.00
Jam Session	1.10
Jam Box MIDI Manager	0.68
K250 Editor/Librarian	2.00
K1000 Ed/Lib	1.00
KbdMover	1.01
KCS Level II	1.00
KidsNotes™	1.20
Lime™	0.40
Listen	2.1.2
Live List™	2.00
M1 File Converter	1.00
M2.2	2.02
Mac Profiler	1.00
MacroMind Director	3.00
Mariah™	1.09
Master List™	2.01
MasterTracks (see Pro 5)	

Programs

Max	2.11
MediaTracks™	1.00
Megalomania	1.0.2
MegaMix	3.10
MetroGnome	1.03
MiBAC™ Jazz	1.5.6
MIDI Logger	1.01
MIDI Mixer 7s Console	1.00
MIDI Terminal™	1.20
Midi Master™	1.00
Midi Mix 3D App	1.00
Midi ReClock1.1	1.80
MidiPaint™	1.03
MIDIPreview™	1.10
MIDISCALES	1.18
MIDIScope™	1.50
MidiTest	2.00
MiniTrax	1.02
MoviePlayer™	1.00
Mozart	2.00
Music Box	1.01
Music Lines	1.10
Music Mouse™	2.03
Music Player	5.10
Music Publisher™	2.52
Music Writer (ConcertWare)	5.14
Music Writer™ (Pyware)	1.10
MusicProse™	2.10
NGtoAI	1.02
Nightingale	0.99beta
NoteWriterII	2.69
ObjectMover	1.00
OMS Setup	1.1.3
One-Step™	1.00
OvalTune	1.1.3
PAN Messenger	2.0.5
PatchBay™	2.01
PatchMaster/PROteus	1.00
Performer™	3.62
PlayAIFF	1.00
Practica Musica	2.28
Pro 4.5.3 ™	4.53
Pro 5™	5.00
ProEDIT	1.00
ProDECK	1.00
Professional Composer™	2.3M
Proteus Ed/Lib	5.41
Proteus Editor	1.07

Programs

Proteus Front-Panel	1.00f2
Protezoa™	2.01
Q-Sheet A/V™	2.00
QLS	3.80
QLS Convert	1.00
ResEdit	2.11
ResExpress	1.00
Resourcerer®	1.05
Rhapsody™	3.00
SampleCell™ Editor	1.10
SBX Librarian	1.00
SeqMover	1.50
SignalEditor II	2.00
Snd Converter	1.21
Sound Apprentice™	1.22
Sound Designer II™	2.01
Sound Installer™	1.30
Sound Mover	1.61R
Sound Utility	3.00
Sound->snd	1.20
Sound-to-Video II	2.10
SoundCapture	4.30
SoundEdit Pro	1.00beta
SoundEdit™	2.03
SoundWave™	1.20
StickyBusiness® 1.3	1.03
Strum	1.00
Studio Vision	1.31
StudioCalc™	9.00
Super Librarian™	3.02
Super Studio Session™	1.00
SuperCard	1.50
SuperEdit	1.50
SuperPlay	4.00
sYbil	2.00
T/M1/M3R Ed/Lib	5.50
TextureSynth™	1.10
Track Chart	1.01
TrackSheet™	3.60
TRAX™	2.00
Turbosynth™	2.00
UpBeat	2.05
Virtual Studio	1.09
Vision	1.32
Watcher	1.00
Widgets	3.04
X-oR	2.00

Extensions

Apple CD-ROM	3.00
CS-1™	1.00
DigiSystem INIT	1.10
DiskExpress™ II	2.07a
Sound Expansion	1.02
IIfx Serial Switch	1.10
MacMike INIT	1.00
MacProteus™ Batteries	1.08
MacRecorder® Driver	1.01
MaxAppleZoom	1.43
MIDI Manager	2.01
MIDI Mangler	1.01
MIDIShare	1.00
MultiClip™	2.1.7
Opcode MIDI INIT	1.01

Extensions

Opcode MIDI System	1.1.1
QuickTime™	1.00
SampleCell INIT (32bit)	1.20
ScreenRecorder™	2.00
SoundMaster	1.72
SpeedyCD	1.11
Stepping Out II	2.02
Suitcase™ II	1.2.11
"Up Your(FCB)s"	1.03
Voice Control	2.20
Voice Impact Pro Sound Driver	2.10
Voice Impact Sound Driver	2.10
Voice Navigator Sound Driver	2.10
Disinfectant INIT	2.8.0

Macworld Authorized Editions

Macworld Guide to Microsoft Word 5
by Jim Heid, *Macworld* magazine's "Getting Started" Columnist

New from the bestselling author of *Macworld Complete Mac Handbook*.

Learn the new Word the easy way with this *Macworld* Authorized Edition.

Highlights:
- Up-to-date for Word 5 — covers all new features
- With step-by-step instructions for mastering everyday word processing tasks
- FREE Illustrated Quick Reference Card includes keyboard shortcuts and type tips

$22.95/$29.95 Canada ■ ISBN: 1-878058-39-8
448 pages. Available now.

Macworld Guide to System 7
by Lon Poole, *Macworld* magazine's "Quick Tips" Columnist

This *Macworld* Authorized Edition is the most recommended guide to System 7.

"You'll find everything you need to know about System 7 in this book."
— Bob Levitus, author of *Dr. Macintosh*

Highlights:
- Optimize the new features of System 7
- Valuable hardware and software compatibility lists
- Scores of undocumented insider tips and secrets
- NEW! System 7.1 Update covers system enhancements and bug fixes

$24.95/$33.95 Canada ■ ISBN: 1-878058-16-9
384 pages. Available now.

Macworld Networking Handbook
by Dave Kosiur, Ph.D., *Macworld* magazine Contributing Editor and **Nancy E.H. Jones**

The *Macworld* Authorized Edition for anyone who manages Mac networks.

Highlights:
- The only practical, hands-on guide that explains Macintosh networking from the ground up
- Design, installation, and management of AppleTalk internets explained simply
- Expert advice on optimizing your network
- Covers Apple-to-IBM, Apple-to-DEC networking

$29.95/$39.95 Canada ■ ISBN: 1-878058-31-2
600 pages. Available June.

Macworld Complete Mac Handbook
by Jim Heid, *Macworld* magazine's "Getting Started" Columnist

The most complete guide to getting started, mastering, and expanding your Mac.

Highlights:
- Loaded with tips and techniques for using the Mac and Mac software better
- For beginners or seasoned veterans
- FREE *Macworld* System 7 Reference Card

$26.95/$35.95 Canada ■ ISBN: 1-878058-17-7
576 pages. Available now.

Macworld Read Me First Book
Edited by Jerry Borrell, *Macworld* magazine's Editor-in-Chief

Macworld's experts recommend hardware and software configurations and offer start-up advice.

Highlights:
- A friendly, authoritative guide for first-time users
- With sections from *Macworld* magazine's most popular experts
- Optimize hardware and software to meet your individual needs

$22.95/$30.95 Canada ■ ISBN: 1-878058-19-3
336 pages. Available now.

IDG BOOKS

Order Form
Order Center: **(800) 762-2974** (7 a.m.–5 p.m., PST, weekdays)
or **(415) 312-0650**
Order Center FAX: **(415) 358-1260**

Quantity	Title & ISBN	Price	Total

Shipping & Handling Charges

Subtotal	U.S.	Canada & International	International Air Mail
Up to $20.00	Add $3.00	Add $4.00	Add $10.00
$20.01–40.00	$4.00	$5.00	$20.00
$40.01–60.00	$5.00	$6.00	$25.00
$60.01–80.00	$6.00	$8.00	$35.00
Over $80.00	$7.00	$10.00	$50.00

In U.S. and Canada, shipping is UPS ground or equivalent. For Rush shipping call (800) 762-2974.

Subtotal _____

CA residents add applicable sales tax _____

IN residents add 5% sales tax _____

Canadian residents add 7% GST tax _____

Shipping _____

TOTAL _____

Ship to:

Name _____

Company _____

Address _____

City/State/Zip _____

Daytime phone _____

Payment: ☐ Check to IDG Books   ☐ Visa   ☐ MasterCard   ☐ American Express

Card # _____   Expires _____

Please send this order form to: IDG Books, 155 Bovet Road, Ste. 610, San Mateo, CA 94402.
Allow up to 3 weeks for delivery. Thank you!

BK=BOBMSB

Power Tools Supplement

I. **Software Disks** including a desk accessory version of the book's index and glossary.
This set of fifteen disks contains numerous utilities and programs for Macintosh musicians.
You may purchase any combination of individual disks or the complete set.

Reference Disks
1) The Macworld Music and Sound Bible Navigation Disk • Online index to the book. Online Macintosh music glossary.
2) The Mac Musician Reference Disk • Help desk accessories for popular music software. MIDI reference stack. Musical reference stack.
3) The Music Database Disk • MacMusic articles database (5 years — 6 magazines). MacMusic products and resources database. MacMusic companies database.
4) The Music Organization Disk (Database Shells) • SoundTracker. SFX Organizer. PAN Messenger tracking database (includes Messenger customizer). Musicians' address book.

Educational Disks
10) Boulanger Stack • Computer-aided instruction in harmony à la Nadia Boulanger's teaching.
11) The Resource Editing Disk • Interactive resource-editing tutorial (ResEdit and Resourcerer). Pre-defined resources to customize your software.
12) Finale Guided Tour • Interactive guided tour to Coda's Finale (requires 4 MB RAM).

Utilities Disks
5) The HyperCard Sound and MIDI Disk • Sample Projects, XCMDs and XFCNs. HyperMIDI Syntax DA and other utilities. Mozart's Musical Dice Game (MIDI and non-MIDI versions).
6) The Music Calculator Disk • Clix to BPM. Notation calculator. Sequencer and Synchronization calculator. Time and Tempo converter.
7) MIDI Rack Designer • Utility for configuring your racks.
8) The Macro Disk • Sets of macros for popular programs.
9) Miscellaneous Third-party Music Shareware • Many of the programs and utilities listed in Chapter 6 and covered in *The Power User Companion*.

Multimedia Disks
13) YAVClips Clip Music • Collection of original 8-bit music clips (no license fees for non-commercial use).
14) YAV MIDI Clips • Pop and classical SMFs in General MIDI format (no license fees for non-commercial use). SMFs of the generated musical examples in Chapters 19 and 20.
15) Synth & Audio Gear Clip Art Disk • Hundreds of devices in object-oriented graphics format, all to scale.

II. **Bimonthly *MuseLetter***

Keeps you up to date on all new developments concerning topics covered in the *Macworld Music & Sound Bible*. Includes product updates and upgrades, new product introductions, on-going power user tips, tutorials, and more user profiles and interviews.

III. **Bytehoven BBS**

(Bulletin Board System)
This is a full-fledged telecommunications service complete with forums, electronic mail, and software libraries of public domain, freeware, and shareware music and general software. Includes telecommunications software.

IV. **Power User Companion to the Macworld Music & Sound Bible**

This 400-page supplemental volume covers the following topics for the Macintosh musician who wants to dig deeper. Cross-referenced to both the *Macworld Music & Sound Bible* and the *Quick Reference Guide*.

Power User Companion To The *Macworld Music & Sound Bible*

• **Power using techniques and strategies including step-by-step tutorials with a complete guide to music utilities**
• **MIDI in HyperCard and SuperCard including sample stacks, scripts, and syntax guides**
• **Icon-based and visual MIDI programming —Max, Megalomania, HookUp!**
• **Advanced MIDI editing techniques applicable to all sequencers**
• **Musicians' guide to modems and telecommunications**
• **"Late-breaking News" and much more!**

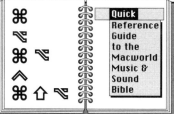

V. **Quick Reference Guide to the Macworld Music & Sound Bible**

This nearly 300-page supplemental volume provides the quickest possible access to the information you need. Cross-referenced to both the *Macworld Music & Sound Bible* and the *Power User Companion*.
• **Quick References for 90 programs covered in the main book**
• **Font reference charts for over 3 dozen music fonts**
• **Additional reference tables and resource guides**

Shipping and Handling

	US	Canada	Europe	Elsewhere
1 to 4 disks	$ 5	7	20	25
5 to 8 disks	$ 6	8	25	30
9 to 12 disks	$ 7	10	30	35
13 to 15 disks (including complete set combo)	$ 8	13	35	40
Power User Companion **or** Quick Reference Guide	$ 5	7	20	25
Power User Companion **and** Quick Reference Guide	$ 7	10	30	35
Everything (I., II., III., IV., and V. combo)	$ 14	21	55	65

Notes

Use the table to calculate shipping and handling.

You may photocopy the coupon or cut off the bottom portion and send it in a normal envelope.

No purchase is necessary to register for additional information and updates.

Optional Questionnaire

The following information will help us to better organize the *MuseLetter* and **Bytehoven BBS** to suit your needs. Please take a moment to complete the form. All responses are kept strictly confidential. Check as many boxes as applicable in each category.

Applications and Interests

- ❏ **MIDI**
- ❏ **Digital Audio**
- ❏ **Composition**
- ❏ **Notation**
- ❏ **Sound Design**
- ❏ **Performance**

- ❏ **Film, Video, Synchronization**
- ❏ **Hard Disk Recording**
- ❏ **Post-production**
- ❏ **Multimedia**
- ❏ **Education, CAI**
- ❏ **Interactive, Algorithmic Music**

- ❏ **CD-ROM**
- ❏ **Research**
- ❏ **Programming**
- ❏ **Music in HyperCard**
- ❏ **Telecommunications**
- ❏ **Power Using**

Computer and Peripherals

Macintosh Model:	_____		RAM _____ MB	❏ Running System 7
Storage:	❏ 800K Floppy	❏ 1.4MB Floppy	❏ Hard Drive	❏ CD-ROM Drive
Monitor:	❏ Color	❏ Gray Scale	❏ Monochrome	❏ NTSC
Modem:	❏ 2400-baud	❏ 9600-bps	❏ 14400-bps	❏ 19200-bps
MIDI Interface:	❏ 16-channel	❏ 32-channel	❏ MIDI Time Piece	❏ Studio 5
Music Gear:	❏ MIDI Keyboard	❏ Sound Module	❏ Digital Audio Card	❏ Direct-to-Hard Disk
Memberships:	❏ Mac Users Group	❏ AFM	❏ CMS	❏ MENC

Fold here

Place stamp here

YAV Digital Music
P.O. Box 1354
Studio City, CA 91614

Please tape bottom and sides if enclosing check or money order.

IDG Books Worldwide Registration Card
Macworld Music & Sound Bible

Fill this out — and hear about updates to this book and other IDG Books Worldwide products!

Name _____

Company/Title _____

Address _____

City/State/Zip _____

What is the single most important reason you bought this book? _____

_____

Where did you buy this book?
- ❏ Bookstore (Name _____)
- ❏ Electronics/Software store (Name_____)
- ❏ Advertisement (If magazine, which? _____)
- ❏ Mail order (Name of catalog/mail order house _____)
- ❏ Other: _____

How did you hear about this book?
- ❏ Book review in: _____
- ❏ Advertisement in: _____
- ❏ Catalog
- ❏ Found in store
- ❏ Other: _____

How would you rate the overall content of this book?
- ❏ Very good   ❏ Satisfactory
- ❏ Good   ❏ Poor
- Why? _____

What chapters did you find most valuable? _____

What chapters did you find least valuable? _____

What kind of chapter or topic would you add to future editions of this book? _____

_____

Please give us any additional comments. _____

_____

Thank you for your help!

❏ I liked this book! By checking this box, I give you permission to use my name and quote me in future IDG Books Worldwide
   promotional materials. Daytime phone number_____ .

❏ FREE! Send me a copy of your computer book and book/disk catalog.

How many computer books do you purchase a year?
- ❏ 1   ❏ 6-10
- ❏ 2-5   ❏ More than 10

What are your primary software applications?
_____
_____
_____

_ _

Fold Here

Place
stamp
here

IDG Books Worldwide, Inc.
155 Bovet Road
Suite 610
San Mateo, CA 94402

Attn: Reader Response / Music & Sound Bible